THE PARALEGAL PROFESSIONAL

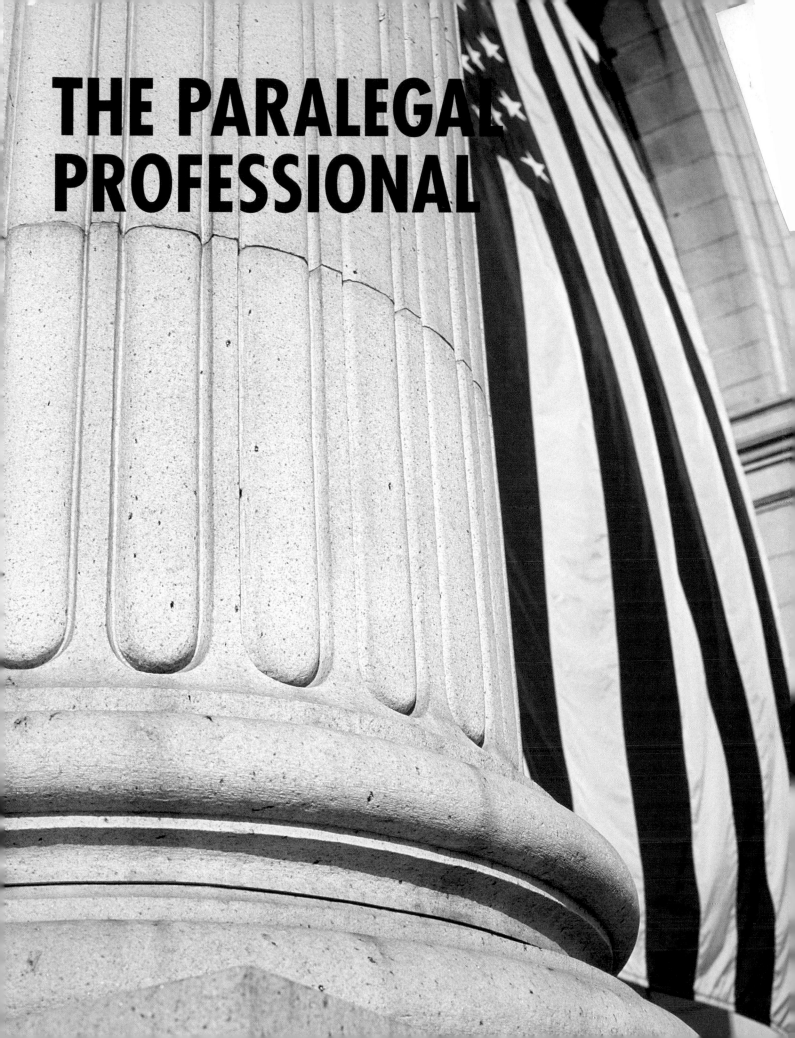

THE PARALEGAL PROFESSIONAL

Second Edition

Henry R. Cheeseman, JD, LLM
CLINICAL PROFESSOR OF LAW
UNIVERSITY OF SOUTHERN CALIFORNIA

Thomas F. Goldman, JD
PROFESSOR OF LAW AND MANAGEMENT
BUCKS COUNTY COMMUNITY COLLEGE

PEARSON

Prentice
Hall

Upper Saddle River, New Jersey 07458

Library of Congress Cataloging-in-Publication Data

Cheeseman, Henry R.
    The paralegal professional / Henry R. Cheeseman, Thomas F. Goldman. — 2nd ed.
        p. cm.
    Includes bibliographical references and index.
    ISBN 0-13-175190-5
    1. Legal assistants—United States—Handbooks, manuals, etc. I. Goldman, Thomas F. II.
Title.

KF320.L4C445 2008
340.023'73—dc22

2006033730

Editor-in-Chief: Vernon R. Anthony
Senior Acquisitions Editor: Gary Bauer
Associate Editor: Linda Cupp
Editorial Assistant: Dan Trudden
Development Editor: Deborah Hoffman
Marketing Manager: Leigh Ann Sims
Marketing Coordinator: Alicia Dysert
Managing Editor—Production: Mary Carnis
Manufacturing Buyer: Ilene Sanford
Production Liaison: Denise Brown
Full-Service Production and Composition: Emily Bush/Carlisle Publishing Services
Permission Coordinator: Lori Bradshaw/Carlisle Publishing Services
Manager of Media Production: Amy Peltier

Media Production Project Manager: Lisa Rinaldi
Director, Image Resource Center: Melinda Patelli
Manager, Rights and Permissions: Zina Arabia
Manager, Visual Research: Beth Brenzel
Manager, Cover Visual Research & Permissions: Karen Sanatar
Image Permission Coordinator: Nancy Seise
Senior Design Coordinator: Mary Siener
Cover Design: John Christiana
Cover Image: Peter Gridley, Getty Images
Interior Design: Janice Bielawa
Printer/Binder: Courier
Cover Printer: Phoenix Color

Photo Credits

Marginal Icon: Jupiter Images - PictureArts Corporation/Brand X Pictures Royalty Free; Pages xii, xv, xvi (left), xvii: Photodisc/Getty Images; Pages vii (top), ix (right), xxxi, xxxv: Ingram Publishing/SuperStock, Inc.; Pages vii (bottom), xiii: Bruce Ayres/Getty Images, Inc./Stone Allstock; Pages viii, x (left), xi (right), xx, xvii: Getty Images; Page ix (left) Jupiter Images - FoodPix - Creatas - Brand X - Banana Stock—PictureQuest/ ER Productions; Page x: Corbis Royalty Free; Page xi (left): Joe Sohm/Chromosohm/The Stock Connection; Page xiv (left): Jack Hollingsworth/Getty Images, Inc./Photodisc; Page xiv (right): © Creasource/Corbis/All Rights Reserved; Page xvi (right): EyeWire Collection/Getty Images/Photodisc; Page 1: SuperStock, Inc./ Ingram Publishing; Page 2: SuperStock, Inc./ Ingram Publishing; Page 38: Jupiter Images - FoodPix - Creatas - Brand X - Banana Stock—PictureQuest/ ER Productions; Page 74: Getty Images, Inc.; Page 128: Corbis Royalty Free; Page 167: Getty Images Inc.—Stone Allstock/ Bruce Ayres; Page 168: The Stock Connection/ Joe Sohm/Chromosohm; Page 198: Getty Images, Inc.; Page 226: Photodisc/Getty Images; Page 270: Robert Clare / Taxi / Getty Images; Page 306: Getty Images, Inc.; Page 346: Getty Images Inc.—Stone Allstock/ Bruce Ayres; Page 390: Getty Images, Inc.—Photodisc/ Jack Hollingsworth; Page 427: Getty Images, Inc.; Page 428: (c) Creasource / CORBIS All Rights Reserved; Page 456: Photodisc/Getty Images; Page 498: Getty Images, Inc.; Page 530: Photodisc/Getty Images; Page 560: Getty Images—Photodisc/EyeWire Collection; Page 586: Getty Images, Inc.; Page 634: Photodisc/Getty Images; Page 688: PhotoEdit Inc./ Michael Newman; Page 718: Photodisc/Getty Images.

Pearson Education Ltd.
Pearson Education Singapore Pte. Ltd.
Pearson Education Canada, Ltd.
Pearson Education—Japan

Pearson Education Australia PTY. Limited
Pearson Education North Asia Ltd.
Pearson Educación de Mexico, S.A. de C.V.
Pearson Education Malaysia Pte. Ltd.

10 9 8 7
ISBN: 0-13-175190-5

Dedicated to the memory of my parents,
Morris and Ethel Goldman, who guided me through life,
encouraged me to pursue an education,
and delighted in my becoming a teacher.

—Thomas Goldman

In memory of
Henry B. and Florence Cheeseman

A grain of sand
has been
ten thousand mountains.

Who are we
to hold it?

—Henry Cheeseman

Contents in Brief

Contents

CHAPTER 3
The Paralegal
Workplace   74

CHAPTER 4
Technology and the
Paralegal   128

PART II
PARALEGAL SKILLS
AND PROCEDURE 167

CHAPTER 5
Sources of American Law
168

CHAPTER 6
The Court System and
Alternate
Dispute Resolution 198

CHAPTER 7
Civil Litigation   226

CHAPTER 8
Administrative Law   270

CHAPTER 9
Interviewing and Investigation Skills 306

CHAPTER 10
Traditional Computer and Internet Legal Research 346

CHAPTER 11
Legal Writing and Critical Legal Thinking   390

PART III
SUBSTANTIVE LEGAL SUBJECTS FOR THE PARALEGAL   427

CHAPTER 12
Torts   428

CHAPTER 13
Contracts and
E-Commerce   456

CHAPTER 14
Property   498

CHAPTER 17
Agency and Employment Law   586

CHAPTER 18
Business Organizations and Bankruptcy Law   634

CHAPTER 19
Criminal Law   688

From the Authors

When we were asked to write this second edition of our textbook, *The Paralegal Professional*, for Pearson Prentice Hall Publishing, we welcomed the opportunity to refine a text that would present essential information for paralegal students in a memorable and exciting way. We hope we have produced a textbook with the best combination of information on paralegal careers and skills needed for success in the field and an overview of substantive law concepts that is easy to read and enjoyable to use.

The second edition has been heavily revised and reorganized based on feedback from a wide range of users and reviewers, resulting in a new text that better serves the needs of students and provides more flexibility in covering substantive law topics. The twenty chapters of *The Paralegal Professional*, Second Edition, are now divided into three Parts:

Part I: The Paralegal Profession,
Part II: Paralegal Skills and Procedures, and
Part III: Substantive Legal Subjects for the Paralegal.

We present the material of our book in a visual format that has been referred to as a "textbook magazine." Topics are presented in a variety of formats designed to impart information in an accessible, understandable manner appropriate for traditional and returning students alike. Among the many changes made to this edition are new chapter opening scenarios that set the stage for chapter topics, new margin annotations, new paralegal applications, new ethical perspective features, new "Advice from the Field" boxes, and many new critical thinking and skill-building exercises.

Our book has been carefully and thoroughly designed to meet the requirements as set forth by the American Bar Association (ABA) and the American Association for Paralegal Education (AAfPE) regarding coverage of paralegal topics, ethical issues, professional skill development, and other educational requirements for an introductory paralegal education course.

The paralegal profession is a dynamic, evolving, and growing field that goes beyond imparting concept knowledge, to developing analytical skills and ethical values that will meet the needs of today's increasingly diverse work environment. This text is written to give paralegal students and professionals the foundation to excel in this field today and in the future.

Henry Cheeseman
Thomas Goldman

About the Authors

Henry R. Cheeseman is an award-winning author of several business-law textbooks published by Prentice Hall Publishing, including the definitive, highly-regarded *Business Law*. Other textbooks published by Professor Cheeseman by Prentice Hall Publishing are *Contemporary Business and Online Commerce Law*, *The Legal Environment of Business and Online Commerce*, *Essentials of Business and Online Commerce*, and *Introduction to Law*. He has earned six degrees, including a Juris Doctor degree from the UCLA School of Law, an LLM degree from Boston University, and an MBA degree from the University of Chicago. Professor Cheeseman is a Clinical Professor of Law and the Director of Legal Studies at the Marshall School of Business, University of Southern California. Students there voted him the best teacher of the year on many occasions, earning him the "Golden Apple" Teacher Award. Professor Cheeseman has also served at the Center for Excellence in Teaching at the University. Recognizing the importance of the paralegal to the practice of law, he has co-authored this new and exciting edition of *The Paralegal Professional*.

Thomas F. Goldman is a Professor of Law and Management, Former Director of the Center for Legal Studies and of the Paralegal Studies Program at Bucks County Community College in Pennsylvania. An accounting and economics graduate of Boston University and of Temple University School of Law, Professor Goldman has an active international law, technology law, and litigation practice. He has worked extensively with paralegals and received the award of the Legal Support Staff Guild. He was elected the Legal Secretaries Association Boss of the Year for his contribution to cooperative education by encouraging the use of paralegals and legal assistants in law offices. He also received the Bucks County Community College Alumni Association Professional Achievement Award. He has been an educational consultant on technology to major corporations and a frequent speaker and lecturer on educational, legal, and technology issues. Appointed to the American Association for Paralegal Education Board of Directors in October 2005, Tom has also served as the Chair of the Technology Task Force initiating the Train the Trainer program.

BUILD A SOLID FOUNDATION FOR YOUR PARALEGAL CAREER!

Written by an award-winning team, *The Paralegal Professional 2e* builds the foundation in substantive and procedural legal knowledge and real-world skills you will need throughout your course of study. The book emphasizes the following:

DEVELOP CRITICAL THINKING AND PROCEDURAL SKILLS!

End of chapter material in this edition has been greatly expanded to focus on developing critical thinking and hands-on skills including the following exercises and assignments:
- Critical thinking and writing case exercises
- Web research exercises
- Ethics analysis and discussion questions
- Collaborative exercises
- Legal analysis and writing cases, cases for briefing
- New portfolio building exercises

LEARN ABOUT TECHNOLOGY APPLICATIONS IN THE LAW OFFICE

To be effective on the job, you will need to become comfortable using computers and common legal office software. Chapter 4, Technology and the Paralegal, introduces you to the types of application programs and their uses commonly found in law offices today.

UNDERSTAND HOW TO HANDLE ETHICAL SITUATIONS IN THE WORKPLACE

The Paralegal Professional 2e text and package is designed to build a strong foundational understanding of ethical principles for paralegals in the introductory course. Resources include: Chapter 2: Ethics, Regulation, and Professional Responsibility, new ethical perspectives boxes integrated throughout the textbook, and 24 Ethics-Related video segments from the new Paralegal Professional Classroom Video Series Segments.

Key Features of the Textbook

▶ NEW PARALEGALS AT WORK CHAPTER OPENERS

These opening scenarios offer a hypothetical fact situation that a professional paralegal could encounter on the job. They are designed to stimulate a student's interest in the material to be covered in the chapter.

▶ PARALEGAL PRACTICE NOTES

The relevance of each chapter topic to the paralegal is set forth in an Introduction to the Paralegal section and new special feature boxes called "The Paralegal and . . ." discuss the relevance of special topics of a chapter to a paralegal.

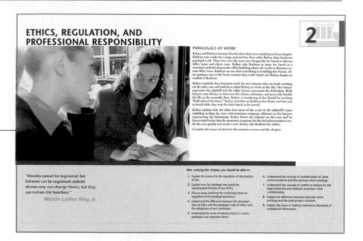

▶ ETHICAL PERSPECTIVES BOXES

ETHICAL *Perspective*

NALA Code of Ethics and Professional Responsibility Canon 7

A legal assistant must protect the confidences of a client and must not violate any rule or statute now in effect or hereafter enacted controlling the doctrine of privileged communications between a client and an

These new boxes present hypothetical fact situations and ethical dilemmas that paralegals might face in their professional careers.

▶ CONTEMPORARY LEGAL ISSUES BOXES

These boxes discuss contemporary legal issues relevant to paralegals, such as the use of technology in the workplace and new laws that affect the paralegal profession.

THE PROCESS OF CHOOSING A SUPREME COURT JUSTICE

In an effort to strike a balance of power between the executive and legislative branches of government, Article II, Section 2 of the U.S. Constitution gives the president the power to appoint Supreme Court justices "with the advice and consent of the Senate."

President George Bush was given the chance to cast a conservative shadow over the Court's decisions when Justice Thurgood Marshall retired in 1991. Marshall, who served 24

▶ MEET THE COURTHOUSE TEAM BOXES

MEET THE COURTHOUSE TEAM

Introduction to the Team

As a paralegal, you will work with a number of different individuals outside of the law office. Many of these people are part of the local, state, and federal court system. Others, though located within the courthouse, are not directly part of the court system but, because of the nature of governmental administration and record keeping, might be related to your job as a paralegal. This text will introduce some of these people to you.

Most courthouses contain offices and personnel involved in administration of the legal process. Generally, the three main areas of law

Discuss the roles of important personnel in the judicial system and the paralegal profession.

▶ NEW ADVICE FROM THE FIELD ARTICLES

These feature professional advice straight from the experts on interviewing skills, developing your portfolio, professional development, handling clients, and more.

Advice from the Field ...

TECHNOLOGY IS A TOOL, NOT A CA

Michael E. Cobo

The latest legal technology products such as animation and courtroom presentation systems can be very alluring to lawyers. After learning about these products, you may

▶ PARALEGAL CHECKLISTS

checklist ✓

■ Address (URL):

■ Name of organization or site:

■ Key subject:

■ Secondary subject:

Checklists help students track their personal progress as well as class and job details.

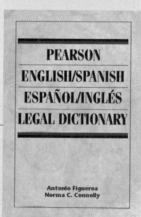
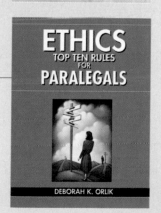

Tools for Teaching!

INSTRUCTOR SUPPLEMENTS

INSTRUCTOR'S MANUAL WITH TOOLKIT FOR NEW INSTRUCTORS

The Instructor's Manual has been dramatically expanded to accommodate the needs of instructors with any level of experience. Whether you are a first time instructor or an experienced hand, this tool contains a wealth of teaching materials including the following:

- **New Instructors Toolkit:**
  - Preparing For Class
  - *"First Day Of Class"* Notes and PowerPoints

- **Sample Syllabi : 10,12,15,16 Week Courses with Templates on CD**
  - Weekly Assignments
  - Weekly Deadlines
  - Drop-Box Formatted Assignments also on CD

- **Using PowerPoint Quick Guide**

- **Using WebCT and BlackBoard Notes**

- **Transition Notes for Users of Miller 3e and Statsky 6e**

- By Chapter
  - **Chapter Outline**
  - **Teaching Notes**
  - **New Law in the Movies Teaching Notes**
  - **New! Outcome Assessment Tools**

PRENTICE-HALL TEST GENERATOR

This computerized test generation system gives you maximum flexibility in preparing tests. It can create custom tests and print scrambled versions of a test at one time, as well as build tests randomly by chapter, level of difficulty, or question type. The software also allows online testing and record-keeping and the ability to add problems to the database.

POWERPOINT LECTURE PRESENTATION PACKAGE

Lecture Presentation screens for each chapter are available online and on the Instructor Resource CD.

INSTRUCTOR RESOURCES CD (IRCD)

The IRCD contains the Instructor's Manual with New Instructor Toolkit, the Prentice-Hall Test Gen, and the PowerPoint Lecture Presentation Package.

THE PARALEGAL PROFESSIONAL CLASSROOM VIDEO SERIES

34 video segments are available for in-class use on DVD and are accessible to students via streaming video in either Blackboard or WebCT courses! (See next spread for a description of the video package.)

ONEKEY DISTANCE LEARNING SOLUTIONS:
CONVENIENCE, SIMPLICITY, SUCCESS

Ready-made **WebCT** and **Blackboard** online courses! If you adopt a OneKey course, student access cards will be packaged with the text. OneKey courses include Research Navigator, a premium online research tool, and access to the Paralegal Professional Classroom Video Series via streaming video.

RESEARCH NAVIGATOR

Pearson's Research Navigator™ is the easiest way for students to start a research assignment or research paper. Complete with extensive help on the research process and four exclusive databases of credible and reliable source material including the EBSCO Academic Journal and Abstract Database, *New York Times* Search by Subject Archive, "Best of the Web" Link Library, and *Financial Times* Article Archive and Company Financials, Research Navigator helps students quickly and efficiently make the most of their research time.

VERSUSLAW® ONLINE LEGAL RESEARCH ACCESS

Pearson Education has teamed-up with VersusLaw® to provide paralegal and legal studies students with on-line legal research access. One-semester subscription access code cards (0-13-118514-4) can be packaged with any Pearson Paralegal Studies title. The VersusLaw® subscription provides students with access that allows them to work from the dorm, home, library, or anywhere there is an Internet connection.

Receive online access to archive and current opinions from the following courts:

- U.S. Supreme Court
- U.S. Circuit Court of Appeals
- Federal District Court
- State Appellate Court
- Tribal Courts
- Foreign Courts

Don't Just Tell Them, Show Them!

THE PARALEGAL PROFESSIONAL
VIDEO SERIES ON DVD

The 2nd Edition of *The Paralegal Professional* is supported by 35 scenario-based video segments that allow you to bring the world of the practicing paralegal into the classroom. Videos cover topics such as resume writing and interviewing for a job, working in a small family firm, the courtroom players and their roles, and paralegals performing various procedures and duties. 24 of the segments present scenarios dealing with common ethical situations that paralegals will encounter on the job making it easy to integrate ethics education throughout the course.

Free to Adopters of Paralegal Professional 2e

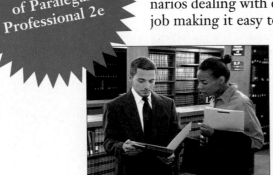

Getting a Job-Related Video Segments:
- Preparing for a Job Interview: Resume Advice
- Preparing for a Job Interview: Interviewing Advice
- Resume Writing Do's and Don'ts
- Interviewing: The Good, The Bad, and the Ugly

Paralegal Practice and Ethics-Related Video Segments:
- UPL Issue: When Friends Ask for Legal Advice
- UPL Issue: Helping the Client without Practicing Law
- UPL Issue: Traditional Exceptions
- UPL Issue: Disclosure of Status
- UPL Issue: Interviewing a Client
- UPL Issue: Working with a Witness
- UPL Issue: Working with Experts
- UPL Issue: Improper Supervision
- UPL Issue: Helping Client Fill Out Forms
- Privilege Issue: Misdirected Email
- Confidentiality Issue: Need to Know Circle
- Confidentiality Issue: Public Information
- Confidentiality Issue: Disclosure of Damaging Information
- Confidentiality Issue: Family Exception?
- Confidentiality Issue: Attorney Client Privilege
- Conflict of Interest Issue: Relationships with Clients
- Conflict of Interest Issue: Independent Paralegal
- Conflict of Interest Issue: Gift to Judge
- Fees and Billing Issue: Contemporaneous Timekeeping
- Fees and Billing Issue: Using Time Effectively
- Zealous Representation Issue: When You Are Asked To Lie
- Zealous Representation Issue: Handling Evidence
- Zealous Representation Issue: Candor to the Court
- Zealous Representation Issue: Signing Documents

Paralegal Practice Video Segments:
- Legal Research: Are Books Obsolete?
- Lillian Harris, Small Family Law Practice
- Independent Paralegal
- Electronic Discovery Process
- Difference Between Civil and Criminal Case
- Meet the Courthouse Team
- Demeanor in the Courtroom

THE PARALEGAL PROFESSIONAL VIDEO SERIES DEMONSTRATION CD

Contact your local representative to receive a demonstration CD containing 5 segments from the series including the teaching notes for each segment. Locate your representative by using the Rep Locator button at www.prenhall.com.

Teaching Notes for the Videos are in the Instructor's Manual!

▶ INTEGRATE ETHICS INSTRUCTION
INTO THE INTRODUCTORY COURSE!

Many paralegal programs struggle with the question of how to integrate dedicated ethics instruction into a paralegal curriculum already packed with coursework. *The Paralegal Professional* 2e text and package is designed to build a strong foundational understanding of ethical principles for paralegals in the introductory course. Resources include:

Chapter 2: Ethics, Regulation, and Professional Responsibility

The fundamental ethics issues and principles are presented in chapter 2.

New Ethical Perspectives Boxes Integrated throughout the Textbook

These new boxes present hypothetical fact situations and ethical dilemmas that highlight situations paralegals might face in their professional careers.

ETHICAL *Perspective*

NALA Code of Ethics and Professional Responsibility Canon 7
A legal assistant must protect the confidences of a client and must not violate any rule or statute now in effect or hereafter enacted controlling the doctrine of privileged communications between a client and an

24 Ethics-Related Paralegal Professional Classroom Video Series Segments

▶ **Need More Coverage of Ethics in a Handy Supplemental Guide?**

ETHICS: TOP TEN RULES FOR PARALEGALS
by Deborah Orlik

If more depth in dealing with ethical issues is desired, this handy guide can be packaged with the textbook at low cost.
(ISBN: 0-13-119321-X)

Acknowledgments

A round of applause to those whose insights contributed to the learning aspects of the book. Special thanks to:

Michael Fitch, for his guidance and encouragement early in the development of the project.

Kathryn Myers, for her generosity and kindness in allowing the use of material on portfolios and for the guidance she unknowingly gave by her example of enthusiasm, dedication, and hard work in support of paralegal education.

Lilian Harris, for her constant encouragement and help in developing materials on family law and the needs of tireless paralegal program directors and faculty to teach students the real-world approach.

Richard Opie, for sharing his ideas and materials.

Joy Smucker, for her encouragement in developing soft skills materials.

Debra Orlik, for help in really understanding the ethics of the paralegal profession.

Bill Mulkeen, for his encouragement and insights into the educational needs of students.

Don Swanson, an independent paralegal, for his expertise in the role of the paralegal in e-discovery and total dedication to help paralegal students by volunteering endless hours to help paralegal educators and authors with real-life experiences and paralegal educational needs.

Members of the AAfPE board who have shared ideas and material and offer guidance in developing the materials for this book to meet the needs of the paralegal student and faculty, including Pamela Bailey, Marissa Campbell, Christine Lissitzyn, Bob LeClair, Ed Husted, and Carolyn Smoot.

The inspiring panelists and speakers at the AAfPE annual and regional meetings over the past five years, who provided insights, guidance, suggestions, and encouragement.

To the officers and members of the local and national professional associations, including NALA, NFPA, NALS, and ALA, for allowing the use of their materials, but mostly for their suggestions regarding topics and real-life issues to be covered.

Paralegal Edie Hannah and Attorney Glenn Hains of Tom Goldman's law office, for their tireless reviews, detail checking, encouragement and support, countless hours on the phone getting materials and networking with other professionals to obtain comments and input to make this textbook relevant to working paralegals as well as to students preparing for the profession.

The students in Tom Goldman's classes, for testing the text and WebCT materials in a class setting and graciously providing suggestions and feedback.

Vivi Wang, Tiffany Lee, and Ashley Anderson, Professor Henry Cheeseman's research assistants at the Marshall School of Business, University of Southern California, for their excellent assistance in conducting legal and paralegal research for this book.

Finally, much gratitude to the reviewers, whose thorough responses helped to complete this project:

FIRST-EDITION REVIEWERS

Chelsea Campbell, Lehman College CUNY
Anderson Castro, Florida International University
Stephanie Delaney, Highline Community College
Linda Hornsby, Florida International University
Nance Kriscenski, Manchester Community College
Linda Cabral Marrero, Mercy College
Leslie Miron, Mercy College
R. Eileen Mitchell, University of New Orleans
Anthony Piazza, Dan N. Myers University
Alex A. Yarborough, Virginia College at Birmingham

SECOND-EDITION REVIEWERS

Special thanks to the reviewers of this text:
Katharine Greenwood, Loyola University
Kathryn L. Myers, Saint Mary-of-the-Woods, Indiana
Mark A. Ciccarelli, Kent State University,
Mercedes P. Alonso-Knapp, Florida International University
Louise B. Gussin, University of Maryland University College
Sue Armstrong, Central Washington University
Victoria H. Lopez, Southwestern College, California
Mary People, Arapahoe Community College, Colorado
Ernest Davila, San Jacinto College North, Texas
Dee Janssen Lammers, Pima Community College, Tucson, Arizona
P. Darrel Harrison, Miramar College, San Diego, California
Deborah Vinecour, SUNY Rockland Community College, New York
Margaret Lovig, Coastline Community College, California
Pierre A. Kleff, Jr., The University of Texas at Brownsville
Tara L. Duncan, Everest College, Phoenix, Arizona
Robin Rossenfeld, Community College of Aurora, Colorado
Wesley K. Sasano, Everest College—Rancho Cucamonga, California
Laura J. Hansen-Brown, Kaplan University, Florida

Henry R. Cheeseman
Thomas F. Goldman

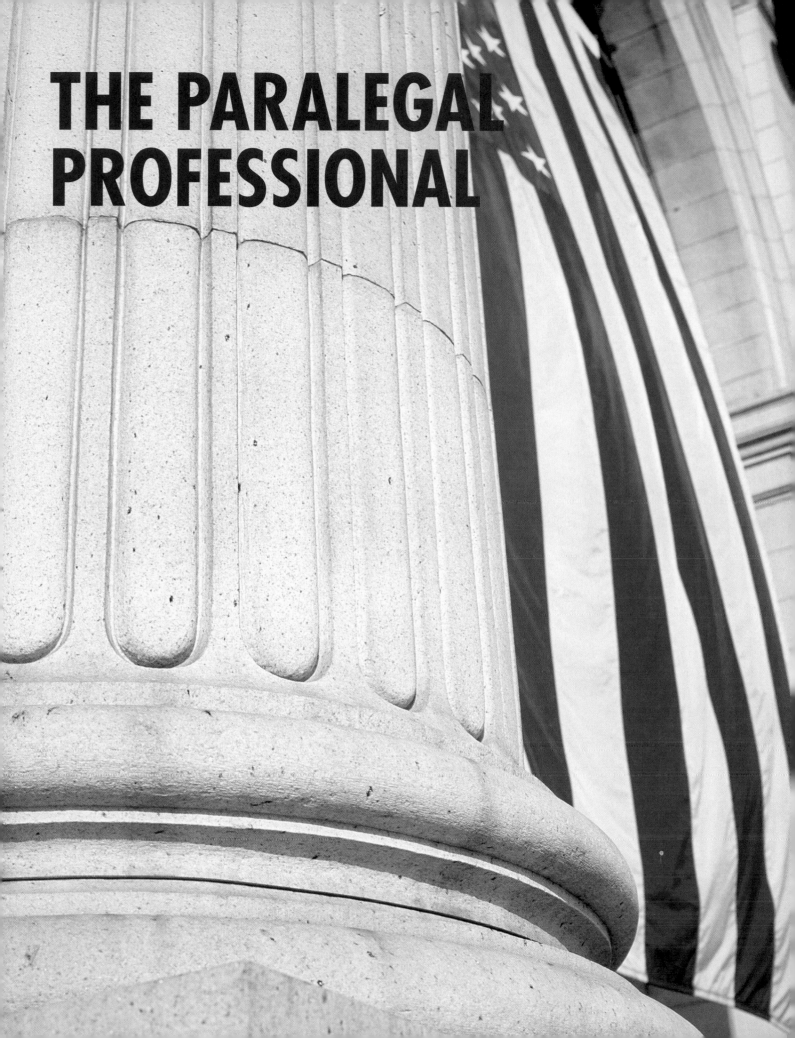

THE PARALEGAL PROFESSIONAL

PART I
The Paralegal Profession

THE PARALEGAL, OR LEGAL ASSISTANT, PROFESSION has seen explosive growth since the late 1960s. In recent years it has evolved into a profession that demands increasingly higher degrees of knowledge and skills for those entering its ranks including knowledge of technology applications, a firm foundation in ethics, and strong people skills. Opportunities and career choices for the paralegal have never been better. Possible employers are as diverse as the duties paralegals are asked to perform. Today's paralegals need specialized skills in many areas. Formal programs of study and continuing education programs have developed to help individuals obtain needed skills. As with other professions, ethical rules and regulations have evolved to help paralegals avoid conflicts and possible malpractice. These topics will be discussed in Part I.

THE PARALEGAL PROFESSION

"The great can protect themselves, but the poor and humble require the arm and shield of the law."

Andrew Jackson

PARALEGALS AT WORK

On the Friday before Thanksgiving, Ariel sits in the bleachers watching her high school alma mater, Lincoln High, take on Newtown. Ariel's brother, Ethan, is a linebacker on the football team and this is his last high school football game.

Ariel graduated from Lincoln in 1995 and went on to get her bachelor's degree with a major in English and a minor in Languages. She spots Mr. Marshall, her high school guidance counselor, and goes over to greet him.

As their conversation continues, Ariel asks Mr. Marshall about the career advice he's given to her brother. Ethan is thinking about a legal career but isn't interested in criminal justice or law enforcement. He's not sure about the time and dedication it takes to get through law school. Mr. Marshall gave Ethan information on local paralegal programs.

Ariel has been working as an editorial assistant for a small publisher of medical books. Although she always has plenty of work to do, she's not challenged in her job. She wants to use the language and writing skills she's developed, as well as have more autonomy and control over her work. Ariel asks Mr. Marshall whether a paralegal career makes sense for her.

Consider the issue involved in this scenario as you read the chapter.

After studying this chapter, you should be able to:

1. Define the term *paralegal*.

2. Explain what paralegals do and their role in the legal profession.

3. Discuss the job opportunities for the paralegal.

4. Explain why education and training are necessary to be recognized as a member of the paralegal profession.

5. Describe the various educational paths available to become a paralegal.

6. Understand the American Bar Association standards for approval of legal assistant education programs.

7. Understand the American Association for Paralegal Education core competencies for paralegal programs.

8. Assess and articulate your background, current skill level, and knowledge.

9. Begin to set goals for your career future.

▶INTRODUCTION FOR THE PARALEGAL

Paralegal (legal assistant)
A person qualified by education, training, or work experience who is employed or retained by a lawyer, law office, corporation, governmental agency, or other entity who performs specifically delegated substantive legal work for which a lawyer is responsible; equivalent term is legal assistant.

The paralegal or legal assistant profession has seen an explosive growth since the late-1960s. Like other professions, this one has evolved over time to meet a need. Prior to the late 1960s, many of the functions of paralegals today were performed by those with titles such as legal secretary, lay assistant, and legal clerk or law clerk (the latter of which usually was reserved for the recent law school graduate who had not yet passed the bar exam).

Opportunities and career choices for the paralegal have never been better. Twenty years ago the paralegal had a limited, behind-the-scenes role with little client contact except possibly as a receptionist or a legal secretary. Today, paralegals are employed in every area of the law. They interview clients, conduct factual investigations, do legal research, prepare legal documents, assist at the counsel table in trials, and even represent clients in some administrative hearings. They are employed in law firms of all sizes, federal, state, and local government, insurance companies, and corporations. ■

WHAT IS A PARALEGAL?

American Bar Association (ABA)
Largest professional legal organization in the United States.

National Federation of Paralegal Associations (NFPA)
Professional organization of state and local paralegal associations founded in 1974.

National Association of Legal Assistants (NALA)
Professional organization for legal assistants that provides continuing education and professional certification for paralegals, incorporated in 1975.

A great deal of confusion has arisen as to what the professional in this field should be called or what the professionals should call themselves. The most popular terms, **paralegal** and **legal assistant**, have been used in most of the United States. These terms were used interchangeably by the **American Bar Association (ABA)**, the **National Federation of Paralegal Associations (NFPA)**, and the **National Association of Legal Assistants (NALA)**. The confusion stems in part from the shift from the title of "secretary" to "administrative assistant" and, in some offices and educational institutions, "law office assistant."

The exact definition of legal assistant has been the subject of discussions by national organizations including the ABA, NFPA, and NALA, as well as many state legislatures, supreme courts, and bar associations. The trend is toward the use of the term *paralegal* and away from using the term *legal assistant*. Originally called the Standing Committee on Legal Assistants, the American Bar Association changed its name to the Standing Committee on Paralegals, in recognition of this trend.

The American Bar Association's 1997 version of the definition, which also has been adopted by the National Association of Legal Assistants, is:

> A legal assistant or paralegal is a person, qualified by education, training, or work experience who is employed or retained by a lawyer, law office, corporation, governmental agency or other entity and who performs specifically delegated substantive legal work for which a lawyer is responsible.

Check the current definition approved by the American Bar Association at www.abanet.org

The National Federation of Paralegal Associations adopted a resolution in 2002 eliminating the term *legal assistant* from its definition of *paralegal* because that term now is being used to refer to positions outside the paralegal definition. Accordingly, NFPA defines a paralegal as follows:

> A paralegal is a person qualified through education, training or work experience to perform substantive legal work that requires knowledge of legal concepts as customarily, but not exclusively performed by a lawyer. This person may be retained or employed by a lawyer, law office, governmental agency or other entity or may be authorized by administrative, statutory or court authority to perform this work.

Review the full NFPA resolution at www.paralegals.org

WHAT DO PARALEGALS DO?

The primary function of paralegals is to assist attorneys in preparing for hearings, trials, meetings, and closings. In many cases paralegals do the preparatory work, helping to draft documents, assisting in the preparation of other documents and forms, coordinating the activities and functions required in some cases, and in many offices maintaining the financial records of the firm.

People tend to think of paralegals as working in a private law office directly under the supervision of attorneys. Actually, employers of the paralegal are just as diverse as the duties they are asked to perform. Many paralegals are employed by the federal government, as well as state and local governments including regulatory bodies. The paralegal's activities might include analyzing legal material for internal use and collecting and analyzing data, as well as preparing information and explanatory material, for use by the general public.

More and more paralegals are coming to the profession from other professions. For example, they may come from nursing, bringing with them a specialized body of knowledge that they combine with the legal skills they learned in a paralegal program. With this expertise they frequently are hired to analyze case materials for trial attorneys, both plaintiff and defense, and also are employed as case analysts and as claims representatives for health insurance companies. Their knowledge of medicine, combined with their legal knowledge, gives them a unique ability to analyze specialized material.

Other specialties can take the same career path. Those with engineering and other bachelor of science degrees bring specialized expertise to the law. A paralegal with a forensic science background, for example, may well be the ideal paralegal to work with criminal defense attorneys and prosecutors.

Prior to the recognition of a separate paralegal profession, individuals typically had acquired specialized knowledge of a narrow legal field through on-the-job training. Someone working with a lawyer—usually a secretary—learned the daily routine

www

Review the Model Standards and Guidelines of the National Association of Legal Assistants at http://www.nala.org/stand.htm

---

NATIONAL ASSOCIATION OF LEGAL ASSISTANTS MODEL STANDARDS AND GUIDELINES

Proper utilization of the services of legal assistants contributes to the delivery of cost effective, high-quality legal services. Legal assistants and the legal profession should be assured that measures exist for identifying legal assistants and their role in assisting attorneys in the delivery of legal services. Therefore, the National Association of Legal Assistants, Inc., hereby adopts these Standards and Guidelines as an educational document for the benefit of legal assistants and the legal profession.

A legal assistant should meet certain minimum qualifications. The following standards may be used to determine an individual's qualifications as a legal assistant:

(1) Successful completion of the Certified Legal Assistant (CLA)/Certified Paralegal (CP) certifying examination of the National Association of Legal Assistants, Inc.;

(2) Graduation from an ABA approved program of study for legal assistants;

(3) Graduation from a course of study for legal assistants which is institutionally accredited but not ABA approved, and which requires not less than the equivalent of 60 semester hours of classroom study;

(4) Graduation from a course of study for legal assistants, other than those set forth in (2) and (3) above, plus not less than six months of in-house training as a legal assistant;

(5) A baccalaureate degree in any field, plus not less than six months in-house training as a legal assistant;

(6) A minimum of three years of law-related experience under the supervision of an attorney, including at least six months of in-house training as a legal assistant; or

(7) Two years of in-house training as a legal assistant.

For purposes of these Standards, "in-house training as a legal assistant" means attorney education of the employee concerning legal assistant duties and these Guidelines. In addition to review and analysis of assignments, the legal assistant should receive a reasonable amount of instruction directly related to the duties and obligations of the legal assistant.

Source: Copyright 1984, adopted 1984; revised 1991, 1997, 2005. Reprinted with permission of the National Association of Legal Assistants, www.nala.org, 1516 S. Boston, #200, Tulsa, OK 74119.

tasks and become knowledgeable about that specific area of law. Many of these individuals became resource sources of information, such as the documentation requirements for real estate settlements, the preparation and filing of estate and trust accountings, and the procedures for preparing and filing cases and appeals. These were the first paralegals.

Today, many of the skills and procedures formerly acquired over an extended time on the job are taught at institutions specializing in the education of paralegals or legal assistants, offering a certificate program, a two-year associate degree program, or a four-year bachelor's degree program.

In 1968 the American Bar Association formed a committee to investigate the use of lay assistants in the legal office. The result was the American Bar Association's forming the Standing Committee on Legal Assistants. The ABA gave this committee jurisdiction over training and standards for the education of legal assistants. Within this jurisdiction the Standing Committee on Legal Assistants monitors trends in the field and recommends to the House of Delegates—the policymaking body of the American Bar Association—training programs that meet its standards for quality education.

Check the latest paralegal statistics in the *Occupational Outlook Handbook* from the Department of Labor, Bureua of Labor Statistics at http://www.bls.gov/oco/home.htm

OPPORTUNITIES FOR PARALEGALS

Paralegals held about 224,000 jobs in 2004, according to the Bureau of Labor Statistics, U.S. Department of Labor, *Occupational Outlook Handbook*, 2006–07 Edition. In May 2004, full-time paralegals had a median annual earnings, including bonuses, of $39,130. Salaries in the industries employing the largest numbers of paralegals in 2002 were:

- Federal government: $59,370
- Local government: $38,260
- Legal services: $37,870
- State government: $34,910

In a 1998 survey by the American Bar Association:

- Almost two-thirds of the lawyers who responded, 65.5 percent, employ legal assistants at their firms; 60.2 percent of respondents actively work with paralegals.
- The general responsibilities most often assigned to paralegals are maintaining client files, drafting correspondence, and performing factual research.
- Legal assistants are more likely to be employed by large firms than small firms.
- Lawyers in smaller firms delegate a wider array of responsibilities to legal assistants than do lawyers in bigger firms.
- Lawyers with business/corporate, probate/estate planning, and litigation practices make more extensive use of paralegals than do lawyers in other practice areas.

The ABA survey demonstrates that clients who choose to work with larger firms are much more likely to have a portion of their work completed by paralegals than those who choose a lawyer from a small firm. Almost all (99 percent) of the lawyers practicing in firms with more than 100 lawyers reported that their firms use legal assistants. By contrast, only 34.8 percent of those working at firms of three or fewer lawyers employ paralegals. Of the lawyers who indicated that their firms do not employ paralegals, 56.8 percent reported that the size of their firm would not support legal assistants, and 44.1 percent said that their secretaries assume tasks that otherwise would be assigned to legal assistants.

Advice from the Field

CHARTING YOUR CAREER IN A NEW LANDSCAPE

Robert Half Legal

The paralegal profession is changing dramatically, as new roles and opportunities emerge and glimpses of further shifts appear on the horizon. It's an exciting time to be pursuing a career in the field, whether you're just starting out or you've been working as a paralegal for years.

One of the most promising developments concerns employment potential. The profession is expected to grow faster than the average for all occupations through 2012, according to projections by the Bureau of Labor Statistics in its *Occupational Outlook Handbook*. The primary reason for this robust growth is the trend among an increasing number of corporate legal departments and law firms to hire paralegals to assume some duties of junior staff attorneys or first-year associates. This move is primarily a cost-saving measure since legal assistants can deliver quality results at lower bill rates than attorneys and other legal personnel.

Within this new landscape, the role of paralegals is rapidly evolving. In response to a survey commissioned by Robert Half Legal, 42 percent of attorneys said that within the next ten years, paralegals will have greater professional autonomy.

To succeed as a paralegal now and in the future, you must create a career plan that enables you to make the most of current developments and stay on top of emerging trends. Your plan should be based on three essential components: technical training, specialization, and the cultivation of advanced interpersonal skills.

Robert Half Legal is a leading staffing service specializing in the placement of legal professionals with law firms and corporate legal departments. Based in Menlo Park, Calif., Robert Half Legal has offices in major cities throughout the United States and Canada. Copyright © Robert Half Legal. Reprinted with permission.

Compensation Issues for the Paralegal

Compensation for paralegals is as varied as the working environments and regional locations. As with most jobs and professions, salaries tend to be higher in large metropolitan areas and lower in small and rural areas. Large firms tend to pay more, and small firms tend to pay less. At times, these variations in compensation can be justified by the costs of working in certain locations, such as higher taxation and the cost of commuting.

www

Full article available at the website of NFPA at http://www.paralegals.org/displaycommon.cfm?an=1&subarticlenbr=564

The Future

The future of the paralegal profession may be determined by clients who are unwilling or unable to pay what they see as inflated fees for lawyers. The future also could be dictated by the courts, which, looking at the fairness of charging higher rates for attorneys' tasks that could properly be delegated to a paralegal would result in a lower charge to the client. Two of the future concerns involving paralegals and billings are the following:

1. The cases in which secretarial or clerical tasks are charged to the client as paralegal fees. These tasks are considered overhead (part of the cost of running the office) and should be performed at no additional cost to the client. This is one of the areas in which the definition of paralegal has come into play in the courts. Courts are allowing charges for paralegal fees but not for secretarial fees.
2. The fairness of charging higher rates for attorneys' performing tasks that could properly be delegated to a paralegal, thereby resulting in a lower charge to the client.

Check the available resources for paralegal students at the different national paralegal organizations:

National Federation of Paralegal Associations

http://www.paralegals.org

National Association of Legal Assistants

http://www.nala.org

Association of Legal Administrators

http://www.alanet.org

International Paralegal Management Association

http://www.paralegalmanagement.org/ipma/

NALS ....the Association for Legal Professionals

http://www.nals.org

For instance, summarizing depositions traditionally has been a task delegated to paralegals. Assume that the paralegal takes two hours to complete the task and the paralegal's time is billed to the client at $75 per hour (don't get excited—that doesn't necessarily have any bearing on what you may be paid); the client would be charged $150. For a lawyer to do the same work, if billed out at $175 per hour, the client would be charged $350. Unless there is good reason for the lawyer to do the work, the decision not to delegate the work to a paralegal seems unfair to the client. A number of court decisions are beginning to draw upon these fundamental questions of the fairness and propriety of attorney billings for their services. As other federal and state courts weigh in on this line of decisions, law firms may have to hire more paralegals.

The U. S. Department of Labor has included the paralegal profession among the fastest growing occupations with employment projected to grow much faster than average for all occupations through 2014. This encompasses additional growth of the occupation as well as the need for individuals to replace existing employees. The Labor Department estimates might be increased further by the de facto requirement found in the court opinions that more paralegals be used to perform services instead of attorneys performing the services.

According to the Department of Labor, occupations requiring a postsecondary vocational award or an academic degree accounted for 25 percent of all jobs in 1998, 29 percent of all jobs in 2000, and will account for 42 percent of total job growth from 2000 to 2010.

The best trained, most skilled individual clearly will be the one to get the job. The challenge in obtaining your first job is to demonstrate that you are the best person for the job. Consider the prospective employer comparing the resumes of a number of paralegal job applicants. One paralegal has a high school diploma and a paralegal certificate. Another applicant has an associate degree or even a bachelor's degree in paralegal studies. Which would you hire?

CAREER PLANNING

Career planning should include educational planning. A sound educational plan builds on a sound foundation, at the base of which are general education courses that will assist in any occupational choice and are acceptable in meeting basic core requirements either for an associate's degree or a bachelor's degree. Occupation-related courses such as paralegal specialty courses should be selected with an eye toward transferability and suitability in a higher-level educational pursuit.

This is not to say that all courses must be transferable from school to school or from associate-degree program to bachelor's- or master's-degree program. Something can be learned from every course you take, including the realization that you do not wish to pursue this area of study further. Think of the people you know who have pursued a career only to discover later that they are not interested in this line of work. One of your early educational goals should be to explore areas of your actual or potential interest. Many students even find a career goal after taking one of the dreaded required courses.

Therefore, you should be prepared to explore new areas of specialty and new technology. It is clearer today than ever that successful paralegals have a good foundation in computer skills. Further, you will have to maintain and build upon these skills as ever more sophisticated online service and resources continues.

ROLE OF THE PARALEGAL

Members of the legal profession and the legal community increasingly see the paralegal as a member of the legal services delivery team. As the paralegals' educational level increases, so will the responsibility given to them. Tasks that were once handled solely by an attorney are now being handled by the paralegal under the supervision of an attorney.

In many areas of law, the cost of legal services has increased. The use of paralegals in many cases permits the delivery of quality legal services at a reduced cost to the client. As concern for access to legal services increases, and discussions about mandatory pro bono service by lawyers expand, so does the possibility of involving paralegals in serving low- and moderate-income populations of the United States.

NATIONAL ASSOCIATIONS OF PARALEGALS

In addition to numerous organizations for local and state paralegals and legal assistants, a number of national paralegal/legal assistant organizations support the profession. Four of these are described briefly below.

National Association of Legal Assistants

National Association of Legal Assistants (NALA) is a leading professional association for legal assistants, providing continuing education and professional certification programs for paralegals. Incorporated in 1975, NALA has a membership of more than 18,000 paralegals, through individual members and through its 90 state- and local-affiliated associations.

National Federation of Paralegal Associations

National Federation of Paralegal Associations (NFPA) is a professional organization of state and local paralegal associations founded in 1974 by eight paralegal associations in response to the growing interest in development of the paralegal profession. NFPA has member associations representing more than 17,000 North American paralegals.

Association of Legal Administrators

The **Association of Legal Administrators (ALA)** was founded in 1971 to provide support to professionals involved in the management of law firms, corporate legal departments, and government legal agencies.

Association of Legal Administrators (ALA)
An association of law office managers.

MEET THE COURTHOUSE TEAM

Introduction to the Team

As a paralegal, you will work with a number of different individuals outside of the law office. Many of these people are part of the local, state, and federal court system. Others, though located within the courthouse, are not directly part of the court system but, because of the nature of governmental administration and record keeping, might be related to your job as a paralegal. This text will introduce some of these people to you.

Most courthouses contain offices and personnel involved in administration of the legal process. Generally, the three main areas of law with separate administrative offices are: civil matters; criminal cases; and wills, probate, and orphans court.

In addition, many courthouses house government offices such as the local tax authorities, recorder of deeds, central records office, district attorney/prosecutor, and public defender.

International Paralegal Management Association

The **International Paralegal Management Association,** formerly known as the Legal Assistant Management Association (LAMA), is a North American management association founded in 1984. It has members in metropolitan communities in the United States and Canada. Its members are managers of legal assistants in law firms, corporate law departments, and governmental, judicial, and legal agencies.

National Association of Legal Secretaries

The **National Association of Legal Secretaries (NALS)** was formed in 1949 with the goal of enhancing the careers of legal secretaries. As the profession evolved, so did NALS. The information needed by legal secretaries was changing along with their job descriptions, and the information provided by NALS paralleled this shift. Diversity of membership reflected a changing legal services industry. NALS determined to go with the new name along with the tag line ". . . the association for legal professionals" in 1999. NALS members represent every area of this industry from paralegals and legal assistants to legal administrators and office managers.

QUALIFICATIONS OF A PARALEGAL

What are the qualifications that permit one to call oneself a paralegal or a legal assistant, and to be billed as a paralegal? The answer is not easy to come by. Just as the practice of law falls to the individual states for regulation, so does regulation of the paralegal profession. Presently regulations lack uniformity, either by statute or by court rules. Without a state law or a court rule, perhaps the most consistent and universal recognition of minimum qualifications are those established by the educational guidelines of the American Bar Association's Standing Committee on Legal Assistants and the **American Association for Paralegal Education (AAfPE),** a national association of legal educators. The minimum educational requirements for certification of the educational institutions' program of study have become the de facto standard of the minimum qualifications to call one a paralegal or legal assistant.

PARALEGAL EDUCATION IN THE UNITED STATES

An estimated 1000 paralegal education programs are available in the United States. Some of these programs have obtained ABA approval of their paralegal education program. More than half of the institutions offering paralegal education programs are members of the American Association for Paralegal Education, which, as a condition of institutional membership, requires substantial compliance with the ABA guidelines for approval of a paralegal program.

The American Bar Association and the American Association for Paralegal Education are voluntary programs. Lack of approval of a program does not necessarily mean that the school or the program is of substandard quality but, rather, that it has chosen not to undergo the cost or process for approval by the ABA or for membership in the AAfPE.

American Bar Association Paralegal Education Standards

The American Bar Association, the largest professional legal organization in the United States, has indicated that one of its highest priorities is to increase access to legal services.

CALIFORNIA REGULATION OF PARALEGALS

While other state legislatures and courts wrestle with the minimum standards, California addressed the requirements in a 2000 amendment to the Business and Professional Code that requires a paralegal to possess at least one of the following:

(1) A certificate of completion of a paralegal program approved by the American Bar Association.

(2) A certificate of completion of a paralegal program at an institution that requires a minimum of 24 semester, or equivalent, units in law-related courses, accredited by a national or regional accreditation organization or approved by the Bureau for Private Postsecondary and Vocational Education.

(3) A baccalaureate or advanced degree and minimum of one year of law-related experience under an attorney who is an active member of the State Bar of California.

(4) A high school diploma or general equivalency diploma and a minimum of three years' law-related experience under the supervision of a California attorney, with this training being completed before December 31, 2003.

Other states might look to the California statute in deciding the question of who is qualified by education, training, or work experience.

Its Standing Committee on Legal Assistants was formed more than 25 years ago to "work within the ABA and with other groups to help make quality legal services more accessible and affordable, primarily by fostering the increasingly effective integration of legal assistants—or paralegals—into the legal services delivery team." The Committee has jurisdiction within the ABA over matters relating to the education, training, and use of legal assistants or legal paraprofessionals. Through its Approval Commission, the committee sets the standards for ABA-approved educational programs for education and training of legal assistants.

In 1974 the committee adopted the first guidelines for approval of legal assistant education programs by the ABA's House of Delegates. These guidelines require that

> the institution shall maintain a program for the education of legal assistants that is designed to qualify its graduates to be employed in law-related occupations, including public and private law practice and/or corporate or government law-related activities. (Guidelines G–301)

The process for ABA approval starts with submission of a self-study report intended

> to provide a comprehensive description of all program components with emphasis on the following areas: organization and administration; financial and other resources; advisory committee; educational program, faculty, and program leadership; admissions and student services; placement; library; and physical plant.

After submission and review of the self-study report, an onsite visit is conducted by a three-member team composed of a representative of the ABA Standing Committee on Legal Assistants, an experienced legal assistant, and an educator from another paralegal program, to verify information provided in the self-study and to acquire supplementary information essential to making an evaluation and recommendation to the House of Delegates at its semi-annual meetings in February and August. On each site visit, the faculty, staff, administration, and students of the institution meet to review various documents such as course outlines, faculty evaluations, placement records, and student files.

FORMAL MISSION STATEMENT OF THE AMERICAN BAR ASSOCIATION

- **Goal I** To promote improvements in the American system of justice.
- **Goal II** To promote meaningful access to legal representation and the American system of justice for all persons regardless of their economic or social condition.
- **Goal III** To provide ongoing leadership in improving the law to serve the changing needs of society.
- **Goal IV** To increase public understanding of and respect for the law, the legal process, and the role of the legal profession.
- **Goal V** To achieve the highest standards of professionalism, competence, and ethical conduct.
- **Goal VI** To serve as the national representative of the legal profession.
- **Goal VII** To provide benefits, programs, and services that promote professional growth and enhance the quality of life of the members.
- **Goal VIII** To advance the rule of law in the world.
- **Goal IX** To promote full and equal participation in the legal profession by minorities, women, and persons with disabilities.
- **Goal X** To preserve and enhance the ideals of the legal profession as a common calling and its dedication to public service.
- **Goal XI** To preserve the independence of the legal profession and the judiciary as fundamental to a free society.

Source: "Formal Mission Statement of the American Bar Association." © 1997 by the American Bar Association. Reprinted with permission.

As stated by the ABA,

> Seeking approval from the American Bar Association is a voluntary process initiated by the institution offering the program. Therefore, the lack of approval does not necessarily mean a paralegal program is not of good quality and reputable.

The ABA Standing Committee Guidelines require that instruction be at the post-secondary level and contain at least 60 semester hours including general educational and legal specialty courses. Of these 60 hours, at least 18 must be general education courses and at least 18 must be legal specialty courses.

For purposes of the Guidelines, a "legal specialty course" is interpreted in Guideline G-303(c)d as a course (1) in a specific area of law, procedure, or legal process, (2) which has been developed for legal assistants and emphasizes legal assistant skills, forms, documents, procedures, and legal principles and theories, and (3) which is pertinent to the legal assistants' performance of a job.

To meet the American Bar Association requirements for approval, the program must (1) have been in operation for at least two academic years, (2) have graduated students, and (3) have satisfied the requirements of the ABA Guidelines for Paralegal Education.

AAfPE Role in Paralegal Education

The American Association Paralegal Education is a national organization of paralegal educators and institutions offering paralegal education programs. It has more than 450 members, of which more than 350 are institutional members.

Since its founding, the AAfPE has become the leading professional organization for paralegal education. Paralegal faculty and program directors represent the institutional members in all aspects of the organization's decision-making. As an organization of paralegal educators, it has strived to set minimum educational standards to ensure that graduates of member institutions are well qualified to enter the workforce.

As the profession has advanced, employers and educators have recognized that successful paralegals must possess certain basic skills. AAfPE looked at the issue and published a report that was approved and adopted by its Board of Directors, the Preamble to which states:

> A person must not only possess a common core of legal knowledge, but also must have acquired vital critical thinking, organizational, communication, and interpersonal skills.

Those entering the profession or seeking to develop the necessary skills and knowledge for professional growth and advancement must have an understanding of the basic skills and knowledge. They might possess some of the skills at one level of competency or another. They might have acquired some of the knowledge. They might need to further develop some skills to higher levels of competency and to gain or update additional knowledge as part of their professional education. In any case, they should look at these core competencies as skills and knowledge that should be continually upgraded and updated. Many of the core competencies can be acquired by completing a paralegal education program, whether a certificate program, associate's degree, bachelor's degree, or other continuing professional education programs and courses.

Individuals must take responsibility for their own professional education and growth. A good starting point is an honest and careful review of one's individual skill levels and knowledge in certain categories. The accompanying box, listing skills and knowledge competencies, is a useful guide.

AAfPE Statement on Academic Quality

Selecting an appropriate educational institution for a basic education or an advanced education can be a difficult task. The AAfPE Statement of Academic Quality is a good starting point for measuring the appropriateness of an institution for an individual's education even if the institution is not a member of the association.

GOALS OF THE AMERICAN ASSOCIATION FOR PARALEGAL EDUCATION

- Promote high standards for paralegal education.
- Provide a forum for professional improvement for paralegal educators.
- Plan, promote, and hold annual conferences and seminars.
- Provide technical assistance and consultation services to institutions, educators, and employers.
- Promote research and disseminate information on the paralegal profession.
- Cooperate with the ABA and other institutions and professional associations in developing an approval process for paralegal education programs.
- Promote the goals of the AAfPE through cooperation with other national, regional, and local groups and organizations interested in paralegal education.

SKILL DEVELOPMENT

- Critical thinking skills
- Organizational skills
- General communication skills
- Interpersonal skills
- Legal research skills
- Legal writing skills
- Computer skills
- Interviewing and investigation skills

ACQUISITION OF KNOWLEDGE

- Organization and operation of the legal system
- Organization and operation of law offices
- The paralegal profession and ethical obligations
- Contracts
- Torts
- Business organizations
- Litigation procedures

The AAfPE Statement on Academic Quality provides, in part:

Paralegal education is a unique academic curriculum, composed of both substantive legal knowledge and professional skills, that incorporates legal theory with an understanding of practical applications. This intellectually demanding course of study is derived from the responsibilities of paralegals as legal professionals. It is the philosophy of this organization that a person is qualified as a paralegal with (1) an associate or baccalaureate degree or equivalent course work; and (2) a credential in paralegal education completed in any of the following types of educational programs: associate degree, baccalaureate degree (major, minor or concentration), certificate, or master's degree. AAfPE recognizes these essential components of quality paralegal education programs:

Curriculum Development
Quality paralegal education programs monitor the responsibilities and competencies expected by employers on an ongoing basis. . . .

Facilities
Quality paralegal education programs have a physical learning environment that provides: (1) access to legal research library facilities that include computer-based resources; (2) classrooms that provide opportunities for interaction among students and between students and the instructor and include the necessary equipment and technology to facilitate learning; (3) a convenient physical location for administration/support staff and the provision of student services; and (4) accessibility pursuant to the Americans with Disabilities Act (ADA) requirements.

Faculty
The faculty of quality paralegal education programs consists of legal professionals and, where appropriate, other similarly qualified persons in good standing in their profession who (1) possess expertise and experience in their subject area; (2) have background working as or with paralegals; (3) can demonstrate teaching ability; (4) hold a graduate degree or possess exceptional expertise in the legal subject to be taught; and (5) are committed to the role of paralegals in the delivery of legal services. . . .

Paralegal Instruction
Quality paralegal education programs maintain standards of excellence and include, either as separate classes or with the overall course of study, the following topics:

ethics, substantive and procedural law, the American legal system, delivery of legal services, law offices and related environments, the paralegal profession, legal research and writing, law-related computer skills, legal interviewing and investigation, and areas of legal practice such as those described in AAfPE's Core Competencies for Paralegal Programs; and offer an experiential learning component, such as internship, practicum, or clinical experience.

Related Competencies
Quality paralegal education programs assist their students in acquiring these essential related competencies, primarily in general education: (1) critical thinking skills (analysis, judgment, research, and problem-solving); (2) communication skills (oral, written, nonverbal, and interpersonal); (3) computer skills; (4) computational skills; (5) understanding of ethics; and (6) organizational skills. Graduates also possess a basic understanding of American history, business, and political systems. (Reprinted with the permission of the AafPE)

Types of Educational Programs

The goal of the educational experience is to get a job and be able to perform at a professional level. The demands on paralegals today require them to have higher-level skills and ability than in the past. Whereas basic typing, office, and business communications skills might have been acceptable for a starting position in a law firm twenty years ago, these are not the skills demanded for those looking for a paralegal position today. The core competencies as set by the AAfPE are essential for getting a job and succeeding in the profession today.

More and more employers today also are asking for transcripts showing the courses taken and the minimum number of hours of study as spelled out in the ABA guidelines, even for graduates of educational institutions that have not obtained ABA certification of their programs. The reality is that many attorneys do not know the educational requirements to obtain a paralegal degree or certificate. And in many cases they do not know the elements of the ABA, NFPA, or NALA definitions of paralegal or legal assistant.

Paralegal/legal assistant educational programs generally fall into two categories: (a) those offering a certificate, and (b) those offering a degree, either an **associate's degree** or a **bachelor's degree.** These programs of study may be offered by a two-year community college or junior college or a four-year college or university. A number of business and private (**proprietary**) schools also offer paralegal/legal assistant programs of study.

Associate's degree
A college degree in science (AS) arts (AA), or applied arts (AAS), generally requiring two years of full-time study.

Bachelor's degree
A college degree generally requiring four years of fulltime study.

Proprietary school
Private, as opposed to public, institution, generally for profit, offering training and education.

Students' educational and professional backgrounds will determine, in many cases, which of the programs to select. Those with bachelor's and higher academic degrees may need only the legal specialty courses. Those who come from a specialty background, such as nursing or one heavy in science courses, may want to broaden their education by taking courses of a general nature in addition to the legal specialty courses.

Certificate Programs

Most educational institutions with paralegal/legal assistant programs, both public and private, offer a certificate. The **certificate** recognizes completion of a program of study that requires less than is required to receive a degree. Some certificates award college credits; some do not. For students who already possess a baccalaureate degree, obtaining additional college credits probably isn't an issue. For students without an undergraduate degree, programs that do not offer college credit still can be valuable but should be considered carefully. At the very least, the actual time spent in the classroom should be equivalent to the minimums of college credit courses.

Certificate
A recognition of the completion of a program of study that requires less than that needed for a degree.

Students' concerns should be for what is acceptable in the community in which they intend to work. Those planning to transfer should consider the acceptability of the course for transferring credit to another credit-granting institution. Even if they have no immediate intent to continue in school, they would be wise to plan ahead and not lose the hours and credits they have earned, in the event they later decide to transfer or go on to obtain a degree.

Many professional paralegal organizations are reporting that a bachelor's degree is becoming more necessary to enter the paralegal field and some programs. The U. S. Attorney's Office, for example, is requiring at least a four-year degree to consider individuals for a paralegal position.

Associate Degree Programs

Many community colleges and junior colleges offer an associate degree in science (AS degree) or in arts (AA degree) or applied arts (AAS degree) in paralegal or legal assistant studies. For many students the two-year community college or junior college programs offer a community-based transition into higher education. For others it is a way of getting back into higher education while working at a full-time job or after being in another occupation.

Support services for returning students or students who need additional help are often available. Many of these schools offer English courses for those for whom English is a second language and those returning to school who need a refresher course or help with study skills after years away from school. This also tends to be a cost-effective educational environment for trying different areas of study before finding an area of concentration.

Baccalaureate Programs

Some of the earliest paralegal programs were built on a model in which a bachelor's degree was the prerequisite for entering the paralegal program of study. A number of programs now offer a bachelor's degree in paralegal studies. One national organization has recommended the bachelor's degree as the minimum qualification to enter the profession. The increase in professional recognition of paralegals has resulted in their gaining more responsibility, as well as a growing demand for the skills required to perform the assigned tasks. As the standing of the paralegal on the legal team rises, so will the demand for those with a broad-based educational background to serve in those positions. Four-year programs of study are attempting to meet that demand by merging traditional four-year study core requirements and legal specialty courses.

Consider the family law attorney or paralegal. In the frequently highly charged emotional environment of custody and divorce, knowledge of family and child psychology is essential. For those in an intellectual-property practice, an understanding of science and engineering is a basic requirement. The four-year timeframe allows more flexibility to explore and build skills and knowledge, as well as to meet the increasing demand for more education for paralegals.

Graduate Programs

A few colleges and universities now offer graduate degrees in legal studies. Others offer advanced degrees in related areas such as legal administration.

Specialty Certificates

Specialty certificates, such as the paralegal certificate or the legal nurse consultant certificate, offer an excellent entry point into a paralegal career. Specialty certificates combined with degrees in other fields of study, such as nursing, journalism, and computer science, are like a capstone program preparing a person for entry into a new career. One of the greatest demands has been for those with a background in nursing combined with a paralegal education. A growing number of colleges are offering a certificate in Legal Nurse Consulting.

www

Detailed information on PACE can be obtained at http://www. paralegals.org/displaycommon. cfm?an=17

Paralegal Certification

The National Federation of Paralegal Associations (NFPA) administers an exam to test the competency level of experienced paralegals known as **Paralegal Advance Competency Exam (PACE)**, which requires that:

> "the paralegal cannot have been convicted of a felony nor be under suspension, termination, or revocation of a certificate, registration, or license by any entity."

- "An associates degree in paralegal studies obtained from an institutionally accredited and/or ABA approved paralegal education program; and six (6) years substantive paralegal experience; OR
- A bachelor's degree in any course of study obtained from an institutionally accredited school and three (3) years of substantive paralegal experience; OR
- A bachelor's degree and completion of a paralegal program with an institutionally accredited school; said paralegal program may be embodied in a bachelor's degree; and two (2) years substantive paralegal experience; OR
- four (4) years substantive paralegal experience on or before December 31, 2000."

Those who successfully pass the exam may use the designation "PACE-Registered Paralegal, or "RP." Continued use of the designation requires 12 additional hours of continuing legal or specialty education every 2 years, with at least one hour of legal ethics.

Since 1976, the National Association of Legal Assistants has conferred the **Certified Legal Assistant (CLA)** designation on those who pass its national certification program's two-day comprehensive examination. In 2004, NALA registered the certification mark CP with the U.S. Patent and Trademark Office for those who prefer the term Certified Paralegal. To be eligible to take the exam requires the following.

1. Graduation from a legal assistant program that is:
   - approved by the American Bar Association; or
   - an associate degree program; or
   - a post-baccalaureate certificate program in legal assistant studies; or
   - a bachelor's degree program in legal assistant studies; or
   - a legal assistant program which consists of a minimum of 60 semester hours (900 clock hours or 90 quarter hours) of which at least 15 semester hours (225 clock hours or 22.5 quarter hours) are substantive legal courses.
2. A bachelor's degree in any field plus one year's experience as a legal assistant. Successful completion of at least 15 semester hours (or 22.5 quarter hours or 225 clock hours) of substantive legal assistant courses will be considered equivalent to one year's experience as a legal assistant.
3. A high school diploma or equivalent plus seven (7) year's experience as a legal assistant under the supervision of a member of the Bar, plus evidence of a minimum of twenty (20) hours of continuing legal education credit to have been completed within a two (2) year period prior to the examination date.

To maintain use of the CLA designation, evidence must be submitted of completion of 50 hours of continuing legal assistant education every five years. For those who have achieved the initial designation, NALA also offers specialist credentials for those practicing in a specific area of law, such as bankruptcy, intellectual property, civil litigation, probate, and estate planning. Successful completion of these examinations permits the additional designation CLAS, Certified Legal Assistant–Specialty.

Paralegal Advanced Competency Exam (PACE)
National Association of Paralegal Association's certification program that requires the paralegal to have two years of experience and a bachelor's degree and have completed a paralegal course at an accredited school.

General information about paralegal certification, including requirements, exam subjects, and testing schedule can be found at http://www.nala.org/cert.htm

Certified Legal Assistant (CLA)
Designation by National Association of Legal Assistants for those who take and pass NALA certification program two-day comprehensive examination.

ALS
The basic certification for legal professional of NALS.

PLS
The advanced certification for legal professionals of NALS.

PP
Professional Paralegal certification of NALS.

NALS offers members and nonmembers the opportunity to sit for three unique certifications dedicated to the legal services profession—ALS, PLS, and PP. The exams are of varying levels and are developed by professionals in the industry.

1. **ALS**—the basic certification for legal professionals exam—covers:
   Part 1: Written Communications
   Part 2: Office Procedures and Legal Knowledge
   Part 3: Ethics, Human Relations, and Judgment
2. **PLS**—the advanced certification for legal professionals exam—covers:
   Part 1: Written Communications
   Part 2: Office Procedures and Technology
   Part 3: Ethics and Judgment
   Part 4: Legal Knowledge and Skills
3. **PP**—Professional Paralegal—for professionals performing paralegal duties. examination eligibility requires five years' experience performing paralegal/legal assistant duties (a candidate may receive a partial waiver of one year if he or she has a postsecondary degree, other certification, or a paralegal certificate; a candidate with a paralegal degree may receive a two-year partial waiver). The exam covers:
   Part 1: Written Communications
   Part 2: Legal Knowledge and Skills
   Part 3: Ethics and Judgment Skills
   Part 4: Substantive Law

A comparison of the various exams— NALS, NALA, and NFPA—is presented in Exhibit 1.1.

Minimum Education

IPMA's position is that a baccalaureate degree should be the minimum requirement for employment as a legal assistant. Legal assistants have assumed many responsibilities formerly handled by lawyers. Working with complex legal issues requires that a legal assistant possess clear writing, researching, and critical thinking abilities. Because a strong academic background is essential, a baccalaureate degree should be the minimum requirement for employment as a legal assistant. IPMA believes this accepted professional standard of academic achievement lends greater credibility and respect to the legal profession.

MAKING A PERSONAL ASSESSMENT AND SETTING GOALS

If you are reading this book, you probably have made at least a tentative career goal to enter the paralegal profession, with the ultimate goal of obtaining a job. It should not be "just a job" but, rather, a job that will give you satisfaction and one that you will get up and go to with anticipation, not dread. The paralegal field offers many and varied specialties. An early goal should be to take courses that will introduce you to the specialty you would enjoy most. Maybe you already are well versed in something that will lead to a specialty, such as nursing, one of the sciences, or law enforcement.

One of the first steps is to assess your own skills. What are your other educational skills? What are your personality traits? Do you like working under deadlines or working with certain groups of people, such as elderly people or those with disabilities?

As you will find out, the paralegal profession offers opportunities in many areas of legal specialty and in many types of working environments. Understanding your interests, skills, and desired working conditions and job locations will help you select the best educational path toward achieving your professional goals.

Exhibit 1.1 **Legal certification comparison chart**

Compares the certification exams offered by: NALS . . . the association for legal professionals National Association for Legal Assistants (NALA), National Federation of Paralegal Associations, Inc. (NFPA)

	Professional Paralegal (PP) —NALS	PLS . . . the advanced certification for legal professionals (PLS)—NALS	Certified Legal Assistant (CLA)— or Paralegal (CP)—NALA	Paralegal (RP)— Paralegal Advanced Competency Exam (PACE) Registered
Organization Established	1929, incorporated in 1949	1929, incorporated in 1949	1975	1974
Certification Established	2004	1960	1976	1996
Membership	5,000 individual members $100 new member[7] ($90/yr after) $45 associate[8] $19 student $750 lifetime	5,000 individual members $100 new member[7] ($90/yr after) $45 associate[8] $19 student $750 lifetime	6,000 individual members $99 new member —active[2] $84 associate[3] $40 student $50 sustaining[4]	15,000 (includes affiliate organizations; no information is available on individual members) $60 new member (paralegal or paralegal supervisor) $50 associate[5] $40 student $100 sustaining[6]
Number Certified	339 (eff. 03/06)	5,355 (eff. 03/06)	13,325 CLA (eff. 02/06) 1,126 CLAS (advanced certification)	580 (eff. 12/05)
Eligibility to Test Education and/or Employment	Five years' experience performing paralegal duties Partial waivers: (1) A two-year waiver for a candidate with a paralegal degree, or (2) A maximum one-year waiver for postsecondary degrees, successful completion of the PLS exam, or other certifications	Three years' experience in the legal field Partial waiver: A maximum one-year waiver for postsecondary degrees, successful completion of the ALS exam, or other certifications	(1) Graduation from legal assistant program approved by ABA or associate degree program or postbaccalaureate certificate program in legal assistant studies, or bachelor's degree program in legal assistant studies, or legal assistant program of 60+ hours, 15 hours in substantive legal courses (2) Bachelor's degree in any field plus one	An associates degree in paralegal studies obtained from an institutionally accredited and/or ABA-approved paralegal education program and six years substantive paralegal experience; OR Bachelor's degree in any course of study obtained from an institutionally accredited school and three years of substantive paralegal experience; OR Bachelor's degree and completion of a paralegal program within an institutionally accredited school (which may be embodied in the bachelor's degree) and a minimum of two years substantive paralegal experience; OR

(continued)

Exhibit 1.1 **Legal certification comparison chart** (*continued*)

	Professional Paralegal (PP) —NALS	PLS . . . the advanced certification for legal professionals (PLS)—NALS	Certified Legal Assistant (CLA)— or Paralegal (CP)—NALA	Paralegal (RP)— Paralegal Advanced Competency Exam (PACE) Registered
			year's experience as legal assistant (15 hours of substantive legal courses equivalent to one year's experience as legal assistant)	Four years substantive paralegal experience completed on or before December 31, 2000
			(3) High school diploma or equivalent plus seven years' experience as a legal assistant under supervision of attorney, plus minimum of 20 hours of CLE within two-year period prior to exam date	
Examination Topics	Part 1—Written Communications: Grammar and word usage, spelling, punctuation, number usage, capitalization, composition and expression Part 2—Legal Knowledge and Skills: Legal research, citations, legal terminology, the court system and ADR, and the legal skills of interviewing clients and witnesses, planning and conducting investigations, and docketing Part 3—Ethics and Judgment: Ethical situations involving contact with clients, the public, coworkers, and subordinates; other ethical considerations for the legal profession; decisionmaking and analytical ability; and ability to recognize	Part 1—Written Communications: Grammar and word usage, punctuation, number usage, capitalization, spelling, and composition and expression Part 2—Office Procedures and Technology: Records management, computer information systems, equipment/ information services, office procedures and practices, office accounting Part 3—Ethics and Judgment: Ethical situations involving contact with clients, the public,	Federal law and procedure, major subject areas include communications, ethics, legal research, human relations and interviewing techniques, judgment and analytical ability, legal terminology. Section on Substantive Law includes five miniexaminations covering the American Legal System and four of the following areas: administrative law, bankruptcy, business, organizations/ corporations, contracts, family law, criminal law and procedure, litigation, probate and estate	Domain 1—Adminstration of client legal matters: conflict checks; develop, organize and maintain client files; develop and maintain calendar/tickler systems; develop/maintain databases; coordinate client services Domain II—Development of client legal matters: client interviews; analyze information; collaborate with counsel; prepare, file, and serve legal documents/exhibits; prepare clients/witnesses for legal proceedings Domain III—Factual/legal research: obtain factual/legal information; investigate/compile facts; Inspect/evaluate evidence; ascertain/analyze legal authority Domain IV—Factual/legal writing: communicate with client/counsel; draft legal analytical documents

Exhibit 1.1 **Legal certification comparison chart** *(continued)*

	Professional Paralegal (PP) —NALS	PLS . . . the advanced certification for legal professionals (PLS)—NALS	Certified Legal Assistant (CLA)— or Paralegal (CP)—NALA	Paralegal (RP)— Paralegal Advanced Competency Exam (PACE) Registered
	Part 4—All areas of substantive law, including administrative; business organizations and contracts; civil procedure and litigation; criminal; family; real property; torts; wills, trusts, and estates; admiralty and maritime; antitrust; bankruptcy; environmental; federal civil rights and employment discrimination; immigration; intellectual property; labor; oil and gas; pension and profit sharing; taxation; water; workers' compensation	coworkers; ethical considerations for legal profession; decision-making and analytical ability; ability to recognize priorities Part 4—Legal Knowledge and Skills: Legal Knowledge: citations, legal research, and the ability to prepare legal documents based on oral instructions and materials; all areas of substantive law	planning, real estate.	Domain V—Office Administration: personnel management; acquire technology; coordinate and utilize vendor services; create and maintain library of legal resources; develop/maintain billing system (Ethics embedded throughout)
Length Sites	one day nationally/most major cities	one day nationally/most major cities	two days nationally/most major cities	four hours—200 questions 200+ Sylvan Learning Centers
Frequency	First Saturday in March July at Regional Meetings only; Last Saturday in September (no waiting period to retest)	First Saturday in March July at Regional Meetings only; Last Saturday in September (no waiting period to retest)	March April July December	Within 90 days of approval of application (six-month waiting period to retest)
Cost Member Nonmember	$200 (retake $50/section) $250 (retake $60/section) PLS Members Part 4: $150 (retake $50) PLS Nonmember Part 4: $200 (retake $60)	$150 (retake $40/section) $200 (retake $50/section)	$225 (retake $50/section) $250 (retake $50/section)	$225 (no section retake) $225 (no section retake)
Recertification Frequency	Every five years	Every five years	Every five years	Every two years
CLE Required	75 hours (five hours legal ethics)	75 hours	50 hours	12 hours (one hour legal ethics)
Topics	Education on PP exam topics, teaching, lecturing, writing, earning college credit, earning other certifications	Education on PLS exam topics or teaching, lecturing, writing, earning college credit, earning other certifications	Legal assistant topics or teaching	Substantive law; specific nature of paralegal profession, i.e., computer skills, research techniques, management skills, etc.; ethics

(continued)

Exhibit 1.1 **Legal certification comparison chart, (continued)**

	Professional Paralegal (PP) —NALS	PLS . . . the advanced certification for legal professionals (PLS)—NALS	Certified Legal Assistant (CLA)— or Paralegal (CP)—NALA	Paralegal (RP)— Paralegal Advanced Competency Exam (PACE) Registered
Costs	$75	$75	$50	$25 (if a topic is not pre-approved by NFPA, individual or speaker may request approval—$25 for a speaker or nonmember; $10 for individual member)
American Council on Education College Credit for Certification	Application in process	Yes, up to 27 credits	None	None

1. 200,000 paralegals nationwide per U.S. Department of Labor, Bureau of Labor Statistics, http://stats.bls.gov (3/21/04)
2. Anyone who completed CLA exam; graduated from ABA program for legal assistants; graduated from legal assistant accredited course not ABA approved/not less than 60 semester hours of study; graduated from legal assistant course/not less than six months of in-house training as legal assistant whose attorney–employer attests individual is qualified as legal assistant ("attorney attests"); or earned baccalaureate degree in any field plus at least six months in-house training as legal assistant whose attorney attests; person with at least three years of law-related experience and at least six months in-house training as a legal assistant whose attorney attests; or person who has a minimum of two years in-house training as a legal assistant whose attorney attests.
3. Attorneys, educators, legal assistant supervisors.
4. Individuals, law firms, corporations and legal assistant program representatives who endorse or promote the legal assistant concept or promote the legal assistant profession.
5. Nonvoting; former paralegal or legal professional other than paralegal
6. Nonvoting; persons, partnerships, corporations, associations supporting purposes and activities of NFPA.
7. Members include those who work for attorneys, e.g., paralegals/legal assistants, secretaries, office managers. court personnel.
8. Educators, judges, attorneys

Legal Certification Comparison Chart prepared by Kathleen L. McRae, PLS, RP and Lyn M. Hurlbutt, PP, PLS, CLA, RP, CPS. © NALS, Inc. All rights reserved. NALS is dedicated to enhancing the competencies and contributions of members in the legal services profession. NALS Resource Center, 314 East Third Street, Suite 210, Tulsa, OK 74120 918.582.5188 918.582.5907 (fax) © NALS, Inc. Reprinted with permission. All rights reserved.

Selecting a Specialty

It is never too early to set career goals; although you will find that your final career path will take many bends and turns as you start your first job and learn about the various areas of practice that are available to you. Your ultimate specialty or employer might result from your educational background, such as journalism or medicine, or an area of special interest such as environmental issues, or possibly just a preference to work with certain types of clients such as the elderly or infirm.

And it is never too late to make a career adjustment. Many successful individuals begin a career later in life. Colonel Sanders started Kentucky Fried Chicken late in life. Schools are full of nontraditional students seeking a career change. In the paralegal field we are seeing more and more nurses who, having worked in the medical field for years, are making a career change to the legal field.

Your decision should be based on a self-evaluation of your likes and dislikes, interests, passions, and any physical or geographic limitations. If you hate to fly, you probably will not want a job that requires travel. If you are not comfortable with strangers,

checklist ☑

☐ My current paralegal job-related skills are:

☐ My special interests are:

☐ My passions are:

☐ My personality traits are:

☐ My geographical work and living desires are:

☐ My willingness to accept responsibility is:

☐ My level of self-motivation is:

you probably will not want a job as a paralegal investigator for a litigation firm. If you like books and research, you might want to work as the firm's librarian or researcher.

Assessing Your Background

As the law has become more specialized, so has the demand for paralegals with more than just paralegal skills. Law firms specializing in an area such as medical malpractice frequently look for paralegals who also have a medical background such as nursing. Firms with large, complex litigation cases often look for someone with computer database skills who can manage the files. Paralegals with journalism experience and training frequently are sought out for their interviewing and writing skills.

Your personal background can be an asset when added to your paralegal certificate or degree. As you begin your professional training, take stock of your entire educational background, special skills, and talents, as well as personal areas of interest.

Doing a self-assessment early in your studies offers you an opportunity to recognize your strengths and develop them and to acknowledge weaknesses that you need to work on to permit your personal and professional growth.

Assessing Your Skills

You may well have a number of personal skills that will benefit you in the future as a paralegal. You might have great interpersonal skills, communicate well orally and in writing, and be a highly motivated person—all qualities of a good paralegal.

Individuals with language skills are particularly in demand in international law, as well as in working with clients who lack English-language skills. The paralegal who understands a second language and the cultural nuances of the client's background can be invaluable.

Assessing Your Interests

What are your personal interests? Are you an active outdoors person in your free time, for whom working on environmental issues would be of high interest and satisfaction? Do you find yourself drawn to volunteering or working in your free time with shut-ins and elderly people?

Selecting Your Electives

Becoming aware of your interests and background knowledge enables you to select the elective course that can qualify you for work in a specialty field of law. Taking electives is a good way to explore an area in which you think you might be interested, without committing to more than one semester or a few credits of study. Many students find new interests and a potential career direction after taking courses in areas they had not considered previously. For example, you may have been reading in newspapers and magazines, and following on television, stories about the high-technology industries and wondered how your career goal as a paralegal might fit into this growth area.

One of the fastest growing fields is that of intellectual property law. In an age of dot coms, computers, and a growing global marketplace, protection of intellectual property has become a critical concern for individuals and companies alike. Taking a three-credit course in intellectual property may well introduce the paralegal student to a new area of interest in a potential growth area of the paralegal profession. This is also true for other emerging areas in the paralegal profession, such as environmental law and legal nurse consulting.

PARALEGAL SKILLS

The skills needed by a paralegal are varied and depend, in some cases, on the nature of the legal specialty in which one works. Common to all paralegals are certain basic skills and attributes including communication skills, initiative, resourcefulness, commitment or "stick-to-itiveness," and self-motivation, among others.

Everyone has goals in life. You might be an accomplished jogger who longs to win the Boston Marathon, or a skilled writer who has visions of writing the great American novel. Achieving most goals requires some set of skills. If your goal is to be a successful paralegal, you will need certain basic skills. You may possess some of these already, and may need to acquire others. Some of the basic skills you already have are

- the ability to read English—unless someone is reading this book to you
- the ability to communicate at some level in writing or speaking
- initiative—because you have signed up for this course or have picked up this book to read and learn about the paralegal profession

In addition, you may have skills such as

- facility with computers and the Internet
- the ability to speak a second or third language
- a background in medicine, engineering, business, or other academic or occupational area

Some other skills are less obvious—resourcefulness, commitment or stick-to-itiveness, analytical skills and interpersonal skills including cultural sensitivity—so we will explore them in more depth. We cannot all run a marathon or type 160 words a minute, but we all can acquire most of the basic skills by making an effort to improve ourselves and attain the knowledge base to achieve most, if not all, of our goals.

Many people achieve much more than they, themselves, and others believed they were capable of achieving—by just plain hard work. If you want something bad enough and are willing to work hard enough, you can achieve your personal and professional goals. A good starting point in achieving your goals is to under-

checklist ✔

☐ My strengths:

☐ How I can capitalize on my strengths:

☐ My weaknesses:

☐ How I can overcome my weaknesses:

stand your strengths and weaknesses, capitalize on the strengths, and work on improving the weaknesses.

Resourcefulness

Resourcefulness is the ability to meet and handle a situation and find solutions to problems. It is one of the most valuable skills anyone can have—and one that is not easily taught. A resourceful person in the office is sometimes referred to as the "can-do" person on the team. This is the person who usually finds some creative way to accomplish what everyone else has given up on. Certainly, creativity is involved—solving the problem by thinking outside the box and not limiting the solution to tried-and-true methods.

The skill of organizing includes the ability to

- categorize
- prioritize
- organize
- utilize time efficiently

When everyone else says, "I can't find this witness," the resourceful person tries a new approach and finds the witness. When others use only the standard telephone directories, the resourceful person uses the cross-reference directory. When local telephone directories do not yield results, resourceful people use the national telephone directories on CD and the online Internet telephone directories.

In the legal workplace the person who gets noticed is the one who finds a way to get the job done in time for the hearing, meeting, or arbitration. This is the person who is willing to use unconventional ways to get the job finished, such as when the power goes out or the computer system crashes just before a deadline. Lawyers want resourceful people on their team and reward them to keep them on the team.

Commitment

Commitment means finishing what one starts out to do or complete. From our childhood we remember the story of the tortoise and the hare (rabbit), in which the tortoise wins the race by being "slow and steady." The tortoise wins in part because of commitment—putting everything into the race and not stopping until the job is done. Many people start jobs and don't finish them. Others start what seems to be an insurmountable task and—to their amazement and maybe ours—finish, and finish well. Taking on an assignment in a law office requires commitment. Team members are expected to finish the task, whether it is researching a case, writing a brief, filing a pleading, or organizing a file.

As a professional, you are expected to finish the tasks within the assigned time-frame. There is no excuse for not doing some tasks, such as filing the complaint with the court before the statute of limitations expires, or getting the brief to the court by the court-imposed deadline. Even a simple thing like getting to court on time requires commitment.

Not everyone has the necessary commitment or wants to take on the responsibility of meeting commitments. You have to decide whether you are willing to make the commitment. Others will be depending on you, and if you do not want to commit, admit it to yourself and to the others who are depending on you, and then choose some other activity or profession. Choosing a profession, whether it is the legal profession, the paralegal profession, the medical profession, or the accounting profession, requires a commitment to serve others. As a professional, you are making a commitment to your clients that you will provide the best professional advice, skill, and effort. They depend on this professionalism and the necessary commitment.

Analytical Skills

Analytical skills allow one to follow a step-by-step process to solve a problem. It could be finding a missing witness by looking in telephone books, or determining that the person is part of a group, such as a professional society or an organization that publishes a membership directory. Solving these types of problems requires analytical skills to figure out, for instance, what made a bottle explode, injuring a client. Determining the actual cause requires a step-by-step analysis of the potential reasons and the narrowing down of possible causes.

One of the basic skills that law students and paralegal students are taught is legal analysis, the ability to identify the facts and legal issues and contrast and compare them to the law and to other cases. This is a skill that develops with time. As you learn the elements of crimes, torts, and other areas of law, you will learn the individual parts of each. In contracts law, you will learn what conduct is a valid acceptance of a contract offer, and in tort law, what constitutes reasonable conduct under the circumstances.

Interpersonal Skills

Vital to paralegal success, as well as to success in other endeavors, is the ability to work with people. To categorize people, coworkers, colleagues, and employers might be unfair, but we all do it. We think—and sometimes say—things like, "He's a pleasure to work with" or, "She has clients eating out of her hand." Conversely, we might say things like, "She's the most negative person I know," or "He's only out for himself." These comments reflect the other person's interpersonal skills (or lack thereof), the ability to work with and communicate with others.

How we relate to others can make the job easier or harder. These others include not just coworkers as members of the legal team but also clients, witnesses, and opposing parties. Obviously, everyone in the firm or on the team must have a level of trust and confidence in the others on the team. People who have a good working relationship accomplish more and enjoy doing it. By contrast, conflict and tension make the job harder and can cause people to take shortcuts and avoid contact, which can result in poor performance and potential malpractice.

Not everyone has the personality to deal with every type of situation and every type of personality—for example, dealing with clients. But everyone on the

---

CREATING AN IMPRESSION

Unless you are intentionally trying to create a different impression, try to

- have a positive attitude
- be diplomatic
- be flexible
- establish good rapport with others
- be a team player
- be resourceful
- be adaptable
- be thorough

legal team has to develop the skills to work with people and recognize when they may have to have someone else handle certain aspects of a case or client. The skill is in recognizing when and how they can affect relationships and results. Some might call this "sensitivity"—to other people's needs, desires, wants, likes, and dislikes.

Cultural differences are discussed later, but in the American culture, for example, people tend to be sensitive to odors—breath, body, environmental. We do not want to offend. Our use of language is another area of sensitivity. We try to avoid using words that we believe will offend the other person in a specific circumstance, such as telling off-color jokes in a religious setting in front of a person of the cloth.

The starting point in working with attorneys, paralegals, and support staff, clients and opposing counsel, court personnel and others, is to be sensitive to issues such as these. What offends you probably offends others. Being sensitive to how others react to your words, conduct, and actions can provide good clues as to what is acceptable and what is not.

In the past, how we related to others and how others perceived us was measured by direct face-to-face contact, telephone contact, and written communications. Today we have to add to those forms of communication the way we write emails and use electronic communications. These technological advances make our communications more immediate. Too many happy faces and frowning faces, such as :) or :(in an email could be interpreted as overfamiliarity. THE USE OF ALL CAPITAL LETTERS might be interpreted as shouting at the reader. Poor spelling and bad grammar in emails are likely to be seen as less than professional or pure sloppiness or carelessness. In the past, letters were dictated, typed, proofread, and then signed. Today we dash off an email without much thought—and sometimes it reflects just that. How our clients view our capabilities and skill now might be measured by that quick email response.

Communication Skills

Communication means expressing ideas effectively. The practice of law requires good communication, both oral and written. The lawyer and the paralegal who work together must be able to communicate assignments and information with clarity and, frequently, brevity. Over time, communication will improve, as each person comes to understand what the other is really asking or saying.

Communication is made complex by subtleties, nuances, and expressions that may require interpretation or explanation. For example, older attorneys who are used to using traditional methods of research may ask the new paralegal (who has a deep understanding of computer research methods and little traditional book experience) to "check the pocket parts." This means checking for the latest update or change to a statute or case law. Or asking a paralegal to "Shepardize" a case may have no meaning to one who has learned only the West system, in which the method for checking other cases is called KeyCiting, or the Loislaw system, which refers to this as GlobalCiting.

Communication can be a major problem in the fast-paced office when the litigation attorney sends a message from court in the middle of a case to the support paralegal at the office, by a two-way pager, after the other side has brought up an unexpected case in argument to the court. Nowadays, we rarely have the luxury of time to develop a common written and oral language base for communication among the paralegal, clients, opposing attorneys, and court personnel. Letters, pleadings, contracts, and other written documents must be clear and accurate. In

COMMUNICATION SKILLS

How well do you

- read with comprehension?
- listen effectively and accurately and interpret nonverbal communication?
- write in clear, concise, and grammatically correct English?
- speak in clear, concise, and grammatically correct English?
- use language to persuade?
- tailor the nature of the communication to maximize understanding in the intended audience, including people with different levels of education and different cultural backgrounds?

Source: American Association for Paralegal Education

checklist ☑

- ☐ Skills I need to acquire:

- ☐ Skills I need to strengthen:

- ☐ Courses I should take:

- ☐ Extracurricular activities for the resume:

- ☐ Interim work experience I should seek:

- ☐ Volunteer activities:

- ☐ Short-term career goals:

- ☐ Long-term career goals:

www

The Kathryn Myers' student portfolio article and other information for students can be found on the American Association for Paralegal Education website at www.aafpe.org

many situations, only one document must carefully communicate the idea, request, or demand.

Oral communication also must be clear and precise. The old adage still holds true: First impressions matter. If a first discussion in person or by telephone is filled with slang and poor grammar, the impression may affect the client's or court's view of the firm's professionalism, ability, and legal skills. It can influence the client's decision to stay with the firm or not, the judge's granting the request, or the court clerk's giving you the help you need.

Advice from the Field ··

THE STUDENT PORTFOLIO

Kathryn Myers, Coordinator, Paralegal Studies, Saint Mary-of-the-Woods College, Paralegal Studies Program

A portfolio is a purposeful collection of student work that is accumulated over time. The material reveals the extent of student learning, achievement, and development. The "portfolio system" is intended to specify knowledge and competence in areas considered necessary to successfully work as a paralegal/ legal assistant while leaving the selection of means of documentation of competency to the individual student. Documentation of knowledge and skill acquisition can take a variety of forms including, but not limited to,

  letters of support

  diaries

  videotapes and audiotapes of work

  pleadings

  memoranda

  course projects

  registration receipts from continuing education and other conferences attended

  proof of membership in professional organizations

  subscriptions to legal publications

Typically, much of the material can be compiled from projects and activities required within courses.

PROCEDURE

The portfolio shall contain documentation of knowledge and skill acquisition based on the Core Competencies established by the American Association for Paralegal Education. Those core competencies are divided into two areas—skill development and acquisition of knowledge. Within those areas are competencies based on:

SKILL DEVELOPMENT

  critical thinking skills

  organizational skills

  general communication skills

  interpersonal skills

  legal research skills

  legal writing skills

  computer skills

  interviewing and investigation skills

ACQUISITION OF KNOWLEDGE

  organization and operation of the legal system

  organization and operation of law offices

  the paralegal profession and ethical obligations

  contracts

  torts

  business organizations

  litigation procedures

It is understood that the areas may overlap somewhat and that these areas do not cover all competencies associated with the program, student growth, or professional success. However, students who perfect these competencies and who perform from this educational base have a foundation for success.

It is suggested that the student purchase a secure container to collect and organize the material [such as] a hanging file folder or file box. This portfolio may be maintained on computer disk; however, you will not have any graded materials if this is the only method of collection you use.

Students should keep a log of all materials completed. When completing each assignment, [they should] enter the document in the log, with a column to check for inclusion in the campus portfolio and another to check for inclusion in the professional portfolio. Some documents may, of course, overlap in their application.

Students are responsible for the contents of their portfolios. The student should periodically review the contents of the portfolio and add or remove materials based on decisions as to the extent to which the contents adequately represent knowledge and skill acquisition in each of the areas outlined below. This portfolio is not intended to be a compilation of senior level work; rather, it is useful to provide work of varying levels of efficiency to show, among other things, growth and improvement.

CONTENT

To be a successful paralegal/legal assistant, the student must possess a common core of legal knowledge as well as acquire vital critical thinking, organizational, communication, and interpersonal skills. Courses in a student's program should provide the student with the means to

(continued)

Advice from the Field ··

(continued)

develop the competencies, which have been divided into the following sections:

Area 1 Understanding the Profession and Its Ethical Obligations

Area 2 Research

Area 3 Legal Writing

Area 4 Basic Skills

Area 5 Acquisition of Legal Knowledge

Area 6 Professional Commitment Beyond Course-work

Area 7 Evaluation of Professional Growth/ Evaluation of Program

Appendix

GUIDELINES FOR SELECTING ENTRIES

When selecting entries, students should bear in mind that each piece is part of a much larger whole and that, together, the artifacts and rationale make a powerful statement about individual professional development. Asking the following questions may help with decision making.

1. What do I want my portfolio to show about me as a paralegal? What are my attributes as a paralegal?
2. What do I want my portfolio to demonstrate about me as a learner? How and what have I learned?
3. What directions for my future growth and development does my self-evaluation suggest? How can I show them in my portfolio?
4. What points have been made by others about me as a paralegal and learner? How can I show them in my portfolio?
5. What effect does my professionalism have upon my peers? How can I show this in my portfolio?
6. What overall impression do I want my portfolio to give a reviewer about me as a learner and as a paralegal?

When decision-making about what to include becomes a challenge, it may be helpful to look at each artifact and ask yourself, "What would including this item add that has not already been said or shown?" Remember that portfolios create representative records of your professional development; they are not intended to be comprehensive.

VALUES AND ATTITUDES

Values and attitudes determine the choices we make in our lives. They cross the boundaries of subject-matter areas. Thus, in this final section of your portfolio, you are asked to look at your own values and attitudes and then write a one- to three-page paper in which you reflect upon your own values. Identify one or more values that are important to you. Explain how they influence your choices as a person, parent, future paralegal, voter, and/or citizen of the global community. Include specific examples.

The following questions may help you choose a topic for your essay: What does it mean to be honest? fair? tolerant? open to new ideas and experiences? respect evidence? Which is more important—decreasing the production of greenhouse gases or preserving jobs? The right to choose how many children we want or controlling world population growth? Freedom to produce pornographic art or the right of children to be sheltered from such experiences? Spending more time with your children or getting a second job so you can buy things you want?

There are no easy answers to these questions. Have fun thinking about your own values. Remember to include specific examples from your own life!

TRANSCRIPTS

Include copies of unofficial transcripts from all colleges and universities that you have attended.

Degree evaluation

Graduation evaluation

Awards or recognitions

Include a copy of your degree evaluation, if you received one.

Include a copy of your graduation evaluation.

Include copies of awards or recognitions you have received.

PROFESSIONAL PORTFOLIO

Modify this inclusive portfolio into a professional portfolio. This professional portfolio will be representative, not comprehensive. Each artifact chosen for inclusion should represent at least one significant aspect of you and/or your

Advice from the Field ·····················

(continued)

accomplishments that can be translated into employability. Use these guidelines to prepare your professional portfolio:

1. Prepare your portfolio as a showcase of your best work—your highest achievements. This will involve selecting from artifacts in your portfolio and adding new ones.
2. Do not send your portfolio when you apply for a job. Rather, include in your cover letter a statement concerning your portfolio. For example: "Throughout my paralegal studies program at _____ College, I developed a professional portfolio that clearly and concisely exhibits my attributes as a paralegal. I would be pleased to share this portfolio with you during an interview."
3. If granted an interview, take your portfolio with you. Be prepared to present the highlights. Practice presenting it effectively. In some instances, you might be asked to present it at the beginning of the interview, and in other instances you might use it as a source of evidence or enhancement of a point you make in the interview. Interviewing practices vary widely from employer to employer. Portfolios are most likely to be reviewed in situations where the employer is familiar with the abilities of a paralegal.
4. If the interviewer(s) is particularly interested and would like to examine your portfolio more closely, offer to leave it if at all possible. You should make explicit arrangements for collecting it and, of course, follow through as planned. It could be that

your portfolio will create the impression that tips the scales in your favor.

5. Remember—it is likely that some people in a position to hire are not familiar with professional portfolios as you know them. Take time to concisely explain that developing your portfolio has been a process of reflection and evaluation that has helped you to know yourself as a paralegal and to establish a foundation for career-long professional development. To some extent, presenting your portfolio will inform the interviewer about both you and the portfolio concept and process.
6. Keep your portfolio up to date. As you continue to gain experience and to grow professionally, alter it to reflect your development. It is not only your first job application that may be enhanced by a well prepared and presented portfolio but developing your portfolio is an excellent foundation for meeting any expectation of continuing legal education.

CONCLUSION

It is my hope and intention that by your creating this portfolio, you have an opportunity to reflect upon your education and to emphasize to yourself and others that you are capable and qualified to perform as a paralegal. It is time to believe in you. Good luck!

Reproduced with permission of Kathryn Myers.

Legal Terminology

ALS basic certification for legal professionals   18

American Association for Paralegal Education (AAfPE)   10

American Bar Association (ABA)   4

Association of Legal Administrators (ALA)   9

Associate's degree   15

Bachelor's degree   15

Certificate   15

Certified Legal Assistant (CLA)   17

International Paralegal Management Association (IPMA)   10

Legal assistant   4

National Association of Legal Assistants (NALA)   4

National Association of Legal Secretaries (NALS)   10

National Federation of Paralegal Associations (NFPA)   4

Paralegal   4

Paralegal Advanced Competency Exam (PACE)   17

PLS advanced certification for legal professionals   18

Professional Paralegal (PP)   18

Proprietary school   15

Summary

CHAPTER *1*   THE PARALEGAL PROFESSION

What Is a Paralegal?

Definition	A paralegal, or legal assistant, is "a person qualified by education, training, or work experience who is employed or retained by a lawyer, law office, corporation, governmental agency or other entity who performs specifically delegated substantive legal work for which a lawyer is responsible."

What Do Paralegals Do?

Functions of Paralegals	The primary function of paralegals is to assist attorneys in preparing for hearings, trials, meetings, and closings.

Opportunities for Paralegals

Compensation Issues for the Paralegal	In 2004, paralegals held about 224,000 jobs in the United States, with median annual earnings of $39,130. The U.S. Department of Labor projects that this profession will continue to be among the fastest growing through the year 2014.

The Future

Career Planning	As courts require the use of paralegals to reduce legal costs, law firms may have to hire more paralegals and delegate work to them in fairness to clients and propriety in billing practice.
Education	1. General education courses 2. Associate's degree or bachelor's degree

Role of the Paralegal

Level of Responsibility	The paralegal is a member of the legal services delivery team with responsibilities commensurate with his or her education and experience.

National Associations of Paralegals

Major Associations	1. National Association of Legal Assistants 2. National Federation of Paralegal Associations 3. Association of Legal Administrators 4. Legal Assistant Management Association

Qualifications of a Paralegal

Minimum Qualifications	Established by the educational guidelines of the American Bar Association's Standing Committee on Paralegals and American Association for Paralegal Education.

Paralegal Education in the United States

Standards	1. American Bar Association Paralegal Education Standards 2. AAfPE in Paralegal Education 3. AAfPE Statement of Academic Quality
Types of Education Programs	1. Certificate programs 2. Associate degree programs 3. Baccalaureate programs 4. Graduate programs 5. Specialty certificates

Paralegal Certification	PACE (Paralegal Advance Competency Exam) of the National Federation of Paralegal Associations CLA (Certified Legal Assistant) of the National Association of Legal Assistants ALS (the basic certification for legal professionals of NALS) PLS (the advanced certification for legal professionals of NALS) PP (Professional Paralegal certification of NALS)

Making a Personal Assessment and Setting Goals

Making a Personal Assessment	1. What are your other educational skills? 2. What are your personality traits? 3. Do you like working under deadlines? 4. Do you like working with certain groups of people? 5. What are your personal interests? 6. Recognize your strengths 7. Acknowledge weaknesses
Setting Goals	Find a career that will give you satisfaction

Paralegal Skills

	1. Depends in some cases, on the nature of the legal specialty in which one works. 2. Resourcefulness 3. Commitment or "stick-to-itiveness" 4. Analytical skills 5. Interpersonal skills 6. Communication skills

▶WORKING THE WEB

1. Download a copy of the latest edition of the ABA Standing Committee on Paralegals *Update Newsletter* at **www.abanet.org/ legalservices/paralegals/home.html**

2. What advice does the ABA Standing Committee on Paralegals offer in its publication on *Getting Started As a Pro Bono Legal Assistant*. **www.abanet.org/ legalservices/paralegals/publications.html**

3. The *Occupational Outlook Handbook* is updated regularly. Download a copy of the current version on Paralegals and Legal Assistants and compare the salary ranges with those in this text. Have they changed? **www.bls.gov/oco/ocos114.htm**

4. One of the significant issues for paralegals over the past years has been whether paralegals are classified as exempt or nonexempt according to the U.S. Department of Labor regulations. Download a copy of the current Overview for Executive, Administrative, Professional, Computer, & Outside Sales Employees, and highlight the information that applies to paralegals. **www.dol.gov/esa/regs/ compliance/whd/fairpay/main.htm**

5. Print out a copy of the Mission Statement or Homepage of each of the major national paralegal associations.
   a. International Paralegal Management Association **www.paralegalmanagement.org**
   b. NALS . . . . the Association for Legal Professionals **http://www.nals.org**
   c. National Federation of Paralegal Associations **www.paralegals.org**
   d. National Association of Legal Assistants **www.nala.org**
   e. Association of Legal Administrators **www.alanet.org**

6. Compare your skills with the list of knowledge or competencies required of principal legal administrators at **http://www.alanet.org/ education/knowledgelist.html**

▶CRITICAL THINKING AND WRITING QUESTIONS

1. How does the American Bar Association define the term "paralegal"?
2. What are the minimum qualifications that a paralegal should meet?
3. What is the role of the paralegal in the legal system?
4. Why should those planning to become paralegals or legal assistants get a well-grounded education and develop the necessary skills?
5. What is the difference between the job of a legal secretary, legal administrator, or legal assistant manager and that of a paralegal?
6. How can one satisfy the court that he or she is qualified as a paralegal and not as a legal secretary?
7. Based on the AAfPE core competencies, what kinds of assignments and tasks should you expect in your paralegal education?
8. Based on the AAfPE core competencies, prepare a plan of action for improving your skills and knowledge.
9. What is the advantage to the paralegal in obtaining the PACE or CLA designation?
10. What educational plan makes the most sense for you? Why?
11. How can a paralegal demonstrate the qualifications for employment as a paralegal?
12. Why would an employer, such as the U.S. Attorney's office, require a four-year degree for those seeking a paralegal position?
13. Complete the checklist "Career Planning" and assess your personal skills and professional goals. Based on your answers, how well prepared are you for a career as a paralegal? What skills need development?
14. How does assessing your interests and skills help in choosing a career path?
15. What skills are required to be a paralegal and why are they important?
16. Complete the "Strengths & Weaknesses" checklist in this chapter.
17. Why are good English writing and speaking skills important for the paralegal?
18. Complete the "My Career Roadmap" checklist in this chapter.
19. How can you use the "Strengths & Weaknesses" checklist in preparing your personal career roadmap?
20. What advantages might a person have in entering the paralegal profession later in life?
21. What actions have you observed in other people that demonstrated their resourcefulness? Have others ever told you that you are resourceful?
22. How can you demonstrate the characteristic of commitment?
23. Start to network by setting up a meeting with a working paralegal and preparing a list of questions to ask at that meeting.

▶ETHICS ANALYSIS AND DISCUSSION QUESTIONS

1. Does your state by statute, regulation, code, ethics rule, or court rule define "Paralegal" or "Legal Assistant?" If it does, what is that definition and where is it so defined? If not, should it formally define the term?
2. Does your state have a statute or court rule on the regulation of the paralegal or legal assistant practice? What are the requirements to practice as a paralegal or legal assistant? Does the law define the practice in some other terminology?
3. Does your state have minimum educational requirements for paralegals? Should there be a set of minimum qualifications?
4. Does having a set of minimum educational requirements eliminate the need for a set of ethical guidelines?

▶DEVELOPING YOUR COLLABORATION SKILLS

Working on your own or with a group of other students assigned by your instructor, review the scenario at the beginning of the chapter discussing the employment options and educational issues involved.

1. Discuss why or why not Ethan and Ariel should consider a paralegal career. What are the advantages or disadvantages? What strengths or skills do Ethan and Ariel bring to this type of career choice?
2. Working individually or in a group, complete the following:
   a. Summarize, in writing, your career advice to Ethan and/or Ariel.
   b. Share your advice with other students or groups. Does your group have any additional advice or recommendations?
   c. Take on the role of Ethan and/or Ariel. Might they have any other questions for Mr. Marshall about the paralegal profession? Make a list of additional questions. Where might Ethan and Ariel get additional information about the paralegal profession?
3. Select a spokesperson who can summarize and present your recommendations in class.

▶PARALEGAL PORTFOLIO EXERCISE

Using a three-ring binder with tabbed sections listed below, start to create a hardcopy portfolio of your work and accomplishments in this course. Please also include any work you are doing in other courses that best represents your growing "skill set." Prepare binder tabs with the headings listed below and insert into your three-ring binder:

A. Understanding the Profession and Its Ethical Obligations

B. Research

C. Legal Writing

D. Basic Skills

E. Acquisition of Legal Knowledge

F. Professional Commitment Beyond Coursework

G. Evaluation of Professional Growth/ Evaluation of Program

H. Appendix

▶LEGAL ANALYSIS AND WRITING CASES

Doe v. Condon   *532 S.E.2d 879(S.C. 2000)*

The Unauthorized Practice of Law and the Paralegal

A paralegal asked the court if he could conduct unsupervised "wills and trusts" seminars for the public, "emphasizing" living trusts during the course of his presentation, answer estate-planning questions from the audience and proposed a fee-splitting arrangement with his attorney–employer.

The South Carolina Supreme Court ruled: "The activities of a paralegal do not constitute the practice of law as long as they are limited to work of a preparatory nature, such as legal research, investigation, or the composition of legal documents, which enables licensed attorney–employer to carry a given matter to a conclusion through his own examination, approval, or additional effort.

. . . The paralegal plays a supporting role to the supervising attorney. Here the roles are reversed. The attorney would support the paralegal. Petitioner would play the lead role, with no meaningful attorney supervision and the attorney's presence and involvement only surfaces on the back end. Meaningful attorney supervision must be present throughout the process. The line between what is and what is not permissible conduct by a non-attorney is sometimes unclear as a potential trap for the unsuspecting client. . . . It is well settled the paralegal may not give legal advice, consult, offer legal explanations, or make legal recommendations."

Questions

1. Why is the practice of law limited to licensed attorneys?
2. What tasks may a paralegal perform?
3. What tasks may a paralegal not perform?
4. Why is the answering of legal questions about the need for a will or a trust the unauthorized practice of law (UPL)?
5. Why is a fee-splitting arrangement between a lawyer and a paralegal prohibited?

Note: If in South Carolina, include the parallel citation: 341 S.C. 22. The Lexis citation for this case is 2000 S.C. LEXIS 125.

▶WORKING WITH THE LANGUAGE OF THE COURT CASE

Missouri v. Jenkins

491 U.S. 274 (1989)
Supreme Court of the United States

Read the following case excerpts. Information on preparing a briefing is provided in Appendix A: How To Brief a Case. In your brief, prepare a written answer to each of the following questions.

1. What is the difference between "market rates" for paralegals and cost to the attorney for paralegal service?

2. Does billing for paralegal services at market rates unfairly benefit the law firm?

(continued)

3. According to this court, how is a reasonable attorney's fee calculated?
4. How does the public benefit from allowing paralegals to be billed at market rates?

5. Does this court believe that a reasonable attorney's fee should include paralegal fees?

Brennan, J., delivered the opinion of the Court.

This is the attorney's fee aftermath of major school desegregation litigation in Kansas City, Missouri. We [are hearing this case to decide] should the fee award compensate the work of paralegals and law clerks by applying the market rate for their work?

I

This litigation began in 1977 as a suit by the Kansas City Missouri School District (KCMSD), the school board, and the children of two school board members, against the State of Missouri and other defendants. The plaintiffs alleged that the State, surrounding school districts, and various federal agencies had caused and perpetuated a system of racial segregation in the schools of the Kansas City metropolitan area. . . . After lengthy proceedings, including a trial that lasted 7½ months during 1983 and 1984, the District Court found the State of Missouri and KCMSD liable. . . . It ordered various intradistrict remedies, to be paid for by the State and KCMSD, including $260 million in capital improvements and a magnet-school plan costing over $200 million.

The plaintiff class has been represented, since 1979, by Kansas City lawyer Arthur Benson and, since 1982, by the NAACP Legal Defense and Educational Fund, Inc. (LDF). Benson and the LDF requested attorney's fees under the Civil Rights Attorney's Fees Awards Act of 1976, 42 U.S.C. § 1988. Benson and his associates had devoted 10,875 attorney hours to the litigation, as well as 8,108 hours of paralegal and law clerk time. For the LDF, the corresponding figures were 10,854 hours for attorneys and 15,517 hours for paralegals and law clerks. Their fee applications deleted from these totals 3,628 attorney hours and 7,046 paralegal hours allocable to unsuccessful claims against the suburban school districts. With additions for postjudgment monitoring and for preparation of the fee application, the District Court awarded Benson a total of approximately $1.7 million and the LDF $2.3 million. . . .

Both Benson and the LDF employed numerous paralegals, law clerks (generally law students working part-time), and recent law graduates in this litigation. The court awarded fees for their work based on Kansas City market rates for those categories. As in the case of the attorneys, it used current rather than historic market rates in order to compensate for the delay in payment. It therefore awarded fees based on hourly rates of $35 for law clerks, $40 for paralegals, and $50 for recent law graduates. [. . .]

III

Missouri's second contention is that the District Court erred in compensating the work of law clerks and paralegals (hereinafter collectively "paralegals") at the market rates for their services, rather than at their cost to the attorney. While Missouri agrees that compensation for the cost of these personnel should be included in the fee award, it suggests that an hourly rate of $15—which it argued below corresponded to their salaries, benefits, and overhead—would be appropriate, rather than the market rates of $35 to $50. According to Missouri, § 1988 does not authorize billing paralegals' hours at market rates, and doing so produces a "windfall" for the attorney.

We begin with the statutory language, which provides simply for "a reasonable attorney's fee as part of the costs." Clearly, a "reasonable attorney's fee" cannot have been meant to compensate only work performed personally by members of the bar. Rather, the term must refer to a reasonable fee for the work product of an attorney.

Thus, the fee must take into account the work not only of attorneys but also of secretaries, messengers, librarians, janitors, and others whose labor contributes to the work product for which an attorney bills her client; and it also must take account of other expenses and profit. The parties have suggested no reason why the work of paralegals should not be similarly compensated, nor can we think of any. We thus take as our starting point the self-evident proposition that the "reasonable attorney's fee" provided for by statute should compensate the work of paralegals, as well as that of attorneys.

The more difficult question is how the work of paralegals is to be valuated in calculating the overall attorney's fee.

The statute specifies a "reasonable" fee for the attorney's work product. In determining how other elements of the attorney's fee are to be calculated, we have consistently looked to the marketplace as our guide to what is "reasonable." In Blum v. Stenson, 465 U.S. 886 (1984), for example, we rejected an argument that attorney's fees for nonprofit legal service organizations should be based on cost. We said: "The statute and legislative history establish that 'reasonable fees' under § 1988 are to be calculated according to the prevailing market rates in the relevant community. . . ." A reasonable attorney's fee under § 1988 is one calculated on the basis of rates and practices prevailing in the relevant market, i.e., "in line with those [rates] prevailing in the community for similar services by lawyers of reasonably comparable skill, experience, and reputation," and one that grants the successful civil rights plaintiff a "fully compensatory fee," comparable to what "is traditional with attorneys compensated by a fee-paying client."

If an attorney's fee awarded under § 1988 is to yield the same level of compensation that would be available from the market, the "increasingly widespread custom of separately billing for the services of paralegals and law students who serve as clerks," all else being equal, the hourly fee charged by an attorney whose rates include paralegal work in her hourly fee, or who bills separately for the work of paralegals at cost, will be higher than the hourly fee charged by an attorney competing in the same market who bills separately for the work of paralegals at "market rates." In other words, the prevailing "market rate" for attorney time is not independent of the manner in which paralegal time is accounted for. Thus, if the prevailing practice in a given community were to bill paralegal time separately at market rates, fees awarded the attorney at market rates for attorney time would not be fully compensatory if the court refused to compensate hours billed by paralegals or did so only at "cost." Similarly, the fee awarded would be too high if the court accepted separate billing for paralegal hours in a market where that was not the custom.

We reject the argument that compensation for paralegals at rates above "cost" would yield a "windfall" for the prevailing attorney. Neither petitioners nor anyone else, to our knowledge, has ever suggested that the hourly rate applied to the work of an associate attorney in a law firm creates a windfall for the firm's partners or is otherwise improper under § 1988, merely because it exceeds the cost of the attorney's services. If the fees are consistent with market rates and practices, the "windfall" argument has no more force with regard to paralegals than it does for associates. And it would hardly accord with Congress' intent to provide a "fully compensatory fee" if the prevailing plaintiff's attorney in a civil rights lawsuit were not permitted to bill separately for paralegals, while the defense attorney in the same litigation was able to take advantage of the prevailing practice and obtain market rates for such work. Yet that is precisely the result sought in this case by the State of Missouri, which appears to have paid its own outside counsel for the work of paralegals at the hourly rate of $35.

Nothing in § 1988 requires that the work of paralegals invariably be billed separately. If it is the practice in the relevant market not to do so, or to bill the work of paralegals only at cost, that is all that § 1988 requires. Where, however, the prevailing practice is to bill paralegal work at market rates, treating civil rights lawyers' fee requests in the same way is not only permitted by § 1988, but also makes economic sense. By encouraging the use of lower cost paralegals rather than attorneys wherever possible, permitting market-rate billing of paralegal hours "encourages cost-effective delivery of legal services and, by reducing the spiraling cost of civil rights litigation, furthers the policies underlying civil rights statutes."

Such separate billing appears to be the practice in most communities today. In the present case, Missouri concedes that "the local market typically bills separately for paralegal services," and the District Court found that the requested hourly rates of $35 for law clerks, $40 for paralegals, and $50 for recent law graduates were the prevailing rates for such services in the Kansas City area. Under these circumstances, the court's decision to award separate compensation at these rates was fully in accord with § 1988.

IV

The courts correctly granted a fee enhancement to compensate for delay in payment and approved compensation of paralegals and law clerks at market rates. The judgment of the Court of Appeals is therefore Affirmed. ■

ETHICS, REGULATION, AND PROFESSIONAL RESPONSIBILITY

"Morality cannot be legislated, but behavior can be regulated. Judicial decrees may not change hearts, but they can restrain the heartless."

Martin Luther King, Jr.

PARALEGALS AT WORK

Kelsey and Kathryn became friends when they were studying to be paralegals. Kathryn now works for a large national law firm while Kelsey does freelance paralegal work. They have over the years met frequently for lunch to discuss office issues and client cases. Kelsey asks Kathryn to meet for lunch at a crowded sandwich shop in the office building where she works to discuss a recent office issue. Kathryn can see that something is troubling her friend. After getting a seat at the lunch counter they order lunch and Kelsey begins to confide in Kathryn.

Kelsey regularly does freelance work for two lawyers who are both working on the same case and both have asked Kelsey to work on the file. One lawyer represents the plaintiff and the other lawyer represents the defendant. Both lawyers want Kelsey to interview the clients, witnesses, and generally handle the file as she normally does. Kelsey is wondering if she should be working "both sides of the fence." Kelsey describes to Kathryn the clients and the case in detail while they wait for their lunch to be served.

Kelsey explains that she often does most of the work on the plaintiff's cases including settling the cases with insurance company adjusters or the lawyers representing the defendants. Kelsey knows the adjuster on this case and he has revealed to her that the insurance company for the defendant wants to settle the case quickly and avoid a trial. Kelsey asks Kathryn for advice.

Consider the issues involved in this scenario as you read the chapter.

After studying this chapter, you should be able to:

1. Explain the reasons for the regulation of the practice of law.

2. Explain how the paralegal may avoid the Unauthorized Practice of Law (UPL).

3. Discuss issues involving the conflicting views on regulation of the paralegal profession.

4. Understand the difference between the attorney's rules of ethics and the paralegal's rules of ethics and the obligations of each profession.

5. Understand the areas of federal practice in which paralegals may represent clients.

6. Understand the concept of confidentiality of client communications and the attorney–client privilege.

7. Understand the concept of conflict of interest for the legal profession and methods to protect client confidentiality.

8. Explain the difference between attorney–client privilege and the work product doctrine.

9. Explain the issues in making inadvertent disclosure of confidential information.

▶INTRODUCTION FOR THE PARALEGAL

Ethical guidelines
Rules of minimally acceptable professional conduct.

ABA Model Rules of Professional Conduct
A recommended set of ethics and professional conduct guidelines for lawyers, prepared by American Bar Association, originally released in 1983; prior release was Model Code of Professional Conduct.

Check the latest version of the ABA Model Rules of Professional Conduct at http://www.abanet.org/cpr/mrpc/model_rules.html

Unauthorized Practice of Law (UPL)
Giving legal advice, if legal rights may be affected, by anyone not licensed to practice law.

Every profession develops a set of guidelines for those in the profession to follow. These may be the rules of practice, such as court rules of procedure; **ethical guidelines**, such as the **ABA Model Rules of Professional Conduct** for lawyers; or statutorily mandated rules, such as professional licensing statutes. By their own efforts, lawyers have developed a combination of organizational guidelines such as the rules of ethics, and have lobbied for licensing regulation of the legal profession through the courts and the legislature.

In developing these guidelines, the paralegal profession is going through a growth phase. Even though these rules and regulations are in the development stage, the paralegal must have some sense of the rules to be followed. The paralegal in many workplaces today is a substitute for the recent law school graduate, frequently referred to as a junior associate, who may not have taken the bar examination and been admitted to practice. In any case, ethics rules must be followed to avoid conflict, potential violation of client rights and statutory regulation, and possible malpractice. ▪

REGULATING THE PRACTICE OF LAW

To protect the public, certain professions, such as law, require state licensure as a method of regulating who can practice. For the lawyer, the rules that must be followed to continue practice are found in the individual states' code or canon of ethics for lawyers, such as the Model Rules of Professional Conduct of the American Bar Association as adopted by many states' highest courts, serious violation of which can result in the loss of the license or right to practice law.

Paralegals, with a few exceptions, have no state license requirement to enter the profession, and no unified code of ethics. State regulations and ethics opinions are neither uniform nor mandatory. At worst, a paralegal runs the risk of a charge of unauthorized practice of law under the state criminal code, and at best the violation of a professional organizations ethics code results in a loss of membership in the organization. The dilemma for the paralegal is knowing when giving advice or helping someone fill in blank forms is the **Unauthorized Practice of Law (UPL)**.

Unauthorized Practice of Law (UPL)

Just as the practice of medicine and other professions is regulated, the practice of law is regulated by state government and court rule in an attempt to protect the public from incompetent and unscrupulous practitioners. To protect the public, certain occupations and professions, such as law, require obtaining a license as a method of regulating and monitoring those who offer services to the public. Obtaining a license may be as simple as completing a form and providing proof that the required education and or experience requirements have been satisfied. The profession of law, in most cases, requires taking a qualifying examination after proving that the required educational background has been obtained. This has not always been the case. In the past, admission was possible by satisfying the court that one had studied or, as it was called, "read" the law and had worked under the supervision of a lawyer.

In some states, prior admission for a required period of time allowed admission to the new jurisdiction without taking the examination. Today's rules generally have eliminated these alternative methods of admission to the practice of law. Even seasoned attorneys seeking admission to other states such as California and Florida must retake the examination for that state as a condition for admission.

This examination is generally called the "bar exam." The term "bar" in bar exam has been attributed to the custom of separating the public by a bar from those allowed to pass the bar and approach the judge or court. Most modern courtrooms continue the tradition with a barrier separating the area where spectators sit from where the lawyers, judges, and juries sit. The bar examination tests the applicant's basic legal knowledge and attempts to assure a minimum standard of competency.

Passing the bar exam is the first step in "getting admitted to practice." Admission usually is a ceremonial swearing-in by the court to which the person is "admitted to practice" upon the recommendation of the state or local bar examiners and the introduction and motion for admission by an existing member of the bar of that court.

Admission to practice before one court does not automatically authorize practice before other courts. Each state has its own rules and standards. Generally, admission to the highest court of the state confers admission to all of the other state and municipal and minor judiciary courts of that state. The right to practice before the various federal courts requires separate application and admission to practice. Admission to federal court is generally granted upon motion of an existing member of the court bar upon submission of proof of admission to practice before the highest court of the state of admission and proof of good character.

For the lawyer, the rules that must be followed in the practice of law are found in the individual code of professional responsibility or canons of ethics, such as the Model Rules of Professional Conduct of the American Bar Association, as adopted by the individual state's highest court. The rules of conduct or ethics are enforced by disciplinary committees and their recommendation to the court for sanctions against offending attorneys. Complaints about breaches of ethical behavior normally are

ILLINOIS SUPREME COURT RULES: ARTICLE VIII. ILLINOIS RULES OF PROFESSIONAL CONDUCT

PREAMBLE

The practice of law is a public trust. Lawyers are the trustees of the system by which citizens resolve disputes among themselves, punish and deter crime, and determine their relative rights and responsibilities toward each other and their government. Lawyers therefore are responsible for the character, competence and integrity of the persons whom they assist in joining their profession; for assuring access to that system through the availability of competent legal counsel; for maintaining public confidence in the system of justice by acting competently and with loyalty to the best interests of their clients; by working to improve that system to meet the challenges of a rapidly changing society; and by defending the integrity of the judicial system against those who would corrupt, abuse or defraud it.

To achieve these ends, the practice of law is regulated by the following rules. Violation of these rules is grounds for discipline. No set of prohibitions, however, can adequately articulate the positive values or goals sought to be advanced by those prohibitions. This preamble therefore seeks to articulate those values in much the same way as did the former canons set forth in the Illinois Code of Professional Responsibility. Lawyers seeking to conform their conduct to the requirements of these rules should look to the values described in this preamble for guidance in interpreting the difficult issues which may arise under the rules.

The policies which underlie the various rules may, under certain circumstances, be in some tension with each other. Wherever feasible, the rules themselves seek to resolve such conflicts with clear statements of duty. For example, a lawyer must disclose, even in breach of a client confidence, a client's intent to commit a crime involving a serious risk of bodily harm. In other cases, lawyers must carefully weigh conflicting values, and make decisions, at the peril of violating one or more of the following rules. Lawyers are trained to make just such decisions, however, and should not shrink from the task. To reach correct ethical decisions, lawyers must be sensitive to the duties imposed by these rules and, whenever practical, should discuss particularly difficult issues with their peers.

referred to a committee for investigation. In some states, minor infractions can subject the lawyer to private reprimand, public reprimand or censure, or in serious cases, temporary or permanent loss of the license to practice law, usually called disbarment.

Breaches of unauthorized practice of law complaint generally are referred to the state attorney or local prosecutor for criminal prosecution as a violation of statute and not a breach of the court rules of ethical behavior. It should be noted that some ethical breaches also may be violations of statute. Attorneys who breach a client's trust by taking the client's fund are guilty of violating an ethical rule and a criminal act of theft.

An appreciation for the system of admission and monitoring of those who seek to practice law can be found in the Preamble to the Illinois Supreme Court Rules of Professional Conduct on the previous page.

The Paralegal and Licensing

There are, with a few exceptions, no state licensing requirements for one to work as a paralegal—unlike the procedures that lawyers must follow to practice law. Some states, such as California, Maine, and North Carolina, have enacted legislation establishing licensure to perform certain functions frequently performed by paralegals. Generally, these are attempting to regulate the unsupervised performance by freelance or independent paralegals, such as document-completion services.

At best, these laws carve out a small part of the practice of law that can be performed by nonlawyers without risking the performance of acts that constitute the unlawful practice of law. But none allow anyone other than a lawyer properly admitted to practice in the jurisdiction to give legal advice or opinions. Even the selection of the correct form is considered a lawyer's function. (See the California Business Code on the next page.) The client must select the forms.

There is a fine line between lawful activity and unlawful practice of law. Recommending or selecting a form that may impact on a person's legal rights is more likely than not to be treated as practicing law and therefore subject the unlicensed person to a charge of UPL.

California is the first state to limit the use of the term "paralegal" to those who meet certain minimum requirements. Whether this will be a trend or not remains to be seen. What is interesting is that the courts look to these kinds of minimum qualifications for paralegals when deciding the question of who is a paralegal and thereby eligible for court approval of fees for legal services.

Although each state is free to define the practice of law differently, the statutes have certain elements in common. Typical of the various states' definitions of the Practice of Law is that of Arizona.

DEFINITION OF PRACTICE OF LAW IN ARIZONA

A. "Practice of law" means providing legal advice or services to or for another by:

(1) preparing any document in any medium intended to affect or secure legal rights for a specific person or entity;
(2) preparing or expressing legal opinions;
(3) representing another in a judicial, quasi-judicial, or administrative proceeding, or other formal dispute resolution process such as arbitration and mediation;
(4) preparing any document through any medium for filing in any court, administrative agency or tribunal for a specific person or entity; or
(5) negotiating legal rights or responsibilities for a specific person or entity...

Source: Rules of the Supreme Court of Arizona, Rule 31, Regulation of the Practice of Law, effective December 1, 2005.

Penalties for the Unauthorized Practice of Law

States such as Pennsylvania have specifically addressed the issue of unauthorized practice of law by paralegals and legal assistants. The Pennsylvania statute on the unauthorized practice of law makes it a misdemeanor for "any person, including, but not limited to, a paralegal or legal assistant who within this Commonwealth, shall practice law . . ." 42 Pa. C.S.A. § 2524

The Pennsylvania statute seems to address concerns that the general public will misinterpret the title of paralegal or legal assistant as denoting a person admitted to practice law in the commonwealth. An unresolved issue in Pennsylvania, and in other states, is to define what specific conduct the courts will hold to be the practice of law. Because the interpretation will vary from state to state, the paralegal must be aware of the local requirements and limitations that define the unauthorized practice of law within that jurisdiction.

In those states that have enacted legislation regulating paralegal activity some guidance is offered by the defined activity that is permitted. For example, California has included within its Business and Professional Code, licensing of persons as "Unlawful Detainer Assistant" and "Legal Document Assistant" and defining the activity permitted.

> **Chapter 5.5. Legal Document Assistants and Unlawful Detainer Assistants**
> **Article 1. General Provisions**
>
> 6400 (a) "Unlawful detainer assistant" means any individual who for compensation renders assistance or advice in the prosecution or defense of an unlawful detainer claim or action, including any bankruptcy petition that may affect the unlawful detainer claim or action.
> (b) "Unlawful detainer claim" means a proceeding, filing, or action affecting rights or liabilities of any person that arises under Chapter 4 (commencing with Section 1159) of Title 3 of Part 3 of the Code of Civil Procedure and that contemplates an adjudication by a court.
> (c) "Legal document assistant" means:
> (1) Any person who is not exempted under Section 6401 and who provides, or assists in providing, or offers to provide, or offers to assist in providing, for compensation, any self-help service to a member of the public who is representing himself or herself in a legal matter, or who holds himself or herself out as someone who offers that service or has that authority. This paragraph does not apply to any individual whose assistance consists merely of secretarial or receptionist services.

AVOIDING UPL: HOLDING ONESELF OUT

With so much uncertainty in what constitutes the unauthorized practice of law the question for every paralegal must be "How Do I Avoid UPL?" Some general guidelines should be followed. A common thread in the law of UPL is the prohibition of holding oneself out as a lawyer when not admitted to practice law. The Florida statute was amended recently to read:

> Any person not licensed or otherwise authorized to practice law in this state who practices law in this state or holds himself or herself out to the public as qualified to practice law in this state, or who willfully pretends to be, or willfully takes or uses any name, title, addition, or description implying that he or she is qualified, or recognized by law as qualified, to practice law in this state, commits a felony of the third degree. . . .
> Chapter 2004-287, Senate Bill 1776.

California, in the Business and Professional Code mentioned above, reinforces the concept of not misleading the public into thinking one is a lawyer when he/she provides limited service, by requiring the following statement to prospective clients:

> (4) The statement: "I am not an attorney" and, if the person offering legal document assistant or unlawful detainer assistant services is a partnership or a corporation, or uses a fictitious business name, "(name) is not a law firm. I/we cannot represent you in court, advise you about your legal rights or the law, or select legal forms for you."

For the paralegal, the first rule must be to inform the parties with whom they are dealing that they are not lawyers. Paralegals must not hold themselves out as being anything more than a paralegal. Parties with whom the paralegal has contact must know the limited role the person plays as a paralegal on the legal team. Other lawyers, members of the legal team, and courthouse staff are put on notice by being informed of the person's status as paralegal. This may be by oral comment, written statement, such as a letter signed using the title "paralegal," or presentment with a business card clearly showing the title of paralegal.

Advising clients, witnesses, and other members of the general public of the role of the paralegal is not as easy. Those who are not properly educated in the role of the paralegal may believe that a paralegal is someone with advanced training and knowledge who can perform some of the functions normally. Those who are not properly educated in the role of the paralegal may believe that a paralegal is someone with advanced training and knowledge who can perform some of the functions normally performed by lawyers, including giving legal advice and opinions. The safest course is to be certain the other party is not misled about the role of the paralegal. Use of the statement from the California Business Code above is a start: "I am not an attorney" . . . "I . . . cannot represent you in court, advise you about your legal rights or the law, or select legal forms for you."

Even this may have its peril when the individual is not aware of the differences in our legal system in the functions of members of the legal team. Some members of the community may come from backgrounds where the distinctions are not clear—for example, those coming from other countries where the legal systems are different and the roles of people in the system are different or where different terms are used for those who perform legal-type functions such as notaries.

For non-native English-speaking people, translation also may play a role in the misunderstanding. To some clients, the paralegal is the "face" or main contact with the law firms. The paralegal may be the first point of contact and the one through whom all documents and information is communicated by the lawyers in the firm.

Paralegals must make it clear that they are paralegals and not lawyers. In a first meeting with anyone—client, witness, opposing counsel or court personnel—the wisest course of action is to advise them of your position as a paralegal. A short, "I am Miss Attorney's paralegal" may be sufficient to put the other party on notice. Business cards and letterhead, where permitted, should clearly state the title of paralegal. Correspondence always should include the title as part of the signature block.

Never allow the other party to think you are anything other than what you are—a professional who is a paralegal. For those who are not familiar with the role of the paralegal, you may have to clarify what the paralegal can and cannot do in your jurisdiction.

Avoiding UPL: Giving Advice

Every UPL statute or rule prohibits anyone other than a lawyer properly admitted to practice in the state or jurisdiction from preparing or expressing legal opinions. Clearly, then, a paralegal cannot give a legal opinion or give legal advice. It sounds easy, but the reality is that paralegals must be on guard constantly to avoid giving legal advice or rendering a legal opinion. Clients and those seeking "a little free advice" may not want to respect the limitations on the paralegal's role in the legal system.

Certain conduct required or requested by an attorney or client should, at the very least, cause the paralegal to pause. A client who asks you to prepare a power of attorney "without bothering the lawyer," or to "go with me to the support conference" should raise a caution flag in the paralegal's mind. Even in a social setting, you may have to repeat the statement, "I am not an attorney"... "I/we cannot represent you in court, advise you about your legal rights or the law, or select legal forms for you."

When is giving advice an unauthorized practice of law? If legal rights may be affected, it probably is legal advice. The question of what advice is legal advice is not easy to answer. Consider the seemingly innocent question, "How should I sign my name?" In most circumstances the answer might be: "Just sign it the way you normally write your name." But when a person is signing a document in a representative capacity—for example as the officer of a corporation or on behalf of another person under a power of attorney—telling the client to "just sign your name" might be giving legal advice because the client's legal rights could be affected if he or she does not indicate representative capacity.

Avoiding UPL: Filling Out Forms

Filling out forms for clients also can be a source of trouble. In some jurisdictions, paralegals are permitted to assist clients in preparing certain documents. Other courts, however, view this assistance as rendering legal advice.

> As a general matter, other courts have held that the sale of self-help legal kits or printed legal forms does not constitute the unauthorized practice of law as long as the seller provides the buyer no advice regarding which forms to use or how the forms should be filled out.
> Fifteenth Jud. Dis. v. Glasgow, M1996-00020-COA-R3-CV (Tenn.App. 12-10-1999)(FN4)

The Florida court addressed this issue in an unlawful practice of law case, holding the UPL consisted of

> . . . a nonlawyer who has direct contact with individuals in the nature of consultation, explanation, recommendations, advice, and assistance in the provision, selection, and completion of legal forms engages in the unlicensed practice of law; . . . [W]hile a nonlawyer may sell certain legal forms and type up instruments completed by clients, a nonlawyer "must not engage in personal legal assistance in conjunction with her business activities, including the correction of errors and omissions. . . ."
> **The Florida Bar**, petitioner, versus **We The People Forms and Service Center of Sarasota, Inc.**, et al., No. SC02—1675

Avoiding UPL: Representing Clients

Knowing when someone may represent a client before a judicial or quasi-judicial board, such as an administrative agency, is a difficult question to answer. The difficulty is in knowing what the individual courts allow or will permit in individual circumstances. Some jurisdictions and administrative agencies do permit those who are not licensed or admitted to practice to appear in court or before administrative law judges or referees on behalf of clients. Typically, these are law students acting under the guidance and supervision of an attorney under limited circumstances, but they may include paralegals. Depending upon the jurisdiction, nature of the action, and level of the court, the paralegal might be permitted to appear with or on behalf of a client—for example, before a Social Security Administration Administrative Law Judge.

Who may represent clients is not a simple question for lawyers, or for paralegals. Representation of parties traditionally has been the role of lawyers. But even lawyers are not always permitted to represent parties. Appropriate admission to practice in the jurisdiction is typically a requirement. A lawyer admitted to practice in one state may not necessarily represent the same client in another state. Lawyers admitted to practice in one jurisdiction, however, may ask the court of another jurisdiction for permission to appear and try a specific case. This is a courtesy generally granted for a single case, and usually when the trial attorney has retained local counsel who will appear as well to advise on local rules and procedures. But the issue of out-of-state counsel is not without other issues. The complexity of the issue is raised in a portion of a report on the Unauthorized Practice of Law prepared by the Nevada Assistant Bar Counsel.

> The Bar has received complaints of out-of-state counsel participating in the pre-litigation mediation procedures. Writing notification letters, engaging in discovery, and appearing at pre-litigation mediations in a representative capacity is generally the practice of law. In Nevada there is no mechanism to obtain authority from the Supreme Court to appear in pre-litigation cases. Therefore, engaging in legal activities involving Nevada disputes and Nevada parties requires a licensed Nevada attorney. . . . (Unauthorized Practice of Law, David A. Clark, Assistant Bar Counsel, September 20, 2001)

If the representation of clients is not clear for members of the bar, it certainly is not clear for members of the paralegal profession. Generally, only duly admitted lawyers in the jurisdiction may represent parties. But this rule has been modified to allow law students in some states to represent parties in certain situations, generally under appropriate supervision.

In some states a nonlawyer employee may represent a business in some proceeding before administrative agencies or before the minor judiciary, such as small claims courts. There is no uniformity of rules when nonlawyers may represent parties or before which agencies or courts. Any appearance before a court must be approached carefully. Even the presentation of a request for continuance of a case may be considered by some courts to be the practice of law.

Appearance on behalf of clients before federal and state administrative agencies is no less lacking in uniformity than appearances before courts. But it frequently is easier to determine the ability to appear as a paralegal representing a client. Some federal agencies specifically permit nonlawyers to appear. Most notable is the Social Security Administration, which allows representation by nonlawyers with few differences from representation by lawyers. The U.S. Patent Office also specifically permits nonlawyer practice. Some states, by specific legislation or administrative rule, also permit representation by nonlawyers.

Avoiding UPL: Guidelines

The National Association of Legal Assistants, Inc. Model Standards and Guidelines for the Utilization of Legal Assistants provides guidelines on conduct that may prevent UPL.

Guideline 1

Legal Assistants Should:

1. Disclose their status as legal assistants at the outset of any professional relationship with a client, other attorneys, a court or administrative agency or personnel thereof, or members of the general public.

Guideline 2

Legal Assistants Should Not:

1. Establish attorney–client relationships; set legal fees; give legal opinions or advice; or represent a client before a court, unless authorized to do so by said court; nor
2. Engage in, encourage, or contribute to any act that could constitute the unauthorized practice of law.

Guideline 3

Legal Assistants May Perform Services for an Attorney in the Representation of a Client, Provided:

1. The services performed by the legal assistant do not require the exercise of independent professional legal judgment;

2. The attorney maintains a direct relationship with the client and maintains control of all client matters;
3. The attorney supervises the legal assistant;
4. The attorney remains professionally responsible for all work on behalf of the client, including any actions taken or not taken by the legal assistant in connection therewith; and
5. The services performed supplement, merge with, and become the attorney's work product.

REGULATING THE PARALEGAL PROFESSION

Regulation and licensing of the paralegal profession has been one of the hottest topics in the legal and paralegal communities. Each state, through its respective legislature and court, regulates and licenses the practice of law. The original UPL issues were simply those of the licensing of attorneys and laws preventing the unauthorized practice of law. With the development of the paralegal profession has come a new set of concerns and controversy surrounding what constitutes the unauthorized practice of law, who should be permitted to render legal services, and under what conditions.

The conflict is between the paralegal profession and the bar organizations, such as the American Bar Association, which does not see the need for the additional time, effort, and cost for certification of paralegals. The ABA position is broadly based on the argument that the public is protected by the attorney's obligation to supervise the paralegal and responsibility to the public.

For the most part, the paralegal profession has sought some level of regulation, certification, or licensure. Somewhere in the middle are increasing numbers of employers of paralegals who want some level of assurance that those they hire who claim to be paralegals are qualified for those positions. As the responsibilities undertaken by paralegals have increased, so have the educational requirements. Within the profession has come a concern that those who hold themselves out as paralegals are truly qualified to perform the work they have undertaken. This is no different from the organized bar monitoring the activities of those holding themselves out as being lawyers.

Exhibit 2.1 provides the states' statutory references for legal assistants and paralegals.

State Licensing Attempts

Individual states have attempted to set up licensing systems. A case in point is the proposal rejected in 1999 by the New Jersey Supreme Court to license traditional paralegals, which had been developed after five years of study by that court's committee on paralegal education and regulation. If it had been approved, this proposal would have made New Jersey the first state to license traditional paralegals.

- California leads the nation in setting stringent educational requirements that may become a model for other states. In 2000 California amended its Business and Professional Code requiring minimum educational standards for paralegals.
- In 2001 the Washington State Bar adopted a rule to establish a Practice of Law Board that authorizes nonlawyers to practice law in limited areas as needed to assure access to affordable legal services. Not until March 2005, however, was a discussion draft of the proposed rule issued.
- After a number of efforts, a Hawaii State Bar Association task force on paralegal certification developed a compromise voluntary certification proposal for consideration by the Hawaii Supreme Court, which recognized the opposition from some segments of the bar.

To some observers it is obvious that the organized bar is fearful in many cases of the incursion of the paralegal profession into the practice of law. For some, the issue

Exhibit 2.1 Statutory references to legal assistants and paralegals

State	Definition	Regulation	Fee Reimbursement	Other
Alabama				§ 36-15-11.1. Paralegal employees for Attorney General.
Alaska				08.08.230. Unlawful practice a misdemeanor; (Use of paralegals not prohibited)
Arkansas				23-91-209 Insurance Commissioner to consider legal services agreements with paralegal personnel; 16-21-1102 DA may hire paralegals
California	§ 6450 Bus. & Prof.	§ 6452 Bus. & Prof.	§ 10953 Prob— Paralegal fees in probate	Sec. 17b-427 Dept of Social Services to have qualified attorney or paralegal to
Connecticut				Sec. 17b-427 Dept of Social Services to have qualified attorney or paralegal to provide Medicare info
Florida			57.104 Computation of attorneys' fees.— legal assistant included; services defined	287.059 Govt contracts for legal fees— paralegal rates to be identified
Georgia				43-38-14 Bona fide legal assistant exempted from Private Detective chapter
Idaho			54-2118 Veterinarian discipline—paralegal fees recoverable 67-1408 AG may bill paralegal fees	
Illinois	5 ILCS 70/1.35		5 ILCS 70/1.35	
Indiana	IC 1-1-4-6		IC 1-1-4-6	IC 1-1-4-6 Legal Services may train attorneys and paralegals in provision of services or advice to eligible clients
Kansas			16-1405 Paralegal fees recoverable in contract action	60-230 Legal Assistant, paralegal be present at deposition
Maine	4 M.R.S.A. § 921	4 M.R.S.A. § 922 Restriction on use of titles	24-A M.R.S.A. § 2393 WC Collection— paralegal fees	
Michigan				333.16233 Dept of Commerce may establish paralegal unit
Minnesota			148.941 Psychologist discipline—paralegal fees recoverable	
Mississippi				§ 43-13-116 Paralegal with Legal Services may represent client in Medicaid eligibility hearing
Montana	37-60-101. Paralegal, Legal Assistant defined in Investigator Statute			37-60-105 paralegal, legal assistant exempt from Private Investigator Statute; 27-2-206 Statute of Limitations on attorney, paralegal, legal intern malpractice
New Mexico			52-3-47 Workers' Comp—paralegal fees recoverable	
New York			§ 8602 N.Y.C.P.L.R. Definitions; § 308-a Agric. & Mkts Paralegal fees recoverable	

State	Definition	Regulation	Fee Reimbursement	Other
North Carolina		**§ 84-37** State Bar may investigate unauthorized use of Paralegal designation		
North Dakota				**43-30-02** Paralegal, legal assistant exempt from Private Investigator Statute
Ohio		**§ 5311.18** Condo lien priorities—paralegal fees recoverable		
Oklahoma		**§ 74-20i** AG contract for legal services to include rates for paralegals, legal assistants		**Title 5 Ch. 1 rule 3.3** CLE credit earned through teaching paralegals, legal assistants
Oregon				**703.411** Paralegal, legal assistant exempt from Investigators' truth and deception detection regs; **Title 51 657.270** Paralegal, legal assistant may represent UC claimant
Pennsylvania				**42 Pa.C.S.A. § 2524** UPL statute applies to paralegals and legal assistants
South Dakota		**16-18-34.1-3** Legal Assistant Qualifications; Ethical uses; Limitations		
Tennessee			**63-1-144** Paralegal fees in Health Professions discipline	**37-5-105** DCS commissioner to report on # of paralegal staff
Texas		**§ 2254.106 GOV'T** Govt contract for legal services to set attorney & paralegal rates		
Utah				**78-3a-912(3)(f)** Attorney may appear through a paralegal at administration GAL hearings **78-7-45** GAL paralegal fees
Vermont				**26 V.S.A. § 3151a** Paralegals exempt from PI statutes; **24 V.S.A. § 5403** Paralegal on land records commission
Washington				**RCW 19.154.030** Paralegals exempt from Immigration Assistant Practices Act
West Virginia			**§ 29-21-13a** Public Defender reimbursement for Paralegals (out of court only)	
Wisconsin				**SCR 22.26** Suspended Attorney not to engage in paralegal work

Courtesy of Professor Richard Opie, Paralegal Program Director, Lakeshore Technical College.

Advice from the Field ···

NORTH CAROLINA STATE BAR PARALEGAL CERTIFICATION PROGRAM

I recommend a visit to the The North Carolina State Bar's Paralegal website (http://www.nccertifiedparalegal.org), for information on the benefits of paralegal certification. The first page is shown below.

PLAN FOR CERTIFICATION OF PARALEGALS

The State Bar's interest in the paralegal profession promotes proper utilization of paralegals and assures that legal services are professionally and ethically offered to the public. The Plan for Certification of Paralegals approved by the NC State Bar and adopted by the NC Supreme Court in 2004 will assist in the development of paralegal standards, raise the profile of the paralegal profession, and standardize the expectations of the public and other legal professionals.

The State Bar has worked diligently with attorneys and paralegals across our state to establish a voluntary North Carolina certification program with requirements that are properly defined and that will ensure the credential has value. Through education and experience, the North Carolina certification plan will assist lawyers and administrators in distinguishing paralegals that meet or exceed the skills required for certification. As multi-skilled professionals, paralegals have a diverse knowledge base and must practice effective interpersonal communi-cation skills to maintain collaborative relationships within the legal team. Paralegals, like attorneys, will continue to be held accountable to the highest of ethical and professional standards.

Paralegals certified by the State Bar may use the following designations:

- North Carolina Certified Paralegal
- North Carolina State Bar Certified Paralegal
- Paralegal Certified by the North Carolina State Bar Board of Paralegal Certification
- NCCP

This site has two brochures that may be downloaded,

NC Certified Paralegal—A Primer for Paralegals

NC Certified Paralegal—A Primer for Attorney

Both brochures review the benefits to the public, to the profession, to attorneys and to paralegals. I think that they give a great overall response to "why" become certified. North Carolina began their certification program July 1, 2005, as of February 2006, the Board received 1489 applications and had certified 762. The current applicants are qualifying under the grandfather clause which ends June 30, 2007.

is loss of income. Others are concerned for the delivery of quality legal services by all those who hold themselves out as being members of the legal profession.

For the paralegal, it is a question of status as well as job opportunities. With the establishment of minimum standards for holding oneself out as a paralegal comes a status that members of a profession are entitled to enjoy. For those who have worked hard to develop the necessary paralegal skills by way of education and experience, it eliminates unqualified individuals from taking jobs that should be performed by qualified individuals. The stated goals of the different groups are not that far apart: delivery of quality legal services at affordable prices with a reasonable standard of living for the legal profession and the paralegal profession.

The traditional role of the attorney in advising and representing clients is limited to those who are admitted to practice as lawyers under the applicable state law. Some exemptions do exist that allow nonlawyers to perform certain services under state law, such as document preparation under California law.

Advice from the Field ··

ETHICS THROUGH THE EYES OF A NON-LAWYER *Betty Wells, PP, PLS, TSC*

Betty Wells, PP, PLS, TSC, is currently employed in the Austin, Texas, office of Cox Smith Matthews Incorporated, a San Antonio law firm. She joined NALS in 1994, is a NALS Life Member, and is serving as webmaster for her local chapter, Corresponding Secretary for her state association, Chair of the NALS Foundation, as well as a non-voting Board Member of NALS. She received the Member of the Year in 1997–98 and 2001–02 from her local chapter, the Legal Professional of the Year award in 1997–98 from her state association and the NALS Award of Excellence in 2003. In 2004–05 she received the Mentor of the Year award from her local chapter.

This article was originally published in the Winter 2002-3 issue of @Law, the NALS magazine for legal professionals. It is printed with the permission of @Law and NALS, the association for legal professionals. © NALS, Inc. Reprinted with permission. All rights reserved.

The American Bar Association and NALS ... *the association for legal professionals* uses this definition for a legal assistant or paralegal: "A legal assistant or paralegal is a person, qualified by education, training or work experience who is employed or retained by a lawyer, law office, corporation, governmental agency or other entity and who performs specifically delegated substantive legal work for which a lawyer is responsible."

In simple language, a legal assistant is a non-lawyer who provides substantive legal services and is supervised by a lawyer. Legal services performed by non-lawyers differ from firm to firm but may include anything from answering the phone to complex research. Just as the description of legal tasks the non-lawyer may be asked to perform varies from firm to firm, so do non-lawyer classifications. In one firm, a legal secretary may simply answer the attorney's phone and revise documents, while in another firm a legal secretary may prepare complex wills and research case law. You may be "classed" as a legal secretary in your firm while you are actually asked to perform "legal assistant or paralegal" work while working under the supervision of an attorney.

Non-lawyers should be aware of how their conduct could affect not only themselves, but also the lawyer and firm for whom they work. Although legal assistants or paralegals are not directly subject to any rules of professional conduct promulgated by courts, legislatures, or government agencies, those non-lawyer personnel could loose [sic] their job for not following the rules of ethical conduct. In addition, the supervising lawyer could be reprimanded, suspended, or even disbarred, depending on the severity of the unethical conduct of the non-lawyer. Legal assistants or paralegals who are members of national and/or local paralegal associations are required to follow the ethical codes of those associations.

Possibly the biggest ethical situation a non-lawyer faces is the unauthorized practice of law ("UPL"). If you are "tenured," you may find you know more about a particular area of the law than some newly "sworn" lawyers. Because of your knowledge, you may get dangerously close to crossing or may have already crossed the UPL line. Tasks a non-lawyer may perform are limited by statutory or court authority, and the lawyer's determination of the non-lawyer's competency. As the legal profession has evolved so has the role of non-lawyers. Today a non-lawyer is well-educated and well-trained with a variety of backgrounds and experience. The practice of law includes accepting cases, setting fees, giving legal advice, preparing or signing legal documents, and appearing before a court or other judicial body in a representative capacity. The unauthorized practice of law occurs when a non-lawyer engages in activities which affect the legal rights and obligations of clients. The biggest risk for a non-lawyer is giving legal advice instead of general legal information especially when the request comes from a family member or friend. Family members are typically the hardest to convince that you cannot give them legal advice, and they can be relentless in their pursuit of advice.

(continued)

Advice from the Field

(continued)

Be aware: Your willingness to dispense legal advice to the family member or friend could potentially result in your unemployment.

How can the non-lawyer avoid UPL? The best way is to always identify oneself as a legal secretary, legal assistant or paralegal who has posed the specific question to a supervising lawyer and as one who is relaying information gleaned from that lawyer. Make certain all legal documents and correspondence that could be considered legal opinion are reviewed, approved and signed by your supervising lawyer or another lawyer in the firm that is familiar with the matter. If you do not know what the UPL provisions are in your state, call your state bar and ask them for the guidelines non-lawyers must follow. Find out today before you are forced to explain what you have done, not only to your employer but to the bar association in your state.

Confidentiality is another area non-lawyers are faced with each and every day. It is important to a lawyer's practice that his clients are able to speak freely with the lawyer's support personnel and for the clients to know the information they are relaying through you will be held in the strictest of confidence. Did the firm where you are employed ask you to sign a confidentiality statement when you were hired? If they did, did they explain to you what client confidentiality meant? If they didn't, ask them for the form and ask them to explain client confidences.

If the firm doesn't have a confidentiality form for non-lawyers, ask them to create one—their malpractice insurance carrier will love you for it. In simple terms, protecting a client's confidence means you do not talk about clients or cases in your firm with anyone, anywhere, especially in public places—the ethics rules require the lawyer to exercise reasonable care to prevent his employees or associates from violating the obligation regarding client confidences or secrets. In other words, the non-lawyer must follow the same rules as the lawyer when it comes to protecting client confidentiality.

Have you ever interviewed for a position at a law firm only to find yourself conflicted out of employment? More and more often, law firms are asking support personnel to provide a list of clients they have worked with. On occasion a non-lawyer has not been hired due to a conflict of interest that cannot be resolved. Have you been hired by a firm, or found yourself doing temp work in a firm and realized you have knowledge from your past job that could change the outcome of the matter on which you are working? Did you immediately go to the supervising lawyer or HR department and tell them of the possibility of a conflict? You should never make the decision that the information you have is inconsequential or take it for granted simply because you are "just a temp." Remember, it is important for you to inform your employer of the potential conflict to avoid potential problems as the matter progresses, not only for you but for the lawyer and their firm as well.

What about receiving legal fees? Can you "troll" for clients and be compensated when your firm is hired? Remember, you are not allowed to set fees, you must not practice law or give the appearance of practicing law, so therefore, you must not accept fees. The reasoning behind this is to protect the lawyer's professional independence of judgment. The obligations of the lawyer to the client do not change simply because you "brought" the client to the firm.

Your unethical behavior may cause you to loose [sic] your job *and* it may cost your employer his or her career. Stay current with ethical requirements in your profession by attending continuing legal education seminars offered by local and state bar associations, as well as through your local, state, and national association. You and your employer will be glad you did.

Federal Practice

Under federal regulations, nonlawyers may represent parties before the Social Security Administration, the Patent Office, and other agencies. A conflict may arise between the federal law and state law that limits the activity. For example, Florida sought unsuccessfully to enjoin a practitioner authorized to practice before the Patent Office, alleging UPL (*Sperry v. Florida*, 373 U.S. 379 (1963)).

Under federal regulation, a paralegal can, without supervision, represent individuals before the Social Security Administration, including appearing before Administrative Law Judges on behalf of clients. Paralegals may appear as representatives of claimants for disability claims; Medicare parts A, B, and C; and cases of overpayment and underpayment.

As representative of a claimant, the paralegal in practice before the Social Security Administration may obtain information, submit evidence, and make statements and arguments. The difference between the paralegal and the attorney is only in the matter of direct versus indirect payment for services. The Social Security Administration pays the attorney directly, whereas the paralegal must bill the client for services rendered. Within the Social Security Administration, paralegals are employed as decision writers and case technicians.

ETHICAL RULES AND OBLIGATIONS

Lawyers generally need to follow only one set of ethics guidelines. Although it may be a set enacted by the state legislature, it usually is one adopted by the supreme court of the state in which they practice.

The most widely adopted is the Model Rules of Professional Conduct, prepared by the American Bar Association and originally released in 1983. The prior release, the Model Code of Professional Conduct (Model Code), is still in use in some jurisdictions. Procedurally, each state reviews the Model Rules or Model Code and adopts the entire recommended set of Model Rules or the Model Code, or portions as it thinks appropriate for its jurisdiction.

Unlike the ABA for lawyers, no single source of ethical rules is set out for the legal assistant. Absent a single unified body of ethical rules, legal assistants must follow state statutes and conduct themselves in conformity with the rules of professional conduct applicable to attorneys and with the ethics opinions of their professional associations. The two major legal assistant organizations providing an ethical code for their members are the National Federation of Paralegal Associations (NFPA) and the National Association of Legal Assistants (NALA).

Although legal assistants are not governed directly by the American Bar Association ethical rules, there is an intertwined relationship between the lawyer, the client, and the paralegal. What the paralegal does or does not do can have a real impact on the lawyer's duty and obligation to the client. Under the Model Rules, the lawyer ultimately is responsible for the actions of the legal assistant

ABA Model Guidelines for the Utilization of Paralegal Services

In 1991, the American Bar Association's policymaking body, the House of Delegates, initially adopted a set of guidelines intended to govern the conduct of lawyers when utilizing paralegals or legal assistants. These guidelines were updated in 2002 to reflect the legal and policy developments that had taken place since 1991.

Attorneys are bound by the ethical code adopted by the state in which they practice. The ethical guidelines for the paralegal are a combination of the ethical rules imposed on the supervising attorney and the paralegal professional association rules imposed on paralegals. As a general rule, whatever the ethical rules forbid the attorney from doing, they also forbid the paralegal from doing. Paralegals, therefore, can look to their state's adopted set of rules, or code, of professional responsibility for guidance in deciding what is appropriate or inappropriate from an ethical perspective.

By definition, the paralegal works under the supervision of an attorney. As such, the paralegal is the agent of the attorney and therefore owes a duty to the supervising attorney similar to that of the traditional agent–servant relationship found in agency law—that of a fiduciary obligation. Among the fiduciary obligations of an agent are the duty to exercise reasonable care, skill, and diligence.

The agent also owes a duty of loyalty to the principal. This includes the obligation to act for the employer's benefit rather than for his or her own benefit or the benefit of another whose interest may be adverse to that of the employer.

ETHICAL *Perspective*

American Bar Association Model Rules of Professional Conduct Rule 1.6, Confidentiality of Information

(a) A lawyer shall not reveal information relating to the representation of a client unless the client gives informed consent, the disclosure is impliedly authorized in order to carry out the representation or the disclosure is permitted by paragraph (b).

See Appendix B for Commentary on Model Rule 1.6.

ABA Model Rules of Professional Conduct, 2004 Edition. © 2003 by the American Bar Association. Reprinted with permission. Copies of the ABA Model Rules of Professional Conduct, 2004 Edition, are available from Service Center, American Bar Association. 321 North Clark Street, Chicago, IL 60610, 1-800-285-2221.

Model guidelines for the utilization of legal assistant services
A set of guidelines by ABA policymaking body, the House of Delegates, intended to govern conduct of lawyers when utilizing paralegals or legal assistants.

By extension of the rule of agency, the paralegal, as a subagent of the supervising attorney, becomes an agent of the client. The attorney is an agent of the client, and the paralegal is a subagent. As an agent of the client, the same duties that are owed to the law firm as the employer are also owed to the client.

One of the questions that arise in firms engaged in corporate practice and in securities practice is whether the paralegal can purchase stock (securities) in a client corporation. Some firms have written policies prohibiting members of the firm, including paralegals, from purchasing the securities (stock) of client corporations. At the forefront is the propriety of using the information leading to the purchase or the transaction in client securities. Among the issues is whether the purchase was made based upon material inside information, information not generally available to the public, the knowledge of which would cause a person to buy or sell a corporate security. Use of material inside information of publicly traded stocks is generally a violation of federal securities laws prohibiting insider transactions.

For the attorney, guidance is available from Model Rule 1.7 and the comments to the Model Rule and under the previous Model Code DR 5–101A, which provides that an attorney must refuse employment when personal interests, including financial interests, might sway professional judgment. To the extent that this rule applies to the attorney, good judgment would dictate that it applies to the paralegal as well.

Uniformity of Paralegal Ethics

The paralegal profession has no unified code of ethics. State regulations and ethics opinions are not uniform. National organizations such as the National Association of Legal Assistants and the National Federation of Paralegal Associations each provide a uniform code of ethical conduct for members.

Ethics Codes of Paralegal Associations

The two leading national paralegal membership organizations are the National Federation of Paralegal Associations and the National Association of Legal Assistants. Each of these groups has formulated a set of ethical guidelines for its respective membership, as well as for others looking for ethical guidance in regulating the paralegal profession.

National Federation of Paralegal Associations

The National Federation of Paralegal Associations, Inc. is a professional organization composed of paralegal associations and individual paralegals throughout the United States and Canada. Members of NFPA have varying backgrounds, experiences, education, and job responsibilities that reflect the diversity of the paralegal profession. NFPA promotes the growth, development, and recognition of the paralegal profession as an integral partner in the delivery of legal services.

In April 1997, NFPA adopted the Model Disciplinary Rules (Model Rules) to make possible the enforcement of the Canons and Ethical Considerations contained in the NFPA Model Code. At present, unlike a violation by an attorney of the state-adopted rules that can result in loss of the right to practice (disbarment), no such sanction exists for the paralegal breach of association rules except loss of membership.

National Association of Legal Assistants

The National Association of Legal Assistants, formed in 1975, is a leading professional association for legal assistants. NALA provides continuing professional education, development, and certification. It may best be known in the profession for its Certified Legal Assistant (CLA) examination. The ABA Standing Committee on Legal Assistants has recognized the CLA designation as a designation marking a high level of professional achievement.

www

The National Associations Ethics Codes and ethical guidelines can be reviewed at:

National Federation of Paralegal Associations:

www.paralegals.org/displaycommon.cfm?an=1&subarticlenbr=330

National Association of Legal Assistants:

www.nala.org/

NALS .... the Association for Legal Professionals:

http://www.nals.org

Association of Legal Administrators:

www.alanet.org

Conflict of Interest

A **conflict of interest** exists if the representation of one client will be adverse to the interest of another client. Conflict of interest may best be explained by the biblical adage that no one can serve two masters. If the master is entitled to complete loyalty, any conflict in loyalties presents a conflict of interest in which neither master can be certain of the loyalty of his or her servant. It's easy to see the conflict that would arise in a lawyer's going to court representing both the plaintiff and the defendant.

Less obvious are situations in which the attorney represents two parties with a common interest, such as a husband and wife purchasing a new home. In most cases, the interests would be the same and no conflict would exist. When these clients are seeking counseling for marital problems, however, the conflict becomes more obvious as one of them seeks a greater share of the common property or other rights and the lawyer is called upon to give legal advice as to the right to the parties. Finally, lawyers clearly cannot represent both husband and wife in court in the marital dissolution trial.

The American Bar Association Model Rules of Professional Conduct provide a guideline in Rule 1.7, Conflict of Interest: General Rule, which provides in part that a lawyer shall not represent a client if the representation of that client will be directly adverse to another client, unless the lawyer reasonably believes the representation will not adversely affect the relationship with the other client; and each client consents after consultation. The essence of the rule is that of loyalty to the client. The 1981 version of the American Bar Association Model Code of Professional Responsibility provides in Canon 5:

> A lawyer should exercise independent professional judgment on behalf of a client.

The ethical considerations comment to Canon 5 states:

> EC–1 The professional judgment of a lawyer should be exercised, within the bounds of the law, solely for the benefit of his client and free of compromising influences and loyalties. Neither his personal interests, the interests of other clients, nor the desires of third persons should be permitted to dilute his loyalty to his client.

Clearly, a lawyer should not accept the employment if the lawyer's personal interests or desires will, or if there is a reasonable probability that they will, adversely affect the advice to be given or services to be rendered to the prospective client. The information that may be considered to create a conflict of interest is not limited solely to that of the attorney representing a client. It also includes the information held by another member of the legal team, including the legal assistant.

The National Federation of Paralegal Associations Model Code of Ethics provides in Canon 8:

> A paralegal shall avoid conflicts of interest and shall disclose any possible conflict to the employer or client, as well as to their prospective employers or clients.

The ultimate obligation to determine the conflict of interest of the paralegal or legal assistant rests with the supervising attorney. Standard procedure in law firms is to check for conflicts of interest within the law firm before accepting a new client or undertaking a new matter for an existing client. Just as other attorneys are asked to review lists of new clients and new matters, so must paralegals check to be certain they do not have a conflict of interest.

Conflicts of interest may arise for paralegals when they change from one employer to another. If the previous employer represented a client or handled certain matters for a client during the period in which the paralegal was employed, a conflict of interest may exist. A more difficult concern for the paralegal is the conflict of interest that can arise from a law firm's representation of family members and personal friends. Paralegals frequently refer family and friends to the attorney or the law firm where they work. The mere relationship or friendship itself might not create conflict, but in some cases could give rise to a claim of undue influence wherein the paralegal may stand to

Conflict of interest
The representation of one client being directly adverse to the interest of another client.

Ethical wall
An environment in which an attorney or a paralegal is isolated from a particular case or client to avoid a conflict of interest or to protect a client's confidences and secrets.

Moonlighting
Working for more than one firm or attorney.

Attorney–client privilege
A rule that says a client can tell his or her lawyer anything about the case without fear that the attorney will be called as a witness against the client.

benefit from the action of the law firm. Examples are the drafting of wills and trusts in which the paralegal may be named as a beneficiary or instances in which the paralegal may be named as the executor of the estate or as a trustee receiving compensation.

Ethical Wall

Law firms use the term "**ethical wall**"—also called a Chinese wall—to describe an environment in which an attorney or a paralegal is isolated from a particular case or client to avoid a conflict of interest or to protect a client's confidences and secrets. By creating this boundary or wall, any potential communications, whether written or oral, are prevented between members of the legal team handling a particular matter or client and the person with whom there may be a conflict of interest.

In an age of consolidation of law firms in many areas, the number of individual employers has diminished while the number of clients has increased. As a result, professionals today may find themselves in firms that were on the opposite side of cases in the past. Creating an ethical wall permits the professional to accept employment with the other firm. It also permits greater mobility by professionals, as they can go to a new firm in which there may have been a conflict.

Moonlighting

Freelance or independent paralegals who work for more than one firm or attorney face the potential problem of conflict of interest. Special caution has to be taken to avoid accepting employment in cases where conflicts may exist. Freelance and independent paralegals are keenly aware of this and generally take precautions to prevent conflicts. The law firms and attorneys for whom they work usually are aware of the potential and also take special precautions to isolate potential conflict situations. Full-time paralegals who seek outside income should pay special attention to potential conflicts that may arise.

Not all of these conflicts are obvious. Consider the case of a paralegal working for a plaintiff's negligence firm handling cases against a major retail store. That paralegal's acceptance of employment at the retail store the firm is suing presents a conflict of interest. Knowledge of the strategy of the case would be of interest to the retail store employer. But divulging the information would breach the confidence of the law firm and the confidence of the law firm's client. Failing to disclose information to the retail store that directly affects its business breaches the duty of loyalty to that employer.

THE DUTY OF CONFIDENTIALITY, ATTORNEY–CLIENT PRIVILEGE, AND WORK PRODUCT DOCTRINE

The three concepts—duty of confidentiality, attorney–client privilege, and work product doctrine—have something in common: they are all connected to the legal profession's obligation to protect the secrets of the client so that the client can provide all the information necessary for the legal team to conduct an effective representation of the client.

Attorney–client privilege is founded on the belief that clients should be able to tell their attorneys everything about their case so the attorney can give proper legal advice to the client. For the attorney, the ABA Model Rules provide in Rule 1.6, Confidentiality of Information, that a lawyer shall not reveal information relating to representation of a client unless the client consents after consultation, except for disclosures that are impliedly authorized. What is confidential information is also defined in the ABA model rules: "all information, regardless of the source, gained in the representation of the client."

In every case there are two sides, each represented by an attorney. The attorney for each party to a case has a competing interest, either to obtain information or to protect information from the other. Attorneys want to protect the information received from their clients, or developed in the process of preparing for litigation. The conflict over protecting or releasing information has intensified in recent years as pri-

> ### RULE 501. GENERAL RULE REGARDING PRIVILEGE
>
> Except as otherwise required by the Constitution of the United States or provided by Act of Congress or in rules prescribed by the Supreme Court pursuant to statutory authority, the privilege of a witness, person, government, State, or political subdivision thereof shall be governed by the principles of the common law as they may be interpreted by the courts of the United States in the light of reason and experience. However, in civil actions and proceedings, with respect to an element of a claim or defense as to which State law supplies the rule of decision, the privilege of a witness, person, government, State, or political subdivision thereof shall be determined in accordance with State law. (Jan. 2, 1975, P.L. 93-595, § 1, 88 Stat. 1933)

THE CLAUS VON BULOW CASE: THE PARALEGAL AND THE CLAIM OF ATTORNEY–CLIENT PRIVILEGE

As stated by the federal court in the case of Claus Von Bulow:

The law is clear in this circuit the person claiming the attorney–client privilege has the burden of establishing all the essential elements thereof. The question is a simple one: Was Reynolds [a friend of Claus Von Bulow claiming that information given to her by the defendant was privileged] an agent of an attorney and has she presented sufficient evidence of this relationship? In other words, were communications made to her, in confidence, in her capacity as an agent of an attorney for the purpose of obtaining legal advice from that attorney? We think not.

The attorney–client privilege is founded on the assumption that encouraging clients to make the fullest disclosure to their attorneys enables the latter to act more effectively. We have recognized that an attorney's effectiveness depends upon his ability to rely on the assistance of various aides, be they secretaries, file clerks, telephone operators, messengers, clerks not yet admitted to the bar, and aides of other sorts. The privilege must include all the persons who act as the attorney's agents.

Source: Von Bulow v. Von Bulow, 811 F. 2d 136 (2d Cir. 1987)

---

vate counsel and government counsel challenge the attorney's obligation to maintain in confidence information obtained directly and through use of agents such as paralegal, and public relations consultants in criminal and civil matters before commencement of litigation. Increased regulatory obligations have created additional obligations on businesses to conduct internal investigations, which has resulted in a new area of federal and state privilege—"the audit privilege."

Increased use of electronic media, such as the Internet email, has created the era of the instant message, and with it the instant inadvertent disclosure of potentially privileged material with the press of a key stroke. Lawyers and paralegals must know how to handle inadvertent disclosure of privileged information and, when possible, prevent a loss of the confidentiality privilege that could result in a potential loss of the case and a possible malpractice claim against the law firm.

Confidentiality

The duty of **confidentiality** is just that for the legal team, a duty. It is a duty imposed on the attorney and each member of the legal team working under the supervision of the attorney to enable clients to obtain legal advice by allowing the client to freely and openly give the members of the legal team all the relevant facts without fear of disclosure of these facts except in limited situations, such as to prevent commission of a crime or to defend against a client's suit.

Attorneys, and the members of the legal team, have a duty to treat client information obtained in the course of representation of a client in confidence under ABA Rule 1.6.[i] Members of the legal team cannot tell anyone the client's information. The duty does not end when the case ends but continues forever and precludes discussing the information with friends, spouses, strangers, or anyone else who might inquire about the case.

The duty of confidentiality also extends to paralegals under ethical guidelines of the major national paralegal organizations such as NALA.[ii] Although these ethical rules are not mandatory on the paralegal, in most states the paralegal's position as an agent creates an obligation to the attorney and to the client.

In the modern practice of law, the attorney must rely on others, such as paralegals, legal secretaries, investigators, law clerks, and the like, to assist in vigorous

Confidentiality
A duty imposed on the attorney to enable clients to obtain legal advice by allowing the client to freely and openly give the attorney all the relevant facts

representation of the client. These "agents" also must be covered by the attorney-client privilege. To do otherwise would require the attorney to guard every document, exhibit, and pretrial memorandum from the eyes of everyone on the legal team and perform every task personally from interviews of clients and witnesses, to the typing of reports and memorandum of law, to the conduct of fact and legal research to the preparation of trial exhibits and documents. This is clearly not desirable or cost effective for the client or the administration of justice.

Attorney–Client Privilege

The attorney–client privilege differs from the duty of confidentiality because it applies only to information obtained from the client—for example, the client's confession of commission of the crime. This privilege is found in the state or federal evidence code. It is a rule of evidence that applies in cases where the Rules of Evidence apply: a court of law, a deposition, or other places where a witness is under oath, such as interrogatories, responses to requests for documents, or grand jury hearings. The attorney–client privilege is a part of both state and federal law. The law of each jurisdiction must be consulted to determine the extent of the privilege.

For example, Pennsylvania is typical of many states in treating the privilege as part of the state common law tradition that has been incorporated in state law (*Commonwealth v. Noll*, 662 A.2d 1123, 1126 (Pa.Super. 1995), appeal denied, 543 Pa. 726, 673 A.2d 333 (1996)). The rules in federal court involving privilege are found in the Federal Rules of Evidence Section 501.[iii]

The "privilege" belongs to the client, not to the attorney. The client may waive the privilege and allow the attorney or paralegal to reveal the information; however, the attorneys or paralegals may not of themselves waive the privilege when asked what the client has told them. In a court proceeding, an appropriate answer to the question of what the client said would be: "I declined to answer because of the attorney–client privilege." If the client had revealed or released the same information to someone else, the privilege is lost. Thus, the client must really keep the information secret for the privilege to apply.

The concept of privilege also extends to persons while acting within certain roles such as:

1. Spouse[iv]
2. Clergy–penitent[v]
3. Doctor–patient[vi]
4. Psychotherapist–patient.[vii]
5. Participants in settlement negotiations[viii]

PRIVILEGES IN THE WORDS OF THE SUPREME COURT

"The privileges between priest and penitent, attorney and client, and physician and patient limit protection to private communication. These privileges are rooted in the imperative need for confidence and trust. The priest-penitent privilege recognizes the human need to disclose to a spiritual counselor, in total and absolute confidence, what are believed to be flawed acts or thoughts and to receive priestly consolation and guidance in return. The lawyer-client privilege rests on the need for the advocate and counselor to know all that relates to the client's reasons for seeking representation if the professional mission is to be carried out. Similarly, the physician must know all that a patient can articulate in order to identify and to treat disease; barriers to full disclosure would impair diagnosis and treatment."

Burger C.J. Trammell v. United States, 445 U.S. 40 (1980)[ix]

Claim of Privilege

Privilege is not automatically invoked. The person claiming the privilege—usually the client—has the burden to establish the existence of the privilege.

> "To sustain a claim of privilege, the party invoking it must demonstrate that the information at issue was a communication between client and counsel or his employee, that it was intended to be and was in fact kept confidential, and that it was made in order to assist in obtaining or providing legal advice or services to the client"[x]

Privilege
A special legal right.

Extension of Attorney–Client Privilege to Others

It is now accepted that the efficient administration of justice requires lawyers to engage others, such as legal assistants, accountants, and other experts. This would not be possible if the privilege did not extend to these agents of the attorney including, most recently, public relations firms.

The U.S. District Court for the Southern District of New York summarized the law, stating:

> "... the privilege in appropriate circumstances extends to otherwise privileged communications that involve persons assisting the lawyer in the rendition of legal services. This principle has been applied universally to cover office personnel, such as secretaries and law clerks, who assist lawyers in performing their tasks. But it has been applied more broadly as well. For example, In *United States v Kovel*, the Second Circuit held that a client's communication with an accountant employed by his attorney were privileged where made for the purpose of enabling the attorney to understand the client situation in order to provide legal advice." (IN RE Grand Jury Subpoenas dated March 24, 2003 directed to (A) Grand Jury Witness Firm and (B) Grand Jury Witness, M11-188 (USDC, S.D.N.Y.) (June 2, 2003)).

Common Interest Privilege

Another variation of privilege is the **common interest privilege**. "The purpose of the common interest privilege is to permit a client to share confidential information with the attorney for another who shares a common legal interest.

> The key consideration is that the nature of the interest be identical, *not similar* [emphasis added], and be legal, not solely commercial.[xi, xii]"

Common interest privilege
To permit a client to share confidential information with the attorney for another who shares a common legal interest.

Work–product doctrine
A qualified immunity from discovery for "work product of the lawyer" except on a substantial showing of "necessity or justification" of certain written statements and memoranda prepared by counsel in representation of a client, generally in preparation for trial.

Work–Product Doctrine

The **work–product doctrine** is different from both the attorney–client privilege and the duty of confidentiality. The attorney–client privilege and the duty of confidentiality relate to the information provided by the clients regardless of whether they involve potential litigation.

FRCP 26 (b) DISCOVERY SCOPE AND LIMITS

Unless otherwise limited by order of the court in accordance with these rules, the scope of discovery is as follows:

(1) In General. Parties may obtain discovery regarding any matter, not privileged, that is relevant to the claim or defense of any party, including the existence, description, nature, custody, condition, and location of any books, documents, or other tangible things and the identity and location of persons having knowledge of any discoverable matter. For good cause, the court may order discovery of any matter relevant to the subject matter involved in the action. Relevant information need not be admissible at the trial if the discovery appears reasonably calculated to lead to the discovery of admissible evidence. All discovery is subject to the limitations imposed by Rule 26(b)(2)(i),(ii), and (iii).

IN THE WORDS OF THE SUPREME COURT

The US Supreme Court recognized the work–product doctrine and its importance saying:

> Proper preparation of a client's case demands that he assemble information, sift what he considers to be the relevant from the irrelevant facts, prepare his legal theories and plan his strategy without undue and needless interference. That is the historical and the necessary way in which lawyers act within the framework of our system of jurisprudence to promote justice and to protect their clients' interests.
>
> This work is reflected, of course, in interviews, statements, memoranda, correspondence, briefs, mental impressions, personal beliefs, and countless other tangible and intangible ways—aptly though roughly termed by the Circuit Court of Appeals in this case as the "work product of the lawyer." Were such materials open to opposing counsel on mere demand, much of what is now put down in writing would remain unwritten.
>
> An attorney's thoughts, heretofore inviolate, would not be his own. Inefficiency, unfairness and sharp practices would inevitably develop in the giving of legal advice and in the preparation of cases for trial. The effect on the legal profession would be demoralizing. And the interests of the clients and the cause of justice would be poorly served.
>
> . . . .where relevant and non-privileged facts remain hidden in an attorney's file and where production of those facts is essential to the preparation of one's case, discovery may be properly had.

Hickman v. Tayler, 329 U.S. 495 (1947) at page 511.

The work–product doctrine provides a limited protection for material prepared by the attorney or those working for the attorney in anticipation of litigation or for trial.

> "The work–product doctrine is narrower than the attorney–client privilege in that it protects only materials prepared "in anticipation of litigation," Fed. R. Civ. P. 26(b) (3), whereas the attorney–client privilege protects confidential legal communications between an attorney and client regardless of whether they involve possible litigation."[xiii]

The work–product doctrine is codified in the Federal Rules of Civil Procedure Rule 26 (B) (3),[xiv] and in Rule 16 (B) (2) of the Federal Rules of Criminal Procedure.[xv]

Exceptions and Limitations to the Work–Product Doctrine

The work–product doctrine has some exceptions. It does not cover documents prepared in the normal operation of the client's business, such as sales reports, data analysis, or summaries of business operations.

> The work–product doctrine does not extend to documents in an attorney's possession that were prepared by a third-party in the ordinary course of business and that would have been created in essentially similar form irrespective of any litigation anticipated by counsel.[xvi]

In other words, the client cannot obtain protection for internal business documents by giving them to the attorney and thereby protect them from discovery by the other side because they are in the possession of the attorney.

Exception to the Third-Party Document Exception

The courts have made an exception to the exception in which a lawyer is trying to find out the other party's strategy by asking about documents already in his/her possession that would not be protected under the third-party exception. To protect the lawyer's trial strategy, the court may impose a privilege where it would not otherwise exist. We, too, have observed that

> "Where a request is made for documents already in the possession of requesting party, with precise goal of warning what the opposing attorney's thinking or strategy may be, even **third-party documents** may be protected." Id[xvii]

Governmental Attorney Exception

The attorney–client privilege does not extend to government attorneys. Individuals and corporations are both subject to criminal liability for their transgressions. Individuals will not talk and corporations will have no incentive to conduct or cooperate in internal investigations if they know that any information disclosed may be turned over to the authorities. . . . A state agency, however, cannot be held criminally liable. . . . A government attorney should have no privilege to shield relevant information from the public citizens to whom she owes ultimate allegiance, as represented by the grand jury.[xviii]

Third-party documents
Documents prepared by a third party in the ordinary course of business that would have been prepared in similar form if there was no litigation.

Inadvertent Disclosure of Confidential Information

Inadvertent disclosure of confidential or privileged information does happen. It may be the slip of the finger in sending an email, an accidental pushing of the wrong number on the speed dial of a fax machine or the sending of a misaddressed envelope.

The admissibility of the inadvertently disclosed documents may hinge on the steps the firm takes before and after the disclosure. Having a proper screening policy in place and monitoring this policy may prevent a claim of negligence.[xix]

The treatment will depend on the individual jurisdiction. The courts follow no single policy.

Judicial Views

There are three judicial views on handling the inadvertent disclosure under the attorney–client privilege: (1.) Automatic waiver; (2.) no waiver; (3.) and balancing test.[xx]

Automatic Waiver
These cases hold that once the confidentiality is breached, the privilege is therefore waived.

No Waiver
There can only be a waiver when a client makes a knowing voluntary waiver of the privilege. Therefore, the attorney's inadvertent disclosure does not constitute a waiver.

Balancing Test
The courts using the balancing test looked to the nature of the methods taken to protect the information, efforts made to correct the error, the extent of the disclosure and fairness. Remedies under this test range from unlimited use of the disclosed materials, to court-ordered return of documents, to disqualification of attorneys who have reviewed inadvertently disclosed privileged documents.

ABA Ethics Opinion

The American Bar Association has issued a formal opinion modifying the long-standing opinion 92-368, which advocated for confidentiality of privileged materials to protect the client, and imposing a burden upon receiving attorneys not to review privileged material and return it following instructions given to them by the disclosing attorney, issuing a clarifying formal opinion 05-437, which states:

> A lawyer who receives a document from opposing parties or their lawyers and knows or reasonably should know that the document was inadvertently sent should promptly notify the sender in order to permit the sender to take protective measures. To the extent that Formal Opinion 92-368 opined otherwise, it is hereby withdrawn.

ETHICAL *Perspective*

One Last Word About Integrity

Model Rule 8.1 states that legal professionals should be persons of integrity. The more integrity each of us brings to the profession, the better the legal system will be. Regardless of a person's expertise or extraordinary gift for the law, the person still will be held to high standards of moral ethical conduct, as has been the case historically. (See also EC8-7)

Ethics: Ten Top Rules for Paralegals, by Deborah K. Orlik. © 2006, Pearson Education, Upper Saddle River, N.J. Reproduced by permission.

Internal Investigations and Evidentiary Privileges

Businesses, and particularly corporations with publicly traded stocks, are under state and federal requirement to take a proactive approach to determine wrongdoing and identify violations of statutes and regulations. These investigations and "audits" create a body of documents all, some, or none of which may be subject to evidentiary privilege.

THE FUTURE

What can you expect in the future? Certainly the demands of employers and courts will dictate that educational requirements be increased as the paralegal becomes a more and more important member of the legal services team. As an organization, the American Association of Legal Administrators, representing the law office administrators who do much of the hiring of paralegals, advocates a four-year degree as a minimum standard.

As courts mandate that certain activities be performed by paralegals and not by lawyers, the demand for better qualified paralegals will follow. The courts will look to credentials and training in making determinations of who may act and bill for services as a paralegal. If lawyers are responsible for the activities delegated to their paralegals, they will insist that paralegals be better trained and qualified.

Hiring decisions in the future may be based on educational minimums. Years of experience as a legal secretary may not count as much as being a graduate of an educational institution with a minimum set of standards such as those of the American Association for Paralegal Education.

Legal Terminology

ABA Model Rules of Professional Conduct   40
Attorney–client privilege   56
Common interest privilege   59
Conflict of interest   55
Confidentiality   57

Ethical guidelines   40
Ethical wall   56
Model Guidelines for the Utilization of Legal Assistant Services   53
Moonlighting   56

Privilege   59
Third-party documents   61
Unauthorized practice of law (UPL)   40
Work-product doctrine   59

Summary

CHAPTER 2   ETHICS, REGULATION, AND PROFESSIONAL RESPONSIBILITY
Regulating the Practice of Law

Unauthorized Practice of Law (UPL)	1. The practice of law is regulated by state government and court rule to protect the public from incompetent and unscrupulous practitioners. 2. The profession of law, in most cases, requires taking a qualifying examination after proving the required educational background has been obtained.
The Paralegal and Licensing	1. With few exceptions, no state licensing requirements exist. 2. Some states have enacted legislation establishing licensure to perform certain paralegal functions.
Definition of Practice of Law	Each state is free to define the practice of law differently. Typical definitions include providing legal advice or services to or for another.

Penalties for the Unauthorized Practice of Law	The specific conduct the courts hold to be the practice of law varies from state to state, including the penalties, which may include criminal prosecution ranging from misdemeanors to felonies.
Avoiding UPL: Holding Oneself Out	Parties with whom the paralegal has contact must know the limited role the person plays on the legal team as a paralegal.
Avoiding UPL: Giving Advice	A paralegal cannot give a legal opinion or give legal advice. If legal rights may be affected, it is probably legal advice.
Avoiding UPL: Filling Out Forms	UPL may consist of a nonlawyer who explains, recommends, advises, and assists in the selection, completion, and corrections of errors and omissions of legal forms.
Avoiding UPL: Representing Clients.	1. Some jurisdictions and administrative agencies do permit those who are not licensed or admitted to practice to appear in court or before administrative law judges or referees on behalf of clients. 2. No uniformity of rules exists outlining when nonlawyers may represent parties or the specific agencies or courts before which nonlawyers can appear. Any appearance before a court must be approved carefully. 3. The presentation of a request for continuance of a case may be considered by some courts to be the practice of law. 4 Some federal agencies specifically permit nonlawyers to appear. Most notable are the Social Security Administration and the U.S. Patent Office.

Avoiding UPL: Guidelines

Guideline 1

Legal assistants should:
1. disclose their status as legal assistants at the outset of any professional relationship with a client, other attorneys, a court or administrative agency or personnel thereof, or members of the general public.

Guideline 2

Legal assistants should not:
1. establish attorney–client relationships; set legal fees, give legal opinions or advice, or represent a client before a court, unless authorized to do so by said court; nor
2. engage in, encourage, or contribute to any act that could constitute the unauthorized practice law.

Guideline 3

Legal assistants may perform services for an attorney in the representation of a client, provided that
1. the services performed by the legal assistant do not require the exercise of independent professional legal judgment;
2. the attorney maintains a direct relationship with the client and maintains control of all client matters;
3. the attorney supervises the legal assistant;
4. the attorney remains professionally responsible for all work on behalf of the client, including any actions taken or not taken by the legal assistant in connection therewith.

Regulating the Paralegal Profession

State Licensing	The traditional role of the attorney in advising and representing clients is limited to those who are admitted to practice as lawyers under the applicable state law. Some exemptions do exist that allow nonlawyers to perform certain services under state law.
Federal Practice	Under federal regulations nonlawyers may represent parties before the Social Security Administration, the Patent Office, and other agencies.

Ethical Rules and Obligations

	1. Lawyers generally need to follow only one set of ethics guidelines. Although it may be a set enacted by the state legislature, it usually is one adopted by the supreme court of the state in which they practice. 2. The most widely adopted is the Model Rules of Professional Conduct. 3. No single source of ethical rules is set out for the paralegal. 4. Absent a single unified body of ethical rules, legal assistants must follow state statutes and conduct themselves in conformity with the rules of professional conduct applicable to attorneys and with the ethics opinions of their professional associations. 5. Case law tells us that the paralegal is subject to the same rules as attorneys. Paralegals, therefore, can look to their state's adopted set of rules, or code, of professional responsibility for guidance in deciding what is appropriate or inappropriate from an ethical perspective.
Uniformity of Paralegal Ethics	At present, unlike a violation by an attorney of the state-adopted rules that can result in loss of the right to practice (disbarment), no such sanction exists for the paralegal breach of association rules except loss of membership.
Paralegal Associations Ethics Codes	1. National Federation of Paralegal Associations, Inc. 2. National Association of Legal Assistants
Conflict of Interest	1. A conflict of interest exists if the representation of one client will be adverse to the interest of another client. 2. Conflicts of interest may arise for paralegals when they change from one employer to another if the previous employer represented a client or handled certain matters for a client during the period in which the paralegal was employed.

Ethical Wall

	This is an environment in which an attorney or a paralegal is isolated from a particular case or client to avoid a conflict of interest or to protect a client's confidences and secrets.

Moonlighting

	Freelance or independent paralegals who work for more than one firm or attorney face the potential problem of conflict of interest.

The Duty of Confidentiality, Attorney–Client Privilege, and the Work Product Doctrine

Confidentiality	This is a duty imposed on the attorney and each member of the legal team working under the supervision of the attorney to enable clients to obtain legal advice by allowing the client to freely and openly give the members of the legal team all the relevant facts without fear of disclosure of these facts except in limited situations, such as to prevent commission of a crime or to defend against a client's suit.

Attorney–Client Privilege	1. This privilege is found in the state or federal evidence code and is a rule of evidence that applies in cases where the Rules of Evidence apply: a court of law, a deposition, or other places where a witness is under oath: such as interrogatories, responses to requests for documents or grand jury hearings.
	2. The "privilege" belongs to the client not to the attorney.
	3. The person claiming the privilege, usually the client, has the burden to establish the existence of the privilege.
Extension of Attorney-Client Privilege to Others	The efficient administration of justice requires the privilege to extend to agents of the attorney. The person claiming the privilege, usually the client, has the burden to establish the existence of the privilege.

Work-Product Doctrine

	1. The work-product doctrine provides a limited protection for material prepared by the attorney or those working for the attorney in anticipation of litigation or for trial.
	2. The work-product doctrine is different from both the attorney–client privilege and the duty of confidentiality. The attorney–client privilege and the duty of confidentiality relate to the information provided by the clients regardless of whether they involve potential litigation.
Exceptions and Limitations to the Work Product Doctrine	Does not cover documents prepared in the normal operation of the client's business, such as sales reports, data analyses, or summaries of business operations.
Exception to the Third-Party Document Exception	Courts have made an exception when a lawyer is trying to find out the other party's strategy by asking about documents already in his/her possession.
Governmental Attorney Exception	Government attorneys should have no privilege to shield relevant information from the public citizens to whom they owe ultimate allegiance, as represented by the grand jury.
Inadvertent Disclosure of Confidential Information	The treatment will depend on the individual jurisdiction. The courts follow no single policy.
Judicial Views	The three judicial views on handling the inadvertent disclosure under the attorney-client privilege are 1. automatic waiver 2. no waiver 3. balancing test
Internal Investigations and Evidentiary Privilege	Internal investigations and audits mandated by state and federal regulation create a body of documents, some, or none of which may be subject to evidentiary privilege.

The Future

	1. The demands of employers and courts will dictate that educational requirements be increased as the paralegal becomes a more and more important member of the legal services team.
	2. The courts will look to credentials and training in making determinations of who may act and bill for services as a paralegal.

WORKING THE WEB

1. Download the latest ethics opinions and guidelines from the NALA website at **www.NALA.org**

2. Download any ethics updates from the NFPA website at **www.paralegal.org**

3. Download a personal reference copy of the Model Rules of Professional Conduct from the ABA Center for Professional Responsibility at **www.abanet.org**

4. Use a web browser or search engine to find the URL (web address) for your state or local bar association website that provides guidance or opinions on legal ethics. Three popular search engines are **www.google.com**, **www.yahoo.com** or **www.ask.com**

5. Use the NFPA website to find the names of agencies that allow nonlawyer practice. **www.paralegals.org/Development/Roles/allow.html**

CRITICAL THINKING AND WRITING QUESTIONS

1. What is the general theory for regulating the practice of law? How is this applied?

2. Why is "just giving advice" potentially the unauthorized practice of law?

3. How would regulation of the paralegal profession assure the public of quality legal services?

4. When may nonlawyers represent clients?

5. How can the paralegal avoid UPL?

6. How do unauthorized-practice-of-law statutes protect the public?

7. Why should the paralegal be familiar with the ABA Model Rules of Professional Conduct?

8. How do the ABA Model Guidelines for the Utilization of Legal Assistant Services define the role of the paralegal in the law office?

9. Do a paralegal's violating the ethics rules of the national paralegal associations have the same impact as violating the ethical rules of attorneys on the right to practice?

10. Would a paralegal dating a client have a conflict of interest caused by compromising influences and loyalties?

11. What is the reason for creating privileged communications?

12. Under what circumstances might a paralegal have a conflict of interest in taking a new job in a law firm?

13. How does an ethical wall protect the client?

14. What is a "Chinese wall"?

15. What are the potential dangers in paralegals' moonlighting?

16. What is a conflict of interest under the Model Rules of Professional Conduct?

17. Does a client have an attorney–client privilege regarding information given to a paralegal during the preparation of a case?

18. What duty does a paralegal owe to the supervising attorney?

19. How is a paralegal an agent of the client?

20. In possible conflict of interest, with whom does the ultimate decision rest?

21. Under what circumstance must a lawyer or a paralegal refuse employment?

22. What is required to invoke the attorney–client privilege?

23. What is covered under the work-product doctrine?

24. Should a paralegal be considered an "other representative" under the Federal Rules of Civil Procedure, Rule 26? Why or why not?

25. What is the audit privilege?

▶ ETHICS ANALYSIS AND DISCUSSION QUESTIONS

1. Are paralegals held to the same standard as attorneys when there is no supervising attorney?
2. What is the paralegal's duty to the client when the paralegal's employer breaches its duty to the client?
3. Who is responsible for the quality of the legal work performed for a client—the attorney or the paralegal?
4. Assume you have graduated from a paralegal program at a local college. While you are looking for a job where your talents can be properly utilized, a friend asks you to help him fill out a set of bankruptcy forms using a computer program he purchased at the local office supply mega warehouse. The program is designed to pick out the exemptions after the requested information is plugged in. [*In Re Kaitangian*, Calif. 218 BR 102 (1998).] Is this the unauthorized practice of law?

Paralegal Ethics in Practice

5. Assume you are offered the opportunity to work with a local law firm providing living trust services to the public. Your responsibility would be to make a presentation to community groups and in other public meetings on the advantages of living trusts. After the general session, any interested person would meet with you and you would fill out the forms, collect the fee, and send the completed form and half the fee collected to the law firm for review and transmittal to the client. You would retain half the amount collected as your fee. [*Cincinnati Bar Assn. v. Kathman*, 92 Ohio St.3d 92 (2001).]

   What ethical issues are involved? Explain.

▶ DEVELOPING YOUR COLLABORATION SKILLS

Working on your own or with a group of other students assigned by your instructor, review the scenario at the beginning of the chapter.

1. In a group or individually, identify all the potential ethical issues involved in this scenario.
2. Imagine that a local lawyer who knows both Kathryn and Kelsey was sitting next to them and overheard their conversation. The lawyer sends a letter to the local Ethics Board. Let one

group represent the Ethics Board, one group represent Kathryn's employer, and another Kelsey's employers.
   a. How should the Ethics Board respond?
   b. How should the employers respond?
3. Write or discuss a summary of the advice the group would give to Kathryn and Kelsey, and the law firms that employ them.

▶ PARALEGAL PORTFOLIO EXERCISE

Prepare a memorandum of law for submission to a potential employer, outlining the existing regulations in your state for paralegals, and the application of any unauthorized

practice of law statutes. Include complete citations to any cases, statutes or regulations, and the Internet address of any state or local ethics sites for lawyers and/or paralegals.

▶LEGAL ANALYSIS AND WRITING CASES

In Re Estate of Devine 263 Ill. App.3d 799 (1994)

A paralegal working in a small office became friendly with a client of the attorney and assisted the client in personal matters outside of the office, including helping him to shop and handle personal finances. In that role, the paralegal was given power to sign checks for the client. After the client died, the paralegal withdrew $165,958 from the joint account with the deceased client. Is a lawyer responsible for the actions of a paralegal?

The court held both the paralegal and the attorney liable for breach of fiduciary duty, holding that if the attorney, who performed work including writing a will leaving a bequest to the attorney and the paralegal, was a fiduciary, so then was the paralegal as a matter of law. Further, the court noted that the law in a number of states holds the attorney liable for a para-

legal's acts including the responsibility for unethical conduct by nonlawyer employees of the lawyer. The Illinois court quoted New York and New Jersey cases holding the employing attorney in violation of the Code of Professional Conduct for failing to properly supervise employed paralegals.

Questions

1. Does this case effectively extend the lawyer's ethical rules to the conduct of paralegals?
2. May a paralegal maintain a personal relationship with a client of the firm?
3. Should a paralegal be as familiar as the supervising (employing) attorney with the ABA Model Rules of Professional Conduct?

Sperry v Florida 373 U.S. 379 (1963)

Petitioner, not a lawyer and not admitted to practice in Florida as a lawyer, was nevertheless authorized to practice before the U.S. Patent Office pursuant to federal statute (35 U.S.C. Sec. 31). The Florida Bar sued to prevent him from representing patent applicants, preparing and prosecuting the patent claims and advising them in the State of Florida.

The Supreme Court, in holding that the Petitioner was permitted to perform tasks incident to prosecuting of patent claims, said, ". . . by virtue of the Supremacy Clause, Florida may not deny to those failing to meet its own qualifications the right to perform the functions within the scope of the federal authority." The Court further stated, ". . . since

patent practitioners are authorized to practice before the Patent Office, the State maintains control over the practice of law within its borders except to the limited extent for the accomplishment of the federal objective."

Questions

1. Does this decision allow anyone to practice before any federal agency without being licensed?
2. What are the prerequisites for nonlawyers to act on behalf of others before federal agencies?
3. What steps would a paralegal have to take to prosecute patent claims?

▶WORKING WITH THE LANGUAGE OF THE COURT CASE

Tegman v. Accident and Medical Investigations

30 P.3d 8 (Wash. Ct. App. 2001)
Court of Appeals of Washington, Division One

Read the following case excerpted from the Court of Appeals opinion. Review and brief the case. In your brief, answer the following questions.

1. How does this court define "the practice of law"?
2. What is the standard or duty of care that this court imposes on a paralegal who does not have a supervising attorney?
3. What action does this court suggest that a paralegal take when it becomes clear that there is no supervising attorney?
4. Why should a paralegal contact the supervising attorney immediately upon being given a case to handle?
5. Based on this case, should a paralegal advise the client that he or she is a paralegal? If so, when? Why?

Becker, Mary K., A.C.J.

Between 1989 and 1991, plaintiffs Maria Tegman, Linda Leszynski, and Daina Calixto were each injured in separate and unrelated automobile accidents. After their accidents, each plaintiff retained G. Richard McClellan and Accident & Medical Investigations, Inc. (AMI) for legal counsel and assistance in handling their personal injury claims.... Each plaintiff signed a contingency fee agreement with AMI, believing that McClellan was an attorney and AMI a law firm. McClellan has never been an attorney in any jurisdiction. McClellan and AMI employed Camille Jescavage, ...[a] licensed attorney....

Jescavage... learned that McClellan entered into contingency fee agreements with AMI's clients and that McClellan was not an attorney. [Attorneys for AMI] settled a number of cases for AMI, and learned that McClellan processed settlements of AMI cases through his own bank account....

In July 1991, McClellan hired Deloris Mullen as a paralegal. Mullen considered Jescavage to be her supervising attorney, though Jescavage provided little supervision. Jescavage resigned from AMI in the first week of September 1991. McClellan told Mullen that her new supervising attorney would be James Bailey. Mullen did not immediately contact Bailey to confirm that he was her supervising attorney. [He] later told Mullen he was not.

While at AMI, Mullen worked on approximately 50–60 cases, including those of [the] plaintiffs.... Mullen was aware of some of McClellan's questionable practices and knew that there were substantial improprieties involved with his operation. Mullen stopped working at AMI on December 6, 1991, when the situation became personally intolerable to her and she obtained direct knowledge that she was without a supervising attorney.

When she left, she did not advise any of the plaintiffs about the problems at AMI. After Mullen left, McClellan settled each plaintiff's case for various amounts without their knowledge or consent, and deposited the funds in his general account by forging their names on the settlement checks.

The "practice of law" clearly does not just mean appearing in court. In a larger sense, it includes "legal advice and counsel, and the preparation of legal instruments and contracts by which legal rights are secured." Mullen contends that her status as a paralegal precludes a finding that she was engaged in the practice of law. She argues that a paralegal is, by definition, someone who works under the supervision of an attorney, and that it is necessarily the attorney, not the paralegal, who is practicing law and owes a duty to the clients. Her argument assumes that she had a supervising attorney.

The trial court's determination that Mullen was negligent was dependent on the court's finding that Mullen knew, or should have known, that she did not have a supervising attorney over a period of several months while she was at AMI.... The label "paralegal" is not in itself a shield from liability. A factual evaluation is necessary to distinguish a paralegal who is working under an attorney's supervision from one who is actually practicing law. A finding that a paralegal is practicing law will not be supported merely by evidence of infrequent contact with the supervising attorney.

As long as the paralegal does in fact have a supervising attorney who is responsible for the case, any deficiency in the quality of the supervision or in the quality of the paralegal's work goes to the attorney's negligence, not the paralegal's.

In this case, Mullen testified that she believed James Bailey was her supervising attorney after Jescavage left. The court found Mullen was not justified in that belief. . . . Mullen testified that she had started to distrust McClellan before he informed her that Bailey would be her supervising attorney. Mullen also testified that she did not contact Bailey to confirm that he was supervising her. Bailey testified at a deposition that he did not share Mullen's clients and she did not consult him regarding any of her ongoing cases. He also said that one of the only conversations he remembers having with Mullen with respect to AMI is one where he told her that he was not her supervising attorney after she raised the issue with him. This testimony amply supports the trial court's finding that Mullen was unjustified in her belief that Bailey was her supervising attorney.

[Mullen] continued to send out demand and representation letters after Jescavage left AMI. Letters written by Mullen before Jescavage's departure identify Mullen as a paralegal after her signature,

(continued)

whereas letters she wrote after Jescavage's departure lacked such identification. Even after Mullen discovered, in late November 1991, that Bailey was not her supervising attorney, she wrote letters identifying "this office" as representing the plaintiffs, neglecting to mention that she was a paralegal and that no attorney was responsible for the case. This evidence substantially supports the finding that Mullen engaged in the practice of law.

Accordingly, we conclude the trial court did not err in following Bowers and holding Mullen to the duty of an attorney. The duty of care owed by an attorney is that degree of care, skill, diligence, and knowledge commonly possessed and exercised by a reasonable, careful, and prudent lawyer in the practice of law in Washington....

The court found that the standard of care owed by an attorney, and therefore also by Mullen, required her to notify the plaintiffs of: (1) the serious problems concerning the accessibility of their files to persons who had no right to see them, (2) the fact that client settlements were not processed through an attorney's trust account but, rather, McClellan's own account, (3) the fact that McClellan and AMI, as nonlawyers, had no right to enter into contingent fee agreements with clients and receive contingent fees, (4) the fact that McClellan was, in fact, engaged in the unlawful practice of law, and that, generally, (5) the clients of McClellan and AMI were at substantial risk of financial harm as a result of their association with AMI. Mullen breached her duty to her clients in all of these particulars.

We conclude the finding is supported by substantial evidence. Accordingly, the trial court did not err in concluding that Mullen was negligent. . . .

Although Mullen was a paralegal, she is held to an attorney's standard of care because she worked on the plaintiffs' cases during a period of several months when she had no supervising attorney. The fact that she did not render legal advice directly does not excuse her; in fact, her failure to advise the plaintiffs of the improper arrangements at AMI is the very omission that breached her duty. Under these circumstances it is not unjust to hold her accountable as a legal cause of the plaintiffs' injuries. As all the elements of negligence have been established, we affirm the judgment against Mullen.

Affirmed.

WE CONCUR: AGID, J., COLEMAN, J.

This case also was scheduled to be published in the Washington Appellate Reports, and if cited in the courts of Washington, would require that citation as well. This case has a Lexis number of 2001 Wash. App. LEXIS 1890. ∎

Rubin v. Enns

23 S.W.3d 382
Tex. App.-Amarillo (7th Dist. 2000)

1. Does the court's "rebuttable presumption" test work? Would any other test work better?
2. Using the court's "rebuttable presumption" test, would there be some temptation on the part of the second law firm to obtain confidential information that the paralegal learned at the first law firm?
3. Do the ethics standards of the American Bar Association and paralegal associations adequately address ethical conflicts that paralegals face? Discuss.

FACTS

Inda Crawford was employed as a legal assistant by the law firm of Hicks, Thomas & Lilienstern (HTL) for a number of years prior to May 1999.

During her employment with the HTL law firm, HTL represented Michael Rubin and other real estate agents in a lawsuit against Westgate Petroleum and other defendants. Crawford worked on this case as a legal assistant for HTL and billed 170 hours of work on the case.

In May 1999, Crawford left her employment at HTL and went to work for the law firm Templeton, Smithee, Hayes, Fields, Young & Heinrich (Templeton). Templeton represented Westgate Petroleum and the other defendants in the previously mentioned lawsuit. Rubin and the other real estate agents in this case filed a writ of mandamus with trial court judge the Honorable Ron Enns to have the Templeton firm disqualified as counsel for Westgate et al. because Crawford had now switched firms.

Rubin argued that because Crawford had previously worked on the case for the HTL firm, the opposing counsel she now worked for should be disqualified from representing the opposing side in the lawsuit. The trial court judge denied the petitioners' writ of mandamus. The petitioners appealed.

ISSUE

Should the writ of mandamus be approved disqualifying a law firm that represents one side of a lawsuit because a legal assistant who worked for the law firm that represented the other side of the lawsuit has now switched firms and works for the law firm sought to be disqualified?

Boyd, Chief Justice

In *Phoenix Founders, Inc. v. Marshall*, 887 S.W.2d 831, 835 (Tex. 1994), the court had occasion to discuss at some length circumstances such as the one before us in which a paralegal has changed employment from a law firm on one side of a case to a law firm on the other side of the case. In doing so, it recognized the countervailing interests involved and noted with approval the ABA suggestion that any restrictions on the nonlawyer's employment should be held to the minimum standard necessary to protect confidentiality of client information. In the course of its discussion, the court held that a paralegal or legal assistant who changes employment and who has worked on a case is subject to a conclusive presumption that confidences and secrets were imparted. While the presumption that a legal assistant obtained confidential information is not rebuttable, the presumption that the information was shared with a new employer is rebuttable.

Such distinction was created to ensure that a nonlawyer's mobility would not be unduly restricted. However, the court emphasized that the only way the rebuttable presumption could be overcome would be (1) to instruct the legal assistant not to work on any matter on which the paralegal worked during the prior employment, or regarding which the paralegal had information relating to the former employer's representation; and (2) "to take other reasonable steps to ensure that the paralegal does not work in connection with the matters on which the paralegal worked during the prior employment, absent client consent."

The trial court also had before it copies of a May 17, 1999, memo from Joe Hayes, managing partner of the Templeton firm, addressed to all the lawyers and staff of the Templeton firm. In the memo, Hayes designated two cases (one of which underlies this proceeding) as those about which Crawford might possess confidential information. In the memo, the recipients were instructed that Texas Disciplinary Rules 1.05(b)(1) and 5.03(a) prohibited them, as Crawford's supervising employers, "from revealing any confidential information she might have regarding the cases." The memo also advised that to satisfy the requirements of the Disciplinary Rules, as well as those set forth by the supreme court in the *In Re American Home Products Corporation* case, the firm was implementing the following six policies and procedures, effective immediately:

1. Inda shall not perform any work or take any action in connection with the *Westgate* case or the *Seger* case [the second, unrelated, case].
2. Inda shall not discuss the *Westgate* case or the *Seger* case, or disclose any information she has concerning these cases, with anyone.
3. No lawyer or staff member shall discuss the *Westgate* case or the *Seger* case with Inda, or in her presence.
4. All computer information relating to the *Westgate* case and the *Seger* case shall be removed from the firm's computer system. No future information concerning either the *Westgate* case or the *Seger* case shall be stored in any electronic medium but, rather, kept solely in hard copy form with the files in the respective case.

(continued)

5. The files in the *Westgate* case and the *Seger* case shall be kept in locked files under my supervision. No one shall have access to those files other than me, and those to whom I have given specific authority to access these files. Inda shall not have access to these files or the area where the files are to be maintained. At the close of each business day, all documents relating to these cases shall be placed in their respective files, which shall be returned to their storage places, which shall then be locked.

6. Inda shall not be given access to any of the files pertaining to the *Westgate* case or the *Seger* case, or their contents. None of the documents pertaining to either of these cases shall be disclosed to Inda, discussed with her, or discussed in her presence.

Our review of the record before the trial court convinces us that we cannot say he abused his discretion in arriving at his decision to deny the motion to disqualify the Templeton law firm. Accordingly, relators' petition seeking mandamus relief must be, and is, denied.

DECISION AND REMEDY

The court of appeals affirmed the trial court's denial of the writ of mandamus, thus permitting Crawford to work for the second law firm, which had imposed sufficient safeguards to assure that confidential information obtained at the first law firm was not disclosed to the second law firm.

The court also may find that the lower court has made an error that can be corrected, by sending the case back to the lower court, and **remand** the case to the lower court, to take additional action or conduct further proceedings. For example, the lower court may be directed to hold further proceedings in which a jury hears testimony related to the issue of damages and makes an award of monetary damages.

An appellate court will reverse a lower court decision if it finds an *error of* law the record. An error of law occurs if the jury was improperly instructed by the trial court judge, prejudicial evidence was admitted at trial when it should have been excluded, prejudicial evidence was obtained through an unconstitutional search and seizure, and the like. An appellate court will not reverse a finding of fact unless such finding is unsupported by the evidence or is contradicted by the evidence. ■

▶ENDNOTES

[i]American Bar Association Model Rules of Professional Conduct Rule 1.6, Confidentiality of Information

(a) **A lawyer shall not reveal information relating to the representation of a client unless the client gives informed consent, the disclosure is impliedly authorized in order to carry out the representation or the disclosure is permitted by paragraph (b).**

[ii]**NALA Code of Ethics and Professional Responsibility** *Canon* **7. A legal assistant must protect the confidences of a client and must not violate any rule or statute now in effect or hereafter enacted controlling the doctrine of privileged communications between a client and an attorney.**

[iii]Rule 501 General Rule

Except as otherwise required by the Constitution of the United States or provided by Act of Congress or in rules prescribed by the Supreme Court pursuant to statutory authority, the privilege of a witness, person, government, State, or political subdivision thereof shall be governed by the principles of the common law as they may be interpreted by the courts of the United States in the light of reason and experience. However, in civil actions and proceedings, with respect to an element of a claim or defense as to which State law supplies the rule of decision, the privilege of a witness, person, government, State, or political subdivision thereof shall be determined in accordance with State law. (Jan. 2, 1975, P.L. 93-595, § 1, 88 Stat. 1933)

[iv]*Trammell v. U.S.* 445 U.S. 40 (1980)

[v]How secrets are kept: Viewing the current clergy-penitent privilege through a comparison with the attorney–client privilege. *Brigham Young University Law* Review, Provo, 2002, Shawn P. Bailey.

[vi]*Conant v. Walters,* 309 F3d 629 (9th Cir. 2002).

[vii]*Jaffe v. Redmond,* 518 US 1 (1996).

[viii]Rule 408 FRE: . . . evidence of conduct or statements made in compromise negotiation is . . . not admissible. Also see *The Goodyear Tire and Rubber Company v Chiles Power Supply, Inc, et al,* 2003 Fed App 0197P (6th Cir)

[ix]*Trammell v. U.S.,* 445 U.S. 40 (1980)

[x]*SR International Bus. Ins. Co v. World Trade Center* Prop No 01 Civ 9291 (S.D.N.Y. 2002), quoting *Browne of New York City, Inc v. Ambase Corp.*

[xi]*International Bus. Ins. Co. v. World Trade Center Prop* No 01 Civ 9291 (S.D.N.Y. 2002), quoting North River Insurance Co. v. Columbia Casualty Company No. 9 Civ 2518, 1995 WL 5792

[xii]Also see the interesting article on the issue of providing privileged information to insurers. Guarding privileged documents poses challenge to "utmost good faith" doctrine, *National Underwriter; Eranger,* April 28, 2003; *Sally Agel; Felton Newell*

[xiii]*Electronic Data Systems Corporation v. Steingraber Case* 4:02 CV 225 USDC, E.D. Texas (2003).

[xiv]**FRCP 26 (b) Discovery Scope and Limits. Unless otherwise limited by order of the court in accordance with these rules, the scope of discovery is as follows:**

(1) In General. **Parties may obtain discovery regarding any matter, not privileged, that is relevant to the claim or defense of any party, including the existence, description, nature, custody, condition, and location of any books, documents, or other tangible things and the identity and location of persons having knowledge of any discoverable matter. For good cause, the court may order discovery of any matter relevant to the subject matter involved in the action. Relevant information need not be admissible at the trial if the discovery appears reasonably calculated to lead to the discovery of admissible evidence. All discovery is subject to the limitations imposed by Rule 26(b)(2)(i), (ii), and (iii).**

[xv]Fed. R. Crim. P. 16.

[xvi]In Re Grand Jury Subpoenas, 318 F. 3d 379 (2nd Cir 2002) at page 385.

[xvii]Id page 385

[xviii]*In Re a Witness,* 288 F.3d 289 (7th Cir.2002) at pages 293–294.

[xix]*VLT Inc. Lucent Technologies,* no 00–11049-PBS (D. Mass. 01/21/03)

[xx]Inadvertent Disclosure: Approaches and Remedies, *The Practical Lawyer,* Philadelphia, April 2001, by Kevin M. McCarthy

THE PARALEGAL WORKPLACE

"A lawyer's time and advice are his stock in trade."

Abraham Lincoln

3

PARALEGALS AT WORK

Law Offices
Goldenberg, Craigie, and Luria

INTEROFFICE MEMO

TO: Natasha Weiser
FROM: Cary Moritz, Office Manager
SUBJECT: Mentoring for New Hires

All of us at Goldenberg, Craigie, and Luria welcome you to our firm. We know you had other job opportunities but believe you will be professionally satisfied and challenged by working here.

The paralegal profession has changed dramatically since I first started in this field, and the one thing we can count on is more change. Please know that you can call on me at any time for advice and guidance. No question is too big or too small.

After all these years I have seen a number of major changes in the profession. When I started out, we were hired based on our keyboarding skills and basically operated as secretaries. Today, more and more lawyers treat us as a part of the legal team and demand as much, if not more, of us than they do new law graduates.

After studying this chapter, you should be able to:

1. Describe the different types of practice arrangements of lawyers and law firms.

2. Explain the organizational structure of law offices.

3. Describe the administrative procedures found in most law offices.

4. Understand the purpose and the importance of conflict-checking in the law office.

5. Explain why knowledge of accounting is important in a law practice.

6. Describe the emerging fields in paralegal specialty practice.

7. Be able to prepare a traditional resume and an electronic resume.

8. Create an effective cover letter submitting your resume for employment.

9. Understand the planning needed for a successful job interview.

In your new job as a paralegal for Goldenberg, Craigie, and Luria, you frequently will represent our firm as the client's first point of contact and be responsible for conducting initial interviews with clients. As you prepare your interview strategies, please use me as a sounding board. It is important to build rapport so clients will feel comfortable sharing sensitive and personal information with someone who is, at first, a complete stranger. As time goes on, clients often become most comfortable with the paralegal assigned to their case.

As a paralegal, you will be expected to follow a case and do much of the administrative work, such as keeping track of the time and costs associated with each case. Bookkeeping and accounting skills can be a real plus! When I first started, I did only litigation work. When the lawyers in my firm found out that I had been a bookkeeper and had taken accounting classes, I was asked not only to work in the estates area but also was given responsibility for some of the in-office accounting. This is something to think about as you look to develop your professional skill set. Getting a Bachelor's degree eventually led to my job as Office Manager. Additional education is always a plus!

Please know that you can count on me to help you succeed in the present and also to plan and prepare for future endeavors here at Goldenberg, Craigie, and Luria.

Consider the issues involved in this scenario as you read the chapter.

▶ INTRODUCTION FOR THE PARALEGAL

As the paralegal profession has evolved, so, too, have the duties and roles of the paralegal within the legal system and elsewhere. The earliest legal assistant was probably a legal secretary who developed specialized skills while working for an attorney in one of the legal specialties. As the need for specialized skills became more obvious, legal assistant programs and paralegal programs were created to teach the requisite skills.

In the classic sense, a paralegal performs those tasks and activities that assist the supervising attorney in representing clients. In the broader view, the paralegal performs many of the same functions that attorneys perform, under the supervision of an attorney but limited by laws and regulations on the unauthorized practice of law (UPL). The paralegal's actual tasks and functions vary according to the type of practice, size of the firm or organization, and skill of the individual paralegal. ■

ARRANGEMENTS AND ORGANIZATION OF LAW OFFICES AND FIRMS

The classic image of the law firm was of the practitioner working alone in a small office in a small town. The more modern view portrayed in movies and on TV is that of a large national or global law firm. In between are small partnerships and other environments—corporations, insurance companies, government agencies, and consulting firms composed of accountants, lawyers, and management consultants. Exhibit 3.1 shows organization charts for four typical types of arrangements in which the paralegal may find work.

Exhibit 3.1 **Typical organization charts for various-sized firms**

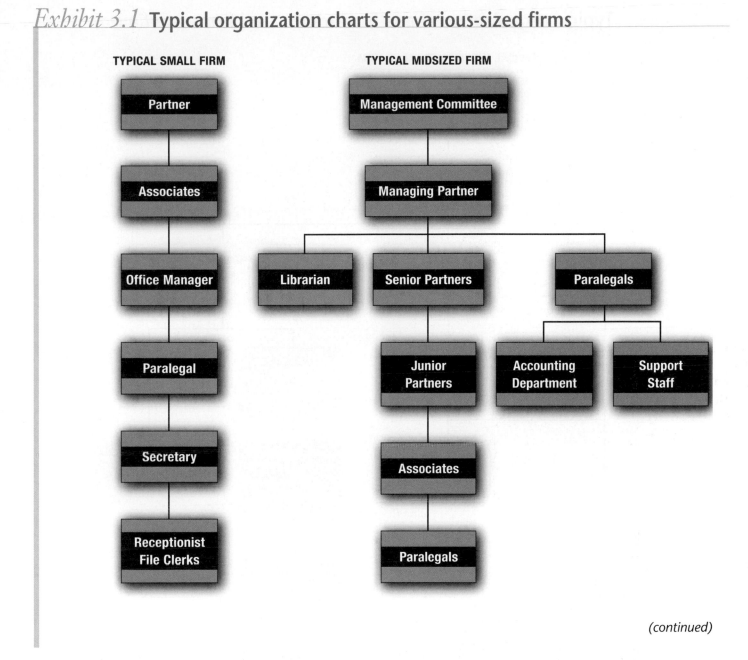

(continued)

Solo Practice

Solo practice refers to one lawyer practicing alone without the assistance of other attorneys. The solo practitioner still exists, not only in small towns but in large metropolitan areas as well. The solo practitioner may well be the employer who most depends on the skills of the paralegal in running the office, working with clients, and assisting at trial. A solo practice offers perhaps the greatest challenge for the paralegal who wishes to be involved in every aspect of a law practice. Tasks that otherwise might be assigned to an associate will fall to the paralegal to perform.

In a litigation practice or a practice in which the attorney is frequently out of the office attending meetings, the paralegal becomes the main point of contact and coordination between clients and the supervising attorney. Jobs that might be done in larger firms by an accounting staff, such as preparation of payroll and maintenance of client escrow accounts, frequently are done by the paralegal in solo practices. Many solo practitioners consider their paralegal to be a key resource in the practice of law.

solo practice
One lawyer practicing alone without the assistance of other attorneys.

Exhibit 3.1 **Typical organization charts for various-sized firms** *(continued)*

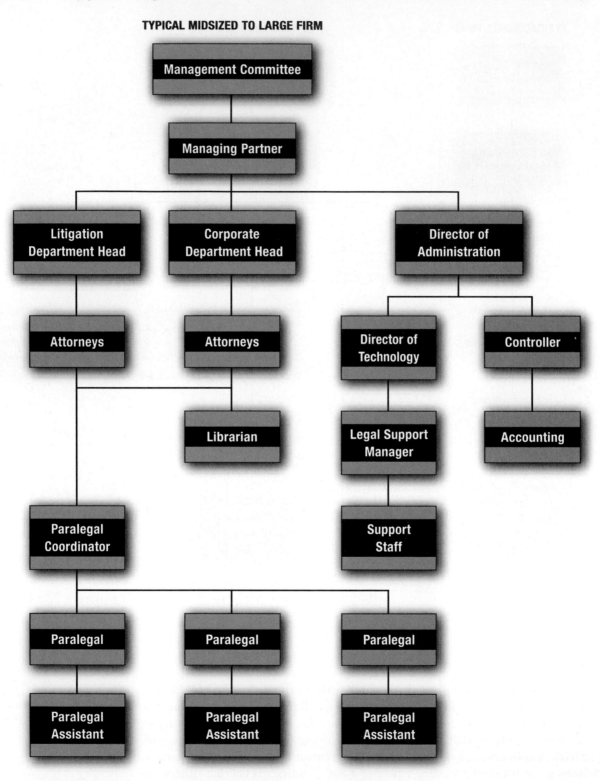

TYPICAL MIDSIZED TO LARGE FIRM

(continued)

Exhibit 3.1 Typical organization charts for various-sized firms (continued)

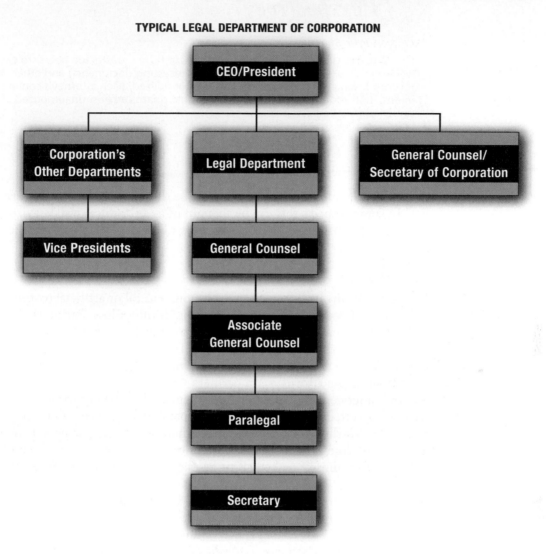

TYPICAL LEGAL DEPARTMENT OF CORPORATION

Source: WAGNER, ANDREA, HOW TO LAND YOUR FIRST PARALEGAL JOB: INSIDERS, 3rd, © 2001. Electronically reproduced by permission of Pearson Education, Inc., Upper Saddle River, New Jersey.

Small Offices

Small-office arrangements range from individual practitioners sharing space to partnerships. For the small practitioner, the cost of maintaining an adequate law library, conference room, office space, and office support services such as photocopy and fax machines is daunting. Therefore, practices frequently share these common services while separating client practices. The lawyers might have a similar type of practice, such as criminal law or family law, or dissimilar practices, such as family law and insurance defense work. Depending upon the arrangement, the practitioners might refer clients back and forth. The responsibility for the client and the client relationship is a personal one for the attorney.

Depending upon the arrangement, personnel, such as the receptionist, secretary, or paralegal, might be shared. In these situations the paralegal must be certain which of the attorneys is the supervising attorney with regard to each client. The paralegal who is working for more than one attorney in a sharing arrangement might be privy

Small offices
Small-office arrangements range from individual practitioners sharing space to partnerships.

ETHICAL *Perspective*

Lawyers Who Share Offices

It is "impermissible for unaffiliated attorneys to have unrestricted access to each other's electronic files (including email and word-processing documents) and other client records. If separate computer systems are not utilized, each attorney's confidential client information should be protected in a way that guards against unauthorized access and preserves client confidences and secrets."

Source: District of Columbia Ethics Opinion 303

to confidential information that may not be shared with the other attorneys in the office. In some respects this can be thought of as an "ethical wall" environment. At the very least, the paralegal and the attorneys must clearly understand the ethical issues involved.

Partnerships

Partnership
Two or more natural or artificial (corporation) persons who have joined together to share ownership and profit or loss.

In a **partnership** arrangement, two or more natural or artificial (corporation) persons have joined together to share ownership and profit or loss. Partnerships in small-office arrangements may take the form of true partnerships, sharing all aspects of the practice, or may be partnerships in name only. In the latter case, the same ethical issues that the paralegal faces in the pure office-sharing arrangement must be considered.

If all of the attorneys are partners with complete responsibility for each other and the practice, paralegals may find themselves working for more than one of the partners. In effect, the partners share the paralegal's services. This can give rise to certain issues for the paralegal when more than one of the partners demand something at the same time with the same sense of urgency. The fact that each of the partners will consider himself or herself to be "boss" can create a delicate situation for the paralegal.

A common solution in many offices is for one of the partners to be the primary supervising attorney for the paralegal, through whom the other partner (or partners) funnels work and requests. From an ethical point of view this solves the problem of who the supervising attorney is for the clients and files on which the paralegal is working and at the same time clarifies the lawyers' responsibilities under the lawyers' Rules of Professional Conduct.

Large Offices

Large law offices
Large law offices are an outgrowth of traditional law offices that have expanded over the years, adding partners and associates along the way.

Historically, what are now viewed as **large law offices** are an outgrowth of traditional law offices that have expanded over the years, adding partners and associates along the way. Initially, the larger law firms were regional, confined to major cities such as New York, Chicago, Philadelphia, and Los Angeles. With the growth of government at the national level, many firms found themselves establishing offices in the nation's capital to service clients appearing before federal agencies.

Continued growth of the national economy and business and corporate clients around the country resulted in many firms establishing offices in other large cities, giving them a presence on each of the coasts as well as central locations such as Chicago, with offices in Washington, D.C., and elsewhere. Growth of the global economy has taken us one step farther, with law firms establishing offices in foreign countries. As a result, the large law firm has taken on the characteristics of many corporations, with firms merging to bring specialty areas of law within one firm while expanding the global availability of legal services.

For the paralegal the large office can be an exciting and dynamic area of practice. Paralegals may be called upon to travel with other members of the legal team or on their own as part of the practice. Even when no travel is required, the paralegal might be called upon to work with clients who have diverse backgrounds, both domestically and internationally. One of the values of the large law firm for clients is the availability of a number of legal specialties within one legal services provider. For the paralegal this offers the opportunity to work in different areas of legal specialty.

Working in a large law firm also has some disadvantages. The larger the firm, the greater is the potential for fewer personal relationships and contacts with clients and other members of the legal team. In some firms, just as in any large organization, "playing politics" becomes very real. A paralegal's status, as well as some of the perks and benefits of the job, may depend on the status of the individual's supervising attorney. At the same time, the opportunities for advancement in a large firm might outweigh the disadvantages.

Large Firms

Unlike the small office, in which the paralegal also might be the bookkeeper, office manager, receptionist, and second chair in litigation, a department within a large firm typically hires support staff for each of these functions. The first contact for a paralegal with a large firm may be with the human resources department as part of the job-application process. Bookkeeping or accounting departments usually handle payroll, check requests, and other financial issues. In the larger firms, even the function of making copies takes place in a duplicating department, and the firm might have a mailroom for handling incoming and outgoing mail.

The large law firm has specialized components. In some ways this is similar to the structure of the English legal system, in which the solicitor deals directly with clients and the barrister litigates the cases. U.S. law firms frequently have litigation specialists who spend their time in the actual litigation of cases while other attorneys within the same firm rarely, if ever, go to court. The role of the latter is to work with clients and, when the need arises, prepare the materials for the litigation department.

Just as the law has become more complex, lawyers also have come to specialize in narrow areas of practice such as environmental law, intellectual property law, health-care law, insurance law, tort law, and family law. This means that paralegals in large law firms also become specialists within their supervising attorney's primary field of law. Large-practice firms encourage clients to use the firm for all of their legal needs, so a lawyer within the firm frequently refers clients to other specialists in the firm while maintaining primary contact with the clients. Some firms have lawyers whose expertise is in getting new clients. These lawyers, often former politicians and government officials, frequently are referred to as the "rainmakers." They use their contacts to obtain clients and then refer the clients to the specialists within the firm.

Compensation for attorneys within large firms is generally based on how much new business the attorney has brought in, as well as how many billable hours the supervising attorneys have been able to bill for themselves and their paralegals. In this kind of environment, the paralegal who is able to maintain relationships with clients is an invaluable asset to the firm.

General Practice

A **general law practice** is one that handles all types of cases. This is what people usually think of as the small-town lawyer, the generalist to whom everyone in town comes for advice. The reality is that the same generalists practice in cities as well as small towns throughout the country. Their practices are as diverse as the law itself, handling everything from adoptions to zoning appeals. As general practitioners, they serve the same function in law as the general family practice doctor does in medicine.

Lawyers in this type of practice often work in several areas of law within the same day—attending a hearing in small-claims court in the morning, preparing a will before lunch, having a luncheon meeting with an opposing attorney to discuss settlement

General law practice
A general law practice is one that handles all types of cases.

of an accident case, then helping someone who is forming a corporation, and finally appearing at a municipal government meeting in the evening to seek a zoning approval. For many, the general practice is the most exciting type of practice, with a continually changing clientele offering all sorts of legal challenges. The paralegal in this environment has the opportunity to work with different types of clients on different types of legal matters on a constant basis. The challenge in this type of practice is to stay current in each of the areas of law of the practice.

SPECIALTY PRACTICE

Specialty practice
A specialty practice is involved in practice in one area of law.

A **specialty practice** is involved in one area of law. Lawyers with specialty backgrounds, such as engineering, might choose to work in patent law or intellectual-property law. Those coming into the legal profession with accounting backgrounds might specialize in tax matters. Others have special interests and passions such as working with senior citizens in an elder law practice, or protecting the interests of children as child advocates, or practicing criminal law.

With the increasing complexity of the law, legal specialists frequently are receiving referrals from attorneys in other specialties or in general practice. The paralegal working for a specialist often acquires such a high level of knowledge in a specific area of law that it rivals that of many general practitioners. One of the dangers for the paralegal with this extent of specialty knowledge is that other attorneys could ask the paralegal questions to which the answers border on, or actually result in, the unauthorized practice of law.

Because the paralegal in a specialty law practice is dependent—as are the supervising attorney and the practice—on referrals from other attorneys, the natural tendency is to accommodate referral attorneys by trying to answer questions of a legal nature. To avoid a potential claim of UPL, the paralegal must diplomatically avoid giving legal advice even to an attorney from another firm.

Maintaining relationships with other law firms and their paralegals and secretaries becomes a primary job function for the paralegal in a specialty practice. The paralegal commonly obtains referrals for the supervising attorney and the firm as a result of relationships developed in professional associations with other paralegals who recommend their friend who works for a lawyer specializing in the area sought.

In many areas of specialty, the paralegal has become a vital team member. Paralegals with specialty skills in specific substantive areas perform services that allow the attorney to concentrate on other substantive issues of law. In addition, the paralegal handles office management tasks and functions. These encompass intraoffice support including coordination between members of the professional team and the client.

 MEET THE COURTHOUSE TEAM

The Courtroom

The first time you enter a courtroom, you may be surprised to find a number of people working as part of the courtroom team. Obviously, a judge is presiding. Less obvious are the support personnel—the people who keep the courtroom organized and handle trial details such as scheduling and processing documents. Also, they sometimes act as the interface between jury and judge. Depending on the state and the court, they are called minutes clerk, bailiff, or court deputy. In addition, there usually is a court reporter whose job is to make a contemporaneous record of the proceeding. Frequently, the judge's law clerk sits in on hearings as well.

Legal Nurse Consultants and Nurse Paralegals

Nurse paralegals or legal nurse consultants are nurses who have gained medical-work experience and combine it with paralegal skills. Becoming a legal nurse consultant or a nurse paralegal is an ideal career opportunity for nurses with clinical nursing experience who want to work in the legal environment. Entry to most education programs requires a current license as a Registered Nurse and a minimum of 2,000 to 6,000 hours of clinical nursing experience, usually one to three years. Some programs are open to those with an associate degree in nursing, but usually a bachelor's degree in nursing is requested or desired.

Nurse paralegals draw upon their knowledge of medical terminology, medical procedures, and nursing practice to decipher medical records for the legal community. The most obvious advantage is their ability to analyze medical records from both medical and legal standpoints. Their experience also enables them to conduct more effective interviews with clients, fact witnesses, and expert witnesses in cases of medical malpractice and cases involving injury and damage investigation. Graduates of these programs often work as independent nurse consultants for law firms and insurance companies. Others find positions with insurance companies and law firms specializing in medical malpractice and personal injury.

Although the ABA considers the nurse paralegal and legal nurse consultant to be part of the paralegal profession, the American Association of Legal Nurse Consultants (AALNC) views this role as a subspecialty of nursing. In March 1998, the then named Standing Committee on Legal Assistants of the American Bar Association, now named the Standing Committee on Paralegals, decided that "legal nurses and legal nurse consultants fall squarely within the ABA definition of 'paralegal/legal assistant.'" By contrast, AALNC has defined the legal nurse consultant as a specialty practitioner of nursing whose education should be developed and presented as specialty nursing curricula by nurse educators in partnership with legal educators.

> **Nurse paralegals or legal nurse consultants**
> Nurses who have gained medical work experience and combine it with paralegal skills.

Further information on Legal Nurse Consulting can be obtained at www.Aalnc.org

Real Estate

Paralegals with real estate experience in sales or from title insurance agencies can perform many of the tasks associated with a real estate practice, such as communicating between buyers and sellers, coordinating the documentation for settlement, and preparing documents for recording purposes. In most jurisdictions, becoming a licensed salesperson or a real estate broker requires completion of a course of study that provides a foundation in the practices and procedures of real estate practice and equips the paralegal with a terminology base that facilitates effective communication with the supervising attorney.

Complex Litigation

Complex litigation takes many forms, from class-action lawsuits to complex product-liability cases. Paralegals working in complex litigation typically oversee the requests for document production and maintain indexes, usually on computer databases, of the paperwork generated from litigation. In large cases the paralegal might supervise a staff of other paralegals or law students in summarizing discovery documents. At trial, these paralegals frequently coordinate the production of exhibits.

> **Complex litigation**
> Cases involving many parties as in a class action or multiple or complex legal issues.

Environmental Law

Environmental law covers everything from toxic waste dumps to protecting of wildlife and the environment. A challenge for the environmental paralegal is in locating and obtaining public records and other documents necessary to establish the areas of concern and claims, some of which predate computer records, such as toxic waste dumps created during World War II and the early 1950s.

> **Environmental Law**
> An area of the law dealing with the protection of the environment.

Intellectual Property

In a survey by The Affiliates, a company providing temporary and full-time legal personnel, 48 percent of the surveyed attorneys indicated **intellectual property** as the fastest growing field in law. The intellectual-property paralegal is concerned with the formalities of protecting intellectual-property interests including patent rights, trade secrets, and copyrights and trademarks. The two main areas are (a) prosecution, which involves establishing the priority of the claims that will result in granting of the patent or copyright, and (b) litigation, which protects those rights against claims by others, such as in patent-infringement cases.

Intellectual property
Protection of intellectual property interests like patents, trademarks and copyrights.

Elder Law

With the aging of the population has come an increased need to protect the rights of the elderly and obtain all the benefits to which they are entitled. This includes simple tasks such as assisting individuals to apply for Social Security benefits, Medicare benefits, or Medicaid benefits. It also entails working with the elderly to create estate plan documents, powers of attorney, and health-care directives. More and more, the paralegal or legal assistant is becoming an advocate for the elderly, in many cases working in a pro bono capacity or through social service agencies. **Elder law** has come to include the additional issues of helping the elderly work through the maze of health care and government benefits.

Elder law
Advocacy for the elderly.

Paralegal Managers

As paralegal staffs have grown, even at some of the smaller firms, the position of **paralegal manager** has emerged. With higher turnover rates and increased specialization comes the associate's need for someone to hire, supervise, train, and evaluate paralegals. In many firms this person is the interface between the paralegal and the attorneys.

As paralegals gain specialized knowledge in specific fields, they find themselves working for different attorneys as their expertise demands. Attorneys, for the most part, do not have the time to handle the nonlegal aspects of managers, such as acting as leader, mentor, employee advocate, supervisor, trainer, evaluator, problem solver, and resource manager.

The largest firms appoint a managing partner to handle the management tasks and human resources issues. In many smaller firms, these duties fall to the individual with the title of paralegal manager. This new specialty is well recognized and supported by its own organization, the International Paralegal Management Association.

Paralegal manager
Someone who hires, supervises, trains, and evaluates paralegals.

Check the latest IPMA News at the IPMA Web site
www.ipma.org

Pro Bono Paralegals

Pro bono means working without compensation on behalf of individuals and organizations that otherwise could not afford legal assistance. Increasingly, the legal profession has taken on the role of working without compensation in legal aid offices and community legal service programs. As members of professional associations, paralegals participate in pro bono activities at varying levels and time commitments. For example, the Massachusetts Paralegal Association supports a number of pro bono projects. In one of these, the Family Law Project, paralegals partner with attorneys to help handle domestic violence cases without compensation. Pro bono work is seen as part of an ethical obligation of the legal profession.

Pro bono
Working without compensation on behalf of individuals and organizations that otherwise could not afford legal assistance.

Government Employment

Federal, state, and local governments are large employers of paralegals, and paralegals are expected to be utilized even further at every level in the future. Many of the federally employed paralegals are found in administrative agencies. A good example is the work of paralegals in the Social Security Administration as decision writers, case schedulers, and case specialists. Just as the private law firm has discovered the value of the paralegal on the legal team, so have government law offices such as the U.S. At-

Government employment
Working for federal, state, and local government agencies and authorities.

THE DUPONT EXPERIENCE

In an effort to reduce costs, DuPont, one of the largest companies in the United States, changed the way it uses legal assistants—elevating the work, positions, and numbers of legal assistants. Legal assistants have been given more responsibility in handling documents, technology, and investigations. In doing so, DuPont reportedly reduced by almost 90 percent the number of outside law firms and services it formerly used.

As of 2000, the DuPont legal department had 51 paralegals working with 140 lawyers. In the DuPont model, the legal department acts as counsel to the other DuPont-owned companies and deals with them as clients much in the way that the outside law firms did in the past.

Source: "Paralegals Are Part of DuPont's Legal Team," by D. L. Hawley, *Legal Assistant Today*, March 4, 2000.

torney's Office and the Office of the Solicitor General. These offices are involved with both criminal prosecutions and civil litigation where the government is a party. Many other agencies that conduct administrative hearings utilize paralegals at all levels.

Legal Departments of Corporations

Many people think of a corporate legal department as a laid-back, conservative environment with little activity other than drafting minutes of meetings and filing corporate records with federal and state governments. The reality today is that, in the global economy, more and more corporations with in-house staffs are engaged in international trade. A whole body of law relates to compliance for imports and exports.

For example, the transfer and sale of certain high-tech equipment and technology must have prior government approval. Sales involving shipments to other countries require letters of credit and currency conversion. International trade creates a host of unique issues related to the laws of the countries with which the domestic corporation may be doing business.

The paralegal is in the middle of these transactions, juggling the requirements from both the legal perspective and the sales/marketing perspective. Paralegals with foreign language skills find themselves in even greater demand in handling communication issues. Those with cultural ties to, or background in, the countries with which the corporation is doing business will find their knowledge frequently tapped to avoid cultural mistakes resulting from miscommunication.

Self-Employment

The paralegal has some opportunities to be self-employed, although state regulation may limit the opportunities or restrict paralegal **self-employment.** Where authorized by federal law, the paralegal may actively represent clients without the supervision of an attorney, such as before the U.S. Patent Office or Social Security Administration. Many paralegals work as freelancers for different attorneys, usually on a case-by-case basis. In addition to the normal ethical obligations regarding confidentiality and conflict of interest, the freelance paralegal must observe the ethical guidelines on advertising in the local jurisdiction and avoid creating the appearance of being available to render legal advice except where authorized.

Networking

Regardless of the size or type of working environment, **networking** is important for the individual. It establishes contact with others with whom questions and information are shared. For the paralegal, networking may be the key to obtaining a job. As you've heard no doubt, it is not what you know but whom you know. Knowing the right person or a person who can refer you to the right person is a valuable asset.

DOCUMENT SPECIALIST OR PARALEGAL?

Under the definition enacted by the Maine legislature, anyone calling himself or herself a paralegal or legal assistant must work under the supervision of an attorney. Independent paralegals no longer can use the title "paralegal" or "legal assistant." This has resulted in some of them changing the name of their freelance business to "document specialist" (*Bangor Daily News,* August 16, 1999).

The California legislature has a law prohibiting self-help legal document service providers from receiving compensation unless the legal document assistant is registered in the county where the service is provided and provides a bond of $25,000.

Self employment
Working independently either as a freelance paralegal for different lawyers or, when authorized by state or federal law, performing services for the public.

Networking
The establishment of contact with others with whom questions and information are shared.

Many paralegals develop a referral list of other paralegals they can call to get a quick answer in their own jurisdiction and in others. Most paralegals facing a deadline are not too proud to call their contacts—whether they are across the street, across the state, or across the country—to meet a deadline or get the necessary form. During interviews, hiring attorneys have been known to ask about the paralegal's networking activity.

PARALEGAL TASKS AND FUNCTIONS

The actual tasks and functions the paralegal performs vary according to the type of practice, size of the firm or organization, and skill of the individual paralegal. Some of the more generic tasks include

- conducting interviews
- maintaining written and verbal contacts with clients and counsel
- setting up, organizing, and maintaining client files
- preparing pleadings and documents
- reviewing, analyzing, summarizing, and indexing documents and transcripts

Advice from the Field ·······························

PARALEGALS: A CRUCIAL COMPONENT TO CLIENT SERVICE

D. Jeffrey Campbell

An often overlooked, yet critically important aspect of a paralegal's performance is the role he or she plays in ensuring high-quality client service. The quality of a lawyer's client service, as distinct from the quality of the lawyer's work product, is often the determining factor in whether or not the lawyer gets repeat business or referrals from a client. Lawyers who fully and skillfully use paralegals to supplement their own efforts to achieve superior client satisfaction will be at a competitive advantage over lawyers who do not use paralegals.

One of the ways in which paralegals can elevate client service is to act as an easily accessible and consistent client contact. While attorneys are often out of the office, and therefore not immediately available to clients, paralegals normally work in the office. Therefore, a paralegal who has good oral communication skills and a working relationship with a client can often respond to client questions and concerns more promptly and effectively than can lawyers. Similarly, paralegals can prepare routine correspondence to clients, following-up on requests for information and forwarding documents for clients' review.

Of course, in order for paralegals to enhance client service in these ways, they must possess good communi-

cation skills. It is therefore important that paralegals' academic experience prepares them for effective written and oral communication. Coursework should provide either formal training in writing and speaking or ample opportunities for written and oral presentations. Through such experience and training, the paralegal gains the knowledge and confidence to interact effectively with clients.

Paralegals with good communication skills can maintain close working relationships with clients, particularly institutional clients, for years. While associates often move from one practice area to another, leave the firm for other professional endeavors, or become partners and develop their own clientele, paralegals often service the same clients for years. Such clients develop a high degree of familiarity with and confidence in these paralegals. Thus, paralegals can and should be key members of the client service team—members who enhance client satisfaction, build client relationships, and help to secure repeat business or referrals for years to come.

"Paralegals: A Crucial Component to Client Services" by Jeffrey Campbell, published in Update, *Volume 5, No. 3, Spring/Summer 2004. © 2004 by the American Bar Association. Reprinted with permission.*

- assisting in preparing witnesses and clients for trial,
- maintaining calendar and tickler systems,
- conducting research, both factual and legal, and
- performing office administrative functions including maintaining time and billing records

Client Interviews

Many paralegals act as the first line of contact with clients. Although paralegals may not ethically or legally give legal advice or set legal fees, they frequently conduct the initial interview with the client. This might involve taking the initial client information and preparing the client data sheet (see Exhibit 3.2) or conducting a more in-depth interview to determine the facts of the matter for the attorney's review. Frequently, the paralegal continues to function as the contact point with the client and the supervising attorney or the law firm. Paralegals frequently establish rapport with clients and earn their confidence.

Exhibit 3.2 **Client data sheet**

CLIENT DATA SHEET

ACTION TAKEN/REQUIRED

1. Client Name:

2. Client/Matter Number:
3. Client Address:

4. Phone: Work:
   Home:
   Fax:
5. Email address:
6. Social Security No.:
7. Date of Birth:
8. Marital Status:
9. Client Contact:
10. Matter:

(a) Adverse Party:
(b) Date of Incident:
(c) Statute of Limitations Period:
(d) Statute of Limitations Date:
11. Opposing Counsel:

12. Opposing Counsel Address:

13. Opposing Counsel Phone:

The paralegal always must be keenly aware of the ethical limitations in dealing with clients. This is especially true when the client develops a high level of confidence in dealing with the paralegal. Clients come to the attorney for advice. When they have confidence in a paralegal, they might tend to ask the paralegal for advice and recommendations instead of "bothering" the attorney. Providing such advice or recommendations may be in violation of UPL restrictions.

For example, to the client, the question, "Should I make my son my power of attorney?" seems simple. But the answer is not so simple and involves many legal consequences, so it must be referred to the supervising attorney. Another UPL might be to help the client complete blank legal forms, such as bankruptcy forms or will forms purchased at a retail store.

Investigations

The paralegal may be asked to act as the direct representative of the supervising attorney in conducting an investigation into a pending case. A paralegal trained in the specific area of law understands the factual needs of a case and the sources of information available. A paralegal who has had the opportunity to observe or work with an attorney and has watched the presentation of evidence in a trial obtains a good sense of what will make good demonstrative evidence, such as models and photographs.

In the case of photos, an understanding of the kind of questions that might be asked in direct examination and cross-examination about the photographs offered as evidence enables the paralegal to be certain that the photographs are taken from the correct angles with the correct landmarks or measurements included. Interviews conducted by the paralegal in preparation for trial could qualify as privileged for the attorney–client privilege just as they do when conducted by attorneys. The paralegal must be aware of how interview material may be used and potentially obtained by opposing parties and act to protect clients' privileged communication with the paralegal as a representative of the supervising attorney.

Legal Writing

Paralegals frequently are called upon to maintain the written communications with clients, opposing attorneys, and the court. These may be in the form of correspondence, memos of law, or briefs for the court. Many paralegals become extremely adept at drafting complaints and supporting memoranda of law and briefs. Although the content is the ultimate responsibility of the supervising attorney, the paralegal with good writing skills is an invaluable asset. Well-written and well-reasoned documentation is easy to review for signature and transmittal and is a major timesaver for the attorney.

Legal Research

In the modern law office, legal research is conducted with hardcopy books and also with electronic media, including extensive use of the Internet. The ability to conduct research into case law, statutory enactments, and regulatory rules and procedures gives the paralegal a major advantage in getting the job in the first place and advancing in most firms. Legal research today requires the ability to use online legal services such as Lexis, Westlaw, VersusLaw, and Loislaw, as well as the ability to find information on government websites and private websites.

What Paralegals in Legal Specialties Do

In addition to the various generic tasks that most paralegals or legal assistants perform, paralegals working in specialty areas find themselves performing additional and more specialized tasks that frequently require special knowledge, education, or skill beyond the basic skills and knowledge required of all paralegals. Some of the tasks that paralegals in specialty practice perform are as follows.

General business practice:

- Draft lease agreements
- Draft partnership agreements
- Draft noncompetition agreements
- Prepare agreements of sale and attend real estate settlements
- Draft contracts for business arrangements and new ventures
- Draft employee agreements

Debtor rights and creditor remedies:

- Draft correspondence complying with state and federal regulations concerning debt collection
- Prepare documentation to support garnishment proceedings
- Arrange for execution and support judgments, including publication of notice of sales and levies on personal property
- Transfer judgments to other jurisdictions
- Prepare, file, and terminate Uniform Commercial Code financing statements
- Assist clients in filing bankruptcy petitions, including the preparation of schedules and proofs of claim
- Prepare Chapter 11 debtor's financial statements
- Attend Chapter 13 confirmation hearings

Corporate practice:

- Determine availability and reserve fictitious or corporate name
- Prepare and file fictitious name registrations
- Prepare articles of incorporation, minutes, and bylaws for corporation
- Prepare, issue, and transfer stock certificates
- Prepare shareholder agreements
- Prepare applications and file for employer identification numbers and tax registration numbers
- Prepare and file annual reports
- Prepare and file articles of dissolution
- Prepare and file securities registrations and required filings with state regulatory agencies and with the United States Securities & Exchange Commission

Environmental law:

- Track information with regard to Superfund sites
- Determine applicability of brown fields to client property
- Research history of properties to determine environmental activity
- Obtain the appropriate information about sites from state and federal environmental agencies
- Obtain documentation and assist in the preparation of environmental audits
- Organize and index documentation

Family law:

- Collect information from clients with regard to marital status and prior marital status
- Interview client and collect information with regard to child support (see Exhibit 3.3)
- Draft prenuptial agreements

Exhibit 3.3 **Child support data form**

_____ v. _____ No. _____

THIS FORM MUST BE FILLED OUT

(If you are self-employed or if you are salaried by a business of which you are owner in whole or in part, you must also fill out the Supplemental Income Statement which appears on the last page of this Income and Expense Statement.)

INCOME AND EXPENSE STATEMENT OF

_____

I verify that the statements made in this Income and Expense Statement are true and correct. I understand that false statements herein are made subject to the penalties of 18 Pa.C.S. §4904 relating to unsworn falsification to authorities.

Date: _____ Plaintiff or Defendant: _____

INCOME

Employer: _____

Address: _____

Type of Work: _____

Payroll Number: _____

Pay Period (weekly, biweekly, etc.): _____

Gross Pay per Pay Period: $ _____

Itemized Payroll Deductions: Federal Withholding $ _____
                              Social Security   _____
                              Local Wage Tax   _____
                              State Income Tax   _____
                              Retirement   _____
                              Savings Bonds   _____
                              Credit Union   _____
                              Life Insurance   _____
                              Health Insurance   _____
                              Other (specify)   _____
                              _____
                              Net Pay per Pay Period $_____

OTHER INCOME: (Fill in Appropriate Column)

	Weekly	*Monthly*	*Yearly*
Interest	$ _____	$ _____	$ _____
Dividends	_____	_____	_____
Pension	_____	_____	_____
Annuity	_____	_____	_____
Social Security	_____	_____	_____
Rents	_____	_____	_____
Royalties	_____	_____	_____
Expense Account	_____	_____	_____
Gifts	_____	_____	_____
Unemployment Comp.	_____	_____	_____
Workmen's Comp.	_____	_____	_____
_____	_____	_____	_____
Total	_____	_____	_____
TOTAL INCOME			$ _____

- Draft divorce complaints and responsive pleadings
- Prepare motions for support
- Prepare motions for custody and visitation
- Prepare property settlement agreements
- Prepare protection-from-abuse petitions

Exhibit 3.4 **Sample Immigration and Naturalization Service Form**

U.S. Department of Justice Immigration and Naturalization Service	**Notice of Entry of Appearance** **as Attorney or Representative**

Appearances - An appearance shall be filed on this form by the attorney or representative appearing in each case. Thereafter, substitution may be permitted upon the written withdrawal of the attorney or representative of record or upon notification of the new attorney or representative. When an appearance is made by a person acting in a representative capacity, his personal appearance or signature shall constitute a representation that under the provisions of this chapter he is authorized and qualified to represent. Further proof of authority to act in a representative capacity may be required. **Availability of Records** - During the time a case is pending, and except as otherwise provided in 8 CFR 103.2(b), a party to a proceeding or his attorney or representative shall be permitted to examine the record of proceeding in a Service office. He may, in conformity with 8 CFR 103.10, obtain copies of Service records or information therefrom and copies of documents or transcripts of evidence furnished by him. Upon request, he/she may, in addition, be loaned a copy of the testimony and exhibits contained in the record of proceeding upon giving his/her receipt for such copies and pledging that it will be surrendered upon final disposition of the case or upon demand. If extra copies of exhibits do not exist, they shall not be furnished free on loan; however, they shall be made available for copying or purchase of copies as provided in 8 CFR 103.10.

In re: Lim Chi	Date: 09-15-2002
	File No. A1357

I hereby enter my appearance as attorney for (or representative of), and at the request of the following named person(s):

Name: Lim chi	☑ Petitioner ☐ Applicant ☐ Beneficiary

Address: (Apt. No.) (Number & Street)	(City)	(State)	(Zip Code)
275 Swamp Road	Newtown	Pa 18940	

Name:	☐ Petitioner ☐ Applicant ☐ Beneficiary

Address: (Apt. No.) (Number & Street)	(City)	(State)	(Zip Code)

Check Applicable Item(s) below:

☑ 1. I am an attorney and a member in good standing of the bar of the Supreme Court of the United States or of the highest court of the following State, territory, insular possession, or District of Columbia

Pennsylvania _____   Supreme Court _____   and am not under a court or administrative agency
                                   Name of Court
order suspending, enjoining, restraining, disbarring, or otherwise restricting me in practicing law.

☐ 2. I am an accredited representative of the following named religious, charitable, social service, or similar organization established in the United States and which is so recognized by the Board:

☐ 3. I am associated with _____
the attorney of record previously filed a notice of appearance in this case and my appearance is at his request. (*If you check this item, also check item 1 or 2 whichever is appropriate.*)

☐ 4. Others (Explain Fully.)

SIGNATURE	COMPLETE ADDRESS 138 North State Street Newtown, pa 18940
NAME (Type or Print) Thomas F. Goldman	TELEPHONE NUMBER 215 555 4321

PURSUANT TO THE PRIVACY ACT OF 1974, I HEREBY CONSENT TO THE DISCLOSURE TO THE FOLLOWING NAMED ATTORNEY OR REPRESENTATIVE OF ANY RECORD PERTAINING TO ME WHICH APPEARS IN ANY IMMIGRATION AND NATURALIZATION SERVICE SYSTEM OF RECORDS:
          Thomas F. Goldman
_____
                    (Name of Attorney or Representative)
THE ABOVE CONSENT TO DISCLOSURE IS IN CONNECTION WITH THE FOLLOWING MATTER:

Name of Person Consenting	Signature of Person Consenting	Date
Lim Chi	*Lim Chi*	

(NOTE: Execution of this box is required under the Privacy Act of 1974 where the person being represented is a citizen of the United States or an alien lawfully admitted for permanent residence.)

This form may not be used to request records under the Freedom of Information Act or the Privacy Act. The manner of requesting such records is contained in 8CFR 103.10 and 103.20 Et.SEQ.

Form G-28 (09/26/00)Y

- Prepare petitions for termination of parental rights
- Prepare adoption petitions

Immigration law:

- Prepare applications and petitions for filing with the Immigration and Naturalization Service (INS) (see Exhibit 3.4 for a sample)

- Coordinate translation of foreign documents
- Prepare immigration and nonimmigration visa applications
- Coordinate activities with clients in foreign jurisdictions seeking visa and entry into the United States
- Assist clients in obtaining work visa to work in foreign countries
- Assist clients in the preparation of documentation to prove claim of marital status for submission to INS

Intellectual property:

- Prepare patent search
- Prepare trademark search
- Prepare applications for patent, trademark, or copyright (Exhibit 3.5 is a sample)
- Assist in preparation of documentation in opposition, interference, infringement, and similar proceedings
- Coordinate activities and filings with foreign patent, trademark, and copyright attorneys and agents
- Work with engineers in preparation of applications and defense of patents and trade secrets
- Draft licensing agreements for intellectual property items

Human resources law:

- Draft plan documents for tax-sheltered employee benefit plans
- Draft deferred compensation plans
- Prepare and file for Internal Revenue Service determination letters of plans
- Prepare and file annual reports including 5500 series Internal Revenue Service forms
- Calculate employer and employee contribution levels and limitations
- Draft, review, and distribute summary plan descriptions

Litigation:

- Investigate factual allegations of case
- Help to locate witnesses and physical evidence
- Draft summons, complaint, answers, and other defenses and responsive pleadings
- Organize and maintain litigation files
- Assist in the preparation of trial notebooks
- Gather, review, summarize, and index documents for use at trial
- Locate and arrange for interviews with expert witnesses
- Prepare written interrogatories
- Assist in preparing and conducting oral depositions, including videotape depositions
- Prepare or obtain subpoenas (see sample in Exhibit 3.6) and arrange for service upon witnesses
- Coordinate, assist, and arrange for trial exhibits
- Obtain jury-pool information, and assist in the selection of appropriate jury members
- Attend trial and assist in the handling of witnesses, exhibits, and evidence
- Prepare contemporaneous summaries of witness statements during trial

Exhibit 3.5 **Copyright form**

FORM TX
For a Nondramatic Literary Work
UNITED STATES COPYRIGHT OFFICE

REGISTRATION NUMBER

TX   TXU

EFFECTIVE DATE OF REGISTRATION

Month   Day   Year

FEE CHANGES
Fees are effective through June 30, 2002. After that date, check the Copyright Office Website at www.loc.gov/copyright or call (202) 707-3000 for current fee information.

DO NOT WRITE ABOVE THIS LINE. IF YOU NEED MORE SPACE, USE A SEPARATE CONTINUATION SHEET.

1 TITLE OF THIS WORK ▼

PREVIOUS OR ALTERNATIVE TITLES ▼

PUBLICATION AS A CONTRIBUTION If this work was published as a contribution to a periodical, serial, or collection, give information about the collective work in which the contribution appeared.   Title of Collective Work ▼

If published in a periodical or serial give: Volume ▼   Number ▼   Issue Date ▼   On Pages ▼

2 a NAME OF AUTHOR ▼

DATES OF BIRTH AND DEATH
Year Born ▼   Year Died ▼

Was this contribution to the work a "work made for hire"?
☐ Yes
☐ No

AUTHOR'S NATIONALITY OR DOMICILE
Name of Country
OR { Citizen of ▶ USA
     Domiciled in ▶

WAS THIS AUTHOR'S CONTRIBUTION TO THE WORK
Anonymous? ☐ Yes ☐ No
Pseudonymous? ☐ Yes ☐ No
If the answer to either of these questions is "Yes," see detailed instructions.

NATURE OF AUTHORSHIP Briefly describe nature of material created by this author in which copyright is claimed. ▼
Sole Author

NOTE
Under the law, the "author" of a "work made for hire" is generally the employer, not the employee (see instructions). For any part of this work that was "made for hire" check "Yes" in the space provided, give the employer (or other person for whom the work was prepared) as "Author" of that part, and leave the space for dates of birth and death blank.

b NAME OF AUTHOR ▼

DATES OF BIRTH AND DEATH
Year Born ▼   Year Died ▼

Was this contribution to the work a "work made for hire"?
☐ Yes
☐ No

AUTHOR'S NATIONALITY OR DOMICILE
Name of Country
OR { Citizen of ▶
     Domiciled in ▶

WAS THIS AUTHOR'S CONTRIBUTION TO THE WORK
Anonymous? ☐ Yes ☐ No
Pseudonymous? ☐ Yes ☐ No
If the answer to either of these questions is "Yes," see detailed instructions.

NATURE OF AUTHORSHIP Briefly describe nature of material created by this author in which copyright is claimed. ▼

c NAME OF AUTHOR ▼

DATES OF BIRTH AND DEATH
Year Born ▼   Year Died ▼

Was this contribution to the work a "work made for hire"?
☐ Yes
☐ No

AUTHOR'S NATIONALITY OR DOMICILE
Name of Country
OR { Citizen of ▶
     Domiciled in ▶

WAS THIS AUTHOR'S CONTRIBUTION TO THE WORK
Anonymous? ☐ Yes ☐ No
Pseudonymous? ☐ Yes ☐ No
If the answer to either of these questions is "Yes," see detailed instructions.

NATURE OF AUTHORSHIP Briefly describe nature of material created by this author in which copyright is claimed. ▼

3 a YEAR IN WHICH CREATION OF THIS WORK WAS COMPLETED This information must be given ▼Year in all cases.

b DATE AND NATION OF FIRST PUBLICATION OF THIS PARTICULAR WORK
Complete this information Month ▶ Day ▶ Year ▶ ◀ Nation
ONLY if this work has been published.   USA

4 COPYRIGHT CLAIMANT(S) Name and address must be given even if the claimant is the same as the author given in space 2. ▼

APPLICATION RECEIVED

ONE DEPOSIT RECEIVED

TWO DEPOSITS RECEIVED

FUNDS RECEIVED

TRANSFER If the claimant(s) named here in space 4 is (are) different from the author(s) named in space 2, give a brief statement of how the claimant(s) obtained ownership of the copyright. ▼
By written agreement.

MORE ON BACK ▶ • Complete all applicable spaces (numbers 5-9) on the reverse side of this page.   DO NOT WRITE HERE
• See detailed instructions.   • Sign the form at line 8.   Page 1 of ____ pages

See instructions before completing this space.

DO NOT WRITE ABOVE THIS LINE

FORM TX

EXAMINED BY

CHECKED BY

☐ CORRESPONDENCE
   Yes

FOR
COPYRIGHT
OFFICE
USE
ONLY

DO NOT WRITE ABOVE THIS LINE. IF YOU NEED MORE SPACE, USE A SEPARATE CONTINUATION SHEET.

5 PREVIOUS REGISTRATION Has registration for this work, or for an earlier version of this work, already been made in the Copyright Office?
☐ Yes ☐ No If your answer is "Yes," why is another registration being sought? (Check appropriate box.) ▼
a. ☐ This is the first published edition of a work previously registered in unpublished form.
b. ☐ This is the first application submitted by this author as copyright claimant.
c. ☐ This is a changed version of the work, as shown by space 6 on this application.
If your answer is "Yes," give: Previous Registration Number ▶   Year of Registration ▶

6 DERIVATIVE WORK OR COMPILATION
Preexisting Material Identify any preexisting work or works that this work is based on or incorporates. ▼   **a**

Material Added to This Work Give a brief, general statement of the material that has been added to this work and in which copyright is claimed. ▼   **b**

7 DEPOSIT ACCOUNT If the registration fee is to be charged to a Deposit Account established in the Copyright Office, give name and number of Account.
Name ▼   Account Number ▼   **a**

CORRESPONDENCE Give name and address to which correspondence about this application should be sent. Name/Address/Apt/City/State/ZIP ▼   **b**

Area code and daytime telephone number ▶ 480-991-7881   Fax number ▶
Email ▶

8 CERTIFICATION* I, the undersigned, hereby certify that I am the
Check only one ▶ {
☐ author
☐ other copyright claimant
☐ owner of exclusive right(s)
☑ authorized agent of
of the work identified in this application and that the statements made by me in this application are correct to the best of my knowledge.
Name of author or other copyright claimant, or owner of exclusive right(s) ▲

Typed or printed name and date ▼ If this application gives a date of publication in space 3, do not sign and submit it before that date.

Handwritten signature (X) ▼   Date ▶
X _____

9 Certificate will be mailed in window envelope to this address:
Name ▼
Number/Street/Apt ▼
City/State/ZIP ▼

YOU MUST:
• Complete all necessary spaces
• Sign your application in space 8

SEND ALL 3 ELEMENTS IN THE SAME PACKAGE:
1. Application form
2. Nonrefundable filing fee in check or money order payable to Register of Copyrights
3. Deposit material

MAIL TO:
Library of Congress
Copyright Office
101 Independence Avenue, S.E.
Washington, D.C. 20559-6000

As of July 1, 1999, the filing fee for Form TX is $30.

*17 U.S.C. § 506(e): Any person who knowingly makes a false representation of a material fact in the application for copyright registration provided for by section 409, or in any written statement filed in connection with the application, shall be fined not more than $2,500.
June 1999—200,000   ☺printed on recycled paper   ☆U.S. GOVERNMENT PRINTING OFFICE: 1999-454-879/49
WEB REV: June 1999

Exhibit 3.6   **Subpoena**

Commonwealth of Pennsylvania
County of Philadelphia

In the matter of:

Henry Thomas
_____
(Plaintiff)   (Demandante)

vs.

Thomas Cheese
_____
(Defendant)   (Demandado)

COURT OF COMMON PLEAS

October _____ Term, Yr. 2007

No. 68-96874 _____

Subpoena

To: Elizabeth Rhodes
_____
(Name of Witness)   (Nombre del Testigo)

1. YOU ARE ORDERED BY THE COURT TO COME TO *(El tribunal le ordena que venga a)*

Court room 654 _____, AT PHILADELPHIA, PENNSYLVANIA ON *(en Filadelfia,*

Pennsylvania el) November 4, 2007 _____, AT *(a las)* 10 O'CLOCK A .M., TO

TESTIFY ON BEHALF OF *(para atestiguar a favor de)* Henry Thomas _____ IN THE ABOVE

CASE, AND TO REMAIN UNTIL EXCUSED *(en el caso arriba mencionado y permanecer hasta que le autoricen irse).*

2. AND BRING WITH YOU THE FOLLOWING *(Y traer con usted lo siguiente):*

_____

_____

NOTICE

If you fail to attend or to produce the documents or things required by this subpoena, you may be subject to the sanctions authorized by Rule 234.5 of the Pennsylvania Rules of Civil Procedure, including but not limited to costs, attorney fees and imprisonment.

AVISO

Si usted falla en comparecer o producir los documentos o cosas requeridas por esta cita, usted estara sujeto a las sanciones autorizadas por la regla 234.5 de las reglas de procedimiento civil de Pensilvania, incluyendo pero no limitado a los costos, remuneracion de abogados y encarcelamiento.

INQUIRIES CONCERNING THIS SUBPOENA SHOULD BE ADDRESSED TO *(Las preguntas que tenga acerca de esta Citacion deben ser dirigidas a):*
ISSUED BY:

Edith Hannah
_____
(Attorney)   *(Abogado/Abogada)*

ADDRESS *(Direccion)* 8 North Broad Street, Philadelphia, PA _____

TELEPHONE NO. *(No. de Telefono)* 215 555 9999 _____

ATTORNEY *(Abogado ID #)* A5B6 _____

BY THE COURT *(Por El Tribunal)*
JOSEPH H. EVERS
PROHONOTARY *(Protonotario)*

PRO _____
(Clerk)   *(Escribano)*

10-200 (Rev. 7/99)   Completed Subpoena must be signed and sealed by the Prothonotary (Room 266 City Hall) before service.

ADMINISTRATIVE PROCEDURES IN LAW OFFICES AND FIRMS

Certain administrative procedures, such as conflict checking and time keeping, are common to most, if not all, law offices. Depending on the size of the law firm and the nature of the practice, a paralegal also may be called upon to perform what might be thought to be accounting or financial activities, such as preparing invoices, maintaining client escrow accounts, maintaining trust accounts, preparing payroll records, preparing court required accounting, and completing real estate settlement forms.

Conflict Checking

Conflict checking is necessary to verify that current and prior representations of parties and matters handled will not present a conflict of interest for the firm in accepting a new client or legal matter. Checking for conflicts of interest is an essential function designed to avoid the ethical violations of representing competing interests. Many offices use computer database software for conflict checking. Names of clients, opposing parties, counsel, and law firms can be quickly searched electronically. Some firms still rely on a manual check of paper lists and file-card indexes containing the names of clients, opposing parties, and opposing attorneys in cases. To determine conflicts where there has been only indirect representation is difficult.

Attorneys and paralegals who change firms may have to do a preliminary conflict check before they accept or start employment. The conflict comes when the former firm and the new firm are, or were, on opposite sides of a case. It may be a conflict for someone who has had access to information about a case to switch to the firm representing the opposing party. Confidential disclosure for the limited purpose of checking for a conflict before starting employment could prevent a serious or perceived ethical breach in the form of a breach of confidentiality or conflict of interest. In some cases, the conflict of interest may result from a financial interest such as stock ownership or investments. Making full disclosure of these potential conflict situations to the supervising attorney or to the appropriate conflict checker with the firm is important.

In many cases, the conflict can be resolved by isolating the individual from information about the case—sometimes called building an ethical wall. An ethical wall, also known as a Chinese wall, is an attempt to shield a paralegal or lawyer from access to information about a case when there is the possibility of a conflict of interest. Most courts permit the establishment of an ethical wall to protect the parties from the conflict of interest or breach of confidentiality.

Conflict checking
Verifying that the attorneys in the firm do not have a personal conflict and have not previously represented and are not currently representing any party with an adverse interest or conflict with the potential client.

ETHICAL *Perspective*

Adequate Screening

"The court does not subscribe to the argument that, as a matter of law, screening would be ineffective when a nonlawyer switches employment to 'the other side.' The ABA opinions indicate that a law firm can set up appropriate screening and administrative procedures to prevent nonlawyers from working on the other side of those common cases and disclosing confidential information."

Source: Connecticut Trial Court, unpublished decision, Devine v. Beinfield, 1997 Ct. Sup. 7674, 1997 Conn Super Lexis 1966, No. CV93 0121721 S (Jul.1, 1997).

LEIBOWITZ V. DIST. CT., 119 NEV. ADV. OP. NO. 57, 39683 (2003) 78 P.3D 515

The Nevada Supreme Court in overturning a 1994 ethics opinion [*Ciaffone v. District Court*, 113 Nev. 1165 (1997), 945 P.2d 950] that prohibited paralegals from working for a firm that represents any client that had an adversarial relationship to any client of the former employer law firm, summarized the rationale for the ethical wall and provided an instructive guide . . .

"... As pointed out by the amici's brief, the majority of professional legal ethics commentators, ethics tribunals, and courts have concluded that nonlawyer screening is a permissible method to protect confidences held by nonlawyer employees who change employment. Nevada is in a minority of jurisdictions that do not allow screening for nonlawyers moving from private firm to private firm."

(continued)

LEIBOWITZ V. DIST. CT. (*continued*)

Imputed disqualification is considered a harsh remedy that "should be invoked if, and only if, the [c]ourt is satisfied that real harm is likely to result from failing to invoke it."

This stringent standard is based on a client's right to counsel of the client's choosing and the likelihood of prejudice and economic harm to the client when severance of the attorney–client relationship is ordered. It is for this reason that the ABA opined in 1988 that screening is permitted for nonlawyer employees, while conversely concluding, through the Model Rules of Professional Conduct, that screening is not permitted for lawyers. The ABA explained that "additional considerations" exist justifying application of screening to nonlawyer employees (*i.e.,* mobility in employment opportunities which function to serve both legal clients and the legal profession) versus the Model Rule's proscription against screening where lawyers move from private firm to private firm. In essence, a lawyer may always practice his or her profession regardless of an affiliation to a law firm. Paralegals, legal secretaries, and other employees of attorneys do not have that option.

We are persuaded that *Ciaffone* misapprehended the state of the law regarding nonlawyer imputed disqualification. We therefore overrule *Ciaffone* to the extent it prohibits screening of nonlawyer employees."

"When a law firm hires a nonlawyer employee, the firm has an affirmative duty to determine whether the employee previously had access to adversarial client files. If the hiring law firm determines that the employee had such access, the hiring law firm has an absolute duty to screen the nonlawyer employee from the adversarial cases irrespective of the nonlawyer employee's actual knowledge of privileged or confidential information.

Although we decline to mandate an exhaustive list of screening requirements, the following provides an instructive minimum:

(1) *"The newly hired nonlawyer [employee] must be cautioned not to disclose any information relating to the representation of a client of the former employer."*
(2) *"The nonlawyer [employee] must be instructed not to work on any matter on which [he or] she worked during the prior employment, or regarding which [he or] she has information relating to the former employer's representation."*
(3) *"The new firm should take . . . reasonable steps to ensure that the nonlawyer [employee] does not work in connection with matters on which [he or] she worked during the prior employment, absent client consent [i.e., unconditional waiver] after consultation."*

In addition, the hiring law firm must inform the adversarial party, or their counsel, regarding the hiring of the nonlawyer employee and the screening mechanisms utilized. The adversarial party may then: (1) make a conditional waiver (*i.e.,* agree to the screening mechanisms); (2) make an unconditional waiver (eliminate the screening mechanisms); or (3) file a motion to disqualify counsel.

However, even if the new employer uses a screening process, disqualification will always be required—absent unconditional waiver by the affected client—under the following circumstances:

(1) *"[W]hen information relating to the representation of an adverse client has in fact been disclosed [to the new employer]"; or, in the absence of disclosure to the new employer,*
(2) *"[W]hen screening would be ineffective or the nonlawyer [employee] necessarily would be required to work on the other side of a matter that is the same as or substantially related to a matter on which the nonlawyer [employee] has previously worked."*

Once a district court determines that a nonlawyer employee acquired confidential information about a former client, the district court should grant a motion for disqualification unless the district court determines that the screening is sufficient to safeguard the former client from disclosure of the confidential information. The district court is faced with the delicate task of balancing competing interests, including: (1) "the individual right to be represented by counsel of one's choice," (2) "each party's right to be free from the risk of even inadvertent disclosure of confidential information," (3) "the public's interest in the scrupulous administration of justice," and (4) "the prejudices that will inure to the parties as a result of the [district court's] decision."

Perspective

Model Rules of Professional Conduct
Client–Lawyer Relationship: Rule 1.5 Fees

(a) A lawyer shall not make an agreement for, charge, or collect an unreasonable fee or an unreasonable amount for expenses. The factors to be considered in determining the reasonableness of a fee include the following:
   (1) the time and labor required, the novelty and difficulty of the questions involved, and the skill requisite to perform the legal service properly;
   (2) the likelihood, if apparent to the client, that the acceptance of the particular employment will preclude other employment by the lawyer;
   (3) the fee customarily charged in the locality for similar legal services;
   (4) the amount involved and the results obtained;
   (5) the time limitations imposed by the client or by the circumstances;
   (6) the nature and length of the professional relationship with the client;
   (7) the experience, reputation, and ability of the lawyer or lawyers performing the services; and
   (8) whether the fee is fixed or contingent.

(b) The scope of the representation and the basis or rate of the fee and expenses for which the client will be responsible shall be communicated to the client, preferably in writing, before or within a reasonable time after commencing the representation, except when the lawyer will charge a regularly represented client on the same basis or rate. Any changes in the basis or rate of the fee or expenses shall also be communicated to the client.

(c) A fee may be contingent on the outcome of the matter for which the service is rendered, except in a matter in which a contingent fee is prohibited by paragraph (d) or other law. A contingent fee agreement shall be in a writing signed by the client and shall state the method by which the fee is to be determined, including the percentage or percentages that shall accrue to the lawyer in the event of settlement, trial or appeal; litigation and other expenses to be deducted from the recovery; and whether such expenses are to be deducted before or after the contingent fee is calculated. The agreement must clearly notify the client of any expenses for which the client will be liable whether or not the client is the prevailing party. Upon conclusion of a contingent fee matter, the lawyer shall provide the client with a written statement stating the outcome of the matter and, if there is a recovery, showing the remittance to the client and the method of its determination.

(d) A lawyer shall not enter into an arrangement for, charge, or collect:
   (1) any fee in a domestic relations matter, the payment or amount of which is contingent upon the securing of a divorce or upon the amount of alimony or support, or property settlement in lieu thereof; or
   (2) a contingent fee for representing a defendant in a criminal case.

(e) A division of a fee between lawyers who are not in the same firm may be made only if:
   (1) the division is in proportion to the services performed by each lawyer or each lawyer assumes joint responsibility for the representation;
   (2) the client agrees to the arrangement, including the share each lawyer will receive, and the agreement is confirmed in writing; and
   (3) the total fee is reasonable.

See Appendix I for Commentary on Model Rule 1.5.

Source: *ABA* Model Rules for Professional Conduct, 2004 Edition. © *2003 by the American Bar Association. Reprinted with permission. Copies of ABA* Model Rules of Professional Conduct, 2004 Edition *are available from Service Center, American Bar Association, 321 North Clark St., Chicago, IL 60610, 1-800-285-2221.*

Time Keeping and Billing

Keeping track of billable time is a critical function to ensure that the law firm will be compensated properly for its advice and efforts on behalf of clients. Tracking time extends beyond just the efforts of attorneys to paralegals and, in some cases, secretaries and clerks.

Billing is the most important function in a law firm. Without billings there is no revenue to pay expenses and salaries. As important as it is, in many offices billing is not treated with enough importance. Time records are the basis for most law firm billings. Without accurate time records, billings cannot be made.

Client expense records, by contrast, are usually well maintained because a check is usually written, which provides a documented record for billing purposes. But the time record must come from the recording of time spent by the attorney, paralegal, or legal team member. This information frequently is maintained manually on pieces of paper called time slips or time records. Client bills are prepared manually from these records.

More frequently, the client billing is prepared using a computer program, such as the popular Timeslips program. Most of these programs allow for random entry of the individual time record information and then automatically sort by client and project or case. These programs also allow for the entry and inclusion in the final billing report or printout of the costs expended in the current period and the costs and fees received from previous billing periods and the application of retainers.

ACCOUNTING IN THE LAW OFFICE

In the law office working environment, your ability to understand basic financial issues makes you a more valuable member of the law office team. A law firm is a business that, as Abraham Lincoln said, deals in time and advice, unlike retail, wholesale, or manufacturing businesses that trade in goods or commodities.

A major function of the legal support staff is to keep track of the time the lawyers and support staff spend on a case and then bill the client for the time expended. Financial account records must be kept accurately both for internal office activities and for matters related to specific clients. Expenses may be associated with specific clients or part of the overall cost of running the office. If accurate records are not kept for the law office operation, it may fail or close.

When the funds involved belong to clients, errors can result in malpractice claims for improperly prepared documentation and the filing of inaccurate court documents and tax returns. At worst, errors may result in a loss or misappropriation of client funds, which can lead to sanctions, including disbarment or even criminal prosecution.

In addition to understanding the internal operations accounting needs of a law firm is the need to understand the accounting and financial affairs of clients. Understanding accounting and financial reports and documents is essential in many areas of law today.

Family Law

Every domestic relations case has concerns related to property settlement, support, and alimony. In today's marital climate, there is an increasing demand for full financial disclosure in prenuptial agreements. A basic understanding of the nature and the sources of the family financial information will enable you to prepare the necessary documents. Exhibit 3.7 shows selected pages from the New Jersey Family Part Case Information.

Commercial Litigation

Commercial litigation has become more complex—in no small matter because of the financial implications of contract breaches and remedies. The tasks of finding, analyzing, and presenting financial matters increasingly fall on litigation paralegals.

Litigation

Even in the simplest of litigation matters, a measure of damages have to be computed. Calculations of wages lost, projection of future losses, and the current or present value may have to be computed or reviewed for accuracy.

Exhibit 3.7 **New Jersey family case information**

PART D - MONTHLY EXPENSES (computed at 4.3 wks/mo.)

Joint Marital Life Style should reflect standard of living established during marriage. Current expenses should reflect the current life style. Do not repeat those income deductions listed in Part C–3.

	Joint Marital Life Style Family, including _____ children	Current Life Style Yours and _____ children
SCHEDULE A: SHELTER		
If Tenant:		
Rent	$_____	$_____
Heat (if not furnished)	$_____	$_____
Electric & Gas (if not furnished)	$_____	$_____
Renter's Insurance	$_____	$_____
Parking (at Apartment)	$_____	$_____
Other Charges (Itemize)	$_____	$_____
If Homeowner:		
Mortgage	$_____	$_____
Real Estate Taxes (if not included w/mortgage payment)	$_____	$_____
Homeowners Ins (if not included w/mortgage payment)	$_____	$_____
Other Mortgages or Home Equity Loans	$_____	$_____
Heat (unless Electric or Gas)	$_____	$_____
Electric & Gas	$_____	$_____
Water & Sewer	$_____	$_____
Garbage Removal	$_____	$_____
Snow Removal	$_____	$_____
Lawn Care	$_____	$_____
Maintenance	$_____	$_____
Repairs	$_____	$_____
Other Charges (Itemize)	$_____	$_____
Tenant or Homeowner:		
Telephone	$_____	$_____
Mobile/Cellular Telephone	$_____	$_____
Service Contracts on Equipment	$_____	$_____
Cable TV	$_____	$_____
Plumber/Electrician	$_____	$_____
Equipment & Furnishings	$_____	$_____
Internet Charges	$_____	$_____
Other (Itemize)	$_____	$_____
TOTAL	$_____	$_____
SCHEDULE B: TRANSPORTATION		
Auto Payment	$_____	$_____
Auto Insurance (number of vehicles)	$_____	$_____
Registration, License	$_____	$_____
Maintenance	$_____	$_____
Fuel and Oil	$_____	$_____
Commuting Expenses	$_____	$_____
Other Charges (Itemize)	$_____	$_____
TOTAL	$_____	$_____

(continued)

Exhibit 3.7 **New Jersey family case information** *(continued)*

PART E - BALANCE SHEET OF ALL FAMILY ASSETS AND LIABILITIES STATEMENT OF ASSETS

Description	Title to Property (H, W, J)	Date of purchase/acquisition. If claim that asset is exempt, state reason and value of what is claimed to be exempt	Value $ Put * after exempt	Date of Evaluation Mo./Day/Yr.

1. Real Property

2. Bank Accounts, CD's

3. Vehicles

4. Tangible Personal Property

5. Stocks and Bonds

6. Pension, Profit Sharing, Retirement Plan(s) 401(k)s, etc. [list each employer]

7. IRAs

8. Businesses, Partnerships, Professional Practices

9. Life Insurance (cash surrender value)

10. Loans Receivable

11. Other (specify)

TOTAL GROSS ASSETS: $_____

TOTAL SUBJECT TO EQUITABLE DISTRIBUTION: $_____

TOTAL NOT SUBJECT TO EQUITABLE DISTRIBUTION: $_____

Maintaining Law Firm Financial Information

Law firms, like any other business, have numerous forms of financial obligations. Utility bills and employees have to be paid on a regular basis. Accurate records have to be maintained to determine which costs are chargeable to individual clients. Office operations frequently involve record keeping for client funds in the form of escrow accounts.

Records of the various receipts and disbursements are used to prepare the firm's tax returns, including quarterly and annual employee withholding and employer tax returns, income tax returns, and informational tax returns, such as reports for non-employee compensation and independent contractors such as freelance paralegals, or reporters and investigators.

Regular use of a systematic system simplifies the completion of financial reports. By using a standard system of accounting, lawyers, bookkeepers, paralegals, and secretarial personnel can easily communicate, contributing information of charges and revenues that are usable for all concerned including the outside accountants and auditors.

Reconstructing the financial information is a common task in many law offices. In many cases, clients deliver piles of financial documents and expect the law office personnel to sort, classify, and organize seemingly unrelated pieces of paper into tax returns, estate tax returns, and documents with which settlements and major decisions will be made. Knowing how to attack the piles of paper can save time, stress, and frustration.

Accounting for Client Retainers and Costs

Law firms frequently request a **retainer**—a payment at the beginning of handling a new matter for a client. This amount may be used to offset the fees for services rendered or costs advanced on behalf of the client. Unless there is some other arrangement, agreed upon in conformity with applicable court rules and ABA guidelines, these funds belong to the law firm only when they have been earned by rendering of the service or actual cost expenditure. Unused amounts may have to be returned to the client and those expended accounted for to the client.

> **Retainer**
> A payment at the beginning of the handling of a new matter for a client. This amount may be used to offset the fees for services rendered or costs advanced on behalf of the client.

Increasingly, under the rules of professional conduct, many states also require a written fee agreement in contingent-fee cases, whereas in other types of cases, it is preferred but not required.

A new approach to providing legal services is sometimes called "unbundled" legal services or discrete task representation. The term refers to a broad range of discrete tasks that an attorney might undertake, such as advice, negotiation, document review, document preparation, and limited representation. A sample retainer agreement under Maine Bar Rule 3.4(I) is shown in Exhibit 3.8.

A lawyer may request a nonrefundable retainer. This is a common practice when the client does not want the law firm to be able to represent the opposing party in a pending legal action. This is seen most commonly in family law or divorce actions. Legal ethics prohibit taking on a client where there is a conflict of interest. In cases of nonrefundable retainers, a statement of application of the funds may or should be made as a matter of the financial accounting practice.

Costs Advanced

Law firms typically pay directly to the court any fees for filing documents for the client. In some cases, the cost of stenographers, expert witnesses, duplication of records, travel, phone, and copying also will be advanced. The firm must keep proper accounting for these items to be able to bill a client properly or charge the amounts expended against prepaid costs or retainers. Good practice is to include in the initial client fee letter the nature and amount of costs that will be charged for these various items.

Exhibit 3.8 **Limited representation agreement**

Date:_____, 20_____
1. The client, _____, retains the attorney, _____, to perform limited legal services in the following matter:
_____ v. _____.

2. The client seeks the following services from the attorney (indicate by writing "yes" or "no"):

a. _____ Legal advice: office visits, telephone calls, fax, mail, e-mail;
b. _____ Advice about availability of alternative means to resolving
the dispute, including mediation and arbitration;
c. _____ Evaluation of client self-diagnosis of the case and advising
client about legal rights and responsibilities;
d. _____ Guidance and procedural information for filing or serving
documents;
e. _____ Review pleadings and other documents prepared by client;
f. _____ Suggest documents to be prepared;
g. _____ Draft pleadings, motions, and other documents;
h. _____ Factual investigation: contacting witnesses, public record
searches, in-depth interview of client;
i. _____ Assistance with computer support programs;
j. _____ Legal research and analysis;
k. _____ Evaluate settlement options;
l. _____ Discovery: interrogatories, depositions, requests for
document production;
m. _____ Planning for negotiations;
n. _____ Planning for court appearances;
o. _____ Standby telephone assistance during negotiations or
settlement conferences;
p. _____ Referring client to expert witnesses, special masters, or
other counsel;
q. _____ Counseling client about an appeal;
r. _____ Procedural assistance with an appeal and assisting with
substantive legal argument in an appeal;
s. _____ Provide preventive planning and/or schedule legal checkups:
t. _____ Other:
_____
_____

3. The client shall pay the attorney for those limited services as follows:
a. Hourly Fee:

The current hourly fee charged by the attorney or the attorney's law firm for services under this agreement are as follows:
i. Attorney: $_____
ii. Associate: $_____
iii. Paralegal: $_____
iv. Law Clerk: $_____

Unless a different fee arrangement is established in clause b. of this paragraph, the hourly fee shall be payable at the time of the service. Time will be charged in increments of one-tenth of an hour, rounded off for each particular activity to the nearest one-tenth of an hour.

b. Payment from Deposit:
For a continuing consulting role, client will pay to attorney a deposit of $_____, to be received by attorney on or before _____, and to be applied against attorney fees and costs incurred by client. This amount will be deposited by attorney in attorney trust account. Client authorizes attorney to withdraw funds from the trust account to pay attorney fees and costs as they are incurred by client. The deposit is refundable. If, at the termination of services under this agreement, the total amount incurred by client for attorney fees and costs is less than the amount of the deposit, the difference will be refunded to client. Any balance due shall be paid within thirty days of the termination of services.

(continued)

Exhibit 3.8 **Limited representation agreement** *(continued)*

c. Costs:

Client shall pay attorney out-of-pocket costs incurred in connection with this agreement, including long distance telephone and fax costs, photocopy expense and postage. All costs payable to third parties in connection with client case, including filing fees, investigation fees, deposition fees, and the like shall be paid directly by client. Attorney shall not advance costs to third parties on client behalf.

4. The client understands that the attorney will exercise his or her best judgment while performing the limited legal services set out above, but also recognizes:

a. the attorney is not promising any particular outcome,
b. the attorney has not made any independent investigation of the facts and is relying entirely on the client limited disclosure of the facts given the duration of the limited services provided, and
c. the attorney has no further obligation to the client after completing the above described limited legal services unless and until both attorney and client enter into another written representation agreement.

5. If any dispute between client and attorney arises under this agreement concerning the payment of fees, the client and attorney shall submit the dispute for fee arbitration in accordance with Rule 9(e)-(k) of the Maine Bar Rules. This arbitration shall be binding upon both parties to this agreement.

WE HAVE EACH READ THE ABOVE AGREEMENT BEFORE SIGNING IT.
Signature of client _____
Signature of attorney _____

Civil Practice: Fee and Cost Billing

In a civil litigation practice, fees may be calculated on an hourly rate, a contingent fee, or a combination of the two. The time records for each member of the firm must be obtained, either from the hard copies of time records or the computer printout of hours spent working on the case. The actual time may be reported to the client chronologically, with all activity by each person who worked on the file integrated with all the others, but may be listed separately by the individual.

The difficulty is in calculating the correct amount for each person at his/her respected hourly rate. It is not unusual to have a senior partner bill at one rate, a junior partner at another rate, and a paralegal at a third rate. It is good practice to calculate the total for each billable person separately, and then collectively. The totals of the individuals, of course, must equal the grand total. Therefore, the comparison acts as a check on mathematical accuracy.

Client bills can be prepared manually from paper copies of time records or other office records. More frequently, the client billing is prepared using a computer program. Most of these programs allow input of the individual time record in a random order that can be sorted automatically by client and project. In addition to the time billing, these programs allow for entry and inclusion in the final billing of costs expended in the current billing period and costs and payments received from previous billing periods and retainers.

Timely Disbursements

As part of the settlement of a case for a client, the opposing side may pay the amount of the cash settlement to the lawyer. These funds must be disbursed to the client and until disbursed, retained in a separate escrow account and not commingled with the lawyers own funds. Records of the receipt and disbursement of these funds must be maintained properly to avoid charges of misuse of client funds.

A lawyer is not required to make disbursements until the draft or check has cleared. A check or draft is deemed cleared when the funds are available for disbursement. But,

Trust accounts
The funds of the client.

IOLTA account
Where the amount is too small to earn interest, court rules require the funds be deposited into a special interest-bearing account, and the interest generally paid to support legal aid projects (Interest on Lawyers Trust Accounts).

SELECTED PROVISIONS OF THE RULES OF PRACTICE AND PROCEDURE IN THE PROBATE COURTS OF THE STATE OF NEW HAMPSHIRE

RULE 108. FIDUCIARY ACCOUNTING STANDARDS

The following standards shall be applicable to all interim and final accountings of Administrators, trustees, guardians and conservators, required or permitted to be filed with the Court.

A. Accounts shall be stated in a manner that is understandable by Persons who are not familiar with practices and terminology peculiar to the administration of estates, trusts, guardianships and conservatorships. . . .

B. A Fiduciary account shall begin with a concise summary of its purpose and content. The account shall begin with a brief statement identifying the Fiduciary, the subject matter, the relationship of Parties interested in the account to the account, and, if applicable, appropriate notice of any limitations on or requirements for action by Parties interested in the account. . . .

C. A Fiduciary account shall contain sufficient information to put parties interested in the account on notice as to all significant transactions affecting administration during the accounting period. . . .

---

lawyers cannot retain the amount for an unreasonable time. The client is entitled to earn the potential interest on the amount to be dispersed. The lawyer is not entitled to keep the amount and earn interest for his/her own account.

Trust Accounts

A **trust account** or fiduciary account contains the client's funds and should never be commingled with those of the firm or the individual attorney. A clear record of all trust transactions must be maintained. When a checking account has been established, the check register is a primary source for creating any required or desired reports. With some larger accounts, checking accounts may not have been set up. Many trust and estate accounts are invested in money market funds, stocks, bonds, and mutual funds.

Keeping a clear record is made more difficult by the potential for periodic increases and decreases in value that are not actually realized—referred to as paper gains and losses. They exist on paper but have not been realized by the actual sale or transfer of the asset. For the attorney, the client or state law must authorize any investments of assets held in trust. Separate records should be maintained showing the activity in each of the trust accounts, including all deposits, interest earned, and disbursements, including bank charges.

IOLTA Accounts

Many states, by court rule, impose an obligation to deposit client funds, when the amount is too small to earn interest, into a special interest-bearing account, the **IOLTA account** (Interest on Lawyers Trust Accounts). Interest generated from these small accounts is paid to the court-designated agency, usually the local legal aid agency, to fund their activities. Because the cost of setting up individual small accounts is greater than the interest earned, or the amount deposited is so small that no interest would accrue to the client, everyone wins by having these funds generate some income for the public good. Reconciliation of this account is simpler because no accounting for the interest to the client has to be made.

Interest-Bearing Escrow Accounts

Lawyers frequently are asked to act as escrow agents or to retain client funds for future disbursements. In some cases the amounts may be significant. Prudent handling of the client's monies dictates that the fiduciary treat them in the same manner as would any prudent investor. If the amount is sufficient to earn interest, the amount earned belongs to the client, not to the attorney, and must be accounted for, to the client.

If earning interest, it is good practice and expected to open up separate accounts for each client. In opening these accounts, the client's Social Security number or other employer identification number should be used. If the law firm maintains the account under its tax identification number, it will have to report interest annually to the client and to the federal and state government.

A significant body of law has emerged to avoid money-laundering. In a law firm this may require reporting when significant amounts of cash are received. The problem is balancing the money-laundering rules and the attorney–client privilege. When amounts in excess of $10,000 are received in cash from a client, current legislation and regulation must be consulted.

To open an account with a financial institution requires a federal identification number. This identification number may be that of the client, the trust, the estate, or other legal entity having a current identification number. In some cases the financial institution may require copies of any documentation that created the client entity, such as the trust documents, death certificate, or decedent's will. The concern of the financial institution is to properly comply with existing regulations on federal withholding and money-laundering or large-deposit reporting obligations. A state requirement is to complete the federal form W-9.

Court Accounting

In addition to the preparation of filing federal and state estate tax returns, the fiduciary often has to file an accounting with the local court that administers or supervises trust and estate matters. These reports are designed to show that the fiduciary has administered the estate or trust properly.

Reports to the court also are required in many jurisdictions in civil cases involving minors. Approval of tort actions involving a minor may be negotiated between the lawyers for the insurance company or defendant and the minor's parent or guardian, subject to the approval of the court. This usually requires submitting a brief accounting of the expenses, including counsel fees, and the proposed disbursements to compensate for out-of-pocket expenses and proposed investments of the proceeds until the minor reaches a set age or by other order of court.

All of the parties are considered as acting as fiduciaries in the best interest of the minor. Local practice and court rules will furthermore dictate the form and methods of fiduciary accounting. The uniform system of accounts has been accepted by some jurisdictions without formal court rule and others by inclusion in the local court rules.

The basic objective of the uniform system of accounts is to present the financial information in a consistent manner that is understandable to the court and all the interested parties. The parties are entitled to full disclosure, clarity, and, when appropriate, supplemental information. Exhibit 3.9 is an example of a uniform system of accounts.

Court accounting
An accounting with the local court that administers or supervises trust and estate matters. These reports are designed to show that the fiduciary has properly administered the estate or trust.

ETHICAL *Perspective*

American Bar Association Model Rules of Professional Conduct
Client–Lawyer Relationship Rule 1.15 Safekeeping Property

(a) A lawyer shall hold property of clients or third persons that is in a lawyer's possession in connection with a representation separate from the lawyer's own property. Funds shall be kept in a separate account maintained in the state where the lawyer's office is situated, or elsewhere with the consent of the client or third person. Other property shall be identified as such and appropriately safeguarded. Complete records of such account funds and other property shall be kept by the lawyer and shall be preserved for a period of [five years] after termination of the representation.

(b) A lawyer may deposit the lawyer's own funds in a client trust account for the sole purpose of paying bank service charges on that account, but only in an amount necessary for that purpose.

(c) A lawyer shall deposit into a client trust account legal fees and expenses that have been paid in advance, to be withdrawn by the lawyer only as fees are earned or expenses incurred.

(d) Upon receiving funds or other property in which a client or third person has an interest, a lawyer shall promptly notify the client or third person. Except as stated in this rule or otherwise permitted by law or by agreement with the client, a lawyer shall promptly deliver to the client or third person any funds or other property that the client or third person is entitled to receive and, upon request by the client or third person, shall promptly render a full accounting regarding such property.

(e) When in the course of representation a lawyer is in possession of property in which two or more persons (one of whom may be the lawyer) claim interests, the property shall be kept separate by the lawyer until the dispute is resolved. The lawyer shall promptly distribute all portions of the property as to which the interests are not in dispute.

See Appendix I for Commentary on Model Rule 1.15.

Source: *ABA* Model Rules for Professional Conduct, 2004 Edition. © 2003 by the American Bar Association. Reprinted with permission. Copies of ABA Model Rules of Professional Conduct, 2004 Edition are available from Service Center, American Bar Association, 321 North Clark St., Chicago, IL 60610, 1-800-285-2221.

Exhibit 3.9 **Model executor's account template sample—Pennsylvania Orphans Court**

ORPHANS' COURT RULES

MODEL EXECUTOR'S ACCOUNT

First and Final Account

FIRST AND FINAL ACCOUNT OF

William C. Doe, Executor

For

ESTATE OF John Doe, Deceased

Date of Death:	November 14, 1978
Date of Executor's Appointment:	November 24, 1978
Accounting for the Period:	November 24, 1978 to November 30, 1979

Purpose of Account: William C. Doe, Executor, offers this account to acquaint interested parties with the transactions that have occurred during his administration.

The account also indicates the proposed distribution of the estate.[1]
It is important that the account be carefully examined. Requests for additional information or questions or objections can be discussed with:

[Name of Executor, Counsel or other appropriate person]
[address and telephone number]

[*Note:* See discussion under Fiduciary Accounting Principle II with respect to presentation of collateral material needed by beneficiaries.]

Note

In Pennsylvania the date of first advertisement of the grant of letters should be shown after the date of the personal representative's appointment.

[1] Optional—for use if applicable.

SUMMARY OF ACCOUNT

	Page	Current Value	Fiduciary Acquisition Value
Proposed Distribution to Beneficiaries[1]	645	$102,974.56	$ 90,813.96
Principal			
Receipts	636		$160,488.76
			2,662.00
Net Gain (or Loss) on Sales or Other Disposition	638		$163,150.76
Less Disbursements:			
Debts of Decedent	639	$ 485.82	
Funeral Expenses	639	1,375.00	
Administration Expenses	639	194.25	
Federal and State Taxes	639	5,962.09	
Fees and Commissions	639	11,689.64	19,706.80
Balance before Distributions			$143,443.96

(continued)

FIDUCIARY ACCOUNTING STANDARDS

Distributions to Beneficiaries	641	52,630.00
Principal Balance on Hand	641	$ 90,813.96
For Information:		
Investments Made	642	
Changes in Investment Holdings	642	
Income		
Receipts	643	$ 2,513.40
Less Disbursements	643	178.67
Balance Before Distributions		$ 2,334.73
Distributions to Beneficiaries	644	2,334.73
Income Balance on Hand		-0-
Combined Balance on Hand		$ 90,813.96

[1]Optional—for use if applicable.

_____

RECEIPTS OF PRINCIPAL

Assets Listed in Inventory (Valued as of Date of Death)			Fiduciary Acquisition Value
Cash:			
First National Bank—checking account	$	516.93	
Prudent Saving Fund Society—savings account		2,518.16	
Cash in possession of decedent		42.54	$ 3,077.63
Tangible Personal Property:			
Jewelry—			
1 pearl necklace			515.00
Furniture—			
1 antique highboy	$	2,000.00	
1 antique side table		60.00	
1 antique chair		55.00	2,115.00
Stocks:			
200 shs. Home Telephone & Telegraph Co., common	$	25,000.00	
50 shs. Best Oil Co., common		5,000.00	
1,000 shs. Central Trust Co., capital		50,850.00	
151 shs. Electric Data Corp., common		1,887.50	
50 shs. Fabulous Mutual Fund		1,833.33	
200 shs. XYZ Corporation, common		6,000.00	90,570.83
Realty:			
Residence— 86 Norwood Road West Hartford, CT			$ 50,000.00
Total Inventory			$146,278.46

Receipts Subsequent to Inventory (Valued When Received)

2/22/79	Proceeds of Sale—Best Oil Co., rights to subscribe received 2/15/79	$ 50.00[1]	
3/12/79	Fabulous Mutual Fund, capital gains dividend received in cash	32.50	
5/11/79	Refund of overpayment of 1978 U.S. individual income tax	127.80	
9/25/79	From Richard Roe, Ancillary Administrator, net proceeds on sale of oil and gas leases in Jefferson Parish, Louisiana	10,000.00	$ 10,210.30

[1]Proceeds of sale of rights may be treated as an additional receipt, as illustrated here, or may be applied in reduction of carrying value as illustrated on page 646 of the Model Trustee's Account. Either method, consistently applied, is acceptable.

Advice from the Field ··

PEOPLE SKILLS CRITICAL TO PROFESSIONAL SUCCESS

Kathleen Call, Executive Director, Robert Half Legal

Kathleen Call is executive director of Robert Half Legal, a leading staffing service specializing in the placement of legal professionals ranging from project attorneys and paralegals to administrators, legal secretaries and other support staff. Robert Half Legal, which works with law firms and corporate legal departments, has offices throughout the United States and Canada.

When you think of which skills will be most important to your career advancement over the next five years, chances are "proficiency with technology" ranks high on your list. Knowledge of key software applications has become a critical success factor in the legal profession. However, to be considered for the best job opportunities in the future, you'll not only need technical competency, but also solid interpersonal skills and problem-solving abilities.

Audio- and video-conferencing, email, corporate Intranets and, of course, the Internet have increased exponentially the amount—and speed—of day-to-day professional communication. The expanded use of technology will make it more important for legal professionals to be able to communicate effectively and articulately.

Another significant development driving the need for strong soft skills is the trend toward a more collaborative workplace. In a team-based office environment, diplomacy, flexibility, persuasiveness and management skills are critical. In a survey we commissioned among executives at the nation's 1,000 largest companies, 79 percent of respondents said self-managed employee work teams will increase productivity for U.S. companies. These productivity gains will only be realized, however, if team members can work together effectively. As a result, firms are placing a premium on excellent interpersonal skills.

WHAT ARE PEOPLE SKILLS?

Since soft skills are intangible and therefore hard to quantify, how do you determine whether you have what it takes to succeed? Our firm has identified a composite of key interpersonal traits represented by the acronym "PEOPLE":

Problem-solving abilities (organization, judgment, logic, creativity, conflict resolution)

Ethics (diplomacy, courtesy, honesty, professionalism)

Open-mindedness (flexibility, open to new business ideas, positive outlook)

Persuasiveness (excellent communication and listening skills)

Leadership (accountability, management and motivational skills)

Educational interests (continuous thirst for knowledge and skills development)

A deficiency in these skills can seriously limit your career prospects, whether you're applying for a new job as a legal assistant or seeking to move upward as an attorney within your current firm. Just as workers who failed to enhance their technical skills were left behind by the digital revolution, those who dismiss the significance of PEOPLE skills can find themselves stagnating in dead-end jobs.

ASSESS YOUR STRENGTHS AND WEAKNESSES

While it's relatively easy to measure the development of your proficiency with technology, it's much more challenging to gauge your progress in enhancing your PEOPLE skills. Again, this is primarily because these qualities are more subjective in nature. Since there are no classes on "flexibility" or "positive outlook" at the typical college or university, how do you acquire and upgrade your interpersonal abilities?

The following steps will help you take an accurate inventory of your strengths and weaknesses:

Honestly evaluate your aptitude in each of the PEOPLE skills. Which seem to come naturally? Is there room for improvement in any area?

Ask trusted friends, family members and coworkers for their opinions. How would they rate your PEOPLE skills?

Advice from the Field ·····························

(continued)

COMMIT TO LEARNING

It takes time and experience to fully develop interpersonal skills, so don't expect to see improvement overnight. Here are some effective strategies to help you continue your progress:

Develop a list of the characteristics you'd most like to develop in yourself. Then brainstorm specific activities that will boost your abilities in your selected areas. For example, if you'd like to refine your leadership skills, volunteer to work on cases that provide the opportunity to supervise others or manage a project from start to finish.

Observe those who demonstrate strong PEOPLE skills in the areas you'd like to improve. How do they apply their abilities in various situations? How are their responses different than what yours would be?

Select a mentor. The best candidate is someone in the legal field whom you admire. Ask your prospective mentor if he or she would advise you, particularly in those PEOPLE skills that you've determined require enhancement. Since it's difficult to see yourself objectively, a mentor's ongoing support and feedback can be invaluable.

Enhance your listening skills. Concentrate on paying close attention to what others are saying. In general, avoid interrupting but ask for clarification when necessary. To prevent misunderstandings, paraphrase information in your own words when you are given complex instructions.

Become a better writer. Read books on effective writing so that you can develop a more concise style, or consider taking a journalism or business writing course. Proofread everything you write, especially e-mail. Because electronic messages are prepared and sent quickly, they can be inadvertently filled with typographical and grammatical errors. In addition, it's important to employ PEOPLE skills in your writing, explaining yourself diplomatically and courteously.

Refine your verbal communication. Know what you want to say before you speak, and use a tone and style appropriate to the audience. When leaving a voice-mail message, organize your thoughts in advance to avoid being vague or rambling. If you're presenting a report to an attorney or client, rehearse a few times so your delivery will be smooth and your message clear.

Become a volunteer. You can acquire stronger leadership and organizational skills through volunteer work. Whether it's becoming involved in a trade association or helping your favorite charity, the skills you develop can be used on the job in a variety of situations.

Seek growth opportunities outside the workplace. Hobbies and leisure-time activities are an enjoyable way to enrich your PEOPLE skills. By coaching your child's soccer team, for example, you'll develop motivational and managerial skills, and become better at dealing with diverse personalities. If you'd like to enhance your creativity, consider taking an art or music class.

Copyright © Robert Half Legal. Reprinted with permission.

PREPARING YOUR RESUME

Resume
A short description of a person's education, a summary of work experience, and other related and supporting information that potential employers use in evaluating a person's qualifications for a position in a firm or an organization.

A **resume** is a short description of a person's education, a summary of work experience, and other related and supporting information that potential employers use in evaluating a person's qualifications for a position in a firm or an organization. Exhibits 3.10 and 3.11 provide examples. You should prepare a resume as you see yourself today. Look at your resume from the perspective of a future employer. What areas do you need to strengthen to demonstrate your ability to perform the type of job you would like to have?

You should look at your resume as being a continuing work in progress. Constantly update your resume to include any new job responsibilities, part-time employment skills and qualifications, and special achievements. Add meaningful items to your resume in the form of courses, skills, and outside interests that will land you that first paralegal job after you complete your training.

After you have gathered all of the necessary information, put it into a proper resume form, then review it. Does the resume reflect the information you want to communicate to a prospective employer? Try to look at it with an open, objective mind.

Exhibit 3.10 Sample functional resume

SARA MARKS

2222 Market Way
Brooklyn, NY 11223
(212) 555-8634 (Home)
(212) 555-9234 (Office)

EDUCATION
Reading College, Brooklyn NY, 2008
 Associate of Science degree, GPA 4.0
  Paralegal Major—ABA-approved program
  Dean's List, Vice President of the Honor Society

EMPLOYMENT HISTORY
Paralegal field work, Brooklyn, NY, 2006 to 2008
 Advisor, Small Claims Court and the Brooklyn Department of Consumer Affairs
 • Assisted claimants with small claim forms
 • Counseled individuals on consumer affairs issues

Registration and admissions clerk, Brooklyn, NY, 2004 to 2006
 Reading College
 • Registered incoming and returning students
 • In charge of organizing the filing system, creating more efficiency in the office
Cosmetologist and Barber, Brooklyn, NY, 2000 to 2004
 • Self-employed
 • Handled all phases of business, including purchasing, bookkeeping, and payroll

SPECIAL SKILLS
 • WordPerfect, Microsoft Office Suite
 • Excellent ability to communicate with general public

PROFESSIONAL AFFILIATIONS
Manhattan Paralegal Association

Excellent references available upon request

Exhibit 3.11 **Sample chronological resume**

MICHAEL C. SMITH

2345 Oregon Street, #A
Portland, OR 98765
(363) 282-7890

EDUCATION
Paralegal Certificate, General Litigation, 2008
University of Portland (ABA approved)
Curriculum included:

Family Law	Paralegal Practices and Procedures
Criminal Law	Legal Research and Writing
Civil Litigation	Estates, Trusts, and Wills

Bachelor of Science Degree,
    Transportation and Distribution Management
    Golden Gate University, San Francisco, CA

EXPERIENCE
Paralegal Practice
- Drafted memos to clients
- Prepared notice of summons
- Conducted research for misdemeanor appeal cases
- Prepared points and authorities for motions
- Observed bankruptcy and family law court proceedings
- Completed necessary documents for probate
- Wrote legal memorandum

Administration and Management
- Participated in new division startup
- Dispatched and routed for the transportation of 80 to 120 special education students daily
- Supervised between 20 and 25 drivers
- Designed and implemented daily operation logs
- Liaison between drivers and school officials or parents
- Evaluated various conditions when assigning routes and equipment

EMPLOYMENT HISTORY

Susan Hildebrand, Attorney, Portland, OR Paralegal Intern	2008
Laidlaw Transit, Inc., San Francisco, CA Dispatch Manager	2002 to 2008
Hayward Unified School District Teaching Assistant	2001 to 2002
San Mateo Union High School District Office Clerk	2000 to 2001

Employers are looking for individuals who demonstrate a good work ethic, willingness to accept responsibility and take direction, and the skills necessary for the job for which they are applying.

Set your roadmap for the job you wish to obtain. What additional educational skills are required? This will determine your future course of study. Work–study programs in your field and cooperative education are good ways of demonstrating on-the-job training. Depending upon your goals, resources, and timeframe, a specialized certificate such as a paralegal certificate, an associate's degree in paralegal studies, or a bachelor's degree in paralegal studies will certainly demonstrate your level of interest and ability to achieve the minimum level of education for the job.

Resume Formats

Many formats may be used in preparing a resume: functional, chronological, reverse chronological, combination, technical, and electronic.

Chronological resume format
Presents education and job history in chronological order with the most recent experience listed first.

Functional resume format
Lists a summary of the individual's qualifications with current experience, and education without any emphasis on dates of employment.

The **chronological resume format** presents education and job history in a time sequence with the most recent experience listed first. An alternative format is the reverse chronological resume format, with the latest job listed last. The **functional resume format** usually gives a summary of the individual's qualifications and current experience and education without emphasizing dates of employment. The combination resume format combines the chronological and functional resume formats.

There are no hard and fast rules for choosing a proper resume format, except perhaps to put your name and contact information at the top. Some suggest that the chronological resume is the form used most commonly in the legal field. Always remember that the main purpose of the resume is to get a job interview and, you hope, employment.

If responding to an ad in the paper, tailor your resume to the job description or to the job listing of the individual employer. You may have to develop resumes in more than one format if the employment opportunities presented require different skill sets. For example, the resume sent to an employer looking for someone with specific computer skills should show that functional skill first. A job description looking for depth of experience probably should use the chronological approach.

Common elements of most resumes include:

- Heading, with your name and contact information
- Career objective, concise and to the point, geared to the job description of the position you seek
- Education, generally at the beginning of the resume if you are a recent graduate, including specific academic honors and awards if applicable to the job
- Experience, including paid and unpaid activities showing the employer the skills you have to offer
- Activities, a brief listing unless directly related to the job description, including professional organizations and educational and volunteer activities

Cover Letters

Cover letter
A brief letter sent with a document identifying the intended recipient and the purpose of the attachment.

Always include a **cover letter** with your resume. This applies to email applications, too. The cover letter creates the first impression. Brief though it is, it represents a sample of your writing skills and ability to communicate in writing. Take the time to be sure it properly reflects who you are and your skills. The cover letter should be brief, as your qualifications will be covered in the accompanying resume.

The cover letter should describe the job you are seeking, summarize your qualifications, request an interview, and express a desire for the job. If possible, address the cover letter directly to the person who is responsible for the hiring decision. Be sure to spell the person's name correctly and include the correct job title.

Just as you may need different resumes for different jobs, you should personalize each letter for each job application.

Creating an Electronic Resume

A growing number of employers are using computers to search the Internet for job applicants and to sort electronically through the resumes they receive. Human resources managers search through resumes received online or through Internet sites by entering a few words or phrases that describe the required skills and qualifications for the position they are trying to fill. Only the resumes in the computer system that

checklist ☑

Personal information

☐ Name

☐ Address

Education

☐ High school
   ☐ Year of graduation

☐ College
   ☐ Year of graduation
   ☐ Degree
   ☐ Gradepoint average or class rank

Work experience

☐ Current or last employer
   ☐ Position(s) held

☐ Prior employer
   ☐ Position held and dates

Specific skills

☐ Office skills   ☐ Computer skills   ☐ Language skills

☐ Other job-related skills

Other

☐ Organizational memberships   ☐ Licenses/certifications

match these electronic sorting terms and phrases are considered for the job offered. To have your resume considered, you will need an electronic resume in addition to the traditional printed resume.

Converting a Traditional Resume into an Electronic Resume

If you plan to send your resume as an attachment to an email, the only way you can be sure the person you are sending it to can read it is if you send it as an ASCII file or in a universally usable format such as Rich text file RTF. If you already have created a resume using a word-processing program, open the file containing your resume and save it as a plain ASCII text file or RTF file. You will want to change the name of the new text file to distinguish it from the file name used for the traditional printed version.

Text-only files cannot accommodate type formatting and special characters, so be sure that your electronic resume appears in one simple font and one font size. You also must remove line justification, tables, rules (lines), and columns. Align all text at the left to avoid indentation problems. Exhibit 3.12 is an example of an electronic resume.

Exhibit 3.12 **Sample electronic resume**

JANE DOE
1234 N. Maple Street
Anytown, USA 90000
Home: (213) 555-1111 * Work: (213) 555-3333
Jane.doe@att.net

LITIGATION PARALEGAL

Education
University of Paralegal Studies, Fremont, CA
Paralegal Specialist Certificate, 2002, Honors graduate
Approved by ABA
Course of study: Legal Research and Writing, Contracts, Torts, Ethics, Litigation Specialization

University of California at Berkeley
Bachelor of Arts Degree in History, 2001
Graduated Cum Laude

Skills and Abilities
• Ability to analyze documents, digest depositions, draft discovery, and prepare cases for trial
• Knowledge of torts and contract law, legal research techniques, and basic civil procedure
• Fluent in French, both written and spoken
• Proficient in Word for Windows, WordPerfect 6.0, and Excel

Legal Internship
Jones, Smith, Smythe and Smooth, Los Angeles, 2001–2002
• Digested depositions for complex litigation case
• Organized multiple documents using several software programs

Work Experience
Los Angeles Unified School District, 1998–1999
Secondary School Teacher
• Arranged classroom materials
• Supervised student teachers
• Chaired English Department
• Created curricula for advanced students

Professional Associations
Los Angeles Paralegal Association
University of Paralegal Studies Alumni Association

References and writing samples available upon request.

The first line of your resume should contain only your full name. Type your street address, phone and fax numbers, and email address on separate lines below your name.

Because many human resource managers search by key words, you'll want to include a key word section near the top of your resume. List nouns that describe your job-related skills and abilities. If you have work experience with specific job titles such as "paralegal," list these key words as well. Also include language proficiency or other specialty qualifications such as "nurse–paralegal" or "fluent in Spanish."

After you have created your resume, save it again as an ASCII plain text file. Email the resume to yourself or to a friend to see how it looks when sent over the Internet.

checklist ☑️

Getting Ready

☐ Write resume.

☐ Make contacts.

☐ Network.

☐ Make appointments from mass mailings, telephone solicitations, and network contacts.

Before the Interview

☐ Know your resume.

☐ Be familiar with a typical application form.

☐ Know something about the company or firm. Check the Martindale Hubbell or Standard and Poor's directories.

☐ Have a list of good questions to ask the interviewer, and know when to ask them.

☐ Rehearse your answers to possible interview questions, then rehearse again.

☐ Plan a "thumbnail" sketch of yourself.

☐ Know the location of the interview site and where to park, or become familiar with the public transportation schedule.

☐ Be at least 10 minutes early.

☐ Go alone.

☐ Bring copies of your resume, list of references, and writing samples in a briefcase or portfolio.

☐ Check local salary ranges for the position.

☐ Be prepared to answer questions regarding your salary expectations.

☐ Try to anticipate problem areas, such as inexperience or gaps in your work history.

☐ Be prepared to handle difficult questions, and know how to overcome objections.

(continued)

INTERVIEWING FOR A JOB

Most students today work at part-time or full-time jobs while pursuing their education. These might be summer jobs, holiday fill-in positions, or full-time jobs. The interview for a part-time, summer, or holiday positions, or the interview for a new full-time position provides an opportunity to perfect your interviewing skills. Interviewing for a job can be highly stressful but careful preparation can reduce the stress and help you put your best foot forward so you can get that dream job you want.

After the interview, you should review what happened and the results of the interview as a way of learning how to improve your interviewing skills. Even if you obtain the job, you'll want to learn what you did correctly that helped you to get the job, as well as what you could have done better, to prepare for future interviews.

checklist

CONTINUED

The Introduction

☐ Dress the part.

☐ Do not smoke, eat, chew gum, or drink coffee prior to or during the interview.

☐ Maintain good eye contact and good posture.

☐ Shake hands firmly.

☐ Establish rapport and be cordial without being overly familiar.

☐ Be positive—convert negatives to positives.

☐ Keep in mind that the first impressions are lasting impressions.

The Interview

☐ Provide all important information about yourself.

☐ Sell yourself—no one else will.

☐ Use correct grammar.

☐ Do not be afraid to say, "I don't know."

☐ Ask questions of the interviewer.

☐ Do not answer questions about age, religion, marital status, or children unless you wish to. Try to address the perceived concern.

☐ Find out about the next interview or contact.

☐ Find out when a decision will be made.

☐ Shake hands at the end of the interview.

After the Interview

☐ Immediately document the interview in your placement file.

☐ Send personalized thank-you letters to each person who interviewed you.

☐ Call to follow up.

Source: *Adapted from* How to Land Your First Paralegal Job, *by Andrea Wagner (Upper Saddle River, NJ: Prentice Hall, 2001), pp. 163–164.*

Advice from the Field ····································

THE PARALEGAL'S PORTFOLIO

Kathryn Myers, Coordinator, Paralegal Studies, Saint Mary-of-the-Woods College, Paralegal Studies Program

INTERVIEW

Q: How did the practice of assembling a portfolio come about?

A: This portfolio is actually based on the old concept of the "artist's portfolio." Anyone who is involved in a "hands-on" profession has utilized this concept for years.

Q: Instead of pictures, what do you mean when you speak of a portfolio for paralegal students?

A: A portfolio for paralegal students consists of two parts. One part is for my use in the program. The students have growth papers for each class, plus a series of other papers. I look at the collection of work to determine whether the paralegal program is doing what it says it will and whether it needs to be changed. I have modified a number of classes based on the material in this portfolio.

The other part is a professional portfolio. The students pull material from the above portfolio and create their own professional portfolio to take on interviews. This contains a copy or copies of their resume, transcripts, selected writing samples, projects, or any other document they believe would be useful at the interview. Employers have been very impressed with this presentation.

Q: Do potential employers ever balk at seeing something that bulky? If so, how would you suggest handling it?

A: This has not been a problem for my students. As indicated earlier, we "create" two portfolios— one program-related and the other for professional purposes. I think this eliminates any problems at the interview.

Q: What is the most important thing about a portfolio?

A: The most important thing in the professional portfolio appears to be that the employer has another tool to assess the quality of the potential employee. Grades do not mean that much anymore. An "A" at [our college] may well come from a more demanding curriculum than an "A" at another institution. There is no basis for comparison unless the employer knows the grading scales/demands of the different programs. However, having a portfolio of material allows the employer to see what an interviewee can do.

Q: With that in mind, what should a paralegal student keep in mind when putting together the portfolio?

A: How a student puts a portfolio together says a lot about the student. I encourage students to incorporate both good and "not so good" work. That shows the employer that the interviewee can learn and can improve. Students collect material as they go through the program rather than waiting until the end.

Students should highlight their growth, their abilities, and their determination. They need to provide documentation that can show abilities that counter any poor grades that might appear on the transcript. This shows potential employers that test-taking is not necessarily the be-all, end-all to grades.

Most of all, the students need to let themselves shine through within the portfolio materials. Each student is unique and each has different talents to highlight. That is the value of the portfolio.

Kathryn Myers is Coordinator, Paralegal Studies, Saint Mary of-the-Woods College, Paralegal Studies Program. Used by permission.

checklist ✔ QUESTIONS TO ASK AT THE INTERVIEW

☐ How does the firm evaluate paralegals?

☐ What is the growth potential for a paralegal in the firm?

☐ Why did the prior paralegal leave?

☐ How is work assigned?

☐ What support services are available to paralegals?

☐ What consideration is given for membership in paralegal associations?

☐ Does the firm provide any assistance for continuing education for paralegals?

checklist ✔ ANALYZING HOW I HANDLED THE INTERVIEW

☐ I arrived early for the interview.

☐ I greeted the interviewer warmly, with a smile and a firm handshake.

☐ I maintained good posture.

☐ I did not smoke or chew gum during the interview.

☐ I spoke clearly, using good grammar.

☐ I demonstrated enthusiasm and interest.

☐ I was able to answer questions asked of me.

☐ I sent a thank-you note within 24 hours after the interview.

Legal Terminology

Chronological resume format 112
Complex litigation 83
Conflict checking 95
Court accounting 105
Cover letter 112
Elder law 84
Environmental law 83
General practice 81
Government employment 84

Intellectual property 84
IOLTA accounts 104
Large law offices 80
Networking 85
Nurse paralegals or legal nurse
consultants 83
Paralegal manager 84
Partnership 80

Pro bono 84
Resume 110
Retainer 101
Self-employment 85
Small office 74
Solo practice 77
Specialty practice 82
Trust accounts 104

Summary

CHAPTER 3   THE PARALEGAL WORKPLACE

Arrangements and Organization of Law Offices and Firms

Solo Practice	One lawyer practicing alone without the assistance of other attorneys
Small Offices	Range from individual practitioners sharing space to partnerships
Partnerships	Two or more natural or artificial (corporation) persons who have joined together to share ownership and profit or loss
Large Offices	An outgrowth of traditional law offices that have expanded over the years, adding partners and associates along the way.
General Practice	Handles all types of cases

Specialty Practice

Nurse Paralegals and Legal Nurse Consultants	Nurses who have gained medical work experience and combine it with paralegal skills
Real Estate	Paralegals with real estate experience in sales or from title insurance agencies
Complex Litigation	Requires document production and maintaining indexes, usually on computer databases, of the paperwork generated from litigation
Environmental Law	Covers everything from toxic waste dumps to protection of wildlife and the environment
Intellectual Property	Concerned with the formalities of protecting intellectual-property interests including patent rights, trade secrets, and copyrights and trademarks
Elder Law	Protecting the rights of the elderly and obtaining all the benefits to which they are entitled
Paralegal Managers	Hire, supervise, train, and evaluate paralegals
Pro Bono Paralegals	Work without compensation on behalf of individuals and organizations that otherwise could not afford legal assistance
Government Employment	Paralegals are found in administrative agencies and federal offices involved with both criminal prosecutions and civil litigation.
Legal Departments of Corporations	Paralegals handle documents, technology, and investigations juggling legal, sales, and marketing perspectives.
Self-Employment	State regulation may limit the opportunities or restrict paralegal self-employment. Where authorized by federal law, the paralegal may actively represent clients without the supervision of an attorney.
Networking	Establishing contact with others to exchange questions and information

PARALEGAL TASKS AND FUNCTIONS

1. Conducting interviews
2. Maintaining written and verbal contacts with clients and counsel
3. Setting up, organizing, and maintaining client files
4. Preparing pleadings and documents
5. Reviewing, analyzing, summarizing, and indexing documents and transcripts
6. Assisting in preparing witnesses and clients for trial
7. Maintaining calendar and tickler systems
8. Conducting research, both factual and legal
9. Performing office administrative functions including maintaining time and billing records

Administrative Procedures in Law Offices and Firms

Conflict Checking	To verify that current and prior representations of parties and matters handled will not present a conflict of interest for the firm in accepting a new client or legal matter
Time Keeping and Billing	Keeping track of billable time

Accounting in the Law Office

Maintaining Law Firm Financial Information	A paralegal needs to understand the internal accounting needs of the firm and to understand and prepare client financial information.
Accounting for Client Retainers and Costs Advanced	A payment at the beginning of the handling of a new matter for a client. This amount may be used to offset the fees for services rendered or costs advanced on behalf of the client.
Civil Practice Fee and Cost Billing	May be calculated on an hourly rate, a contingent fee, or a combination of the two.
Timely disbursements	Lawyers cannot retain settlement funds for an unreasonable time.
Trust accounts	The client's funds
IOLTA Accounts	Where the amount is too small to earn interest, court rules require that the funds be deposited into a special interest-bearing account, and the interest generally paid to support legal aid projects (Interest on Lawyers Trust Accounts).
Court Accounting	An accounting with the local court that administers or supervises trust and estate matters; these reports are designed to show that the fiduciary has properly administered the estate or trust.
Interest Bearing Escrow Accounts	If the amount held for a client is sufficient to earn substantial interest it should be deposited in an interest bearing account for the benefit of the client.

Preparing Your Resume

Resume Formats	Brief description of a person's education, a summary of work experience, and other related and supporting information that potential employers use in evaluating a person's qualifications for a position in a firm or an organization Chronological Resume Format 1. Presents education and job history in chronological order with the most recent experience listed first Functional Resume Format 2. Gives a summary of the individual's qualifications with current experience, and education without emphasizing dates of employment
Cover Letters	The cover letter creates the first impression, and is a sample of your writing skills and ability to communicate in writing.
Creating an Electronic Resume	A growing number of employers use computers to search the Internet for job applicants, sorting resumes electronically.
Converting a Traditional Resume into an Electronic Resume	Traditional word processing documents may not be readable in electronic form and need to be converted to a readable format.

Interviewing for a Job

Interview Program	Careful interview preparation can help to eliminate some of the stress and help you put your best foot forward

WORKING THE WEB

1. Download the Tips for Networking Success from the NALS website at **http://www.nals.org/students/reading/networkingsuccess.html**

2. Review some of the job opportunities posted on the American Alliance of Paralegals. What are the common qualifications? **http://aapipara.org/Jobbank.htm**

3. Check and download from the websites of the various paralegal professional associations information on paralegal occupational opportunities:
   a. National Association of Legal Assistants at **www.nala.org**
   b. National Federation of Paralegal Associations at **www.paralegals.org**
   c. Legal Assistant Management Association at **www.lamanet.org**
   d. American Association of Legal Nurse Consultants at **www.aalnc.org**
   e. The American Association of Nurse Attorneys at **www.taana.org**
   f. American Corporate Legal Assistants Association at **www.aclaa.org**

4. What paralegal opportunities are posted at **www.monster.com**

5. What online resources are available to help in creating resumes:
   a. Purdue University at **www.owl.English.purdue.edu**
   b. College of William and Mary at **www.wm.edu/csrv/career/stualum/resmdir**

6. What online career sources are available at:
   a. Career Resource Library at **www.labor.state.ny.us**
   b. America's Job Bank at **www.ajb.dni.us/index.html**
   c. Wall Street Journal at **www.careers.wsj.com**
   d. CareerWEB at **www.employmentguide.com**

7. What law firms in your area have a website that offers employment opportunities? Use the Martindell-Hubbell Legal Directory to find the law firms.

CRITICAL THINKING AND WRITING QUESTIONS

1. What are the different forms of practice arrangements that lawyers use?
2. What are the advantages and disadvantages of working for a lawyer in solo practice?
3. What are the advantages and disadvantages of working in a small multi-lawyer office or partnership?
4. What are the advantages and disadvantages of working in large law offices or firms?
5. Would working in a specialty practice be less stressful than working in a general practice?
6. What are the advantages and disadvantages of working in a corporate legal department?
7. Why would a law firm want to hire nurse paralegals?
8. What additional costs might a paralegal incur in working in a large-city practice in contrast to a small-town office?
9. Why would a paralegal who specializes in one legal field be at greater risk for unauthorized practice of law?
10. Other than revealing potential employment opportunities, what advantages does networking have for a paralegal?
11. Are interviews conducted by paralegals privileged?
12. Why is doing a conflict check important?
13. Is it necessary to do a conflict check before starting employment at a new law firm? Why?
14. When is an ethical wall required?
15. What steps should be taken to ensure that a proper ethical screen is in place?
16. Why is accurate time keeping important to the paralegal and the law firm?
17. What is a retainer?
18. What is an IOLTA account, and what is the reason behind maintaining IOLTA?

19. What is the purpose of filing a court accounting?
20. What is the objective of the Uniform System of Accounts?
21. Prepare the resume you would like to have five years from now. How would this resume help you in selecting courses, extracurricular activities, and interim employment?
22. Prepare your current resume in print form. What format did you use? Why?
23. Convert a print resume to an electronic resume. Email a copy to your instructor if requested.
24. How does assessing your interests and skills help in preparing your personal resume?

▶ETHICS ANALYSIS AND DISCUSSION QUESTIONS

1. In changing jobs from one firm to another, how does the paralegal avoid a conflict of interest?
2. What ethical and UPL problems do freelance paralegals face that those working in a single firm do not?
3. What ethical issues might arise in determining the paralegal's supervising attorney when the paralegal is working in a small firm of three attorneys?
4. Say you are working as a paralegal in a small law office, shared by three attorneys, each of whom is a solo practitioner. To save money, they share a law library and a fax machine, and they use a common computer network with separate workstations but with a common file server to save files because it has an automatic backup system. You work for each of the lawyers as the need arises, answering phones and generally performing paralegal services. [District of Columbia Ethics Opinion 303.] What issues of confidentiality should be considered? As the office paralegal, do you have any conflict of interest problems?

Paralegal Ethics in Practice

5. You hold a bachelor's degree in paralegal studies from a prestigious college. You want to work as an independent paralegal. May you advertise in the local newspaper and put a sign on the door of your office that uses the term "paralegal," according to your state law?

▶DEVELOPING YOUR COLLABORATION SKILLS

Working on your own or with a group of other students assigned by your instructor, review the scenario at the beginning of the chapter discussing the changes and the opportunities in the paralegal profession.

1. Dividing the class into groups of three, one person will play the role of Cary Moritz and another the role of Natasha Weiser; the third person will act as recorder and presenter.
2. Role-play Natasha's first day on-the-job. She receives the memo from Cary and goes to her office to offer her thanks.
   a. What additional questions could Natasha ask Cary?
   b. What additional advice could Cary offer?
3. The recorder keeps detailed notes of the conversation.
4. Once the role-play is completed, the group summarizes the expectations that Natasha and Cary would have of the other in their working relationship.
5. Now it is Natasha's turn to prepare a memo thanking Cary and summarizing their conversation.

▶PARALEGAL PORTFOLIO EXERCISE

Develop your resume, using the functional format to prepare the resume you would like to have when you finish your education as a paralegal. List the skills you expect to develop or learn before you apply for your desired paralegal position.

▶LEGAL ANALYSIS AND WRITING CASES

Jean v. Nelson 863 F.2d 759 (11th Cir. 1988)

Reimbursement for Paralegal Time under Federal Statute

The district court awarded, and the 11th Circuit Court of Appeals upheld, reimbursement for time spent by paralegals and law clerks where the work normally was done by an attorney. The hourly rate awarded was $40, the rate at which the law firm whose paralegals and clerks were involved bills its clients.

The government challenges the rate awarded, and contends that paralegal time is compensational only at the actual cost to the plaintiff's counsel. In the context of a Title VII case, [the court] held that paralegal time is recoverable as "part of a prevailing party's award for attorney's fees and expenses, [but] only to the extent that the paralegal performs work traditionally done by an attorney. To hold otherwise would be counterproductive because excluding reimbursement for such work might encourage attorneys to handle entire cases themselves, thereby achieving the same results at a higher overall cost."

Questions

1. Does this rationale encourage lawyers to use paralegals?
2. Does this decision facilitate the availability of lower-cost quality legal services?
3. Should an attorney be allowed to charge more than out-of-pocket costs for paralegal services?

In Re Busy Beaver Bldg. Centers, Inc. 19 F.3d 833 (3rd Cir. 1994)

Paralegal Fees Based on Skill Level

In deciding the propriety of awarding paralegal fees in bankruptcy cases, the court held:

As is true with recently graduated attorneys, entry-level paralegals perform the more mundane tasks in the paralegal work spectrum, some of which may resemble those tasks generally deemed "clerical" in nature. Yet, even with these tasks, paralegals may have to bring their training or experience to bear, thereby relieving attorneys of the burden of extensive supervision and ensuring the proper completion of tasks involving the exercise, or potential exercise, of some paraprofessional judgment. Of course, the appropriate rate the attorney will command for paralegal services will ordinarily parallel the paralegal's credentials and the degree of experience, knowledge, and skill the task at hand calls for. . . . [P]urely clerical or secretarial tasks should not be billed at a paralegal rate, regardless of who performs them.

The short of it is that the market-driven approach of the [bankruptcy act] § 330 permits compensation for relatively low-level paralegal services if and only if analogous non-bankruptcy clients agree to pay for the same, and then only at that rate. [T]hose services not requiring the exercise of professional legal judgment . . . must be included in "overhead."

We cannot agree that in all cases the general ability of a legal secretary to perform some particular task determines whether a paralegal or a legal secretary is the appropriate, most efficient, employee to perform it at any given instant. At times temporal constraints may foreclose the delegation option. At other times a paralegal—or, for that matter, an attorney—can more productively complete a clerical task, such as photocopying documents, than can a legal secretary.

Questions

1. How can the attorney prove the skill level of paralegals when seeking compensation for paralegal services?
2. Will this kind of reasoning by the court force attorneys to hire more skilled paralegals?
3. Would the existence of a certificate or degree in paralegal studies be useful in proving that the person who worked on a case was a paralegal?

TECHNOLOGY AND THE PARALEGAL

"Laws too gentle are seldom obeyed; too severe, seldom executed."

Benjamin Franklin, Poor Richard's Almanack (1756)

After studying this chapter, you should be able to:

1. Explain the functions of the components of a computer system in the law office.

2. Describe the types of software and the functions they perform in a law office.

PARALEGALS AT WORK

Edith Hannah and Glenn Hains, Attorneys at Law, have decided to combine their practices to create the Hannah Hains Law Office. Miss Hannah has had a thriving practice for 35 years, and Mr. Hains has been in practice for only 5 years. Both attorneys rely heavily on their paralegal staff to run their businesses. Edward Martin has worked for Miss Hannah for 35 years, and Cary Moritz has been with Mr. Hains for only 3 years.

When Edward first visited the Hains office, he was surprised to see how small the Hains library was compared to Miss Hannah's library. Edward was proud of their legal library, even though it did take a lot of time to keep it up-to-date. He also noticed that the Hains office had many fewer filing cabinets and boxes and no large ledger books.

Edward sat down next to Cary's workstation and asked: "Where do you store all of your files? We have at least a dozen heavy fireproof file cabinets and a rented warehouse room full of boxes of closed files. I've heard of the paperless office, but you must have records somewhere and how do you do legal research without a decent law library?"

Cary: "Well, Edward, most of our clients' files are electronic, and we don't have many actual hard copies of our files or copies of law books. We can access almost everything we need to research cases online. We use the Internet and online research subscriptions to find all of the latest cases, statutes, and regulations. While we are talking about technology, what type of accounting system are you using?"

Edward: "We use ledger books to keep track of time records, financial accounts, and client financial records. We're proud of our detailed accounting system. How do you do it? Wait . . . don't tell me—you do it on the computer."

Cary: "Edward, we have computer software to track cases, client information, deadlines, accounting information, and escrow accounts. Just wait till you see it! Having everything on our own network really makes life easier when you need to prepare a report for the court or a client. Could you hold a minute? . . . You'll have to excuse me. That was an instant message I just received on my cell phone. My boss wants me to bring a file to him in the courthouse."

When they combine their offices, do you think they will have any problems combining files, clients, and office procedures? Consider the issues involved in this scenario as you read this chapter.

3. Describe the features of the electronic courtroom and the paperless office.

4. Describe how a computer network is used by a law firm.

5. Explain the importance and the steps that may be taken to maintain computer and network security.

6. Describe how the computer is used to conduct factual and legal research.

7. Explain how to find and download information and documents using the Internet.

▶INTRODUCTION FOR THE PARALEGAL

The increased use of the computer in the law office has changed the way in which many traditional law office procedures are performed. The computer and the Internet are used more and more not just for the traditional document preparation but also for maintaining client databases, keeping office and client accounting records, and engaging in electronic communications.

Computers also are being used more often to share information in digital format between remote offices, courthouses, government agencies, and clients. Computer files are shared today by use of the Internet as well as in the form of CDs, DVDs, and attachments to emails. In the past, paper had to be physically copied and sent, frequently by costly messenger service or express mail service. Today, large files can be quickly exchanged electronically, almost instantaneously, anywhere in the world, without any paper (hardcopy). Where formerly the physical safety of the delivery of paper documents were concerns, the security and confidentiality of documents sent in electronic format are increasing concerns.

The paralegal is the member of the legal team who is most likely to spend time in the office using the Web and the Internet for more than just pure legal research. Access to most government information is obtained online through Internet websites. Private service providers, such as the yellow pages and white pages for finding businesses and individuals, is handled most efficiently through Web search engines such as Google and Yahoo. The involvement puts the paralegal in potentially the best position to have meaningful input into development of the firm's website, as seeing and using many websites gives one a sense of the best and the worst features of a website. With legal firms increasing development and use of websites, only the best of these retain clients and attract new clients.

The paralegal of today must have a working familiarity with computers and the types of computer programs used in the law office. Not too many years ago, the average law office had a typewriter, an adding machine, and a duplicating machine of some type. Paper was king, with every document typed, edited, retyped—and frequently retyped again. In each instance, a paper copy was produced, delivered to the supervising attorney for review and additional changes. It then was returned for retyping and eventually sent to the client, the opposing counsel, or filed with the court. File cabinets abounded in the law office, and the storage of paper files created back rooms, warehouses, and other storage locations filled with box after box of paper. The trend is toward eliminating paper in the law office through the use of computer technology and software. ■

COMPUTER HARDWARE

Computer hardware is the term used to describe the tangible or physical parts of a computer system that must have a power source to operate (electrical outlet or battery), including:

> the computer (**CPU**)
>
> computer monitors
>
> printers
>
> fax machines
>
> printer–copier–scanner combinations.

Just as the automobile depends on fuel to continue to operate, so is the computer dependent on a power source to operate. Computers cannot remember data or information that appears on the computer screen (work in process) after the power is

Computer hardware
Hardware is the term that encompasses all of the tangible or physical items including computers, monitors, printers, fax machines, duplicators, and similar items that usually have either an electrical connection or use batteries as a power source.

Computer processing unit (CPU)
The computer chip and memory module that perform the basic computer functions.

turned off—unless it has been saved to a permanent memory device. Some permanent memory devices that do not require power to retain data are:

the floppy disk
tape drive
hard disk drive
CDs
DVDs
memory cards
USB memory devices

Uninterruptible power sources (UPS) battery back-up systems for the computer are used frequently to guard against loss of the "work-in-process" files when there is a short term power loss or long term outage. The length of time the computer will continue to work after loss of its permanent power supply depends on the size of the battery in the UPS, and may be as short as a few minutes or as long as an hour or more. The UPS is designed to allow time to save the current files and shut down the computer normally in the event of a major power outage.

Older models of computers, many of which are still found in many law offices, are large, ugly metal boxes connected to large, bulky, and heavy desktop monitors, sometimes taking up half of a desk top. Newer models are smaller and less obtrusive. In some offices the computer system consists of a portable laptop computer, weighing as little as 3–4 pounds and the size of a large book, used at the user's desk with a docking station to connect it to a flat-screen monitor, external keyboard and mouse, Internet connection and network. With the reduction in size have come increased speed and functionality. On older models, opening more than one document uses most of the computer system resources, slowing them down or even "freezing" or stopping the processing of data. The newer models typically run well while allowing the display of multiple documents from multiple applications all running at the same time—word files, Excel spreadsheets, calendering programs and time keeping applications. Exhibit 4.1 shows a monitor display of four programs running at the same time.

The ability to perform multiple functions simultaneously is in part the result of the increase in processing speed permitted by newer central processing units (CPUs) and the availability of inexpensive dynamic computer memory, the temporary computer memory that stores work-in-process.

OPERATING SYSTEMS

The **operating system** is a basic set of instructions to the computer on how to handle basic functions, such as how to process input from "input devices" such as the keyboard and the mouse, the order in which to process information, and what to show on the computer monitor. The operating system is like the ringmaster of a circus, directing the flow of performers and the timing of the performance.

The two most popular computer systems are the PC, or personal computer, and the Apple. The original designs of these two systems were built around different central processor system chips manufactured by different companies—Intel in the case of the PC, and Motorola in the case of Apple. Each computer system requires its own unique operating system.

Although both computer systems have advocates, the PC has a dominant position in the legal and business communities where the main use is text and mathematical computations in the form of word processing and spreadsheet use. The Apple

Operating system
The operating system is a basic set of instructions to the computer on how to handle basic functions—how to process input from "input devices" such as the keyboard and mouse, the order in which to process information, and what to show on the computer monitor.

Exhibit 4.1 **4-page display in Microsoft office suite**

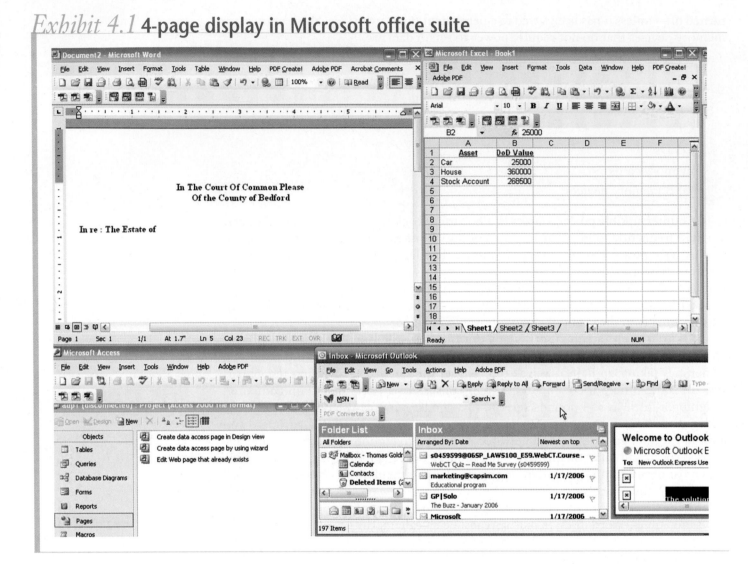

Computer software
Software refers to programs containing sets of instructions that tell the computer and the other computer-based electronic devices what to do and how to do it.

system achieved the dominant position in the graphic and artistic communities, and to some extent among computer game players. New models of both systems have **computer software** that permits the other computer system software to run on the competitive machine.

Apple announced in 2006 that it was going to utilize the same CPU manufacturer as the PC manufacturers use, creating the expectation that new Apple Computers will allow the use of software for both systems on its computers without any additional software to interpret the software instruction of the other system.

Microsoft Windows™ is the most commonly used computer operating system for the personal computer. A number of different versions of the Windows operating system are found in the workplace with the latest versions, such as Windows XP, designed to take advantage of increased computer operating speeds and better on screen graphics. The original PC operating systems did not provide for the graphic user interface, or GUI, which everyone has come to expect. Over time the PC and the Apple systems have come to have similar appearances, and software is generally provided by most software companies for both systems, sometimes on the same CD.

Among the newer computer operating systems gaining followers is the Linux operating system. This is an operating system offered by its developer as an alternative to the Microsoft operating system, provided without a licensing or royalty fee, with the agreement that any improvements will be made available without fee to anyone using the Linux operating system.

APPLICATIONS SOFTWARE

Applications Software programs are those that perform specific tasks, such as prepare documents, sort information, perform computations, and create and present graphic displays. These are the software programs used in the management of the law office and the management of client cases.

Word Processing

Written communication and document preparation are at the heart of every law office. It may be preparation of letters to clients, other counsel or the court, or contracts and agreements, or pleadings. To achieve written clarity and accuracy frequently means writing, rewriting and correcting the same document, sometimes multiple times and by a number of different members of the legal team. The ability to easily make even minor changes in language has a direct impact on the willingness of those reviewing the document to suggest changes and make them in the final document. Computerized word processing makes this possible. Word processing files are sent electronically to the appropriate members of the legal team for review. Changes or revisions are frequently made to the electronic file copy by the reviewer. Where multiple parties may be working on a document, changes made to the original document by each person on the legal team may be monitored by using built in features such as MS Word's **"Track Changes"** tool. This feature shows the original text, the deleted text and the new text by a series of lines that show as a strike through the deleted text and by margin notes on the document. When the final document is completed it may be sent by e-mail, fax (frequently directly from the computer without any intermediate paper), and in some jurisdictions filed electronically with the court. Exhibit 4.2 shows the original word file, the changes inserted and old text with a strike through it, and the final version with the changes still showing in the margin of the document.

Today the most commonly used software program in the law office is the word processor. Although many different word processing programs are available, the legal community most commonly uses either WordPerfect™ or Microsoft Word™. In addition to the usual typing functions, these programs have built-in software tools that check spelling and grammar and allow customized formatting using a variety of type sizes and font styles in the same document—functions that have not been possible with a typewriter. Some offices even use different programs, each with its own file format.

Application software
Applications programs are software that perform generic tasks such as word processing.

Track changes
Track Changes, as found in MS word, shows the original text, the deleted text, and the new text as well as a strike through for deleted text, underlining or highlighting of new text, as well as margin notes on the document.

ETHICAL *Perspective*

Document Comparison Software

When using Track Changes or similar comparison programs, be sure to remove the history of the changes and other information from the document before sending it to the opposing counsel, the client, or the court. The history of changes and other document information is called *metadata*.

The history of the changes may offer the reader insight into the strategy of the case—for example, showing the final price the client is willing to pay, which appeared in the original draft and not the first offer that appeared in the final version sent to the opposing party. Word Help offers instructions on how to remove this information. WordPerfect X3 allows documents to be saved without the metadata, using a file save option—**Save without Metadata**—making it easy to quickly remove private or sensitive data that can be hidden in, but easily extracted from, office productivity documents.

Exhibit 4.2 **Microsoft Word track changes**

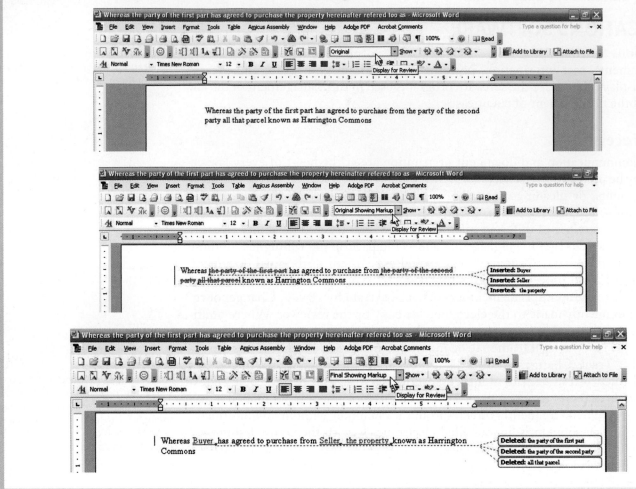

File extension
When a file is saved, a file extension (a period followed by three characters) is added to the end of the filename to identify the program or format in which the file has been saved.

Most word processing programs allow the opening and saving of files in the file formats of other word processing programs. When a file is saved, a **file extension** (a period followed by characters) is added to the end of the file name that identifies the program or format in which the file has been saved.

For example:

the file name NAME	the extension EXT
Microsoft Word	filename.doc
WordPerfect	filename.wpd
Microsoft Works	filename.wps
Web documents	filename.htm
Generic (rich text file) word processing format	filename.rtf
Generic (text file) word processing format	filename.txt

The newer versions of WordPerfect even permit simulation of the Microsoft Word workspace. Word processor files are saved with the document properties such as type font and type size, and document formatting details. The saved files also include instructions to the computer on how to display the document, security features, and hidden information such as the "Track Changes information."

Exhibit 4.3 **Excel spreadsheet**

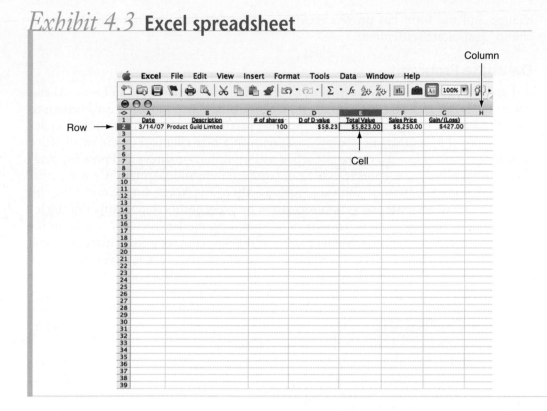

Spreadsheet Programs

Many areas of legal practice involve the calculation and presentation of financial information. For example, in family law practice, the preparation of family and personal balance sheets and income and expense reports are routinely prepared for support and equitable distribution hearings; estate lawyers must submit an "accounting," to the court for approval, showing details of how the fiduciary handled the financial affairs of the estate or trust; and litigation firms must prepare documentation showing the receipts and disbursements of cases, sometime for court approval.

As shown in Exhibit 4.3, in an estate, the calculation involved may be as simple as multiplying the number of shares owned by a decedent by the value on the date of death (D of D), then calculating the profit or loss when the stock was sold. Without a computerized spreadsheet, all of the calculations would have to be done manually, using a multicolumn form known as a spreadsheet or accountant's working papers. The information then has to be typed in a report format for submission to the court, the beneficiaries, or the taxing authorities.

Using a computerized spreadsheet such as Microsoft Excel or Corel Quattro Pro, the numbers are entered in cells, as identified in Exhibit 4.3, and a formula assigned to the cell in which the result is to be displayed, such as "multiply column c by column d," and the result displayed in column e. The computerized spreadsheet, when laid out in the format acceptable to the court, can be printed without reentering the data, or copied into word documents using a simple "Cut and Paste" operation.

The use of computer spreadsheets reduces the errors associated with manual mathematical calculations and errors in retyping the information. Caution must be taken to make sure that the formula is accurate and performs the desired calculation. Even expert spreadsheet users use a set of sample numbers to test the formulas, knowing what the result should be, based on prior use or calculations.

Many offices save spreadsheet templates in the same way that sample forms are saved in word processing. For example, a real estate settlement spreadsheet with formulas and headings may be saved without numbers. Because the formulas do not

Spreadsheet programs
Programs that permit the calculation and presentation of financial information in a grid format of rows and columns.

change and the form has proven accurate, it may be used as a template for other clients' real estate settlements.

Database Programs

A **database program** is a repository of information of all types that can be sorted and presented in a desired meaningful manner. Some offices use a manual card system to keep track of the names of clients and opposing parties, these cards are searched to determine possible conflicts of interest in representing new clients. For the small office this system works. But for the larger office with multiple attorneys and possibly multiple offices, timely entry and searching of large amounts of information is not realistic. Computerized database software, such as Microsoft Access and Corel DB, will facilitate timely, accurate access to information by every authorized member of the legal team. For example, information may be stored on the law firm's server in an information database that includes the names, addresses, contact information, personal data such as birthdates of every client, every opposing party, every fact witness and expert witness, and every opposing counsel with whom any member of the firm has ever had contact in litigation, contract negotiations, or counseling session, or met in any business or legal setting. With a few keystrokes, a list can be prepared for manually checking for conflicts of interest, or a computer search can be performed with a printout of any matter or litigation where a name appears.

In addition to the obvious use in avoiding accepting a client with a potential conflict of interest, the information frequently is used in maintaining client relations. Many firms use the information to send birthday and anniversary greetings and updates on specific changes in the law for which the client has consulted the firm previously.

PRESENTATION GRAPHICS PROGRAMS

It has been said that a picture is worth a thousand words. Presentation graphics software programs, such as WordPerfect Presentation X3 (see Exhibit 4.4) and Microsoft PowerPoint, are being used to used to create high-quality slide shows and drawings. These graphic presentations can include text, data charts, and graphic objects.

Exhibit 4.4 **WordPerfect Presentation X3**

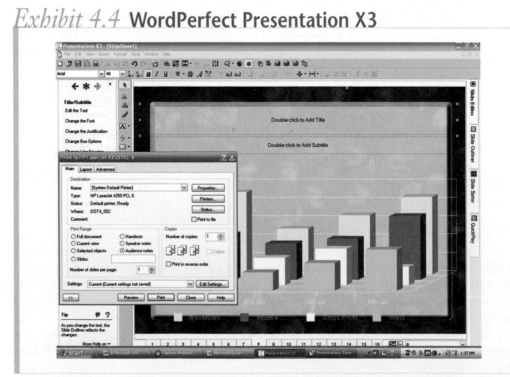

One of the advantages of these programs is their flexibility. They can be used to prepare and present the graphic presentation electronically, using a computer, with or without a projector, and to print out paper copies for distribution. Presentation programs typically provide stock templates of graphics, artwork, and layout as a sample that the user can easily modify. More advanced users can add sound clips to the presentation, include still photos, and incorporate custom graphics from other programs, as well as video clips.

Office Suites Software

Office software suites are sets of commonly used office software programs that manage data; database programs; manipulate financial or numeric information, spreadsheet programs; or display images and graphics and presentation graphics programs. Some of the tools in the two most common program suites, Microsoft Office and Corel WordPerfect, are:

	Microsoft Office	Corel Wordperfect Office X3
Word processor	Word	WordPerfect
Spreadsheet	Excel	Quattro Pro
Database	Access	Paradox
Presentation graphics	PowerPoint	Presentation X3
Graphics	Visio	Presentation Graphics X3

Office software suites
This software consists of commonly used office software programs that manage data and database programs; manipulate financial or numeric information, spreadsheet programs; or display images and graphics presentation graphics programs.

The software suites usually are delivered on one CD, enabling all the programs to be loaded at one time, which simplifies and saves installation time. With common features and appearance, it is easier to switch between programs and copy information between the programs, like copying part of a spreadsheet into a word processing document.

SPECIALTY APPLICATION PROGRAMS

Every year, computers become more powerful, operating faster with more operating and storage memory. Software programs are getting more powerful and capable of performing more complex functions on more data. Whereas older models of computers can perform only basic word processing and data management, newer, more powerful computers can perform complex functions seamlessly, thereby permitting management of law office functions and management of cases and litigation.

Specialty application programs combine many of the basic functions found in software suites, word processing, database management, spreadsheets, and graphic presentations to perform law office case and litigation management. They simplify the operation with the use of customized input screens and preset report generators.

Legal specialty software programs fall generally into the following categories:

Office management

Case management

Litigation support

Transcript management

Trial presentation

Specialty applicaton programs
Specialty programs combine many of the basic functions found in software suites, word processing, database management, spreadsheets and graphic presentations to perform law office, case, and litigation management.

For a self running video demo of Tabs 3, go to http://www.tabs3.com/products/video.html Information on the features of Abacuslaw may be found at http://www.abacuslaw.com

Of the office management specialty application programs, the most basic are the time and billing programs. These provide a standard input screen to record the time spent on a client's case, store the information and, with a request for an invoice for a given client, automatically sort the data, apply the billing rates, and print out an invoice.

Exhibit 4.5 **Sample Tabs 3 time entry form**

Among the popular programs in this group are:

Tabs 3 from Software Technology, Inc.,

Abacuslaw from Abacus Data Systems Inc.

ProLaw from Thomson Elite

PCLaw from LexisNexis

Timeslips from Sage

Exhibit 4.5 is an example of an application input screen.

Early versions of time reporting software are limited to time keeping. With faster computers and greater memory capacity, most of these programs have other features integrated into them, such as accounting functions to track costs and expenses, and practice management functions such as calendar and contact management.

Exhibit 4.6 shows the multiple functions integrated in Abacuslaw Accounting.

www

Details and additional sample screen graphics about PCLaw are available at http://www.pclaw.com/

Case and litigation management
Case and litigation management programs are used to manage documents and the facts and issues of cases.

Case and Litigation Management Software

Paper has long been the bane of the litigation attorney. Even simple cases can involve hundreds of pages of documents. Complex litigation may involve millions of documents and hundreds of witnesses and, in the case of class action litigation, potentially millions of clients. Keeping track of all of the documentation and parties is an overwhelming task even with a large staff of assistants and endless rows of organized file cabinets and file boxes.

Before the availability of fast computers with inexpensive memory-running case and litigation management software, most case management work was done manually, usually by a team of paralegals and junior associate attorneys. In two of the most notable cases—the IBM antitrust suit and the Ford Pinto negligence suit—

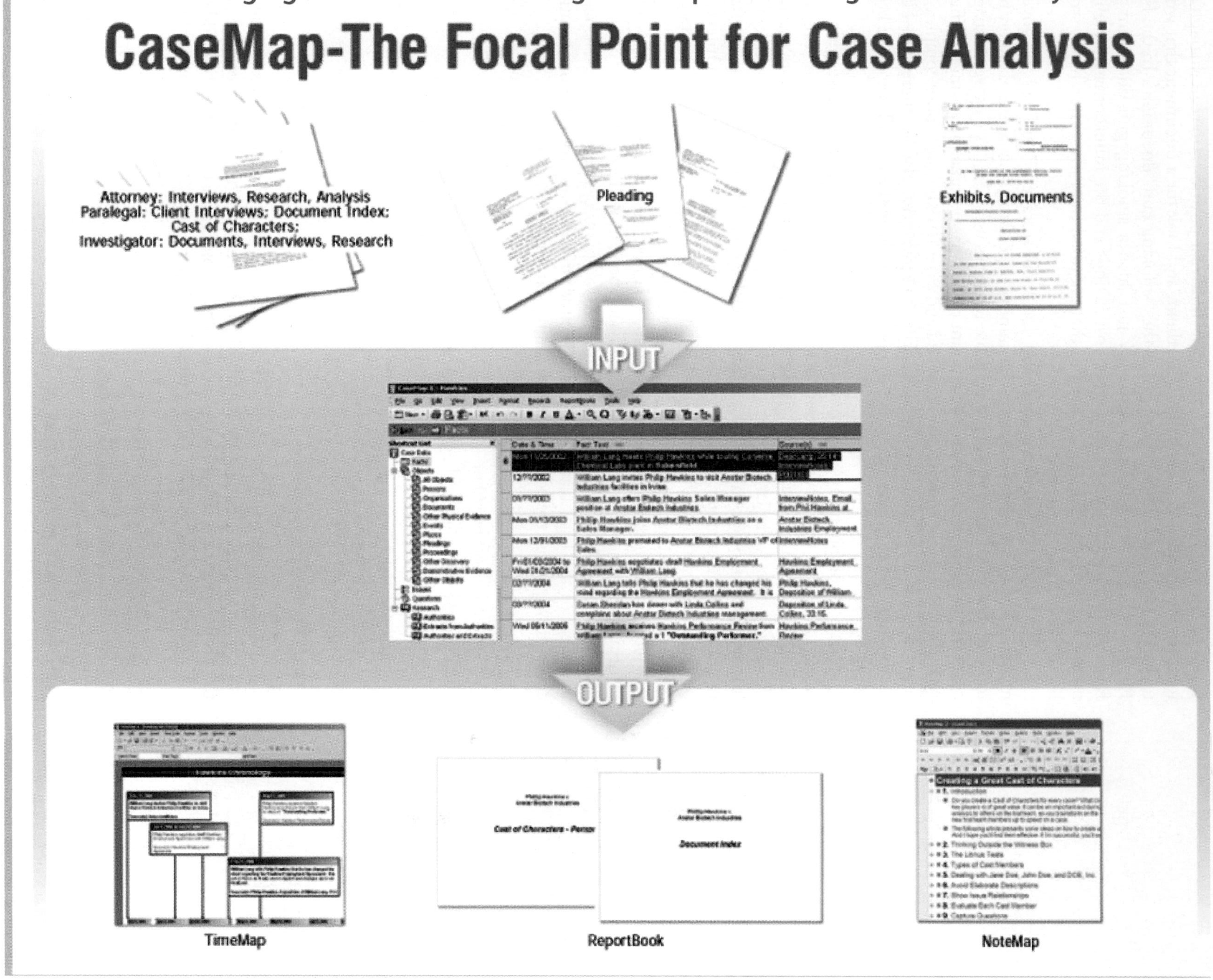

Exhibit 4.6 Managing case information using CaseMap case management and analysis software

teams of law students were hired, some for multiyear positions, to read through and identify the documents, manually index them, and look for a document that would make the case, sometimes referred to as the "smoking gun" document. In the Ford Pinto case, in a serendipitous discovery just such a smoking gun document was found, which detailed the engineering cost savings and the inherent risk by eliminating a specific part that led to the fire that engulfed the Pinto when it was struck by another car from the rear.

The use of computers for email and document storage by business and government has caused a massive increase in the number of potential documents that may have to be reviewed, tracked, and made available to opposing counsel in a case. Managing cases and litigation with the massive amount of data has become increasingly difficult. As the numbers of documents has increased and cases have become more complex, the number of members of the legal team working on a given case also has increased. These factors have led to greater use of the computer to manage the case files and the litigation process.

In pre-computer days, attorneys frequently concentrated on one case, personally working on all of the documentation, pleadings, and discovery, and learning every detail of the case in anticipation of trying the case with little backup support except in the largest cases in the larger firms. The legal-team approach to case management and litigation has allowed, in some ways, for specialization within the legal team. Some members of the litigation team may specialize in discovery of documents. Others may be concerned with locating, interviewing, and preparing witnesses. Still others concentrate on investigative matters and legal research.

Effective case management, therefore, requires some central repository of the information gathered by each of the team members, as well as the ability of each to access the case information input by others. Computer systems today even permit members of the legal team to access the same information from remote locations across town, across the country, and sometimes around the world.

A typical case file contains documentation of the:

Interview of the client

Interviews of fact and expert witnesses

Investigation reports

Expert reports

Research memoranda

Pleadings

Trial preparation material

The trial team frequently has to quickly find a document or information on a specific issue from among potentially thousands of pages of documents. With a computer and the proper specialty software program, this is possible. Some of the litigation and case management specialty software programs found in the law office are discussed below.

CaseMap

CaseMap™ from Lexis-Nexis® CaseSoft is a case management and analysis software tool that acts as a central repository for critical case knowledge. As facts are gathered, parties identified, and documents and research assembled, they may be entered into the program, allowing for easy organization and exploration of the facts, the cast of characters, and the issues by any member of the legal team.

Typical of integrated software applications, CaseMap allows seemless transfer of data to other programs such as TimeMap™, a timeline graphic program, and word processor programs. It also allows for creating specialty reports and documents including trial notebook information. Exhibit 4.6 shows the flow of information in a typical case, using CaseMap as a case management tool.

Demonstration versions of CaseSoft products and Webinar tutorials on their use can be found at http://www.casesoft.com/ student.shtml

Summation

The Summation family of products, from CT Summation, Inc. (a Wolters Kluwer business) and similar software applications programs are classified as litigation support systems. As the number of documents increases in a case, the ability to locate relevant documents in a timely fashion becomes more and more critical. Managing the documents is critical to successful litigation outcomes. In cases involving potentially millions of documents, it is essential to be able to find the relevant information quickly, sometimes in the middle of the direct or cross-examination of a witness.

Summation-type programs allow for easy search and retrieval of all of the evidence, whether documents, testimony, photographs, or electronic files, with a single command. Documents associated with a case are stored on the computer in electronic folders. These folders may be set up to include transcripts, pleadings, text files (from OCR or otherwise), casts of characters, and core databases. Some versions of these programs are designed to work on stand-alone systems such as a laptop carried into court. Others permit concurrent use by many users over a network, and some permit remote access over the Internet.

View an online demo of Summation®LG at http://info.summation.com/demo/modules.htm

Concordance

Concordance, by Dataflight Software® Inc. is a litigation support system program that provides document management. Early versions of Concordance were limited to storing and handling 4 gigabytes of data, or approximately 280,000 documents. The newer version allows the management of 128 times that amount, or more than 35 million documents. Like other document support tools, Concordance has a powerful search engine that allows searches by word, phrase, date, email address, or document type, as well as Boolean, using the fuzzy and wild card searches.

A Boolean search uses connectors between words such as AND, OR, or NOT to narrow the search. A fuzzy or fuzzy string search is the name for a search that looks for strings or letters or characters that approximately match some given pattern. A wildcard search allows the use of a "wild" character such as the symbol * to replace a letter in the search word that allows you to search for plurals or variations of words using a wildcard character. It also is a good way to search if you do not know the spelling of a word. For example: Book* finds Booking and Books.

Learn more about Concordance at http://www.dataflight.com

Trial Director

Trial Director, from InData, and similar trial presentation programs are electronic and trial-presentation software applications. More and more courtrooms are providing, or allowing litigants to provide for their trial, computer-based electronic display systems. Some see this as nothing more than a logical outgrowth of the multimedia presentations that started with the use of chalkboards, movie clips, and slide projectors.

Modern trial presentations frequently include videotaped depositions and the presentation of images, photos, videos, and portions of documents. These may be on personal monitors or large screen displays.

Managing the hundreds of individual components in the courtroom can be a trial nightmare unless they are organized and easily accessed for presentation. Trial Director and similar programs allow the legal team to organize and control the documents, depositions, photographs, and other data as exhibits for trial, and then display them as evidence as and when needed in depositions and trial. Exhibit 4.7 shows sample screens from Trial Director.

An interactive demo of Trial Director showing how trial presentation software can be used in litigation at http://www.indatacorp.com/flash/tdstutorial.swf

ELECTRONIC COURTROOM AND PAPERLESS OFFICE

Computer technology is changing the way that law offices and court systems perform traditional functions. The ease of creating documents, including traditional letters and contracts and electronic communications in the form of emails, has resulted

Exhibit 4.7 **Trial Director sample screens**

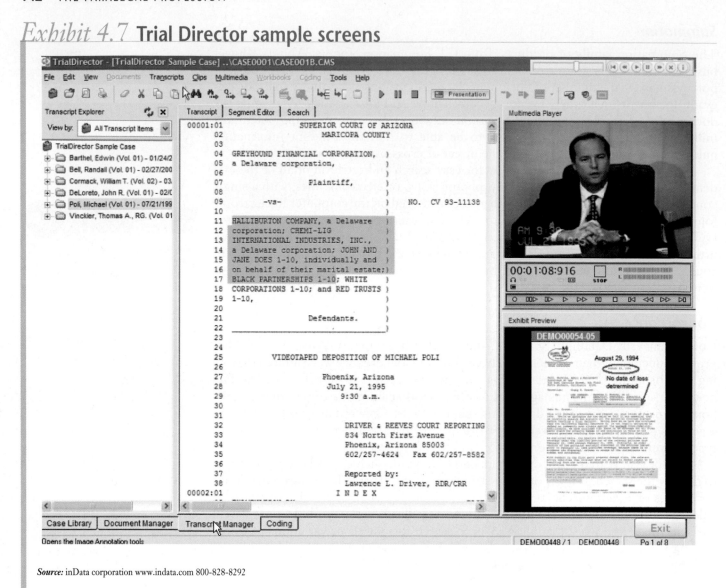

Source: inData corporation www.indata.com 800-828-8292

in a document explosion. At the same time, cases are coming to trial faster because of the demand for "quicker justice," which allows time to prepare and present a case in court. The result has been growth in the use of electronic documentation and computerized case management and the use of computers in litigation.

The Electronic Courtroom

Increasingly, judges are embracing the use of electronics and computer-based systems in the courts. The initial reluctance to allow the "new fangled" technology is giving way to acceptance of tools that enhance the speedy administration of justice. One of the earliest uses of technology in the courtroom was the playing of videotaped depositions of expert witnesses on TV monitors in court.

To get experts to testify is difficult when the schedule for their testimony is uncertain because of uncertain trial schedules. Many experts, such as noted surgeons and medical forensics experts, have active lucrative practices and demand compensation that can range in the thousands of dollars per hour for time lost waiting to testify. The average litigant can rarely afford this litigation cost. A videotape, or electronic recording, of a deposition can be used in trial as a cost effective method of presenting expert witnesses or for witnesses who for reasons of health or distance, could not otherwise be available to testify personally at a trial.

Exhibit 4.8 U.S. tax court electronic (north) courtroom

Source: Reprinted with permission of US Tax Court

As judicial budgets allow, courtrooms are being outfitted with computers and audio visual presentation systems. Exhibit 4.8 shows the U.S. Tax Court's electronic courtroom in Virginia. Computerized courtrooms can be seen frequently on Court TV televised trials, in which computer terminals are present at each lawyer's table, the judge's bench, for each of the court support personnel, and monitors for the jury.

Litigation support software is used in trial to display documentary evidence, graphic presentations, and simulations of accident cases. Relevant portions of documents can be displayed for everyone to see at the same time without passing paper copies to everyone, as the witness testifies and identifies the document. Lawyers can rapidly search depositions and documents, sometimes in the tens of thousands of pages, on their laptop computer to find pertinent material for examination or cross-examination of witness.

The electronic courtroom also is used in many jurisdictions in criminal cases for preliminary matters in which the judge is located at a central location, and the defendants at various lock-up facilities with video cameras and monitors recording and displaying the parties to each other.

Acrobat tutorials "Introduction to PDFs" "Acrobat 101" and "Acrobat 201" may be found at www.casesoft.com/student.htm

THE PAPERLESS OFFICE

To some people, the ideal office is one that has no paper documents, or hardcopy, as they are sometimes referred to. The office where documents are created and stored electronically is sometimes referred to as the **"paperless office,"** or "electronic office." Difficult as it may seem for some who have grown up in the paper world, the paperless office is rapidly approaching reality. In the traditional office, documents are created electronically with word processing software, or received by fax or email and then printed. In the paperless office, documents are created using computer-based word processor programs such as Microsoft Word or Corel WordPerfect. These electronic files then are sent electronically to the attorney for review.

The reviewer frequently makes changes or revisions to the electronic file copy and when multiple parties are working on a document; changes made to the original

Paperless office
The paperless office is one in which documents are created and stored electronically.

document by each person on the legal team may be monitored by using built-in features such as Track Changes in MS Word. This feature shows the original text, the deleted text, and the new text by a strike-through the deleted text, underlining of new text, and by margin notes on the document. When the final document is completed, it may be sent by email, fax (frequently directly from the computer without any intermediate paper) and, in some jurisdictions, filed electronically with the court.

Electronic portability requires inexpensive portable computer memory, a computer to store and transport the documents, and small, lightweight computers to display them. Conversion of existing paper documents requires the availability of scanners and software that converts the documents to an acceptable format that cannot be easily changed.

The paperless law office indeed is becoming the norm with the advent of modern scanning technology, secured methods for transmission of documents, accepted protocols for use of electronic replacements for paper documents, and rules of court permitting electronic submission of documents.

Portable Document Format (PDF)

The ability to save documents in a format that cannot be easily changed through use of the computer is one of the basic requirements of a system that allows for electronic documentation. Anyone who has received a word processing document file knows that they may change it, save it, and present it as an original. Now, documents may be saved in a graphic image format or portable document format (PDF), developed by Adobe Systems. The recipient cannot easily or readily change these graphic images.

Although creating documents in PDF format requires specialty software such as Adobe Acrobat, everyone can download a free Adobe Reader to view these documents. With the acceptance of this format has come a willingness to scan and store documents electronically in this format, eliminating or returning to the client the original paper copies. Companies such as Adobe Systems frequently provide free, limited versions of their programs, downloadable from their website, that allow the opening and reading of files created using their proprietary software formats, such as Adobe's PDF file format.

Many websites that provide programs using these proprietary formats, such as the Internal Revenue Service forms website, contain links to these programs. They are limited in that they allow the user to open and read the files but do not allow changes or the creation of new document files, which requires the full version of the program.

Scanning

Scanning and storing of paper documents has become easier with the development of software such as PaperPort by Nuance. This software provides easy-to-use, high-speed scanning and document capture. As a document management software application, it allows for organizing, finding, and sharing paper and digital documents, which permits the elimination of paper documents.

The original scanning hardware was costly and frequently unreliable. Modern scanners provide double-sided (front and back) scanning of documents with a high degree of accuracy at a relatively low cost. Scanning today has become a common feature in office printers and copy machines. Double-sided scanning is found today in multifunction devices featuring printing, scanning, copying, and faxing, at prices under $100. These devices, when coupled with application software such as PaperPort, allow virtually anyone to create electronic documents.

OCR

Obviously, at times, documents have to be converted from a graphic image to a format that allows for editing or other use in an office suite of applications. These software applications have come to be referred to as OCR, or optical character recognition. Products such as OmniPage, by Nuance, provide document-conversion

Use of
unauthorize
as "**hacking**
formation i
tegrity of th
computer vi
by deleting

Firewalls

A **firewall** i
work system
cess withou
system for c
network or
designed to
Internet tha

A firew
access to the
such as a co
on the firm'
nection to b
planned bef
any issue ma

Encryptio

Encryption
computer in
nology is lik
ily enter the
enter and ta
that it lets c
tion code ca

Encryptio

Confidentia
by the send
intercepted
rithms (mat
word or en
determine t

To un
grams, thinl
provided by
gage. As the
more numb
combination
and effort. I
gram, a basi
three-numb
designed to
ber combin:
required.

or city. Many firm
as a center-city and
from the courthou

With high-s
nected to form a "
works allows acces
to the network, in
documents on a p
of the legal team r

THE INTERN

In its most basic fo
ing more than a gr
the connections for
networked togethe
connected to other
the frequently shar
the connections and
main control comp

The **local are**
as Microsoft Wind
net Explorer—whi
puters with shared
Explorer screen,
providers (ISPs) p
nect to their servic
wired, or by dedic
device called a **mo**
these connections
(modulates) the inf
transferred electro

MO

Modulate

At the receivi
lates) the signal int
ISP service, speeds
the modem and the

Exhibit 4.10

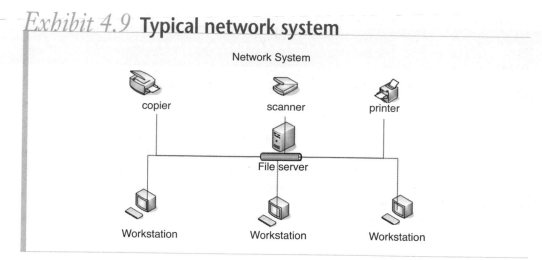

Exhibit 4.9 **Typical network system**

solutions by permitting any scanned page, PDF file, or other image or document file to be converted quickly and accurately into one of a number of different editable formats including Microsoft Word or Corel WordPerfect.

NETWORKS

The first computers in law offices, as we said, generally consisted of a computer, a monitor, and a printer. In the contemporary law office this is called a **workstation**. A network is a group of workstations connected together. This may be as little as two workstations, or in large law firms, hundreds of workstations and other peripheral devices such as shared printers and fax machines all connected through a network file server. Exhibit 4.9 is a typical computer network system in a law office.

A **network file server** is generally a separate computer that acts as the traffic cop of the system, controlling the flow of information between workstations and the file server and other peripheral devices and requests to use the resources of the system or access data stored on the system.

Like the computer that requires an operating system to run, the server requires network operating software that tells it how to communicate with the connected workstations and peripherals devices. These computers and devices are referred to as "connections."

Network Rights and Privileges

Network software programs have security protocols that limit access to the file server, peripherals such as printers, or other workstations. These rights to access the server and the other devices are sometimes called "**network rights and privileges**." The rights or privileges determine who has access to the server, the data stored on the server, and the flow of information between connections.

Network Administrator

Generally the person with the highest level access is called the **network administrator**. Law offices that use network servers generally use these servers as the central repository for all electronic files. Although an individual workstation can store documents or data on the workstation, it is usually stored centrally. This offers a level of protection by limiting access to those who have the proper authorization, most often requiring a password for access. It also makes backing up data easier.

The ability to limit access to files on a file server is one method to ensure confidentiality in a large office. File access can be limited by password-protecting files and granting password access only to those with a need to access and work on those specific files. Because each file or set of files, called folders, can be password-protected

Computer network
A network is a set of workstations connected together.

Workstation
A computer connected to a network that is used for access consisting of a monitor, input device and computer.

Network file server
A separate computer in a network that acts like as the traffic cop of the system controlling the flow of data.

Network rights and privileges
Rights or privileges determine who has access to the server, the data stored on the server, and the flow of information between connections.

Network administrator
The network administrator usually is the person with the highest-level access to the network file server.

Advice

TECH

Micha

The late
and cou
to lawy
be anxi
that tec
solution
sue is: V
to prese

A
result in
fortable
ultimate
cessful a
O
sults car
with the
egy. The
more ef
T
sage, no
tunity to
exhibit l
displaye
chronol

Backup of data
Making a copy of critical
grams in case of a loss c
computer files.

Wide area network
A wide area network is
networks. Each network
it were a connection on

Wireless network
A wireless network uses
nology instead of wires
ing to the network.

ETHICAL *Perspective*

Ohio Rule
Law-Relate

Ohio lawye
participate
law-related
provides th
the arrang
prohibited
referrals or
engaged i
unauthoriz
law. (Ohio
Board of C
Grievances
opinion 2(

che

☐ Sele

☐ Sele
sele

☐ Clic
requ

☐ Sele

ETHICAL *Perspective*

Interception of Electronic Communications

Interception or monitoring of email communications for purposes other than assuring quality of service or maintenance is illegal under the Electronic Communications Privacy Act of 1986, as amended in 1994. [18 U.S.C. B2511(2)(a)(i)]

Computer viruses
Viruses are programs that attack and destroy computer programs, internal computer operating systems, and occasionally the hard disk drives of computers.

ETHICAL *Perspective*

With the increased freedom of communication comes an increased risk of eavesdropping by unauthorized parties accessing the wireless signals. Security measures, such as encryption and access restricted by password, are essential to prevent ethical breaches in confidentiality. Use of public access points, such as the coffee shop with wireless access, the airport lounge, or other public location, invites the curious to eavesdrop and look over the shoulder at the screen of the laptop user. With the growing availability of Internet access on airplanes, the eyes of the adjoining seatmate may be those of a member of the opposing team traveling to the same destination on the same case.

Computer Viruses

Unfortunately, some computer-knowledgeable people take sadistic pleasure in developing and disseminating programs that attack and destroy computer programs, internal computer-operating systems, and occasionally even the hard disk drives of computers. These programs are known as **computer viruses**. Viruses range from those that create minor inconvenience to those that can destroy data and cause computer shutdowns.

Some simple precautions can prevent disaster. A virus-protection program, such as those sold by Norton, McAfee, and others, is as important to have on your computer as the computer operating system itself. This should be the first program loaded on a new computer.

Anti-virus programs scan the computer to identify the presence of viruses, and the better programs eliminate the virus. Every disk should be scanned with a virus program before being used. Files that are downloaded from other computers or over the Internet also should be checked. As good as these programs are, they quickly go out of date as new viruses are created and unleashed. Therefore, these virus checking programs should be updated regularly.

WHAT'S NEXT?

The trend in computers and related computer devices has been toward miniaturization and portability. Smaller devices are becoming more powerful than some desktop systems. Even the telephone has been reduced to a pocket-size wireless communication device that is also capable of taking and displaying photo images, documents, and emails— many functions that formally were reserved to large, wired computer devices.

Hardware in many offices today includes the wireless telephone and the laptop computer with wireless capability. These tools allow constant communication and enable work to be performed virtually anywhere—home, courthouse, airport lounge, or coffee shop. The connection to the office may be by wireless network using the cell phone, or by a wireless connection with built-in wireless network hardware on the computer, or using an adapter card plugged into the computer that uses a wireless Internet connection.

Unlike a few years ago, wires are not necessary to access networks or to set up network connections. Today they may be set up using wireless technology in a wireless network. Just as the cell phone has enabled communications without wires, so has wireless technology allowed networks to be set up where workstations, servers, and peripherals connect over a wireless connection. Remote access is also possible by the use of wireless Internet connection using laptops and other personal computing devices including cell phones with built-in web or Internet access.

Members of the legal team working on cases out of the office can connect with the office file server to retrieve documents, work on them, and send them to other members of the team anywhere in the world. If hardcopy is needed, documents may be printed on any printer accessible over the Internet, including printers in remote office locations, public access points in airports, clients' offices, and courthouses.

Members of the team can work collaboratively from multiple locations as if in the same physical location through software conferencing programs that allow the sharing of files while communicating and seeing each other on the same screen using small desktop cameras or cameras built in to laptop computers. The same remote access technology allows for the taking of witness statements from remote locations while the parties can see each other or view exhibits on the computer screen.

Wireless computer networks are like cell phone networks. Both use radio waves to transmit signals to a receiver. Cell phone systems use cell towers located at strate-

Exhibit 4.15 **Typical wireless Internet access hotspot**

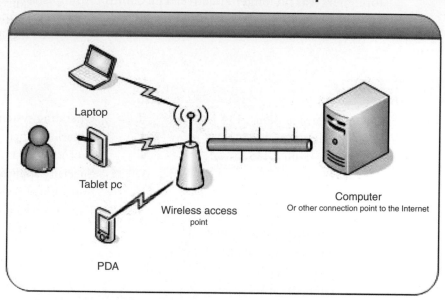

gic points all over the world to receive the signals from the cell phone subscriber's cellular device. The wireless network uses wireless access points, which are essentially receivers of radio signals that convert them so they can be transmitted over a connecting wire to a computer or other connection to the Internet.

Unlike cell phone towers, these access points are more limited. With the exception of a few cities that have access points over a large portion of the city, such as San Francisco, New Orleans, and Philadelphia, these access points are local, often with a range limited to a few hundred feet. Many of these access points are provided in coffee shops, airport lounges, hotels, libraries, and bookstores without charge or at a nominal fee to encourage customers to use the facility instead of a competitor's.

With the growth of wireless "hotspot" locations, the wire connection has been cut. Lawyers and their paralegals may be connected anywhere in the world and send documents electronically back and forth with the same ease as sending them within the same building.

Export of Encryption Technology Worldwide

Software companies in the United States led the development of encryption technology. For years, the U.S. government permitted American software companies to sell its encryption software domestically but prohibited export of the most powerful encryption technology to foreigners. The U.S. government worried that powerful encryption and data-scrambling technology would fall into the hands of criminals and terrorists who would use it to protect their illegal and clandestine activities.

Based on this fear, President Bill Clinton issued an executive order prohibiting the export of much of the most powerful encryption technology developed in the United States. These export restrictions remained in effect during most of the 1990s. In September 1999, after much lobbying by software companies located in the United States, the Administration changed its export policy to allow the export of the most powerful American-made encryption technology.

The export rule was changed because criminals and terrorists could obtain similar data-scrambling technology from software producers in other countries.

Therefore, the American policy prohibiting the export of encryption technology to foreigners was no longer effective. The Clinton Administration's export controls on encryption technology were lifted for all countries except Iran, Iraq, Syria, Sudan, North Korea, and Cuba—countries with a history of terrorist activities.

Legal Terminology

Summary

CHAPTER 4

Computer Hardware

TECHNOLOGY AND THE PARALEGAL

Computer Hardware	Hardware is the term that encompasses all of the tangible or physical items including computers, monitors, printers, fax machines, duplicators, and similar items that usually have either an electrical connection or use batteries as a power source.

Operating Systems

	The operating system is a basic set of instructions to the computer on how to handle basic functions—how to process input from "input devices" such as the keyboard and mouse, the order in which to process information, and what to show on the computer monitor.

Computer Software

	Software refers to programs containing sets of instructions that tell the computer and the other computer-based electronic devices what to do and how to do it.

Applications Programs

Applications Software Programs	Applications programs are software that perform generic tasks such as word processing.
Word Processor Programs	Programs for creating written documents in electronic format
Track Changes	Track Changes, as found in MS word, shows the original text, the deleted text, and the new text as well as a strike through for deleted text, underlining or highlighting of new text, as well as margin notes on the document.

Files Extensions	When a file is saved, a file extension (a period followed by three characters) is added to the end of the filename to identify the program or format in which the file has been saved.
Spreadsheet Programs	Programs that permit the calculation and presentation of financial information in a grid format of rows and columns.
Database Programs	A database program is an electronic repository of information of all types that can be sorted and presented in a meaningful manner.
Office Software Suites	This software consists of commonly used office software programs that manage data and database programs; manipulate financial or numeric information, spreadsheet programs; or display images and graphics, presentation graphics programs.
Specialty Application Programs	Specialty programs combine many of the basic functions found in software suites, word processing, database management, spreadsheets and graphic presentations to perform law office, case, and litigation management.
Case and Litigation Management Software	Case and litigation management programs are used to manage documents and the facts and issues of cases.

The Electronic Courtroom

	The use of electronics and computer-based systems are used in the electronic courtroom.

Paperless Office

	The paperless office is one in which documents are created and stored electronically.

Networks

Workstation	A workstation generally consists of a computer, a monitor, and a printer.
Computer Network	A network is a set of workstations connected together.
Network Server	The network file server generally is a separate computer that acts as the traffic cop of the system controlling the flow of information, and requests to use the resources of the system or data, between the connected workstations and other peripherals that are part of the network. These servers usually are the central repository for all electronic files.
Network Rights and Privileges	Rights or privileges determine who has access to the server, the data stored on the server, and the flow of information between connections.
Network Administrator	The network administrator usually is the person with the highest-level access to the network file server.
Backup of Data	Backing up data—making copies of files—regularly is an essential function to prevent loss of critical files and office data in the event of a disaster.
Wide Area Network	A wide area network is a network of networks. Each network is treated as if it were a connection on the network.
Wireless Network	A wireless network uses wireless technology instead of wires for connecting to the network.

The Internet

What Is It?	The Internet or the World Wide Web is a group of computers linked together with the added ability to search all the connections for information.

Online Computer Resources

Internet Browsers	An Internet or Web browser is a software program that allows a person to use a computer to access the Internet. The two most popular Web browsers are Microsoft Internet Explorer and Netscape.
Search Engines	An Internet search engine is a program designed to take a word or set of words and locate websites on the Internet.
Addresses and Locations	The modern equivalent of a person's telephone number is the email address. Pages on the Internet also have addresses known as the Uniform Resource Locator (URL), made up of three parts: protocol, computer, and path.

Formats of Available Information

File Attachments	The attachment is a popular method for transmitting text files, and occasionally graphic images, by attaching the file to an email.
Receiving and Downloading Files and Attachments	The method for downloading files and attachments is the same. They are downloaded into a directory (a folder), which in Windows usually is called My Download Files or My Files. If there is no existing folder, Windows Explorer can be used to create a file with a name, such as Download.

Computer Viruses

Definition	Viruses are programs that attack and destroy computer programs, internal computer operating systems, and occasionally the hard disk drives of computers.
Precautions	Virus-protection programs such as Norton or McAfee should be updated regularly.

Electronic Filing of Pleadings

Courts	Many courts have established procedures for the electronic filing of pleadings. Each court is free to set up its own rules and procedures and must be consulted before attempting to use this service.
IRS	The Internal Revenue Service and some states have combined in a joint effort to allow the filing of both the federal and state individual income tax returns.

Encryption

Definition	Encryption is technology that allows computer users to put a "lock" around information to prevent discovery by others.

What's Next

	The trend in computers and related computer devices has been toward miniaturization and portability, with increased use of wireless technology that will enable the legal team to work collaboratively from multiple locations as if in the same physical location, using software conferencing programs that allow the sharing of files while communicating and seeing each other on the same screen.

▶ WORKING THE WEB

1. Download the latest 1040 tax form and instructions from the Internal Revenue Service website at **www.irs.gov**.

2. Use one of the search engines listed below to find information on your school or local government:
   a. AltaVista: **http://www.altavista.com**
   b. Ask Jeeves: **http://www.ask.com**
   c. Dogpile: **http://www.dogpile.com**
   d. Excite: **http://www.excite.com**
   e. Google: **http://www.google.com**
   f. MetaCrawler: **http://www.metacrawler.com**
   g. Netscape: **http://www.netscape.com**
   h. Yahoo!: **www.yahoo.com**

3. Use the Google search engine to find information on how firewalls work, and print out the first page of the results. Using one of the results, print out a copy of the information that is most responsive to the search, and write a short summary describing what a firewall does. **http://www.Google.com**

4. Use a search engine of your choice to run a search for legal research resources. Print a copy of the first 10 results. Mark each result you think will be useful in the future as a paralegal and state why.

5. Prepare a step-by-step list of how to find the Code of Federal Regulations on the Government Printing Office website. **http://www.access.gpo.gov**

6. Prepare a list of the legislative information available from the Library of Congress online. **http://www.LOC.gov**

7. Use any search engine or browser search tool to find the document "How our Laws are Made," as revised and updated by Charles W. Johnson-Parliamentarian, on a federal government website. Hint: use quotation marks around the names. Print out the specific query you used and the URL of the source where the document was found.

8. Print out a copy of the results of the search for "firewall" using Yahoo, and compare the results to the result from Google. How many of the first 20 listings are the same?

▶ CRITICAL THINKING AND WRITING QUESTIONS

1. How can the computer and the Internet increase a paralegal's productivity?

2. What is meant by the term "computer hardware"?

3. What is the danger in using the word processing feature "Track Changes"?

4. What are applications software programs? Give an example.

5. What are the advantages of using office suite programs?

6. How can database programs be used to avoid ethical issues?

7. How can legal office management programs help prevent malpractice?

8. What is meant by the "paperless office"? What changes in law office administration have encouraged this?

9. What is the function of a network server?

10. Why is making a backup essential in a law office?

11. What is the advantage to the legal team in having a wide area network or wireless network?

12. How has the availability of the high speed Internet impacted the use of the Internet in the law office?

13. What is an Internet browser? How is this different from Windows Explorer?

14. How reliable are forms and documents obtained over the Internet?

15. What advantages does knowing how to use the Internet provide the paralegal in the law office?

16. What are the limitations of using a website to attract new clients to your state?

17. Do cross-jurisdictional boundary websites present any problems for the law firm using the Internet? If so, why?

18. What are some of the ways in which using an Internet browser can assist the paralegal working on a file or a case? How are URLs used in conducting Internet searches?

19. What copyright issues must a paralegal consider in using the Internet to prepare written documents and reports?

20. How can authenticity of information obtained on the Internet be validated? Explain the issues in downloading information?

21. What is the purpose of a firewall? What are the implications to the law office of not having a firewall?

22. What is a computer virus, and what should a paralegal do to protect the firm against computer viruses?

23. Should encryption software be used regularly in transmitting files electronically? Why?

24. Why would the legal team want to use encryption when transmitting a document?

25. What is a wireless access point? How could this be used in a law firm?

26. What ethical issues arise in the use of "hotspots" or public access points?

ETHICS ANALYSIS AND DISCUSSION QUESTIONS

1. What are the ethical issues related to a law firm website that is available around the world when the firm is licensed to practice only in one jurisdiction?

2. Explain the ethical implication of the following: "In today's society, with the advent of the information superhighway, federal and state legislation and regulations, as well as information regarding industry trends, are easily accessed."

3. What are the ethical issues of erroneously sending or receiving by email or fax a confidential trial strategy memorandum?

4. What ethical issues arise for the law firm when it does not maintain an off-premises copy of files and client records? Does a major catastrophe, such as the flooding caused by Hurricane Katrina in New Orleans in 2005, excuse not having backup files and records?

5. What role do security protocols have in ethical compliance?

6. What ethical issues are involved in combining law practices as discussed in the opening scenario? What specific steps should be taken? Explain how these steps will prevent ethical breaches.

7. You are working in a sophisticated law firm that has the latest computers and software. You have not been trained in the use of the firm's computer encryption software for transmitting email and other electronic documents to clients and other offices of the firm. You live a few blocks from the office and consent to stay late on Friday night before a major holiday weekend when everyone has left early to avoid the rush hour traffic.

   A client calls and asks for a copy of the trial strategy memorandum for a major case to take with him for review over the weekend. He advises that he is getting ready to get on a plane but has a computer with him that has reverse encryption software the firm gave him and tells you he wants to read the memo while he is on the plane for the next 14 hours on his way to Tokyo. He hangs up and you do not have his cell phone number. You send the email without using the encryption software. [*U.S. v. Thomas*, 74 F.3d. 701 (1996), ABA Ethics Opinion, Utah ethics Opinion 00-01.] Have you breached any rules on client confidentiality by sending unencrypted email containing confidential client information?

DEVELOPING YOUR COLLABORATION SKILLS

Working on your own or with a group of other students assigned by your instructor, review the scenario at the beginning of the chapter that deals with combining a paper-based office and an electronic office.

1. Divide into two teams, one team playing the role of the junior paralegal and the other the senior paralegal. Put yourself in that person's place, and make a list of the benefits of the type of office system (electronic or paper) that they are accustomed to working in.

2. Share your list with the other team. As a group, decide what systems/practices you think will be most efficient and effective to use in the combined office to perform the following activities:
   - Manage conflicts of interest
   - Perform legal research
   - Manage cases
   - Handle client files
   - Communicate with clients
   - Manage financial accounts

3. As a group, identify areas of ethical concern in a merger, and discuss how best to handle these issues.

PARALEGAL PORTFOLIO EXERCISE

Prepare a memo for a potential law office manager, outlining the advantages and disadvantages of the paperless office. What security and confidentiality issues must be considered? What potential solutions or office procedures should be put in place? Reference and cite any applicable ethical rules or opinions from your local or state court or bar association.

LEGAL ANALYSIS AND WRITING CASES

Issue: Are Images Displayed on the Internet as a Result of a Search Protected by Copyright?

Defendant operates a "visual search engine" on the Internet that allows a user to obtain a list of related Web content in response to a search query entered by the user. Unlike other Internet search engines, defendant's search engine, the "Ditto" crawler, retrieves images instead of descriptive text. It produces a list of reduced, "thumbnail" pictures related to the user's query. By clicking on the desired thumbnail, a user could view the "image attributes" window displaying the full-size version of the image, a description of its dimensions, and an address for the website where it originated. By clicking on the address, the user could link to the originating website for the image. The search engine works by maintaining an indexed database of approximately two million thumbnail images obtained through a "crawler"—a computer program that travels the Web in search of images to be converted into thumbnails and added to the index.

Plaintiff Kelly is a photographer specializing in photographs of California Gold Rush country and photographs related to the works of Laura Ingalls Wilder. He does not sell the photographs independently, but his photographs have appeared in several books. Plaintiff also maintains two websites, one of which (www.goldrush1849.com) provides a "virtual tour" of California's Gold Rush country and promotes plaintiff's book on the subject. The other (www.showmethegold.com) markets corporate retreats in California's Gold Rush country. Thirty-five of plaintiff's images were indexed by the Ditto crawler and put in defendant's image database. As a result, these images were made available in thumbnail form to users of defendant's visual search engine. After being notified of plaintiff's objections, Ditto removed the images from its database.

Plaintiff filed a copyright-infringement action. One of the questions of first impression is whether the display of copyrighted images by a "visual search engine" on the Internet constitutes fair use under the Copyright Act. The court found that defendant never held out plaintiff's work as its own, or even engaged in conduct specifically directed at plaintiff's work. Plaintiff's images were swept up along with two million others available on the Internet, as part of defendant's efforts to provide its users with a better way to find images on the Internet. Defendant's purposes were and are inherently transformative, even if its realization of those purposes was at times imperfect. Where, as here, a new use and new technology are evolving, the broad transformative purpose of the use weighs more heavily than the inevitable flaws in its early stages of development.

Questions

1. As the use of the Internet matures, will courts view use of information from the Web differently?
2. What are the implications in taking material off the Internet and including it in reports, memos, and briefs?
3. Would the decision have been different if the items were copyrighted legal forms also located by a "crawler" and displayed as a visual image such as a PDF file?

▶ WORKING WITH THE LANGUAGE OF THE COURT CASE

CoStar Group Inc. v. LoopNet, Inc.

164 F. Supp. 2d 688 (D.C. Md. 2001)
United States District Court, Maryland

Read, and if assigned, brief this case. In your brief, include answers to the following questions.

1. What is a "contributory infringer" under the Digital Millennium Copyright Act?
2. Who is an online service provider as defined by the Digital Millennium Copyright Act (DMCA)?
3. When does a service provider lose its immunity under the DMCA?
4. What is a "safe harbor" under the DMCA?
5. What conduct takes a service provider out of the safe harbor?

Deborah K. Chasanow

I. Background

Plaintiffs CoStar Group, Inc. and CoStar Realty Information, Inc. (collectively CoStar) filed suit against LoopNet, Inc. (LoopNet) alleging copyright infringement. CoStar is a national provider of commercial real estate information services . . . which includes photographs. . . .

LoopNet is an Internet-based company offering a service through which a user . . . may post a listing of commercial real estate available for lease. . . . To include a photograph, . . . it is uploaded into a separate "folder," . . . where it is reviewed by a LoopNet employee to determine that it is . . . a photograph of commercial property and that there is no obvious . . . violation of LoopNet's terms and conditions. If the photograph meets LoopNet's criteria . . . it is automatically posted. . . . CoStar claims that over 300 of its copyrighted photographs have appeared on LoopNet's site (the number has increased over time). . . .

(continued)

Application of copyright law in cyberspace is elusive and perplexing. The World Wide Web has progressed far faster than the law and, as a result, courts are struggling to catch up. Legislatures and courts endeavor in this growing area to maintain the free flow of information over the Internet while still protecting intellectual property rights. . . .

CONTRIBUTORY COPYRIGHT INFRINGEMENT

1. Overview

It is, today, a given that: one who, with knowledge of the infringing activity, induces, causes, or materially contributes to the infringing conduct of another, may be held liable as a "contributory" infringer. . . . Put differently, liability exists if the defendant engages in "personal conduct that encourages or assists the infringement." . . .

CoStar does not claim that LoopNet had knowledge of its users' infringements prior to its giving notice. . . . Given the nature of the infringements in this case, it was impossible for LoopNet to have knowledge of the alleged infringement before receiving notice from CoStar. CoStar does not attach a copyright notice to its photos and even CoStar's own expert could not identify a CoStar photo simply by reviewing it. . . . Thus, LoopNet cannot be charged with . . . knowledge before receiving claims of infringement from CoStar. . . . CoStar does not claim that LoopNet had knowledge of infringement prior to receiving notice from CoStar. [T]here remain . . . disputes about [its] knowledge . . . after receiving the claims of infringement. CoStar alleges that once it gave LoopNet notice that its photographs were being infringed, LoopNet can be charged with knowledge of continuing infringements. . . .

The DMCA was enacted both to preserve copyright enforcement in the Internet and to provide immunity to service providers from copyright infringement liability for "passive," "automatic" actions in which a service provider's system engages through a technological process initiated by another without the knowledge of the service provider. . . . The DMCA's protection of an innocent service provider disappears at the moment the service provider loses its innocence, i.e., at the moment it becomes aware that a third party is using its system to infringe. At that point, the Act shifts responsibility to the service provider to disable the infringing matter, "preserving the strong incentives for service providers and copyright owners to cooperate to detect and deal with copyright infringements that take place in the digital networked environment."

The DMCA seeks to strike a balance by shielding online service providers from liability in damages as long as they remove or prevent access to infringing material. . . . The initial inquiry is whether LoopNet can be considered a service provider for the purposes of the DMCA.

a. Service Provider
In order to qualify for the safe harbor in the DMCA, LoopNet must meet the definition of "online service provider." Under § 512 (k)(1)(A), a service provider is "an entity offering the transmission, routing, or providing of connections for digital online communications, between or among points specified by a user, of material of the user's choosing, without modification to the content of the material as sent or received." 17 U.S.C. § 512(k)(1)(A)(1998). . . . For the other safe harbor provisions, including (c), which is at issue here, the definition is broader: "a provider of online services or network access, or the operator of facilities therefore.". . .

"Online services" is surely broad enough to encompass the type of service provided by LoopNet that is at issue here. The term is, of course, only a threshold to the protections of the Act. Even if LoopNet qualifies as a service provider, it must meet the other criteria.

b. Stored at the Instance of the User
A service provider is only protected from liability by the DMCA, "for infringement of copyright by reason of its storage at the direction of user of material." 17 U.S.C. § 512(c)(1). . .[The photographs at issue] are uploaded at the volition of the user and are subject. . . to a mere screening to assess whether they are commercial property and to catch any obvious infringements. . . . Although humans are involved rather than mere technology, they serve only as a gateway and are not involved in a selection process. . . Therefore, this threshold requirement is met and LoopNet is not disqualified from the safe harbor on these grounds.

c. Knowledge
The safe harbor protects service providers from liability unless they have knowledge of copyright infringement. There are three types of knowledge of infringement that can take a service provider out of

the safe harbor: (1) the service provider can have actual knowledge of infringement; (2) it can be aware of facts which raise a "red flag" that its users are infringing; or (3) the copyright owner can notify the service provider in a manner "substantially" conforming with § 512 (c)(3) that its works are being infringed. . . . The service provider does not automatically lose its liability shield upon receiving notice, but "the Act shifts responsibility to the service provider to disable the infringing matter. . . ."

. . . LoopNet received notification of claimed infringement . . . so the adequacy of LoopNet's removal policy must be assessed to determine whether LoopNet is protected by the safe harbor.

d. Adequacy of Termination and "Take Down" Policy
Once a service provider has received notification of a claimed infringement as described in [the Act]. . .the service provider can remain in the safe harbor if it "responds expeditiously to remove, or disable access to, the material that is claimed to be infringing or to be the subject of infringing activity." 17 U.S.C. § 512 (c)(1)(C) (1998). . . .

There are several material factual disputes remaining as to whether the removal of allegedly infringing photographs was satisfactorily expeditious and whether LoopNet's termination policy was reasonable and effective. CoStar's infringement claims are based on the posting of specific photographs. Additionally, Loopnet's knowledge of the alleged infringements and its "take down" and termination policies have changed over time in fairly significant ways. In order to resolve this issue, the factfinder will have to focus on each photo and the policy in effect prior to the posting of each photo. Hence, neither party is entitled to summary judgment on this issue. . . .

3. Liability for Contributory Infringement

With regard to the photographs that were infringed before the safe harbor applied. . . and in case LoopNet's termination policy and take down of infringing photographs is found to be inadequate so as to remove it from the safe harbor, the analysis shifts from the DMCA back to contributory infringement. The determination of contributory infringement liability turns on a different issue of knowledge than the

standard used to determine LoopNet's eligibility for the safe harbor. Here, the question is whether CoStar's notice of claimed infringement was sufficient to satisfy the knowledge prong of the test for contributory infringement either by providing actual knowledge, a "red flag" that infringement was occurring, or constructive knowledge.

. . . [T]he fact finder must determine along a continuum the adequacy of the policy in place prior to the posting of each specific photograph. Therefore, neither party is entitled to summary judgment on this issue.

e. Preemption of Non-Copyright Claims
. . . The Copyright Act preempts state law that is "equivalent to any of the exclusive rights within the general scope of copyright as specified by section 106." 17 U.S.C. § 301(a) (1996) . . . "To determine whether a state claim is preempted by the Act, courts must make a two-part inquiry: (1) the work must be within the scope of the subject matter of copyright, and (2) the state law rights must be equivalent to any exclusive rights within the scope of federal copyright." *Fischer v. Viacom Intern Corp.*, 115 F. Supp. 2d 535. 540 (D.Md. 2000). . . . The critical question, then, is whether Costar's unfair competition claim contains an additional element or whether it is based solely on the alleged copying.

. . . Essentially, CoStar's claim is that LoopNet is exhibiting as its own photographs on its website that CoStar has an exclusive right to exhibit or license for exhibition. This type of reverse passing off is, in effect, a "disguised copyright infringement claim." . . . Therefore, this claim does not satisfy the "extra-element" test and so is equivalent to CoStar's claim under the Copyright Act. Accordingly, it is preempted. . . .

V. Conclusion

For the foregoing reasons; by separate order, both motions concerning the safe harbor defense of the DMCA will be denied,. . . both motions concerning contributory infringement will be denied, . . . summary judgment will be granted in favor of LoopNet on the . . . preemption of the state law claims. ■

PART II

Paralegal Skills and Procedure

THE ASPIRING PARALEGAL PROFESSIONAL must develop a set of skills to allow them to understand and work in a supporting role as part of the legal team in the law office, the court, the administrative agency and in the alternative dispute resolution working environment. Excellent verbal and written skills are crucial for paralegals who will be interviewing clients and witnesses and the general public. Paralegals must develop an ability to think critically and analytically when performing legal research and in writing briefs, memorandum of the law and in general correspondence. Today's paralegal must be familiar with the use of technology to conduct legal and factual research using a digital library and internet research services, as well as how to use traditional print sources of information. Part II covers the procedural aspects of the American legal system and the basic skills needed to be successful on the job.

SOURCES OF AMERICAN LAW

"The nation's armour of defence against the passions of men is the Constitution. Take that away, and the nation goes down into the field of its conflicts like a warrior without armour."

Henry Ward Beecher,
Proverbs from Plymouth
Pulpit, (1887)

PARALEGALS AT WORK

As a paralegal, you are working for a large law firm that specializes in handling constitutional law issues for clients. You work for Vivian Kang, a senior partner of the law firm. One day Ms. Kang calls you into her office and tells you that a new client, Mr. Hayward Storm, has retained the law firm. Ms. Kang asks you to sit in with her during an interview with Mr. Storm. Mr. Storm arrives on the day of the interview, and Ms. Kang, Mr. Storm, and you go into the conference room.

Mr. Storm tells the following story: For more than twenty years he has been on radio and television, primarily as a disc jockey and talk show host. Mr. Storm most recently hosted television shows where he did outlandish things such as using vulgar language, having guests appear on the show nude, telling disgusting jokes, and doing other things that offend many people. Mr. Storm also hosted a radio show in which he used profanity and offensive language. The Federal Communications Commission (FCC), a federal government agency, is responsible for regulating radio and television. Mr. Storm tells you that the FCC has fined him and his employer for his engaging in such conduct over the television and radio airwaves.

In addition, Mr. Storm explains that he will be leaving regular radio and television, which is regulated by the FCC, and has been hired to be a disc jockey for satellite radio broadcasts. He is making this change because satellite radio currently is not regulated by the FCC. Mr. Storm plans to continue his usual offensive programming on satellite radio and says he will expand his extreme language and conduct because satellite radio is not regulated by the FCC but is concerned that Congress will enact a federal statute granting the FCC power to regulate satellite radio.

Consider the issues involved in this scenario as you read the chapter.

After studying this chapter, you should be able to:

1. Define *law* and describe the functions of law.
2. Describe the fairness and flexibility of the law.
3. Explain how English common law was adopted in the United States.
4. List and describe the sources of law in the United States.
5. Describe the concept of federalism and the doctrine of separation of powers.
6. Define and apply important clauses of the U.S. Constitution.
7. Explain the Bill of Rights and its freedoms.

▶ INTRODUCTION FOR THE PARALEGAL

A paralegal must have a foundation in the basic sources of the law of the United States. Our society makes and enforces laws that govern the conduct of the individuals, businesses, and other organizations that function within it. In the words of Judge Learned Hand, "Without law we cannot live; only with it can we insure the future which by right is ours. The best of men's hopes are enmeshed in its success" (*The Spirit of Liberty*, 1960).

Although U.S. law is based primarily on English common law, other legal systems, such as Spanish and French civil law, also influenced it. The sources of law in this country are the U.S. Constitution, state constitutions, federal and state statutes, ordinances, administrative agency rules and regulations, executive orders, and judicial decisions by federal and state courts.

Paralegals need to know the history of the law in the United States and how the law developed to be what it is today. Every person in the United States, and paralegals in particular, should have knowledge of this country's constitutional framework and most important provisions of the U.S. Constitution. This chapter addresses the nature and definition of law, the history and sources of law, and the U.S. Constitution. ■

WHAT IS LAW?

The law consists of rules that regulate the conduct of individuals, businesses, and other organizations within society. Laws are intended to protect persons and their property from unwanted interference from others and forbid persons from engaging in certain undesirable activities.

Law
That which must be obeyed and followed by citizens subject to sanctions or legal consequences; a body of rules of action or conduct prescribed by controlling authority, and having binding legal force.

The concept of **law** is broad. Although it is difficult to state a precise definition, *Black's Law Dictionary*, 5th edition, gives one that is sufficient for this text:

> Law, in its generic sense, is a body of rules of action or conduct prescribed by controlling authority, and having binding legal force. That which must be obeyed and followed by citizens subject to sanctions or legal consequences is a law.

Fairness of the Law

On the whole, the American legal system is one of the most comprehensive, fair, and democratic systems of law ever developed and enforced. Nevertheless, some misuses and oversights of our legal system—including abuses of discretion and mistakes by judges and juries, unequal applications of the law, and procedural mishaps—allow some guilty parties to go unpunished.

checklist ✓

FUNCTIONS OF THE LAW

The law is often described by the functions it serves within a society. The primary functions served by U.S. law are:

1. Keeping the peace, which includes making crimes out of certain activities.
2. Shaping moral standards (e.g., enacting laws that discourage drug and alcohol abuse).
3. Promoting social justice (e.g., enacting statutes that prohibit discrimination in employment).
4. Maintaining the status quo (e.g., passing laws that prevent the forceful overthrow of government).
5. Facilitating orderly change (e.g., passing statutes only after considerable study, debate, and public input).
6. Facilitating planning (e.g., designing commercial laws to allow businesses to plan their activities, allocate their productive resources, and assess the risks they take).
7. Providing a basis for compromise (approximately 90 percent of all lawsuits are settled prior to trial).
8. Maximizing individual freedom (e.g., the rights of freedom of speech, religion, and association granted by the First Amendment to the U.S. Constitution).

THE INTERNET AND THE LAW

Every year paralegal and other students arrive on college campuses and unpack an array of items—clothes, books, furniture, decorations, and their computers. Students today are judged by their computer and Internet savvy. More than 90 percent of college students now own personal computers.

The Internet has revolutionized campus life. Computer kiosks abound around college campuses, occupying space in libraries and dorm rooms. Traditional libraries have become obsolete for many students as they conduct their research online. More than 70 percent of college students check out the Web daily, communicate through email, pick up course assignments, download course notes, and socialize online. Wired to modern technology, today's college students are the leaders of the e-generation.

Universities and colleges now are rated not only on how well they are connected with alumni but also on how well they are connected to computer technology. Some universities have installed software that allows their students to sit anywhere on campus with their laptops and plug into the school's computers. The computer no longer is just a study tool. It has become totally integrated into the students' lives. The new generation of students studies online, shops online, and even dates online.

With this new technology comes one other thing that a student should know about: e-commerce and Internet law. The number of legal questions pertaining to this new technology is endless.

In *Standefer v. United States* [447 U.S. 10, 100 S.Ct. 1999 (1980)] the Supreme Court *affirmed* (let stand) the criminal conviction of a Gulf Oil Corporation executive for aiding and abetting the bribery of an Internal Revenue Service agent. The agent had been acquitted in a separate trial. In writing the opinion of the Court, Chief Justice Warren Burger stated, "This case does no more than manifest the simple, if discomforting, reality that different juries may reach different results under any criminal statute. That is one of the consequences we accept under our jury system."

Flexibility of the Law

One of the main attributes of American law is its flexibility. The law is generally responsive to cultural, technological, economic, and social changes. For example, laws that are no longer viable—such as those that restricted the property rights of women—are often repealed.

Two things most people should never see made: sausages and laws.

An old saying

Sometimes it takes years before the law reflects the norms of society. Other times, society is led by the law. The Supreme Court's landmark 1954 decision in *Brown v. Board of Education* [347 U.S. 483, 74 S.Ct. 686 98 L.Ed. 873, 1954 U.S. Lexis 2094 (1954)] is an example of the law leading the people. The Court's decision overturned the old "separate but equal" doctrine that condoned separate schools for Black children and White children. U.S. law evolves and changes along with the norms of society, technology, and the growth and expansion of commerce in the United States and the world.

Laws cannot be written in advance to anticipate every dispute that could arise in the future. Therefore, *general principles* are developed to be applied by courts and juries to individual disputes. This flexibility in the law leads to some uncertainty in predicting results of lawsuits. The following quote by Judge Jerome Frank addresses the value of the adaptability of law (*Law and the Modern Mind*, 1930):

The law always has been, is now, and will ever continue to be, largely vague and variable. And how could this be otherwise? The law deals with human relations in their most complicated aspects. The whole confused, shifting helter-skelter of life parades before it—more confused than ever, in our kaleidoscopic age.

Men have never been able to construct a comprehensive, eternalized set of rules anticipating all possible legal disputes and formulating in advance the rules which would apply to them.

Situations are bound to occur which were never contemplated when the original rules were made. How much less is such a frozen legal system possible in modern times?

The constant development of unprecedented problems requires a legal system capable of fluidity and pliancy. Our society would be straightjacketed were not the courts, with the able assistance of the lawyers, constantly overhauling the law and adapting it to the realities of ever-changing social, industrial, and political conditions; although changes cannot be made lightly, yet rules of law must be more or less impermanent, experimental and therefore not nicely calculable.

Much of the uncertainty of law is not an unfortunate accident; it is of immense social value.

BROWN v. BOARD OF EDUCATION

When the original thirteen states ratified the Constitution of the United States of America in 1788, they created a democratic form of government and granted certain rights to its people. But all persons were not treated equally, as many people, including drafters of the Constitution such as Thomas Jefferson, owned Black slaves. More than 75 years passed before the Civil War was fought between the northern states and the southern Confederate states over the preservation of the Union and slavery. Slavery was abolished by the Thirteenth Amendment to the Constitution in 1865. In addition, the Fourteenth Amendment of 1868 provided that no state shall "deny to any person within its jurisdiction the equal protection of the laws." The original intent of this amendment was to guarantee equality to freed slaves.

But equality was denied to Blacks for years to come. This included discrimination in housing, transportation, education, jobs, service at restaurants, and other activities. In 1896, the U.S. Supreme Court decided the case of *Plessy v. Ferguson*. In that case, the state of Louisiana had a law that provided for separate but equal accommodations for Black and White railway passengers. A Black passenger challenged the state law. The Supreme Court held that the "separate but equal" state law did not violate the Equal Protection Clause of the Fourteenth Amendment. The "separate but equal" doctrine then was applied to all areas of life, including public education. Thus, Black and White children attended separate schools often with unequal facilities.

Not until 1954 did the U.S. Supreme Court decide a case that challenged the separate but equal doctrine as it applied to public elementary and high schools. In *Brown v. Board of Education*, a consolidated case that challenged the separate school systems of four states—Kansas, South Carolina, Virginia, and Delaware—the Supreme Court decided to revisit the separate but equal doctrine announced by its forbears in another century. This time a unanimous Supreme Court, in an opinion written by Chief Justice Earl Warren, reversed prior precedent and held that the separate but equal doctrine violated the Equal Protection Clause of the Fourteenth Amendment to the Constitution. In its opinion, the Court stated:

We cannot turn the clock back to 1868 when the Amendment was adopted, or even to 1896 when Plessy v. Ferguson *was written. Today, education is perhaps the most important function of state and local governments.*

We conclude that in the field of public education the doctrine of "separate but equal" has no place. Separate educational facilities are inherently unequal. Therefore, we hold that the plaintiffs and others similarly situated for whom actions have been brought are, by reason of the segregation complained of, deprived of the equal protection of the laws guaranteed by the Fourteenth Amendment.

After *Brown v. Board of Education* was decided, court orders and federal army enforcement were required to integrate many of the public schools in this country. The *Brown v. Board of Education* case demonstrates that one Supreme Court case can overrule prior Supreme Court cases to promote justice. [*Brown v. Board of Education of Topeka*, 347 U.S. 483, 74 S.Ct. 686, 98 L.Ed. 873 1954 U.S. Lexis 2094 (1954)]

PARALEGALS AND LEGAL ASSISTANTS: TRAINING, OTHER QUALIFICATIONS, AND ADVANCEMENT

United States Department of Labor Bureau of Labor Statistics

There are several ways to become a paralegal. The most common is through a community college paralegal program that leads to an associate's degree. The other common method of entry, mainly for those who already have a college degree, is through a program that leads to a certification in paralegal studies. A small number of schools also offer bachelor's and master's degrees in paralegal studies. Some employers train paralegals on the job, hiring college graduates with no legal experience or promoting experienced legal secretaries. Other entrants have experience in a technical field that is useful to law firms, such as a background in tax preparation for tax and estate practice or in criminal justice, nursing, or health administration for personal injury practice.

An estimated 1,000 colleges and universities, law schools, and proprietary schools offer formal paralegal training programs. Approximately 260 paralegal programs are approved by the American Bar Association (ABA). Although many programs do not require such approval, graduation from an ABA-approved program can enhance one's employment opportunities. The requirements for admission to these programs vary. Some require certain college courses or a bachelor's degree, others accept high school graduates or those with legal experience, and a few schools require standardized tests and personal interviews.

Paralegal programs include 2-year associate degree programs, 4-year bachelor's degree programs, and certificate programs that can take only a few months to complete. Most certificate programs provide intensive and, in some cases, specialized paralegal training for individuals who already hold college degrees, while associate's and bachelor's degree programs usually combine paralegal training with courses in other academic subjects. The quality of paralegal training programs varies; the better programs usually include job placement services. Programs generally offer courses introducing students to the legal applications of computers, including how to perform legal research on the Internet. Many paralegal training programs also offer an internship in which students gain practical experience by working for several months in a private law firm, the office of a public defender or attorney general, a bank, a corporate legal department, a legal aid organization, or a government agency. Experience gained in internships is an asset when one is seeking a job after graduation. Prospective students should examine the experiences of recent graduates before enrolling in a paralegal program.

Although most employers do not require certification, earning a voluntary certificate from a professional society may offer advantages in the labor market. The National Association of Legal Assistants (NALA), for example, has established standards for certification requiring various combinations of education and experience. Paralegals who meet these standards are eligible to take a 2-day examination, given three times each year at several regional testing centers. Those who pass this examination may use the Certified Legal Assistant (CLA) designation. The NALA also offers an advanced paralegal certification for those who want to specialize in other areas of the law. In addition, the Paralegal Advanced Competency Exam, administered through the National Federation of Paralegal Associations, offers professional recognition to paralegals with a bachelor's degree and at least 2 years of experience. Those who pass this examination may use the Registered Paralegal (RP) designation.

Paralegals must be able to document and present their findings and opinions to their supervising attorney. They need to understand legal terminology and have good research and investigative skills. Familiarity with the operation and applications of computers in legal research and litigation support also is important. Paralegals should stay informed of new developments in the laws that affect their area of practice. Participation in continuing legal education seminars allows paralegals to maintain and expand their knowledge of the law.

Because paralegals frequently deal with the public, they should be courteous and uphold the ethical standards of the legal profession. The National Association of Legal Assistants, the National Federation of Paralegal Associations, and a few States have established ethical guidelines for paralegals to follow.

Paralegals usually are given more responsibilities and require less supervision as they gain work experience. Experienced paralegals who work in large law firms, corporate legal departments, or government agencies may supervise and delegate assignments to other paralegals and clerical staff. Advancement opportunities also include promotion to managerial and other law-related positions within the firm or corporate legal department. However, some paralegals find it easier to move to another law firm when seeking increased responsibility or advancement.

Source: www.bls.gov

Read the opinion of Chief Justice Warren of the U.S. Supreme Court in *Brown v. Board of Education* at http://www.nationalcenter.org/brown.html

Schools of Jurisprudential Thought

The philosophy or science of the law is referred to as **jurisprudence**. Several different philosophies have been advanced about how the law developed, ranging from the classical natural theory to modern theories of law and economics and critical legal studies. Legal philosophers can be grouped into the following major categories.

- The **natural law school of jurisprudence** postulates that the law is based on what is "correct." Natural law philosophers emphasize a *moral theory of law*—that is, law should be based on morality and ethics. People "discover" natural law through reasoning and choosing between good and evil.

    Documents such as the U.S. Constitution, the Magna Carta, and the United Nations Charter reflect this theory.
- The **historical school of jurisprudence** believes that the law is an aggregate of social traditions and customs that have developed over the centuries. Changes in the norms of society will be reflected gradually in the law. The law is an evolutionary process. Thus, historical legal scholars look to past legal decisions (precedent) to solve contemporary problems.
- The **analytical school of jurisprudence** maintains that the law is shaped by logic. Analytical philosophers believe that results are reached by applying principles of logic to the specific facts of the case. The emphasis is on the logic of the result rather than how the result is reached.
- The **sociological school of jurisprudence** asserts that the law is a means of achieving and advancing certain sociological goals. Followers of this philosophy, known as *realists*, believe that the purpose of law is to shape social behavior. Sociological philosophers are unlikely to adhere to past law as precedent.
- The philosophers of the **command school of jurisprudence** believe that the law is a set of rules developed, communicated, and enforced by the ruling party rather than reflecting the society's morality, history,

checklist ✓   SCHOOLS OF JURISPRUDENTIAL THOUGHT

SCHOOL	PHILOSOPHY
Natural law school	Postulates that law is based on what is "correct." Emphasizes a moral theory of law—that is, law should be based on morality and ethics.
Historical school	Believes that law is an aggregate of social traditions and customs.
Analytical school	Maintains that law is shaped by logic.
Sociological school	Asserts that the law is a means of achieving and advancing certain sociological goals.
Command school	Believes that the law is a set of rules developed, communicated, and enforced by the ruling party.
Critical legal studies school	Maintains that legal rules are unnecessary and that legal disputes should be solved by applying arbitrary rules based on fairness.
Law and economics school	Holds that the central concern of legal decision-making should be to promote market efficiency.

Exhibit 5.1 **Declaration of Independence**

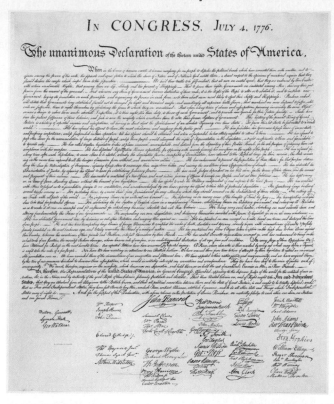

logic, or sociology. This school maintains that the law changes when the ruling class changes.

- The **critical legal studies school of jurisprudence** proposes that legal rules are unnecessary and are used as an obstacle by the powerful to maintain the status quo. Critical legal theorists (the "*crits*") argue that legal disputes should be solved by applying arbitrary rules based on broad notions of what is "fair" in each circumstance. Under this theory, subjective decision-making by judges would be permitted.

- The **law and economics school** proposes that promoting market and economic efficiency should be the central goal of legal decision making. This school is called the "Chicago School" of jurisprudence because it had its roots at the University of Chicago. This school proposes, for example, that free-market principles, cost–benefit analysis, and supply-and-demand theories should be used to determine the passage of legislation and the outcome of lawsuits.

The Declaration of Independence is provided as Exhibit 5.1.

HISTORY OF AMERICAN LAW

When the American colonies were first settled, the English system of law was generally adopted as the system of jurisprudence. This was the foundation from which American judges developed a common law in the United States.

English **common law** was law developed by judges who issued their opinions when deciding a case. The principles announced in these cases became precedent for

Common law

Developed by judges who issued their opinions when deciding a case. The principles announced in these cases became precedent for later judges deciding similar cases.

ADOPTION OF ENGLISH COMMON LAW IN AMERICA

All the states of the United States of America (except Louisiana) base their legal systems primarily on the English *common law*.

In the United States, the law, equity, and merchant courts have been merged. Thus, most U.S. courts permit the aggrieved party to seek both law and equitable orders and remedies.

The importance of common law to the American legal system is described in the following excerpt from Justice William Douglas's opinion in the 1841 case of *Penny v. Little* [4 Ill. 301, 1841 Ill. Lexis 98 (Ill. 1841)]:

The common law is a beautiful system, containing the wisdom and experiences of ages. Like the people it ruled and protected, it was simple and crude in its infancy, and became enlarged, improved, and polished as the nation advanced in civilization, virtue, and intelligence. Adapting itself to the conditions and circumstances of the people and relying upon them for its administration, it necessarily improved as the condition of the people was elevated. The inhabitants of this country always claimed the common law as their birthright, and at an early period established it as the basis of their jurisprudence.

---

later judges deciding similar cases. The English common law can be divided into cases decided by the law courts, chancery or equity courts, and merchant courts.

Law Courts

Prior to the Norman Conquest of England in 1066, each locality in England was subject to local laws as established by the lord or chieftain in control of the local area. There was no countrywide system of law. After 1066, William the Conqueror and his successors to the throne of England began to replace the various local laws with one uniform system of law.

To accomplish this, the king or queen appointed loyal followers as judges in all local areas. These judges were charged with administering the law in a uniform manner in what were called **law courts**. Law at this time tended to emphasize form (legal procedure) over the substance (merit) of the case. The only relief available in law courts was a monetary award for damages.

Chancery (Equity) Courts

Because of the at-times unfair results and the limited remedy available in the law courts, a second set of courts—the **Court of Chancery** (or **equity court**)—was established, under the authority of the Lord Chancellor. Those who believed that the decision of the law court was unfair or that the law court could not grant an appropriate remedy could seek relief in the Court of Chancery.

The Chancery Court inquired into the merits of the case rather than emphasize legal procedure. The Chancellor's remedies were called *equitable remedies* because they were shaped to fit each situation. Equitable orders and remedies of the Court of Chancery took precedence over the legal decisions and remedies of the law courts.

Merchant Courts

As trade developed in the Middle Ages, the merchants who traveled around England and Europe developed certain rules to solve their commercial disputes. These rules, known as the "law of merchants" or the *law merchant*, were based upon common trade practices and usage. Eventually, a separate set of courts, called the **merchant court**, was established to administer these rules. In the early 1900s, the merchant court was absorbed into the regular law court system of England.

THE PARALEGAL AND SOURCES OF THE LAW

The laws of the United States are extremely complex. Throughout history, our legal institutions have evolved and grown. With this growth has come the adoption and passage of thousands of laws originating from many different sources. A paralegal must have a sound understanding of the source of the laws of this country.

Sources of law in the United States include the following:

- Constitution of the United States of America
- statutes enacted by the U.S. Congress
- judicial decisions of the Supreme Court of the United States and other federal courts
- federal administrative agency rules and decisions
- state constitutions
- statutes enacted by the fifty states
- judicial decisions of state courts
- state administrative agency rules and decisions
- laws and judicial decisions of the District of Columbia and United States territories
- local laws, such as those of counties, cities, and municipalities.

Paralegals must have knowledge of the source of the laws that govern their work assignments. Paralegals often are called upon to conduct legal research to find relevant laws and judicial decisions that affect the cases or projects to which they are assigned. A thorough working knowledge of the sources of the law that affect the jurisdiction in which the paralegal practices is necessary. This chapter provides a detailed discussion of the sources of law in this country.

SOURCES OF LAW IN THE UNITED STATES

In more than 200 years since the founding of this country and adoption of the English common law, U.S. lawmakers have developed a substantial body of law. The sources of modern law in the United States are the U.S. and state constitutions, treaties, statutes and ordinances (codified law), administrative agency rules and regulations, executive orders, and judicial decision.

Constitutions

The **Constitution of the United States of America** is the *supreme law of the land*. This means that any law—federal, state, or local—that conflicts with the U.S. Constitution is unconstitutional and, therefore, unenforceable.

The principles enumerated in the Constitution are extremely broad, because the founding fathers intended them to be applied to evolving social, technological, and economic conditions. The U.S. Constitution often is referred to as a "living document" because it is so adaptable.

The U.S. Constitution established the structure of the federal government by creating three branches of government and giving them the following powers:

1. **Legislative branch** (Congress: Senate and House of Representatives):
2. **Executive branch** (President): power to enforce the law
3. **Judicial branch** (courts): power to interpret and determine the validity of the law

Powers not given to the federal government by the U.S. Constitution are reserved to the states. States also have their own constitutions, often patterned after the U.S. Constitution, though many are more detailed. State constitutions establish the legislative, executive, and judicial branches of state government and establish the powers

Constitution of the United States of America
The supreme law of the United States. *The Constitution of the United States of America establishes the structure of the federal government, delegates powers to the federal government, and guarantees certain fundamental rights.*

of each branch. Provisions of state constitutions are valid unless they conflict with the U.S. Constitution or any valid federal law.

Treaties

Treaty
A compact made between two or more nations.

The U.S. Constitution provides that the President, with the advice and consent of the U.S. Senate, may enter into **treaties** with foreign governments. Treaties become part of the supreme law of the land. With increasing international economic relations among nations, treaties will become an even more important source of law affecting business in the future.

Codified Law

Statute
Written law enacted by the legislative branch of the federal and state governments that establishes certain courses of conduct that the covered parties must adhere to.

Statutes are written laws that establish certain courses of conduct to which the covered parties must adhere. The U.S. Congress is empowered by the Commerce Clause and other provisions of the U.S. Constitution to enact **federal statutes** to regulate foreign and interstate commerce. Federal statutes include antitrust laws, securities laws, bankruptcy laws, labor laws, equal employment opportunity laws, environmental protection laws, consumer protection laws, and such. State legislatures enact **state statutes**, which include corporation laws, partnership laws, workers' compensation laws, the Uniform Commercial Code, and the like. The statutes enacted by the legislative branches of the federal and state governments are organized by topic into code books, often called **codified law**.

Read the "History" section of the Sarbanes-Oxley Act for an example of how a federal statute is enacted, at http://en.wikipedia.org/wiki/sarbanes-oxley

State legislatures often delegate lawmaking authority to local government bodies, including cities and municipalities, countries, school districts, water districts, and so on. These governmental units are empowered to adopt **ordinances**. Examples of ordinances are traffic laws, local building codes, and zoning laws. Ordinances are also codified.

Administrative Agencies

The legislative and executive branches of federal and state governments are empowered to establish **administrative agencies** to enforce and interpret statutes enacted by Congress and state legislatures. Many of these agencies regulate business. For example, Congress has created the Securities and Exchange Commission (SEC) and the Federal Trade Commission (FTC), among others.

The U.S. Congress or the state legislatures usually empower these agencies to adopt administrative rules and regulations to interpret the statutes that the agency is authorized to enforce. These rules and regulations have the force of law. Administrative agencies usually have the power to hear and decide disputes. Their decisions are called *orders*. Because of their power, administrative agencies often are informally called the "fourth branch" of government.

Executive Orders

The executive branch of government, which consists of the President of the United States and state governors, is empowered to issue executive orders.

This power is derived from express delegation from the legislative branch and is implied from the U.S. Constitution and state constitutions. For example, on October 8, 2001, President George W. Bush by Executive Order established within the Executive Office of the President an Office of Homeland Security to be headed by the Assistant to the President for Homeland Security.

Judicial Decisions

Judicial decision
A ruling about an individual lawsuit issued by federal and state courts.

When deciding individual lawsuits, federal and state courts issue **judicial decisions**. In these written opinions, the judge or justice usually explains the legal reasoning used to decide the case. These opinions often include interpretations of statutes, ordinances, administrative regulations, and the announcement of legal principles used to decide the case. Many court decisions are printed (reported) in books available in law libraries.

checklist ☑   SOURCES OF LAW IN THE UNITED STATES

SOURCE OF LAW	DESCRIPTION
Constitutions	The U.S. Constitution establishes the federal government and enumerates its powers. Powers not given to the federal government are reserved to the states. State constitutions establish state government and enumerate their powers.
Treaties	The U.S. President, with the advice and consent of the U.S. Senate, may enter into treaties with foreign countries.
Codified law (statutes and ordinances)	Statutes are enacted by the U.S. Congress and state legislatures. Ordinances, enacted by municipalities and local government agencies, establish courses of conduct that the covered parties must follow.
Administrative agency rules and regulations	Administrative agencies are created by the legislative and executive branches of government. They may adopt rules and regulations that regulate the conduct of covered parties.
Executive orders	Executive orders, issued by the U.S. President and government of states, regulate the conduct of covered parties.
Judicial decisions	Courts decide controversies. A court issues decisions that state the holding of the case and the rationale the court used in reaching that decision.

Priority of Law in the United States

Again, the U.S. Constitution and treaties take precedence over all other laws. Federal statutes take precedence over federal regulations, and valid federal law takes precedence over any conflicting state or local law. State constitutions rank as the highest state law, and state statutes take precedence over state regulations. Valid state law takes precedence over local laws.

The Doctrine of *Stare Decisis*

Based on the common law tradition, past court decisions become precedent for deciding future cases. Lower courts must follow the precedent established by higher courts. That is why all federal and state courts in the United States must follow the precedents established by U.S. Supreme Court decisions.

The courts of one jurisdiction are not bound by the precedent established by the courts of another jurisdiction, although they may look to each other for guidance. Thus, state courts of one state are not required to follow the legal precedent established by the courts of another state.

Adherence to precedent is called *stare decisis* ("to stand by the decision"). The doctrine of *stare decisis* promotes uniformity of law within a jurisdiction, makes the court system more efficient, and makes the law more predictable for individuals and businesses. A court may change or reverse its legal reasoning later if a new case is presented to it and change is warranted.

Stare decisis
Latin: "to stand by the decision." Adherence to precedent.

The doctrine of *stare decisis* is discussed in the following excerpt from Justice Musmanno's decision in *Flagiello v. Pennsylvania* 208 A.2d 193, 1965 Pa. Lexis 442 (Pa.1965)].

> *Without* stare decisis, *there would be no stability in our system of jurisprudence.* Stare decisis *channels the law. It erects lighthouses and flies the signals of safety. The ships of jurisprudence must follow that well-defined channel which, over the years, has been proved to be secure and worthy.*

THE PARALEGAL AND THE CONSTITUTION

The Constitution of the United States of America is one of the most important documents ever drafted. The U.S. Constitution created a new country, one that was not ruled by kings, queens, monarchs, or dictators. The country was created as the world's first democracy—a crucial change in the history of the world.

The Constitution has been continually implemented since its ratification more than two centuries ago. The Constitution is considered a "living document" that has been interpreted by the United States Supreme Court and other courts to apply to an ever changing society.

Citizens of the United States should have an understanding of the U.S. Constitution, and this is even more important for paralegals. Paralegals should be renaissance men and women, who have an understanding of this country's founding, its Constitutional protections, and the current debates concerning the application of the Constitutional language in these modern times.

This chapter provides a detailed discussion of these provisions and protections of the Constitution:

- Supremacy clause
- Commerce clause
- Freedom of speech
- Freedom of religion
- Due process clause
- Equal protection clause

The U.S. Constitution has many other important provisions as well. Paralegals should be fully informed citizens, and because of their position, understand how the Constitution created the federal government, built in checks and balances, granted powers to the federal government, and established protections for us against unconstitutional intrusions into our lives by the government. The Constitution of the United States of America is set forth in its entirety in Appendix F to this book.

Exhibit 5.2 The Constitution of the United States

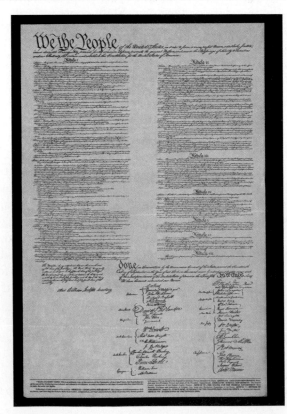

CONSTITUTION OF THE UNITED STATES OF AMERICA

Prior to the American Revolution, each of the thirteen original colonies operated as a separate sovereignty under the rule of England. In September 1774, representatives of the colonies met as a Continental Congress. In 1776, the colonies declared their independence from England, and the American Revolution ensued.

The Constitutional Convention was convened in Philadelphia in May 1787, with the primary purpose of strengthening the federal government. After substantial debate, the delegates agreed to a new U.S. Constitution, reported to Congress in September 1787. State ratification of the Constitution was completed in 1788. Since that time, many amendments, including the Bill of Rights, have been added to the Constitution.

The U.S. Constitution serves two major functions:

1. It creates the three branches of the federal government (executive, legislative, and judicial) and allocates powers to these branches.
2. It protects individual rights by limiting the government's ability to restrict those rights.

The Constitution itself provides that it may be amended to address social and economic changes.

Federalism and Delegated Powers

The U.S. form of government is referred to as **federalism,** which means that the federal government and the 50 state governments share powers. When the states ratified the Constitution, they *delegated* certain powers to the federal government. These **delegated powers,** also called **enumerated powers**, authorize the federal government to deal with national and international affairs. State governments have powers that are not specifically delegated to the federal government by the Constitution and are empowered to deal with local affairs.

Doctrine of Separation of Powers

The first three Articles of the Constitution divide the federal government into three branches:

1. Article I of the Constitution establishes the legislative branch of government, which is bicameral—consisting of the Senate and the House of Representatives—collectively referred to as *Congress*. Each state is allocated two senators. The number of representatives to the House of Representatives is determined by the population of each state. The current number of representatives is determined from the 2000 census.
2. Article II of the Constitution establishes the executive branch of government by providing for the election of the President and Vice President. The President is not elected by popular vote but, instead, by the *electoral college*, whose representatives are appointed by state delegations.
3. Article III establishes the judicial branch of the government in the Supreme Court and provides for the creation of other federal courts by Congress.

Checks and Balances

Certain **checks and balances** are built into the Constitution to ensure that no one branch of the federal government becomes too powerful. Some of the checks and balances in our system of government are as follows:

1. The judicial branch has authority to examine the acts of the other two branches of government and determine whether these acts are constitutional.
2. The executive branch can enter into treaties with foreign governments only with the advice and consent of the Senate.
3. The legislative branch is authorized to create federal courts and determine their jurisdiction and to enact statutes that change judicially made law.

Read the article, "The Power of the Courts — Marbury v. Madison, 1803." At the top of the page shown, click on the sixth icon from the left), at http://archives.gov/national-archives-experience/charters/charters.html
What was the decision in this case?

The Constitution of the United States is not a mere lawyers' document: it is a vehicle of life, and its spirit is always the spirit of age.—

Woodrow Wilson,
Constitutional Government in the United States 69 (1927)

Read the section "How It Works" and answer the following question: "If no candidate for President receives an absolute electoral majority, how is the President of the United States elected?" at http://en.wikipedia.org/wiki/u.s._electoral_college

ETHICAL *Perspective*

Ms. Jennifer Adams is hired as a paralegal at a law firm with expertise in real estate development law. She recently left a paralegal position at another law firm to take the new paralegal position with the current law firm.

At the new firm, Ms. Adams is assigned to work as the paralegal for Mr. Humberto Cruz, a senior partner of the law firm. Mr. Cruz is an expert in complex real estate transactions representing clients in the purchase, development, and leasing of large shopping malls. One client whom Mr. Cruz represents is Modern Properties L.P., a limited partnership that constructs and operates retail shopping malls across the country.

One day Mr. Cruz asks Ms. Adams to attend a meeting with himself and the president of Modern Properties L.P. At the meeting, the president of Modern Properties L.P. discloses a dispute that the partnership has with a tenant, Third National Bank, concerning the lease of a building by Third National Bank at a mall constructed and operated by Modern Properties L.P. The president explains that Third National Bank has filed a lawsuit against Modern Properties L.P. concerning this dispute. The president further explains that the partnership wants Mr. Cruz to represent the partnership in this lawsuit.

Ms. Adams realizes that her prior law firm represented Third National Bank in many lawsuits, and that she had worked as the paralegal on several of the cases involving Third National Bank. During the course of this work, she became privy to confidential information about Third National Bank, including its financial condition, operations, and legal strategy.

Does Ms. Adams have a conflict of interest? If so, what should she do? Several provisions of the *Model Code of Ethics and Professional Responsibility and Guidance for Enforcement* (Model Code) of the National Federation of Paralegal Associations, Inc. (NFPA) provide guidance. Section EC-1.6(b) states: "A paralegal shall avoid conflicts of interest that may arise from previous assignments, whether for a present or past employer or client."

Section EC-1.6(f) states: "A paralegal shall not participate in or conduct work on any matter where a conflict of interest has been identified." State and local paralegal codes of ethics and professional responsibility contain similar prohibitions.

Thus, Ms. Adams must immediately disclose the fact that she previously worked on cases involving Third National Bank at the prior law firm where she was employed, and that because of that employment she possesses confidential information about Third National Bank. Because of this conflict of interest, Ms. Adams must excuse herself from working on the *Third National Bank v. Modern Properties L.P.* case.

Supremacy Clause

Supremacy Clause
A clause of the U.S. Constitution that establishes that the federal Constitution, treaties, federal laws, and federal regulations are the supreme law of the land.

The **Supremacy Clause** establishes that the federal Constitution, treaties, federal laws, and federal regulations are the supreme law of the land [Article VI, Section 2]. State and local laws that conflict with valid federal law are unconstitutional. The concept of federal law taking precedence over state or local law is called the **preemption doctrine**.

Congress may expressly provide that a specific federal statute *exclusively* regulates a specific area or activity. No state or local law regulating the area or activity is valid if there is such a statute. More often, though, federal statutes do not expressly provide for exclusive jurisdiction. In these instances, state and local governments have *concurrent jurisdiction* to regulate the area or activity. But any state or local law that "directly and substantially" conflicts with valid federal law is preempted under the Supremacy Clause.

Commerce Clause

Commerce Clause
A clause of the U.S. Constitution that grants Congress the power "to regulate commerce with foreign nations, and among the several states, and with Indian tribes."

The **Commerce Clause** of the U.S. Constitution grants Congress the power "to regulate commerce with foreign nations, and among the several states, and with Indian tribes" [Article I, Section 8, clause 3]. Because this clause authorizes the federal gov-

FOREIGN COMMERCE CLAUSE

The Commerce Clause of the U.S. Constitution gives the federal government the exclusive power to regulate commerce with foreign nations. Direct and indirect regulation of foreign commerce by state or local governments that discriminates against foreign commerce violates the Foreign Commerce Clause and is therefore unconstitutional.

Consider the following examples: The state of Michigan is the home of General Motors Corporation, Ford Motor Company, and Chrysler Corporation—the three largest automobile manufacturers in the United States. Suppose the Michigan state legislature enacts a law imposing a 100 percent tax on any automobile imported from a foreign country that is sold in Michigan but does not impose the same tax on domestic automobiles sold in Michigan. The Michigan tax violates the Foreign Commerce Clause and, therefore, is unconstitutional and void.

But if Michigan enacts a law that imposes a 100 percent tax on all automobiles sold in Michigan, domestic and foreign, the law does not discriminate against foreign commerce and therefore does not violate the Foreign Commerce Clause. But if the federal government enacts a 100 percent tax on all foreign automobiles but not domestic automobiles sold in the United States, that law would be valid.

ernment to regulate commerce, it has a greater impact on business than any other provision in the Constitution. Among other things, this clause is intended to foster the development of a national market and free trade among the states.

The Commerce Clause also gives the federal government the authority to regulate **interstate commerce**. Originally, the courts interpreted this clause to mean that the federal government could regulate only commerce that moved *in* interstate commerce. The modern rule, however, allows the federal government to regulate activities that *affect* interstate commerce.

Under the *effects on interstate commerce test*, the regulated activity does not itself have to be in interstate commerce. Thus, any **intrastate** (local) **commerce** that has an effect on interstate commerce is subject to federal regulation. Theoretically, this test subjects a substantial amount of business activity in the United States to federal regulation.

For example, in the famous case of *Wickard, Secretary of Agriculture v. Filburn* [317 U.S. 111, 63 S.Ct. 82, 87 L.Ed. 122, 1942 U.S. Lexis 1046 (U.S.)] a federal statute limited the amount of wheat a farmer could plant and harvest for home consumption. Filburn, a farmer, violated the law. The U.S. Supreme Court upheld the statute on the grounds that it prevented nationwide surpluses and shortages of wheat. The Court reasoned that wheat grown for home consumption would affect the supply of wheat available in interstate commerce.

State Police Power

The states did not delegate all power to regulate business to the federal government. They retained the power to regulate intrastate and much interstate business activity that occurs within their borders. This is commonly referred to as states' **police power**.

Police power permits states (and, by delegation, local governments) to enact laws to protect or promote the *public health, safety, morals, and general welfare*. This includes the authority to enact laws that regulate the conduct of business. Zoning ordinances, state environmental laws, corporation and partnership laws, and property laws are enacted under this power.

BILL OF RIGHTS AND OTHER AMENDMENTS

In 1791, the states approved the 10 amendments commonly referred to as the **Bill of Rights**, and they became part of the U.S. Constitution. The Bill of Rights guarantees certain fundamental rights to natural persons and protects these rights from intrusive

Bill of Rights
The first 10 amendments to the Constitution. They were added to the U.S. Constitution in 1791.

Exhibit 5.3 **Bill of Rights**

government action. Most of these rights, or "freedoms," also have been found applicable to so-called artificial persons (i.e., corporations).

The First Amendment to the Constitution guarantees the rights of free speech, assembly, and religion. Because these rights are continually litigated and are frequent subjects of U.S. Supreme Court opinions, they are singled out for discussion in the following paragraphs.

In addition to the Bill of Rights, seventeen amendments have been added to the Constitution. Two important clauses from these amendment—the Due Process Clause and the Equal Protection Clause—are discussed in the following paragraphs.

Freedom of Speech

Freedom of speech
The right to engage in oral, written, and symbolic speech protected by the First Amendment.

One of the most honored freedoms guaranteed by the Bill of Rights is the **freedom of speech** of the First Amendment. Many other constitutional freedoms would be meaningless without it. The First Amendment's Freedom of Speech Clause protects speech only, not conduct. The U.S. Supreme Court places speech into three categories: (1) fully protected, (2) limited protected, and (3) unprotected speech.

Fully Protected Speech

Fully protected speech is speech that the government cannot prohibit or regulate. Political speech is an example of such speech. For example, the government could not enact a law forbidding citizens from criticizing the current administration. The First Amendment protects oral, written and symbolic speech.

Limited Protected Speech

The Supreme Court has held that certain types of speech are only **limited protected speech** under the First Amendment. Although the government cannot forbid this

Find the Bill of Rights at http://www.archives.gov/ national-archives-experience/ charters/charters.html

I disapprove of what you say, but I will defend to the death your right to say it.—

Voltaire

type of speech, it can subject this speech to restrictions of time, place, and manner. The following types of speech are accorded limited protection:

- *Offensive speech* is speech that offends many members of society. (It is not the same as obscene speech, however.) The Supreme Court has held that offensive speech may be restricted by the government under time, place, and manner restrictions. For example, the Federal Communications Commission (FCC) can regulate the use of offensive language on television by limiting such language to times when children would be unlikely to be watching (e.g., late at night).
- *Commercial speech*, such as advertising, was once considered unprotected by the First Amendment. The Supreme Court's landmark decision in *Virginia State Board of Pharmacy v. Virginia Citizens Consumer Council, Inc.* [425 U.S. 748, 96 S. Ct. 1817, 48 L.Ed.2d 346, 1976 U.S. Lexis 55 (U.S.)] changed this rule. In that case, the Supreme Court held that a state statute prohibiting a pharmacist from advertising the price of prescription drugs was unconstitutional because it violated the Freedom of Speech Clause. But, the Supreme Court held that commercial speech is subject to proper time, place, and manner restrictions. For example, a city could prohibit billboards along its highways for safety and aesthetic reasons as long as other forms of advertising (e.g., print media) were available.

Unprotected Speech

The Supreme Court has held that the following types of speech are **unprotected speech** under the First Amendment and may be totally forbidden by the government:

Unprotected speech
Speech that is not protected by the First Amendment and may be forbidden by the government.

- Dangerous speech (including such things as yelling "fire" in a crowded theater when there is no fire)
- Fighting words that are likely to provoke a hostile or violent response from an average person
- Speech that incites the violent or revolutionary overthrow of the government; the mere abstract teaching of the morality and consequences of such action is protected
- Defamatory language
- Child pornography
- Obscene speech

The definition of *obscene speech* is quite subjective. One Supreme Court justice stated, "I know it when I see it" [Justice Stewart in *Jacobellis v. Ohio*, 378 U.S. 184, 84 S.Ct. 1676 12 L.Ed.2d 793, 1964 U.S. Lexis 822 (U.S.)]. In *Miller v. California*, the Supreme Court determined that speech is obscene under the following circumstances.

1. The average person, applying contemporary community standards, would find that the work, taken as a whole, appeals to the prurient interest.
2. The work depicts or describes, in a patently offensive way, sexual conduct specifically defined by the applicable state law.
3. The work, taken as a whole, lacks serious literary, artistic, political, or scientific value. [413 U.S. 15, 93 S.Ct. 2607, 37 L.Ed.2d 419, 1973 U.S. Lexis 149 (U.S.)]

States are free to define what constitutes obscene speech. Movie theaters, magazine publishers, and so on are often subject to challenges that the materials they display or sell are obscene and, therefore, not protected by the First Amendment.

FREE SPEECH IN CYBERSPACE

Once or twice a century a new medium seems to come along that presents new problems in applying freedom-of-speech rights. This time it is the Internet. Congress enacted the *Computer Decency Act* to regulate the Internet. This statute made it a felony to knowingly make "indecent" or "patently offensive" materials available on computer systems, including the Internet, to persons under 18 years of age.

The Act provided for fines, prison terms, and loss of licenses for anyone convicted of violating its terms. Immediately, cyberspace providers and users filed lawsuits challenging these provisions of the Act as violating their free speech rights granted under the First Amendment to the Constitution. Proponents of the Act countered that these provisions were necessary to protect children from indecent materials.

The U.S. Supreme Court also came down on the plaintiff's side. The Court overturned the Computer Decency Act, finding that the terms "indecent" and "patently offensive" were too vague to define and criminally enforce. The Supreme Court reasoned that limiting the content on the Internet to what is suitable for a child resulted in unconstitutional limiting of adult speech. The Court stated that parents can regulate their children's access to the Internet and can install blocking and filtering software programs to protect their children from seeing adult materials.

The Supreme Court declared emphatically that the Internet must be given the highest possible level of First Amendment free-speech protection. The Supreme Court stated, "As the most participatory form of mass speech yet developed, the Internet deserves the highest protection from government intrusion." The Court also reasoned that because the Internet is a global medium, there would be no way to prevent indecent material from flowing over the Internet from abroad.

Source: Reno v. American Civil Liberties Union, 117 S.Ct. 2329 (1997); *United States v. Playboy Entertainment Group, Inc.*, 120 S.Ct. 1878 (2000)

Freedom of Religion

The U.S. Constitution requires federal, state, and local governments to be neutral toward religion. The First Amendment actually contains two separate religion clauses:

Establishment Clause
A clause to the First Amendment that prohibits the government from either establishing a state religion or promoting one religion over another.

1. The **Establishment Clause** prohibits the government from either establishing a state religion or promoting one religion over another. Thus, it guarantees that there will be no state-sponsored religion. The Supreme Court used this clause as its reason for ruling that an Alabama statute that authorized a one-minute period of silence in schools for "meditation or voluntary prayer" was invalid [*Wallace v. Faffree*, 472 U.S. 38, 105 S.Ct. 2479 86 L.Ed.2d 29, 1985 U.S. Lexis 91]. The Court held that the statute endorsed religion.

Free Exercise Clause
A clause to the First Amendment that prohibits the government from interfering with the free exercise of religion in the United States.

2. The **Free Exercise Clause** prohibits the government from interfering with the free exercise of religion in the United States. Generally, this clause prevents the government from enacting laws that either prohibit or inhibit individuals from participating in or practicing their chosen religion. For example, in *Church of Lukumi Babalu Aye, Inc. v. City of Hialeah, Florida* [508 U.S. 520, 113 S.Ct. 2217, 124 L.Ed.2d 472, 1993 U.S. Lexis 4022 (U.S.)], the U.S. Supreme Court held that a city ordinance that prohibited ritual sacrifices of animals (chickens) during church services violated the Free Exercise Clause. Of course, this right to be free from government intervention in the practice of religion is not absolute. For example, human sacrifices are unlawful and are not protected by the First Amendment.

Due Process Clause

The **Due Process Clause** provides that no person shall be deprived of "life, liberty, or property" without due process of the law. It is contained in both the Fifth and the Fourteenth Amendments. The Due Process Clause of the Fifth Amendment applies to federal government action; that of the Fourteenth Amendment applies to state and local government action. The government is not prohibited from taking a person's life, liberty, or property, but the government must follow due process to do so. There are two categories of due process: *substantive* and *procedural*.

Due Process Clause
A clause that provides that no person shall be deprived of "life, liberty, or property" without due process of the law.

Substantive Due Process

Substantive due process requires that government statutes, ordinances, regulations, or other laws be clear on their face and not overly broad in scope. The test of whether substantive due process is met is whether a "reasonable person" could understand the law to be able to comply with it. Laws that do not meet this test are declared *void for vagueness*.

Suppose, for example, that a city ordinance made it illegal for persons to wear "clothes of the opposite sex." Such an ordinance would be held unconstitutional as void for vagueness because a reasonable person could not clearly determine whether his or her conduct violates the law.

Procedural Due Process

Procedural due process requires that the government give a person proper *notice* and *hearing* of the legal action before that person is deprived of his or her life, liberty, or property. The government action must be fair.

For example, if the government wants to take a person's home by eminent domain to build a highway, the government must (1) give the homeowner sufficient notice of its intention, and (2) provide a hearing. Under the **Just Compensation Clause** of the Fifth Amendment, the government must pay the owner just compensation for taking the property.

www

How does Louisiana law differ from the other 49 states? Go to:
http://www.la-legal.com/history_louisiana_law.htm

Equal Protection Clause

The **Equal Protection Clause** of the Fourteenth Amendment to the Constitution, as interpreted by the U.S. Supreme Court, provides that state, local, and federal governments cannot deny to any person the "equal protection of the laws." The clause

Equal Protection Clause
A clause that provides that state, local, and federal governments cannot deny to any person the "equal protection of the laws."

THE CIVIL LAW SYSTEM

One of the major legal systems that has developed in the world, in addition to the Anglo–American common law system, is the Romano–Germanic **civil law system.** This legal system, commonly called the *civil law*, dates to 450 B.C., when Rome adopted the Twelve Tables, a code of laws applicable to the Romans. A compilation of Roman law, called the *Corpus Juris Civilis* (the Body of Civil Law), was completed in A.D. 534. Later, two national codes—the French Civil Code of 1804 (the Napoleonic Code) and the German Civil Code of 1896—became models for countries that adopted civil codes.

In contrast to the Anglo–American common law, in which laws are created by the judicial system as well as by congressional legislation, the Civil Code and parliamentary statutes that expand and interpret it are the sole sources of the law in most civil law countries. Thus, the adjudication of a case is simply the application of the Code or the statutes to a specific set of facts. In some civil law countries, court decisions do not have the force of law.

Today, Austria, Belgium, Greece, Indochina, Indonesia, Japan, Latin America, the Netherlands, Poland, Portugal, South Korea, Spain, Sub-Saharan Africa, Switzerland, and Turkey follow the civil law.

THE PARALEGAL'S UNAUTHORIZED PRACTICE OF LAW

Columbus Bar Association v. Purnell
94 Ohio St. 3d 126, 760 N.E.2d 817 (2002)
Supreme Court of Ohio

Per Curiam. LOC. R. 75.8(A)(2) of the Probate Division of the Common Pleas Court of Franklin County requires that an independent paralegal "shall be registered for each case in which the independent paralegal is performing services," identifying, *inter alia*, a supervising attorney. That attorney must sign the registration, certifying that the independent paralegal is qualified to perform the services and that the supervising attorney will supervise and be responsible for all services of the paralegal.

On September 22, 1999, Respondent, Dellwin Purnell, filed an independent paralegal registration in the Probate Court in connection with the personal injury claim of a minor, Kyle Petersen. The form was not signed by a supervising attorney. On September 24, 1999, Respondent filed an "application to settle a minor's claim" in the Probate Court, striking the words "Attorney" and "Attorneys" from the form language "reasonable attorney fee for the attorney's services" and substituting therefor the phrase, "reasonable paralegal fee for the services." The application indicated that the fee would be $3,500 and that a Fee Agreement between Respondent and the minor's parent was attached to the application.

In a letter to Liberty Mutual Insurance Company, dated October 16, 1998, Respondent had indicated that he was engaged to "represent Kyle Petersen in a claim for personal injuries." On January 24, 2000, the probate judge found Respondent in contempt for representing himself as a paralegal without a supervising attorney.

On September 13, 2000, Relator, Columbus Bar Association, filed a complaint charging Respondent with the unauthorized practice of law. Respondent failed to answer, and on December 4, 2000, Relator filed a motion for default. The matter was referred to the Board of Commissioners on the Unauthorized Practice of Law ("Board"), which granted the motion. The Board found the facts as stated and concluded that Respondent's conduct constituted rendering legal services for another by a person not admitted to the practice of law in Ohio. The Board recommended that Respondent be prohibited from engaging in the unauthorized practice of law in the future.

On review of the record, we adopt the findings, conclusion, and recommendation of the Board. A paralegal who, without the supervision of an attorney, advises and represents a claimant in a personal injury matter is engaged in the unauthorized practice of law.

---

prohibits governments from enacting laws that classify and treat similarly situated persons differently. The clause is designed to prohibit invidious government discrimination. Natural persons and businesses are protected.

The Equal Protection Clause has not been interpreted literally by the U.S. Supreme Court. The Supreme Court has held that some government laws that treat people or businesses differently are constitutional. The Supreme Court has adopted three different standards for determining whether a government action that treats some persons or businesses differently than others is lawful:

1. *Strict scrutiny test.* Any government activity or regulation that classifies persons based on a *suspect class* (i.e., race) is reviewed for lawfulness using a strict scrutiny test. Under this standard, most government classifications of persons based on race are found to be unconstitutional. For example, a government rule that permitted persons of one race, but not of another race, to receive government benefits such as Medicaid, would violate this test. But affirmative action

programs that give racial minorities a "plus factor" when considered for public university admission is lawful, as long as it does not constitute a quota system.

2. **Intermediate scrutiny test.** The lawfulness of government classifications based on *protected classes* other than race (such as sex or age) are examined using an intermediate scrutiny test. Under this standard, the courts determine whether the government classification is "reasonably related" to a legitimate government purpose. For example, a rule prohibiting persons over a certain age from military combat would be lawful, but a rule prohibiting persons over a certain age from acting as government engineers would not be. With regard to a person's gender, the U.S. Supreme Court has held that the federal government can require males, but not females, to register with the military for a possible draft.

3. **Rational basis test.** The lawfulness of all government classifications that do not involve suspect or protected classes is examined using a rational basis test. Under this test, the courts will uphold government regulation as long as there is a justifiable reason for the law. This standard permits much of the government regulation of business. For example, providing government subsidies to farmers but not to those in other occupations is permissible.

Legal Terminology

Administrative agencies   178

Analytical school of jurisprudence   174

Bill of Rights   183

Court of Equity (or equity court)   176

Checks and balances   181

Civil law system   187

Codified law   178

Command school of jurisprudence   174

Commerce Clause   182

Commercial speech   185

Common law   175

Constitution of the United States of America   177

Critical legal studies school of jurisprudence   175

Delegated powers   181

Due Process Clause   187

Enumerated powers   181

Equal Protection Clause   187

Establishment Clause   186

Executive branch   177

Fairness of the law   170

Federal statutes   178

Federalism   181

Flexibility of the law   171

Free Exercise Clause   186

Freedom of speech   184

Fully protected speech   184

Historical school of jurisprudence   174

Intermediate scrutiny test   189

Interstate commerce   183

Intrastate commerce   183

Judicial branch   177

Judicial decisions   178

Jurisprudence   174

Just Compensation Clause   182

Law   170

Law and economics school of jurisprudence   175

Law court   176

Legislative branch   197

Limited protected speech   184

Merchant court   176

Natural school of jurisprudence   174

Obscene speech   185

Offensive speech   185

Ordinances   178

Police power   183

Precedent   175

Preemption doctrine   182

Procedural due process   187

Rational basis test   189

Separation of powers   181

Sociological school of jurisprudence   174

Stare decisis   179

State statutes   178

Statute   178

Strict scrutiny test   188

Substantive due process   187

Supremacy Clause   182

Treaties   178

Unprotected speech   185

CHAPTER 5   SOURCES OF AMERICAN LAW

What Is Law?

Definition	Law consists of a body of rules of action or conduct prescribed by controlling authority and having binding legal force.
Functions of Law	1. Keep the peace 2. Shape moral standards 3. Promote social justice 4. Maintain the status quo 5. Facilitate orderly change 6. Facilitate planning 7. Provide a basis for compromise 8. Maximize individual freedom
Fairness	Although the American legal system is one of the fairest and most democratic systems of law, abuses and mistakes in the application of the law still occur.
Flexibility	The law must be flexible to meet social, technological, and economic changes.

Schools of Jurisprudential Thought

Natural Law	Postulates that law is based on what is "correct"; it emphasizes a moral theory of law—that is, law should be based on morality and ethics.
Historical	Believes that law is an aggregate of social traditions and customs
Analytical	Maintains that law is shaped by logic
Sociological	Asserts that the law is a means of achieving and advancing certain sociological goals
Command	Believes that the law is a set of rules developed, communicated, and enforced by the ruling party
Critical Legal Studies	Maintains that legal rules are unnecessary and that legal disputes should be solved by applying arbitrary rules based on fairness
Law and Economics	Believes that promoting market efficiency should be the central concern of legal decision making

History of American Law

English Common Law	English common law (judge-made law) forms the basis of the legal systems of most states in this country. Louisiana bases its law on the French civil code.

Sources of Law in the United States

Constitutions	The U.S. Constitution establishes the federal government and enumerates its powers. Powers not given to the federal government are reserved to the states. State constitutions establish state governments and enumerate their powers.
Treaties	The President, with the advice and consent of the Senate, may enter into treaties with foreign countries.
Codified Law	1. *Statutes* are enacted by Congress and state legislatures. 2. *Ordinances* and statutes are passed by municipalities and local government bodies to establish courses of conduct that must be followed by covered parties.
Administrative Agencies	Administrative agencies are created by the legislative and executive branches of government; they may adopt rules and regulations that govern the conduct of covered parties.

Executive Orders	Executive orders, issued by the President and governors of states, regulate the conduct of covered parties.
Judicial Decisions	Courts decide controversies by issuing decisions that state the holding of each case and the rationale the court used to reach that decision.

Doctrine of Stare Decisis

Definition	*Stare decisis* means "to stand by the decision." This doctrine provides for adherence to precedent.

Constitution of the United States of America

Scope	The Constitution consists of seven articles and 26 amendments. It establishes the three branches of the federal government, enumerates their powers, and provides important guarantees of individual freedom. The Constitution was ratified by the states in 1788.

Basic Constitutional Concepts	1. *Federalism:* The Constitution created the federal government, which shares power with the state governments.
	2. *Delegated powers:* When the states ratified the Constitution, they delegated certain powers, called *enumerated powers*, to the federal government.
	3. *Reserved powers:* Those powers not granted to the federal government by the Constitution are reserved to the states.
	4. *Separation of powers:* Each branch of the federal government has separate powers.
	   a. Legislative branch—power to make the law
	   b. Executive branch—power to enforce the law
	   c. Judicial branch—power to interpret the law
	5. *Checks and balances:* Certain checks and balances are built into the Constitution to ensure that no one branch of the federal government becomes too powerful.

Supremacy Clause

	The Supremacy Clause stipulates that the U.S. Constitution, treaties, and federal law (statutes and regulations) are the *supreme law of the land*. State or local laws that conflict with valid federal law are unconstitutional. This is called the *preemption doctrine*.

Commerce Clause

	1. *Commerce Clause:* Authorizes the federal government to regulate commerce with foreign nations, among the states, and with Indian tribes. 2. *Interstate commerce:* Under the broad *effects test*, the federal government may regulate any activity (even intrastate commerce) that *affects* interstate commerce. 3. *Police Powers:* Power reserved to the states to regulate commerce.

Bill of Rights

	The Bill of Rights consists of the first 10 amendments to the Constitution. They establish basic individual rights. The Bill of Rights was ratified in 1791.

Freedom of Speech

	Freedom of Speech Clause of the First Amendment guarantees that the government shall not infringe on a person's right to speak. Protects oral, written, and symbolic speech. This right is not absolute—that is, some speech is not protected and other speech is granted only limited protection. The U.S. Supreme Court has placed speech in the following three categories:
	1. **Fully protected speech**. Speech that cannot be prohibited or regulated by the government
	2. **Limited protected speech**. Types of speech that are granted only limited protection under the Freedom of Speech Clause—that is, they are subject to governmental *time, place, and manner restrictions*:
	   a. Offensive speech
	   b. Commercial speech

3. *Unprotected speech*. Speech that is not protected by the Freedom of Speech Clause:
   a. Dangerous speech
   b. Fighting words
   c. Speech that advocates the violent overthrow of the government
   d. Defamatory language
   e. Child pornography
   f. Obscene speech

Freedom of Religion

There are two religion clauses in the First Amendment. They are:
1. *Establishment Clause*. Prohibits the government from establishing a state religion or promoting religion
2. *Free Exercise Clause*. Prohibits the government from interfering with the free exercise of religion. This right is not absolute: for example, human sacrifices are forbidden.

Due Process Clause

Due Process Clause provides that no person shall be deprived of "life, liberty, or property" without due process. Two categories of due process:
1. *Substantive due process:* Requires that laws be clear on their face and not overly broad in scope. Laws that do not meet this test are *void for vagueness*.
2. *Procedural due process:* Requires that the government give a person proper *notice* and *hearing* before that person is deprived of his or her life, liberty, or property. An owner must be paid *just compensation* if the government takes his or her property.

Equal Protection Clause

Equal Protection Clause prohibits the government from enacting laws that classify and treat "similarly situated" persons differently. This standard is not absolute and the government can treat persons differently in certain situations. The U.S. Supreme Court has applied the following tests to determine if the Equal Protection Clause has been violated:
1. *Strict scrutiny test*. Applies to *suspect classes* (e.g., race, national origin)
2. *Intermediate scrutiny test*. Applies to other *protected classes* (e.g., sex, age)
3. *Rational basis test*. Applies to government classifications that do not involve a suspect or protected class

▶ WORKING THE WEB

1. Go to the website **http://www. usconstitution.net/const.html**. Scroll down to "Amendment 7." When was this amendment ratified? What does this amendment provide? Explain.
2. Visit the website **http://www.archives. gov/national-archives-experience/ charters/charters.html**. A page entitled "The Charters of Freedom—A New World is at Hand" will appear on your computer screen. Do the following exercises:
   a. On the page shown, click on the third icon from the left. Read the article entitled, "The Spirit of the Revolution—The Declaration of Independence." What did the Declaration of Independence do? Explain.
   b. On the page shown, click on the sixth icon from the left. Read the article "The Constitutional Convention—Creation of the Constitution." How many states were required to ratify the Constitution for it to be enacted?
   c. At the top of the page shown, click on the second-to-the-last icon from the right. Read the article "Expansion of Rights and Liberties—The Right of Suffrage." What amendment to the U.S. Constitution gave women the right to vote? What year was this amendment ratified?
3. Visit the website **http://www.senate.gov/**. Click on the word "Senators." Who are the two senators who represent your state in the U.S. Senate? Go to each senator's website

and email the senator, expressing your view on a legal issue in which you are interested.

4. Visit the website **http://www.house.gov/**. Who is the person who represents your home district? Go to that representative's website and read about his or her position

on a current legal issue. What is the issue, and what is your representative's view on it?

5. Go to **http://google.com**. Choose a country in which you are interested and search for a treaty of this country (e.g., "China treaty"). Briefly describe this treaty.

▶ CRITICAL THINKING AND WRITING QUESTIONS

1. Define the "law." Is this an easy concept to define? Why?
2. What functions does the law serve? Which of these functions do you think is the most important?
3. Is the law always fair? Give an example of where you think the law was applied unfairly.
4. Should the language of the U.S. Constitution be applied in its original meaning, or should it be applied in a more expansive sense? Explain.
5. What is the power of the legislative branch of government? What is a statute?
6. Do you think that the U.S. Supreme Court makes law when it interprets the U.S. Constitution? Explain.
7. What is the doctrine of *stare decisis*? Why is this doctrine important?
8. What does the doctrine of federalism provide?
9. What does the doctrine of separation of powers provide? Can you give any examples where the separation of the powers of the three branches of government is blurred?
10. What does the doctrine of checks and balances provide? Can you give any examples where one branch of the

government checks the power of another branch of the government?
11. What does the Supremacy Clause provide? What would be the consequences if the Supremacy Clause did not exist? Explain.
12. What does the Commerce Clause of the U.S. Constitution do? Explain.
13. The First Amendment to the U.S. Constitution contains the Freedom of Speech Clause. Explain the difference between fully protected speech, partially protected speech, and unprotected speech.
14. The U.S. Constitution guarantees freedom of religion. Explain the difference between the Establishment Clause and the Free Exercise Clause. Can you give an example of a legitimate government restriction of a possible religious practice?
15. What is the difference between substantive due process and procedural due process? Explain.
16. What does the Equal Protection Clause provide? Explain the differences between the (a) strict scrutiny test, (b) intermediate scrutiny test, and (c) rational basis test.

▶ ETHICS ANALYSIS AND DISCUSSION QUESTIONS

1. Are there any ethical issues in allowing one's personal feelings to be expressed in working on a case? What if you have strong feelings against the client's position?
2. Does the American system of law depend on the legal team to put aside its personal beliefs and work diligently on unpopular cases or issues? How does this ensure equal justice and allow for change in the system?
3. You are working in a law firm for an attorney who has had a series of strokes that have caused a permanent reading disability and memory impairment. Do you have any ethical obligation to the attorney's clients? Do you have any ethical obligation to the firm and to the attorney? [Philadelphia Ethics Opinion 2002-12 (2000); also, see Texas Ethics Opinion 522 (1997)].

▶ DEVELOPING YOUR COLLABORATION SKILLS

With a group of other students, selected by you or as assigned by your instructor, review Paralegals at Work at the beginning of the chapter. As a group, discuss the following questions.

1. Does the Freedom of Speech Clause of the First Amendment protect Mr. Storm's past conduct over regular radio and television? Discuss why or why not.

2. To what extent does the FCC have power to regulate satellite radio content or to make regulations that forbid, for instance, the kind of activities that Mr. Storm encourages on his radio show?
3. A future meeting is scheduled between Ms. Kang and Mr. Storm, which you are to attend. Make a list of some of the issues you would recommend to be researched before this next meeting with Mr. Storm.

▶ PARALEGAL PORTFOLIO EXERCISE

Research and find an article that discusses a Federal Communication Commission (FCC) clash with a radio, cable, or television station regarding the subject matter that it may broadcast. Write a memorandum, no longer than two pages, that discusses this dispute and the outcome of the case.

▶ LEGAL ANALYSIS AND WRITING CASES

Youngstown Co. v. Sawyer, Secretary of Commerce

343 U.S. 579, 72 S.Ct. 863, 96 L.Ed.2d 1153, 1952 U.S. Lexis 2625 (U.S.) (1952)

FACTS

In 1951, a dispute arose between steel companies and their employees about the terms and conditions that should be included in a new labor contract. At the time, the United States was engaged in a military conflict in Korea that required substantial steel resources from which to make weapons and other military goods.

On April 4, 1952, the steelworkers' union gave notice of a nationwide strike called to begin at 12:01 A.M. on April 9. The indispensability of steel as a component in weapons and other war materials led President Dwight D. Eisenhower to believe that the proposed strike would jeopardize the national defense and that governmental seizure of the steel mills was necessary to ensure the continued availability of steel. Therefore, a few hours before the strike was to begin, the President issued. Executive Order 10340, which directed the Secretary of Commerce to take possession of most of the steel mills and keep them running. The steel companies obeyed the order under protest, and brought proceedings against the President.

Question

1. Was the seizure of the steel mills constitutional?

Bonito Boats, Inc. v. Thunder Craft Boats, Inc.

489 U.S. 141, 109 S.Ct. 971, 103 L.Ed.2d 118, 1989 U.S. Lexis 629 (U.S.) (1989)

FACTS

Article 1, Section 8, Clause 8 of the U.S. Constitution grants Congress the power to enact laws to give inventors the exclusive right to their discoveries. Pursuant to this power, Congress enacted federal patent laws that establish the requirements to obtain a patent. Once a patent is granted, the patent holder has exclusive rights to use the patent.

Bonito Boats, Inc. developed a hull design for a fiberglass recreational boat that it marketed under the trade name Bonito Boats Model 5VBR. The manufacturing process involved creating a hardwood model that was sprayed with fiberglass to create a mold. The mold then served to produce the finished fiberglass boats for sale. Bonito did not file a patent application to protect the utilitarian or design aspects of the hull or the manufacturing process.

After the Bonito 5VBR was on the market for six years, the Florida legislature enacted a statute prohibiting the use of a direct molding process to duplicate unpatented boat hulls and forbade the knowing sale of hulls so duplicated. The protection afforded under the state statute was broader than that provided for under the federal patent statute.

Subsequently, Thunder Craft Boats, Inc. produced and sold boats made by the direct molding process. Bonito sued Thunder Craft under Florida law.

Question

1. Is the Florida statute valid?

Heart of Atlanta Motel v. United States

379 U.S. 241, 85 S.Ct. 348, 13 L.Ed.2d 258, 1964 U.S. Lexis 2187 (U.S.) (1964)

FACTS

The Heart of Atlanta Motel, in the state of Georgia, has 216 rooms available to guests. The motel is readily accessible to interstate highways 75 and 85 and to state highways 23 and 41. The motel solicits patronage from outside the state of Georgia through various national advertising media, including magazines of national circulation, and it maintains more than 50 billboards and highway signs within the state. Approximately 75 percent of the motel's registered guests are from out of state.

Congress enacted the Civil Rights Act of 1964, which made it illegal for public accommodations to discriminate against guests based on their race. Prior to that, the Heart of Atlanta Motel had refused to rent rooms to Blacks. After the Act was passed, it alleged that it intended to continue not to rent rooms to Blacks. The owner of the motel brought an action to have the Civil Rights Act of 1964 declared unconstitutional, alleging that Congress, in passing the Act, had exceeded its powers to regulate commerce under the Commerce Clause of the U.S. Constitution.

Question

1. Who wins?

Rostker, Director of the Selective Service v. Goldberg

453 U.S. 57, 101 S.Ct. 2646, 69 L.Ed.2d 478, 69 L.Ed.2d 478, 1981 U.S. Lexis 126 (U.S.) (1981)

FACTS

In 1975, after the war in Vietnam, the U.S. government discontinued draft registration for men in this country. In 1980, after the Soviet Union invaded Afghanistan, President Jimmy Carter asked Congress for funds to reactivate draft registration. President Carter suggested that males and females alike be required to register. Congress allocated funds only for the registration of males. Several men who were subject to draft registration brought a lawsuit that challenged the law as being unconstitutional in violation of the Equal Protection Clause of the U.S. Constitution. The U.S. Supreme Court upheld the constitutionality of the draft registration law, reasoning as follows.

> The question of registering women for the draft not only received considerable national attention and was the subject of wide-ranging public debate, but also was extensively considered by Congress in hearings, floor debate, and in committee. The

foregoing clearly establishes that the decision to exempt women from registration was not the "accidental by-producer of a traditional way of thinking about women."

> This is not a case of Congress arbitrarily choosing to burden one of two similarly situated groups, such as would be the case with an all-black or all-white, or an all-Catholic or all-Lutheran, or an all-Republican or all-Democratic registration. Men and women are simply not similarly situated for purposes of a draft or registration for a draft.

Justice Marshall dissented, stating that "The Court today places its imprimatur on one of the most potent remaining public expressions of 'ancient canards about the proper role of women.' It upholds a statute that requires males but not females to register for the draft, and which thereby categorically excludes women from a fundamental civic obligation. I dissent."

Question

1. Was the decision fair? Was the law a "progressive science" in this case? Was it ethical for males, but not females, to have to register for the draft?

Engine Manufacturers Association v. South Coast Air Quality Management District

541 U.S. 246, 124 S.Ct. 1756 158 L.Ed.2d 529, 2004 U.S. Lexis 3232 (U.S.) (2004)

FACTS

The Clean Air Act, a federal statute, establishes national air pollution standards for fleet vehicles such as buses, taxicabs, and trucks. The South Coast Air Quality Management District (South Coast) is a political entity of the state of California. South Coast establishes air pollution standards for the Los Angeles, California, metropolitan area. South Coast enacted Fleet Rules that prohibited the purchase or lease by public and private fleet operators of vehicles that do not meet stringent air pollution standards set by South Coast.

South Coast's fleet emission standards are more stringent than those set by the federal Clean Air Act.

The Engine Manufacturers Association (Association), a trade association that represents manufacturers and sellers of vehicles, sued South Coast, claiming that South Coast's Fleet Rules are preempted by the federal Clean Air Act. The U.S. District Court and the U.S. Court of Appeals upheld South Coast's Fleet Rules. The Association appealed to the U.S. Supreme Court.

Question

1. Are South Coast's Fleet Rules preempted by the federal Clean Air Act?

Van Orden v. Perry, Governor of Texas

125 S.Ct. 2854 162 L.Ed.2d 607, 2005 U.S. Lexis 5215 (U.S.) (2005)

FACTS

The 22 acres surrounding the Texas State Capital contains seventeen monuments and twenty-one historical markers. The monuments and markers commemorate the people and historical events of Texas. Some of the monuments are: Heroes of the Alamo, confederate Soldiers, a Texas Cowboy, Texas Pioneer Women, Disabled Veterans, and Texas Police Officers. One monument is a 6-feet high and 3-feet wide monument on which is carved an eagle grasping an American flag, an eye inside a pyramid, Stars of David, Greek letters, and the Ten Commandments. This monument has been on the grounds for more than 40 years.

Thomas Van Orden, a native Texan and resident of Austin, Texas, where the Texas State Capitol is located, sued to have the Ten Commandments' monument removed, alleging that the monument violated the Establishment Clause of the U.S. Constitution. The U.S. District Court held that the monument did not violate the Establishment Clause, finding that the monument had a secular purpose. The U.S. Court of Appeals affirmed. Van Orden appealed to the U.S. Supreme Court.

Question

1. Does the monument containing the Ten Commandments, which is located with other monuments on the grounds of the Texas State Capital, violate the Establishment Clause?

Grutter v. Bollinger, Dean of the University of Michigan Law School

539 U.S. 306, 123 S.Ct. 2325, 156 L.Ed.2d 304, 2003
U.S. Lexis 4800 (U.S.) (2003)

FACTS

In 1996, Barbara Grutter, a Caucasian resident of the state of Michigan, applied to the Law School of the University of Michigan, a state government–supported institution. She had a 3.8 undergraduate gradepoint average and a 161 LSAT score. The Law School rejected her application. The Law School received 3,500 applications for a class of 350 students. The Law School used race as one of the factors in considering applicants for admission to law school. The race of minority applicants, defined as Blacks, Hispanics, and Native Americans, was considered as a "plus factor" in considering their applications to law school. Caucasians and Asians were not given such a plus factor. The Law School stated that it used race as a plus factor to obtain a critical mass of underrepresented minority students, to create diversity at the school.

Grutter brought a class action lawsuit against the Law School of the University of Michigan, alleging that its use of a minority's race as a plus factor in admissions violated the Equal Protection Clause of the Fourteenth Amendment to the U.S. Constitution. The District Court held that the Law School's use of race as a factor in admissions violated the Equal Protection Clause. The Court of Appeals reversed. The U.S. Supreme Court granted certiorari to hear the appeal.

Question

1. Does the University of Michigan Law School's use of race as a plus factor in accepting minority applicants for admission to the Law School violate the Equal Protection Clause of the Fourteenth Amendment to the U.S. Constitution?

▶ WORKING WITH THE LANGUAGE OF THE COURT CASE

Lee v. Weisman

505 U.S. 577, 112 S.Ct. 2649 120 L.Ed.2d. 467, 1992
U.S. Lexis 4364 Supreme Court of the United States

Read the following case, excerpted from the U.S. Supreme Court's opinion. Review and brief the case. In your brief, answer the following questions.

1. Who are the plaintiff and defendant?
2. What does the Establishment Clause provide?
3. What test did the court use to determine if the practice violates the Establishment Clause?
4. Was the fact that the prayer was nonsectarian important to the Supreme Court's decision?
5. Is nonsectarian prayer permitted under the Establishment Clause?
6. How close was the vote by the justices in this case?

Kennedy, Justice (joined by Blackmun, Stevens, O'Conner, and Souter)

Deborah Weisman graduated from Nathan Bishop Middle School, a public school in Providence, Rhode Island, at a formal ceremony in June 1989. She was about 14 years old. For many years it has been the policy of the Providence school committee and the Superintendent of Schools to permit princi-

pals to invite members of the clergy to give invocations and benedictions at middle school and high school graduations. Many, but not all, of the principals elected to include prayers as part of the graduation ceremonies. Acting for himself and his daughter, Deborah's father, Daniel Weisman, objected to any prayers at Deborah's middle school graduation, but to no avail. The school principal, petitioner Robert E. Lee, invited a rabbi to deliver prayers at the graduation exercises for Deborah's class. Rabbi Leslie Gutterman, of the Temple Beth El in Providence, accepted.

It also has been the custom of Providence school officials to provide invited clergy with a pamphlet entitled "Guidelines for Civic Occasions," prepared by the National Conference of Christians and Jews. The Guidelines recommended that public prayers at nonsectarian civic ceremonies be composed with "inclusiveness and sensitivity," though they acknowledge that "prayer of any kind may be inappropriate on some civic occasions." The principal gave Rabbi Gutterman the pamphlet before the graduation and advised him that the invocation and benediction should be nonsectarian.

Deborah's graduation was held on the premises of Nathan Bishop Middle School on June 29, 1989. Four days before the ceremony, Daniel Weisman, in his individual capacity as a Providence taxpayer and as next friend of Deborah, sought a temporary restraining order in the United States District Court for the District of Rhode Island to prohibit school officials from including an invocation or a benediction in the graduation ceremony. The court denied the motion for lack of adequate time to consider it. Deborah and her family attended the graduation, where the prayers were recited.

In July 1989, Daniel Weisman filed an amended complaint seeking a permanent injunction barring petitioners, various officials of the Providence public schools, from inviting the clergy to deliver invocations and benedictions at future graduations.

The case was submitted on stipulated facts. The District Court held that petitioners' practice of including invocations and benedictions in public school graduations violated the Establishment Clause of the First Amendment, and it enjoined petitioners from continuing the practice. The court applied the three-part Establishment Clause test. Under that test, to satisfy the Establishment Clause a governmental practice must (1) reflect a clearly secular purpose, (2) have a primary effect that neither advances nor inhibits religion, and (3) avoid excessive government entanglement with religion. On appeal, the United States Court of Appeals for the First Circuit affirmed.

These dominant facts mark and control the confines of our decision: State officials direct the performance of a formal religious exercise at promotional and graduation ceremonies for secondary schools. Even for those students who object to the religious exercise, their attendance and participation in the state-sponsored religious activity are in a fair and real sense obligatory, though the school district does not require attendance as a condition for receipt of the diploma.

The controlling precedents as they relate to prayer and religious exercise in primary and secondary public schools compel the holding here that the policy of the city of Providence is an unconstitutional one. It is beyond dispute that, at a minimum, the Constitution guarantees that government may not coerce anyone to support or participate in religion or its exercise, or otherwise act in a way which "establishes a state religion or religious faith, or tends to do so."

We are asked to recognize the existence of a practice of nonsectarian prayer within the embrace of what is known as the Judeo-Christian tradition, prayer which is more acceptable than one which, for example, makes explicit references to the God of Israel, or to Jesus Christ, or to a patron saint. If common ground can be defined which permits once conflicting faiths to express the shared conviction that there is an ethic and a morality which transcend human invention, the sense of community and purpose sought by all decent societies might be advanced. But though the First Amendment does not allow the government to stifle prayers which aspire to these ends, neither does it permit the government to undertake that task for itself.

The sole question presented is whether a religious exercise may be conducted at a graduation ceremony in circumstances where, as we have found, young graduates who object are induced to conform. No holding by this Court suggests that a school can persuade or compel a student to participate in a religious exercise. That is being done here, and it is forbidden by the Establishment Clause of the First Amendment.

For the reasons we have stated, the judgment of the Court of Appeals is affirmed. ■

THE COURT SYSTEM AND ALTERNATE DISPUTE RESOLUTION

"I was never ruined but twice; once when I lost a lawsuit, and once when I won one."

Voltaire

6

PARALEGALS AT WORK

You have applied for a position as a paralegal at a law firm that specializes in litigation. Most of the law firm's practice is in the area of tort litigation, particularly representing plaintiffs in negligence cases. The firm has scheduled an interview with you. On the day you arrive for the interview, you are called into the office of Mrs. Harriet Green, a senior partner in the firm. Ms. Green wants to determine your knowledge of judicial and nonjudicial dispute resolution. Ms. Green informs you that she will tell you the facts of a case and will ask you several questions about the case.

Ms. Green explains that Ms. Heather Andersen has retained the law firm as the plaintiff to represent her in an accident case. Ms. Green explains that Ms. Andersen was driving her automobile on the main road of your city when Mr. Joseph Burton, driving another automobile, ran a red light and hit Ms. Andersen's vehicle, causing her severe physical injuries, as well as pain and suffering. The law firm plans to file a lawsuit for the tort of negligence on behalf of Ms. Andersen, the plaintiff, against Mr. Burton, the defendant. Ms. Andersen is a resident of your state. Mr. Burton is a resident of another state who was visiting your state when the accident occurred.

Ms. Green asks you the following questions: "What is a complaint?" "In what court or courts can our law firm file the complaint on behalf of Ms. Andersen?" "If we lose the case at trial, to what court can our law firm, on behalf of Ms. Andersen, appeal the trial court's decision?" "After the case is filed in the court, is there any way of resolving the case in favor of Ms. Andersen before the case goes to trial?"

Consider the issues involved in this scenario as you read the chapter.

After studying this chapter, you should be able to:

1. Describe the state court systems.
2. Describe the federal court system.
3. Explain subject-matter jurisdiction of federal and state courts.
4. Describe *in personam* jurisdiction of courts.
5. Explain the use of arbitration, mediation, and negotiation.
6. Explain the use of other nonjudicial methods of alternative dispute resolution.

▶ INTRODUCTION FOR THE PARALEGAL

A paralegal often assists attorneys who represent clients in the courts of this country. The court systems and the procedure to bring and defend a lawsuit are complicated, and a paralegal should be knowledgeable of court systems and how a lawsuit proceeds to trial and is decided in court.

Also, some parties to a dispute will choose to settle a case, or have the case reviewed or determined by a private party rather than by the courts. Thus, a paralegal should be knowledgeable of the manner and procedures for having disputes resolved outside of the court system.

The two major court systems in the United States are: (1) the federal court system, and (2) the court systems of the 50 states and the District of Columbia. Each of these systems has jurisdiction to hear different types of lawsuits. The process of bringing, maintaining, and defending a lawsuit is called **litigation**. Litigation is a difficult, time-consuming, and costly process that must comply with complex procedural rules. Although it is not required, most parties employ a lawyer to represent them when they are involved in a lawsuit.

Several forms of *nonjudicial* dispute resolution have developed in response to the expense and difficulty of bringing a lawsuit. These methods, collectively called alternative dispute resolution (ADR), are being used more and more often to resolve commercial disputes.

Paralegals are especially valuable in providing support to lawyers who are engaged in litigation and alternative dispute resolution. Paralegals interview clients, prepare documents submitted to courts, conduct legal research, and assist lawyers during trial and alternative dispute resolution.

This chapter focuses on the various court systems, the jurisdiction of courts to hear and decide cases, the litigation process, and alternative dispute resolution. ■

STATE COURT SYSTEMS

Each state and the District of Columbia have separate court systems. Most state court systems include:

- Limited-jurisdiction trial courts
- General-jurisdiction trial courts
- Intermediate appellate courts
- A supreme court (or highest state court)

Limited-Jurisdiction Trial Courts

State **limited-jurisdiction trial courts**, which sometimes are referred to as *inferior trial courts*, hear matters of a specialized or limited nature. Examples of these courts in many states are traffic courts, juvenile courts, justice-of-the-peace courts, probate courts, family law courts, and courts that hear misdemeanor criminal law cases and civil cases involving lawsuits of less than a certain dollar amount. Because these courts are trial courts, evidence can be introduced and testimony given. Most limited-jurisdiction courts keep a record of their proceedings. Their decisions usually can be appealed to a general-jurisdiction court or an appellate court.

Many states also have created **small-claims courts** to hear civil cases involving small dollar amounts (e.g., $5,000 or less). Generally, the parties must appear individually and cannot have a lawyer represent them. The decisions of small claims courts are often appealable to general-jurisdiction trial courts or appellate courts.

General-Jurisdiction Trial Court

Every state has a **general-jurisdiction trial court**. These courts often are called **courts of record** because the testimony and evidence at trial are recorded and stored for future reference. These courts hear cases that are not within the jurisdiction of

The law wherein, as in a magic mirror, we see reflected, not only our own lives, but the lives of all men that have been! When I think on this majestic theme, my eyes dazzle.

Oliver Wendell Holmes
The Law, Speeches 17 (1913)

General-jurisdiction trial court (courts of record)
A court that hears cases of a general nature that are not within the jurisdiction of limited-jurisdiction trial courts.

limited-jurisdiction trial courts, such as felonies, civil cases above a certain dollar amount, and so on. Some states divide their general-jurisdiction courts into two divisions, one for criminal cases and another for civil cases.

General-jurisdiction trial courts hear evidence and testimony. The decisions these courts hand down are appealable to an intermediate appellate court or the state supreme court, depending on the circumstances.

Intermediate Appellate Court

In many states, **intermediate appellate courts** (also called appellate courts or *courts of appeal*) hear appeals from trial courts. These courts review the trial court record to determine any errors at trial that would require reversal or modification of the trial court's decision. Thus, the appellate court reviews either pertinent parts or the entire trial court record from the lower court. No new evidence or testimony is permitted. The parties usually file legal briefs with the appellate court, stating the law and facts that support their positions. Appellate courts usually grant a short oral hearing to the parties.

Appellate court decisions are appealable to the state's highest court. In less populated states that do not have an intermediate appellate court, trial court decisions can be appealed directly to the state's highest court.

Intermediate appellate court
An intermediate court that hears appeals from trial courts.

Highest State Court

Each state has a **highest state court** in its court system. Most states call this highest court the *supreme court*. The function of a state supreme court is to hear appeals from intermediate state courts and certain trial courts. The highest court hears no new evidence or testimony. The parties usually submit pertinent parts of or the entire lower court record for review. The parties also submit legal briefs to the court and typically are granted a brief oral hearing. Decisions of state supreme courts are final, unless a question of law is involved that is appealable to the U.S. Supreme Court. Exhibit 6.1 depicts a typical state court system.

Highest state court
The top court in a state court system; it hears appeals from intermediate state courts and certain trial courts.

COST–BENEFIT ANALYSIS OF A LAWSUIT

In most civil lawsuits, every party is responsible for paying their own attorneys' fees, whether the party wins or loses. This is called the "American rule." The court can award lawyers' fees to the winning party if a statute so provides, or the parties have so agreed (e.g., in a contract), or the losing party has acted maliciously or pursued a frivolous case.

An attorney in a civil lawsuit can represent the plaintiff on an hourly, project, or contingency-fee basis. Hourly fees usually range from $75 to $500 per hour, depending on the type of case, the lawyer's expertise, and the locality of the lawsuit. Under a *contingency fee arrangement*, the lawyer receives a percentage of the amount recovered for the plaintiff upon winning or settling the case. Contingency fees normally range from 20 to 50 percent of the award or settlement, with the average being about 35 percent. Lawyers for defendants in lawsuits are typically paid on an hourly basis.

The choice of whether to bring or defend a lawsuit should be analyzed like any other business decision. This includes performing a **cost–benefit analysis** of the lawsuit. For the plaintiff, it may be wise not to sue. For the defendant, it may be wise to settle. In deciding whether to bring or settle a lawsuit, the following factors should be considered.

- The probability of winning or losing.
- The amount of money to be won or lost.
- Lawyers' fees and other costs of litigation.
- Loss of time by managers and other personnel.
- The long-term effects on the relationship and reputation of the parties.
- The amount of prejudgment interest provided by law.
- The aggravation and psychological costs associated with a lawsuit.
- The unpredictability of the legal system and the possibility of error.
- Other factors unique to the parties and lawsuit.

THE PARALEGAL AND THE COURT SYSTEMS

Paralegals are an extremely fortunate group of individuals because many of them get to work in a special environment—the court system. Even if a paralegal does not work directly within the court system, he or she still should have a fundamental knowledge of the court systems of the United States and how they work.

This country has two major sets of court systems: the federal court system and the state court system. And within the state court system, each of the fifty states, the District of Columbia, and each of the territories have their own court systems. And within the federal court system and each of these other court systems are various levels of courts, covering a range that includes specialized courts, general-jurisdiction trial courts, courts of appeal, and supreme courts.

A paralegal who works for litigation attorneys must have a detailed knowledge of the court systems that serve the relevant jurisdiction that he or she works in. Paralegals who work in positions that are not directly involved in supporting lawsuits in court should still have knowledge of the court systems in case they are called upon to assist in this area of the practice of law.

This chapter covers the federal courts and state courts of the United States.

Exhibit 6.1 Typical state court system

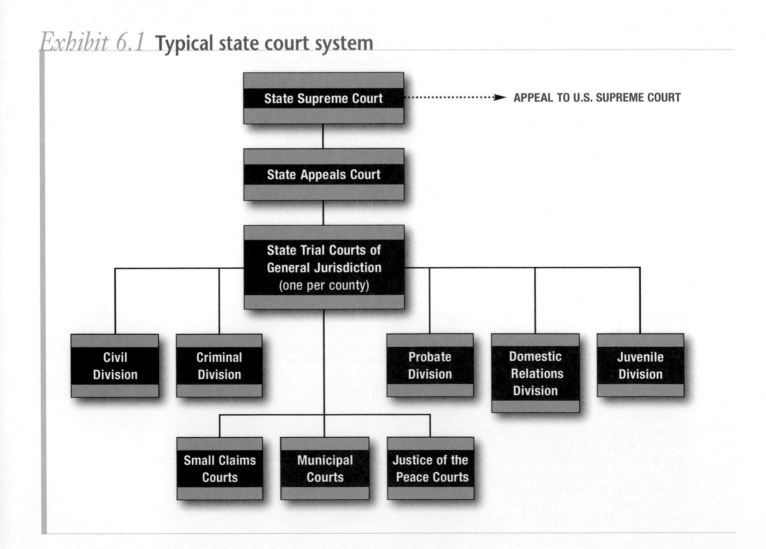

FEDERAL COURT SYSTEM

Article III of the U.S. Constitution provides that the federal government's judicial power is vested in one "supreme court." This court is the U.S. Supreme Court. The Constitution also authorizes Congress to establish "inferior" federal courts in the **federal court system**. Pursuant to this power, Congress has established special federal courts, the U.S. district courts, and the U.S. courts of appeal. Federal judges are appointed for life by the President with the advice and consent of the Senate (except bankruptcy court judges, who are appointed for 14-year terms, and U.S. Magistrate Judges, who are appointed for an 8-year term).

We're the Jury, dread our fury!
William S. Gilbert
Trial by Jury

Special Federal Courts

The **special federal courts** established by Congress have limited jurisdiction. They include:

- **U.S. Tax Court:** Hears cases involving federal tax laws
- **U.S. Court of Federal Claims:** Hears cases brought against the United States
- **U.S. Court of International Trade:** Hears cases involving tariffs and international commercial disputes
- **U.S. Bankruptcy Court:** Hears cases involving federal bankruptcy laws

U.S. District Courts

The **U.S. District Courts** are the federal court system's trial courts of general jurisdiction. The District of Columbia and each state have at least one federal district court; the more populated states have more than one. The geographical area that each court serves is referred to as a *district*. At present there are 96 federal district courts. The federal district courts are empowered to impanel juries, receive evidence, hear testimony, and decide cases. Most federal cases originate in federal district courts.

U.S. District Courts
The federal court system's trial courts of general jurisdiction.

U.S. Courts of Appeals

The **U.S. Courts of Appeals** are the federal court system's intermediate appellate courts. The federal court system has 13 circuits. **Circuit** refers to the geographical area served by a court. Eleven are designated by a number, such as the "First Circuit," "Second Circuit," and so on. The Twelfth Circuit court is located in Washington, D.C., and is called the District of Columbia Circuit.

As appellate courts, these circuit courts hear appeals from the district courts located in their circuit, as well as from certain special courts and federal administrative agencies. The courts review the record of the lower court or administrative agency proceedings to determine if any error would warrant reversal or modification of the lower court decision. No new evidence or testimony is heard. The parties file legal briefs with the court

U.S. Courts of Appeals
The federal court system's intermediate appellate courts.

www

Find the location of the U.S. District Court that hears lawsuits that originate in your city at http://www.uscourts.gov/courtsofappeals.html

MEET THE COURTHOUSE TEAM

U.S. Magistrate Judge

Magistrate judges are appointed by the U.S. district court to serve an 8-year term. Their duties fall into four general categories: (1) conducting most of the initial proceedings in criminal cases; (2) trying certain criminal misdemeanor cases; (3) trying civil cases with the consent of a party; and (4) conducting a wide variety of other proceedings referred to them by district judges.

Exhibit 6.2 **Federal circuit courts of appeals**

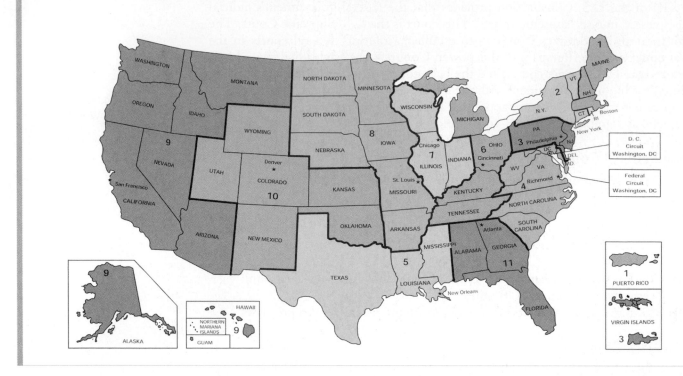

U.S. Court for the Federal Circuit:
www.fedcir.gov/

and are given a short oral hearing. Appeals usually are heard by a three-judge panel. After the panel renders a decision, a petitioner can request a review *en banc* by the full court.

The Thirteenth Circuit court of appeals was created by Congress in 1982. Called the **Court of Appeals for the Federal Circuit** and located in Washington, D.C., this court has special appellate jurisdiction to review the decisions of the Court of Federal Claims, the Patent and Trademark Office, and the Court of International Trade. This court of appeals was created to provide uniformity in the application of federal law in certain areas, particularly patent law.

The map in Exhibit 6.2 shows the 13 federal circuit courts of appeals.

U.S. Supreme Court

The highest court in the land is the **Supreme Court of the United States** located in Washington, D.C. This court is composed of nine justices who are nominated by the President and confirmed by the Senate. The President appoints one justice as **chief justice**, responsible for the administration of the Supreme Court. The other eight justices are **associate justices**.

U.S. Supreme Court
The Supreme Court was created by Article III of the U.S. Constitution. The Supreme Court is the highest court in the land. It is located in Washington, DC.

The **U.S. Supreme Court**, which is an appellate court, hears appeals from federal circuit courts of appeals and, under certain circumstances, from federal district courts, special federal courts, and the highest state courts. The Supreme Court hears no evidence or testimony. As with other appellate courts, the lower court record is reviewed to determine whether an error has been committed that warrants a reversal or modification of the decision. Legal briefs are filed, and the parties are granted a brief oral hearing. The Supreme Court's decision is final.

Exhibit 6.3 illustrates the federal court system.

The U.S. Constitution gives Congress the authority to establish rules for the appellate review of cases by the Supreme Court, except in the rare case where manda-

Exhibit 6.3 **Federal court system**

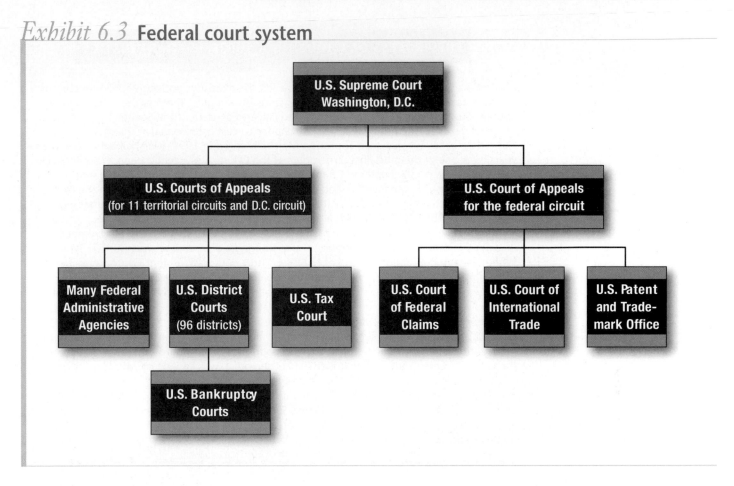

tory review is required. Congress has given the Supreme Court discretion to decide what cases it will hear.

A petitioner must file a **petition for certiorari** asking the Supreme Court to hear the case. If the Court decides to review a case, it will issue a **writ of certiorari**. Because the Court issues only about 150 to 200 opinions each year, writs usually are granted only in cases involving constitutional and other important issues.

Each justice of the Supreme Court, including the chief justice, has an equal vote. The Supreme Court can issue the following types of decisions:

- **Unanimous decision.** If all of the justices voting agree as to the outcome and reasoning used to decide the case, it is a unanimous opinion. Unanimous decisions are precedent for later cases.
- **Majority decision.** If a majority of the justices agree to the outcome and reasoning used to decide the case, it is a majority opinion. Majority decisions are precedent for later cases.
- **Plurality decision.** If a majority of the justices agree to the outcome of the case, but not to the reasoning for reaching the outcome, it is a plurality opinion. A plurality decision settles the case but is not precedent for later cases.
- **Tie decision.** Sometimes the Supreme Court sits without all nine justices present, because of illness or conflict of interest, or because a justice has not been confirmed to fill a vacant seat on the court. In the case of a tie vote, the lower court decision is affirmed. These votes are not precedent for later cases.

Petition for certiorari
A petition asking the Supreme Court to hear one's case.

Writ of certiorari
An official notice that the Supreme Court will review one's case.

THE PROCESS OF CHOOSING A SUPREME COURT JUSTICE

In an effort to strike a balance of power between the executive and legislative branches of government, Article II, Section 2 of the U.S. Constitution gives the president the power to appoint Supreme Court justices "with the advice and consent of the Senate."

President George Bush was given the chance to cast a conservative shadow over the Court's decisions when Justice Thurgood Marshall retired in 1991. Marshall, who served 24 years, was one of the most liberal members of the Court. Also, he had been the only Black person to serve on the Supreme Court. In 1991, President Bush nominated Clarence Thomas, a Black conservative serving as a judge of the U.S. Court of Appeals in the District of Columbia, to replace Marshall. After a heated political debate, Clarence Thomas was confirmed by the U.S. Senate with a 52–48 vote in October 1991.

The election of Bill Clinton as President swung the pendulum back to the Democrats. President Clinton got an early opportunity to nominate a candidate when Justice Byron R. White, a Democrat-appointed member of the Court, retired. President Clinton nominated Judge Ruth Bader Ginsburg to serve on the Supreme Court. Justice Ginsburg was considered a moderate liberal. Ginsburg was approved by a bipartisan vote of the Senate and took office for the Supreme Court's 1993–94 term.

George W. Bush, a Republican, became president of the United States in January 2001. In 2005, then presiding Chief Justice Rehnquist of the U.S. Supreme Court died. President Bush nominated John G. Roberts Jr., a circuit court justice, to be the next Chief Justice of the U.S. Supreme Court. Justice Roberts, a conservative, was easily confirmed by the Senate to the post as Chief Justice of the Supreme Court.

In 2005, Justice Sandra Day O'Conner, the centrist vote of the Court, resigned from the Supreme Court. President Bush nominated Samuel A. Alito, Jr., a conservative circuit of appeals justice, to fill the vacancy. After contentious hearings, Justice Alito was confirmed by a 58–42 vote of the Senate and took office as a justice of the U.S. Supreme Court.

---

www

Go to the website http://www. supremecourtus.gov

Read the section entitled "The Court and Its Procedures." When is the Court's term?

A justice who agrees with the outcome of a case but not the reason proffered by other justices can issue a **concurring opinion**, setting forth his or her reasons for deciding the case. A justice who does not agree with a decision can file a **dissenting opinion** that sets forth the reasons for his or her dissent.

JURISDICTION OF FEDERAL AND STATE COURTS

Article III, Section 2, of the U.S. Constitution sets forth the jurisdiction of federal courts. Federal courts have *limited jurisdiction* to hear cases involving:

Federal question
A case arising under the U.S. Constitution, treaties, or federal statutes and regulations.

Diversity of citizenship
A case between (1) citizens of different states, (2) a citizen of a state and a citizen or subject of a foreign country, and (3) a citizen of a state and a foreign country where a foreign country is the plaintiff.

- **Federal questions:** Cases arising under the U.S. Constitution, treaties, and federal statutes and regulations. Federal question cases that can be brought in federal court have no dollar-amount limit.
- **Diversity of citizenship:** Cases between (a) citizens of different states, (b) a citizen of a state and a citizen or subject of a foreign country, and (c) a citizen of a state and a foreign country where the foreign country is the plaintiff. A corporation is considered to be a citizen of the state in which it is incorporated and in which it has its principal place of business. The reason for providing diversity of citizenship jurisdiction was to prevent state court bias against nonresidents. The federal court must apply the appropriate state's law in deciding the case. The dollar amount of the controversy must exceed $75,000. If this requirement is not met, the action must be brought in the appropriate state court.

Federal courts have **exclusive jurisdiction** to hear cases involving federal crimes, antitrust, bankruptcy, patent and copyright cases, suits against the United States, and most admiralty cases. State courts cannot hear these cases.

"I'LL TAKE YOU TO THE U.S. SUPREME COURT!"

In theory, in the United States you can appeal your legal case all the way to the U.S. Supreme Court. In reality, however, the chance of ever having your case heard by the highest court in the land is slim to none.

Each year, more than 8,000 petitioners ask the Supreme Court to hear their cases. These petitioners usually pay big law firms from $50,000 to $200,000 or more to write the appeal petition. In recent years, the Supreme Court has accepted fewer than 100 of these cases for full review each term.

Each of the nine Supreme Court justices has three law clerks—recent law school graduates usually chosen from the elite law schools across the country—who assist them. The justices rarely read the appellate petitions but instead delegate this task to their law clerks. A clerk then writes a short memorandum, discussing the key issues raised by the appeal, and recommends to the justices whether they should grant or deny a review. The justices meet once a week to discuss what cases merit review. The votes of four justices are necessary to grant an appeal and schedule an oral argument before the Court ("rule of four"). Written opinions by the justices usually are issued many months later.

So what does it take to win a review by the Supreme Court? The U.S. Supreme Court usually decides to hear cases involving major constitutional questions such as freedom of speech, freedom of religion, and due process. The Court, therefore, rarely decides day-to-day legal issues such as breach of contract, tort liability, or corporation law unless they involve more important constitutional or federal law questions. Often a case is not heard unless there was a "split" in the circuit courts of appeal—that is, several circuit courts have decided the legal issue differently. The Supreme Court's ruling resolves the split among the circuit courts.

So the next time you hear someone say, "I'll take you to the U.S. Supreme Court!" just say, "Not!"

State and federal courts have **concurrent jurisdiction** to hear cases involving diversity of citizenship and federal questions over which federal courts do not have exclusive jurisdiction (e.g., cases involving federal securities laws). If a plaintiff brings a case involving concurrent jurisdiction in state court, the defendant can remove the case to federal court. If a case does not qualify to be brought in federal court, it must be brought in the appropriate state court.

Standing to Sue

To bring a lawsuit, a plaintiff must have **standing to sue**. That is, the plaintiff must have some stake in the outcome of the lawsuit.

Consider this example: Linda's friend Jon is injured in an accident caused by Emily. Jon refuses to sue. Linda cannot sue Emily on Jon's behalf because she does not have an interest in the result of the case.

Courts hear and decide actual disputes involving specific controversies. Hypothetical questions will not be heard, and trivial lawsuits will be dismissed.

Types of Jurisdiction

A court must have **jurisdiction** to hear and decide a case. The two types of jurisdiction are: (1) subject-matter jurisdiction, and (2) *in personam, in rem,* or *quasi in rem* jurisdiction.

1. *Subject-matter jurisdiction.* Some courts have only limited jurisdiction. To hear and decide a case, a court must have **subject-matter jurisdiction** over the type of case. For example, federal courts have jurisdiction to hear only certain types of cases (discussed later in this

Subject-matter jurisdiction
Jurisdiction over the subject matter of a lawsuit.

chapter) and certain state courts, such as probate courts and small-claims courts, can hear only designated types of cases. If a court does not have subject-matter jurisdiction, it cannot hear the case.

2. *In personam, in rem* and *quasi in rem jurisdictions.* Jurisdiction over the person is called ***in personam*** **jurisdiction**, or **personal jurisdiction**. By filing a lawsuit with a court, a **plaintiff** gives the court *in personam* jurisdiction over himself or herself. The court also must have *in personam* jurisdiction over the **defendant**, which usually is obtained by having that person served a summons within the territorial boundaries of the state, called **service of process**.

Service of process usually is accomplished by personally serving the summons and complaint on the defendant. If this is not possible, alternative forms of notice, such as mailing the summons or publishing a notice in a newspaper, may be permitted. A corporation is subject to personal jurisdiction in the state in which it is incorporated, has its

In personam **jurisdiction**
Jurisdiction over the parties to a lawsuit.

ETHICAL *Perspective*

Mr. Antonio Alvarez is a paralegal in a law firm and works directly with Ms. Gloria Dawson, a partner in the law firm. In addition to her law practice with the law firm, Ms. Dawson volunteers to work one evening per week at a domestic abuse center that serves females and their children.

At the center, Ms. Dawson interviews domestic abuse victims and pursues whatever legal actions that can be taken to assist the victims and their families. This often includes doing the legal work for obtaining restraining orders, government assistance, and spousal and child support. All of Ms. Dawson's services at the domestic abuse center are provided *pro bono*, that is, for free.

One day Ms. Dawson asks her paralegal, Mr. Alvarez, if he would be interested in volunteering to help her one night each month at the domestic abuse shelter. Ms. Dawson explains that she could use Mr. Alvarez's assistance as a paralegal to help conduct interviews, prepare documents, and obtain government and other assistance for the domestic abuse victims and their families. Mr. Alvarez would be under the supervision of Ms. Dawson while working at the center.

Does a paralegal owe an ethical duty to provide *pro bono* services to the public? Section EC-1.4(c) of the *Model Code of Ethics and Professional Responsibility and Guidance for Enforcement* (Model Code) of the National Federation of Paralegal Associations, Inc. (NFPA) states

> *A paralegal shall support and participate in the delivery of Pro Bono Publico services directed toward implementing and improving access to justice, the law, the legal system or the paralegal and legal professions.*

State and local paralegal ethics codes and codes of professional responsibility emphasize the importance of *pro bono* activities by paralegals as well.

Section EC-1.4(d) of NFPA's Model Code provides:

> *A paralegal should aspire annually to contribute twenty-four (24) hours of Pro Bono Publico services under the supervision of an attorney or as authorized by administrative, statutory or court authority to:*
>
> 1. *persons of limited means; or*
> 2. *charitable, religious, civic, community, governmental and educational organizations in matters that are designed primarily to address the legal needs of persons with limited means; or*
> 3. *individuals, groups or organizations seeking to secure or protect civil rights, civil liberties or public rights.*

Mr. Alvarez agrees to assist Ms. Dawson at the domestic abuse shelter one evening each month. As a paralegal, would you agree to provide *pro bono* services to those in need of help?

principal office, and is doing business. A party who disputes the jurisdiction of a court can make a **special appearance** in that court to argue against the imposition of jurisdiction. Service of process is not permitted during such an appearance.

A court may have jurisdiction to hear and decide a case because it has jurisdiction over the property of the lawsuit: This is called *in rem* **jurisdiction** ("jurisdiction over the thing"). For example, a state court would have jurisdiction to hear a dispute over the ownership of a piece of real estate located within the state. This is so even if one or more of the disputing parties lives in another state or states.

Sometimes a plaintiff who obtains a judgment against a defendant in one state will try to collect the judgment by attaching property of the defendant that is located in another state. This is permitted under *quasi in rem* **jurisdiction**, or **attachment jurisdiction**.

Long-Arm Statutes

In most states, a state court can obtain jurisdiction over persons and businesses located in another state or country through the state's **long-arm statute**. These statutes extend a state's jurisdiction to nonresidents who were not served a summons within the state. The nonresident must have had some *minimum contact* with the state [*International Shoe Co. v. Washington*, 326 U.S. 310, 66 S.Ct. 154, 90 L.Ed. 95, 1945 U.S. Lexis 1447 (1945)]. In addition, maintenance of the suit must uphold the traditional notions of fair play and substantial justice.

The exercise of long-arm jurisdiction is generally permitted over nonresidents who have (1) committed torts within the state (e.g., caused an automobile accident in the state), (2) entered into a contract either in the state or that affects the state (and allegedly breached the contract), or (3) transacted other business in the state that allegedly caused injury to another person.

In rem jurisdiction
Jurisdiction to hear a case because of jurisdiction over the property of the lawsuit.

Quasi in rem (attachment) jurisdiction
Jurisdiction allowed a plaintiff who obtains a judgment in one state to try to collect the judgment by attaching property of the defendant located in another state.

Long-arm statute
A statute that extends a state's jurisdiction to nonresidents who were not served a summons within the state.

THE PARALEGAL AND ALTERNATIVE DISPUTE RESOLUTION

The growth in using alternative dispute resolution to solve disputes has been phenomenal. Alternative dispute resolution is just that—an alternative to using the litigation process and court systems to resolve disputes.

The major form of alternative dispute resolution is arbitration. The United States Supreme Court has upheld the use of arbitration in many types of disputes. Arbitration is used particularly in contract disputes, because many contracts contain arbitration clauses— that is, the parties to the contract have agreed in their contract not to use the court systems to solve their disputes. Instead, they have expressly agreed that an arbitrator, and not a jury, will resolve their dispute.

Most major companies have placed arbitration agreements in their contracts. For example, arbitration clauses appear in contracts to purchase goods, to lease automobiles, to employ services, and in other types of contracts. Also, arbitration clauses are included by employers in many employment contracts. Thus, if an employee has a dispute with his or her employer, the dispute goes to arbitration for resolution because the employee has given up his or her right to use the court system by agreeing to the arbitration clause.

Mediation also has become an indispensable method of helping to solve disputes. In mediation, the mediator does not act as a decision-maker but, instead, acts as a facilitator to try to help the disputing parties reach a settlement of their dispute. Mediation often is used in family law matters, particularly in helping reach a settlement in divorce cases.

Paralegals who work for lawyers in business law-related matters, contract disputes, and family law matters should have a thorough understanding of alternative dispute resolution. Paralegals often are called upon to help attorneys prepare for arbitration, mediation, and other forms of alternative dispute resolution. This chapter addresses the major forms of alternative dispute resolution.

OBTAINING JURISDICTION IN CYBERSPACE

Obtaining personal jurisdiction over a defendant located in another state has always been a difficult issue for the courts. States have enacted long-arm statutes that permit the courts located in one state to reach out and make people in another state come to court and defend themselves. To make sure that this is not overly burdensome the U.S. Supreme Court has held that out-of-state defendants must have had certain "minimum contacts" with the state before they are made to answer to a lawsuit there [*International Shoe Co. v. Washington*, 326 U.S. 310, 66 S.Ct. 154 (1945)].

Today, with the advent of the Internet and the ability of persons and businesses to reach millions of people in other states electronically, applying the *International Shoe* minimum-contacts standard is even more difficult.

Several courts have decided cases involving the reach of a state's long-arm statute to obtain jurisdiction over someone in another state because of his or her Internet activities. In one case: Zippo Manufacturing Company (Zippo) sued Zippo Dot Com, Inc. (Dot Com) in federal district court in Pennsylvania. Zippo manufactures its well-known line of Zippo tobacco lighters in Bradford, Pennsylvania, and sells them worldwide. Dot Com, a California corporation with its principal place of business and its servers located in Sunnyvale, California, operates an Internet website that transmits information and sexually explicit material to its subscribers. Of Dot Com's 140,000 paying subscribers worldwide, 3,000 are located in Pennsylvania.

Zippo sued Dot Com in federal district court in Pennsylvania for trademark infringement. Dot Com alleged that it was not subject to personal jurisdiction in Pennsylvania. The district court applied the *International Shoe* "minimum-contacts" standard and held that Dot Com was subject to personal jurisdiction under the Pennsylvania long-arm statute and ordered Dot Com to defend itself there [*Zippo Manufacturing Company v. Zippo Dot Com, Inc.*, 952 F.Supp. 1119 (W.D.Pa. 1997)]

Parties to a contract may include a **forum-selection clause** that designates a certain court to hear any dispute concerning nonperformance of the contract.

Venue

Venue
A concept that requires lawsuits to be heard by the court with jurisdiction that is nearest the location in which the incident occurred or where the parties reside.

Venue requires lawsuits to be heard by the court with jurisdiction nearest the location in which the incident occurred or where the parties reside. For example, Harry, a Georgia resident, commits a felony crime in Los Angeles County, California. The California Superior Court, located in Los Angeles, is the proper venue because the crime was committed there, the witnesses are probably from the area, and so on.

Occasionally, pretrial publicity may prejudice jurors located in the proper venue. In these cases, a **change of venue** may be requested so a more impartial jury can be found. The courts generally frown upon *forum shopping* (i.e., looking for a favorable court without a valid reason).

ALTERNATIVE DISPUTE RESOLUTION

Negotiation

Negotiation
A procedure in which the parties to a dispute engage in negotiations to try to reach a voluntary settlement of their dispute.

The simplest form of alternative dispute resolution is engaging in negotiation between the parties to try to settle a dispute. **Negotiation** is a procedure whereby the parties to a dispute engage in negotiations to try to reach a voluntary settlement of their dispute. Negotiation may take place either before a lawsuit is filed, after a lawsuit is filed, or before other forms of alternative dispute resolution are engaged in.

In a negotiation, the parties, who often are represented by attorneys, negotiate with each other to try to reach an agreeable solution to their dispute. During negotiation proceedings, the parties usually make offers and counteroffers to one another. The parties or their attorneys also may provide information to the other side that would assist the other side in reaching an amicable settlement.

Many courts require that the parties to a lawsuit engage in settlement discussions prior to trial to try to negotiate a settlement of the case. The judge must be assured that a settlement of the case is not possible before he or she permits the case to go to trial. Judges often convince the parties to engage in further negotiations if the judge determines that the parties are not too far apart in the negotiations of a settlement.

If a settlement of the dispute is reached through negotiation, a settlement agreement is drafted that contains the terms of the agreement. A **settlement agreement** is an agreement that is voluntarily entered into by the parties to a dispute that settles the dispute. Each side must sign the settlement agreement for it to be effective. The settlement agreement usually is submitted to the court, and the case will be dismissed based on execution of the settlement agreement.

Settlement agreement
An agreement voluntarily entered into by the parties to a dispute that settles the dispute.

Use of the court system to resolve business and other disputes can take years and cost thousands, if not millions, of dollars in legal fees and expenses. In commercial litigation, the normal business operations of the parties are often disrupted. To avoid or lessen these problems, businesses are increasingly turning to methods of **alternative dispute resolution (ADR)** and other aids to resolving disputes. The most common form of ADR is negotiation. Other forms of ADR are *mediation, conciliation, minitrial, fact-finding*, and a *judicial referee*.

Alternative dispute resolution (ADR)
Methods of resolving disputes other than litigation.

Arbitration

In **arbitration**, the parties choose an impartial third party to hear and decide the dispute. This neutral party is called the **arbitrator:** Arbitrators usually are selected from members of the American Arbitration Association (AAA) or another arbitration association. Labor union agreements, franchise agreements, leases, and other commercial contracts often contain **arbitration clauses** that require disputes arising out of the contract to be submitted to arbitration. If there is no arbitration clause, the parties can enter into a **submission agreement**, whereby they agree to submit a dispute to arbitration after the dispute arises.

Arbitration
A form of ADR in which the parties choose an impartial third party to hear and decide the dispute.

The benefits of arbitration are that it is less expensive than litigation, is completed faster than a lawsuit, and is decided by a person who is knowledgeable in the area of law that is in dispute. Some consumers and employees who are subject to arbitration agreements argue that arbitration unfairly favors businesses and employers over them.

Exhibit 6.4 is the form for a Demand for Arbitration.

Federal Arbitration Act

The Federal Arbitration Act (FAA) was originally enacted by Congress in 1925 to reverse the longstanding judicial hostility to arbitration agreements that had existed as English common law and had been adopted by American courts [9 U.S.C. Sections 1 et. seq.]. The Act provides that arbitration agreements involving commerce are valid, irrevocable, and enforceable contracts, unless some grounds exist at law or equity (e.g., fraud, duress) to revoke them. The FAA permits one party to obtain a court order to compel arbitration if the other party has failed, neglected, or refused to comply with an arbitration agreement.

About half of the states have adopted the **Uniform Arbitration Act**, which promotes the arbitration of disputes at the state level. Many federal and state courts have instituted programs to refer legal disputes to arbitration or another form of alternative dispute resolution.

ADR Providers

ADR services usually are provided by private organizations or individuals who qualify to hear and decide certain disputes. For example, the **American Arbitration Association (AAA)** is the largest private provider of ADR services. The AAA employs persons who are qualified in special areas of the law to provide mediation and arbitration services in those areas. These persons are called **neutrals**.

Exhibit 6.4 **Demand for arbitration**

American Arbitration Association
Dispute Resolution Services Worldwide

_____ARBITRATION RULES
(ENTER THE NAME OF THE APPLICABLE RULES)
Demand for Arbitration

MEDIATION: If you would like the AAA to contact the other parties and attempt to arrange mediation, please check this box. ☐
There is no additional administrative fee for this service.

Name of Respondent	Name of Representative (if known)
Address:	Name of Firm (if applicable):
	Representative's Address

City	State	Zip Code	City	State	Zip Code
Phone No.		Fax No.	Phone No.		Fax No.
Email Address:			Email Address:		

The named claimant, a party to an arbitration agreement dated _____, which provides for arbitration under the
_____Arbitration Rules of the American Arbitration Association, hereby demands arbitration.

THE NATURE OF THE DISPUTE

Dollar Amount of Claim $	Other Relief Sought: ☐ Attorneys Fees ☐ Interest ☐ Arbitration Costs ☐ Punitive/ Exemplary ☐ Other _____

AMOUNT OF FILING FEE ENCLOSED WITH THIS DEMAND (please refer to the fee schedule in the rules for the appropriate fee) $

PLEASE DESCRIBE APPROPRIATE QUALIFICATIONS FOR ARBITRATOR(S) TO BE APPOINTED TO HEAR THIS DISPUTE:

Hearing locale_____ (check one) ☐ Requested by Claimant ☐ Locale provision included in the contract

Estimated time needed for hearings overall: _____hours or _____days	Type of Business: Claimant _____ Respondent_____

Is this a dispute between a business and a consumer? ☐Yes ☐No
Does this dispute arise out of an employment relationship? ☐Yes ☐No

If this dispute arises out of an employment relationship, what was/is the employee's annual wage range? Note: This question is required by California law. ☐Less than $100,000 ☐ $100,000 - $250,000 ☐ Over $250,000

You are hereby notified that copies of our arbitration agreement and this demand are being filed with the American Arbitration Association's Case Management Center, located in (check one) ☐ Atlanta, GA ☐ Dallas, TX   ☐ East Providence, RI ☐ Fresno, CA ☐ International Centre, NY, with a request that it commence administration of the arbitration. Under the rules, you may file an answering statement within the timeframe specified in the rules, after notice from the AAA.

Signature (may be signed by a representative) Date:	Name of Representative
Name of Claimant	Name of Firm (if applicable)
Address (to be used in connection with this case):	Representative's Address:

City	State	Zip Code	City	State	Zip Code
Phone No.		Fax No.	Phone No.		Fax No.
Email Address:			Email Address:		

To begin proceedings, please send two copies of this Demand and the Arbitration Agreement, along with the filing fee as provided for in the Rules, to the AAA. Send the original Demand to the Respondent.
Please visit our website at www.adr.org if you would like to file this case online. AAA Customer Service can be reached at 800-778-7879

Source: Reprinted with permission of American Arbitration Association.

For example, if parties have a contract dispute involving an employment contract, a construction contract, an Internet contract, or other commercial contract or business dispute, the AAA has a special group of neutrals that can hear and decide these cases. Other mediation and arbitration associations are located throughout the United States and internationally.

ADR Procedure

An arbitration agreement often describes the specific procedures that must be followed for a case to proceed to and through arbitration. If one party seeks to enforce an arbitration clause, that party must give notice to the other party. The parties then select an arbitration association or arbitrator as provided in the agreement. The parties usually agree on the date, time, and place of the arbitration. This can be at the arbitrator's offices, at a law office, or at any other agreed-upon location.

At the arbitration, the parties can call witnesses to give testimony, and introduce evidence to support their case and refute the other side's case. Rules similar to those followed by federal courts usually are adhered to at the arbitration. Often, each party pays a filing fee and other fees for the arbitration. Sometimes the agreement provides that one party will pay all of the costs of the arbitration. Arbitrators are paid by the hour or day, or other agreed-upon method of compensation.

Decision and Award

After the hearing is complete, the arbitrator reaches a decision and issues an **award**. The parties often agree in advance to be bound by an arbitrator's decision and remedy. This is called **binding arbitration**. In this situation, the decision and award of the arbitrator cannot be appealed to the courts. If the arbitration is not binding, the decision and award of the arbitrator can be appealed to the courts. This is called **nonbinding arbitration**. Courts usually give great deference to an arbitrator's decision and award.

If a decision and award has been rendered by an arbitrator but a party refuses to abide by the arbitrator's decision, the other party may file an action in court to have the arbitrator's decision enforced. For example, assume that there has been a contract dispute between NorthWest Corporation and SouthEast Corporation that goes to binding arbitration. The arbitrator issues a decision that awards SouthEast Corporation $5 million against NorthWest Corporation. If NorthWest Corporation fails to pay the award, SouthEast Corporation can file an action in court to have the award enforced by the court.

Mediation

Mediation is a form of negotiation in which a neutral third party assists the disputing parties in reaching a settlement of their dispute. The neutral third party is called a **mediator**. The mediator usually is a person who is an expert in the area of the dispute, or a lawyer or retired judge. The mediator is selected by the parties as provided in

Mediation
A form of negotiation in which a neutral third party assists the disputing parties in reaching a settlement of their dispute.

Mediator
A neutral third party who assists the disputing parties in reaching a settlement of their dispute. The mediator cannot make a decision or an award.

ONLINE ADR

Several services now offer **online arbitration**. Most of these services allow a party to a dispute to register the dispute with the service and then notify the other party by email of the registration of the dispute. Most online arbitration requires the registering party to submit an amount that the party is willing to accept or pay to the other party in the online arbitration. The other party is afforded the opportunity to accept the offer. If that party accepts the offer, a settlement has been reached. The other party, however, may return a **counteroffer**. The process continues until a settlement is reached or one or both of the parties remove themselves from the online ADR process.

Also, several websites offer **online mediation** services. In an online mediation, the parties sit before their computers and sign onto the site. Two chat rooms are assigned to each party. One chat room is used for private conversations with the online mediator, and the other chat room is for conversations with both parties and the mediator.

Online arbitration and mediation services charge fees for their services. The fees are reasonable. In an online arbitration or mediation, a settlement can be reached rather quickly without paying lawyers' fees and court costs. The parties also are acting through a more objective online process than meeting face-to-face or negotiating over the telephone, either of which could conclude with verbal arguments.

their agreement, or as otherwise selected by the parties. Unlike an arbitrator, however, a mediator does not make a decision or an award.

A mediator's role is to assist the parties in reaching a settlement. The mediator usually acts as an intermediary between the parties. In many cases the mediator will meet with the two parties at an agreed-upon location, often the mediator's office or one of the offices of the parties. The mediator then will meet with both parties, usually separately, to discuss their side of the case.

After discussing the facts of the case with both sides, the mediator will encourage settlement of the dispute and will transmit settlement offers from one side to the other. In doing so, the mediator points out the strengths and weaknesses of each party's case and gives his or her opinion to each side why they should decrease or increase their settlement offers. The mediator's job is to facilitate settlement of the case.

The mediator gives his or her opinion to the parties as to what he or she believes to be a reasonable settlement of the case, and usually proposes settlement of the dispute. The parties are free to accept or reject such proposal. If the parties agree to a settlement, a settlement agreement is drafted that expresses their agreement. Execution of the settlement agreement ends the dispute. The parties, of course, must perform their duties under the settlement agreement.

Exhibit 6.5 is the form for a Request for Mediation.

Conciliation

Conciliation

A form of dispute resolution in which a conciliator transmits offers and counteroffers between the disputing parties in helping to reach a settlement of their dispute.

Conciliator

A third party in a conciliation proceeding who assists the disputing parties in reaching a settlement of their dispute. The conciliator cannot make a decision or an award.

Conciliation is another form of alternative dispute resolution. In conciliation, a party named a **conciliator** helps the parties to try to reach a resolution of their dispute. Conciliation often is used when the parties refuse to face each other in an adversarial setting. The conciliator schedules meetings and appointments during which information can be transferred between the parties. A conciliator usually carries offers and counteroffers for a settlement back and forth between the disputing parties. A conciliator cannot make a decision or an award.

Although the role of a conciliator is not to propose a settlement of the case, many often do. In many cases, conciliators are neutral third parties, although in some circumstances the parties may select an interested third party to act as the conciliator. If the parties reach a settlement of their dispute through the use of conciliation, a settlement agreement is drafted and executed by the parties.

Minitrial

Minitrial

A voluntary private proceeding in which the lawyers for each side present a shortened version of their case to representatives of the other side, and usually to a neutral third party, in an attempt to reach a settlement of the dispute.

A **minitrial** is a voluntary private proceeding in which the lawyers for each side present a shortened version of their case to the representatives of the other side. The representatives of each side who attend the minitrial have the authority to settle the dispute. In many cases, the parties also hire a neutral third party, often someone who is an expert in the field concerning the disputed matter or a legal expert, who presides over the minitrial. After hearing the case, the neutral third party often is called upon to render an opinion as to how the court would most likely decide the case.

During a minitrial, the parties get to see the strengths and weaknesses of their own position and that of the opposing side. Once the strengths and weaknesses of both sides are exposed, the parties to a minitrial often settle the case. The parties also often settle a minitrial based on the opinion rendered by the neutral third party. If the parties settle their dispute after a minitrial, they will enter into a settlement agreement setting forth their agreement.

Minitrials serve a useful purpose in that they act as a substitute for the real trial, but they are much briefer and not as complex and expensive to prepare for. By exposing the strengths and weaknesses of both sides' cases, the parties usually are more realistic regarding their own position and the merits of setting the case prior to an expensive, and often more risky, trial.

Exhibit 6.5 **Request for mediation**

American Arbitration Association
Dispute Resolution Services Worldwide

REQUEST FOR MEDIATION

Name of Responding Party	Name of Representative (if known)
Address:	Name of Firm (if applicable)
	Representative's Address:

City	State	Zip Code	City	State	Zip Code
Phone No.		Fax No.	Phone No.		Fax No.
Email Address:			Email Address:		

The undersigned party to an agreement contained in a written contract dated _____, providing for mediation under the
_____ Mediation Procedures of the American Arbitration Association, hereby requests mediation

THE NATURE OF THE DISPUTE

CLAIM OR RELIEF SOUGHT (amount, if any):

AMOUNT OF FILING FEE ENCLOSED WITH THIS REQUEST: $

Mediation locale_____ (check one) ☐ Requested by Filing Party ☐ Locale provision included in the contract

Type of Business: Filing Party _____   Responding Party_____

You are hereby notified that copies of our mediation agreement and this request are being filed with the American Arbitration Association's Case Management Center, located in (check one) ☐ Atlanta, GA ☐ Dallas, TX ☐ East Providence, RI ☐ Fresno, CA ☐ International Centre, NY, with a request that it commence administration of this mediation.

Signature (may be signed by a representative) Date:	Name of Representative
Name of Filling Party	Name of Firm (if applicable)
Address (to be used in connection with this case):	Representative's Address:

City	State	Zip Code	City	State	Zip Code
Phone No.		Fax No.	Phone No.		Fax No.
Email Address:			Email Address:		

To begin proceedings, please send two copies of this Request and the Mediation Agreement, along with the filing fee as provided for in the Rules, to the AAA. Send the original Request to the responding party.

Please visit our website at www.adr.org if you would like to file this case online. AAA Customer Service can be reached at 800-778-7879

Source: Reprinted with permission of American Arbitration Association.

Fact-Finding

In some situations, called fact-finding, the parties to a dispute will employ a neutral third party to act as a fact-finder to investigate the dispute. The fact-finder is authorized to investigate the dispute, gather evidence, prepare demonstrative evidence, and prepare reports of his or her findings.

A fact-finder is not authorized to make a decision or award. In some cases, a fact-finder will recommend settlement of the case. The fact-finder presents the evidence

---

UNITED STATES SUPREME COURT UPHOLDS ARBITRATION CLAUSE

In October 1995, Saint Clair Adams was hired as a sales counselor by Circuit City Stores, Inc., a national retailer of consumer electronics. Adams signed an employment contract that included the following arbitration clause:

I agree that I will settle any and all previously unasserted claims, disputes or controversies arising out of or relating to my application or candidacy for employment, employment and/or cessation of employment with Circuit City, *exclusively* by final and binding *arbitration* before a neutral Arbitrator. By way of example only, such claims include claims under federal, state, and local statutory or common law, such as the Age Discrimination in Employment Act. Title VII of the Civil Rights Act of 1964, the Americans with Disabilities Act, the law of contract and the law of tort.

Two years later Adams filed an employment discrimination lawsuit against Circuit City in court. Circuit City sought to enjoin the court proceeding and to compel arbitration, pursuant to the Federal Arbitration Act (FAA). The district court granted Circuit City's request. The court of appeals reversed, holding that employment contracts are not subject to arbitration. The U.S. Supreme Court granted certiorari to hear the appeal. The U.S. Supreme Court decided the case as follows.

The U.S. Supreme Court held that employment contracts including the one in this case between Circuit City and Adams are subject to arbitration if an arbitration agreement has been executed. The Supreme Court reversed the decision of the Court of Appeals and remanded the case.

Source: *Circuit City Stores, Inc. v. Adams.* 532 U.S. 105, 121 S.Ct. 1302, 149 L.Ed.2d 234 2001 U.S. 2459 Supreme Court of the United States

---

and findings to the parties, who then may use such information in negotiating a settlement if they wish.

Judicial Referee

If the parties agree, the court may appoint a **judicial referee** to conduct a private trial and render a judgment. Referees, who often are retired judges, have most of the powers of a trial judge, and their decisions stand as a judgment of the court. The parties usually reserve their right to appeal.

Legal Terminology

Summary

CHAPTER 6

JUDICIAL AND ALTERNATIVE DISPUTE RESOLUTION

State Court Systems

Limited-Jurisdiction Trial Court	This state court hears matters of a specialized or limited nature (e.g., misdemeanor criminal matters, traffic tickets, civil matters under a certain dollar amount). Many states have created small-claims courts that hear small-dollar-amount civil cases (e.g., under $5,000) in which parties cannot be represented by lawyers.
General-Jurisdiction Trial Court	This is a state court that hears cases of a general nature that are not within the jurisdiction of limited-jurisdiction trial courts.
Intermediate Appellate Court	This state court hears appeals from state trial courts. The appellate court reviews the trial court record in making its decision; no new evidence is introduced at this level.
Highest State Court	Each state has a highest court in its court system. This court hears appeals from appellate courts and, where appropriate, trial courts. This court reviews the record in making its decision; no new evidence is introduced at this level. Most states call this court the *supreme court*.

Federal Court System

Federal Courts	The following are included:
	1. *Special Federal Courts:* federal courts that have specialized or limited jurisdiction. They include:
	  a. *U.S. tax court:* hears cases involving federal tax laws
	  b. *U.S. claims court:* hears cases brought against the United States
	  c. *U.S. Court of International Trade:* hears cases involving tariffs and international commercial disputes
	  d. *U.S. bankruptcy courts:* hear cases involving federal bankruptcy law
	2. *U.S. District Courts:* federal trial courts of general jurisdiction that hear cases that are not within the jurisdiction of specialized courts. Each state has at least one U.S. district court per state; more populated states have several district courts. The area served by one of these courts is called a *district*.

	3. *U.S. Courts of Appeals:* intermediate federal appellate courts that hear appeals from district courts located in their circuit, and in certain instances from special federal courts and federal administrative agencies. There are 12 geographical *circuits* in the United States. Eleven serve areas composed of several states, and another is located in Washington, DC. A thirteenth circuit court—the *Court of Appeals for the Federal Circuit*—is located in Washington, DC, and reviews patent, trademark, and international trade cases. 4. *U.S. Supreme Court:* highest court of the federal court system; hears appeals from the circuit courts and, in some instances, from special courts and U.S. district courts. The Court, located in Washington, DC, comprises nine justices, one of whom is named Chief Justice.
Decisions by U.S. Supreme Court	*Petition of certiorari and writ of certiorari:* To have a case heard by the U.S. Supreme Court, a petitioner must file a *petition for certiorari* with the Court. If the Court decides to hear the case, it will issue a *writ of certiorari.*
Voting by the U.S. Supreme Court	1. *Unanimous decision:* All of the justices agree as to the outcome and reasoning used to decide the case; the decision becomes precedent. 2. *Majority decision:* A majority of justices agrees as to the outcome and reasoning used to decide the case; the decision becomes precedent. 3. *Plurality decision:* A majority of the justices agrees to the outcome but not to the reasoning; the decision is not precedent. 4. *Tie decision:* If there is a tie vote, the lower court's decision stands; the decision is not precedent. 5. *Concurring opinion:* A justice who agrees as to the outcome of the case but not the reasoning used by other justices may write a concurring opinion setting forth his or her reasoning. 6. *Dissenting opinion:* A justice who disagrees with the outcome of a case may write a dissenting opinion setting forth his or her reasoning.

Jurisdiction of Federal and State Courts

Limited Jurisdiction	Federal courts may hear the following cases: 1. *Federal question:* cases arising under the U.S. Constitution, treaties, and federal statutes and regulations; no dollar-amount limit 2. *Diversity of citizenship:* cases between (a) citizens of different states, and (b) citizens of a state and a citizen or subject of a foreign country; federal courts must apply the appropriate state law in such cases. The controversy must exceed $75,000 for the federal court to hear the case.
Jurisdiction of State Courts	State courts hear some cases that may be heard by federal courts. 1. *Exclusive jurisdiction:* Federal courts have exclusive jurisdiction to hear cases involving federal crimes, antitrust, and bankruptcy; patent and copyright cases; suits against the United States; and most admiralty cases. State courts may not hear these matters. 2. *Concurrent jurisdiction:* State courts have concurrent jurisdiction to hear cases involving diversity of citizenship cases and federal question cases over which the federal courts do not have exclusive jurisdiction. The defendant may have the case removed to federal court.
Standing to Sue	To bring a lawsuit, the plaintiff must have some stake in the outcome of the lawsuit.
Subject-Matter Jurisdiction	The court must have jurisdiction over the subject matter of the lawsuit; each court has limited jurisdiction to hear only certain types of cases.

In Personam Jurisdiction (or Personal Jurisdiction)	The court must have jurisdiction over the parties to a lawsuit. The plaintiff submits to the jurisdiction of the court by filing the lawsuit there. Personal jurisdiction is obtained over the defendant by serving that person *service of process*.
In Rem Jurisdiction	A court may have jurisdiction to hear and decide a case because it has jurisdiction over the property at issue in the lawsuit (e.g., real property located in the state).
Quasi In Rem Jurisdiction (or Attachment Jurisdiction)	A plaintiff who obtains a judgment against a defendant in one state may utilize the court system of another state to attach property of the defendant's located in the second state.
Long-Arm Statutes	These statutes permit a state to obtain personal jurisdiction over an out-of-state defendant as long as the defendant had the requisite minimum contact with the state. The out-of-state defendant may be served process outside the state in which the lawsuit has been brought.
Venue	A case must be heard by the court that has jurisdiction nearest to where the incident at issue occurred or where the parties reside. A *change of venue* will be granted if prejudice would occur because of pretrial publicity or another reason.
Forum-Selection Clause	This clause in a contract designates the court that will hear any dispute that arises out of the contract.

Alternative Dispute Resolution (ADR)

ADR	ADR consists of *nonjudicial* means of solving legal disputes. ADR usually saves time and money required by litigation.
Negotiation	

Arbitration	1. Arbitration is a form of ADR where an impartial third party, called the arbitrator, hears and decides the dispute. The arbitrator makes an award. The award is appealable to a court if the parties have not given up this right. Arbitration is designated by the parties pursuant to:
	   a. *Arbitration clause:* Agreement contained in a contract stipulating that any dispute arising out of the contract will be arbitrated.
	   b. *Submission agreement:* Agreement to submit a dispute to arbitration after the dispute arises.
	2. Federal Arbitration Act (FAA) is a federal statute that provides that arbitration agreements involving commerce are valid, irrevocable, and enforceable contracts, unless some grounds exist at law or equity (e.g., fraud, duress) to revoke them.

Mediation	In mediation, a neutral third party, called a *mediator*, assists the parties in trying to reach a settlement of their dispute. The mediator does not make an award.
Conciliation	In conciliation, an interested third party, called a *conciliator*, assists the parties in trying to reach a settlement of their dispute. The conciliator does not make an award.
Minitrial	A minitrial is in a short session, the lawyers for each side present their case to representatives of each party who has the authority to settle the dispute.
Fact-finding	In fact-finding, the parties hire a neutral third person, called a *fact-finder*, to investigate the dispute and report his or her findings to the adversaries.
Judicial Referee	With the consent of the parties, the court can appoint a judicial referee (usually a retired judge or lawyer) to conduct a private trial and render a judgment. The judgment stands as the judgment of the court and may be appealed to the appropriate appellate court.

▶ WORKING THE WEB

1. Visit the website **http://www.clickNsettle. com**. What services are offered by this website? What are the costs of using this site's services?

2. Visit the website **http://www. internetneutral.com**. What services are offered by this site? What are the costs of these services?

3. Visit the website **http://www. supremecourtus.gov**. Go to the section entitled "About the Supreme Court." Find the biographies of the current justices of the U.S. Supreme Court. List the current justices. Which justice is the Chief Justice? For each justice, list which president nominated the justice to the Supreme Court and to which political party that President belonged.

4. Visit the website **http://www.abanet.org/ published/preview/briefs/home.html**. Select one of the case names. Find the

"Petitioner's Brief" for the selected case and either print out or write down the "Question Presented" for that case.

5. Visit the website **http://www.law.cornell. edu/supct/index.html**. Find the most recent decision of the U.S. Supreme Court. Read the case heading and the summary of the case. Who are the parties? What issue was presented to the Supreme Court? What was the decision of the Supreme Court?

6. Go to the website **http://www.adr.org**. overview. Read "A Brief Overview of the American Arbitration Association." Define a "neutral."

7. Find the homepage for the courts in your state. What are the names of the courts in your state? Draw a diagram of the courts of your state. Include limited-jurisdiction courts, general-jurisdiction trial courts, appellate courts, and the highest state court.

▶ CRITICAL THINKING AND WRITING QUESTIONS

1. Describe the difference between state limited-jurisdiction courts and general-jurisdiction courts.

2. What are the functions of the state intermediate courts and the highest state courts? Explain.

3. List the special federal courts, and describe the types of cases that each of these courts can hear.

4. What is the function of U.S. District Courts? How many are there?

5. What is the function of U.S. Courts of Appeals? How many U.S. Courts of Appeals are there? How does the Court of Appeals for the Federal Circuit differ from the other U.S. Courts of Appeals?

6. What is the function of the U.S. Supreme Court? How many justices does the Supreme Court have? How does the Chief Justice differ from Associate Justices?

7. Explain the difference between the following types of decisions by the U.S. Supreme Court: (1) unanimous decision, (2) majority decision, (3) plurality decision, and (4) tie decision. Which types of decision or decisions establish precedent? What are concurring opinions and dissenting opinions?

8. Explain the difference between a federal court's jurisdiction to hear a case based on (1) federal question jurisdiction and (2) diversity of citizenship jurisdiction.

9. Explain the difference between subject-matter jurisdiction and *in personam* jurisdiction. Explain the difference between *in rem jurisdiction* and *quasi in rem* jurisdiction.

10. What is a long-arm statute? What is the purpose of a long-arm statute?

11. What is venue? When can a change of venue be granted?

12. What is the difference between judicial dispute resolution and nonjudicial alternative dispute resolution? Why would one be preferred over the other, and who would have a preference?

13. Define arbitration. Describe how the process of arbitration works. What is an award?

14. Describe the difference between mediation and conciliation. How do these differ from arbitration?

15. Describe minitrial and fact-finding.

▶ ETHICS ANALYSIS AND DISCUSSION QUESTIONS

1. May a paralegal represent a client in court?

2. Are a paralegal's time records or calendar subject to the attorney–client privilege?

3. You have been appointed as a trustee of a client's children's educational trust. You need to petition the court for a release of the funds for noneducational purposes—paying the taxes on the trust income. [*Ziegler v. Harrison Nickel*, 64 Cal. App. 4th 545; 1998 Lexis 500.] May you appear alone as the trustee and represent the trust in the court proceedings? Would a nonlawyer, nonparalegal be permitted to appear?

▶ DEVELOPING YOUR COLLABORATION SKILLS

With a group of other students, selected by you or as assigned by your instructor, review the Paralegals at Work at the beginning of the chapter. As a group, discuss the questions posed in the opening scenario.

1. What is a complaint?
2. In what court or courts can the complaint on behalf of Ms. Andersen, the plaintiff, be filed?
3. If the plaintiff loses the case at trial, to what court can the trial court's decision be appealed?
4. After the case is filed in the court, can the case be resolved in any way in favor of the plaintiff before the case goes to trial?

▶ PARALEGAL PORTFOLIO EXERCISE

Based on the facts of the case described in the Opening Scenario, prepare and complete the following documents as well as you can from the facts of the scenario.

1. A complaint to file the case on behalf of the plaintiff against the defendant in the appropriate trial court of your state.

2. The defendant's answer to the complaint.

▶ LEGAL ANALYSIS AND WRITING CASES

Ashcroft, Attorney General v. The Free Speech Coalition

535 U.S. 234, 122 S.Ct. 1389, 152 L.Ed.2d 403 2002 U.S. Lexis 2789 (U.S.)

FACTS

In 1996, Congress enacted the Child Pornography Prevention Act (CPPA). Section 2256(8)(B) of the act prohibits "any visual depiction, including any photograph, film, video, picture, or computer-generated image or picture" that "is, or appears to be, of a minor engaging in sexually explicit conduct." This section includes computer-generated images known as "virtual child pornography." A first-time offender may be imprisoned for 15 years; repeat offenders face prison sentences up to 30 years. The Free Speech Coalition, a trade association for the adult-entertainment industry, sued the United States, alleging that Section 2256(8)(B) violated their constitutional free speech rights. The District Court granted summary judgment to the United States government, but the court of appeals reversed. The U.S. Supreme Court granted certiorari.

Question

1. Does Section 2256(8)(B), which criminalizes virtual child pornography, violate the Freedom of Speech Clause of the First Amendment to the U.S. Constitution?

Carnival Cruise Lines, Inc. v. Shute

499 U.S. 585, 111 S.Ct. 1522, 113 L.Ed.2d 622 1991 U.S. Lexis 2221 (U.S.)

FACTS

Mr. and Mrs. Shute, residents of the state of Washington, purchased passage for a seven-day cruise on the *Tropicale*, a cruise ship operated by the Carnival Cruise Lines, Inc. (Carnival). They paid the fare to the travel agent, who forwarded the payment to Carnival's headquarters in Miami, Florida. Carnival prepared the tickets and sent them to the Shutes. Each ticket consisted of five pages, including contract terms. The ticket contained a forum-selection clause that designated the state of Florida as the forum for any lawsuits arising under or in connection with the ticket and cruise.

The Shutes boarded the *Tropicale* in Los Angeles, which set sail for Puerto Vallarta, Mexico. While the ship was on its return voyage and in international waters off the Mexican coast, Mrs. Shute was injured when she slipped on a deck mat during a guided tour of the ship's galley. Upon return to

Washington, she filed a negligence lawsuit against Carnival in U.S. district court in Washington, seeking damages. Carnival filed a motion for summary judgment contending that the suit could be brought only in a court located in the state of Florida. The District Court granted Carnival's motion. The court of appeals reversed, holding that Mrs. Shute could sue Carnival in Washington. Carnival appealed to the U.S. Supreme Court.

Question

1. Is the forum-selection clause in Carnival Cruise Line's ticket enforceable?

Allison v. ITE Imperial Corp.

729 F.Supp. 45 1990 U.S. Dist. Lexis 607 (S.D. Miss.)

FACTS

James Clayton Allison, a resident of Mississippi, was employed by the Tru-Amp Corporation as a circuit breaker tester. As part of his employment, Allison was sent to inspect, clean, and test a switch gear located at the South Central Bell Telephone Facility in Brentwood, Tennessee. On August 26, 1988, he attempted to remove a circuit breaker manufactured by ITE Corporation (ITE) from a bank of breakers when a portion of the breaker fell off. The broken piece fell behind a switching bank and, according to Allison, caused an electrical fire and explosion. Allison was severely burned in the accident. Allison brought suit against ITE in Mississippi state court, claiming more than $50,000 in damages.

Question

1. Can this suit be removed to federal court?

AMF Inc. v. Brunswick Corp.

621 F.Supp. 456 1985 U.S. Dist. Lexis 14205 (E.D.N.Y.)

FACTS

AMF Incorporated and Brunswick Corporation both manufacture electric and automatic bowling center equipment. In 1983 the two companies became involved in a dispute over whether Brunswick had advertised certain automatic scoring devices in a false and deceptive manner. The two parties settled the dispute by signing an agreement that any future problems between them involving advertising claims would be submitted to the National Advertising Council for arbitration. In March 1985, Brunswick advertised a new product, Armor Plate 3000, a synthetic laminated material used to make bowling lanes. Armor Plate 3000 competed with wooden lanes produced by AMF. Brunswick's advertisements claimed that bowling centers could save up to $500 per lane per year in maintenance and repair costs if they would switch to Armor Plate 3000 from wooden lanes. AMF disputed this claim and requested arbitration.

Question

1. Is the arbitration agreement enforceable?

Calder v. Jones

465 U.S. 783, 104 S.Ct. 1482, 79 L.Ed.2d 804 1984 U.S. Lexis 41 (U.S.)

FACTS

The National Enquirer, Inc., a Florida corporation, has its principal place of business in Florida. It publishes the *National Enquirer*, a national weekly newspaper with a circulation of more than 5 million copies. About 600,000 copies, almost twice the level of the next highest state, are sold in California. On October 9, 1979, the *Enquirer* published an article about Shirley Jones, an entertainer. Jones, a California resident, filed a lawsuit in California state court against the *Enquirer* and its president, a resident of Florida. The suit sought damages for alleged defamation, invasion of privacy, and intentional infliction of emotional distress.

Question

1. Are the defendants subject to suit in California?

Burnham v. Superior Court of California

495 U.S. 604, 110 S.Ct. 2105, 109 LEd.2d 631 1990 U.S. Lexis 2700 (U.S.)

FACTS

Dennis and Francis Burnham were married in 1976 in West Virginia. In 1977, the couple moved to New Jersey, where their two children were born. In July 1987, the Burnhams decided to separate. Mrs. Burnham, who intended to move to California, was to have custody of the children. Mr. Burnham agreed to file for divorce on grounds of "irreconcilable differences." In October 1987, Mr. Burnham threatened to file for divorce in New Jersey on grounds of "desertion." After unsuccessfully demanding that Mr. Burnham adhere to the prior agreement, Mrs. Burnham brought suit for divorce in California state court in early January 1988. In late January, Mr. Burnham visited California on a business trip. He then visited his children in the San Francisco Bay area, where his wife resided. He took the older child to San Francisco for the weekend. Upon returning the child to Mrs. Burnham's home, he was served with a California court summons and a copy of Mrs. Burnham's divorce petition. He then returned to New Jersey. Mr. Burnham made a special appearance in the California court and moved to quash the service of process.

Question

1. Did Mr. Burnham act ethically in trying to quash the service of process? Did Mrs. Burnham act ethically in

having Mr. Burnham served on his visit to California? Is the service of process good?

▶WORKING WITH THE LANGUAGE OF THE COURT CASE

Adler v. Duval County School Board

112 F.3d 1475 1997 U.S. App. Lexis 10000
United States Court of Appeals, Eleventh Circuit

Read the following case, excerpted from the court of appeals opinion. Review and brief the case. In your brief, answer the following questions.

1. What is the doctrine of mootness?
2. What was the action the plaintiffs complained of?
3. When would the plaintiffs have had to file and have their case heard for the court to rule on their claim?
4. How would bringing the cases as a class action have allowed the court to hear the case under the Case or Controversy requirement?
5. How does this case differ from the case of *Lee v. Weisman* in Chapter 5?

Tjoflat, Circuit Judge

Appellants are four former high school students in the Duval County, Florida, school system who brought this action under 42 U.S.C. § 1983 (1994), alleging that a Duval County school policy permitting student-initiated prayer at high school graduation ceremonies (the "policy") violated their rights under the First and Fourteenth Amendments.

On June 7, 1993, three of the appellants graduated from Mandarin, one of the schools in the Duval County system. A fourth appellant graduated in June 1994. Because all four appellants have graduated, we find that to the extent they seek declaratory and injunctive relief, their case is moot. The only justiciable controversy in this case is the appellants' claim for money damages. We affirm the District Court's grant of summary judgment for the appellees on this claim, but we do so without reviewing the merits of the District Court's constitutional analysis. We begin by noting that appellants' claims for declaratory and injunctive relief are moot. All appellants have graduated, and none is threatened with harm from possible prayers in future Duval County graduation ceremonies. . . .

Article III of the Constitution limits the jurisdiction of the federal courts to the consideration of certain "Cases" and "Controversies." . . . The doc-

trine of mootness is derived from this limitation because an action that is moot cannot be characterized as an active case or controversy. "[A] case is moot when the issues presented are no longer 'live' or the parties lack a legally cognizable interest in the outcome." Any decision on the merits of a moot case would be an impermissible advisory opinion.

To apply the doctrine of mootness to this case, we must distinguish the appellants' claims for equitable relief from their claim for money damages. . . .

Equitable relief is a prospective remedy, intended to prevent future injuries. In contrast, a claim for money damages looks back in time and is intended to redress a past injury. The plaintiff requests money damages to redress injuries caused by the defendant's past conduct and seeks equitable relief to prevent the defendant's future conduct from causing future injury. When the threat of future harm dissipates, the plaintiff's claims for equitable relief become moot because the plaintiff no longer needs protection from future injury. This is precisely what happened in this case.

Appellants argue that, despite their graduation from high school, their claims for declaratory and injunctive relief are not moot because the original injury is "capable of repetition, yet evading review." This exception to the mootness doctrine is narrow. In the absence of a class action, the "capable of repetition, yet evading review" doctrine is limited to the

(continued)

situation where two elements combine: (1) the challenged action [is] in its duration too short to be fully litigated prior to its cessation or expiration, and (2) there is a reasonable expectation that the same complaining party will be subjected to the same action again. This case does not satisfy the second element. Because the complaining students have graduated from high school, there is no reasonable expectation that they will be subjected to the same injury again.

Having disposed of the appellants' claims for equitable relief, we are left with their claim for money damages, which we now address. Because the appellants' claim for money damages does not depend on any threat of future harm, this claim remains a live controversy. We accordingly turn our focus to the basis for the appellants' claim for damages. The complaint alleges that a "senior class chaplain" delivered a prayer at the June 7, 1993, Mandarin graduation ceremony at which appellants Adler, Jaffa, and Zion graduated. The only past injury for which the appellants could seek redress is being subjected to this prayer at their graduation ceremony. To prove that the appellees caused this injury, the appellants alleged in their complaint that the prayer was "a direct consequence" of the school's policy. In their answer, the appellees admitted that a student said the prayer, but denied that the prayer was a consequence of the policy.

The only issue the appellants raise on appeal is whether the District Court erred in holding the policy constitutional. While the constitutionality of the policy may have been central to the now moot issue of whether equitable relief is warranted to prevent the policy from being implemented at future graduations, it does not dispose of the issue of whether the appellants should be awarded money damages for being subjected to the prayer at their graduation. In other words, any claim for damages does not depend on the constitutionality of the policy in the abstract or as applied in other Duval County schools.

Even if the policy is unconstitutional, the defendants might not be liable if, for example, they did not implement the policy at the ceremony in question or if the prayer would have been delivered without the policy. On the other hand, if the District Court was correct in finding the policy constitutional, defendant Epting, Mandarin's principal, might nonetheless be liable if he implemented the policy in an unconstitutional manner.

The constitutionality of the policy, therefore, has little independent relevance to the appellants' damages claim. Whether they are entitled to damages depends entirely on the circumstances under which the prayer was delivered at their graduation ceremony. In order to prevail, the appellants must have some theory connecting the individual defendants to the prayer. For these reasons, even if we were to find fault with the district court's constitutional analysis of the policy, this conclusion by itself would not answer the question of whether the court erred in granting the appellees summary judgment on the damages claim. The appellants offer no other grounds in their briefs for finding trial court error.

After considering the appellants' briefs and oral argument, we are convinced that they either fail to understand the basis for their damages claim or do not seriously seek damages. They have offered us no connection between the prayer and their damages claim; their briefs offer no indication as to any of the circumstances surrounding the Mandarin graduation prayer. They failed to argue that the prayer was a "direct consequence" of the policy, or any other theory connecting the defendants' actions to the Mandarin prayer. Their briefs do not even include the allegation made in their complaint that a prayer was delivered at Mandarin.

For all these reasons, we hold that they have waived their damages claim on appeal. We therefore affirm the District Court's order to the extent it denied the appellants' motion for summary judgment and granted the appellees' motions for summary judgment on the appellants' damages claim. For the foregoing reasons, we *vacate* the district court's order granting the appellees summary judgment on the appellants' claims for declaratory and injunctive relief and *remand* the case with instructions that the District Court dismiss those claims. We *affirm* the District Court's denial of the appellants' motion for summary judgment and its grant of summary judgment for the appellees on the appellants' damages claim. It is *so ordered*.

UPDATE TO CASE

After a rehearing en banc the court, upon a majority vote of the judges of the court, issued a subsequent opinion on June 3, 1999, and on March 15, 2000 on further proceeding the Court ruled that the policy on prayer did not violate the Establishment Clause.

On June 19, 2000, the Supreme Court rendered a decision in *Santa Fe Independent School District v. Doe*, 530 U.S. 290, which invalidated a Texas school board's policy permitting students to vote on a prayer subject to officials' approval at home football games. The Duval Court proceeded to rehear the case based on the *Santa Fe* decision and ruled again in favor of the Duval School Board because the prayer there was not subject to official approval or input [*Adler v. Duval County Sch. Bd.*, 250 F.3d 1330, 2001 U.S. App. Lexis 8880 (11th Cir.)]. ■

CIVIL LITIGATION

"Discourage litigation. Persuade your neighbors to compromise whenever you can. Point out to them how the nominal winner is often a real loser—in fees, and expenses, and waste of time. As a peacemaker, the lawyer has a superior opportunity of being a good man. There will still be business enough."

Abraham Lincoln, Notes on the Practice of Law (1850)

PARALEGALS AT WORK

You are a paralegal for a law firm in your city. One of the law firm's major clients is MicroHard Corporation. MicroHard Corporation is an extremely successful developer of computer software, including office management software, an Internet browser, and other sophisticated software. MicroHard Corporation wanted to enter into a merger whereby it would purchase Raspberry Inc., a corporation that has developed Berry-Pod, a small handheld device whose software allows a user to listen to downloaded music, watch videos, view stored photographs, send and receive email, and is a cellular telephone. The written merger agreements were drawn and signed by MicroHard Corporation and Raspberry, Inc. However, Raspberry, Inc. has refused to go through with the merger although all necessary board of directors, shareholders, and government approvals have been obtained.

As a paralegal, you have been called into the meeting of the senior partners of your law firm with the chief executives of MicroHard Corporation. The meeting is to discuss what legal action MicroHard Corporation should take against Raspberry, Inc. At the meeting, it is determined that your law firm will represent MicroHard Corporation and bring a breach of written contract lawsuit against Raspberry, Inc. Vivian Blackstone, senior partner of the law firm, asks you to be the paralegal who will assist her in preparing and bringing the lawsuit on behalf of MicroHard Corporation.

Questions include: What document or documents should your law firm prepare on behalf of MicroHard Corporation and file with the court and serve on Raspberry, Inc. to start the lawsuit. What document will Raspberry Inc. file and serve on MicroHard Corporation to defend the lawsuit? What methods could be used to uncover all of the information and documents that will be necessary to pursue this lawsuit against Raspberry Inc.?

Consider the issues involved in this scenario as you read the chapter.

After studying this chapter, you should be able to:

1. Outline the litigation process.

2. Define the term *pleading* and describe a complaint and summons.

3. Describe an answer and cross-complaint.

4. Explain how depositions, interrogatories, and production of documents are used in discovery.

5. List and describe the stages in a trial.

6. Explain how verdicts and judgments are rendered at trial.

7. Describe how a case is appealed and what decisions can be rendered by an appellate court.

▶ INTRODUCTION FOR THE PARALEGAL

Paralegals often work for lawyers who specialize in litigating lawsuits. These could be civil lawsuits that seek monetary damages or other remedies, or could be criminal cases. The paralegal could work either for the plaintiff's lawyer or for the defendant's lawyer. The bringing, maintaining, and defense of a lawsuit comprise the litigation process, or **litigation**.

Civil litigation involves legal action to resolve disputes between parties, as contrasted with criminal litigation, which is brought by the government against a party accused of violating the law. The parties to civil litigation may be individuals, businesses, or in some cases, government agencies. Although the fundamental process is the same, the court and the procedure may vary.

Many lawyers specialize in civil litigation, in which a plaintiff sues a defendant to recover money damages or other remedy for the alleged harm the defendant causes the plaintiff. This may be an automobile accident case, a suit alleging a breach of a contract, a claim of patent infringement, or any of a myriad of other civil wrongs.

In a civil case, either party can appeal the trial court's decision once a final judgment is entered. In a criminal case, only the defendant can appeal. The appeal is made to the appropriate appellate court.

A paralegal often spends considerable time researching, preparing documents, interviewing clients, and consulting with the attorney on civil litigation matters. This chapter discusses civil litigation and the appellate process. ■

PLEADINGS

Pleadings
The paperwork that is filed with the court to initiate and respond to a lawsuit.

The paperwork that is filed with the court to initiate and respond to a lawsuit is referred to as the **pleadings**. The major pleadings are the complaint, the answer, the cross-complaint, and the reply.

Complaint

Plaintiff
The party who files the complaint.

Complaint
The document the plaintiff files with the court and serves on the defendant to initiate a lawsuit.

The party who is suing—the **plaintiff**—must file a **complaint**, also called a plaintiff's original petition or summons in some jurisdictions, with the proper court. The content and form of the complaint will vary depending on local court's procedural rules. Many courts follow the federal practice of "notice pleading." Other state courts follow the traditional form requiring detailed allegations of the basis for the action.

A complaint must name the parties to the lawsuit, allege the ultimate facts and law violated, and state the remedy desired and the "prayer for relief" to be awarded by the court. The complaint can be as long as necessary, depending on the case's complexity. Exhibit 7.1 is a sample state trial court complaint filed in Pennsylvania. Exhibit 7.2 is a federal complaint. Exhibit 7.3 is a bilingual notice to plead a complaint.

Summons

Summons
A court order directing the defendant to appear in court and answer the complaint.

Defendant
The party who files the answer.

Once a complaint has been filed with the court, the court issues a **summons,** a court order directing the **defendant** to appear in court and answer the complaint. A fundamental requirement is that notice be given to the defendant. A sheriff, another government official, or a private process server may serve the complaint and, where required, the summons on the defendant. In some cases, the defendant may be served by other means, such as by publication when the defendant cannot otherwise be found to be served personally.

Exhibit 7.1 **Sample state**

IN THE COURT OF COMMON PLEAS OF BUCKS COUNTY, PA.
CIVIL ACTION-LAW

COUNTY LINE FENCE CO., INC.   :   NO.
2051 W. County Line Road
Warrington, PA 18976   :

         V.   ATTORNEY I.D. #12204

WAYNE YARNELL   :
5707 Dunbar Court
Bensalem, PA 19020   :

<u>COMPLAINT</u>

1. Plaintiff is County Line Fence Company, Inc., a Pennsylvania corporation duly authorized to do business in Pennsylvania, with a place of business at 2051 W. County Line Road, Warrington, Bucks County, Pennsylvania.

2. Defendant, WAYNE YARNELL, is an adult individual residing at 5707 Dunbar Court, Bensalem, Pennsylvania.

3. On or about April 30, 2002, Defendant entered into a contract with the Plaintiff for a 140 ft. Bufftech fence to be installed on Defendant's property at 5707 Dunbar Court, Bensalem, PA 19020. (See Exhibit "A")

4. Plaintiff properly and adequately installed the fencing per the contract.

5. Defendant agreed to pay a total of $5,300.00 for the fence.

6. Demand was made upon the Defendant by Plaintiff for payment of the amount due for fencing and installation.

7. In spite of the demand for payment, Defendant has failed and refused, and continues to fail and refuse to pay Plaintiff the balance due.

WHEREFORE, Plaintiff demands judgment in the amount of $5,300.00, together with attorneys fees, costs of suit and any additional amounts as the court deems proper.
THOMAS F. GOLDMAN & ASSOCIATES

Thomas F. Goldman

Thomas F. Goldman, Esquire
Attorney for Plaintiff

Exhibit 7.2 **Complaint filed in federal court**

UNITED STATES DISTRICT COURT
FOR THE DISTRICT OF COLUMBIA

UNITED STATES OF AMERICA	) CASE NUMBER 1:01CV01660
	) JUDGE: Ricardo M. Urbina
	) DECK TYPE: General Civil
Plaintiff,	) DATE STAMP: 08/01/2002
	)
v.	)
	) Civ. No.
	) COMPLAINT FOR CIVIL
ENHANCED SERVICES BILLING, INC.	) PENALTIES, PERMANENT
BILLING CONCEPTS, INC.,	) INJUNCTION, CONSUMER
Delaware Corporations,	) REDRESS AND OTHER
both with their principal place of business at	) EQUITABLE RELIEF
7411 John Smith Drive, Suite 200	)
San Antonio, Texas 78229,	)
	)
NEW CENTURY EQUITY HOLDINGS CORP.	)
A Delaware Corporation,	)
10101 Reunion Place, Suite 450	)
San Antonio, Texas 78216	)
	)
	)
Defendants.	)

Plaintiff, the United States of America, acting upon notification and authorization to the Attorney General by the Federal Trade Commission ("FTC" or "Commission"), for its complaint alleges that:

1. Plaintiff brings this action under Sections 5(a)(1), 5(m)(1)(A), 9, 13(b), 16(a) and 19 of the Federal Trade Commission Act, 15 U.S.C. §§45(a)(1),

Exhibit 7.2 **Complaint filed in federal court** *(continued)*

45(m)(1)(A), 49, 53(b), 56(a) and 57b, and the Telephone Disclosure and Dispute Resolution Act of 1992 ("TDDRA"), 15 U.S.C. §§ 5701 *et. seq.*, to obtain injunctive relief and consumer redress for violations of Section 5(a)(1) of the Federal Trade Commission Act, 15 U.S.C. § 45(a)(1), and to obtain monetary civil penalties, consumer redress and injunctive and other relief for Defendants' violations of the Commission's Trade Regulation Rule Pursuant to the Telephone Disclosure and Dispute Resolution Act of 1992 ("900-Number Rule"), 16 C.F.R. Part 308.

JURISDICTION AND VENUE

2. This court has jurisdiction over this matter under 28 U.S.C. §§ 1331, 1337(a), 1345 and 1355 and under 15 U.S.C. §§ 45(m)(1)(A), 49, 53(b), 56(a), 57b, 5721 and 5723. This action arises under 15 U.S.C. § 45(a)(1).

3. Venue in the District of Columbia is proper under 15 U.S.C. § 53(b) and 28 U.S.C. §§ 1391(b) and (c) and 1395(a).

DEFENDANTS

4. Defendant Enhanced Services Billing, Inc. is a Delaware corporation with its principal place of business at 7411 John Smith Drive, Suite 200, San Antonio, Texas 78229. Enhanced Services Billing, Inc. provides or provided billing and collection services for vendors who market Internet Web sites, psychic memberships, voice mail and hospital telephone and television rental, and other enhanced services. Enhanced Services Billing, Inc. was incorporated on March 17, 1994. Enhanced Services Billing, Inc. transacts or has transacted business in this district.

5. Defendant Billing Concepts, Inc. is a Delaware corporation with its principal place of business at 7411 John Smith Drive, Suite 200, San Antonio, Texas 78229. Billing Concepts, Inc. provides or provided billing and collection services for vendors who market . . .

Exhibit 7.3 **Bilingual notice to plead a complaint**

IN THE COURT OF COMMON PLEAS
OF PHILADELPHIA COUNTY, PENNSYLVANIA
CIVIL ACTION LAW

KATHRYN KELSEY   : NO.

    vs.   : ATTORNEY I.D. NO.

KATHRYN CARROLL   : COMPLAINT IN EQUITY

COMPLAINT – CIVIL ACTION

NOTICE

You have been sued in court. If you wish to defend against the claims set forth in the following pages, you must take action within twenty (20) days after this complaint and notice are served, by entering a written appearance personally or by attorney and filing in writing with the court your defenses or objections to the claims set forth against you. You are warned that if you fail to do so the case may proceed without you and a judgment may be entered against you by the court without further notice for any money claimed in the complaint or for any other claims or relief requested by the plaintiff. You may lose money or property or other rights important to you.

You should take this paper to your lawyer at once. If you do not have a lawyer or cannot afford one, go to or telephone the office set forth below to find out where you can get legal help.

Philadelphia Bar Association
Lawyer Referral and
Information Service
One Reading Center
Philadelphia, Pennsylvania 19107
215-238-1701

AVISO

Le han demandado a usted en la corte. Si usted quiere defenderse de estas demandas expuestas en las paginas siguientes, usted tiene veinte (20) dias de plazo al partir de la fecha de la demanda y la notificacion. Hace falta asentar una compancia escrita o en persona o con un abogado y entregar a la corte en forma escrita sus defensas o sus objeciones a las demandas en contra de su persona. Sea avisado que si usted no se defiende, la corta tomara medidas y puede continuar la demanda en contra suya sin previo aviso o notificacion. Ademas, la corte puede decidir a favor del demandante y requiere que usted cumpla con todas las provisiones de esta demanda. Usted puede perer dinero o sus propiedades u oetros derechos importantes para usted.

Lieva esta demanda a un abogado immediatamente. Si no tiene abogado o si no tiene el dinero suficiente de pagartal servicio, vaya en persona o llame por telefono a la oficina cuya direccion se encuentra escrita abajo para averiguar donde se puede conseguir asistencia legal.

Asociacion de Licenciados de Filadelfia
Servicio de Referencia e
Informacion Legal
One Reading Center
Filadelfia, Pennsylvania 19107
215-238-1701

THE PARALEGAL AND CIVIL LITIGATION

Civil litigation is an area in which a paralegal's talents can shine. The paralegal's analytical ability, expertise in legal research, ability to draft pleadings and documents, and other skills are truly put to the test. Paralegals who choose to work in the litigation field must have excellent knowledge of the various facets of the litigation process, the rules of evidence, and court procedure.

A paralegal's first introduction to a new lawsuit will be when a client employs the law firm for whom the paralegal works to represent the client in a civil lawsuit. The client may be either the plaintiff or the defendant. Many times the paralegal's first work assignment is to sit in on conferences between the attorney and the client, and to take notes of pending issues.

Then the paralegal usually is notified to "start a file" for the lawsuit. This means obtaining available evidence, documents, and others items relevant to the case. Each attorney has his or her own system for preparing a case for trial (or settlement), and the paralegal has his or her own way of preparing the file as well.

The paralegal often is assigned to help draft the pleadings for the case. In addition, the paralegal may interview the client, contact the client for information, draft documents to obtain production of documents and other evidence, and assist in the preparation of depositions to be taken or attended by his or her supervising attorney.

At this stage, the paralegal is involved in the case as much as his or her supervising attorney. Because of their knowledge of a case, paralegals can be indispensable in the proper preparation for lawyer–client meetings, discovery, depositions, and settlement conferences.

If the case is to go to trial, the paralegal usually is called upon to help conduct the legal research that will be placed in the brief of the case to be submitted to the court. The paralegal's responsibility is to help organize the case for trial, and to use all available technology to prepare the case for trial.

At trial, the paralegal becomes indispensable in assisting the attorney present his or her case on behalf of the client. The paralegal usually gets the same "rush" as the lawyer going to trial.

This chapter discusses the phases of civil litigation that will be important to a paralegal working in this area of the law.

Cross-Complaint and Reply

A defendant who believes that he or she has been injured by the plaintiff can file a **cross-complaint**, or counterpetition as it is called in some jurisdictions, against the plaintiff in addition to an answer. In the cross-complaint, the defendant (now the **cross-complainant**) sues the plaintiff (now the **cross-defendant**) for damages or some other remedy. The original plaintiff must file a **reply**, or **answer** to the cross-complaint. Exhibit 7.4 is a sample state answer. The reply—which can include affirmative defenses—must be filed with the court and served on the original defendant.

Exhibit 7.5 illustrates the pleadings process.

Cross-complaint
Filed by the defendant against the plaintiff to seek damages or some other remedy.

Reply
Filed by the original plaintiff to answer the defendant's cross-complaint.

Intervention and Consolidation

If other persons have an interest in a lawsuit, they may step in and become parties to the lawsuit—called an **intervention**. For instance, a bank that has made a secured loan

Exhibit 7.4 **Sample state answer**

DATZ and GOLDBERG

BY: MARC C. BENDO, ESQUIRE

IDENTIFICATION NO. 80075   ATTORNEY FOR   DEFENDANT

1311 SPRUCE STREET

PHILADELPHIA, PENNSYLVANIA 19107

(215) 545-7960

COUNTY LINE FENCE CO., INC.
2051 W. County Line Road
Warrington, PA 18976

vs.

WAYNE YARNALL
5707 Dunbar Court
Bensalem, PA 19020

COURT OF COMMON PLEAS

BUCKS COUNTY DIVISION

TERM

NO. 99004879-23-1

ANSWER OF DEFENDANT, WAYNE YARNALL, TO PLAINTIFF'S CIVIL ACTION WITH
NEW MATTER

1. Denied. Plaintiff is without knowledge or information sufficient to form a belief as to the truth or falsity of this averment. Accordingly, same is denied with strict proof demanded at time of Trial.

2. Admitted. By way of further answer, however, Plaintiff's Civil Action has misspelled Defendant's proper name, which is Wayne Yarnall.

3. Denied. These allegations constitute conclusions of law to which no response is required pursuant to the applicable Pennsylvania Rules of Civil Procedure . . .

Exhibit 7.5 **Pleadings process**

```
┌─────────────┐    complaint     ┌─────────────┐
│  Plaintiff  │ ───────────────▶ │  Defendant  │
│             │ ◀─────────────── │             │
└─────────────┘     answer       └─────────────┘


┌─────────────┐  cross-complaint ┌─────────────────┐
│  Plaintiff  │ ◀─────────────── │   Defendant     │
│(cross-      │                  │(cross-          │
│ defendant)  │ ───────────────▶ │ complainant)    │
└─────────────┘      reply       └─────────────────┘
```

E-FILINGS IN COURT

When litigation ensues, the clients, lawyers, and judges involved in the case usually are buried in paper—pleadings, interrogatories, documents, motions to the court, briefs, and memoranda; the list goes on and on. By the time a case is over, reams of paper are stored in dozens, if not hundreds, of boxes. Further, court appearances, no matter how small the matter, must be made in person. For example, lawyers often wait hours for a 10-minute scheduling or other conference with the judge. Additional time is required to drive to and from court, which in an urban area may amount to hours.

The technology currently is available for implementing electronic filing—*e-filing*—of pleadings, briefs, and other documents related to a lawsuit. E-filing would include using CD-ROMs for briefs, scanning evidence and documents into a computer for storage and retrieval, and emailing correspondence and documents to the court and the opposing counsel. Scheduling and other conferences with the judge or opposing counsel could be held via telephone conferences and email.

Some courts have instituted e-filing already. For example, in the Manhattan bankruptcy court, e-filing is now mandatory. Other courts around the world are doing the same. Companies such as Microsoft and LexisNexis have developed systems to manage e-filings of court documents. Some forward-thinking judges and lawyers envision a day when the paperwork and hassle are reduced or eliminated in a "virtual courthouse."

on a piece of real estate can intervene in a lawsuit between parties who are litigating ownership of the property.

If several plaintiffs have filed separate lawsuits stemming from the same fact situation against the same defendant, the court can initiate a **consolidation** of the cases into one case if it would not cause undue prejudice to the parties. Suppose, for example, that a commercial airplane crashes, killing and injuring many people. The court could consolidate all of the lawsuits against the defendant airplane company.

Statute of Limitations

Some crimes, such as murder, have no limitation on the time in which a defendant can be charged. In civil actions, however, the plaintiff must bring suit within a certain period of time after the action that gives rise to the complaint or lose the right to use the courts to enforce the civil right and remedy. This period is called the **statute of limitations**.

www

Locate the U.S. District Court that serves the county or parish in which you live. Go to that court's website and find and review the "Court Forms" for that court. http://uscourts.gov/

Statute of limitations
A law that establishes the period during which a plaintiff must bring a lawsuit against a defendant.

Exhibit 7.6 **Sample interrogatory (continued)**

OTHER EXPENSES*

3. If you have incurred any bills or expenses in connection with the injuries or diseases which you suffered because of the accident referred to in the Complaint, identify each such bill or expense, the service for which the bill or expense was incurred, and the identity of the person who rendered the bill or who was involved in the expense.

PRIOR OR SUBSEQUENT INJURIES OR DISEASES

4. Either prior to or subsequent to the accident referred to in the Complaint, have you ever suffered any injuries or diseases in those portions of the body claimed by you to have been affected by the accident referred to in the Complaint?

   If so, identify:

   (a) The injuries or diseases you suffered;

   (b) The date and place of any accident, if such an injury or disease was caused by an accident;

   (c) All hospitals, doctors or practitioners who rendered treatment or examinations because of any such injuries or diseases;

   (d) Anyone against whom a claim was made, and the Court, term or number of any claim or lawsuit that was filed, in connection with any such injuries or diseases.

EARNINGS BEFORE THE ACCIDENT*

5. For the period of three years immediately preceding the date of the accident referred to in the complaint, state:

   (a) The name and address of each of your employers or, if you were self-employed during that period, each of your business addresses and the name of the business while self-employed;

   (b) The dates of commencement and termination of each of your periods of employment or self-employment;

   (c) A detailed description of the nature of your occupation in each employment or self-employment;

   (d) The amount of income from employment and self-employment for each year. (Attach your federal income tax return for each year.)

EARNINGS AFTER THE ACCIDENT*

6. If you have engaged in one or more gainful occupations subsequent to the date of the accident referred to in the Complaint, state:

   (a) The name and address of each of your employers or if you were self-employed, each of your business addresses and the name of the business while self-employed;

   (b) The dates of commencement and termination of each of your periods of employment or self-employment;

   (c) A detailed description of the nature of your occupation in each employment or self-employment;

   (d) The wage, salary or rate of earnings received by you in each employment or self-employment. (Attach your federal income tax return for each year subsequent to the accident);

   (e) The dates of all absences from your occupation resulting from the injuries and diseases suffered in this accident. Set forth the amount of any earnings or other benefits lost by you because of such absences.

LIMITATIONS OF DUTIES AND ACTIVITIES AFTER THE ACCIDENT

7. State whether, as a result of this accident, you have been unable to perform any of your customary occupational duties or social or other activities in the same manner as prior to the accident, stating with particularity (a) the duties and/or activities you have been unable to perform, (b) the periods of time you have been unable to perform, and (c) the names and last known addresses of all persons who have knowledge thereof.

Exhibit 7.6 Sample interrogatory *(continued)*

WITNESSES AND THOSE WITH KNOWLEDGE OF ACCIDENT

8. (a) Identify each person who (1) was a witness to the accident through sight or hearing and/or (2) has knowledge of facts concerning the happening of the accident or conditions or circumstances at the scene of the accident prior to, after, or at the time of the accident.

   (b) With respect to each person identified in the answer to the interrogatory above, state that person's exact location and activity at the time of the accident.

STATEMENTS

9. Have you or has anyone acting on your behalf obtained from any person any statement (as defined by the Rules of Civil Procedure) concerning this action or its subject matter?
   If so, identify:

   (a) Each such person;

   (b) When, where, by whom and to whom each statement was made, and whether it was reduced to writing or otherwise recorded;

   (c) Any person who has custody of any such statements that were reduced to writing or otherwise recorded.

STATEMENTS MADE BY PARTY TO WHOM INTERROGATORY IS ADDRESSED*

10. Have you given any statement (as defined by the Rules of Civil Procedure) concerning this action or its subject matter?
    If so, identify:

    (a) Each person to whom a statement was given;

    (b) When and where each statement was given;

    (c) Any person who has custody of any such statements that were reduced to writing or otherwise recorded.

DEMONSTRATIVE EVIDENCE*

11. Do you or does anyone acting on your behalf know of the existence of any photographs, motion pictures, video recordings, maps, diagrams or models of the site of the accident, the parties or any other subject matter involved in this action?
    If the answer is in the affirmative, identify:

    (a) The date(s) when they were made and what they are;

    (b) The name and address of the person making them;

    (c) The subject that each represents or portrays.

TRIAL PREPARATION MATERIAL

12. Have you or has anyone on your behalf conducted any investigations of the accident which is the subject matter of the complaint?
    If the answer is in the affirmative, identify:

    (a) Each person, and the employer of each person, who conducted any investigation;

    (b) The dates of the investigations;

    (c) All notes, reports or other documents prepared during or as a result of the investigations and the identity of the persons who have possession thereof.

(continued)

Exhibit 7.6 **Sample interrogatory *(continued)***

EXPERTS*

13. (a) State the name and address of each person whom you expect to call as an expert witness at trial and state the subject matter on which the expert is expected to testify.

   (b) For each such expert, have the expert state the substance of the facts and opinions to which the expert is expected to testify and summarize the grounds for each such opinion.

   (c) Set forth the qualifications of each expert, listing the schools attended, years of attendance, degrees received, and experience in any particular field of specialization or expertise.

INSURANCE

14. (a) State whether you are covered by any type of insurance including any excess or umbrella insurance, in connection with this accident.

   If the answer is in the affirmative, state the following with respect to each policy:

   (b) The name of the insurance carrier which issued each policy of insurance;

   (c) The name insured under each policy and the policy number;

   (d) The type of each policy and the effective dates;

   (e) The amount of coverage provided for injury to each person, for each occurrence, and in the aggregate for each policy;

   (f) Each exclusion, if any, in the policy which is applicable to any claim thereunder and the reasons why you or the company claims the exclusion is applicable.

   (g) Whether you have made a claim under the policy and if so set forth the nature of the claim, the amount recovered and the date of recovery.

NONSTANDARD INTERROGATORIES

15. State your full name, address, date of birth and social security number.

16. Have you ever used any names other than the one listed above? If yes, state all names used and when each additional name was used.

17. To the extent known to you, your attorney or other representative, set forth the name and home and business address of the following:

   (a) Those who actually saw the accident;

   (b) Those who were present at or near the scene at the time of the accident;

   (c) Those who have any knowledge of, or information concerning the circumstances and manner in which the accident occurred or the nature of the injuries sustained in the accident.

18. At the time of the accident or immediately thereafter, did you have any conversation with or make any statements to any of the parties or witnesses, or did any of them make any statements to you or in your presence? If so state the substance of any such conversation or statement and in whose presence it took place.

19. If you, your representative, attorney, consultant, surety, indemnitor, insurer or agent obtained a statement or statements as defined in Pennsylvania Rules of Civil Procedure 4003.4(1) and (2), concerning this action and/or its subject matter from any party to this action, any witness, or any person not a party to this action then state:

   (a) The name and address of the person who gave such statement, including the name and address of each person's employer;

   (b) The date each statement was given;

   (c) The name and address of the person who obtained each statement;

Exhibit 7.6 **Sample interrogatory (*continued*)**

(d) The date when each statement was obtained;

(e) The place where each statement was obtained;

(f) Whether each statement is written, signed by the person making it or if there is a stenographic, mechanical, electrical or other recording, or a transcription thereof;

(g) The names and addresses of all persons and/or entities who presently have custody of each original statement identified in your answer above;

(h) Please attach to your Answer to Interrogatories a copy or like reproduction of each statement identified in your answer above.

20. State the exact date, time and place the accident occurred and describe in detail how you claim the accident occurred.

21. State:

(a) The exact portion of the highway where the accident occurred;

(b) The positions of the respective vehicles prior to impact;

(c) Distance from you when you first observed the other vehicle;

(d) Positions of vehicles after impact;

(e) What part of your vehicle came in contact with what part of the other vehicle;

(f) The weather and road conditions at the time of the accident;

(g) If weather was inclement, state whether windshield wipers were in use at the time of the collision;

(h) What type of traffic signals controlled the place where the accident occurred;

(i) Speed of all vehicles immediately prior to impact;

(j) Lighting conditions at time of accident, including whether any artificial light illuminated place of accident. If there were artificial lights, state type and distance from accident.

22. State the name and address of the owner of the vehicle in which you were traveling.

23. State the registration number, year, make and model of above vehicle.

24. With regard to the vehicle listed above, state the name, address, age and driver's license number of operator of vehicle.

25. State whether the vehicle or any part thereof in which you were traveling at the time of the accident was defective, or not in safe working order. Identify defects, if any:

26. State whether repairs were made to the vehicle after accident. If yes, identify name and address of person/business making repairs, date and type of work performed. Attach copy of repair bill.

27. State where you were coming from and where you were going at time of the accident.

28. State how long you had been traveling and approximately how many miles traveled prior to the accident.

29. State whether you had been at the location of the accident previously; if yes, approximately how many times.

30. State whether you had consumed any alcohol, medication or drugs within 24 hours of the accident. If so, identify substance and when, where, and amount consumed.

31. State whether you have a prescription for any corrective lenses. If so, identify type of prescription and whether you were wearing same at time of accident.

32. Please identify your driver's license number and the State which issued the license. Identify any restriction on your license.

33. If your driver's license has ever been revoked, suspended or withdrawn, state where, when and for what offense.

34. State when you first experienced pain following accident.

35. State nature of pain experienced.

(continued)

Exhibit 7.6 **Sample interrogatory** *(continued)*

36. State name and address of family physician.
37. State name and address of all physicians, clinics, hospitals, therapists, etc. where you sought consultation or treatment within five (5) years prior or subsequent to this accident and reason for consultation and/or treatment.
38. Did you know any of the witnesses or the individuals in any of the other vehicles involved in this accident or any of the witnesses to the occurrences?
    (a) If answer is yes, state name(s) of individual(s) you knew, how long you knew the individual(s) and the nature of your relationship with the individual(s) named.
    (b) As to the individual(s) named in 38(a) who were in another vehicle involved in this accident, did you know the individual(s) would be traveling near you on the highway?
39. As to each party traveling in the vehicle you were in, state your relationship (i.e., friend, relative, stranger, etc.).
40. As to each party named in #39, state how long you have known this person.
41. As to each witness, state your relationship (i.e., friend, relative, stranger, etc.) and where each witness was at the time of the accident.
42. State whether or not you knew or had ever before seen any of the occupants of the other vehicle(s) involved in this accident. If yes, state:
    (a) Who it is you knew or had seen prior to this accident;
    (b) How you know the person(s) identified;
    (c) For what length of time prior to the accident you knew this person(s);
    (d) Whether you knew the individual(s) named above would be traveling near you;
    (e) Whether you were traveling to the same location for the same purpose.
43. State whether or not you reside in a household where a relative owns a motor vehicle. Identify this individual and his/her relationship to you.
    (a) Identify the vehicle owned by year, make, model, license and vehicle identification number.
    (b) State whether this vehicle is insured. If yes, attach a copy of the declaration page indicating whether or not the limited tort option was selected.
44. State whether or not the police were called to the locale of the accident. If yes, state:
    (a) Who called police;
    (b) Whether or not the police responded to the call;
    (c) How long it took the police to respond;
    (d) The name(s) and badge(s) of the officer(s);
    (e) Whether you left the location prior to the police arrival;
    (f) Whether you provided your name to the police;
    (g) What, if anything, you told police;
    (h) Whether or not a police report was prepared. If answer is yes, please attach a copy of the police report and/or identify police department involved and police reference number for accident report.
45. If you were taken to the hospital for treatment, state how and by whom you were transported.

THOMAS F. GOLDMAN & ASSOCIATES
BY: _____

Exhibit 7.7 **Sample request for production of documents**

THOMAS F. GOLDMAN & ASSOCIATES
138 N. State Street
Newtown, PA 18940
(123) 555-1234

KATHRYN KELSEY	:	COURT OF COMMON PLEAS
	:	PHILADELPHIA COUNTY
vs.	:	APRIL TERM, 2002
KATHRYN CARROLL	:	NO. 1259

REQUEST TO PRODUCE UNDER PA R.C.P. 4033 and 4009
<u>DIRECTED TO PLAINTIFFS</u>

Within thirty (30) days of service, please produce for inspection and copying at the office of THOMAS F. GOLDMAN & ASSOCIATES, 138 North State Street, Newtown, Pennsylvania 18940, the following:

1. All photographs and/or diagrams of the area involved in this accident or occurrence, the locale or surrounding area of the site of this accident or occurrence, or any other matter or things involved in this accident or occurrence.

2. All property damage estimates rendered for any object belonging to the Plaintiffs which was involved in this accident or occurrence.

3. All property damage estimates rendered for any object belonging to the Defendant which was involved in this accident or occurrence.

4. All statements concerning this action or its subject matter previously made by any party or witness. The statements referred to here are defined by Pa. R.C.P. 4003.4.

5. All transcriptions and summaries of all interviews conducted by anyone acting on behalf of the Plaintiff or Plaintiff's insurance carrier of any potential witness and/or person(s) who has any knowledge of the accident or its surrounding circumstances.

6. All inter-office memorandum between representative of Plaintiffs' insurance carrier or memorandum to Plaintiffs' insurance carrier's file concerning the manner in which the accident occurred.

7. All inter-office memorandum between representative of Plaintiffs' insurance carrier or memorandum to Plaintiffs' insurance carrier's file concerning the injuries sustained by the Plaintiffs.

8. A copy of any written accident report concerning this accident or occurrence signed by or prepared by Plaintiff for Plaintiffs' insurance carrier or Plaintiff's employers.

9. A copy of the face sheet of any policy of insurance providing coverage to Plaintiffs for the claim being asserted by Plaintiff in this action.

10. All bills, reports, and records from any and all physicians, hospitals, or other health care providers concerning the injuries sustained by the Defendants from this accident or occurrence.

11. All photographs and/or motion pictures of any and all surveillance of Defendant performed by anyone acting on behalf of Plaintiff, Plaintiffs' insurer and/or Plaintiffs' attorney.

12. All photographs taken of Plaintiffs' motor vehicle which depict any damage to said vehicle which was sustained as a result of this accident.

13. All photographs taken of defendant's motor vehicle which depict any damage to said vehicle which was sustained as a result of this accident.

14. Any and all reports, writings, memorandum, Xeroxed cards and/or other writings, lists or compilations of the Defendant and others with similar names as indexed by the Metropolitan Index Bureau, Central Index Bureau or other Index Bureau in possession of the Plaintiffs or the Plaintiffs' insurance carrier.

E-DISCOVERY

The use of email, electronic retention of records, establishment of websites, selling goods and services online, and other digital technologies has exploded in conducting business. This technology is used extensively in conducting personal affairs as well. Therefore, in many lawsuits, much of the evidence is in digital form. The winning or losing of lawsuits may lie in the ability of a party to conduct electronic discovery.

Modern discovery practices permit the electronic discovery of evidence. Most federal and state courts have adopted rules that permit the e-discovery of emails, electronically stored data, e-contracts, and other electronic records. E-discovery is fast becoming a burgeoning part of the preparation of a case for trial or settlement.

The lawyer and the paralegal must have a sound understanding of permissible e-discovery. Courts have resoundingly permitted the discovery of emails and electronic databases where relevant to a court case. A party seeking e-discovery must prepare the proper requests for such discovery as required by court rules.

In addition to discovery of email and electronic information, courts permit the use of electronic interrogatories to be proffered to the other side, as well as the electronic response to such e-interrogatories. Some courts also permit the taking of depositions electronically. This requires that the questions by the lawyers and answers of the deponent be communicated electronically by email.

Federal and state courts have established rules of evidence that require the parties to a lawsuit not to destroy or delete documents or other evidence that is relevant to the pending lawsuit. This prohibition is particularly important when the documents and evidence are digital. The destruction or deletion of e-evidence may subject the violating party to civil and criminal penalties.

In the case where digital evidence has been destroyed or deleted from electronic files, it may be possible to reconstruct the evidence. The use of computer experts will be necessary to find the missing evidence and digitally reconstruct it.

E-discovery will continue to increase as an important feature in many lawsuits. The recovery of emails, mining of electronic databases, and reconstructing thought-to-be destroyed electronic evidence will play an ever more important part of discovery in current and future lawsuits. E-discovery is clearly an important part of the digital law office and the virtual courtroom.

PRETRIAL MOTIONS

Pretrial motion
A motion a party can make to try to dispose of all or part of a lawsuit prior to trial.

Parties to a lawsuit can make several **pretrial motions** to try to dispose of all or part of a lawsuit prior to trial. The two major pretrial motions are the motion for judgment on the pleadings and the motion for summary judgment.

Motion to Dismiss

A defendant can file a **motion to dismiss** the plaintiff's complaint for failure to state a claim for which relief can be granted. A motion to dismiss is sometimes called a *demurrer*. A motion to dismiss a case alleges that even if the facts as presented in the plaintiff's complaint are true, there is no reason to continue the lawsuit. For example, a motion to dismiss would be granted if the plaintiff alleges that the defendant was negligent but the facts as alleged do not support a claim of negligence.

A motion to dismiss can be filed with the court prior to the defendant's having filed an answer in the case. If the motion to dismiss is denied, the defendant is given further time to answer. If the court grants the motion to dismiss, the defendant does not have to file an answer. The plaintiff usually is given time to file an amended complaint. If the plaintiff fails to file an amended complaint, judgment will be entered against the plaintiff. If the plaintiff files an amended complaint, the defendant must answer the complaint or file a new motion to dismiss.

Motion for Judgment on the Pleadings

Once the pleadings are complete, either party can make a **motion for judgment on the pleadings**. This motion alleges that if all of the facts presented in the pleadings are true, the party making the motion would win the lawsuit when the proper law is applied to these facts. In deciding this motion, the judge cannot consider any facts outside the pleadings.

Motion for Summary Judgment

The trier of the fact (i.e., the jury, or, if no jury, the judge) determines *factual issues*. A **motion for summary judgment** asserts that there are no factual disputes to be decided by the jury and that the judge should apply the relevant law to the undisputed facts to decide the case. Motions for summary judgment, which can be made by either party, are supported by evidence outside the pleadings. Affidavits from the parties and witnesses, documents (e.g., a written contract between the parties), depositions, and such are common forms of evidence.

If, after examining the evidence, the court finds no factual dispute, it can decide the issue or issues raised in the summary judgment motion. This may dispense with the entire case or with part of the case. If the judge finds that a factual dispute exists, the motion will be denied and the case will go to trial.

SETTLEMENT CONFERENCE

Federal court rules and most state court rules permit the court to direct the attorneys or parties to appear before the court for a **pretrial hearing**, or **settlement conference**. One of the major purposes of these hearings is to facilitate settlement of the case. Pretrial conferences often are held informally in the judge's chambers. If no settlement is reached, the pretrial hearing is used to identify the major trial issues and other relevant factors.

More than 90 percent of all cases are settled before they go to trial. In cases that do proceed to trial, the trial judge may advise the attorneys of the rules or timetable of the individual judge. The judges also will advise the attorneys of any deadlines for discovery and the deadline for submitting any final motions with regard to what may be offered at the trial, called *motions in limine*.

In a number of jurisdictions, cases are referred to arbitration or other forms of alternative dispute resolution. Depending on the amount of money in controversy, some cases are required to be submitted before court-approved panels of attorneys sitting as arbitrators of the dispute. In other courts, the litigants may elect to have the case heard before an arbitration panel. Appeal rights from arbitration panel decisions vary, but cases typically may be appealed *de novo* to the trial court as if no arbitration had occurred, except possibly the payment of an appeal fee to cover part of the cost of the arbitration.

Exhibit 7.8 shows the sequence of key events before trial.

TRIAL

Pursuant to the Seventh Amendment to the U.S. Constitution, a party to an action at law is guaranteed the right to a **jury trial** in cases in federal court. Most state constitutions contain a similar guarantee for state court actions. If either party requests a jury, the trial will be by jury. If both parties waive their right to a jury, the trial will be without a jury. In non-jury trials, the judge sits as the **trier of fact.** These trials also are called *waiver trials* or **bench trials.** At the time of trial, the parties usually submit to the judge **trial briefs** containing legal support for their side of the case.

Trier of fact
The jury in a jury trial; the judge where there is not a jury trial.

Exhibit 7.8 **Key events before trial**

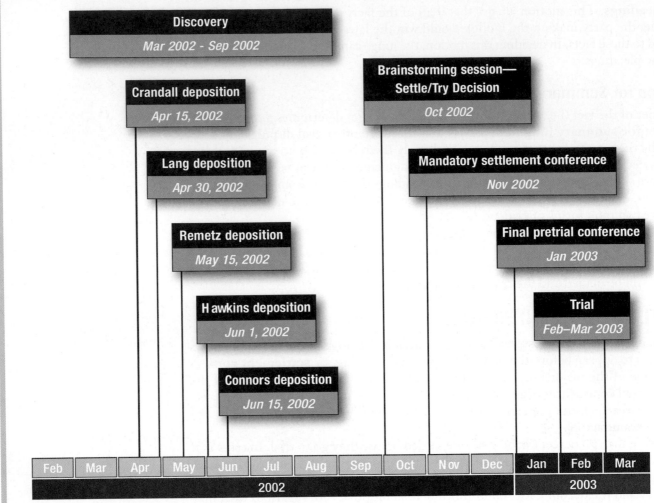

Prepared with TimeMap, courtesy of CaseSoft, a division of DataQuest.

Trials usually are divided into the following phases:

- Jury selection
- Opening statements
- Plaintiff's case
- Defendant's case
- Rebuttal and rejoinder
- Closing arguments
- Jury instructions
- Jury deliberation
- Entry of judgment

Jury Selection

In **jury selection**, the pool of the potential jurors usually is selected from voter or automobile registration lists. Potential jurors are asked to fill out a questionnaire such as that shown in Exhibit 7.9. Individuals are selected to hear specific cases through the process called **voir dire** ("to speak the truth"). Lawyers for each party and the judge can ask questions of prospective jurors to determine if they would be biased in their

Voir dire
Process whereby prospective jurors are asked questions by the judge and attorneys to determine if they would be biased in their decision.

Exhibit 7.9 **Sample jury questionnaire**

JURY QUESTIONNAIRE

(Please Print)

NAME _____   JUROR NO. _____

    (Last)   *(First)*   *(Middle initial)*

SECTION OF CITY _____

    (Currently)   *(Other sections of city lived in within past ten years)*

Marital Status   ☐ Married   ☐ Single   ☐ Divorced   ☐ Separated   ☐ Widowed

Occupation _____

    (Currently)   *(Other occupations within past ten years)*

Occupation of   ☐ Spouse *(or deceased spouse)*   ☐ Other

_____

    (Currently)   *(Other occupations within past ten years)*

No. of Male Children _____ Ages _____

No. of Female Children _____ Ages _____

Your Level of Schooling Completed _____

Race   ☐ White   ☐ Hispanic   ☐ Black   ☐ Other

STOP HERE
Writing below this line is prohibited until the juror video is shown

---

QUESTIONS TO BE ANSWERED IN THE JURY ASSEMBLY ROOM

1. Do you have any physical or psychological disability or are you presently taking any medication?   ❑ YES   ❑ NO

2. (a) Have you ever been a juror before?   ❑ YES   ❑ NO

    (b) If so, were you ever on a hung jury?   ❑ YES   ❑ NO

Questions 3 through 15 apply to criminal cases only

3. Do you have any religious, moral or ethical beliefs that would prevent you from sitting in judgment in a criminal case and rendering a fair verdict?   ❑ YES   ❑ NO

4. Have you or anyone close to you ever been a victim of a crime?   ❑ YES   ❑ NO

5. Have you or anyone close to you ever been charged with or arrested for a crime, other than a traffic violation?   ❑ YES   ❑ NO

6. Have you or anyone close to you ever been an eyewitness to a crime, whether or not it ever came to Court?   ❑ YES   ❑ NO

(continued)

Exhibit 7.9 **Sample jury questionnaire** *(continued)*

7. Have you, or has anyone close to you, ever worked as a police officer or in other law enforcement jobs? This includes prosecutors, public defenders, private criminal defense lawyers, detectives, and security or prison guards. ❏ YES ❏ NO

8. Would you be more likely to believe the testimony of a police officer or any other law enforcement officer just because of his job? ❏ YES ❏ NO

9. Would you be less likely to believe the testimony of a police officer or any other law enforcement officer just because of his job? ❏ YES ❏ NO

10. Would you have any problem following the Court's instruction that the defendant in a criminal case is presumed to be innocent until proven guilty beyond a reasonable doubt? ❏ YES ❏ NO

11. Would you have any problem following the Court's instruction that the defendant in a criminal case does not have to take the stand or present evidence, and it cannot be held against the defendant if he or she elects to remain silent? ❏ YES ❏ NO

12. Would you have any problem following the Court's instruction in a criminal case that just because someone is arrested, it does not mean that the person is guilty of anything? ❏ YES ❏ NO

13. In general, would you have any problem following and applying the judge's instructions on the law? ❏ YES ❏ NO

14. Would you have any problem during jury deliberations in a criminal case discussing the case fully but still making up your own mind? ❏ YES ❏ NO

15. Is there any other reason you could not be a fair juror in a criminal case? ❏ YES ❏ NO

Questions 16 through 24 apply to civil cases only

16. Have you or anyone close to you ever sued someone, been sued, or been a witness? ❏ YES ❏ NO

17. Have you or anyone close to you been employed as a lawyer or in a law-related job? ❏ YES ❏ NO

18. Have you or anyone close to you been employed as a doctor or nurse or in a medical-related job? ❏ YES ❏ NO

19. In a civil case, would you have any problem following the Court's instruction that the plaintiff has the burden or proof, but unlike in a criminal case, the test is not beyond a reasonable doubt but "more likely than not"? ❏ YES ❏ NO

20. In a civil case, would you have any problem putting aside sympathy for the plaintiff and deciding the case solely on the evidence? ❏ YES ❏ NO

21. In a civil case, would you have any problem following the Court's instruction to award money for damages for things like pain and suffering, loss of life's pleasures, etc., although it is difficult to put a dollar figure on them? ❏ YES ❏ NO

22. Would you have any problem during jury deliberations in a civil case discussing the case fully but still making up your own mind? ❏ YES ❏ NO

23. Is there any reason in a civil case that you cannot follow the Court's instructions on the law? ❏ YES ❏ NO

24. Is there any reason in a civil case that you cannot otherwise be a fair juror? ❏ YES ❏ NO

decision. Jurors can be "stricken for cause" if the court believes that the potential juror is too biased to render a fair verdict. Lawyers may also use preemptory challenges to exclude a juror from sitting on a particular case without giving any reason for the dismissal.

Once the appropriate number of jurors is selected (usually six to twelve jurors), they are impaneled to hear the case and are sworn in. The trial is ready to begin. In cases in which the Court is concerned for the safety of the jury, such as a high-profile murder case, it can **sequester,** or separate it from the outside world. Jurors are paid minimum fees for their service. Courts can hold people in contempt and fine or jail them for willful refusal to serve as a juror.

Opening Statements

Each party's attorney is allowed to make an **opening statement** to the jury. In opening statements, attorneys usually summarize the main factual and legal issues of the case and describe why they believe their client's position is valid. The information given in this statement is not considered as evidence. It is the attorney's opportunity to tell the trier of fact what he or she intends to tell the jury through witnesses and evidence.

Plaintiff's Case

Plaintiffs bear the **burden of proof** to persuade the trier of fact of the merits of their case. This is called the **plaintiff's case.** The plaintiff's attorney calls witnesses to give testimony. After a witness has been sworn in, the plaintiff's attorney examines (questions) the witness. This is called **direct examination.** Documents and other evidence can be introduced through each witness.

After the plaintiff's attorney has completed his or her questions, the defendant's attorney can question the witness in **cross-examination.** The defendant's attorney can ask questions only about the subjects that were brought up during the direct examination. After the defendant's attorney completes his or her questions, the plaintiff's attorney can ask questions of the witness in **redirect examination.** The defendant's attorney then can ask questions of the witness again. This is called **recross examination.** Exhibit 7.10 illustrates this sequence for examining witnesses.

Plaintiff's case
Process by which the plaintiff calls witnesses and introduces evidence to prove the allegations contained in his or her complaint.

Defendant's Case

After the plaintiff has concluded his or her case, the **defendant's case** proceeds. The defendant's case must

1. rebut the plaintiff's evidence.
2. prove any affirmative defenses asserted by the defendant.
3. prove any allegations contained in the defendant's cross-complaint.

The defendant's witnesses are examined in much the same way as the plaintiff's attorney cross-examines each witness. This is followed by redirect and recross examination.

Defendant's case
Process by which the defendant calls witnesses and introduces evidence to (1) rebut the plaintiffs evidence, (2) prove affirmative defenses, and (3) prove allegations made in a cross-complaint.

Rebuttal and Rejoinder

After the defendant's attorney has completed calling witnesses, the plaintiff's attorney can call witnesses and put forth evidence to rebut the defendant's case. This is called a **rebuttal.** The defendant's attorney can call additional witnesses and introduce other evidence to counter the rebuttal. This is called the **rejoinder.**

Closing Arguments

At the conclusion of the evidence, each party's attorney is allowed to make a **closing argument** to the jury. Each attorney tries to convince the jury to render a verdict for

Exhibit 7.10 Sequence for examining witnesses

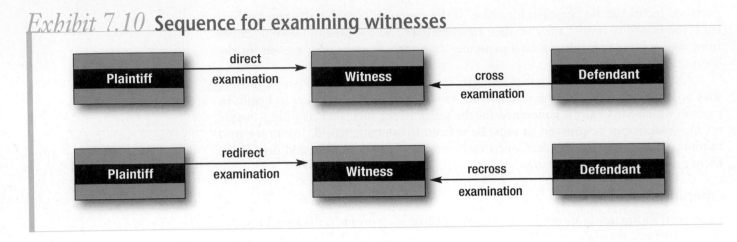

his or her clients by pointing out the strengths in the clients' case and the weaknesses in the other side's case.

Information given by the attorneys in their closing statements is not evidence. It is a chance for the attorneys to tell the jury what they said they would tell the jury through witnesses and evidence in the opening statements and how they had done that during the trial.

Jury Instructions

Jury instructions (charges)
Instructions given by the judge to the jury that informs them of the law to be applied in the case.

Once the closing arguments are completed, the judge reads **jury instructions**, or **charges** to the jury. These instructions inform the jury about what law to apply in deciding the case (see Exhibit 7.11). For example, in a criminal trial the judge will read the jury the statutory definition of the crime charged. In an accident case, the judge will read the jury the legal definition of *negligence*.

Jury Deliberation

Verdict
Decision reached by the jury.

The jury then goes into the jury room to deliberate its findings. **Jury deliberation** can take from a few minutes to many weeks. After deliberation, the jury announces its **verdict.** In civil cases, the jury also assesses damages. In criminal cases, the judge assesses penalties.

Entry of Judgment

Judgment
The official decision of the court.

After the jury has returned its verdict, in most cases the judge enters **judgment** to the successful party, based on the verdict. This is the official decision of the court. But the court may overturn the verdict if it finds bias or jury misconduct. This is called a **judgment notwithstanding the verdict**, or **judgment n.o.v.**, or **j.n.o.v.**, for the Latin *judgment non obstante verdicto*.

In a civil case, the judge may reduce the amount of monetary damages awarded by the jury if he or she finds the jury to have been biased, emotional, or inflamed. This is called **remittitur**: The trial court usually issues a **written memorandum** setting forth the reasons for the judgment. This memorandum, together with the trial transcript and evidence introduced at trial, constitutes the permanent *record* of the trial court proceeding.

APPEAL

Appeal
The act of asking an appellate court to overturn a decision after the trial court's final judgment has been entered.

In a civil case, either party can **appeal** the trial court's decision once a final judgment is entered. In a criminal case, only the defendant can appeal. The appeal is made to the appropriate **appellate court** (see Exhibit 7.12). A notice of appeal must be filed

Exhibit 7.11 Sample jury instructions

6.01J (Civ) PROPERTY DAMAGE

The plaintiff is entitled to be compensated for the harm done to his (her) property. If you find that the property was a total loss, damages are to be measured by either its market value or its special value to plaintiff, whichever is greater. If the property was not a total loss, damages are measured by (the difference in value before and after the harm) (the reasonable cost of repairs) and you may consider such evidence produced by defendant by way of defense to plaintiff's claim. In addition, plaintiff is entitled to be reimbursed for incidental costs or losses reasonably incurred because of the damage to the property, such as (rental of a replacement vehicle during repairs), (towing charges), (loss of use of the property), (etc.).

SUBCOMMITTEE NOTE

Damage to property is covered generally by Restatement of Torts, §§ 927 and 928. Section 927 provides for damages to be measured by the "market value" or "damages based upon its special value to [plaintiff] if that is greater than its market value." Restatement of Torts, § 927, Comment c (1934). Section 928 provides, in the case of damages not amounting to total destruction, damages measured by "the difference between the value of the chattel before the harm and the value after the harm or, at plaintiff's election, the reasonable cost of repair or restoration." This accounts for the parenthesized phrases (the difference in value before and after the harm) and (the reasonable cost of repairs).

Incidental costs will depend on the nature of the property damage. Rental of a substitute vehicle has long been recognized as one such compensable item. *Bauer v. Armour & Co.*, 84 Pa.Super. 174 (1924). Compensation for loss of use is specifically authorized by Restatement of Torts, § 928(b), in the case of less than total loss. The Subcommittee can see no logical reason why such damages should not be awarded under Section 927 in the case of total loss. *Nelson v. Johnson*, 55 D. & C. 2d 21 (Somerset C.P. 1970). Any further expense, proximately resulting from the loss or damage is recoverable under general provisions of tort law. *Nelson v. Johnson, supra,* at 33–34.

In the case of damage to automobiles, however, the appellate courts have adhered to the ancient rule requiring testimony of the one who supervised or made the repairs, prior to admission of damage estimates. *Mackiw v. Pennsylvania Threshermen & Farmers Mut. Cas. Ins. Co.*, 201 Pa.Super. 626, 193 A.2d 745 (1963). This rule has been criticized as time-consuming and "technical" by the very courts adhering to it. *Mackiw, supra,* 193 A.2d at 745. It further creates an intolerable burden on the courts, in a period when backlog has led to "compulsory" arbitration in many counties of cases valued below $10,000. E.g., *Loughery v. Barnes*, 181 Pa.Super. 352, 124 A.2d 120 (1956) (appeal after verdict of $341.30 for property damage); *Wilk v. Borough of Mt. Oliver*, 152 Pa.Super. 539, 33 A.2d 73 (1943) (new trial ordered after verdict of $175). The Subcommittee therefore adopts a rule requiring only the submission of a repair bill or estimate in proof of damages to automobiles (such bill being submitted prior to trial to defense counsel); should defendant wish to challenge such an estimate, he may do so through cross-examination and through the introduction of evidence in his own case. See *Watsontown Brick Co. v. Hercules Powder Co.*, 265 F.Supp. 268, 275 (M.D.Pa.), *aff'd*, 387 F.2d 99 (3rd Cir. 1967) (after introduction of damage evidence, burden shifts to defendant to show reduction).

Absent stipulation, the issue of reasonable compensation remains a jury issue.

6.01F (Civ) FUTURE PAIN AND SUFFERING

The plaintiff is entitled to be fairly and adequately compensated for such physical pain, mental anguish, discomfort, inconvenience and distress as you believe he (she) will endure in the future as a result of his (her) injuries. [. . .]

Exhibit

Settle

Descr

Trial

Jury S

Open

Plaint

Defer

Rebu

Closir

Jury I

Jury I

Entry

Appe

Appel

Appellant
The appealing
known as *petit*

Appellee
The respondir
Also known as

Briefs
Documents su
attorneys to th
gal support for

Briefs

Oral

Actio

Affir

Rever

Rema

ADMINISTRATIVE LAW

"I should regret to find that the law was powerless to enforce the most elementary principles of commercial morality."

*LORD HERSCHELL,
REDDAWAY v. BANHAM
(1896)*

PARALEGALS AT WORK

You are a paralegal for a large law firm that represents clients in proceedings before federal government agencies. One of your clients is Medic Pharmaceutical Corporation, a large pharmaceutical company that invents, patents, and markets prescription drugs in the United States and worldwide. Ms. Phoebe Jones is the senior law partner you work for at the firm.

One day Ms. Jones explains that Medic Pharmaceutical Corporation has employed the law firm to represent it in a highly classified administrative law case. Ms. Jones tells you the following facts: Medic Pharmaceutical Corporation has invented a new drug it calls "Paean." The new drug cures the common cold. This is one of the most important inventions of all time and will make Medic Pharmaceutical Corporation the richest corporation in the world. Shareholders of the corporation will increase their investment one-hundred fold if the new drug receives the necessary government approval and comes to market.

Ms. Jones explains that Medic Pharmaceutical Corporation has employed the law firm to represent the corporation in proceedings at the U.S. Food and Drug Administration (FDA). The FDA is a federal government administrative agency whose approval must be obtained before a new prescription drug can be sold to the public. Ms. Jones is the lead attorney of the law firm that will represent Medic Pharmaceutical Corporation in its proceedings at the FDA. Ms. Jones informs you that you will be assisting her in this matter. Ms. Jones also explains to you that this is a highly confidential matter.

Consider the issues involved in this scenario as you read the chapter.

After studying this chapter, you should be able to:

1. Describe general government regulation.
2. Describe specific government regulation.
3. Define an *administrative agency*.
4. Explain the scope of the Administrative Procedure Act.
5. Describe the legislative powers of administrative agencies.
6. Describe the judicial powers of administrative agencies.
7. Describe the executive powers of administrative agencies.
8. List the responsibilities of the Federal Food and Drug Administration and other government agencies.

▶INTRODUCTION FOR THE PARALEGAL

Many paralegals work for lawyers who engage in a practice of law that deals with governmental administrative agencies and government regulation. These matters could include filing applications for licenses from federal and state administrative agencies, appearing at hearings before these agencies, or appealing from decisions rendered by administrative agencies. Paralegals who assist lawyers in this area of the law should have a knowledge of how administrative agencies work.

The federal government's ability to create administrative agencies is implied in the U.S. Constitution. Congress and the executive branch of government have created more than 100 federal **administrative agencies**. These agencies are intended to provide resources and expertise in dealing with complex commercial organizations and businesses. In addition, state governments have created many state administrative agencies. Since the 1960s, the numbers of administrative agencies and the regulations they produce have increased substantially. Because of their importance, administrative agencies are informally referred to as the *fourth branch of government*. (In reality, they only have the powers delegated from the actual branches of government.) Federal and state administrative agencies have adopted and enforced thousands of rules and regulations regarding business operations.

This chapter discusses administrative agencies and government regulation. ■

ADMINISTRATIVE LAW AND AGENCIES

The government's record-keeping and reporting requirements form a large part of administrative law. Other government regulations concern proper business purpose and conduct, entry restrictions into an industry, government rate setting, and the like.

General Government Regulation

General government regulation
Government regulation that applies to many industries collectively.

Most government regulation applies to many businesses and industries collectively. For example, the National Labor Relations Board (NLRB) is empowered to regulate the formation and operation of labor unions in most industries, the Occupational Safety and Health Administration (OSHA) is authorized to formulate and enact safety and health standards for the workplace, the Consumer Product Safety Commission (CPSC) is empowered to establish mandatory safety standards for products sold in the United States, and the Securities and Exchange Commission (SEC) is authorized to enforce federal securities laws that apply to issuers of and persons who trade in securities.

Specific Government Regulation

Specific government regulation
Government regulation that applies to individual industries.

The U.S. Congress and the executive branch have created some administrative agencies to monitor certain regulated industries. For example, the Federal Communications Commission (FCC) regulates the operation of television and radio stations, the Interstate Commerce Commission (ICC) regulates railroads, the Federal Aviation Administration (FAA) regulates commercial airlines, and the Office of the Comptroller of the Currency (OCC) regulates national banks. Although a detailed discussion of these agencies and the laws they administer is beyond the scope of this book, the reader should know that they exist.

Administrative Agencies

Administrative agencies are established with the overall goal of creating a body of professionals who are experts in a specific field. These experts have delegated authority to regulate an individual industry or a specific area of commerce. Federal, state, and local governments create administrative agencies ranging from large, complex federal agencies, such as the Department of Health and Human Services, to local zoning

DO-NOT-CALL REGISTRY

Two federal administrative agencies—the Federal Trade Commission (FTC) and the **Federal Communications Commission (FCC)** are accorded heroes' status by consumers for creating the **Do-Not-Call Registry**, on which consumers can place their names and free themselves from most unsolicited commercial telephone calls. The FTC and the FCC found their authority to adopt their coordinated do-not-call rules in several federal statutes.

(1) The **Telephone Consumer Protection Act of 1991**, which authorized the FCC to establish a national database of consumers who objected to receiving commercial sales calls.

(2) The **Telemarketing and Consumer Fraud and Abuse Prevention Act of 1994**, which authorized the FTC to prohibit sales calls that a reasonable consumer would consider abusive to his or her privacy.

(3) After the Do-Not-Call Registry was put in place, in 2003 Congress enacted an **Act to Ratify the Authority of the Federal Trade Commission to Establish a Do-Not-Call Registry**.

In 2003, the FTC and the FCC promulgated administrative rules that created the Do-Not-Call Registry. A person can place himself or herself on the Do-Not-Call Registry by calling toll-free 888-382-1222 or registering online, at www.donotcall.gov. Wire-connected phones and wireless cell phones both can be registered. Telemarketers have 3 months from the date on which a consumer signs up for the registry to remove the customer's phone number from their sales call list. Customer registration remains valid for five years and can be renewed. Charitable and political organizations are exempt from the registry.

Also, an "established business relationship" exception allows businesses to call customers for 10 months after they sell or lease goods or services to that person or conduct a financial transaction with that person. The Do-Not-Call Registry allows consumers to designate specific companies not to call them, including those that otherwise qualify for the established business relationship exemption.

Telemarketers, who claimed they would lose substantial business and have to fire millions of workers, sued to have the Do-Not-Call Registry declared unconstitutional as a violation of their constitutional right to free speech. A U.S. District Court in Colorado agreed with the telemarketers. On appeal, however, the U.S. Court of Appeals for the Tenth Circuit reversed, holding that the Do-Not-Call Registry did not violate telemarketers' free speech rights. The Court of Appeals stated, "The Do-Not-Call Registry lets consumers avoid unwanted sales pitches that invade the home via telephone." [*Mainstream Marketing Services, Inc. v. Federal Trade Commission*, 358 F.3d 1228, 2004 U.S. App. Lexis 2564 (2004)]

boards. Many administrative agencies are given the authority to adopt rules and regulations that enforce and interpret statutory law.

Administrative law combines substantive and procedural law. Each administrative agency is empowered to administer a specific statute or statutes. For example, the Securities and Exchange Commission (SEC) is authorized to enforce the Securities Act of 1933, the Securities Exchange Act of 1934, and other federal statutes dealing with securities markets. These statutes are the **substantive law** that the agency enforces. Administrative agencies are often criticized for creating too much "red tape" for businesses and individuals.

Federal Administrative Agencies

The most pervasive government regulations have developed from the statutes enforced by and the rules and regulations adopted by **federal administrative agencies**. Most federal administrative agencies—including the Justice Department, the Department of Housing and Urban Development, the Labor Department, the Transportation Department, and the Commerce Department—are part of the executive branch of government.

Federal administrative agencies
Agencies established by legislative and executive branches of federal and state governments.

DEPARTMENT OF HOMELAND SECURITY

On September 11, 2001, the World Trade Center buildings in New York City were destroyed and the Pentagon in Washington, D.C. was damaged by terrorist attacks. After the attacks, President George W. Bush issued an Executive Order creating the Office of Homeland Security. The President called for the Office to be made into a Cabinet-level agency. Congress responded by enacting the **Homeland Security Act of 2002**, which created the Cabinet-level **Department of Homeland Security (DHS)**. The DHS is the largest government reorganization in more than 50 years.

The Act placed 22 existing federal agencies with more than 180,000 employees under the umbrella of the DHS. The DHS is the second largest government agency (the Department of Defense is the largest). The DHS contains the Bureau of Customs and Border Protection, the Bureau of Citizenship and Immigration Services, the U.S. Secret Service, the Federal Emergency Management Agency (FEMA), the Federal Computer Incident Response Center, the National Domestic Preparedness Office, the U.S. Coast Guard, and portions of the Federal Bureau of Investigation (FBI), Treasury Department, Commerce Department, Justice Department, and other federal government agencies.

The mission of the DHS is to prevent domestic terror attacks, reduce vulnerability to terror attacks, minimize the harm caused by such attacks, and assist in the recovery if a terrorist attack occurs. The DHS provides services in the following critical areas:

(1) border and transportation security, including protecting airports, seaports, and borders, and providing immigration and visa processing;

(2) chemical, biological, radiological, and nuclear countermeasures, including metering the air for biological agents and developing vaccines and treatments for biological agents;

(3) information analysis and infrastructure protection, including protection of communications systems, power grids, transportation networks, telecommunications, and cyber systems; and

(4) emergency preparedness and response to terrorist incidents, including training first responders and coordinating government disaster relief.

See Exhibit 8.1 for a diagram of the Department of Homeland Security.

Congress has established many **federal administrative agencies**. These agencies are independent of the executive branch and have broad regulatory powers over key areas of the national economy.

State Administrative Agencies

All states have created administrative agencies to enforce and interpret state law. For example, most states have a corporations department to enforce state corporations law, a banking department to regulate the operation of banks, fish and game departments, and workers' compensation boards. **State administrative agencies** also have a profound effect on business. Local governments and municipalities create administrative agencies, such as zoning commissions, to administer local law.

Administrative Procedure Act

In 1946, Congress enacted the **Administrative Procedure Act (APA)** [5 U.S.C. Sections 551 et seq.], which established certain administrative procedures that federal administrative agencies must follow in conducting their affairs. For example, the APA establishes notice and hearing requirements, rules for conducting agency adjudicative actions, and procedures for rule making. In addition, most states have enacted administrative procedural acts that govern state administrative agencies.

Delegation of Powers

Because the U.S. Constitution does not stipulate that administrative agencies are a separate branch of the government, the legislative or executive branch must create them. When an administrative agency is created, it is delegated certain powers. Under

Find out the threat advisory for the risk of terrorist attacks today at http://dhs.gov/dhspublic/

Administrative Procedure Act (APA)
An act that establishes certain administrative procedures that federal administrative agencies must follow in conducting their affairs.

Exhibit 8.1 **Department of Homeland Security**

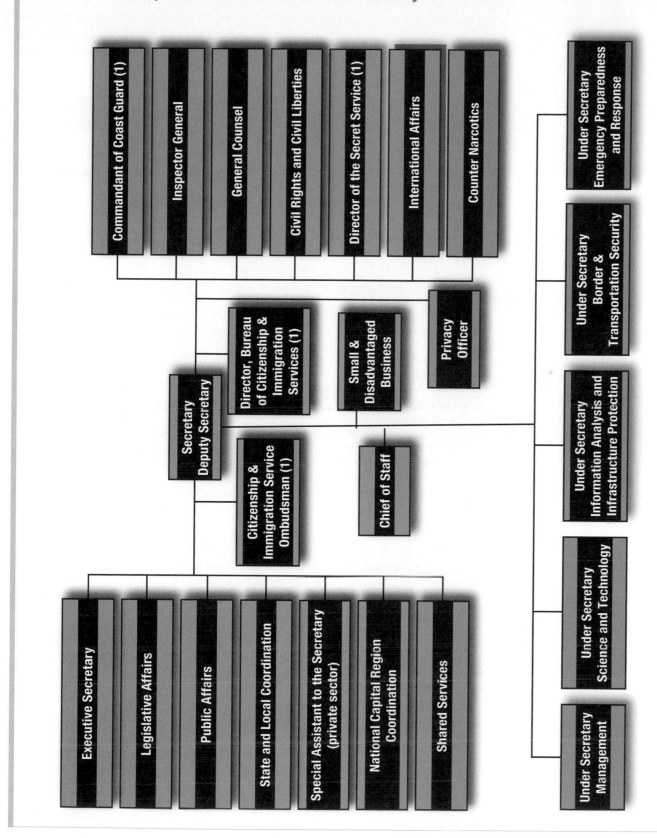

the **delegation doctrine** the agency has only the legislative, judicial, and executive powers that are delegated to it.

Thus, an agency can adopt a rule or regulation (a legislative function), prosecute a violation of the statute or rule (an executive function), and adjudicate the dispute (a judicial function). The courts generally have upheld this combined power of admin-

THE PARALEGAL AND ADMINISTRATIVE LAW

Lawyers increasingly employ paralegals in areas of law that involve practice before administrative agencies. Administrative law has become extremely important for businesses and individuals alike. Administrative agencies govern many aspects of general business operations, specific industries, and our personal lives as well.

The number of administrative agencies in this country is staggering. The federal government alone has dozens of administrative agencies. These range from agencies whose powers apply to the country and economy in general, to agencies that regulate specific industries. Some of the major federal administrative agencies are:

- Environmental Protection Agency (EPA): regulates air, water, hazardous waste, and other types of pollution.
- Equal Employment Opportunity Commission (EEOC): enforces many antidiscrimination laws that affect businesses, employees, disabled persons, and others.
- Federal Trade Commission (FTC): enforces many consumer protection laws.
- Food and Drug Administration (FDA): regulates the safety of foods, drugs, cosmetics, and medicinal devices.
- Federal Communications Commission (FCC): regulates radio, television, cable, and other broadcast media.
- National Labor Relations Board (NLRB): regulates labor union formation, elections, bargaining with employers, and other labor issues.
- Securities Exchange Commission (SEC): regulates the issuance, sale, and purchase of securities, including stocks and bonds.
- Department of Homeland Security (DHS): responsible for coordinating certain federal agencies in protecting the country against terrorism and other threats.

In addition to federal administrative agencies, there are thousands of state and local administrative agencies. These include state administrative agencies that regulate corporations, agencies that license and regulate financial institutions, state environmental protection agencies, and other state administrative agencies. At the local level, cities and municipalities have administrative agencies that regulate construction, set building codes, establish zoning regulations, issue water permits, and so forth.

Paralegals often work for lawyers who specialize in making appearances before specific federal, state, and local administrative agencies. For example, lawyers must prepare applications for submission to the Federal Communications Commission (FCC) to obtain a license for a client to operate a radio, television, or cable company. Lawyers must prepare applications for submission to the Federal Food and Drug Administration (FDA) to obtain approval for a client to market a new drug. Lawyers must prepare applications to be submitted to a state banking commission to obtain a license for a client to operate a new commercial bank.

The federal government has enacted the Administrative Procedure Act (APA), which establishes rules for legal practice before federal administrative agencies. The state has similar administrative procedures acts/at the state level. In addition, each administrative agency has its own rules and regulations for submitting applications and appearing at hearings before the administrative agency.

Paralegals who work for lawyers specializing in certain administrative law practices must become familiar with that agency's rules and procedures. Paralegals often are called upon to assist in drafting documents that will be submitted to administrative agencies and preparing cases that will be heard and decided by these agencies. Thus, paralegals often become experts in areas of administrative law and, therefore, can be indispensable to lawyers who practice before administrative agencies.

istrative agencies as being constitutional. If an administrative agency acts outside the scope of its delegated powers, it is an unconstitutional act.

LEGISLATIVE POWERS OF ADMINISTRATIVE AGENCIES

Administrative agencies usually are delegated certain legislative powers. These include rule making and licensing powers.

Substantive Rule Making

Many federal statutes expressly authorize an administrative agency to issue **substantive rules**. A substantive regulation is much like a statute: It has the force of law, and the persons and businesses it covers must adhere to it.

Violators may be held civilly or criminally liable, depending on the rule. All substantive rules are subject to judicial review.

A federal administrative agency that proposes to adopt a substantive rule must follow procedures set forth in the APA. This means that the agency must do the following:

1. Publish a general notice of the proposed rule making in the *Federal Register*. The notice must include
   a. the time, place, and nature of the rule-making proceeding.
   b. the legal authority pursuant to which the rule is proposed.
   c. the terms or substance of the proposed rule or a description of the subject and issues involved.
2. Give interested persons an opportunity to participate in the rule-making process. This may involve oral hearings.
3. Review all written and oral comments. Then the agency announces its *final rule making* in the matter. This procedure often is referred to as *notice-and-comment rule making*, or *informal rule making*.
4. Require, in some instances, *formal rule making*. Here, the agency must conduct a trial-like hearing at which the parties may present evidence, engage in cross-examination, present rebuttal evidence, and such.

Substantive rule
A rule issued by an administrative agency that has much the same power as a statute: It has the force of law and must be adhered to by covered persons and businesses.

Interpretive Rule Making

Administrative agencies can issue **interpretive rules** which explain existing statutory language. These rules do not establish new laws, and neither public notice nor public participation is required.

Statements of Policy

Administrative agencies also can issue **statements of policy.** These statements announce a proposed course of action that an agency intends to follow in the future. These statements do not have the force of law. Again, public notice and participation are not required.

Licensing Powers

Statutes often require the issuance of a government **license** before a person can enter certain types of industries (e.g., the operation of banks, television and radio stations, commercial airlines) or professions (e.g., doctors, lawyers, dentists, certified public accountants, contractors). Most administrative agencies have the power to determine whether to grant licenses to applicants.

Applicants usually must submit detailed applications to the appropriate administrative agency. In addition, the agency usually accepts written comments from interested parties and holds hearings on the matter. The administrative agency's decision is subject to judicial review. The courts, however, generally defer to the expertise of administrative agencies in licensing matters.

Ethical Requirements for Attorneys Who Hire Paralegals

The Colorado Bar Association has promulgated a set of ethical requirements for an attorney who hires paralegals. These ethical requirements are:

1. A lawyer shall ascertain the paralegal's abilities, limitations and training, and must limit the paralegal's duties and responsibilities to those that can be competently performed in view of those abilities, limitations and training.
2. A lawyer shall educate and train paralegals with respect to the ethical standards which apply to the lawyer.
3. A lawyer is responsible for monitoring and supervising the conduct of paralegals to prevent the violation of the ethical standards which apply to the lawyer, and the lawyer is responsible for assuring that paralegals do not do anything which the lawyer could not do.
4. A lawyer shall continuously monitor and supervise the work of paralegals in order to assure that the services rendered by the paralegals are performed competently and in a professional manner.
5. A lawyer is responsible for assuring that the paralegal does not engage in the unauthorized practice of law.
6. A lawyer shall assume responsibility for the improper conduct of paralegals and must take appropriate action to prevent recurrence of improper behavior or activities.
7. Paralegals who deal directly with lawyers' clients must be identified to those clients as non-lawyers, and the lawyer is responsible for obtaining the understanding of the clients with respect to the role of and the limitations which apply to those assistants.

EXECUTIVE POWERS OF ADMINISTRATIVE AGENCIES

Good government is an empire of laws.

John Adams
Thoughts on Government (1776)

Administrative agencies usually are granted **executive powers**, the authority to investigate and prosecute possible violations of statutes, administrative rules, and administrative orders. To perform these functions successfully, the agency often must obtain information from the persons and businesses under investigation, as well as from other sources. If the required information is not supplied voluntarily, the agency may issue an administrative subpoena to search the business premises. As discussed shortly, however, these powers are subject to certain constitutional constraints.

Administrative Subpoena

Administrative subpoena
An order that directs the subject of the subpoena to disclose the requested information.

An **administrative subpoena** is an order that directs the subject of the subpoena to disclose the requested information. Judicial enforcement may be sought if the party does not comply with the subpoena and the agency can prove that it has reasonable grounds to believe that the information sought will prove to be a violation of the law. "Fishing expeditions" are prohibited. If a party ignores a judicial order to enforce an administrative subpoena, the party may be held in contempt of court.

Administrative Searches

Sometimes a physical inspection of a business premise is crucial to the investigation. Most inspections by administrative agencies are considered "searches" subject to the Fourth Amendment of the U.S. Constitution. The Fourth Amendment protects persons (including businesses) from unreasonable search and seizures.

Searches by administrative agencies are generally considered to be reasonable within the meaning of the Fourth Amendment if

- the party voluntarily agrees to the search.
- the search is conducted pursuant to a validly issued **search warrant.**
- a warrantless search is conducted in an emergency situation.

- the business is part of a special industry in which warrantless searches are automatically considered valid (such as liquor or firearm sales).
- the business is part of a hazardous industry and a statute expressly provides for nonarbitrary warrantless searches (such as coal mines).

Evidence from an unreasonable search and seizure ("tainted evidence") may be inadmissible in court, depending on the circumstances of the case.

JUDICIAL POWERS OF ADMINISTRATIVE AGENCIES

Many administrative agencies have the judicial authority to adjudicate cases through an administrative proceeding. Such a proceeding is initiated when an agency serves a complaint on a party the agency believes has violated a statute or administrative rule or order. The person on whom the complaint is served is called the respondent.

In adjudicating cases, an administrative agency must comply with the **Due Process Clause** of the U.S. Constitution (and the state constitution, where applicable). **Procedural due process** requires that the respondent be given (1) proper and timely notice of the allegations or charges against him or her, and (2) an opportunity to present evidence on the matter. **Substantive due process** requires that the statute or rule that the respondent is charged with violating be clearly stated.

Procedures for Administrative Adjudication

Administrative law judges (ALJs) preside over administrative proceedings and decide questions of law and fact concerning the case. There is no jury. The ALJ is an employee of the administrative agency.

Administrative law judges (ALJ)
A judge, presiding over administrative proceedings, who decides questions of law and fact concerning the case.

checklist ✓ POWERS OF ADMINISTRATIVE AGENCIES

POWER	DESCRIPTION
Legislative Powers	
1. Substantive rule making	Adopting rules that advance the purpose of the statutes the agency is empowered to enforce. These rules have the force of law, and public notice and participation are required.
2. Interpretive rule making	Adopting rules that interpret statutory language. These rules do not establish new laws, and neither public notice nor participation is required.
3. Statements of policy	Announcing a proposed course of action the agency plans to take in the future. These statements do not have the force of law, and public participation and notice are not required.
4. Licensing	Granting licenses to applicants (e.g., television station licenses, bank charters) and to suspend or revoke licenses.
Executive Powers	
	To prosecute violations of statutes and administrative rules and orders, including the power to investigate suspected violations, issue administrative subpoenas, and conduct administrative searches.
Judicial Powers	
	To adjudicate cases through an administrative proceeding, including the power to issue a complaint, hold a hearing by an administrative law judge (ALJ), and issue an order deciding the case and assessing remedies.

Exhibit

U.S. S

Government in the Sunshine Act

The **Government in the Sunshine Act** [5 U.S.C. Section 552(b)] was enacted to open certain federal administrative agency meetings to the public. Only federal administrative agencies that are headed by two or more persons appointed by the President are subject to this Act. Exceptions to this rule are meetings (1) about things that are exempt from disclosure under the Freedom of Information Act, (2) where a person is accused of a crime, (3) concerning an agency's issuance of a subpoena, (4) where attendance of the public would significantly frustrate implementation of a proposed agency action, and (5) concerning day-to-day operations. Decisions by federal administrative agencies to close a meeting to the public are subject to judicial review in the proper U.S. district court.

Government in the Sunshine Act
An act that was enacted to open certain federal administrative agency meetings to the public.

Equal Access to Justice Act

Congress enacted the **Equal Access to Justice Act** [5 U.S.C. Section 504] to protect persons from harassment by federal administrative agencies. Under this Act, a private party who is the subject of an unjustified federal administrative agency action can sue to recover attorneys' fees and other costs. The courts generally have held that the agency's conduct must be extremely outrageous before they will make an award under this Act. A number of states have similar statutes.

Privacy Act

The federal **Privacy Act** [5 U.S.C. Section 552(a)] stipulates that federal administrative agencies can maintain only information about an individual that is relevant and necessary to accomplish a legitimate agency purpose. The Act affords individuals the right to have access to agency records concerning themselves and to correct these records. Many states have enacted similar privacy acts.

FEDERAL ADMINISTRATIVE AGENCIES

The federal executive and legislative branches of the government have created hundreds of federal administrative agencies. Each agency is delegated the power to regulate a certain part of the economy or a specific industry.

Several of the most important federal administrative agencies are discussed in the following paragraphs. These include the Federal Food and Drug Administration (FDA), the Equal Opportunity Employment Commission (EEOC), the Consumer Product Safety Commission (CPSC), the Federal Trade Commission (FTC), and the Environmental Protection Agency (EPA).

Food and Drug Administration (FDA)

The **Food and Drug Administration (FDA)** is a federal administrative agency that is involved in the regulation of food, drugs, cosmetics, and medicinal devices. The first federal statute regulating the wholesomeness of food and drug products was enacted in 1906. A much more comprehensive act—the federal **Food, Drug and Cosmetic Act (FDCA)** [21 U.S.C. Section 301]—was enacted in 1938. This Act, as amended, provides the basis for regulation of much of the testing, manufacture, distribution, and sale of foods, drugs, cosmetics, and medicinal products and devices in the United States. The FDA can seek search warrants and conduct inspections; obtain orders for the seizure, recall, and condemnation of products; seek injunctions; and seek criminal penalties against willful violations. The U.S. Department of Justice has the authority to bring lawsuits to enforce the FDCA.

Before certain food additives, drugs, and medicinal devices can be sold to the public, they must receive FDA approval. An applicant must submit an application to the FDA that contains relevant information about the safety and uses of the product.

Food and Drug Administration (FDA)
A federal administrative agency that administers and enforces the federal Food, Drug, and Cosmetic Act (FDCA) and other federal consumer protection laws.

Food, Drug, and Cosmetic Act (FDCA)
A federal statute enacted in 1938 that provides the basis for the regulation of much of the testing, manufacture, distribution, and sale of foods, drugs, cosmetics, and medicinal products.

After considering the evidence, the FDA will either approve or deny the application. The FDA can sue and obtain a seizure order and injunction against further sales of unapproved items.

Regulation of Food

The federal government has enacted a comprehensive set of statutes that regulates the manufacture, processing, distribution, and sale of food. These laws are intended to (1) ensure the wholesomeness of food, (2) encourage accuracy in labeling and packaging, and (3) prevent injury to health.

Adulterated Food

The FDCA prohibits the shipment, distribution, or sale of **adulterated food**. Food is deemed adulterated if it consists in whole or in part any "filthy, putrid, or decomposed substance" or if it is otherwise "unfit for food." Note that food does not have to be entirely pure to be distributed or sold; it only has to be unadulterated.

Misbranded Food

The FDCA also prohibits false and misleading labeling of food products called **misbranded food**. In addition, it mandates affirmative disclosure of information on food labels, including the name of the food, the name and place of the manufacturer, and a statement of ingredients. A manufacturer may be held liable for deceptive labeling or packaging.

Go to the FDA website. Click on "Contact FDA." Select the Topic "Food (Including Dietary Supplements)." Then click on "Food Labeling." Find the definitions for "Healthy," "Reduced," and Fresh." http://www.fda.gov/

Regulation of Drugs

The FDCA gives the FDA the authority to regulate the testing, manufacture, distribution, and sale of **drugs**. The *Drug Amendment to the FDCA*, enacted in 1962, give

---

A HIDDEN SOURCE OF PROTEIN IN PEANUT BUTTER

You take a big bite of a peanut butter sandwich and savor the taste. It has been processed by a food manufacturer and inspected by the federal government, so you think it is pure peanut butter. Not necessarily. Under federal FDA guidelines, peanut butter may contain up to 30 insect fragments per 3½ ounces and still be considered "safe" for human consumption.

The FDA has set ceilings or "action levels" for certain contaminants, or "defects," as the FDA calls them, for various foods. Several of these action levels are

Golden raisins—35 fly eggs per 8 ounces
Popcorn—two rodent hairs per pound
Shelled peanuts—20 Insects per 100 pounds
Canned mushrooms—20 maggots per 3½ ounces
Tomato juice—10 fly eggs per 3½ ounces

The FDA can mount inspections and raids to enforce its action levels. If it finds that the federal tolerance system has been violated, it can seize the offending food and destroy it at the owner's expense. For example, in the Great Peanut Raid of 1991, the FDA seized 8.5 million pounds of peanuts shipped to the United States from foreign countries. The FDA found that these peanuts contained illegal levels of contamination and sent them back to their home countries.

The courts have upheld the presence of some contamination in food as lawful under the Food, Drug, and Cosmetic Act. For example, in one case the court found that 28 insect parts in 9 pounds of butter did not violate the Act. The court stated, "Few foods contain no natural or unavoidable defects. Even with modern technology, all defects in foods cannot be eliminated" [*United States v. Capital City Foods, Inc.*, 345 F.Supp. 277 (N.D. 1972)].

Exhibit 8.4 **Application to market a new drug, biologic, or an antibiotic drug for human use**

| Next Page | Export Data | Import Data | Reset Form |

DEPARTMENT OF HEALTH AND HUMAN SERVICES
FOOD AND DRUG ADMINISTRATION

APPLICATION TO MARKET A NEW DRUG, BIOLOGIC, OR AN ANTIBIOTIC DRUG FOR HUMAN USE
(Title 21, Code of Federal Regulations, Parts 314 & 601)

Form Approved: OMB No. 0910-0338
Expiration Date: September 30, 2008
See OMB Statement on page 2.

FOR FDA USE ONLY

APPLICATION NUMBER

APPLICANT INFORMATION

NAME OF APPLICANT

DATE OF SUBMISSION

TELEPHONE NO. *(Include Area Code)*

FACSIMILE *(FAX) Number (Include Area Code)*

APPLICANT ADDRESS *(Number, Street, City, State, Country, ZIP Code or Mail Code, and U.S. License number if previously issued):*

AUTHORIZED U.S. AGENT NAME & ADDRESS *(Number, Street, City, State, ZIP Code, telephone & FAX number)* IF APPLICABLE

PRODUCT DESCRIPTION

NEW DRUG OR ANTIBIOTIC APPLICATION NUMBER, OR BIOLOGICS LICENSE APPLICATION NUMBER *(If previously issued)*

ESTABLISHED NAME *(e.g., Proper name, USP/USAN name)*

PROPRIETARY NAME *(trade name)* IF ANY

CHEMICAL/BIOCHEMICAL/BLOOD PRODUCT NAME *(If any)*

CODE NAME *(If any)*

DOSAGE FORM:

STRENGTHS:

ROUTE OF ADMINISTRATION:

(PROPOSED) INDICATION(S) FOR USE:

APPLICATION DESCRIPTION

APPLICATION TYPE *(check one)*
☐ NEW DRUG APPLICATION (CDA, 21 CFR 314.50) ☐ ABBREVIATED NEW DRUG APPLICATION (ANDA, 21 CFR 314.94)
☐ BIOLOGICS LICENSE APPLICATION (BLA, 21 CFR Part 601)

IF AN NDA, IDENTIFY THE APPROPRIATE TYPE ☐ 505 (b)(1) ☐ 505 (b)(2)

IF AN ANDA, OR 505(b)(2), IDENTIFY THE REFERENCE LISTED DRUG PRODUCT THAT IS THE BASIS FOR THE SUBMISSION

Name of Drug   Holder of Approved Application

TYPE OF SUBMISSION *(check one)* ☐ ORIGINAL APPLICATION ☐ AMENDMENT TO A PENDING APPLICATION ☐ RESUBMISSION
☐ PRESUBMISSION ☐ ANNUAL REPORT ☐ ESTABLISHMENT DESCRIPTION SUPPLEMENT ☐ EFFICACY SUPPLEMENT
☐ LABELING SUPPLEMENT ☐ CHEMISTRY MANUFACTURING AND CONTROLS SUPPLEMENT ☐ OTHER

IF A SUBMISSION OF PARTIAL APPLICATION, PROVIDE LETTER DATE OF AGREEMENT TO PARTIAL SUBMISSION:

IF A SUPPLEMENT, IDENTIFY THE APPROPRIATE CATEGORY ☐ CBE ☐ CBE-30 ☐ Prior Approval (PA)

REASON FOR SUBMISSION

PROPOSED MARKETING STATUS *(check one)* ☐ PRESCRIPTION PRODUCT (Rx) ☐ OVER THE COUNTER PRODUCT (OTC)

NUMBER OF VOLUMES SUBMITTED   THIS APPLICATION IS ☐ PAPER ☐ PAPER AND ELECTRONIC ☐ ELECTRONIC

ESTABLISHMENT INFORMATION (Full establishment information should be provided in the body of the Application.)
Provide locations of all manufacturing, packaging and control sites for drug substance and drug product (continuation sheets may be used if necessary). Include name, address, contact, telephone number, registration number (CFN), DMF number, and manufacturing steps and/or type of testing (e.g. Final dosage form, Stability testing) conducted at the site. Please indicate whether the site is ready for inspection or, if not, when it will be ready.

Cross References (list related License Applications, INDs, NDAs, PMAs, 510(k)s, IDEs, BMFs, and DMFs referenced in the current application)

FORM FDA 356h (10/05)   PAGE 1 OF 4

the FDA broad powers to license new drugs in the United States. After a new drug application is filed, the FDA holds a hearing and investigates the merits of the application. This process can take many years. The FDA may withdraw approval of any previously licensed drug, or speed up the approval process for experimental drugs that hold promise in treating incurable diseases (e.g., AIDS).

This law requires all users of prescription and nonprescription drugs to receive proper directions for use (including the method and duration of use) and adequate warnings about any related side effects. The manufacture, distribution, or sale of adulterated or misbranded drugs is prohibited.

Exhibit 8.4 is a Department of Health and Human Services application to market a new drug, biologic, or an antibiotic drug.

Exhibit 8.4 **Application to market a new drug, biologic, or an antibiotic drug for human use** *(continued)*

Previous Page   Next Page

This application contains the following items: *(Check all that apply)*

☐ 1. Index

☐ 2. Labeling *(check one)*   ☐ Draft Labeling   ☐ Final Printed Labeling

☐ 3. Summary (21 CFR 314.50 (c))

☐ 4. Chemistry section

☐   A. Chemistry, manufacturing, and controls information (e.g., 21 CFR 314.50(d)(1); 21 CFR 601.2)

☐   B. Samples (21 CFR 314.50 (e)(1); 21 CFR 601.2 (a)) (Submit only upon FDA's request)

☐   C. Methods validation package (e.g., 21 CFR 314.50(e)(2)(i); 21 CFR 601.2)

☐ 5. Nonclinical pharmacology and toxicology section (e.g., 21 CFR 314.50(d)(2); 21 CFR 601.2)

☐ 6. Human pharmacokinetics and bioavailability section (e.g., 21 CFR 314.50(d)(3); 21 CFR 601.2)

☐ 7. Clinical Microbiology (e.g., 21 CFR 314.50(d)(4))

☐ 8. Clinical data section (e.g., 21 CFR 314.50(d)(5); 21 CFR 601.2)

☐ 9. Safety update report (e.g., 21 CFR 314.50(d)(5)(vi)(b); 21 CFR 601.2)

☐ 10. Statistical section (e.g., 21 CFR 314.50(d)(6); 21 CFR 601.2)

☐ 11. Case report tabulations (e.g., 21 CFR 314.50(f)(1); 21 CFR 601.2)

☐ 12. Case report forms (e.g., 21 CFR 314.50 (f)(2); 21 CFR 601.2)

☐ 13. Patent information on any patent which claims the drug (21 U.S.C. 355(b) or (c))

☐ 14. A patent certification with respect to any patent which claims the drug (21 U.S.C. 355 (b)(2) or (j)(2)(A))

☐ 15. Establishment description (21 CFR Part 600, if applicable)

☐ 16. Debarment certification (FD&C Act 306 (k)(1))

☐ 17. Field copy certification (21 CFR 314.50 (l)(3))

☐ 18. User Fee Cover Sheet (Form FDA 3397)

☐ 19. Financial Information (21 CFR Part 54)

☐ 20. OTHER *(Specify)*

CERTIFICATION

I agree to update this application with new safety information about the product that may reasonably affect the statement of contraindications, warnings, precautions, or adverse reactions in the draft labeling. I agree to submit safety update reports as provided for by regulation or as requested by FDA. If this application is approved, I agree to comply with all applicable laws and regulations that apply to approved applications, including, but not limited to the following:

1. Good manufacturing practice regulations in 21 CFR Parts 210, 211 or applicable regulations, Parts 606, and/or 820.
2. Biological establishment standards in 21 CFR Part 600.
3. Labeling regulations in 21 CFR Parts 201, 606, 610, 660, and/or 809.
4. In the case of a prescription drug or biological product, prescription drug advertising regulations in 21 CFR Part 202.
5. Regulations on making changes in application in FD&C Act section 506A, 21 CFR 314.71, 314.72, 314.97, 314.99, and 601.12.
6. Regulations on Reports in 21 CFR 314.80, 314.81, 600.80, and 600.81.
7. Local, state and Federal environmental impact laws.

If this application applies to a drug product that FDA has proposed for scheduling under the Controlled Substances Act, I agree not to market the product until the Drug Enforcement Administration makes a final scheduling decision.

The data and information in this submission have been reviewed and, to the best of my knowledge are certified to be true and accurate.

Warning: A willfully false statement is a criminal offense, U.S. Code, title 18, section 1001.

SIGNATURE OF RESPONSIBLE OFFICIAL OR AGENT	TYPED NAME AND TITLE	DATE:
Sign		

ADDRESS *(Street, City, State, and ZIP Code)*	Telephone Number

Public reporting burden for this collection of information is estimated to average 24 hours per response, including the time for reviewing instructions, searching existing data sources, gathering and maintaining the data needed, and completing and reviewing the collection of information. Send comments regarding this burden estimate or any other aspect of this collection of information, including suggestions for reducing this burden to:

Department of Health and Human Services
Food and Drug Administration
Center for Drug Evaluation and Research
Central Document Room
5901-B Ammendale Road
Beltsville, MD 20705-1266

Department of Health and Human Services
Food and Drug Administration
Center for Biologics Evaluation and Research (HFM-99)
1401 Rockville Pike
Rockville, MD 20852-1448

An agency may not conduct or sponsor, and a person is not required to respond to, a collection of information unless it displays a currently valid OMB control number.

FORM FDA 356h (10/05)   PAGE 2 OF 4

Save Data   Print

Regulation of Cosmetics

The FDA's definition of cosmetics includes substances and preparations for cleansing, altering the appearance of, and promoting the attractiveness of a person. For example, eye shadow and other facial makeup are cosmetics subject to FDA regulation. Ordinary household soap is expressly exempted from this definition.

The FDA has issued regulations that require cosmetics to be labeled, to disclose ingredients, and to contain warnings if they are carcinogenic (cancer-causing) or otherwise dangerous to a person's health. The manufacture, distribution, or sale of adulterated or misbranded cosmetics is prohibited. The FDA may remove from commerce

Exhibit 8.5 **Cosmetic product ingredient statement**

Save As...	Print	Next Page	Reset Form

DEPARTMENT OF HEALTH AND HUMAN SERVICES FOOD AND DRUG ADMINISTRATION COLLEGE PARK, MD 20740-3835	Form Approved: OMB NO. 0910-0030. Expiration Date: December 31, 2008. See Burden Statement on Reverse of Part I.

COSMETIC PRODUCT INGREDIENT STATEMENT

(In accordance with 21 CFR 720)

Read Instruction Booklet Before Completing. Type entries in CAPITAL LETTERS.

TYPE OF SUBMISSION: ☐ ORIGINAL ☐ AMENDED ☐ DISC ☐ BASE

FOR FDA USE ONLY ON ORIGINAL SUBMISSIONS

FDA CPIS NO.   FILING DATE

F _ _ _ _ _ _ _   _ _ – _ _ _ _ – _ _

NOTE: This report is authorized by Public Law 21 U.S.C. 371(a); 21 CFR 720. While you are not required to respond, your cooperation is needed to make the results of this voluntary program comprehensive, accurate, and timely.

01. NAME OF MANUFACTURER / PACKER / DISTRIBUTOR *(On Label)*

11. NAME OF MANUFACTURER / PACKER *(Private Labeler)*

02. KIND OF BUSINESS ☐ MFR ☐ PKR ☐ DISTR

03. NAME OF PARENT COMPANY *(If any)*

12. NAME OF PARENT COMPANY *(If any)*

04. COMPLETE MAILING ADDRESS:

13. COMPLETE MAILING ADDRESS:

14. IS THIS STATEMENT FILED BY COMPANY 01 OR COMPANY 11?
(Please check one) ☐ COMPANY 01 ☐ COMPANY 11

15. PRODUCT CATEGORY CODE: ___ ___ ___

BRAND NO.	16. BRAND NAME OF COSMETIC PRODUCT	17. TYPE OF ACTION	18. DATE OF ACTION
01			
02			
03			
04			
05			
06			
07			
08			

19. TYPE NAME AND TITLE OF AUTHORIZED INDIVIDUAL	20. TELEPHONE NO. ( )	21. SIGNATURE AND DATE

FORM FDA 2512 (6/06)   CONTINUE COSMETIC PRODUCT INGREDIENT STATEMENT ON FORM FDA 2512a

EF PSC Graphics (301) 443-1090

Page ___ of ___ Pages

cosmetics that contain unsubstantiated claims of preserving youth, increasing virility, growing hair, and the like.

Exhibit 8.5 is a statement of ingredients in a cosmetic product.

Regulation of Medical Devices

In 1976, Congress enacted the Medicinal Device Amendment to the FDCA. This amendment gave the FDA authority to regulate medicinal devices, such as heart pacemakers, kidney dialysis machines, defibrillators, surgical equipment, and other diagnostic, therapeutic, and health devices. The mislabeling of such devices is prohibited and the FDA is empowered to remove "quack" devices from the market.

Perspective

Paralegal Disciplinary Committees Investigate Paralegal Misconduct

Most state and local paralegal associations have created disciplinary committees that investigate and decide allegations of paralegal misconduct. The state and local paralegal associations set forth the requirements to sit on this committee, how many committee members there will be, and how the committee members are appointed or elected.

Paralegal associations establish procedures for reporting suspected paralegal misconduct and provide methods for investigating alleged violations. After concluding its investigation, the committee can dismiss the charge or refer the matter for hearing before a designated tribunal of the paralegal association.

The paralegal under investigation must be notified of the allegations. Usually, a hearing is held, at which time the paralegal may appear and give testimony. The parties have the right to call witnesses and introduce evidence in support of their case.

At the completion of the hearing, the tribunal makes a decision and must present a written decision to the parties. Upon a finding of misconduct, the tribunal may impose certain penalties, including:

- reprimanding the paralegal
- ordering counseling
- requiring attendance at an ethics course
- ordering probation
- suspending the paralegal's license
- revoking the paralegal's license
- imposing a fine

If a criminal violation is found, the paralegal association is obligated to report it to the appropriate government authorities.

U.N. BIOSAFETY PROTOCOL FOR GENETICALLY ALTERED FOODS

Many food processing firms in the United States and across the world genetically modify some foods by adding genes from other organisms to help crops grow faster or to ward off pests. In the past, food processors did not notify consumers that they were purchasing genetically modified agricultural products. Although the companies insist that genetically altered foods are safe, consumers and many countries began to demand that these foods be clearly labeled so buyers could decide for themselves. When most large food processors balked at this idea, the consumers went to their lawmakers.

The most concerned countries in the world regarding this issue were in Europe. Led by Germany, many European countries wanted to require genetically engineered food products to be labeled as such and to be transported separately from nonaltered agricultural products. Some European countries wanted genetically altered foods to be banned completely. The United States—a major exporter of agricultural products and the leader in the development of biotech foods—argued that these countries were using this issue to erect trade barriers to keep U.S.-produced food products out of their countries in violation of international trade treaties and conventions administered by the World Trade Organization (WTO), which had reduced or eliminated many international trade restrictions.

In January 2000, a compromise was reached when 138 countries, including the United States, agreed to the United Nations-sponsored Biosafety Protocol. After much negotiation, the countries agreed that all genetically engineered foods would be clearly labeled with the phrase "May contain living modified organisms." This allows consumers to decide on their own whether to purchase altered food products. In addition, the boxes and containers in which the goods are shipped must be clearly marked as containing genetically altered food products. This compromise assures that biosafety labeling rules will coexist with the free-trade agreements of the WTO.

EMAIL CAN CAUSE A HOSTILE WORK ENVIRONMENT

The use of email in business has dramatically increased efficiency and information sharing among employees. Managers and workers alike can communicate with each other, send documents, and keep each other apprised of business developments. In many organizations, email has replaced the telephone as the most-used method of communication and has eliminated the need for many meetings. This is a boon for business. But the downside is that email has increased the exposure of businesses to sexual and racial harassment lawsuits.

Email often sets the social tone of an office and has been permitted to be slightly ribald. At some point, however, email conduct becomes impermissible and crosses the line to actionable sexual or racial harassment. The standard of whether email creates an illegal hostile work environment is the same as that for measuring harassment in any other context. The offensive conduct must be severe and cannot consist of isolated or trivial remarks and incidents. And, as in other harassment cases, an employer may raise the defense that requires two elements:

(1) The employer exercised reasonable care to prevent and correct the behavior.
(2) The plaintiff employee unreasonably failed to take advantage of any preventive or corrective opportunities provided by the employer or to avoid the harm.

Email differs from many other incidents of harassment because it is subtle and insidious. Unlike the situation with paper pin-up calendars in plain view, an employer does not readily see email messages. Obscenity pulled off the Internet or scanned into a computer can be sent as an attachment to an email message. Because email is hidden, to detect offensive messages, employers must take action to review email messages on its network.

Courts generally have held that employees do not have an expectation of privacy of email. Stored email is the property of the employer, which may review it freely. Employers also can use software to scan and filter email messages that contain any of a predefined list of objectionable words or phrases or certain "to" or "from" headers. Employers also can use software programs to scan graphics and block X-rated pictures.

Email not only has increased the possibility of there being sexual or racial harassment on the job, but it has also become the smoking gun that undermines a company's attempt to defend such cases. Therefore, employers must adopt policies pertaining to the use of email by their employees and make their employees aware that certain email messages constitute sexual or racial harassment and violate the law.

OTHER FEDERAL ADMINISTRATIVE AGENCIES

Foremost among the other federal administrative agencies are the Equal Employment Opportunity Commission, the Consumer Product Safety Commission, the Federal Trade Commission, and the Environmental Protection Agency.

Equal Opportunity Employment Commission (EEOC)

Starting in the 1960s, Congress began enacting a comprehensive set of federal laws that eliminated major forms of employment discrimination. These laws, which were passed to guarantee **equal employment opportunity** to all employees and job applicants, have been broadly interpreted by the federal courts, particularly the U.S. Supreme Court. States have also enacted antidiscrimination laws.

The **Equal Employment Opportunity Commission (EEOC)** is the federal administrative agency that is responsible for enforcing most federal antidiscrimination laws. Members of the EEOC are appointed by the U.S. President. The EEOC is empowered to conduct investigations, interpret the statutes, encourage conciliation between employees and employers, and bring suit to enforce the law. The EEOC also can seek injunctive relief.

Equal Employment Opportunity Commission (EEOC)
A federal administrative agency responsible for enforcing most federal antidiscrimination laws.

Visit the EEOC website to find out what laws it administers, at http://www.eeoc.gov/

STATE LEMON LAWS PROTECT CONSUMERS

In the past, consumers who purchased automobiles and other vehicles that developed nagging mechanical problems had to try to convince the dealers or manufacturer to correct the problem. If the problem was not corrected, the consumer's only recourse was to seek redress through costly and time-consuming litigation. Today, most states have enacted **lemon laws**, which give consumers a new weapon in this battle.

Lemon laws provide a procedure for consumers to follow to correct recurring problems in vehicles. Lemon laws establish an administrative procedure that is less formal than a court proceeding. Most of these laws require that an arbitrator decide the dispute between a consumer and car dealer. Lemon laws stipulate that if the dealer or manufacturer does not correct a recurring defect in a vehicle within a specified number of tries (e.g., four tries) within a specified period of time (e.g., two years), the purchaser can rescind the purchase and recover a full refund of the vehicle's purchase price.

To properly invoke a state's lemon law, a consumer should take the following steps:

(1) Notify the car dealer immediately of any mechanical or other problems that develop in the vehicle.

(2) Take the vehicle back to the dealer for the statutory number of times to give the dealer the opportunity to correct the defects.

(3) File a claim with the appropriate state agency, seeking arbitration of the claim if the defect is not corrected during the number of times and time period established by the state's lemon law.

(4) Attend the arbitration hearing and present evidence to substantiate the claim that the vehicle suffered from a defect that the dealer or manufacturer did not correct within the statutorily presented period.

Consumer Product Safety Commission (CPSC)

In 1972, Congress enacted the **Consumer Product Safety Act (CPSA)**, which created the **Consumer Product Safety Commission (CPSC)**. The CPSC is an independent federal administrative agency empowered to adopt rules and regulations to interpret and enforce the CPSA, conduct research on the safety of consumer products, and collect data regarding injuries caused by consumer products. Certain consumer products, including motor vehicles, boats, aircraft, and firearms, are regulated by other government agencies.

Because the CPSC regulates potentially dangerous consumer products, it issues product safety standards for consumer products that pose an unreasonable risk of injury. If a consumer product is found to be imminently hazardous—that is, its use can cause an unreasonable risk of death or serious injury or illness—the manufacturer can be required to recall, repair, or replace the product or take other corrective action.

Alternatively, the CPSC can seek injunctions, bring actions to seize hazardous consumer products, seek civil penalties for knowing violations of the act or CPSC rules, and seek criminal penalties for knowing and willful violations of the act or of CPSC rules. A private party can sue for an injunction to prevent violations of the Act or of CPSC rules and regulations.

Consumer Product Safety Commission (CPSC)
A federal administrative agency responsible for enforcing most federal consumer safety laws.

Visit the CPSC website to see what this federal administrative agency is empowered to do, at http://www.cpsc.gov/

Federal Trade Commission (FTC)

The **Federal Trade Commission Act (FTC Act)** was enacted in 1914 and the **Federal Trade Commission (FTC)** was created the following year. The FTC is empowered to enforce the FTC Act, as well as other federal consumer protection statutes.

Section 5 of the FTC Act prohibits *unfair and deceptive practices*. The Act has been used extensively to regulate business conduct. This section gives the FTC the

Federal Trade Commission (FTC)
A federal administrative agency responsible for enforcing the Federal Trade Commission Act.

WHAT DOES "MADE IN AMERICA" MEAN?

Many goods contain the label "Made in America." What does this label really mean? In 1998, the Federal Trade Commission (FTC), the administrative agency charged with protecting consumers from deception, issued new standards that define "Made in America." These standards try to balance domestic-origin claims and the global marketplace.

The 1998 FTC guidelines require goods that are "substantially made" in the United States to bear the "Made in America" label. This new test rejects the "wholly domestic" 100 percent standard. Instead, the FTC states that a marketer may claim the "Made in America" label if either of the following "safe harbor" rules are met:

(1) At least 75 percent of the total cost of manufacturing the product is U.S. manufacturing cost.
(2) The final product was last "substantially transformed" in the United States. This rule requires that the manufacturing process results in a new and different article of commerce having a name, character, and use different from what existed prior to processing. For example, using foreign steel to make a new automobile qualifies, but adding a tail light to an already-made automobile would not.

The FTC guidelines also permit marketers to make qualified claims of U.S. origin even when their products would not meet the rules for the unqualified "Made in America" label. For example, a product assembled in the United States but made primarily with foreign parts could be labeled "Made in USA of foreign parts."

The labeling law is designed to protect consumers from false "Made in USA" claims. The FTC is empowered to seek sanctions against violators and to turn over fraudulent cases to the U.S. Department of Justice for criminal prosecution.

authority to bring an administrative proceeding to attack a deceptive or unfair practice. If, after a public administrative hearing, the FTC finds a violation of Section 5, it may order a cease-and-desist order, an affirmative disclosure to consumers, corrective advertising, or something similar. The FTC may sue in state or federal court to obtain compensation on behalf of consumers.

Environmental Protection Agency (EPA)

In the 1970s, the federal government began enacting statutes to protect our nation's air and water from pollution. Federal legislation also was enacted to regulate hazardous wastes and to protect wildlife. In many instances, states enacted their own environmental laws that now coexist with federal law as long as they do not directly conflict with the federal law or unduly burden interstate commerce. These laws provide both civil and criminal penalties.

The development of such a vast body of law in such a short time is unprecedented in U.S. history. Environmental protection is one of the most important, and costly, issues facing business and society today.

In 1970, Congress created the **Environmental Protection Agency (EPA)** to coordinate the implementation and enforcement of the federal environmental protection laws. The EPA has broad rule-making powers to adopt regulations to advance the laws that it is empowered to administer. The agency also has adjudicative powers to hold hearings, make decisions, and order remedies for violations of federal environmental laws. In addition, the EPA can initiate judicial proceedings in court against suspected violators of federal environmental laws.

Environmental Impact Statement

The **National Environmental Policy Act (NEPA)** became effective January 1, 1970 [42 U.S.C. Sections 4321 et seq.]. The NEPA mandates that the federal government

Environmental Protection Agency (EPA)
A federal administrative agency responsible for enforcing most federal environmental protection laws.

Visit the EPA website, scroll to "Your Air Quality," and click on the map. Another screen page will pop up. Click on "More" and find the area closest to where you live. What is the air quality rating today? http://www.epa.gov/

consider the "adverse impact" of proposed legislation, rule making, or other federal government action on the environment before implementing the action.

The NEPA and rules adopted thereunder require that an **Environmental Impact Statement (EIS)** be prepared for all proposed legislation or major federal action that significantly affects the quality of the human environment. The purpose of the EIS is to provide enough information about the environment to enable the federal government to determine the feasibility of the project. The EIS also is used as evidence in court whenever a federal action is challenged as violating the NEPA or other federal environmental protection laws. Examples of actions that require an EIS include proposals to build a new federally funded highway, to license nuclear plant, and the like.

The EIS must (1) describe the affected environment, (2) describe the impact of the proposed federal action on the environment, (3) identify and discuss alternatives to the proposed action, (4) list the resources that will be committed to the action, and (5) contain a cost–benefit analysis of the proposed action and alternative actions. Expert professionals, such as engineers, geologists, and accountants, may be consulted during preparation of the EIS.

After an EIS is prepared, it is subject to public review, and the public has 30 days in which to submit comments to the EPA. After the comments have been received and reviewed, the EPA will issue an order stating whether the proposed action may proceed. Decisions of the EPA are appealable to the appropriate U.S. Court of Appeals.

Most states and many local governments have enacted laws that require an EIS to be prepared regarding proposed state and local government action, as well as private development.

Air Pollution

One of the major problems facing this country is **air pollution**. The **Clean Air Act** was enacted in 1963 to assist states in dealing with air pollution. The act was amended in 1970 and 1977 and, most recently, by the **Clean Air Act Amendments of 1990** [42 U.S.C. Sections 7401 et seq.]. The Clean Air Act, as amended, provides comprehensive regulation of air quality in this country.

Substantial amounts of air pollution are emitted by **stationary sources** (e.g., industrial plants, oil refineries, public utilities). The Clean Air Act requires states to identify major stationary sources and develop plans to reduce air pollution from these sources. Automobile and other vehicle emissions are a major source of air pollution in this country. In an effort to control emissions from these **mobile sources**, the Clean Air Act requires air pollution controls to be installed on motor vehicles. Emission standards have been set for automobiles, trucks, buses, motorcycles, and airplanes. In addition, the Clean Air Act authorizes the EPA to regulate air pollution caused by fuel and fuel additives.

The Clean Air Act directs the EPA to establish **national ambient air quality standards (NAAQS)** for certain pollutants. These standards are set at two different levels: primary (to protect human beings) and secondary (to protect vegetation, matter, climate, visibility, and economic values). Specific standards have been established for carbon monoxide, nitrogen oxide, sulfur oxide, ozone, lead, and participate matter.

Although the EPA establishes air quality standards, the states are responsible for their enforcement. The federal government has the right to enforce these air pollution standards if the states fail to do so. Each state is required to prepare a *State Implementation Plan* (SIP) that sets out how the state plans to meet the federal standards. The EPA has divided each state into *air quality control regions (AQCRs)*. Each region is monitored to ensure compliance.

Water Pollution

Water pollution affects human health, recreation, agriculture, and business. Pollution of waterways by industry and humans has caused severe ecological and environmental problems, including making water sources unsafe for drinking water, fish,

Environmental Impact Statement (EIS)
A document that must be prepared by the federal government, which analyzes the adverse impact that a federal government action will have on the environment.

Air pollution
Pollution caused by factories, homes, vehicles, and the like that affects the air.

Water pollution
Pollution of lakes, rivers, oceans, and other bodies of water.

birds, and animals. The federal government has enacted a comprehensive scheme of statutes and regulations to prevent and control water pollution.

In 1948, Congress enacted the **Federal Water Pollution Control Act (FW-PCA)** to regulate water pollution. This act has been amended several times. As amended, it is simply referred to as the **Clean Water Act** [33 U.S.C. Sections 1251 et seq.] and is administered by the EPA.

Pursuant to the Clean Water Act, the EPA has established water quality standards that define which bodies of water can be used for public drinking water, recreation (such as swimming), propagation of fish and wildlife, and agricultural and industrial uses.

States are primarily responsible for enforcing the provisions of the Clean Water Act and EPA regulations adopted thereunder. If a state fails to do so, the federal government may enforce the Act.

The Clean Water Act regulates the following types of water pollution:

- *Point sources of water pollution.* The Clean Water Act authorizes the EPA to establish water pollution control standards for **point sources** of water pollution (mines, manufacturing plants, paper mills, electric utility plants, municipal sewage plants, and other stationary sources of water pollution). Dischargers of pollutants are required to keep records, maintain monitoring equipment, and keep samples of discharges.

- *Thermal pollution.* The Clean Water Act expressly forbids **thermal pollution** because the discharge of heated waters or materials into the nation's waterways may upset the ecological balance, decrease the oxygen content of water, and harm fish, birds, and animals that use the waterways. Sources of thermal pollution (e.g., electric utility companies, manufacturing plants) are subject to the provisions of the Clean Water Act and regulations adopted by the EPA.

- *Wetlands.* **Wetlands** are defined as areas that are inundated or saturated by surface water or ground water that support vegetation typically adapted for life in saturated soil conditions. Wetlands include swamps, marshes, bogs, and similar areas that support birds, animals, and vegetative life. The Clean Water Act forbids the filling or dredging of wetlands unless a permit has been obtained from the **Army Corps of Engineers (Corps)**. The Corps is empowered to adopt regulations and conduct administrative proceedings in enforcing the Act.

Thermal pollution
Pollution created by heated water or material being discharged into waterways. It upsets the ecological balance and decreases the oxygen content.

Toxic Substances

Many chemicals used for agricultural, industrial, and mining uses contain **toxic substances** that cause cancer, birth defects, and other health-related problems in human beings, as well as injury or death to birds, animals, fish, and vegetation. Many chemical compounds used in the manufacture of products are toxic (e.g., PCBs, asbestos). Hundreds of new chemicals and chemical compounds that may be toxic are discovered each year.

In 1976, Congress enacted the **Toxic Substances Control Act** [15 U.S.C. Sections 2601 et seq.]. and gave the EPA authority to administer the Act. The Act requires manufacturers and processors to test new chemicals to determine their effects on human health and the environment and to report the results to the EPA before they can be marketed. The EPA may limit or prohibit the manufacture and sale of toxic substances, or it may remove them from commerce if it finds that they pose an imminent hazard or an unreasonable risk of injury to human health or the environment. The EPA also requires special labeling of toxic substances.

Toxic substances
Chemicals used for agricultural, industrial, and mining uses that cause injury to humans, birds, animals, fish, and vegetation.

Hazardous Waste

Wastes, which often contain hazardous substances that can harm the environment or pose a danger to human health, are generated by agriculture, mining, industry, other

THE SUPERFUND

In 1980, Congress enacted the **Comprehensive Environmental Response, Compensation, and Liability Act (CERCLA)**, which is commonly called the **Superfund** [42 U.S.C. Sections 9601 et seq.]. The CERCLA, significantly amended in 1986, is administered by the EPA. The Act gave the federal government a mandate to deal with hazardous wastes that have been spilled, stored, or abandoned. The Superfund provides for the creation of a government fund to finance the clean-up of hazardous waste sites (hence the name *Superfund*). The fund is financed through taxes on chemicals, feedstocks, motor fuels, and other products that contain hazardous substances.

The Superfund requires the EPA to (1) identify sites in the United States where hazardous wastes have been disposed, stored, abandoned, or spilled, and (2) rank these sites regarding the severity of the risk. When it ranks the sites, the EPA considers factors such as the types of hazardous waste, toxicity of the wastes, types of pollution (air, water, land, or other pollution), number of people potentially affected by the risk, and other factors. The hazardous waste sites with the highest ranking are put on a National Priority List. The sites on this list receive first consideration for clean-up. The EPA has the authority to clean up hazardous priority or nonpriority sites quickly to prevent fire, explosion, contamination of drinking water, or other imminent danger.

The EPA can order a responsible party to clean up a hazardous waste site. If that party fails to do so, the EPA can clean up the site and recover the cost of the clean-up. The Superfund imposes strict liability—that is, liability without fault. The EPA can recover the cost of the clean-up from (1) the generator who deposited the wastes, (2) the transporter of the wastes to the site, (3) the owner of the site at the time of the disposal, and (4) the current owner and operator of the site. The Superfund permits states and private parties who clean up hazardous waste sites to seek reimbursement from the fund.

---

businesses, and households. Wastes consist of garbage, sewage, industrial discharges, old equipment, and such. The mishandling and disposal of **hazardous wastes** can produce air, water, and **land pollution**.

In 1976, Congress enacted the **Resource Conservation and Recovery Act (RCRA)** [42 U.S.C. Sections 6901 et seq.], regulating the disposal of new hazardous wastes. This Act, which has been amended several times, authorizes the EPA to regulate facilities that generate, treat, store, transport, and dispose of hazardous wastes. States have the primary responsibility for implementing standards established by the Act and EPA regulations.

The Act defines hazardous waste as solid waste that may cause or significantly contribute to an increase in mortality or serious illness or pose a hazard to human health or the environment if improperly managed. The EPA has designated as hazardous, substances that are toxic, radioactive, or corrosive, or that ignite, and the EPA can add to the list of hazardous wastes as needed.

The EPA also establishes standards and procedures for the safe treatment, storage, disposal, and transportation of hazardous wastes. Under the Act, the EPA is authorized to regulate underground storage facilities, such as underground gasoline tanks.

Hazardous waste
Substances that may cause or significantly contribute to an increase in mortality or serious illness or pose a hazard to human health or the environment if managed improperly.

Endangered Species

Many species of animals are endangered or threatened with extinction. The reduction of certain species of wildlife may be caused by environmental pollution, real estate development, and/or hunting. The **Endangered Species Act** was enacted in 1973. [16 U.S.C. Sections 1531 et seq.]. The Act, as amended, protects *endangered* and *threatened* species of animals. The Secretary of the Interior is empowered to declare a form of wildlife as *endangered* or *threatened*. The Act requires the EPA and the Department of Commerce to designate *critical habitats* for each endangered and threatened species.

Real estate and other development in these areas is prohibited or severely limited. The Secretary of Commerce is empowered to enforce the provisions of the Act as to marine species.

In addition, the Act, which applies to both government and private persons, prohibits the *taking* of any endangered species. *Taking* is defined as an act intended to "harass, harm, pursue, hunt, shoot, wound, kill, trap, capture, or collect" an endangered animal.

Legal Terminology

Summary

CHAPTER 8   ADMINISTRATIVE LAW

Administrative Law and Agencies

General Government Regulation	The government enacts laws that regulate businesses and industries collectively.
Specific Government Regulation	The government also enacts laws that regulate certain industries only.
Administrative Agencies	Created by federal and state legislative and executive branches; consist of professionals having expertise in a certain area of commerce, who interpret and apply designated statutes
Rules and Regulations	Administrative agencies are empowered to adopt rules and regulations that interpret and advance the laws they enforce.
Administrative Procedure Act (APA)	The APA establishes procedures (e.g., notice, hearing) for federal agencies to follow in conducting their affairs. States have enacted their own procedural acts to govern state agencies.
Delegation Doctrine	When an administrative agency is created, it is delegated certain legislative, judicial, and executive powers. If an administrative agency acts outside the scope of its delegated powers, it is an unconstitutional act.

Legislative Powers of Administrative Agencies

Substantive Rule Making	Administrative agencies have the power to adopt substantive rules that have the force of law and must be adhered to by covered persons and businesses.
Interpretive Rule Making	Administrative agencies make rules that interpret existing statutory language.
Statement of Policy	A statement of policy announces a proposed course of action that an agency intends to follow in the future.
Licensing Powers	Administrative agencies are authorized to issue licenses before a person or business can enter certain types of industries.

Executive Powers of Administrative Agencies

Administrative Subpoena	An administrative subpoena is an order that directs the subject of the subpoena to disclose the requested information.
Administrative Search	An administrative search is inspection of business premises, subject to the Fourth Amendment's protection against unreasonable search and seizure.

Judicial Powers of Administrative Agencies

Complaint	The administrative agency serves a complaint on the party (the respondent) it believes has violated the law.
Administrative Law Judge (ALJ)	The ALJ is an employee of the administrative agency who presides over the administrative proceeding; decides questions of law and fact, issues a decision in the form of an order.

Judicial Review of Administrative Agency Actions

Petitioner	The petitioner is the party appealing the decision of an administrative agency.
Conditions for Judicial Review	1. The case must be *ripe for review*. 2. The petitioner must have *exhausted all administrative remedies*. 3. The *final-order rule* requires that the decision of the administrative agency must be final before judicial review can be sought.

| Immunity | Administrative agency employees are immune from lawsuits for personal liability regarding actions and decisions they make while performing their agency duties. |

Public Disclosure of Agency Actions

Freedom of Information Act	The FOIA is a federal law that gives the public access to most documents in the possession of federal administrative agencies. It also requires federal administrative agencies to publish agency procedures, rules, regulations, interpretations, and other information in the *Federal Register*.
Government in the Sunshine Act	This federal law opens certain federal administrative agency meetings to the public.
Equal Access to Justice Act	This federal law protects persons from harassment by federal administrative agencies and provides certain penalties for its violation.
Privacy Act	The Privacy Act (a) restricts information a federal administrative agency can maintain about an individual, and (b) gives individuals the right to access agency records concerning themselves.

Federal Administrative Agencies

Food and Drug Administration (FDA)	The FDA is the federal administrative agency empowered to interpret and enforce the Food, Drug, and Cosmetic Act and other federal consumer protection laws.
Food, Drug, Cosmetic Act (FDCA)	The FDCA is a federal statute that regulates the testing, manufacture, distribution, and sale of foods, food additives, drugs, cosmetics, and medicinal products.
Powers of the FDA	The FDA has the power to approve or deny applications by private companies to distribute drugs, food additives, and medicinal devices to the public.
Regulation of Food, Drugs, Cosmetics, and Medical Devices	The FDA prohibits the shipment, distribution, or sale of *adulterated* or *misbranded* food, drugs, cosmetics, and medicinal devices.

Other Federal Administrative Agencies

Equal Employment Opportunity Commission (EEOC)	The EEOC is the administrative agency responsible for enforcing most federal antidiscrimination laws.
Consumer Product Safety Commission (CPSC)	The CPSC is the administrative agency responsible for enforcing most federal consumer safety laws
Federal Trade Commission (FTC)	The FTC is the administrative agency responsible for enforcing the Federal Trade Commission Act.
Environmental Protection Agency (EPA)	The EPA is the federal administrative agency responsible for enforcing most federal environmental protection laws. The following are regulated by the EPA: 1. **Air pollution.** Pollution caused by factories, homes, vehicles, and the like that affects the air. 2. **Water pollution.** Pollution of lakes, rivers, oceans, and other bodies of water.

3. **Thermal pollution**. Heated water or material discharged into waterways that upsets the ecological balance and decreases the oxygen content
4. **Wetlands**. Areas that are inundated or saturated by surface or groundwater that support vegetation typically adapted for life in such conditions
5. **Toxic substances**. Chemicals used for agricultural, industrial, and mining uses that cause injury to humans, birds, animals, fish, and vegetation
6. **Hazardous waste**. Solid waste that may cause or significantly contribute to an increase in mortality or serious illness or pose a hazard to human health or the environment if improperly managed

▶ WORKING THE WEB

1. Go to the Web site **http://www.fda.gov/**. This is the website for the Federal Food and Drug Administration (FDA). Click on one of the "Hot Topic" subject matters that interests you and write a one-page report on that information.

2. Using the Food and Drug Administration (FDA) website **http://www.fda.gov/**, click on the word "Forms." Choose a "Subject" and locate an FDA form. Print the form and write a brief description of what the form is used for.

3. Go to the Web site **http://www.cpsc.gov/**. This is the website for the federal Consumer Product Safety Commission (CPSC). Click on "Recent Recalls" for the most current month. Find a recall of a product that interests you and write a half-page report describing the product and its recall.

4. Go to the website **http://google.com**. Search for your state to find an article about a recall of a consumer product in your state, under either federal or state law.

5. View the Federal Trade Commission (FTC) website at **http://www.ftc.gov/**. Click on the words "For Consumers" and then click on "ID Theft." Write a one-page report on what identity theft is and what you should do if you are a victim of identity theft.

▶ CRITICAL THINKING AND WRITING QUESTIONS

1. What is an administrative agency? Who creates administrative agencies?
2. What is the purpose of an administrative agency? Explain.
3. Describe the difference between general government regulation and specific government regulation. Give an example of each.
4. What is the Department of Homeland Security? Who created this agency? What are its main purposes?
5. What is the Administrative Procedure Act (APA)? What are its functions?
6. Describe the difference between substantive rules, interpretative rules, and statements of policy.
7. What is an administrative subpoena? Describe situations in which administrative searches are permitted. Are warrantless administrative searches ever allowed? Explain.
8. What is an administrative law judge (ALJ)? What does an ALJ do? What is an order?
9. Are administrative agency actions subject to judicial review? If so, what requirements must be met? What does the final order rule provide?
10. Describe what the following federal statutes provide: (1) Freedom of Information Act, (2) Government in the Sunshine Act, (3) Equal Access to Justice Act, and (4) Privacy Act.
11. Describe the Food and Drug Administration (FDA). What does it regulate? Give some examples.
12. Describe the Equal Opportunity Employment Commission (EEOC). What does it regulate? Give some examples.
13. Describe the Consumer Product Safety Commission (CPSC). What does it regulate? Give some examples.
14. Describe the Federal Trade Commission (FTC). What does it regulate? Give some examples.
15. Describe the Environmental Protection Agency (EPA). What does it regulate? Give some examples.

flooded by the operation of the Tellico Dam. The snail darter was not found anywhere else in the world. It feeds exclusively on snails and requires substantial oxygen, both supplied by the fast moving waters of the Little Tennessee River. The impounding of the water behind the Tellico Dam would destroy the snail darter's food and oxygen supplies, thus causing its extinction. Evidence was introduced showing that the TVA could not, at any time, successfully transplant the snail darter to any other habitat.

Also in 1973, Congress enacted the Endangered Species Act (Act). The act authorizes the Secretary of the Interior (Secretary) to declare species of animal life *endangered* and to identify the *critical habitat* of these creatures. When a species or its habitat is so listed, Section 7 of the Act mandates that the Secretary take such action as is necessary to ensure that actions of the federal government do not jeopardize the continued existence of such endangered species. The Secretary declared the snail darter an endangered species and the area that would be affected by the dam its critical habitat.

Congress continued to appropriate funds for the construction of the dam, which was completed at a cost of over $100 million. In 1976, a regional association of biological scientists, a Tennessee conservation group, and several individuals filed an action seeking to enjoin the TVA from closing the gates of the dam and impounding the water in the reservoir on the grounds that those actions would violate Section 7 of the Act by causing the extinction of the snail darter. The District Court filed in favor of the TVA. The Court of Appeals reversed and remanded, with instructions to the District court to issue a permanent injunction halting the operation of the Tellico Dam. The TVA appealed to the U.S. Supreme Court.

Question

1. Would the TVA be in violation of the Endangered Species Act if it were to operate the Tellico Dam?

Federal Communications Commission v. Midwest Video Corporation 440 U.S. 689, 99.S.Ct. 1435 59 L.Ed.2d 692, 1979 U.S. Lexis 82 (U.S.)

FACTS

The Federal Communications Commission (FCC) is a federal administrative agency that is empowered to enforce the Communications Act of 1934. This Act, as amended, gives FCC power to regulate broadcasting of radio and television. The Act provides that "broadcasting shall not be deemed a common carrier." In *United States v. Midwest Video Corporation* [406 U.S. 649, 92 S.Ct. 1860 (1972)], the U.S. Supreme Court held that FCC also has the power to regulate cable television.

In May 1976, FCC promulgated rules requiring cable television operators that have 3,500 or more subscribers to

(1) develop a 20-channel capacity, (2) make four channels available for use by public, educational, local, governmental, and leased-access users (with one channel assigned to each), (3) make equipment available for those utilizing these public-access channels, and (4) limit the fees that cable operators could charge for their services.

Question

1. Do these rules exceed the statutory authority of FCC?

Bowman Transportation, Inc. v. Arkansas—Best Freight System, Inc. 419 U.S. 281, 95 S.Ct. 438 42 L.Ed.2d 447, 1974 U.S. Lexis 51 (U.S.)

FACTS

The Interstate Commerce Commission (ICC) is a federal administrative agency empowered to regulate motor carriers involved in interstate commerce. Trucking companies must apply to ICC and obtain a license before they can offer trucking services on a route. The Interstate Commerce Act empowers ICC to grant an application for a license if it finds that (1) the applicant is fit, willing, and able to properly perform the service proposed, and (2) the service proposed is or will be required by the present or future "public convenience or necessity."

Thirteen motor carriers applied to offer trucking services between points in the Southwest and Southeast. After reviewing the applications and extensive written evidence (including the testimony of more than 900 witnesses), ICC granted licenses to three of the applicants. Arkansas-Best Freight Systems, Inc., a rejected applicant, brought an action seeking to annul ICC's order.

Question

1. Should ICC's grant of the licenses be overturned on appeal?

United States v. Gel Spice Co., Inc. 601 F.Supp. 1205 1984 U.S. Dist. Lexis 21041 (E.D.N.Y)

FACTS

Barry Engel owned and operated Gel Spice Co., Inc., which specialized in the importation and packaging of various food spices for resale. All of the spices that Gel Spice imported were unloaded at a pier in New York City and taken to a warehouse on McDonald Avenue. Storage and repackaging of the spices took place in the warehouse.

Between July 1976 and January 1979, the McDonald Avenue warehouse was inspected four times by investigators from the FDA. The investigators found live rats in bags of basil leaves, rodent droppings in boxes of chili peppers, and mammalian urine in bags of sesame seeds. The investigators produced additional evidence that showed that spices packaged and sold from the warehouse contained insects, rodent excreta pellets, rodent hair, and rodent urine. The FDA brought criminal charges against Engel and Gel Spice.

Question

Are they guilty?

Donovan, Secretary of Labor v. Dewey 452 U.S. 594, 101 S.Ct. 2534 69 L.Ed.2d 262, 1980 U.S. Lexis 58 (U.S.)

FACTS

The Federal Mine Safety and Health Act of 1977 requires the Secretary of Labor to develop detailed mandatory health and safety standards to govern the operation of the nation's mines. The Act provides that federal mine inspectors are to inspect underground mines at least four times a year and surface mines at least twice a year to ensure compliance with these standards and to make the following inspections to determine whether previously discovered violations have been corrected. The Act also grants mine inspectors "a right of entry to, upon or through any coal or other mine" and states that "no advance notice of an inspection shall be provided to any person."

In July 1978, a federal mine inspector attempted to inspect quarries owned by Waukesha Lime and Stone Company (Waukesha) to determine whether all 25 safety and health violations uncovered during a prior inspection had been corrected. Douglas Dewey, Waukesha's president, refused to allow the inspector to inspect the premises without first obtaining a search warrant.

Question

1. Are the warrantless searches of stone quarries authorized by the Mine Safety and Health Act constitutional? Did Dewey act ethically in refusing to allow the inspections?

INTERVIEWING AND INVESTIGATION SKILLS

"It is the spirit and not the form of law
that keeps justice alive."

Earl Warren

9

PARALEGALS AT WORK

Sara had been working for only a few weeks as a paralegal intern for a small, boutique litigation law firm. Mrs. Weiser, one of the two paralegals supporting the two trial attorneys, told Sara about her long-planned Alaskan cruise that she would be taking with her husband for their 25th anniversary. The reality of the situation started to set in when Sara was advised that the cruise would start from Anchorage the next day and Mrs. Weiser was scheduled to leave within the hour to catch a plane. Sara's concerns heightened when she and Mrs. Weiser reviewed the office calendar and it became obvious that Sara would be alone in the office. The attorneys and the other full-time paralegal were involved in a major medical malpractice case in another state for at least the next two weeks. Clearly, Sara would be in charge of the office, answering the phone and taking care of anyone who came in. Somewhat troubling would be the lack of any contact with Mrs. Weiser for the duration of the cruise, or contact with the other paralegal or attorneys during the trial day.

The instructions left no doubt that Sara would be busy when she was told: "Now remember—we advertise on TV, and Mr. Elliott expects us to screen potential clients without bothering him with loser cases. I've left a couple of files for you to work on while I'm gone. The Morales case just came in. It's an accident case that happened a few years ago, and you need to get her in for an initial interview—get all the necessary facts and see what else we have to do to move it along and either settle it or start suit. Oh, by the way, you do speak Spanish, don't you? Mrs. Morales is from Puerto Rico.

"The LaCorte case is on the trial list for next month. We don't have an expert yet who can substantiate our theory of the case. See what you can find. Oh, and you'd better get that case organized so they can start trial immediately in case the current trial lasts longer than the expected three weeks. All the material is in piles or in boxes in Mr. Martin's office. Prepare a trial notebook, or you can try that new case management software program we just got that is

---

After studying this chapter, you should be able to:

1. Explain the potential issues involved in a screening interview.

2. Describe the issues in preparing for and conducting an interview.

3. Explain the steps and process of conducting an investigation.

4. List and describe sources for obtaining information.

5. Explain the function of the trial notebook and its relationship to case management.

supposed to make life easier. I'm sure, with your computer skills, that you can get it up and running and use it to get the case ready for trial."

Consider the issues involved in this scenario as you read the chapter.

▶ INTRODUCTION FOR THE PARALEGAL

Communication skills are at the heart of paralegals' ability to conduct successful interviews and investigations. The paralegal must be prepared to be the first point of contact with the client. In some practices, clients are interviewed first by the supervising attorney and then referred to the paralegal for a detailed factual interview. In other practices, the paralegal is the first one to meet with the client and conduct the initial interview before referring the client to the supervising attorney.

The paralegal must be able to interview clients, fact witnesses, expert witnesses, investigators, and others, including public records custodians who may have access to information necessary for the preparation of a case. The skill of the interviewer or investigator can determine the accuracy and completeness of the information obtained—and ultimately the outcome of the case. The impressions created and the relationship developed with a new client may be the deciding factor in whether the client stays with the firm or seeks other counsel. Professional relationships developed with public officials, public custodians of records, hospital records librarians, police investigators, and similar independent investigators can make the paralegal's job much easier and ultimately benefit the client. ■

INTERVIEWS

Any contact that a paralegal has with a client, or prospective client, constitutes an interview. It may involve limited contact, such as a **screening interview**, or an in-depth initial fact-gathering interview. In each case, the paralegal usually is the first point of contact with the client for the firm. The impression the paralegal makes is the impression the firm makes. As someone once said, we have only one opportunity to make a good first impression.

The initial contact with a client is what is sometimes called a screening interview. This usually begins with an initial telephone call to the firm, although a person may appear at the reception desk, looking for an attorney and wanting to determine if the firm is interested in taking the case, and usually what it will cost.

Also, paralegals frequently make the initial contact with potential witnesses. Again this may be a telephone call to set up a meeting or a telephone interview. The initial meeting with potential witnesses may be in the office or in the field at the witness' home or place of business. The initial contact with a potential witness, just as with a potential client, may set the tone for the interview and the willingness of the person to cooperate.

Screening interview
Limited first contact with a prospective new client.

Screening Interview

Many clients come to a law firm or lawyer from a referral source, such as a current or former client. This source of clients acts as a potential screening. The individual probably has been told by the referral source something about the nature of the practice, the kind of work being done for the referring person, and the perceived reputation or ability of the lawyer or firm. Other potential clients find the firm's name and phone number in the telephone book, on a website listing of attorneys, or from another law firm advertisement or promotional piece.

Finally, some people simply appear at the office door and ask for an appointment or basic information about the firm's ability or interest in taking a case. In smaller offices the paralegal is the one who often takes these calls, doubling as receptionist–phone operator.

IMPLIED ATTORNEY CLIENT RELATIONSHIP

Implied attorney–client relationship may result when a prospective client divulges confidential information during a consultation with an attorney for the purpose of retaining the attorney, even if actual employment does not result." Pro-Hand Servs.

Source: *Trust v. Monthei,* 49 P.3d 56, 59 (Mont.2002).

The initial contact is filled with potential landmines. If the paralegal solicits too much information or the prospective client volunteers too much information, an **implied attorney–client relationship** may be created. If too little information is obtained, the attorney will not have enough information to decide if he or she wants to talk to the potential client. Therefore, the paralegal or receptionist has to decide how much information to take and how much information to give.

First Meeting

At the very least, it is prudent for the paralegal to advise the potential client that paralegal are not lawyers, and that only a lawyer can give legal advice. Also, anything said to the paralegal may not be subject to the **attorney–client privilege**.

The prospective client may want a quick answer to the question, "Do I have a case? The answer requires a legal analysis that only the attorney can make. The attorney–employer probably does not want to be bothered with most such early contacts but also does not want to lose a good case. Should the paralegal give advice or have this person speak with a lawyer? Most of these potential problems can be avoided by having a policy or strategy in place. Most offices have a policy on the fee for an initial interview. Many offer a no-cost initial interview to determine the validity of a case and any potential conflict of interests that might require the office to decline a case. In some cases, a nominal fee is charged. This may be a flat rate or an hourly rate. In many jurisdictions, referrals from the local lawyer referral office or legal aid office are charged at a token fee, sometimes as little as $5, or in indigent cases, no fee as part of the local pro bono program. The paralegal must ask the firm's policy before attempting to give and receive information from potential clients.

Implied attorney client relationship
Implied attorney–client relationship may result when a prospective client divulges confidential information during a consultation with an attorney for the purpose of retaining the attorney, even if actual employment does not result.

Attorney client privilege
A client's right to have anything told to a lawyer while seeking legal advice, kept confidential in most instances.

ETHICAL *Perspective*

ABA Model Rules of Professional Conduct
Rule 1.18 Duties to Prospective Client

(a) A person who discusses with a lawyer the possibility of forming a client–lawyer relationship with respect to a matter is a prospective client.

(b) Even when no client–lawyer relationship ensues, a lawyer who has had discussions with a prospective client shall not use or reveal information learned in the consultation, except as Rule 1.9 would permit with respect to information of a former client.

(c) A lawyer subject to paragraph (b) shall not represent a client with interests materially adverse to those of a prospective client in the same or a substantially related matter if the lawyer received information from the prospective client that could be significantly harmful to that person in the matter, except as provided in paragraph (d). If a lawyer is disqualified from representation under this paragraph, no lawyer in a firm with which that lawyer is associated may knowingly undertake or continue representation in such a matter, except as provided in paragraph (d).

(d) When the lawyer has received disqualifying information as defined in paragraph (c), representation is permissible if:
    (1) both the affected client and the prospective client have given informed consent, confirmed in writing, or:
    (2) the lawyer who received the information took reasonable measures to avoid exposure to more disqualifying information than was reasonably necessary to determine whether to represent the prospective client; and
        (i) the disqualified lawyer is timely screened from any participation in the matter and is apportioned no part of the fee therefrom; and
        (ii) written notice is promptly given to the prospective client.

See Appendix I for Commentary on Model Rule 1.18.

Source: *ABA* Model Rules for Professional Conduct, 2004 Edition. © 2003 by the American Bar Association. Reprinted with permission. Copies of ABA Model Rules of Professional Conduct, 2004 Edition are available from Service Center, American Bar Association, 321 North Clark St., Chicago, IL 60610, 1-800-285-2221.

Implied Attorney–Client Relationship

If too much information is taken, the potential client may think he or she now has a lawyer. The courts have ruled on the side of the prospective client, holding that an implied attorney–client relationship exists. In this "implied" relationship, the client is entitled to expect the same degree of confidentiality under the attorney–client privilege. In this situation, a **conflict of interest** may result if the firm is already representing another party in the same matter, which would result in disqualification of the attorney or the establishment of an **ethical wall** to prevent access to information by members of the legal team with a conflict.

One of the biggest potential areas of potential malpractice is to miss a **statute of limitations** on a client's case. The statute of limitations is a time period within which a case must be filed with the court or the right to use the court for resolution of the case is lost. The statute of limitation is based on statute, and each jurisdiction has the power to set its own statute of limitation for each type of case. For example, in many states the time limit for filing a tort action arising out of an automobile action is two years, and a contract action six years, but in some states the suit must be filed in as little as 30 days. To a client seeking a new lawyer for an appeal, the timeframe may not be important. But to the lawyer, it is potentially critical to prevent malpractice, especially when the timeframe is short, such as when the court has allowed a time limit for an appeal of 10 to 45 days, after which time the court order is not appealable barring special relief by the court.

The timing of the statute of limitations deadline always must be considered when taking the initial call or during the first contact with the potential client. If a court holds that an implied attorney–client relationship exists after the statute of limitations has run out (expired), the failure of the attorney to have taken action may be held to be malpractice and subject the lawyer to pay what would have been recovered if the case had gone forward and a recovery obtained. As the first point of potential

Conflict of interest
Representation of another with conflicting rights.

Ethical wall
A artificial barrier preventing anyone not authorized who may have a conflict of interest from accessing client information.

Statute of limitations
A time limit within which a case must be brought or lose the right to seek redress in court.

IN THE WORDS OF THE COURT

Identity of Clients

. . . the identity of an attorney's clients is sensitive personal information that implicates the clients' rights of privacy. "[E]very person [has the right] to freely confer with and confide in his attorney in an atmosphere of trust and serenity. . . ." (Willis v. Superior Court (1980) 112 Cal.App.3d 277, 293.)

Clients routinely exercise their right to consult with counsel, seeking to obtain advice on a host of matters that they reasonably expect to remain private. A spouse who consults a divorce attorney may not want his or her spouse or other family members to know that he or she is considering divorce.

Similarly, an employee who is concerned about conduct in his workplace, an entrepreneur planning a new business endeavor, an individual with questions about the criminal or tax consequences of his or her acts, or a family member who desires to rewrite a will may consult an attorney with the expectation that the consultation itself, as well as the matters discussed therein, will remain confidential until such time as the consultation is disclosed to third parties, through the filing of a lawsuit, the open representation of the client in dealing with third parties or in some other manner.

Upon such public disclosure of the attorney-client relationship, the client's privacy concerns regarding the fact of the consultation evaporate and there is no longer a basis for preventing the attorney from identifying the client. (See Satterlee v. Bliss (1869) 36 Cal. 489, 501.) However, until such a public disclosure occurs, the client's identity is itself a matter of privacy, subject to the protection against involuntary disclosure through compelled discovery against the attorney.

Source: Hooser v. Superior Court of San Diego County, 84 Cal.App.4th 997 (2000) 101 Cal.Rptr.2d 341.

client contact, the paralegal must be prepared to take appropriate action and refer the matter to the supervising attorney.

Some calls are not from potential clients but, rather, from those attempting to get information about the representation of other clients. This is not unusual. Particularly in family law cases, a party may call as if seeking representation but in reality is trying to find out if the other party has retained the firm.

PREPARING FOR THE INTERVIEW

The first step in preparing for an interview or conducting an investigation is to understand the outcome desired. One of the desired outcomes in an initial interview with a new client is to instill confidence in the firm and its personnel. The fundamentally desired outcome of any interview is to obtain all of the relevant facts for the case that has been assigned. Understanding the goals of the interview or investigation, the background or cultural issues of the individual, and the nature of the situation will help in structuring a successful interview.

Occasionally an interview has to be conducted without time for preparation, such as when the paralegal is asked to fill in for someone else at the last moment.

Investigation Checklists

The investigation checklist (Exhibit 9.1) should not be viewed as a static document. The checklist should start with a listing of all of the parties involved who should be interviewed, including initial fact witnesses. As additional parties and witnesses are interviewed, more people may have to be added to the list. Exhibit 9.2 is a witness information form. Investigation of locations and physical evidence may result in the need to examine other locations and evidence. Initial interviews also may result in the need to add one or more expert witnesses to the investigation checklist.

A checklist can be a valuable tool to be certain that all the information required for a certain type of case or other legal matter is obtained during the initial interview. The same checklist offers a good foundation for developing a more detailed interview plan when there is time for preparation.

Physical surroundings, clothing, and appearance are important in preparing for interviews and investigations. They merit your attention.

Physical Surroundings

The physical surroundings in the interview location can set the tone for the interview. Depending upon the purpose of the interview and the person being interviewed, the paralegal may wish to create either a formal or an informal environment. You probably can remember a situation in which someone interviewed you from across a desk. Didn't you feel a certain formality and possibly subservience to the interviewer? Contrast that situation with sitting in an informal setting with a low coffee table and living room-style chairs. This setting gives the meeting a more personal tone.

Putting a client at ease may be easier in the informal setting, whereas dealing with opposing counsel might be better handled in the formal, "across the desk" meeting. In most cases, the paralegal will want to create the impression of a competent professional, although in some situations, creating a more casual and less professional impression may be beneficial. Some witnesses are more cooperative and helpful when they feel as if they are the ones in charge and are helping the paraprofessional.

Dress and Appearance

Remember the old saying, "First impressions count"? The impression a paralegal makes when walking into the room for the initial interview may set the stage for the entire relationship with the client or witness. Clothing, posture, and manner of greeting create the first impression.

Exhibit 9.1 **Investigation checklist for auto accident**

INVESTIGATION CHECKLIST

Client name

Phone (hm)   (wk)   (cell)

Current address

Prior address(es)

Date of birth   Place of birth

Social Security No.

VEHICLE CLIENT OPERATING/PASSENGER

Owner and type of motor vehicle

Insurance Co.   Policy number

Insurance company contact   Phone

Date of incident   Time of day   Weather conditions

Location of incident

City, State   County   Municipality

Opposing party

Address

Phone (hm)   (wk)   (cell)

Owner and type of motor vehicle

Insurance Co.   Policy number

FACT WITNESSES

Name   Address

Name   Address

Name   Address

Name of ambulance

Name of hospital

Police report issued   Copy ordered

Photographs of scene taken

Name of treating physicians

EXPERT WITNESSES

Name   Address

Name   Address

Summary of cause of action

Attach detailed accident/incident description, accident reports and diagrams.

Exhibit 9.2 **Witness information form**

Witness Information

CLIENT PERSONAL DATA

Client Name	Case No.	File No.

Address	City, State, Zip	Phone

CASE DATA

File Label	Case Issue	Date

Responsible Attorney(s)

WITNESS DATA

Witness Name

Aliases, if any	US Citizen ☐ Yes ☐ No

Current Address	City, State, Zip	Phone

Past Address(es)

Date & Place of Birth	Sex	Race	Age	Current Marital Status ☐ Single ☐ Divorced

Name of Spouse	Number/Former Marriages	Number/Children	☐ Married ☐ Widowed ☐ Separated

Name of Children (natural & adopted)	Age	Name	Age

Current Employer

Address	City, State, Zip	Phone

Job Title	Supervisor	From	To

Previous Employer

Address	City, State, Zip	Phone

Job Title	Supervisor	From	To

Education/Name of School	City/State	From	To	Degree
High School				
College				
Technical/Other				

Witness for ☐ Plaintiff ☐ Defendant	Type of Witness ☐ Expert ☐ Character ☐ Eye Witness	Have you ever been a party or witness in a court suit? ☐ No ☐ Yes

If yes, where & when

OTHER PERTINENT DATA

Form 9557 - 9/96 EXCOM Madison, WI Printed in U.S.A.

Clothing sends a nonverbal message about the person and the firm or business. The impression a person makes upon walking into the room can enhance or destroy credibility. In the practice of law, or in a corporate law department, the unexpected can become the norm. Many attorneys, male and female alike, keep a "going-to-court suit" in the office just in case they need to have a more professional appearance at a moment's notice. When the new client comes in, they can change quickly while the receptionist or secretary buys them time to change to the "power" outfit.

A client may be offended by a paralegal's "casual Friday" appearance, believing that the paralegal is not taking the matter seriously. The working paralegal, however, usually doesn't have time to change when the unexpected arises, often being the one to "buy time" for the attorney. Therefore, paralegals always must be prepared to make a good impression and tailor their appearance appropriately as the situation warrants. In the case of field interviews, a casual appearance may be preferred to put the potential witness at ease.

Check religious holiday dates at
http://www.interfaithcalendar.org/

Communication Skills in a Multicultural Society*

Those with whom paralegals communicate can be addressed in many ways. Clients, witnesses, and others with whom the paralegal comes in contact should never be stereotyped. At the same time, paralegals should be aware of the gender, religious, and ethic sensitivities of people. Paralegals' skills as interviewers depend on their ability to appreciate the differences in how and why individuals act and react differently. They must not assume that everyone in each category believes and acts the same and have to be sensitive to issues that may cause a person not to communicate as might have been anticipated from first impressions of them. We will point out some general differences in the way men and women communicate, followed by some cultural background considerations.

Gender Differences

A man, in comparison to a woman, is more likely to

- have been socialized to perform more aggressively and boast of his successes;
- have learned from childhood games that winning is desirable;
- be motivated by competition;
- view conflict as impersonal, a necessary part of working relationships;
- be impressed by power, ability, and achievement;
- hear only the literal words and miss the underlying emotion;
- not express his true feelings through facial expressions;
- have a more direct communication style.

A woman is more likely to

- have been socialized to work cooperatively and to be modest about her success;
- have learned from childhood games to compromise and collaborate, and continue to be motivated by affiliation;
- compete primarily with herself—with her own expectations of what she should be able to accomplish;
- take conflict personally;
- be impressed by personal disclosure and professional courage;
- have the ability to focus on several projects at the same time;

---

*This section on communication skills is adapted from *Crosstalk: Communicating in a Multicultural Workplace*, by Sherron Kenton and Deborah Valentine, 1997. Reprinted with permission of the Authors.

- be proficient at decoding nonverbal meanings and likely to display her feelings through facial expression and body language;
- have an indirect style, except with other women of equal rank.

Considering the receiver's attitudes about the paralegal:

- Man-to-man: He may afford the paralegal instant credibility based on the same gender.
- Woman-to-woman: She may expect the paralegal to be friendly, nurturing, and concerned and may afford the paralegal instant credibility based on same-gender assumptions.
- Paralegal man-to-woman. She may expect that the paralegal will not really listen to her.
- Paralegal woman-to-man: He may expect the paralegal to be friendly and nurturing, even passive-dependent. Any aggressive behavior or deviation from his expectation could cause him discomfort and confusion, or produce negative responses. He may simply disregard the female paralegal.

Cultural Sensitivity

The culturally sensitive person is aware of the reasons for differences in the way people behave, based on religious and ethnic background and belief system. As the cultural makeup of the United States has become more diverse, the need for cultural awareness and sensitivity in the legal and paralegal professions has grown. Just as men and women are said to be different in some ways, so are Europeans, Asians, Latinos, and Africans who have not fully assimilated into the culture of the country.

Interviewing a Latino male, for example, may require a different approach than interviewing an Asian female. Even subtleties of eye contact can affect an interview. Whereas Americans view eye contact as a sign of sincerity, some Asian cultures view this as aggressive. In developing communication skills, paralegals must become sensitive to how they are perceived and learn to fashion their approach to maximize accuracy of communication.

The effectiveness of paralegals also is influenced by how well they "read" the cultural backgrounds of those with whom they interact. This involves manner of speaking, dressing, and acting, and whether one is a man or a woman in that culture. What is heard may not be what was intended. What is perceived may not be what the other person perceives, because of cultural differences that affect the interpretation of words and body language. We will briefly highlight some general characteristics of four cultural groups.

European background. Generally, the countries of Western Europe, including Scandinavia, comprise the group of European background. This group is extraordinarily large and complex, which limits attempts to make cultural generalities. In terms of gender differences, men and women with roots in the European culture may have different initial reactions to the paralegal and attitudes about the topic. Male and female listeners alike tend to perceive men as having more credibility than women of equal rank, experience, and training. Men tend to be more credible to other men, and women may be more credible to other women.

Now consider the cultural implications of graphic pictures of physical injuries from car crashes. These photos are acceptable in the United States, but Germans tend to dislike the sight of blood and the British are likely to be offended by violence.

According to Kenton and Valentine, if the paralegal appears to be European–American, receivers of communication may be concerned that the paralegal will:

- reject their opinions;
- take advantage of them or hold them back;

- consider them different in a negative way;
- deny them equal opportunities.

Latino background.   Collectively, Latin America encompasses 51 countries generally considered to be those south of the U.S. border: Mexico and the countries of Central America, South America, and the Caribbean islands. With so vast an area, many differences can be expected from country to country and even from city to city. The languages, too, are not the same. Portuguese is spoken in Brazil, and the Spanish that is spoken in South America differs from the Spanish spoken in Puerto Rico. The Latino–American population has moved closer to becoming the largest minority group in the United States. According to Kenton and Valentine, individuals with roots in the Latino culture tend to:

- value family and loyalty to family;
- honor nationalism;
- exhibit a strong sense of honor;
- have a fatalistic view of the world;
- express passion in speech, manner, and deed.

Asian background.   More than 30 countries can be considered Asian—among them, China, Malaysia, Japan, the Philippines, India, and Korea. They, too, demonstrate vast differences from culture to culture. Some generalizations may be made, however. Asian cultures generally consider that being direct and to the point are rude, and relationships are considered top priority. The Japanese, for example, tend to prefer an indirect style of communication. In communicating with people who have an Asian background, then, it might be best to begin with pleasantries about the weather, sports, or inquire about the well-being of the individual and his or her family.

Roots in the African culture.   African Americans represent the largest ethnic group in the United States. A distinction should be made between African Americans of recent immigration with stronger cultural ties to the African culture and African Americans with long family ties within the United States whose cultural roots are American. According to Kenton and Valentine, some of the African core beliefs and cultural values that may influence attitudes and behavior are:

- a holistic worldview;
- emotion and expressiveness;
- a keen sense of justice or fairness.

CONDUCTING THE INTERVIEW

In the first meeting, the paralegal must make clear that he or she is a paralegal and not an attorney. During the first few minutes of the interview, paralegals must build a relationship with the interviewees, explain the reason for the interview, and eliminate any barriers that would prevent obtaining the necessary information. Sometimes the interviewees seem to be fully cooperative when in fact they are not cooperating. Or the subject matter may be embarrassing, or they may have a fear of authority figures, or they might be uncomfortable using certain terms necessary to describe the situation.

Effective interviewers learn the verbal and nonverbal cues that help them understand the reasons for interviewees' reluctance to answer questions. In some situations the solution is first to ask easy questions, such as the person's name and address. Once interviewees start speaking, they have less trouble answering well thought-out questions that build logically on the previous information.

This is not always the case, though. In times of great stress, clients have been known to read the name from a nameplate in the office and state it as their own name! The interviewer must be careful to avoid embarrassing the interviewee and have prepared questions that can be answered easily and thereby help the person gain composure, such as, "My records show that you live at 123 South Main Street. Is that correct?" Or "How do you spell your name?"

Listening Skills

A good interviewer must master the skill of listening. Most of us hear the words being said but may not be listening to *what* is being said. Instead of concentrating on what is being said, listeners may be more concerned with the next question they want to ask, or emotionally influenced by the speaker's message, or distracted by the speaker's physical behavior.

Interviewing clients and witnesses requires listening to what is being said in the context of the speaker's cultural makeup. It also requires an understanding of the type of witness—friendly, hostile, or expert—and the witnesses' bias toward the client or the type of case for which they are being interviewed. Fact witnesses may not want to get involved, or be hostile witnesses, saying what they either think you want to hear or what will move their agenda along. Fact witnesses in criminal matters involving members of different races or religions may not be as concerned for the truth as they are for "someone paying" for committing the crime. Bias and cultural identity may influence what is said.

The professional interviewer must listen to what is really being said in a nonjudgmental impartial manner.

When listening, the paralegal must focus on what is said and not how it is said. Some people are not articulate, and the facts may be lost if a person doesn't listen carefully. Others may try to shock or put off the paralegal by buzz words designed to get a reaction. In sports, this is referred to as "trash talk"—saying things to get the listener to react emotionally and lose concentration.

Good listeners avoid distractions. They do not allow themselves to lose focus because of environmental distractions such as noise or activity in the area of the interview, or a speaker's annoying physical habits, such as tapping the fingers or legs, or speech impediments, such as stuttering. Think about how hard it is to concentrate on what is being said in a large classroom. Good listeners focus on the message and block out distractions.

Further, good interviewers do not make assumptions about the facts of the case. They listen with an open mind. Making assumptions about people or facts can lead to attempts to make the facts fit the interviewer's preconceived notions. Sometimes the facts are not what they first seem to be. Look at the number of people released from

checklist ✓

LISTENING SKILLS

- Empathize with the person, and try to put yourself in his or her place to help you see the point.
- Don't interrupt; allow time for the person to say what he or she is trying to say.
- Leave your emotions behind, and control your anger. Emotions will prevent you from listening well.
- Get rid of distractions.
- Don't argue mentally.
- Don't antagonize the speaker. This could cause someone to conceal important ideas, emotions, and attitudes.
- Avoid jumping to conclusions. This can get you into trouble. For example, don't assume that the speaker is using the words in the same way that you are interpreting them. If you are unsure, ask for clarification.

© Student Counseling Service, Texas A&M University.

For more information on Listening Skills see the Texas A & M Website at http://www.scs.tamu.edu/selfhelp/elibrary/listening_skills.asp

Leading question
A question which suggests the answer.

Open-ended question
Questions that usually do not have a yes or no answer.

Narrative opportunity
A question that allows the giving of a full explanation.

Moral obligation
An obligation based on one's own conscience.

Ethical obligation
A minimum standard of conduct usually within one's profession.

jail after DNA evidence proves they did not do the crime everyone assumed they committed. Fact witness may have been interviewed and been given a version of the incident that the DNA does not prove to be correct, and the person is innocent.

Leading Questions

Leading questions are those that suggest the desired answer. In conducting a cross-examination, lawyers in trial frequently use leading questions to force the witness to answer in a desired manner. An obvious example is, "Have you stopped kicking your dog?"

On direct examination, an attorney might ask a more direct and neutral question: "Have you ever kicked your dog?"

Leading questions do not lead to open-ended answers but are directed toward a desired answer: "You ran the red light, didn't you?"

Open-Ended Questions

Open-ended questions are designed to give interviewees an opportunity to tell their story without the limitation of yes-or-no answers. Open-ended questions create a **narrative opportunity** for the witness. For example: "Tell me about your life"; "Tell me about your life since the accident."

In fact interviews, the witness should receive the opportunity for open-ended narrative answers. Asking a question to solicit an answer that you desire may cut off information that is essential to your case. For example, you may want to know whether your client was at the scene of an accident, and therefore you ask the witness, "Did you see my client at the scene of the accident?" The answer to this question may be "yes" or "no." A better question would be, "Who was present at the scene of the accident?" This kind of question may lead to additional information on additional witnesses you may want to interview.

Similarly, the question, "How fast were the cars going prior to the impact?" is much better than, "Were the cars speeding before the impact?" In this context, the term "speeding" may be interpreted as exceeding the speed limit instead of going too fast for the conditions.

With the witness's statements from the interview in hand at the time of trial, the trial attorney might appropriately ask a leading question such as, "My client wasn't present at the scene of the accident, was she?" Or, "Isn't it true that the defendant was speeding before the impact?" With knowledge of the prior statement, there should be no surprise in the answer at trial. If there is, the prior statement can be used to impeach the credibility of the witness, if desired, as part of the trial strategy.

At times, the interviewer may want to focus clients or witnesses by asking questions that give them a perspective of time or place, such as, "What did you observe at noon on Saturday?" or, "Tell me what happened on September 11, 2001." The tragedy of that day will haunt the memories of Americans and most of the rest of the world, so little stimulus will be needed to elicit where they were and what they observed. This is true of most traumatic events in people's lives—the loss of a loved one, the birth of a child, or a serious accident in which they were injured. Other days and times tend to blur and have to be brought to the consciousness of the witness by questions such as, "Let's think back to August 19, 2001" and, "What happened to you that day?"

MORAL VERSUS ETHICAL CONSIDERATIONS

At times in the investigation of a case, it is necessary to consider the difference between a moral consideration and an ethical consideration. A **moral obligation** is one based on one's own conscience or a person's perceived rules of correct conduct, generally in the person's own community. Some communities, for instance, may consider it to be morally improper to ask someone to give information about another person. An **ethical obligation**, for members of the legal team including those acting on behalf of a supervising attorney, are the responsibilities of the legal profession under the ABA Model Rules of Professional Conduct, including thoroughness in representing a client.

Is it ethically improper to ask someone to tell the truth surrounding the facts of a case that may lead to a neighbor, relative, or friend being subjected to liability for his or her actions? For the paralegal and the legal team, the primary ethical obligation is the duty to the client. Some members of the legal team, for example, may be offended to ask a mother to testify against a child. This is a moral issue for the mother, in which the results may cause financial hardship or ruin upon awarding a verdict for causing injury as the result of negligent conduct, but ethics may require this course of conduct for the paralegal.

PRIVILEGED COMMUNICATION

Certain forms of communication are considered privileged and not usable at trial unless the privilege is waived. Forms of **privileged communication** are:

1. Attorney–client communications
2. Doctor–patient communications
3. Priest–penitent communications
4. Spousal communications during marriage

Each of these privileges can be waived but the waiver must come from the client, the patient, the penitent, or the spouse making the statement with the belief that it is privileged. Changes in some of the rules of ethics, and by statute, may permit certain otherwise privileged communications to be revealed to prevent harm or injury to another. The spouse, the priest, or the doctor may have a moral issue in revealing what was communicated.

When the paralegal is acting on behalf of the attorney, communications between a client and the paralegal have the same privilege as those between the client and the attorney. Information gathered from the client as part of representation of the client and necessary for rendering competent legal advice is privileged. The paralegal, therefore, is in the same position as the attorney, the doctor, the priest, or the spouse to whom the confidential information has been communicated. Each must

---

ETHICAL *Perspective*

Model Rules of Professional Conduct

Client–Lawyer Relationship Rule 1.6 Confidentiality of Information

(a) A lawyer shall not reveal information relating to the representation of a client unless the client gives informed consent, the disclosure is impliedly authorized in order to carry out the representation or the disclosure is permitted by paragraph (b).....

Privileged communication
A communication that the person has a right to be kept confidential based on the relationship with the other part such as attorney and client.

FEDERAL RULES OF CIVIL PROCEDURE 26 F.R.C.P. 26(b)(4)

(4) TRIAL PREPARATION: EXPERTS

(A) A party may depose any person who has been identified as an expert whose opinions may be presented at trial. If a report from the expert is required under subdivision (a)(2)(B), the deposition shall not be conducted until after the report is provided.

(B) A party may, through interrogatories or by deposition, discover facts known or opinions held by an expert who has been retained or specially employed by another party in anticipation of litigation or preparation for trial and who is not expected to be called as a witness at trial, only as provided in Rule 35(b) or upon a showing of exceptional circumstances under which it is impracticable for the party seeking discovery to obtain facts or opinions on the same subject by other means.

(C) Unless manifest injustice would result, (i) the court shall require that the party seeking discovery pay the expert a reasonable fee for time spent in responding to discovery under this subdivision; and (ii) with respect to discovery obtained under subdivision (b)(4)(B) of this rule the court shall require the party seeking discovery to pay the other party a fair portion of the fees and expenses reasonably incurred by the latter party in obtaining facts and opinions from the expert.

carefully guard the confidential information and not inadvertently or intentionally reveal the information. In some cases, such as when another person's life may be in danger, these people may be compelled by a court to testify even when they believe it is a violation of their moral duty to another person from whom they have received information.

EXPERT WITNESSES

Expert witness
A person qualified by education or experience to render an opinion based on a set of facts.

Expert witnesses are individuals whose background, education, and experience are such that courts recognize them as qualified to give opinions based on a set of facts. The expert witness may be a doctor certified by a board of medical experts or a scientist or engineer specializing in an area of science such as flammability of fabrics. The report of these experts may be advice based on the facts of a potential case to determine whether there is sufficient evidence to believe that a wrong has occurred or malpractice committed. Without this report, the lawyers may be obligated to advise clients that they have no actionable cause of action.

There is no clear rule on whether what is revealed to an expert in the preparation of a case is protected as part of the attorney–client privilege in the same manner as that revealed to a member of the trial team, including other attorneys, paralegals, and secretarial staff working on the case with the primary trial attorney. Almost certainly, anything revealed to an expert who is listed as an expert witness on the list of witnesses to be called at trial is discoverable.

Some law firms retain an expert to advise them but do not use that expert to testify. The advice and information provided by these experts to help in the preparation for trial may come under the privilege. Although the privilege is the client's, the paralegal and others on the legal team must be careful not to divulge privileged or confidential material without authorization.

The expert retained for background trial advice must have as much confidence in the legal team as the legal team has in the expert's advice and integrity. Some experts fear that the legal team will give them only selected information. With the limited information provided, they might give an expert opinion that is not what they would have given if they had received the complete set of facts.

Exhibit 9.3 indicates factors to be considered in arranging for an expert witness.

checklist ✓   DEPOSING EXPERT WITNESSES

Ask an expert witness these ten questions at deposition, even if you don't have time to ask anything else:

- What opinions have you formed in this matter?
- What did you do to reach those opinions?
- How did you do that?
- Why did you do that?
- What results did you get?
- How did the results affect your opinion?
- Are there reliable authorities in this field?
- What assumptions did you make in your work?
- What tasks didn't you do?
- Is this your current and accurate resume?

Source: From David M. Malone and Paul J. Zwier, *Expert Rules: 100 (and more) Points You Need to Know About Expert Witnesses,* 2nd ed. Copyright © NITA, 2001. Reprinted by permission.

Exhibit 9.3 **Expert witness form**

EXPERT WITNESS CHECKLIST

BACKGROUND

Full name   Date of birth

Business address

Business telephone number   Business fax number

Business email address   Business website

Locations of prior offices

Home address

Home telephone number

EDUCATION

Schools attended   Dates of attendance

Degrees or honors awarded

Continuing education courses

WORK HISTORY

Place of employment   Dates of employment

Job description

Reasons for leaving

Specific area of expertise

Published articles and books

Professional affiliations

Professional magazines subscribed to

Licenses and jurisdictions

Litigations or disciplinary action

PRIOR LEGAL EXPERIENCE

Ratio of plaintiff/defense cases

Prior clients including date (plaintiff or defendant)

Types of investigations with dates

Deposition testimony given with dates

Court testimony with dates

Legal references

AVAILABILITY

Vacation plans and dates   Potential meeting dates

INVESTIGATING CLAIMS

The legal team must gather all of the relevant information about a cause of action before making a recommendation to a client to file a lawsuit or respond to a claim of wrongdoing. In most cases, before the first interview with the client is conducted, the paralegal has some indication of the area of law or the nature of the claim. It may be from a telephone interview when the client calls for an appointment, or from the referral from the supervising attorney to the paralegal to conduct the interview and investigation. If paralegals specialize in certain areas of law, they are likely to understand the underlying elements of the claims or rights the client wishes to assert. Those in general practice and those entering a new area have to understand the rules of law as they apply to that issue.

For example, in a product liability case, understanding traditional, or common-law, of negligence is not enough. One also must understand the law of **strict liability** for product defect cases as found in the **Restatement of the Law Third, Torts**: Product Liability. Where negligence requires a breach of duty, strict liability is without fault in cases where the doctrine applies. An interview conducted strictly considering negligence as the basis for a legal action could improperly result in the client's being advised that he or she does not have a claim when, under the no-fault strict liability concept for defective products, an action might exist.

The first step is to determine the legal basis of a client's claim. With an understanding of the legal basis of the claim and the applicable law, an investigative plan can be prepared to obtain the necessary witness statements, locate physical evidence, and obtain photographs, reports, and other evidence for use in preparation for and at trial. Where a claim of negligence is to be made, photographic evidence may be essential in demonstrating the nature of the hazard.

For example, when a client has injured himself or herself as result of a fall in a store, photographs showing the hazardous condition should be obtained as quickly as possible. In the case of strict liability involving a product defect that caused injury or loss, preservation of the defective product or photographic documentation of the defect becomes essential as a matter of proof. Knowing what elements of the action must be proven dictates what evidence must be located in the form of witnesses, photographs, and physical evidence. Knowing the elements of the claim will ensure that the proper questions are asked in the interview, which then will dictate the necessary investigation steps.

One of the most useful tools in the gathering of information about a case is the digital camera. Digital photographs may be shared on computer networks or by Internet transfer to other members of the legal team, clients, and possible witnesses. It also is useful to take pictures of potential witnesses so other members of the legal team may recognize them later at the time of depositions and trial. If the photographs are going to be used at trial, it should be kept in mind that the photographer may be called to authenticate them.

A Defense Perspective

Most people quite naturally think of a lawsuit from the plaintiff's perspective. Most people think in terms of the violation of rights and resulting injury. In a perfect world, only legitimate actions would be filed and the law would provide a perfect remedy for all wrongs. But not every plaintiff is in the right, and some have been known to file frivolous or even fraudulent lawsuits.

The balance in the American legal system is achieved by a vigorous defense on behalf of the defendant. A plaintiff may claim, for example, that she slipped and was injured as a result of the negligence of a storeowner. The defendant storeowner might be innocent of any wrongdoing or breach of any duty. It is well to remember that for every plaintiff there is a defendant, and for each party there is a law firm, an attorney, and a paralegal.

For more information in the changes in the revised Restatement of the Law Third, visit the American Law Institute http://www.ali.org./ali/promo6081.htm

Strict liability
Liability without fault.

Restatement of the law third torts
A legal treatise with suggested rules of laws relating to torts.

Obtaining Official Reports

Most incidents giving rise to litigation have associated official reports. In the negligence action, it may be a police accident or incident report, emergency medical services report, fire department call report, or incident reports of safety violations by federal, state, or local authorities. These reports are filed in a central depository as public records. A useful starting point is to obtain any official reports associated with the case. These reports frequently indicate time, place, and the names of fact witnesses. In some cases, detailed diagrams or photographs may accompany the reports. Exhibit 9.4 is an example of a police accident report form.

Fact Analysis

Analyzing the facts starts with interviewing the clients and their recitation of the time, place, circumstances, and other people involved as participants or witnesses. Exhibit 9.5 is a sample client interview form. A complete analysis usually requires further field investigation of the location, the object involved, such as an automobile, and interviews of the parties and witnesses. One person's perception may not be reality. A client's recollection and description of the physical surroundings may not be proven by the investigator's visit to the location. What one person describes as a narrow, congested walkway may actually be a standard-width open sidewalk.

The ultimate trier of fact will be the jury, a panel of arbitrators, or a judge acting as the trier of fact. Therefore, analysis of the facts must be sufficient to justify the position taken and the presentation made in pursuing a client's claim or its defense in **arbitration** or in trial.

Locations

Careful analysis of a claim includes verification of the physical aspects of the actual location where the cause of action occurred. Ask any group of people to describe a location, and you're likely to get as many different descriptions as there are people in the group. How the person viewed the location, from the south, from the north, east, or west, may influence their description. Or the driver's view from behind the wheel of a large tractor– trailer might be different from the view from behind the wheel of a small sports car.

Investigation of a case should involve a trip to the location where the incident occurred. The trier of fact will be relying upon the plaintiff's and defendant's counsels to describe in their presentation the characteristics of the physical location. They also will be looking at the location from an impartial, neutral point of view, usually without prior familiarity with the location. The diagrams usually presented at trial are those of an aerial view with its sterile, one-dimensional presentation. Photographs from the points of view of all the participants can make the difference in understanding the duties and responsibilities of the litigants. Unlike diagrams of the location, these photographs more typically will be from the point of view of the plaintiff, defendant, or witness at ground level, or from behind the wheel of a vehicle, or looking out of a building window.

Satellite photos are available of locations around the world. Earth Google™ offers a Web access to images that may be modified to add desired descriptions such as street names, points of interest, including lodgings, restaurants, schools, churches, and many others by the click of the computer mouse. Images from before a loss such as Hurricane Katrina combined with images taken after the devastation may be helpful in submitting claims for damages.

Tangible Evidence

Tangible evidence consists of the physical objects that may have caused the injury. These may include items as small as a giveaway toy from a fast-food restaurant swallowed by a 2-year-old, to a bottle that exploded, to a large automobile whose brakes failed or

Arbitration
A form of ADR in which the parties choose an impartial third party to hear and decide the dispute.

Find your home on Google Earth at http://earth.google.com

Exhibit 9.4 **Sample police accident report form**

COMMONWEALTH OF PENNSYLVANIA
POLICE ACCIDENT REPORT

XX. REFER TO OVERLAY SHEETS   REPORTABLE ☐   NON - REPORTABLE ☐   PENNDOT USE ONLY

POLICE INFORMATION

1. INCIDENT NUMBER	
2. AGENCY NAME	
3. STATION/ PRECINCT	4. PATROL ZONE
5. INVESTIGATOR	BADGE NUMBER
6. APPROVED BY	BADGE NUMBER
7. INVESTIGATION DATE	8. ARRIVAL TIME

ACCIDENT INFORMATION

9. ACCIDENT DATE	10. DAY OF WEEK
11. TIME OF DAY	12. NUMBER OF UNITS
13. # KILLED	14.# INJURED	15. PRIV. PROP. ACCIDENT Y ☐ N ☐

16. DID VEHICLE HAVE TO BE REMOVED FROM THE SCENE?
UNIT 1   UNIT 2
Y ☐ N ☐   Y ☐ N ☐

17. VEHICLE DAMAGE
0 - NONE   UNIT 1 ☐
1 - LIGHT
2 - MODERATE
3 - SEVERE   UNIT 2 ☐

18. HAZARDOUS MATERIALS Y ☐ N ☐
19. PENNDOT PROPERTY Y ☐ N ☐

ACCIDENT LOCATION

20. COUNTY	CODE
21. MUNICIPALITY	CODE

PRINCIPAL ROADWAY INFORMATION

22. ROUTE NO. OR STREET NAME
23. SPEED LIMIT | 24. TYPE HIGHWAY | 25. ACCESS CONTROL

INTERSECTING ROAD:

26. ROUTE NO. OR STREET NAME
27. SPEED LIMIT | 28. TYPE HIGHWAY | 29. ACCESS CONTROL

IF NOT AT INTERSECTION:

30. CROSS STREET OR SEGMENT MARKER
31. DIRECTION FROM SITE N S E W | 32. DISTANCE FROM SITE FT. MI.
33. DISTANCE WAS MEASURED ☐ ESTIMATED ☐
34. CONSTRUCTION ZONE ☐ | 35. TRAFFIC CONTROL DEVICE PRINCIPAL ☐ INTERSECTING ☐

UNIT # 1

36. LEGALLY PARKED? Y ☐ N ☐	37. REG. PLATE	38. STATE
39. PA TITLE OR OUT-OF-STATE VIN	
40. OWNER	
41. OWNER ADDRESS	
42. CITY, STATE & ZIPCODE	
43. YEAR	44. MAKE
45. MODEL - (NOT BODY TYPE)	46. INS. Y ☐ N ☐ UNK ☐
47. BODY TYPE	48. SPECIAL USAGE	49. VEHICLE OWNERSHIP
50. INITIAL IMPACT POINT	51. VEHICLE STATUS	52. TRAVEL SPEED
53. VEHICLE GRADIENT	54. DRIVER PRESENCE	55. DRIVER CONDITION
56. DRIVER NUMBER	57. STATE
58. DRIVER NAME	
59. DRIVER ADDRESS	
60. CITY, STATE & ZIPCODE	
61. SEX	62. DATE OF BIRTH	63. PHONE
64. COMM. VEH. Y ☐ N ☐	65. DRIVER CLASS	66. DRIVER SS #
67. CARRIER	
68. CARRIER ADDRESS	
69. CITY, STATE & ZIPCODE	
70. USDOT #	ICC #	PUC #
72. VEH. CONFIG.	73. CARGO BODY TYPE	74. GVWR
75. NO. OF AXLES	76. HAZARDOUS MATERIALS	77. RELEASE OF HAZ MAT Y ☐ N ☐ UNK ☐

UNIT # 2

36. LEGALLY PARKED? Y ☐ N ☐	37. REG. PLATE	38. STATE
39. PA TITLE OR OUT-OF-STATE VIN	
40. OWNER	
41. OWNER ADDRESS	
42. CITY, STATE & ZIPCODE	
43. YEAR	44. MAKE
45. MODEL - (NOT BODY TYPE)	46. INS. Y ☐ N ☐ UNK ☐
47. BODY TYPE	48. SPECIAL USAGE	49. VEHICLE OWNERSHIP
50. INITIAL IMPACT POINT	51. VEHICLE STATUS	52. TRAVEL SPEED
53. VEHICLE GRADIENT	54. DRIVER PRESENCE	55. DRIVER CONDITION
56. DRIVER NUMBER	57. STATE
58. DRIVER NAME	
59. DRIVER ADDRESS	
60. CITY, STATE & ZIPCODE	
61. SEX	62. DATE OF BIRTH	63. PHONE
64. COMM. VEH. Y ☐ N ☐	65. DRIVER CLASS	66. DRIVER SS #
67. CARRIER	
68. CARRIER ADDRESS	
69. CITY, STATE & ZIPCODE	
70. USDOT #	ICC #	PUC #
72. VEH. CONFIG.	73. CARGO BODY TYPE	74. GVWR
75. NO. OF AXLES	76. HAZARDOUS MATERIALS	77. RELEASE OF HAZ MAT Y ☐ N ☐ UNK ☐

AA-45 (1/92)   PAGE: CENTER FOR HIGHWAY SAFETY

Exhibit 9.4 **Sample police accident report form** (*continued*)

78. RESPONDING EMS AGENCY	INCIDENT #:
79. MEDICAL FACILITY	ACCIDENT DATE:

80. PEOPLE INFORMATION

A	B	C	D	E	F	G	NAME	ADDRESS	H	I	J	K	L	M

81. ILLUMINATION [ ]   82. WEATHER [ ]

83. ROAD SURFACE [ ]

84. PENNSYLVANIA SCHOOL DISTRICT
(IF APPLICABLE)

85. DESCRIPTION OF DAMAGED PROPERTY

OWNER

ADDRESS

PHONE

86. DIAGRAM

87. NARRATIVE - IDENTIFY PRECIPITATING EVENTS, CAUSATION FACTORS, SEQUENCE OF EVENTS, WITNESS STATEMENTS, AND PROVIDE ADDITIONAL DETAILS. LIKE INSURANCE INFORMATION AND LOCATION OF TOWED VEHILCES, IF KNOWN.

INSURANCE INFORMATION	COMPANY		INSURANCE INFORMATION	COMPANY	
UNIT 1	POLICY NO		UNIT 2	POLICY NO	

88. WINTESSES	NAME	ADDRESS	PHONE
	NAME	ADDRESS	PHONE

	89. VIOLATIONS INDICATED	90. SECTION NUMBERS (ONLY IF CHARGED)	TC NTC
UNIT 1			[ ] [ ]
UNIT 2			[ ] [ ]

	91. PROBABLE USE	92. TYPE TEST	93. RESULTS			91. PROBABLE USE	92. TYPE TEST	93. RESULTS		94. INVESTIGATION COMPLETE ?
UNIT 1			0.___ ___%	[ ] NO TEST [ ] REFUSE [ ] UNK	UNIT 2			0.___ ___%	[ ] NO TEST [ ] REFUSE [ ] UNK	YES [ ] NO [ ]

AA-45 (1/92)   PAGE: CENTER FOR HIGHWAY SAFETY

Exhibit 9.5 **Initial client interview form**

CLIENT INTERVIEW CHECKLIST

CLIENT PERSONAL INFORMATION

Name _____

Address _____

City _____ State _____ Zip _____

Phone (hm) _____ (wk) _____ (cell) _____

How long at this address _____

Date of birth _____ Place of birth _____

Social Security No. _____

Prior address _____

City _____ State _____ Zip _____

Dates at this address _____

Employer: _____

Job description _____

Marital status _____ Maiden name _____

Spouse's name _____ Date of birth _____

Child's name _____ Date of birth _____

Child's name _____ Date of birth _____

Child's name _____ Date of birth _____

CASE INFORMATION

Case referred by _____

Case type: ☐ Appeal ☐ Business ☐ Corporate ☐ Estate ☐ Litigation
            ☐ Municipal ☐ Real Estate ☐ Tax ☐ Trust ☐ Other

Opposing party(ies) _____

Opposing party _____

Address _____

Opposing attorney _____

Address _____

Date of incident _____ Statute of limitation date _____

Summary of facts _____

_____

_____

_____

---

whose seatbelts snapped. In some cases, the tangible evidence is essential to proving negligence or an element of strict liability in tort.

Much has been written about the effects of the plaintiffs' and defendants' failure to preserve critical evidence of this type. In some cases, failure to preserve the evidence has resulted in loss of the case by the plaintiff, and in other cases by the defendant.

Exhibit 9.6 **Sample timeline using LexisNexis CaseSoft TimeMap**

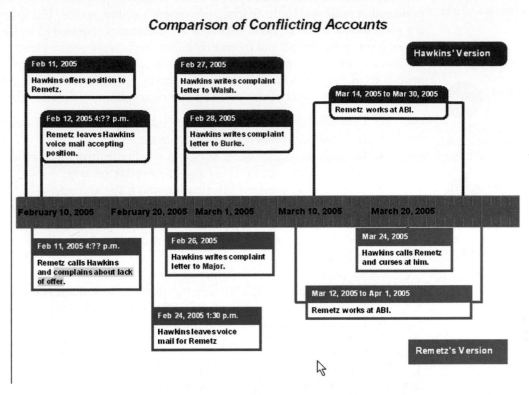

Timeline created using Time Map, from DecisionQuest, CaseSoft (www.casesolt.com). Copyright LexisNexis® Case Soft.

It is important to understand the local rules with regard to **spoliation of evidence** and its effect on a cause of action. In determining the proper penalty for spoliation of evidence, courts are most likely to consider [*Schroeder v. Department of Transportation*, 551 Pa. 243, 710 A.2d 23, 26 (1998)]:

1. The degree of fault of the party who altered or destroyed the evidence.
2. The degree of prejudice suffered by the opposing party.
3. The availability of a lesser sanction that will protect the opposing party's rights and deter future similar conduct.

Spoliation of evidence
Destruction of evidence.

Following a Timeline

Causes of action should be viewed from the events leading up to the incident to the events and occurrences following the incident. (See Exhibit 9.6 for a comparison of conflicting accounts.) Few things in life that give rise to a potential claim occur in a vacuum. Usually some facts lead up to the incident and others follow the incident. The question may be, "Given the time in which the parties allege this happened, could this really have happened?" For example, could the parties have driven the 30 miles in 20 minutes through crowded rush-hour traffic on city streets? In a food-poisoning case, could ingestion of the food at noon have caused the reaction claimed by 1:00 P.M. The claimant might have been negligent, or the first perceived wrong-doer perhaps was not the correct person, as most food-poisoning cases require 6 to 12 hours from ingestion of the tainted food until onset of symptoms of the illness.

The starting point is the time of the alleged injury. Also important, from a fault standpoint or defense standpoint, is what happened that led up to the incident. From the damages standpoint, what happened after the incident, including treatment and subsequent changes in the person's life or lifestyle, is important.

The CPSC FOIA Request form can be completed online at https://xapps.cpsc.gov/FOIA/pages/requestentry.jsp

FREEDOM OF INFORMATION ACT (FOIA)

Freedom of Information Act
A federal statute permitting access to federal agency records.

Obtain a copy of the latest CPSC FOIA report at http://www.cpsc.gov/LIBRARY/FOIA/foia.html

For information or making an FOIA request to the Department of Justice is available at www.usdoj.gov/ 04foia/

The **Freedom of Information Act** is a federal statute designed to open to the public the information possessed by the federal government and its agencies. The federal government is a good source of information. Many of the documents required to be filed are available through the government, and frequently online, such as corporate filings with the Securities and Exchange Commission. Other information may be available by request, under the provisions of the Freedom of Information Act (FOIA), 5 U.S.C. § 552. Some limitations apply to the information available. The general exceptions, as found in the statute, are:

1. Classified documents concerning national defense and foreign policy.
2. Internal personnel rules and practices.
3. Exemptions under other laws that require information to be withheld, such as patent applications and income-tax returns.
4. Confidential business information and trade secrets.
5. Intra-agency and inter-agency internal communications not available by law to a party in litigation.
6. Protection of privacy of personnel and medical files and private lives of individuals.
7. Law-enforcement investigatory files.
8. Examination, operation, or condition reports of agencies responsible for the regulation and supervision of financial institutions.
9. Geological and geophysical information and data including maps concerning wells.

Many federal agencies do not require a formal FOIA request. Some federal agencies, such as the National Transportation Agency, make information available online (Exhibit 9.7). Other agencies, such as the Consumer Product Safety Commission

Exhibit 9.7 **FOIA information available online from NTSB**

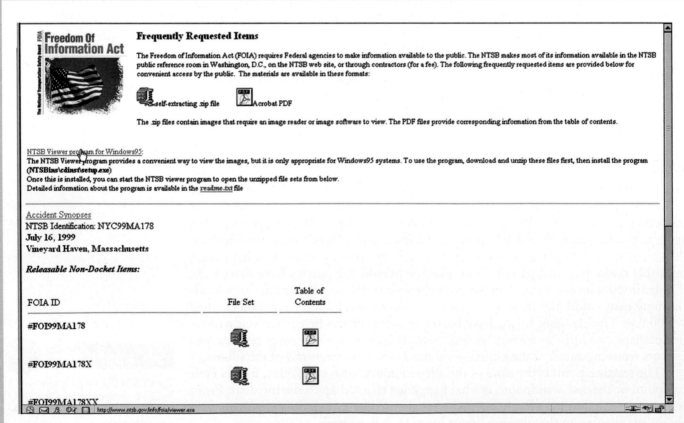

Exhibit 9.8 **Online Freedom of Information Request form for USPSC.**

US Consumer Product Safety Commission

▶ Consumer Safety   ▶ About CPSC   ▶ Library - FOIA   ▶ Business

New FOIA Request Form
Requestor Information

Name Prefix:

* Last Name:

* First Name:

Phone No:

* Email Address:

If you represent a company or firm, enter it below, otherwise enter personal information.

Company Name:

Website:

* Mailing Address:

* City:

* State:

* ZIP Code:

* Country: United States

Request Detail

* Range of Search Request: 2002   * To   2005

* Subject:

* Request Type:

* Type of Requestor:

Product Description:

Brand/Model:

* Remarks:

* Some requests will include fees. Please check if you accept any fees associated with this request.

Submit   Clear

* Indicates Required Field
Questions on submitting a FOIA request should be directed to aheggs@cpsc.gov

(CPSC), permit requests to be made on the CPSC website (see Exhibit 9.8). The CPSC site also is helpful in finding information about defective products that may be a cause of a client's injuries. Limitations are placed on the information that an agency may disclose under applicable federal law. An example is shown in the CPSC limitation (Exhibit 9.9).

LOCATING WITNESSES

Most witnesses can be located by use of directories. The Web has also become a valuable tool for locating witnesses.

Directories

Investigators usually keep a collection of telephone books of the areas in which they work. Rarely today does a person not have a telephone of some sort, even if it is an unlisted number. In addition to the standard-issue telephone directories, the cross-reference directory (also known as a "criss-cross directory") is a standard tool; these list phone numbers by address or by phone number instead of by name. Therefore, an address may be checked for a corresponding phone number—for example, determining the phone number located at 123 Main Street, or using the phone numbers listed at an address to determine the physical location or billing address of the phone.

Exhibit 9.9 **Simplified online FOIA form to request information not already available from National Transportation Safety Board(NTSB)**

Freedom of Information Act (FOIA) Request
Be sure to read what's available under FOIA before making a request.

Please specify as much detail as possible about the item(s) you are requesting. Depending on the complexity of your request, turnaround could range from 3 weeks to 1 year or more. For assistance, please contact the Records Management Division at (800) 877-6799 or (202) 314-6551.

First Name: _____ Email Addr: _____

Last Name: _____ Phone No: _____

Street: _____

City: _____ Business/Affiliation: _____

State: [▾] Zip: _____ Country: _____

Transportation: [- Select Mode - ▾]

Please describe your request or comment below - be specific about dates, locations, etc., where applicable:

_____

CPSC LIMITATIONS OF FOIA DISCLOSURE

15 U.S.C. § 2055. Public disclosure of information release date: 2005-08-01

"(a) Disclosure requirements for manufacturers or private labelers; procedures applicable

(1) Nothing contained in this Act shall be construed to require the release of any information described by subsection (b) of section 552 of title 5 or which is otherwise protected by law from disclosure to the public.

(2) All information reported to or otherwise obtained by the Commission or its representative under this Act which information contains or relates to a trade secret or other matter referred to in section 1905 of title 18 or subject to section 552 (b)(4) of title 5 shall be considered confidential and shall not be disclosed.

(3) The Commission shall, prior to the disclosure of any information which will permit the public to ascertain readily the identity of a manufacturer or private labeler of a consumer product, offer such manufacturer or private labeler an opportunity to mark such information as confidential and therefore barred from disclosure under paragraph (2).

(4) All information that a manufacturer or private labeler has marked to be confidential and barred from disclosure under paragraph (2), either at the time of submission or pursuant to paragraph (3), shall not be disclosed, except in accordance with the procedures established in paragraphs (5) and (6)....″

Telephone directories are not limited to just the United States but typically are published in most parts of the world in one form or another. Companies and businesses also can be located by use of commercial or industrial telephone directories, both domestically and internationally.

In addition to telephone directories, directories are published by trade organizations, professional groups, and educational institutions. These directories may be limited to membership but can be useful in cases where the name and the association are known, but not the city, state, or country where the person can be found.

Exhibit 9.10 **Online search window from Martindale–Hubbell**

The Web

As paper is replaced by electronic media, directories are being placed online. Search engines can help locate individuals, businesses, and organizations on the Internet. Communications companies and other private firms offer a number of online white pages for individuals and yellow pages for businesses. Many organizations and publishers of professional directories now offer their print directories online. An example is the Web version of Martindale–Hubbell for attorneys (see Exhibit 9.10). These services may change or cancel their Web address and others may be added, so the list of websites has to be kept up to date.

Experts can be located using the Lexis Nexis/Martindale–Hubbell free website at http://resources. martindale.com/mhes/index.jsp

INTERVIEWS, INVESTIGATIONS, AND TRIALS

It is never too soon to start preparing for trial. Trial preparation starts with the first client contact and gathering the first document. Good preparation for trial includes an assessment of how well clients and witnesses will react in depositions or in court under the pressure of cross-examination and how they will be perceived by opposing counsel, the judge, or the jury. Will they come across sympathetically as being truthful and likeable? Or will they appear sneaky, unpleasant, and trying to hide the truth? These observational notes may be of great interest when the legal team must decide whether to settle or try the case.

A practical consideration in deciding whether to try a case before a jury is how the parties will appear to the jury. If the client appears to be sympathetic and deserving and the opposing party unsympathetic and having adequate financial resources, a jury may try to reward the client with a finding unsupported by the facts or evidence.

Effectively managing a case may involve reviewing, sorting, and marking for identification hundreds or even thousands of documents, photographs, and other graphics. Careful tracking and handling should start at the beginning of the case management process. Good case management requires a thoughtful process for storing, handling, examining, evaluating, and indexing every page. In the computer age, case

NTSB EXEMPTIONS

The four most common exemptions under which the NTSB withholds information are:

(1) 5 USC 552 (b)(5), draft reports and staff analyses (see 49 CFR 801.54);

(2) 5 USC 552 (b)(6), personal information, where a personal interest in privacy outweighs a public interest in release; this includes graphic photographs of injuries in accidents and autopsy reports (see 49 CFR 801.55);

(3) 5 USC 552 (b)(4), Trade Secrets and/or confidential financial/commercial information submitted by private persons or corporations to the NTSB in the course of an investigation (see 49 CFR 801.59); and

(4) 5 USC 552 (b)(3), information protected from release by another statute (see 49 CFR 801.53). This includes information such as:

- Cockpit Voice Recorder (CVR) tapes. Release of the tapes is prohibited by 49 USC 1114(c). However, the Board will release a CVR transcript [edited or unedited], the timing of such release is also controlled by statute - 49 USC 1114(c)(B);
- Voluntarily provided safety-related information. 49 USC 1114(b)(3) prohibits the release of such information if it is not related to the exercise of the Board's accident or incident investigation authority and if the Board finds that the disclosure would inhibit the voluntary provision of that type of information; and
- Records or information relating to the NTSB's participation in foreign aircraft accident investigations. 49 USC 1114(e) prohibits the release of this information before the country conducting the investigation releases its report or 2 years following the accident, whichever occurs first.

Check frequently requested information at the NTSB website http://www.ntsb.gov/info/foia.htm

management includes making decisions on the appropriateness and potential use of electronic display technologies, as well as the fallback on traditional paper exhibit preparation. Demonstrative evidence, physical items, such as defective products in a strict liability action or an automobile in a motor vehicle accident, may have to be obtained and preserved for examination by expert witnesses or for use at trial.

There are almost as many different approaches to setting up case files and managing cases as there are legal teams. One of the traditional approaches includes the case notebook or case **trial notebook**. Summary information about the case is maintained in a notebook with tabs for each major activity, party, expert, or element of proof needed. A sample of the sections is shown in Exhibit 9.11. With the use of a trial notebook comes the responsibility to maintain the case file and file boxes or file cabinets into which the hardcopies of documents, exhibits, and physical evidence are maintained. If only one

Trial notebook
A summary of the case tabbed for each major activity, witness or element of proof.

VIDEO GUIDELINES

Bruce W. Kauffman, J.

Chambers Policies and Procedures

13. VIDEOTAPED TESTIMONY

All videotape recordings should be conducted with an acute sensitivity that the videotape may be shown to a jury. Skillful organization of the testimony, elimination of unnecessary objections, and conservation of time are strongly urged. Videotaped testimony should begin with the witness being sworn. Whenever a deposition or videotape is to be used, a transcript of the testimony and all exhibits should be furnished to the Court in advance. Objections should be submitted to the Court well in advance of the tapes being offered so that the tapes may be appropriately edited.

The complete set of General Guidelines for Judge Bruce Kauffman may be viewed at www.paed.uscourts.gov/documents /procedures/kaupol.pdf

Exhibit 9.11 **Sample case file tabs**

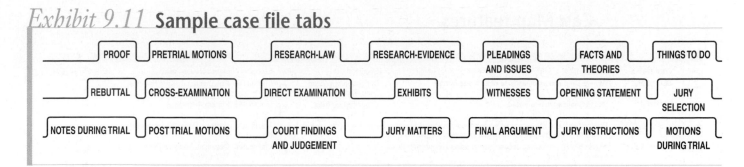

PROOF	PRETRIAL MOTIONS	RESEARCH-LAW	RESEARCH-EVIDENCE	PLEADINGS AND ISSUES	FACTS AND THEORIES	THINGS TO DO
REBUTTAL	CROSS-EXAMINATION	DIRECT EXAMINATION	EXHIBITS	WITNESSES	OPENING STATEMENT	JURY SELECTION
NOTES DURING TRIAL	POST TRIAL MOTIONS	COURT FINDINGS AND JUDGEMENT	JURY MATTERS	FINAL ARGUMENT	JURY INSTRUCTIONS	MOTIONS DURING TRIAL

trial or case notebook is kept for the team, someone working on the case must take responsibility to be certain that there is no duplication of effort and that the most current activities are entered. When multiple copies are used, each trial notebook must be updated regularly, again to be sure that there is no duplication of effort and that current activity information is made available for all members of the legal team.

Case and Practice Management Software

The legal team may work on a number of cases at the same time, and each case may be in a different stage of preparation for trial. With the team approach to handling cases, each member of the team must be able to access case information and know what the other members of the team have done and what still needs to be done. In the traditional paper file case management approach, the physical file is the repository of everything from interview notes, to pleadings and exhibits. To work on the case, the physical file has to be located and the needed folder removed. In the **"paperless" office**, everything, in theory, is available on the computer screen. Documents are scanned into an electronic format and saved on the computer, pleadings and notes are saved as word-processor files, and transcripts of depositions and court hearings are stored in electronic form. For the case with voluminous paperwork and days or weeks of deposition transcripts, only by use of computer file software can relevant documents or appropriate deposition notes be accessed quickly and efficiently.

A number of software programs can be used to manage the law office and the cases within the office. They generally provide what is sometimes referred to as case management, or practice management. Practice management programs have evolved out of the early programs that tracked time spent on cases, sometimes with a calendar component that could be used to track deadlines such as the statute of limitations for a case. Modern programs may include practice management functions such as time and cost tracking, calendaring, conflict checking, scheduling, and contact management. Others allow for management of the individual cases, tracking of documents, parties, issues, and events.

Paperless office
An office with electronic documents.

Software

Case management software is evolving constantly as the various vendors try to meet the demands and needs of their respective customers. Some nonlegal-specific software has case or practice management-type functions. Microsoft Outlook provides a combination contact manager, calendar–scheduler, task "to do" list, and email function. More sophisticated programs such as Practice Manager from Tabs3 provide the same functions, as well as outlining, billing, integrated research management, timelines, and other functions. LexisNexis CaseSoft provides individual programs that can share data, including CaseMap, TimeMap, TextMap, and NoteMap. One of the features of CaseMap is the ability to organize a case by facts, objects or parties, chronology, as shown in Exhibit 9.12, and then seamlessly create timelines from the chronological information by using the TimeMap program (see Exhibit 9.13). Summation's litigation support software allows transcripts, documents, issues, and events to be managed using computer technology.

Exhibit 9.12 **CaseMap features**

	Date & Time	Fact Text	Source(s)	Key	Status +	Linked Issues	Eval by CA	Eval
Main	06/??/1999	William Lang makes decision to reduce size of staff.	Deposition of William Lang, 43:19	☐	Undisputed	Age Discrim Against Hawkins	↘	
Facts	07/??/1999	Susan Sheridan is terminated.	Deposition of Philip Hawkins	☐	Undisputed	Pattern & Practice	↓	
Obje cts	Sun 07/04/1999	Philip Hawkins allegedly makes derogatory remarks about Linda Collins to Karen Thomas during Anstar Biotech Industries Fourth of	Interview Notes	☑	Disputed by:	Hawkins Deserved Termination	↗	
	Mon 07/12/1999	Anstar Biotech Industries second quarter sales announced. Sales have dropped by 8%.		☐	Undisputed	Demotion, Hawkins Deserved Termination	→	
Issue s	Fri 07/30/1999	Philip Hawkins demoted to sales manager.	Deposition of Philip Hawkins, p. 24, I15.	☐	Undisputed	Demotion	↘	
	Thu 08/05/1999 #1	Philip Hawkins and William Lang meet.	????	☐	Undisputed	Age Discrim Against Hawkins	→	
	Thu 08/05/1999 #2	Philip Hawkins alleges that William Lang tells him "The old wood must be trimmed back hard."	Complaint, p. 8; Deposition of Philip...	☑	Disputed by: Us	Pattern & Practice, Demotion	↓	
	Mon 08/09/1999	Philip Hawkins transferred to Anstar Biotech Industries office in Fresno.	Deposition of Philip Hawkins, p.43, I18.	☐	Undisputed	Transfer, Hawkins Deserved Termination	↘	
	09/23/1999	Philip Hawkins writes letter to William Lang complaining about the way he's being treated and alleging plan to eliminate older staff	Hawkins Letter of 9/23/99	☐	Undisputed	Wrongful Termination, Age Discrim Against Hawkins	↘	
	Fri 11/12/1999	Reduction in force takes place. 55 Anstar Biotech Industries employees are let go including Philip Hawkins.		☑	Undisputed	Wrongful Termination, Age Discrim Against Hawkins	↓	
	Mon 11/22/1999	Philip Hawkins files suit.	Complaint	☐	Undisputed		→	
	Tue 12/14/1999	Philip Hawkins turns down job offer from Converse Chemical Labs.	Rumor William Lang heard	☐	Prospective	Failure to Mitigate	↗	
	01/??/2000	Philip Hawkins meets with Susan Sheridan	Rumor William Lang heard	☐	Prospective		?	
	01/??/2000	Philip Hawkins is diagnosed as suffering Post Traumatic Stress Disorder.		☐		Mental Anguish	↗	

Exhibit 9.13 **TimeMap features**

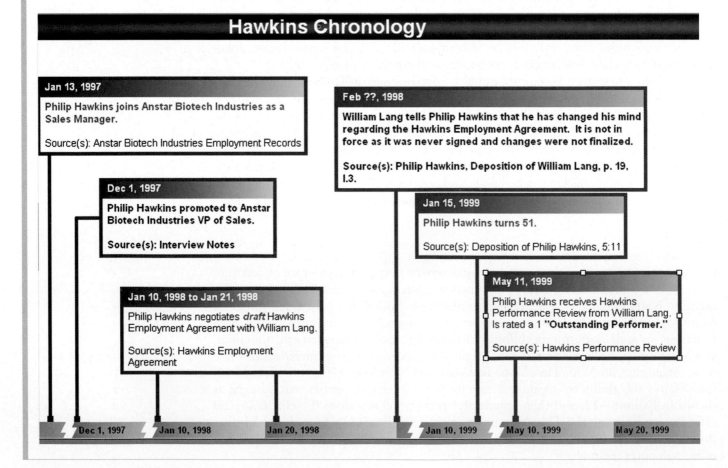

Advice from the Field ···

THE 10 AREAS OF INFORMATION YOU SHOULD ALWAYS HAVE AT YOUR FINGERTIPS

Neal R. Bevans

The ultimate paralegal resource guide is the place you save every important piece of information you have gathered in your daily work as a paralegal. This resource should contain telephone numbers, e-mails, important dates, notes about attorneys and judges and much more. The couple of hours you spend creating it will save you hundreds of hours throughout your career, give you a competitive edge and make you an invaluable member of your legal team. In fact, having all of this information at your fingertips will make you seem almost superhuman.

If putting together your own paralegal resource guide sounds unusual, it isn't. Legal professionals have been creating their own handy references for decades. When I first started out as a lawyer, a senior partner at my firm had a ragged manila file folder on his credenza containing copies of complaints he previously used in a wide variety of cases. When he needed a new complaint, he would pull out some of those old pleadings and reuse them. Your system might be a similar large file folder on your desk. Perhaps you keep everything stored in a database on your laptop, or in a network folder. Whatever method you currently use to hang on to your important information, you need to pull it all together and put it in one place. Let these 10 categories be your guide to organizing your resources and making your job easier.

1. COMPLETE CONTACT INFORMATION

Although there are a lot of telephone database programs available, including some basic software programs that came with most computers, many people find simple solutions are better.

A telephone reference is easy to create in any word processing program. The nice thing, about using Corel WordPerfect or Microsoft Word to create these tables is these programs already are running on your computer, you can keep the files open while you work on other materials, you can constantly update your entries and alphabetizing them is a breeze. For instance, Janice Johnson, a paralegal for attorney Russ Becker in Morganton N.C., said she uses a client list she originally created using WordPerfect. Her basic client list includes a chart consisting of the client's name, phone numbers, postal and e-mail addresses and notes.

Johnson said she encourages clients to contact her via e-mail. "I can check on e-mail in an extremely timely manner without having an interruption while a client is in my office," she said. "I also can respond back without getting caught on a call that ends up going entirely too long, Also, I have a word-for-word record of what information was given to the client through the e-mail contacts."

BlackBerry wireless devices are another great way to store contact information and have become very popular among law firms. Dana Martin, a paralegal at Greenbaum, Doll & McDonald, with offices in Ohio, Kentucky, Tennessee and the District of Columbia, likes the fact that with her BlackBerry, she can retrieve her e-mail anywhere, anytime. "We have Microsoft Outlook and [the BlackBerry] gives wireless access to that and my address book." She said she takes the BlackBerry with her wherever she goes.

The notes category is where your telephone reference really shines. You might not think having a notes section is important, but little details about your contacts really can help.

Denise Cunningham, a paralegal for attorney M. Lynne Osterholt in Louisville, Ky., said she lists personal information for many of her contacts. "Along with the addresses, I also put in other information, like birthdays and anniversaries."

Little, personal details, such as remembering a client's birthday or the names of a client or contact's children, can help build personal relationships and provide you with substantial help when you need it most. For instance, one client might be able to help you locate another client who is missing or unavailable. Personal relationships with courthouse personnel will put you on the inside track when it comes to things as simple as when to schedule a hearing or earn you a warning phone call when your firm forgets to file appropriate paperwork in a case.

2. ONE CENTRAL CALENDAR

Everyone knows having a calendar isn't a luxury, it's an absolute necessity. With so much to do and so little time to do it, your calendar must be accurate, easy to access

(continued)

Moral Versus Ethical Considerations

Moral Obligations	Based on one's own conscience or perceived rules of correct conduct, generally in the person's own community.
Ethical Obligations	Obligations of legal profession under ABA Model Rules of Professional Conduct, including thoroughness in representing a client.

Privileged Communications

Forms of communication	Attorney–client communications Doctor–patient communications Priest–penitent communications Spousal communications during marriage
Waivers	Privileges can be waived, but the waiver must come from the client, the patient, the penitent, or the spouse making the statement with the belief that it is privileged.

Investigating Claims

Expert Witnesses

Definition	Expert witnesses are individuals whose background, education, and experience are such that courts will recognize them as qualified to give opinions based on a set of facts.

Freedom of Information Act (FOIA)

Definition	FOIA is a federal statute designed to open to the public the information in the possession of the federal government and its agencies.

Locating Witnesses

Directories	1. Phone books 2. Cross-reference directories 3. Membership directories
The Web	Search engines can help locate individuals, businesses, and organizations on the Internet.

Interviews, Investigations, and Trials

Trial preparation	Trial preparation starts with the first client contact and the gathering of the first document. Good preparation for trial includes an assessment of how well clients and witnesses will react in depositions or in court under the pressure of cross-examination and how they will be perceived by opposing counsel, the judge, or the jury.
Case Management	Good case management requires a thoughtful process for storing, handling, examining, evaluating, and indexing every page. In the computer age, case management involves decisions on the appropriateness and potential use of electronic display technologies, as well as the fallback on traditional paper exhibit preparation.
Traditional Case Management	Traditional approaches includes the case notebook or case trial notebook.
Case and Practice Management Software	A number of software programs can be used to manage the law office and the cases within the office, in what is sometimes referred to as case management or practice management.

▶ WORKING THE WEB

1. Use MapQuest to printout a map of the local area around your school. **www.Mapquest.com**

2. Use the Mapquest directions feature to obtain driving directions from your home to your school's main entrance. Don't worry if you live a long distance from your school. Print out the directions and related maps anyway.

3. Repeat items 1 and 2 using Yahoo! Maps. **http://maps.yahoo.com.** and Mapblast from MSN **www.mapblast.com.** Which gives you the most information?

4. Obtain a satellite image of your school from Google Earth. **http://earth.google.com.** How might this be more helpful in investigating a case than the other maps available on the Internet?

5. Use Findlaw to locate an accounting expert in your state. **www.findlaw.com.** Print out a list of experts listed.

6. Use the LexisNexis Martindale–Hubbell website to locate an expert witness for a patent intellectual property case involving electronics. Print out a copy of the contact information you find.

7. Using the search function of your computer browser, find and print out a copy of Rule 26 of the Federal Rules of Civil Procedure.

8. Download a trial copy of TimeMap from CaseSoft: **http://www.casesoft.com/ student.shtml**

9. Prepare a timeline of the assignments and exams for the courses you currently are taking. Print a copy of the timeline.

10. Assume you have been asked to work on the case of a pedestrian struck by a car going north on the west side of the Flat Iron Building in Manhattan (New York City). Print out a satellite image of the location showing the building and the traffic flow using Earth Google at **www.earth.google.com.** Note that you will have to download the Earth Google viewer. Check with your instructor before downloading on a school computer. What is the proper direction of the vehicle traffic? Was the crosswalk visible? Were any other potential images available? Prepare a short report memorandum about your findings.

▶ CRITICAL THINKING AND WRITING QUESTIONS

1. What are the legal and ethical issues involved for the paralegal when the potential client says he or she just wants a quick answer to the question, "Do I have a case?" Explain fully, including references to your state statute.

2. What is a screening interview? What potential ethical and malpractice issues are involved?

3. How is the implied attorney–client relationship created? What are the critical issues for the law firm when this relationship is established?

4. Does the attorney have a duty to keep the names of clients confidential? Explain the ethical rules that apply.

5. What are the ethical and or legal implications of not advising a party that you are a paralegal and not a lawyer?

6. What is the difference between listening and hearing? Explain.

7. How can stereotypes prevent hearing what is said in interviews?

8. What effect do cultural issues play in the interview process? Explain.

9. What are the strategic reasons for using leading questions and using open-ended questions? Give an example of when each would be better used than the other type.

10. In representing a client, is it acceptable or required to ignore an ethical or moral consideration? Explain, giving an example and reason for breaching each.

11. Explain fully the ultimate reason for conducting a thorough investigation of a case. What ethical issues dictate how an investigation is to be conducted?

12. How can the Internet be used to effectively conduct an investigation of a case? Explain, using examples of traditional methods that also could be used.

13. Using the Facts in the *Palsgraf* case in Appendix A, prepare a list of witnesses who might be called in that case. Prepare an interview checklist for each of the witnesses.

14. Using the Facts in the *Palsgraf* case in AppendixA, prepare an investigative checklist, including a list of the evidence that should be gathered in the case, including a list and description of any photographs needed.

15. In conducting an interview, when would it be appropriate to dress in "Friday casual" attire?

16. Why is it important to visit the site of the accident in a motor-vehicle case being prepared for trial?

17. Under what circumstances might it be advisable for someone other than you in the firm to handle an interview with a client or witness?

18. Why would someone feel a moral obligation not to answer questions in an interview?

19. Why would a law firm hire an expert witness and not call that person as a witness at trial?

20. How useful is the Freedom of Information Act in obtaining state or local government documents? Explain.

21. Can a client restrict the use of information obtained as part of the investigation in preparation for trial even if doing so will have adverse consequences in the opinion of the attorney? Why or why not?

22. What are the issues and potential problems in using a trial notebook?

23. How does the use of case management software improve the effectiveness of the legal team? Who has the ultimate responsibility for managing the case file when using case management software?

ETHICS ANALYSIS AND DISCUSSION QUESTIONS

1. Review the opening scenario of this chapter. What are the ethical issues involved? Prepare a suggested policy, referencing the specific ethics code sections, to present to the supervising attorney of the firm. Address the issues of how to answer the phone and what should and should not be said. Your instructor may provide you with specifics, such as the fee for an initial consultation.

DEVELOPING YOUR COLLABORATION SKILLS

Working on your own or with a group of other students assigned by your instructor, review the scenario at the beginning of the chapter and the discussion that takes place between Sara and Mrs. Weiser.

1. a. Prepare a list of questions Sara should prepare before starting work. Discuss who should be asked and what action she should or should not take.
   b. What are the ethical issues facing Sara?
   c. What are the potential malpractice issues facing the firm?

2. Write a summary of the advice the group would give to Sara.

3. Form groups of three. Designate one person who will act as Sara, one as a potential client, and the third as a supervising paralegal.
   a. As the paralegal interviewer for the client who has just walked in the door of the office after being injured in an accident, use the facts of the Palsgraf case in the Appendix or one assigned by your instructor.
   b. As the client, you want to be sure that you have a case and that the fee is acceptable.
   c. As the supervising paralegal, comment on the interview, what issues were raised, and what you would have done differently.

PARALEGAL PORTFOLIO EXERCISE

Using the current information for your area or jurisdiction, complete the Investigation Information Source Checklist. Print out a copy for your portfolio.

▶LEGAL ANALYSIS AND WRITING CASES

Limitations on Obtaining Information in Criminal Cases Under the FOIA

The FOIA can be a good source of information in criminal cases as well as civil litigation. As with discovery-limitation exemptions in civil cases, additional exemptions exist under the Act in criminal cases. Landano was convicted in New Jersey state court for murdering a police officer during what may have been a gang-related robbery. In an effort to support his claim in subsequent state court proceedings that his rights were violated by withholding material exculpatory evidence, he filed Freedom of Information Act requests with the Federal Bureau of Investigation (FBI) for information it had compiled in connection with the murder investigation.

When the FBI redacted some documents and withheld others, Landano filed an action, seeking disclosure of the contents of the requested files. The court held that the government is not entitled to a presumption that all sources supplying information to the FBI in the course of a criminal investigation are confidential sources within the meaning of Exemption 7(D). Further, a source should be deemed "confidential" if the source furnished information with the understanding that the FBI would not divulge the communication except to the extent it thought necessary for law-enforcement purposes.

Questions

1. Does this unfairly subject an informant to potential harassment?

2. Does limiting information unfairly prevent the defendant from receiving a fair trial?

3. Does the limitation effectively limit any usefulness in making a request under the FOIA?

Department of Justice v. Landano, 508 U.S. 165 (1993)

Spoliation of Evidence
IN RE DAIMLERCHRYSLER AG SECURITIES LITIGATION, (USDC Del. 2003)
Civil Action No. 00-993-JJF

Defendants requested relief in the form of sanctions against the plaintiff for the spoliation of evidence contending that a personal assistant to one of the Plaintiffs, Jaclyn Thode, had destroyed documents that she used to prepare a list of meetings and/or conversations prepared at the request of general counsel, who had failed to instruct her to preserve the documents used in making the list. The court in ruling on the defendant's motion concluded that sanctions were not warranted as a result of the alleged spoliation of evidence. The un-rebutted deposition testimony and affidavit of Ms. Thode establish that she discarded her handwritten notes after converting them into typewritten form, consistent with her practice in the past. Ms. Thode had no information or understanding about the substance of the litigation and no information as to the purpose of counsels' request, and thus she had no reason to alter or omit any information from the documents and that she acted unintentionally when she discarded the steno pads and pink message notes. The Court also found the Defendants did not suffer any prejudice, because they had a complete and accurate chronology of the contents of the documents that were discarded. The court cited *Son, Inc. v. Louis & Nashville R.R. Co.*, 695 F.2d 253, 259 (7th Cir.1982) (finding that destruction of evidence was not intentional where handwritten notes were discarded after being typed and person handling evidence had no reason to omit or alter necessary information).

Questions

1. Should the investigation of a case where documents include transcription include inquiry to the source of transcripted notes? Why or why not?

2. Why would not knowing the purpose of creating the notes matter in determining the potential spoliation of evidence?

3. What advice would you give to someone who has the responsibility of transcribing or keeping minutes of meetings?

TRADITIONAL COMPUTER AND INTERNET LEGAL RESEARCH

"This trial is a travesty; it's a travesty of a mockery of a sham of a mockery of a travesty of two mockeries of a sham. I move for a mistrial."

Woody Allen, Bananas

PARALEGALS AT WORK

As the managing partner of a large multinational law firm, Mr. Mulkeen was preparing for an executive committee meeting with the senior partners from the firm offices around the world. As with all law firms, cost saving was high on the agenda. The diverse group of partners ranged from young partners on the fast track to senior partners concerned more with developing client contacts than working on cases directly. Some firm's newer offices specialize in specific areas of law, such as the five-person health care group in a distant city to the 500-lawyer office in a major metropolitan area.

One of the major cost items on the firm's income statement was designated for the law library. Some partners wanted to expand the library, and others wanted to cut it. Mr. Mulkeen wanted to try to gain a consensus and keep as many members of the firm and support staff happy and have the necessary input from a cross-section of the firm. He invited a cross-section of the firm to a meeting to discuss the issue and get feedback. At the meeting, he indicated that the firm was at something of a crossroads in making a decision about the direction of the firm's law library, what to keep, what to get rid of, and to what to commit resources to. The cost of the space for the library, in the rental cost per square foot, was a major issue for the firm, as well as the increasing cost of law reporters and upkeep services.

Mr Hains, a senior partner with the firm more than 25 years, reminded everyone that when he started with the firm, it didn't have as many resources as it had currently and that the law book collection was a point of pride he frequently pointed to with new clients. He said the firm could research case law in most jurisdictions where it had offices back to volume one of the law reports and that the firm had all of the state and federal statutes and codes. He indicated that research could be done on weekends if necessary, and pages copied out of the books. He said he didn't feel comfortable eliminating any of the hardbound volumes, and that there is something to be said for

After studying this chapter, you should be able to:

1. Systematically analyze a research assignment.
2. Create a legal research plan.
3. Explain the differences between conducting legal research using a traditional paper law library and computer-based law resources.
4. Use publisher-specific and generalized legal terminology to create search queries using the computerized resources and traditional book resources.
5. Explain the differences between primary resources, secondary resources, and finding tools.
6. Explain the need for, and the methods of, updating legal research.
7. Read and use legal citations.

thumbing through the pages to find something even if you are not sure what you are looking for.

As one of the senior paralegals, Kathryn indicated that she didn't use the library that much, that it was mostly a place for her to spread things out. She said that she and her supervising attorney did most of their research at their desks, using computers to access the Internet and online research services. She felt limited, she said, in using the hourly-fee research services for research because the cost could not always be billed to the client and the bookkeeping people were critical about not passing on the fees. Kathryn's final point was that the litigation team was always in court or trying cases out of town, so the in-house library didn't really do the litigation team much good anyway.

Kevin, one of the long-term secretaries, expressed concern with eliminating the current library. He explained that in working for one of the general-practice attorneys, many times it was necessary to get up to speed on a new area of law and he had to browse through some of the encyclopedias and treatises just to understand the basic issues and terminology. He said he couldn't do this using the computer—at least until the issues and terminology were understood.

Consider the issues involved in this scenario as you read the chapter.

▶ INTRODUCTION FOR THE PARALEGAL

One of the most important skills a paralegal can develop is the ability to find current relevant information in a timely manner. Knowing where to look is just as important as knowing what to look for. Clients expect their legal counsel to use the latest law in advising them. The paralegal is expected to be able to understand the relevant facts and find the current statutory law and case law. The frequent changes in court decisions and statutory enactments present a challenge to the legal profession. Traditional law libraries consisting of printed text may not have available the latest case, statute, or regulation for days or weeks because of the time required to assemble, print, and send out updates. Internet and computer technology allows for more rapid distribution. Many courts now issue the electronic version of court opinions at the same time as the printed version. Instant availability is certainly a benefit if the paralegal is working on a similar case.

Although the ability to obtain current case law is important, in many cases an older common law case may still be precedent. The problem is that some electronic or online services, such as Versuslaw, may not have included the older cases in their database of available cases. When that happens, being able to find the case the old-fashioned way by checking through the books is a valuable skill. When using an electronic case service such as Versuslaw, the dates of the available cases should be checked to be certain that they cover the time period needed for the search. ■

LEGAL RESEARCH

Legal research
The process for finding the answer to a legal question.

Legal research is a process for finding the answer to a legal question. In practice, the desired answer is usually the answer to a legal question involving a specific set of facts. The answer may include federal, state, and local statutory law, administrative agency regulation, and case law. Before starting, you have to have a clear picture of the legal question and what the person giving you the research assignment needs. With this in mind, proceeding in a systematic way will save time and ensure that all research avenues have been considered. A systematic approach begins with planning the research and knowing what issues must be addressed and covered.

CREATING A RESEARCH PLAN

The first step in legal research is setting up a research plan. The research plan helps to focus on the issues, sources, and methods for finding the answer and controlling law. A few basic questions should be considered in setting up the research plan.

1. What is the issue or legal question?
   - a statute or regulation, or
   - a legal question involving a set of facts
2. What is the appropriate search terminology?
   - words
   - phrases
   - legal terms
   - popular names of statutes or cases
3. What type of research material is available?
   - traditional
   - computer
4. What jurisdiction or jurisdictions are involved?
   - federal
   - state
   - local
5. What is the controlling law?
   - statutory
   - regulatory
   - case law
6. What are the types of resources to be used?
   - primary
   - secondary
   - finding tools
7. Where is the needed research material located?
   - in-house traditional materials
   - fee-based legal services
   - free Web-based remote libraries

What Is the Issue or Legal Question?

Legal research is like a puzzle to be solved. Understanding the question is essential. A lot of time may be wasted if the paralegal takes the wrong research path, because the framer of the question has not been clear or the researcher is not clear on the information needed. At times the question is framed with some specificity:

Find the statute . . .
Get me the case of . . .

More often, however, the question is:

Based on these facts, what is the law about . . . ?

Researchers first must understand the facts that apply to the case they are asked to research. Unlike the cases in textbooks and court opinions, the **relevant facts** and the specific area of substantive or procedural law in real life usually are not so clear. The initial interview information may have focused on what the client or the interviewer thought was the applicable law. Further research may indicate other areas of law that must be considered.

For example, what may seem to be a simple rear-end automobile accident caused by negligent driving may be in actuality a case of product liability caused by a manufacturing defect by the automobile manufacturer or the supplier of a defectively manufactured part, such as the tires. To analyze a case properly, the researcher must know

Relevant facts
Facts crucial to the case and having legal significance.

the factual elements of a negligence case and of a product liability case. The researcher must understand the facts of the case at hand. Some facts are crucial to the case; others may or may not be important or have no legal significance.

What Is the Appropriate Search Terminology?

Knowing the legal terminology used in the indexes of the research materials is critical. Publishers of legal materials do not always use the same words or legal terms to index the same rules of law. For example, one publisher uses the term "infant" to identify people under the age of majority that another publisher indexes under "minor." Consider the legal question: "What are the contract rights of a person under the age of majority?" Using "minor" will not produce the desired results in some published materials where the information is listed under "infant." Print research materials require finding material based on a printed index of individual words as selected by the editors of the service.

Computer research is not as dependent on an index of terms and may require a completely different set of words or legal terms. Most computer research allows for searches of words found in the documents using a text search of requested words in the **search query**, in which the computer looks through the entire document for every instance of the desired words.

Search query
Specific words used in a computerized search.

What Type of Research Material Is Available?

Traditionally, the law library has consisted of books in paper form, case reporters, legal encyclopedias, legal dictionaries, and a host of finding tools including paper card indexes and digests. Some modern law libraries are completely electronic, using online computer services such as Westlaw, Lexis, and Loislaw. Other libraries combine traditional paper-based materials and electronic materials.

Paralegal students who grew up in the era of the ever-available online research sources provided by some high schools and colleges frequently ask why they need to learn how to use a traditional "paper" law library. In the working world, not every office has access to all the latest computer resources, or the same ones. Ask anyone who has tried a case out of town or in a different courthouse and had to check an unexpected case or resource about the availability of resources or lack of them.

At times, paralegals accompany the lawyer to court. During the trial, they may be asked to slip out of the courtroom and conduct a quick bit of legal research. They may not be able to use a computer for legal research. In some courthouses, computers cannot be connected to outgoing phone lines for security reasons, and even cell phones are retained at the security desk. Other courthouses do not have a public computer terminal available in the law library. In these situations, the paralegal must conduct the research quickly and accurately using traditional book methods. In short, the paralegal must be able to find the information needed when the familiar resources are not available.

Computer research requires the use of appropriate search words to complete a successful search. As with any profession, the legal profession has its own vocabulary. These include words defined by the courts over the years to have specific meaning when used in a legal sense. For example, the legal definition of the term "holder" is "a person to whom a negotiable instrument has been properly negotiated." To the layperson, it may mean people holding something in their hands—not necessarily a negotiable instrument, or with any legal formality. Other words have a different meaning for a number of different groups. For example, to the medical community, the word "head" means the top of a person's body; to the sailor it means a bathroom; and to a bartender it means the top of a beer.

People in all areas of life develop words and phrases that help them understand their fields of interest. In creating laws, legislatures use language in special ways that may not be clear to laypersons or even legal researchers who are not accustomed to the terminology of the lawmakers. The people who create indexes to legal references, such as the professional indexers from the Library of Congress and the indexers of the numerous private legal publications, each have their own vocabulary and method of indexing material. For example, West Publishing Company editors index material using the 450 West Digest Topics (see Exhibit 10.1).

Unless the paralegal understands what items are included under each index classification, it is difficult to find the items even with a fast computer search engine. The word "holder," for example, is listed in the *West Digest* index as being under "Statutes," but the word "holder" as defined above, is actually found under the West Digest Topic "Bills and Notes." *Black's Law Dictionary* defines the same word in the language of the negotiable instrument law. Using the West Topic heading "Bills and Notes" and "holder" in a computer search will not return cases of negotiable instrument holders. But using the terms "negotiable instrument" and "holder" as the search words in a computer search will yield the desired result. Because paralegals cannot be sure whether the research will be done using a traditional paper library or a computer search, they must understand how each resource files the information.

Knowing how to use both traditional and computer methods, and recognizing the strengths and weaknesses of each system, is important in conducting searches. Traditional research may be better when general background research is needed and the paralegal isn't familiar with an area of law. Indexing systems are grouped by concept, and once paralegals get into the right area of law they can browse easily. The ability to flip pages back and forth when they are generally in the right area is particularly helpful in statutory research, as many of the computer-based systems perform that task slowly, if at all—and assuming the paralegal can figure out how the index has been developed to create the computer search term. In contrast, for a narrow, fact-based question, or if the research already has a citation or case name to work from, computer-based research usually is the best approach. Success in research depends on recognizing the best tools for a specific problem and using them efficiently.

What Jurisdiction or Jurisdictions Are Involved?

Research may involve federal, state, or local law. Some questions point to a certain jurisdiction—for example, "What is the age of majority in Florida?" Others are not as clear, "What law controls the situation of an unruly passenger on a flight from Los Angeles to Philadelphia?" Here the paralegal must consider jurisdictional issues related to California, Pennsylvania, and federal statutes. Or consider the case of the driver from Georgia who is driving a truck belonging to a South Carolina company and has an accident in Alabama. The legal team working on that case might want to know the law in each jurisdiction before deciding where to file suit. Focusing on a single jurisdiction or a minimum number of jurisdictions reduces the number of traditional volumes of books necessary and saves online computer search time.

What Is the Controlling Law?

The controlling law is found in primary sources of the law—statutes, regulations, and case law. Knowing which set of materials to use, the statutes of the jurisdiction, the regulation of a certain administrative agency, or the courts of a specific jurisdiction will save time in doing the research. Possibly, the controlling law is a local city, county, or parish ordinance, such as a zoning ordinance or a local plumbing code. Irrelevant sources can be eliminated from consideration and the source of the needed material located if not available onsite or online.

What Are the Types of Resources to Use?

Law libraries usually have primary and secondary sources of the law. A **primary source** is the actual law itself, which includes the statutes and the case law. The cases you have been briefing in this text are primary sources. **Secondary sources** are not

Primary source of law
The actual law itself.

Secondary source of law
Writings about the law.

Exhibit 10.2 Research materials

PRIMARY SOURCES	SECONDARY SOURCES	FINDING TOOLS
Constitutions	Legal dictionaries	Digests
Statutes	Legal encyclopedias	Citators
Court decisions	Treatises	Indexes
Common-law cases	Law reviews	
Administrative regulations	Textbooks	
Ordinances	Legal periodicals	
Court rules		

Finding tools
Publications used to find primary and secondary sources.

the laws themselves but, instead, are writings about the law, such as legal encyclopedias and digests. This textbook is a secondary source. A third set of resources is referred to as finding tools—publications, such as digests or the *Index to Legal Periodicals*, used to find primary and secondary sources. Frequently, sources contain both secondary sources and **finding tools** in one publication, such as the *American Law Reports*. Some services combine all three into one service or publication. Exhibit 10.2 delineates primary and secondary sources and finding tools.

Ultimately, the primary sources of law are the ones that will be used in preparing the legal memo or brief. Secondary sources are useful, efficient ways to get an overview of an area of law or learn the terminology used in a certain field of law of which you are not familiar. The torts specialist suddenly asked to research an issue related to a different area of law, such as negotiable instruments, may be lost trying to remember the terminology and rules applicable from courses taken long ago.

Secondary sources such as encyclopedias can supply a quick review and point the research to the appropriate primary sources such as the *Uniform Commercial Code* as adopted by the state in question. Legal dictionaries frequently list cases that have defined the words in legal terms that can be a starting point for case research.

Where Is the Needed Research Material Located?

It would be nice to have a complete law school level print and electronic library available onsite to use for legal research. The reality is that law libraries are costly to acquire and maintain. The cost of the materials can run into the hundreds of dollars per volume, and the annual upkeep services not much less for pocket parts, supplemental volumes, and new case reporters. Space in office complexes is another factor. Office space is expensive, and as a library grows, more of the expensive floor space must be used for books instead of people. Finally the cost of filing the updates and keeping the space orderly must be considered. If the collection is large enough, a full-time librarian may be needed. In smaller offices these tasks take the time of paralegals that could be spent performing billable services for clients.

These cost and availability issues have spurred the adoption of electronic libraries such as the fee-based online services provided by Loislaw, Lexis, Westlaw, and VersusLaw, and the free online services provided by some colleges and universities such as the Cornell School of Law. Virtually all primary material is available online. Some certain proprietary secondary materials, such as encyclopedias, are available from some sources and not others. Depending on the resources needed to complete an assignment, the paralegal may have to locate the needed material at a remote library such as a bar association library or a law school library.

Creating a List of Research Terms

The paralegal should create a list of words for online searches and a separate list for traditional print sources. The list should be updated as the paralegal performs research, adding or deleting words and phrases and annotating the list with citations for future research. The word list should be developed from the facts of the question, the parties, locations, case-specific goods and services, and status and relationships between them.

Consider the case of the off-duty police officer who has just come from a doctor's visit for high blood pressure and been given a medicine to reduce his blood pressure. He is involved in a rear-end collision with a van of school children returning from a fundraiser selling candy. The driver is one of the mothers, who is also a teacher in the school. A skateboarder darts in front of one of the vehicles.

checklist ✓   RESEARCH PLAN: WORDS AND PHRASES

CONCEPTS AND ISSUES	GENERIC WORDS AND PHRASES	TEXT-BASED RESEARCH TERMS	COMPUTER-BASED RESEARCH TERMS
Persons			
Status			
Relationship			
Occupation			
Group			
Class			
Item(s) Involved			
Location(s)			
Subject Matter			
Jurisdiction			
Federal			
State			
City			
Locality			
Cause of Action			
Tort			
Contract			
Family Law			
Commercial			
Relief Sought			
Injunction			
Damages			
Compensatory			
Punitive			
Mandamus			
Defenses			

What are some of the words and terms with which to start researching the issue of liability? As with most cases, each person has multiple roles or status that must be considered: teacher, parent, driver, police officer, student, child, principal, agent of school, agent of other parents, patient.

Further, the situation may have been caused by any of a number of factors, road conditions, and weather issues, time of day, speed, medical issues, carelessness, and distracted driver. And what about the vehicles' braking ability, recalls of vehicles, and airbag deployment issues? Obviously not every issue relates in every case. Before starting the research, the researcher must identify the relevant terms that apply to the case being researched. The time spent creating the list will save time chasing deadends or irrelevant issues. In creating the word list, the researcher should think of words, legal terms, and phrases and consider alternatives to those words—synonyms, antonyms, and related terms. Appropriate language may be found using secondary sources and finding tools such as legal dictionaries and legal encyclopedias and treatises.

Executing the Research Plan

Having laid out a plan of action based on answers to the preliminary questions, the research plan now can be executed. As with the execution of any plan, detours can be expected. The law is in a constant evolutionary state as new statutes are enacted and new case interpretations are handed down. During the research process, the researcher must look for changes and potential changes from pending legislation and cases on appeal. Word lists and citation must be updated and new search paths followed.

The time spent creating the list of terms, phrases, and or search terms will save time when the research plan is executed. In looking for a statute, knowing the subject matter of the desired law, such as "blood alcohol level for driving," or the popular name of the law, such as "Sarbanes-Oxley," will save time by focusing the search on a specific statutory index or popular name index.

Not every search term will result in a successful search; some may lead to other search terms. The research plan should be executed in a systematic way using a checklist of the terms and research materials. The search is updated with citations, both successful and unsuccessful. When the inevitable circular search brings the researcher back to a previous result, this indicates a deadend, so the researcher can proceed on a more fruitful path.

When the time comes to finalize the research in a written document, the researcher will have the citation references and will not have to go back and find the material again. In the event of additional, similar research assignments, the researcher will have a ready reference to pick up the search and proceed quickly, using relevant terms and citations.

FINDING THE LAW

Legislative branch
The part of the government that consists of Congress (the Senate and the House of Representatives).

Judicial branch
The court system.

Bicameral
In the American system a legislature of a house of representatives and a senate.

Finding "the law" should be an easy thing to accomplish. We go to the original source and look at it. But what is the original source, and how is it located in a modern law library? The law is found in the statutes and regulations passed by the **legislative branch** and the case law in court decisions of the **judicial branch.** In the United States, laws are created at the federal, state, and local levels. At the federal legislative level laws are passed by the United States Congress, which is a **bicameral** legislative body—meaning that there are two legislative houses, the House of Representatives and the Senate. At the state government level, all of the state legislatures are bicameral except Nebraska. Local governing bodies include cities, towns, and boroughs. At the judicial level, both federal and state courts create case law through their issuing of court decisions. The law also is found in the regulations enacted by administrative agencies as a result of the authority granted to them by the legislative branch of government, whether federal, state, or local.

checklist ☑

PRIMARY SOURCES	SECONDARY SOURCES
Case	Encyclopedia—National
• Name	• Name
• Citation	• Key or descriptive word
Federal statute	Encyclopedia—State
• Federal citation	• Name
• Popular name	• Key or descriptive word
State (name)	Treatises
• State citation	• Name
• Popular name	• Citation
Local jurisdiction name	Restatement of law
• Local citation	• Name
• Popular name	• Citation
Administrative regulations	Periodicals
• Federal agency name	• Citation
• Citation	
	Practice Books
State agency name	• Name
• Citation	• Citation
Local agency name	Dictionary
• Citation	• Name
Constitution	Digest
• Federal citation	• Name
• State citation	• Citation

Generally, the assignment is to find the current controlling law. Occasionally the research assignment is to find the law that was in control at a point in the past, such as what the blood alcohol limit was last year when the client was cited for driving under the influence. In this case, we might start by asking:

Is there a statute?

Are there administrative regulations?

Is there case law on point?

If there is a statute in the applicable jurisdiction, it will be controlling. Regulations enacted to enforce the statute also will be controlling subject to compliance with the statutory authority under which they are enacted. Case law may exist to clarify and explain the law under the facts of the cases decided by the courts.

Primary Sources and Authority

Primary sources are the law. Primary sources include constitutions, both federal and state. Primary law includes statutes enacted by the legislative branch of government pursuant to the constitutional limitations and the regulations of the administrative agencies established by the legislature to carry out the statutory enactments. Court rules and court decisions are sources of primary law from the judicial branch of government. Exhibit 10.3 lists the primary sources at the federal level.

Mandatory and Persuasive Authority

Mandatory authority
Court decisions that are binding on all lower courts.

Start with primary sources that are **mandatory authority.** Primary authority is the law itself. It is the constitution, the enactments of the legislative branch of government, and the case law decisions of the judicial branch of government. Mandatory authority is legal authority that the courts must follow. In addition to statutes and administrative regulations and ordinances, it includes case law from higher courts. The highest court in the United States is the United States Supreme Court. The decisions of the Supreme Court are mandatory on all lesser federal and state courts. The decisions of the highest appellate court of a state are mandatory authority for all lesser courts of that state.

Persuasive authority
Court decisions the court is not required to follow but are well reasoned and from a respected court.

If mandatory authority cannot be found, the researcher should search for **persuasive authority,** authority the courts are not required to follow but is from a re-

Exhibit 10.3 **Federal primary sources**

SOURCE	JURISDICTION	LOCATION	URL
Constitution	United States Constitution	U.S. Const. art 1, § 10,cl.3	http://www.gpoaccess.gov/constitution/index.html
Statutes	United States Code	19 U.S.C. § 2411 (2004)	http://www.gpoaccess.gov/uscode/index.html
Administrative Regulations	Code of Federal Regulations	31 C.F.R. § 515.329 (2002)	http://www.gpoaccess.gov/cfr/index.html
Highest Appellate Court	US Supreme Court	*Brown v. Bd. Of Educ.,* 349 U.S. 294 (1955)	http://www.supremecourtus.gov/opinions/opinions.html
Intermediate Appellate Court	US Court of Appeals	*McHenry v. Fla. Bar,* 21 F.3d 1038 (11th Cir. 1994)	http://www.uscourts.gov/courtlinks/
Trial Court	US District Court	*U.S. v. Chairse,* 18 F. Supp. 2d 1021 (D. Minn. 1998)	http://www.uscourts.gov/courtlinks/
Federal Rules of Civil Procedure		Fed. R. Civ. P. 26	http://www.law.cornell.edu/rules/frcp/
Federal Rules of Criminal Procedure		Fed. R. Crim. P. 21(a)	http://www.law.cornell.edu/rules/frcrmp/

Source: Citations in ALWD Citation format. Copyright © ALWD. Reprinted with permission.

spected source and well reasoned. Decisions of some state courts traditionally have been looked at as being so well reasoned that other courts in other states have been persuaded to follow the legal reasoning in deciding cases for which their own state did not have any previously decided cases or statutes on point.

A good example of a persuasive opinion is that of Justice Cardozo in the New York Court of Appeals case of *Palsgraf* v. *Long Island Railroad Company*, 248 N.Y. 339 (1928) (see Appendix A, How To Brief a Case). Many courts, even today, find the logic and reasoning of Justice Cardozo persuasive and he is frequently quoted by courts in other states.

Constitutions

The United States Constitution is the ultimate primary law that sets the guidelines, limits, and authority of the federal government and the state governments. The individual state constitutions are the ultimate law for the individual state, and set the guidelines, the limits, and the authority of the state government and the local governing bodies of the state. The constitutions are primary sources, the original writing or primary source of law. Finding the United States Constitution is probably the easiest task in legal research. It is reproduced in many publications, including many textbooks, is available in virtually every public library, and is easily available on the Internet from many sources including the National Archives. Finding the Constitution for individual states however, is not as easy. Although some are posted on general-interest websites, most require access to specialty legal research websites, or to the paper version, generally found in the bound volumes of the state statutes.

View a high-resolution version of the original copy of the U.S. Constitution at www.archives.gov

Statutes

Statutes enacted by the legislative branch of government are primary sources of the law. The statute of the United States—the United States Code—is available online from a number of free sources including the U.S. Government Printing Office. Many states currently make available their state statutes online through an official state website. Until a few years ago, this free-access source was generally limited to state legislators. Caution should still be the rule in using Web-based resources. Some unofficial sites have posted websites that appear to be an official primary source of the law but in reality are not complete or up-to-date.

Court Decisions

Court decisions also are primary authority. The U.S. Supreme Court and some federal courts provide their current opinions and decisions online. Notably, the Legal Information Institute at Cornell University provides free access to the U.S. Supreme Court opinions, as well as many others. Other court decisions generally are not available from free Web sources and require the use of a paid subscription or fee-based services such as Lexis, Westlaw, Loislaw, and VersusLaw. Exhibit 10.4 shows the homepage of U.S. Courts with judiciary links.

Courts such as the U.S. Supreme Court issue opinions from the "bench" called **bench opinions** and a **slip opinion** that is sent for printing. This second version may contain corrections in the bench opinion. See the U.S. Supreme Court comments on the difference in Exhibit 10.5.

The actual court language is a primary source of the law. The **case syllabus**, summaries, interpretations, or abstracts of the points of law presented by the editorial staff of the publishers of the case law, usually called **headnotes**, are not the primary source of law; rather they are explanations, interpretations, or comments that help the reader understand the legal concepts. As such, they are secondary sources. Note

Read the latest U.S. Supreme Court opinion at http://www.supremecourtus.gov Visit the homepage of the Legal Information Institute at Cornell University Law School to see the information provided. www.cornell.lii.edu

Bench opinions
The initial version of a decision issued from the bench of the court.

Syllabus
In a court opinion a headnote for the convenience of the reader.

Slip opinion
A copy of the opinion sent to the printer.

Headnotes
The syllabus or summary of the points of law prepared by the editorial staff of a publisher.

Exhibit 10.4 **U.S. courts website**

Source: Administrative Office of the U.S. Courts, Washington, D.C.

www

Search and View Full Text of Supreme Court Decisions Issued between 1937 and 1975 at www.fedworld.gov/supcourt

the cautionary comment in the syllabus of the Supreme Court case in Exhibit 10.6. Contrast the syllabus of the case with the opinion of the court in Exhibit 10.7.

Legal dictionaries and encyclopedias use headnotes—short, single-concept definitions and summaries, to provide basic information. When doing research, it should be kept in mind that these short "snippets" are taken out of the context of the case in which they were presented. None of the factual or procedural background is presented that caused the statement to be made.

Taking court statements out of the context in which the case was presented and relying on headnotes or summaries can present many problems for the researcher—the most obvious of which is accuracy. Was the headnote or summary copied correctly from the final version of the opinion? Judges have been known to correct errors in the language of opinions. Did the editor writing the note use the final version of the opinion? More important—does this statement accurately reflect the majority view, or does it reflect a minority or dissenting view? Was it the actual decision on the point

Exhibit 10.5 **Supreme Court explanation on differences between bench and slip opinions**

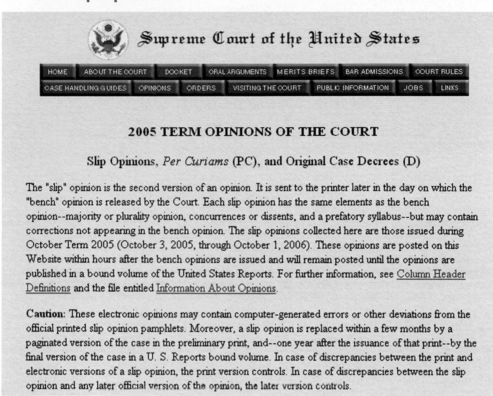

Supreme Court of the United States

| HOME | ABOUT THE COURT | DOCKET | ORAL ARGUMENTS | MERITS BRIEFS | BAR ADMISSIONS | COURT RULES |
| CASE HANDLING GUIDES | OPINIONS | ORDERS | VISITING THE COURT | PUBLIC INFORMATION | JOBS | LINKS |

2005 TERM OPINIONS OF THE COURT

Slip Opinions, *Per Curiams* (PC), and Original Case Decrees (D)

The "slip" opinion is the second version of an opinion. It is sent to the printer later in the day on which the "bench" opinion is released by the Court. Each slip opinion has the same elements as the bench opinion--majority or plurality opinion, concurrences or dissents, and a prefatory syllabus--but may contain corrections not appearing in the bench opinion. The slip opinions collected here are those issued during October Term 2005 (October 3, 2005, through October 1, 2006). These opinions are posted on this Website within hours after the bench opinions are issued and will remain posted until the opinions are published in a bound volume of the United States Reports. For further information, see Column Header Definitions and the file entitled Information About Opinions.

Caution: These electronic opinions may contain computer-generated errors or other deviations from the official printed slip opinion pamphlets. Moreover, a slip opinion is replaced within a few months by a paginated version of the case in the preliminary print, and--one year after the issuance of that print--by the final version of the case in a U. S. Reports bound volume. In case of discrepancies between the print and electronic versions of a slip opinion, the print version controls. In case of discrepancies between the slip opinion and any later official version of the opinion, the later version controls.

Source: Supreme Court of the United States.

of law before the court and, therefore, the "**holding**" of the court having precedential weight, or merely comments having no precedential authority because they are not related directly to the court decision and, therefore, are what are referred to as **dicta.** Contrast the headnote and the full court opinion in the case in Exhibit 10.8.

Doing legal research requires finding the most current and accurate statement of the legislative enactments and of the court. Presenting editorial headnotes, judges' dicta, or a dissenting opinion as accurate current legal authority is a potential career-ending course of action. The members of your legal team may rely on the potentially erroneous information and prepare the case, its prosecution or defense strategy, on the

Holding
The actual decision on the specific point of law the court was asked to decide.

Dicta
Court comments on issues not directly related to the holding and therefore not having precedential effect.

ETHICAL *Perspective*

Model Rules of Professional Conduct
Advocate Rule 3.3 Candor Toward the Tribunal

(a) A lawyer shall not knowingly:
    (1) make a false statement of fact or law to a tribunal or fail to correct a false statement of material fact or law previously made to the tribunal by the lawyer;
    (2) fail to disclose to the tribunal legal authority in the controlling jurisdiction known to the lawyer to be directly adverse to the position of the client and not. . .

See Appendix B for Commentary and complete Model Rule 3.3.

Source: ABA Model Rules for Professional Conduct, 2004 Edition. © 2003 by the American Bar Association. Reprinted with permission. Copies of ABA Model Rules of Professional Conduct, 2004 Edition *are available from Service Center, American Bar Association, 321 North Clark St., Chicago, IL 60610, 1-800-285-2221.*

Exhibit 10.6 **Sample of U.S. Supreme Court syllabus**

Syllabus

NOTE: Where it is feasible, a syllabus (headnote) will be released, as is being done in connection with this case, at the time the opinion is issued.
The syllabus constitutes no part of the opinion of the Court but has been prepared by the Reporter of Decisions for the convenience of the reader.
See United States v. Detroit Timber & Lumber Co., 200 U.S. 321, 337.

SUPREME COURT OF THE UNITED STATES

ROPER, SUPERINTENDENT, POTOSI CORRECTIONAL CENTER v. SIMMONS

CERTIORARI TO THE SUPREME COURT OF MISSOURI

No. 03—633. Argued October 13, 2004—Decided March 1, 2005

At age 17, respondent Simmons planned and committed a capital murder. After he had turned 18, he was sentenced to death. His direct appeal and subsequent petitions for state and federal postconviction relief were rejected. This Court then held, in *Atkins* v. *Virginia*, 536 U.S. 304, that the Eighth Amendment, applicable to the States through the Fourteenth Amendment, prohibits the execution of a mentally retarded person. Simmons filed a new petition for state postconviction relief, arguing that *Atkins'* reasoning established that the Constitution prohibits the execution of a juvenile who was under 18 when he committed his crime. The Missouri Supreme Court agreed and set aside Simmons' death sentence in favor of life imprisonment without eligibility for release. It held that, although *Stanford* v. *Kentucky*, 492 U.S. 361, rejected the proposition that the Constitution bars capital punishment for juvenile offenders younger than 18, a national consensus has developed against the execution of those offenders since *Stanford*.

Held: The Eighth and Fourteenth Amendments forbid imposition of the death penalty on offenders who were under the age of 18 when their crimes were committed. Pp. 6—25.

(a) The Eighth Amendment's prohibition against "cruel and unusual punishments" must be interpreted according to its text, by considering history,

Source: Supreme Court of the United States

PADILLA v. LEVER, 03-56259 (9TH CIR. 2005)

What exactly constitutes "dicta" is hotly contested and judges often disagree about what is or is not dicta in a particular case. See *United States v. Johnson*, 256 F.3d 895, 914-16 (9th Cir. 2001) (en banc) (Kozinski, J., concurring). In Johnson, Judge Kozinski explained that, "where a panel confronts an issue germane to the eventual resolution of the case, and resolves it after reasoned consideration in a published opinion, that ruling becomes the law of the circuit, regardless of whether doing so is necessary in some strict logical sense." Id. at 914; accord *Cetacean Cmty. v. Bush*, 386 F.3d 1169, 1173 (9th Cir. 2004) (quoting Johnson); *Miranda B. v. Kitzhaber*, 328 F.3d 1181, 1186 (9th Cir. 2003) (per curiam) (same).

Only "[w]here it is clear that a statement is made casually and without analysis, where the statement is uttered in passing without due consideration of the alternatives, or where it is merely a prelude to another legal issue that commands the panel's full attention, it may be appropriate to re-visit the issue in a later case." Johnson, 256 F.3d at 915. Nevertheless, "any such reconsideration should be done cautiously and rarely — only where the later panel is convinced that the earlier panel did not make a deliberate decision to adopt the rule of law it announced." Id. If, however, "it is clear that a majority of the panel has focused on the legal issue presented by the case before it and made a deliberate decision to resolve the issue, that ruling becomes the law of the circuit and can only be overturned by an en banc court or by the Supreme Court." Id. at 916; see also Cetacean Cmty., 386 F.3d at 1173; Miranda B., 328 F.3d at 1186.

This understanding of binding circuit authority was further articulated in *Barapind v. Enomoto*, 400 F.3d 744 (9th Cir. 2005) (en banc) (per curiam), where we said that when a panel has "addressed [an] issue and decided it in an opinion joined in relevant part by a majority of the panel," the panel's decision becomes "law of the circuit." Id. at 750-51 (footnote omitted).

Exhibit 10.7 Sample opinion of the U.S. Supreme Court

Opinion of the Court

NOTICE: This opinion is subject to formal revision before publication in the preliminary print of the United States Reports.Readers are requested to notify the Reporter of Decisions, Supreme Court of the United States, Washington, D. C. 20543, of any typographical or other formal errors, in order that corrections may be made before the preliminary print goes to press.

SUPREME COURT OF THE UNITED STATES

No. 03–633

DONALD P. ROPER, SUPERINTENDENT, POTOSI CORRECTIONAL CENTER, PETITIONER v. CHRISTOPHER SIMMONS

ON WRIT OF CERTIORARI TO THE SUPREME COURT OF MISSOURI

[March 1, 2005]

Justice Kennedy delivered the opinion of the Court.

This case requires us to address, for the second time in a decade and a half, whether it is permissible under the Eighth and Fourteenth Amendments to the Constitution of the United States to execute a juvenile offender who was older than 15 but younger than 18 when he committed a capital crime. In *Stanford* v. *Kentucky*, 492 U.S. 361 (1989), a divided Court rejected the proposition that the Constitution bars capital punishment for juvenile offenders in this age group. We reconsider the question.

I

At the age of 17, when he was still a junior in high school, Christopher Simmons, the respondent here, committed murder. About nine months later, after he had turned 18, he was tried and sentenced to death. There is little doubt that Simmons was the instigator of the crime. Before its commission Simmons said he wanted to murder someone. In chilling, callous terms he talked about his plan, discussing it for the most part with two friends, Charles Benjamin and John Tessmer, then aged 15 and 16 respectively. Simmons proposed to commit burglary and murder by breaking and entering, tying up a

Source: Supreme Court of the United States

inaccurate information. Notwithstanding the potential effect on the trial of the case, at best it may result in a severe reprimand or dismissal from employment. Presenting the erroneous information to the court is an ethical violation.

It does not matter to the court that it was prepared by someone other than the attorney presenting the case, the brief, or the oral argument. It is a breach of the duty of candor to the court by the attorney.

This is not to say that dissenting opinions and dicta may not be presented or argued to the court. Many of the finest jurists have issued dissenting views that became the law in future cases. And dicta in another case may well be a valid argument in a current case. The researcher's duty is to make clear the source of the information, whether from a primary or a secondary source.

Secondary Sources

Secondary sources explain the law. Trying to understand a new area of law can be difficult. Secondary sources are useful sources of information to learn about the history of an area of law, the issues involved, and in some situations the direction the law may be taking. A secondary source may be the editorial headnotes of a case or an in-depth scholarly interpretation, such as a treatise, a law review, or an article in a scholarly journal or other periodical.

Exhibit 10.8 **Regional reporter sample page**

Reference to Volume and Name of Reporter ⟶ | ⟵ Case Name

COM. v. ZAENGLE ⟵ Case Name   Pa. 1335 ⟵ Reporter Page Number
Cite as 497 A.2d 1335 (Pa.Super. 1985)

Kevin A. Hess, Asst. Dist. Atty., Carlisle, ⟵ Lawyers
for Commonwealth, appellee.

Before WICKERSHAM, OLSZEWSKI, ⟵ Judges Who Heard Case
AND HOFFMAN, JJ.

COMMONWEALTH of Pennsylvania
v.
John Stephen ZAENGLE, Appellant.
Superior Court of Pennsylvania.
Argued April 3, 1984.

Date of Opinion ⟶ Filed Aug. 16, 1985.

Beginning of West's Editor Summary ⟶ Defendant was convicted in the Court of Common Pleas, Criminal Division, Cumberland County, No. 886 Criminal 1982, Keller, J., of one count of driving while under the influence and three counts of homicide by vehicle, and he appealed his sentences. The Superior Court remanded for resentencing, 332 Pa.Super. 137, 480 A.2d 1224, and State appealed. The Supreme Court, 497 A.2d 1330, remanded for proceedings consistent with *Commonwealth v. Frisbie*. The Superior Court, No. 175 Harrisburg 1983, Olszewski, J., held that imposing multiple sentences upon defendant for the multiple deaths which resulted from his single violation of the homicide by vehicle statute was permissible.

End of Summary ⟶ Sentences reinstated.

West Digest Topic and Corresponding West Key Number ⟶ Criminal Law 984(7)
Legislature authorized multiple sentences for multiple deaths resulting from a single violation of homicide by vehicle statute, 75 Pa.C.S.A. § 3732.

Lawyers ⟶ Taylor P. Andrews, Public Defender, Carlisle, for appellant.

OLSZEWSKI, Judge:

By order of the Supreme Court, 497 ⟵ Beginning of Court's Opinion
A.2d 1330, this case has been remanded for proceedings consistent with *Commonwealth v. Frisbie*, 506 Pa. 461, 485 A.2d 1098 (1984). *Frisbie* holds that, where legislatively authorized, the imposition of multiple sentences upon a defendant whose single unlawful act injures multiple victims is legal. In the instant case, appellee driving drunk killed three people. The test of legislative authorization under *Frisbie* looks to the language of the statute defining the offense. *See id.* at 466, 485 A.2d at 1100 (comparing the language of 18 Pa.C.S. Sec 2705 with that of 18 Pa.C.S. Sec. 2707 and 2710). The operative language in 75 Pa.C.S. Sec. 3732 penalizes "(a)ny person who unintentionally causes *the death of another person*." (Emphasis added.) Applying the *Frisbie* analysis to the facts of this case, we conclude that the legislature did authorize multiple sentences for multiple deaths resulting from a single violation of 75 Pa.C.S. Sec. 3732. Accord *Commonwealth v. Zaengle*, 332 Pa.Super. 137, 141, 480 A.2d 1224, 1228 (1984) (Olszewski J., dissenting).

The sentences imposed by the trial court are reinstated.

Legal Dictionaries

Legal dictionaries, as opposed to general English or other specialized dictionaries, define words and phrases as used in the law. The "law," as with most professions, trades, and occupations, has developed its own specialized vocabulary. Each specialized area of law further develops a specialized terminology. Lawyers in specialty fields, such as antitrust law, use terms that have developed specialized meaning through case decisions such as the antitrust law term "tying arrangement," used to describe the situation in which one product can be purchased only with another product. This term comes

Exhibit 10.9 **Black's Law Dictionary, sample page**

confesses in open court. U.S. Const. Art. IV, § 2, cl. 2.

tying, *adj. Antitrust.* Of or relating to an arrangement whereby a seller sells a product to a buyer only if the buyer purchases another product from the seller <tying agreement>.

tying arrangement. *Antitrust.* **1.** A seller's agreement to sell one product or service only if the buyer also buys a different product or service. The product or service that the buyer wants to buy is known as the *tying product* or *tying service*; the different product or service that the seller insists on selling is known as the *tied product* or *tied service.* Tying arrangements may be illegal under the Sherman or Clayton Act if their effect is too anticompetitive. **2.** A seller's refusal to sell one product or

service unless the buyer also buys a different product or service. — Also termed *tying agreement; tie-in; tie-in arrangement.* Cf. RECIPROCAL DEALING.

tying product. See TYING ARRANGEMENT (1).

tyranny, *n.* Arbitrary or despotic government; the severe and autocratic exercise of sovereign power, whether vested constitutionally in one ruler or usurped by that ruler by breaking down the division and distribution of governmental powers. — **tyrannical, tyrannous,** *adj.*

tyrant, *n.* A sovereign or ruler, legitimate or not, who wields power unjustly and arbitrarily to oppress the citizenry; a despot.

Source: Black's Law Dictionary, 7e, 1995. Reprinted with permission of Thomson/West Publishing.

from the 1947 antitrust case of *International Salt v. United States*, which held that a patent is presumed to give the patent holder "market power" (another legal term), making it illegal to "tie the sale of the patented product to the sale of another." Without an understanding of the basic terminology and legal concepts, it is hard to conduct proper legal search using either traditional books or computer-based services. Exhibit 10.9 is a sample page from *Black's Law Dictionary*, illustrating the term "tying."

Secondary Sources-Legal Encyclopedias

Legal encyclopedias, like legal dictionaries, can provide the needed background to understand an area enough to start the research. They can provide an overview of the concepts and history of an area of law, the legal issues involved, and the terminology. The annotations (lists of case citations) can provide a starting point for case law research. National encyclopedias such as *Corpus Juris Secondum* (CJS) and *American Jurisprudence* (AM JUR) provide cases from all jurisdictions for reference and research. Exhibit 10.10 is a sample page from *American Jurisprudence*.

State-specific encyclopedias generally limit case references or citations to that jurisdiction. Where the research is on a new area of law for the jurisdiction, the national coverage may provide information on persuasive authority from other jurisdictions. Exhibit 10.11 is a sample page from a secondary source, *Corpis Juris Secondum*, a national legal encyclopedia.

Treatises, Law Reviews, and Legal Periodicals

Some secondary sources are authoritative or of sufficient scholarly value to be persuasive to the court. For example, the treatise on Torts by Prosser is frequently used in argument as persuasive and accepted as such by most courts. In new areas of the law, such as cyber law, or emerging and changing areas such as privacy rights, courts frequently welcome a well reasoned scholarly article from a law review or other legal journal that make a clear and convincing argument with well researched and reasoned thought. In some instances, these article are like the **amicus curia** briefs submitted to the court by interested parties that have no actual standing as a party but have a clear interest in the outcome. Examples are Planned Parenthood and a national right-to-life organization in abortion-rights cases.

Amicus curia
Briefs submitted by interested parties who do not have standing in the action as a "friend of the court."

Exhibit 10.10 **American Jurisprudence, sample page**

is infected with a contagious disease[90] or has been dangerously exposed to such a disease.[91]

§ 317. —Children infected with the AIDS virus

Acquired Immune Deficiency Syndrome (AIDS) disables victims of the disease by collapsing their immune systems, making them unable to fight infection.[92] State education authorities, rather than local school authorities, are the appropriate parties to promulgate regulations concerning the right of AIDS-infected children to attend public school, since the state's power to regulate on the issue, inferable from its broad grant of authority to supervise the schools, pre-empts any rights of local authorities under their statutory discretion to exclude children from school to prevent the spread of contagious disease.[93]

◆ *Caution:* State statutes and local health regulations concerning contagious diseases in general, which make no specific reference to AIDS, do not apply to the decision whether AIDS-infected students should be allowed to attend public school.[94]

Procedures for determining whether AIDS-infected children should be excluded from a public school have withstood a due process challenge, one court having upheld the constitutionality of a plan which provided for an impartial decision by a medical panel, proper notice, and the opportunity to call and cross-examine witnesses.[95] However, distinguishing between students known to be infected with AIDS and students who were unidentified carriers of AIDS-related complex or asymptomatic carriers is constitutionally unacceptable since the proposed exclusion from public school of only the known AIDS-infected children constitutes an equal protection violation.[96]

◆ *Practice Guide:* Numerous organizations, both medical and educational, have formulated guidelines on when AIDS carriers should be segregated from the rest of the population. In cases concerning the right of a student with AIDS to attend school, courts have received evidence of the guidelines

---

90. Kenney v. Gurley, 208 Ala. 623, 95 So. 34, 26 A.L.R. 813 (1923); Nutt v. Board of Education of City of Goodland, Sherman County, 128 Kan. 507, 278 P. 1065 (1929).

As to the right to public education, generally, see §§ 242 et seq.

Forms: Answer—Defense—School district providing home teaching to student with contagious or infectious disease pending determination whether student's attendance at school would be danger to others. 22 Am Jur Pl & Pr Forms (Rev), Schools, Form 182.

91. Bright v. Beard, 132 Minn. 375, 157 N.W. 501 (1916).

92. Board of Educ. of City of Plainfield, Union County v. Cooperman, 105 N.J. 587, 523 A.2d 655, 38 Ed. Law Rep. 607, 60 A.L.R.4th 1 (1987).

Law Reviews: AIDS in public schools: Resolved issues and continuing controversy, 24 J Law and Educ 1:69 (1995).

Students with AIDS: Protecting an infected child's right to a classroom education and

developing a school's AIDS policy, 40 S Dakota LR 1:72 (1995).

93. Board of Educ. of City of Plainfield, Union County v. Cooperman, 105 N.J. 587, 523 A.2d 655, 38 Ed. Law Rep. 607, 60 A.L.R.4th 1 (1987).

94. District 27 Community School Bd. by Granirer v. Board of Educ. of City of New York, 130 Misc. 2d 398, 502 N.Y.S.2d 325, 32 Ed. Law Rep. 740 (Sup. Ct. 1986).

95. Board of Educ. of City of Plainfield, Union County v. Cooperman, 105 N.J. 587, 523 A.2d 655, 38 Ed. Law Rep. 607, 60 A.L.R.4th 1 (1987).

Forms: Complaint, petition, or declaration—To enjoin expulsion of student who tested positive for AIDS virus—By guardian. 22 Am Jur Pl & Pr Forms (Rev), Schools, Form 177.

96. District 27 Community School Bd. by Granirer v. Board of Educ. of City of New York, 130 Misc. 2d 398, 502 N.Y.S.2d 325, 32 Ed. Law Rep. 740 (Sup. Ct. 1986).

537

Source: American Jurisprudence, 2e, 2000. Reprinted with permission of Thomson/West Publishing.

Exhibit 10.11 **Page from *Corpis Juris Secundum*—a legal encyclopedia**

§§ 58–59   SOCIAL SECURITY   81 C.J.S.

individual who died fully insured,[65] and have physical or mental impairments which, under regulations promulgated for the purpose, are deemed to be of such severity as to preclude engaging in any gainful activity.[66] The requirements for obtaining disability benefits by such persons are more restrictive than requirements for the insured individual himself.[67] The physical impairment necessary to a finding of disability is placed on a level of severity to be determined administratively,[68] and the regulations adopted to carry out the statutory provisions have been upheld.[69]

A claim for disability is judged solely by medical criteria,[70] without regard to non-medical factors[71] such as age, education, and work experience,[72] in contrast to the considerations given to an insured individual's age, education, and work experience, in determining his ability to engage in substantial gainful activity, as discussed supra § 56. An individual cannot qualify for disability insurance benefits unless suffering from an impairment listed in the appendix to the regulations applicable to disabilities, or from one or more unlisted impairments that singly or in combination are the medical equivalent of a listed impairment.[73] The benefits are to be paid only for a disabling medical impairment,[74] and not simply for the inability to obtain employment.[75]

§ 59.   Benefits of Disabled Child

A disabled child of an insured individual who is, or would have been, eligible for social security benefits, may be entitled to disability insurance benefits.

Research Note

Status as child eligible for benefits under statute generally is discussed supra § 41.

Library References

Social Security and Public Welfare ⬤123, 140.5.

Under the provisions of the Social Security Act,[76] disabled children of retired or disabled insured individuals, and of insured individuals who have died, may be paid benefits if they have been disabled since before they reached twenty-two years of age, and if they meet the other conditions of eligibility.[77] The purpose of the provision is to provide a measure of income and security to those who have lost a wage-earner on whom they depended,[78] or to provide support for the dependents of a disabled wage earner,[79] and not to replace only that support enjoyed by the child prior to the onset of disability.[80] The liberal perspective of the Act applies to the award of children's disability benefits.[81]

In order to be entitled to recover benefits under this provision, the child must have been disabled,[82] as defined elsewhere in the Act,[83] prior to attaining a specified age,[84] and must be un-

---

65. U.S.—Sullivan v. Weinberger, C.A. Ga., 493 F.2d 855, certiorari denied 95 S.Ct. 1958, 421 U.S. 967, 44 L.Ed.2d 455.

66. U.S.—Wokojance v. Weinberger, C. A.Ohio, 513 F.2d 210, certiorari denied 96 S.Ct. 106, 423 U.S. 856, 46 L.Ed.2d 82.

Hendrix v. Finch, D.C.S.C., 310 F. Supp. 513.

Baby sitting; domestic work
U.S.—Dixon v. Weinberger, C.A.Ga., 495 F.2d 202.

Time impairment manifest
U.S.—Sullivan v. Weinberger, C.A.Ga., 493 F.2d 855, certiorari denied 95 S.Ct. 1958, 421 U.S. 967, 44 L.Ed.2d 455.

67. U.S.—Wokojance v. Weinberger, C. A.Ohio, 513 F.2d 210, certiorari denied 96 S.Ct. 106, 423 U.S. 856, 46 L.Ed.2d 82.

Solis v. U. S. Secretary of Health, Ed. and Welfare, D.C.Puerto Rico, 372 F.Supp. 1223—Truss v. Richardson, D. C.Mich., 338 F.Supp. 741—Nickles v. Richardson, D.C.S.C., 320 F.Supp. 777.

68. U.S.—Gillock v. Richardson, D.C. Kan., 322 F.Supp. 354.

69. U.S.—Sullivan v. Weinberger, C.A. Ga., 493 F.2d 855, certiorari denied 95 S.Ct. 1958, 421 U.S. 967, 44 L.Ed.2d 455.

Gunter v. Richardson, D.C.Ark., 335 F.Supp. 907—Zanoviak v. Finch, D.C. Pa., 314 F.Supp. 1152—Frasier v. Finch, D.C.Ala., 313 F.Supp. 160, affirmed, C. A., 434 F.2d 597.

70. U.S.—Wokojance v. Weinberger, C. A.Ohio, 513 F.2d 210, certiorari denied 96 S.Ct. 106, 423 U.S. 856, 46 L.Ed.2d 82.

71. U.S.—Sullivan v. Weinberger, C.A. Ga., 493 F.2d 855, certiorari denied 95 S.Ct. 1958, 421 U.S. 967, 44 L.Ed.2d 455.

72. U.S.—Gillock v. Richardson, D.C. Kan., 322 F.Supp. 354.

73. U.S.—Wokojance v. Weinberger, C. A.Ohio, 513 F.2d 210, certiorari denied 96 S.Ct. 106, 423 U.S. 856, 46 L.Ed.2d 82.

Gillock v. Richardson, D.C.Kan., 322 F.Supp. 354—Hendrix v. Finch, D.C.S. C., 310 F.Supp. 513.

74. U.S.—Sullivan v. Weinberger, C.A. Ga., 493 F.2d 855, certiorari denied 95 S.Ct. 1958, 421 U.S. 967, 44 L.Ed.2d 455.

75. U.S.—Sullivan v. Weinberger, C.A. Ga., 493 F.2d 855, certiorari denied 95 S.Ct. 1958, 421 U.S. 967, 44 L.Ed.2d 455.

76. 42 U.S.C.A. § 402(d).

77. U.S.—Lowe v. Finch, D.C.Va., 297 F.Supp. 667—Blevins v. Fleming, D.C. Ark., 180 F.Supp. 287.

78. U.S.—Ziskin v. Weinberger, D.C. Ohio, 379 F.Supp. 124.

79. U.S.—Jimenez v. Weinberger, Ill., 94 S.Ct. 2496, 417 U.S. 628, 41 L.Ed.2d 363, appeal after remand, C.A., 523 F.2d 689, certiorari denied 96 S.Ct. 3200.

80. U.S.—Jimenez v. Weinberger, Ill., 94 S.Ct. 2496, 417 U.S. 628, 41 L.Ed.2d 363, appeal after remand, C.A., 523 F.2d 689, certiorari denied 96 S.Ct. 3200.

81. U.S.—Ziskin v. Weinberger, D.C. Ohio, 379 F.Supp. 124.

82. U.S.—Ziskin v. Weinberger, D.C. Ohio, 379 F.Supp. 124.

83. 42 U.S.C.A. § 423.

84. U.S.—Ziskin v. Weinberger, D.C. Ohio, 379 F.Supp. 124—Moon v. Richardson, D.C.Va., 345 F.Supp. 1182.

Finding Tools

Finding tools help to "find" the law. Finding the right case, statute, or regulation can be difficult, particularly if the correct term or phrase is not used to conduct the search. As mentioned previously, West Publishing might use the phrase "Bills and Notes" and another publisher might us the term "holder" to refer to the same cases and material on negotiable instruments.

Indexes and Digests

Indexes and digests offer a way of finding the material.

Citator
An index of cases.

1. Indexes and citators. Among the more useful sets of indexes and **citators** are those that cross-reference material. Some indexes use the commonly used or popular name of a case or statute to provide the citation or reference to the original source. For example, the commonly used or popular name for the statement of rights read to criminal defendants when arrested is "Miranda Rights." Using a popular name index provides the citation to the case in which the U.S. Supreme Court made mandatory the reading of these rights to defendants—*Miranda v Arizona* 384 US 436 (1966).
2. Legal digests provide lists of cases in subject topic format, with cases generally in chronological order from the earliest to the latest. Digests do not offer the detailed analysis found in encyclopedias. Exhibit 10.12 is a sample page from *West's Digest*.

PERSONAL RESEARCH STRATEGY

Over time, each paralegal develops a personal search strategy based on the nature of the problem or issue to be researched and the resources available. When a legal issue is well defined and a specific case or statute is in question, it may be possible to start with the original primary source. More likely, though, the research assignment will be less defined and may be just a set of facts describing a situation. A possible area of relevant law may be suggested. This could be a specific area of law such as "driving too fast for conditions," or a general area of law such as "personal injury from an automobile accident."

The facts will determine the area of law. If the paralegal is unfamiliar with the area of law, the relevant facts may not be obvious. Secondary sources provide a good reference source to acquire a general understanding about an area of law. As the paralegal learns more about the specifics of the area of law and the essential elements of causes of actions, the relevant facts should become clearer. One of the advantages of using the traditional book form of research is the ability to flip pages back and forth and scan many items that can lead to a specific point of law. This is sometimes referred to as "the serendipity of research."

Computer search engines can lead to specific case law and statutes. The challenge is in how to construct the search query or question. If you do not know the relevant facts to include, the resulting report may not be accurate. Computers, for the most part, are limited to finding only the things the search query specifically asks for. Learning the relevant facts to create the proper question may involve using the print resources first to determine the relevant facts or the proper terminology. For example, in a fair-use doctrine case of alleged copyright violation, is the status of the alleged violator as a nonprofit organization relevant?

Always verify that the law and cases cited in the research and memo of law is current law or current authority. Look for pending cases and legislation that might change the answer to the legal question. Look in legal journals, periodicals, and legal newspapers, as well as newspapers of general circulation, for cases that are on appeal

Exhibit 10.12 *West's Digest,* sample page

CRIMINAL LAW

SUBJECTS INCLUDED

Acts and omissions in violation of law punishable as offenses against the public

Nature and elements of crime in general

Capacity to commit crime, nature and extent of responsibility therefore in general, and responsibility of principals, accessories, etc.

Jurisdiction over and place of prosecution of crimes

Limitation of time for prosecution

Preliminary complaints, warrants, examination and commitment

Arraignment and pleas

Evidence in criminal proceedings

Trial, and acquittal or conviction

Motions in arrest of judgment and for new trial

Judgment or sentence and final commitment

Review on appeal, writ of error or certiorari

Prosecution and punishment of successive offenses or of habitual criminals

Modes of punishment and prevention of crime in general

SUBJECTS EXCLUDED AND COVERED BY OTHER TOPICS

Arrest, see ARREST

Bail, see BAIL

Constitutional rights and privileges of accused not peculiar to matters within scope of this topic, see CONSTITUTIONAL LAW, INDICTMENT AND INFORMATION, JURY, SEARCHES AND SEIZURES, WITNESSES and other specific topics

Convicts, disabilities and regulation, see CONVICTS

Costs in criminal prosecutions, see COSTS

Extradition of fugitives, see EXTRADITION AND DETAINERS

Fines in general, see FINES

Grand juries and inquisitions by them, see GRAND JURY

Habeas corpus to obtain discharge from imprisonment, see HABEAS CORPUS

Included offenses, conviction under indictment for broader offense, see INDICTMENT AND INFORMATION

Indictments or other accusations, see INDICTMENT AND INFORMATION and specific topics relating to particular offenses

Injunction against commission of crime, see INJUNCTION

Judgment of acquittal, conviction or sentence, effect as adjudication, see JUDGMENT

Jury trial, right to and waiver, and qualifications and selection of jurors, see JURY

Juvenile offenders, special rules and proceedings, see INFANTS

that involve the same legal issues. Check the legislative services for pending legislation that may have an impact on the case. Research that is concerned with giving clients advice on future actions may depend on knowing the changes that may occur that will change the basic parameters of the law. For example, can I have a smoking section in my new restaurant? Are the tax rates for estate planning going to change next year?

A FINAL WORD ON EXECUTING THE LEGAL RESEARCH PLAN

We emphasize this final piece of advice: Know when to ask for help. Everyone on the legal team who has done legal research has at one time or another hit a research dead-end. Sometimes taking a few minutes to ask a question will yield the "magic" word, term, or phrase that will result in the answer you seek.

USING PRINTED LEGAL REFERENCE WORKS

Most legal references have a set of common features. They generally have a section, usually in the introduction, that explains the coverage and how to use the specific book or service. This usually includes the abbreviations used throughout the work (see Exhibit 10.13), and the method of pagination—for example, standard page numbering or use of section numbers. A table of contents at the beginning of the work (see Exhibit 10.14) provides a general list of major topics. The index at the end of the work provides the detailed coverage. Multivolume sets might have a separate set of volumes containing the index. Each volume also might contain an index for the specific volume.

Most legal words also contain a table of cases that are mentioned in the text. This is a useful feature when a case seems to be on point or relevant and the paralegal wants to research the area of law and other cases on the same issue. A table of statutes also may be included, to help the researcher find cases or discussions of a statute.

Exhibit 10.13 **Sample list of abbreviations**

ABBREVIATIONS

A.   *Atlantic Reporter*
A.2d   *Atlantic Reporter, Second Series*
Abb.   *Abbott's Circuit Court Reports, U.S.*
Abb.Adm.   *Abbott's Admiralty Reports, U.S.*
Adams L.J.   *Adams County Legal Journal*
Add.   *Addison's Reports*
Am.Dec.   *American Decisions*
Am.L.J., N.S.   *American Law Journal, New Series*
Am.L.J.,O.S.   *American Law Journal, Hall's*
Am.L.Reg., N.S.   *American Law Register, New Series*
Am.L.Reg., O.S.   *American Law Register, Old Series*
Am.Rep.   *American Reports*
Am.St.Rep.   *American State Reports*
Ann.Cas.   *American & English Annotated Cases*
Ashm.   *Ashmead's Reports*
Baldw.   *Baldwin's Reports, U.S.*
Beaver   *Beaver County Legal Journal*
Ben.   *Benedict's Reports, U.S.*
Berks   *Berks County Legal Journal*
Binn.   *Binney's Reports*

Binns' Just.   *Binns' Justice*
Biss.   *Bissell's Reports, U.S.*
Black   *Black's United States Supreme Court Reports*
Blair   *Blair County Law Reports*
Blatchf.C.C.   *Blatchford's Reports, U.S.*
Bond   *Bond's Reports, U.S.*
B.R.   *Bankruptcy reports*
Bright.E.C.   *Brightly's Election Cases*
Bright.N.P.   *Brightly's Nisi Prius Reports*
Browne   *P.A. Browne's reports*
Brock.   *Brockenbrough's Reports, U.S.*
Bucks   *Bucks County Law Reporter*
C.A.   *United States Court of Appeals*
C.C.A.   *United States Circuit Court of Appeals*
Cambria   *Cambria County Legal Journal*
Cambria C.R.   *Cambria County Reports*
Camp.   *Campbell's Legal Gazette Reports*
Cent.   *Central Reporter*
C.C.   (see Pa.C.C.) *County Court Reports*
Chest.   *Chester County Reports*

Source: From Purdon's *Pennsylvania Statutes Annotated,* © 1994 by West Group, a Thomson Company. Reproduced with permission.

Exhibit 10.14 **Sample table of contents**

Source: *From Pennsylvania Estate Planning and Drafting, 2/E,* by Robert J. Weinberg. © George T. Bisel Company, Inc.. Reproduced by permission.

WHEN ARE COURT DECISIONS PRECEDENTS?

There is a controversy with regard to the use of **unpublished opinions** in other court proceedings. In reviewing the issue, the Court in Anastoff made the following observations:

"Before concluding, we wish to indicate what this case is not about. It is not about whether opinions should be published, whether that means printed in a book or available in some other accessible form to the public in general. Courts may decide, for one reason or another, that some of their cases are not important enough to take up pages in a printed report. Such decisions may be eminently practical and defensible, but in our view they have nothing to do with the authoritative effect of any court decision.

The question presented here is not whether opinions ought to be published, but whether they ought to have precedential effect, whether published or not. We point out, in addition, that "unpublished" in this context has never meant "secret." So far as we are aware, every opinion and every order of any court in this country, at least of any appellate court, is available to the public. You may have to walk into a clerk's office and pay a per-page fee, but you can get the opinion if you want it. Indeed, most appellate courts now make their opinions, whether labeled "published" or not, available to anyone on line."

Anastasoff v. U.S. *223 F. 3d 898 (8th cir. 2000)*

Unpublished opinions
Cases which the court does not feel have precedential effect and are limited to a specific set of facts.

Updates

Print material is updated in a number of ways. One of the most frequent is the use of **pocket parts**, so called because they are slipped into a pocket in the back of the print volume. Usually these are annual updates, but they may be produced more or less frequently depending on the publisher and the need for updates. Also used are supplemental pamphlets, usually paperbacks, to supplement the annual updates. Some are issued monthly, and others quarterly or semi-annually.

It is essential that the pocket part or supplement be consulted. In statutory research, the main volumes may be many years old and sections of the law repealed. The pocket parts or other supplements, not the main volume, contain the latest information. For this reason, some researchers look at the pocket part first, before consulting the main volume. More and more frequently, additional updates are provided online. The paralegal must learn how each resource is updated and the frequency of the updates. Exhibit 10.15 is a sample pocket part supplement.

Pocket parts
An update to a book that is a separate document that slips into a pocket in the back of the main volume.

Versus Law Research Manual:
www.versuslaw.com/Support/
R–Manual_Preface.asp

CONSTRUCTING A COMPUTER SEARCH QUERY

Constructing a search query requires one to select a computer search index, then to create the query.

Creating a Computer Search

Lexis: www.lexisnexis.com/
Westlaw: www.westlaw.com/about/
VersusLaw: www.versuslaw.com
Loislaw: www.loislaw.com

The three primary full-service online providers of computer research services—Lexis, Loislaw, and Westlaw—provide a broad range of legal materials including cases, statutes, and regulations. In addition, a limited-service search provider, VersusLaw, specializes in providing cases and limited access to additional items, such as the *Code of Federal Regulations*.

In using a limited-service provider, it is important to check the coverage dates and content. In some cases the same information is available at other sources, such as the *United States Code* and the *Code of Federal Regulations*, which are available online through the GPO Access website. In all cases, researchers must be certain that they have checked all the latest update sources.

Exhibit 10.15 **Sample pocket part supplement**

13 Pa.C.S.A. § 1105   COMMERCIAL CODE

DIVISION 1
GENERAL PROVISIONS

CHAPTER 11

SHORT TITLE, CONSTRUCTION, APPLICATION
AND SUBJECT MATTER OF TITLE

§ 1105. Territorial application of title; power of parties to choose applicable law

Notes of Decisions

Bankruptcy 6

_____

1. In general

In re Eagle Enterprises, Inc., Bkrtcy.E.D.Pa. 1998, 223 B.R. 290, [main volume] affirmed 237 B.R. 269.

2. Law governing

When parties agree to apply foreign law, pursuant to which their contract to "lease" goods kept in Pennsylvania will be deemed a true "lease," despite fact that contract does not permit lessor to terminate agreement but affords him an option to purchase goods for nominal consideration, Pennsylvania law will not give effect to that choice. In re Eagle Enterprises, Inc., E.D.Pa.1999, 237 B.R. 269.

4. Third parties

In re Eagle Enterprises, Inc., Bkrtcy.E.D.Pa. 1998, 223 B.R. 290, [main volume] affirmed 237 B.R. 269.

6. Bankruptcy

While Chapter 7 debtor and equipment lessor were generally free, under Pennsylvania statute, to agree what law would govern their rights and duties, debtor and equipment lessor could not impose their choice of law on Chapter 7 trustee, as party who never agreed to choice-of-law provision, in order to prevent trustee from challenging parties' characterization, as equipment "lease," of agreement which required debtor to pay alleged rent throughout full term of lease, and which then allowed debtor to acquire equipment at end of lease for nominal consideration of one dollar, merely because lease would allegedly have been recognized as true lease under law of foreign country that parties chose to govern their agreement. In re Eagle Enterprises, Inc., E.D.Pa.1999, 237 B.R. 269.

CHAPTER 12

GENERAL DEFINITIONS AND PRINCIPLES OF INTERPRETATION

§ 1201. General definitions

Notes of Decisions

11. Lease or lease intended as security

Under Pennsylvania law, "lease" transaction in which "lessee" cannot terminate "lease" during its term, but may thereafter become owner of "leased" goods for no additional or nominal additional consideration, does not create lease, but rather a security interest. In re Eagle Enterprises, Inc., E.D.Pa.1999, 237 B.R. 269.

When parties agree to apply foreign law, pursuant to which their contract to "lease" goods kept in Pennsylvania will be deemed a true "lease," despite fact that contract does not permit lessor to terminate agreement but affords him an option to purchase goods for nominal consideration, Pennsylvania law will not give effect to that choice. In re Eagle Enterprises, Inc., E.D.Pa.1999, 237 B.R. 269.

13. Security interest

Revised Pennsylvania statute defining term "security interest" seeks to correct shortcomings

of its predecessor by focusing inquiry of lease/security interest analysis on economics of the transaction, rather than on intent of the parties. In re Kim, Bkrtcy.E.D.Pa.1999, 232 B.R. 324.

Whether, under Pennsylvania law, lease or security interest is created by a particular transaction is no longer within exclusive control of the parties and subject to possible manipulation through artful document drafting; rather, issue is to be determined by reference to uniform criteria set forth in revised statute defining term "security interest." In re Kim, Bkrtcy.E.D.Pa.1999, 232 B.R. 324.

In determining whether debtor's lease was a disguised security interest or a true lease under Pennsylvania law, bankruptcy court was required to consider entire "transaction" and was not constrained to look solely to documents signed by the parties which were designated "lease" or which made use of terms commonly found in leases, but could examine both parol and extrin-

4

Search Method and Query

Each of the online providers uses words to find and retrieve documents. As part of the publication process, indexes are prepared of every word in the document, the words are tabulated for frequency, and a word index is prepared. The search you create searches this index. VersusLaw uses a full-text retrieval method that searches every word except "stop words"—words that are used too commonly in documents to be used in a search, such as "the," "not," "of," and "and."

Creating the Query

When you conduct a search, you are asking the search engine to find the indexed words you have chosen. These may be legal specialty words or common English words. Single words may be in any of the Internet or legal search engines. Frequently you will be looking for more detailed information. Using combinations of words in the search can narrow the search results. Usually, the most productive search contains a combination of words, which may consist of terms such as "strict liability," "legal malpractice," "automobile accident," or "reckless indifference," for example.

Using Connectors

Connectors
Instructions in a search query on how to treat the words in the query.

Connectors are instructions to the search engine to look for documents containing combinations of words. Connectors may be thought of as instructions to the search engine: Find me documents in which the words "strict" AND "liability" appear. The word AND is a connector that instructs the search not to return the documents in which only one of the words is found. Exhibit 10.16 shows a Loislaw search with the AND connector.

The connector OR instructs the search engine to find either term—the word "strict" OR the word "liability"—and retrieve the documents. Exhibit 10.17 depicts a Lexis search with the OR connector. The NOT connector instructs the search to eliminate certain words. For example, you may wish to review documents in which the word "malpractice" is found but *not* those with the word "medical."

In some cases it might be assumed that there will be other words between the desired terms, such as in the phrase "Paralegals are bound by the ethics of their profession." The NEAR connector helps to locate documents where the terms are near each other; for example: find "paralegal" NEAR "ethics." The NEAR connector

Exhibit 10.16 **Loislaw Search with AND connector**

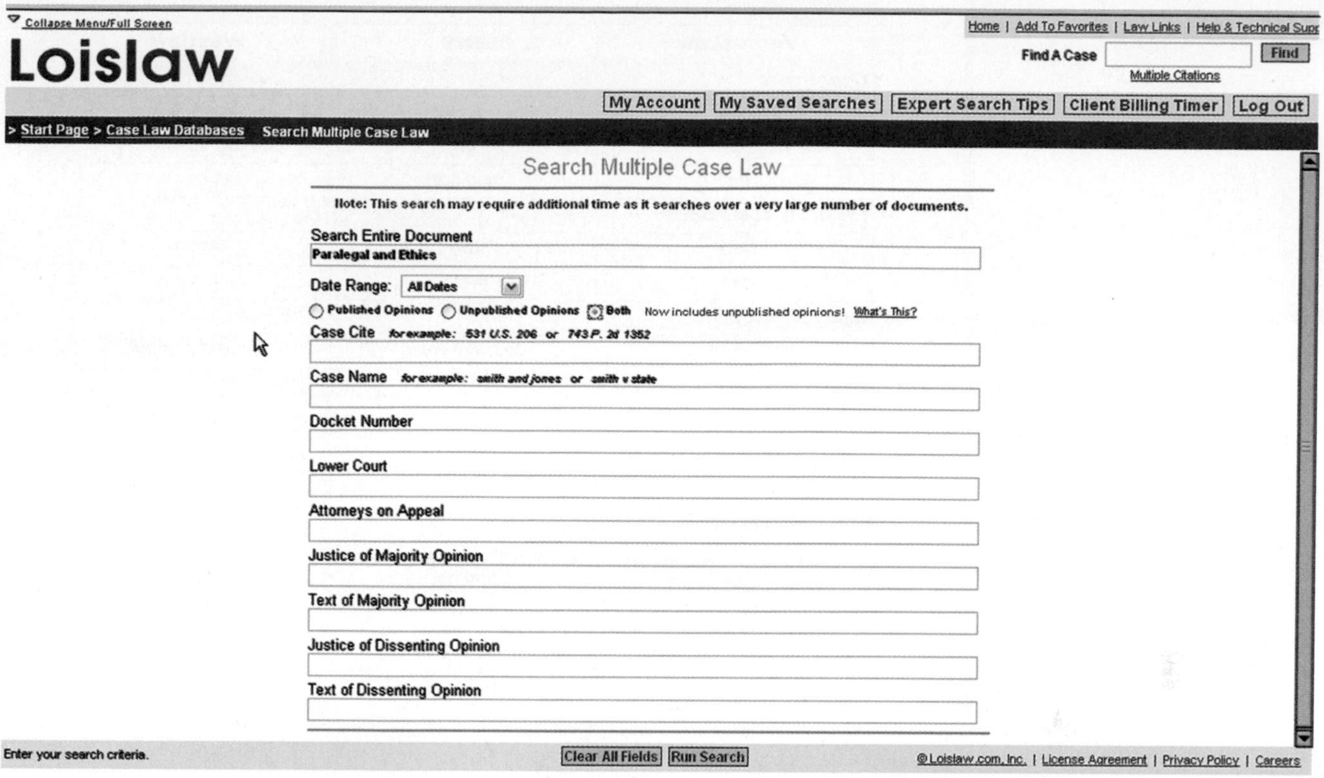

Source: Reproduced with permission of Aspen Publishers, Loislaw screen shot.

Exhibit 10.17 **Lexis Search with OR connector**

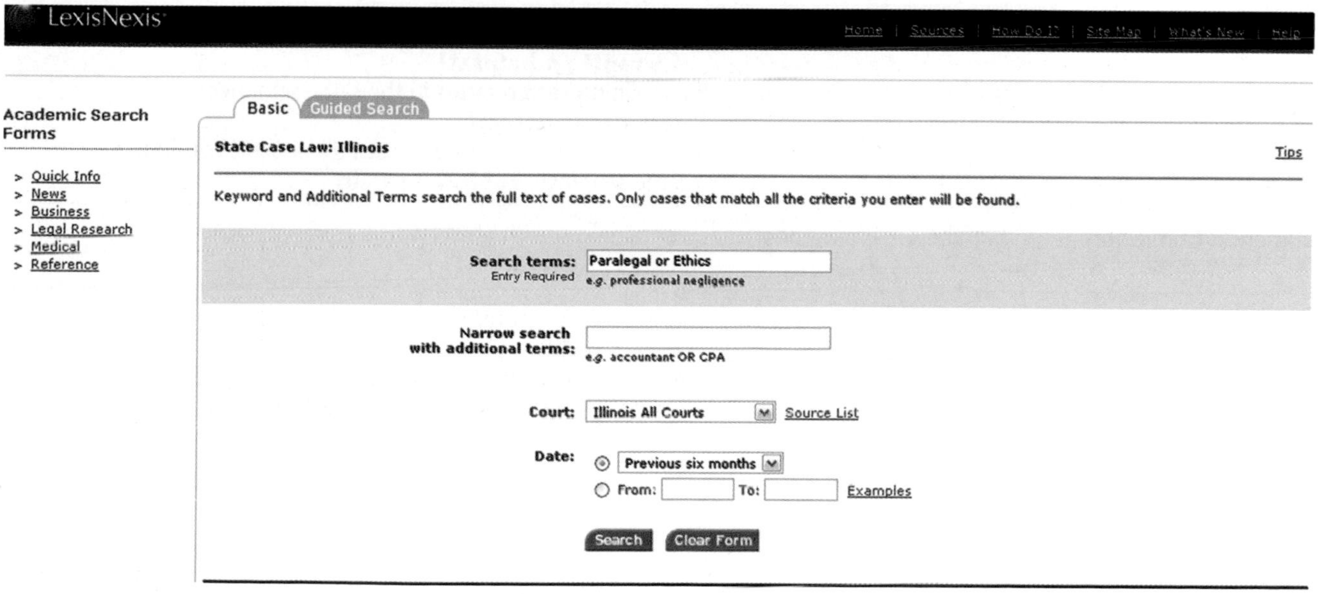

Source: The Legal Intelligencer, April 7, 2006, vol. P, 2431, p.7.

Exhibit 10.18 **Comparison grid from VersusLaw**

VersusLaw	LEXIS	Westlaw
Connectors		
and	and	and, &
or	or	or, *space*
not	and not	but not, %
Proximity operators		
w/n	w/n	w/n, /n
w/n	pre/n	pre/n, +n
Exact phrase match		
unlawful entry	unlawful entry	"unlawful entry"
Wild Cards - end of root words		
*	!	!
Wild Cards - single character		
?	*	*
Order of operators		
proximity operators, not, and, or	or, proximity operators, and, and not	or, proximity operators, and, but not

Exhibit 10.19 **Westlaw guide to connectors**

USING CONNECTORS

Connector	You type	Westlaw retrieves documents
AND	&	containing both search terms: **work-place & safety**
OR	a space	containing either search term or both search terms: **landlord lessor**
Grammatical Connectors	/p	containing search terms in the same paragraph: **warrant! /p habitat!**
	/s	containing search terms in the same sentence: **danger! /s defect!**
	+s	in which the first term precedes the second within the same sentence: **capital +s gain**
Numerical Connectors	/n (where *n* is a number)	containing search terms with *n* terms of each other: **issues /5 fact**
	+n (where *n* is a number)	in which the first term precedes the second by *n* terms: **20 + 5 1080**
BUT NOT	%	not containing the term or terms following the percent symbol (%): **tax taxation % tax taxation /3 income**

allows the paralegal to search for words near each other by specifying the number of words apart that is acceptable.

Exhibit 10.18 gives a comparison of these concepts, by VersusLaw, and Exhibit 10.19 gives a guide to connectors from Westlaw.

UPDATING LEGAL RESEARCH

The legal team always must use the most current statutory and case law in advising clients and arguing cases to the court. One of the features of the American legal system is its constant change. Courts attempt to meet the needs of a changing society by reviewing prior case law and, when appropriate, overruling or modifying it as the contemporary American view of justice dictates. The American legal system concept of *stare decisis* provides that we use prior case law as **precedent** but change the law as American society changes. Occasionally, existing case law may be held unconstitutional, such as happened with the landmark case of *Roe v. Wade*.

Knowing if the case law being used in a legal argument is the current case law is a vital part of the lawyer's obligation to the client and to the court. Up to the moment before the arguments are made to the court or the brief is submitted, a case that the attorney or the opponent is using as a basis for a legal argument may be overturned. The ethical obligation of candor to the court and of professional competency requires the use of current case law.

Thus, an essential part of legal research for paralegals is to verify that they have the latest case or statute. The process is complicated by the method by which changes in statutes or case law are released to the public. Ultimately, new statutes and new case law are reported in a published form, both in paper and electronically, but not all publications are able to disseminate the information daily. Paper versions take time to print and distribute. Not all electronic versions are posted immediately. Therefore, it becomes important to know how quickly the reporting or electronic services of the law firm or practice distribute post-statutory changes and new cases. More and more courts have their own websites and release case opinions electronically along with the print versions to the public and publishing companies. For example, you can check decisions of the U.S. Supreme Court daily.

What is difficult is knowing if the new cases or new statutes affect the case being researched. When the court specifically mentions a case being cited in a memo of law or a court brief, the paralegal has to know if the new case follows the older case law, reverses it, or in some way differs from the older case.

As soon as a case is entered into an electronic case law database, such as Westlaw, Lexis, Loislaw, or VersusLaw, a general search can be made for references to the case name or citation. Before it is entered, the same search will not show the newest reference. Even a reference to the case will not tell whether the case law has changed, only that another case has referred to it. Someone must actually read the case to see how the court has used it or referred to it in the opinion.

Shepard's

Long a standard tool of legal research in law libraries, *Shepard's Citations* is a multivolume set of books listing cases and statutes by their respective citations and giving the citation of every other case in which the listed case was mentioned. The listings originally were compiled by editors who physically read through every case reported to find citations. These then were reported by case citation, with every other mention of the case reported by its citation in chronological fashion, with notations indicating if the opinion was reversed, affirmed, followed, overruled, and so on. The process of using *Shepard's* to check legal citations came to be called "Shepardizing"—a term that many legal assistants still use, even when using other citation-checking services such as Westlaw's KeyCite. An advantage to the *Shepard's Citator* is the editorial symbol system used to indicate how the new case affects the case being checked, as shown in Exhibit 10.20.

The problem with the traditional paper form of *Shepard's* is the lag in time for the print version to be prepared and sent out to subscribers. *Shepard's* now provides the same service online through the Lexis service; subscribers can obtain the latest case information, to the day, by calling a toll-free number. One of the difficulties in using the print version of *Shepard's* is the number of hardbound volumes and

Stare decisis
The legal principle that prior case law should apply unless there is a substantial change in society necessitating a change in the case law.

Precedent
Prior case law that is controlling.

Exhibit 10.20 **Shepard's symbols showing effects of new cases**

Shepard's Signal		Positive	Positive treatment indicated. Includes:
⬤ Warning	Strong negative treatment indicated. Includes: • Overruled by • Questioned by • Superceded by • Revoked • Obsolete • Rescinded		• Followed • Affirmed • Approved
		Ⓐ Citing References with Analysis	Other cases cited the case and assigned some analysis that is not considered positive or negative. Includes: • Appeal denied by • Writ of certiorari denied
▲ Caution	Possible negative treatment indicated. Includes: • Limited • Criticized by • Clarified • Modified • Corrected	Ⓘ Citation Information	References have not applied any analysis to the citation. For example the case was cited by law reviews, ALR® Annotations, or in other case law not warranting an analysis. Example: Cited By

Source: Screen capture is reprinted with the permission of LexisNexis. LexisNexis, the Knowledge Burst Logo and *Shepard's* are registered trademarks and *Shepard's Signal* is a trademark of Reed Elsevier Properties, Inc., used with the permission of LexisNexis.

paperback updates required to be consulted, and finding the latest update pamphlet if someone has misfiled it in the law library. Exhibit 10.21 is an example of the print version case presentation in *Shepard's*.

Many educational institutions and public libraries subscribe to the Web-based LexisNexis Academic Universe. *Shepard's* citation service (see Exhibit 10.22) usually is available for the U.S. Supreme Court as part of the service, but other federal and state *Shepard* citation services may not be included because of the cost of the additional license fees involved.

GlobalCite™

GlobalCite
Loislaw's tool for searching cases containing references to another case.

Loislaw's **GlobalCite** provides a reverse chronological list of the case law, the statutes in the order of the highest number of citation occurrences, the regulations listed in relevancy order, and reference to other databases in the Loislaw library. Exhibit 10.23 shows a GlobalCite screen.

KeyCite™

KeyCite
Westlaw's tool for searching cases containing references to another case.

KeyCite is the Westlaw online citation update service. The Westlaw KeyCite is a combination citator and case finder. Unlike other similar services, KeyCite uses the West Key number system and West Headnotes.

V. CITE™

V.Cite
VersusLaw's tool for searching cases containing references to another case.

V. Cite, VersusLaw's new citation tool, will produce a list of all cases within the selected jurisdictions that have cited the case being searched. The list that a V. Cite

Exhibit 10.21 **Example of print version case presentation in *Shepard's***

—157— **Oregon v Plowman 1992**	—558— **Oregon v Plowman 1992**	—558— **Oregon v Plowman 1992**
(838P2d558)	(314Ore157)	(314Ore157)
s 107OrA782	s 813P2d1114	s 813P2d1114
cc 314Ore170	cc 813P2d1115	cc 813P2d1115
e 315Ore375	cc 838P2d566	cc 838P2d566
315Ore380	840P2d1324	840P2d1324
317Ore^{4}258	e 840P2d1325	e 840P2d1325
317Ore451	841P2d650	841P2d650
f 317Ore452	e 845P2d1285	e 845P2d1285
j 317Ore472	845P2d1289	845P2d1289
f 318Ore488	j 851P2d1147	j 851P2d1147
318Ore492	j 852P2d888	j 852P2d888
d 318Ore497	854P2d959	854P2d959
116OrA189	855P2d^{4}625	855P2d^{4}625
e 116OrA192	857P2d107	Calif
h 116OrA265	f 857P2d108	17CaR2d296
j 119OrA303	j 857P2d119	e 19CaR2d448
j 120OrA333	f 871P2d458	e 19CaR2d449
121OrA384	871P2d461	Iowa
j 128OrA14	d 871P2d463	500N W 42
71OLR689	j 874P2d1348	
22A5268n		

Shepard's Oregon Citations, *Oregon Reports division,* shows citations from:

• *state reports*
• Oregon Law Review
• *annotations*
(*ALR*® 5th)

Shepard's Oregon Citations, *Oregon Cases division, shows citations from Oregon as published in the* Pacific Reporter.

Shepard's Pacific Reporter Citations, *P.2d division, shows citations from all cases published in a West regional reporter.*

search produces will include cases that have cited the initial case, which most likely will discuss similar issues. Using the added V. Cite feature allows the appending of a specific term to the search request. For example, including the word "damages" in the "additional query information" section of the V. Cite form will restrict the search to cases that cite the searched case and also discuss "damages."

PARALLEL CITATIONS

Most cases are reported in more than one service or set of books. A **parallel citation** is a cite to the same material, usually a case, in another source. Frequently a state has an official publication, such as the court's own publication, and a private publication, such as the *West Reporter*. In some cases, *West* was and is the official reporter, and there may not be a parallel print source. One of the many uses of *Shepard's* is to find the parallel citation to other locations for the same case.

Shepard's also provides update information on statutory citations. Amendments and repeals of statutory information are listed in *Shepard's*. Citations to any cases in which the statute has been cited also are listed, with information on how the case law considered the statute.

Parallel citation
The citation to the same case in a diffent publication.

Exhibit 10.22 **LexisNexis Total Shepard's® Table of Authorities**

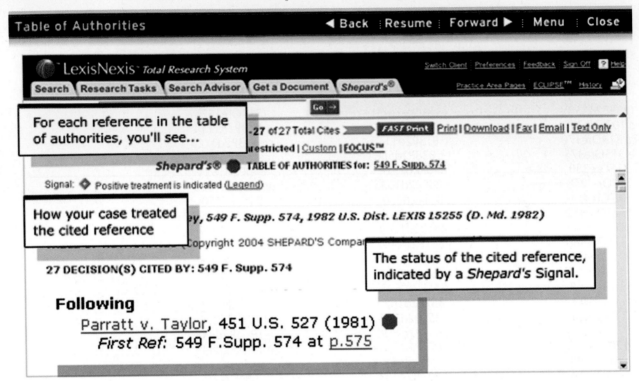

Exhibit 10.23 **GlobalCite screen**

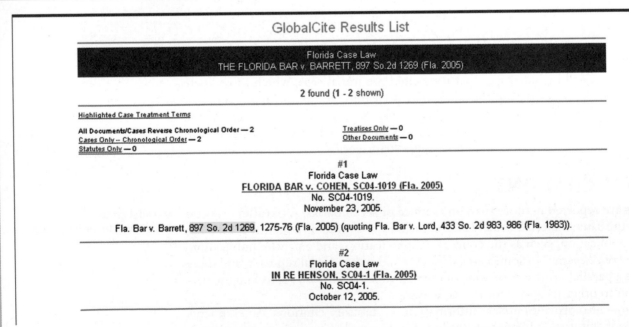

checklist ✓

RESEARCH SEARCH ITEMS

☐ Client: ☐ Date:

☐ Issue:

☐ Search terms and phrases:

☐ Search combinations used:

checklist ✓

RESEARCH SOURCES CHECKED

CHECKED SOURCE	CITATION	POCKET PART CHECKED ▼	WEB LOCATION
Primary Sources			
State statute			www.
USC			www.
USCA			www.
CFR			www.
Local ordinance			www.
			www.
Secondary Sources			
State digest			www.
Federal digest			www.
ALR			www.
			www.
Encyclopedia			www.
State			www.
C.J.S.			www.
Periodicals			www.
Treatises			www.

Legal Terminology

Summary

CHAPTER 10

TRADITIONAL COMPUTER AND INTERNET LEGAL RESEARCH

Legal Research

Definition	Legal research is a process for finding the answer to a legal question.
Creating a Research Plan	The research plan helps to focus on the issues, sources, and methods for finding the answer and controlling law.
What Is the Issue or Legal Question?	What are the relevant facts or statutory materials?
What Is the Appropriate Search Terminology?	Print research materials require finding material based on a printed index of individual words as selected by editors of the service. Computer research allows for searches of words found in the documents using a text search of requested words in the search query.
What Type of Research Material Is Available?	The paralegal must be able to find the information needed when the familiar resources are not available. Paralegals cannot be sure whether the research will be done using a traditional paper library or a computer search; they must understand how each resource files the information.
What Jurisdiction or Jurisdictions Are Involved?	Focusing on a single jurisdiction or a minimum number of jurisdictions reduces the numbers of traditional volumes of books necessary and saves online computer search time.
What Is the Controlling Law?	Knowing which set of materials to use, the statutes of the jurisdiction, the regulation of a given administrative agency, or the courts of a given jurisdiction will save time in doing the research.
What Are the Types of Resources to Be Used?	1. Primary sources of law are used in preparing the legal memo or brief. 2. Secondary sources are useful, efficient ways to get an overview of an area of law or learn the terminology of a particular field of law in which the paralegal is not familiar. 3. Finding tools are publications containing tools for finding both primary and secondary sources.
Where Should the Needed Research Material Be Located?	The needed material may have to be located at a remote library such as a bar association library or a law school library.
Creating a List of Research Terms	Separate lists should be created for online searches and traditional print sources.

Executing the Research Plan	As with the execution of any plan, detours can be expected, as the law is in a constant evolutionary state. New statutes are enacted, and new case interpretations are handed down. During the research process, the researcher must look for changes and potential changes from pending legislation and cases on appeal.

Finding the Law

The Controlling Law	The controlling law may be found at federal, state, or local legislative or judicial levels.
Primary Sources and Authority	Primary sources include the law, constitutions, statutes, regulations, court rules, and case decisions.
Mandatory and Persuasive Authority	1. Mandatory authority is legal authority that the courts must follow. 2. Persuasive authority is legal authority the courts are not required to follow but is from a respected source and well reasoned.
Constitutions	Constitutions are primary sources that set the guidelines, limits, and authority of the federal government and the state governments.
Statutes	Statutes are enacted by the legislative branch of government.
Court Decisions	The actual court language is a primary source of the law. The syllabus, summaries, interpretations, or abstracts of the points of law presented by the editorial staffs of the publishers of the case law—usually called headnotes—are not the primary source of law.
Secondary Sources	Secondary sources explain the law. 1. Legal dictionaries, as opposed to general English or other specialized dictionaries, define words and phrases as used in the law. 2. Legal encyclopedias provide the background to understand the area enough to start the research. They provide an overview of the concepts and history of an area of law, the legal issues involved, and the terminology. 3. Treatises, Law Reviews, and Legal Periodicals are authoritative or of sufficient scholarly value to be persuasive to the court.
Finding Tools	Finding tools help to "find" the law. 1. Digests provide lists of cases in a subject topic format, with cases generally in chronological order. 2. Indexes and citators cross-reference material, such as by the commonly used or popular name of a case or statute.

Personal Research Strategy

	Over time, each paralegal develops a personal search strategy based on the nature of the problem or issue to be researched and the resources available. Methods of verifying that the law and cases cited in your research and memo of law is current law or current authority, and methods for looking for pending cases and legislation that might change the answer to the legal question.
Final word on executing the legal research plan	Know when to ask for help.

Using Printed Legal Reference Works

Common Features	Table of abbreviations Table of contents in the front Index of terms in the back Table of cases and citations
Updates	Print material is frequently updated with pocket parts, usually issued annually, slipped into the back of the volume in a pocket. Paperback supplements are issued annually, quarterly, or monthly. Online updates from the publishers are increasingly available for some materials.

Computer Research

Query Search	A combination of words, phrases and connectors used to search for a desired answer
Constructing a Computer Search Query	Each online provider uses words to find and retrieve documents. As part of the publication process, indexes are prepared of every word in the document, the words are tabulated for frequency, and a word index is prepared. The search created searches this index.
Creating a Computer Search	The search engine is used to find the indexed words the paralegal has chosen; they may be legal specialty words or common English words. Using combinations of words in the search can narrow the search results.
Search Method and Query Connectors in Legal Research	AND instructs the search not to return documents in which only one of the words is found. OR instructs the search engine to find either term. NEAR may be used to find the occurrence of desired words within a set number of words of each other.
Updating Legal Research	1. Shepard's: A multivolume set of books listing cases and statutes by their respective citations and giving the citation of every other case in which the listed case was mentioned; checking citations is often called "Shepardizing." 2. GlobalCite (Loislaw): Provides a reverse chronological list of the case law, a list of statutes in the order of the highest number of citation occurrences, regulations in relevancy order, and reference to other databases in Loislaw library 3. KeyCite (Westlaw): Online citation update service 4. V. CITE (VersusLaw) Online citation tool
Parallel Citation	A citation to the same material, usually a case, in another source
Statutory Law Updates	*Shepard's* provides updated information on amendments and repeals of statutory information. Citations to any cases in which the statute has been cited are also listed, with information on how the case law considered the statute.

▶WORKING THE WEB

1. Use the Government Printing Office website to find and print out the summary purpose of 21 CFR 404, or any other section assigned by your instructor. **www.gpoaccess.gov**

2. Make a list of the available federal primary sources available on the Government Printing Office website.

3. From the sitemap of the VersusLaw website, print out for your future computer searches the printable version of the *Versuslaw Research Manual* **http://www.versuslaw.com/features/sitemap.htm**

4. Use the Legal Information Institute at the Cornell University website to find title 44 C.F.R. 201 and print out the list of key responsibilities of FEMA and state and local/tribal governments. **http://lii.law.cornell.edu/**. Does this site provide direct access or a link to another source? Explain. What primary federal sources does this site offer?

5. Conduct a search for information on paralegal ethics using two different search engines, and print out a copy of the first page of each result. Are they the same? What is the difference in results and order of presentation? Possible search engines include: Google, **www.google.com**; Yahoo, **www.yahoo.com**; Ask Jeeves, **www.ask.com**; Findlaw, **www.findlaw.com**.

6. If you have access to Loislaw, NexisLexis, Westlaw, or VersusLaw, conduct a search for paralegal ethics cases for your jurisdiction. Prepare a list of authorities cited in the search.

7. Print out the current list of opinions of the U.S. Supreme Court at **http://www.supremecourtus.gov**.

8. Print out the complete version of Rule 3.3, Candor Toward the Tribunal, of the *ABA Model Rules of Professional Conduct* at **http://www.abanet.org/cpr/mrpc/mrpc_toc.html**.

9. Under the theory of *stare decisis*, on which courts would the decisions of a court have a binding effect? Would a decision in a case be binding on future cases if the decision were available only in the clerks' office?

10. Would your answer be the same if the decision were available in the clerk's office at first but then available in printed form or online at a later date? When would the decision become effective as precedent?

11. Where is the "law" found?

12. Who makes the "law" under the United States system?

13. What is meant by a "bicameral" legislature?

14. In legal research, what is meant by "primary source?"

15. What is a "treatise?" Is it a primary source? Explain.

16. What is a headnote in legal research? Is it a primary source? Explain.

17. What is dicta? What is its effect on other courts? Explain.

18. Of what weight do courts give secondary sources? Explain fully.

19. Why are finding tools important to the legal researcher? Give an example of how a finding tool might be used.

20. On which courts would the decisions of a court have binding effect under the theory of *stare decisis*?

21. Would a decision in a case be binding on future cases if the decision were available only in the clerks' office?

22. Would your answer be the same if the decision were available in the clerk's office at first but then available in printed form or online at a later date? When would the decision become effective as precedent?

23. Do unpublished opinions have precedential effect? Explain.

▶ CRITICAL THINKING AND WRITING QUESTIONS

1. Using the facts in the *Palsgraph* case in Appendix A, prepare a search query using connectors to locate the law or a similar case in your jurisdiction. Run the search using an online legal research service, if available.

2. Why does a paralegal have to be familiar with both traditional and electronic research tools and methods?

3. Why does the paralegal have to know how quickly changes in statutory and case law are updated by online and traditional primary and secondary sources?

4. Why is knowledge of the underlying law in an area important in constructing a question for online research?

5. How can a researcher be certain that a case that seems to be on point is still the current case law?

6. Why should secondary sources not be relied upon in citing binding authority?

7. Why would a researcher use a traditional paper resource before using an online research tool?

8. How does the use of connectors help in conducting online research? Give an example.

9. Why might an identical search query return different results?

10. Why must researchers clearly understand the question they are being asked to research? How can they be certain they do?

▶ ETHICS ANALYSIS AND DISCUSSION QUESTIONS

1. Is there an ethical obligation under the Model Rules to perform legal research competently? Explain.

2. What is the ethical obligation under the Model Rules to provide the court with legal authority that is not favorable to your client's legal position?

3. What is the ethical obligation to "Shepardize" cases and statutes before submitting a brief or memo of law to the court?

For answers, look at American Bar Association Rule 3.3, Candor Toward the Tribunal, and Rule 1.1, Competence (ABA *Model Rules of Professional Conduct*, 2002).

Confidentiality

There are few certainties in the area of ethics, for paralegals or in any profession. What qualifies as ethical conduct is in most cases based on state law and court interpretation applied to a set of facts. The citation listed below represents one legal opinion and is provided as a research starting point. Do not assume that the same rule applies in your jurisdiction. For the following:

- Prepare a written statement based on your state law.
- Use your state bar association website as a starting point.

You are waiting for a fax needed for a case on which you are working. While you are standing by the fax machine, a fax comes in from an attorney at an opposing firm containing a letter about settlement that was clearly intended for the attorney's client and not for opposing counsel. Your best friend in the office is the paralegal who is working on that case at the other law office. She is stressed out by the case and made the mistake of dialing your fax number. From your reading of the letter it appears the information will be of major help in your law office winning the case. [*ABA Formal Ethics Opinion, State Compensation Insurance Fund v. The WPS, Inc.*, 70 CA 4644; 82 C.R.2 799 (1999)] Do you quietly return the fax to your friend and say nothing to anyone? Do you read it carefully to be sure of the contents? Do you return it to opposing counsel? Do you tell your supervising attorney about the letter? The contents?

▶ DEVELOPING YOUR COLLABORATION SKILLS

Working on your own or with a group of other students assigned by your instructor, review the scenario at the beginning of the chapter and discuss the different views on law libraries, including traditional versus computer legal research.

1. Write a summary of the potential advantages and disadvantages of each point of view.

2. Prepare a report to the executive committee, considering the different views of members of the firm with a solution that might satisfy most users of the firm's library.

3. The group is divided into two teams. One team will conduct a research assignment using traditional methods and the other will use computer research tools.
   a. Each team is to complete the Research Sources Checked checklist and prepare a copy for the members of the other team and your instructor.
   b. After you have completed the research, prepare a short memorandum of law to submit to your instructor.

4. Complete a second research project with each team now using the other approach to research. The traditional methods team now will use computer tools, and the computer tools team will conduct the research using traditional tools. Prepare a short memorandum and complete the Research Sources Checked checklist.

5. Based on your experience doing traditional and computer research, what recommendations would you make to the managing partner in the opening scenario?

▶ PARALEGAL PORTFOLIO EXERCISE

Complete the "Web Location" section portion of the Research Sources Checked checklist. When preparing the list, include alternative sources where available. Print a copy for your portfolio for future use and a copy for your instructor.

▶ LEGAL ANALYSIS AND WRITING CASES

American Geophysical Union v. Texaco Inc. 37 F.3d 881 (2d Cir. 1994)

Copying of Material for Future Research and Law Library Archives from Copyrighted Magazines and Journals

Most researchers understand that misuse of copyright material may subject them to liability under the copyright laws. The case of *American Geophysical Union v. Texaco* illustrates the potential liability in regularly copying copyrighted articles for personal archives. Researchers of Texaco regularly made copies of articles for future reference from the works of the plaintiff and 82 other publishers of scientific and technical journals. Texaco raised the defense of "fair use" as permitted under the copyright law.

Fair use as a defense depends on four tests: (1) the purpose and character of the use—including whether for nonprofit educational purposes or commercial use; (2) the nature of copyright work—the law generally recognizes a greater need to disseminate factual works than works of fiction or fantasy; (3) amount and substantiality of portion used—was the quantity used reasonable in relation to the purpose of the copying? (4) effect on potential market or value—will the copying have an impact on the sale of the works, and is there an efficient mechanism for the licensing of the works?

Questions

1. How does copyright law apply to a student copying copyrighted materials while doing research for a class project?

2. Would the answer be the same if the student were doing the research as part of an assignment while working in a law office?

3. Does it matter if the work copied is a court case or an article by an expert in automobile airbags liability? Why?

LEGAL WRITING AND CRITICAL LEGAL THINKING

"Justice is the end of government. It is the end of civil society. It ever has been, and ever will be pursued, until it be obtained, or until liberty be lost in the pursuit."

James Madison

PARALEGALS AT WORK

Amanda Chen had worked for the law firm of Douglas and Myers only a few weeks when the senior partner, who specialized in mergers and acquisitions, asked her to sit in on the initial meeting of a long-term client and the client's daughter. One of the more senior paralegals on staff told Amanda that her role was to take notes. The partner never took notes. He conducted the interview, asked the questions, and didn't want anyone else to interfere.

After escorting the client and the client's daughter, Bill and Tonya Johnson, from the reception area to the partner's office, Amanda was asked to take a seat in the corner and record the meeting notes. Bill Johnson made it clear that he was paying the bill and that he expected his attorney to get the charges of driving under the influence against Tonya dropped. Tonya acknowledged that she had been drinking at a country western bar and knew she was well over the legal drinking limit. She had tested her alcohol level on a breath analyzer that the bar made available to its patrons.

Upon leaving the bar, Tonya went out to her car, got in, started it, and then fell asleep at the wheel. A police officer found her in this condition, woke her, and took her to the hospital for a blood alcohol test. The officer cited her for operating a vehicle while under the influence of alcohol, based on her .09% blood alcohol reading.

After the clients left, the partner told Amanda to prepare a memorandum of law that he could use to get the charges against the client's daughter dismissed.

After doing a little research, Amanda realized that the law was against the client's getting the charges dismissed. Furthermore, in the meeting with her father and the partner, Tonya had admitted to being intoxicated. Based on the advice from the other paralegals, Amanda was concerned about putting anything negative into the memo and decided to write a memo presenting a case for dismissal.

Consider the issues involved in this scenario as you read the chapter.

After studying this chapter, you should be able to:

1. Explain the process of critical legal thinking.

2. Define the ethical duty of candor.

3. Describe the similarities and differences between a memorandum of law and a court brief.

4. Explain the reasons for the various citation format rules.

5. Explain and describe the need for, and how to use, proper citation format.

▶INTRODUCTION FOR THE PARALEGAL

Legal writing and critical legal thinking are intertwined. Legal writing can take a number of forms, memos, letters, opinions, memoranda of law for internal purposes, and briefs for the court. The differences in presentation are determined by the intended audience. The similarities are in the needs for clarity and accuracy. Preparation of these documents starts with an understanding of the material facts of a case and identifying the legal issues. Critical legal thinking is used to identify what is material, what law applies, and then to apply the law to the facts and come to a conclusion that answers the issue or issues presented. ■

CRITICAL LEGAL THINKING

Critical legal thinking The process of identifying the issue, the material facts, and the applicable law and applying the law to come to a conclusion.

Issue The legal matter in dispute.

Critical legal thinking is the process of identifying the **issue**—the legal matter in dispute—presented by a case, identifying the material (also called key or relevant) facts in the case and the applicable law, and then applying the law to the facts to come to a conclusion that answers the issue or issues presented. Critical legal thinking is the thought process that puts the pieces of the legal puzzle together. The critical thinking process starts with a clear understanding of the facts of the client's case and identifying the legal issues in that case.

Before starting the research, one must have a clear picture of all the material facts. Part of the interview with the client is to determine all the facts. Some of what the client thinks are important facts may in fact not be relevant in deciding the legal issue. And some of the facts that seemed unimportant to the client may in fact be relevant and on which the outcome may depend. For example, it may not seem important that the client was struck by a driver going north. It may be a material fact when it is determined that the street was a one-way street going south.

Consider the timeline on a contract case. Assume that a client signed an employee noncompetition contract three months after starting employment. State law may deny the enforceability of the covenant not to compete unless entered into before commencing employment or unless contemporary, full and adequate consideration is given for signing the agreement after commencing employment.

Understanding the relevant facts enables a review of the court cases and the statutory law to determine applicability to the client case. A difference of one fact may make all the difference in the world in the outcome of the case. Consider the case of the client charged with killing King Kong. The facts indicate that King Kong is not a human being. The murder statute of the jurisdiction defines murder as the taking of the life of a human being by another human being; therefore, the statute has not been violated. Other statutes may have been violated, but not the murder statute. The client may be guilty of hunting out of season, hunting without a license, or killing an endangered species, but not murder.

For these issues, additional facts, immaterial in the murder prosecution, may become material. The material facts also would be different in the civil action by the owner of the animal in a suit for damages for loss of an irreplaceable item. What is relevant as a fact depends on the type of case—civil or criminal—and the wrong committed or the right violated.

The American justice system is based on the statutory law and case law. Just as in the criminal law issues discussed above, factual analysis requires determining the elements of the crime, looking at the statute, and applying the facts. It may be necessary to look at case law for precedent on the definition of an operative fact. For example, all states have laws prohibiting driving under the influence of alcohol. Some of these statutes also use the terms "vehicle" and "operating." One of the material facts for the researcher to determine is what is defined as a vehicle and what conduct is defined as "operating."

ALASKA CASE LAW

WHITING v. STATE, A-8755 (Alaska App. 10-12-2005)

MANNHEIMER, Judge.

Michael T. Whiting appeals his conviction for felony driving under the influence, . . . the facts . . . : Whiting and his girlfriend and his girlfriend's six-year-old son decided to go fishing in Gastineau Channel. Whiting piloted a skiff into the channel and then turned the motor off. The three occupants of the skiff fished while the skiff drifted in the channel; Whiting sat in the rear of the skiff near the motor. While Whiting was fishing, he was also drinking alcoholic beverages.

A Coast Guard vessel approached the skiff . . . , discovered that he was under the influence. Whiting claimed that he had been sober when he piloted the boat into the channel, and that he did not become intoxicated until after he stopped the motor and the fishing began.

. . . Whiting's argument hinges on his assertion that the statutory definition of driving under the influence, AS 28.35.030(a) does not include the situation where an intoxicated person is in control of a watercraft whose engine is not running. Whiting's assertion is incorrect. . . . this Court held that "operating" a watercraft includes being in control of the watercraft, even if its engine is not running.

We addressed essentially the same argument in *Kingsley v. State*, 11 p. 3d 1001 (Alaska App. 2000). The defendant in *Kingsley* drove his car into a snow berm, where it became stuck. Kingsley turned the engine off and decided to remain in the car. According to Kingsley, it was only then that he consumed a bottle of whiskey and became intoxicated.

Kingsley argued that, under these circumstances, he was not intoxicated when he was operating the vehicle, and he was never in "control" of the vehicle after he became intoxicated. We rejected this narrow definition of "control".

As Kingsley acknowledges in his brief to this court, a person who engages the engine of a vehicle and allows it to run is not merely exercising physical control over the vehicle but is also "operating" it. Thus, if the engine of Kingsley's vehicle had been running when the police arrived, the State might have proved that Kingsley was operating the vehicle while intoxicated. But the State had to prove only that Kingsley was in actual physical control of the vehicle while intoxicated.

. . . A person's attempt to operate a vehicle may furnish convincing proof that the person is in actual physical control of the vehicle, but a person may exercise actual physical control over a vehicle without making active attempts to operate it.

Whiting was the one who had piloted the skiff into the channel, and Whiting remained primarily in the rear of the skiff, nearest the motor, while his girlfriend and her son sat in the front of the skiff. Under these facts, as a matter of law, Whiting was in physical control of the skiff, and he was therefore operating the skiff for purposes of the DUI statute.

Defense counsel must look carefully to try to differentiate the client's fact pattern from decided cases. Slight variations in facts can be important in successfully arguing a case, or at least make a compelling argument.

Facts are pieces of information or details that in actuality or reality exist, or have occurred, as opposed to someone's theory, supposition, or conjecture. Facts, in the law, are the circumstances of an event, motion, occurrence, or state of affairs, rather than interpretations of its significance. The car was going south on State Street at 55 miles per hour as shown on the radar unit. These are facts. Supposition, conjecture, or theory, and not fact is the statement of the witness that everyone speeds down the street in front of their house, that the defendant has done it before, that they heard the car driven by the defendant while they were in the house watching TV facing away from the street, and that they heard the car going south at 55 mph.

Facts
Information or details.

Material facts
A fact significant or essential to the issue.

Immaterial facts
A fact not essential to the matter or issue at hand.

Facts may be divided into **material** (relevant) **facts** and **immaterial** (irrelevant) **facts**. A material fact is a fact that is significant or essential to the issue or matter at hand. An immaterial fact is one that is not essential to the matter at issue. Some facts, while not material, may lead to material facts. Consider the case of the person coming from the doctor's office, driving within the speed limit, who strikes another car in the rear at a red stoplight. Is the fact that he was coming from a doctor's office a material fact in the accident? It may be if he were given medication that caused blurred vision or drowsiness and if the doctor told him not to drive or operate any machinery. Certainly knowing this fact leads to the discovery of other relevant facts.

LEGAL WRITING

There are as many writing styles as there are writers. Writers of novels have a style of writing that may devote pages to setting a stage for the characters and more pages developing the characters. Readers probably come to expect this and look forward to long paragraphs building the scene and setting the stage for the plot.

Writers of short stories are more like skilled legal writers. They must quickly and accurately set the stage in few words and tell the story in a short space. Skilled legal writers are those that can explain, persuade, and state facts for the record accurately, concisely, and clearly. The purpose of writing is to communicate. If the writing does not communicate the subject to the reader, it has not served its purpose. Unlike the novelist or poet, the legal writer must follow a set of guidelines dictated by ethical concerns for honesty and candor, while at the same time clearly present the answer to clients that they may not want to hear, or persuade the court to the advocated point of view.

WRITING STYLES

Memorandum
A working legal document for the legal team for use in preparation and presentation of a case.

Both the brief and the memorandum may be on the exact same set of facts, legal issue, and applicable law, but the writing style is totally different. The **memorandum** is a working document for the legal team to be used in the preparation and presentation of a case. As a result, it has to be an objective analysis of the case, including factual subtleties and analysis of the applicable law with any alternate interpretations. The brief written for the court is designed to provide written advocacy of the client's position and must be written to convince the court to adopt a position favorable to the client.

checklist ✓

MEMORANDUM OF LAW TEMPLATE

- ☐ To:
- ☐ From:
- ☐ Date:
- ☐ Subject:
- ☐ Facts
- ☐ Issue(s)
- ☐ Discussion
- ☐ Conclusion

Duty of Candor

Above all is an obligation to be honest with the court, called the **duty of candor**. The legal team has an ethical obligation not to mislead the court. Just one brief that intentionally distorts or hides the truth or intentionally misleads the court can destroy a legal career. Even if it doesn't result in sanctions, suspension, or disbarment, judges talk with their colleagues, and a bad reputation for integrity to the court is hard to correct. At the least, the court always will remember that the attorney did shoddy work and may give more credibility to the opposing side in the future, even if later cases by the offending attorney are better prepared and more accurately on point.

Duty of candor
Honesty to the court.

PREPARING OFFICE MEMORANDUM

In doing research and preparing the memorandum of law, the legal assistant must be careful to include all the relevant applicable statutes and case law. Some paralegals are intimidated by the gruff and even downright nasty attitude of certain lawyers, particularly trial counsel in the middle of a stressful case. The paralegals are afraid the lawyer will "shoot the messenger." The reality is that the attorney *must* know the weaknesses in the case along with the strengths. Nothing is more upsetting to the attorney, whether in court or in a meeting with a client or opposing counsel, than to be surprised by a case, facts, or law that has not been covered in the office memorandum of law.

Office memoranda are frequently indexed by subject and filed in the office for future reference. If the same or a similar fact pattern requires research, these provide a good starting point and can be a major time-saver. So that a memorandum may be indexed properly, the facts upon which the conclusion is based must be clearly stated. All statutes, regulations, and cases must be cited properly so anyone reading the memorandum in the future can look them up. Listing relevant websites used in the preparation also is helpful.

Starting Point

The starting point for the legal researcher is to understand the specific assigment. What is it that the researcher has been asked to research? For the memorandum of law, it usually is to answer a question:

> What is the current law on . . . ?
> What happens if . . . ?
> What is the procedure for . . . ?

Before starting an assignment, the paralegal must be certain what is really being asked. Any questions should be resolved by asking the person for whom this is being prepared: "What does the attorney expect?" Where the paralegal's knowledge of the subject area is sufficient, he or she may know that certain facts may change the outcome—such as the requirement in some states that a subscribing witness to a decedent's will cannot be a beneficiary. Before starting, paralegals must be sure to have all the relevant facts, then restate what they believe they are being asked to research in the form of a statement of the question. For example: "You have asked for the law on the rights of individuals to . . . ."

Part of the skill in legal writing is using analytical skills to find the similarities and differences in cases that can be used as persuasive argument for the position being presented for the client. This is the critical legal thinking aspect of the legal writing process. And writing is a process. It requires research, analysis, organization, writing, editing, and proofreading. Sometimes it requires starting over when the final document when viewed from the position of the ultimate reader does not communicate the necessary information or tell the story.

ETHICAL *Perspective*

ABA Model Rules of Professional Conduct
Rule 3.3 Candor Toward The Tribunal

(a) A lawyer shall not knowingly: . . .

(b) fail to disclose to the tribunal legal authority in the controlling jurisdiction known to the lawyer to be directly adverse to the position of the client and not disclosed by opposing counsel; or . . .

The Model rules of professional conduct require candor to the court. This includes the obligation to present opposing case law is relevant to the case at hand. It is not ethically acceptable to hide negative precedent from the court. This does not mean the advocate cannot present persuasive arguments for changing the case law.

See Appendix B for Commentary and complete Model Rule 3.3.

Source: *ABA* Model Rules for Professional Conduct, 2004 Edition. © *2003 by the American Bar Association. Reprinted with permission. Copies of ABA* Model Rules of Professional Conduct, 2004 Edition *are available from Service Center, American Bar Association, 321 North Clark St., Chicago, IL 60610, 1-800-285-2221.*

In the legal working environment, time to rethink, re-research and rewrite is a luxury. The pressure is on developing good skills to minimize the time necessary to produce an acceptable document, whether it is a letter, an office memorandum, or a court brief.

Memorandum of Law Format

A memo is frequently prepared by the supervising attorney with a request for research and an office memorandum of a specific subject or case. A sample of an assignment memo is shown in Exhibit 11.1. Frequently, the assignment is given in a face-to-face meeting. When the assignment is made orally, it is a good idea to confirm the specific assignment if there is any question of the details required.

The format or template for office memoranda is fairly standard, as shown in the Memorandum of Law Template. Some offices may add, for identification purposes, headings such as office file numbers or client identifiers. Some offices that maintain a paper format include subject matter legal terms or areas of law so they can be filed and retrieved if future cases require a memorandum on the same subject. Copies of memorandum are increasingly stored electronically as word processor files. These electronic files can be searched using a search function such as the file search function in Microsoft Word shown in Exhibit 11.2.

When taking an assignment to do research and write a memorandum, a few basics have to be remembered. The attorney, in all probability, will not redo the research or do much more than refer to the material submitted with the memorandum. The memorandum must be an unbiased presentation of the law as it exists, clearly presented. If the content of the memorandum is not accurate and complete, the attorney relying on the analysis and discussion may be, at the least, embarrassed by the opposing counsel or, worst, by the court.

Points to remember in preparing a memorandum of law are:

- **Never** rely on case law headnotes. Headnotes are not a primary source of the law.
- **Always** check the language of the court cases. It is the primary authority.
- **Check** the dates of the cases and of the statutes. Be sure they are current law.
- **Shepardize** (GlobalCite, KeyCite, V.Cite) the cases you used and relied on to be certain they have not been overruled by a later case or law.
- **Don't** be afraid to show the cases and law against your client's position.
- **Cite all** sources used. Never plagiarize.

Exhibit 11.1 Assignment memo

MEMORANDUM

To: Edith Hannah
From: Glenn Hains
Date: January 23, 2006
File   Number: GH 06-1002
Re: Commonwealth of Pennsylvania vs. Kevin Dones

Our client was stopped by a police officer at the bottom of the hill on route 332 in Northhampton Township, at 3:30 on Sunday afternoon, January 15, 2006. He was riding a bicycle south on route 332 and was given a citation for speeding. The police used a radar unit and claimed a speed of 35 mph in a 25 mph zone. He administered a field sobriety test, which gave a reading over the legal limit, and client was given a citation for driving under the influence. He tells me he was riding a bike because his license was suspended for a previous DUI.

Please prepare a brief memorandum of law, with citations and cases.

Exhibit 11.2 Word search function

Source: Microsoft product screen shots reprinted with permission from Microsoft Corporation.

■ **Analyze** opposing case law for any differences that may give the attorney a chance to argue that the negative cases are different in some factual or legal way.

■ **Ask,** if you don't understand the issues or question involved. It is better to admit that you are having a problem with the research than to give the attorney wrong, incomplete, or unintelligible information.

The format of the memorandum of law is determined by the nature of the assignment, the number of issues, and the ultimate use that will be made of the memorandum, as well as personal preferences of the person making the assignment.

The components of a memorandum of law and the components of a court opinion (case) are similar. Exhibit 11.3 presents a comparison.

Some case opinions have a brief summary or syllabus of the case that is prepared by an editor, such as the West editors or Supreme Court editors, which is not an official part of the case but is provided for reader convenience. Some attorneys prefer to have a Brief Answer under the Statement of the Assignment in a Memorandum of Law. The brief answer is generally a shortened version of the main points of the conclusion.

Samples of a traditional memorandum of law and one prepared for internal government use are shown in Exhibits 11.4 and 11.5.

If you have ever "briefed" a case you will notice the similarity to the list of items shown in the comparison above. A sample of a case and a case brief is provided in Appendix A: How to Brief a Case.

Facts

Paralegals, of course, must have a clear statement of the facts from which to work. The facts relied upon in writing the memo must be part of the ultimate final memorandum. Other people may read the memorandum. They need to understand the specific facts upon which the analysis is based, particularly if they read it at a time when the paralegal is not available to answer questions, such as the middle of a case, out ill, on vacation, or after the paralegal has left the firm. It also is frequently necessary to recite other facts not relied upon and the reason for not considering them—that the result would be different. An example is a notation that this fact pattern is based upon the participants' all being over the age of majority for contracting, or over the age to purchase and consume alcoholic beverages.

Exhibit 11.3 Components of memorandum of law and court opinion

COURT OPINIONS	MEMORANDUM OF LAW
Caption: Parties, citation, relevant dates	**Heading:** Assigning party, client, file number
Judicial history: Prior proceeding (how the case got to this court)	**Statement of the assignment:** History of what happened and why the client sought representation
Issue: Legal question before the court	**Issue:** Legal issues of clients raised in statement of assignment
Facts: Relevant facts used to decide case	**Statement of facts:** Relevant facts
Analysis and discussion: Discussion of the facts, rules of law, issues, judicial reasons for decision	**Analysis and discussion:** Discussion of each issue, how the applicable law applies, what relevant facts impact the decision.
Conclusion: Holding of the Court	**Conclusion:** Restatement of the conclusion to each issue analyzed and discussed above, summarizing the main points.

Exhibit 11.4 **Sample memorandum of law prepared by leading legal research provider**

MEMORANDUM OF LAW

TO: Ellen Holroyd, Esq.

FROM: ██████████████████

DATE: January 29, 2004

RE: SEC Definitions of Terms Under the Sarbanes-Oxley Act of 2002

QUESTION PRESENTED

With regard to its regulations promulgated pursuant to the Sarbanes-Oxley Act of 2002, how does the Security and Exchange Commission define the concepts "material violation", "credible evidence", and "reasonable behavior" by an attorney?

DISCUSSION

Section 307 of the Sarbanes-Oxley Act of 2002 ("Sarbanes-Oxley") requires the Securities and Exchange Commission ("SEC") to "prescribe minimum standards of professional conduct for attorneys appearing and practicing before the Commission in any way in the representation of issuers." Implementation of Standards of Professional Conduct for Attorneys, Securities Act Release No. 33,8185, 68 Fed. Reg. 6,296 (Feb. 6, 2003.) According to the SEC, these standards "must include a rule requiring an attorney to report evidence of a material violation of securities laws or breach of fiduciary duty or similar violation by the issuer." Id., at 6,296. This memorandum discusses the definitions embraced by the SEC for "material violation," "credible evidence," and "reasonable behavior" by an attorney, three concepts found in the regulations adopted by the SEC pertaining to Sarbanes-Oxley.

(continued)

Exhibit 11.7 **Comparison of selected ALWD third edition rules and bluebook 18th edition rules** *(continued)*

RULE	ALWD CITATION	BLUEBOOK CITATION	DIFFERENCES
Footnotes and endnotes **ALWD:** Rule 7 **BB:** Rule 3.2(b)–(c)	n. 7 nn. 12–13	n. 7 nn. 12–13	ALWD requires a space after n. or nn. abbreviation.
Supra* and *infra **ALWD:** Rule 10 **BB:** Rule 3.5	*Supra* n. 45.	*Supra* note 45.	Under ALWD, abbreviate note as "n." and place a space after the period.
***Id*.** **ALWD:** Rule 11.3 **BB:** B5.2, Rules 4.1, 10.9 & 12.9	*Id.* at 500.	*Id.* at 500.	Basically similar rules. ALWD eliminates the "5 *id.* in a row" rule found in Bluebook Rule 10.9. In the ALWD Manual, *id.* cannot be used with Practitioner and Court documents. Rule 29.6.
Cases **ALWD:** Rule 12 **BB:** B5 & Rule 10	*Brown v. Bd. of Educ.*, 349 U.S. 294, 297 (1955). *MBNA Am. Bank, N.A. v. Cardoso*, 707 N.E.2d 189 (Ill. App. 1st Dist. 1998). [required inclusion of district court information]	*Brown v. Bd. of Educ.*, 349 U.S. 294, 297 (1955). *MBNA Am. Bank, N.A. v. Cardoso*, 707 N.E.2d 189 (Ill. App. Ct. 1st Dist. 1998). [permissive inclusion of district information]	Under ALWD, case names are always italicized or underlined. Under ALWD, you do not have to abbreviate words in case names. For those who want to abbreviate, Appendix 3 provides a longer list of words that are abbreviated. ALWD requires division and district information for state appellate courts, and eliminates "Ct." from most court abbreviations. For cases cited from Westlaw or LexisNexis, ALWD does not require the docket number of the case. ALWD also requires two asterisks to identify multiple pages of a pinpoint cite.
Constitutions **ALWD:** Rule 13 **BB:** B7 & Rule 11	U.S. Const. amend. V.	U.S. Const. amend. V.	No substantial differences.
Statutes **ALWD:** Rule 14	18 U.S.C. § 1965 (2000).	18 U.S.C § 1965 (2000).	No substantial differences.

Exhibit 11.7 **Comparison of selected ALWD third edition rules and bluebook 18th edition rules** *(continued)*

RULE	ALWD CITATION	BLUEBOOK CITATION	DIFFERENCES
BB: B6.1.1, B6.1.2 & Rule 12			
Legislative Materials **ALWD:** Rules 15 & 16 **BB:** B6.1.6 & Rule 13	Sen. Res. 146, 109th Cong. (2005).	S. Res. 146, 109th Cong. (2005).	ALWD abbreviates Senate as "Sen." instead of "S." to avoid confusion with other abbreviations. Most forms are relatively consistent.
Court Rules **ALWD:** Rule 17 **BB:** B6.1.3 & Rule 12.8	Fed. R. Civ. P. 11.	Fed. R. Civ. P. 11.	No substantial differences.
Administrative Materials **ALWD:** Rules 19 and 20 **BB:** B6.1.4 & Rule 14.2	34 C.F.R. § 607.1 (2006). 70 Fed. Reg. 10868 (Mar. 5, 2005).	34 C.F.R. § 607.1 (2006). 70 Fed. Reg. 10868 (Mar. 5, 2005).	C.F.R. citation is the same. Both require an exact date for Fed. Reg. citations. ALWD includes guidance about how to cite C.F.R. references found on unofficial electronic databases, such as Westlaw and LexisNexis. Rule 19.1(d).
Books and Treatises **ALWD:** Rule 22 **BB:** B8 & Rule 15	Charles Alan Wright, Arthur R. Miller & Mary Kay Kane, *Federal Practice and Procedure* vol. 7A, § 1751, 10–17 (3d ed., West 2005). OR Charles Alan Wright et al., *Federal Practice and Procedure* vol. 7A, § 1751, 10–17 (3d ed., West 2005).	7A Charles Alan Wright, Arthur R. Miller & Mary Kay Kane, *Federal Practice and Procedure* § 1751, at 10–17 (3d ed. 2005). OR 7A Charles Alan Wright et al., *Federal Practice and Procedure* § 1751, at 10–17 (3d ed. 2005).	ALWD places volume information after the title, just like any other subdivisions. ALWD separates subdivisions separated with a comma, but no "at." ALWD requires that the publisher be included, no matter what type of document. ALWD uses et al. for three authors or more, compared with the Bluebook which uses et al. for two authors or more.
Legal Periodicals **ALWD:** Rule 23 **BB:** B9 & Rule 16	Geoffrey P. Miller, *Bad Judges*, 83 Tex. L. Rev. 431 (2004). Margaret Graham Tebo, *Duty Calls*, 91 ABA J. 35 (Apr. 2005).	Geoffrey P. Miller, *Bad Judges*, 83 Tex. L. Rev. 431 (2004). Margaret Graham Tebo, *Duty Calls*, A.B.A. J., Apr. 2005, at 35.	ALWD eliminates most distinctions between Consecutively and non-consecutively paginated articles. Include longer date for non-consecutively paginated journals, but do so within the parenthetical.

(continued)

Exhibit 11.7 **Comparison of selected ALWD third edition rules and bluebook 18th edition rules** *(continued)*

RULE	ALWD CITATION	BLUEBOOK CITATION	DIFFERENCES
	Carrie Ann Wozniak, Student Author, *Difficult Problems Call for New Solutions: Are Guardians Proper for Viable Fetuses of Mentally Incompetent Mothers in State Custody?* 34 Stetson L. Rev. 193 (2004).	Carrie Ann Wozniak, Comment, *Difficult Problems Call for New Solutions: Are Guardians Proper for Viable Fetuses of Mentally Incompetent Mothers in State Custody?* 34 Stetson L. Rev. 193 (2004).	ALWD uses the term "Student Author" to replace Note, Comment, Recent Development, etc.
	Jodi Wilgoren, *Prosecution Lays out Case for Harsh Sentencing of B.T.K. Killer in Gory Detail*, 154 N.Y. Times A14 (Aug. 18, 2005).	Jodi Wilgoren, *Prosecution Lays out Case for Harsh Sentencing of B.T.K. Killer in Gory Detail*, N.Y. Times, Aug. 18, 2005, at A14.	
A.L.R. Annotations **ALWD**: Rule 24 **BB**: Rule 16.6.6	Carolyn Kelly MacWilliam, *Individual and Corporate Liability for Libel and Slander in Electronic Communications, Including E-mail, Internet and Websites*, 3 A.L.R.6th 153 (2005).	Carolyn Kelly MacWilliam, Annotation, *Individual and Corporate Liability for Libel and Slander in Electronic Communications, Including E-mail, Internet and Websites*, 3 A.L.R.6th 153 (2005).	ALWD eliminates the "Annotation" reference.
Legal Dictionaries **ALWD**: Rule 25 **BB**: Rule 15.8	*Black's Law Dictionary* 87 (Bryan A. Garner ed., 8th ed., West 2004).	*Black's Law Dictionary* 87 (8th ed. 2004).	ALWD treats dictionaries like books.
Legal Encyclopedias **ALWD**: Rule 26 **BB**: Rule 15.8	98 C.J.S. *Witnesses* § 397 (2002). 68 Am. Jur. 2d *Schools* §§ 20–24 (2000 & Supp. 2005).	98 C.J.S. *Witnesses* § 397 (2002). 68 Am. Jur. 2d *Schools* §§ 20–24 (2000 & Supp. 2005).	No substantial differences; however, ALWD provides expanded coverage and includes a list of many abbreviations for state encyclopedias.
Internet **ALWD**: Rule 40 **BB**: Rule 18.2.3	Fed. Jud. Ctr., *History of the Federal Judiciary*, http://www.fjc.http://www.fjc.gov/history/home.nsf (accessed Aug. 18, 2005).	Federal Judicial Center, *History of the Federal Judiciary* (visited Aug. 18, 2005), at http://www.fjc.gov/history/home.nsf.	ALWD permits the abbreviation of an organizational author's name, to save space. ALWD uses "accessed" instead of "visited" to be consistent with non-legal citation guides. The Bluebook contains different formats for material that appears only on the Web and for material that appears on the Web and in other medium. The position of the date parenthetical moves depending on the type of information cited.

Exhibit 11.7 **Comparison of selected ALWD third edition rules and bluebook 18th edition rules** *(continued)*

RULE	ALWD CITATION	BLUEBOOK CITATION	DIFFERENCES
Signals **ALWD**: Rule 44 **BB**: B4 & Rule 1.2	Signals are *e.g., accord, see, see also, cf., contra, compare . . . with, but see, but cf.,* and *see generally.*	Signals are *e.g., accord, see, see also, cf., contra, compare . . . with, but see, but cf.,* and *see generally.*	Under ALWD, all signals may be separated with semicolons. Under the Bluebook, a new citation sentence must start when there is a new type of signal. (Signals are categorized by type in the Bluebook—supportive, comparative, contradictory, or background—whereas in ALWD, the signals are ordered individually.) ALWD does not use any punctuation after a signal.
Order of Cited Authority **ALWD**: Rule 45 **BB**: B4.5 & Rule 1.4	ALWD lists federal, state, and foreign court cases first by jurisdiction, then in reverse chronological order.	Federal (appellate and trial) court cases are ordered in reverse chronological order. State court cases are first, alphabetized by state, and then ranked within each state.	Minor differences in the order when looking at the list of specific sources: (1) Under ALWD, statutes (federal and state) come before rules of evidence and procedure, whereas in the Bluebook, federal statutes and rules of evidence and procedure come before state statutes and rules of evidence and procedure. (2) Under the ALWD, the student-authored articles are classified with all other material in law reviews, law journals, and other periodicals, whereas in the Bluebook, the student-authored articles are separate, and cited after the non-student-authored articles.
Quotations **ALWD**: Rule 47 **BB**: B12 & Rule 5	ALWD says to block indent passages if they contain at least fifty words OR if they exceed four lines of typed text.	The *Bluebook* says to block indent passages if they contain at least 50 words.	ALWD does not require you to count the exact number of words in long quotations.

Source: Copyright © 2005, Darby Dickenson. Reprinted with permission.

The Universal Citation Format represents an attempt to solve this problem. The difficulty with some courts is the requirement that the Universal Citation Format be used only until the hardcopy is published, at which time the traditional citation must be used. As a result, you may see the following citation format within documents:

Jones v. Smith, 1999 Pennsylvania Superior 1, _____Pa Super_____, _____A2d_____(1999)

in which the blank spaces are provided to insert the ultimate volume and page number in the print version when it is available. Exhibit 11.8 lists court name abbreviations.

Exhibit 11.8 Federal court name abbreviations

Court	Abbrev.
United States Supreme Court	U.S.

UNITED STATES COURTS OF APPEALS

First Circuit	1st Cir.
Second Circuit	2d Cir.
Third Circuit	3d Cir.
Fourth Circuit	4th Cir.
Fifth Circuit	5th Cir.
Sixth Circuit	6th Cir.
Seventh Circuit	7th Cir.
Eighth Circuit	8th Cir.
Ninth Circuit	9th Cir.
Tenth Circuit	10th Cir.
Eleventh Circuit	11th Cir.
D.C. Circuit	D.C. Cir.
Federal Circuit	Fed. Cir.

UNITED STATES DISTRICT COURTS

Middle District of Alabama	M.D. Ala.
Northern District of Alabama	N.D. Ala.
Southern District of Alabama	S.D. Ala.
District of Alaska	D. Alaska
District of Arizona	D. Ariz.
Eastern District of Arkansas	E.D. Ark.
Western District of Arkansas	W.D. Ark.
Central District of California	C.D. Cal.
Eastern District of California	E.D. Cal.
Northern District of California	N.D. Cal.
Southern District of California	S.D. Cal.
District of the Canal Zone	D.C.Z.

(Note: The D.C.Z. ceased to exist on March 31, 1982.)

District of Colorado	D. Colo.
District of Connecticut	D. Conn.
District of Delaware	D. Del.
District of D.C.	D.D.C.
Middle District of Florida	M.D. Fla.
Northern District of Florida	N.D. Fla.
Southern District of Florida	S.D. Fla.
Middle District of Georgia	M.D. Ga.
Northern District of Georgia	N.D. Ga.
Southern District of Georgia	S.D. Ga.
District of Guam	D. Guam
District of Hawaii	D. Haw.
District of Idaho	D. Idaho
Central District of Illinois	C.D. Ill.

Northern District of Illinois	N.D. Ill.
Southern District of Illinois	S.D. Ill.
Northern District of Indiana	N.D. Ind.
Southern District of Indiana	S.D. Ind.
Northern District of Iowa	N.D. Iowa
Southern District of Iowa	S.D. Iowa
District of Kansas	D. Kan.
Eastern District of Kentucky	E.D. Ky.
Western District of Kentucky	W.D. Ky.
Eastern District of Louisiana	E.D. La.
Middle District of Louisiana	M.D. La.
Western District of Louisiana	W.D. La.
District of Maine	D. Me.
District of Maryland	D. Md.
District of Massachusetts	D. Mass.
Eastern District of Michigan	E.D. Mich.
Western District of Michigan	W.D. Mich.
District of Minnesota	D. Minn.
Northern District of Mississippi	N.D. Miss.
Southern District of Mississippi	S.D. Miss.
Eastern District of Missouri	E.D. Mo.
Western District of Missouri	W.D. Mo.
District of Montana	D. Mont.
District of Nebraska	D. Neb.
District of Nevada	D. Nev.
District of New Hampshire	D.N.H.
District of New Jersey	D.N.J.
District of New Mexico	D.N.M.
Eastern District of New York	E.D.N.Y.
Northern District of New York	N.D.N.Y.
Southern District of New York	S.D.N.Y.
Western District of New York	W.D.N.Y.
Eastern District of North Carolina	E.D.N.C.
Middle District of North Carolina	M.D.N.C.
Western District of North Carolina	W.D.N.C.
District of North Dakota	D.N.D.
District of the Northern Mariana Islands	D.N. Mar. I.
Northern District of Ohio	N.D. Ohio
Southern District of Ohio	S.D. Ohio
Eastern District of Oklahoma	E.D. Okla.
Northern District of Oklahoma	N.D. Okla.
Western District of Oklahoma	W.D. Okla.
District of Oregon	D. Or.
Eastern District of Pennsylvania	E.D. Pa.
Middle District of Pennsylvania	M.D. Pa.
Western District of Pennsylvania	W.D. Pa.
District of Puerto Rico	D.P.R.

Exhibit 11.8 Federal court name abbreviations *(continued)*

District of Rhode Island	**D.R.I.**	United States Air Force Court of Criminal Appeals	**A.F. Crim. App.**
District of South Carolina	**D.S.C.**	United States Army Court of Criminal Appeals	**Army Crim. App.**
District of South Dakota	**D.S.D.**	United States Coast Guard Court Of Criminal Appeals	**Coast Guard Crim. App.**
Eastern District of Tennessee	**E.D. Tenn.**	United States Navy-Marine Corps Court of Criminal Appeals	**Navy-Marine Crim. App.**
Middle District of Tennessee	**M.D. Tenn.**		
Western District of Tennessee	**W.D. Tenn.**		
Eastern District of Texas	**E.D. Tex.**		
Northern District of Texas	**N.D. Tex.**		
Southern District of Texas	**S.D. Tex.**		
Western District of Texas	**W.D. Tex.**	**BANKRUPTCY COURTS**	
District of Utah	**D. Utah**		
District of Vermont	**D. Vt.**	Each United States District Court has a corresponding bankruptcy court. To cite a bankruptcy court, add Bankr. to the district court abbreviation.	
Eastern District of Virginia	**E.D. Va.**		
Western District of Virginia	**W.D. Va.**		
District of the Virgin Islands	**D.V.I.**	*Examples:*	
Eastern District of Washington	**E.D. Wash.**	Bankr. N.D. Ala.	
Western District of Washington	**W.D. Wash.**	Bankr. D. Mass.	
Northern District of West Virginia	**N.D.W. Va.**		
Southern District of West Virginia	**S.D.W. Va.**	**OTHER FEDERAL COURTS**	
Eastern District of Wisconsin	**E.D. Wis.**		
Western District of Wisconsin	**W.D. Wis.**	Court of Federal Claims	**Fed. Cl.**
District of Wyoming	**D. Wyo.**	Court of Customs and Patent Appeals	**Cust. & Pat. App.**
		Court of Claims	**Ct. Cl.**
MILITARY COURTS		Claims Court	**Cl. Ct.**
		Court of International Trade	**Ct. Intl. Trade**
United States Court of Appeals for the Armed Forces	**Armed Forces App.**	Tax Court	**Tax**
United States Court of Veterans Appeals	**Vet. App.**		

Source: Reprinted with permission of Aspen Publishers, from ALWD Citation Manual: A Professional System of Citation.

Other Citation Formats

Many states, including Pennsylvania, have adopted as their official citation format one that originally was created by publishers such as West Publishing Company. These sometimes are referred to as **vendor-specific citation formats**. The West Publishing Company format is based on the West Regional Reporter system and its publications of federal material.

New methods of electronic information technology, in the form of databases, CD-ROMs, and the Internet, have created a number of problems with the traditional citation format. Some of the vendors have claimed copyright protection for their pagination systems.

In 1985, West Publishing Company, in a case against Mead Data Central, argued successfully that the wholesale use of its *pagination* by a competing online publisher infringed upon West's copyright interest in the arrangement of cases in its court reports. And in a 1998 case involving Matthew Bender & Company and West Publishing Company, the Second Circuit held that West's pagination was not protected by copyright. Obviously, all claims to a pagination system or citation system that is vendor-specific will result in some action to protect the corporate claim for copyright, trademark, or potential patent for some electronic methodology.

Cite Checking

Cite checking is the process of verifying that the proper citation format has been used in a document. The term also means checking the referenced case or statute to determine that it is valid and that it has not been repealed or overturned. The strictness

Vendor-specific citation format
Citation format of a legal publisher adopted by a court.

Cite checking
The process of verifying proper citation format in a document.

Exhibit 11.9 American Association of Law Libraries universal case citation

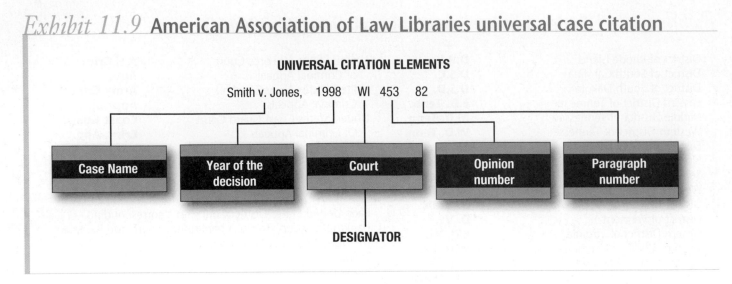

with which the citation rules must be applied, as well as the method—*Bluebook, ALWD Citation Manual*, or Universal Citation Format—depends on the wishes and demands of the attorney for whom the document is prepared or the court or judge to whom it is submitted. Some courts view the presentation of improper citation format with a jaundiced eye, just as they view improper punctuation, improper spelling, and bad grammar. Others are upset if the citation to the paper references or online legal research service available to them is not used.

Bluebook and ALWD Compared

Which citation format is used depends on the local custom and courts in which the firm or supervising attorney practices (and the wishes of your instructors!). The two forms used most commonly—the *Bluebook* and the *ALWD Manual*—have a number of similarities. Both of these documents are divided into parts and rules—the *Bluebook* into three parts and the *ALWD Manual* into seven parts.

The parts are further divided into rules. The *Bluebook* has 20 basic rules, and the *ALWD* 50 rules. Most of the rules have a common pattern, and some are the same, such as *Bluebook* Rule 12–Statutes, and *ALWD* Rule 14 on the method of citing the United States Code: 18 U.S.C. § 1965 (1994). Others are minor variations in presentation, such as *Bluebook* Rule 10.2.2, which provides, "Do not abbreviate 'United States,'" and *ALWD* Rule 12.2(g) "United States as party: Cite as U.S. Omit 'America.'"

Sample *Bluebook* citation formats:

Rule 11 Constitutions:	U.S.Const.art.I, § 9, cl.2.
Rule 10 Cases:	United States v Shaffer Equip. Co., 11 F.3d 450 (4th Cir. 1993)
Rule 12 Statutes:	42 U.S.C. § 1983 (1994)

Sample *ALWD* citation formats:

Rule 13 Constitutions:	U.S. Const.art. IV, § 5(b)
Rule 12 Cases:	Brown v. Bd. Of Educ., 349 U.S. 294
	U.S. v. Chairse, 18 F.Supp. 2d 1021
	(D. Minn. 1998)
Rule 14 Statutory Codes:	
Session Laws, SlipLaws:	18 U.S.C. § 1965 (1994)

Advice from the Field ••

PROFESSIONAL COMMUNICATION *by Kathryn L. Myers, Associate Professor and Coordinator of Paralegal Studies at Saint Mary-of-the-Woods College in Saint Mary-of-the-Woods, IN.*

There are countless misunderstandings, conflicts, and disagreements in every organization in the United States. Effective listening skills are almost extinct in many firms, and gossip among colleagues has become commonplace. The result is lost productivity, hurt feelings, hidden agendas, loss of innovative ideas, and mistrust among coworkers.

The importance of professional communication skills in dealing with these problems cannot be overstressed. *The Wall Street Journal* recently reported a study involving more than one hundred Fortune 500 executives who ranked interpersonal communication first, across the board, as the most valuable skill they considered in hiring or promotion decisions. Lack of interpersonal communication skills impedes professional effectiveness in influencing persuading, and negotiating, all of which are crucial to success.

Professional communication may take the form of written communication, active listening, or nonverbal communication, all of which require interpersonal communication skills. All three skills work together to define professional communication, but this article focuses specifically on written communication.

Writing intimidates many people, but there are times when writing is the best way to communicate and often is the only way to get a message across. Good writers must have access to at least one quality writing guide. Some good choices are: *The Elements of Style,* by William Strunk, Jr., and E.B. White for lawyers, paralegals, and others engaged in formal writing; *The Bedford Handbook,* by Diana T. Hacker; *How 10: A Handbook for Office Professionals,* by James L. and Lyn R. Clark; and *The Associated Press Stylebook* for traditional journalists is the professional bible.

The following tips are offered as examples of what careful writers must consider.

BE CAUTIOUS

Written communication is more concrete than verbal communication and is less forgiving of errors. Once something is written and sent, it cannot be taken back; and it cannot be nuanced or explained away as readily as can be done with the spoken word.

Communicators in writing must meet the challenges of spelling, grammar, punctuation, and style in addition to the actual wording (rhetoric). Modern technology superficially makes writing seem easier by providing grammar and spelling checks, but these tools are not failsafe. They may actually contribute to egregious errors if the writer is not carefully involved with the writing and proofreading the material for sense.

REMEMBER THE ABCS OF WRITING

Accuracy—Proof and reproof
Brevity—Keep sentences short
Clarity—Use active voice for clear meaning

BEWARE OF COMMON ERRORS

Commas—Use commas after each part of full dates (*e.g.,* "Wednesday, July 13, 2005," or "July 13, 2005," unless the year falls at the end of the sentence. No comma is used with a calendar date expressed alone (*e.g.,* "February 14.") Do not use commas where the year stands by itself (*e.g.,* "the year 2005 was special.")

Restrictive words, phrases, or clauses modify the main idea and are essential to its meaning. These are not set off by commas. Nonrestrictive words, phrases, or clauses, however, do not significantly change the meaning of the sentence and are set off by commas. Place commas inside quotation marks and parentheses.

Semicolons—Use semicolons when there are two or more independent clauses that do not have coordinating conjunctions, or when the clauses are joined by a transitional expression such as "however." Also use them to separate clauses in a series which have internal commas. Place semicolons outside quotation marks and parentheses.

Colons—Use colons after independent clauses that introduce a formal list or enumeration of items, but not if a verb of being precedes the list. Use a colon after a business salutation and to introduce formal quotations (*e.g.,* the court held: "no offense was proven . . .")

Dashes—Use dashes instead of commas to achieve greater pause and emphasis to what follows. Also

(continued)

Advice from the Field ·····································

(continued)

use them in place of commas with parenthetical expressions or appositives that contain internal commas.

Ellipsis—An ellipsis is a series of three periods to indicate one or more words are missing from the middle of a sentence in the quoted text. If the missing text is at the end of a sentence, this fact is indicated with a fourth period—the sentence period—at the end of the series.

Quotation Marks—Quotation marks are used to show directly quoted speech or text as well as the titles of published articles. Quotations of 50 words or more do not use quotation marks but, rather, are written as separate paragraph(s), single spaced, and indented on the right and left margins greater than the normal text.

Apostrophe—The apostrophe is used to indicate a missing letter in a contraction (*e.g.*, "it's" for "it is" or "don't" for "do not") or to denote singular possession (*e.g.*, "Mary's"), or plural possession (*e.g.*, "the companies' policies.") "Its" is the correct (albeit counterintuitive) possessive form of "it." No apostrophe is used. All possessive case pronouns (my, your, yours, their, its, whose, theirs, ours) are written without apostrophes.

When there is joint ownership, the apostrophe attaches to the last noun (*e.g.*, "it was Dick and Jane's home"). With individual possession where there are two or more nouns, each noun shows ownership (*e.g.*, "it was either Dick's or Jane's").

WATCH YOUR GRAMMAR

Active Voice—Using action verbs and active voice provides clear and readable sentences.

Noun/Pronoun Agreement—A singular noun (legal assistant) must have a singular pronoun (his/her). Plural nouns (legal assistants) must have plural pronouns (their). Avoid confusion by writing in the plural form when possible.

Subjective Case—Use the subjective case of a pronoun (I, he, she, you, we, they, who, it, whoever) for the subject, for the complement of a "being" verb, and after the infinitive "to be" when this verb does not have a subject directly preceding it.

Objective Case—Use the objective case of a pronoun (me, him, her, you, us, them, whom, it, whomever) as the direct or indirect object of a verb, the object of a preposition, the subject of any infinitive, the object of the infinitive "to be" when it has a subject directly preceding it, and the object of any other infinitive.

Noun/Verb Agreement—Singular nouns take singular verbs. Know the difference among present, past,

and future tenses. Do not switch verb tenses in documents unless the material requires the switch.

Identifiers (Modifiers)—Place identifiers (modifiers) (*e.g.*, adjectives and adverbs) as close as possible to the words they identify (modify).

Proper Pairs—Certain words (correlative conjunctions) must be used in pairs (*e.g.*, either/or, neither/nor, not only/but also).

Clichés, Slang, and Jargon—Avoid clichés: use them only when there is a sound reason to believe that a particular cliché will strengthen your rhetoric. Use slang and "legalese" only when it would be awkward for the reader not to do so, and only if you are sure the reader will understand the reference. A judge, for example, expects to read some amount of legalese. He or she likely would be disappointed to see none at all in a trial brief.

Spelling—Use your spelling checker, but proofread to make sure you do not have correct spelling of the wrong word (*e.g.*, "she was soaking in the tube.") Great care should be taken to spell the names of people and companies correctly.

Acronyms and Abbreviations—Except for acronyms and abbreviations in common usage and which are self-explanatory in context (*e.g.*, "the Hon. James Parker" or "she is an interpreter with NATO"), give full titles and names when the acronym or abbreviation first is mentioned. Err on the side of spelling it out if there is any doubt.

Numbers—In general, single-digit numbers should be written as words; double digit, as numerals in written materials unless the number is used to begin a sentence (*e.g.*, "I had only 10 reference books when I began five years ago.")

Source Acknowledgement—The source of borrowed material of any kind must be attributed with quotation marks if directly quoted, or by attribution if not directly quoted (*e.g.*, "I shall return," Gen. MacArthur promised, or, "General Douglas MacArthur promised he would be back"). In formal research and in legal writing, complete citations must be provided according to the legal convention or the style prescribed by the particular publication.

LETTERS

Correspondence is a primary form of communication between the law firm and the world. It is vital that correspondence be crafted well to properly reflect both the reputation of the law office and your own professional-

Advice from the Field ·····················

ism. Correspondence must be free of grammar and spelling errors, and the research and analysis must be absolutely correct.

There are different types of letters for different purposes: informational letters, opinion letters, and demand letters, to name a few. Although paralegals would not sign their names to opinion or demand letters, it is quite common for them to draft substantial portions of this correspondence.

There are certain parts to a letter that are necessary for successful correspondence.

Format—There are three primary formats: 1) full block, 2) modified block with blocked paragraphs, and 3) modified block with indented paragraphs.

Letterhead—Preprinted letterhead needs no additional information; but subsequent pages need to contain an identification of the letter, or a header including the name of the addressee, the date, and the page number.

Date—The full date appears below the letterhead at the left or right margin depending on the format used.

Method of Delivery—This appears at the left margin below the date if delivery other than U.S. Postal Service is used.

Recipient's Address Block—The inside address is placed at the left margin and should include:

The recipient

The recipient's title (if any)

The name of the business (if appropriate)

The address

Reference Line—Usually introduced with "Re:" the reference line identifies the subject of the letter. Depending upon office requirements, it may contain case identification.

Salutation—Legal correspondence generally is formal; and the salutation is followed with a colon, such as "Dear Ms. Myers:" You can use the first name if you know the person well, although it is a safer practice to remain formal. It is best to address the letter to a named individual. This may mean calling the recipient business and identifying a person to whom the letter should be addressed.

Body—The body of the letter should have three components:

1. Introduction: For normal business letters, your letter should start with an overall summary, showing in the first paragraph why the letter is relevant to the reader. Don't make reader go past the first paragraph to find out why the letter was sent.
2. Main section: The body of the letter needs to explain the reason for the correspondence, including any relevant background and current information. Make sure the information flows logically to make your points effectively.
3. Requests/instructions: The closing of the letter is the final impression you leave with the reader. End with an action point such as, "I will call you later this week to discuss the matter."

Closing—Following the body of the letter, the closing consists of a standard statement and/or an action item.

Signature and Title—Clearly identify the writer by name and title.

Initials of Drafter—This is a reference to the author (KLM) and the typist (sbk).

Enclosure Notation—"Enc." or "Encs." notations are used to identify one or more enclosures.

Copies to Others—The traditional "cc" notation, formerly meaning "carbon copy," now means "courtesy copy" and is used universally. Some writers, however, will use only "c" or "copy to," along with the name(s), to identify others receiving copies of the document.

PROOFREADING

Even when you believe your draft is exactly what you want, read it one more time. This rule is for everything you write whether it is a memorandum, letter, proposal, or some other document. It is true no matter how many drafts you have written.

Use both the grammar and spelling checker on your computer, paying very close attention to every word highlighted. Do not place total faith in your computer. Instead, have both a printed dictionary and a thesaurus nearby to double-check everything your computer's editing tools highlight, because the computer tools are not always reliable.

Make sure your document is clear and concise. Is there anything that could be misinterpreted? Does it raise questions or fail to make the point you need to make? Can

(continued)

Advice from the Field ⋯⋯⋯⋯⋯⋯⋯⋯⋯⋯⋯⋯⋯

(continued)

you reduce the number of words or unnecessarily long words? Do not use a long word when a short one works as well; do not use two words when one will do; and do not waste the reader's time with unnecessary words or phrases.

Is your written communication well organized? Does each idea proceed logically from one paragraph to the next? Make sure written communications are easy to read, contain the necessary information, use facts where needed, and avoid information that is not relevant. Be sure to specify the course of action you expect, such as a return call or an order.

Close appropriately, whether formally or informally, according to the nature of the communication.

This may seem obvious, but it is sometimes overlooked and can make written communications look amateurish. This diminishes your chances of meeting your written communication's goals.

Communication is vital to the success of any workplace; and in the legal arena, professionals live or die by the communicated word. Well-crafted documents are a positive step toward being a successful professional.

Reprinted with permission of the National Association of Legal Assistants and Kathryn L. Myers. The article originally appeared in the May 2005 issue of FACTS & FINDINGS, the quarterly journal for legal assistants. The article is reprinted here in its entirety. For further information, contact NALA at www.nala.org or phone 918-587-6828.

Legal Terminology

Summary

CHAPTER *11*   LEGAL WRITING AND CRITICAL LEGAL THINKING

Critical Legal Thinking: Definitions

Critical Legal Thinking	The process of identifying legal issues, determining the relevant facts, and applying the applicable law to come to a conclusion that answers the legal question the issues present. The paralegal must understand the audience for whom the document is being prepared: the client, the supervising attorney and other members of the legal team, or the court.
Facts	Facts are pieces of information or details that in actuality or reality exist, or have occurred, as opposed to someone's theory, supposition, or conjecture. A fact is, in the law, the circumstances of an event, motion, occurrence, or state of affairs, rather than an interpretation of its significance.
Material (relevant) Fact	A material fact is a fact that is significant or essential to the issue or matter at hand.
Immaterial (irrelevant) Fact	An immaterial fact is one that is not essential to the matter at issue.

Legal Writing

Standards	1. The language used must be clear to the intended reader. 2. The writer must make an honest presentation of the facts and argument. 3. Arguments advocating a new interpretation to the existing law, as well as the current law, must be clearly stated. 4. The ethical obligation to the court must be obeyed, including the presentation of adverse authority in the jurisdiction. 5. Factual variation must be presented, and the sources used clearly identified by proper citation in a format acceptable to the reader.
Duty of Candor	There is an obligation to be honest with the court and not to mislead the court.

Office Memorandum

Purpose	1. The memorandum is a working document for the legal team to be used in preparation and presentation of a case. 2. The paralegal must understand the specific assignment. For the memorandum of law, it usually is the answer to a question. 3. Office memoranda are frequently indexed by subject and filed in the office for future reference; if the same or a similar fact pattern requires research, it is a good starting point and can be a major time-saver. 4. The facts relied upon in writing the memo must be a part of the final memorandum; other people who read the memorandum need to understand the specific facts. 5. A memorandum must present both sides of the issue, and in that respect be a neutral, unbiased, objective presentation of applicable laws as they apply to the facts of the case. Issues that the opposing attorney or the judge may raise should be considered and presented. A good analysis includes a discussion of how the fact pattern may differ in cases that are not on point.
Preparing Court Briefs	Written for the court, the brief provides written advocacy of the client's position and must be written to convince the court to adopt a position favorable to the client.

Citations

Purpose	A citation should allow someone else to find the case or other material mentioned in a document, and the form of citation must do this. The format must be generally accepted and used by others in the legal community.

Traditional Sources (Print) Citation Format	The basic paper or traditional citation form is: Volume • Book or Series • Page e.g., 232 Atlantic 2d 44 232 refers to the volume in the Atlantic 2d series reporter service of West Publishing Company, and 44 refers to the page on which the authority may be found.
Bluebook Citation Format	Bluebook has been the generally accepted authority for proper citation form unless the rules of a particular court dictated a different citation format.
ALWD Citation Format	This citation format authority was written by Association of Legal Writing Directors.
Universal Citation Format	Traditionally, paper or book-based citation used information based on internal page numbers. Universal Citation Format relies upon the courts to provide numbered paragraphs in their opinions.
Cite Checking	Documents must be checked to verify that they use the proper citation format and that the referenced cases and statutes are valid and the cases have not been repealed or overturned. The strictness with which the citation rules must be applied, as well as the method—*Bluebook*, *ALWD*, or Universal Citation Format—depends on the wishes and demands of the attorney for whom the document is being prepared, or the court or judge to whom it is submitted.

▶ WORKING THE WEB

1. Summarize in a memo the requirements for briefs submitted to the United States Supreme Court, and the citation to the applicable rule. **http://www.supremecourtus.gov/ctrules/rulesofthecourt.pdf** or **http://www.law.cornell.edu/ rules/supct/overview.html**

2. Use the Internet to find the information to prepare an internal office memorandum on the requirements for filing briefs in your jurisdiction's highest court. For example, in California at **http://www.courtinfo.ca.gov/rules/titleone/title1-1-59.htm**, or Kansas at **http://www.kscourts.org/ctruls/ctrul610.htm**

3. The Legal Law Institute at Cornell Law School offers a number of sources for the legal writer, including citation information. Use the LII website to download the section from Introduction to Basic Legal Citation by Peter W. Martin—"Who Sets Citation Norms"—at **http://www.law.cornell.edu/citation/1-600.htm**

4. Use the homepage link from the Web page in question 3, and download your personal copy of the reference document.

5. If you are using the ALWD manual for citation rules, download a copy of the latest updates at **www.alwd.org**.

▶ CRITICAL THINKING AND WRITING QUESTIONS

1. What is critical legal thinking? Explain and give an example.

2. Why is it important to have all the material facts before beginning the research to prepare a memorandum of law?

3. What is meant by "material facts?" Give an example of a material fact.

4. What is meant by an "immaterial fact?" Give an example.

5. What is the goal of legal writing?

6. Why should headnotes not be used in legal writing?

7. How important is it to shepardize the cases in a memorandum of law or brief? When should this be done? Why?

8. How are the memorandum of law and the court brief similar, and different? Explain fully.

9. Contrast and compare the fact situation in the opening scenario and the Alaskan case of *Whiting v. State* in the chapter. What are the similarities, and what are the points that could be used to argue that the law does not apply.

10. How does the general duty to inform the court preserve the integrity of the judicial process? (*Hazel-Atlas Glass Co. v. Hartford-Empire Co.*, 322 U.S. 238)
11. Are sanctions against attorneys for failing to observe a duty of candor to the court an appropriate remedy? [*Beam v. IPCO Corp.*, 838 F.2d 242 (7th Cir. 1998)]
12. What are the relevant facts in the *Palsgraf v. LIRR* case found in Appendix A? What facts are interesting but not relevant facts? Create a computer search query using the facts in the *Palsgraf* case, and search the case law of your jurisdiction using these relevant facts. Prepare a short brief of the latest case you find, including proper *Bluebook* and *ALWD* citation format.

13. What questions should a paralegal ask before preparing a memo of law or a brief?
14. Why should both sides of a case be presented in an office memo of law?
15. Why would an attorney request that all parallel citations be listed for each case listed in a memo of law?
16. How would knowing the intended audience influence the writing of a memo of law or a legal brief?
17. What level of confidentiality should be attached to the preparation and handling of a memo of law? Why?

ETHICS ANALYSIS AND DISCUSSION QUESTIONS

1. What are the ethical issues in failing to properly cite authorities used in a document?
2. What are the ethical obligations in arguing to the court for a change in the law and not the current law?
3. What are the ethical obligations to the client when analysis of the law indicates there is no valid claim?
4. Assume you have been working for a legal specialist in estate law for a number of years and have taken a number of advanced courses in the field. You are highly regarded in the paralegal community as the person to call for help in the field. Your supervising attorney decides to take a three-week bicycle trip through the Swiss Alps and leaves you in charge of the office.

   During his absence, you give a talk to a local senior citizens group on the advantages of preparing a will. You meet with most of the people in the audience after the talk and tell them a simple will can be prepared for $25 (your office's standard fee) and proceed to take the information from them for a will. You prepare the individual wills and send copies marked **DRAFT** to each person, along with an invoice for the $25 fee with a note to return the fee if they wish to have the will completed. Everyone accepts and sends in the fee.

   Upon his return, the attorney looks over the wills, tells you they are "letter perfect" and says "It's just what

   I would have done." [*Cincinnati Bar v. Kathman*, 92 Ohio St. 92 (2001) quoting *People v. Cassidy*, 884 P.2d 309 (Colo. 1994).] What are the legal and ethical issues?

5. It is the week between Christmas and New Year's Day. You are the only one covering the office while all of the lawyers and support personnel are on vacation. A client who is traveling in Asia calls and asks you to fax to his hotel a copy of an opinion letter prepared by your supervising attorney. You helped prepare the opinion letter and know that it contains a summary of the facts, including details about the opposing parties, case strategy, and potential violations of law. May you send it? What are the ethical issues, if any?
6. You are working for the local prosecutor as a paralegal. The District Attorney asks you to prepare an office memorandum of law on the question: Is there any duty to advise the court of any changes in the law or facts after the case has been presented.
7. You prepared a memorandum of law for the firm's trial attorney, and a brief for the court that was used in the case that started today. Closing arguments will be made tomorrow. You now discover that there is case law that is favorable to the other side that effectively overturns the case law you used in the memo of law and brief. What do you do? Are there any ethical issues? Explain fully.

DEVELOPING YOUR COLLABORATION SKILLS

Working on your own or with a group of other students assigned by your instructor, review the scenario at the beginning of the chapter.

1. Divide the group into two teams.
   a. One team is to prepare a memo for the court in the form of a brief.
   b. One team is to prepare a memo of law for the partner.

   c. After the memos are finished, each group should compare and write a report on the differences between the memos.

2. As a group, prepare a memo that Henry might prepare for the supervising paralegal or other attorney on the handling of the interview and any concerns or recommendations.
3. Discuss any ethical concerns that Henry might have, based on the interview and the potential handling of the case.

TORTS

"Negligence is not actionable unless it involves the invasion of a legally protected interest, the violation of a right. Proof of negligence in the air, so to speak, will not do."

C. J. Cardozo, Palsgraf v. Long Island Railroad Co. (1928)

PARALEGALS AT WORK

As a paralegal, you work for a law firm that represents clients in tort actions against automobile insurance companies and other defendants. Most of the law firm's business comes from automobile accident cases. Your firm specializes in representing the injured plaintiffs in these negligence and product liability lawsuits.

You work for Mr. Joshua Berk, senior litigator for the firm. One day Mr. Berk invites you in to his office. He explains that the firm has just been retained by a plaintiff, Mrs. Helen Sheen, to represent her and her daughter Jessica in a lawsuit. Mr. Berk explains that you will be assisting him in preparation of the case.

Mr. Berk explains the following facts of the case: Two months ago Mrs. Helen Sheen and her husband, Mr. Patrick Sheen, were driving on the Interstate 10 freeway to Las Vegas in their one-year old SUV (sports utility vehicle) manufactured by DaimlerChrysler Group. Mrs. Sheen was driving the SUV, Mr. Sheen was in the passenger's seat, and their 4-year old daughter Jessica was in the back seat of the car. Mrs. Sheen, Mr. Sheen, and Jessica were wearing their seat belts.

While in the State of Nevada, and about 20 miles from Las Vegas, Mrs. Sheen heard the steering wheel of the SUV rattle and then felt it loosen in her hands. Mrs. Sheen lost control of the vehicle and the vehicle flipped over several times before coming to a stop upside down and 40-feet from the freeway. Mr. Sheen died in the accident.

Jessica suffered severe back injuries from the accident that will require at least $100,000 of surgeries over the next year. Her future injuries from the accident are unknown at this time. Mrs. Sheen was not physically injured in the accident, but suffers severe emotional distress caused by the accident.

Investigators of the accident scene have determined that Mrs. Sheen was driving at the legal speed limit of 70 miles per hour. Investigation also has shown that one of the bolts holding the steering wheel in place had broken off, causing the steering wheel to become loose and unmanageable at the time of the accident. The steering wheel and steering wheel column for the SUV was manufactured by the sub-manufacturer Steering Columns Corporation and installed in the DaimlerChrysler SUVs.

Consider the issues involved in this scenario as you read the chapter.

After studying this chapter, you should be able to:

1. List and describe intentional torts against persons.

2. List and describe intentional torts against property.

3. Describe the torts of invasion of privacy and misappropriation of the right to publicity.

4. List and explain the elements necessary to prove negligence.

5. Apply special negligence doctrines such as negligence per se, negligent infliction of emotional distress, and *res ipsa loquitur*.

6. Describe and apply the doctrine of strict liability to product liability cases.

7. Explain when punitive damages are awarded in strict liability actions.

▶ INTRODUCTION FOR THE PARALEGAL

Many paralegals work for lawyers who represent clients involved in automobile accidents and other negligence or intentional tort cases. These are civil lawsuits in which the plaintiff is usually seeking to recover monetary damages from the defendant or the defendant's insurance company. In this type of case, the paralegal may be working for the plaintiff's lawyer, the defendant's lawyer, or lawyers at the defendant's insurance company.

Tort is the French word for a "wrong." Tort law protects a variety of injuries and provides remedies for them. Under tort law, an injured party can bring a civil lawsuit to seek compensation for a wrong done to the party or to the party's property. Many torts originate in common law. The courts and legislatures have extended tort law to reflect changes in modern society.

Tort damages are monetary damages sought from the offending party, intended to compensate the injured party for the injury suffered. These may consist of past and future medical expenses, loss of wages, pain and suffering, mental distress, and other damages caused by the defendant's tortious conduct. If the victim of a tort dies, his or her beneficiaries can bring a *wrongful death action* to recover damages from the defendant. Punitive damages, which are awarded to punish the defendant, may be recovered in intentional tort and strict liability cases. Other remedies, such as injunctions, may be available, too.

Tort lawsuits make up a substantial portion of the civil lawsuits in the United States. Therefore, a paralegal should have knowledge of the major tort principles and the elements of each tort. This chapter covers various tort laws, including intentional torts, negligence, and strict liability. ∎

INTENTIONAL TORTS

Intentional torts
A category of torts that requires that the defendant possessed the intent to do the act that caused the plaintiff's injuries.

The law protects a person from unauthorized touching, restraint, or other contact. In addition, the law protects a person's reputation and privacy. Violations of these rights are actionable as **intentional torts**. The law also recognizes certain intentional torts against real and personal property. Internal torts are discussed in the paragraphs that follow.

Assault

Assault is (1) the threat of immediate harm or offensive contact, or (2) any action that arouses reasonable apprehension of imminent harm. Actual physical contact is unnecessary. For example, suppose a 6-foot 5-inch, 250-pound male makes a fist and threatens to punch a 5-foot, 100-pound woman. If the woman is afraid that the man will physically harm her, she can sue him for assault. If she is a black-belt karate champion and laughs at the threat, there is no assault because the threat does not cause any apprehension.

Battery

Thoughts much too deep for tears subdue the Court When I assumpsit bring, and godlike waive a tort.
J. L. Adolphus The Circuiteers (1885)

Battery is unauthorized and harmful or offensive physical contact with another person. Basically, the interest protected here is each person's reasonable sense of dignity and safety. For example, intentionally hitting someone is considered battery because it is harmful. Note that there does not have to be direct physical contact between the victim and the perpetrator. If an injury results, throwing a rock, shooting an arrow or a bullet, knocking off a hat, pulling a chair out from under someone, and poisoning a drink are all instances of actionable battery. The victim need not be aware of the harmful or offensive contact (e.g., it may take place while the victim is asleep). Assault and battery often occur together, although they do not have to (e.g., the perpetrator hits the victim on the back of the head without any warning).

THE PARALEGAL AND TORTS

A substantial number of lawsuits in the United States involve torts. Therefore, a substantial number of paralegals work for lawyers who practice in this area of the law. A tort occurs when one party violates a duty owed to another party and injures that party. The injured party often brings a civil lawsuit to recover monetary damages and other remedies.

The most familiar form of a tort is negligence. And the most common form of negligence occurs in automobile accidents. Attorneys representing clients who have been injured in automobile accidents usually have a volume practice—that is, the lawyer handles a large number of cases. The defense law firms who represent the insurance companies also have large caseloads of negligence automobile lawsuits.

Paralegals who work for either the plaintiff lawyers or the defense lawyers in automobile injury cases are responsible for handling a large caseload. Paralegals who work for plaintiff lawyers are typically called upon to draft complaints, requests for discovery, and other documents associated with the case. Paralegals who work for defense law firms have parallel duties of drafting answers, requests for discovery, and other documents associated with the cases. Paralegals who work on automobile tort cases become experts and often do much of the work on these cases, under the supervision of the attorney, of course.

Because 90 percent of these cases settle, there is usually not much opportunity to conduct legal research concerning these cases. More complex cases, and those that do go to trial, however, may require legal research by the paralegal to help the attorney prepare the brief for the case.

Among the many other types of torts are professional malpractice (e.g., medical malpractice by doctors), defamation of character, intentional infliction of emotional distress, invasion of privacy, misappropriation of the right to publicity, malicious prosecution, negligent infliction of emotional distress, liability of landowners, and other forms of intentional and unintentional torts. These tort cases usually are more complex and, therefore, require more expertise of the paralegals who work for the plaintiff and defense lawyers who represent clients in these cases. Again, paralegals are called upon to draft complaints, answers, requests and responses to discovery, and other documents associated with these more complex cases. Because of the more complex nature of these cases, paralegals often are assigned to conduct research concerning the legal issues involved in these cases.

The area of torts will remain an important area for the employment of paralegals. Therefore, paralegals should have knowledge of the various types of intentional and unintentional torts.

Sometimes a person acts with the intent to injure one person but actually injures another. The **doctrine of transferred intent** applies to these situations. Under this doctrine, the law transfers the perpetrator's intent from the target to the actual victim of the act. The victim then can sue the defendant.

False Imprisonment

The intentional confinement or restraint of another person without authority or justification and without that person's consent constitutes **false imprisonment**. The victim may be restrained or confined by physical force, barriers, threats of physical harm, or the perpetrator's false assertion of legal authority (i.e., *false arrest*). A threat of future harm or moral pressure is not considered false imprisonment. The false imprisonment must be complete. For example, merely locking one door to a building when other exits are not locked is not false imprisonment. A person is not obliged to risk danger or an affront to his or her dignity by attempting to escape.

Shoplifting causes substantial losses to merchants each year. Almost all states have enacted **merchant protection statutes**, also known as the *shopkeeper's privilege*.

Merchant protection statute
A state statute that allows merchants to stop, detain, and investigate suspected shoplifters without being held liable for false imprisonment if (1) there are reasonable grounds for the suspicion, (2) suspects are detained for only a reasonable time, and (3) investigations are conducted in a reasonable manner.

Trespass to Land

Interference with an owner's right to exclusive possession of land constitutes the tort of **trespass to land**. There does not have to be any interference with the owner's use or enjoyment of the land; the ownership itself is what counts. Thus, unauthorized use of another person's land is trespass even if the owner is not using it. Actual harm to the property is not necessary.

Examples of trespass to land are entering another person's land without permission, remaining on the land of another after permission to do so has expired (e.g., a guest refuses to leave), or causing something or someone to enter another's land (e.g., one person builds a dam that causes another person's land to flood). A person who is pushed onto another's land or enters that land with good reason is not liable for trespass. For example, a person may enter another person's land to save a child or a pet from harm.

Trespass to and Conversion of Personal Property

The tort of **trespass to personal property** occurs whenever one person injures another person's personal property or interferes with that person's enjoyment of his or her personal property. The injured party can sue for damages. For example, breaking another's car window is trespass to personal property.

Depriving a true owner of the use and enjoyment of his or her personal property by taking over such property and exercising ownership rights over it constitutes the tort of **conversion of personal property**. Conversion also occurs when someone who originally is given possession of personal property fails to return it (e.g., fails to return a borrowed car). The rightful owner can sue to recover the property. If the property was lost or destroyed, the owner can sue to recover its value.

LIABILITY FOR FRIVOLOUS LAWSUITS

Entrepreneurs and others often believe they have a reason to sue someone to recover damages or other remedies. If the plaintiff has a reason to bring the lawsuit and does so but the plaintiff does not win the lawsuit, he or she does not have to worry about being sued by the person he or she sued. But a losing plaintiff does have to worry about being sued by the defendant in a second lawsuit for **malicious prosecution** if certain elements are met.

In a lawsuit for malicious prosecution, the original defendant sues the original plaintiff. In this second lawsuit, which is a *civil* action for damages, the original defendant is the plaintiff and the original plaintiff is the defendant. The courts do not look favorably on malicious prosecution lawsuits because they think these inhibit the original plaintiff's incentive to sue. Thus, to succeed in a malicious prosecution lawsuit, the courts require the plaintiff to prove all of the following:

- The plaintiff in the original lawsuit (now the defendant) instituted or was responsible for instituting the original lawsuit.
- There was no *probable cause* for the first lawsuit; that is, it was a frivolous lawsuit.
- The plaintiff in the original action brought it with *malice*. [Caution: This is a difficult element to prove.]
- The original lawsuit was terminated in favor of the original defendant (now the plaintiff).
- The current plaintiff suffered injury as a result of the original lawsuit.

A successful case of malicious prosecution involves proof of malicious conduct, which is an intentional tort. Therefore, punitive damages can be awarded in a malicious prosecution case. The moral of the story is simple: Make sure you have probable cause for instituting an action before bringing a lawsuit.

UNINTENTIONAL TORTS—NEGLIGENCE

Under the doctrine of **unintentional tort**, commonly referred to as **negligence**, a person is liable for harm that is the *foreseeable consequence* of his or her actions. Negligence is defined as "the omission to do something which a reasonable man would do, or doing something which a prudent and reasonable man would not do" [*Blyth v. Birmingham Waterworks Co.*, 11 Exch. 781, 784 (1856)]. Consider this example: A driver who causes an automobile accident because he or she fell asleep at the wheel is liable for any resulting injuries caused by his or her negligence.

Unintentional tort/negligence
A doctrine that says a person is liable for harm that is the foreseeable consequence of his or her actions.

Elements of Negligence

To be successful in a negligence lawsuit, the plaintiff must prove that (1) the defendant owed a *duty of care* to the plaintiff, (2) the defendant *breached* this duty of care, (3) the plaintiff suffered *injury*, and (4) the defendant's negligent act *caused* the plaintiff's injury. Each of these elements is discussed in the paragraphs that follow.

Duty of Care

To determine whether a defendant is liable for negligence, it first must be ascertained whether the defendant owed a **duty of care** to the plaintiff. Duty of care refers to the obligation we all owe each other—the duty not to cause any unreasonable harm or risk of harm. For example, each person owes a duty to drive his or her car carefully, not to push or shove on escalators, not to leave skateboards on the sidewalk, and the like. Businesses owe a duty to make safe products, not to cause accidents, and so on.

Duty of care
The obligation we all owe each other not to cause any unreasonable harm or risk of harm.

The courts decide whether a duty of care is owed in specific cases by applying a **reasonable person standard**. Under this test, the courts attempt to determine how an *objective, careful, and conscientious person would have acted in the same circumstances*, and then measure the defendant's conduct against this standard. The defendant's subjective intent ("I didn't mean to do it") is immaterial in asserting liability. Certain impairments do not affect the reasonable person standard. For instance, there is no reasonable alcoholics standard.

Defendants with specific expertise or competence are measured against a **reasonable professional standard**. This standard is applied in much the same way as the reasonable person standard. For example, a brain surgeon is measured against a reasonable brain surgeon standard rather than a lower reasonable doctor standard. Children are generally required to act as a *reasonable child* of similar age and experience would act.

Negligence is the omission to do something which a reasonable man would do, or doing something which a prudent and reasonable man would not do.
B. Alderson Blyth v. Birmingham
Waterworks Co. (1856)

Breach of Duty

Once a court finds that the defendant actually owed the plaintiff a duty of care, it must determine whether the defendant breached this duty. A **breach of the duty of care** is the failure to exercise care. It is the failure to act as a reasonable person would act. A breach of this duty may consist of either an action (e.g., throwing a lit match on the ground in a forest and causing a fire) or failure to act when there is a duty to act (e.g., a firefighter who refuses to put out a fire). Generally, passersby are not expected to rescue others gratuitously to save them from harm.

Breach of the duty of care
Failure to exercise care or to act as a reasonable person would act.

Injury to Plaintiff

Even though a defendant's act might have breached a duty of care owed to the plaintiff, this breach is not actionable unless the plaintiff suffers **injury**. For example, a business's negligence causes an explosion and fire at its factory at night. No one is injured and there is no damage to the neighbor's property. The negligence is not actionable.

The damages recoverable depend on the effect of the injury on the plaintiff's life or profession. Now suppose two men injure their hands when a train door malfunctions.

OUCH! THE COFFEE'S TOO HOT!

Studies have shown that people don't care about how good their coffee tastes if it is hot. So restaurants, coffee shops, and other sellers make their coffee hot. McDonald's ended up in hot water for making its coffee *too* hot. Consider this case.

Stella Liebeck, an 81-year-old resident of Albuquerque, New Mexico, visited a drive-through window of a McDonald's restaurant with her grandson. Her grandson, the driver of the vehicle placed the order. When it came, he handed a cup of hot coffee to Liebeck. As her grandson drove away from the drive-through window, Liebeck took the lid off the coffee cup she held in her lap. The coffee spilled on Liebeck, who suffered third degree burns on her legs, groin, and buttocks. She required medical treatment, was hospitalized, and has permanent scars from the incident.

Liebeck sued McDonald's for selling coffee that was too hot and for failing to warn her of the danger of the hot coffee it served. McDonald's rejected Liebeck's pretrial offer to settle the case for $300,000.

At trial, McDonald's denied that it had been negligent and asserted that Liebeck's own negligence—opening a hot-coffee cup on her lap—caused her injuries. The jury heard evidence that McDonald's enforces a quality-control rule that requires its restaurants and franchises to serve coffee at 180 to 190 degrees Fahrenheit. Evidence showed that this was 10 to 30 degrees hotter than coffee served by competing restaurant chains, and approximately 40 to 50 degrees hotter than normal house-brewed coffee.

Based on this evidence, the jury concluded that McDonald's acted recklessly and awarded Liebeck $200,000 compensatory damages (reduced by $40,000 for her own negligence), and $2.7 million punitive damages. After the Trial Court judge reduced the amount of punitive damages to $480,000, the parties reached an out-of-court settlement for an undisclosed amount. As a result of this case, McDonald's and other purveyors of coffee have reduced the temperature at which they sell coffee and have placed warnings on their coffee cups.

The first man is a professional basketball player. The second is a college professor. The first man can recover greater damages.

Causation

Causation
The two types of causation that must be proven are (1) causation in fact (actual cause) and (2) proximate cause (legal cause).

A person who commits a negligent act is not liable unless this act was the *cause* of the plaintiff's injuries. Courts have divided **causation** into two categories—causation in fact and proximate cause—and require each to be shown before the plaintiff may recover damages.

1. *Causation in fact*. The defendant's negligent act must be the **causation in fact** (or **actual cause**) of the plaintiff's injuries. For example, suppose a corporation negligently pollutes the plaintiff's drinking water. The plaintiff dies of a heart attack unrelated to the polluted water. Although the corporation has acted negligently, it is not liable for the plaintiff's death. There was a negligent act and an injury, but there was no *cause-and-effect* relationship between them. If, instead, the plaintiff had died from the pollution, there would have been causation in fact and the polluting corporation would have been liable. If two (or more) persons are liable for negligently causing the plaintiff's injuries, both (or all) can be held liable to the plaintiff if acts by each of them are substantial factors in causing the plaintiff's injuries.

2. *Proximate cause*. Under the law, a negligent party is not necessarily liable for all damages set in motion by his or her negligent act. Based on public policy, the law establishes a point along the damage chain after which the negligent party is no longer responsible for the consequences of his or her actions. This limitation on liability is referred to

as **proximate cause**, or **legal cause**. The general test of proximate cause is *foreseeability*. A negligent party who is found to be the actual cause—but not the proximate cause—of the plaintiff's injuries is not liable to the plaintiff. Situations are examined on a case-by-case basis.

The landmark case establishing the doctrine of proximate cause is *Palsgraf v. Long Island Railroad Company* [248 N.Y. 339, 162 N.E. 99, 1928 N.Y. Lexis 1269 (1928)]. Helen Palsgraf was standing on a platform waiting for a passenger train. The Long Island Railroad Company owned and operated the trains and employed the station guards. As a man carrying a package wrapped in a newspaper tried to board the moving train, railroad guards tried to help him. As they did so, the package was dislodged from the man's arm, fell to the railroad tracks, and exploded. The package contained hidden fireworks. The explosion shook the railroad platform, causing a scale on the platform to fall on Palsgraf, injuring her. She sued the railroad for negligence. Justice Cardoza denied her recovery, finding that the railroad was not the proximate cause of her injuries.

SPECIAL NEGLIGENCE DOCTRINES

The courts have developed many *special negligence doctrines*. The most important of these are discussed in the paragraphs that follow.

Professional Malpractice

Professionals, including doctors, lawyers, architects, accountants, and others, owe a duty of ordinary care in providing their services. This duty is known as the *reasonable professional standard*. A professional who breaches this duty of care is liable for the injury that his or her negligence causes. This liability is commonly referred to as **professional malpractice**.

Consider these examples. A doctor who amputates a wrong leg is liable for *medical malpractice*. A lawyer who fails to file a document with the court on time causing the client's case to be dismissed is liable for *legal malpractice*. An accountant who fails to use reasonable care, knowledge, skill, and judgment when providing auditing and other accounting services to a client is liable for *accounting malpractice*.

Professionals who breach this duty are liable to their patients or clients. They also may be liable to some third parties.

Negligent Infliction of Emotional Distress

Some jurisdictions have extended the tort of emotional distress to include the **negligent infliction of emotional distress**. The most common examples of this involve bystanders who witness the injury or death of a loved one that is caused by another's negligent conduct. Under this tort, the bystander, even though not personally physically injured, can sue the negligent party for his or her own mental suffering.

Generally, to be successful in this type of case, the plaintiff must prove that (1) a relative was killed or injured by the defendant, (2) the plaintiff suffered severe emotional distress, and (3) the plaintiff's mental distress resulted from a sensory and contemporaneous observance of the accident. Some states require that the plaintiff's mental distress be manifested by some physical injury; other states have eliminated this requirement.

Negligence Per Se

Statutes often establish duties that one person owes to another. Violating a statute that proximately causes an injury is **negligence per se**. The plaintiff in such an action must prove that (1) a statute existed, (2) the statute was enacted to prevent the type of injury suffered, and (3) the plaintiff was within a class of persons the statute meant to protect.

Negligence per se
Tort where the violation of a statute or ordinance constitutes the breach of the duty of care.

Consider this example: Most cities have an ordinance that places the responsibility for fixing public sidewalks in residential areas on the homeowners whose homes front the sidewalk. A homeowner is liable if he or she fails to repair a damaged sidewalk in front of his or her home and a pedestrian trips and is injured because of the damage. The injured party does not have to prove that the homeowner owed the duty because the statute establishes that.

Res Ipsa Loquitur

Res ipsa loquitur

Tort where the presumption of negligence arises because (1) the defendant was in exclusive control of the situation, and (2) the plaintiff would not have suffered injury but for someone's negligence. The burden switches to the defendant(s) to prove they were not negligent.

If a defendant is in control of a situation in which a plaintiff has been injured and has superior knowledge of the circumstances surrounding the injury, the plaintiff might have difficulty proving the defendant's negligence. In such a situation, the law applies the doctrine of *res ipsa loquitur* (Latin for "the thing speaks for itself"). This doctrine raises a presumption of negligence and switches the burden to the defendant to prove that he or she was *not* negligent. *Res ipsa loquitur* applies in cases where the following elements are met:

1. The defendant had exclusive control of the instrumentality or situation that caused the plaintiff's injury.
2. The injury ordinarily would not have occurred "but for" someone's negligence.

Consider this example: Haeran goes in for major surgery and is given anesthesia to put her to sleep during the operation. Sometime after the operation, it is discovered that a surgical instrument has been left in Haeran during the operation. She suffers severe injury because of the left-in instrument. Haeran would be hard-pressed to identify which doctor or nurse had been careless and left the instrument in her body. In this case, the court can apply the doctrine of *res ipsa loquitur* and place the presumption of negligence on the defendants. Any defendant who can prove that he or she did not leave the instrument in Haeran escapes liability; any defendant who does not disprove his or her negligence is liable. Other typical *res ipsa loquitur* cases involve commercial airplane crashes, falling elevators, and the like.

Good Samaritan Law

Good Samaritan law

A state statute that relieves medical professionals from liability for ordinary negligence when they stop and render aid to victims in emergency situations.

In the past, exposure to liability made many doctors, nurses, and other medical professionals reluctant to stop and render aid to victims in emergency situations, such as highway accidents. Almost all states have enacted a **Good Samaritan law** that relieves medical professionals from liability for injury caused by their ordinary negligence in such circumstances.

Good Samaritan laws protect medical professionals only from liability for their *ordinary negligence*, not for injuries caused by their gross negligence or reckless or intentional conduct. Most Good Samaritan laws protect licensed doctors and nurses and laypersons who have been certified in CPR. Good Samaritan statutes generally do not protect laypersons who are not trained in CPR—that is, they are liable for injuries caused by their ordinary negligence in rendering aid.

Consider this example: Sam is injured in an automobile accident and is unconscious in his automobile alongside the road. Doctor Pamela Heathcoat, who is driving by the scene of the accident, stops, pulls Sam from the burning wreckage, and administers first-aid. In doing so, Pamela negligently breaks Sam's shoulder. If Pamela's negligence is ordinary negligence, she is not liable to Sam because the Good Samaritan law protects her from liability. If Pamela was grossly negligent or reckless in administering aid to Sam, she is liable to him for the injuries she caused.

It is a question of fact for the jury to decide whether a doctor's conduct was ordinary negligence or gross negligence or recklessness. If Cathy, a layperson not trained in CPR, had rendered aid to Sam and caused Sam injury because of her ordinary negligence, the Good Samaritan law would not protect her and she would be liable to Sam.

Dram Shop Act

Many states have enacted a **Dram Shop Act** that makes a tavern and bartender civilly liable for injuries caused to or by patrons who are served too much alcohol. The alcohol must be either served in sufficient quantity to make the patron intoxicated or served to an already intoxicated person. Both the tavern and the bartender are liable to third persons injured by the patron and for injuries the patron suffered. They also are liable for injuries caused by or to minors served by the tavern, regardless of whether the minor is intoxicated.

Guest Statute

Many states have enacted a **guest statute** providing that if a driver voluntarily and without compensation gives a ride in a vehicle to another person (e.g., a hitchhiker), the driver is not liable to the passenger for injuries caused by the driver's ordinary negligence. If the passenger pays compensation to the driver, however, the driver owes a duty of ordinary care to the passenger and will be held liable. The driver is always liable to the passenger for wanton and gross negligence—for example, injuries caused because of excessive speed.

> *No court has ever given, nor do we think ever can give, a definition of what constitutes a reasonable or an average man.*
>
> Lord Goddard C.J.R. v. McCarthy
> (1954)

Fireman's Rule

Under the **fireman's rule**, a firefighter who is injured while putting out a fire may not sue the party whose negligence caused the fire. This rule has been extended to police officers and other government workers. The bases for this rule are that (1) people might not call for help if they could be held liable; (2) firefighters, police officers, and other such workers receive special training for their jobs; and (3) these workers have special medical and retirement programs paid for by the public.

Danger-Invites-Rescue Doctrine

The law recognizes a **danger-invites-rescue doctrine**. Under this doctrine, a rescuer who is injured while going to someone's rescue can sue the person who caused the dangerous situation. For example, a passerby who is injured while trying to rescue children from a fire set by an arsonist can bring a civil suit against the arsonist.

Social Host Liability

Several states have adopted the **social host liability** rule. This rule provides that a social host is liable for injuries caused by guests who are served alcohol at a social function (e.g., a birthday party, a wedding reception) and later cause injury because they are intoxicated. The injury may be to a third person or to the guest himself or herself. The alcohol served at the social function must be the cause of the injury. A few states have adopted statutes that relieve social hosts from such liability.

Liability of Landowners

Owners and renters of real property owe certain duties to protect visitors from injury while on the property. A landowner's and tenant's liability generally depends on the visitor's status. Visitors fall into the following two categories:

1. *Invitees and licensees.* An **invitee** is a person who has been expressly or impliedly invited onto the owner's premises for the *mutual benefit* of both parties (e.g., guests invited for dinner, the mail carrier, and customers of a business). A **licensee** is a person who, *for his or her own benefit*, enters the premises with the express or implied consent of the owner (e.g., Avon representative, encyclopedia salesperson, Jehovah's Witnesses). An owner owes a **duty of ordinary care** to invitees and licensees. An owner is liable if he or she negligently causes injury to an invitee or licensee. For example, a homeowner is liable if she leaves a

Duty of ordinary care
The duty an owner or renter of real property owes an invitee or a licensee to prevent injury or harm when the invitee or licensee steps on the owner's premises.

garden hose across the walkway on which an invitee or a licensee trips and is injured.

2. *Trespassers.* A **trespasser** is a person who has no invitation, permission, or right to be on another's property. Burglars are a common type of trespasser. Generally, an owner does not owe a duty of ordinary care to a trespasser. For example, if a trespasser trips and injures himself on a bicycle the owner negligently left out, the owner is not liable. An owner, however, does owe a **duty not to willfully or wantonly injure** a trespasser. Thus, an owner cannot set traps to injure trespassers.

Duty not to willfully or wantonly injure
The duty an owner or renter of real property owes a trespasser to prevent intentional injury or harm to the trespasser when the trespasser is on his or her premises.

A few states have eliminated the invitee–licensee–trespasser distinction. These states hold that owners and renters owe a duty of ordinary care to all persons who enter the property.

Liability of Common Carriers and Innkeepers

The common law holds common carriers and innkeepers to a higher standard of care than most other businesses. **Common carriers** and **innkeepers** owe a **duty of utmost care**—rather than a duty of ordinary care—to their passengers and guests. For example, innkeepers must provide security for their guests. The concept of utmost care is applied on a case-by-case basis. Obviously, a large hotel must provide greater security to guests than a "mom-and-pop" motel has to provide. Some states and cities have adopted specific statutes and ordinances relating to this duty.

DEFENSES TO NEGLIGENCE

A defendant in a negligence lawsuit may raise several defenses to the imposition of liability. These defenses are discussed in the following paragraphs.

Superseding or Intervening Event

Under negligence, a person is liable only for foreseeable events. Therefore, an original negligent party can raise a **superseding (or intervening) event** as a defense to liability. For example, assume that an avid golfer negligently hits a spectator with a golf ball, knocking the spectator unconscious. While lying on the ground waiting for an ambulance to come, the spectator is struck by a bolt of lightning and killed. The golfer is liable for the injuries caused by the golf ball. He is not liable for the death of the spectator, however, because the lightning bolt was an unforeseen intervening event.

Assumption of the Risk

If a plaintiff knows of and voluntarily enters into or participates in a risky activity that results in injury, the law recognizes that the plaintiff assumed, or took on, the risk involved. Thus, the defendant can raise the defense of **assumption of the risk** against the plaintiff. This defense assumes that the plaintiff (1) had knowledge of the specific risk, and (2) voluntarily assumed that risk. For example, under this theory, a race car driver assumes the risk of being injured or killed in a crash.

Assumption of the risk
A defense a defendant can use against a plaintiff who knowingly and voluntarily enters into or participates in a risky activity that results in injury.

Contributory Negligence

Under the common law doctrine of **contributory negligence**, a plaintiff who is partially at fault for his or her own injury cannot recover against the negligent defendant. For example, suppose a driver who is driving faster than the speed limit negligently hits and injures a pedestrian who is jaywalking. The jury finds that the driver is 80 percent responsible for the accident and the jaywalker is 20 percent responsible. The pedestrian suffered $100,000 in injuries. Under the doctrine of contributory negligence, the pedestrian cannot recover any damages from the driver.

ETHICAL *Perspective*

Duty – Disclose Information That Could Result in Bodily Harm

Ms. Vivi Phan is a paralegal who works for a large law firm that represents major corporate clients. One of the clients that the law firm represents is the IceStone Corporation, which manufactures and sells automobile tires. IceStone Corporation is a major supplier of automobile tires to automobile manufacturers, which place IceStone tires on the automobiles, SUVs, and trucks they sell to the public.

IceStone Corporation designed and manufactured a new automobile tire it calls Ice-Track. IceStone Corporation advertises the tires as having new technology that makes vehicles ride safer, as well as being longer-lasting than tires made by other tire manufacturers. Millions of Ice-Track tires are purchased and placed on new and used vehicles that are sold around the world.

After one year, IceStone Corporation has received thousands of complaints from vehicle owners who allege that their Ice-Track tires easily shred and explode, causing accidents in which drivers and passengers have been killed or injured. Many lawsuits have been filed against IceStone Corporation, alleging product defects in the Ice-Track tires.

IceStone Corporation determines, after a secret internal investigation, that the Ice-Track tires most likely shred and explode when the temperature drops below 32 degrees Fahrenheit. Therefore, most of the accidents involving Ice-Track tires have occurred in the northern areas of the United States and the world that have colder climates. IceStone Corporation does not make this information available to the public.

Ms. Phan is assigned by the law firm to work on the hundreds of product liability lawsuits that IceStone Corporation now faces concerning the defect in its Ice-Track tires. At one of the meetings with the lawyers of your firm and the executives of IceStone Corporation that Ms. Phan attends, the executives of the IceStone Corporation disclose a cost–benefit analysis they have prepared showing that it will be cheaper for the corporation to let the existing Ice-Track tires remain on vehicles without a recall and pay monetary damages to injured victims and the heirs of deceased victims than to recall and replace the defective tires. The lawyers and the executives agree to this strategy and decide not to recall any of the defective tires.

Does Ms. Phan, who has heard this strategy, have any ethical duties to disclose this confidential strategy? Section EC-1.5(d) of the *Model Code of Ethics and Professional Responsibility and Guidance for Enforcement* (Model Code) of the National Federation of Paralegal Associations, Inc. (NFPA) provides guidance. This section states:

> *A paralegal may reveal confidential information only after full disclosure and with the client's written consent; or when required by law or court order; or when necessary to prevent the client from committing an act that could result in death or serious bodily harm.*

In this case, although the information revealed at the meeting is confidential, Ms. Phan owes a duty to disclose this information because it is necessary to prevent the client, IceStone Corporation, from committing an act that will result in deaths and bodily injury to consumers driving vehicles equipped with the Ice-Track tires. Ms. Phan must disclose these confidential facts to the authorities.

* Reprinted by permission from The National Federation of Paralegal Associations, Inc., www.paralegals.org.

The doctrine of contributory negligence has one major exception: The defendant has a duty under the law to avoid the accident if at all possible. This rule is known as the *last clear chance rule*. For example, a driver who sees a pedestrian walking across the street against a "Don't Walk" sign must avoid hitting him or her if possible. When deciding cases involving this rule, the courts consider the attentiveness of the parties and the amount of time each had to respond to the situation.

Comparative Negligence

As seen, application of the doctrine of contributory negligence could reach an unfair result where a party only slightly at fault for his or her injuries could not recover from an otherwise negligent defendant. Many states have replaced the doctrine of contributory

Comparative negligence
A doctrine under which damages are apportioned according to fault.

negligence with the doctrine of **comparative negligence**. Under this doctrine, damages are apportioned according to fault. When the comparative negligence rule is applied to the previous example, the result is much fairer. The plaintiff–pedestrian can recover 80 percent of his or her damages (or $80,000) from the defendant–driver. This is an example of *pure comparative negligence*. Several states have adopted *partial comparative negligence*, which provides that a plaintiff must be less than 50 percent responsible for causing his or her own injuries to recover under comparative negligence; otherwise, contributory negligence applies.

STRICT LIABILITY AND PRODUCT LIABILITY

In the landmark case *Greenmun v. Yuba Power Products, Inc.* [59 Cal.2d 57, 27 Cal.Rptr. 697, 377 P.2d 897, 1963 Cal. Lexis 140 (1963)], the California Supreme Court adopted the **doctrine of strict liability in tort** as a basis for **products liability** actions. Most states now have adopted this doctrine as a basis for product liability actions. The doctrine of strict liability removes many of the difficulties for the plaintiff associated with other theories of product liability. In the remainder of this chapter, we will examine the scope of the strict liability doctrine.

Products liability
The liability of manufacturers, sellers, and others for the injuries caused by defective products.

Restatement of Torts

The doctrine of strict liability is not part of the Uniform Commercial Code (UCC). The most widely recognized articulation of the doctrine is found in Section 402A of the Restatement (Second) of Torts, which provides:

(1) One who sells any product in a defective condition unreasonably dangerous to the user or consumer or to his property is subject to liability for physical harm thereby caused to the ultimate user or consumer, or to his property, if
    (a) the seller is engaged in the business of selling such a product, and
    (b) it is expected to and does reach the user or consumer without substantial change in the condition in which it is sold.
(2) The rule stated in Subsection (1) applies although
    (a) the seller has exercised all possible care in the preparation and sale of his product, and
    (b) the user or consumer has not bought the product from or entered into any contractual relation with the seller.

Liability Without Fault

Unlike negligence, strict liability does not require the injured person to prove that the defendant breached a duty of care. **Strict liability** *is imposed irrespective of fault*. A seller can be found strictly liable even though he or she has exercised all possible care in the preparation and sale of his or her product.

Strict liability
A tort doctrine that makes manufacturers, distributors, wholesalers, retailers, and others in the chain of distribution of a defective product liable for the damages caused by the defect *irrespective of fault*.

    The doctrine of strict liability applies to sellers and lessors of products who are engaged in the business of selling and leasing products. Casual sales and transactions by nonmerchants are not covered. Thus, a person who sells a defective product to a neighbor in a casual sale is not strictly liable if the product causes injury.
    Strict liability applies only to products, not services. In hybrid transactions involving both services and products, the dominant element of the transaction dictates whether strict liability applies. For example, in a medical operation that requires a blood transfusion, the operation would be the dominant element and strict liability would not apply. Strict liability may not be disclaimed.

All in the Chain of Distribution Are Liable

Chain of distribution
All manufacturers, distributors, wholesalers, retailers, lessors, and subcomponent manufacturers involved in a transaction.

All parties in the **chain of distribution** of a defective product are strictly liable for the injuries caused by that product. Thus, all manufacturers, distributors, wholesalers, retailers, lessors, and subcomponent manufacturers may be sued under this doctrine. This view is based on public policy. Lawmakers presume that sellers and lessors will insure against the risk of a strict liability lawsuit and spread the cost to their consumers by raising the price of products.

Consider this example: Suppose a subcomponent manufacturer produces a defective tire and sells it to a truck manufacturer. The truck manufacturer places the defective tire on one of its new-model trucks. The truck is distributed by a distributor to a retail dealer. Ultimately, the retail dealer sells the truck to a buyer. The defective tire causes an accident in which the buyer is injured. All of the parties in the tire's chain of distribution can be sued by the injured party. In this case, the liable parties are the subcomponent manufacturer, the truck manufacturer, the distributor, and the retailer.

A defendant who has not been negligent but who is made to pay a strict liability judgment can bring a separate action against the negligent party in the chain of distribution to recover its losses. In the preceding example, the retailer could sue the manufacturer to recover the strict liability judgment assessed against it. Exhibit 12.1 compares the doctrines of negligence and strict liability.

Parties Who Can Recover for Strict Liability

Because strict liability is a tort doctrine, privity of contract between the plaintiff and the defendant is not required. The doctrine applies even if the injured party had no contractual relations with the defendant. Under strict liability, sellers and lessors are liable to the ultimate user or consumer. Users include the purchaser or lessee, family members, guests, employees, customers, and persons who passively enjoy the benefits of the product (e.g., passengers in automobiles).

Exhibit 12.1 **Doctrines of negligence and strict liability compared**

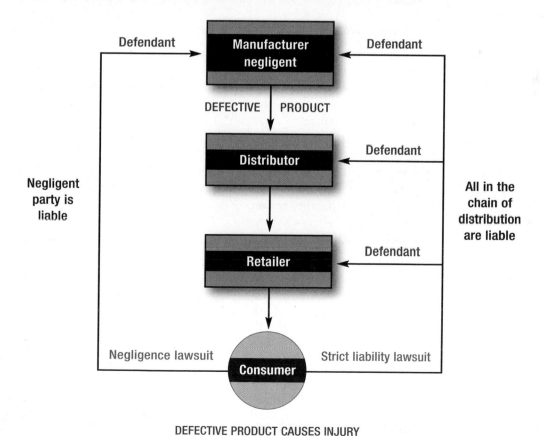

DEFECTIVE PRODUCT CAUSES INJURY

Most jurisdictions have judicially or statutorily extended the protection of strict liability to bystanders. The courts have stated that bystanders should be entitled to even greater protection than a consumer or user. This is because consumers and users have the chance to inspect for defects and to limit their purchases to articles manufactured by reputable manufacturers and sold by reputable retailers, whereas bystanders do not have the same opportunity.

Damages Recoverable for Strict Liability

The damages recoverable in a strict liability action vary by jurisdiction. Damages for personal injuries are recoverable in all jurisdictions that have adopted the doctrine of strict liability, although some jurisdictions limit the dollar amount of the award. Property damage is recoverable in most jurisdictions, but economic loss (e.g., lost income) is recoverable in only a few jurisdictions. **Punitive damages** are generally allowed if the plaintiff can prove that the defendant either intentionally injured him or her or acted with reckless disregard for his or her safety.

Defects

> **Defect**
> Something wrong, inadequate, or improper in manufacture, design, packaging, warning, or safety measures of a product.

To recover for strict liability, the injured party must show that the product that caused the injury had a **defect.** (Remember that the injured party does not have to prove who caused the product to become defective.) A product can be found to be defective in many ways. The most common types of defects are *defects in manufacture*, *failure to warn*, *defects in design*, and *defects in packaging*. These defects are discussed in the following paragraphs.

Defect in Manufacture

A **defect in manufacture** occurs when the manufacturer fails to (1) properly assemble a product, (2) properly test a product, or (3) adequately check the quality of the product.

Failure to Warn

Certain products are inherently dangerous and cannot be made any safer and still accomplish the task for which they are designed. For example, certain useful drugs cause side effects, allergies, and other injuries to some users. Many machines and appliances include dangerous moving parts which, if removed, would defeat the purpose of the machine or appliance.

Manufacturers and sellers of such products are under a *duty to warn* users about the product's dangerous propensities. A proper and conspicuous warning placed on the product insulates the manufacturer and others in the chain of distribution from strict liability. **Failure to warn** of these dangerous propensities is a defect that will support a strict liability action.

Defect in Design

> **Defect in design**
> A flaw that occurs when a product is improperly designed.

A **defect in design** can support a strict liability action. Design defects that have supported strict liability awards include toys that are designed with removable parts that could be swallowed by children, machines and appliances designed without proper safeguards, and trucks and other vehicles designed without warning devices to let people know that the vehicle is backing up.

In evaluating the adequacy of a product's design, the courts apply a risk–utility analysis and consider the gravity of the danger posed by the design, the likelihood that injury will occur, the availability and cost of producing a safer alternative design, the social utility of the product, and other factors.

Defect in Packaging

Manufacturers owe a duty to design and provide safe packages for their products. This duty requires manufacturers to provide packages and containers that are tamperproof

GM HIT WITH PUNITIVE DAMAGES

On Christmas Eve, Patricia Anderson was driving her Chevrolet Malibu automobile, which was manufactured by the General Motors (GM) Corporation, home from church. Her four young children, ages 1 through 9, and a neighbor were also in the car. The Chevy Malibu was stopped at a stoplight at 89th Place and Figueroa Street in Los Angeles when a drunken driver plowed his car into the back of the Malibu at 50 to 70 mph. The Malibu burst into flames as its gas tank ruptured and ignited. Although no one died in the crash, the occupants of the Malibu were severely burned. Many required substantial and multiple skin grafts.

The two injured women and four injured children sued GM for product liability. They alleged that the fuel tank of the Chevy Malibu was defectively designed and placed too close to the rear bumper. The accident victims produced evidence showing that GM knew the car's fuel-tank design was unsafe but had not changed the design because of cost.

The Chevy Malibu was one of GM's A-Class cars, which also include the Pontiac Grand Am, the Oldsmobile Cutlass, and the Chevrolet Monte Carlo, all of which have similar fuel-tank designs. The plaintiffs produced GM memos that said it would cost GM $8.59 per vehicle to produce and install a safer fuel tank design, but that it would cost the company only an estimated $2.40 per car not to fix the cars and pay damages to injured victims.

After a 10-week trial, the jurors returned a verdict of $107 million in compensatory damages to the plaintiffs for injuries, disfigurement, and pain and suffering caused to them by the accident. The jury then tacked on $4.9 billion as punitive damages to punish GM. This was the largest amount ever awarded in a personal-injury lawsuit. GM asked the trial judge to throw out the trial, claiming that the jury was prejudiced by repetitive personal attacks on GM as a "soulless company" and its lawyers as "hired guns" who consumed "cappuccinos and designer muffins." GM did not convince the judge that such animosity influenced the jury.

In its post-trial motions, GM argued that the award of damages, specifically the $4.8 billion of punitive damages, was the result of bias and prejudice of the jury and asked the trial court judge to reduce the award of damages. This the Trial Court judge did. He let stand the compensatory damages award but reduced the award of punitive damages to $1 billion.

or that clearly indicate if they have been tampered with. Certain manufacturers, such as drug manufacturers, owe a duty to place their products in containers that cannot be opened by children. A manufacturer's failure to meet this duty subjects that manufacturer and others in the chain of distribution of the product to strict liability for **defect in packaging.**

Other Product Defects

Other product defects can prove the basis for a strict liability action. **Failure to provide adequate instructions** for either the safe assembly or safe use of a product is a defect that subjects the manufacturer and others in the chain of distribution to strict liability.

Other defects include inadequate testing of products, inadequate selection of component parts of materials, and improper certification of the safety of a product. The concept of defect is an expanding area of the law.

Legal Terminology

Actual cause 436	Breach of duty of care 435	Common carrier 440
Assault 430	Causation 436	Comparative negligence 442
Assumption of the risk 440	Causation in fact 436	Contributory negligence 440
Battery 430	Chain of distribution 442	Conversion of personal property 434

Summary

CHAPTER *12* TORTS

Intentional Torts

Assault	Assault is the threat of immediate harm or offensive contact, or any action that arouses reasonable apprehension of imminent harm.
Battery	Battery is the unauthorized and harmful or offensive physical contact with another person. *Transferred intent doctrine:* If a person intends to injure one person but actually harms another person, the law transfers the perpetrator's intent from the target to the actual victim.
False Imprisonment	Intentional confinement or restraint of another person without authority or justification and without that person's consent
Merchant Protection	Merchant protection statutes permit businesses to stop, detain, and investigate suspected shoplifters (and not be held liable for false imprisonment) if the following requirements are met. 1. There are reasonable grounds for the suspicion. 2. Suspects are detained for only a reasonable time. 3. Investigations are conducted in a reasonable manner.
Defamation of Character	When the defendant makes an untrue statement of fact about the plaintiff that is published to a third party, it is defamation of character. Truth is an absolute defense. Types of defamation: 1. *Slander:* Oral defamation 2. *Libel:* Written defamation Public-figure plaintiffs must prove the additional element of *malice*.
Misappropriation of the Right to Publicity	Also called *tort of appropriation*, this tort means appropriating another person's name or identity for commercial purposes without that person's consent.
Invasion of the Right to Privacy	Unwarranted and undesired publicity of a private fact about a person is invasion of privacy. The fact does not have to be untrue. Truth is not a defense.

Intentional Infliction of Emotional Distress	Also known as *tort of outrage*, this is extreme and outrageous conduct intentionally or recklessly done that causes severe emotional distress. Some states require that the mental distress be manifested by physical injury.
Malicious Prosecution	A successful defendant in a prior lawsuit can sue the plaintiff if the first lawsuit was frivolous.
Trespass to Land	Trespass to land interferes with a landowner's right to exclusive possession of his or her land.
Trespass to Personal Property	In this form of trespass, a person injures another person's personal property or interferes with that person's enjoyment of his or her property.
Conversion of Personal Property	Conversion of personal property means taking over another person's personal property and depriving him or her of the use and enjoyment of the property.

Unintentional Torts—Negligence

Definition	Negligence is defined as the omission to do something that a reasonable person would do, or doing something that a prudent and reasonable person would not do.

Elements of Negligence	To establish negligence, the plaintiff must prove:
	1. The defendant owed *a duty of care* to the plaintiff.
	2. The defendant *breached this duty*.
	3. The plaintiff suffered *injury*.
	4. The defendant's negligent act *caused* the plaintiff's injury. Two types of causation must be shown:
	  a. *Causation in fact* (or *actual cause*): The defendant's negligent act was the actual cause of the plaintiff's injury.
	  b. *Proximate cause* (or *legal cause*): The defendant is liable only for the *foreseeable* consequences of his or her negligent act.

Special Negligence Doctrines

Professional Malpractice	Doctors; lawyers, architects, accountants, and other professionals owe a duty of ordinary care in providing their services. They are judged by a *reasonable professional standard*. Professionals who breach this duty are liable to clients and some third parties for *professional malpractice*
Negligent Infliction of Emotional Distress	A person who witnesses a close relative's injury or death may sue the negligent party who caused the accident, to recover damages for any emotional distress the bystander suffered. To recover for *negligent infliction of emotional distress*, the plaintiff must prove: 1. A relative was killed or injured by the defendant. 2. The plaintiff suffered severe emotional distress. 3. The plaintiff's mental distress resulted from a sensory and contemporaneous observance of the accident. Some states require that the mental distress be manifested by physical injury.
Negligence *Per Se*	A statute or ordinance establishes the duty of care. A violation of the statute or ordinance constitutes a breach of this duty of care.
Res Ipsa Loquitur	A presumption of negligence is established if the defendant had exclusive control of the instrumentality or situation that caused the plaintiff's injury and the injury would not have ordinarily occurred but for someone's negligence. The defendants may rebut this presumption.
Good Samaritan Laws	Good Samaritan laws relieve doctors and other medical professionals from liability for ordinary negligence when they render medical aid in emergency situations.
Dram Shop Act	A dram shop act is a state statute that make taverns and bartenders liable for injuries caused to or by patrons who are served too much alcohol and cause injury to themselves or others.

Guest Statute	A guest statute provides that a driver of a vehicle is not liable for ordinary negligence to passengers whom he or she gratuitously transports. The driver is liable for gross negligence.
Fireman's Rule	Firefighters, police officers, and other government employees who are injured in the performance of their duties cannot sue the person who negligently caused the dangerous situation that caused the injury.
Danger-Invites-Rescue Doctrine	A person who is injured while going to someone's rescue may sue the person who caused the dangerous situation.
Social Host Liability	Some states make social hosts liable for injuries caused by guests who are served alcohol at a social function and later cause injury because they are intoxicated.
Liability of Landowners	Landowners (and tenants) owe the following duties to persons who come upon their property: 1. *Invitees:* Duty of ordinary care 2. *Licensees:* Duty of ordinary care 3. *Trespassers:* Duty not to willfully and wantonly injure trespassers
Liability of Common Carriers and Innkeepers	Common carriers and innkeepers owe a *duty of utmost care*, rather than the duty of ordinary care, to protect their passengers and patrons from injury.

Defenses to Negligence

Superseding Event	An intervening activity by another person that caused the plaintiff's injuries, which relieves the defendant from liability
Assumption of the Risk	A defendant is not liable for the plaintiff's injuries if the plaintiff had knowledge of a specific risk and voluntarily assumed that risk. States have adopted one of the following two rules that affect a defendant's liability if the plaintiff had been partially at fault for causing his or her own injuries: 1. *Contributory negligence*: A plaintiff cannot recover anything from the defendant. 2. *Comparative negligence*: Damages are apportioned according to the parties' fault. Also called *comparative fault*.

Strict Liability and Product Liability

Strict Liability	A manufacturer or seller who sells a defective product is liable to the ultimate user who is injured thereby. All in the chain of distribution are liable irrespective of fault. Sometimes called *vertical liability*.
Products Liability	Products liability is the liability of manufacturers, sellers, and others for the injuries caused by defective products.
Defect	To recover for strict liability, the injured party must show that the product that caused the injury was defective. The most common types of defects are: 1. Defect in manufacture 2. Failure to warn 3. Defect in design 4. Defect in packaging 5. Failure to provide adequate instructions

WORKING THE WEB

1. Visit the website **http://en.wikipedia.org/wiki/negligence.html**. On the right side of the screen, pick a negligence issue that interests you and click on this subject. Read the material that is available and write a half-page report about this negligence issue.

2. Visit the website **http://www.atra.org.html**. Click on "State and Federal Reform," then click on your state. Write a one-page report describing recent tort reforms in your state.

3. Go to the website **http://www.google.com/html** or similar Internet search engine. Using an Internet search, find your state's Good Samaritan law. Print out this law or write a half-page brief of this law.

4. Go to the website **http://stellaawards.com/html**. Subscribe to receive True Stella Awards case write-ups free. Many of these case write-ups are about tort cases. For the next tort case that you receive from this site, write a half-page report describing this case.

5. Visit the website **http://en.wikipedia.org/wiki/intentional_torts.html**. On the right side of the screen, pick an intentional tort issue that interests you and click on this subject. Read the material that is available and write a half-page report about this negligence issue.

CRITICAL THINKING AND WRITING QUESTIONS

1. Define the word *tort*.
2. What is an *intentional* tort?
3. Define and differentiate assault and battery.
4. Define false imprisonment. What do merchant protection statutes provide? What requirements must be met to be protected by a merchant protection statute?
5. Describe the following intentional torts: (a) defamation of character, (b) misappropriation of the right to publicity, (c) invasion of the right to privacy, and (d) intentional infliction of emotional distress.
6. What is negligence? What elements must be proven to find negligence? Describe duty of care and breach of duty of care.
7. For a plaintiff to win a tort lawsuit, must the plaintiff have suffered injury? Explain.
8. What is the difference between causation in fact (actual cause) and proximate cause (legal cause)?
9. Describe the following special negligence doctrines: (a) professional malpractice, (b) negligence per se, (c) *res ipsa loquitur*, and (d) negligent infliction of emotional distress.
10. Describe Good Samaritan laws. What public policy do these laws serve?
11. Define the following parties: (a) invitees, (b) licensees, and (c) trespassers. Describe the liability of landowners and tenants to each of these persons.
12. Describe the following two defenses to negligence: (a) superseding event, and (b) assumption of the risk.
13. Describe the difference between contributory negligence and comparative negligence. Give an example of each.
14. Describe the doctrine of strict liability. To what type of lawsuit does this doctrine apply? Describe how strict liability differs from negligence.
15. Describe the following types of product defects and give an example of each: (a) defect in manufacture, (b) failure to warn, (c) defect in design, and (d) defect in packaging.

ETHICS ANALYSIS AND DISCUSSION QUESTIONS

1. What ethical obligation does the legal team have to inform clients, even when the client does not ask for advice, of actions they should take to avoid liability in light of decisions like the one in the case against McDonald's for damages from hot coffee?
2. What is the "reasonable professional standard" for a paralegal?
3. As a recent graduate with school loans to pay, you also work at a local food market at night. You are working on a slow Tuesday evening and instead of walking the aisle of the store, you take a coffee break in the back of the store. A customer slips on a small bunch of grapes, which are in the aisle, breaking a bone in the leg. The injured customer is also a long-time client of the law firm where you work. Is there any conflict of interest? How can the conflict be resolved?

▶DEVELOPING YOUR COLLABORATION SKILLS

Working on your own or with a group of other students assigned by your instructor, review the scenario at the beginning of the chapter. As a group, discuss the following questions.

1. Does the legal doctrine of negligence apply to this case? What are the elements of negligence that Mrs. Sheen must prove to win a negligence case? Who would the defendants be in a negligence lawsuit?

2. What does the doctrine of strict liability provide? Is the doctrine of strict liability applicable to this case? What type of defect could be asserted in a strict liability lawsuit in this case? Who would be defendants in a strict liability lawsuit?

3. What type of injuries could the plaintiffs assert, and what type of damages could the plaintiffs recover in this case? Explain. Would punitive damages be available in this case?

▶PARALEGAL PORTFOLIO EXERCISE

1. Prepare a memorandum, no longer than three pages, that discusses the doctrine of strict liability as used in product liability cases, the different types of defects that can be asserted in a strict liability case, and the types of damages that can be awarded in strict liability cases.

▶LEGAL ANALYSIS AND WRITING CASES

James v. Meow Media, Inc.

300 F.3d 683
United States Court of Appeals, Sixth Circuit

FACTS

Michael Carneal was a 14-year-old freshman student at Heath High School in Paducah, Kentucky. Carneal regularly played the violent interactive video and computer games *Doom, Quake, Castle Wolfenstein, Rampage, Nightmare Creatures, Mech Warrior, Resident Evil, and Final Fantasy.* These games involved the player shooting virtual opponents with computer guns and other weapons. Carneal also watched videotaped movies, including one called *The Basketball Diaries,* in which a high-school student protagonist dreams of killing his teacher and several of his fellow classmates. On December 1, 1997, Carneal brought a .22-caliber pistol and five shotguns to the lobby of Heath High School and shot several of his fellow students, killing three and wounding many others. The three students killed were Jessica James, Kayce Steger, and Nicole Hadley.

The parents of the three dead children ("James") sued the producers and distributors of the violent video games and movies that Carneal had watched previous to the shooting. The parents sued to recover damages for wrongful death, alleging that the defendants were negligent in producing and distributing such games and movies to Carneal. The U.S. district court applied Kentucky law and held that the defendants did not owe or breach a duty to the plaintiffs and therefore were not liable for negligence. The plaintiffs appealed.

Question

1. Did the defendant video and movie producers and distributors owe a duty of care to the plaintiffs by selling and licensing violent video games and movies to Carneal, who killed the three students?

Cheong v. Antablin

16 Cal. 4th 1063, 68 Cal.Rptr.2d 859 946 P.2d 817 (1997)
Supreme Court of California

FACTS

On April 11, 1991, Wilkie Cheong and Drew R. Antablin, long-time friends and experienced skiers, skied together at Alpine Meadows, a resort near Tahoe City, California. While skiing, Antablin accidentally collided with Cheong, causing injury to him. Cheong sued Antablin to recover damages for negligent skiing. The trial court granted Antablin's motion for summary judgment, holding that the doctrine of assumption of risk barred Cheong's claim and dismissed the lawsuit. The court of appeals affirmed. Cheong appealed to the California Supreme Court.

Question

1. Does the doctrine of assumption of risk bar recovery?

Shoshone Coca-Cola Bottling Co. v. Dolinski

420 P.2d 855 Supreme Court of Nevada

FACTS

Leo Dolinski purchased a bottle of Squirt, a soft drink, from a vending machine at a Sea and Ski plant, his place of employment. Dolinski opened the bottle and consumed part of its contents. He immediately became ill. Upon examination, it was found that the bottle contained the decomposed body of a mouse, mouse hair, and mouse feces. Dolinski visited a doctor and was given medicine to counteract nausea. Dolinski suffered physical and mental distress from consuming the decomposed mouse and possessed an aversion to soft drinks. The Shoshone Coca-Cola Bottling Company (Shoshone) manufactured and distributed the Squirt bottle.

Dolinski sued Shoshone, basing his lawsuit on the doctrine of strict liability. The state of Nevada had not previously recognized the doctrine of strict liability. However, the trial court adopted the doctrine of strict liability, and the jury returned a verdict in favor of the plaintiff. Shoshone appealed.

Question

1. Should the state of Nevada judicially adopt the doctrine of strict liability? If so, was there a defect in the manufacture of the Squirt bottle that caused the plaintiff's injuries?

Lakin v. Senco Products, Inc.

925 P.2d 107
Court of Appeals of Oregon

FACTS

Senco Products, Inc. (Senco) manufactures and markets a variety of pneumatic nail guns, including the SN325 nail gun, which discharges 3.25-inch nails. The SN325 uses special nails designed and sold by Senco. The SN325 will discharge a nail only if two trigger mechanisms are activated; that is, the user must both squeeze the nail gun's finger trigger and press the nail gun's muzzle against a surface, activating the bottom trigger for safety. The SN325 can fire up to nine nails per second if the trigger is continuously depressed and the gun is bounced along the work surface, constantly reactivating the muzzle safety/trigger.

On December 1, 1990, John Lakin was using a Senco SN325 nail gun to help build a new home. When attempting to nail 2×4s under the eaves of the garage, Lakin stood on tiptoe and raised a 2×4 over his head. As he held the board in position with his left hand and the nail gun in his right hand, he pressed the nose of the SN325 up against the board, depressed the safety, and pulled the finger trigger to fire the nail into the board. The gun fired the first nail and then, in a phenomenon known as "double firing," immediately discharged an unintended second nail that struck the first nail. The gun recoiled violently backward toward Lakin and, with Lakin's finger still on the trigger, came into contact with his cheek. That contact activated the safety/trigger, causing the nail gun to fire a third nail. This third nail went through Lakin's cheekbone and into his brain.

The nail penetrated the frontal lobe of the right hemisphere of Lakin's brain, blocked a major artery, and caused extensive tissue damage. Lakin was unconscious for several days and ultimately underwent multiple surgeries. He suffers permanent brain damage and is unable to perceive information from the left hemisphere of the brain. He also suffers partial paralysis of the left side of his body. Lakin has undergone a radical personality change and is prone to violent outbursts. He is unable to obtain employment. Lakin's previously warm and loving relationship with his wife and four children has been permanently altered. He can no longer live with his family and instead resides in a supervised group home for brain-injured persons.

Lakin and his wife sued Senco for strict liability based on design defect. The trial court found Senco liable and awarded $3.6 million to Lakin, $457,000 to his wife, and $4 million in punitive damages against Senco. Senco appealed.

Question

1. Is Senco liable to Lakin for strict liability based on a design defect in the SN325 that allowed it to double-fire?

Manning v. Grimsley

643 F.2d 20
1981 U.S. App. Lexis 19782 (1st Cir. 1981)

FACTS

On September 16, 1975, the Baltimore Orioles professional baseball team was at Boston's Fenway Park to play the Boston Red Sox. Ross Grimsley was a pitcher for the visiting Baltimore club. During one period of the game, Grimsley was warming up in the bullpen, throwing pitches to a catcher. During this warmup, Boston spectators in the stands heckled Grimsley.

After Grimsley had completed warming up and the catcher had left from behind the plate in the bullpen, Grims-ley wound up as if he were going to throw the ball in his hand at the plate, then turned and threw the ball at one of the hecklers in the stand. The ball traveled at about 80 miles an hour, passed through a wire fence protecting the spectators, missed the heckler that Grimsley was aiming at, and hit another spectator, David Manning; Jr., causing injury. Manning sued Grimsley and the Baltimore Orioles.

Question

1. Are the defendants liable?

Johnson v. Kmart Enterprises, Inc.

297 N.W.2d 74 1980
Wisc. App. Lexis 3197 (Wis. App. 1980)

FACTS

At about 7:30 P.M. on September 8, 1976, Deborah A. Johnson entered a Kmart store located in Madison, Wisconsin, to purchase some diapers and several cans of motor oil. She took her young child along to enable her to purchase the correct-size diapers, carrying the child in an infant seat that the mother had purchased at Kmart two or three weeks previously. A large Kmart price tag was still attached to the infant seat. Johnson purchased the diapers and oil and some children's clothes. She was in a hurry to leave because it was 8:00 P.M., her child's feeding time, and she hurried through the checkout lane. She paid for the diapers, the oil, and the clothing.

Just after leaving the store, she heard someone ask her to stop. She turned around and saw a Kmart security officer. He showed her a badge and asked her to come back into the store, which she did. The man stated, "I have reason to believe that you have stolen this car seat." Johnson explained that she had purchased the seat previously. She demanded to see the manager, who was called to the scene. When Johnson pointed out that the seat had cat hairs, food crumbs, and milk stains on it, the man said, "I'm really sorry. There's been a terrible mistake. You can go." Johnson looked at the clock when she left, which read 8:20 P.M. Johnson sued Kmart for false imprisonment.

Question

1. Is Kmart liable?

Karns v. Emerson Electric Co.

817 F.2d 1452
1987 U.S. App. Lexis 5608 (1987)

FACTS

The Emerson Electric Co. manufactures and sells a product called the Weed Eater Model XR-90. The Weed Eater is a multipurpose weed-trimming and brush-cutting device. It consists of a handheld gasoline-powered engine connected to a long drive shaft, at the end of which can be attached various tools for cutting weeds and brush. One such attachment is a 10-inch circular sawblade capable of cutting through growth up to 2 inches in diameter. When this sawblade is attached to the Weed Eater, approximately 270 degrees of blade edge are exposed when in use.

The owner's manual contained the following warning: "Keep children away. All people and pets should be kept at a safe distance from the work area, at least 30 feet, especially when using the blade."

Donald Pearce, a 13-year-old boy, was helping his uncle clear an overgrown yard. The uncle was operating a Weed Eater XR-90 with the circular sawblade attachment. When Pearce stooped to pick up something off the ground about 6 to 10 feet behind and slightly to the left of where his uncle was operating the Weed Eater, the sawblade on the Weed Eater struck something near the ground. The Weed Eater kicked back to the left and cut off Pearce's right arm to the elbow. Pearce, through his mother, Charlotte Karns, sued Emerson to recover damages under strict liability.

Question

1. Is Emerson liable?

Luque v. McLean, Trustee

8 Cal.3d 136, 104 Cal.Rptr. 443 501 P.2d 1163, 1972 Cal. Lexis 245 (Cal. 1972)

FACTS

Celestino Luque lived with his cousins Harry and Laura Dunn in Millbrae, California. The Dunns purchased a rotary lawn mower from Rhoads Hardware. The lawn mower was manufactured by Air Capital Manufacturing Company and was distributed by Garehime Corporation. On December 4, 1965, neighbors asked Luque to mow their lawn. While Luque was cutting the lawn, he noticed a small carton in the path of the lawn mower. Luque left the lawn mower in a stationary position with its motor running and walked around the side of the lawn mower to remove the carton. As he did so, he suddenly slipped on the wet grass and fell backward.

Luque's left hand entered the unguarded hole of the lawn mower and was caught in the revolving blade, which turns at 175 miles per hour and 100 revolutions per second. Luque's hand was severely mangled and lacerated. The word *Caution* was printed above the unguarded hole on the lawn mower.

Luque sued Rhoads Hardware, Air Capital, and Garehime Corporation for strict liability. The defendants argued that strict liability does not apply to *patent* (obvious) defects.

Question

1. Was it ethical for the defendants to argue that they were not liable for patent defects? Would patent defects ever be corrected if the defendants' contention were accepted by the court? Who wins?

▶WORKING WITH THE LANGUAGE OF THE COURT

Braun v. Soldier of Fortune Magazine, Inc.

968 F.2d 1110 1992 U.S. App. Lexis 18556 (1992)
United States Court of Appeals, Eleventh Circuit

Read the following case, excerpted from the Court of Appeals opinion. Review and brief the case. In your brief answer the following questions:

1. Who are the plaintiffs? What are they suing for?
2. When does a magazine owe a duty to refrain from publishing an advertisement?
3. Was the advertisement the proximate cause of the plaintiff's injuries?
4. Should the award of punitive damages have been reduced?

Anderson, Circuit Judge

In January 1985, Michael Savage submitted a personal service advertisement to Soldier of Fortune (SOF). After several conversations between Savage and SOF's advertising manager, Joan Steel, the following advertisement ran in the June 1985 through March 1986 issues of SOF:

> GUN FOR HIRE: 37-year-old professional mercenary desires jobs. Vietnam Veteran. Discrete [sic] and very private. Body guard, courier, and other special skills. All jobs considered. Phone (615) 436-9785 (days) or (615) 436-4335 (nights), or write: Rt. 2, Box 682 Village Loop Road, Gatlinburg, TN 37738.

Savage testified that, when he placed the ad, he had no intention of obtaining anything but legitimate jobs. Nonetheless, Savage stated that the overwhelming majority of the 30 to 40 phone calls a week he received in response to his ad sought his participation in criminal activity such as murder, assault, and kidnapping. The ad also generated at least one legitimate job as a bodyguard, which Savage accepted.

In late 1984 or early 1985, Bruce Gastwirth began seeking to murder his business partner, Richard Braun. Gastwirth enlisted the aid of another business associate, John Horton Moore, and together they arranged for at least three attempts on Braun's life, all of which were unsuccessful. Responding to Savage's SOF ad, Gastwirth and Moore contacted him in August 1985 to discuss plans to murder Braun.

On August 26, 1985, Savage, Moore, and another individual, Sean Trevor Doutre, went to Braun's suburban Atlanta home. As Braun and his 16-year-old son Michael were driving down the driveway, Doutre stepped in front of Braun's car and fired several shots into the car with a MAC 11 automatic pistol. The shots hit Michael in the thigh and wounded Braun as well. Braun managed to roll out of the car, but Doutre walked over to Braun and killed him by firing two more shots into the back of his head as Braun lay on the ground.

On March 31, 1988, appellees Michael and Ian Braun filed this diversity action against appellants in the United States District Court for the Middle District of Alabama, seeking damages for the wrongful death of their father. Michael Braun also filed a separate action seeking recovery for the personal injuries he received at the time of his father's death. The district court consolidated these related matters.

Trial began on December 3, 1990. Appellees contended that, under Georgia law, SOF was liable for their injuries because SOF negligently published a personal service advertisement that created an unreasonable risk of the solicitation and commission of violent criminal activity, including murder. To show that SOF knew of the likelihood that criminal activity would result from placing an ad like Savage's, appellees introduced evidence of newspaper and magazine articles published prior to Braun's murder which described links between SOF and personal service ads and a number of criminal convictions including murder, kidnapping, assault, extortion, and attempts thereof. Appellees also presented evidence that, prior to SOF's acceptance of Savage's ad, law enforcement officials had contacted SOF staffers on two separate occasions in connection with investigations of crimes.

In his trial testimony, SOF president Robert K. Brown denied having any knowledge of criminal activity associated with SOF's personal service ads at any time prior to Braun's murder in August 1985. Both Jim Graves, a former managing editor of SOF, and Joan Steel, the advertising manager who accepted Savage's advertisement, similarly testified that they were not aware of other crimes connected with SOF ads prior to running Savage's ad. Steel further testified that she had understood the term "Gun for Hire" in Savage's ad to refer to a "bodyguard or protection service-type thing" rather than to any illegal activity.

The jury returned a verdict in favor of appellee and awarded compensatory damages on the wrongful death claim in the amount of $2,000,000. The jury also awarded appellee Michael Braun $375,000 in compensatory damages and $10,000,000 in punitive damages for his personal injury claim.

To prevail in an action for negligence in Georgia, a party must establish the following elements:

1. A legal duty to conform to a standard of conduct raised by the law for the protection of others against unreasonable risks of harm,
2. a breach of this standard,
3. a legally attributable causal connection between the conduct and the resulting injury, and
4. some loss or damage flowing to the plaintiff's legally protected interest as a result of the alleged breach of the legal duty.

To the extent that SOF denies that a publisher owes any duty to the public when it publishes personal service ads, its position is clearly inconsistent with Georgia law. We believe, however, that the crux of SOF's argument is not that it had no duty to the public but that, as a matter of law, there is a risk to the public when a publisher prints an "unreasonable" advertisement only if the ad openly solicits criminal activity.

SOF further argues that imposing liability on publishers for the advertisements they print indirectly threatens core, noncommercial speech to which the Constitution accords its full protection. Supreme Court cases discussing the limitations the First Amendment places on state defamation law indicate that there is no constitutional infirmity in Georgia law holding publishers liable under a negligence standard with respect to the commercial advertisements they print. Past Supreme Court decisions indicate, however, that the negligence standard the First Amendment permits is a "modified" negligence standard. The Court's decisions suggest that Georgia law may impose tort liability on publishers for injury caused by the advertisements they print only if the ad on its face, without the need to investigate, makes it apparent that there is a substantial danger of harm to the public.

We conclude that the First Amendment permits a state to impose upon a publisher liability for compensatory damages for negligently publishing a commercial advertisement where the ad on its face, and without the need for investigation, makes it apparent that there is a substantial danger of harm to the public. The absence of a duty requiring publishers to investigate the advertisements they print and the requirement that the substance of the ad itself must warn the publisher of a substantial danger of harm to the public guarantee that the burden placed on publishers will not impermissibly chill protected commercial speech.

Our review of the language of Savage's ad persuades us that SOF had a legal duty to refrain from publishing it. Savage's advertisement (1) emphasized the term "Gun for Hire," (2) described Savage as a "professional mercenary," (3) stressed Savage's willingness to keep his assignments confidential and "very private," (4) listed legitimate jobs involving the use of a gun—bodyguard and courier—followed by a reference to Savage's "other special skills," and (5) concluded by stating that Savage would consider "all jobs."

The ad's combination of sinister terms makes it apparent that there was a substantial danger of harm to the public. The ad expressly solicits all jobs requiring the use of a gun. When the list of legitimate jobs—i.e., bodyguard and courier—is followed by "other special skills" and "all jobs considered," the implication is clear that the advertiser would consider illegal jobs. We agree with the district court that "the language of this advertisement is such that, even though couched in terms not explicitly offering criminal services, the publisher could recognize the offer of criminal activity as readily as its readers obviously did." We find that the jury had ample grounds for finding that SOF's publication of Savage's ad was the proximate cause of Braun's injuries.

For the foregoing reasons, we affirm the District Court's judgment.

CONTRACTS AND E-COMMERCE

"The movement of the progressive societies has hitherto been a movement from status to contract."

—Sir Henry Maine,
Ancient Law

PARALEGALS AT WORK

You are a paralegal who works for Mr. Andrew Copan, a lawyer who represents small businesses. A significant part of Mr. Copan's practice is the drafting of contracts for the business clients when they are dealing with individuals and other businesses. Mr. Copan also engages in civil litigation and represents his clients bringing or defending contract-related cases in court.

One of Mr. Copan's clients is Jewelry Associates Corporation, a small corporation that is in the retail jewelry business. The business has three owners. The business buys jewels in overseas markets and sells the jewels in a retail store serving customers.

One day, the three owners of Jewelry Associates Corporation make an appointment to see Mr. Copan to discuss several business matters. As his paralegal, Mr. Copan asks you to sit in on the meeting, which you do. At the meeting, the three owners explain that they have found a new source of jewels, which is a foreign company located in the country of Sri Lanka. The owners ask Mr. Copan to draft a contract that will be used between Jewelry Associates Corporation and the foreign company. Jewelry Associates Corporation will be the buyer, and the foreign company will be the seller of jewels. The owners ask Mr. Copan to research the law applicable to the situation and prepare a contract for this transaction.

The owners further explain that they have obtained the Web address jewelryjewelry.com and that they want to begin selling jewelry through e-commerce. They disclose that they are having a website designed, and that they need an online contract drafted for the sale of jewelry online. They ask Mr. Copan to draft the necessary online contract that will be placed on the website.

In addition, the owners of Jewelry Associates Corporation disclose that the business currently leases its retail store space from an owner of the building housing their retail store, but that their lease will be over in nine months. The

---

After studying this chapter, you should be able to:

1. List the elements necessary to form a valid contract.

2. Define an offer and an acceptance.

3. Define consideration and analyze whether contracts are lacking in consideration.

4. Identify illegal contracts that are contrary to statutes and that violate public policy.

5. List and describe the contracts that must be in writing under the Statute of Frauds.

6. Describe compensatory, consequential, and liquidated damages.

7. Define sales contracts governed by Article 2 of the UCC and lease contracts governed by Article 2A of the UCC.

8. Describe the writing, signature, and other special requirements for Internet contracts.

9. Define e-commerce and describe the formation and enforcement of e-contracts.

owners disclose that their corporation entered into a contract with Real Estate Developers Inc. to purchase a building and land to which they will transfer their retail business. The clients disclose, however, that Real Estate Developers Inc. now has refused to go through with the contract and has refused to sell Jewelry Associates Corporation the building and land. The owners ask Mr. Copan what course of action to take to obtain the building.

After the clients have left, Mr. Copan asks you, as his paralegal, to assist him in conducting the legal research necessary for these matters, and to prepare first drafts of the contracts discussed at the meeting.

Consider the issues involved in this scenario as you read the chapter.

▶ INTRODUCTION FOR THE PARALEGAL

The law of contracts makes up a substantial portion of many lawyers' practices. Lawyers rely heavily on the help of paralegals in drafting and reviewing contracts. Lawyers are called upon to prepare and review all sorts of contracts, including contracts for the sale of personal property and real property, commercial sales and lease contracts, licenses, and other contracts.

Contracts are the basis of many of our daily activities. They provide the means for individuals and businesses to sell and otherwise transfer property, services, and other rights. The purchase of goods is based on sales contracts; the hiring of employees is based on service contracts; and the lease of apartments is based on rental contracts. In addition, electronic contracts—e-contracts—are formed using email and the Internet. The list is almost endless. Without enforceable contracts, commerce would collapse.

Contracts are voluntarily entered into by parties. The terms of the contract become *private law* between the parties. The courts are obliged to give legal effect to such contracts according to the true interests of the parties.

This chapter covers the study of traditional contract law and e-contracts. ■

FORMATION OF A CONTRACT

A **contract** is an agreement that is enforceable by a court of law or equity. A simple and widely recognized definition is:

> "A contract is a promise or a set of promises for the breach of which the law gives a remedy or the performance of which the law in some way recognizes a duty. [Restatement (Second) of Contracts, Section 1].

Most contracts are performed without the aid of the court system. This usually is because the parties feel a moral duty to perform as promised. Although some contracts, such as illegal contracts, are not enforceable, most are **legally enforceable**. This means that if a party fails to perform a contract, the other party may call upon the courts to enforce the contract.

Every contract involves at least two parties. The **offeror** is the party who makes an offer to enter into a contract. The **offeree** is the party to whom the offer is made (see Exhibit 13.1). In making an offer, the offeror promises to do—or to refrain from doing—something. The offeree then has the power to create a contract by accepting the offeror's offer. A contract is created if the offer is accepted. No contract is created if the offer is not accepted.

Legally enforceable
A contract in which if one party fails to perform as promised, the other party can use the court system to enforce the contract and recover damages or other remedy.

Offeror
The party who makes an offer to enter into a contract.

Offeree
The party to whom an offer to enter into a contract is made.

Exhibit 13.1 **Parties to a contract**

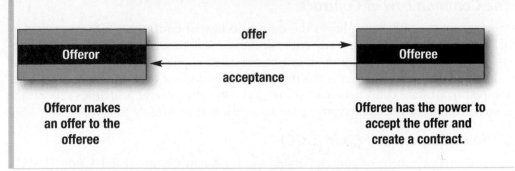

offer

Offeror → ← **Offeree**

acceptance

Offeror makes an offer to the offeree

Offeree has the power to accept the offer and create a contract.

THE PARALEGAL AND CONTRACTS

The words "paralegal" and "contracts" can almost be used simultaneously. There is no area of substantive law that paralegals are involved in more than contracts. Contracts make the world go round. The list of contracts in an individual's life and those of businesses are staggering.

Contracts are used to support most commercial transactions. Business contracts consist of those for the sale and lease of goods and the provision of services. Lawyers that practice in the area of business law are consistently called upon to draft contracts for their clients. And business contracts may be those for smaller business, such as sole proprietorships and general partnerships, to those between Fortune 500 companies such as Microsoft Corporation and Intel Corporation.

Contracts are needed for the sale, transfer, and lease of real property. Lawyers involved in the practice of real estate law must draft contracts for these transfers of interests in real estate. These include short contracts for simple matters such as an apartment lease, to long detailed contracts for construction of shopping malls, the building of skyscrapers, and other real estate matters.

Other contracts are needed to sell, lease, or transfer ownership of any property. Contracts are required for the settlement of divorce cases, agreements between owners of business, the creation of franchises, the licensing of intellectual property (e.g., patents, copyrights), the mergers of large corporations, and so on. In addition, the provision of services, such as that of architects, lawyers, doctors, consultants, and other professionals, require contracts between the client and the professional.

Paralegals are indispensable in assisting lawyers in drafting and reviewing contracts for individuals and businesses that are clients of the law firm that the paralegal works for. A paralegal must be familiar with general contract law principles. In addition, paralegals also must become familiar with specific types of contracts that the lawyer they work for practices in. So, a paralegal who works for a lawyer that practices in the real estate field must be familiar with real estate contracts. A paralegal that works for a lawyer that practices family law must be familiar with the specifics of divorce settlement agreements. And so on.

Many lawsuits are brought concerning contracts. For example, a client of the law firm the paralegal works for may have reason to bring a lawsuit against the other contracting party for breach of contract. On the other hand, a client of the law firm may find itself being sued for an alleged breach of a contract. This is where a paralegal's skill in conducting interviews, uncovering evidence, preparing the file for trial, and conducting contract law research is needed. Paralegals with an expertise in contract law are called upon to support lawyers who litigate contract disputes.

Paralegals that are familiar with contract law, drafting contracts, and researching contract law are in substantial demand. This demand will continue as the number and complexity of contracts increase in importance to individuals and businesses.

Sources of Common Law

The Common Law of Contracts

Common law of contracts
Contract law developed primarily by state courts.

A major source of contract law is the **common law of contracts**. The common law of contracts developed from early court decisions that became precedent for later decisions. A limited federal common law of contracts applies to contracts made by the federal government. The larger and more prevalent body of common law has been developed from state court decisions. Thus, although the general principles remain the same throughout the country, there is some variation from state to state.

Uniform Commercial Code (UCC)

Uniform Commercial Code (UCC)
A comprehensive statutory scheme that includes laws covering aspects of commercial transactions.

Another major source of contract law is the **Uniform Commercial Code (UCC)**. The UCC, which was first drafted by the National Conference of Commissioners on Uniform State Laws in 1952, has been amended several times. Its goal is to create a uniform system of commercial law among the 50 states. Provisions of the UCC normally take precedence over the common law of contracts (Chapters 18–21).

The UCC is divided into nine main articles. Every state has adopted at least part of the UCC. In the area of contract law, two of the major provisions of the UCC are:

1. *Article 2 (Sales).* This article prescribes a set of uniform rules for the creation and enforcement of contracts for the sale of goods. These contracts are often referred to as **sales contracts**. For example, the sale of equipment is a sales contract subject to Article 2 of the UCC.
2. *Article 2A (Leases).* This article prescribes a set of uniform rules for the creation and enforcement of contracts for the lease of goods. These contracts are referred to as **lease** contracts. For example, the lease of an automobile is a lease subject to Article 2A of the UCC.

Elements of a Contract

To be an enforceable contract, the following four basic requirements must be met:

1. *Agreement.* To have an enforceable contract, there must be an agreement between the parties.

E-CONTRACTS ACT

As we entered the twenty-first century, a new economic shift brought the United States and the rest of the world into the Information Age. Computer technology and the use of the Internet increased dramatically. A new form of commerce—electronic commerce, or e-commerce—is flourishing. All sorts of goods and services are now sold over the Internet. You can purchase automobiles and children's toys, participate in auctions, purchase airline tickets, make hotel reservations, and purchase other goods and services over the Internet.

Much of the new cyberspace economy is based on electronic contracts and the licensing of computer information. E-commerce created problems for forming contracts over the Internet, enforcing e-commerce contracts, and providing consumer protection. To address these problems, the National Conference of Commissioners on Uniform State Laws (a group of lawyers, judges, and legal scholars) drafted the Uniform Computer Information Transactions Act (UCITA).

The UCITA establishes uniform legal rules for the formation and enforcement of electronic contracts and licenses. The UCITA addresses most of the legal issues that are encountered while conducting e-commerce over the Internet. The UCITA is a model act that does not become law until a state legislature adopts it as a statute for the state. Since its promulgation in July 1999, many states have adopted the UCITA in whole or part. Because of the need for uniformity of e-commerce rules, the UCITA is becoming the basis for the creation and enforcement of cyberspace contracts and licenses.

2. **Consideration.** The promise must be supported by a bargained-for consideration that is legally sufficient.
3. **Contractual capacity.** The parties to a contract must have the capacity to contract.
4. **Lawful object.** The object of the contract must be lawful, or legal.

The text of this chapter discusses these requirements in greater detail:

Agreement

Agreement is the manifestation by two or more persons of the substance of a contract. It requires an *offer* and *acceptance*. The process of reaching an agreement usually proceeds as follows: Prior to entering into a contract, the parties may engage in preliminary negotiations about price, time of performance, and such. At some point during these negotiations, one party makes an **offer**. The person who makes the offer is called the offeror and the person to whom the offer is made is called the offeree. The offer sets forth the terms under which the offeror is willing to enter into the contract. The offeree has the power to create an agreement by accepting the offer.

Requirements of the offer.   Section 24 of the Restatement (Second) of Contracts defines an offer as:

> "The manifestation of willingness to enter into a bargain, so made as to justify another person in understanding that his assent to that bargain is invited and will conclude it."

To be effective:

1. The offeror must *objectively intend* to be bound by the offer.
2. The terms of the offer must be definite or reasonably *certain*.
3. The offer must be *communicated* to the offeree.

> *A contract is a mutual promise.*
> William Paley
> *The Principles of Moral and Political Philosophy (1784)*

agreement
The manifestation by two or more persons of the substance of a contract.

offer
The manifestation of willingness to enter into a bargain, so made as to justify another person in understanding that his assent to that bargain is invited and will conclude it.

> *An honest man's word is as good as his bond.*
> Don Quixote

A CONTRACT IS A CONTRACT IS A CONTRACT

Mighty Morphin Power Rangers was a phenomenal success as a television series. The Power Rangers battled to save the universe from all sorts of diabolical plots and bad guys. They also were featured in a profitable line of toys and garments bearing the Power Rangers logo. The Power Rangers' name and logo became known to millions of children and their parents worldwide. The claim of ownership of the logo for the Power Rangers ended up in a battle itself, this time in a courtroom.

David Dees was a designer working as d/b/a David Dees Illustration. Saban Entertainment, Inc. (Saban) which owned the copyright and trademark to Power Ranger figures and the name "Power Ranger," hired Dees as an independent contractor to design a logo for the Power Rangers. The contract signed by the parties was entitled "Work-for-Hire/Independent Contractor Agreement." The contract was drafted by Saban with the help of its attorneys; Dees signed the agreement without the representation of legal counsel.

Dees designed the logo used for the Power Rangers and was paid $250 to transfer his copyright ownership in the logo. Subsequently, Dees sued Saban to recover damages for copyright and trademark infringement. Saban defended, arguing that a contract is a contract is a contract, and Dees was bound by the agreement he had signed.

The Trial Court agreed with Saban, finding that the "Work-for-Hire/Independent Contractor Agreement" was an enforceable contract between the parties and that Dees had transferred his ownership interests in the logo to Saban. Dees appealed. The Court of Appeals affirmed the judgment for Saban, stating. "The disputed agreement transferred plaintiff's copyright in the Mighty Morphin Power Rangers' logo with as much specificity as the law requires." The court found that a contract is a contract is a contract, at least in this case. Dees' appeal to the U.S. Supreme Court was denied. [*Dees, d/b/a David Dees Illustration v. Saban Entertainment, Inc.,* 131 F.3d 146 (1997)]

Consider the following examples: A question such as "Are you interested in selling your building for $2 million?" is not an offer. It is an invitation to make an offer or an invitation to negotiate. But the statement "I will buy your building for $2 million" is a valid offer because it indicates the offeror's present intent to contract.

Suppose the owner of Company A has lunch with the owner of Company B. In the course of their conversation, Company A's owner exclaims in frustration, "For two dollars I'd sell the whole computer division!" A valid contract cannot result from that offer made in anger.

Revocation of an offer by the offeror.   Under the common law, an offeror may revoke (i.e., withdraw) an offer any time prior to its acceptance by the offeree. Generally, an offer can be so revoked even if the offeror promised to keep the offer open for a longer time. The **revocation** may be communicated to the offeree by the offeror or by a third party and made by (1) the offeror's express statement (e.g., "I hereby withdraw my offer") or (2) an act of the offeror that is inconsistent with the offer (e.g., selling the goods to another party). Most states provide that a revocation is not effective until it is actually received by the offeree or the offeree's agent.

Offers made to the public may be revoked by communicating the revocation by the same means used to make the offer. For example, if a reward offer for a lost watch was published in two local newspapers each week for four weeks, notice of revocation must be published in the same newspapers for the same length of time. The revocation is effective against all offerees, even those who saw the reward offer but not the notice of revocation.

Rejection of an offer by the offeree.   An offer is terminated if the offeree rejects it. Any subsequent attempt by the offeree to accept the offer is ineffective and is construed as a new offer that the original offeror (now the offeree) is free to accept or reject. A **rejection** may be evidenced by the offeree's express words (oral or written) or conduct. Generally, a rejection is not effective until it is actually received by the offeror.

Consider this example: Harriet Jackson, sales manager of IBM Corporation, offers to sell 1,000 computers to Ted Green, purchasing manager of General Motors Corporation, for $250,000. The offer is made on August 1. Green telephones Jackson to say that he is not interested. This rejection terminates the offer. If Green later decides that he wants to purchase the computers, an entirely new contract must be formed.

Counteroffer by the offeree.   A counteroffer by the offeree simultaneously terminates the offeror's offer and creates a new offer. For example, suppose that Fei Jia says to Harold Brown, "I will sell you my house for $700,000." Brown says, "I think $700,000 is too high; I will pay you $600,000. Brown has made a counteroffer. The original offer is terminated, and the counteroffer is a new offer that Jia is free to accept or reject.

Option contracts.   An offeree can prevent the offeror from revoking his or her offer by paying the offeror compensation to keep the offer open for an agreed-upon period of time. This is called an **option contract**, in which the offeror agrees not to sell the property to anyone but the offeree during the option period. The death or incompetency of either party does not terminate an option contract unless it is for the performance of a personal service.

Consider this example: Anne Mason offers to sell a piece of real estate to Harold Greenberg for $1 million. Mr. Greenberg wants time to make a decision, so he pays Ms. Mason $20,000 to keep her offer open to him for 6 months. At any time during the option period, Mr. Greenberg may exercise his option and pay Ms. Mason the $1 million purchase price. If he lets the option expire, however, Ms. Mason may keep the $20,000 and sell the property to someone else.

Revocation
Withdrawal of an offer by the offeror which terminates the offer.

Rejection
Express words or conduct by the offeree that rejects an offer. Rejection terminates the offer.

Counteroffer
A response by an offeree that contains terms and conditions different from or in addition to those of the offer. A counteroffer terminates an offer.

checklist ✓

TERMINATION OF AN OFFER

ACTION	DESCRIPTION
• Revocation	The offeror *revokes* (withdraws) the offer any time prior to its acceptance by the offeree.
• Rejection	The offeree rejects the offer by his or her words or conduct.
• Counteroffer	A counteroffer by the offeree creates a new offer and terminates the offeror's offer.

Acceptance. **Acceptance** is a manifestation of assent by the offeree to the terms of the offer in a manner invited or required by the offer as measured by the objective theory of contracts. Recall that generally (1) unilateral contracts can be accepted only by the offeree's performance of the required act, and (2) a bilateral contract can be accepted by an offeree who promises to perform (or, where permitted, by performance of) the requested act.

Only the offeree has the legal power to accept an offer and create a contract. Third persons usually do not have the power to accept an offer. If an offer is made individually to two or more persons, each has the power to accept the offer. Once an offeree accepts the offer, though, it terminates as to the other offerees. An offer that is made to two or more persons jointly must be accepted jointly.

The offeree's acceptance must be **unequivocal**. For an acceptance to exist, the offeree must accept the terms as stated in the offer. This is called the **mirror image rule**. Generally, a "grumbling acceptance" is a legal acceptance. For example, a response such as "Okay, I'll take the car, but I sure wish you would make me a better deal" creates an enforceable contract. An acceptance is equivocal if certain conditions are added to the acceptance. For example, if the offeree responds, "I accept, but only if you repaint the car red." There is no acceptance in this case.

Express and implied contracts. An actual contract (as distinguished from a quasi-contract, discussed later in this chapter) may be either *express* or *implied-in-fact*.

1. **Express contracts** are stated in oral or written words. Examples of such contracts include an oral agreement to purchase a neighbor's bicycle and a written agreement to buy an automobile from a dealership.
2. **Implied-in-fact contracts** are implied from the conduct of the parties. Implied-in-fact contracts leave more room for questions. The following elements must be established to create an implied-in-fact contract:
   a. The plaintiff provided property or services to the defendant.
   b. The plaintiff expected to be paid by the defendant for the property or services and did not provide the property or services gratuitously.
   c. The defendant was given an opportunity to reject the property or services provided by the plaintiff but failed to do so.

Consideration

Consideration is a necessary element for a contract to exist. Consideration is defined as the thing of value given in exchange for a promise. Consideration can come in many forms.

Acceptance
A manifestation of assent by the offeree to the terms of the offer in a manner invited or required by the offer as measured by the objective theory of contracts.

Mirror image rule
A rule that states that for an acceptance to exist, the offeree must accept the terms as stated in the offer.

Express contract
An agreement that is expressed in written or oral words.

Implied-in-fact contract
A contract in which agreement between parties has been inferred from their conduct.

Consideration
Something of legal value given in exchange for a promise.

CONTRACT FRAUD

Contracting parties must be careful not to be taken by fraud. Basically if a deal sounds "too good to be true," it is a signal that the situation might be fraudulent. Other frauds are difficult to detect. If there is fraud, the innocent party can get out of the contract and recover his or her losses. To prove **contract fraud,** the following elements must be shown:

(1) The wrongdoer made a false representation of material fact.
(2) The wrongdoer intended to deceive the innocent party.
(3) The innocent party justifiably relied on the misrepresentation.
(4) The innocent party was injured.

MATERIAL MISREPRESENTATION OF FACT

A misrepresentation may occur by words (oral or written) or by the conduct of the party. To be actionable as fraud, the misrepresentation must be of a past or existing material fact. This means that the misrepresentation must have been a significant factor in inducing the innocent party to enter into the contract. It does not have to be the sole factor. Statements of opinion or predictions about the future generally do not form the basis for fraud.

INTENT TO DECEIVE

To prove fraud, the person making the misrepresentation must either have had knowledge that the representation was false or made it without sufficient knowledge of the truth. This is called *scienter* ("guilty mind"). The misrepresentation must have been made with the intent to deceive the innocent party. Intent can be inferred from the circumstances.

RELIANCE ON THE MISREPRESENTATION

A misrepresentation is not actionable unless the innocent party to whom the misrepresentation was directed acted upon it. Further, an innocent party who acts in reliance on the misrepresentation must justify his or her reliance. Justifiable reliance generally is found unless the innocent party knew that the misrepresentation was false or was so extravagant as to be obviously false. For example, reliance on a statement such as, "This diamond ring is worth $10,000, but I'll sell it to you for $100" would not be justified.

INJURY TO THE INNOCENT PARTY

To recover damages, the innocent party must prove that the fraud caused economic injury. The measure of damages is the difference between the value of the property as represented and the actual value of the property. This measure of damages gives the innocent party the "benefit of the bargain." In the alternative, the buyer can rescind the contract and recover the purchase price.

Illegality—contracts contrary to public policy. Certain contracts are illegal because they are **contracts contrary to public policy**. Although *public policy* eludes a precise definition, the courts have held contracts to be contrary to public policy if they have a negative impact on society or interfere with the public's safety and welfare.

STATUTE OF FRAUDS—WRITING REQUIREMENT

Statute of frauds
A state statute that requires certain types of contracts to be in writing.

All states have enacted a **Statute of Frauds** that requires certain types of contracts to be in *writing*. This statute is intended to ensure that the terms of important contracts are not forgotten, misunderstood, or fabricated.

Generally, an **executory contract** that is not in writing even though the Statute of Frauds requires it to be is unenforceable by either party. (If the contract is valid in all other respects, however, it may be voluntarily performed by the parties.) The Statute of Frauds usually is raised by one party as a defense to enforcement of the

ETHICAL *Perspective*

Duty Not to Engage in Fraudulent Billing Practices

Mr. Richard Pease works as a paralegal for a large law firm with more than 800 attorneys. The law firm has offices located throughout the United States, as well as in other countries.

The law firm has established annual billing goals for both attorneys and paralegals. When making decisions for promotions, payment of bonuses, and keeping one's employment at the firm the law firm considers meeting this billing-hour goal. At his level, Mr. Pease is responsible for billing 1,600 hours per year.

Although intending to reach the 1,600 hours of billing time, during the first 10 months of the current year, Mr. Pease spent too much time during office hours conversing with friends on the telephone and playing games on the Internet.

In October of the current year, Mr. Pease realizes that he will not reach the 1,600 hours unless he works additional overtime for the next several months. Instead of doing this, however, Mr. Pease decides to "book" additional time on some of the files he has been working on but without actually doing the work. Thus, for the months of November and December, Mr. Pease records time that he has not worked. By doing so, Mr. Pease makes his 1,600 hours billed for the year. Mr. Pease justifies his actions by telling himself that he will work hours on these clients' files next year but not bill them for those hours.

The *Model Code of Ethics and Professional Responsibility and Guidance for Enforcement* of the National Federation of Paralegal Associations, Inc. (NFPA) states:

> *EC-1.2(c) A paralegal shall ensure that all time keeping and billing records prepared by the paralegal are thorough, accurate, honest, and complete.*

Source: *Reprinted by permission from The National Federation of Paralegal Associations, Inc., www.paralegals.org*

> *EC-1.2(d) A paralegal shall not knowingly engage in fraudulent billing practices. Such practices may include, but are not limited to: inflation of hours billed to a client or employer; misrepresentation of the nature of tasks performed; and/or submission of fraudulent expense and disbursement documentation.*

Source: *Reprinted by permission from The National Federation of Paralegal Associations, Inc., www.paralegals.org*

Mr. Pease's conduct of billing for hours that he has not worked violates the paralegal's professional rules of conduct. In addition, Mr. Pease's conduct constitutes fraud, which could be actionable as a crime.

contract by the other party. But if an oral contract that should have been in writing under the Statute of Frauds is already **executed** (fully performed), neither party can seek to rescind the contract on the ground of noncompliance with the Statute of Frauds. Contracts that are required to be in writing under the Statute of Frauds are discussed next.

Contracts Involving Interests in Real Property

Any contract that transfers an ownership interest in real property must be in writing to be enforceable under the Statute of Frauds. Real property includes the land itself, buildings, trees, soil, minerals, timber, plants, crops, fixtures, and things permanently affixed to the land or buildings. Certain personal property that is permanently affixed to the real property—for example, built-in cabinets in a house—are *fixtures* that become part of the real property.

Other contracts that transfer an ownership interest in land must be in writing under the Statute of Frauds. For example, borrowers often give a lender an interest in real property as security for the repayment of a loan. This must be done through a written *mortgage* or *deed of trust*. A lease is the transfer of the right to use real property for a specified period of time. Most Statutes of Frauds require leases for a term of more than one year to be in writing.

A verbal contract isn't worth the paper it's written on.

Samuel Goldwyn

One-Year Rule

According to the Statute of Frauds, an executory contract that cannot be performed by its own terms within one year of its formation must be in writing. This **one-year rule** is intended to prevent disputes about contract terms that otherwise may occur toward the end of a long-term contract. If performance of the contract is possible within the one-year period, the contract may be oral.

Formality of the Writing

Many written commercial contracts are long, detailed documents that have been negotiated by the parties and drafted and reviewed by their lawyers. Other written contracts are preprinted forms that are prepared in advance to be used in recurring situations.

To be legally binding, a written contract does not have to be either drafted by a lawyer or formally typed. Regarding the **formality of the writing**, the law generally requires only a writing containing the essential terms of the parties' agreement. Under this rule, any writing—letters, telegrams, invoices, sales receipts, handwritten agreements written on scraps of paper, and such—can be an enforceable contract.

Required Signature

The Statute of Frauds and the UCC require the written contract, whatever its form, to be signed *by the party against whom the enforcement is sought*. The signature of the person who is enforcing the contract is not necessary. Thus, a written contract may be enforceable against one party but not the other party.

Generally, the signature may appear anywhere on the writing. In addition, it does not have to be a person's full legal name. The person's last name, first name, nickname, initials, seal, stamp, engraving, or other symbol or mark (e.g., an X) that indicates the person's intent can be binding. The signature may be affixed by an authorized agent.

PERFORMANCE AND BREACH

In contracts, parties make certain promises to each other. These promises may be classified as *covenants* or *conditions*. Performance may be classified as complete performance, substantial performance (minor breach), or inferior performance (material breach). A **breach of contract** occurs when a contracting party fails to perform an absolute duty owed under the contract.

Breach of contract
A contracting party's failure to perform an absolute duty owed under a contract.

Covenants

A **covenant** is an unconditional promise to perform. Nonperformance of a covenant is a breach of contract that gives the other party the right to sue. *For example*: if Medcliff Corporation borrows $100,000 from a bank and signs a promissory note to repay this amount plus 10 percent interest in one year, this promise is a covenant. It is an unconditional promise to perform.

Covenant
An unconditional promise to perform.

Conditions Precedent

If the contract requires the occurrence (or nonoccurrence) of an event before a party is obligated to perform a contractual duty, there is a **condition precedent**. The happening (or nonhappening) of the event triggers the contract or duty of performance. If the event does not occur, no duty to perform arises, because there is a failure of condition.

Consider this example: Suppose X Company offers Joan Andrews a job as an industrial engineer upon her graduation from college. If Ms. Andrews graduates, the condition has been met. If the employer refuses to hire Ms. Andrews at that time, she

Condition precedent
A condition that requires the occurrence of an event before a party is obligated to perform a duty under a contract.

can sue the employer for breach of contract. But if Ms. Andrews does not graduate, X company is not obligated to hire her, because there has been a failure of condition.

Complete Performance

Most contracts are discharged by the **complete performance** of the contracting parties. Complete performance occurs when a party to a contract renders performance exactly as required by the contract. A fully performed contract is called an **executed contract**.

Tender of performance also discharges a party's contractual obligations. Tender is an unconditional and absolute offer by a contracting party to perform his or her obligations under the contract.

Consider this example: Suppose Ashley's Dress Shops, Inc., contracts to purchase dresses from a dress manufacturer for $25,000. Ashley's has performed its obligation under the contract once it tenders the $25,000 to the manufacturer. If the manufacturer fails to deliver the dresses, Ashley's can sue it for breach of contract.

Complete performance
A situation in which a party to a contract renders performance exactly as required by the contract. Complete performance discharges that party's obligations under the contract.

Substantial Performance (Minor Breach)

Substantial performance occurs when there has been a **minor breach** of contract. It occurs when a party to a contract renders performance that deviates only slightly from complete performance. The nonbreaching party may (1) convince the breaching party to elevate his or her performance to complete performance, or (2) deduct the cost to repair the defect from the contract price and remit the balance to the breaching party, or (3) sue the breaching party to recover the cost to repair the defect if the breaching party has already been paid.

Consider this example: Suppose Donald Trump contracts with Big Apple Construction Co. to have Big Apple construct an office building for $50 million. The architectural plans call for installation of three-ply windows in the building. Big Apple constructs the building exactly to plan except that it installs two-ply windows. There has been substantial performance. It would cost $300,000 to install the correct windows. If Big Apple agrees to replace the windows, its performance is elevated to complete performance and Trump must remit the entire contract price. But if Trump has to hire someone else to replace the windows, he may deduct this cost of repair from the contract price and remit the difference to Big Apple.

Substantial performance
Performance by a contracting party that deviates only slightly from complete performance.

Minor breach
A breach that occurs when a party renders substantial performance of his or her contractual duties.

Interior Performance (Material Breach)

Inferior performance occurs when there has been a **material breach** of a contract. A material breach results when a party fails to perform certain express or implied obligations that impair or destroy the essence of the contract. Because there is no clear line between a minor breach and a material breach, determination is made on a case-by-case basis. Where there has been a material breach of a contract, the nonbreaching party has two choices:

1. The nonbreaching party may *rescind* the contract, seek restitution of any compensation paid under the contract to the breaching party, and be discharged from any further performance under the contract.
2. The nonbreaching party may treat the contract as being in effect and sue the breaching party to recover *damages*.

Inferior performance
A situation in which a party fails to perform express or implied contractual obligations and impairs or destroys the essence of the contract.

Material breach
A breach that occurs when a party renders inferior performance of his or her contractual duties.

Consider this example: Suppose a university contracts with a general contractor to build a new three-story building with classroom space for 1,000 students. But the completed building can support the weight of only 500 students because the contractor used inferior materials. The defect cannot be repaired without rebuilding the entire structure. Because this is a material breach, the university may rescind the contract and require removal of the building. The university is discharged of any obligations

checklist ✓

TYPE OF PERFORMANCE	LEGAL CONSEQUENCE
• Complete performance	The contract is discharged.
• Substantial performance (minor breach)	The nonbreaching party may recover damages caused by the breach.
• Inferior performance (material breach)	The nonbreaching party may either (1) rescind the contract and recover restitution or (2) affirm the contract and recover damages.

under the contract and is free to employ another contractor to rebuild the building. Alternatively, the university could accept the building and deduct from the contract price the damages caused by the defect.

REMEDIES

Monetary damages
An award of money.

The most common remedy for a breach of contract is an award of **monetary damages**. This is often called the "law remedy." Monetary damages are of three types: compensatory, consequential, and liquid. But if a monetary award does not provide adequate relief, the court may order any one of several **equitable remedies**, including specific performance, injunction, reformation, and quasi-contract. Equitable remedies are based on the concept of fairness.

Types of Monetary Damages
Compensatory Damages

Compensatory damages
An award of money intended to compensate a nonbreaching party for loss of the bargain. Compensatory damages place the nonbreaching party in the same position as if the contract had been fully performed by restoring the "benefit of the bargain."

Compensatory damages are intended to compensate a nonbreaching party for the loss of the bargain. They place the nonbreaching party in the same position as if the contract has been fully performed by restoring the "benefit of the bargain."

Consider this example: Suppose Lederle Laboratories enters into a written contract to employ a manager for three years at a salary of $6,000 per month. Before work is to start, the manager is informed that he will not be needed. This is a material breach of contract.

Assume that the manager finds another job, but it pays only $5,000 a month. The manager may recover $1,000 per month for 36 months (total $36,000) from Lederle Laboratories as compensatory damages. These damages place the manager in the same situation as if the contract with Lederle had been performed.

Consequential Damages

Consequential damages
Foreseeable damages that arise from circumstances outside the contract. To be liable for these damages, the breaching party must know or have reason to know that the breach will cause special damages to the other party.

In addition to compensatory damages, a nonbreaching party sometimes can recover *special* or **consequential damages** from the breaching party. Consequential damages are *foreseeable* damages that arise from circumstances outside the contract. To be liable for consequential damages, the breaching party must know or have reason to know that the breach will cause special damages to the other party.

Consider this example: Suppose Soan-Allen Co., a wholesaler, enters into a contract to purchase 1,000 men's suits for $150 each from the Fabric Manufacturing Co., a manufacturer. Prior to contracting, the wholesaler tells the manufacturer that the suits will be resold to retailers for $225. The manufacturer breaches the contract by failing to manufacture the suits. The wholesaler cannot get the suits manufactured by

checklist ✓

TYPE OF DAMAGE	DESCRIPTION
• Compensatory	Damages that compensate a nonbreaching party for the loss of a bargain. It places the nonbreaching party in the same position as if the contract had been fully performed.
• Consequential	Damages that compensate a nonbreaching party for foreseeable special damages. The breaching party must have known or should have known that these damages would result from the breach.
• Liquidated	An agreement by the parties in advance that sets the amount of damages recoverable in case of breach. These damages are lawful if they do not cause a penalty.

anyone else in time to meet his contracts. He can recover $75,000 of lost profits on the resale contracts (1,000 suits × $75 profit) as consequential damages from the manufacturer because the manufacturer knew of this special damage to Soan-Allen Co. if it were to breach the contract.

Liquidated Damages

Under certain circumstances, the parties to a contract may agree in advance to the amount of damages payable upon a breach of contract. These are called **liquidated damages**. To be lawful, the actual damages must be difficult or impracticable to determine, and the liquidated amount must be reasonable in the circumstances. An enforceable liquidated damage clause is an exclusive remedy even if actual damages are later determined to be different.

A liquidated damage clause is considered a *penalty* if actual damages are clearly determinable in advance or the liquidated damages are excessive or unconscionable. If a liquidated damage clause is found to be a penalty, it is unenforceable. The nonbreaching party then may recover actual damages.

Liquidated damages
Damages to which parties to a contract agree in advance should be paid if the contract is breached.

Mitigation of Damages

If a contract has been breached, the law places a duty on the innocent non-breaching party to take reasonable efforts to mitigate (i.e., avoid and reduce) the resulting damages. The extent of **mitigation of damages** required depends on the type of contract involved. For example, if an employer breaches an employment contract, the employee owes a duty to mitigate damages by trying to find substitute employment. The employee is required only to accept comparable employment. In determining the comparability of jobs, the courts consider factors such as compensation, rank, status, job description, and geographical location.

Mitigation of damages
A nonbreaching party's legal duty to avoid or reduce damages caused by a breach of contract.

Specific Performance

An award of **specific performance** orders the breaching party to *perform* the acts promised in the contract. The courts have the discretion to award this remedy if the subject matter of the contract is unique. This remedy is available to enforce land contracts because every piece of real property is considered unique. Works of art, antiques, items of sentimental value, rare coins, stamps, heirlooms, and such also fit the requirement for uniqueness. Most other personal property does not. Specific performance of personal-service contracts is not granted because the

Specific performance
A remedy that orders the breaching party to perform the acts promised in the contract. Specific performance usually is awarded in cases where the subject matter is unique, such as in contracts involving land, heirlooms, and paintings.

checklist ☑   TYPES OF EQUITABLE REMEDIES

TYPE OF EQUITABLE REMEDY	DESCRIPTION
• Specific performance	A court orders the breaching party to perform the acts promised in the contract. The subject matter of the contract must be unique.
• Reformation	A court rewrites a contract to express the parties' true intentions. It is usually used to correct clerical errors.
• Injunction	A court prohibits a party from doing a certain act. Injunctions are available in contract actions only in limited circumstances.

courts would find it difficult or impracticable to supervise or monitor performance of the contract.

Injunction

Injunction
A court order that prohibits a person from doing a certain act.

An **injunction** is a court order that prohibits a person from doing a certain act. To obtain an injunction, the requesting party must show that he or she will suffer irreparable injury unless the injunction is issued.

For example: Suppose a professional football team enters into a five-year employment contract with a "superstar" quarterback. The quarterback breaches the contract and enters into a contract to play for a competing team. Here, the first team can seek an injunction to prevent the quarterback from playing for the other team.

Reformation

Reformation
An equitable doctrine that permits the court to rewrite a contract to express the parties' true intentions.

Reformation is an equitable doctrine that permits the court to *rewrite* a contract to express the parties' true intentions. For example, suppose a clerical error is made during the typing of the contract and both parties sign the contract without discovering the error. If a dispute later arises, the court can reform the contract to correct the clerical error to read what the parties originally intended.

Quasi-contract

Quasi-contract
An equitable doctrine whereby a court may award monetary damages to a plaintiff for providing work or services to a defendant even though no actual contract existed.

A **quasi-contract** (also called an *implied-in-law contract*) is an equitable doctrine that permits the recovery of compensation even though no enforceable contract exists between the parties because of lack of consideration, the Statute of Frauds has run out, or the like. Such contracts are imposed by law to prevent unjust enrichment. Under quasi-contract, a party can recover the reasonable value of the services or materials provided. For example, a physician who stops to render aid to an unconscious victim of an automobile accident may recover the reasonable value of his services from that person.

EQUITY

Equity
A doctrine that permits judges to make decisions based on fairness, equality, moral rights, and natural law.

Recall that two separate courts developed in England: the courts of law and the Chancery Courts (or courts of equity). The equity courts developed a set of maxims based on fairness, equality, moral rights, and natural law that were applied in settling disputes. **Equity** was resorted to when (1) an award of money damages "at law" would not be the proper remedy or (2) fairness required the application of equitable principles.

Today, in most states of the United States, the courts of law and equity have been merged into one court. In an action "in equity," the judge decides the equitable issue; there is no right to a jury trial in an equitable action. The doctrine of equity is sometimes applied in contract cases.

UNCONSCIONABLE CONTRACT

The general rule of freedom of contract holds that if (1) the object of a contract is lawful and (2) the other elements for the formation of a contract are met, the courts will enforce a contract according to its terms. Although it is generally presumed that parties are capable of protecting their own interests when contracting, it is a fact of life that dominant parties sometimes take advantage of weaker parties. As a result, some lawful contracts are so oppressive or manifestly unfair that they are unjust.

To prevent the enforcement of such contracts, the courts developed the equitable doctrine of unconscionability, which is based on public policy. A contract found to be unconscionable under this doctrine is called an **unconscionable contract**, or a *contract of adhesion*.

The courts are given substantial discretion in determining whether a contract or contract clause is unconscionable. There is no single definition of *unconscionability*. The doctrine may not be used merely to save a contracting party from a bad bargain.

The following elements must be shown to prove that a contract or clause in a contract is unconscionable:

- The parties possessed severely unequal bargaining power.
- The dominant party unreasonably used its unequal bargaining power to obtain oppressive or manifestly unfair contract terms.
- The adhering party had no reasonable alternative.

If the court finds that a contract or contract clause is unconscionable, it may (1) refuse to enforce the contract, (2) refuse to enforce the unconscionable clause but enforce the remainder of the contract, or (3) limit the applicability of any unconscionable clause so as to avoid any unconscionable result. The appropriate remedy depends on the facts and circumstances of each case. Note that because unconscionability is a matter of law, the judge may opt to decide the case without a jury trial.

UNIFORM COMMERCIAL CODE (UCC)

One of the major frustrations of businesspersons conducting interstate business is that they are subject to the laws of each of the states in which they operate. To address this problem, in 1949 the National Conference of Commissioners on Uniform State Laws promulgated the Uniform Commercial Code (UCC). The UCC is a model act that contains uniform rules that govern commercial transactions. To create this uniformity, individual states had to enact the UCC as their commercial law statute. In fact, they did. Every state (except Louisiana, which has adopted only parts of the UCC) enacted the UCC as a commercial statute.

The UCC is divided into articles, with each article establishing uniform rules for a specific facet of commerce in the United States. The articles of the UCC are

Article 1	General provisions
Article 2	Sales
Article 2A Revised	Leases
Article 3	Negotiable instruments
Article 4	Bank deposits and collections
Article 4A	Wire transfers
Article 5	Letters of credit
Article 6	Bulk transfers
Article 7	Documents of title

Article 8	Investment securities
Article 9	Secured transactions

The UCC is being revised continually to reflect changes in modern commercial practices and technology.

Article 2 (Sales) of the UCC

Article 2 (Sales) of the UCC
An article of the UCC that governs the sale of goods.

Article 2 (Sales) of the UCC applies to *transactions in goods*—that is, the sale of goods [UCC 2-102]. All states except Louisiana have adopted some version of Article 2 of the UCC. A **sale** consists of the passing of title from a seller to a buyer for a price [UCC 2-106(1)]. For example, the purchase of the book is a sale subject to Article 2. This is so whether the book was paid for by cash, check, credit card, or another form of consideration.

Article 2 establishes a uniform law covering the formation, performance, and default of sales contracts.

Goods are defined as tangible things that are movable at the time of their identification to the contract [UCC 2-105(1)]. Examples of goods are specially manufactured goods and the unborn young of animals.

Money and intangible items, such as stocks, bonds, and patents, are not tangible goods. Therefore, they are not subject to Article 2.

Real estate is not subject to Article 2 either, because it is not movable [UCC 2-105(1)]. Minerals, structures, growing crops, and other things that are severable from real estate may be classified as goods subject to Article 2, however. For example, the sale and removal of a chandelier in a house is a sale of goods subject to Article 2 because its removal would not materially harm the realty. But the sale and removal of the furnace would be a sale of real property because its removal would cause material harm [UCC 2-107(2)].

Contracts for the provision of services—including legal services, medical services, dental services, and such—are not covered by Article 2. Sometimes, however, a sale involves the provision of both a service and a good in the same transaction. This is referred to as a *mixed sale*. Article 2 applies to mixed sales only if the goods are the predominant part of the transaction. The UCC provides no guidance for deciding cases based on mixed sales. Therefore, the courts decide these issues on a case-by-case basis.

Contracts must not be the sports of an idle hour, mere matters of pleasantry and badinage, never intended by the parties to have any serious effect whatever.

Lord Stowell
Dalrymple v. Dalrymple (1811)

Article 2A (Leases) of the UCC

Personal property leases are a billion-dollar industry. Consumer rentals of automobiles and equipment, and commercial leases of such items as aircraft and industrial machinery, fall into this category.

Article 2A (Leases) of the UCC
An article of the UCC that governs the lease of goods.

Article 2A (Leases) of the UCC was promulgated in 1987. This article, cited as the Uniform Commercial Code—Leases, directly addresses personal property leases [UCC 2A-101]. It establishes a comprehensive, uniform law covering the formation, performance, and default of leases in goods [UCC 2A-102, 2A-103(h)].

Article 2A is similar to Article 2. In fact, many Article 2 provisions were changed to reflect leasing terminology and practices and carried over to Article 2A. Many states have adopted Article 2A, and many more are expected to do so in the future.

A lease is a transfer of the right to the possession and use of the named goods for a set term in return for certain consideration [UCC 2A-103(1)(i)(x)]. The leased goods can be anything from a hand tool leased to an individual for a few hours to a complex line of industrial equipment leased to a multinational corporation for a number of years.

In an ordinary lease, the **lessor** is the person who transfers the right of possession and use of goods under the lease [UCC 2A-103(1)(p)]. The **lessee** is the person who acquires the right to possession and use of goods under a lease [UCC 2A-103(1)(n)].

Most of the disputes in the world arise from words.

Lord Mansfield
C. J. Morgan v. Jones (1773)

A **consumer lease** is one with a value of $25,000 or less between a lessor regularly engaged in the business of leasing or selling and a lessee who leases the goods primarily for a personal, family, or household purpose [UCC 2A-103(1)(e)].

A **finance lease** is a three-party transaction consisting of the lessor, the lessee, and the **supplier** (or vendor) [UCC 2A-103(1)(g)].

Consider this example: The Row Chemical Company decides to use robotics to manufacture most of its products. It persuades Zand Corp. to design the robotic equipment that will meet its needs. To finance the purchase of the equipment, Row Chemical goes to City Bank, which purchases the robotics equipment from Zand Corp. and leases it to Row Chemical. City Bank is the lessor, Row Chemical is the lessee, and Zand Corp. is the supplier.

Offer

A contract for the sale or lease of goods may be made in any manner sufficient to show agreement, including conduct by both parties that recognizes the existence of a contract [UCC 2-204,(1), 2A-204(1)]. Under the UCC, an agreement sufficient to constitute a contract for the sale or lease of goods may be found even though the moment of its making is undetermined [UCC 2-204 (2), 2A-204 (2)].

Open Terms

Sometimes the parties to a sale or lease contract leave open a major term in the contract. The UCC is tolerant of open terms. According to UCC 2-204(3) and 2A-204(3), the contract does not fail because of indefiniteness if (1) the parties intended to make a contract and (2) there is a reasonably certain basis for giving an appropriate remedy. In effect, certain **open terms** are permitted to be "read into" a sales or lease contract. This rule is commonly referred to as the **gap-filling rule**.

Some examples of terms that are commonly left open are:

Gap-filling rule
A rule that says an open term can be "read into" a sales or lease contract.

- *Open price term.* If a sales contract does not contain a specific price— an open price term—a "reasonable price" is implied at the time of delivery. The contract may provide that a price is to be fixed by a market rate (e.g., a commodities market), as set or recorded by a third person or agency (e.g., a government agency), or by another standard, either upon delivery or on a set date. If the agreed-upon standard is unavailable when the price is to be set, a reasonable price is implied at the time of delivery of the goods [UCC 2-305(1)].

  A seller or buyer who reserves the right to fix a price must do so in good faith [UCC 2-305(2)]. When one of the parties fails to fix an open price term, the other party may opt either (1) to treat the contract as canceled or (2) to fix a reasonable price for the goods [UCC 2-305(3)].

- *Open payment term.* If the parties to a sales contract do not agree on payment terms, payment is due at the time and place at which the buyer is to receive the goods. If delivery is authorized and made by way of document of title, payment is due at the time and place at which the buyer is to receive the document of title, regardless of where the goods are to be received [UCC 2-310].

- *Open delivery term.* If the parties to a sales contract do not agree to the time, place, and manner of delivery of the goods, the place for delivery is the seller's place of business. If the seller does not have a place of business, delivery is to be made at the seller's residence. If identified goods are located at some other place and both parties know of this fact at the time of contracting, that place is the place of delivery [UCC 2-308].

  Where goods are to be shipped but the shipper is not named, the seller is obligated to make the shipping arrangements. Such arrangements must be made in good faith and within limits of commercial reasonableness [UCC 2-311(2)].

■ *Open time term.* If the parties to a sales contract do not set a specific time of performance for any obligation under the contract, the contract must be performed within a reasonable time. If the sales contract provides for successive performance over an unspecified period of time, the contract is valid for a reasonable time [UCC 2-309].

■ *Open assortment term.* If the assortment of goods to a sales contract is left open, the buyer is given the option of choosing those goods. For example, suppose Macy's contracts to purchase 1,000 dresses from Liz Claiborne, Inc. The contract is silent as to the assortment of colors of the dresses. The buyer may pick the assortment of colors for the dresses from the seller's stock. The buyer must make the selection in good faith and within limits set by commercial reasonableness [UCC 2-311(2)].

UCC Firm Offer Rule

Recall that the common law of contracts allows the offeror to revoke an **offer** any time prior to its acceptance. The only exception allowed by the common law is an *option contract* (i.e., where the offeree pays the offeror consideration to keep the offer open).

The UCC recognizes another exception, which is called the **firm offer rule.** This rule states that a merchant who (1) offers to buy, sell, or lease goods and (2) gives a written and signed assurance on a separate form that the offer will be held open cannot revoke the offer for the time stated or, if no time is stated, for a reasonable time. The maximum amount of time permitted under this rule is three months [UCC 2-205, 2A-205].

Consider this example: On June 1, a merchant–seller offers to sell a Mercedes-Benz to a buyer for $50,000. The merchant–seller signs a written assurance to keep that offer open until August 30. On July 1, the merchant–seller sells the car to another buyer. On August 21, the original offeree tenders $50,000 for the car. The merchant–seller is liable to the original offeree for breach of contract.

Acceptance

Both common law and the UCC provide that a contract is created when the offeree (i.e., the buyer or lessee) sends an acceptance to the offeror, not when the offeror receives the acceptance. For example, a contract is made when the acceptance letter is delivered to the post office. The contract remains valid even if the post office loses the letter.

Unless otherwise unambiguously indicated by language or circumstance, an offer to make a sales or lease contract may be accepted in any manner and by any reasonable medium of acceptance [UCC 2-206(1)(a), 2A-206(1)].

Consider this example: A seller sends a telegram to a proposed buyer, offering to sell certain goods to the buyer. The buyer responds by mailing a letter of acceptance to the seller. In most circumstances, mailing the letter of acceptance would be considered reasonable. If the goods were extremely perishable or if the market for the goods were volatile, however, a faster means of acceptance (such as a telegram) might be warranted.

UCC Statute of Frauds

The UCC includes Statute of Frauds provisions that apply to all sales and lease contracts. All contracts for the sale of goods costing $500 or more (the 2003 amendments to the UCC changes this amount to $5,000 or more) and lease contracts involving payments of $1,000 or more must be in writing [UCC 2-201(1), 2A-201(1)]. The writing must be sufficient to indicate that a contract has been made between the parties. Except as discussed in the paragraphs that follow, the writing must be signed by the party against whom enforcement is sought or by his or her author-

UCC ADDITIONAL TERMS: "BATTLE OF THE FORMS"

Under common law's mirror image rule, an offeree's acceptance must be on the same terms as the offer. The inclusion of additional terms in the acceptance is considered a counteroffer rather than an acceptance. Thus, the offeror's original offer is extinguished.

When merchants negotiate sales contracts, they often exchange preprinted forms. These "boilerplate" forms usually contain terms that favor the drafter. Thus, an offeror who sends a standard form contract as an offer to the offeree may receive an acceptance drafted on the offeree's own form contract. This scenario—commonly called the **battle of the forms**—raises important questions: Is there a contract? If so, what are its terms? The UCC provides guidance in answering these questions.

Under UCC 2-207(2), if both parties are merchants, any additional terms contained in an acceptance become part of the sales contract unless (1) the offer expressly limits acceptance to the terms of the offer, (2) the additional terms materially alter the terms of the original contract, or (3) the offeror notifies the offeree that he or she objects to the additional terms within a reasonable time after receiving the offeree's modified acceptance.

The most important point in the battle of the forms is that there is no contract if the additional terms so materially alter the terms of the original offer that the parties cannot agree on the contract. The courts make this fact-specific determination on a case-by-case basis.

ized agent or broker. If a contract falling within these parameters is not written, it is unenforceable.

Consider this example: A seller orally agrees to sell her computer to a buyer for $550. When the buyer tenders the purchase price, the seller asserts the Statute of Frauds and refuses to sell the computer to him. The seller is correct. The contract must be in writing to be enforceable because the contract price for the computer exceeds $499.99.

UCC Written Confirmation Rule

If both parties to an oral sale or lease contract are merchants, the Statute of Frauds requirement can be satisfied if (1) one of the parties to an oral agreement sends a written confirmation of the sale or lease within a reasonable time after contracting and (2) the other merchant does not give written notice of an objection to the contract within 10 days after receiving the confirmation. The **UCC written confirmation rule** is true even though the party receiving the written confirmation has not signed it. The only stipulations are that the confirmation be sufficient and that the party to whom it was sent have reason to know its contents [UCC 2-201(2)].

Consider this example: A merchant–seller in Chicago orally contracts by telephone to sell goods to a merchant–buyer in Phoenix for $25,000. Within a reasonable time after contracting, the merchant–seller sends a sufficient written confirmation to the buyer. The buyer, who has reason to know the contents of the confirmation, fails to object to the contents of the confirmation in writing within 10 days after receiving it. The Statute of Frauds has been met, and the buyer cannot thereafter raise it against enforcement of the contract.

Good Faith and Reasonableness

Generally, the common law of contracts only obligates the parties to perform according to the express terms of their contract. There is no breach of contract unless the parties fail to meet these terms.

Recognizing that certain situations may develop that are not expressly provided for in a contract or that strict adherence to the terms of a contract without doing more may not be sufficient to accomplish the contract's objective, the Uniform Commercial

checklist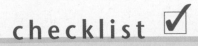

POSSESSION OF GOODS AT TIME OF BUYER'S BREACH	SELLER'S OR LESSOR'S REMEDIES

• Goods in the possession of the seller	1. Withhold delivery of the goods [UCC 2-703(a),2A-523(1)(c)].
	2. Demand payment in cash if the buyer is insolvent [UCC 2-702(1), 2A-525(1)].
	3. Resell or re-lease the goods and recover the difference between the contract or lease price and the resale or re-lease price [UCC 2-706, 2A-527].
	4. Sue for breach of contract and recover as damages either
	  a. the difference between the market price and the contract price [UCC 2-708(1), 2A-528(1)], or
	  b. lost profits [UCC 2-708(2), 2A-528(2)].
	5. Cancel the contract [UCC 2-703(f), 2A-523(1)(a)].

• Goods in the possession of a carrier or bailee	1. Stop goods in transit [UCC 2-705(1), 2A-526(1)].
	  a. Carload, truckload, planeload, or larger shipment if the buyer is solvent.
	  b. Any size shipment if the buyer is insolvent.

• Goods in the possession of the buyer	1. Sue to recover the purchase price or rent [UCC 2-709(1), 2A-529(1)].
	2. Reclaim the goods [UCC 2-507(2), 2A-525(2)].
	  a. The seller delivers goods in cash sale, and the buyer's check is dishonored.
	  b. The seller delivers goods in a credit sale, and the goods are received by an insolvent buyer.

Code (UCC) adopts two broad principles that govern the performance of sales and lease contracts: good faith and reasonableness.

UCC 1-203 states: "Every contract or duty within this Act imposes an obligation of good faith in its performance or enforcement." Although both parties owe a duty of good faith in the performance of a sales or lease contract, merchants are held to a higher standard of good faith than nonmerchants. Nonmerchants are held to the subjective standard of honesty in fact whereas merchants are held to the objective standard of fair dealing in the trade [UCC 2-103(1)(b)].

The words *reasonable* and *reasonably* are used throughout the UCC to establish the duties of performance by the parties to sales and lease contracts. For example, unless otherwise specified, the parties must act within a "reasonable" time [UCC 1-204(1)(2)]. As another example, if the seller does not deliver the goods as contracted, the buyer may make "reasonable" purchases to cover (i.e., obtain substitute performance) [UCC 2-712(1)].

The term *commercial reasonableness is* used to establish certain duties of merchants under the UCC. Articles 2 and 2A of the UCC do not specifically define the terms *reasonable* and *commercial reasonableness*. Instead, these terms are defined by reference to the course of performance or the course of dealing between the parties, usage of trade, and such.

Note that the concepts of good faith and reasonableness extend to the "spirit" of the contract as well as the contract terms. The underlying theory is that the parties are

checklist ☑   BUYER'S AND LESSEE'S REMEDIES

SITUATION	BUYER'S OR LESSEE'S REMEDY
• Seller or lessor refuses to deliver the goods or delivers nonconforming goods that the buyer or lessee does not want.	1. Reject nonconforming goods [UCC 2-601, 2A-509]. 2. Revoke acceptance of nonconforming goods [UCC 2-608, 2A-517(1)]. 3. Cover [UCC 2-712, 2A-518]. 4. Sue for breach of contract and recover damages [UCC 2-713, 2A-519]. 5. Cancel the contract [UCC 2-711(1), 2A-508(1)(a)].
• Seller or lessor tenders nonconforming goods and buyer or lessee accepts them.	1. Sue for ordinary damages [UCC 2-714(1), 2A-516(1)]. 2. Deduct damages from the unpaid purchase or rent price [UCC 2-714(1), 2A-516(1)].
• Seller or lessor refuses to deliver the goods and buyer or lessee wants them.	1. Sue for specific performance [UCC 2-716(1), 2A-521(1)]. 2. Verify the goods [UCC 2-716(3), 2A-521(3)]. 3. Recover the goods from an insolvent seller or lessor [UCC 2-502, 2A-522].

more apt to perform properly if their conduct is to be judged against these principles. This is a major advance in the law of contracts.

E-COMMERCE

Use of the Internet and the World Wide Web to sell goods and services through **e-commerce** is commonplace today. E-commerce also is refered to as **online commerce**. Businesses and individuals sell goods and services over the Internet through websites and registered domain names. Consumers and businesses can purchase or sell almost any good or service they want over the Internet, using their own sites or sites such as Amazon.com, eBay, and others. In addition, software and information may be licensed either by physically purchasing the software or information and installing it on a computer or by merely downloading the software or information directly into the computer.

E-commerce
The sale of goods and services by computer over the Internet.

E-Contract

Email and the Web have exploded as a means of personal and business communication. In the business environment, email and the Web are sometimes the methods used to negotiate and agree on contract terms and to send and agree to a final contract. Are email and Web contracts enforceable? Assuming that all the elements to establish a contract are present, an email or **Web contract** is valid and enforceable. These are typically called **e-contracts**. The main problem in a lawsuit seeking to enforce an e-contract is evidence, but this problem, which exists in almost all lawsuits, can be overcome by printing out the e-contract and its prior email or Web negotiations, if necessary.

E-contract
A contract that is entered into by email and over the World Wide Web.

E-Contracts Writing Requirement

In 2000, the federal government enacted the **Electronic Signature in Global and National Commerce Act**. This is a federal statute enacted by Congress and, therefore, has national reach. The Act is designed to place the world of electronic commerce on a par with the world of paper contracts in the United States.

> One of the main features of the Act is that it recognizes electronic contracts as meeting the writing requirement of the Stature of Frauds for most contracts. Statutes of Frauds are state laws that require certain types of contracts to be in writing. The 2000 federal Act provides that electronically signed contracts cannot be denied effect

Electronic Signature in Global and National Commerce Act
A federal statute that recognizes that electronic contracts, or e-contracts, meet the writing requirement of the Statute of Frauds and gives electronic signatures, or e-signatures, the same force and effect as pen-inscribed signatures on paper.

THE PARALEGAL AND E-COMMERCE

As a paralegal, you have witnessed the explosive growth of electronic commerce, or e-commerce, around the world. You can find almost anything being sold over the Internet through Web pages. Large companies and small companies alike, as well as individuals, are selling and buying over the Internet.

When someone sells and purchases something over the Internet, they usually enter into an e-contract, also called a Web contract or online contract. Originally, state contract law solely regulated the formation and performance of e-contracts. This led to an often nonuniform application of law to e-contracts.

Some of the common law of contracts and provisions of the Uniform Commercial Code (UCC) did not directly apply to e-contracts. To alleviate this problem, the UCC has been updated to apply to sales and leases made over the Internet. Modern changes to the UCC have helped considerably in bringing uniform contract rules to electronic commerce. A uniform law for e-contracts also has been promulgated and is being adopted in whole or part by state legislatures.

A special kind of contracting that is especially suited for online commerce is licensing. Many companies transfer software, data, information technology, and other forms of intellectual property over the Internet through the use of licenses. Special rules of licensing apply to these **e-licenses**. A model act, called the Uniform Computer Information Transactions Act (UCITA), has been promulgated to apply to e-licenses. Many states have adopted this Act or provisions similar to this Act that create more uniform contract law for e-licenses.

In addition, the federal government has stepped in and enacted federal statutes to bring uniformity to e-commerce transactions. The major law in this area is the Electronic Signature in Global and National Commerce Act. This federal act establishes special rules that recognize electronic contracts, or e-contracts, and signatures. The federal government is expected to continue to adopt laws as is necessary to bring more uniform law to the area of e-commerce.

Paralegals have a unique opportunity to become experts in this relatively new area of the law. E-contracts and e-licenses face special rules in their formation, performance, and enforcement. In addition, many lawsuits involving e-contracts and e-licenses will be litigated in the courts. Paralegals will be needed to assist lawyers in drafting e-contracts and e-licenses, as well as assisting in the litigation of disputes involving e-commerce.

because they are in electronic form or delivered electronically. The Act also provides that record retention requirements are satisfied if the records are stored electronically.

The federal law was passed with several provisions to protect consumers.

1. Consumers must consent to receiving electronic records and contracts.
2. To receive electronic records, consumers must be able to demonstrate that they have access to the electronic records.
3. Businesses must tell consumers that they have the right to receive hardcopy documents of their transaction.

E-Signatures

In the past, signatures have been hand-applied by the person signing the document. No more. In the electronic commerce world, it is now, "What is your mother's maiden name?" "Slide your smart card in the sensor," or "Look into the iris scanner." But are electronic signatures sufficient to form an enforceable contract? In 2000, the federal government stepped into the breach and enacted the Electronic Signature in Global and National Commerce Act.

One of the main features of this federal law is that it recognizes an *electronic signature* or **e-signature**. The Act gives an e-signature the same force and effect as a pen-inscribed signature on paper. The act is technology neutral, however, in that the law does not define or decide which technologies should be used to create a legally binding signature in cyberspace.

Loosely defined, a **digital signature** is some electronic method that identifies an individual. The challenge is to make sure that someone who uses a digital signature is the person he or she claims to be. The Act provides that a digital signature basically can be verified in one of three ways:

1. By something the signatory knows; such as a secret password, pet's name, and so forth
2. By something a person has, such as a "smart card," which looks like a credit card and stores personal information
3. By biometrics, which uses a device that digitally recognizes fingerprints or the retina or iris of the eye

The verification of electronic signatures is creating a need for scanners and methods for verifying personal information.

E-License

Intellectual property and information rights are extremely important assets of many individuals and companies. Software programs, data, copyrights, and such constitute valuable intellectual property and information rights.

The owners of intellectual property and information rights often wish to transfer limited rights in the property or information to parties for specified purposes and limited duration. The agreement that is used to transfer such limited rights is called a **license**. The parties to a license are the licensor and the license. The **licensor** is the party who owns the intellectual property or information rights and obligates himself or herself to transfer rights in the property or information to the licensee. The **licensee** is the party who is granted limited rights in or access to the intellectual property of information rights. A licensing arrangement is illustrated in Exhibit 13.2.

In 1999 the National Conference of Commissioners on Uniform State Laws (a group of lawyers, judges, and legal scholars) drafted the **Uniform Computer Information Transactions Act (UCITA)**. This model act establishes a uniform and comprehensive set of rules that govern the creation, performance, and enforcement of computer information transactions. A computer information transaction is an agreement to create, transfer, or license computer information or information rights [UCITA Section 102(a)(11)].

The UCITA does not become law until a state's legislature enacts it as a state statute. States have adopted the UCITA or laws similar to the UCITA as their law for computer transactions and the licensing of informational rights.

Licensing Agreement

A licensor and a licensee usually enter into a written **licensing agreement** that expressly states the terms of their agreement. Licensing agreements tend to be very detailed and

License
A contract that transfers limited rights in intellectual property and informational rights.

Licensor
An owner of intellectual property or informational rights who transfers rights in the property or information to the licensee.

Licensee
A party who is granted limited rights in or access to intellectual property or informational rights owned by a licensor.

Uniform Computer Information Transactions Act (UCITA)
A model state law that creates contract law for the licensing of information technology rights.

Licensing agreement
A detailed and comprehensive written agreement between a licensor and a licensee that sets forth the express terms of their agreement.

Exhibit 13.2 **Parties to a license**

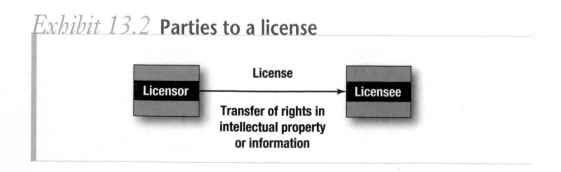

comprehensive contracts. This is primarily because of the nature of the subject matter and the limited uses granted in the intellectual property or informational rights.

The parties to a contract for the licensing of information owe a duty to perform the obligations stated in the contract. If a party fails to perform as required, there is a breach of the contract. Breach of contract by one party to a licensing agreement gives the non-breaching party the right to recover damages or other remedies.

Counteroffers Ineffectual Against Electronic Agents

In today's e-commerce, many sellers use electronic agents to sell goods and services. An **electronic agent** is any telephonic or computer system that has been established by a seller to accept orders. Voice mail and Web page order systems are examples of electronic agents.

In the past, when humans dealt with each other face-to-face, by telephone, or in writing, their negotiations might have consisted of an exchange of several offers and counteroffers until agreed-upon terms were reached and a contract was formed. Each new counteroffer extinguished the previous offer and became a new, viable offer. Most electronic agents do not have the ability to evaluate and accept counteroffers or to make counteroffers.

The UCITA recognizes this limitation and provides that a contract is formed if an individual takes action that causes the electronic agent to confer performance or promise benefits on the individual. Thus, counteroffers are not effective against electronic agents.

Consider this example: "Birdie" is an electronic ordering system for placing orders for electronic information sold by the Green Company, a producer of computer software and electronic information. Freddie Calloway dials the Green Company's toll-free telephone number and orders new software for $1,000, using the Birdie voice mail electronic ordering system.

Freddie enters the product code and description, his mailing address and credit card information, and other data needed to complete the transaction, but at the end of the order states, "I will accept this software if, after two weeks of use, I am satisfied with the software." Because Freddie has placed the order with an electronic agent, Freddie has ordered the software, and his counteroffer is ineffectual.

Electronic Errors

The UCITA provides that consumers are not bound by their unilateral **electronic errors** if the consumer:

1. Promptly, upon learning of the error, notifies the licensor of the error.
2. Does not use or receive any benefit from the information, or make the information or benefit available to a third party.
3. Delivers all copies of the information to the licensor or destroys all copies of the information, pursuant to reasonable instructions from the licensor.
4. Pays all shipping, reshipping, and processing costs of the licensor.

The UCITA does not relieve a consumer of his or her electronic error if the other party provides a reasonable method to detect and correct or avoid the error. Thus, many sellers establish methods whereby the buyer must verify the information and purchase order a second time before an electronic order is processed.

Consider this example: Kai, a consumer, intends to order 10 copies of a videogame over the Internet from Cybertendo, a videogame producer. In fact, Kai makes an error and orders 110 games. The electronic agent maintaining Cybertendo's website's ordering process electronically disburses 110 games.

Men keep their agreements when it is an advantage to both parties not to break them.

Solon
(c. 600 B.C.)

The next morning Kai discovers his mistake and immediately e-mails Cybertendo, describing the mistake and offering to return or destroy the copies at his expense. When Kai receives the games, he returns the 110 copies unused.

Under the UCITA, Kai has no contract obligation for 110 copies but bears the cost of returning them to Cybertendo or destroying them if Cybertendo instructs him to do so. But if Cybertendo's website's electronic ordering system had asked Kai to confirm his order of 110 copies of the purchase order and Kai had confirmed the original order of 110 copies, Kai would have had to pay for the 110 copies even if his confirmation had been in error.

Electronic Self-Help

Just like traditional contracts, electronic licenses can be breached by licenses. If a breach occurs, the licensor can recover damages and other remedies. A licensor can resort to **electronic self-help** if a breach occurs—for example, if the licensee fails to pay the license fee. Such electronic self-help can consist of activating disabling bugs and timebombs that have been embedded in the software or information that will prevent the licensee from further using the software or information. The UCITA provides that a licensor is entitled to use electronic self-help only if the following requirements are met:

Law cannot stand aside from the social changes around it.

William J. Brennan, Jr.

1. The licensee must agree specifically to the inclusion in the license of self-help as a remedy. It must have a specific self-help option to which the licensee assents.
2. The licensor must give the licensee at least 15 days' notice prior to the disabling action. The notice period allows the licensee to make lawful adjustments to minimize the effects of the licensor's self-help or to seek a judicial remedy to combat the use of the self-help.
3. The licensor may not use self-help if it would cause a breach of the peace, risk personal injury, cause significant damage or injury to information other than the licensee's information, result in injury to the public health or safety, or cause grave harm to national security.

A licensor who violates these provisions and uses self-help improperly is liable for damages. This liability cannot be disclaimed.

UNITED NATIONS CONVENTION ON CONTRACTS FOR THE INTERNATIONAL SALE OF GOODS (CISG)

Businesspersons who engage in international commerce face the daunting task of trying to comply with the laws of many nations. To ease this burden, more than 60 countries are signatories to the **United Nations Convention on Contracts for the International Sale of Goods (CISG)**. This treaty took more than 50 years to negotiate and incorporates rules from all the major legal systems of the world.

The CISG establishes uniform rules for the formation and enforcement of contracts involving the international sale of goods. Many of its provisions are remarkably similar to the provisions of the American UCC. The CISG applies if the buyer and seller have their places of business in different countries and both nations are parties to the convention.

The contracting parties may agree to exclude (i.e., opt out of) the CISG and let other laws apply. The parties to any international contract can agree that the CISG controls, even if one or both of their countries are not signatories to the convention.

Advice from the Field ··

THE PARALEGAL PROFESSION IS NO LONGER IN "INFANCY"
What Comes with "Middle Age?"
Carl Alvarado, Los Angeles Paralegal Association

In a profession whose educational financing already seems to rival the national defense budget, and surely runs parallel to the cost of sending 10 astronauts to the moon and back, this "middle aged profession" seems to have become much more demanding academically as well. I speak from experience, having already pursued this same type of education years ago in one State, only to have to re-educate myself by more current standards in another. One way to account for these higher costs and the more stringent class work is the almost mandatory requirement to pursue only paralegal curriculum approved by the American Bar Association. Suffice to say, those paralegals who have not received their certificate or paralegal diploma from an ABA approved program aren't necessarily *underqualified*, but it is what most law firms are looking for at the onset of just about every interview. Without it, just getting your foot in the door adds new meaning to the word "challenge" while seeking employment in the legal job market.

Nowadays I seem to have way too much homework, way too many cram sessions, too little sleep, and no social life to speak of. Mind you, I'm just trying to maintain a B average, even though it feels as if I'm putting out better than A average effort. And don't even get me started on the cost. At a time when maybe 3 or 4 books, plus tuition and school supplies, for a couple of measly paralegal courses tallies just over $1,400.00, I am now left pulling lint out of my pockets instead of any kind of loose change. And I can't help but cringe at the financial obligation of having to pay even more money for such occupational enhancements we'll call *gasp!* regulation fees!!! Like it or not though, the paralegal profession is definitely headed that way; toward regulation and toward those highly touted ABA approved programs which confirm only the most legitimate paralegal training and education of its kind. This is all fine and good, as the public is better served I'm sure, but it sure makes for a tough road to hoe.

Allow me to digress for a moment to an old television series starring Raymond Burr as Perry Mason. For those of you who can remember that far back, try and recall that Perry always had a sidekick named Paul who was always at Mr. Mason's beckoned call from one episode to the next. Paul, as it turned out, was my first recollection of just what the heck a paralegal is, and does, from time to time as Perry's bonafide legal assistant. . .well, sort of. Given the fact that this particular TV series was first aired sometime during the late 50's or early 60's, when the profession itself was barely a glint in the eye of the American Bar Association, try and recall what the *World* population might have been at that time. Just how many people in the world or just in the U.S. alone, do you think were actually employed as *paralegals*? I went on the internet and discovered that the worldwide human population then, was just over three billion, with our U.S. population just under several hundred million and maybe, just maybe, there were probably a thousand people employed as *paralegals* in the entire U.S. at that time. Jump back to the present day census of paralegal professionals and, more likely than not, I bet that number is equivalent to a population the entire size of Texas.

My point is this; given the middle aged status of our astute profession as it stands today, with so many good paralegals out there and so many people in this already overpopulated world of ours who call themselves *Good Paralegals*, how do you keep tabs on all of them? How do you insure that the quality of their service and training as legal professionals is adequate? How do you enforce the fact that they abide by the ethical standards now required for modern day legal representation? How do you distinguish John Doe who is an outstanding paralegal living in Minnesota, from John Doe who is a mediocre paralegal living in Iowa? How do you weed out the qualified good apples from the under-qualified not so goods? I'm referring of course to those paralegal professionals who are not part of the same regulation process, and who think the acronym "ABA" stands for, "**A**lways **B**roke. . .**A** lot !?!?!" And all this. . .because our world just had to get bigger.

Well, one sure way of ensuring some sort of supervision over the dominion of thousands, is to implement regulatory protocol on a national level. This basically boils down to assigning numbers to the names of all those individuals who can effectively prove that they have paid for (tuition and books remember. . .?) and are in fact qualified as (with a C grade or better. . .) *Good Apples*, with certifiable proof that they have graduated

Advice from the Field ·······························

from a regulated and probably more standardized ABA program.

Hectic isn't it? Bothersome you say? Well maybe, but stop and think for a moment of what might happen to this profession if it doesn't progress toward the process of regulation and/or our most current ABA watch dog authority. Cheap, fly by night Paralegal programs, all claiming legitimate accreditation and training, could ostensibly spring up everywhere. Oh sure, they're accredited alright, but not by the Southern Association of Colleges and Schools as required in this State nor are they approved by the supervisory capacity of the American Bar Association. More than likely they'll be accredited by an independent association of old guys we'll call, *Investors*, who brained stormed an idea one night to capitalize on the hopes and dreams of people who want to be paid good money, quickly. Young people especially, as enthusiastic as they are and looking for the same good paying position as the rest of us, all jump on this fly by night bandwagon. They earn their little fly by night certificate/diploma and are then promptly thrown into the lion's maw of the legal workforce immediately after they graduate. They have high expectations these young people, for they believe they have been effectively trained and educated at their comparatively cheap little fly by night, non affiliated business college. All too quickly do they discover that they have no legitimate concept or understanding of what's expected of them under the watchful and ethical eye of their legal employers. Certain legal terms and procedures all too familiar to paralegal trainees who were effectively taught these things under a more regulated ABA program, elude the fly by nighters. Their high hopes are dashed as they become disillusioned and downright angry at the foolishness of their expectations. They continue to mope along from one job interview to the next and from one legal placement position to the next, only to eventually leave the profession altogether. . .bitter, angry and still financially in debt to an illegitimate, albeit comparatively cheap, paralegal program that promised them the world, but couldn't deliver. Not to be smug mind you but. . .HA! YOU GET WHAT YOU PAY FOR!!!

Consider too, the consequences suffered by your average law firm client. Here's a guy who comes into a legal office, also with high expectations, seeking legitimate counsel and legal support, only to discover that the services provided for by the average, non-regulated fly by nighter are anything but adequate, seemingly not effective, and probably down right ILLEGAL!!! All the while these fly by night graduates continue on, not pursuing any sort of regulated schooling, thereby circumventing the ABA process until a lawsuit ensues. This in turn, does no one any good and in the end only disgruntled people, (would be paralegals and clientele alike) remain, with nothing less than a very bad disposition about the legal profession (my profession) as a whole.

So, you get the picture of where I'm going with this? I don't want people coming into my law firm thinking my constituents are bad, or corrupt, or dysfunctional, or inadequate, I want people to think this occupation I've chosen, and all those associated with it, are good. . .no wait, not just good. . .but GREAT!

Now, there was a time when I truly felt the only real reason regulation, tougher schooling, and ABA approval were coming about, was simply to line the coffers of some big wig legal organization that was sitting somewhere at the very top of the State's legal food chain. I had a similar perspective in order to account for the higher tuition costs in college as well. I envisioned a bunch of greedy old curmudgeons wringing their hands and slathering at the mouth at the cash flow of these new *required* regulation and tuition fees that I felt sure were flowing into their greased and greedy little fingers. My perspectives may have been a little narrow minded at the time I'll admit, but that was probably because I was tired of eating corn flakes and milk for dinner, having just paid for my books and tuition at school earlier that day. Still, like most good paralegal students before me, I eventually began to understand and come to terms with the importance of "paying my dues" so to speak, which is why I also understand the importance of regulating this occupation, coupled with the associated cost for *legitimate* paralegal training. It's an inevitable process that had to come about as our world got bigger and the expectations of our clients became higher. There's peace of mind with that, as opposed to pieces of a mind which is what I'm usually left with just after finals.

Understand also, that most legal employers who are hiring out there realize that the quality of a person's character is sometimes determined by what he or she may have had to sacrifice to get where they're at. With that in mind, they usually pay accordingly. However, never let money be the ONLY reason you stay interested in this profession. What each of us is paid per hour is important to

(continued)

Advice from the Field ··········

(continued)

be sure, but make sure that this is your occupation of choice first, and that you are willing to accept this constant, on going process of both personal and professional self improvement. Stay aware and up to date of the ethical standards now coming about. Do this, before ever deciding what your own self worth is, however top dollar you feel that may be. Do this, and you will also come to realize that it won't be corn flakes and milk forever.

So, to reiterate. . .never settle for mediocrity in school or in life, realize and accept the importance of just where this profession is headed insofar as regulating all *Good Paralegals* and those pesky ABA standards are concerned, then accept the fact that if you raise the bar on the requirements of good education and conduct, we all rise to the occasion as professional team players. And that, boys and girls, has been the gist of this entire writing.

As for me, I'm going out to celebrate and buy myself a steak for dinner tonight. . .uh, right after I finish reading chapter 7 in preparation for my litigation test, and writing that term paper for my legal ethics class. Just my luck though, that green patch of moss in my wallet isn't a dollar bill. . . *begins sniveling. . . .* I'm so tired of corn flakes and milk!!!

"The Paralegal Professional is No Longer in Infancy," by Carl D. Alvarado, Editor for the Los Angeles Paralegal Association (LAPA).

Legal Terminology

Summary

CHAPTER *13*
Formation of a Contract

CONTRACTS AND COMMERCIAL LAW

Definition	A contract is a promise or set of promises for the breach of which the law gives a remedy or the performance of which the law in some way recognizes a duty.
Parties to a Contract	1. *Offeror*: Party who makes an offer to enter into a contract. 2. *Offeree*: Party to whom the offer is made.
Sources of Contract Law	1. Common law of contracts (law) 2. Uniform Commercial Code (law) 3. Restatement (Second) of Contracts (advisory only, not law)
Elements of a Contract	1. Agreement 2. Consideration 3. Contractual capacity 4. Lawful object
Agreement	1. *Offer*: Manifestation by one party of a willingness to enter into a contract. 2. *Offeror*: Party who makes an offer. 3. *Offeree*: Party to whom an offer is made. This party has the power to create an agreement by accepting the terms of the offer.
Termination of an Offer by Action of the Parties	1. *Revocation*: The offeror may *revoke* (withdraw) an offer any time prior to its acceptance by the offeree. 2. *Rejection*: An offer is terminated if the offeree rejects the offer by his or her words or conduct. 3. *Counteroffer*: A counteroffer by the offeree terminates the offeror's offer (and creates a new offer).
Acceptance	Manifestation of assent by the offeree to the terms of the offer. Acceptance of the offer by the offeree creates a contract.
Option Contract	A contract that is created if an offeree pays the offeror compensation to keep an offer open for an agreed upon period of time. The offeror cannot sell the property to anyone else during the *option period*.
Express and Implied Contracts	1. *Express contract*: A contract expressed in oral or written words. 2. *Implied-in-fact contract*: A contract implied from the conduct of the parties.

Consideration	Thing of value given in exchange for a promise. May be tangible or intangible property, performance of a service, forbearance of a legal right, or another thing of value.
Gift Promises	Promises to make gifts that are unenforceable because they lack consideration. Also called *gratuitous promise*.
Capacity to Contract	1. *Infancy doctrine*: Minors under the age of majority may *disaffirm* (cancel) most contracts they have entered into with adults. The contract is *voidable* by the minor but not by the adult. 2. *Mental incompetence*: Contracts by persons who are insane are *voidable* by the insane person but not by the competent party to the contract. 3. *Intoxicated persons*: Contracts by *intoxicated* persons are *voidable* by the intoxicated person but not by the competent party to the contract.
Lawful Object	An illegal contract is *void*. Therefore, the parties cannot sue for nonperformance. If the contract has been executed, the court will *leave the parties where it finds them*. 1. Contracts that violate statutes are illegal, void, and unenforceable. 2. Contracts that violate public policy are illegal, void, and unenforceable.

Statute of Frauds

Writing Requirement	A state statute requires the following contracts to be in writing: 1. *Contracts involving the transfer of interests in real property*: Includes contracts for the sale of land, buildings, and items attached to land, mortgages, leases for a term of more than one year, and express easements. 2. Contracts that cannot be performed within one year of their formation (*one-year rule*). 3. *Contracts for the sale of goods* costing $500 or more (UCC 201). (The 2003 amendments to the UCC changes this contract to $5,000 or more)
Sufficiency of the Writing	1. *Formality of the writing*: A written contract does not have to be formal or drafted by a lawyer to be enforceable. Informal contracts, such as handwritten notes, letters, invoices, and the like, are enforceable contracts. 2. *Required signature*: The party against whom enforcement of the contract is sought must have signed the contract. The signature may be the person's full legal name, last name, first name, nickname, initials, or other symbol.
Electronic Signatures	*Electronic Signature in Global and National Commerce Act (E-Sign Act)*: A federal statute that recognizes and gives electronic signatures—e-signatures—the same force and effect as a pen-inscribed signature on paper. The act is technology-neutral in that the law does not define or decide which technologies should be used to create a legally binding signature in cyberspace.

Performance and Breach

Covenant	A covenant is an unconditional promise to perform. Nonperformance of a covenant is a breach of contract that gives the other party the right to sue.
Conditions Precedent	Conditions precedent require the occurrence or nonoccurrence of an event before a party is obligated to perform.
Levels of Performance	1. *Complete performance*: A party renders performance exactly as the contract requires. That party's contractual duties are discharged. 2. *Substantial performance*: A party renders performance that deviates only slightly from complete performance. There is a *minor breach*. The non-breaching party may recover damages caused by the breach.

3. *Inferior performance*: A party fails to perform express or implied contractual duties that impair or destroy the essence of the contract.
There is a *material breach*. The non-breaching party may either (1) rescind the contract and recover restitution or (2) affirm the contract and recover damages.

Remedies

Types of Monetary Damages	1. *Compensatory damages*: Damages that compensate a non-breaching party for loss of the contract. Restore the "benefit of the bargain" to the non-breaching party as if the contract had been fully performed. 2. *Consequential damages*: Foreseeable damages that arise from circumstances outside the contract and of which the breaching party either knew or had reason to know. Also called *special damages*. 3. *Liquidated damages*: Damages payable upon breach of contract that are agreed on in advance by the contracting parties. Liquidated damages substitute for actual damages.
Mitigation of Damages	The duty the law places on a non-breaching party to take reasonable efforts to avoid or reduce the resulting damages from a breach of contract. To mitigate a breach of an employment contract, the non-breaching party must only accept "comparable" employment.
Specific Performance	Specific performance is a court order that requires the breaching party to perform his or her contractual duties. It is available only if the subject matter of the contract is *unique*.
Injunction	An injunction is a court order that prohibits a person from doing a certain act. The requesting party must show that he or she will suffer irreparable injury if the injunction is not granted.
Reformation	Reformation permits the court to rewrite a contract to express the parties true intention. Available to correct clerical and mathematical errors.
Quasi-contract	A quasi-contract permits the court to order recovery of compensation even though no enforceable contract exists between the parties. It is used to prevent unjust enrichment. Also called an *implied-in-law contract* or *quantum meruit*.

Unconscionable Contracts

Definition	Unconscionable contracts are oppressively unfair or unjust. Also called *contracts of adhesion*.
Elements	1. The parties possessed severely unequal bargaining power. 2. The dominant party unreasonably used its power to obtain oppressive or manifestly unfair contract terms. 3. The adhering party had no reasonable alternative.
Remedies	Where a contract or contract clause is found to be unconscionable, the court may do one of the following: 1. Refuse to enforce the contract. 2. Refuse to enforce the unconscionable clause but enforce the remainder of the contract. 3. Limit the applicability of any unconscionable clause so as to avoid any unconscionable result.

Equity

	Equity is a doctrine that permits judges to make decisions based on fairness, equality, moral rights, and natural law.

Uniform Commercial Code (UCC)

Definition	The UCC is a comprehensive statutory scheme that includes laws covering most aspects of sales and lease contracts of goods.
Article 2 (Sales)	Article 2 of the UCC applies to sales transactions in goods.
Article 2A (Leases)	Article 2A of the UCC applies to personal property leases of goods.
Open Terms	If the parties leave open a major term in a sales or lease contract, the UCC gap-filling rule permits the following terms to be read into the contract: 1. Price term 2. Payment term 3. Delivery term 4. Time term 5. Assortment term
UCC Firm Offer Rule	The UCC firm-offer rule says that a merchant who (1) makes an offer to buy, sell, or lease goods and (2) assures the other party in a separate writing that the offer will be held open cannot revoke the offer for the time stated, or if no time is stated, for a reasonable time.
Additional Terms	If both parties to a sales contract are merchants, the UCC permits an acceptance of a sales contract to contain additional terms and still to act as an acceptance rather than a counteroffer in certain circumstances.
UCC Statute of Frauds	The UCC Statute of Frauds requires contracts for the sale of goods costing $500 or more and lease contracts involving payments of $1,000 or more to be in writing.
UCC Written Confirmation Rule	If both parties to an oral sales or lease contract are merchants, the Statute of Frauds requirements are satisfied if (1) one of the parties sends a *written confirmation* of the sale to the other within a reasonable time after contracting and (2) the other merchant does not give written notice of an objection to the contract within 10 days after receiving the confirmation.

E-Commerce

Definition	Electronic commerce, or e-commerce, is the use of the Internet and the World Wide Web to sell goods and services. Also called *online commerce*.
E-Contract	An electronic contract is entered into by e-mail or only the Internet for the sale or lease of goods, other property, or services.
Electronic Signature in Global and National Commerce Act	This federal act applies to e-commerce and does the following: 1. *Writing:* The federal act recognizes that e-contracts meet the writing requirements of the Statutes of Fraud. 2. *E-signature:* The federal act gives electronic signatures the same force and affect as pen-inscribed signatures on paper.
E-License	The electronic license is a contract that is entered into by e-mail or over the Internet that transfers limited rights in intellectual property and informational rights. 1. *Licensor:* An owner of intellectual property or informational rights who transfers rights in the property or information to the licensee. 2. *Licensee:* A party who is granted limited rights in or access to intellectual property or information rights owned by a licensor.
Uniform Computer Information Transactions Act (UCITA)	The UCITA is a model act issued by the National Conference of Commissioners on Uniform State Laws that establishes a uniform and comprehensive set of rules that govern the creation, performance, and enforcement of computer information transactions.
Licensing Agreement	A licensing agreement is a detailed and comprehensive written agreement between a licensor and a licensee that sets forth the express terms of their agreement.

Counteroffer Rule	The UCITA provides that counteroffers are not effective against electronic agents. This is because most electronic agents do not have the ability to evaluate and accept counteroffers or make counteroffers.
Electronic Errors	The UCITA provides that consumers are not bound by their unilateral electronic errors if the consumer: 1. Promptly, upon learning of the error, notifies the other party of the error. 2. Does not use or receive any benefit from the information, or make the information or benefit available to a third party. 3. Delivers all copies of the information to the third party or destroys all copies of the information pursuant to reasonable instructions from the other party. 4. Pays all shipping, reshipping, and processing costs of the other party.
Electronic Self-Help	The UCITA provides that if an electronic license has been breached by a licensee, the licensor can resort to electronic self-help such as activating disabling bugs and time bombs that have been embedded in the software or information that will prevent the licensee from further using the software or information. A licensor is entitled to use electronic self-help only if the following requirements are met.

▶ WORKING THE WEB

1. Visit the website **http://www.lectlaw.com/ formb/html**. Click on the words "Contract, Sale of Goods." Print this form and review the form.

2. Using the website **http://www.google.com/ html** or other Internet search engine, locate an article about a Microsoft software licensing agreement. Write a one-page report on the specifics of the licensing agreement.

3. Visit the website **http://cisg.law.pace.edu/ html**, which is the website for the Institute of International Commercial Law. Click on

"CISG-AC Opinion no 1." Write a one-page report about what Sections 11.1, 13.1, and 13.2 provide.

4. Visit the website **http://lectlaw.com/forma/ html**. Click on the words "Fee Agreement— Contingent." Read this form in its entirety. What type of form contract is this?

5. Using the website **http://www.google.com/ html** or other Internet search engine, locate an article about a recent contract dispute. Write a one-page report on the specifics of this contract dispute.

▶ CRITICAL THINKING AND WRITING QUESTIONS

1. Define a contract.
2. Define an offer. Who is the offeror? Who is the offeree?
3. What are the four elements necessary for an enforceable contract?
4. Describe the common law of contracts. Describe the Uniform Commercial Code (UCC).
5. Explain the following: (a) revocation of an offer, (b) rejection of an offer, and (c) counteroffer. What is the effect of each?
6. What is an acceptance? Explain the mirror image rule.

7. Describe the following: (a) express contract, and (b) implied-in-fact contract. Give an example of each.
8. Define an option contract. When would one be used?
9. What is consideration? Give an example.
10. Define a gift promise. Give an example. Is it enforceable? Explain.
11. Define capacity to contract. Explain the enforceability of contracts made by (a) minors (the infancy doctrine), (b) mentally incompetent persons, and (c) intoxicated persons.

12. Define lawful object. What is an illegal contract? What is the effect of an illegal contract?

13. Explain the difference between the illegality of (a) contracts contrary to statutes and (b) contracts contrary to public policy. Give an example of each.

14. What is the Statute of Frauds. What is the effect if the Statute of Frauds is not met?

15. What types of contracts does the Statute of Frauds cover? Give examples. What does the UCC Statute of Frauds provide?

16. What is contract fraud? What are the elements to prove fraud? What is the legal effect of contract fraud?

17. Describe the difference between: (a) covenant and (b) condition precedent.

18. Define complete performance? What is the effect of complete performance? Give an example. Define tender of delivery.

19. Describe substantial performance. Is there a breach of the contract? Give an example.

20. Define inferior performance. Is this a breach of contract? Give an example.

21. Explain the following types of monetary damages: (a) compensatory damages and (b) consequential damages. Give an example of each.

22. Define liquidated damages. Give an example.

23. What does mitigation of damages require? Give an example.

24. Describe the following types of equitable remedies: (a) specific performance, (b) injunction, and (c) reformation. Give an example of each.

25. Define quasi-contract (implied-in-law contract). Give an example.

26. Define an unconscionable contract. Give an example. If the court finds a contract to be unconscionable, what remedies may the court order?

27. What is Article 2 (Sales) of the Uniform Commercial Code? What type of contracts does it cover? Give an example.

28. What is Article 2A (Leases) of the Uniform Commercial Code? What type of contracts does it cover? Give an example.

29. What is e-commerce? Explain (a) e-contract and (b) e-license.

30. What is the Electronic Signature in Global and National Commerce Act? Explain how this statute (a) affects the Statute of Frauds for e-contracts, and (b) gives affect to e-signatures.

31. What is the Uniform Computer Information Transactions Act (UCITA)?

32. Describe the United Nations Convention on Contracts for the International Sale of Goods (CISG).

ETHICS ANALYSIS AND DISCUSSION QUESTIONS

1. Is it ethical to copy into your word processor, and use as your own, a standard-form real estate contract that contains a copyright notice from the state association of realtors?

2. You have been asked to witness the signature of a client's spouse who is not present. Are there any ethical issues?

3. You are a paralegal not otherwise licensed to practice law. Because of your substantial expertise, you are requested to prepare a complex set of legal documents for a former client. You enter into a fee agreement and are paid upon completion of the work. The "clients" then seek return of the funds paid, claiming they did not understand the significance of the UPL law in the state. [*Vista Designs v. Silverman*, 774 So.2d 884 (Fla.App. 4 Dist. 2001).] Can you be compelled to return the fee paid? Has the client breached its contract?

DEVELOPING YOUR COLLABORATION SKILLS

With a group of other students, selected by you or as assigned by your instructor, review the Opening Scenario at the beginning of the chapter. As a group, discuss the following questions.

1. Discuss the possible terms that should be included in the contract between Jewelry Associates Corporation and the foreign jewel supplier in Sri Lanka.

2. Regarding Jewelry Associates Corporation's online contract, would such a contract meet the Statute of Frauds? Will a customer's online signature be valid?

3. In the dispute where Real Estate Developers Inc. refuses to honor its contract with Jewelry Associates Corporation, what course of action would you suggest? Is any contract remedy available that could get the property for Jewelry Associates Corporation? Explain.

▶PARALEGAL PORTFOLIO EXERCISE

Find a sample buy–sell agreement between owners of a business where the owners agree that if one of them leaves the business or dies, the remaining owners will purchase his or her shares, either by paying the leaving partner or by paying the beneficiaries or heirs of a deceased owner.

Using this sample agreement, draft the buy–sell agreement for the three owners of Jewelry Development Corporation referred to in the Opening Scenario. (Make up the three names of the owners.)

▶LEGAL ANALYSIS AND WRITING CASES

Cooper v. Smith

800 N.E.2d 372 Court of Appeals of Ohio

FACTS

In May 2001, Lester Cooper suffered serious injuries that caused him to be hospitalized for an extended time. While he was hospitalized, Julie Smith, whom Cooper had met the year before, and Janet Smith, Julie's mother, made numerous trips to visit him. Although Julie was married to another man at the time, a romantic relationship developed between Cooper and Julie. While in the hospital, Cooper proposed marriage to Julie, and she accepted. Julie obtained a divorce from her husband in October 2001. Cooper ultimately received a $180,000 settlement for his injuries.

After being released from the hospital, Cooper moved into Janet's house and lived with Janet and Julie. Over the next couple of months, Cooper purchased a number of items for Julie, including a diamond engagement ring, a car, a com-

puter, a tanning bed, and horses. On Julie's request, Cooper paid off Janet's car. Cooper also paid for various improvements to Janet's house, such as having a new furnace installed and having wood flooring laid in the kitchen.

By December 2001, the settlement money had run out and Julie had not yet married Cooper. In the summer of 2002, Julie and Cooper had a disagreement, and Cooper moved out of the house. Julie returned the engagement ring to Cooper. Cooper sued Julie and Janet to recover the gifts or the value of the gifts he gave them. The magistrate who heard the case dismissed Cooper's case, and the Trial Court affirmed the dismissal of the case. Cooper appealed.

Question

1. Can Cooper recover the gifts or the value of the gifts he gave to Julie and Janet Smith?

Flood v. Fidelity & Guaranty Life Insurance Co.

394 So.2d 1311 Court of Appeals of Louisiana

FACTS

Ellen and Richard Alvin Flood, who were married in 1965, lived in a mobile home in Louisiana. Richard worked as a maintenance man, and Ellen was employed at an insurance agency. Evidence at trial showed that Ellen was unhappy with her marriage. Ellen took out a life insurance policy on the life of her husband and named herself as beneficiary. The policy was issued by Fidelity & Guaranty Life Insurance Company (Fidelity).

In June 1972, Richard became unexpectedly ill. He was taken to the hospital, where his condition improved. After a visit at the hospital from his wife, however, Richard died. Ellen was criminally charged with the murder of her hus-

band by poisoning. Evidence showed that six medicine bottles at the couple's home, including Tylenol and paregoric bottles, contained arsenic. The court found that Ellen had fed Richard ice cubes laced with arsenic at the hospital.

Ellen was tried and convicted of the murder of her husband. Ellen, as beneficiary of Richard's life insurance policy, requested Fidelity to pay her the benefits. Fidelity refused to pay the benefits and returned all premiums paid on the policy. This suit followed. The District Court held in favor of Ellen Flood and awarded her the benefits of the life insurance policy. Fidelity appealed.

Question

1. Was the life insurance policy an illegal contract that is void?

Ryno v. Tyra

752 S.W.2d 148 Court of Appeals of Texas

FACTS

R. D. Ryno, Jr. owned Bavarian Motors, an automobile dealership in Fort Worth, Texas. On March 5, 1981, Lee Tyra discussed purchasing a 1980 BMW M-1 from Ryno for $125,000. Ryno then suggested a double-or-nothing coin flip, to which Tyra agreed. If the seller Ryno won the coin flip, Tyra would have to pay $250,000 for the car; if the

buyer Tyra won the coin flip he would get the car for free. When Tyra won the coin flip, Ryno said, "It's yours," and handed Tyra the keys and German title to the car. Tyra drove away in the car.

This suit ensued as to the ownership of the car. The Trial Court held in favor of Tyra. Ryno appealed.

Question

1. Was there an illegal contract? Who owns the car?

Wilson v. Western National Life Insurance Co.

235 Cal.App.3d 981, 1 Cal.Rptr.2d 157
1249 (1991) California Court of Appeals

FACTS

Daniel and Doris Wilson were husband and wife: On August 13, 1985, Daniel fainted from a narcotics overdose and was rushed, unconscious, to the hospital. Doris accompanied him. Daniel responded to medication used to counteract a narcotics overdose and recovered. The emergency room physician noted that Daniel probably had incurred a heroin overdose and that Daniel had multiple puncture sites on his arms.

On October 8, 1985, an agent for Western National Life Insurance Company (Western) met with the Wilsons in their home for the purpose of taking their application for life insurance. The agent asked questions and recorded the Wilsons' responses on a written application form. Daniel answered the following questions:

		Yes	No
13.	In the past 10 years, have you been treated or joined an organization for alcoholism or drug addiction? If "Yes," explain on the reverse side.	**Yes**	No X
17.	In the past 5 years, have you consulted or been treated or examined by any physician or practitioner?	**Yes**	No X

Both of the Wilsons signed the application form and paid the agent the first month's premium. Under insurance law and the application form, the life insurance policy took effect immediately. Daniel Wilson died from a drug overdose two days later. Western rescinded the policy and rejected Doris Wilson's claim to recover the policy's $50,000 death benefit for Daniel's death, alleging failure to disclose the August 13, 1985 incident. Doris sued to recover the death benefits. The Trial Court granted summary judgment for Western. Doris appealed.

Question

1. Was there concealment of a material fact that justified Western's rescission of the life insurance policy?

Bobby Floars Toyota, Inc. v. Smith

269 S.E.2d 320 (N.C.App. 1980)

FACTS

Infancy Doctrine. Charles Edwards Smith, a minor, purchased an automobile from Bobby Floars Toyota on August 15, 1973. Smith executed a security agreement to finance part of the balance due on the purchase price, agreeing to pay off the balance in 30 monthly installments. On September 25, 1973, Smith turned 18, the age of majority. Smith made 10 monthly payments after turning 18. He then decided to disaffirm the contract and stopped making the payments. Smith claims that he may disaffirm the contract entered into when he was a minor. Toyota argues that Smith had ratified the contract since attaining the age of majority.

Question

1. Who is correct?

Welch v. Metro-Goldwyn-Mayer Film Co.

207 Cal.App.3d 164, 254 Cal.Rptr. 645 (Cal.App. 1989)

FACTS

Damages. Raquel Welch, a movie actress, appeared in about 30 films between 1965 and 1980. Considered a sex symbol, her only serious dramatic role was as a roller derby queen in *Kansas City Bomber*.

About 1980, Michael Phillips and David Ward developed a film package based on the John Steinbeck novella *Cannery Row*. In early 1981, Metro-Goldwyn-Mayer Film Co. (MGM) accepted to produce the project and entered into a contract with Welch to play the leading female character, a prostitute named Suzy. At 40 years old, Welch relished the chance to direct her career toward more serious roles. Welch was to receive $250,000 from MGM, with payment being divided into weekly increments during filming.

Filming began on December 1, 1980. On December 22, 1980, MGM fired Welch and replaced her with another actress, Debra Winger. Welch sued MGM to recover the balance of $194,444 that remained unpaid under the contract.

Question

1. Who wins?

Liz Claiborne, Inc. v. Avon Products, Inc.

530 N.Y.S.2d 425, 141 A.D.2d 329 (N.Y. Sup.App. 1988)

FACTS

Specific Performance. Liz Claiborne, Inc., is a large maker of women's better sportswear in the United States and a well-known name in fashion, with sales of more than $1 billion a year. Claiborne distributes its products through 9,000 retail outlets in the United States. Avon Products, Inc. is a major producer of fragrances, toiletries, and cosmetics, with sales of more than $3 billion a year. Claiborne, who desired to promote its well-known name on perfumes and cosmetics, entered into a joint venture with Avon whereby Claiborne would make available its name, trademarks, and marketing experience and Avon would engage in the procurement and manufacture of the fragrances, toiletries, and cosmetics. The parties would equally share the financial requirements of the joint venture.

In 1986, its first year of operation, the joint venture had sales of more than $16 million. In the second year, sales increased to $26 million, making it one of the fastest-growing fragrance and cosmetic lines in the country. In 1987, Avon sought to "uncouple" the joint venture. Avon thereafter refused to procure and manufacture the line of fragrances and cosmetics for the joint venture. When Claiborne could not obtain the necessary fragrances and cosmetics from any other source for the fall/Christmas season, Claiborne sued Avon for breach of contract, seeking specific performance of the contract by Avon.

Question

1. Is specific performance an appropriate remedy in this case?

Walgreen Co. v. Sara Creek Property Co.

966 F.2d 273 (7th Cir. 1992)

FACTS

Walgreen Company operated a pharmacy in the Southgate Mall in Milwaukee since 1951, when the mall opened. Its lease, signed in 1971 and carrying a 30-year term, contains an exclusivity clause in which the landlord, Sara Creek Property Company, promised not to lease space in the mall to anyone else who wants to operate a pharmacy or a store containing a pharmacy.

In 1990, after its anchor tenant went broke, Sara Creek informed Walgreen that it intended to lease the anchor tenant space to Phar-Mor Corporation. Phar-Mor, a "deep discount" chain, would occupy 100,000 square feet, of which 12,000 square feet would be occupied by a pharmacy the same size as Walgreen's. The entrances to the two stores would be within a few hundred feet of each other.

Walgreen sued Sara Creek for breach of contract and sought a permanent injunction against Sara Creek's leasing the anchor premises to Phar-Mor.

Question

1. Do the facts of this case justify issuing a permanent injunction? Did Sara Creek act ethically in not living up to the contract?

Ms. Trump's property to reach his property that the prior owner of his property had used for 20 years. The dirt road runs from the highway that is north of Ms. Trump's, Mrs. Gasper's, and Mr. Jones's properties. The south side of each of the three properties is the lake and beach. The dirt road runs from the highway beginning about one-third of the way from the east lot line with Mr. Jones, traverses across Ms. Trump's property, and arrives at the front of Mr. Jones's property at the beach on Mr. Jones's property about 20 feet across the lot line with Ms. Trump's property. The neighbor and Ms. Trump have no formal written agreement, however.

Ms. Trump asks Mr. Klapova to look into these matters for her and to advise her if she has any legal problems concerning the proposed sale of her property. Consider the issues involved in this scenario as you read the chapter.

▶ INTRODUCTION FOR THE PARALEGAL

Private ownership of property forms the foundation of our economic system. As such, a comprehensive body of law has been developed to protect property rights. The law protects the right of property owners to use, sell, dispose of, control, and prevent others from trespassing on their rights.

Many lawyers practice in the area of real estate law. A paralegal often is called upon to assist an attorney in preparing the necessary documents for the sale of real property and for the recording of transfers of real property.

This chapter covers the topics of personal property, real property, and landlord–tenant relationships. ■

PERSONAL PROPERTY

The two kinds of property are real property and personal property.

1. Real property includes land and property that is permanently attached to it. For example, minerals, crops, timber, and buildings that are attached to land are generally considered real property.
2. **Personal property** (sometimes referred to as *goods* or *chattels*) consists of everything that is not real property.

Personal property
Tangible property such as automobiles, furniture, and equipment, and intangible property such as securities, patents, and copyrights.

Real property can become personal property if it is removed from the land. For example, a tree that is part of a forest is real property; a tree that is cut down is personal property.

Personal property can be either tangible or intangible. **Tangible property** includes physically defined property, such as goods, animals, and minerals. **Intangible property** represents rights that cannot be reduced to physical form, such as stock certificates, certificates of deposit, bonds, and copyrights.

Personal property that is permanently affixed to land or buildings is called a *fixture*. Such property, which includes things such as heating systems and storm windows, is categorized as real property. Unless otherwise agreed, fixtures remain with a building when it is sold. Personal property (e.g., furniture, pictures, and other easily portable household items) may be removed by the seller prior to sale.

Purchase or Production

Personal property has no locality.
Lord Loughborough C.J.
Sill v. Worswick (1971)

The most common method of acquiring title to personal property is by *purchasing* the property from its owner. For example, Urban Concrete Corporation owns a large piece of equipment. City Builders, Inc., purchases the equipment from Urban Concrete for $50,000. Urban Concrete signs over the title to the equipment to City Builders. City Builders is now the owner of the equipment.

ETHICAL *Perspective*

Duty Not to Engage in the Unauthorized Practice of Law

Mr. Kenneth Fields is an attorney who practices law in the credit and bankruptcy area. Mr. Fields' clients are mainly individuals who file for bankruptcy. Ms. Nedra Harrington, an experienced paralegal in the bankruptcy law area, is hired by Mr. Fields as his paralegal.

Several months after Ms. Harrington's employment, Mr. Fields opens a second law office in another part of the city to attract additional clients. Mr. Fields spends Mondays, Wednesdays, and Fridays at his first office, and Tuesdays and Thursdays at the new second office. Both offices are successful in attracting clients.

Mr. Fields assigns Ms. Harrington to work at the office that he is not working at—that is, when he is working at the first office, Ms. Harrington is assigned to work at the second office. Mr. Fields directs Ms. Harrington to sign up as many clients as she can who come into the office she is covering.

Mr. Fields instructs Ms. Harrington to answer any questions that potential clients or clients may have regarding how unsecured credit, credit card debt, secured credit, and assets are handled under bankruptcy law, and to answer any other questions that they may have. Mr. Fields tell Ms. Harrington that because she is an expert in credit and bankruptcy law, she should give whatever advice she thinks is pertinent to a client's case.

The issue is whether Ms. Harrington would be engaged in the unauthorized practice of law. Section EC-1.8(a) of the *Model Code of Ethics and Professional Responsibility and Guidance for Enforcement* (Model Code) of the National Federation of Paralegal Associations, Inc. (NFPA) states:

A paralegal shall comply with the applicable legal authority governing the unauthorized practice of law in the jurisdiction in which the paralegal practices.

Source: *Reprinted by permission from The National Federation of Paralegal Associations, Inc., www.paralegals.org*

Bankruptcy law permits a paralegal to complete the forms necessary for a bankruptcy filing. The law does not allow a paralegal to give legal advice, however. Mr. Fields' instructions to Ms. Harrington are to give legal advice to potential and actual clients. Therefore, such conduct violates a paralegal's professional code of conduct. Ms. Harrington must inform Mr. Fields of this and refuse to give legal advice to potential and actual clients.

Production is another common method of acquiring ownership in personal property. Thus, a manufacturer that purchases raw materials and produces a finished product owns that product.

Gift

A **gift** is a voluntary transfer of property without consideration. The lack of consideration is what distinguishes a gift from a purchase. The person making a gift is called the **donor**. The person who receives the gift is called the **donee**. The three elements of a valid gift are:

1. ***Donative Intent.*** For a gift to be effective, the donor must have intended to make a gift. Donative intent can be inferred from the circumstances or language used by the donor. The courts also consider factors such as relationship of the parties, size of the gift, and mental capacity of the donor.
2. ***Delivery.*** Delivery must occur for there to be a valid gift. Although *physical delivery* is the usual method of transferring personal property, it sometimes is impracticable. In such circumstances, *constructive delivery* (or *symbolic delivery*) is sufficient. For example, if the property being gifted is kept in a safe-deposit box, physically giving the key to the

Gift
A voluntary transfer of title to property without payment of consideration by the donee. To be a valid gift, three elements must be shown: (1) *donative intent*, (2) *delivery*, and (3) *acceptance*.

Donor
A person who gives a gift.

Donee
A person who receives a gift.

donee is enough to signal the gift. Most intangible property is transferred by written conveyance (e.g., conveying a stock certificate represents a transfer of ownership in a corporation).

3. *Acceptance.* Acceptance usually is not a problem because most donees readily accept gifts. In fact, the courts presume acceptance unless there is proof that the gift was refused. Nevertheless, a person cannot be forced to accept an unwanted gift.

A gift made during a person's lifetime that is an irrevocable present transfer of ownership is a **gift *inter vivos***. A **gift *causa mortis*** is a gift made in contemplation of death. A gift *causa mortis* is established when (1) the donor makes a gift in anticipation of approaching death from some existing sickness or peril and (2) the donor dies from such sickness or peril without having revoked the gift. A gift *causa mortis* can be revoked by the donor up until the time he or she dies. A gift *causa mortis* takes precedence over a prior conflicting will.

Consider this example: Suppose Sandy is a patient in the hospital. She is to have a major operation from which she may not recover. Prior to going into surgery, Sandy removes her diamond ring and gives it to her friend Pamela, stating, "In the event of my death, I want you to have this." This gift is a gift causa mortis. If Sandy dies from the operation, the gift is effective and Pamela owns the ring. If Sandy lives, the requisite condition for the gift (her death) has not occurred; therefore, the gift is not effective, and Sandy can recover the ring from Pamela.

Uniform Gift to Minors Act

Uniform Gift to Minors Act or Revised Uniform Gift to Minors Act
Acts that establish procedures for adults to make gifts of money and securities to minors.

All states have adopted in whole or part the **Uniform Gift to Minors Act** or the **Revised Uniform Gift to Minors Act**. These laws establish procedures for adults to make irrevocable gifts of money and securities to minors. Gifts of money can be made by depositing the money in an account in a financial institution with the donor or another trustee (such as another adult or bank) as custodian for the minor. Gifts of securities can be made by registering the securities in the name of a trustee as custodian for the minor. The laws give custodians broad discretionary powers to invest the money or securities for the benefit of the minor.

Will or Inheritance

Title to personal property is frequently acquired by **will** or **inheritance**. If the person who dies has a valid will, the property is distributed to the **beneficiaries** pursuant to the provisions of that will. Otherwise the property is distributed to the **heirs**, as provided in the relevant state's inheritance statute.

Mislaid Property

Mislaid property
Property that an owner voluntarily places somewhere and then inadvertently forgets.

Property is called **mislaid property** when its owner voluntarily places the property somewhere and then inadvertently forgets it. It is likely that the owner will return for the property upon realizing that it was misplaced.

The owner of the premises where the property is mislaid is entitled to take possession of the property against all except the rightful owner. This right is superior to the rights of the person who finds it. Such possession does not involve a change of title. Instead, the owner of the premises becomes an involuntary bailee of the property (bailments are discussed later in this chapter) and owes a duty to take reasonable care of the property until it is reclaimed by the owner.

Consider this example: Suppose Felicity is on a business trip and stays in a hotel during her trip. Felicity accidentally leaves her diamond engagement ring in the hotel room she has stayed in and checks out of the hotel. The engagement ring

ESTRAY STATUTES

Most states have enacted **estray statutes** that permit a finder of *mislaid* or *lost* property to clear title to the property if

(1) The finder reports the found property to the appropriate government agency and then turns over possession of the property to this agency,

(2) Either the finder or the government agency posts notices and publishes advertisements describing the lost property, and

(3) A specified time (usually a year or a number of years) has passed without the rightful owner's reclaiming the property.

Many state estray statutes require that the government receive a portion of the value of the property. Some statutes provide that title cannot be acquired in found property that is the result of illegal activity. For example, title has been denied to finders of property and money deemed to have been used for illegal drug purchases.

Consider the following case: While hunting on unposted and unoccupied property in Oceola Township, Michigan, Duane Willsmore noticed an area with branches arranged in a crisscross pattern. When he kicked aside the branches and sod, he found a watertight suitcase in a freshly dug hole. Willsmore informed the Michigan state police of his find. A state trooper and Willsmore together pried open the suitcase and discovered $383,840 in cash. The state police took custody of the money, which was deposited in an interest-bearing account.

Michigan's estray statute provides that the finder and the township in which the property was found must share the value of the property if the finder publishes required notices and the true owner does not claim the property within one year. Willsmore published the required notices and brought a declaratory judgment action seeking determination of ownership of the money. After one year had gone by and the rightful owner had not claimed the briefcase, the court ordered that Willsmore and the Township of Oceola were equal one-half owners of the briefcase, and its contents.

Source: Willsmore v. Township of Oceola, Michigan, *308 N.W.2d 796, (1981 Mich.App. Lexis 2993 Mich.App. 1981)]*

is mislaid property, and the hotel has a duty to return it to Felicity, its rightful owner.

Lost Property

Property is considered **lost property** when its owner negligently, carelessly, or inadvertently leaves it somewhere. The finder obtains title to such property against the whole world except the true owner. The lost property must be returned to its rightful owner, whether he or she discovers the loser's identity or the loser finds him or her. A finder who refuses to return the property is liable for the tort of conversion and the crime of larceny. Many states require the finder to conduct a reasonable search (e.g., place advertisements in newspapers) to find the rightful owner.

Consider this example: If a commuter finds a laptop computer on the floor of a subway station in New York City, the computer is considered lost property. The finder can claim title to the computer against the whole world except the true owner. If the true owner discovers that the finder has her computer, she may recover it from the finder. If there is identification of the owner on the computer (e.g., name, address, and telephone number), the finder owes a duty to contact the rightful owner and give back the computer.

Exhibit 14.1 is a synopsis of mislaid and lost property.

Lost property
Property that the owner leaves somewhere because of negligence, carelessness, or inadvertence.

Exhibit 14.1 Mislaid and lost property

Type of Property	Ownership Rights
Mislaid property	The owner of the premises where property is mislaid is entitled to possession but does not acquire title. He or she holds the property as an involuntary bailee until the owner reclaims it.
Lost property	The finder acquires title to the property against the whole world except the true owner; the owner may reclaim his or her property from the finder.

BAILMENTS

Bailment
A transaction in which an owner transfers his or her personal property to another to be held, stored, delivered, or for some other purpose. Title to the property does not transfer.

Bailor
The owner of property in a bailment.

Bailee
A holder of goods who is not a seller or a buyer (e.g., a warehouse or common carrier).

A **bailment** occurs when the owner of personal property delivers his or her property to another person to be held, stored, or delivered, or for some other purpose. In a bailment, the owner of the property is the **bailor** and the party to whom the property is delivered for safekeeping, storage, or delivery (e.g., warehouse or common carrier) is the **bailee** (see Exhibit 14.2).

A bailment is different from a sale or a gift because title to the goods does not transfer to the bailee. Instead, the bailee must follow the bailor's directions concerning the goods. For example, suppose Hudson Corp. is relocating its offices and hires American Van Lines to move its office furniture and equipment to the new location. American Van Lines (the bailee) must follow Hudson's (the bailor) instructions regarding delivery. The law of bailments establishes the rights, duties, and liabilities of parties to a bailment.

Mutual Benefit Bailments

Mutual benefit bailments are bailments that *benefit both parties*. The bailee owes a **duty of reasonable care**, or **ordinary care**, to protect the bailed goods. This means that the bailee is liable for any goods that are lost, damaged, or destroyed because of his or her negligence.

Consider this example: Suppose ABC Garment Co. delivers goods to Lowell, Inc., a commercial warehouseman, for storage. A fee is charged for this service. ABC Garment Co. receives the benefit of having its goods stored, and Lowell, Inc., receives the benefit of being paid compensation for storing the goods. In this example, Lowell, Inc. (the bailee) owes a duty of ordinary care to protect the goods.

Exhibit 14.2 Parties to a bailment

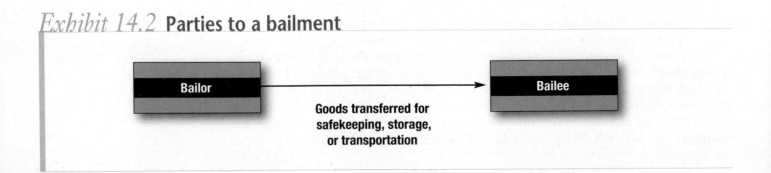

Bailor → Bailee

Goods transferred for safekeeping, storage, or transportation

THE PARALEGAL AND REAL PROPERTY

Many paralegals work in positions for lawyers who practice in the area of real estate law. Most real estate law is state law and, therefore, is state-specific. In addition to having general knowledge of real estate law, then, paralegals must have significant knowledge of the intricacies of the real estate law of the state in which they work.

A paralegal often is involved in drafting and completing documents for real estate transactions. This includes the purchase and sale of single-family houses, condominiums, cooperatives, and other housing units. Although the buyer and the seller usually use real estate brokers to represent them, lawyers often are involved in representing clients in these transactions. The paralegal must know the specific documents required in these transactions.

Lawyers, and therefore their paralegals, often are involved in the purchase, sale, or transfer of vacant real property. This might involve a single buyer or multiple buyers. In these transactions, paralegals usually are called upon to prepare documents and otherwise assist the lawyers on both the seller's and the buyer's side in completing the transaction.

Paralegals frequently are called upon to use their expertise in complex real estate transactions. These include transactions where a developer is going to develop an entire housing tract, shopping mall, office building, or commercial building. Each of these types of development requires substantial work by lawyers representing clients on both sides of the transaction. These real estate transactions require paralegals who also have knowledge of the complex real estate law.

Another facet of real estate law in which paralegals assist lawyers is the area of leasing. Some leases are simple—for example, the lease of an apartment. The lawyer for the owner of the property usually drafts the lease for the landowner. Other leases are extremely complex. For example, leases on large office building space and commercial properties are negotiated individually by both sides, usually using their lawyers. The lawyers then draft the leases and other documents necessary to complete an agreed-upon lease transaction. Paralegals often assist lawyers in representing clients in these complicated lease transactions.

Paralegals who work in the real estate area often acquire expertise in specific types of real estate transactions. Many paralegals learn the intricate procedures, documents, and law that are necessary to complete real estate transactions handled by the lawyers for whom they work.

REAL PROPERTY

Property and ownership rights in real property play an important part in this country's society and economy. Individuals and families own or rent houses, farmers and ranchers own farmland and ranches, and businesses own or lease commercial and office buildings. **Real property** includes the following:

> **Real property**
> The land itself as well as buildings, trees, soil, minerals, timber, plants, and other things permanently affixed to the land.

1. *Land and buildings.* **Land** is the most common form of real property. A landowner usually purchases the **surface rights** to the land—that is, the right to occupy the land. The owner may use, enjoy, and develop the property as he or she sees fit, subject to any applicable government regulations. **Buildings** constructed on land—such as houses, apartment buildings, manufacturing plants, and office buildings—are real property. Things such as radio towers, bridges, and the like are considered real property as well.

2. *Subsurface rights.* The owner of land possesses **subsurface rights** (or **mineral rights**), to the earth located beneath the surface of the land. These rights can be valuable. For example, gold, uranium, oil, or natural

Fixtures
Goods that are affixed to real estate so as to become part thereof.

Estate (estate in land)
Ownership rights in real property; the bundle of legal rights of the owner to possess, use, and enjoy the property.

Freehold estate
An estate in which the owner has a present possessory interest in the real property.

Fee simple absolute (fee simple)
A type of ownership of real property that grants the owner the fullest bundle of legal rights that a person can hold in real property.

Fee simple defeasible (qualified fee)
A type of ownership of real property that grants the owner all the incidents of a fee simple absolute except that it may be taken away if a specified condition occurs or does not occur.

gas may lie beneath the surface of land. Theoretically, mineral rights extend to the center of the earth. In reality, mines and oil wells usually extend only several miles into the earth. Subsurface rights may be sold separately from surface rights.

3. *Plant life and vegetation.* **Plant life and vegetation** growing on the surface of land are considered real property. This includes natural plant life (e.g., trees) and cultivated plant life (e.g., crops). When land is sold, any plant life growing on the land is included unless the parties agree otherwise. Plant life that is severed from the land is considered personal property.

4. *Fixtures.* Certain personal property is associated so closely with real property that it becomes part of the realty. These items are called **fixtures**. For example, kitchen cabinets, carpeting, and doorknobs are fixtures, but throw rugs and furniture are personal property. Unless otherwise provided, if a building is sold, the fixtures are included in the sale. If the sale agreement is silent as to whether an item is a fixture, the courts make their determinations on the basis of whether the item can be removed without causing substantial damage to the realty.

Freehold Estates

A person's ownership rights in real property are called an **estate in land**, or **estate**. An estate is defined as the bundle of *legal rights* that the owner has to possess, use, and enjoy the property. The type of estate that an owner possesses is determined from the deed, will, lease, or other document that transferred the ownership rights to him or her.

A **freehold estate** is one in which the owner has a *present possessory interest* in the real property; that is, the owner may use and enjoy the property as he or she sees fit, subject to any applicable government regulation or private restraint. The two types of freehold estates are *estates in fee* and *life estates*.

Estates in Fee

A **fee simple absolute** (or **fee simple**) is the highest form of ownership of real property because it grants the owner the fullest bundle of legal rights that a person can hold in real property. This **estates in fee** is the type of ownership that most people connect with "owning" real property. A fee simple owner has the right to exclusively possess and use his or her property to the extent that the owner has not transferred any interest in the property (e.g., by lease).

A **fee simple defeasible**, or **qualified fee**, grants the owner all the incidents of a fee simple absolute except that it may be taken away if a specified *condition* occurs or does not occur. For example, a conveyance of property to a church "as long as the land

---

AIR RIGHTS

Common law provided that the owners of real property owned that property from the center of the earth to the heavens. This rule has been eroded by modern legal restrictions such as land-use control laws, environmental protection laws, and air navigation requirements. Even today, however, the owners of land may sell or lease air space parcels above their land.

An **air-space parcel** is a three-dimensional cube of air above the surface of the earth. Air-space parcels are valuable property rights, particularly in densely populated metropolitan areas where building property is scarce. For example, many developments have been built in air-space parcels in New York City. The most notable are Madison Square Garden and Two Penn Plaza, which were built in air-space parcels above Penn Station.

is used as a church or for church purposes" creates a qualified fee. The church has all of the rights of an owner of a fee simple absolute except that its ownership rights are terminated if the property is no longer used for church purposes.

Life Estate

A **life estate** is an interest in real property that lasts for the life of a specified person, usually the grantee. For example, a conveyance of real property "to Anna for her life" creates a life estate. A life estate also may be measured by the life of a third party (e.g., "to Anna for the life of Benjamin"). This is called an **estate** *pur autre vie*. A life estate may be defeasible (e.g., "to John for his life, but only if he continues to occupy this residence"). Upon the death of named person, the life estate terminates and the property reverts to the grantor or the grantor's estate or other designated person.

A life tenant is treated as the owner of the property during the duration of the life estate. He or she has the right to possess and use the property except to the extent that it would cause permanent *waste* of the property. A life tenant may sell, transfer, or mortgage his or her estate in the land. The mortgage, however, cannot exceed the duration of the life estate. A life tenant is obligated to keep the property in repair and to pay property taxes.

Future Interests

A person may be given the right to possess property in the *future* rather than in the present. This right is called a **future interest**. The two forms of future interests are *reversion* and *remainder* (see Exhibit 14.3).

1. *Reversion.* A **reversion** is a right of possession that returns to the *grantor* after the expiration of a limited or contingent estate. Reversions do not have to be stated expressly because they arise automatically by law. For example, if a grantor conveys property "to M. R. Harrington for life," the grantor has retained a reversion in the property. That is, when Harrington dies, the property reverts to the grantor or, if he or she is not living, then to his or her estate.

2. *Remainder.* If the right of possession returns to a *third party* upon the expiration of a limited or contingent estate, it is called a **remainder**. The person who is entitled to the future interest is called a **remainderman**. For example, a conveyance of property "to Joe for life, remainder to Meredith" is a *vested* remainder—the only contingency to Meredith's possessory interest is Joe's death.

Life estate
An interest in land for a person's lifetime; upon that person's death, the interest will be transferred to another party.

Property is an instrument of humanity. Humanity is not an instrument of property.

Woodrow Wilson
Speech (1912)

Future interest
The interest that the grantor retains for him- or herself or a third party.

Reversion
A right of possession that returns to the grantor after the expiration of a limited or contingent estate.

Remainder (remainderman)
A right of possession that returns to a third party upon the expiration of a limited or contingent estate.

Exhibit 14.3 **Future interests**

Concurrent Ownership

Co-ownership (concurrent ownership)
A situation in which two or more persons own a piece of real property. Also called *concurrent ownership*.

When two or more persons own a piece of real property, it is called **co-ownership** or **concurrent ownership**. The following forms of co-ownership are recognized: *joint tenancy*, *tenancy in common*, *tenancy by the entirety*, *community property*, *condominium*, and *cooperative*.

Joint Tenancy

Joint tenancy
A form of co-ownership that includes the right of survivorship.

To create a **joint tenancy**, words that clearly show a person's intent to create a joint tenancy must be used. Language such as "Marsha Leest and James Leest, as joint tenants" is usually sufficient. The most distinguishing feature of a joint tenancy is the co-owners' **right of survivorship**. This means that upon the death of one of the co-owners or **joint tenants** the deceased person's interest in the property passes automatically to the surviving joint tenants. Any contrary provision in the deceased's will is ineffective.

Consider this example: Jones, one of four people who own a piece of property in joint tenancy, executes a will leaving all of his property to a university. Jones dies. The surviving joint tenants—not the university—acquire his interest in the piece of property. Each joint tenant has a right to sell or transfer his or her interest in the property, but such conveyance terminates the joint tenancy. The parties then become tenants in common.

Tenancy in Common

Tenancy in common
A form of co-ownership in which the interest of a surviving tenant in common passes to the deceased tenant's estate and not to the co-tenants.

In a **tenancy in common**, the interests of a surviving **tenant in common** pass to the deceased tenant's estate and not to the co-tenants. A tenancy in common may be created by express words, such as "Iran Cespedes and Joy Park, as tenants in common." Unless otherwise agreed, a tenant in common can sell, give, devise, or otherwise transfer his or her interest in the property without the consent of the other co-owners.

Consider this example: Lopez, one of four tenants in common who own a piece of property, has a will that leaves all of his property to his granddaughter. When Lopez dies, the granddaughter receives his interest in the tenancy in common, and the granddaughter becomes a tenant in common with the three other owners.

Tenancy by the Entirety

Tenancy by the entirety
A form of co-ownership of real property that can be used only by married couples.

Tenancy by the entirety is a form of co-ownership of real property that can be used only by married couples. This type of tenancy must be created by express words, such as "Harold Jones and Maude Jones, husband and wife, as tenants by the entireties." A surviving spouse has the right of survivorship.

Tenancy by the entirety is distinguished from a joint tenancy in that neither spouse may sell or transfer his or her interest in the property without the other spouse's consent. Only about half of the states recognize a tenancy by the entirety.

Community Property

Community property
A form of ownership in which each spouse owns an equal one-half share of the income of both spouses and the assets acquired during the marriage.

Nine states—Arizona, California, Idaho, Louisiana, Nevada, New Mexico, Texas, Washington, and Wisconsin—recognize a form of co-ownership known as **community property**. This method of co-ownership applies only to married couples and is based on the notion that a husband and wife should share equally in the fruits of the marital partnership.

Under these laws, each spouse owns an equal one-half share of the income of both spouses and the assets acquired during the marriage regardless of who earns the income. Property that is acquired through gift or inheritance either before or during marriage remains separate property.

checklist  SUMMARY OF CONCURRENT OWNERSHIP

FORM OF OWNERSHIP	RIGHT OF SURVIVORSHIP	TENANT MAY UNILATERALLY TRANSFER HIS OR HER INTEREST
Joint tenancy	Yes. Deceased tenant's interest passes automatically to co-tenants.	Yes. Tenant may transfer his or her interest without the consent of co-tenants. Transfer severs joint tenancy.
Tenancy in common	No. Deceased tenant's interest passes to his or her estate.	Yes. Tenant may transfer his or her interest without the consent of co-tenants. Transfer does not sever tenancy in common.
Tenancy by the entirety	Yes. Deceased tenant's interest passes automatically to his or her spouse.	No. Neither spouse may transfer his or her interest without the other spouse's consent.
Community property	Yes. When a spouse dies, the surviving spouse automatically receives one-half of the community property. The other half passes to the heirs of the deceased spouse as directed by a valid will or by state intestate statute if there is no will.	No. Neither spouse may transfer his or her interest without the other spouse's consent.

When a spouse dies, the surviving spouse automatically receives one-half the community property. The other half passes to the heirs of the deceased spouse as directed by will or by state intestate statute if there is no will.

During the marriage, neither spouse can sell, transfer, or gift community property without the consent of the other spouse. Upon a divorce, each spouse has a right to one-half of the community property.

The location of the real property determines whether community property law applies. For example, if a married couple who lives in a non–community property state purchases real property located in a community property state, community property laws apply to that property.

Consider this example: A husband and wife have community property assets of $1.5 million and the wife dies with a will. The husband automatically has a right to receive $750,000 of the community property. The remaining $750,000 passes as directed by the wife's will. Any separate property owned by the wife, such as jewelry she inherited, also passes in accordance with her will. Her husband has no vested interest in that property.

Condominium

The **condominium** is a common form of ownership in multiple-dwelling buildings. Purchasers of a condominium (1) have title to their individual units, and (2) own the common areas (e.g., hallways, elevators, parking areas, and recreational facilities) as tenants in common with the other owners. Owners may sell or mortgage their units without the permission of the other owners. Owners are assessed monthly fees for maintenance of common areas. In addition to dwelling units, the condominium form of ownership is offered for office buildings, boat docks, and such.

Property has its duties as well as its rights.

Benjamin Disraelli Sybil, Bk. II, Ch. XI (1845)

Condominium
A common form of ownership in a multiple-dwelling building in which the purchaser has title to the individual unit and owns the common areas as a tenant in common with the other condominium owners.

Cooperative

Cooperative
A form of co-ownership of a multiple-dwelling building in which a corporation owns the building and the residents own shares in the corporation.

A **cooperative** is a form of co-ownership of a multiple-dwelling building in which a corporation owns the building and the residents own shares in the corporation. Each cooperative owner then leases a unit in the building from the corporation under a renewable, long-term, proprietary lease. Individual residents may not secure loans with the units they occupy. The corporation may borrow money on a blanket mortgage, and each shareholder is jointly and severally liable on the loan. Usually, cooperative owners may not sell their shares or sublease their units without the approval of the other owners.

TRANSFER OF OWNERSHIP OF REAL PROPERTY

Deed
A writing that describes a person's ownership interest in a piece of real property.

Grantor
The party who transfers an ownership interest in real property.

Grantee
The party to whom an interest in real property is transferred.

Ownership of real property may be transferred from one person to another. Title to real property may be transferred by sale, tax sale, gift, will, or inheritance. **Deeds** are used to convey real property by sale or gift. The seller or donor is called the **grantor**. The buyer or recipient is called the **grantee**. A deed may be used to transfer a fee simple absolute interest in real property or any lesser estate (e.g., life estate).

State laws recognize different types of deeds that provide differing degrees of protection to grantees. A **warranty deed** contains the greatest number of warranties and provides the most protection to grantees. A **quitclaim deed** provides the least amount of protection because the grantor conveys only whatever interest he or she has in the property.

Sale of Real Estate

Sale
The passing of title from a seller to a buyer for a price. Also called a *conveyance*.

A **sale** or conveyance is the most common method for transferring ownership rights in real property. An agreement for the sale of real property under the state Statute of Frauds must be in writing to be enforceable. Exhibit 14.4 shows the parties to a real estate sale. The seller delivers a deed to the buyer and the buyer pays the purchase price at the closing or settlement.

A copy of an agreement form for the sale of real estate is set forth in Exhibit 14.5. A **settlement statement** is shown in Exhibit 14.6.

Exhibit 14.4 **Parties and documents in a real estate transaction**

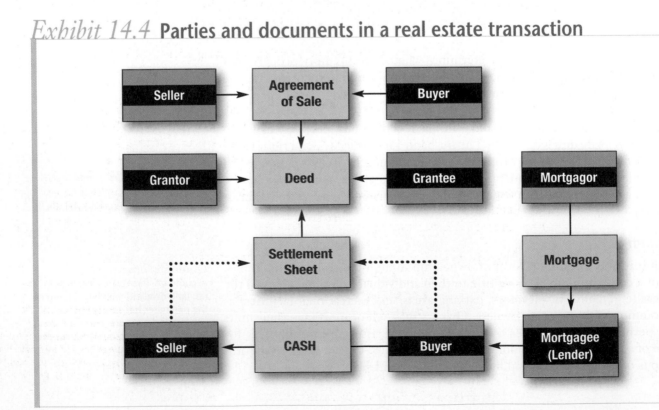

Exhibit 14.5 **Agreement for the sale of real property**

COPIES	
1. White	Seller
2. Yellow	Agent
3. Pink	Buyer
4. Blue	Mortgagee
5. Gold	
6. Green	Buyer's copy at time of signing

AGREEMENT FOR THE SALE OF REAL ESTATE
COPYRIGHT PENNSYLVANIA ASSOCIATION OF REALTORS® 1973

S & C 1969A Residential
(Rev. 7-90)

┌─────────AGENT FOR THE SELLER─────────┐ ┌─────────SUBAGENT FOR SELLER─────────┐

└─────────PA. LICENSED BROKER─────────┘ └─────────PA. LICENSED BROKER─────────┘

This Agreement, this .... day of .... A.D. ....

1. PRINCIPALS (1-78) Between ....

....

(residing at ....

.... Zip Code ....) hereinafter called Seller,

and ....

(residing at ....

.... Zip Code ....) hereinafter called Buyer.

2. PROPERTY (4-89) Seller hereby agrees to sell and convey to Buyer, who hereby agrees to purchase:
ALL THAT CERTAIN lot or piece of ground with buildings and improvements thereon erected, if any, known as:

....

.... in the .... of ....

County of .... **State of** ...., **Zip Code** ....

Zoning Classification

Failure of this agreement to contain the zoning classification (except in cases where the property [and each parcel thereof, if subdividable] is zoned solely or primarily to permit single-family dwellings) shall render this agreement voidable at the option of the Buyer, and, if voided, any deposits tendered by the Buyer shall be returned to the Buyer without any requirement for court action.

3. TERMS (3-85) (A) Purchase Price ....

.... **Dollars**

 which shall be paid to the Seller by the Buyer as follows:

    (B) Cash or check at signing this agreement: .... $..................

    (C) Cash or check to be paid on or before: .... 19...... $..................

    (D) .... $..................

    (E) Cash or certified check at time of settlement: .... $_____

                           TOTAL $..................

    (F) Written approval of Seller to be on or before: .... 19......

    (G) Settlement to be made on or before: .... 19......

    (H) Conveyance from Seller will be by fee simple deed of special warranty.

    (I) Payment of transfer taxes will be divided equally between Buyer and Seller.

    (J) The following shall be apportioned pro-rata as of and at time of settlement: taxes as levied and assessed, rents, interest on mortgage assumptions, condominium fees and homeowner association fees, if any, water and or sewer rents, if any, together with any other lienable municipal services.

4. MORTGAGE CONTINGENCY (4-89) This sale is NOT contingent upon any mortgage financing except as hereinafter provided.

    (A) Mortgage terms required by Buyer. Amount of mortgage loan $ ...., Term .... years,
        Type of mortgage ....
        Interest rate............. %; **however, Buyer agrees to accept the interest rate as may be committed by the mortgage lender, not to exceed a maximum interest rate of** .... %.

    (B) Within ten(10) days of Seller's approval of this agreement, Buyer shall make a completed mortgage application to a responsible mortgage lending institution through the office of Subagent for the Seller, if any, otherwise through the office of Agent for the Seller, **who for the purposes of negotiating for the said mortgage loan, shall be considered the Agent for the Buyer.**

    (C) (1) Buyer will, upon receipt of a mortgage commitment, promptly provide a copy to Seller, Agent and/or Subagent, if any.
        (2) Mortgage commitment date ...., ... If a written commitment is not received
            by the above date, **Buyer agrees to extend the commitment date until Seller terminates this agreement in writing.**
        (3) Should the mortgage commitment:
            (a) not be valid until the date of settlement, or
            (b) be conditioned upon the **sale and settlement of any other property,** or
            (c) contain any other condition not specified in this Agreement,
            Seller has the option to terminate this Agreement in writing.
        (4) In the event that the Seller terminates this agreement as specified in paragraphs 4(C) (2) or (3), OR
            (a) the mortgage commitment is not obtained by or valid until the date of settlement, or
            (b) the mortgage commitment is conditioned upon the **sale and settlement of any other property** which do not occur by the date of settlement, or
            (c) the mortgage commitment contains any other condition not specified in this Agreement which the Buyer is unable to satisfy by the date of settlement,
            the Buyer shall not be required to purchase the property and all deposit monies paid on account shall be returned to the Buyer, except any payments made by Buyer as described in Paragraph 7(C) (1), (2), and (3).

    (D) Seller hereby agrees to permit inspections by authorized appraisers, reputable certifiers and/or Buyer as may be required by the lending institution or insuring agencies.

5. SPECIAL CLAUSES

(continued)

Exhibit 14.5 Agreement for the sale of real property *(continued)*

6. NOTICES & ASSESSMENTS (7-90)

(A) Seller represents as of the approval date of this agreement, that no public improvement, condominium or homeowner association assessments have been made against the premises which remain unpaid and that no notice by any government or public authority has been served upon the Seller or anyone on the Seller's behalf, including notices relating to violations of zoning, housing, building, safety or fire ordinances which remain uncorrected unless otherwise specified herein.

(B) If required by law, Seller shall deliver to Buyer on or before settlement, a certification from the appropriate municipal department or departments disclosing notice of any uncorrected violation of zoning, housing, building, safety or fire ordinances.

(C) Buyer is advised that access to a public road may require issuance of a highway occupancy permit from the Department of Transportation.

(D) Seller will be responsible for any notice of improvements or assessments received on or before the date of Seller's approval of this agreement, unless improvements consist of sewer or water lines not in use.

(E) Buyer will be responsible for any notice served upon Seller after the approval date of this agreement and for the payment thereafter of any public improvement, condominium or homeowner association assessments.

7. TITLE AND COSTS (1-86)

(A) The premises are to be conveyed free and clear of all liens, encumbrances, and easements, EXCEPTING HOWEVER, the following: existing building restrictions, ordinances, easements of roads, easements visible upon the ground, privileges or rights of public service companies, if any; otherwise the title to the above described real estate shall be good and marketable and such as will be insured by a reputable Title Insurance Company at the regular rates.

(B) In the event the Seller is unable to give a good and marketable title and such as will be insured by a reputable Title Company, subject to aforesaid, Buyer shall have the option of taking such title as the Seller can give without abatement of price or of being repaid all monies paid by Buyer to the Seller on account of the purchase price and the Seller will reimburse the Buyer for any costs incurred by the Buyer for those items specified in paragraph 7(C) items (1), (2), (3), and in paragraph 7(D); and in the latter event there shall be no further liability or obligation on either of the parties hereto and this agreement shall become NULL AND VOID and all copies will be returned to Seller's Agent for cancellation.

(C) The Buyer will pay for the following:

(1) The premium for mechanics lien insurance and/or title search, or fee for cancellation of same, if any.
(2) The premiums for flood insurance and/or fire insurance with extended coverage, insurance binder charges or cancellation fee, if any.
(3) Appraisal fees and charges paid in advance to mortgagee if any.
(4) Buyer's normal settlement costs and accruals.

(D) Any survey or surveys which may be required by the Title Insurance Company or the abstracting attorney, for the preparation of an adequate legal description of the premises (or the correction thereof), shall be secured and paid for by the Seller. However, any survey or surveys desired by the Buyer or required by his/her mortgagee shall be secured and paid for by the Buyer.

8. FIXTURES, TREES, SHRUBBERY, ETC. (1-81) All existing plumbing, heating and lighting fixtures (including chandeliers) and systems appurtenant thereto and forming a part thereof, and other permanent fixtures, as well as all ranges, laundry tubs, T.V. antennas, masts and rotor systems, together with wall to wall carpeting, screens, storm sash and/or doors,shades, awnings, venetian blinds, couplings for automatic washers and dryers, etc., radiator covers, cornices, kitchen cabinets, drapery rods, drapery rod hardware, curtain rods, curtain rod hardware, all trees, shrubbery, plantings now in or on property, if any, unless specifically excepted in this agreement, are included in the sale and purchase price. None of the above mentioned items shall be removed by the Seller from the premises after the date of this agreement. Any remaining heating and/or cooking fuels stored on the premises at time of settlement are also included under this agreement. Seller hereby warrants that he will deliver good title to all of the articles described in this paragraph, and any other fixtures or items of personalty specifically scheduled and to be included in this sale.

9. DEPOSIT AND RECOVERY FUND (4-89) Deposits, regardless of the form of payment and the person designated as payee, shall be paid to Agent for the Seller who shall retain them in an escrow account until consummation or termination of this Agreement in conformity with all applicable laws and regulations. Agent for the Seller may, at his or her sole option, hold any uncashed check tendered as deposit, pending the acceptance of this offer. Buyer and Seller agree that, in the event the Agent and/or Subagent are/is joined in litigation for the return of deposit monies, the Agent's and/or Subagent's attorneys fees and costs will be paid by the party joining the Agent or Subagent.
A Real Estate Recovery Fund exists to reimburse any persons who have obtained a final civil judgment against a Pennsylvania real estate licensee owing to fraud, misrepresentation, or deceit in a real estate transaction and who have been unable to collect the judgement after exhausting all legal and equitable remedies. For complete details about the Fund, call (717) 783-3658.

10. POSSESSION AND TENDER (3-85)

(A) Possession is to be delivered by deed, keys and physical possession to a vacant building (if any) broom clean, free of debris at day and time of settlement, or by deed and assignment of existing lease(s) at time of settlement if premises are tenant occupied at the signing of this agreement, unless otherwise specified herein. Buyer will acknowledge existing lease(s) by initialing said lease(s) at time of signing of this agreement of sale if tenant occupied.

(B) Seller will not enter into any new leases, written extension of existing leases, if any, or additional leases for the premises without expressed written consent of the Buyer.

(C) Formal tender of an executed deed and purchase money is hereby waived.

(D) Buyer reserves the right to make a pre-settlement inspection of the subject premises.

11. MAINTENANCE AND RISK OF LOSS (3-85)

(A) Seller shall maintain the property (including all items mentioned in paragraph #8 herein) and any personal property specifically scheduled herein in its present condition, normal wear and tear excepted.

(B) Seller shall bear risk of loss from fire or other casualties until time of settlement. In the event of damage to any property included in this sale by fire or other casualties, not repaired or replaced prior to settlement, Buyer shall have the option of rescinding this agreement and receiving all monies paid on account or of accepting the property in its then condition together with the proceeds of any insurance recovery obtainable by Seller. Buyer is hereby notified that he may insure his equitable interest in this property as of the time of the acceptance of this agreement.

12. RECORDING (3-85) This agreement shall not be recorded in the Office for the Recording of Deeds or in any other office or place of public record and if Buyer causes or permits this agreement to be recorded, Seller may elect to treat such act as a breach of this agreement.

13. ASSIGNMENT (3-85) This agreement shall be binding upon the parties, their respective heirs, personal representatives, guardians and successors, and to the extent assignable, on the assigns of the parties hereto, it being expressly understood, however, that the Buyer shall not transfer or assign this agreement without the written consent of the Seller.

14. DEFAULT-TIME OF THE ESSENCE (1-79) The said time for settlement and all other times referred to for the performance of any of the obligations of this agreement are hereby agreed to be of the essence of this agreement. Should the Buyer:

(A) Fail to make any additional payments as specified in paragraph #3, or

(B) Furnish false or incomplete information to the Seller, the Seller's Agent, or the mortgage lender, concerning the Buyer's legal or financial status, or fail to cooperate in the processing of the mortgage loan application, which acts would result in the failure to obtain the approval of a mortgage loan commitment, or

(C) Violate or fail to fulfill and perform any other terms or conditions of this agreement,

then in such case, all deposit money and other sums paid by the Buyer on account of the purchase price, whether required by this agreement or not, may be retained by the Seller: (1) On account of the purchase, or (2) As monies to be applied to the Seller's damages, or (3) As liquidated damages for such breach, as the Seller may elect, and in the event that the Seller elects to retain the monies as liquidated damages in accordance with paragraph #14(3), the Seller shall be released from all liability or obligations and this agreement shall be NULL AND VOID and all copies will be returned to the Seller's Agent for cancellation.

15. AGENT(S) (3-85) It is expressly understood and agreed between the parties that the named Agent, Broker, and any Subagent, Broker and their salespeople, employees, officers and or partners, are Agent(s) for the Seller, not the Buyer, however, the Agent(s) may perform services for the Buyer in connection with financing, insurance and document preparation.

16. REPRESENTATIONS (3-85) It is understood that Buyer has inspected the property, or hereby waives the right to do so and has agreed to purchase it as a result of such inspection and not because of or in reliance upon any representation made by the Seller or any other officer, partner or employee of Seller, or by the Agent, Subagent, if any, of the Seller, their salespeople and employees, officers and or partners.
The Buyer has agreed to purchase it in its present condition unless otherwise specified herein. It is further understood that this agreement contains the whole agreement between the Seller and the Buyer and there are no other terms, obligations, covenants, representations, statements or conditions, oral or otherwise of any kind whatsoever concerning this sale. Furthermore, this agreement shall not be altered, amended, changed or modified except in writing executed by the parties.

APPROVAL BY BUYER BUYER ....(SEAL)

WITNESS AS
TO BUYER .... BUYER ....(SEAL)

WITNESS AS
TO BUYER .... BUYER ....(SEAL)

APPROVAL BY SELLER

Seller hereby approves the above contract this .... day of .... A.D. ....

and in consideration of the services rendered in procuring the Buyer, Seller agrees to pay the named Agent a fee of ....

of/from the herein specified sale price. In the event Buyer defaults hereunder, any monies paid on account shall be divided .... Seller,

...................., Agent, but in no event will the sum paid to the Agent be in excess of the above specified Agent's fee.

WITNESS AS
TO SELLER .... SELLER ....(SEAL)

WITNESS AS
TO SELLER .... SELLER ....(SEAL)

AGENT BY: .... SELLER ....(SEAL)

TO: .... (Agent) Date ....

In conjunction with the purchase of the premises described in this agreement of sale attached hereto, I/We hereby authorize your firm to perform the services as indicated below by my/our initials.

A. Order Title insurance in any reputable title insurance company ....(INITIALS)

B. Order insurance in the amount of $ .... ☐ Homeowners ☐ Fire & Extended Coverage ☐ Flood ....(INITIALS)

C. ....(INITIALS)

Exhibit 14.6 **Settlement statement**

A. **Settlement Statement**	U.S. Department of Housing and Urban Development	OMB Approval No. 2502-0265

B. Type of Loan

1. ☐ FHA 2. ☐ FmHA 3. ☐ Conv. Unins. 4. ☐ VA 5. ☐ Conv. Ins.	6. File Number:	7. Loan Number:	8. Mortgage Insurance Case Number:

C. Note: This form is furnished to give you a statement of actual settlement costs. Amounts paid to and by the settlement agent are shown. Items marked "(p.o.c.)" were paid outside the closing; they are shown here for informational purposes and are not included in the totals.

D. Name & Address of Borrower: Ethan & Ariel Marshall 52 Moritz Way Anyplace, PA 55555	E. Name & Address of Seller: Sara and Natasha Elliot 138 Weisser Place Anyplace, PA 55555	F. Name & Address of Lender: 4th National Bank OneSouth Main St. Newcity, PA 44444

G. Property Location: 1 Zollinger Way	H. Settlement Agent: Roberts	
	Place of Settlement: Newcity	I. Settlement Date: 08-19-2002

J. Summary of Borrower's Transaction		K. Summary of Seller's Transaction	
100. Gross Amount Due From Borrower		**400. Gross Amount Due To Seller**	
101. Contract sales price	150000	401. Contract sales price	150000
102. Personal property		402. Personal property	
103. Settlement charges to borrower (line 1400)	21000	403.	
104.		404.	
105.		405.	
Adjustments for items paid by seller in advance		*Adjustments for items paid by seller in advance*	
106. City/town taxes 08-19-2002 to 12-31-2002	650	406. City/town taxes 08-19-2002 to 12-31-2002	650
107. County taxes to		407. County taxes to	
108. Assessments to		408. Assessments to	
109.		409.	
110.		410.	
111.		411.	
112.		412.	
120. Gross Amount Due From Borrower	152750	**420. Gross Amount Due To Seller**	150650
200. Amounts Paid By Or In Behalf Of Borrower		**500. Reductions In Amount Due To Seller**	
201. Deposit or earnest money		501. Excess deposit (see instructions)	
202. Principal amount of new loan(s)		502. Settlement charges to seller (line 1400)	9000
203. Existing loan(s) taken subject to		503. Existing loan(s) taken subject to	
204.		504. Payoff of first mortgage loan	75000
205.		505. Payoff of second mortgage loan	
206.		506.	
207.		507.	
208.		508.	
209.		509.	
Adjustments for items unpaid by seller		*Adjustments for items unpaid by seller*	
210. City/town taxes to		510. City/town taxes to	
211. County taxes to		511. County taxes to	
212. Assessments to		512. Assessments to	
213.		513.	
214.		514.	
215.		515.	
216.		516.	
217.		517.	
218.		518.	
219.		519.	
220. Total Paid By/For Borrower	135000	**520. Total Reduction Amount Due Seller**	84000
300. Cash At Settlement From/To Borrower		**600. Cash At Settlement To/From Seller**	
301. Gross Amount due from borrower (line 120)	152750	601. Gross amount due to seller (line 420)	150650
302. Less amounts paid by/for borrower (line 220)	(135000)	602. Less reductions in amt. due seller (line 520)	(84000)
303. Cash ☑ From ☐ To Borrower	17750	**603. Cash** ☑ To ☐ From Seller	

Section 5 of the Real Estate Settlement Procedures Act (RESPA) requires the following: • HUD must develop a Special Information Booklet to help persons borrowing money to finance the purchase of residential real estate to better understand the nature and costs of real estate settlement services; • Each lender must provide the booklet to all applicants from whom it receives or for whom it prepares a written application to borrow money to finance the purchase of residential real estate; • Lenders must prepare and distribute with the Booklet a Good Faith Estimate of the settlement costs that the borrower is likely to incur in connection with the settlement. These disclosures are manadatory.

Section 4(a) of RESPA mandates that HUD develop and prescribe this standard form to be used at the time of loan settlement to provide full disclosure of all charges imposed upon the borrower and seller. These are third party disclosures that are designed to provide the borrower with pertinent information during the settlement process in order to be a better shopper.

The Public Reporting Burden for this collection of information is estimated to average one hour per response, including the time for reviewing instructions, searching existing data sources, gathering and maintaining the data needed, and completing and reviewing the collection of information.

This agency may not collect this information, and you are not required to complete this form, unless it displays a currently valid OMB control number.

The information requested does not lend itself to confidentiality.

Recording Statutes

Recording statute
A state statute that requires a mortgage or deed of trust to be recorded in the county recorder's office of the county in which the real property is located.

Every state has a **recording statute** that provides that copies of deeds and other documents concerning interests in real property (e.g., mortgages, liens, easements) may be filed in a government office where they become public records open to viewing by the public. Recording statutes are intended to prevent fraud and to establish certainty in the ownership and transfer of property. Instruments usually are filed in the *county recorder's office* of the county in which the property is located. A fee is charged to record an instrument.

Persons interested in purchasing the property or lending on the property check these records to determine if the grantor or borrower actually owns the property and whether any other parties (e.g., lienholders, mortgages, easement holders) have an interest in the property. The recordation of a deed is not required to pass title from the grantor to the grantee. Recording the deed gives *constructive notice* to the world of the owner's interest in the property.

Quiet title action
An action brought by a party seeking an order of the court declaring who has title to disputed property. By its decision, the court "quiets title."

A party who is concerned about his or her ownership rights in a parcel of real property can bring a **quiet title** action to have a court determine the extent of those rights. Public notice of the hearing must be given so that anyone claiming an interest in the property may appear and be heard. After the hearing, the judge declares who has title to the property—that is the court "quiets title" by its decision.

Marketable Title

Marketable title
Title to real property that is free from any encumbrances or other defects that are not disclosed but would affect the value of the property. Also called *good title*.

Marketable title means that the title is free from any encumbrances, defects in title, or other defects that are not disclosed but would affect the value of the property. A buyer of real property can purchase **title insurance** from a title insurance company. The **title insurance policy** lists any defects in the title of the property, if any, and ensures against unlisted defects in title.

The title insurer must reimburse the insured for any losses caused by undiscovered defects in the title. Each time a property is transferred, a new title insurance policy must be obtained. Exhibit 14.7 shows the opening two pages of a title insurance policy.

Adverse Possession

Adverse possession
A situation in which a person who wrongfully possesses someone else's real property obtains title to that property if certain statutory requirements are met.

In most states, a person who wrongfully possesses someone else's real property obtains title to that property if certain statutory requirements are met. This is called **adverse possession.** Property owned by federal and state governments is not subject to adverse possession.

REGISTRAR OF DEEDS

Records of all transfers of real estate, claims against real estate, and the form of mortgages and means are generally maintained in a separate office under the direction of the Registrar, or Recorder, of Deeds. The **Registrar of Deeds** may be an elected or appointed official and is responsible for recording documents related to the transfer of real estate, and documents related to claims against property in the form of mortgages and liens. These records may be hardcopy or electronic copies, or a combination.

The Registrar of Deeds office is concerned with the authenticity of the deeds filed and proper authentication by way of notarization. In filing documents, it is necessary to determine the standards of the individual office with regard to the form of the notarization and any additional paperwork required before it will accept the document for recording.

This office also may collect the taxes as an agent for the taxing authority, whether local or state, and additional paperwork is required in this regard. The Registrar also generally charges a fee for filing documents, which may include additional charges when the pages exceed a certain number. It is always best to check with the office to determine the number and amounts of the checks, drafts, or other forms of payment required.

Exhibit 14.7 Title insurance policy

FIRST AMERICAN TITLE INSURANCE COMPANY

OWNERS FORM

SCHEDULE A

Policy Number	Date of Policy	Amount of Insurance
00000000000	January 1, 2002	$200,500.00

File Number ABC 12345

1. Name of Insured on the Owner's Policy:

   Mary Jane Smith

2. The estate or interest in the land described in this Schedule and which is encumbered by the insured mortgage is Fee Simple.

3. The estate or interest referred to herein is at Date of Policy vested in the insured:

   The Insured by virtue of a Deed from Thomas Jones dated 12/31/2001 and recorded 1/1/2002 in Bucks County in Land Record Book 1111 page 111.

4. The land herein described is encumbered by the following mortgage or trust deed, and assignments:

   $150,500.00 Mary Jane Smith to Country Bank dated 12/31/2001 and recorded 1/1/2002 in Bucks County in land Record Book 1111 page 222.
   and the mortgage or trust deeds, if any, shown in Schedule B hereof.

5. The land referred to in this policy is situated in the State of Pennsylvania, County of Bucks and is described as follows:

   See attached Exhibit "A"
   Commonly known as:

   County Parcel Number 12-12-12-12-12
   123 Main Street
   Main Township
   Bucks County, Pennsylvania

PA - 3

Form No. FA 13
(10-17-92)
ALTA Owner's Policy

POLICY OF TITLE INSURANCE

ISSUED BY

First American Title Insurance Company

SUBJECT TO THE EXCLUSIONS FROM COVERAGE, THE EXCEPTIONS FROM COVERAGE CONTAINED IN SCHEDULE B AND THE CONDITIONS AND STIPULATIONS, FIRST AMERICAN TITLE INSURANCE COMPANY, a California corporation, herein called the Company, insures, as of Date of Policy shown in Schedule A, against loss or damage, not exceeding the Amount of Insurance stated in Schedule A, sustained or incurred by the insured by reason of:

1. Title to the estate or interest described in Schedule A being vested other than as stated therein;
2. Any defect in or lien or encumbrance on the title;
3. Unmarketability of the title;
4. Lack of a right of access to and from the land.

The Company will also pay the costs, attorneys' fees and expenses incurred in defense of the title, as insured, but only to the extent provided in the Conditions and Stipulations.

First American Title Insurance Company

BY *Parker J. Kennedy* PRESIDENT

ATTEST *Mark R. Arneson* SECRETARY

BY _____ COUNTERSIGNED

Under this doctrine, the transfer of the property is involuntary and does not require delivery of a deed. For a person to obtain title under adverse possession, the wrongful possession must be

- ■ *For a statutorily prescribed period of time.* In most states, this period is between 10 and 20 years.
- ■ *Open, visible, and notorious.* The adverse possessor must occupy the property so as to put the owner on notice of the possession.
- ■ *Actual and exclusive.* The adverse possessor must physically occupy the premises. The planting of crops, grazing of animals, or building of a structure on the land constitutes physical occupancy.
- ■ *Continuous and peaceful.* The occupancy must be uninterrupted for the required statutory period. Any break in normal occupancy terminates the adverse possession. This means that the adverse possessor may leave the property to go to work, to the store, on a vacation, and such. The adverse possessor cannot take the property by force from an owner.
- ■ *Hostile and adverse.* The possessor must occupy the property without the express or implied permission of the owner. Thus, a lessee cannot claim title to property under adverse possession.

If the elements of adverse possession are met, the adverse possessor acquires clear title to the land. But title is acquired only as to the property actually possessed and occupied during the statutory period, and not the entire tract. For example, an adverse possessor who occupies one acre of a 200,000-acre ranch for the statutory period of time acquires title to only the one acre.

Easements

Easement
A given or required right to make limited use of someone else's land without owning or leasing it.

An **easement** is an interest in land that gives the holder the right to make limited use of another's property without taking anything from it. Typical easements include common driveways, party walls, right-of-ways, and such.

Easements may be *expressly* created by (1) grant (in which an owner gives another party an easement across his or her property), called **easement by grant**, or (2) **reservation** (where an owner sells land he or she owns but reserves an easement on the land). They also may be (1) **easements by implication** in which an owner subdivides a piece of property with a well, path, road, or other beneficial appurtenant that serves the entire parcel, or (2) **easements by necessity**; for example, "landlocked" property has an implied easement across surrounding property to enter and exit the landlocked property. Easements also can be created by adverse possession.

Exhibit 14.8 shows a dominant and servient easement with a common driveway. Exhibit 14.9 shows a landlocked real property and **easement by necessity**.

LANDLORD–TENANT RELATIONSHIP

Landlord–tenant relationships are common in the United States because (1) more than half of the population rent their homes, and (2) many businesses lease office space, stores, manufacturing facilities, and other commercial property. The parties to the relationship have certain legal rights and duties governed by a mixture of real estate and contract law.

A landlord–tenant relationship is created when the owner of a freehold estate (i.e., an estate in fee or a life estate) transfers a right to exclusively and temporarily possess the owner's property. The tenant receives a **nonfreehold estate** in the property—that is, the tenant has a right to possession of the property but not title to the property.

Exhibit 14.10 shows the parties to a lease.

Exhibit 14.8 **Dominant and servient easement**

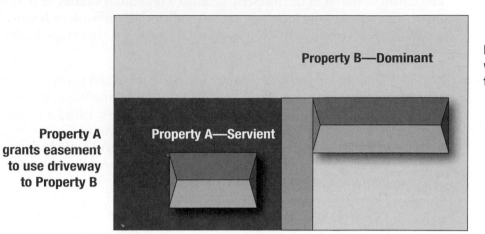

Property B—Dominant

**Property B
with house on
the property line**

**Property A
grants easement
to use driveway
to Property B**

Property A—Servient

Exhibit 14.9 **Easement by necessity**

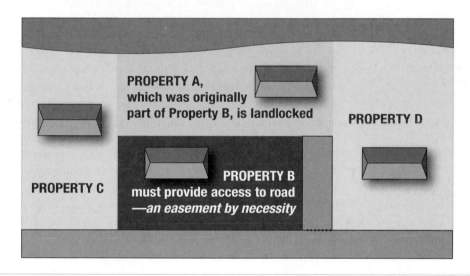

**PROPERTY A,
which was originally
part of Property B, is landlocked**

PROPERTY D

PROPERTY C

**PROPERTY B
must provide access to road
—*an easement by necessity***

Exhibit 14.10 **Parties to a lease**

Lease

Landlord
(lessor)

**Owner–landlord owns
title to the real property**

**Tenant acquires a
nonfreehold estate in the
real property that gives
the tenant a right to
possession of the property**

Leasehold
A tenant's interest in property.

Landlord
An owner who transfers a leasehold.

Tenant
The party to whom a leasehold is transferred.

Tenancy for years
A tenancy created when the landlord and the tenant agree on a specific duration for a lease.

Periodic tenancy
A tenancy created when a lease specifies intervals at which payments are due but does not specify the length of the lease.

Tenancy at will
A tenancy created by a lease that may be terminated at any time by either party.

Tenancy at sufferance
A tenancy created when a tenant retains possession of property after the expiration of another tenancy or a life estate without the owner's consent.

Types of Tenancy

The tenant's interest in the property is called a **leasehold estate,** or **leasehold**. The owner who transfers the leasehold estate is called the **landlord,** or **lessor**. The party to whom the leasehold estate is transferred is called the **tenant,** or **lessee**. *Tenancies* are of four types:

1. *Tenancy for years.* A **tenancy for years** is created when the landlord and the tenant agree on a specific duration for the lease. Any lease for a stated period—no matter how long or short—is called a tenancy for years. Examples of these arrangements range from office space leased in a high-rise office building on a 30-year lease to a cabin leased for the summer. A tenancy for years terminates automatically, without notice, upon expiration of the stated term.

2. *Periodic tenancy.* A **periodic tenancy** is created when a lease specifies intervals at which payments are due but does not specify the duration of the lease. A lease that states, "Rent is due on the first day of the month" establishes a periodic tenancy. Many such leases are created by implication. A periodic tenancy may be terminated by either party at the end of any payment interval but adequate notice of the termination must be given. At common law, the notice period equaled the length of the payment period. Therefore, a month-to-month tenancy requires a one-month notice of termination.

3. *Tenancy at will.* A lease that may be terminated at any time by either party is termed a **tenancy at will**. A tenancy at will may be created expressly (e.g., "to tenant as long as landlord wishes") but more likely is to be created by implication. Most states have enacted statutes requiring minimum advance notice for the termination of a tenancy at will. The death of either party terminates a tenancy at will.

4. *Tenancy at sufferance.* A **tenancy at sufferance** is created when a tenant retains possession of the property after the expiration of another tenancy or a life estate without the owner's consent. That is, the owner suffers the *wrongful possession* of his or her property by the holdover tenant. This is not really a true tenancy but merely the possession of property without right. Technically, a tenant at sufferance is a tres-

checklist ✓

TYPES OF TENANCY	DESCRIPTION
Tenancy for years	Continues for the duration of the lease and then terminates automatically without requiring notice. It does not terminate upon the death of either party.
Periodic tenancy	Continues from payment interval to payment interval. It may be terminated by either party with adequate notice. It does not terminate upon the death of either party.
Tenancy at will	Continues at the will of the parties and may be terminated by either party at any time with adequate notice. It terminates upon the death of either party.
Tenancy at sufferance	Arises when a tenant wrongfully occupies real property after the expiration of another tenancy or life estate. It continues until the owner either evicts the tenant or holds him or her over for another term. It terminates upon the death of the tenant.

passer. A tenant at sufferance is liable for the payment of rent during the period of sufferance. To evict a holdover tenant, most states require an owner to go through certain legal proceedings, called *eviction proceedings* or *unlawful detainer actions*. A few states allow owners to use self-help to evict a holdover tenant as long as force is not used.

The Lease

The rental agreement between the landlord and the tenant is called the **lease**. Leases generally can be either oral or written, except that most statutes of frauds require written leases for periods of time longer than one year. The lease must contain the essential terms of the parties' agreement. The lease frequently is a form contract prepared by the landlord and presented to the tenant. This is particularly true of residential leases. Other leases are negotiated between the parties. For example, a bank's lease of a branch office would be negotiated with the owner of the building. Lease forms typically are considerably longer than two pages.

Lease
A transfer of the right to the possession and use of real property for a set term in return for certain consideration; the rental agreement between a landlord and a tenant.

Implied Warranty of Habitability

The courts of many jurisdictions hold that an **implied warranty of habitability** applies to residential leases for their duration. This warranty provides that the leased premises must be fit, safe, and suitable for ordinary residential use. On the one hand, unchecked rodent infestation, leaking roofs, and unworkable bathroom facilities have been held to breach the implied warranty of habitability. On the other hand, a small crack in the wall or some paint peeling from a door does not breach this warranty.

Implied warranty of habitability
A warranty that provides that leased premises must be fit, safe, and suitable for ordinary residential use.

If the landlord's failure to maintain or repair the leased premises affects the tenant's use or enjoyment of the premises, state statutes and judicial decisions provide various remedies. Generally, the tenant may (1) withhold from his or her rent the amount by which the defect reduced the value of the premises to him or her, (2) repair the defect and deduct the cost of repairs from the rent due for the leased premises, (3) cancel the lease if the failure to repair constitutes constructive eviction, or (4) sue for damages for the amount the landlord's failure to repair the defect reduced the value of the leasehold.

LAND USE CONTROL

Generally, the ownership of property entitles the owner to use his or her property as he or she wishes. Such use, however, is subject to limitations imposed by government regulation. These limitations are collectively referred to as **land use control**, or **land use regulation**. Several forms of land use regulation are discussed in the following paragraphs.

Land use control or land use regulation
The collective term for the laws that regulate the possession, ownership, and use of real property.

Zoning

Most counties and municipalities have enacted **zoning ordinances** to regulate land use. Zoning ordinances generally (1) establish use districts within the municipality (i.e., areas are generally designated residential, commercial, or industrial); (2) restrict the height, size, and location of buildings on a building site; and (3) establish aesthetic requirements or limitations for the exterior of buildings.

Zoning ordinances
Local laws that are adopted by municipalities and local governments to regulate land use within their boundaries.

A **zoning commission** usually formulates zoning ordinances, conducts public hearings, and makes recommendations to the city council, which must vote to enact an ordinance. Once a zoning ordinance is enacted, the zoning ordinance commission enforces it. If landowners believe that a zoning ordinance is illegal or that it has been applied unlawfully to them or their property, they may institute a court proceeding seeking judicial review of the ordinance or its application.

An owner who wishes to use his or her property for a use different from that permitted under a current zoning ordinance may seek relief from the ordinance by obtaining a **variance**. To obtain a variance, the landowner must prove that the ordinance

Advice from the Field

AT A CROSSROAD. . .

Michelle DeVera, freelance journalist, bachelor's degree in journalism and English from California State University, Long Beach.

Life has many detours. Finding the right one can be as difficult as navigating your way through a steep, rocky, mountain pass. Not only do you have to be wary of hazardous road conditions, but you also have to be able to handle the unexpected turns and surprises.

Deciding to switch careers can be one of those dark, desolate detours filled with jagged unfamiliarity. As you stand at the cross in the road with the option to follow along the same, well-known path or go down the road less traveled, what are you going to do?

When Randie English faced the same question 18 years ago, her marriage was ending. Since high school, English's sole occupation for 16 years had been raising her three children as a stay-at-home mom. As a new single parent, English knew she had to do something, and becoming a paralegal not only offered her a worthwhile career but it also became a key factor in her current success as a law book sales manager.

Being a paralegal "gave me a basic understanding of how the law works," English said, adding that her paralegal background provided that understanding. "You have to be able to understand what the book is and what the book can do for you. If you don't know what discovery is or can't answer an attorney's question, how can you help the customer?"

But in 1988, without a college education, her choices were limited. Under the guidance of both her brother and brother-in-law, who were academic counselors at a local community college, she decided to become a paralegal and uprooted her family from their Canadian home to attend Highline Community College in Washington.

By 1990, English had completed the American Bar Association (ABA) accredited paralegal program and had interned in a variety of legal fields including probation, prosecution, and personal injury. Her internship at the law firm of Adler Giersch eventually turned into a full-time paralegal position. For the next 3½ years, English worked with a staff of about four attorneys and 10 legal assistants handling personal injury cases as a case manager. Her duties were to manage the file up to the point of litigation under the supervision of an attorney. "When I first started it, I loved it," English said.

Conducting the initial client interviews refined her listening skills, as well as her ability to read body language—important attributes to have for success in sales and as a people manager, she said. "To sell, you must see and/or hear the hidden signals in body language and in voice tone; what a person says, and what a person doesn't say are all-important clues," English added. "To manage people, you must also hear and see. What does the employee really mean? What do they want? What do they think they heard me say? Listening always goes beyond just hearing the words."

Randie English says her paralegal skills made possible her success as a legal publishing sales manager. Besides a general understanding of the law, English says her paralegal experience taught her to "remain calm in a storm."

Although English had contact with the clients, she is a "people person" and said she hungered for more one-on-one interactions. "Paralegals were given a great deal of responsibility along with opportunities to improve their knowledge," she said. "We worked in paralegal–attorney teams and created teams from all levels of the firm, to handle specific issues, including developing a mission statement. . . . In my current position, I have a great deal of decision-making authority. My paralegal career helped me gain the confidence to claim that authority."

By the time the firm had downsized in 1994, English had lightened her caseload to the point where she didn't have any active cases and started dabbling in public relations. Because she had stopped serving her function as a paralegal and the firm could no longer sustain a public relations department, English was laid off.

"At that point, we were the first ones to go," she said. "I [decided] to start thinking about what else I could do besides [be a] paralegal. When you've worked in one particular area, you're likely to be hired in that field again. I didn't know if I'd enjoy it again," English said.

Since all of her children had graduated from high school, English seized the opportunity to concentrate on herself. She sold her house and headed south for California. She stayed with family and spent the next year contemplating a new limitless future. Going back to school and working part-time seemed like her best bet until she found an ad in the local newspaper for a receptionist position at James Publishing Inc., an independent law book publisher based in Costa Mesa, Calif.

Advice from the Field ••

(continued)

Once the employer saw her resume and cover letter dripping with legal assistant experience, he offered English a job as an account representative. "He called me and sold me on the company," she said. English excelled in her new career selling law books via telephone, and in 1997 she was promoted to manager of the outbound telephone sales department where she hires and trains account representatives. She also determines promotions and travels across the nation putting together book exhibits at law-related events, such as annual state bar meetings.

Her occupation as a sales manager wouldn't have been possible without her experience as a paralegal, however. Besides acquiring a general knowledge of law, English said other skills she transferred over were knowing how a law firm operates, working with people, verbal and written communication, time management, and prioritizing.

"I learned how to remain calm in a storm while working as a paralegal—an invaluable skill," English said.

"At a Crossroad . . ." by Michelle DeVera, As seen in the September/October 2000 issue of Legal Assistant Today. *Copyright 2000 James Publishing Inc. Reprinted courtesy of* Legal Assistant Today *magazine. For subscription information call (800) 394-2626, or visit www.legalassistanttoday.com.*

causes an undue hardship by preventing him or her from making a reasonable return on the land as zoned. Variances usually are difficult to obtain.

Zoning laws act prospectively; that is, uses and buildings that already exist in the zoned area are permitted to continue even though they do not fit within new zoning ordinances. These are called **nonconforming uses**. For example, if a new zoning ordinance is enacted, making an area a residential zone, an existing funeral parlor is a nonconforming use.

Compensable Taking of Real Property

The government may use its power of **eminent domain** to acquire private property for public purposes. However, the Due Process Clause of the U.S. Constitution (and state constitutions, where applicable) requires the government to allow the owner to make a case for keeping the property. The **Just Compensation Clause** of the Fifth Amendment to the U.S. Constitution requires the government to compensate the property owner (and possibly others, such as lessees) when it exercises the power of eminent domain.

Anyone who is not satisfied with the compensation offered by the government can bring an action to have the court determine the compensation to be paid. Often, the government's action is not considered a "taking," even if it causes economic losses to property owners and others.

Consider this example: Assume that ITT has acquired a large piece of property, with the intention of erecting a commercial building at some future time. Now suppose the government wants to build a new highway that passes through the property owned by ITT. The government can use its power of eminent domain to acquire the property. There has been a "taking," so the government must pay ITT just compensation. Suppose, instead, that the government enacts a zoning law that affects ITT's property by restricting building in the area to single-family housing. Although ITT would suffer a substantial economic loss, the zoning law, nevertheless, probably would not constitute a "taking" requiring the payment of compensation.

Eminent domain
The government's power to take private property for public use, provided that just compensation is paid to the private property holder.

Just Compensation Clause
A clause of the U.S. Constitution that requires the government to compensate the property owner, and possibly others, when the government takes property under its power of eminent domain.

Legal Terminology

Summary

CHAPTER *14* PROPERTY
Personal Property

Definition	Personal property is everything that is not real property; sometimes referred to as *goods* or *chattels*.
Types of Personal Property	1. *Tangible property*: Physically defined property such as goods, animals, and minerals. 2. *Intangible property*: Rights that cannot be reduced to physical form, such as stock certificates, bonds, and copyrights.

Acquiring Ownership of Personal Property	Ownership to personal property may be acquired by the following means:
	1. *Purchase:* A person can purchase property from its rightful owner.
	2. *Production:* A person can produce a finished product from raw materials and supplies.
	3. *Gift:* A gift is a voluntary transfer of property by its owner to a donee without consideration. The three elements necessary to create a valid gift are:
	  a. Donative intent.
	  b. Delivery.
	  c. Acceptance.
	4. *Will or inheritance:* Gifts made to beneficiaries of a will, and inheritances stipulated in an inheritance statute.

Types of Gifts	1. *Gift inter vivos:* These gifts are made during a donor's lifetime. 2. *Gift causa mortis:* These gifts are made in anticipation of death.

Mislaid and Lost Personal Property	1. *Mislaid property:* Mislaid property is personal property that an owner voluntarily places somewhere and then inadvertently forgets. The owner of the premises where the property is mislaid does not acquire title to the property but has the right of possession against all except the rightful owner. The rightful owner can reclaim the property.
	2. *Lost Property:* Lost property is personal property that an owner leaves somewhere because of negligence or carelessness. The finder obtains title to the property against the whole world except the true owner. The rightful owner can reclaim the property.
	3. *Estray statutes:* These state statutes permit a finder of mislaid or lost property to obtain title to the property. To obtain clear title, the finder must:
	  a. Report the find to the appropriate government agency and turn over possession of the property to the agency.
	  b. Post and publish required notices.
	  c. Wait the statutorily required time (e.g., one year) without the rightful owner claiming the property.

Bailments

Description	Bailments occur when the owner of personal property delivers the property to another person to be held, stored, or delivered, or for some other purpose.
Parties	1. *Bailor:* Owner of the property 2. *Bailee:* Party to whom the property is delivered
Mutual Benefit Bailment	A mutual benefit bailment arises when both parties benefit from the bailment. This includes commercial bailments. The bailee owes a duty of *reasonable care* (or *ordinary care*) and is liable for *ordinary negligence*.

Real Property

Nature of Real Property	Real property is immovable; it includes land, buildings, subsurface rights, air rights, plant life, and fixtures.
Freehold Estates	Estates where the owner has a present possessory interest in the real property.
Types of Fees	Estates in Fee 1. *Fee simple absolute* (or *fee simple*): Highest form of ownership 2. *Fee simple defeasible* (or *qualified fee*): Estate that ends if a specified condition occurs
Life Estates	A life estate is an interest in real property that lasts for the life of a specified person; called an *estate pour autre vie* if the time is measured by the life of a third person.
Future Interest	Future interest means the right to possess real property in the future rather than currently. Two types:
	Reversion: Right to possession that returns to the grantor after the expiration of a limited or contingent estate. Remainder: Right to possession that goes to a third person after the expiration of a limited or contingent estate; the third person is called a *remainderman*.

Concurrent Ownership	When two or more persons jointly own real property, it is called concurrent ownership. Joint Tenancy: Owners may transfer their interests without the consent of co-owners; transfer severs the joint tenancy. Under the *right of survivorship*, the interest of a deceased owner passes to his or her co-owners. Tenancy in Common: Owners may transfer their interests without the consent of co-owners; transfer does not sever the tenancy in common. Interest of a deceased owner passes to his or her estate. Tenancy by the Entirety: Form of co-ownership that can be used only by a married couple; neither spouse may transfer his or her interest without the other spouse's consent. A surviving spouse has the right of survivorship.
Community Property	Form of co-ownership that applies only to a married couple; neither spouse may transfer his or her interest without the other spouse's consent. When a spouse dies, the surviving spouse automatically receives one-half of the community property. Condominium: Owners have title to their individual units and own the common areas as tenants in common; owners may transfer their interests without the consent of other owners. Cooperative: A corporation owns the building, and the residents own shares of the corporation. Usually, owners may not transfer their shares without the approval of the other owners.

Transfer of Ownership of Real Property

Sale of Real Estate	An owner sells his or her property to another for consideration.
Recording Statutes	Recording statutes permit copies of deeds and other documents concerning interests in real property (e.g., mortgages, liens) to be filed in a government office, where they become public record. This puts third parties on notice of recorded interests.
Marketable Title	A marketable title is a title free of encumbrances, defects in title, or other defects.
Deed	A deed is an instrument used to convey real property by sale or gift. 1. *Warranty deed:* provides the most protection to the grantee because the grantor makes warranties against defect in title. 2. *Quitclaim deed:* provides least amount of protection to the grantee because the grantor transfers only the interest he or she has in the property.
Easement	An interest in land that gives the holder the right to make limited use of another's property without taking anything from it (e.g., driveways, party walls).
Adverse Possession	A person who occupies another's property acquires title to the property if the occupation has been: 1. for a statutory period of time (in many states, 10 to 20 years). 2. open, visible, and notorious. 3. actual and exclusive. 4. continuous and peaceful. 5. hostile and adverse.

Landlord–Tenant Relationship

Definition	A landlord–tenant relationship is created when an owner of a freehold estate transfers a right to another to exclusively and temporarily possess the owner's property.
Types of Tenancy	1. *tenancy for years:* tenancy for a specified period of time 2. *Periodic tenancy:* tenancy for a period of time determined by the payment interval 3. *Tenancy at will:* tenancy that may be terminated at any time by either party 4. *Tenancy at sufferance:* tenancy created by the wrongful possession of property
Lease	The rental agreement between the landlord and the tenant that contains the essential terms of the parties' agreement.
Implied Warranty of Habitability	An implied warranty of habitability provides that leased premises must be fit, safe, and suitable for ordinary residential use.

Land-Use Control

Zoning	*Zoning ordinances* are laws adopted by local governments that restrict use of property, set building standards, and establish architectural requirements. 1. *Variance:* Permits an owner to make a nonzoned use of his or her property; requires permission from a zoning board. 2. *Nonconforming use:* A nonzoned use that is permitted (grandfathered in) when an area is rezoned.
Compensable Taking of Property	Eminent domain is the power and process by which the government acquires private property for public purposes. The Just Compensation Clause of the U.S. Constitution mandates that the government compensate the property owner and possibly others (e.g., renters) just compensation when the government exercises its power of eminent domain.

▶ WORKING THE WEB

1. Using the website **http://www.google.com/html** or similar Internet search engine, or the Internet legal search services Westlaw or LexisNexis, find the estray statute for your state. What requirements must be met for a finder to obtain title to mislaid or lost property that he or she finds?

2. Using the website **http://www.google.com/html** or similar Internet search engine, find a listing of houses or property that is for sale in your area. Compare home prices. Are the prices higher or lower than you thought they would be?

3. Using the website **http://www.google.com/html** or similar Internet search engine, or the Internet legal search services Westlaw or LexisNexis, find information about a conservation easement in your state. Write a one-page report about this easement.

4. Using the website **http://www.google.com/html** or similar Internet search engine, or the Internet legal search services Westlaw or LexisNexis, find the law for your state for transferring property to minors. Write a one-page report on your state's requirements for transferring property to minors.

5. Visit the website **http://nationalatlas.gov/printable/image/pdf/fedlands/id.pdf.** The map will show the lands owned by the federal government in the state of Idaho. Substitute your state's two letter code (e.g., al for Alabama, ny for New York) where the "id" appears in the website, and find the map showing the lands that are owned by the federal government in your state. Does the federal government own land in your area? If so, what department or bureau of the federal government owns the land?

▶ CRITICAL THINKING AND WRITING QUESTIONS

1. Define personal property. What is the difference between tangible and intangible personal property? Give an example of each.

2. What is the difference between a gift *inter vivos* and a gift *causa mortis*?

3. What does the Uniform Gift to Minors Act and the Revised Uniform Gift to Minors Act provide? Explain.

4. What is the difference between mislaid property and lost property? Give an example of each.

5. Describe an estray statute. What is the purpose of an estray statute? Explain how an estray statute works.

6. Define a bailment. Who is the bailor? Who is the bailee?

7. Define real property. What is land? What are buildings? What are surface rights?

8. Describe subsurface rights (or mineral rights). Give an example.

9. What are fixtures? Give an example.

10. What is an estate in land (estate)? Define a freehold estate.

11. Define a fee simple absolute (or fee simple). Define a fee simple defeasible (or qualified fee).

12. What is a life estate? Give an example.

13. What is a future interest? What is the difference between a reversion and a remainder? Give an example of each.

14. What is concurrent ownership (co-ownership)?

15. Define joint tenancy. Define the right of survivorship.

16. Define tenancy in common. How does the real property of a deceased tenant in common pass upon her or his death?

17. Define tenancy by the entirety. Who can have a tenancy by the entirety?
18. Define community property. Give an example.
19. What is a condominium? What is a cooperative?
20. Define the following: (a) deed, (b) warranty deed, (c) quit-claim deed. Who are the grantor and the grantee?
21. Describe a recording statute. What does the Registrar of Deeds do? Explain.
22. Describe a quiet title action. What is its purpose?
23. What does the legal doctrine of adverse possession provide? What elements have to be met for adverse possession to occur? Give an example.
24. What is title insurance? What protection does title insurance provide?
25. What is an easement? Describe the difference between the following types of easements: (a) easement by grant, (b) easement by reservation, (c) easement by implication, and (d) easement by necessity.
26. Define *landlord*. Define *tenant*.
27. Describe the following types of tenancies: (a) tenancy for years, (b) periodic tenancy, (c) tenancy at will, and (d) tenancy at sufferance.
28. Define the implied warranty of habitability. Give an example of its breach.
29. What is land use control?
30. Define zoning. What does a zoning ordinance do? Give an example of zoning.
31. What is a variance? What is a nonconforming use?
32. Define eminent domain. What is a "taking?" What does the Just Compensation Clause of the U.S. Constitution require?

▶ ETHICS ANALYSIS AND DISCUSSION QUESTIONS

1. Does the preparation of a report for a client showing the history of the ownership of a property, as shown in public records, and claims against the property, as shown in public records, constitute the practice of law?
2. In your jurisdiction is priority given to real estate based upon the time of filing of deeds? Is the failure to promptly file a deed malpractice?
3. As an experienced paralegal, you have investigated many complex cases and developed a reputation for discovering little-known facts and obtaining information not normally obtained by investigators. A law firm proposes to have its client hire you to conduct the investigation of a complex and troublesome environmental case involving a major corporation that appears to be hiding information. [*Ethics Opinion 510, Texas Professional Ethics Committee Opinions.*] Can you accept the case with your compensation based on a contingent fee if paid directly from the client from his or her award, if any? From the firm? Can you accept a "substantial" bonus from the law firm?

▶ DEVELOPING YOUR COLLABORATION SKILLS

Working on your own or with a group of other students assigned by your instructor, review the Paralegals at Work at the beginning of the chapter. As a group, discuss the following questions.

1. From the facts of the case, make a drawing of the properties owned by Ms. Trump, Mrs. Gasper, and Mr. Jones. Draw the beach side and the highway side of the properties. Also draw Mrs. Gasper's fence line, and the dirt road that runs across Ms. Trump's property to reach Mr. Clive's property.
2. What is the zoning restriction on Ms. Trump's property? What would have to be obtained for this property for it to be able to be developed as a resort by the proposed purchaser?
3. What problem is caused by Mrs. Gasper's fence line? In a quiet title action *Trump v. Gasper*, who do you think would win? Why?
4. What problem is caused by the dirt road that traverses Ms. Trump's property to reach Mr. Jones's property? In a quiet title action *Trump v. Jones*, who do you think would win? Why?
5. For the proposed purchaser to be sure that the property has no other problems, what would you advise him to do? Explain.
6. If the proposed purchaser actually purchases the property from Ms. Trump, what should he purchase to protect him if other parties later come forward claiming ownership rights in the property?

▶ PARALEGAL PORTFOLIO EXERCISE

Prepare a memorandum, no longer than three pages, that does the following two things: (1) describes the requirements for title to property to be obtained by the doctrine of adverse possession in your state; (2) finds two cases in your state where the doctrine of adverse possession has been asserted to try to obtain title to property, and discuss the results of the cases.

▶LEGAL ANALYSIS AND WRITING CASES

Sisters of Charity of the Incarnate Word v. Meaux

122 S.W.3d 428 Court of Appeals of Texas

FACTS

The Sisters of Charity of the Incarnate Word d/b/a St. Elizabeth Hospital of Beaumont, operates a health and wellness center. Phil Meaux was a paying member of the health center. The rules of the center, which Meaux had been given, state. "The Health & Wellness Center is not responsible for lost or stolen items." A sign stating "We cannot assure the safety of your valuables" was posted at the check-in desk. The wellness center furnished a lock and key to case members but had a master key to pen lockers in case a member forgot or lost his or her key.

On January 19, 2000, Meaux went to the wellness center, placed his clothes and an expensive Rolex watch and a money clip with $400 cash in the locker assigned him. Upon returning from swimming, Meaux discovered that his locker had been pried open, and his watch and money had been stolen by some unknown person. Meaux sued the Sisters of Charity, alleging that a bailment had been created between him and the Sisters and that the Sisters, as bailee, were negligent and therefore liable to him for the value of his stolen property.

The Trial Court held in favor of Meaux and awarded him $19,500 as the value of the stolen property, plus interest and attorneys' fees. The Sisters of Charity appealed.

Question

1. Was a bailment created between Meaux and the Sisters of Charity?

Cunningham v. Hastings

556 N.E.2d 12 Court of Appeals of Indiana

FACTS

On August 30, 1984, Warren R. Hastings and Joan L. Cunningham, who were unmarried, purchased a house together. Hastings paid $45,000 down payment toward the purchase price out of his own funds. The deed referred to Hastings and Cunningham as "joint tenants with the right of survivorship." Hastings and Cunningham occupied the property jointly. After their relationship ended, Hastings took sole possession of the property. Cunningham filed a complaint seeking partition of the real estate. Based on its determination that the property could not be split, the trial court ordered it to be sold. The Trial Court further ordered that $45,000 of the sale proceeds be paid of Hastings to reimburse him for his down payment and that the remainder of the proceeds be divided equally between Hastings and Cunningham. Cunningham appealed, alleging that Hastings should not have been given credit for the down payment.

Question

1. Is Cunningham entitled to an equal share of the proceeds of the sale of the real estate?

Witt v. Miller

845 S.W.2d. 665 Court of Appeals of Missouri

FACTS

Edward and Mary Shaughnessey purchased a 16-acre tract in St. Louis county in 1954. Subsequently, they subdivided 12 acres into 18 lots offered for sale and retained possession of the remaining 4-acre tract. In 1967, Charles and Elaine Witt purchased lot 12, which is adjacent to the 4-acre tract. The Witts constructed and moved into a house on their lot. In 1968, they cleared an area of land that ran the length of their property and extended 40 feet onto the 4-acre tract. The Witts constructed a pool and a deck, planted a garden, made a playground for their children, set up a dog run and built a fence along the edge of the property line, which included the now-disputed property. Neither the Witts nor the Shaughnesseys realized that the Witts had encroached on the Shaughnesseys' property.

In February 1988, the Shaughnesseys sold the 4-acre tract to Thomas and Rosanne Miller. When a survey showed the encroachment, the Millers demanded that the Witts remove the pool and cease using the property. When the Witts refused to do so, the Millers sued to quiet title. The Witts defended, arguing that they had obtained title to the disputed property by adverse possession. The Trial Court held that there was no adverse possession and ruled in favor of the Millers. The Witts appealed.

Question

1. Had the elements for adverse possession been met?

Kelo v. City of New London, Connecticut

545 U.S. 469, 125 S.Ct. 2655, 162 L.Ed. 2d 439, 2005 U.S. Lexis 5011 Supreme Court of the United States

FACTS

The City of New London is located in southeastern Connecticut at the junction of the Thames River and the Long Island Sound. The city has suffered decades of economic decline, including the closing in 1996 of the federal military base in the Fort Trumbull area of the city. In 1998 the city's unemployment was nearly double that of the state, and the city's population of 24,000 was the lowest since 1920.

To remedy the situation, state and local officials targeted the City of New London for economic revitalization. The government created the New London Development Corporation

(NLDC) to assist the city in planning economic redevelopment. The NLDC finalized an integrated redevelopment plan for 90 acres in the Fort Trumbull area of the city. The redevelopment plan included a waterfront conference hotel, restaurants, stores, a marina, 80 new residences, and office buildings. These projects were to be constructed and owned by private developers and parties selected by the city. The stated purpose was to make the city more attractive, create jobs, and increase tax revenue.

The city purchased from private owners most of the land needed for the redevelopment. When Susette Kelo and other home owners in the redevelopment district (collectively Kelo) refused to sell their properties, the NLDC initiated eminent domain actions to take their properties. The properties themselves were well kept and were not blighted. Kelo defended, arguing that the taking violated the "public use" requirement of the Fifth Amendment to the U.S. Constitution. The state Trial Court held for Kelo. The State Supreme Court held that the taking of private property by the NLDC was valid. The U.S. Supreme Court agreed to hear the case.

Question

1. Does the city's decision to take property for the purpose of economic development satisfy the "public use" requirement of the Fifth Amendment to permit Kelo's property to be taken by eminent domain?

Naab v. Nolan

327 S.E.2d 151, 1985 W.Va. Lexis 476 (WV 1985)

FACTS

In 1973, Joseph and Helen Naab purchased a tract of land in a subdivision of Williamstown, West Virginia. At the time of purchase, the property had both a house and a small concrete garage. Evidence showed that the garage had been erected sometime prior to 1952 by one of the Naabs' predecessors in title. In 1975, Roger and Cynthia Nolan purchased a lot contiguous to that owned by the Naabs. The following year, the Nolans had their property surveyed. The survey indicated that one corner of the Naabs' garage encroached 1.22 feet onto the Nolans' property and the other corner encroached 0.91 feet over the property line. The Nolans requested that the Naabs remove the garage from their property. When the Naabs refused, the lawsuit ensued.

Question

1. Who wins?

Hill v. Pinelawn Memorial Park, Inc.

282 S.E.2d 779, 1981 N.C. Lexis 1326 (N.C. 1981)

FACTS

On October 13, 1972, Johnnie H. Hill and his wife, Clara Mae, entered into an installment sales contract with Pinelawn Memorial Park (Pinelawn) to purchase a mausoleum crypt. They made it clear they wanted to buy crypt "D," which faced eastward toward Kinston. The Hills paid $1,035 down payment and continued to make $33.02 monthly payments.

On February 13, 1974, William C. Shackleford and his wife, Jennie L., entered into an agreement with Pinelawn to purchase crypt D. They paid $1,406 down payment and two annual installments of $912. The Hills were first put on notice of the second contract when they visited Pinelawn in February 1977 and saw the Shackleford name on crypt D. The Hills then tendered full payment to Pinelawn for crypt D.

On April 25, 1977, the Hills sued Pinelawn and the Shacklefords. They demanded specific performance on the contract and the deed to crypt D. Upon being served with summons, the Shacklefords discovered that they had no deed to the crypt and demanded one from Pinelawn. Pinelawn delivered them a deed dated August 18, 1977, which the Shacklefords recorded in the County Register on September 9, 1977.

Question

1. Who owns crypt D?

Love v. Monarch Apartments

771 P.2d 79, 1989 Kan.App. Lexis 219 (Kan.App. 1989)

FACTS

Sharon Love entered into a written lease agreement with Monarch Apartments for apartment 4 at 441 Winfield in Topeka, Kansas. Shortly after moving in, she experienced serious problems with termites. The walls swelled, clouds of dirt came out, and when she checked on her children one night, she saw termites flying around the room. She complained to Monarch, which arranged for the apartment to be fumigated. When the termite problem persisted, Monarch moved Love and her children to apartment 2. Upon moving in, Love noticed that roaches crawled over the walls, ceilings, and floors of the apartment. She complained, and Monarch called an exterminator, who sprayed the apartment. When the roach problem persisted, Love vacated the premises.

Question

1. Did Love lawfully terminate the lease?

Souders v. Johnson

501 So.2d 745, 1987 Fla.App. Lexis 6579 (Fla.App. 1987)

FACTS

When Dr. Arthur M. Edwards died, leaving a will disposing of his property, he left to his stepson, Ronald W. Souders, the villa-type condominium in which he lived, its "contents," and $10,000. Edwards left the residual of his estate to other named legatees. In administering the estate, certain stock certificates, passbook savings accounts, and other bank statements were found in Edwards' condominium. Souders claimed that these items belonged to him because they were "contents" of the condominium. The other legatees opposed Souders' claim, alleging that the disputed property was intangible property and not part of the contents of the condominium.

The value of the property was as follows: condominium, $138,000; furniture in condominium, $4,000; stocks, $377,000; and passbook and other bank accounts, $124,000.

Question

1. Who is entitled to the stocks and bank accounts? Do you think Souders acted ethically in this case?

WORKING WITH THE LANGUAGE OF THE COURT CASE

Case for Briefing: Walker v. Quillen

1993 Del. Lexis 105
Supreme Court of Delaware

Read the following case, excerpted from the Court of Appeals opinion. Review and brief the case. In your brief answer the following questions:

1. Who were the plaintiffs (appellees)? Who was the defendant (appellant)?
2. Describe the tract of land owned by the plaintiffs and defendant.
3. What was the issue in this case? How did the court decide this issue?

Moore, Justice

Pursuant to Supreme Court Rule 25(a), appellees, Elizabeth Star Ayres and Clara Louise Quillen, have moved to affirm a judgment of the Court of Chancery granting an implied easement in favor of appellees' servient estate, as against the dominant estate of appellant, Irvin C. Walker ("Walker"). The appellees contend that sufficient evidence supports the findings of the Court of Chancery and that there was no abuse of discretion in granting the implied easement. We agree and affirm.

The appellees own in fee simple absolute a tract of land in Sussex County known as "Bluff Point." The tract is surrounded on three sides by Rehoboth Bay and is landlocked on the fourth side by Walker's land. At one time, the two tracts in question were held by a common owner. In 1878, Bluff Point was sold in fee simple absolute apart from the other holdings, thereby landlocking the parcel. A narrow dirt road, which traverses Walker's land, connects Bluff Point to a public road and is its only means of access.

Under the doctrine of implied easement or easement by necessity, the Court of Chancery found that the appellees were entitled to cross over a portion of Walker's land for access to Bluff Point. The court also found that water access, even if a reasonable substitute for land access, was not feasible because of the shallowness of the water surrounding Bluff Point. There is ample evidence in the record to support the finding that the two tracts originated from the unified holdings of one owner, and that an implied easement was created by the severance that landlocked Bluff Point. The record also sufficiently supports the finding that navigable access to Bluff Point was not feasible. Now, therefore, it is ordered that the judgment of the Court of Chancery be, and the same hereby is, affirmed. ■

ESTATE PLANNING AND ELDER LAW

"When you have told someone you have left him a legacy, the only decent thing to do is to die at once."

Samuel Butler

PARALEGALS AT WORK

You are a paralegal for Mr. Patrick O'Rourke, an expert in estate planning law. As the paralegal for Mr. O'Rourke, you conduct research, attend client conferences, and prepare estate planning documents for Mr. O'Rourke's review.

One day Mr. O'Rourke asks you to sit in on a client conference. The clients are Ms. Harriet Huntington and Mr. Theodore Huntington. At the meeting, the Huntingtons disclose the following information: Ms. Huntington is 45 years old, and Mr. Huntington is 50 years old. They have been married 15 years. Mr. Huntington owns his own business, a successful retail store. Ms. Huntington works as a manager at a large software company. Mr. Huntington earns about $150,000 per year, and Ms. Huntington earns about $250,000 per year. They have three children, ages 13, 10, and 7.

During the course of their marriage, the Huntingtons have accumulated the following assets: A home that is worth $1,000,000 with a $300,000 mortgage, securities of $500,000, and cash savings in bank accounts totaling $100,000. Ms. Huntington and Mr. Huntington each has a pension at work, and each has a life insurance policy for $1,000,000. Together they have accumulated two automobiles, furniture, and jewelry worth $50,000.

The Huntingtons explain that they currently do not have any wills or trusts. They explain that they would like to have Mr. O'Rourke advise them on matters of estate planning and prepare the necessary documents to effectuate the plans they agree to. The Huntingtons explain that they each want the other to receive all of their property if one of them should die. They explain further that they want to have control over their assets during their lifetime and receive all of the income from their property during their life. But they would like to avoid probate.

Both Mr. and Ms. Huntington explain their personal wish that certain life saving measures not be taken on their behalf should they become severely ill or

After studying this chapter, you should be able to:

1. List and describe the requirements for making a valid will.

2. Describe how a will can be changed and revoked.

3. Explain the effect of entering into a mutual will.

4. Identify how property is distributed under intestacy statutes if a person dies without a will.

5. Describe the process of probate.

6. Explain a living will.

7. Define *trust* and identify the parties to a trust.

injured. They also each want the other to make health care decisions for them if they are unable to do so.

The Huntingtons ask Mr. O'Rourke to develop an estate plan for them. As Mr. O'Rourke's paralegal, you will assist him in developing the estate plan for the Huntingtons and help him prepare the necessary documents to implement the estate plan.

Consider the issues involved in this scenario as you read the chapter.

▶ INTRODUCTION FOR THE PARALEGAL

Many paralegals work for lawyers who represent clients in estate planning. Paralegals often assist lawyers in drafting wills, trusts, and other estate planning documents. Paralegals who work in this field also assist lawyers in the transfers of assets pursuant to trust and living trust arrangements, as well as assist in handling matters of probate. Clients also often want living trusts and health care proxies completed while they are living.

Wills transfer property upon a person's death. When that person dies, his or her property is distributed as provided in the will. If a person dies without a will, state law provides how the deceased person's property is distributed. A person may transfer property to a trust while he or she is living. Some trusts are living trusts—the trust is created for the benefit of the beneficiaries while they are living. Other trusts are established to go into effect when a person dies. In addition, many people sign a living will and health care *proxy* that states their wishes should an accident or illness disable them so they no longer can make decisions themselves and appoint someone else to make any necessary decisions for them.

A paralegal working in the estate planning field must have knowledge of wills, trusts, living trusts, living wills, health care proxies, probate, and other matters related to estate planning. This chapter covers all of the legal issues and documents associated with estate planning. ■

WILLS

A **will** is a declaration of how a person wants his or her property to be distributed upon his or her death. It is a *testamentary* deposition of property. The person who makes the will is called the **testator** (or **testatrix**). The persons designated in the will to receive the testator's property are called **beneficiaries**. Exhibit 15.1 shows the parties to a will.

Requirements for Making a Will

Every state has a **Statute of Wills** that establishes the requirements for making a valid will in that state. These requirements are:

- *Testamentary capacity*. The testator must have been of legal age and "sound mind" when the will was made. The courts determine **testamentary capacity** on a case-by-case basis. The legal age for executing a will is set by state statute.
- *Writing*. Wills must be in writing to be valid (except for dying declarations, discussed later in this chapter). The writing may be formal or informal. Although most wills are typewritten, they can be handwritten (see the discussion of holographic wills). The writing may be on legal paper, scratch paper, envelopes, napkins, or other paper. A will may incorporate additional documents by reference.
- *Testator's signature*. Wills must be signed.

Will
A declaration of how a person wants his or her property to be distributed upon death.

Testator or testatrix
The person who makes a will.

Beneficiary
A person or organization designated in the will that receives all or a portion of the testator's property at the time of the testator's death.

Statute of Wills
A state statute that establishes the requirements for making a valid will.

Exhibit 15.1 **Parties to a will**

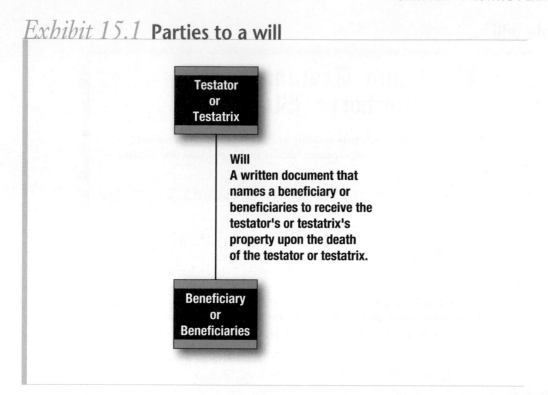

Testator or Testatrix

Will
A written document that names a beneficiary or beneficiaries to receive the testator's or testatrix's property upon the death of the testator or testatrix.

Beneficiary or Beneficiaries

Most jurisdictions require the testator's signature to appear at the end of the will. This is to prevent fraud that could occur if someone were to add provisions to the will below the testator's signature. Generally, courts have held that initials ("R.K.H."), a nickname ("Buffy"), title ("mother"), or even an "X" is a valid signature on a will if it can be proven that the testator intended it to be his or her signature.

Attestation by Witnesses

Wills must be attested to by mentally competent witnesses. Although state law varies, most states require two or three witnesses to **attestation**. The witnesses do not have to reside in the jurisdiction in which the testator is domiciled. Most jurisdictions stipulate that interested parties (e.g., a beneficiary under the will or the testator's attorney) cannot be witnesses. If an interested party has attested to a will, state law either voids any clauses that benefit such person or voids the entire will.

Witnesses usually sign the will following the signature of the testator. This is called the **attestation clause.** Most jurisdictions require that each witness attest to the will in the presence of the other witnesses.

A will that meets the requirements of the Statute of Wills is called a *formal will*. A sample will is shown as Exhibit 15.2.

Attestation
The action of a will being witnessed by the required number of competent people.

Changing a Will

A will cannot be amended by merely striking out existing provisions and adding new ones. **Codicils** are the legal way to change an existing will. A codicil is a separate document that must be executed with the same formalities as a will. In addition, it must incorporate by reference the will it is amending. The codicil and the will then are read as one instrument. A codicil is shown as Exhibit 15.3.

Codicil
A separate document that must be executed to amend a will. It must be executed with the same formalities as a will.

Revoking a Will

A will may be revoked by acts of the testator. A will is revoked if the testator intentionally burns, tears, obliterates, or otherwise destroys it. A properly executed

Exhibit 15.2 **Sample will**

Last Will and Testament of Florence Winthorpe Blueblood

I, FLORENCE WINTHORPE BLUEBLOOD, presently residing at Boston, County of Suffolk, Massachusetts, being of sound and disposing mind and memory, hereby make, publish, and declare this to be my Last Will and Testament.

FIRST. I hereby revoke any and all Wills and Codicils previously made by me.

SECOND. I direct that my just debts and funeral expenses be paid out of my Estate as soon as practicable after my death.

THIRD. I am presently married to Theodore Hannah Blueblood III.

FOURTH. I hereby nominate and appoint my husband as the Personal Representative of this my Last Will and Testament. If he is unable to serve as Personal Representative, then I nominate and appoint Mildred Yardly Winthorpe as Personal Representative of this my Last Will and Testament. I direct that no bond or other security be required to be posted by my Personal Representative.

FIFTH. I hereby nominate and appoint my husband as Guardian of the person and property of my minor children. In the event that he is unable to serve as Guardian, then I nominate and appoint Mildred Yardly Winthorpe Guardian of the person and property of my minor children. I direct that no bond or other security be required to be posted by any Guardian herein.

SIXTH. I give my Personal Representative authority to exercise all the powers, rights, duties, and immunities conferred upon fiduciaries under law with full power to sell, mortgage, lease, invest, or reinvest all or any part of my Estate on such terms as he or she deems best.

SEVENTH. I hereby give, devise, and bequeath my entire estate to my husband, except for the following specific bequests:

I give my wedding ring to my daughter, Hillary Smythe Blueblood.

I give my baseball card collection to my son, Theodore Hannah Blueblood IV.

In the event that either my above-named daughter or son predeceases me, then and in that event, I give, devise, and bequeath my deceased daughter's or son's bequest to my husband.

EIGHTH. In the event that my husband shall predecease me, then and in that event, I give, devise and bequeath my entire estate, with the exception of the bequests in paragraph SEVENTH, to my beloved children or grandchildren surviving me, per stirpes.

NINTH. In the event I am not survived by my husband or any children or grandchildren, then and in that event, I give, devise, and bequeath my entire estate to Harvard University.

IN WITNESS WHEREOF, I Florence Winthorpe Blueblood, the Testatrix, sign my name to this Last Will and Testament this 3rd day of January, 2007.

_____
(Signature)

Signed, sealed, published and declared by the above-named Testatrix, as and for her Last Will and Testament, in the presence of us, who at her request, in her presence and in the presence of one another, have hereunto subscribed our names as attesting witnesses, the day and year last written above.

Witness   *Address*

_____   _____

_____   _____

_____   _____

Disinherit: The prankish action of the ghosts in cutting the pockets out of trousers.

Frank McKinney Hubbard
The Roycroft Dictionary (1923)

subsequent will revokes a prior will if it specifically states that it is the testator's intention to do so. If the second will does not expressly revoke the prior will, the wills are read together. If any will provisions are inconsistent, the provisions in the second will controls.

Wills can be revoked by operation of law. For example, divorce or annulment revokes disposition of property to the former spouse under the will. The remainder of

Exhibit 15.3 **Sample codicil**

SECOND CODICIL TO
THE LAST WILL AND TESTAMENT OF
SARA ELLIOTT

I, SARA ELLIOTT, of Scottsdale, Maricopa County, Arizona, declare this to be a Second Codicil to my Last Will and Testament dated March 13, 2000, and the Codicil to my Last Will and Testament dated June 22, 2002.

ARTICLE FIRST: I hereby revoke Article Third of my Will dated March 13, 2000, as amended by the Codicil of June 22, 2002, and substitute the following:

    (a) I devise and bequeath all my jewelry to my daughter, Kaylee E. Sam, presently of Mesa, Arizona.

    (b) I devise and bequeath the house and real property located at 1840 Norwood Place, Clearwater, Florida, to my daughter, Kaylee E. Sam, presently of Mesa, Arizona.

ARTICLE SECOND: I do hereby reaffirm all other provisions of my Last Will and Testament dated March 13, 2000, as amended by my First Codicil to my Last Will and Testament dated June 22, 2002.

IN WITNESS WHEREOF, I have hereunto set my hand this _____ day of _____ 2007.

_____

SARA ELLIOTT

The preceding instrument consisting of two typewritten pages, identified by the signature of the testatrix, was on the date thereof, signed, published and declared by SARA ELLIOTT in the presence of us who, in her presence and at her request and in the presence of each other, have subscribed our names as witnesses hereto.

_____

    (Name)   *(Address)*

_____

    (Name)   *(Address)*

_____

    (Name)   *(Address)*

---

the will is valid. The birth of a child after a will has been executed does not revoke the will but does entitle the child to receive his or her share of the parents' estate as determined by state statute.

MEET THE COURTHOUSE TEAM

Registrar of Wills

Initiation of the proceedings involving wills and the administration of estates may be delegated to the Registrar of Wills, who may be an elected official or one appointed to oversee the authentication of wills. The process, usually referred to as probate, starts with filing of the will and any codicils to the will with the court. Typically this involves presenting the will together with a death certificate to the court-designated officers.

The named executor or executrix—or administrator where no executor is available or named in the will—usually must appear at the same time and acknowledge his or her willingness to act as the executor or administrator. Depending upon the requirements of the local jurisdiction, the subscribing witnesses to the will also may be required to appear to authenticate their signatures and the will and the signature of the deceased.

Filing fees are part of the process, and appropriate checks for payment are generally required. Fees may vary depending upon the size of the probate estate. Additional forms may be required with regard to the assets and their values. In some jurisdictions, the Registrar of Wills or his or her agents may come to the attorney's office or to other locations as a convenience to the parties or where the parties, by virtue of age or disability, are unable to go to the courthouse.

SPECIAL TYPES OF WILLS

The law recognizes some types of wills that do not meet all of the requirements discussed above. Two special types of wills admitted by the courts are holographic wills and noncupative wills.

Holographic Wills

Holographic wills are entirely handwritten and signed by the testator. The writing may be in ink, pencil, crayon, or some other writing instrument. Many states recognize the validity of such wills even though they are not witnessed.

Noncupative Wills

Noncupative wills are oral wills made before witnesses. These wills are usually valid only if they are made during the testator's last illness. They sometimes are called **deathbed wills** or **dying declarations**.

TESTAMENTARY GIFTS

In a will, a gift of real estate by will is called a **devise**. A gift of personal property by will is called a **bequest** or **legacy**. Gifts in wills can be specific, general, or residuary.

- *Specific gifts:* specifically named pieces of property, such as a ring, a boat, or a piece of real estate.
- *General gifts:* gifts that do not identify the specific property from which the gift is to be made, such as a cash amount that can come from any source in the decedent's estate.
- *Residuary gifts:* established by a **residuary clause** in the will. The clause might state, for example, "I give my daughter the rest, remainder, and

---

Holographic will
Will that is entirely handwritten and signed by the testator.

Deathbed will
Oral will that is made dying declaration before a witness during the testator's last illness.

residual of my estate." This means that any portion of the estate left after the debts, taxes, and specific and general gifts have been paid belongs to the decedent's daughter.

A person who inherits property under a will or an intestacy statute takes the property subject to all of the outstanding claims against it (e.g., liens, mortgages). A person can **renounce an inheritance**—and often does—when the liens or mortgages against the property exceed the value of the property.

Videotaped Wills

Many will contests involve written wills.

The contesters allege things such as mental incapacity of the testator at the time the will was made, undue influence, fraud, or duress. Although the written will speaks for itself, the mental capacity of the testator and the voluntariness of his or her actions cannot be determined from the writing alone.

To prevent unwarranted will contests, a testator can use a **videotaped will** to supplement a written will. Videotaping a will that can withstand challenges by disgruntled relatives and alleged heirs involves a certain amount of planning.

The following procedure should be followed. A written will should be prepared to comply with the state's Statute of Wills. The video session should not begin until after the testator has become familiar with the document. The video should begin with the testator reciting the will verbatim. Next, the lawyer should ask the testator questions to demonstrate the testator's sound mind and understanding of the implications of his or her actions. The execution ceremony—the signing of the will by the testator and the attestation by the witnesses—should be the last segment on the film. The videotape then should be stored in a safe place.

With the testator's actions crystallized on videotape, a judge or jury will be able to determine the testator's mental capacity at the time the will was made and the voluntariness of his or her testamentary gifts. In addition, fraudulent competing wills will fall in the face of such proof.

Simultaneous Deaths

Sometimes people who would inherit property from each other die simultaneously. If it is impossible to determine who died first, the question becomes one of inheritance. The **Uniform Simultaneous Death Act** provides that each deceased person's property is distributed as if he or she survived.

Consider this example: Suppose a husband and wife make wills leaving their entire estate to each other. Assume that the husband and wife are killed simultaneously in an airplane crash. Here, the husband's property would go to his relatives and the wife's property would go to her relatives.

Joint and Mutual Wills

If two or more testators execute the same instrument as their will, the document is called a **joint will.** A joint will may be held invalid as to one testator but not the other(s).

Mutual or **reciprocal will** are developed when two or more testators execute separate wills that make testamentary dispositions of their property to each other on the condition that the survivor leave the remaining property on his or her death as agreed by the testators. The wills usually are separate instruments with reciprocal terms. Because of their contractual nature, mutual wills cannot be revoked unilaterally after one of the parties has died.

Undue Influence

A will may be found to be invalid if it was made as a result of **undue influence** on the testator. Undue influence can be inferred from the facts and circumstances

Undue influence
Occurs where one person takes advantage of another person's mental, emotional, or physical weakness and unduly persuades that person to make a will; the persuasion by the wrongdoer must overcome the free will of the testator.

THE PARALEGAL AND ELDER LAW

A relatively new area of the law that paralegals can work in is called elder law. Many lawyers and the paralegals who work for them specialize in this area of law, which provides legal services to the elderly in society.

Elder law cannot be found in one place. It is a composite of many areas of the law, including providing estate planning, giving tax advice, drafting wills and trusts, preparing living wills and health care proxies, representing clients in Medicaid, Social Security, and disability matters, and other areas of the law affecting the elderly.

Many lawyers specialize in estate planning—that is, planning how the estate of a client will be distributed when the client dies. Estate planning requires detailed knowledge of state and federal inheritance laws and tax laws. Attorneys working in this field advise clients as to the best means of accomplishing their goals.

Paralegals assist lawyers in estate planning. This may consist of attending meetings, obtaining information from clients, and conducting legal research. Paralegals also assist lawyers in drafting wills, trust agreements, and other documents required to effectuate the client's estate plan.

In today's modern world, many individuals want to direct how their medical care will be handled if they are not able to make such decisions. Persons who do not want their life prolonged indefinitely by artificial means can sign a living will in advance, setting forth their wishes. In addition, people can sign a health care proxy naming individuals to make medical decisions if they are unable to do so. Paralegals assist lawyers in drafting living wills, health care proxies, and other related documents in this field of law.

A relatively new area of the law is the use of living trusts. Persons establish living trusts while they are alive. A living trust is a method of holding property during a person's lifetime and distributing the property upon a person's death. Living trusts have become a major form of estate planning. Paralegals assist lawyers in this area of the law and preparing the documents necessary to create the living trusts.

Another area of elder law involves advising clients about their rights under government programs. Such programs include Social Security benefits, Medicaid benefits, and other government-sponsored benefits for the elderly. Paralegals often are called upon to assist lawyers in obtaining such benefits for elderly clients.

The specialized and complex area of elder law provides substantial employment opportunities for paralegals. Paralegals who work in this field must have detailed knowledge of the state and federal laws, regulations, procedures, forms, applications, and other documents necessary to carry forth the estate planning wishes and other goals of clients that are represented by the lawyer the paralegal works for.

surrounding the making of the will. For example, if an 85-year-old woman leaves all of her property to the lawyer who drafted her will and ignores her blood relatives, the court is likely to presume undue influence.

Undue influence is difficult to prove by direct evidence, but it may be proved by circumstantial evidence. The elements that courts examine to find the presence of undue influence include the following.

- The benefactor and beneficiary are involved in a relationship of confidence and trust.
- The will contains substantial benefit to the beneficiary.
- The beneficiary caused or assisted in effecting execution of the will.
- There was an opportunity to exert influence.
- The will contains an unnatural disposition of the testator's property.
- The bequests constitute a change from a former will.
- The testator was highly susceptible to the undue influence.

PROBATE

When a person dies, his or her property must be collected, debts and taxes paid, and the remainder of the estate distributed to the beneficiaries of the will or the heirs under the state intestacy statute. This process is called **settlement of the estate** or **probate**. The process and procedures for settling an estate are governed by state statute. A specialized state court, called the probate court, usually supervises the administration and settlement of an estate.

A *personal representative* must be appointed to administer the estate during its settlement phase. If the testator's will names the personal representative, that person is called an **executor** or **executrix**.

The **Uniform Probate Code (UPC)** was promulgated to establish uniform rules for creating wills, administering estates, and resolving conflicts in estate settlements. These rules provide a speedy, efficient, and less expensive method than many existing state laws for settling estates. Only about one-third of the states have adopted all or part of the UPC.

Probate (settlement of estate)
The process of a deceased's property being collected, debts and taxes being paid, and the remainder of the estate being distributed.

Lineal Descendants

A testator's will may state that property is to be left to his or her **lineal descendants** (children, grandchildren, great-grandchildren, etc.) either *per stirpes* or *per capita*. The difference between these two methods is discussed in the following paragraphs.

Lineal descendants
The testator's children, grandchildren, great-grandchildren, and so on.

Per Stirpes Distribution

Pursuant to *per stirpes* distribution, the lineal descendants *inherit by representation of their parent*; that is, they split what their deceased parent would have received. If their parent is not deceased, they receive nothing.

Consider this example: Suppose Anne dies without a surviving spouse and she had three children, Bart, Beth, and Bruce. Bart, who survives his mother, has no children. Beth has one child, Carla, and they both survive Anne. Bruce, who predeceased his mother, had two children, Clayton and Cathy; and Cathy, who predeceased Anne, had two children, Deborah and Dominic, both of whom survive Anne.

If Anne leaves her estate to her lineal descendants *per stirpes*, Bart and Beth each get one-third, Carla receives nothing because Beth is alive, Clayton gets one-sixth, and Deborah and Dominic each get one-twelfth. Exhibit 15.4 illustrates this example.

Per stirpes distribution
A distribution of the estate that makes grandchildren and great-grandchildren of the deceased inherit by representation of their parent.

The power of making a will is an instrument placed in the hands of individuals for the prevention of private calamity.

Jeremy Bentham
Principles of the Civil Code (1748)

Per Capita Distribution

Pursuant to *per capita* distribution, the lineal descendants *equally share the property of the estate*. That is, children of the testator share equally with grandchildren, great-grandchildren, and so forth.

Consider this example: Suppose the facts are the same as in the previous example, except that Anne leaves her estate to her lineal descendants *per capita*. In this case, all of the surviving lineal descendants—Bart, Beth, Carla, Clayton, Deborah, and Dominic—share equally in the estate. That is, they each get one-sixth of Anne's estate. See Exhibit 15.5.

Per capita distribution
A distribution of the estate that makes each grandchild and great-grandchild of the deceased inherit equally with the children of the deceased.

Ademption and Abatement

If a testator leaves a specific gift of property to a beneficiary, but the property is no longer in the estate of the testator when he or she dies, the beneficiary receives nothing. This doctrine is called the doctrine of **ademption**.

Ademption
A principle that says if a testator leaves a specific devise of property to a beneficiary, but the property is no longer in the estate when the testator dies, the beneficiary receives nothing.

Exhibit 15.4 **Example of *per stirpes* distribution**

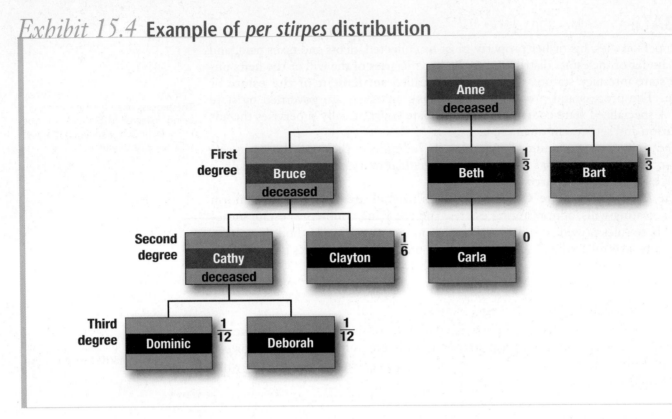

Exhibit 15.5 **Example of *per capita* distribution**

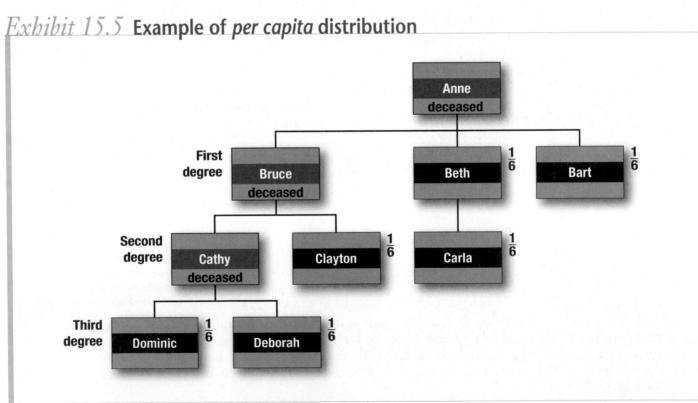

Abatement
If the property the testator leaves is not sufficient to satisfy all the beneficiaries named in a will and there are both general and residuary bequests, the residuary bequest is abated first (i.e., paid last).

If the testator's estate is not large enough to pay all the devises and bequests, the doctrine of **abatement** applies. The doctrine works as follows:

- If a will provides for both general and residuary gifts, the residuary gifts are abated first. For example, suppose a testator executes a will when he owns $500,000 of property that leaves (1) $100,000 to the Red Cross,

checklist ☑ COMPARISON OF DYING WITH AND WITHOUT A VALID WILL

SITUATION	PARTIES WHO RECEIVE DECEASED'S PROPERTY
Deceased dies with a valid will	*Beneficiaries* named in the will.
Deceased dies without a valid will	*Heirs* set forth in the applicable state intestacy statute. If no heirs, the deceased's property escheats to the state.

(2) $100,000 to a university, and (3) the residue to his niece. Suppose that when the testator dies, his estate is worth only $225,000. Here, the Red Cross and the university each receive $100,000 and the niece receives $25,000.

■ If a will provides only for general gifts, the reductions are proportionate. For example, suppose a testator's will leaves $75,000 to two beneficiaries, but the estate is only $100,000. Each beneficiary would receive $50,000.

Intestate Succession

If a person dies without a will, or his or her will fails for some legal reason, that person dies **intestate**. In this case, the deceased person's property is distributed to his or her relatives pursuant to the state's **intestacy statute**.

Relatives who receive property under these statutes are called **heirs**. Although intestacy statutes differ from state to state, the general rule is that the deceased's real property is distributed according to the intestacy statute of the state where the real property is located and the deceased's personal property is distributed according to the intestacy statute of the state where the deceased had his or her permanent residence.

Intestacy statutes usually leave the deceased's property to his or her heirs in this order: spouse, children, lineal heirs (e.g., grandchildren, parents, brothers and sisters), collateral heirs (e.g., aunts, uncles, nieces, nephews), and other next of kin (e.g., cousins). If the deceased has no surviving relatives, the deceased's property **escheats** (goes) to the state. In-laws do not inherit under most intestacy statutes. If a child dies before his or her parents, the child's spouse does not receive the inheritance.

To avoid the distribution of an estate as provided in an intestacy statute, a person should have a properly written, signed, and witnessed will that distributes the estate property as the testator wishes.

Intestate
The state of having died without leaving a will.

Intestacy statute
A state statute that specifies how a deceased's property will be distributed if he or she dies without a will or if the last will is declared void and there is no prior valid will.

LIVING WILL AND HEALTH CARE PROXY

Technological breakthroughs have greatly increased the life span of human beings. This same technology, however, permits life to be sustained long after a person is "brain dead." Some people say they have a right to refuse such treatment. Others argue that human life must be preserved at all costs. In 1990, the U.S. Supreme Court was called upon to decide the **right to die** issue. [*Cruzan v. Director, Missouri Department of Health*, 497 U.S. 261, 110 S.Ct. 2841, 111 L.Ed.2d 224, 1990 U.S. Lexis 3301 (1990)].

In the *Cruzan* case, the U.S. Supreme Court acknowledged that the right to refuse medical treatment is a personal liberty protected by the due process clause of the U.S. Constitution. The Court stated that this interest must be expressed through clear and convincing proof that the patient did not want to be sustained by artificial means.

The clear message of the Supreme Court's opinion is that people who do not want their lives prolonged indefinitely by artificial means should sign **a living will** that stipulates their wishes before catastrophe strikes and they become unable to express it themselves because of an illness or an accident. The living will should state which life-saving measures the signor does and does not want. In addition, the signor can specify that he or she wants to have any such treatments withdrawn if doctors determine that there is no hope of a meaningful recovery. The living will provides clear and convincing proof of a patient's wishes with respect to medical treatment.

In a living will or in a separate document usually called a **health care directive** or **health care proxy**, the maker should name someone, such as a spouse or another relative or trusted party, to be his or her **health care agent** to make all health care decisions in accordance with his or her wishes in the living will. An alternative person also should be named in case the originally designated health care agent is unable or chooses not to serve in that capacity.

A well known example of a person not having a living will and health care proxy was the Terri Shiavo case. In February 1990, Terri collapsed and was placed on life support systems. For 15 years, Terri remained in a vegetative state. Her husband wanted Terri to be taken off life support systems, but her parents did not. After years of legal battles that included more than fifty trial and appellate court hearings, in April 2005 the Florida Supreme Court ordered Terri to be taken off life support systems. Days later she died.

Much of the legal battle concerned what Terri's intention would have been about staying on, or being removed from, life support systems. If Terri would have had a living will and health care proxy, her intentions would have been clear. A living will and health care proxy is set forth in Exhibit 15.6.

TRUSTS

Trust
A legal arrangement established when one person transfers title to property to another person to be held and used for the benefit of a third person.

Settlor, trustor, or transferor
Person who creates a trust.

Trustee
Person or entity that holds legal title to the trust *corpus* and manages the trust for the benefit of the beneficiary or beneficiaries.

Trust *corpus* or trust *res*
The property and assets held in trust.

Income beneficiary
Person or entity to be paid income from the trust.

Remainder beneficiary
Person or entity to receive the trust *corpus* upon termination of the trust.

A **trust** is a legal arrangement under which one person—the **settlor, trustor,** or **transferor**—delivers and transfers legal title to property to another person, bank, or other entity called the **trustee** to be held and used for the benefit of a third person or entity (the **beneficiary** of a trust). The property and assets held in trust is called the **trust *corpus*** or **trust *res***. The trust has legal title to the trust *corpus*, and the beneficiary has equitable title. Unlike wills, trusts are not public documents, so property can be transferred in privacy.

A trust can be created and become effective during a trustor's lifetime, or it can be created during a trustor's lifetime to become effective upon the trustor's death.

During the existence of the trust, the trustee collects money owed to the trust, pays taxes and necessary expenses of the trust, makes investment decisions, pays the income to the income beneficiary, and keeps necessary records of transactions.

Trusts often provide that any trust income is to be paid to a person or entity called the **income beneficiary**. The person or entity to receive the trust corpus upon the termination of the trust is called the **remainder beneficiary**. The income beneficiary and the remainder beneficiary can be the same person or different persons. The designated beneficiary can be any identifiable person, animal (such as a pet), charitable organization, or other institution or cause that the settlor chooses. There can be multiple income and remainder beneficiaries. An entire class of persons—for example, "my grandchildren"—can be named.

A trust can allow the trustee to invade (use) the trust *corpus* for certain purposes. These purposes can be named (e.g., "for the beneficiary's college education"). The trust agreement usually specifies how the receipts and expenses of the trust are to be divided between the income beneficiary and the remainder beneficiary.

Generally, the trustee has broad management powers over the trust property. Thus, the trustee can invest the trust property to preserve its capital and make it productive. The trustee must follow any restrictions on investments contained in the trust agreement or state statute.

Exhibit 15.7 shows the parties to a trust.

Exhibit 15.6 **Sample living will and health care proxy**

Living Will and Health Care Proxy

I. Living Will Including Statement Concerning Right to Die

Death is as much a reality as birth, growth, maturity and old age—it is the one certainty of life. If the time comes when I, John Doe, can no longer take part in decisions for my own future, let this statement stand as an expression of my wishes and directions to my Health Care Agent and others while I am still of sound mind. I intend, without otherwise limiting the absolute authority granted to my Health Care Agent in this instrument, that this instrument be binding upon my Health Care Agent.

If the situation should arise in which there is no reasonable expectation of my recovery from extreme physical or mental disability, including, but not limited to, a circumstance where there is no reasonable expectation that I will recover consciousness, commonly referred to as "brain dead," I direct that I be allowed to die and not be kept alive by medications, artificial means, including but not limited to artificial nutrition and hydration, or "heroic measures." Without limiting the generality of the foregoing, I hereby consent in such situation to an order not to attempt cardiopulmonary resuscitation. I do, however, ask that medication be mercifully administered to me to alleviate suffering even though this may shorten my remaining life and retard my consciousness.

II. Health Care Proxy

I hereby appoint my spouse, Jane Doe, to be my health care agent to make any and all health care decisions in accordance with my wishes and instructions as stated above and as otherwise known to her. In the event the person I appoint above is unable, unwilling or unavailable to act as my Health Care Agent, I hereby appoint my twin brother, Jack Doe, as my health care agent.

This health care proxy shall take effect in the event that I become unable to make my own health care decisions. I hereby revoke any prior health care proxy given by me to the extent it purports to confer the authority herein granted. I understand that, unless I revoke it, this health care proxy will remain in effect indefinitely.

Although I do not know today the exact circumstances that will exist when my Health Care Agent is called upon to make a decision or decisions on my behalf, I have selected my Health Care Agent with the confidence that such person understands my feelings in these matters and will make the decision I will want made considering the circumstances as they exist at the time. It is my intention, therefore, that the decision of my Health Care Agent be taken as a final and binding decision of mine, and will be the conclusive interpretation of the wishes I have made known in this document.

III. Waiver and Indemnity

To the extent permitted by law, I, for myself and for my heirs, executors, legal representatives and assigns, hereby release and discharge and agree to indemnify and hold harmless my Health Care Agent from and against any claim or liability whatsoever resulting from or arising out of my Health Care Agent's reliance on my wishes and directions as expressed herein. To induce any third party to act hereunder, I hereby agree that any third party receiving a duly executed copy or facsimile of this instrument may act hereunder, and that revocation or termination by me hereof shall be ineffective as to such third party unless and until actual notice or knowledge of such revocation shall have been received by such third party, and, to the extent permitted by law, I, for myself and for my heirs, executors, legal representatives and assigns, hereby release and discharge and agree to indemnify and hold harmless any such third party from and against any claims or liability whatsoever that may arise against such third party by reason of such third party having relied on the provisions of this instrument.

I understand the full import of this directive and I am emotionally and mentally competent to make this directive.

Signed _____

The declarant has been personally known to me and I believe him or her to be of sound mind.

Witness _____

Witness _____

Exhibit 15.7 **Parties to a trust**

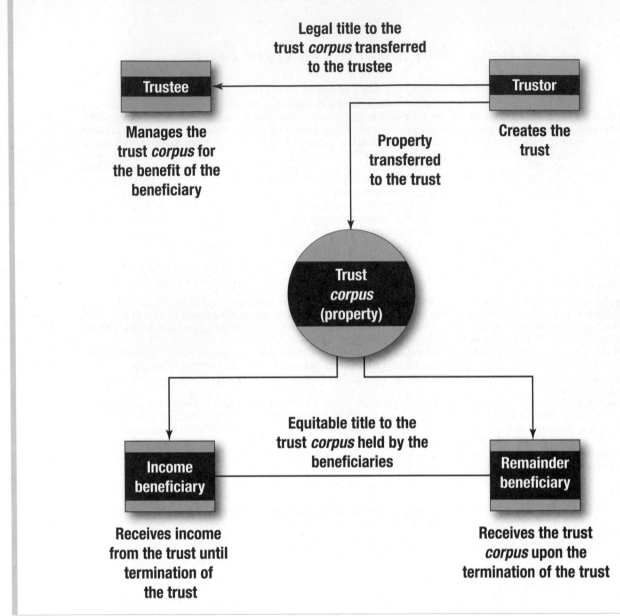

Express Trust

Express trust
A trust created voluntarily by the settlor.

Inter vivos **trust**
A trust that is created while the settlor is alive.

Testamentary trust
A trust created by will: the trust comes into existence when the settlor dies.

An **express trust** is created voluntarily by the settlor. It usually is written. The agreement is called a *trust instrument* or *trust agreement*. Express trusts fall into two categories:

1. *inter vivos* **trust**, created while the settlor is alive. The settlor transfers legal title of property to a named trustee to hold, administer, and manage for the benefit of named beneficiaries.
2. **testamentary trust**, created by will. The trust comes into existence when the settlor dies. If the will that establishes the trust is found to be invalid, the trust is also invalid.

Consider this example: Suppose grandmother creates a trust and places assets in the trust that consist of stocks, bonds, bank accounts, and an apartment building. In the trust document, grandmother designates her daughter to receive the income from the trust (e.g., dividends, interest, and rental income) until the daughter dies, and upon the

ASSISTED SUICIDE UPHELD BY THE U.S. SUPREME COURT

In 1994, the voters of the state of Oregon approved a ballot measure that enacted the Oregon Death with Dignity Act (ODWDA). The Act exempts state-licensed physicians who prescribe and dispense lethal doses of drugs to assist terminally ill patients to commit suicide. To be eligible for doctor-assisted suicide, the patient's attending physician must give his or her opinion that the patient suffers from an incurable and irreversible disease that will cause death within six months. A second opinion must be obtained from a consulting physician that supports the attending physician's opinion. The patient may choose to voluntarily ingest a lethal dose of prescription medicine prescribed or dispensed by the physician. Oregon physicians may prescribe and dispense the medication but may not administer the medication.

In 1970, the federal government enacted the Controlled Substances Act (CSA). The purpose of this Act was to combat drug abuse and control the distribution of controlled substances. The Act makes it a crime to distribute and dispense controlled substances without authority to do so. The drugs the Oregon physicians prescribed for assisted suicides are regulated under the CSA. In 2001, the U.S. Attorney General issued an Interpretive Rule stating that the use of controlled substances to assist suicide was not a legitimate medical practice.

The state of Oregon challenged the Interpretive Rule in federal District Court. The District Court held for Oregon and issued a permanent injunction prohibiting enforcement of the Rule. The Court of Appeals affirmed this decision. The U.S. Supreme Court agreed to hear the federal government's appeal.

In the case, the Supreme Court addressed the issue of whether the federal Controlled Substances Act authorized the U.S. Attorney General to prohibit physician-assisted suicides permitted by Oregon Law. In its opinion, the Supreme Court stated:

> In deciding whether the CSA can be read as prohibiting physician-assisted suicide, we look to the statute's text and design. The statute and our case law amply support the conclusion that Congress regulates medical practice insofar as it bars doctors from using their prescription-writing powers as a means to engage in illicit drug dealing and trafficking as conventionally understood. Beyond this, however, the statute manifests no intent to regulate the practice of medicine generally. The silence is understandable given the structure and limitations of federalism, which allows states great latitude under their police powers to legislate as to the protection of the lives, limbs, health, comfort, and quiet of all persons.
>
> Rather than simply decriminalizing assisted suicide, the ODWDA limits its exercise to the attending physicians of terminally ill patients, physicians who must be licensed by Oregon's Board of Medical Examiners. In the face of the CSA's silence on the practice of medicine generally, and its recognition of state regulation of the medical profession, it is difficult to defend the U.S. Attorney General's declaration that the statute impliedly criminalizes physician-assisted suicide.

The U.S. Supreme Court held that the federal Controlled Substances Act does not prohibit physician-assisted suicide as provided for under Oregon law. The Supreme Court affirmed the decisions of the court of appeals and the district court.

Source: Gonzales, Attorney General v. Oregon, 126 S.Ct. 904, 1963 L.Ed.2d 748 (2006).

daughter's death the trust corpus is to be divided equally among grandmother's three granddaughters. Grandmother names Country Bank the trustee. This is a testamentary trust. Grandmother is the trustor, Country Bank is the trustee, the daughter is the income beneficiary, and the three granddaughters are the remainder beneficiaries.

Constructive Trust

A **constructive trust** is an equitable trust that is implied by law to avoid fraud, unjust enrichment, and injustice. In constructive trust arrangements, the holder of the actual title to property (i.e., the trustee) holds the property in trust for its rightful owner.

Constructive trust
An equitable trust that is implied by law to avoid fraud, unjust enrichment, and injustice.

A constructive trust is the formula through which the conscience of equity finds expression.

Cardozo, J.
Beatty v. Guggenheim Exploration Co.
(1919)

Consider this example: Suppose Thad and Kaye are partners. Assume Kaye embezzles partnership funds and uses the stolen funds to purchase a piece of real estate. In this case, the court can impose a constructive trust under which Kaye (who holds actual title to the land) is considered a trustee who is holding the property in trust for Thad, its rightful owner.

Resulting Trust

Resulting trust
A trust that is implied from the conduct of the parties.

A **resulting trust** is implied from the conduct of the parties. For example, suppose Henry is purchasing a piece of real estate but cannot attend the closing. He asks his brother, Gregory, to attend the closing and take title to the property until he can return. In this case, Gregory holds the title to the property as trustee for Henry until he returns.

Special Types of Trusts

Trusts may be created for special purposes. Three types of special trusts that are fairly common are:

1. **charitable trusts**, created for the benefit of a segment of society or society in general. An example is a trust that is created for the construction and maintenance of a public park.
2. **spendthrift trusts**, designed to prevent a beneficiary's personal creditors from reaching his or her trust interest. All control over the trust

ETHICAL *Perspective*

Ms. Vivian Zhong works as a paralegal for a law firm that specializes in the area of elder law, estates, and trusts. The lawyers of the firm engage in estate planning for clients, draft wills and trusts, and represent clients in other areas of elder law. As required by law, the law firm has established trust funds at banks where clients' funds are kept on deposit during the period that a will or trust is being administered by the law firm.

Mr. Richard Hawthorne is a partner of the law firm. Mr. Hawthorne currently is going through a divorce and has several children in college whom he helps support. Mr. Hawthorne, who needs money to support himself and his family, falsifies records at the law firm and misappropriates $200,000 from a trust fund administered by the law firm.

Ms. Zhong, who is the paralegal assigned to assist in administering the trust fund, discovers Mr. Hawthorne's misappropriation of the funds from the trust. Ms. Zhong faces the dilemma of whether to report Mr. Hawthorne's misappropriation of the trust funds, and if so, to whom.

Section EC-1.2(f) of the *Model Code of Ethics and Professional Responsibility and Guidance for Enforcement* (Model Code) of the National Federation of Paralegal Associations, Inc. (NFPA) provides guidance. Section EC-1.2(f) states:

> *A paralegal shall advise the proper authority of nonconfidential knowledge of any dishonest or fraudulent acts by any person pertaining to the handling of the funds, securities, or other assets of a client. The authority to whom the report is made shall depend on the nature and circumstances of the possible misconduct (e.g., ethics committees of law firms, corporations and/or paralegal associations, local or state bar associations, local prosecutors, administrative agencies, etc.). Failure to report such knowledge is in itself misconduct and shall be treated as such under these rules.*

Source: *Reprinted by permission from The National Federation of Paralegal Associations, Inc., www.paralegals.org*

Applying this section to the facts of this case, Ms. Zhong owes a duty to report Mr. Hawthorne's misappropriation of the funds from the trust account to the ethics committee of the law firm, and if there is no such committee, then to the senior partners of the law firm. Ms. Zhong has a duty to report Mr. Hawthorne's misappropriation to government authorities if she sees that the partners of the firm are taking no action against Mr. Hawthorne to recover the funds and to report Mr. Hawthorne's activities to the bar association and appropriate government authorities.

is removed from the beneficiary. Personal creditors still can go after trust income that is paid to the beneficiary, however.

3. **totten trusts**, created when a person deposits money in a bank account in his or her own name and holds it as a trustee for the benefit of another person. A totten trust is a tentative trust because (a) the trustee can add or withdraw funds from the account, and (b) the trust can be revoked at any time prior to his or her death or prior to completing delivery of the funds to the beneficiary.

Termination of a Trust

A trust is irrevocable unless the settlor reserves the right to revoke it. Most trusts fall into the first category. Usually, a trust either contains a specific termination date or provides that it will terminate upon the happening of an event (e.g., when the remainder beneficiary reaches a certain age). Upon termination, the trust *corpus* is distributed as provided in the trust agreement.

LIVING TRUSTS

Living trusts have become a popular method for holding property during a person's lifetime and distributing the property upon that person's death. A living trust works as follows: During his or her life, a person establishes a living trust, which is a legal entity used for estate planning. A living trust also is referred to as a **grantor's trust** or a **revocable trust.** The person who creates the trust is called the **grantor**, or the **trustor**.

Benefits of a Living Trust

The primary purpose of using a living trust is to avoid probate associated with using a will. If a person dies with a will, the will must be probated so the deceased's assets can be properly distributed according to the will. A probate judge is named to oversee the probate process, and all documents, including the will, are public record. By contrast, a living trust is private.

When the grantor dies, the assets are owned by the living trust and therefore are not subject to probate proceedings. In addition, if real property is owned in more than one state and a will is used, ancillary probate must be conducted in the other state. If a living trust is used, ancillary probate is avoided.

Living trusts often are promoted for claimed benefits that do not exist. The true facts are that a living trust:

- does not reduce estate taxes any more than a will does.
- does not reduce the grantor's income taxes. All the income earned by the trust is attributed to the grantor, who must pay income taxes on the earnings just as if the trust did not exist.
- does not avoid creditors. Thus, creditors can obtain liens against property in the trust.
- is subject to property division upon divorce.
- is usually not cheaper than a will. Both require payments to lawyers and usually to accountants and other professionals to draft and probate a will or draft and to manage a living trust.
- does not avoid controversies upon the grantor's death. Like wills, living trusts can be challenged for lack of capacity, undue influence, duress, and other legal grounds.

Funding and Operation of a Living Trust

To fund a living trust, the grantor transfers title to his or her property to the trust. This property is called the trust *corpus*. Bank accounts, stock certificates, real estate,

Living trust
A method for holding property during a person's lifetime and distributing the property upon that person's death. Also called a *grantor's trust* and a *revocable trust*.

Grantor (trustor)
The person who creates a living trust. Also called the *trustor*.

The law relating to public policy cannot remain immutable, it must change with the passage of time. The wind of change blows on it.

L.J. Danckwerts
Nagle v. Feilden (1966)

personal property, intangible property, and other property owned by the grantor must be retitled to the trust's name.

For example, the grantor must execute deeds transferring title to real estate to the trust. Once property is transferred to the trust, the trust is considered funded. A living trust is revocable during the grantor's lifetime. Thus, a grantor can later change his or her mind and undo the trust and retake title of the property in his or her own name.

A living trust names a trustee who is responsible for maintaining, investing, buying, or selling trust assets. The trustee is usually the grantor. Thus, the grantor who establishes the trust does not lose control of the property placed in the trust and may manage and invest trust assets during his or her lifetime. The trust should name a *successor trustee* to replace the grantor–trustee if the grantor becomes incapacitated or too ill to manage the trust.

Beneficiaries

A living trust names a beneficiary or beneficiaries who are entitled to receive income from the living trust while it is in existence and to receive the property of the trust when the grantor dies. Usually the grantor is the income beneficiary, who receives the income from the trust during his or her lifetime. Upon the death of the grantor, assets of the trust are distributed to the remainder beneficiary or beneficiaries named in the trust. The designated trustee has the fiduciary duties of identifying assets, paying creditors, paying income and estate taxes, transferring assets to named beneficiaries, and rendering an accounting.

Pour-Over Will

Pour-over will
A will that, upon the grantor's death, distributes the grantor's property that is not in the living will.

A **pour-over will** is necessary to distribute any property acquired in the name of the grantor after the living trust is established or any property that was not transferred to the trust in the first place. The pour-over will transfers this property to the trust upon the grantor's death, and it then is distributed to the named beneficiaries of the trust. A pour-over will is subject to probate and is therefore public. A pour-over will usually is created at the same time that the living trust is established.

A living trust is a legitimate planning tool for many people. A person should seek professional advice from and have an attorney draft the living trust, pour-over will, and other necessary documents.

ASPIRATIONAL STANDARDS FOR THE PRACTICE OF ELDER LAW

Excerpts from National Academy of Elder Law Attorneys

PREAMBLE

In the past 20 years, Elder Law has developed as a separate specialty area because of the unique and complex issues faced by older persons. Elder Law includes helping such persons and their families with planning for incapacity and long-term care, Medicaid and Medicare, including coverage of nursing home and home care, health and long-term care insurance, and health care decision making. It also includes the drafting of special needs and other trusts, the selection of long-term care providers, home care and nursing home problem solving, retiree health and income benefits, retirement housing, and fiduciary services or representation.

In these and other areas, the Elder Law Attorney is often asked to advocate for clients with diminished capacity. Family members and persons with fiduciary responsibilities become involved. The traditional client–attorney relationship is not always clear. Issues such as

**ASPIRATIONAL STANDARDS FOR THE
PRACTICE OF ELDER LAW** *(continued)*

substituted judgment, best interests, and "who is the client?" present problems not regularly faced by other lawyers.

In recognizing Elder Law as a specialty practice area to meet the legal needs of older persons and persons with disabilities and their families, the National Academy of Elder Law Attorneys (NAELA) was founded in 1987. The following Guidelines set out Aspirational Standards of professionalism and ethical behavior for Elder Law Attorneys. They are the product of study and deliberation by NAELA members and, specifically, NAELA's Professionalism and Ethics Committee.

A. Client Identification
The Elder Law Attorney:
   (1) Gathers all information and takes all steps necessary to identify who the client is at the earliest possible stage and communicates that information to the persons immediately involved.
   (2) Meets with the identified prospective or actual client in private at the earliest possible stage so that the client's capacity and voice can be engaged unencumbered. If the attorney determines that it is clearly not in the best interest of the client for the attorney to meet privately with the client, the attorney takes other steps to ensure that the client's wishes are identified and respected.
   (3) Utilizes an engagement agreement, letter or other writing(s) that:
      • identifies the client(s);
      • describes the scope and objectives of representation;
      • discloses any relevant foreseeable conflicts among the clients;
      • explains the lawyer's obligation of confidentiality and confirms that the lawyer will share information and confidences among the joint clients;
      • sets out the fee arrangement (hourly, flat fee, or contingent); and
      • explains when and how the client–attorney relationship may end.
   (4) Oversees the execution of documents that directly affect the interests of an individual only after establishing a client-attorney relationship with the individual.

B. Potential Conflict of Interest
Elder Law Attorneys are frequently approached by families who seek counsel or representation on behalf of one or more persons. If there is no apparent conflict of interest, joint representation may be a preferred form of representation that will further shared goals, common interests, family harmony, economic efficiency, consistency of action, and enhanced likelihood of serving the best interests of the clients. However, because the potential for conflicts always exists whenever two or more persons are represented, the Elder Law Attorney:
   (1) In representing multiple family members ensures that the family members understand who are the clients and whether the representation is Joint (i.e., confidences are shared) or Separate. As used in these Standards, separate representation means representing persons in separate matters where confidences are not shared; joint representation (sometimes referred to as common representation) means representation of multiple clients in the same matter.
   (2) Undertakes joint representation, as permitted by state rules of professional conduct, only after obtaining the consent of the parties after having reviewed with them the advantages and disadvantages of such representation—including the relevant foreseeable conflicts of interest and risks of such representation—in a manner that will be best understood by each person to be represented.
   (3) Treats family members who are not clients as unrepresented persons but accords them involvement in the client's representation so long as it is consistent with the client's wishes and values, and the client consents to the involvement.
   (4) Accepts payment of client fees by a third party only after determining that payment by the third party will not influence the attorney's independent professional judgment on behalf of the client, informing the client who consents to the payment by a third party, and ensuring that the parties understand and agree to the ethical ground rules for third party payment (i.e., non-interference

(continued)

ASPIRATIONAL STANDARDS FOR THE PRACTICE OF ELDER LAW *(continued)*

by the payer, independence of judgment by the attorney on behalf of the client, and confidentiality).

(5) May also serve as a fiduciary for the client, if it is in the client's best interest and if the client gives informed consent after full disclosure.

(6) In representing a client who is a fiduciary under a power of attorney, trust, or conservatorship/guardianship, ensures that the client understands that the duties of both the fiduciary and the attorney ultimately are governed by the known wishes and best interest of the principal.

C. Confidentiality

The Elder Law Attorney:

(1) Carefully explains the obligation of confidentiality to the client and involved parties as early as possible in the representation to avoid misunderstanding, and to ascertain and respect the client's wishes regarding the disclosure of confidential information.

(2) Establishes as a prerequisite to any joint representation a clear understanding and agreement that the attorney shall keep no client secrets from any other client in that joint representation.

(3) Strictly adheres to the obligation of client confidentiality, especially in representation that may involve frequent contacts with family members, care takers, or other involved parties who are not clients.

D. Competent Legal Representation

The Elder Law Attorney:

(1) Recognizes the special range of client needs and professional skills unique to the practice of Elder Law and holds himself or herself out as an Elder Law Attorney only after ensuring his or her professional competence in handling elder law and disability related matters.

(2) Approaches client matters in a holistic manner, recognizing that legal representation of clients often is enhanced by the involvement of other professionals, support groups, and aging network resources.

(3) Regularly pursues continuing professional education and peer collaboration in Elder Law. Continuing education should include a broad range of Elder Law related subjects as well as an understanding of the physical, cognitive, and psycho-social challenges of aging and disability, and the skills needed to serve persons who are physically or mentally challenged.

(4) Ensures adequate training and supervision of legal and non-legal staff with a corresponding emphasis on the knowledge and skills needed to best serve persons facing the challenges of aging and disability.

E. Client Capacity

The Elder Law Attorney:

(1) Respects the client's autonomy and right to confidentiality even with the onset of diminished capacity.

(2) Develops and utilizes appropriate skills and processes for making and documenting preliminary assessments of client capacity to undertake the specific legal matters at hand.

(3) Adapts the interview environment, timing of meetings, communications and decision-making processes to maximize the client's capacities.

(4) Takes appropriate measures to protect the client when the attorney reasonably believes that the client: (1) has diminished capacity, (2) is at risk of substantial physical, financial or other harm unless action is taken, and (3) cannot adequately act in the client's own interest.

(5) When taking appropriate measures to protect the client:

is guided by the wishes and values of the client and the client's best interests;

seeks to minimize the intrusion into the client's decision-making autonomy and maximizes the client's capacity;

respects the client's family and social connections; and

considers a range of actions other than court proceedings and adult protective services.

ASPIRATIONAL STANDARDS FOR THE PRACTICE OF ELDER LAW *(continued)*

(6) Discloses client confidences only when essential to taking protective action and to the extent necessary to accomplish the intended protective action.

(7) Recommends guardianship or conservatorship only when all possible alternatives will not work.

(8) In representing a fiduciary for a person with diminished capacity:
- is guided by the known wishes and best interests of the person with diminished capacity, and
- may disclose otherwise confidential information, in the event a conflict arises between the fiduciary and the person with diminished capacity, if necessary to avoid substantial harm to the interests of the person with diminished capacity.

F. Communication and Advocacy

The Elder Law Attorney:

(1) Works to minimize barriers to effective communication with and representation of older persons or persons with disabilities.

(2) Maintains direct communication with the client, even when the client chooses to involve others in the process, and especially when significant decisions are to be made.

(3) Advises clients of their options, the practical and legal consequences of each option, and the likelihood of success in pursuing each option.

(4) Strives to address clients, whether in person, on the telephone, or through correspondence, in ways they can readily understand.

(5) Advocates within the law, courses of action chosen by the client.

(6) Provides counsel and representation regarding critical life planning decisions, such as long term care planning that may involve repositioning of assets. In such cases, the Elder Law Attorney should:
- strive to ascertain the client's fundamental values in order to be responsive to the goals and objectives of the client;
- endeavor to preserve and promote the client's dignity, self-determination, and quality of life in the face of competing interests and difficult alternatives;
- counsel the client about the full range of long-term care issues, options, risks, consequences, and costs relevant to the client's circumstances;
- counsel the client regarding asset preservation strategies as appropriate in light of the client's needs, personal values, and alternatives available; and
- counsel the client about the estate planning and tax implications of such estate and asset preservation strategies.

Source: Copyright © The National Academy of Elder Law Attorneys (NAELA). Reprinted with permission.

MURDER, SHE WROTE

Most states, by statute or court decision, provide that a person who murders another person cannot inherit the victim's property. This rule, often called the **murder disqualification doctrine**, is based on the public policy that a person should not benefit from his or her wrongdoing.

Walter A. Gibbs married Delores Christenson in 1964. The couple were divorced in 1973. Gibbs married Delores's twin sister, Darlene Wahl. That marriage ended in divorce in 1980.

During the winter of 1988–89, Delores, Darlene, and Darlene's new husband, Jerry Phillips, lived together. Delores contacted Gibbs, who was older than 80 years at the time, at the nursing home where he resided. In February 1989, Delores, Darlene, and Jerry moved Gibbs to his house and moved in with him. The group lived together as a "family" for about one year.

(continued)

MURDER, SHE WROTE (continued)

Gibbs had a will that named his first cousin, Bernice Boettner, as sole beneficiary. In January 1990, Delores located an attorney who drafted a new will for Gibbs, and she procured two witnesses for the will's execution. The will disinherited Gibbs's relations and left his entire estate, worth about $175,000, to Delores. Gibbs executed the will on January 5, 1990.

On January 8, 1990, Darlene and Jerry discussed killing Gibbs to "activate the will." On the morning of April 1, 1990, Darlene got a pillow from her bedroom and gave it to Jerry. Delores sat at the kitchen table approximately 17 feet from Gibbs's bed. Darlene held Gibbs's arms while Jerry smothered him.

In January 1991, Delores, Darlene, and Jerry were indicted on charges of murder, conspiracy to commit murder, and aiding and abetting murder. Jerry pleaded guilty to conspiracy to commit second-degree murder. Darlene was convicted of murder and sentenced to life in prison. Delores was acquitted of all charges.

Delores offered Gibbs's will for probate. Boettner filed a petition to revoke the probate of Gibbs's will and an application to disqualify Delores as the beneficiary as a willful slayer of Gibbs. Delores argued in defense that she should be allowed to inherit Gibbs's estate because she had not been criminally convicted. The Trial Court held that Delores qualified as a willful slayer under the murder disqualification statute even though she had not been convicted at her criminal trial. The state supreme court affirmed. Gibbs's prior will, which left his estate to Boettner, was admitted to probate. [*In the Matter of the Estate of Walter A. Gibbs*, 490.N.W.2d 504, 1992 S.D. Lexis 127 (S.D. 1992)]

Legal Terminology

Summary

CHAPTER 15   WILLS, TRUSTS, AND ESTATES

Wills

Definition	A will is a declaration of how a person wants his or her property to be distributed upon his or her death.
Parties to a Will	1. *Testator or testatrix*: The person who makes a will. 2. *Beneficiary*: The person designated in the will to receive the testator's property. There may be multiple beneficiaries. 3. *Executor or executrix*: The person named in a will to administer the testator's estate during settlement of the estate.
Requirements for Making a Will	1. *Statute of Wills*: a state statute that establishes the requirements for making a valid will. 2. The normal requirements for making a will are: 　a. *testamentary capacity* (legal age and "sound mind"). 　b. *in writing*. 　c. *testator's signature*. 　d. *attestation by witnesses* (mentally competent and uninterested).
Changing a Will	1. *Codicil*: a legal way to change an existing will 2. must be executed with the same formalities as a will

Special Types of Wills

Holographic Will	A holographic will is entirely handwritten and is signed by the testator. Most states recognize the validity of these wills even though they are not witnessed.
Noncupative Will	A noncupative will is an oral will made by dying persons before witnesses. Many states recognize these oral wills. Also called a *deathbed will* or a *dying declaration*.

Testamentary Gifts

Types of Gifts	1. Specific gift: gift of a specifically mentioned piece of property (e.g., a ring) 2. General gift: gift that does not identify the specific property from which the gift is to be made (e.g., gift of cash) 3. Residuary gift: gift of the remainder of the testator's estate after the debts, taxes, and specific and general gifts have been paid
Videotaped Will	
Simultaneous Deaths	
Ademption	If a testator leaves a specific gift but the property is no longer in the estate when the testator dies, the beneficiary of that gift receives nothing.
Abatement	If the testator's estate is insufficient to pay the stated gifts, the gifts are abated (reduced) in the following order: (1) residuary gifts, then (2) general gifts proportionately.
Lineal Descendants	1. *Per stirpes* distribution: Lineal descendants inherit by representation of their parent; they split what their deceased parent would have received.
	2. *Per capita* distribution: Lineal descendants equally share the property of the estate without regard to degree.

Types of Testamentary Gifts

Simultaneous Deaths	Uniform Simultaneous Death Act provides that if people who would inherit property from each other die simultaneously, each deceased person's property is distributed as if he or she had survived.
Joint Will	Two or more testators execute the same instrument as their will.
Mutual or Reciprocal Will	Two or more testators execute separate wills that leave property in favor of the other on condition that the survivor leave the remaining property upon his or her death as agreed by the testators.
Undue Influence	A will may be found to be invalid if it was made under undue influence, in which one person takes advantage of another person's mental, emotional, or physical weakness and unduly persuades that person to make a will.
Intestate Succession	1. *Intestacy statute*: State statute that stipulates how a deceased's property will be distributed if he or she dies without leaving a will or if the will fails for some legal reason. 2. *Heirs*: Relatives who receive property under an intestacy statute. 3. *Escheat*: If no heirs, deceased's property goes to the state, under intestacy statutes.

Probate

Definition	Legal process of settling a deceased person's estate
Administrator or Administratrix	Person named to administer the estate of a deceased person who dies intestate. An administrator also is named if an executor is not named in a will or the executor cannot or does not serve.

Living Will and Health Care Proxy

Right to Die	The right to die is a personal liberty protected by the U.S. Constitution.
Living Will	A living will is a document signed by a person that stipulates his or her wishes to not have his or her life prolonged by artificial means.
Health Care Directive	A health care proxy, or directive, is a document that names a person as a health care agent who has the authority to make health care decisions for the maker of the health care directive in accordance with the maker's wishes. Also called a *health care proxy*.

Trusts

Definition	A trust is a legal arrangement whereby one person delivers and transfers legal title to property to another person to be held and used for the benefit of a third person.
Trust Corpus	*Trust corpus* is the property that is held in trust, also called *trust res*.

Parties	1. *Settlor*: Person who establishes a trust; also called a *trustor* or *transferor*.
	2. *Trustee*: Person to whom *legal title* of the trust assets is transferred; responsible for managing the trust assets as established by the trust and law.
	3. *Beneficiary*: Person for whose benefit a trust is created; holds *equitable title* to the trust assets. There can be multiple beneficiaries, including:
	  a. *Income beneficiary*: person to whom trust income is to be paid
	  b. *Remainder beneficiary*: person who is entitled to receive the *trust corpus* upon termination of the trust

Express Trusts	Express trusts are voluntarily created by the settlor. Two types are: 1. Inter vivos *trust*: Created while the settlor is alive; also called a *living trust*. 2. *Testamentary trust*: Created by will and comes into existence when the settlor dies.
Constructive trust	Constructive trusts are equitable trusts imposed by law to avoid fraud, unjust enrichment, and injustice.

Resulting Trust	Resulting trusts are created from the conduct of the parties.
Special Types of Trusts	1. *Charitable trust*: A trust created for the benefit of a segment of society or society in general. 2. *Spendthrift trust*: A trust whereby the creditors of the beneficiary cannot recover the trust's assets to satisfy debts owed to them by the beneficiary. 3. *Totten trust*: A trust created when a person deposits money in a bank account in his or her own name and holds it as a trust for the benefit of another person.

Living Trusts

Definition	A living trust is a legal entity used for estate planning. Also called a *grantor's trust, revocable trust,* or *inter vivos trust.*
Trust Corpus	The *trust corpus* is the property that is placed in a living trust to fund the trust.
Parties	1. *Grantor.* A person who establishes a living trust 2. *Trustee.* A person who is responsible for maintaining, investing, buying, and selling trust assets 3. *Income beneficiary.* A person who is entitled to receive income from a living trust 4. *Remainder beneficiary.* A person who is entitled to receive the assets of a trust upon the death of the grantor
Pour-Over Will	A pour-over-will is necessary to distribute to the trust upon the grantor's death, any of the grantor's property not in the living trust at the time of the grantor's death.
Murder Disqualification	A person who murders another person cannot inherit the victim's property.

▶ WORKING THE WEB

1. Using Internet search engines such as **http://www.google.com.html** or Internet legal search services such as Westlaw or LexisNexis, find your state's will statute. What are the requirements for completing a valid will in your state? What are the attestation requirements? Write a one-page report on your findings. If you can, print out a sample will and attach it to your report.

2. Using Internet legal search services such as Westlaw or LexisNexis or Internet search engines such as **http://www.google.com.html**, find your state's intestacy statute. Make a list, in descending order of heirs, of how the property of a deceased person will be distributed if he or she dies without a will. When does the property escheat to the state?

3. Using Internet search engines such as **http://www.google.com.html** or Internet legal search services such as Westlaw or LexisNexis, find your state's living trust statute. What are the requirements for completing a valid living trust in your state?

Write a one-page report on your findings. If you can, print out a sample living trust and attach it to your report.

4. Using Internet legal search services such as Westlaw or LexisNexis or Internet search engines such as **http://www.google.com.html**, find your state's living will statute. What are the requirements for completing a valid living will in your state? Also find your state's health care directive (health care proxy) statute. What are the requirements for completing a valid health care directive in your state? Write a one-page report on your findings. If you can, print out a sample living will and sample health care directive and attach these to your report.

5. Using the Internet search engine **http://www.google.com.html** or other Internet search engines, find articles that discuss Ms. Anna Nicole Smith's will challenge to her husband Howard Marshall's will. Write a one-page report on the case and the court decisions in the case.

CRITICAL THINKING AND WRITING QUESTIONS

1. What is a will? What are the requirements for making a will?
2. Define a beneficiary of a will.
3. What is a codicil? What is a subsequent will?
4. Define holographic will and nuncupative will.
5. What is a devise (or legacy)? Describe the following types of devises: (a) specific gift, (b) general gift, and (c) residuary gift.
6. Define a lineal descendant. Explain the difference between *per capita* and *per stirpes* distribution of property to lineal descendants.
7. What is the difference between abatement and ademption?
8. What is a joint (or mutual) will?
9. Explain the doctrine of undue influence. Give an example.
10. What does it mean for a person to die intestate? Describe what an intestacy statute does? Who is an heir? What is escheat?
11. Describe a living will. What is a heath care directive (or proxy)?
12. What is a trust? Define settlor (trustor or transferor). What is *trust corpus* (trust res)? Define an income beneficiary and a remainder beneficiary.
13. Define the following types of trusts: (a) express trust, (b) constructive trust, (c) resulting trust, (d) charitable trust, (e) spendthrift trust, and (f) totten trust.
14. Describe a living will and what it accomplishes. Describe a health care directive (health care proxy) and what it accomplishes.
15. What is a living (grantor's or revocable) trust? Define the following parties: grantor (trustor), trustee, and beneficiary. What are the benefits of establishing a living trust?

ETHICS ANALYSIS AND DISCUSSION QUESTIONS

1. Is there a conflict of interest regarding representing both husband and wife in a divorce?
2. Is the preparation of divorce papers by a paralegal in an uncontested divorce the unauthorized practice of law in your jurisdiction?
3. As a paralegal, you have gained substantial expertise in the education of children with disabilibies. [*Arons v. New Jersey State Bd. of Educ.*, 842 F.2d 58 (3d Cir. 1988).] May you act as a lay advocate on behalf of parents of children with disabilities in administrative hearings to determine the children's appropriate educational placement? May you receive fees for representation in those proceedings?

DEVELOPING YOUR COLLABORATION SKILLS

With a group of other students, selected by you or as assigned by your instructor, review the Paralegals and Work at the beginning of the chapter. As a group, discuss the following questions.

1. Would you recommend that the Huntingtons establish a will? How can they be sure that each one of them will abide by the same will provisions?
2. Would a trust serve the Huntingtons' needs and wishes? Explain.
3. Would a living trust accomplish the Huntingtons' goals? Explain.
4. What should the Huntingtons do to accomplish their wishes regarding health decisions upon serious illness or accident?
5. How would the Huntingtons' property be distributed if they were to die without a will or trust in place?

PARALEGAL PORTFOLIO EXERCISE

Review the Paralegals at Work at the beginning of the chapter. Prepare a joint will for Mr. and Ms. Huntington that meets your state's will requirements. Have another person and you sign the will as if you were Mr. and Ms. Huntington, and have the proper attestation of the will as required in your state.

▶LEGAL ANALYSIS AND WRITING CASES

Opperman v. Anderson

782 S.W.2d 8, 1989 Tex.App. Lexis 3175
Court of Appeals of Texas

FACTS

On September 26, 1983, Ethel M. Ramchissel executed a will that made the following bequests: (1) one-half of the stock she owned in Pabst Brewing Company (Pabst) to Mary Lee Anderson, (2) all of the stock she owned in Houston Natural Gas Corporation (Houston Natural Gas) to Ethel Baker and others (Baker), and (3) the residue and remainder of her estate to Boysville, Inc.

Later, the following events happened. First, in response to an offer by G. Heilman Brewing Company to purchase Pabst, Ramchissel sold all of her Pabst stock and placed the cash proceeds in a bank account to which no other funds have been added. Second, pursuant to a merger agreement between Internorth, Inc. and Houston Natural Gas, Ramchissel converted her Houston Natural Gas stock to cash and placed the cash in a bank account to which no other funds have been added.

When Ramchissel died on April 4, 1987, her will was admitted into probate. The Probate Court awarded the money in the two bank accounts to Anderson and Baker, respectively. This appeal ensued.

Question

1. Were the bequests to Anderson and Baker specific bequests that were adeemed when the stock was sold?

In the Matter of the Estate of Jansa

670 S.W.2d 767 1984 Tex.App. Lexis 5503
(Tex.App. 1984)

FACTS

On or about June 10, 1959, Martha Jansa executed a will naming her two sons as executors of her will and leaving all of her property to them. The will was properly signed and attested to by witnesses. Thereafter, Martha died. When Martha's safe deposit box at a bank was opened, the original of this will was discovered along with two other instruments that were dated after the will. One was a handwritten document that left her home to her grandson, with the remainder of her estate to her two sons; this document was not signed. The second document was a typed version of the handwritten one; this document was signed by Martha but was not attested to by witnesses.

Question

1. Which of the three documents should be admitted to probate?

Woods v. Woods

397 S.E.2d 291, 1900 Ga. Lexis 404 (GA 1990)

FACTS

Martha L. Woods and Henry R. Woods, who lived in Georgia, were married on February 21, 1987. Both of them had been married previously and their respective spouses had died. Each had accumulated separate estates. Prior to departing on an automobile trip to Wichita, Kansas, they executed an instrument entitled "Agreement," dated March 27, 1987. It stated: "It is agreed that in the event of an accident or disaster which would result in the death of one of us, the surviving party is to retain ownership in the other's real and personal property until the time of his or her death."

On April 5, 1987, they returned safely from their trip and did not subsequently execute another will. Henry died on June 11, 1988, as a result of a disease.

Question

1. Should the March 27, 1987, agreement be admitted into probate?

In re Estate of Potter

469 So.2d 957 1985 Fla.App. Lexis 14338 (Fla.App. 1985)

FACTS

Mrs. Mildred D. Potter executed a will providing that, upon her death, her residence in Pompano Beach, Florida, was to go to her daughter and an equivalent amount of cash to her son. Evidence showed that Mrs. Potter's intent was to treat the daughter and son equally in the distribution of her estate. When she died, her will was admitted into probate. At the time, she still possessed her home in Pompano Beach. Unfortunately, assets were insufficient to pay Mrs. Potter's son the equivalent amount of cash.

Question

1. Can the son share in the value of the house so that his inheritance is equal to his sister's?

Jones v. Jones

718 S.W.2d 416 1986 Tex.App. Lexis 8929 (Tex.App. 1986)

FACTS

In 1967, Homer and Edna Jones, husband and wife, executed a joint will that provided: "We will and give to our survivor, whether it be Homer Jones or Edna Jones, all property and estate of which the first of us that dies may be seized and possessed. If we should both die in a common catastrophe, or upon the death of our survivor, we will and give all property and estate then remaining to our children, Leonida Jones Eschman, daughter, Sylvia Marie Jones, daughter, and Grady V. Jones, son, share and share alike."

Homer died in 1975, and Edna Jones received his entire estate under the 1967 will. In 1977, Edna executed a new will that left a substantially larger portion of the estate to her daughter, Sylvia Marie Jones, than to the other two children. Edna Jones died in 1982. Edna's daughter Sylvia introduced the 1977 will for probate. The other two children introduced the 1967 will for probate.

Question

1. Did Edna act ethically in this case? Who wins?

▶ WORKING WITH THE LANGUAGE OF THE COURT CASE

In re Estate of Vallerius

629 N.E.2d 1185 1994 Ill.App. Lexis 267 (1994)
Appellate Court of Illinois

Read the following case, excerpted from the Court of Appeals opinion. Review and brief the case. In your brief, answer the following questions.

1. Who was to inherit Adella Vallerius's property upon her death?
2. What criminal acts did Douglas and Craig White commit?
3. Who is Renie White? Whose property did she inherit, and why?
4. Who was to inherit Renie White's property upon her death?
5. Were Douglas or Craig White permitted to inherit either Adella's or Renie's property upon her death?

Lewis, Presiding Justice

On December 22, 1987, Douglas White murdered his grandmother, Adella G. Vallerius. On the same day, at the same time, and in the same house, Douglas' brother, Craig White, murdered his grandmother's friend, Carroll Pieper. Douglas was convicted of Mrs. Vallerius' murder. Craig entered a negotiated plea of guilty to, and was convicted of, the murder of Carroll Pieper. Craig testified for the State in Douglas' murder trial as part of his negotiated guilty plea.

Mrs. Vallerius died testate, naming Douglas and Craig as her sole beneficiaries. Mrs. Vallerius' only heir was her daughter, Renie White, Douglas and Craig's mother. On January 11, 1988, Mrs. Vallerius' will was admitted to probate. In compliance with the terms of the will, Douglas White and Dennis Johnson were appointed legal representatives of Mrs. Vallerius' estate. About 2½ months after Mrs. Vallerius was murdered, on March 7, 1988, Renie White died, intestate, of natural causes. She left as her only heirs her two sons, Douglas and Craig.

On March 12, 1990, the appellees, Peter M. Vallerius, Glenna F. Giacoletto, Lawrence Joe Davis, Helen L. Vallerius, Gail Kadavi, Iione V. Henry, Janis Murray, Terrie L. Illies, and Duffy Joe Vallerius, filed a petition to intervene and to consolidate the estates of Mrs. Vallerius and Renie White and an "Objection to Distribution" in the estate of Mrs. Vallerius, wherein they alleged that "Douglas Keith White and Craig Steven White, having intentionally and unjustifiably caused the death of Adella G. Vallerius, cannot lawfully receive any property, benefit or other interest" by reason of her death, through the estate of Mrs. Vallerius or through the estate of Renie White.

After an evidentiary hearing on the appellees' objection to distribution, the court entered an order granting the appellees' request. The trial court found that the issue in the case was whether Douglas and Craig could receive any property or interest by reason of the death of Mrs. Vallerius, whether through her estate or the estate of Renie White. The court determined that, under both statute and common law, the public policy of Illinois has long been to prevent wrongdoers from profiting from intentionally committed wrongful acts. The court further found that the petitioner-objectors (appellees herein) had sustained their burden of proof, by clear and convincing evidence, that Douglas and Craig intentionally caused the death of their grandmother, Mrs. Vallerius.

Appellants argue that the law does not preclude a murderer from inheriting property from a person other than the victim. The obvious intent of the law is that persons like Douglas and Craig White must not profit from their brutal murder of their grandmother. The fact that there is an intervening estate should not expurgate the wrong of the murderer.

The appellants argue that Craig cannot be held accountable for Douglas' murder of Mrs. Vallerius, since Craig did not actually swing the sledgehammer that killed Mrs. Vallerius but only killed Carroll Pieper after Douglas killed Mrs. Vallerius. Appellants argue that even though Craig "may have borne criminal responsibility for the actions of Douglas White under the criminal accountability statute," Craig cannot be denied his right of inheritance from his mother.

Craig White cannot be permitted to receive any benefit by reason of the death of Mrs. Vallerius, whether through her estate directly or indirectly through the estate of her daughter, Renie White. If we were to allow Craig White to receive any property, benefit, or interest from the estate of Renie White, our decision would directly contravene the state's unambiguous mandate that he not receive any property by reason of his grandmother's death in any capacity or by any circumstance. ■

FAMILY LAW

"The happiest moments of my life have been the few which I have passed at home in the bosom of my family."

Thomas Jefferson,
Letter to
Francis Willis, Jr. 1790

PARALEGALS AT WORK

As a paralegal, you work for Ms. Sara Khan, a lawyer who specializes in family law and domestic relations issues. Specializing in family law, you often are assigned to investigate and discover information pertinent to clients' cases, conduct legal research on family law issues, and draft documents for review by Ms. Khan before they are submitted to the family law court. You also attend meetings of Ms. Khan and her clients wherein the clients are interviewed to obtain relevant information about their family law matter.

One day Ms. Jennifer Aston, a new client, arrives at the law office. Ms. Khan invites you to sit in on the initial meeting with Ms. Aston. At the meeting, Ms. Aston discloses that she wants to obtain a divorce from her spouse, Mr. Bret Pit. At the meeting, Ms. Aston tells the following facts about her marriage. Mrs. Aston and Mr. Pit met after she graduated from medical school. They have been married 15 years. Ms. Aston is now 45 years old, and Mr. Pit is 42 years old. They have two children: Kayla, their 10-year-old daughter born to the spouses, and Jason, an adopted son who is 6 years old.

Ms. Aston discloses the following facts about her and her spouse's financial situation: Ms. Aston is a medical doctor who earns $500,000 per year. Mr. Pit is an actor/waiter who earns $50,000 per year. They have a joint bank account into which both of their earnings are deposited. During the course of their marriage, they have accumulated the following assets from their earnings: (1) the house where they live with their children, valued at $1,000,000 and with a $300,000 mortgage (loan) against it; (2) $1,800,000 of securities in the stock market; (3) a $200,000 savings account at a bank; (4) two automobiles, each valued at $25,000; and (5) personal property, including furniture, valued at $150,000.

Ms. Aston reveals these additional facts: During the course of the marriage, she inherited $1,000,000 of securities from her grandmother. Ms. Aston has kept these securities in her own name. The securities have increased to $1,600,000 in value at this time. Mr. Pit has no separate property.

After studying this chapter, you should be able to:

1. Define *marriage* and enumerate the legal requirements of marriage.

2. Explain adoption and describe how adoption proceedings work.

3. Define *divorce* and *no-fault divorce*, and describe divorce proceedings.

4. Describe how assets are distributed upon the termination of marriage.

5. Explain the requirements for awarding spousal support.

6. Explain child custody, visitation rights, joint custody of children, and child support.

Ms. Khan asks Ms. Aston if there is a prenuptial agreement, and Ms. Aston states that there is no such agreement. Ms. Aston explains that she wants to keep the house and retain custody of the two children.

Consider the issues involved in this scenario as you read the chapter. Keep in mind all the divorce, division of property, child custody, child support, spousal support, and other issues that would relate to Ms. Aston's divorce case.

▶ INTRODUCTION FOR THE PARALEGAL

Family law and domestic relations is a broad area of the law, involving premarital issues, prenuptial agreements, marriage, dissolution of marriage, division of property upon dissolution of marriage, spousal and child support payments, child custody, and other family law issues.

Paralegals often work in the family law and domestic relations area. Those who work in this area of the law are called upon to interview clients, investigate and obtain relevant information, draft letters and documents to be sent to clients, and prepare legal forms that will be submitted to the family law or domestic relations court. The paralegal must report to and submit letters, documents, and forms to the supervising attorney for approval and often signature.

This chapter provides the paralegal with an introduction to the issues most commonly encountered in a family law legal practice. ■

PREMARRIAGE ISSUES

Prior to marriage, several legal issues may arise. These include promises to marry, engagement, and prenuptial agreements.

Promise to Marry

In the nineteenth century, many courts recognized an action for breach of a **promise to marry**. This usually would occur if a man proposed marriage, the woman accepted, and then the man backed out before the marriage took place. The lawsuit was based on a breach-of-contract theory.

Today, most courts do not recognize a breach of a promise-to-marry lawsuit. The denial of such lawsuits is based on current social norms. If, however, the potential groom backs out late, after many of the items for the pending marriage were purchased or contracted for (e.g., flowers, rental of a reception hall), he may be responsible for paying these costs.

Engagement

As a prelude to getting married, many couples go through a period of time known as **engagement**. The engagement usually begins when the male proposes marriage to the female, and if the female accepts, he gives her an engagement ring (usually a diamond ring). In these modern times, a female also may propose marriage to a male. During an engagement, the female is called the **fiancée** and the male is called the **fiancé**. The engagement period runs until the wedding is held or the engagement is broken off. If the couple get married, they often exchange wedding band rings at the marriage ceremony.

Sometimes the engagement is broken off prior to the wedding. Then the issue becomes: Who gets the engagement ring if the engagement is broken off? Some states follow a **fault rule**, which works as follows:

- If the prospective groom breaks off the engagement, the prospective bride gets to keep the engagement ring.
- If the prospective bride breaks off the engagement, she must return the engagement ring to the prospective groom.

The fault rule is sometimes difficult to apply. Questions often arise as to who broke off the engagement, which then requires a trial to decide the issue.

The modern rule and trend is to abandon the fault rule and adopt an **objective rule**: If the engagement is broken off, the prospective bride must return the engagement ring, regardless of who broke off the engagement. This objective rule is clear and usually avoids litigation unless the female refuses to return the ring.

Objective rule
A rule stating that if an engagement is broken off, the prospective bride must return the engagement ring, regardless of which party broke off the engagement.

Prenuptial Agreements

In today's society, many spouses sign prenuptial agreements in advance of their marriage. **Prenuptial agreements**—also called **premarital agreements**—are contracts that specify how property will be distributed upon termination of the marriage or death of a spouse. To be enforced, a prenuptial agreement must be in writing.

Prenuptial agreements often are used where both parties to a marriage have their own career and have accumulated assets prior to the marriage, or one of the spouses

Prenuptial agreement
A contract entered into prior to marriage that specifies how property will be distributed upon the termination of the marriage or death of a spouse.

THE PARALEGAL AND FAMILY LAW

With the divorce rate in this country around 50 percent, a substantial number of lawyers and paralegals work in the family law area. A paralegal in the family law area usually is involved in a broad spectrum of legal issues.

A divorce case is a lawsuit. Therefore, the legal rules and procedures involving the court system apply. Paralegals must know these procedures for the state in which they work. For example, a divorce case usually involves investigating finances and other issues concerning the divorce, preparing notices for discovery of evidence, drafting interrogatories, and preparing other documents needed in the divorce case.

Most divorces are settled before they go to trial. This often requires negotiation between the parties and their lawyers to reach an acceptable settlement agreement. The paralegal frequently sits in on many of the meetings and negotiation sessions between the parties and their attorneys.

If a settlement is reached, the paralegal often is called upon to prepare a draft of the settlement agreement. This will require substantial knowledge of the law of the state, as well as of the facts of the individual divorce case. In addition, the paralegal may be assigned to prepare the documents associated with the settlement of a divorce case, such as deeds and documents to transfer real property, securities, bank accounts, and other property necessary to complete the divorce.

In many divorce cases, custody battles over children arise. The lawyers will represent the parties in these custody disputes, and their paralegals will assist the lawyers in preparing for these disputes. Other issues in divorce cases may include visitation rights, child support payments, and alimony, among others. Again, the paralegal must be familiar with these legal issues, and the procedures and documents associated with these issues.

In many instances, the parties sign a prenuptial agreement prior to marriage. These agreements establish the rights of parties should the parties separate. The paralegal often is responsible for preparing drafts of prenuptial agreements and other documents necessary to support the prenuptial agreement.

Other issues in the family law area concern the adoption of children, contracts for surrogate mothers, proceedings to determine the capacity of parents, spouses, and other loved ones, the appointment of conservators, and other family law matters. These areas usually require the expertise of family law lawyers and their paralegals.

One current area of the law pertains to the rights and duties of same-sex partners. These couples require legal representation in many family law issues. These may include the drafting of legal documents, adoption of children, separation of the partners, division of assets upon separation of partners, and other issues. In addition, lawyers are called upon to represent same-sex partners in cases to establish legal rights and duties, and to eliminate laws that treat same-sex partners different from heterosexual partners.

The family law area provides a wealth of opportunities for well-trained and knowledgeable paralegals.

has significant assets prior to the marriage. Prenuptial agreements also are often used where there are children from a prior marriage and the agreement guarantees that these children will receive a certain share of the assets of the remarrying spouse if he or she dies or the marriage is terminated.

For a prenuptial agreement to be enforceable, each party must make full disclosure of all his or her assets and liabilities and each party should be represented by his or her own attorney. Prenuptial agreements must be entered into voluntarily, without threats or undue pressure. They must provide for the fair distribution of assets and must not be unconscionable. Generally, courts will enforce a properly negotiated prenuptial agreement even if the agreement provides for an unequal distribution of assets and eliminates financial support of a spouse in case the marriage is terminated.

Courts will not enforce a prenuptial agreement in the following circumstances:

- One of the parties was not represented by an attorney.
- One of the parties failed to make full disclosure of his or her assets and liabilities.
- The agreement was entered into at the "last moment," immediately prior to the marriage.
- The terms of the agreement are unfair or unconscionable.
- The agreement violates public policy (for example, if a party is forced to live on government assistance if the agreement is enforced).

Sometimes the parties enter into an agreement during the marriage, setting forth the distribution of property upon death or termination of the marriage. This is called an **antenuptial agreement**. The courts apply the same standards for enforceability as in prenuptial agreements.

MARRIAGE

Each state has marriage laws that recognize a legal union between a man and a woman. **Marriage** confers certain legal rights and duties upon the spouses, as well as upon the children born of the marriage. A couple wishing to marry must meet the legal requirements established by the state in which they are to be married. The following paragraphs discuss the legal rights and duties of spouses.

Marriage Requirements

State law establishes certain **marriage requirements** that must be met before two people can be married. Most states require that the parties be a man and a woman. The parties must be of a certain age (usually 18 years of age). States will permit younger persons to be married if they have the consent of their parents or if they are emancipated from their parents. **Emancipation** means that the person is not supported by his or her parents and provides for himself or herself.

All states provide that persons under a certain age, such as 14 or 15 years of age, cannot be married. States also prohibit marriages between persons who are closely related, usually by blood. For example, a brother could not marry his sister or half-sister. Cousins may marry in some states. Another requirement of marriage is that neither party currently is married to someone else.

Marriage License

To be legally married, certain legal procedures must be followed. State law requires that the parties obtain a **marriage license** issued by the state. Marriage licenses usually are obtained at the county clerk's office. Some states require that the parties take a blood test prior to obtaining a license to determine if the parties have certain diseases, particularly sexually transmitted diseases.

Some states require that, in addition to a marriage license, there must be some sort of **marriage ceremony**. This ceremony usually is held in front of a justice of the peace or similar government officer, or at a church, temple, or synagogue, in front of a minister, priest, or rabbi. At the ceremony, the parties exchange wedding vows, in which they make a public statement that they will take each other as wife and husband.

After the wedding ceremony, the marriage license is recorded. Some states require a waiting period between the time the marriage license is obtained and when the wedding ceremony takes place.

Financial Support

Most states require a spouse to provide **financial support** to the other spouse and their children during their marriage. This includes providing for the necessities such as food, shelter, clothing, and medical care. A spouse is obligated only up to the level he or she is able to provide. In some states this duty exists even if the spouses are living apart. The spouses are free to agree on additional duties in separate contracts. Contracts to provide sex violate public policy and therefore are illegal.

Common-Law Marriage

Several states recognize a form of marriage called a **common-law marriage**. A common law marriage is one in which the parties have not obtained a valid marriage license, nor have they participated in a legal marriage ceremony. Instead, a common-law marriage is recognized if the following requirements are met: (1) The parties are eligible to marry; (2) the parties voluntarily intend to be husband and wife; (3) the parties must live together; and (4) the parties hold themselves out as husband and wife.

Common-law marriage
A type of marriage recognized in some states where a marriage license has not been issued but certain requirements are met.

Two misconceptions about common-law marriages are: (1) cohabitation is not sufficient in and of itself to establish a common-law marriage, and (2) the length of time the parties live together is not sufficient alone to establish a common-law marriage. For example, couples who immediately live together and intend a common-law marriage have one, whereas couples who live together a long time but do not intend a common-law marriage do not have one.

When a state recognizes a common-law marriage and the necessary requirements are met to establish one, the couple has a legal and formal marriage. All the rights and duties of a normal licensed marriage apply. As such, a court decree of divorce must be obtained to end a common-law marriage.

PARENTS AND CHILDREN

In many instances, a major purpose of marriage is to have children. Couples who have children have certain legal rights and duties that develop from their parental status.

Parents' Rights and Duties

Parents have the obligation to provide food, shelter, clothing, medical care, and other necessities to their children until a child reaches the age of 18 or until emancipation. A child becomes emancipated if he or she leaves the parents and lives voluntarily on his or her own. The law imposes certain **parents' duties** as well. For example, a parent must see to it that the child attends school until 16 or 18 years of age, depending on the state, unless the child is home-schooled. Parents may be legally responsible for a child beyond the age of majority if the child has a disability.

Also, **parents' right** to control the behavior of a child is legally mandated. Parents have the right to select the schools for their children and the religion they will practice. Parents have the right to use corporal punishment (physical punishment) as long as it does not rise to the level of child abuse. For example, mild slapping or spanking is legally permitted.

SAME-SEX MARRIAGES

Same-sex partners have been fighting for years to obtain the same rights as heterosexual couples to marry. In most states, same-sex couples do not have the same rights to marry as heterosexual couples. This is because most state marriage statutes are expressly drafted to permit only couples of different sexes to marry.

Same-sex partners have been lobbying their state legislatures and bringing lawsuits in the courts to change marriage statutes to permit them to marry. In these lawsuits, same-sex partners allege that the state statutes permitting heterosexual partners to marry but not same-sex partners causes discrimination that violates equal-protection clauses of state constitutions and the U.S. Constitution.

The state of Massachusetts now permits same-sex partners to marry. Most other states have not done so. Several states have enacted statutes that permit same-sex partners to join in a **civil union**. These civil union statutes grant same-sex partners most of the rights granted to heterosexual partners under marriage statutes. Same-sex partners will continue their fight to persuade states to change their marriage statutes to permit same-sex couples to marry.

Many employers provide the same health, pension, and other employment benefits to same-sex partners as they do to heterosexual married couples. The granting of same-sex partners such employment rights will continue to increase in the future.

In 1996, the federal government enacted the **Defense of Marriage Act (DOMA)** [28 U.S.C. Section 1738C], which bars same-sex couples from enjoying federal benefits (e.g., Social Security benefits, Veterans' benefits, and such) that otherwise would be accorded heterosexual married couples. Same-sex partners argue that this part of DOMA violates the Equal Protection Clause of the U.S. Constitution by treating same-sex partners differently than heterosexual married couples.

DOMA also provides that states cannot be forced to recognize same-sex marriages performed in other states. For example, if a same-sex couple gets lawfully married in Massachusetts and moves to another state that does not recognize same-sex marriages, this new state does not have to recognize the partner's same-sex marriage from Massachusetts.

The battle for recognizing **same-sex marriages** and the granting of rights to same-sex partners equal to heterosexual couples will continue to be waged in state and federal legislatures, as well as state and federal courts.

Child neglect occurs when a parent fails to provide a child with the necessities of life or other basic needs. The state may remove a child, either temporarily or permanently, from situations of child neglect. A parent's refusal to obtain medical care for a child can be punished as a crime.

Paternity Actions

Paternity action
A legal proceeding that determines the identity of the father of a child.

If there is any question as to who the father of a child is, called **paternity**, a **paternity action** may be filed in court to determine the true identity of the father. Most of these actions are filed by a mother against a man whom the mother claims to be the father of the child. This often is done to seek financial assistance from the father for the child's upbringing.

Paternity lawsuits sometimes are brought by the government if the mother is receiving welfare payments. In these cases, the government seeks to recover the financial assistance payments made to the mother and to establish the father's financial responsibility in the future. Sometimes a paternity action is brought by a male to prove that he is not the father of a child.

At other times, a father will bring a paternity action to establish that he is the biological father of a child. This is usually done when the father seeks to obtain legal rights, such as custody or visitation rights, concerning the child. Most states have a **father's registry** in which a male may register as the father of a child. This requires that the father be notified of a planned adoption of the child so the father may appear and oppose the adoption.

In most states, the law presumes that the husband of a wife who bears a child is the legal father of the child. In about half of the states, a husband who believes that he is not the father can bring a lawsuit to prove that he is not the father. The other half of the states do not permit such actions.

A male can be proven to be or not to be the father of a child through DNA testing. Also, a male may prove that he is not the father of a child if he had no access to the mother at the time of pregnancy or if he is impotent or had a vasectomy prior to the pregnancy.

Parent's Liability for a Child's Wrongful Act

Generally, parents are not liable for their children's negligent acts. For example, if a child negligently injures another child while they are playing, the parents of the child who caused the injury are not liable. Parents are liable if their negligence caused their child's act. For example, if a parent lets a child who does not have a driver's license drive an automobile and the child-driver injures someone, the parents are liable.

About half of the states have enacted **child liability statutes** that make the parents financially liable for the intentional torts of their children. This liability usually is limited to a specified dollar amount, such as $5,000.

Surrogacy

A relatively new area of the law has to do with reproductive medicine. This includes **surrogacy** and fertilized embryos. Several cases highlight the legal questions that arise.

The first case is the famous Baby M case, *In re Baby M*, 109 N.J. 396, 537 A. 2d 1227, 1988 N.J. Lexis (N.J.). In that case, William and Elizabeth Stern contracted with Mary Beth Whitehead whereby Ms. Whitehead was artificially inseminated with Mr. Stern's sperm and agreed to give the baby to the Sterns after the child was born, at which time Mrs. Stern would adopt the baby. Ms. Whitehead was compensated $10,000 by the Sterns.

When the baby was born, Ms. Whitehead decided to keep the baby. The Sterns sued Ms. Whitehead for breach of contract. The New Jersey Supreme Court held that the **surrogacy contract** violated public policy and could not be enforced because it represented baby selling. The court decided, however, that it was in the child's best interests to place the baby in the Sterns' custody but awarded visitation rights to Ms. Whitehead.

In the second case, *Anna J.v. Mark C.*, 286 Cal.Rptr 369, 1991 Cal. App. Lexis 1162 (Cal.App.), a contract was executed whereby a fertilized embryo formed from the husband's sperm and the wife's egg was implanted in the womb of a surrogate mother. When the nonbiological surrogate mother refused to turn over the baby to the biological parents, the biological parents sued. In this case, the court enforced the contract and ruled in favor of the biological parents. The court held that the surrogate mother had no legal rights concerning the child she had borne.

As these cases suggest, surrogate parenting is an unsettled area of the law. As medical science expands, so must the law in delineating the rights and duties of biological and surrogate parents of children born using advanced medical technology.

Adoption

Adoption occurs when a person becomes the legal parent of a child who is not his or her biological child. Thus, a married couple can adopt a child together, a single parent can adopt a child, and a spouse can adopt the child of his or her new spouse.

Adoption
A situation in which a person becomes the legal parent of a child who is not his or her biological child.

The process for adoption is complicated and is regulated by state law. Basically, the procedure for adoption consists of the following requirements:

- All procedures of the state law for adoption are met.
- The biological parents' legal rights as parents are terminated by legal decree or death.
- A court formally approves the adoption.

The two main ways by which persons can become adoptive parents are *agency adoptions* and *independent adoptions*.

Agency Adoption

Agency adoption
An adoption that occurs when a person adopts a child from a social service organization of a state.

An **agency adoption** occurs when a person adopts a child from a social service organization of a state. The state often obtains jurisdiction over children who are born out of wedlock and the biological parents give up the child for adoption by terminating their parental rights. The state also may obtain jurisdiction over a child if the child has been permanently removed from parents who are judged unsuitable to be parents, or where parents are deceased and no relative wants or qualifies to become the child's parents.

In the past, the identity of the biological parents of adopted children was kept confidential in an agency adoption. Currently, many states allow for disclosure of the identity of the biological parents in certain circumstances. Usually, the court will notify the other side—either the child or the biological parent—that the other wishes to meet with them. If both sides consent, the meeting will be arranged.

Open Adoption

In many cases today, **open adoption** procedures are being used. In these cases, the biological and **adoptive parents** are introduced prior to the adoption. The **biological parents** may screen the prospective adoptive parents to assure that the adoptive parents are suitable for the child. In many instances, the adoptive and biological parents remain in contact with each other, and the biological parents are given visitation rights to see the child.

Independent Adoption

Independent adoption
An adoption in which there is a private arrangement between the biological parents and adoptive parents.

An **independent adoption** occurs when there is a private arrangement between the biological and adoptive parents. Often, an intermediary, such as a lawyer, doctor, or private adoption agency, introduces the two parties. The biological parents and the adoptive parents enter into a private arrangement for adoption of the child. Adoptive parents usually pay intermediaries a fee for their services, as well as paying the costs of the adoption.

Many divorced people who have children remarry. Often, a new stepparent formally adopts the child or children of his or her new spouse. To do so, the child's other biological parent must relinquish his or her legal rights concerning the child. This can be done voluntarily or by order of the court if it is deemed to be in the best interests of the child.

Court Approval of Adoption

In both agency adoptions and independent adoptions, the court must approve the adoption before it is legal. The court will consider the home environment, financial resources, and family stability of the adoptive parents, as well as their religious beliefs, ages, and other factors. The decision of the court will be based on the best interests of the child. Although preference usually is given to couples, single parents can adopt children. States vary as to whether they permit homosexual couples to adopt children.

MEET THE COURTHOUSE TEAM

Family Law Judges

Many states have specialized courts that handle family law matters. These courts most often are called Family Law Courts. Other states provide that family law matters be heard and decided by their courts of general jurisdiction. In these cases, the courts that hear family law matters typically are a separate division of the general court system.

Judges that hear family law matters usually are referred to as Family Law Judges. These judges are experts in family law issues. In the course of their work, these judges hear and decide matters of paternity, annulments, divorce, division of property upon divorce, child custody, child visitation rights, child support, conservatorship, and other family law cases.

Because of the number of family law issues that arise in society, family law judges hear and decide a significant number of cases. Family law judges will continue to be an integral part of each state's judicial system.

Once the court approves an adoption, the adoptive couple is subject to a probation period which usually is six months or one year. During this time, government social workers investigate whether the adoptive parents are caring for the adopted child properly. If they are not, the court can remove the child from the adoptive parents.

Foster Care

A child may become the responsibility of the state under several circumstances. The first is if a child's parents or parent dies and there are no relatives to take the child or no other arrangements have been made for the care of the child. Another situation occurs if the state institutes a proceeding to remove a child from the parents' or parent's custody based upon the parent being unfit to care for the child or because the child is in danger (such as from child abuse).

Today, the primary means of caring for children under the state's jurisdiction is to place children in **foster care**. This is usually a temporary arrangement. The state pays the **foster family** for the care given to the **foster child**. This temporary arrangement will be terminated if the child is returned to his or her biological parents or if the child is legally adopted. Sometimes the **foster parents** will legally adopt a child who has been placed in their care.

TERMINATION OF MARRIAGE

Once a state has recognized the marital status of a couple, only the state can terminate this marital status. This is so even if the couple separate and live apart from one another. As long as they are married, they continue to have certain legal rights and duties to one another. The law recognizes two methods for **marriage termination**: *annulment and divorce*.

Annulment

An **annulment** is an order of the court declaring that a marriage did not exist. The order invalidates the marriage. Annulments are granted rarely now that most states recognize no-fault divorces.

Annulment
An order of the court declaring that a marriage did not exist.

Certain grounds must be asserted to obtain a legal annulment. One is that the parties lacked capacity to consent. Examples are:

1. One of the parties was a minor and had not obtained his or her parents' consent to marry.
2. One of the parties was mentally incapacitated at the time of marriage.
3. A party was intoxicated at the time of the marriage.
4. The marriage was never consummated.

Marriage also can be annulled if the parties are too closely related to one another or there was bigamy (one of the parties was already married). A marriage also can be annulled if there was duress or fraud leading to the marriage (e.g., one of the parties declared that he or she could conceive children when the person knew in fact that he or she could not).

Many annulments are sought because of a person's religion. For example, a Roman Catholic cannot be remarried in the church if he or she is divorced. An annulment would allow for a subsequent marriage in the church. A person also may be required to go through a procedure to seek an annulment from the church. A legal annulment and a religious annulment are two separate and distinct procedures.

The law considers children born of a marriage that is annulled to be legitimate. When a marriage is annulled, issues of child support, child custody, spousal support, and property settlement must be agreed upon by the couple or decided by the court.

Divorce

Divorce
An order of the court that terminates a marriage.

The most common option used by married partners to terminate their marriage is divorce. **Divorce** is a legal proceeding whereby the court issues a decree that legally orders a marriage terminated.

Traditionally, a married person who sought a divorce had to prove that the other person was *at fault* for causing a major problem with continuing the marriage. An **at-fault divorce** requires the petitioning party to allege grounds for seeking the divorce. Grounds for granting a divorce consisted of adultery, physical or emotional abuse, abandonment, substance or alcohol abuse, or insanity.

No-fault divorce
A divorce recognized by the law of a state whereby neither party is blamed for the divorce.

Beginning in the 1960s, states began to recognize **no-fault divorce**. A spouse wishing to obtain a divorce merely had to assert **irreconcilable differences** with his or her spouse. In a no-fault divorce, neither party is blamed for the divorce. Today, every state recognizes no-fault divorce. A spouse still may decide to assert that the other party was at fault for causing the divorce in those states that consider fault when deciding how to divide **marital assets** and award spousal support.

Divorce Proceedings

Petition for divorce
A document filed with the proper state court that commences a divorce proceeding.

A divorce proceeding is commenced by a spouse filing a **petition for divorce** with the proper state court. The petition must contain required information, such as the names of the spouses, date and place of marriage, names of minor children, and reason for the divorce. The petition must be served on the other spouse. This spouse then has a certain period of time (usually 20 to 30 days) to file an answer to the petition.

If the spouses do not reach a settlement of the issues involved in the divorce—such as property division, custody of the children, and spousal and child support—the case will go to trial. The parties are permitted to conduct discovery, which includes taking depositions and obtaining the production of documents. If the case goes to trial, each side is permitted to call witnesses, including expert witnesses (e.g., financial experts), to testify on his or her behalf. Both parties also are allowed to introduce evidence that will support their claims.

Many states require a certain waiting period from the date a divorce petition is filed to the date the court grants a divorce. A typical waiting period is six months. The public policy for this waiting period is to give the parties time for reconciliation. After the waiting period has passed, a court will enter a **decree of divorce,** which is a court order terminating the marriage. The parties then are free to marry again. The decree of divorce may be granted even if the other issues concerning the divorce, such as division of property or support payments, have not yet been settled or tried.

Decree of divorce
A court order that terminates a marriage.

If there is a showing that one partner is likely to injure the other spouse, a court may issue a **restraining order.** This places limitations on the ability of the dangerous partner to go near the innocent partner.

Pro se Divorce

In a *pro se* **divorce**, the parties do not have to hire lawyers to represent them but may represent themselves in the divorce proceeding. Most states permit *pro se*—commonly

ETHICAL *Perspective*

Duty to Provide Pro Bono *Services to the Public*

Mr. Antonio Alvarez is a paralegal in a law firm and works directly with Ms. Gloria Dawson, a partner in the law firm. In addition to her law practice with the law firm, Ms. Dawson volunteers to work one evening per week at a domestic abuse center that serves females and their children.

At the center, Ms. Dawson interviews domestic abuse victims and pursues whatever legal actions can be taken to assist the victims and their families. This includes doing the legal work for obtaining restraining orders, government assistance, and spousal and child support. All of Ms. Dawson's services at the domestic abuse center are provided *pro bono*, that is, for free.

One day Ms. Dawson asks her paralegal, Mr. Alvarez, if he would be interested in volunteering to help her one night each month at the domestic abuse shelter. Ms. Dawson explains that she could use Mr. Alvarez's assistance as a paralegal to help conduct interviews, prepare documents, and obtain government and other assistance for the domestic abuse victims and their families. Mr. Alvarez would be under the supervision of Ms. Dawson while working at the center.

Does a paralegal owe an ethical duty to provide *pro bono* services to the public? Section EC-1.4(c) of the *Model Code of Ethics and Professional Responsibility and Guidance for Enforcement* (Model Code) of the National Federation of Paralegal Associations, Inc. (NFPA) states:

> *A paralegal shall support and participate in the delivery of Pro Bono Publico services directed toward implementing and improving access to justice, the law, the legal system or the paralegal and legal professions.*

State and local paralegal ethics codes and codes of professional responsibility emphasize the importance of *pro bono* activities by paralegals as well.

Section EC-1.4(d) of NFPA's Model Code provides:

> *A paralegal should aspire annually to contribute twenty-four (24) hours of Pro Bono Publico services under the supervision of an attorney or as authorized by administrative, statutory or court authority to:*

> 1. *persons of limited means; or*
> 2. *charitable, religious, civic, community, governmental, and educational organizations in matters that are designed primarily to address the legal needs of persons with limited means; or*
> 3. *individuals, groups, or organizations seeking to secure or protect civil rights, civil liberties or public rights.*

Reprinted by permission from The National Federation of Paralegal Associations, Inc., www.paralegals.org

Mr. Alvarez agrees to assist Ms. Dawson at the domestic abuse shelter one evening each month. As a paralegal, would you agree to provide *pro bono* services to those in need of help?

Source: *Section EC 1.4 (c) of Model Code of Ethics and Professional Responsibility and Guidance for Enforcement (Model Code) of National Federation of Paralegal Associations, Inc. (NFPA). Used by permission.*

called "do-it-yourself"—divorces. If substantial assets are at stake in the divorce, or if there are other complicated issues involving child custody, child support, or spousal support, the parties usually hire lawyers to represent them in the divorce proceeding.

Divorce Settlement

Approximately 90 percent of divorce cases are settled between the parties prior to trial. The parties often engage in negotiations to try to settle a divorce lawsuit in order to save the time and expense of a trial and to reach a **divorce settlement** that is acceptable to each side. These negotiations usually are conducted between the parties with the assistance of each of their attorneys.

Some divorcing parties use mediation to try to reach a settlement of the issues involved in terminating their marriage. Some states have mandatory mediation before divorcing couples can use the court to try the case. In **mediation,** a neutral third party—an attorney, a retired judge, or other party—acts as a **mediator** between the parties. A mediator is not empowered to make a decision but, instead, acts as a go-between and facilitator to try to help the parties reach an acceptable settlement of the issues. Mediation tends to be successful because it forces the parties to consider all facets of the case, even the position of the opposing side.

Settlement agreement
A written document signed by divorcing parties that evidences their agreement settling property rights and other issues of their divorce.

If a settlement is reached, a **settlement agreement** is drafted, usually by the attorneys. After being signed by the parties, the settlement agreement is presented to the court. The court will accept the terms of the settlement agreement if the judge believes the settlement is fair and that the rights of the parties and minor children are properly taken care of. If a case is not settled, the case will go to trial.

DIVISION OF ASSETS AND SPOUSAL SUPPORT

Upon termination of a marriage, the parties may own certain assets, including property owned prior to marriage, gifts and inheritances received during marriage, and assets purchased with income earned during marriage. In most cases, the parties reach a settlement as to how these assets are to be divided. If no settlement agreement is reached, the court will order the **division of assets.**

Separate Property

Separate property
Property owned by a spouse prior to marriage, as well as inheritances and gifts received by a spouse during the marriage.

In most states, each spouse's separate property is awarded to the spouse who owns the separate property. **Separate property** includes property owned by a spouse prior to the marriage as well as inheritances and gifts received during the marriage. In most states, upon the termination of a marriage, each spouse is awarded his or her separate property.

But if separate property is commingled with marital property during the course of the marriage, or if the owner of the separate property changes title to the separate property by placing the other spouse's name on title to the property (e.g., real estate), the separate property is considered a marital asset.

Marital Property

Marital property
Property acquired during the course of marriage using income earned during the marriage, and separate property that has been converted to marital property.

Marital property consists of property acquired during the course of the marriage, using income earned by the spouses during the marriage and separate property that has been converted to marital property.

Different states adhere to two major legal theories when dividing marital assets upon the termination of a marriage. These are the theories of *equitable distribution* and *community property*.

Equitable Distribution

Equitable distribution
A law used by many states where the court orders a *fair distribution* of marital property to the divorcing spouses.

In states that follow the rule of **equitable distribution**, the court may order the **fair distribution** of property. The fair distribution of property does not necessarily mean the equal distribution of property. In determining the fair distribution of property, the court may consider factors such as:

- Length of the marriage
- Occupation of each spouse
- Standard of living during the marriage
- Wealth and income-earning ability of each spouse
- Which party is awarded custody of the children
- Health of the individuals
- Other factors relevant to the case

In most states, the house is awarded most often to the parent who is granted custody of the children. A court may order the house to be sold and the proceeds divided fairly between the individuals.

Community Property

Under the doctrine of **community property**, all property acquired during the marriage using income earned during the marriage is considered marital property. It does not matter which spouse earned the income or which spouse earned the higher income. Money placed in pension funds, stock options, the value of businesses, the value of professional licenses, and such, are considered community property.

In community-property states, marital property is divided *equally* between the individuals. An **equal division** of property does not necessarily mean that each piece of property is sold and the proceeds divided equally between the individuals. Typically, each asset of the marital asset is valued using appraisers and expert witnesses. The court then awards the property to the spouses. If one spouse is awarded the house, the other spouse is awarded other property of equal value.

Community property
A law used by some states in which the court orders an *equal division* of marital property to the divorcing spouses.

Division of Debts

Upon termination of the marriage, individuals often have debts that must be divided. How these debts are divided depends on the type of debt and on state law. In most states, each spouse is personally liable for his or her own premarital debts and the other spouse is not liable for these debts. This is because the debt was incurred prior to the marriage. Student loans are a good example of this type of debt.

Debts that are incurred during the marriage for necessities and other joint needs, including but not limited to shelter, clothing, automobiles, medical expenses, and such, are **joint marital debts** and are the joint responsibility of each spouse. The court may distribute these debts equally upon termination of the marriage. Spouses are jointly liable for taxes incurred during their marriage.

If a debt is not paid by the spouse to whom the court has distributed the debt, the third-party creditor may recover payment of the debt from the other spouse, however. This individual's only recourse is to recover the amount paid from his or her prior spouse.

Words pay no debts.

William Shakespeare
Troilus and Cressida, Act III

checklist ✓

DIVISION OF MARITAL PROPERTY

LAW	DESCRIPTION
• Equitable distribution	The marital property is distributed fairly. This does not necessarily mean the equal distribution of the property.
• Community property	The marital property is divided *equally* between the parties.

Advice from the Field ••••••••••••••••••••••••••••••••••••

THE FAMILY LAW PARALEGAL

The family law paralegal plays an extremely important role in the delivery of legal services to people who are involved in divorce proceedings. These clients for the most part have had little or no experience in legal proceedings and do not understand the legal process. They are frightened about their future and know their lives are about to change dramatically, for better or worse. They must open their personal life history to virtual strangers and expose themselves to the naked truth of their marital discord and failure.

People are most vulnerable at this point in their lives, coupled with the abundant free advice from family and friends who are not impartial and who purport to know the law. Everyone knows someone who has been through a divorce, and talk is cheap. Some people may have been referred to your office because you "got" their friend the marital home and that is what they want, too. Ironically, if your attorney has the reputation of being a "shark," it often is valued as a good thing.

The paralegal frequently is the first person to have initial contact with a prospective client, as the paralegal may schedule the appointment, take down preliminary new client information, and make the client feel welcome while he or she is waiting for the appointment. Don't be surprised if the prospective client asks you a question such as, "How many cases has your attorney won?" It takes experience to respond, giving a positive opinion of the attorney without answering the question. This question should not be answered, as one of the best-kept secrets of the family law practitioner is that there are no winners or losers in matrimonial cases handled by competent counsel. The cases are settled fairly and equitably under the totality of circumstances, or proceed to trial where the court will make the decision, after days, weeks, and sometime months of testimony. The attorney will make the determination during the initial interview as to whether the firm will take the case.

A frequently asked question is, "Should the paralegal be present during the initial interview"? Most attorneys respond in the negative. It is difficult enough for the prospective client to reveal intimate details of his or her marriage to one stranger, let alone a second one who is present. The best practice is for the attorney to be retained and for a Retainer Agreement to be fully executed before the paralegal begins work on the file.

The experienced paralegal will be able to prepare all the pleadings and paperwork necessary to litigate the case. No matter how much the paralegal knows about the case, only the attorney can make court appearances. However, the paralegal may be asked to prepare the case for trial and assist counsel at trial. As the case proceeds, the paralegal may be in direct communication with the clients to obtain detailed confidential information necessary to complete extensive paperwork. The divorce proceeding is "paper-intensive," and the paralegal will be privy to highly confidential information.

Attorney–client privilege extends to the paralegal, and the paralegal is bound by the same rule of confidentiality as the attorney. After a long day at work, the paralegal may go home to an inquisitive spouse or friend who will want to discuss the happenings of the day. Remember—,the attorney–client privilege extends to the paralegal, and what happens in the office must stay in the office!

Upon the termination of a marriage, it is wise for the individuals to notify prior creditors that they will no longer be responsible for the other's debts. This is particularly true if the individuals have joint credit cards.

Spousal Support

Spousal support
Payments made by one divorced spouse to the other divorced spouse. Also called *alimony*.

In some cases where a marriage is terminated, a court may award **spousal support**—also called **alimony**—to one of the divorced spouses. The other divorced spouse typically is ordered to pay the alimony in monthly payments. The parties may agree to the amount of alimony to be paid. If they do not reach an agreement, the court will determine whether the payment of alimony is warranted and, if so, the amount of alimony to be paid. In the past, alimony usually has been awarded to the female. Today, with the female often earning more than the male, the male has been awarded alimony in some cases.

Alimony is usually awarded for a specific period of time. This is called **temporary alimony** or **rehabilitation alimony**. This alimony is designed to provide the receiving individual with payment for a limited time during which the individual can obtain the necessary education or job skills necessary to enter the job force. Alimony also is awarded in cases where a parent, usually the female, is needed to care for a child with a disability and must remain home to care for the child. The amount of alimony is based on the needs of the individual who will receive the alimony and the income and ability of the other individual to pay.

Spousal support payments terminate if the former spouse dies, remarries, or otherwise becomes self-sufficient. Spousal support awards may be modified by the court if circumstances change. This occurs if the paying individual loses his or her job, or his or her income decreases, if the receiving individual's income increases, or similar circumstances. A party wishing to have a spousal support award changed must petition the court to *modify* the award of spousal support.

The award of **permanent alimony**—sometimes called **lifetime alimony**—is usually awarded only if the individual to receive the alimony is of an older age and if that individual has been a homemaker who has little opportunity to obtain job skills to enter the workplace. Permanent alimony must be paid until the individual receiving it dies or remarries.

CHILD CUSTODY AND CHILD SUPPORT

When a marriage is terminated, the custody of a child or children must be decided. In addition, child support may be awarded. These issues are discussed next.

Child Custody

When a couple terminates their marriage and they have children, the issue of who is legally and physically responsible for raising the children must be decided, either by settlement or by the court. The legal term **custody** is used to describe who has legal responsibility for raising a child. **Child custody** is one of the most litigated issues of a divorcing couple.

Traditionally, the court almost always granted custody of a child to the mother. Today, with fathers taking a more active role in childrearing, and with many mothers working, this is not always the case.

In **child custody disputes**, where both parents want custody of a child, the courts will determine what is in the **best interests of the child** in awarding custody. Some of the factors that a court considers are:

Child custody
The awarding of legal custody of a child to a parent based on the best interests of the child. The parent awarded custody is called the *custodial parent*.

- The ability of each parent to provide for the emotional needs of the child.
- The ability of each parent to provide for the needs of the child, such as education.
- The ability of each parent to provide a stable environment for the child.
- The ability of each parent to provide for the special needs of a child if the child has a disability or requires special care.
- The desire of each parent to provide for the needs of the child.
- The wishes of the child. This factor is given more weight the older the child is.
- The religion of each parent.
- Other factors the court deems relevant.

The awarding of custody to a **custodial parent** is not permanent. Custody may be altered by the court if circumstances change.

The parent who is awarded custody has **legal custody** of the child. This usually includes physical custody of the child. The custodial parent has the right to make day-to-day decisions and major decisions concerning the child's education, religion, and other such matters.

The court will not award custody to a parent, and sometimes not to either parent, if it is in the child's best interest not to be awarded to a parent, or if there has been **child abuse,** or because of other extenuating circumstances. In such cases, the court may award custody to other relatives, such as grandparents, or place the child in a foster home.

Joint Custody

Most states now permit joint custody of a child. **Joint custody** means that both parents are responsible for making major decisions concerning the child, such as his or her education, religion, and other major matters.

Parents sometimes are awarded **joint physical custody** of the child as well. This means that the child will spend a certain portion of time being raised by each parent. For example, the child may spend every other week with each parent, or the weekdays with one parent and the weekends with another parent. These arrangements are awarded only if the child's best interests are served—for example, the child remaining in the same school while in the physical custody of each parent.

Visitation Rights

If the parents do not have joint custody of a child, the noncustodial parent typically is awarded **visitation rights**. This means that the noncustodial parent is given the right to visit the child for limited periods of time, as determined by a settlement agreement or by the court.

If the court is concerned about the safety of a child, the court may grant only supervised visitation rights to a noncustodial parent. This means that a court-appointed person must he present during the noncustodial parent's visitation with the child. This usually is done if there has been a history of child abuse or there is a strong possibility that the noncustodial parent may kidnap the child.

Child Support

Child support
Payments made by the noncustodial parent to help pay for the financial support of his or her children.

The noncustodial parent is obligated to contribute to the financial support of his or her natural and adopted children. This includes the child's costs for food, shelter, clothing, medical expenses, and other necessities of life. This payment is called **child support**. The custodial and noncustodial parents may agree to the amount of child support. If they do not, the court will determine the amount of child support to be paid.

In awarding child support, the court considers several factors, including the number of children, needs of the children, net income of the parents, standard of living of the children prior to termination of the marriage, any special medical or other needs of the children, and other factors that the court deems relevant. The duty to pay child support usually continues until a child reaches the age of majority or graduates from high school, or emancipates himself or herself by voluntarily choosing to live on his or her own.

To help in the determination of child support, about half of the states have adopted a formula for computing the amount of child support, based on a percentage of the noncustodial parent's income. A court is permitted to deviate from the formula if a child has special needs, such as if the child has a disability or requires special educational assistance.

An award of child support may be *modified* if conditions change. For example, an award of child support may be decreased if the noncustodial parent loses his or her job. Or the amount of child support may be modified if the child's needs change, such as if the child needs special care because of a disability. The parent wishing to obtain modification of child support must petition the court to change the award of child support.

Family Support Act

In the past, many noncustodial parents failed to pay child support when due. This often required long and expensive legal procedures by the custodial parent to obtain child support payments. To remedy this situation, the federal government enacted the **Family Support Act**. This federal law, effective in 1994, provides that all original or modified child support orders require automatic wage withholding from a noncustodial parent's income. The Family Support Act was designed primarily to prevent noncustodial parents from failing to pay required support payments.

Assume that a court order requires a noncustodial parent to pay 25 percent of his or her gross monthly income for child support. In this case, the court will order that noncustodial parent's employer to deduct this amount from that parent's income and send a check in this amount to the custodial parent. The noncustodial parent receives a check for the remainder of his or her income.

Legal Terminology

Adoption 567
Adoptive parents 567
Agency adoption 567
Alimony 574
Annulment 569
Antenuptial agreement 564
At-fault divorce 570
Best interests of the child 575
Biological parents 567
Child abuse 576
Child custody 575
Child custody disputes 575
Child liability statute 567
Child neglect 566
Child support 576
Civil union 566
Common-law marriage 565
Community property 573
Custodial parent 575
Custody 575
Decree of divorce 571
Defense of Marriage Act (DOMA) 566
Division of assets 572
Divorce 570
Divorce settlement 572
Emancipation 564
Engagement 562

Equal division 573
Equitable distribution 572
Fair distribution 572
Family Support Act 577
Father's registry 566
Fault rule 562
Fiancé 562
Fiancée 562
Financial support 565
Foster care 569
Foster child 569
Foster family 569
Foster parent 569
Independent adoption 567
Irreconcilable differences 570
Joint custody 576
Joint physical custody 576
Joint marital debts 573
Legal custody 576
Lifetime alimony 575
Marital assets 570
Marital property 572
Marriage 564
Marriage ceremony 565
Marriage license 564
Marriage requirements 564
Marriage termination 569

Mediation 572
Mediator 572
No-fault divorce 570
Objective rule 563
Open adoption 567
Parents 565
Parents' duties 565
Parents' right 565
Paternity 566
Paternity action 566
Permanent alimony 575
Petition for divorce 570
Premarital agreement 563
Prenuptial agreement 563
Pro se divorce 571
Promise to marry 562
Rehabilitation alimony 575
Restraining order 571
Same-sex marriage 566
Separate property 572
Settlement agreement 572
Spousal support 574
Surrogacy 567
Surrogacy contract 567
Temporary alimony 575
Visitation rights 576

Summary

CHAPTER 16   FAMILY LAW

Premarriage Issues

Promise to marry	A promise by one person to marry is made to another person. The courts usually do not enforce such promises as contracts.
Engagement	The engagement is a period of time that begins when one person asks another person to marry him or her, and ends when the parties get married or terminate their engagement. The prospective bride is called the *fiancée*, and the prospective groom is called the *fiancé*. Most often, the male is the one who gives the female an engagement ring to signify their engagement. Females also may give males engagement rings.
Terminated Engagement	If a party ends the engagement, states apply one of the following rules regarding return of the engagement ring. a. *Fault rule*: If the prospective groom breaks off the engagement, the prospective bride may keep the ring. If the prospective bride breaks off the engagement, the ring must be returned to the prospective groom. b. *Objective rule*: If the engagement is broken off, the prospective bride must return the ring to the prospective groom irrespective as to which party broke off the engagement.
Prenuptial Agreement	A prenuptial agreement is a contract entered into by prospective spouses prior to marriage, specifying how property will be distributed upon termination of the marriage or death of a spouse.
Antenuptial Agreement	An antenuptial agreement is a contract entered into by prospective spouses during marriage, specifying how property will be distributed upon termination of the marriage or death of a spouse.

Marriage

Marriage	Marriage has been defined as a legal union between a male and a female that confers certain duties and rights upon the spouses. Some states permit the marriage of spouses of the same sex.
Marriage License	A marriage license is a legal document issued by the state, certifying that two people are married.
Marriage Ceremony	A marriage ceremony is held before a designated government official, or at a church, temple, synagogue, mosque, or other place of worship before a minister, priest, rabbi, or mullah. At the ceremony, the parties exchange wedding vows.
Common-Law Marriage	A common-law marriage is a type of marriage recognized by several states, wherein two people who have not been officially married are considered married if certain requirements are met, such as living together for a specified period of time.
Same-Sex Marriage	Same-sex marriage is a marriage between two people of the same sex. Several states permit same-sex marriages. Some other states permit *civil unions* between persons of the same sex.

Parents and Children

Emancipation	Emancipation occurs if a child leaves the parents and voluntarily lives on his or her own. The child then is responsible for providing his or her own livelihood.
Paternity Action	A paternity action is a legal proceeding in which the court identifies the true identity of the father of a child.

Surrogacy	Surrogacy is a situation in which a woman agrees to be artificially inseminated with the sperm of a male and to give the baby up to the sperm donor (and his spouse, if he has a spouse) upon the birth of the child. The contract between the birth mother and the father (and spouse) is called a *surrogacy agreement*.

Adoption	Adoption occurs when a person becomes the legal parent of a child who is not his or her biological child.
	1. *Agency adoption*:
	   A person adopts a child from a social organization of a state.
	2. *Open adoption*:
	   The biological mother is introduced to the adoptive parent or parents prior to the adoption.
	3. *Independent adoption*:
	   The biological mother or parents enter into a private arrangement with the adoptive parent or parents for the adoption of the child.

Foster Care	Foster care is an arrangement in which a child is placed temporarily with a foster family. The state government pays the foster family a fee for caring for the foster child.

Termination of Marriage

Annulment	An annulment is an order of the court declaring that a marriage did not exist.
Divorce	A divorce is an order of the court that terminates a marriage. A *decree of divorce* is issued by the court that terminates the divorce. 1. *At-fault divorce*: a divorce recognized by the law of a state that requires the petitioning party to allege and prove grounds for obtaining a divorce. 2. *No-fault divorce*: a divorce recognized by the law of a state where neither party is blamed for the divorce; the petitioning party merely has to assert irreconcilable differences.
Pro Se Divorce	*Pro se* denotes a divorce proceeding in which the parties do not hire an attorney but instead represent themselves in the divorce action.
Divorce Settlement	Prior to going to court, the parties sometimes settle their divorce voluntarily. The *settlement agreement* is the written document signed by the divorcing parties that evidences their agreement to settle property rights and other issues of their divorce.

Division of Assets and Spousal Support

Separate Property	Separate property is the property owned by a spouse prior to marriage, as well as inheritances and gifts received by the spouse during the marriage.
Marital Property	Marital property is the property acquired during the course of marriage using income earned during the marriage, plus property that has been converted into marital property. Two methods are: 1. A method used by some states where the court orders *equitable* (fair) *distribution* of marital property to the divorcing spouses. This does not necessarily mean the equal distribution of marital property. 2. A method used by some states where the court orders an *equal distribution* of marital property to the divorcing spouses.
Division of Debts	*Joint marital debts* incurred during the marriage are the joint responsibility of divorcing spouses. The court may distribute these debts to individual divorcing spouses, but if that spouse does not pay the debt, the creditor can seek payment from the other divorced spouse.

Spousal Support	Spousal support is an amount of money ordered by a court to be paid by one divorcing spouse to another divorcing spouse for a period of time during and after the divorce is final. Also called *alimony* of which there are two types: 1. *Temporary alimony*: An amount ordered by the court to be paid to one divorcing spouse to the other divorcing spouse for a limited period of time. Also called *rehabilitation alimony*. 2. *Permanent alimony*: An amount ordered by the court to be paid to one divorcing spouse to the other divorcing spouse until the receiving spouse dies or remarries. Sometimes called *lifetime alimony*.

Child Custody and Child Support

Child Custody	The awarding of child custody to a parent is based on the best interests of the child. The parent awarded custody is called the *custodial parent*. The other parent is called the *noncustodial parent*.
Joint Custody	Joint custody means that both divorcing parents are responsible for making major decisions concerning the child.
Joint Physical Custody	Joint physical custody means that the child of divorcing parents spends a certain amount of time being raised by each parent.
Visitation Rights	Visitation rights confer to the noncustodial parent the right to visit his or her child for limited periods of time.
Child Support	Child support consists of payments made by the noncustodial parent to help pay for the financial support of his or her children.
Family Support Act	The Family Support Act is a federal statute that provides for the automatic withholding of child support payments from a noncustodial parent's income.

▶ WORKING THE WEB

1. Using **http://google.com** or similar Internet search engine, find the marriage requirements for your state. Write a one-page report describing the requirements for getting married in your state.

2. Go to the website **http://en.wikipedia.org/wiki/cohabitation_agreement**. What is a cohabitation agreement? When would such an agreement be used? Write a one-page report describing a cohabitation agreement, and the advantages and disadvantages of using one.

3. **Using http://google.com** or similar Internet search engine, find the law or an article about the law of dividing marital property upon divorce in your state. Does your state follow the equitable distribution rule or the community property rule for dividing marital property?

4. Go to the website **http://www/fbi.gov/hq/cid/cac/recovery.htm**. Read this page regarding the federal crimes associated with not paying child support. Write a one-page report discussing these federal crimes and the penalties for committing these crimes.

5. Choose a country, and using the website **http://google.com** or similar Internet search engine, find information about adopting a child from that country. Write a one-page report discussing the adoption services available and the requirements for adopting a child from that country.

CRITICAL THINKING AND WRITING QUESTIONS

1. What is a promise to marry? Is such a promise enforceable?
2. What is engagement? Who gets the engagement ring if the engagement is broken off, under (a) the fault rule, and (b) the objective rule.
3. Describe a prenuptial agreement. Under what circumstances will prenuptial agreements not be enforced?
4. Define marriage. What are the legal requirements to be able to be married? Define a marriage license.
5. What is a common-law marriage?
6. What is same-sex marriage? In which states are same-sex marriages recognized?
7. Describe a parent's rights and duties toward his or her children?
8. What is a paternity action? What is a father's registry?
9. Define a surrogacy contract. Who are the parties to a surrogacy contract?
10. Describe the following: (a) agency adoption, (b) open adoption, and (c) independent adoption.
11. Define and describe foster care.
12. What is an annulment? What are the requirements for obtaining an annulment?
13. Define divorce. Describe the difference between (a) at-fault divorce, and (b) no-fault divorce.
14. Describe the following: (a) petition for divorce, (b) decree of divorce, and (c) *pro se* divorce.
15. Describe a divorce settlement. What is a settlement agreement?
16. Describe the difference between (a) separate property, and (b) marital property.
17. Describe the rule of equitable distribution. Describe the doctrine of separate property.
18. What is spousal support? Explain the difference between (a) temporary alimony or rehabilitation alimony, and (b) permanent alimony or lifetime alimony.
19. Describe (a) child custody, (b) joint custody, (c) joint physical custody, and (d) visitation rights.
20. What is child support?
21. What does the Family Support Act provide?

ETHICS ANALYSIS AND DISCUSSION QUESTIONS

1. What are the ethical obligations of a paralegal regarding discussing facts about a client's divorce with others? Explain.
2. As a paralegal, can you give any advice to clients of your law firm regarding the procedures for obtaining a divorce in your state? What are the limits of the information that you can tell a client about such procedures?
3. As a paralegal, the attorney you work for has requested that you research how to adopt a child from another country. You find out this information. The client calls to see if you have found out this information. As a paralegal, are you at liberty to share this information with the client? Explain.

DEVELOPING YOUR COLLABORATION SKILLS

With a group of other students, selected by you or as assigned by your instructor, review the Paralegals at Work at the beginning of the chapter. As a group, discuss the following questions.

1. Discuss the requirements for obtaining a divorce in your state.
2. What is the difference between marital property and separate property?
3. Does your state follow the equitable distribution doctrine or the community property doctrine for dividing marital property? How would marital and separate property be divided in your state?
4. Do you think either of the divorcing parties would receive spousal support? If so, who and how much?
5. Under the law, who most likely would be awarded custody of the two children? Why? Would child support be warranted in this case?
6. What type of visitation rights would most likely be granted to the noncustodial parent?
7. Would you recommend that Ms. Aston, represented by Ms. Khan, should seek mediation to try to settle the divorce issues with Mr. Pit? Why or why not?

▶PARALEGAL PORTFOLIO EXERCISE

Refer to the Paralegals and Work at the beginning of the chapter. Prepare a memorandum, no longer than three pages, that describes how the property of Ms. Aston and Mr. Pit would be distributed under (1) the rule of equi-table distribution, and (2) the rule of community property. Make any assumptions you think are necessary, but be sure to list those assumptions in your memorandum.

▶LEGAL ANALYSIS AND WRITING CASES

Neville v. Neville

734 So.2d 352 (1999)
Court of Appeals of Mississippi

FACTS

George Neville and Tina Neville were married in 1988. At the time, George was 31 years old and a practicing attorney; Tina was a 23-year-old medical student. After 7 years, Tina became a licensed physician. In 1995, George filed for divorce from Tina because she was having an adulterous affair with another doctor. At the time of the divorce, George was earning $55,000 per year practicing law; Tina was earning $165,000 per year as a physician.

The divorce was filed in Mississippi, where the couple lived. Mississippi follows the doctrine of equitable distribu-tion. George sought to have Tina's medical license and med-ical practice valued as an ongoing business, and he claimed a portion of the value. The court refused George's request and instead applied the doctrine of equitable distribution and awarded him rehabilitative alimony of $1,400 per month for 120 months. The aggregate amount of the alimony was $168,000. George appealed this award, alleging on appeal that Tina's medical license and practice should be valued and that he should receive a portion of this value.

Question

1. Under the doctrine of equitable distribution, was the Trial Court's award fair, or should George win on appeal?

Johnston v. Johnston

649 N.E.2d 799 (1995)
Appeals Court of Masschusetts

FACTS

Ronald R. and Edith Johnston were married in 1967 and had three sons, who ranged in age from 12 to 16 when the parties separated in 1986. Edith filed for divorce the same year. The Johnstons owned a primary residence worth $186,000, with no mortgage on it. Ronald was a successful entrepreneur. He owned Depot Distributors, Inc., a business involved in sell-ing and installing bathroom cabinets. He also owned several other businesses. Ronald's income was $543,382 in 1985, $820,439 in 1986, $1,919,713 in 1987, and $1,462,712 in 1988. Ronald invested much of his income in commercial and residential real estate, which was held in his name only. At the time of the divorce trial in 1991, the real estate was valued at $11,790,000 and was subject to mortgages of $4,966,343.

After their separation, Ronald engaged in certain trans-fers of property and distributions of property, in violation of the court's order, that obfuscated his income and net worth. The Trial Court judge therefore accepted Edith's appraisals of the value of the real estate. The trial court judge applied the equitable distribution doctrine of Massachusetts and awarded Edith real estate totaling $2,446,000, the family res-idence, and alimony of $1,200 per month. The trial court judge awarded Ronald real estate valued at $9,314,000 sub-ject to mortgages of $4,966,343, for a net value of $4,347,657. The judge characterized this as a roughly 60-40 split of the real estate (i.e., 60 percent for Ronald and 40 per-cent for Edith). Ronald appealed the split of real estate and the award of alimony as violating the equitable distribution doctrine.

Question

1. Under the doctrine of equitable distribution, was the Trial Court's award fair, or should Ronald win on appeal?

Schweinberg v. Click

627 So.2d 548 (1993)
Court of Appeal of Florida

FACTS

Randolph J. Schweinberg and Sandra Faye Click were married on January 26, 1973. On March 12, 1986, Sandra Click moved out of the couple's home, and the couple was divorced on December 2, 1986. At the time of the divorce, the couple had two minor children, Randolph II and Russell. Randolph II had cerebral palsy and walked with difficulty. The children lived with Randolph after Sandra moved out. Randolph was a sergeant in the United States Air Force, stationed in South Carolina; however, he considered Florida as his permanent home.

In the divorce proceeding, the court awarded custody of the two minor children to Randolph. The two children were doing well in school, and the court found that Randolph II needed the emotional support provided by his brother Russell. Sandra was permitted visitation rights to see the children. Sandra later married a new husband, who previously had been convicted of lewd and lascivious behavior on a female child and was under court supervision for 15 years.

On December 19, 1991, Sandra petitioned the court to modify the custody order to grant her custody of the two minor children. The trial court granted the petition and awarded custody to Sandra. Randolph appealed the trial court's decision.

Question

1. Under the best interests test, should Randolph or Sandra be awarded custody of the two minor children?

Chadwick v. Janecka, Prison Warden, Pennsylvania

312 F.3d 597 (2002)
United States Court of Appeals, Third Circuit

FACTS

In 1992, Mrs. Barbara Chadwick filed for divorce from Mr. H. Beatty Chadwick in Pennsylvania. During an equitable distribution conference in 1993, Mr. Chadwick informed the divorce court that he had transferred more than $2.5 million of the marital estate to pay an alleged debt he owed to Maison Blanche, Ltd., a Gibraltar partnership. It later was discovered that the principals of Maison Blanche had transferred $995,726 to a bank account in Switzerland in Mr. Chadwick's name and had purchased $869,106 of insurance annuity contracts in Mr. Chadwick's name. Mr. Chadwick redeemed these annuity contracts and received the money. In addition, $550,000 in stock certificates in Mr. Chadwick's name had been "lost."

The divorce court ordered Mr. Chadwick to return the $2,502,000 to an account under the jurisdiction of the court. When Mr. Chadwick refused, the court held Mr. Chadwick in civil contempt of court and ordered him jailed. During a seven-year period of incarceration, Mr. Chadwick applied 14 times to be released from prison, and each request was denied. Mr. Chadwick filed another request to be released from prison, alleging that he should be released because of the unlikelihood that he would comply with the divorce court's order to turn over the money and that, therefore, the civil contempt order has lost its coercive effect.

The District Court agreed and granted Mr. Chadwick's petition to be released from prison. The government appealed the case to the U.S. Court of Appeals.

Question

1. Did Mr. Chadwick act ethically in this case? Should Mr. Chadwick be released from prison?

Baker v. State of Vermont

744 A.2d 864 (1999)
Supreme Court of Vermont

FACTS

The plaintiffs are three same-sex couples who have lived together in committed relationships for periods ranging from 4 to 25 years. Two of the couples have raised children together. Each couple applied for a marriage license from their respective town clerks in the Vermont towns they lived in, and each was refused a marriage license because the Town Clerk determined that same-sex couples were ineligible to marry under Vermont law that permitted opposite-sex couples to marry.

The plaintiffs filed this lawsuit against the State of Vermont and the three towns, seeking declaratory judgment that the refusal to issue the plaintiffs marriage licenses violated the Vermont Constitution. The Vermont Trial Court upheld the state's and the towns' decision to refuse to grant marriage licenses to the plaintiffs. The plaintiffs appealed to the Vermont Supreme Court.

Question

1. May the State of Vermont exclude same-sex couples from the benefits and protections that its laws provide to opposite-sex married couples?

▶ WORKING WITH THE LANGUAGE OF THE COURT CASE

Troxel v. Granville

530 U.S. 57, 120 S.Ct. 2054,
147 L.Ed.2d 49 (2000)
Supreme Court of the United States

Read the following case, excerpted from the U.S. Supreme Court opinion. Review and brief the case. In your brief, answer the following questions.

1. Who were the original plaintiffs?
2. What rights did the plaintiffs seek? What law did the plaintiffs assert that gave them this right?
3. Who is the defendant?
4. What rights did the original defendant seek? What law did the defendant assert that gave her this right?

5. What was the decision of the U.S. Supreme Court? What law did the Supreme Court apply in reaching its decision?

Section 26.10.160(3) of the Revised Code of Washington permits "any person" to petition a superior court for visitation rights "at any time," and authorizes that court to grant such visitation rights whenever "visitation may serve the best interest of the child." Petitioners Jenifer and Gary Troxel petitioned a Washington Superior Court for the right to visit their grandchildren, Isabelle and Natalie Troxel. Respondent Tommie Granville, the mother of Isabelle and Natalie, opposed the petition. The case ultimately reached the Washington Supreme Court, which held that Section 26.10.160(3) unconstitutionally interferes with the fundamental right of parents to rear their children.

Tommie Granville and Brad Troxel shared a relationship that ended in June 1991. The two never married, but they had two daughters, Isabelle and Natalie. Jenifer and Gary Troxel are Brad's parents, and thus the paternal grandparents of Isabelle and Natalie. After Tommie and Brad separated in 1991, Brad lived with his parents and regularly brought his daughters to his parents' home for weekend visitation. Brad committed suicide in May 1993. Although the Troxels at first continued to see Isabelle and Natalie on a regular basis after their son's death, Tommie Granville informed the Troxels in October 1993 that she wished to limit their visitation with her daughters to one short visit per month.

In December 1993, the Troxels commenced the present action by filing, in the Washington Superior Court for Skagit County, a petition to obtain visitation rights with Isabelle and Natalie. The

Troxels filed their petition under Washington statute Wash. Rev. Code Section 26.10.160(3) (1994). Section 26.10.160(3) provides: "Any person may petition the court for visitation rights at any time including, but not limited to, custody proceedings. The court may order visitation rights for any person when visitation may serve the best interest of the child."

At trial, the Troxels requested two weekends of overnight visitation per month and two weeks of visitation each summer. Granville did not oppose visitation altogether, but instead asked the court to order one day of visitation per month with no overnight stay. In 1995, the Superior Court issued an oral ruling and entered a visitation decree ordering visitation one weekend per month, one week during the summer, and four hours on both of the petitioning grandparents' birthdays.

Granville appealed, during which time she married Kelly Wynn. Before addressing the merits of Granville's appeal, the Washington Court of Appeals remanded the case to the Superior Court. Granville's husband formally adopted Isabelle and Natalie.

The Washington Court of Appeals reversed the lower court's visitation order and dismissed the Troxels' petition for visitation, holding that nonparents lack standing to seek visitation under Section 26.10.160(3) unless a custody action is pending. In the Court of Appeals' view, that limitation on nonparental visitation actions was consistent with the constitutional restrictions on state interference with parents' fundamental liberty interest in the care, custody, and management of their children.

The Washington Supreme Court granted the Troxels' petition for review and affirmed. The Washington Supreme Court agreed with the Court of Appeals' ultimate conclusion that the Troxels could not obtain visitation of Isabelle and Natalie pursuant to Section 26.10.160(3). The court rested its decision on the Federal Constitution, holding that Section 26.10.160(3) unconstitutionally infringes on the fundamental right of parents to rear their children.

We granted certiorari and now affirm the judgment. Specifically, we are asked to decide whether Section 26.10.160(3), as applied to Tommie Granville and her family, violates the Federal Constitution. The Fourteenth Amendment provides that no State shall "deprive any person of life, liberty, or property, without due process of law."

The liberty interest at issue in this case—the interest of parents in the care, custody, and control of their children—is perhaps the oldest of the fundamental liberty interests recognized by this Court.

We have recognized the fundamental right of parents to make decisions concerning the care, custody, and control of their children.

Section 26.10.160(3), as applied to Granville and her family in this case, unconstitutionally infringes on that fundamental parental right. The Washington nonparental visitation statute is breathtakingly broad. According to the statute's text, *any person* may petition the court for visitation rights *at any time*, and the court may grant such visitation rights whenever visitation may serve *the best interest of the child*. 26.10.160(3). That language effectively permits any third party seeking visitation to subject any decision by a parent concerning visitation of the parent's children to state-court review. Once the visitation petition has been filed in court and the matter is placed before a judge, a parent's decision that visitation would not be in the child's best interest is accorded no deference. Section 26.10.160(3) contains no requirement that a court accord the parent's decision any presumption of validity or any weight whatsoever. Instead, the Washington statute places the best-interest determination solely in the hands of the judge. Should the judge disagree with the parent's estimation of the child's best interests, the judge's view necessarily prevails. Thus, in practical

effect, in the State of Washington a court can disregard and overturn *any* decision by a fit custodial parent concerning visitation whenever a third party affected by the decision files a visitation petition, based solely on the judge's determination of the child's best interests.

Turning to the facts of this case, the record reveals that the Superior Court's order was based on precisely the type of mere disagreement we have just described and nothing more. The Superior Court's order was not founded on any special factors that might justify the State's interference with Granville's fundamental right to make decisions concerning the rearing of her two daughters.

The Troxels did not allege, and no court has found, that Granville was an unfit parent. That aspect of the case is important, for there is a presumption that fit parents act in the best interests of their children. Accordingly, so long as a parent adequately cares for his or her children (*i.e.*, is fit), there will normally be no reason for the State to inject itself into the private realm of the family to further question the ability of that parent to make the best decisions concerning the rearing of that parent's children.

We note that there is no allegation that Granville ever sought to cut off visitation entirely. Rather, the present dispute originated when Granville informed the Troxels that she would prefer to restrict their visitation with Isabelle and Natalie to one short visit per month and special holidays.

In the Superior Court proceedings Granville did not oppose visitation but instead asked that the duration of any visitation order be shorter than that requested by the Troxels. While the Troxels requested two weekends per month and two full weeks in the summer, Granville asked the Superior Court to order only one day of visitation per month (with no overnight stay) and participation in the Granville family's holiday celebrations.

The combination of these factors demonstrates that the visitation order in this case was an unconstitutional infringement on Granville's fundamental right to make decisions concerning the care, custody, and control of her two daughters. Accordingly, we hold that Section 26.10.160(3), as applied in this case, is unconstitutional. ■

AGENCY AND EMPLOYMENT LAW

"Let every eye negotiate for itself, and
trust no agent."

William Shakespeare,
Much Ado About Nothing

PARALEGALS AT WORK

You are an attorney for Ms. Francis Brown, a renowned attorney in the area of employment law. You have been Ms. Brown's paralegal for more than ten years. One day Ms. Brown calls you into her office to sit in on a conference with a new client, Ms. Maria Rodriquez. Ms. Rodriquez has hired Ms. Brown to determine whether she has an employment law case against her employer, Retro Bank, N.A., a private bank that has hundreds of branch offices across the United States. During the conference, Ms. Rodriquez explains her situation.

Ms. Rodriquez has worked for Retro Bank for fifteen years. She started as an assistant branch manager and was promoted to Branch Manager and Assistant Vice President seven years ago. Ms. Rodriquez is still an Assistant Vice President and branch manager in a branch office located in the Hispanic community. Ms. Rodriquez explains that she had earned a bachelor's degree in business administration from the Wharton School, University of Pennsylvania, just before starting with the bank.

Several months ago Ms. Rodriquez applied for a promotion to District Manager of a region of the bank. The bank advertised this open position. One other candidate applied for the position. Mr. Rich Huntington, a white male, had graduated with a master in Business Administration (MBA) degree from a university and has worked as a branch manager for three years.

The candidate to be promoted to the new District Manager position would be in charge of at least ten branch offices, and the promotion to this position would include the title "Vice President" and a salary increase of $50,000 per year. The requirements for the new position were a bachelor's degree, experience as a bank branch manager for three or more years, passing a financial analysis test, and an interview with the President and the Board of Directors of the bank. Ms. Rodriquez and Mr. Huntington both passed the financial test.

At the interview, the president and board members of the bank asked Ms. Rodriquez questions about her job experience and management style. Ms. Rodriquez

---

After studying this chapter, you should be able to:

1. Describe how express, implied, and apparent agencies are created.

2. Identify and describe the principal's liability for the tortuous conduct of an agent.

3. Explain how state workers' compensation programs work and describe the benefits available.

4. Describe the scope of coverage of Title VII of the Civil Rights Act of 1964.

5. Describe the scope of coverage of the Age Discrimination in Employment Act.

6. Describe the protections afforded by the Americans with Disabilities Act.

7. Describe how a labor union is organized and employers' rights to strike and picket.

found several question somewhat troubling—questions about the ages of her two children (4 and 6), whether she would be willing to attend charity events on some evenings to promote the bank, and whether traveling on bank business would cause any problems with her family. Later, Ms. Rodriquez was told that she did not receive the promotion, that Mr. Huntington had received the promotion.

Ms. Rodriquez wants to know if she has any cause to sue Retro Bank. She said she had heard that the bank promoted majority-race males over minority-race females in the past, particularly for positions as District Managers, including oversight of bank branches in primarily white areas. Currently the bank has forty District Managers. Only four of the District Managers are females, and none of them are minorities.

Consider the issues involved in this scenario as you read the chapter.

▶ INTRODUCTION FOR THE PARALEGAL

Paralegals often work for lawyers who specialize in employment law matters. Lawyers in this area of practice negotiate and draft employment contracts, advise businesses on compliance with federal and state worker protection and antidiscrimination laws, and represent businesses and employees in the litigation of employment law disputes. Paralegals who work in this area must have an understanding of agency law, federal and state employment statutes, and administrative law that affects the employment relationship.

If individuals and businesses had to conduct all of their business personally, the scope of their activities would be severely curtailed. The use of agents (or agency), which allows one person to act on behalf of another, solves this problem. Among the many examples of agency relationships are a salesperson who sells goods for a store, an executive who works for a corporation, a partner who acts on behalf of a partnership, an attorney who is hired to represent a client, and a real estate broker who is employed to sell a house. Agency is governed by a large body of common law, known as *agency law*.

The United States Congress has enacted many federal statutes that provide protections and benefits for employees. For example, Congress has enacted federal statutes establishing worker safety rules, providing for the payment of minimum wages, and prohibiting discrimination based on race, sex, religion, age, disability, and other protected classes. States have enacted similar laws.

Employment law is a burgeoning area of the law. Paralegals will be called on to conduct research, assist lawyers in the preparation and review of employment contracts, and prepare for litigation in this exciting area of the law. Agency and employment law are discussed in this chapter. ■

AGENCY LAW

Agency relationships are formed by the mutual consent of a principal and an agent. Section 1(1) of the Restatement (Second) of Agency defines *agency* as a *fiduciary relationship* "which results from the manifestation of consent by one person to another that the other shall act in his behalf and subject to his control, and consent by the other so to act." The Restatement (Second) of Agency is the reference source of the rules of agency. A party who employs another person to act on his or her behalf is called a **principal**. A party who agrees to act on behalf of another is called an **agent**. The principal–agent relationship is commonly referred to as an **agency**. This relationship is depicted in Exhibit 17.1.

Any person who has the capacity to contract can appoint an agent to act on his or her behalf. Generally, persons who lack contractual capacity, such as insane persons and minors, cannot appoint an agent. But, the court can appoint a legal guardian or other representative to handle the affairs of insane persons, minors, and others who lack capacity to contract. With court approval, these representatives can enter into enforceable contracts on behalf of the persons they represent.

Principal
A party who employs another person to act on his or her behalf.

Agent
A party who agrees to act on behalf of another.

Agency
A principal–agent relationship; the fiduciary relationship "which results from the manifestation of consent by one person to another that the other shall act in his behalf and subject to his control, and consent by the other so to act."

Exhibit 17.1 **The principal-agent relationship**

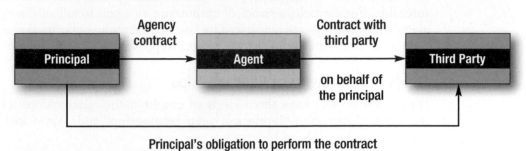

THE PARALEGAL AND EMPLOYMENT LAW

The paralegal who works in the employment law area can be involved in many different areas. Employment law consists of an array of state and federal laws. A paralegal who works in the employment law field must have good knowledge of the state and federal laws that apply to employers and employees in the state in which they work.

The law of agency applies to employers and employees, as well as to other employment relationships. Principals generally are liable for the torts of their agents, and usually are liable for the contracts entered into by agents on behalf of the principal while the agent is acting within the scope of his or her employment.

Employers often are sued by third parties either to recover for the negligence and other torts committed by employees, or to enforce contracts that their employees have entered. Agency law is an area of the law in which paralegals are needed to support attorneys, particularly when an attorney is representing the employer, employee, or third party in lawsuits involving agency and employment law matters.

In the employment law area, attorneys are called upon to negotiate and draft employment contracts. Attorneys sometimes are hired by corporations and other businesses to draft form employment contracts that the employer requires employees to sign. In other cases, attorneys represent either the executive or the employer in negotiating complex employment law agreements—bonuses, stock option plans, and the like. Paralegals usually prepare drafts of these employment contracts for the attorneys.

Paralegals often work for attorneys who represent clients who must comply with complex federal and state worker safety and protection statutes. These include workers' compensation laws, the federal Occupational Safety and Health Act, the federal Fair Labor Standards Act, and other state and federal laws. Attorneys represent employers and employees in administrative proceedings and lawsuits involving these safety laws. Paralegals must understand these laws and regulatory procedures. Paralegals often draft documents required to comply with these laws, conduct research, and perform other tasks for lawyers involved in this area of employment law.

One exciting area of employment law for paralegals is the compliance and enforcement of equal opportunity in employment laws. A major federal statute in this area is Title VII of the Civil Rights Act of 1964, which prohibits employment discrimination based on race, national origin, color, religion, and sex. Other federal antidiscrimination statutes include the Equal Pay Act, the Age Discrimination in Employment Act, and the Americans with Disabilities Act, among others. States also have statutes that prohibit job discrimination.

In the area of equal opportunity in employment laws, paralegals may be engaged in researching statutes, regulations, or case law, preparing documents to be submitted to government administrative agencies that enforce these laws, or preparing for lawsuits involving equal opportunity in employment laws. If there is an administrative hearing or a lawsuit, a paralegal is called upon by his or her attorney to help prepare the case for the hearing or lawsuit.

The area of employment law covers a vast array of employment opportunities for paralegals. This is a growing area of the law, so there will be even more need in the future for paralegals who are qualified for positions in employment law.

An agency can be created only to accomplish a lawful purpose. Agency contracts that are created for illegal purposes or are against public policy are void and unenforceable. For example, a principal cannot hire an agent to kill another person. Some agency relationships are prohibited by law. For example, unlicensed agents cannot be hired to perform the duties of certain licensed professionals (e.g., doctors and lawyers).

Kinds of Employment Relationships

Businesses usually have three kinds of employment relationships: (1) employer–employee relationships; (2) principal–agent relationships; and (3) principal–independent contractor relationships.

Employer–Employee Relationship

Employer–employee relationship

A relationship that results when an employer hires an employee to perform some form of physical service.

An **employer–employee relationship** exists when an employer hires an employee to perform some form of physical service. For example, a welder on General Motors Corporation's assembly line is employed in an employer–employee relationship because he performs a task.

An employee is not an agent unless he or she is specifically empowered to enter into contracts on the principal employer's behalf. Employees may enter into only the contracts that are within the scope of their employment. The welder in the example is not an agent, because he cannot enter into contracts on behalf of General Motors Corporation. If the company empowers him to enter into contracts, he becomes an agent.

Principal–Agent Relationship

Principal–agent relationship

A relationship in which an employer hires an employee and gives that employee authority to act and enter into contracts on his or her behalf.

A **principal–agent relationship** is formed when an employer hires an employee and gives that employee authority to act and enter into contracts on his or her behalf. The extent of this authority is governed by any express agreement between the parties and implied from the circumstances of the agency. For example, the president of a corporation usually has the authority to enter into major contracts on the corporation's behalf, but a supervisor on the corporation's assembly line may have the authority only to purchase the supplies necessary to keep the line running.

Principal–Independent Contractor Relationship

Independent contractor

A person or business that is not an employee and is employed by a principal to perform a certain task on his or her behalf.

A **principal–independent contractor relationship** exists when principals employ outsiders—persons and businesses who are not employees—to perform certain tasks on their behalf. These persons and businesses are called **independent contractors**. Professionals and tradespeople who typically act as independent contractors include doctors, dentists, stockbrokers, architects, certified public accountants, real estate brokers, and plumbers.

A principal can authorize an independent contractor to enter into contracts. Principals are bound by the authorized contracts of their independent contractors. For example, if a client authorizes an attorney to settle a case within a certain dollar amount and the attorney does so, the settlement agreement is binding.

Formation of the Agency Relationship

An agency and the resulting authority of an agent can arise in any of four ways: (1) express agency, (2) implied agency, (3) apparent agency, and (4) agency by ratification. Each of these types of agencies is discussed in the following pages.

Express Agency

Express agency

An agency that occurs when a principal and an agent expressly agree to enter into an agency agreement with each other.

The most common form of agency is **express agency**. In an express agency, the agent has the authority to contract or otherwise act on the principal's behalf as expressly stated in the agency agreement. In addition, the agent may possess certain implied or apparent authority to act on the principal's behalf (as discussed later in this chapter).

checklist 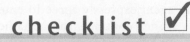   SUMMARY OF EMPLOYMENT RELATIONSHIPS

TYPE OF RELATIONSHIP	DESCRIPTION
• Employer–employee	The employer has the right to control the physical conduct of the employee.
• Principal–agent	The agent has the authority to act on behalf of the principal as authorized by the principal and implied from the agency. An employee is often the agent of his or her employer.
• Principal–independent contractor	The principal has no control over the details of the independent contractor's conduct. An independent contractor usually is not an agent of the principal.

EMPLOYMENT-AT-WILL

Employees who are offered express employment contracts for a definite term cannot be discharged in violation of the contract. Most employees, however, do not have employment contracts; their status is termed **employment-at-will**.

Under common law, an at-will employee could be discharged by an employer at any time for any reason. This laissez-faire doctrine gave the employer great flexibility in responding to its changing needs. It also caused unfair results for some employees. Today, there are many statutory, contract, public policy, and tort exceptions to the at-will doctrine. These exceptions are:

- *Statutory exception*. Federal and state statutes that restrict the employment-at-will doctrine include federal labor laws that prohibit employers from discharging employees who are members of labor unions in violation of labor laws or collective bargaining agreements. Title VII and other federal and state antidiscrimination laws that prohibit employers from engaging in race, sex, religious, age, disability, or other forms of discrimination are additional examples of such laws.
- *Contract exception*. The courts have held that an implied-in-fact contract can be created between an employer and an employee. Implied-in-fact contracts develop from the conduct of the parties. For example, a company bulletin, handbook, or personnel policy might mention that employees who do their jobs properly will not be discharged. This can be construed as an implied promise that an employee can be discharged only for good cause. Thus, the employer's ability to discharge an employee at will is removed. An employee who is discharged in violation of an implied-in-fact contract can sue the employer for breach of contract.
- *Public policy exception*. The most used common-law exception to the employment-at-will doctrine is the *public policy exception*. This rule states that an employee cannot be discharged if such discharge violates the public policy of the jurisdiction. Examples of violations of public policy are discharging an employee for serving as a juror, refusing to do an act in violation of the law (e.g., refusing to engage in dumping of toxic wastes in violation of environmental protection laws), refusing to engage in illegal research (e.g., research that violates patent laws or animal protection laws), and refusing to distribute defective products.

An employee who has been wrongfully discharged can sue his or her employer for damages and other remedies (reinstatement, back pay, and such). Punitive damages may be recovered if the employer has engaged in fraud or other intentional conduct.

Express agency occurs when a principal and an agent expressly agree to enter into an agency agreement with each other. Express agency contracts can be either oral or written unless the Statute of Frauds stipulates that they must be written. For example, in most states a real estate broker's contract to sell real estate must be in writing.

If the principal and agent enter into an **exclusive agency contract**, the principal cannot employ any agent other than the exclusive agent. If the principal does so, the exclusive agent can recover damages from the principal. If an agency is not an exclusive agency, the principal can employ more than one agent to try to accomplish a stated purpose. When multiple agents are employed, the agencies with all of the agents terminate when any one of the agents accomplishes the stated purpose.

Power of attorney
An express agency agreement that is often used to give an agent the power to sign legal documents on behalf of the principal.

A **power of attorney** is one of the most formal types of express agency agreements. It is often used to give an agent the power to sign legal documents, such as deeds to real estate, on behalf of the principal. The two kinds of powers of attorney are (1) **general power of attorney**, which confers broad powers on the agent to act in any matters on the principal's behalf; and (2) **special power of attorney**, which limits the agent to acts specifically enumerated in an agreement. The agent is called an **attorney-in-fact** even though he or she does not have to be a lawyer. Powers of attorney must be written, and usually they must be notarized. A general power of attorney is shown in Exhibit 17.2.

Implied Agency

In many situations, a principal and an agent do not expressly create an agency. Instead, the agency is implied from the conduct of the parties. This type of agency is referred to as **implied agency**. The extent of the agent's authority is determined from the facts and circumstances of the particular situation. Implied authority can be conferred by

1. industry custom,
2. prior dealing between the parties,
3. the agent's position, and
4. the acts deemed necessary to carry out the agent's duties.

The court may deem other factors relevant as well. Implied authority cannot conflict with express authority or with stated limitations on express authority.

Often, even an express agency agreement does not provide enough detail to cover all contingencies that may arise in the future regarding the performance of the agency. In this case, the agent possesses certain implied authority to act. This implied authority sometimes is referred to as *incidental authority*. Certain emergency situations may arise in the course of an agency. If the agent cannot contact the principal for instructions, the agent has implied emergency powers to take all actions reasonably necessary to protect the principal's property and rights.

Apparent Agency

Apparent agency
Agency that arises when a principal creates the appearance of an agency that in actuality does not exist.

Apparent agency, or **agency by estoppel,** arises when a principal creates the appearance of an agency that in actuality does not exist. Where an apparent agency is established, the principal is estopped from denying the agency relationship and is bound to contracts entered into by the apparent agent while acting within the scope of the apparent agency. Note that the principal's action—not the agent's—is what creates an apparent agency.

Consider this example: Suppose Georgia Pacific, Inc., interviews Albert Iorio for a sales representative position. Mr. Iorio, accompanied by Jane Franklin, the national sales manager, visits retail stores located in the open sales territory. While visiting one store, Jane tells the store manager, "I wish I had more sales reps like Albert." Nevertheless, Albert is not hired. If Albert later enters into contracts with the store on

Exhibit 17.2 **Sample general power of attorney**

POWER OF ATTORNEY

Know All Men by These Presents: That _____ the undersigned (jointly and severally, if more than one) hereby make, constitute and appoint _____ My true and lawful Attorney for me and in my name, place and stead and for my use and benefit:

(a) To ask, demand, sue for, recover, collect and receive each and every sum of money, debt, account, legacy, bequest, interest, dividend, annuity and demand (which now is or hereafter shall become due, owing or payable) belonging to or claimed by me, and to use and take any lawful means for the recovery thereof by legal process or otherwise, and to execute and deliver a satisfaction or release therefor, together with the right and powers to compromise or compound any claim or demand;

(b) To exercise any or all of the following powers as to real property, any interest therein and/or any building thereon: To contract for, purchase, receive and take possession thereof and of evidence of title thereto; to lease the same for any term or purpose, including leases for business, residence, and oil and/or mineral development; to sell, exchange, grant or convey the same with or without warranty; and to mortgage, transfer in trust, or otherwise encumber or hypothecate the same to secure payment of a negotiable or non-negotiable note or performance of any obligation or agreement;

(c) To exercise any or all of the following powers as to all kinds of personal property and goods, wares and merchandise, chosen in action and other property in possession or in action: To contract for, buy, sell, exchange, transfer and in any legal manner deal in and with the same and to mortgage, transfer in trust, or otherwise encumber or hypothecate the same to secure payment of a negotiable or non-negotiable note or performance of any obligation or agreement;

(d) To borrow money and to execute and deliver negotiable or non-negotiable notes therefor with or without security, and to loan money and receive negotiable or non-negotiable notes therefor with such security as said Attorney shall deem proper;

(e) To create, amend, supplement and terminate any trust and to instruct and advise the trustee of any trust wherein I am or may be trustor or beneficiary; to represent and vote stock, exercise stock rights, accept and deal with any dividend, distribution or bonus, join in any corporate financing reorganization, merger, liquidation, consolidation or other action and the extension, compromise, conversion, adjustment, enforcement or foreclosure, singly or in conjunction with others of any corporate stock, bond, note, debenture or other security; to compound, compromise, adjust, settle and satisfy any obligation secured or unsecured, owing by or to me and to give or accept any property and/or money whether or not equal to or less in value than the amount owing in payment, settlement or satisfaction thereof;

(f) To transact business of any kind or class and as my act and deed to sign, execute, acknowledge and deliver any deed, lease, assignment of lease covenant, indenture, indemnity, agreement, mortgage, deed of trust, assignment of mortgage or of the beneficial interest under deed of trust, extension or renewal of any obligation, subordination or waiver of priority, hypothecation, bottomry, charter-party, bill of lading, bill of sale, bill, bond, note, whether negotiable or non-negotiable, receipt, evidence of debt, full or partial release or satisfaction of mortgage, judgment and other debt, request for partial or full reconveyance of deed of trust and such other instruments in writing of any kind or class as may be necessary or proper in the premises.

Giving and Granting unto my said Attorney full power and authority to do and perform all and every act and thing whatsoever, requisite, necessary or appropriate to be done in and about the premises as fully to all intents, and purposes as I might or could do it personally present, hereby ratifying all that my said Attorney shall lawfully do or cause to be done by virtue of these presents. The powers and authority hereby conferred upon my said Attorney shall be applicable to all real and personal property or interests therein now owned or hereafter required by me and whenever situate.

My said Attorney is empowered hereby to determine in said Attorney's sole discretion the time when, purpose for and manner in which any power herein conferred upon said Attorney shall be exercised, and the conditions, provisions and covenants of any instrument or document which may be executed by said Attorney pursuant hereto and in the acquisition or disposition of real or personal property, my said Attorney shall have exclusive power to fix the terms thereof for cash, credit and/or property, and if on credit with or without security.

The undersigned, if a married person, hereby further authorizes and empowers my said Attorney, as my duly authorized agent, to join in my behalf, in the execution of any instrument by which any community real property or any interest therein, now owned or hereafter acquired by my spouse and myself, or either of us, is sold, leased, encumbered, or conveyed.

When the context to requires, the masculine gender includes the feminine and/or neuter, and the singular number includes the plural.

Witness my hand this _____ day of _____ 20_____ STATE OF CALIFORNIA, COUNTY OF _____ SS.

On _____ before me, the undersigned, a Notary Public in and for said State personally appeared _____

personally known to me (or proved to me on the basis of satisfactory evidence) to be the person _____ whose name _____ subscribed to the within instrument and acknowledge that _____ executed the same.

WITNESS my hand and official seal.

Signature _____

Name *(Typed or Printed)* _____

(This area for official seal)

APPARENT AGENCY: FRANCHISING

Franchising has become a major form of conducting business in the United States. In a franchise agreement, one company (called the franchisor) licenses another company (called the franchisee) to use its trade name, trademarks and service marks, and trade secrets. Many fast-food restaurants, gas stations, motels and hotels, and other businesses are operated in this fashion.

The franchisor and franchisee are independently owned businesses. A principal–agent relationship usually is not created by the franchise. If no express or implied agency is created, the franchisor normally would not be civilly liable for the tortious conduct (e.g., negligence) of the franchisee. Liability could be imposed on the franchisor, however, if an apparent agency is shown. Consider the following case.

HOWARD JOHNSON CASE

The Howard Johnson Company (HJ) operates a chain of hotels, motels, and restaurants across the United States. Approximately 75 percent of the HJ motor lodges are owned and operated by franchisees licensed by HJ to do business under the "Howard Johnson" trade name and trademarks. The rest are company-owned.

Orlando Executive Park, Inc. (OEP) is a corporate franchisee that owns and operates an HJ motor lodge franchise in Orlando, Florida. The motor lodge is part of a large complex known as "Howard Johnson's Plaza," located off Interstate 4. The motor lodge contains approximately 300 guest rooms in six separate buildings.

P.D.R. (name withheld by the court), a 35-year-old married woman and mother of a young child, worked as a supervisor for a restaurant chain. Her work occasionally required her to travel and stay overnight in Orlando.

On October 22, 1975, P.D.R. stopped to stay at the HJ motor lodge in Orlando. At approximately 9:30 P.M. P.D.R. registered for her previously reserved room at the lodge. The registration form did not inform her that the hotel was an HJ franchisee. P.D.R. parked her car in the motor lodge parking lot and proceeded with her suitcase to her ground-floor room in Building A, which was located directly behind the registration office. P.D.R. then went back to her car to get some papers.

After obtaining the papers from her car, P.D.R. returned to Building A. As she proceeded down an interior hallway of the building toward her room, she was accosted by a man she had previously seen standing behind the registration office. The man struck her in the throat and neck and choked her until she became semiconscious. When P.D.R. fell to the floor, her assailant sat on top of her and stripped her of her jewelry. He then dragged her down the hallway and beneath a secluded stairway, where he brutally beat her. The assailant then disappeared into the night and has never been identified.

P.D.R. suffered serious physical and psychological injury, including memory loss, mental confusion, and an inability to tolerate and communicate with people. Within one year of the assault, she lost her job. P.D.R. suffers permanent injury that requires expensive, long-term medical and psychiatric treatment. P.D.R. brought a tort action against OEP and HJ and sought actual and punitive damages against both of them.

NEGLIGENCE OF THE INDEPENDENT CONTRACTOR

The jury had little trouble finding that OEP had breached its duty of care and was liable. Evidence showed that other criminal activity had occurred previously on the premises but that OEP had failed to warn guests, including P.D.R., of the danger. In fact, OEP management actively discouraged criminal investigations by the sheriff's deputies, thus minimizing any deterrent effect they may have had. Further evidence showed that the dark and secluded stairwell area where P.D.R. was dragged was a security hazard that should have been boarded up or better lit.

LIABILITY OF THE PRINCIPAL

The jury also found HJ liable to P.D.R. under the doctrine of apparent agency. The appellate court stated:

APPARENT AGENCY: FRANCHISING *(continued)*

While OEP might not be HJ's agent for all purposes, the signs, national advertising, uniformity or building design and color schemes allow the public to assume that this and other similar motor lodges are under the same ownership. An HJ official testified that it was the HJ marketing strategy to appear as a chain that sells a product across the nation.

"There was sufficient evidence for the jury to reasonably conclude that HJ represented to the traveling public that it could expect a particular level of service at a Howard Johnson Motor Lodge. The uniformity of signs, design and color schemes easily leads the public to believe that each motor lodge is under common ownership or conforms to common standards, and the jury could find that they are intended to do so."

The appellate court upheld an award of $750,000 compensatory damages against OEP and HJ jointly.

Source: [*Orlando Executive Park, Inc. v. P.D.R.,* 402 So.2d 442, 1981 Fla. App. Lexis 20565 (Fla. App.)].

checklist ✓   FORMATION OF AGENCY RELATIONSHIPS

TYPE OF AGENCY	DEFINITION	ENFORCEMENT OF THE CONTRACT
Express	Authority is expressly given to the agent by the principal.	Principal and third party are bound to the contract.
Implied	Authority is implied from the conduct of the parties, custom and usage of trade, or act incidental to carrying out the agent's duties.	Principal and third party acts are bound to the contract.
Apparent	Authority created when the principal leads a third party into believing that the agent has authority.	Principal and third party are bound to the contract.
By ratification	Acts of the agent committed outside the scope of his or her authority.	Principal and third party are not bound to the contract unless the principal ratifies the contract.

behalf of Georgia Pacific and Jane has not controverted the impression of Albert she left with the store manager, the company will be bound to the contracts.

Agency by Ratification

Agency by ratification occurs when (1) a person misrepresents himself or herself as another's agent when in fact he or she is not, and (2) the purported principal ratifies (accepts) the unauthorized act. In such cases, the principal is bound to perform and the agent is relieved of any liability for misrepresentation.

Consider this example: Bill Levine sees a house for sale and thinks his friend Sherry Maxwell would want it. Bill enters into a contract to purchase the house from the seller and signs the contract "Bill Levine, agent for Sherry Maxwell." Because Bill is not Sherry Maxwell's agent, she is not bound to the contract. If, however, Sherry agrees

Agency by ratification
An agency that occurs when (1) a person misrepresents him or herself as another's agent when in fact he or she is not and (2) the purported principal ratifies the unauthorized act.

Advice from the Field ·······································

THE PARALEGAL PROFESSION: POISED FOR EXPLOSIVE GROWTH

D. Jeffrey Campell, Standing Committee on Legal Assistants

The paralegal profession is on the verge of dynamic change and explosive growth. General business conditions, the economics of law practice, and the relative unavailability of challenging and stimulating job opportunities in other fields are converging to make this a pivotal point in the progress of the paralegal profession. SCOLA is excited about these changes, and about working with other organizations to direct those changes and the future of the paralegal profession.

. . . [T]here is an increasing realization within the business community and among law firms that the overall price of legal services must be reduced. This reality applies across a wide spectrum of consumers of legal services, from large corporations, to small and privately held companies, to individuals. The increased use of paralegals is one of the few strategies that will, in the long run, reduce the real cost of legal services. Much of the work that is done by junior associates (and in some cases by senior lawyers) in law firms can be performed just as well or better by experienced paralegals. Hourly rates charged for associate attorney time typically are 50 to 100 percent higher than rates charged for paralegal time on the same task.

Thus, from the client's perspective, there is absolutely no justification for having an associate perform such tasks when they can be done by a paralegal. In serving the best interests of their clients, law firms should fundamentally change their staffing of matters to emphasize paralegals much more heavily and reserve for attorneys those duties that truly require the education, training, and experience of a lawyer. Conversely, clients should insist that their counsel effectively staff matters so as to achieve optimal results at the lowest possible cost.

Law firm economics similarly mandates the increased use of paralegals. As clients exert ever-greater pressure on billing rates, and the cost of associate attorneys continues to escalate, increased utilization of paralegals provides one of the few opportunities for long-term profit growth. Increasing the use of paralegals or, in other words, increasing the ratio of paralegals to lawyers, is a powerful way to increase average revenue per lawyer. The only other two meaningful ways to do this are by increasing hourly rates and by increasing average client billable hours.

As noted above, clients are becoming more and more resistant to large increases in hourly rates. Likewise, the personal and social values of many of today's "Generation X" associates make it very difficult to increase average client billable hours. Therefore, firms that seek long-term growth in revenue per lawyer must re-examine their historic methods of practice management and staffing so as to ensure a greater use of paralegals.

The increased utilization of paralegals, which is so beneficial to both clients and law firms, is not possible, of course, unless there is a pool of educated and talented paralegals to fill the need. This is where the final element of today's exciting environment fits in. Enrollment in paralegal education programs is up! As other areas of the economy have suffered, more and more entrants to the job market have focused on the paralegal profession as an attractive career opportunity. This increase in enrollment, and therefore in the available pool of well educated paralegal job applicants, provides legal employers with the opportunity to meet their clients' needs and to plan for the long-term economic health of their firms.

Thus, all the pieces are in place for explosive growth in the utilization of paralegals: client demand, economic necessity, and an available and growing pool of well qualified paralegals. But even with these strong forces at play, much needs to be done to ensure that the full benefits of paralegal utilization are realized.

First, paralegal educators must see that paralegals receive the education needed to enable them, at or shortly after graduation, to provide valuable services to attorneys and clients. Second, individual attorneys and law firm leaders must be educated concerning the substantive capabilities of paralegals and the ways in which they can contribute to client service and economic performance. Third, clients must be shown how paralegals can meet their need for reduction in cost without reduction in service. Finally, paralegals must be indoctrinated with the fact that they are integral to the success of the legal team—they must be taught to demonstrate initiative, to focus on client service, and to add value to their clients and their employers in all that they do. Only then will they be viewed as true partners in the delivery of legal services.

SCOLA is excited about each of these educational challenges. We are committed to working with AAfPE and individual paralegal educators to continually improve the quality of paralegal education. We are also developing

Advice from the Field ······································

(continued)

seminars for attorneys on a number of topics relating to the increased use of paralegals, including ethical issues arising from working with paralegals, the economic benefits of paralegal utilization, and the substantive use of paralegals in various practice areas. These programs will be designed for use both as local and state bar CLE programs and as in-house training programs for law firms and corporate law departments.

We look forward to working with the Legal Assistant Management Association and the Association of Legal Administrators in promoting these programs and in advancing other efforts to educate lawyers and law firm managers on the topic of paralegal utilization. Finally,

SCOLA would like to work with the national paralegal associations to help instill in paralegals the importance of their role in the larger legal profession.

Through these collective efforts we can make the most of the opportunities facing the paralegal profession in this dynamic time. We can unleash an unprecedented growth in paralegal services that will benefit not only clients and the legal profession, but also paralegals themselves.

"The Paralegal Professional: Poised for Explosive Growth" by D. Jeffrey Campbell, published in SCOLA Update, Volume 5, No. 1/2, Fall 2002/Winter 2003. ©2003 *by the American Bar Association. Reprinted with permission.*

to purchase the house, there is an agency by ratification. The ratification "relates back" to the moment Bill Levine entered into the contract. Upon ratification of the contract, Sherry Maxwell is obligated to purchase the house.

Contract Liability to Third Parties

A principal who authorizes an agent to enter into a contract with a third party is liable on the contract. Thus, the third party can enforce the contract and recover damages if the principal fails to perform it.

The agent also can be held liable on the contract in certain circumstances. Imposition of such liability depends upon whether the agency is classified as (1) *fully disclosed*, (2) *partially disclosed*, or (3) *undisclosed*.

Fully Disclosed Agency

A **fully disclosed agency** results if the third party entering into the contract knows (1) that the agent is acting as an agent for a principal, and (2) the actual identity of the principal. The third party has the requisite knowledge if the principal's identity is disclosed to the third party by either the agent or some other source.

In a fully disclosed agency, the contract is between the principal and the third party. Thus, the principal, who is called a fully disclosed principal, is liable on the contract. The agent, however, is not liable on the contract, because the third party relied on the principal's credit and reputation when the contract was made. An agent is liable on the contract if he or she guarantees that the principal will perform the contract.

The agent's signature on a contract entered into on the principal's behalf is important. It can establish the agent's status and, therefore, his or her liability. For instance, in a fully disclosed agency, the agent's signature must clearly indicate that he or she is acting as an agent for a specifically identified principal. Examples of proper signatures include "Allison Adams, agent for Peter Perceival," "Peter Perceival, by Allison Adams, agent," and "Peter Perceival, by Allison Adams."

Fully disclosed agency
An agency in which the contracting third party knows (1) that the agent is acting for a principal and (2) the identity of the principal.

Consider this example: Poran Kawamara decides to sell her house and hires Mark Robbins, a real estate broker, to list and sell the house for a price of $1 million. They agree that Mark will disclose the existence of the agency and the identity of the principal to interested third parties. This is a fully disclosed agency. Mark shows the house to Heather, a prospective buyer, and discloses to Heather that he is acting as an agent for Poran. Heather makes an offer for the house at the $1 million asking price. Mark signs the contract with Heather on behalf of Poran by signing, "Mark Robbins, agent for Poran Kawamara." Poran is liable on the contract with Heather, but Mark is not liable on the contract with Heather.

Partially Disclosed Agency

Partially disclosed agency
An agency in which the contracting third party knows that the agent is acting for a principal but does not know the identity of the principal.

A **partially disclosed agency** occurs if the agent discloses his or her agency status but does not reveal the principal's identity and the third party does not know the principal's identity from another source. The nondisclosure may be because (1) the principal instructs the agent not to disclose his or her identity to the third party, or (2) the agent forgets to tell the third party the principal's identity. In this kind of agency, the principal is called a partially disclosed principal.

In a partially disclosed agency, both the principal and the agent are liable on third-party contracts. This is because the third party must rely on the agent's reputation, integrity, and credit because the principal is unidentified. If the agent is made to pay the contract, the agent can sue the principal for indemnification. The third party and the agent can agree to relieve the agent's liability.

Consider these examples: Assume that a principal employs an agent to purchase a business on its behalf. The principal and the agent expressly agree that the agent will disclose the existence of the agency to third parties but will not disclose the identity of the principal. The agent finds a business that is for sale, and he discloses to the seller that he is acting as an agent but does not disclose the identity of the principal. The seller agrees to sell the business, and the agent signs "Allison Adams, agent." This is a partially disclosed agency. The principal is liable on the contract with the third-party seller; the agent is also liable on the contract with the third-party seller.

If, instead, a principal and an agent agree that the agent will represent the principal to purchase a business and that the agent will disclose the existence of the agency and the identity of the principal to third parties, this is a fully disclosed agency. Suppose the agent finds a suitable business for the principal and contracts to purchase the business on behalf of the principal but the agent mistakenly signs the contract with the third party "Allison Adams, agent." This is a partially disclosed agency. The principal is liable on the contract with the third party, but the agent is also liable.

Undisclosed Agency

Undisclosed agency
An agency in which the contracting third party does not know of either the existence of the agency or the principal's identity.

An **undisclosed agency** occurs when the third party is unaware of either the existence of an agency or the principal's identity. The principal is called an **undisclosed principal**. Undisclosed agencies are lawful. They often are used when the principal thinks the terms of the contract would be changed if his or her identity were known. For example, a wealthy person may use an undisclosed agency to purchase property if he thinks the seller would raise the price of the property if his identity were revealed.

In an undisclosed agency, both the principal and the agent are liable on the contract with the third party. This is because the agent, by not divulging that he or she is acting as an agent, becomes a principal to the contract. The third party relies on the reputation and credit of the agent in entering into the contract. If the principal fails to perform the contract, the third party can recover against the principal or the agent.

of *respondea*
theory of **vic**
his or her er
was personal

This d
to derive cer
should bear
of an agent

Frolic and

Agents some
own interest
a detour to
commonly r
frolic and d
ally liable fo
lieved of lia
minor, howe
conduct.

Conside
ment for his
with his auto
the way from
who is suppo
friend and is
mine its out

The "Com

Under the c
agents and e
"coming an
bile or other
ating expens
agents and
agents on th

che

AGENT'S

• Intentio

• Neglige

If the agent is made to pay the contract, he or she can recover indemnification from the principal.

Consider these examples: Assume that The Walt Disney Company wants to open a new theme park in Chicago but has to first acquire land for the park. Disney employs an agent to work on its behalf to acquire the needed property, with an express agreement that the agent will not disclose the existence of the agency to a third-party seller. If a seller agrees to sell the needed land and the agent signs her name "Allison Adams" without disclosing the existence of the agency, it is an undisclosed agency. Disney is liable on the contract with the third-party seller, and so is the agent.

Suppose instead that Disney hires an agent to purchase land on its behalf and they agree that the agent will represent Disney in a fully disclosed agency—that is, the agent is to disclose the existence of the agency and the identity of the principal to the third-party seller. If the agent locates a third-party seller who is willing to enter into a contract to sell the land but the agent mistakenly signs the contract "Allison Adams" without disclosing the agency to the third party, it is an undisclosed agency. Disney is liable on the contract with the third-party seller, and the agent is also liable.

Agent Exceeding the Scope of Authority

An agent who enters into a contract on behalf of another party impliedly warrants that he or she has the authority to do so. This is called the agent's **implied warranty of authority**. If the **agent exceeds the scope of his or her authority,** the principal is not liable on the contract unless the principal ratifies it. The agent, however, is liable to the third party for breaching the implied warranty of authority. To recover, the third party must show (1) reliance on the agent's representation, and (2) ignorance of the agent's lack of status.

Consider these example: Suppose Sam, Sara, Satchel, Samantha, and Simone form a rock bank called SSSS. SSSS is a voluntary association without any legal status. Sam enters into a contract with Rocky's Musical Instruments to purchase instruments and equipment for the band on credit and signs the contract "Sam, for SSSS." When SSSS fails to pay the debt, Rocky's can sue Sam and recover. Sam must pay the debt because he breached his implied warranty of authority when he acted as an agent for a **nonexistent principal**—that is, the purported principal was not a legal entity on which liability could be imposed.

checklist ✓   CONTRACT LIABILITY OF PRINCIPALS AND AGENTS TO THIRD PARTIES

TYPE OF AGENCY	PRINCIPAL LIABLE	AGENT LIABLE
• Fully disclosed	Yes	No, unless the agent (1) acts as a principal, or (2) guarantees the performance of the contract
• Partially disclosed	Yes	Yes, unless the third party relieves the agent's liability
• Undisclosed	Yes	Yes
• Nonexistent	No, unless the principal ratifies the contract	Yes, the agent is liable for breaching the implied warranty of authority

TERMINATION OF AN AGENCY

An agency contract is similar to other contracts in that it can be terminated either by an act of the parties or by operation of law. These different methods of termination are discussed next. Note that once an agency relationship is terminated, the agent no longer can represent the principal or bind the principal to contracts.

Termination by Acts of the Parties

The parties to an agency contract can terminate an agency contract by agreement or by their actions. The four methods of termination of an agency relationship by acts of the parties are:

1. *Mutual agreement.* As with any contract, the parties to an agency contract can mutually agree to terminate their agreement. By doing so, the parties relieve each other of any further rights, duties, obligations, or powers provided for in the agency contract. Either party can propose the termination of an agency contract.

2. *Lapse of time.* Agency contracts are often written for a specific period of time. The agency terminates when the specified time period elapses. Suppose, for example, that the principal and agent enter into an agency contract "beginning January 1, 2002, and ending December 31, 2005." The agency automatically terminates on December 31, 2005. If the agency contract does not set forth a specific termination date, the agency terminates after a reasonable time has elapsed. The courts often look to the custom of an industry in determining the reasonable time for termination of the agency.

3. *Purpose achieved.* A principal can employ an agent for the time it takes to accomplish a certain task, purpose, or result. Such agencies automatically terminate once they are completed. Suppose a principal employs a licensed real estate broker to sell his house. The agency terminates when the house is sold and the principal pays the broker the agreed-upon compensation.

4. *Occurrence of a specified event.* An agency contract can specify that the agency exists until a specified event occurs. The agency terminates when the specified event happens. For example, if a principal employs an agent to take care of her dog until she returns from a trip, the agency terminates when the principal returns from the trip.

Wrongful Termination of an Agency or Employment Contract

Generally, agency and employment contracts that do not specify a definite time for their termination can be terminated at will by either the principal or the agent without liability to the other party. When a principal terminates an agency contract, it is called a *revocation of authority.* When an agent terminates an agency, it is called a *renunciation of authority.*

Unless an agency is irrevocable, both the principal and the agent have an individual power to unilaterally terminate any agency contract. Note that having the power to terminate an agency agreement is not the same as having the right to terminate it. The unilateral termination of an agency contract may be wrongful. If the principal's or agent's termination of an agency contract breaches the contract, the other party can sue for damages for **wrongful termination of an agency.**

Consider this example: A principal employs a licensed real estate agent to sell his house. The agency contract gives the agent an exclusive listing for three months. After one month, the principal unilaterally terminates the agency. The principal has the power to do so, and the agent can no longer act on behalf of the principal. Because the

---

It is difficult to imagine any grounds, other than our own personal economic predilections, for saying that the contract of employment is any the less an appropriate subject of legislation than are scores of others, in dealing with which this Court has held that legislatures may curtail individual freedom in the public interest.

—Justice Stone
Dissenting Opinion, Morehead v. New York, *298 U.S. 587, 56 S.Ct. 918 (1936)*

Work-related
A test that says
intentional tor
time or space,
for any injury
intentional tor

Wrongful termination of an agency
The termination of an agency contract in violation of the terms of the agency contract. In this situation, the nonbreaching party may recover damages from the breaching party.

principal did not have the right to terminate the contract, however, the agent can sue him and recover damages (i.e., lost commission) for wrongful termination.

WORKERS' COMPENSATION

Many types of employment are dangerous, and each year many workers are injured on the job. At common law, employees who were injured on the job could sue their employer for negligence. This time-consuming process placed the employee at odds with his or her employer. In addition, there was no guarantee that the employee would win the case. Ultimately, many injured workers—or the heirs of deceased workers—were left uncompensated.

Workers' compensation acts were enacted in response to the unfairness of that result. These acts create an administrative procedure for workers to receive compensation for injuries that occur on the job—**workers' compensation.** First, the injured worker files a claim with the appropriate state government agency (often called the workers' compensation board or commission). Next, that entity determines the legitimacy of the claim. If the worker disagrees with the agency's findings, he or she may appeal the decision through the state court system. Workers' compensation benefits are paid according to preset limits established by statute or regulation. The amounts that are recoverable vary from state to state.

Workers' compensation acts
Laws that compensate workers and their families if workers are injured in connection with their jobs.

Workers' Compensation Insurance

States usually require employers to purchase insurance from private insurance companies or state funds to cover workers' compensation claims. Some states permit employers to self-insure if they demonstrate that they have the ability to pay workers' compensation claims. Many large companies self-insure. Workers can sue an employer in court to recover damages for employment-related injuries if the employer does not carry workers' compensation insurance or does not self-insure if permitted to do so.

Employment-Related Injury

To be compensable under workers' compensation, the claimant must prove that the injury arose out of and in the course of his or her employment, that it is an **employment-related injury.** An accident that occurs while an employee is actively working is clearly within the scope of this rule. Accidents that occur at a company cafeteria or while on a business lunch for an employer are covered. Accidents that happen while the employee is at an off-premises restaurant during his or her personal lunch hour are not covered. Many workers' compensation acts include stress as a compensable work-related injury.

Exclusive Remedy

Workers' compensation is an **exclusive remedy.** Thus, workers cannot sue their employers in court for damages. The one exception to this rule is: If an employer intentionally injures a worker, the worker can collect workers' compensation benefits and sue the employer. Workers' compensation acts do not bar injured workers from suing responsible third parties to recover damages.

OCCUPATIONAL SAFETY AND HEALTH ACT

In 1970, Congress enacted the **Occupational Safety and Health Act** to promote safety in the workplace. Virtually all private employers are within the scope of the act, but federal, state, and local governments are exempt. Industries regulated by other federal safety legislation are also exempt. The Act also established the **Occupational**

Occupational Safety and Health Act
A federal act enacted in 1970 that promotes safety in the workplace.

Find the address of the office of the federal Occupational Safety and Health Administration (OSHA) that serves your area. http://www.osha.gov/html

Safety and Health Administration (OSHA), a federal administrative agency within the Department of Labor that is empowered to enforce the act. The Act imposes record keeping and reporting requirements on employers and requires them to post notices in the workplace, informing employees of their rights under the Act.

Specific and General Duty Standards

OSHA is empowered to adopt rules and regulations to interpret and enforce the Occupational Safety and Health Act. OSHA has adopted thousands of regulations to enforce the safety standards established by the Act. These include the following:

- *Specific duty standards.* Many of the OSHA standards address safety problems of a **specific duty** nature. For example, OSHA standards establish safety requirements for equipment (e.g., safety guards), set maximum exposure levels to hazardous chemicals, regulate the location of machinery, establish safety procedures for employees, and the like.
- *General duty standards.* The Act imposes a general duty on an employer to provide a work environment free from recognized hazards that are causing or are likely to cause death or serious physical harm to employees. This is so even if no specific regulation applies to the situation.

OSHA is empowered to inspect places of employment for health hazards and safety violations. If a violation is found, OSHA can issue a *written citation* that requires the employer to abate or correct the situation. Contested citations are reviewed by the Occupational Safety and Health Review Commission. Its decision is appealable to the Federal Circuit Court of Appeals. Employers who violate the Act, OSHA rules and regulations or OSHA citations are subject to both civil and criminal penalties. Exhibit 17.3 shows the OSHA notice that should be posted in workplaces where there are teenage workers.

FAIR LABOR STANDARDS ACT

Fair Labor Standards Act (FLSA)
A federal act enacted in 1938 to protect workers that prohibits child labor and establishes minimum wage and overtime pay requirements.

In 1938, Congress enacted the **Fair Labor Standards Act (FLSA)** to protect workers. The FLSA applies to private employers and employees engaged in the production of goods for interstate commerce.

Child Labor

The FLSA forbids the use oppressive **child labor** and makes it unlawful to ship goods produced by businesses that use oppressive child labor. The Department of Labor has adopted the following regulations that define lawful child labor.

1. Children under the age of 14 cannot work except as newspaper deliverers.
2. Children ages 14 and 15 may work limited hours in nonhazardous jobs approved by the Department of Labor (e.g., restaurants and gasoline stations).
3. Children ages 16 and 17 may work unlimited hours in nonhazardous jobs.

The Department of Labor determines which occupations are hazardous (e.g., mining, roofing, working with explosives). Children who work in agricultural employment and child actors and performers are exempt from these restrictions. Persons age 18 and older may work at any job, whether it is hazardous or not.

Minimum Wage and Overtime Pay Requirements

The FLSA establishes minimum wage and overtime pay requirements for workers. Managerial, administrative, and professional employees are exempt from the Act's wage and hour provisions. As outlined in the following paragraphs, the FLSA requires

Exhibit 17.3 **Notice to teen workers & Occupational Safety and Health Administration (OSHA)**

Teen Workers!
You have a right to a safe
and healthy workplace

- Know your work-place rights.
- Talk to your employer about safety and health issues at work.
- Stay alert and work safely.
- Get safety and health training.
- Visit the OSHA Teen Workers website at www.osha.gov/teens

 **OSHA** Occupational
Safety and Health
Administration
U.S. Department of Labor

OSHA is the federal agency that helps assure the safety and health
of all workers, including teens, on the job. OSHA provides information,
resources and guidance to employers and employees.

For more information, talk to your employer or call:
1-800-321-OSHA
www.osha.gov/teens
(TTY) 1-877-889-5627

 Back to Top   www.osha.gov   www.dol.gov

employers to pay covered workers at least the minimum wage for their regular work hours and to provide overtime pay:

- *Minimum wage.* The **minimum wage** is set by Congress and can be changed. As of 2006, it was set at $5.15 per hour. The Department of Labor permits employers to pay less than the minimum wage to students and apprentices. An employer may reduce minimum wages by an amount equal to the reasonable cost of food and lodging provided to employees.
- *Overtime pay.* Under the FLSA, an employer cannot require nonexempt employees to work more than 40 hours per week unless they are paid one-and-a-half times their regular pay for each hour worked in excess of 40 hours. Each week is treated separately. For example, if an employee works 50 hours one week and 30 hours the next, the employer owes the employee 10 hours of **overtime** pay for the first week.

TITLE VII OF THE CIVIL RIGHTS ACT OF 1964

After substantial debate, Congress enacted the **Civil Rights Act of 1964. Title VII** of that Act (entitled the Fair Employment Practices Act) was intended to eliminate job discrimination based on the following *protected classes:* (1) *race,* (2) *color,* (3) *religion,*

Title VII of the Civil Rights Act of 1964
A title of a federal statute enacted to eliminate job discrimination based on five protected classes: *race, color, religion, sex, and national origin.*

(4) *sex*, or (5) *national origin* [42 U.S.C. Sections 2000e et seq.]. As amended by the Equal Employment Opportunity Act of 1972, Section 703(a)(2) of Title VII provides in pertinent part that: It shall be an unlawful employment practice for an employer

1. to fail or refuse to hire or to discharge any individual, or otherwise to discriminate against any individual with respect to his compensation, terms, conditions, or privileges of employment, because of such individual's race, color, religion, sex, or national origin; or
2. to limit, segregate, or classify his employees or applicants for employment in any way which would deprive or tend to deprive any individual of employment opportunities or otherwise adversely affect his [or her] status as an employee, because of such individual's race, color, religion, sex, or national origin.

Equal Employment Opportunity Commission (EEOC)

Equal Employment Opportunity Commission (EEOC)
A federal administrative agency responsible for enforcing most federal antidiscrimination laws.

The **Equal Employment Opportunity Commission (EEOC)** is a federal agency responsible for enforcing most federal antidiscrimination laws. Members of the EEOC are appointed by the U.S. President. The EEOC is empowered to conduct investigations, interpret the statutes, encourage conciliation between employees and employers, and bring suit to enforce the law. The EEOC also can seek injunctive relief. Exhibit 17.4 shows a map of the fifteen districts of the EEOC.

Scope of Coverage of Title VII

Title VII prohibits discrimination in hiring, decisions regarding promotion or demotion, payment of compensation and fringe benefits, availability of job training and apprenticeship opportunities, referral systems for employment, decisions regarding dismissal, work rules, and any other "term, condition, or privilege" of employment. Any employee of covered employers, including undocumented aliens, may bring actions for employment discrimination under Title VII.

Racial discrimination in any form and in any degree has no justifiable part whatever in our democratic way of life. It is unattractive in any setting but it is utterly revolting among a free people who have embraced the principles set forth in the Constitution of the United States.

Judge Murphy
Dissenting opinion, Korematsu v. U.S.
(1944)

Race, Color, and National Origin Discrimination

Title VII of the Civil Rights Act of 1964 was enacted primarily to prohibit **race discrimination, color discrimination,** and **national origin discrimination** in employment. *Race* refers to broad categories such as Black, Caucasian, Asian, and American Indian. *Color* refers to the color of a person's skin. *National origin* refers to the country of a person's ancestors or cultural characteristics.

Exhibit 17.5 sets forth the EEOC's description of race and color discrimination.

Religious Discrimination

Religious discrimination
Discrimination against a person solely because of his or her religion or religious practices.

Title VII prohibits employment discrimination based on a person's religion. Religions include traditional religions, other religions that recognize a supreme being, and religions based on ethical or spiritual tenets. Many **religious discrimination** cases involve a conflict between an employer's work rule and an employee's religious beliefs (e.g., when an employee is required to work on his or her religious holiday).

The right of an employee to practice his or her religion is not absolute. Under Title VII, an employer is under a duty to *reasonably accommodate* the religious observances, practices, or beliefs of its employees if it does not cause an *undue hardship* on the employer. The courts must apply these general standards to specific fact situations. In making their decisions, the courts must consider factors such as the number of employees of the employer, the importance of the employee's position, and the availability of alternative workers.

Rights matter most when they are claimed by unpopular minorities.

Michael Kirby, J.
Sydney Morning Herald
(November 30, 1985)

Exhibit 17.6 sets forth the EEOC's description of religion, ethnicity, and country of origin discrimination.

Exhibit 17.4 **Fifteen districts of the Equal Employment Opportunity Commission (EEOC)**

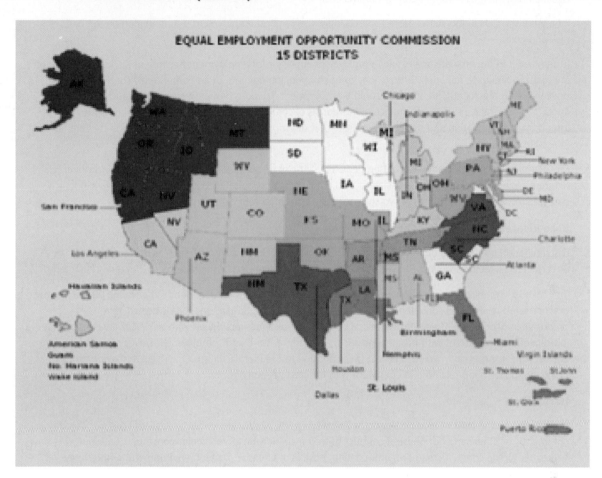

District Offices

Atlantic District Office	Memphis District Office
Birmingham District Office	Miami District Office
Charlotte District Office	New York District Office
Chicago District Office	Philadelphia District Office
Dallas District Office	Phoenix District Office
Houston District Office	San Francisco District Office
Indianapolis District Office	St. Louis District Office
Los Angeles District	

Source: Equal Employment Opportunity Commission (EEOC)

Exhibit 17.5 **Race/color discrimination**

Equal employment opportunity commission (EEOC)

Title VII of the Civil Rights Act of 1964 protects individuals against employment discrimination on the basis of race and color.

It is unlawful to discriminate against any employee or applicant for employment because of his/her race or color in regard to hiring, termination, promotion, compensation, job training, or any other term, condition, or privilege of employment. Title VII also prohibits employment decisions based on stereotypes and assumptions about abilities, traits, or the performance of individuals of certain racial groups. Title VII prohibits both intentional discrimination and neutral job policies that disproportionately exclude minorities and that are not job-related.

Equal employment opportunity cannot be denied because of marriage to or association with an individual of a different race; membership in or association with ethnic based organizations or groups; or attendance or participation in schools or places of worship generally associated with certain minority groups.

Race-Related Characteristics and Conditions

Discrimination on the basis of an immutable characteristic associated with race, such as skin color, hair texture, or certain facial features violates Title VII, even though not all members of the race share the same characteristic.

Title VII also prohibits discrimination on the basis of a condition which predominantly affects one race unless the practice is job related and consistent with business necessity. For example, since sickle cell anemia predominantly occurs in African-Americans, a policy which excludes individuals with sickle cell anemia must be job-related and consistent with business necessity. Similarly, a "no-beard" employment policy may discriminate against African-American men who have a predisposition to pseudofolliculitis barbae (severe shaving bumps) unless the policy is job-related and consistent with business necessity.

Harassment

Harassment on the basis of race and/or color violates Title VII. Ethnic slurs, racial "jokes," offensive or derogatory comments, or other verbal or physical conduct based on an individual's race/color constitutes unlawful harassment if the conduct creates an intimidating, hostile, or offensive working environment, or interferes with the individual's work performance.

Segregation and Classification of Employees

Title VII is violated where minority employees are segregated by physically isolating them from other employees or from customer contact. Title VII also prohibits assigning primarily minorities to predominantly minority establishments or geographic areas. It is also illegal to exclude minorities from certain positions or to group or categorize employees or jobs so that certain jobs are generally held by minorities. Coding applications/resumes to designate an applicant's race, by either an employer or employment agency, constitutes evidence of discrimination where minorities are excluded from employment or from certain positions.

Pre-Employment Inquiries

Requesting pre-employment information which discloses or tends to disclose an applicant's race suggests that race will be unlawfully used as a basis for hiring. Solicitation of such pre-employment information is presumed to be used as a basis for making selection decisions. Therefore, if members of minority groups are excluded from employment, the request for such pre-employment information would likely constitute evidence of discrimination.

However, employers may legitimately need information about their employees' or applicants' race for affirmative action purposes and/or to track applicant flow. One way to obtain racial information and simultaneously guard against discriminatory selection is for employers to use "tear-off sheets" for the identification of an applicant's race. After the applicant completes the application and the tear-off portion, the employer separates the tear-off sheet from the application and does not use it in the selection process.

Source: Equal Employment Opportunity Commission (EEOC)

Exhibit 17.6 Religion, ethnicity, or country of origin discrimination

Anger at those responsible for the tragic events of September 11 should not be misdirected against innocent individuals because of their religion, ethnicity, or country of origin. Employers and labor unions have a special role in guarding against unlawful workplace discrimination.

Title VII of the Civil Rights Act of 1964 prohibits workplace discrimination based on religion, national origin, race, color, or sex. At this time, employers and unions should be particularly sensitive to potential discrimination or harassment against individuals who are—or are perceived to be—Muslim, Arab, Afghani, Middle Eastern, or South Asian (Pakistani, Indian, etc.).

The law's prohibitions include harassment or any other employment action based on any of the following:

- Affiliation: Harassing or otherwise discriminating because an individual is affiliated with a particular religious or ethnic group. For example, harassing an individual because she is Arab or practices Islam, or paying an employee less because she is Middle Eastern.
- Physical or cultural traits and clothing: Harassing or otherwise discriminating because of physical, cultural, or linguistic characteristics, such as accent or dress associated with a particular religion, ethnicity, or country of origin. For example, harassing a woman wearing a hijab (a body covering and/or head-scarf worn by some Muslims), or not hiring a man with a dark complexion and an accent believed to be Arab.
- Perception: Harassing or otherwise discriminating because of the perception or belief that a person is a member of a particular racial, national origin, or religious group whether or not that perception is correct. For example, failing to hire an Hispanic person because the hiring official believed that he was from Pakistan, or harassing a Sikh man wearing a turban because the harasser thought he was Muslim.
- Association: Harassing or otherwise discriminating because of an individual's association with a person or organization of a particular religion or ethnicity. For example, harassing an employee whose husband is from Afghanistan, or refusing to promote an employee because he attends a Mosque.

Harassment

Employers must provide a workplace that is free of harassment based on national origin, ethnicity, or religion. They may be liable not only for harassment by supervisors, but also by coworkers or by non-employees under their control. Employers should clearly communicate to all employees—through a written policy or other appropriate mechanism—that harassment such as ethnic slurs or other verbal or physical conduct directed toward any racial, ethnic, or religious group is prohibited and that employees must respect the rights of their coworkers. An employer also should have effective and clearly communicated policies and procedures for addressing complaints of harassment and should train managers on how to identify and respond effectively to harassment even in the absence of a complaint.

Religious Accommodation

Title VII requires an employer to reasonably accommodate the religious practices of an employee or prospective employee, unless doing so would create an undue hardship for the employer. Some reasonable religious accommodations that employers may be required to provide workers include leave for religious observances, time and/or place to pray, and ability to wear religious garb.

Source: Equal Employment Opportunity Commission (EEOC)

Sex Discrimination

Although the prohibition against **sex discrimination** applies equally to men and women, the overwhelming majority of Title VII sex discrimination cases are brought by women. An example of such discrimination is the old airline practice of ignoring the marital status of male flight attendants but hiring only single female flight attendants.

In 1978, the **Pregnancy Discrimination Act** was enacted as an amendment to Title VII. This amendment forbids employment discrimination because of "pregnancy, childbirth, or related medical conditions." Thus, a work rule that prohibits the hiring of pregnant women violates Title VII.

Sex discrimination
Discrimination against a person solely because of his or her sex.

Exhibit 17.7 **Sexual harassment**

Sexual harassment is a form of sex discrimination that violates Title VII of the Civil Rights Act of 1964.

Unwelcome sexual advances, requests for sexual favors, and other verbal or physical conduct of a sexual nature constitutes sexual harassment when submission to or rejection of this conduct explicitly or implicitly affects an individual's employment, unreasonably interferes with an individual's work performance, or creates an intimidating, hostile, or offensive work environment.

Sexual harassment can occur in a variety of circumstances, including but not limited to the following:

- The victim as well as the harasser may be a woman or a man. The victim does not have to be of the opposite sex.
- The harasser can be the victim's supervisor, an agent of the employer, a supervisor in another area, a coworker, or a non-employee.
- The victim does not have to be the person harassed but could be anyone affected by the offensive conduct.
- Unlawful sexual harassment may occur without economic injury to or discharge of the victim.
- The harasser's conduct must be unwelcome.

It is helpful for the victim to directly inform the harasser that the conduct is unwelcome and must stop. The victim should use any employer complaint mechanism or grievance system available.

When investigating allegations of sexual harassment, EEOC looks at the whole record: the circumstances, such as the nature of the sexual advances, and the context in which the alleged incidents occurred. A determination on the allegations is made from the facts on a case-by-case basis.

Prevention is the best tool to eliminate sexual harassment in the workplace. Employers are encouraged to take steps necessary to prevent sexual harassment from occurring. They should clearly communicate to employees that sexual harassment will not be tolerated. They can do so by establishing an effective complaint or grievance process and taking immediate and appropriate action when an employee complains.

Source: Equal Employment Opportunity Commission (EEOC)

Sexual harassment
Lewd remarks, touching, intimidation, posting of pinups, and other verbal or physical conduct of a sexual nature that occur on the job.

Click on your state on the map to find the address of the federal Equal Employment Opportunity Commission (EEOC) that serves your area. http://www.eeoc.gov/offices/html

Bona fide occupational qualification (BFOQ)
Lawful employment discrimination that is based on a protected class (other than race or color) and is *job-related* and a *business necessity*. This exception is narrowly interpreted by the courts.

Sexual Harassment

In the modern work environment, coworkers sometimes become sexually interested or involved with each other voluntarily. On other occasions, though, a coworker's sexual advances are not welcome.

Refusing to hire or promote someone unless he or she has sex with the manager or supervisor is sex discrimination that violates Title VII. Other forms of conduct, such as lewd remarks, touching, intimidation, posting pinups, and other verbal or physical conduct of a sexual nature, constitute **sexual harassment** and violate Title VII. To determine what conduct creates a hostile work environment, the U.S. Supreme Court stated [*Harris v. Forklift Systems, Inc.*, 510 U.S. 17, 114 S. Ct. 367, 126 L.Ed.2d 295, 1999 U.S. Lexis 7155 (1993)]:

> We can say that whether an environment is "hostile" or "abusive" can be determined only by looking at all the circumstances. These may include the frequency of the discriminatory conduct; its severity; whether it is physically threatening or humiliating, or a mere offensive utterance; and whether it unreasonably interferes with an employee's work performance.

Exhibit 17.7 sets forth the EEOC's description of sexual harassment. Exhibit 17.8 sets forth a company's policies against sexual harassment.

Bona Fide Occupational Qualification (BFOQ)

Discrimination based on protected classes (other than race or color) is permitted if it is shown to be a **bona fide occupational qualification (BFOQ)**. To be legal, a BFOQ must be both *job-related* and a *business necessity*. For example, allowing only women to

Exhibit 17.8 **Company's policies against sexual harassment**

Many businesses have taken steps to prevent sexual harassment in the workplace. For example, some businesses have explicitly adopted policies (see below) forbidding sexual harassment, implemented procedures for reporting incidents of sexual harassment, and conducted training programs to sensitize managers and employees about the issue.

Statement of Prohibited Conduct

The management of Company considers the following conduct to illustrate some of the conduct that violates Company's Sexual Harassment Policy:

A. Physical assaults of a sexual nature, such as

   1. Rape, sexual battery, molestation, or attempts to commit these assaults.

   2. Intentional physical conduct that is sexual in nature, such as touching, pinching, patting, grabbing, brushing against another employee's body, or poking another employee's body.

B. Unwanted sexual advances, propositions, or other sexual comments, such as

   1. Sexually oriented gestures, noises, remarks, jokes, or comments about a person's sexuality or sexual experience directed at or made in the presence of any employee who indicates or has indicated in any way that such conduct is unwelcome in his or her presence.

   2. Preferential treatment or promises of preferential treatment to an employee for submitting to sexual conduct, including soliciting or attempting to solicit any employee to engage in sexual activity for compensation or reward.

   3. Subjecting, or threats of subjecting, an employee to unwelcome sexual attention or conduct or intentionally making performance of the employee's job more difficult because of the employee's sex.

C. Sexual or discriminatory displays or publications anywhere in Company's workplace by Company employees, such as

   1. Displaying pictures, posters, calendars, graffiti, objects, promotional materials, reading materials, or other materials that are sexually suggestive, sexually demeaning, or pornographic, or bringing into Company's work environment or possessing any such material to read, display, or view at work.

      A picture will be presumed to be sexually suggestive if it depicts a person of either sex who is not fully clothed or in clothes that are not suited to or ordinarily accepted for the accomplishment of routine work in and around the workplace and who is posed for the obvious purpose of displaying or drawing attention to private portions of his or her body.

   2. Reading or otherwise publicizing in the work environment materials that are in any way sexually revealing, sexually suggestive, sexually demeaning, or pornographic.

   3. Displaying signs or other materials purporting to segregate an employee by sex in any area of the workplace (other than restrooms and similar semi-private lockers/changing rooms).

be locker-room attendants in a women's gym is a valid BFOQ, but prohibiting males from being managers or instructors at the same gym would not be a BFOQ.

EQUAL PAY ACT

Discrimination often takes the form of different pay scales for men and women performing the same job. The **Equal Pay Act of 1963** protects both sexes from pay discrimination based on sex. This Act covers all levels of private-sector employees and state and local government employees. Federal workers are not covered, however.

Equal Pay Act of 1963
A federal statute that protects both sexes from pay discrimination based on sex. It extends to jobs that require equal skill, equal effort, equal responsibility, and similar working conditions.

The Act prohibits disparity in pay for jobs that require *equal skill* (i.e., equal experience), *equal effort* (i.e., mental and physical exertion), *equal responsibility* (i.e., supervision and accountability), or *similar working conditions* (e.g., dangers of injury, exposure to the elements). To make this determination, the courts examine the actual requirements of jobs to determine whether they are equal and similar. If two jobs are determined to be equal and similar, an employer cannot pay disparate wages to members of different sexes.

Employees can bring a private cause of action against an employer for violating the Act. Back pay and liquidated damages are recoverable. In addition, the employer must increase the wages of the discriminated-against employee to eliminate the unlawful disparity of wages. The wages of other employees may not be lowered.

The Equal Pay Act expressly provides four criteria that justify a differential in wages. These defenses include payment systems that are based on

1. Seniority
2. Merit (as long as there is some identifiable measurement standard)
3. Quantity or quality of product (commission, piecework, or quality-control–based payment systems are permitted)
4. "Any factor other than sex" (including shift differentials, i.e., night versus day shifts) The employer bears the burden of proving these defenses.

FAMILY AND MEDICAL LEAVE ACT

In February 1993, Congress enacted the **Family and Medical Leave Act.** This law guarantees workers unpaid time off from work for medical emergencies. The Act, which applies to companies with 50 or more workers as well as federal, state, and local governments, covers about half of the nation's workforce. To be covered by the Act, an employee must have worked for the employer for at least one year and have performed more than 1,250 hours of service during the previous 12-month period.

Covered employers are required to provide up to 12 weeks of unpaid leave during any 12-month period as a result of the

1. birth of, and care for, a son or daughter
2. placement of a child for adoption or in foster care
3. serious health condition that makes the employee unable to perform his or her duties.
4. care for a spouse, child, or parent with a serious health problem.

Leave because of the birth of a child or the placement of a child for adoption or foster care cannot be taken intermittently unless the employer agrees. Other leaves may be taken on an intermittent basis. The employer may require medical proof of claimed serious health conditions.

An eligible employee who takes leave must, upon returning to work, be restored to either the same or an equivalent position with equivalent employment benefits and pay. The restored employee is not entitled to the accrual of seniority during the leave period, however. A covered employer may deny restoration to a salaried employee who is among the highest-paid 10 percent of that employer's employees if the denial is necessary to prevent "substantial and grievous economic injury" to the employer's operations.

AGE DISCRIMINATION IN EMPLOYMENT ACT

In the past, some employers discriminated against employees and prospective employees based on their age. For example, employers often refused to hire older workers. The **Age Discrimination in Employment Act (ADEA)**, which prohibits certain age discrimination practices, was enacted in 1967 [29 U.S.C. Sections 621–634].

ADEA prohibits age discrimination in all employment decisions, including hiring, promotions, payment of compensation, and other terms and conditions of employment. Originally, ADEA prohibited employment discrimination against persons

Age Discrimination In Employment Act (ADEA)
A federal statute that prohibits age discrimination practices against employees who are age 40 and older.

Perspective

Attorney Sanctioned for Ordering a Paralegal to Falsify a Document

OPINION BY: Randall T. Shepard

Pursuant to Ind. Admission and Discipline Rule 23, Section 11, the Indiana Supreme Court Disciplinary Commission and the respondent have submitted for approval a *Statement of Circumstances and Conditional Agreement for Discipline* stipulating a proposed discipline and agreed facts as summarized below:

Respondent, a sole practitioner, represented a defense client in a personal injury case. Respondent requested that plaintiff sign medical release forms for all of his medical records from the preceding ten years. Plaintiff signed release forms for ten of his physicians. In examining the released records, respondent learned that she did not have release forms for additional unnamed treating physicians. Respondent instructed her paralegal to alter one of the release forms plaintiff had signed by adding the name of an unnamed physician, and to alter the execution date of the document, which had expired some months before.

Respondent sent the altered release to the physician without identifying herself as an adverse party involved in litigation with the physician's patient. The altered form resulted in respondent learning of a relevant preexisting condition that would have been discoverable through authorized discovery procedures. Respondent shared this information with plaintiff's counsel on the day respondent received the information, which also happened to be the day the matter was set for mediation. The matter settled during the mediation.

Respondent violated Indiana Professional Conduct Rules:

4.3 Acting in a manner such that an unrepresented person might misunderstand the lawyer's role in the matter, by soliciting patient medical records from plaintiff's doctor using an altered consent form and without identifying herself as counsel adverse to the doctor's patient.

4.4 Using methods of obtaining evidence that violate the legal rights of another, by altering a consent form to obtain an opposing party's medical records, and without providing prior notice to opposing counsel, thereby depriving the opposing party of the opportunity to object.

8.4(c) Engaging in conduct involving dishonesty, fraud, deceit or misrepresentation, by obtaining the medical records of an opposing party in litigation without providing notice to opposing counsel and by altering a previously executed consent form with the intent to mislead a third party into believing that plaintiff had provided consent to their being disclosed.

Thirty (30) days suspension from the practice of law, effective May 1, 2005, with automatic reinstatement to the practice of law thereafter.

Source: In the Matter of Blumenthal, 825 N.E.2d 374 (2005), Supreme Court of Indiana

between 40 and 65 years of age. In 1978, its coverage was extended to persons up to 70 years of age. Further amendments completely eliminated an age ceiling, so ADEA now applies to employees who are age 40 and older.

AMERICANS WITH DISABILITIES ACT

The **Americans with Disabilities Act (ADA)**, signed into law on July 26, 1990 [42 U.S.C. Sections 1201 et seq.], is the most comprehensive piece of civil rights legislation since the Civil Rights Act of 1964. ADA imposes obligations on employers and providers of public transportation, telecommunications, and public accommodations to accommodate individuals with disabilities.

Title I of ADA prohibits employment discrimination against qualified individuals with disabilities in regard to job application procedures, hiring, compensation, training, promotion, and termination. It requires an employer to make reasonable accommodations to individuals with disabilities that do not cause undue hardship to the

Americans with Disabilities Act (ADA)
A federal statute that imposes obligations on employers and providers of public transportation, telecommunications, and public accommodations to accommodate individuals with disabilities.

Exhibit 17.9 Spanish instructions for filing a charge of job discrimination

Presentación de una acusación de discriminación de empleo

Comisión para la Igualdad de Oportunidades de Empleo de los Estados Unidos

Leyes sobre la igualdad de oportunidades de empleo

Si usted opina que un empleador, una agencia de empleo o un sindicato ha discriminado contra usted al solicitar un empleo o al ejercer un cargo por motivo de raza, color, sexo, religión, origen nacional, edad o discapacidad, puede presentar una acusación de discriminación ante la Comisión para la Igualdad de Oportunidades de Empleo de los Estados Unidos.

La EEOC hace cumplir las siguientes leyes federales contra la discriminación de empleo:

* El Título VII de la Ley de Derechos Civiles de 1964 (Título VII) prohíbe la discriminación de empleo por motivo de raza, color, religión, sexo u origen nacional;
* la Ley de Igualdad de Salarios de 1963 (*Equal Pay Act* EPA) protege a hombres y mujeres que desempeñen sustancialmente el mismo trabajo en el mismo establecimiento contra la discriminación de salarios por motivo del sexo;
* la Ley contra la Discriminación de Empleo por Motivo de Edad de 1967 (*Age Discrimination in Employment Act* ADEA) protege a los individuos de 40 años de edad o más contra la discriminación de empleo por motivo de edad;
* el Título I de la Ley de los Ciudadanos Americanos con Discapacidades de 1990 (*Americans with Disabilities Act* ADA) prohíbe la discriminación de empleo contra individuos calificados con discapacidades; y
* la Ley de los Derechos Civiles de 1991 proporciona indemnización monetaria en los casos de discriminación intencional en el empleo.

Según el Título VII, la ADA y la ADEA, es ilícito discriminar en cualquier aspecto del empleo, incluyendo contratación, despido, salario, asignación, transferencia, ascenso, despido involuntario, reintegro, prestaciones suplementarias, planes de jubilación, licencia, o cualquier otro plazo o condición de empleo.

Estas leyes prohíben el hostigamiento sexual, así como el hostigamiento por motivo de raza, color, religión, sexo, origen nacional, discapacidad o edad y la discriminación por motivo de embarazo. Es ilícito también tomar represalias contra un individuo por presentar una acusación de discriminación, tomar parte en una investigación o por oponerse a prácticas discriminatorias.

Los empleadores cubiertos

El Título VII y la ADA cubren a todos los empleadores privados, los gobiernos estatales y locales, y las instituciones educativas que emplea a 15 o más individuos. La ADEA cubre a todos los empleadores privados, los gobiernos estatales y locales, y las instituciones educativas con 20 o más empleados. Estas leyes cubren también a las agencias de empleo públicas y privadas, los sindicatos y los comités obrero-patronales que controlan el aprendizaje o la capacitación.

La EPA protege a todos los empleados cubiertos por la Ley Federal de Salarios y Horarios (Ley de Normas Laborales Justas). Esta ley cubre a casi todos los empleadores.

El Título VII, la ADEA y la EPA cubren también al gobierno *federal*. Además, la Sección 501 de la Ley de Rehabilitación de 1973, tal como está enmendada, que la EEOC hace cumplir y que incorpora los requisitos de no discriminación en el empleo de la ADA, cubre al gobierno federal. *Si desea mayor información sobre cómo presentar una reclamación de discriminación en un empleo federal, comuníquese con la oficina de la EEOC de la agencia federal donde tuvo lugar la supuesta discriminación.*

Presentación de una acusación de discriminación de empleo

Toda persona que opine que se han infringido sus derechos de empleo tiene el derecho a presentar una acusación de discriminación ante la EEOC. Cualquier otra persona, grupo o institución puede también presentar una acusación en nombre de otra persona.

Exhibit 17.9 **Spanish instructions for filing a charge of job discrimination**
(continued)

Se puede presentar una acusación por correo o personalmente en la oficina de la EEOC más cercana. En el directorio telefónico de su zona puede figurar el número de teléfono de dicha oficina bajo *"U.S. Government"* (Gobierno de los Estados Unidos). También se puede comunicar con esa oficina llamando al teléfono 1-800-669-4000 (voz) o 1-800-669-6820 (TTY) (para los que tengan una discapacidad auditiva). Además, puede hallar los números de teléfono, así como información sobre como presentar una acusación, en el lugar electrónico de la EEOC en Internet: **www.eeoc.gov**

La parte acusadora es la responsable de mantener informada a la EEOC de cualquier cambio en su dirección postal o número de teléfono mientras se tramite la acusación.

Plazo para presentar la acusación

La acusación se deberá presentar ante la EEOC en el plazo de 180 días a partir de la fecha de la supuesta infracción para proteger los derechos de la parte acusadora. Este plazo de 180 días se puede extender a 300 días si es que la acusación está también cubierta por ciertas leyes estatales y locales contra la discriminación. Según todas las leyes que hace cumplir la EEOC, salvo la EPA, la acusación se debe presentar a la EEOC antes de llevarla a un tribunal.

Estos plazos no se aplican a las reclamaciones según la EPA. Sin embargo, puesto que muchas de las reclamaciones según la EPA también presentan cuestiones de discriminación sexual conforme al Título VII, es posible que sea preferible presentar la acusación conforme a las dos leyes dentro de los plazos prescritos.

Trámite para una acusación de discriminación

Cuando se presenta una acusación, la EEOC informa al empleador dentro del plazo de diez días. La acusación recibe la más pronta atención cuando los hechos parecen indicar la posibilidad de que efectivamente la discriminación ocurrió. Los demás cargos se investigarán posteriormente, de acuerdo a la disponibilidad de los recursos, si más información se considera necesaria. La EEOC puede también cerrar el caso en cualquier momento si opina que más investigación no demostrará que se han infringido las leyes contra la discriminación.

Las acusaciones se podrán escoger para el programa de mediación de EEOC si tanto la parte acusadora como el empleador se interesan en esta opción. La mediación es una alternativa a la investigación y puede solucionar una acusación rápidamente. La participación en el programa de mediación es confidencial y es de carácter voluntario. La tramitación de la acusación se reanudará si la mediación fallara.

- La EEOC podrá resolver la acusación en cualquier momento durante la investigación, si tanto la parte acusadora como el empleador están de acuerdo. Si no hubiese resolución temprana, la tramitación seguirá su curso.
- Después de la investigación pertinente, la EEOC podrá decidir que hubo discriminación o podrá cerrar la acusación porque la evidencia no demostró discriminación.
- Si se cierra la acusación, la EEOC entregará a la parte acusadora un "Aviso del derecho a entablar juicio".
- Si se encuentra discriminación, la EEOC procurará un desagravio a la parte acusadora mediante conciliación.
- Si la conciliación no tuviese éxito, la EEOC podrá entablar un juicio contra el empleador.
- Si la parte acusadora no estuviese satisfecha con las gestiones de la EEOC, la parte acusadora tendrá el derecho de entablar su propio juicio contra el empleador dentro el plazo de 90 días después de haber recibido el "Aviso del Derecho a Entablar Juicio".

Desagravios disponibles cuando se encuentra discriminación

Los desagravios disponibles para la discriminación de empleo podrían incluir contratación, reintegro, ajuste razonable, ascenso, pago retroactivo, pago anticipado u otras medidas que resarcirán "plenamente" a la persona (la condición en que se encontraría si no hubiese ocurrido la discriminación). Los desagravios podrían incluir también el pago de los honorarios de los abogados, los honorarios de los peritos y las costas del tribunal.

(continued)

Exhibit 17.9 **Spanish instructions for filing a charge of job discrimination** *(continued)*

Según a la mayoría de las leyes que hace cumplir la EEOC, los daños por discriminación **intencional** se podrían hacer disponibles para pérdidas pecuniarias reales, para pérdidas pecuniarias futuras y por sufrimiento mental e inconvenientes causados. También se pueden procurar daños punitivos si el empleador infringió la ley a sabiendas e intencionalmente.

Números de teléfono y recursos de la EEOC

Para obtener asistencia o mayor información de la oficina local de la EEOC más cercana a usted, llame al teléfono 1-800-669-4000 (voz) o 1-800-669-6820 (TTY) (para los que tengan una discapacidad auditiva).

Para obtener publicaciones a título gratuito, comuníquese con el Centro de Distribución de Publicaciones (*Publications Distribution Center*) de la EEOC llamando al número de teléfono 1-800-669-3362 (voz), 1-800-800-3302 (TTY) (para los que tengan una discapacidad auditiva), ó 513-489-8692 (fax).

Podrá también hallar información sobre las leyes que hace cumplir la EEOC en el sitio electrónico de la EEOC en Internet: **www.eeoc.gov**

Este folleto está disponible en braille, letra de imprenta grande, audio cinta y archivo electrónico en disco para computadora. Puede recibir las publicaciones de la EEOC en formatos de fácil acceso, previa solicitud al Centro de Distribución de Publicaciones.

Se permite duplicar esta publicación de la EEOC.

Comisión para la Igualdad de Oportunidades de Empleo de los Estados Unidos

Source: Equal Employment Opportunity Commission (EEOC)

All about me may be silence and darkness, yet within me, in the spirit, is music and brightness, and color flashes through all my thoughts.

Helen Keller
The Open Door (1957)

employer. Reasonable accommodations may include making facilities readily accessible to individuals with disabilities, providing part-time or modified work schedules, acquiring equipment or devices, modifying examination and training materials, and providing qualified readers or interpreters.

Employers are not obligated to provide accommodations that would impose an *undue burden*, or actions that would require significant difficulty or expense. The courts consider factors such as the nature and cost of accommodation, the employer's overall financial resources, and the employer's type of operation. Obviously, what may be a significant difficulty or expense for a small employer may not be an undue hardship for a large employer.

CIVIL RIGHTS ACT OF 1866

Civil Rights Act of 1866
A federal statute enacted after the Civil War that says all persons "have the same right . . . to make and enforce contracts . . . as is enjoyed by white persons." It prohibits racial and national origin employment discrimination.

The **Civil Rights Act of 1866** was enacted after the Civil War. **Section 1981** of this act states that all persons "have the same right . . . to make and enforce contracts . . . as is enjoyed by white persons." This law was enacted to give African Americans, just freed from slavery, the same right to contract as Caucasians. Section 1981 expressly prohibits racial discrimination; it also has been held to forbid discrimination based on national origin.

Employment decisions are covered by Section 1981 because the employment relationship is contractual. Although most racial and national origin employment discrimination cases are brought under Title VII, there are two reasons that a complainant would bring the action under Section 1981:

1. A private plaintiff can bring an action without going through the procedural requirements of Title VII.
2. There is no cap on the recovery of compensatory or punitive damages.

LABOR UNION LAW

Prior to the Industrial Revolution, employees and employers had somewhat equal bargaining power. Once the country became industrialized in the late 1800s, large corporate employers had much more bargaining power than their employees. In the early 1900s, members of the labor movement lobbied Congress to pass laws to protect their rights to organize and bargain with management. During the Great Depression of the 1930s, several statutes were enacted to give workers certain rights and protections. Other statutes have been added since then. The major federal statutes in this area are:

- *Norris-LaGuardia Act.* Enacted in 1932, this Act stipulates that it is legal for employees to organize and form labor unions.
- *National Labor Relations Act (NLRA).* This Act, also known as the Wagner Act, was enacted in 1935. The NLRA establishes the right to employees to form, join, and assist labor organizations; to bargain collectively with employers; and to engage in concerted activity to promote these rights.
- *Labor–Management Relations Act.* In 1947, Congress enacted the Labor–Management Relations Act (the Taft-Hartley Act). This Act (1) expands the activities that labor unions can engage in, (2) gives employers the right to engage in free speech efforts against unions prior to a union election, and (3) gives the president of the United States the right to seek an injunction (for up to 80 days) against a strike that would create a national emergency.
- *Labor–Management Reporting and Disclosure Act.* Congress enacted the Labor–Management Reporting and Disclosure Act of 1959 (the Landrum-Griffin Act). This Act regulates internal union affairs and establishes the rights of union members.
- *Railway Labor Act.* The Railway Labor Act of 1926, as amended in 1934, covers employees of railroad and airline carriers.

Today, approximately 12 percent of private-sector wage and salary workers belong to labor unions: Many government employees also belong to unions.

> No private business monopoly, producer organization or cartel wields the market (and physical) power or commands the discipline over its members which many unions have achieved.
>
> Gottfried Haberler
> *Economic Growth and Stability (1974)*

Find the office of the Federal National Labor Relations Board (NLRB) that serves your area. http://www.nlrb.gov/html

National Labor Relations Board (NLRB)

The NLRA created the **National Labor Relations Board (NLRB)**. The NLRB is an administrative body composed of five members appointed by the President and approved by the Senate. The NLRB oversees union elections, prevents employers and unions from engaging in illegal and unfair labor practices, and enforces and interprets certain federal labor laws. The decisions of the NLRB are enforceable in court.

National Labor Relations Board (NLRB)
A federal administrative agency that oversees union elections, prevents employers and unions from engaging in illegal and unfair labor practices, and enforces and interprets certain federal labor laws.

Organizing a Union

Section 7 of the NLRA gives employees the right to join together and form a union. Section 7 provides that employees shall have the right to self-organization; to form, join, or assist labor organizations; to bargain collectively through representatives of their own choosing; and to engage in other concerted activities for the purpose of collective bargaining or other mutual aid protection.

Section 8(a) of the NLRA makes it an **unfair labor practice** for an employer to interfere with, coerce, or restrain employees from exercising their statutory right to form and join unions. Threats of loss of benefits for joining the union, statements such as "I'll close this plant if a union comes in here," and the like are unfair labor practices. Also, an employer may not form a company union. Section 8(b) of the NLRA prohibits unions from engaging in unfair labor practices that interfere with a union election. Coercion, physical threats, and such are unfair labor practices.

Section 7 of the NLRA
A law that gives employees the right to join together and form a union.

Collective bargaining
The act of negotiating contract terms between an employer and the members of a union.

Strike
Cessation of work by union members to obtain economic benefits or correct an unfair labor practice.

Picketing
The action of strikers walking in front of the employer's premises carrying signs announcing their strike.

Management and union may be likened to that serpent of the fables who on one body had two heads that fighting with poisoned fangs, killed themselves.

Peter Drucker
The New Society (1951)

Strong responsible unions are essential to industrial fair play. Without them the labor bargain is wholly one-sided.

Louis D. Brandeis

Once a union has been elected, the employer and the union discuss the terms of employment of union members and try to negotiate a contract that embodies these terms. The act of negotiating is called **collective bargaining**, and the resulting contract is called a **collective bargaining agreement**. The employer and the union must negotiate with each other in good faith.

Strikes and Picketing

The NLRA gives union management the right to recommend that the union call a **strike** if a collective bargaining agreement cannot be reached. Before there can be a strike, though, a majority vote of the union's members must agree to the action.

Striking union members often engage in **picketing** in support of their strike. Picketing usually takes the form of the striking employees and union representatives walking in front of the employer's premises carrying signs announcing their strike. Picketing is used to put pressure on an employer to settle a strike. The right to picket is implied from the NLRA.

Picketing is lawful unless it

1. is accompanied by violence,
2. obstructs customers from entering the employer's place of business,
3. prevents nonstriking employees from entering the employer's premises, or
4. prevents pickups and deliveries at the employer's place of business.

An employer may seek an injunction against unlawful picketing.

Several types of strikes have been held to be illegal and are not protected by federal labor laws, Illegal strikes take the form of:

- *Violent strikes.* In **violent strikes**, striking employees cause substantial damage to property of the employer or a third party. Courts usually tolerate a certain amount of isolated violence before finding that the entire strike is illegal.
- *Sit-down strikes.* In **sit-down strikes**, striking employees continue to occupy the employer's premises. Such strikes are illegal because they deny the employer's statutory right to continue its operations during the strike.
- *Partial or intermittent strikes.* In **partial** or **intermittent** strikes, employees strike part of the day or workweek and work the other part. This type of strike is illegal because it interferes with the employer's right to operate its facilities at full operation.

A union is required to give an employer a 60-day notice before commencing a strike. This is called **cooling-off period**. This mandatory cooling-off period is designed to give the employer and the union time to negotiate a settlement of the union grievances and avoid a strike. Any strike without a proper 60-day notice is illegal. Illegal strikers may be discharged by the employer, with no rights to reinstatement.

Crossover and Replacement Workers

Individual members of a union do not have to honor a strike. They may (1) choose not to strike, or (2) return to work after joining the strikers for a time. Employees who choose either of these two options are known as **crossover workers**.

Once a strike begins, the employer may continue operations by using management personnel and hiring **replacement workers** to take the place of the striking employees. Replacement workers can be hired on either a temporary or a permanent basis. If replacement workers are given permanent status, they do not have to be dismissed when the strike is over.

PARALEGALS AND LEGAL ASSISTANTS EMPLOYMENT

Paralegals and legal assistants held about 224,000 jobs in 2004. Private law firms employed 7 in 10 paralegals and legal assistants; most of the remainder worked for corporate legal departments and various levels of government. Within the Federal Government, the U.S. Department of Justice is the largest employer, followed by the Social Security Administration and the U.S. Department of the Treasury. A small number of paralegals own their own businesses and work as freelance legal assistants, contracting their services to attorneys or corporate legal departments.

Employment for paralegals and legal assistants is projected to grow much faster than average for all occupations through 2014. Employers are trying to reduce costs and increase the availability and efficiency of legal services by hiring paralegals to perform tasks formerly carried out by lawyers. Besides new jobs created by employment growth, additional job openings will arise as people leave the occupation. Despite projections of rapid employment growth, competition for jobs should continue as many people seek to go into this profession; however, experienced, formally trained paralegals should have the best employment opportunities.

Private law firms will continue to be the largest employers of paralegals, but a growing array of other organizations, such as corporate legal departments, insurance companies, real estate and title insurance firms, and banks hire paralegals. Corporations in particular are boosting their in-house legal departments to cut costs. Demand for paralegals also is expected to grow as an expanding population increasingly requires legal services, especially in areas such as intellectual property, health care, international law, elder issues, criminal law, and environmental law.

Paralegals who specialize in areas such as real estate, bankruptcy, medical malpractice, and product liability should have ample employment opportunities. The growth of prepaid legal plans also should contribute to the demand for legal services. Paralegal employment is expected to increase as organizations presently employing paralegals assign them a growing range of tasks and as paralegals are employed increasingly in small and medium-size establishments. A growing number of experienced paralegals are expected to establish their own businesses.

Job opportunities for paralegals will expand in the public sector as well. Community legal-service programs, which provide assistance to the poor, elderly, minorities, and middle-income families, will employ additional paralegals to minimize expenses and serve the most people. Federal, state, and local government agencies, consumer organizations, and the courts also are expected to continue to hire paralegals in increasing numbers.

To a limited extent, paralegal jobs are affected by the business cycle. During recessions, the demand declines for some discretionary legal services, such as planning estates, drafting wills, and handling real estate transactions. Corporations are less inclined to initiate certain types of litigation when falling sales and profits lead to fiscal belt tightening. As a result, full-time paralegals employed in offices adversely affected by a recession may be laid off or have their work hours reduced. During recessions, by contrast, corporations and individuals are more likely to face other problems that require legal assistance, such as bankruptcies, foreclosures, and divorces. Paralegals, who provide many of the same legal services as lawyers at a lower cost, tend to fare relatively better in difficult economic conditions.

Source: United States Department of Labor Bureau of Labor Statistics

PLANT CLOSING ACT

Often a company would choose to close a plant without giving its employees prior notice of the closing. To remedy this situation, on August 4, 1988, Congress enacted the **Worker Adjustment and Retraining Notification (WARN) Act**, also called the **Plant Closing Act.** The Act, which covers employers with 100 or more employees, requires employers to give their employees 60 days' notice before engaging in certain plant closings or layoffs.

(continued)

PLANT CLOSING ACT (continued)

If the employees are represented by a union, the notice must be given to the union; if they are not, the notice must be given to the employees individually.

The actions covered by the act are:

- **Plant closings.** A plant closing is a permanent or temporary shutdown of a single site that results in a loss of employment of 50 or more employees during any 30-day period.
- **Mass layoffs.** A mass layoff is a reduction of 33 percent of the employees or at least 50 employees during any 30-day period.

An employer is exempted from having to give such notice if the closing or layoff is caused by business circumstances that were not reasonably foreseeable as of the time the notice would have been required.

Legal Terminology

Summary

CHAPTER *17*   EMPLOYMENT LAW
Agency Law

Definition	Agency is a fiduciary relationship that results from the manifestation of consent by one person to act on behalf of another person with that person's consent.
Parties	1. *Principal*: party who employs another person to act on his or her behalf 2. *Agent*: party who agrees to act on behalf of another person
Kinds of Employment Relationships	Employer–employee relationship: An employer hires an employee to perform some form of physical service. An employee is not an agent unless the principal authorizes him or her to enter into contracts on the principal's behalf. Principal–agent relationship: An employer hires an employee and authorizes the employee to enter into contracts on the employer's behalf. Principal–independent contractor relationship: A principal employs a person who is not an employee of the principal. The independent contractor has authority to enter into only those contracts authorized by the principal.
Formation of the Agency Relationship	1. Express agency: The principal and the agent expressly agree in words to enter into an agency agreement. The agency contract may be oral or written unless the Statute of Frauds requires it to be in writing. 2. Implied agency: An agency is inferred from the conduct of the parties. 3. Apparent agency: A principal creates an appearance of an agency that in actuality does not exist. Also called *agency by estoppel* or *ostensible agency*. 4. Agency by ratification: A person misrepresents himself or herself as another's agent when he or she is not and the purported principal ratifies (accepts) the unauthorized act.
Contract Liability to Third Parties	1. Fully disclosed agency: The third party entering into the contract knows that the agent is acting for a principal and knows the identity of the principal. The principal is liable on the contract; the agent is not liable on the contract. 2. Partially disclosed agency: The third party knows that the agent is acting for a principal but does not know the identity of the principal. Both the principal and the agent are liable on the contract. 3. Undisclosed Agency: The third party does not know that the agent is acting for a principal. Both the principal and the agent are liable on the contract.

Tort Liability of Principals and Agents to Third Parties

Description	Principals are liable for the *tortious conduct* of an agent who is acting within the *scope of his or her authority*. Liability is imposed for misrepresentation, negligence, and intentional torts.
Intentional Torts	States apply one of the following rules: 1. *Motivation test*: The principal is liable if the agent's intentional tort was committed to promote the principal's business. 2. *Work-related test*: The principal is liable if the agent's intentional tort was committed within a work-related time or space. Agents are personally liable for their own tortious conduct.

Negligence	Principals are liable for the negligent conduct of agents acting within the scope of their employment. Special negligence doctrines include: 1. *Frolic and detour*: Principals are generally relieved of liability if the agent's negligent act occurred on a substantial frolic and detour from the scope of employment. 2. *"Coming and going" rule*: Principals are not liable if the agent's tortious conduct occurred while on the way to or from work. 3. *Dual-purpose mission*: If the agent is acting on his or her own behalf and on behalf of the principal, the principal is generally liable for the agent's tortious conduct.
Independent Contractor	Generally, principals are not liable for the tortious conduct of independent contractors. Exceptions to the rule are for: 1. *Nondelegable duties.* 2. *Special risks.* 3. *Negligence in selecting an independent contractor.* Independent contractors are personally liable for their own torts.

Termination of an Agency

Termination by Acts of the Parties	The following *acts of the parties* terminate agency contracts: 1. *Mutual agreement* 2. *Lapse of time* 3. *Purpose achieved* 4. *Occurrence of a specified event*
Wrongful Termination of an Agency Contract	If an agency is for an agreed-upon term or purpose, the *unilateral termination* of the agency contract by either the principal or the agent constitutes the *wrongful termination* of the agency. The breaching party is liable to the other party for damages caused by the breach.

Workers' Compensation

Workers' Compensation Acts	Workers' compensation acts are state statutes that create an administrative procedure for workers to receive payments for job-related injuries.
Workers' Compensation Insurance	Most states require employers to carry private or government-sponsored *workers' compensation insurance*. Some states permit employers to self-insure.
Employment-Related Injury	To be compensable under workers' compensation, the claimant must prove that the injury arose out of and in the course of his or her employment.
Exclusive Remedy	Workers' compensation is an exclusive remedy. Thus, workers cannot sue their employers to recover damages for job-related injuries.

Occupational Safety and Health Act

Descriptions	1. *Occupational Safety and Health Act*: a federal statute that requires employers to provide safe working conditions 2. *Occupational Safety and Health Administration (OSHA)*: federal administrative agency that administers and enforces the Occupational Safety and Health Act
Duty Standards	OSHA enforces the following duty standards on employers: 1. *Specific duty standards*: OSHA safety standards established for specific equipment (e.g., chain saw) or a specific industry (e.g., mining) 2. *General duty standards*: OSHA standards that impose a general duty on employers to provide safe working conditions

Fair Labor Standards Act (FLSA)

Description Protections	*Fair Labor Standards Act (FLSA)*: federal statute that protects workers.
	1. *Child labor*: The FLSA forbids the use of illegal child labor. The U.S. Department of Labor defines illegal child labor.
	2. *Minimum wage*: Workers must be paid a minimum wage. The federal minimum wage is $5.15 per hour. The minimum wage can be changed by Congress.
	3. *Overtime pay*: An employer cannot require employees to work more than 40 hours per week unless they are paid 1.5 times their regular pay for each hour worked in excess of 40 hours.

Title VII of the Civil Rights Act of 1964

Description	Title VII of the Civil Rights Act of 1964 is a federal statute that prohibits job discrimination based on the (1) race, (2) color, (3) religion, (4) sex, or (5) national origin of the job applicant.
Scope of Coverage of Title VII	*Employment decisions subject to Title VII*: Decisions regarding hiring; promotion; demotion; payment of salaries, wages, and fringe benefits; job training and apprenticeships; work rules; or any other "term, condition, or privilege of employment."
Protected Classes	Title VII prohibits employment discrimination based on the following protected classes: 1. *Race*: broad class based on common physical characteristics 2. *Color*: skin color 3. *National origin*: a person's national heritage 4. *Sex*: male or female 5. *Religion*: discrimination solely because of a person's religious beliefs or practices. An employer has a duty to *reasonably accommodate* an employee's religious beliefs if it does not cause an *undue hardship* on the employer.
Sexual Harassment	Sexual harassment consists of lewd remarks, touching, intimidation, posting pinups, and other verbal or physical conduct of a sexual nature that occurs on the job. Sexual harassment that creates a *hostile work environment* violates Title VII [*Meritor Savings Bank v. Vinson*, 477 U.S. 57 (1986)].

Equal Pay Act

Description	The Equal Pay Act is a federal statute that forbids pay discrimination for the same job based on the sex of the employee performing the job, where the job requires equal skill, effort, responsibility, and working conditions.
Criteria that Justify a Differential in Wages	The Equal Pay Act expressly provides the following four criteria that justify a differential in wages for the same job: 1. Seniority 2. Merit (based on a measurable standard) 3. Quantity or quality of product (e.g., commission, piecework) 4. "Any factor other than sex" (e.g., night shift)

Family and Medical Leave Act

Description	The Family and Medical Leave Act is a federal statute that guarantees covered workers unpaid time off from work for the birth or adoption of a child, serious health problems of the worker, and serious health problems of a spouse, child, or parent.

Age Discrimination in Employment Act (ADEA)

Description	ADEA is a federal statute that prohibits employment discrimination against applicants and employees who are 40 years of age and older.

Americans with Disabilities Act (ADA)

Description	ADA is a federal law that imposes obligations on employers and providers of public transportation, telecommunications, and public accommodations to accommodate individuals with disabilities.
Title I of ADA	Title I of ADA is a federal law that prohibits employment discrimination against qualified individuals with disabilities. It requires employers to make *reasonable accommodations* for employees with disabilities that do not cause *undue hardship* to the employer.

Civil Rights Act of 1866

Section 1981	Section 1981 of the Civil Rights Act of 1866, enacted after the Civil War, states that all persons "have the same right . . . to make and enforce contracts . . . as enjoyed by white persons."
Protected Class	Section 1981 prohibits discrimination because of *race* or *national origin* concerning employment contracts.
Remedies	A successful plaintiff can recover compensatory and punitive damages. There is no monetary cap on compensatory and punitive damages.

Labor Union Law

National Labor Relations Act (NLRA)	The NLRA is a federal statute that established the right of employees to form, join, and assist labor unions.
National Labor Relations Board (NLRB)	The NLRB is a federal administrative agency empowered to administer federal labor law, oversee union elections, and decide labor disputes.
Unfair Labor Practice	1. *Employer*: Section 8(a) of the NLRA makes it an *unfair labor practice* for an employer to interfere with, coerce, or restrain employees exercising their right to form and join unions. 2. *Labor union*: Section 8(b) makes it an *unfain labor practice* for a union to interfere with a union election.
Collective Bargaining	1. *Collective bargaining*: a process whereby a union and an employer negotiate the terms and conditions of employment for the covered employee union members 2. *Collective bargaining agreement*: a contract between an employer and a labor union that results from collective bargaining

Strikes and Picketing	1. *Strike*. A strike is cessation of work by union members in obtaining economic benefits, correcting for the purpose of an unfair labor practice, or preserving their work. The NLRA gives employees the right to strike.
	2. *Cooling-off period*. A labor union must give an employer at least 60 days' prior notice of a strike—called the *cooling-off period*.
	3. *Picketing*. Striking employees and union organizers may picket—walk around the employer's premises, usually carrying signs, notifying the public of their grievance against the employer.
	4. *Illegal strikes and picketing*. The following types of picketing and strikes are illegal:
	  a. *Illegal picketing*: Picketing that is accompanied by violence, or obstructs customers, nonstriking workers, or suppliers from entering the employer's premises.
	  b. *Violent strike*: A strike in which striking employees cause substantial damage to the employer's or a third party's property.
	  c. *Sit-down strike*. A strike in which the striking employees occupy and refuse to leave the employer's premises.
	  d. *Partial or intermittent strike*. A strike in which the striking employees strike for only parts of each day or week.

Plant Closing Act	The *Worker Adjustment and Retraining Notification (WARN) Act* is a federal statute that requires employers with 100 or more employees to give their employees 60 days notice before engaging in certain plant closings or layoffs. Also called the *Plant Closing Act*.

▶ WORKING THE WEB

1. Visit the website **http://www.eeoc.gov/html**, the site of the federal Equal Employment Opportunity Commission (EEOC). Under the category "Discrimination by Types," find the description of "Pregnancy Discrimination." Write a one-page report on pregnancy discrimination.

2. Visit the website **http://www.osha.gov/html**, the website of the federal Occupational Safety and Health Administration (OSHA). Find an OSHA workplace safety rule that interests you. Write a one-page report that describes the rule.

3. Visit the website **http://www.nlrb.gov/html**, the website of the federal National Labor Relations Board (NLRB). Find a recent decision of the NLRB for the current year and write a one-page report summarizing the facts of the case and the NLRB's decision in the case.

4. Visit the website **http://www.eeoc.gov/html**, the website of the federal Equal Employment Opportunity Commission (EEOC). Click on the category "News." Find a current case or news event that interests you and write a one-page report on the case or news item.

5. Visit the website **http://www.dol.gov/html**, the website of the U.S. Department of Labor (DOL). Click on "Wages." On the next page click on "minimum wage." On the next page click on "states." On the next page click on "Current State Minimum Wage Rates." On the map that is shown, click on your state. Based on federal and state law, what is the minimum wage for your state?

▶ CRITICAL THINKING AND WRITING QUESTIONS

1. Define an agency, a principal, and an agent.
2. Define an independent contractor. What elements are examined to determine if a person or party is an independent contractor?
3. What is an employee-at-will? Can an at-will employee be easily terminated? Explain.
4. Describe the differences among the following: (1) express agency, (2) implied agency, and (3) agency by ratification.
5. What is an apparent agency? Give an example.
6. What is power of attorney? What is the difference between a general power of attorney and a special power of attorney? Who is an attorney-in-fact?
7. Explain the contract liability of a principal and an agent in the following types of agencies: (1) fully disclosed agency, (2) partially disclosed agency, and (3) undisclosed agency.
8. Describe the tort liability of a principal for the intentional torts of an agent under each of the following tests: (1) motivation test, and (2) work-related test.
9. Define the term *respondeat superior*. Describe vicarious liability.
10. What is the principal's liability for an agent's negligence? What does "scope of authority" mean?
11. Describe a principal's liability for the torts of an agent under the following special doctrines: (1) frolic and detour, (2) "coming and going" rule, and (3) dual-purpose mission.
12. Describe the wrongful termination of an agency. Give an example.
13. What is workers' compensation? Describe the following: (1) work-related injury, and (2) exclusive remedy.
14. What does the Occupational Safety and Health Act require? Describe the difference between specific duty standards and general duty standards.
15. What are the Fair Labor Standards Act (FLSA) requirements concerning (1) child labor, (2) minimum wage, and (3) overtime pay?
16. What does Title VII of the Civil Rights Act of 1964 provide? What are the protected classes under Title VII?
17. What is the difference between race discrimination and national heritage discrimination? Give an example of each.

18. What is a bona fide occupational qualification (BFOQ)? Give an example.
19. Define sexual harassment. Give an example.
20. Define religious discrimination prohibited by Title VII. What is the duty of an employer concerning protecting the religious preferences of employees? Give an example.
21. What does the Equal Pay Act provide? Give an example.
22. What is age discrimination? What age group is protected by the Age Discrimination in Employment Act?
23. What does the Americans with Disabilities Act (ADA) provide? What is the duty of an employer concerning protecting employees under this ADA? Give an example.
24. What benefits does the Family Medical Leave Act provide? Explain.
25. What does the Civil Rights Act of 1866 provide? Elaborate.
26. Define a labor union. What benefit does the National Labor Relations Act (NLRA) provide to workers?
27. Describe the following: (1) unfair labor practice, (2) collective bargaining, (3) strike, (4) cooling-off period, and (5) picketing.
28. What does the Plant Closing Act provide? Explain.

▶ ETHICAL ANALYSIS AND DISCUSSION QUESTIONS

1. What ethical issues may be involved when a paralegal acts under a power of attorney for a client of the firm?
2. Is a paralegal who is investigating the facts of a case acting as an agent for the client or for the law firm? Does the answer change the ethical obligations of the paralegal?
3. A corporate client is concerned about testimony that an employee may give in a pending civil action even though the corporation has not been named as a defendant [Colorado Bar Association Ethics Opinion 79.] May a paralegal attend depositions for the sole purpose of taking notes on testimony given or taken in the action?

▶ DEVELOPING YOUR COLLABORATION SKILLS

Working on your own or with a group of other students assigned by your instructor, review Paralegals at Work at the beginning of the chapter. As a group, discuss the following questions.

1. What are the protected classes under Title VII of the Civil Rights Act of 1964? Does Ms. Rodriquez fall under any of these protected classes? If so, which one(s)?
2. Does Ms. Rodriquez have a legitimate Title VII sex discrimination claim against her employer, Retro Bank? Explain.
3. Does Ms. Rodriquez have a legitimate Title VII national origin discrimination claim against her employer, Retro Bank? Explain.

▶ PARALEGAL PORTFOLIO EXERCISE

Using the website http://google.com/html or similar Internet website, or the Internet legal services Westlaw or LexisNexis, or law books, find a sample general power of attorney for your state. Complete this form as if you are the principal and someone you choose is the attorney-in-fact. Complete the form, meeting all of the state's requirements for creating a valid general power of attorney.

▶LEGAL ANALYSIS AND WRITING CASES

Edgewater Motels, Inc. v. Gatzke and Walgreen Co.

277 N.W.2d 11 (1979) Supreme Court of Minnesota

FACTS

Arlen Gatzke (Gatzke) was a district manager for the Walgreen Company (Walgreen). In August 1979, Gatzke was sent to Duluth, Minnesota, to supervise the opening of a new Walgreen store. In Duluth, Gatzke stayed at the Edgewater Motel (Edgewater). While in Duluth, Gatzke was "on call" 24 hours a day to other Walgreen stores located in his territory.

About midnight on the evening of August 23, 1979, Gatzke, after working 17 hours that day, went with several other Walgreen employees to a restaurant and bar to drink. Within one hour's time, Gatzke had consumed three "doubles" and one single brandy Manhattan. About 1:30 A.M., he went back to the Edgewater Motel and filled out his expense report. Soon thereafter a fire broke out in Gatzke's motel room. Gatzke escaped, but the fire spread and caused extensive damage to the motel. Evidence showed that Gatzke smoked two packs of cigarettes a day. An expert fire reconstruction witness testified that the fire started from a lit cigarette in or next to the wastepaper basket in Gatzke's room.

Edgewater Motels, Inc. sued Gatzke and Walgreen. The parties stipulated that the damage to the Edgewater Motel was $330,360. The jury returned a verdict against defendants Gatzke and Walgreen. The court granted Walgreen's post-trial motion for judgment notwithstanding the verdict. Plaintiff Edgewater and defendant Gatzke appealed.

Question

1. Was Gatzke's act of smoking within his "scope of employment," making his principal, the Walgreen Company, vicariously liable for his negligence?

International Union, United Automobile, Aerospace and Agricultural Implement Workers of America, UAW v. Johnson Controls, Inc.

499 U.S. 187, 111 S.Ct. 1196 113 L.Ed.2d 158 (1991) Supreme Court of the United States

FACTS

Johnson Controls, Inc. (Johnson Controls), manufactures batteries. Lead is the primary ingredient in the manufacturing process. Exposure to lead entails health risks, including risk of harm to any fetus carried by a female employee. To protect unborn children from such risk, Johnson Controls adopted an employment rule that prevents pregnant women and women of childbearing age from working at jobs involving lead exposure. Only women who were sterilized or could prove they could not have children were not affected by the rule. Consequently, most female employees were relegated to lower-paying clerical jobs at the company.

Several female employees field a class action suit, challenging Johnson Controls's fetal-protection policy as sex discrimination in violation of Title VII. The District Court held that the policy was justified as a bona fide occupational qualification (BFOQ) and granted summary judgment to Johnson Controls. The Court of Appeals affirmed. The plaintiffs appealed to the U.S. Supreme Court.

Question

1. Is Johnson Controls's fetal-protection policy a BFOQ?

PGA Tour, Inc. v. Martin

532 U.S. 661, 121 S.Ct. 1879 149 L.Ed.2d 904 (2001) Supreme Court of the United States

FACTS

The PGA Tour, Inc., is a nonprofit entity that sponsors professional golf tournaments. The PGA has adopted a set of rules that apply to its golf tour. One rule requires golfers to walk the course during PGA-sponsored tournaments. Casey Martin is a talented amateur golfer who won many high school and university golf championships. Martin has contracted Klippel-Trenaunay-Weber syndrome, a degenerative circulatory disorder that obstructs the flow of blood from his right leg to his heart. The disease is progressive and has atrophied his right leg. Walking causes Martin pain, fatigue, and anxiety, with significant risk of hemorrhaging.

When Martin turned professional, he qualified for the PGA Tour. He made a request to use a golf cart while playing in PGA tournaments. When the PGA denied his request, Martin sued the PGA for violation of the Americans with Disabilities Act (ADA) for not making reasonable accommodations for his disability. The District Court sided with Martin and ordered the PGA to permit Martin to use a golf cart. The Court of Appeals affirmed. The U.S. Supreme Court agreed to hear the PGA's appeal.

Question

1. Does the ADA require PGA Tour, Inc., to accommodate Casey Martin, a professional golfer with a disability, by permitting him to use a golf cart while playing in PGA-sponsored golf tournaments?

Grinder v. Bryans Road Building & Supply Co., Inc.

432 A.2d 453 1981 Md. Lexis 246 (Md.App. 1981)

FACTS

G. Elvin Grinder of Marbury, Maryland, was a building contractor who, prior to May 1, 1973, did business as an individual and traded as "Grinder Construction." Grinder maintained an open account, on his individual credit, with Bryans Road Building & Supply Co., Inc. Grinder would purchase materials and supplies from Bryans on credit and later pay the invoices.

On May 1, 1973, G. Elvin Grinder Construction, Inc., a Maryland corporation, was formed with Grinder personally owning 52 percent of the stock of the corporation. Grinder did not inform Bryans that he had incorporated, and he continued to purchase supplies on credit from Bryans under the name "Grinder Construction."

In May 1978, after certain invoices were not paid by Grinder, Bryans sued Grinder personally to recover. Grinder asserted that the debts were owed by the corporation. Bryans amended its complaint to include the corporation as a defendant.

Question

1. Who is liable to Bryans?

Largey v. Intrastate Radiotelephone, Inc.

136 Cal.App.3d 660, 186 Cal.Rptr. 520, 1982 Cal.App. Lexis 2049 (Cal.App. 1982)

FACTS

Intrastate Radiotelephone, Inc., a public utility, supplies radiotelephone utility service to the general public for radiotelephones, pocket pagers, and beepers. Robert Kranhold, an employee of Intrastate, was authorized to use his personal vehicle on company business. On the morning of March 9, 1976, when Kranhold was driving his vehicle to Intrastate's main office, he negligently struck a motorcycle driven by Michael S. Largey, causing severe and permanent injuries to Largey. The accident occurred at the intersection where Intrastate's main office is located.

Evidence showed that Kranhold acted as a consultant to Intrastate, worked both in and out of Intrastate's offices, had no set hours of work, often attended meetings at Intrastate's offices, and went to Intrastate's offices to pick up things or drop off things. Largey sued Intrastate for damages.

Question

1. Is Intrastate liable?

Huddleston v. Roger Dean Chevrolet, Inc.

845 F.2d 900 1988 U.S. App. Lexis 6823 (11th Cir. 1988)

FACTS

Shirley Huddleston became the first female sales representative of Roger Dean Chevrolet, Inc. (RDC) in West Palm Beach, Florida. Shortly after she began working at RDC, Philip Geraci, a fellow sales representative, and other male employees began making derogatory comments to and about her, expelled gas in her presence, called her a whore, and such. Many of these remarks were made in front of customers. The sales manager of RDC participated in the harassment. On several occasions, Huddleston complained about this conduct to RDC's general manager.

Question

1. Was Title VII violated?

Dothard, Director, Department of Public Safety of Alabama v. Rawlinson

433 U.S. 321, 97 S. Ct. 2720 53 L.Ed.2d 786, 1977 U.S. Lexis 143 (1977)

FACTS

Dianne Rawlinson, 22 years old, is a college graduate whose major course of study was correctional psychology. After graduation, she applied for a position as a correctional counselor (prison guard) with the Alabama Board of Corrections. Her application was rejected because she failed to meet the minimum 120-pound weight requirement of an Alabama statute that also established a height minimum of 5 feet 2 inches. In addition, the Alabama Board of Corrections adopted Administrative Regulation 204, which established gender criteria for assigning correctional counselors to maximum-security prisons for "contact positions." These are correctional counselor positions that require continual close physical proximity to inmates. Under this rule, Rawlinson did not qualify for contact positions with male prisoners in Alabama maximum-security prisons.

Rawlinson brought this class action lawsuit against Dothard, who was the director of the Department of Public Safety of Alabama.

Question

1. Does either the height–weight requirement or the contact position rule constitute a bona fide occupational qualification that justifies the sexual discrimination in this case? Does society owe a duty of social responsibility to protect women from dangerous job positions? Or is this "romantic paternalism?"

▶WORKING WITH THE LANGUAGE OF THE COURT CASE

District of Columbia v. Howell

607 A.2d 501 1992 D.C. App. Lexis 109 (D.C.Pap. 1992)
United States Court of Appeals. District of Columbia

Read the following case, excerpted from the Court of Appeals opinion. Review and brief the case. In your brief, answer the following questions:

1. Was A. Louis Jagoe hired by the District of Columbia as an employee or as an independent contractor?
2. Describe the accident. Who was injured?
3. Normally, an employer is not liable for the tortious conduct of an independent contractor it has hired. What is the "special risks" exception to this rule?
4. What damages were awarded to the plaintiff?

Farrell, Associate Judge

The Murch School Summer Discovery Program was designed to provide hands-on education for gifted and talented eight- and nine-year-old children. The program originated in 1985 when Mrs. Gill, the Murch School principal, attended a reception at Mount Vernon College arranged by Greg Butta, a Ph.D. candidate at the American University, to advertise the success of a summer program he had conducted at Mount Vernon. The program interested Mrs. Gill, and after several discussions Butta sent her a formal proposal for conducting a similar program at the Murch School. Gill proposed changes to the proposal, then solicited and received approval for the program from the Assistant Superintendent for the District of Columbia Public Schools.

Butta hired the staff for the summer program, including some of the instructors who had taught in the Mount Vernon program. Mrs. Gill, however, reviewed all of the instructors' resumes, had veto authority over their hiring, and interviewed most of the staff, including A. Louis Jagoe, before the hiring was made final. Jagoe, who was hired to teach chemistry to the eight- and nine-year-olds in the program, held a master's degree in chemistry and was a Ph.D. candidate at the American University. Before the first general staff meeting, he told Butta that as part of the class he would do a luminescence experiment and a "cold-pack" experiment and wanted to make sparklers with the children. Jagoe and Butta discussed the safety of the sparkler experiment only in regard to the location where the children would be allowed to light the sparklers.

On August 1, 1985, a staff meeting was held at which Gill, Butta, and all instructors and counselors were present. Each instructor gave a brief talk about what he or she intended to do in class. Several instructors testified that Jagoe told the group, including Mrs. Gill, that he planned to make sparklers as one of the chemistry experiments. Gill, who was in and out of the meeting, did not remember hearing Jagoe discuss the experiment, although notes she took at the meeting reflect that she heard him discuss the luminescence and cold-pack experiments and asked him questions about these. Gill spoke and emphasized the "hands-on" nature of the program and her hopes for its success.

One child attending the program was nine-year-old Dedrick Howell, whose parents enrolled him after receiving the school brochure in the mail. The accident occurred on August 12, 1985. At the beginning of the chemistry class, Jagoe distributed his "recipe" for sparklers to the children and also wrote it on the blackboard. Along with other chemical ingredients, the recipe called for the use of potassium perchlorate as the oxidizing agent. Potassium perchlorate was described at trial as an extremely unstable and highly volatile chemical often used to make rocket fuel. Commercially made sparklers are not made with potassium perchlorate.

The children scooped the chemicals, including the potassium perchlorate, out of jars and, using pestles, ground up the mixture in mortars. While they were combining the chemicals, Jagoe ignited three different chemical mixtures at the front of the room with a butane lighter. Butta was present for one of the ignitions when he entered the room to drop off metal hangers for use in the experiment. Mrs. Gill also entered the room at one point, and saw the children working at tables wearing goggles or glasses. She also saw Jagoe at the front of the room lighting the chemicals with a fire extinguisher on the table next to him.

The children continued to grind the material while a counselor, Rebecca Seashore, distributed pieces of metal hangers to be dipped into the mixture at a later time. Dedrick Howell was specifically told not to dip the hanger into the material until instructed to do so. Moments later the chemicals exploded in front of Dedrick. The chemicals burned at 5000 degrees Fahrenheit, and Dedrick was burned over 25% of his body including his hands, arms, chest, and face.

An employer generally is not liable for injuries to third parties caused by an independent contractor over whom (or over whose work) the employer has reserved no control. There are exceptions to the rule, however, one of which is that one who employs an independent contractor to do work involving a special danger to others which the employer knows or has reason to know to be inherent in or normal to the work, or which he contemplates or has reason to contemplate when making the contract, is subject to liability for physical harm caused to such others by the contractor's failure to take reasonable precautions against such danger.

It is sufficient that work of any kind involves a risk, recognizable in advance, of physical harm to others which is inherent in the work itself, or normally to be expected in the ordinary course of the usual or prescribed way of doing it, or that the employer has special reason to contemplate such a risk under the particular circumstances under which the work is to be done.

The sparkler experiment combined flammable, combustible chemicals, open flames, and children; for that very reason, presumably, the children had been equipped with goggles. Though sparklers are explosives of a lesser order, conducting controlled explosions is a textbook example of an inherently dangerous activity. It was not unreasonable for the jury to conclude that the manufacture of sparklers by nine-year-old children was an inherently dangerous activity.

Therefore, the jury was well within its authority in finding that Jagoe was an independent contractor performing inherently dangerous work of which the District had actual or constructive knowledge.

The judgment is affirmed as to liability and as to the award of $8 million in damages both for pain and suffering and for past medical expenses. ■

BUSINESS ORGANIZATIONS AND BANKRUPTCY LAW

"The biggest corporation, like the humblest private citizen, must be held to strict compliance with the will of the people."

Theodore Roosevelt

PARALEGALS AT WORK

As a paralegal, you work for Mr. Abraham Weinstein, a well-known business attorney. One day Mr. Weinstein asks you to come into the conference room for a meeting with him. During the meeting, Mr. Weinstein informs you that he has been retained by new clients, Ms. Sophia Lopez and four other persons, who want to form a new business venture.

Mr. Weinstein informs you that the five prospective owners each will invest $300,000 in the new business. The business will open and operate a new men's clothing store called Victor's Secret. The store will sell upscale casual clothes, formal clothes, undergarments, perfume, and other accessories for men. The owners plan to open the first store six months from now, and then plan to expand and open one additional store each year for the next five years.

Mr. Weinstein explains to you that the owners would like to form a type of business organization in which they will have limited liability—that is, they will have no personal liability beyond their capital in the business. They also want to have flow-through taxation—that is, the entity will pay no taxes and all of the gains and losses of the business will flow-through to their individual tax returns. In addition, the five owners want two of the owners, Ms. Lopez and Ms. Genevieve Cross, to manage the business; the other three owners do not want to manage the business but only want to remain owners and investors.

Mr. Weinstein asks you to compare the different forms of business organizations available and determine which type or types of organizations best meet the owners' requirements.

Consider the issues involved in this scenario as you read the chapter.

After studying this chapter, you should be able to:

1. Define a *sole proprietorship* and explain the liability of a sole proprietor.

2. Define *general partnership* and describe how general partnerships are formed.

3. Define *limited partnership* and distinguish between limited and general partners.

4. Define *limited liability partnership (LLP)* and describe the limited liability of partners of an LLP.

5. Define *limited liability company (LLC)* and describe the limited liability of owners of an LLC.

6. Define *corporation* and describe the process of forming a corporation.

7. Explain the functions of shareholders, directors, and officers in managing the affairs of a corporation.

8. Identify the major forms of bankruptcy permitted under federal bankruptcy law.

9. Describe the major changes to federal bankruptcy law made by the Bankruptcy Abuse Prevention and Consumer Protection Act of 2005.

▶ INTRODUCTION FOR THE PARALEGAL

Many paralegals work for lawyers who represent various forms of businesses. These consist of lawyers who represent entrepreneurs and other small business owners, as well as lawyers who represent the largest multinational corporations in the world. Corporations and other forms of business employ lawyers to represent the business in all sorts of matters ranging from starting the entity, to advising the business as to compliance with the law, to representing the business and their owners or managers in bringing or defending lawsuits.

Among the many different types of business organizations are *sole proprietorships*, *general partnerships*, *limited partnerships*, *limited liability partnerships (LLPs)*, *limited liability companies (LLCs)*, and *corporations*. These are collectively referred to as *business organizations*. An entrepreneur must make a choice as to which type of business to form and operate. Once formed, these business organizations employ lawyers to represent them in their ongoing business transactions.

Paralegals often assist lawyers in representing corporations and other business organizations. This ranges from drafting the original documents to form a business, as well as assisting the lawyer in representing businesses and their management in many other ways. Therefore, a paralegal working in this field must have knowledge of the law of business organizations. This chapter covers the law regarding the formation and operation of corporations and other forms of business. ■

SOLE PROPRIETORSHIP

Sole proprietorship
A form of business in which the owner is actually the business; the business is not a separate legal entity.

The **sole proprietorship** is the simplest form of **business organization.** The owner, called a **sole proprietor,** is the business; there is no separate legal entity. Sole proprietorships are the most common form of business organization in the United States. Many small businesses—and a few large ones—operate this way.

Operating a business as a sole proprietorship has these advantages:

1. Ease and low cost of formation.
2. The owner's right to make all management decisions concerning the business, including those involving hiring and firing employees.
3. The sole proprietor owns all of the business, with the right to receive all of the ownership of business's profits.
4. Ease of transfer or sale if and when the owner desires to do so; no other approval (such as from partners or shareholders) is necessary.

This business form has disadvantages, too, among them:

1. The sole proprietor's access to capital is limited to personal funds plus any loans he or she can obtain.
2. The sole proprietor is legally responsible for the business's contracts and the torts he or she or any of his or her employees commits in the course of employment.

Creation of a Sole Proprietorship

It is easy to create a sole proprietorship. There are no formalities, and no federal or state government approval is required. Some local governments require all businesses, including sole proprietorships, to obtain a license to do business within the city. If no other form of business organization is chosen, the business is a sole proprietorship by default.

d.b.a. ("Doing Business As")

A sole proprietorship can operate under the name of the sole proprietor or a *trade name*. For example, the author of this book can operate a sole proprietorship under the name "Henry R. Cheeseman" or under a trade name such as "The Big Cheese."

Operating under a trade name is commonly designated as a **d.b.a. (doing business as)** (e.g., Henry R. Cheeseman, doing business as "The Big Cheese").

Most states require all businesses that operate under a trade name to file a **fictitious business name statement** (or *certificate of trade name*) with the appropriate government agency. The statement must contain the name and address of the applicant, the trade name, and the address of the business. Most states also require that notice of the trade name be published in a newspaper of general circulation serving the area in which the applicant does business.

These requirements are intended to disclose the real owner's name to the public. Noncompliance can result in a fine. Some states prohibit violators from maintaining lawsuits in the state's courts. A sample fictitious business name statement is shown in Exhibit 18.1.

Locate the website for your state's fictitious business name statement. Print out this form and make a note of this Web site.
http://google.com.html

Exhibit 18.1 Sample fictitious business name statement

Return To:	PUBLISH IN:
Name: Kerry Fields, Esq. Address: 115 S. Chaparral Court City: Anaheim, CA 92808 Telephone # (714) 283-0140 Cust. Ref. # 53247	COUNTY CLERK'S FILING STAMP
☒ First Filing ☐ Renewal Filing Current Registration No.	

FICTITIOUS BUSINESS NAME STATEMENT

THE FOLLOWING PERSON(S) IS (ARE) DOING BUSINESS AS:

1	Fictitious Business Name(s) The Big Cheese
2	Street address & Principal place of Business in California 1000 Exposition Boulevard Los Angeles California Zip Code 90089
3	Full name of Registrant (if corporation - incorporated in what state) Henry R. Cheeseman
	Residence Address City State Zip Code 575 Barrington Ave. Los Angeles California 90049
	Full Name of Registrant (if corporation - incorporated in what state)
	Residence Address City State Zip Code
	Full name of Registrant (if corporation - incorporated in what state)
	Residence Address City State Zip Code
	Full name of Registrant (if corporation - incorporated in what state)
	Residence Address City State Zip Code
4	This Business is conducted by: (check one only) (X) an Individual ( ) a general partnership ( ) joint venture ( ) a business trust ( ) co-partners ( ) husband and wife ( ) a corporation ( ) a limited partnership ( ) an unincorporated association other than a partnership ( ) other—*(please specify)* _____
5	The registrant commenced to transact business under the fictitious business name or names listed above on _____
6	**a.** Signed: *[signature]* Henry R. Cheeseman SIGNATURE TYPE OR PRINT NAME _____ SIGNATURE _____ TYPE OR PRINT NAME _____ SIGNATURE _____ TYPE OR PRINT NAME	**b.** If Registrant a corporation sign below: _____ CORPORATION NAME _____ SIGNATURE & TITLE _____ TYPE OR PRINT NAME

This statement was filed with the County Clerk of ___ Los Angeles ___ County on date indicated by file stamp above.

NOTICE THIS FICTITIOUS NAME STATEMENT EXPIRES FIVE YEARS FROM THE DATE IT WAS FILED IN THE OFFICE OF THE COUNTY CLERK. A NEW FICTITIOUS BUSINESS NAME STATEMENT MUST BE FILED BEFORE THAT TIME. THE FILING OF THIS STATEMENT DOES NOT OF ITSELF AUTHORIZE THE USE IN THIS STATE OF A FICTITIOUS BUSINESS NAME IN VIOLATION OF THE RIGHTS OF ANOTHER UNDER FEDERAL, STATE, OR COMMON LAW (SEE SECTION 14400 ET SEQ., BUSINESS AND PROFESSIONS CODE).	I HEREBY CERTIFY THAT THIS COPY IS A CORRECT COPY OF THE ORIGINAL STATEMENT ON FILE IN MY OFFICE. _____ Helen Pitts COUNTY CLERK BY ___ Deborah Cantrell ___ DEPUTY FILE NO. ___ 081646

Personal Liability of Sole Proprietors

The sole proprietor bears the entire risk of loss of the business; the owner will lose his or her entire capital contribution if the business fails. In addition, the sole proprietor has unlimited **personal liability** (see Exhibit 18.2). Therefore, creditors may recover claims against the business from the sole proprietor's personal assets (e.g., home, automobile, bank accounts).

Consider this example: Suppose Ken Smith opens a clothing store called The Rap Shop and operates it as a sole proprietorship. Smith files the proper statement and publishes the necessary notice of the use of the trade name. He contributes $25,000 of his personal funds to the business and borrows $100,000 in the name of the business from a bank. Assume that after several months Smith closes the business because it was unsuccessful. At the time it is closed, the business has no assets, owes the bank $100,000, and owes rent, trade credit, and other debts of $25,000. Here, Smith is personally liable to pay the bank and all of the debts from his personal assets.

Exhibit 18.2 Sole proprietorship

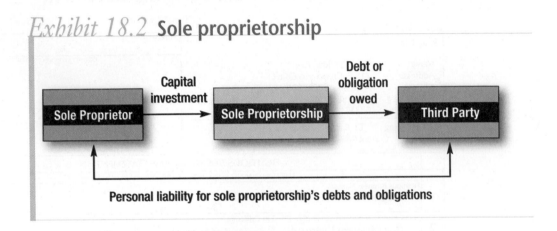

Personal liability for sole proprietorship's debts and obligations

THE PARALEGAL AND SMALL BUSINESS

Many paralegals work for lawyers who represent small businesses and their owners. Small businesses are everywhere in this country. For example, most businesses in small towns and cities are operated by local businesspersons. This includes the local department store, restaurants, insurance agencies, automobile repair shops, the local bank, plumbers, and so forth. The small businesses in local communities comprise a substantial amount of work for lawyers.

In addition, thousands of small businesses operate in large cities. These include small businesses serving specific areas of the larger metropolitan area in which they are located. In large cities, many of the small businesses serve ethnic communities as well. Thousands of small businesses located in large cities require the services of lawyers.

In smaller communities, small businesses are more likely to rely on local attorneys to handle their legal needs. These attorneys tend to be sole practitioners or attorneys who work for smaller law firms. The attorneys are members of the local community and are well known, often friends or acquaintances of their clients. Small businesses in large cities tend to rely on smaller law firms to handle their legal affairs, although some use larger law firms as well.

Small businesses often require the services of lawyers. For instance, to get started, entrepreneurs need advice as to the type of legal form under which their business should operate. Some of these businesses are sole proprietorships, general partnerships, limited partnerships, limited liability companies, limited liability partnerships, or small corporations.

(continued)

THE PARALEGAL AND SMALL BUSINESS *(continued)*

The lawyer representing such clients must advise these clients as to the form of organization that would best suit the clients' needs, and the paralegal must have knowledge of these different forms of organization as well.

Paralegals for small law firms that represent small businesses are often called upon to draft the necessary legal documents to start the business. If it is to be a small corporation or a limited liability company, the paralegal will draft the initial articles of incorporation or articles of organization, plus other documents such as bylaws, minutes of the first meeting of the owners, and such. If a type of partnership is chosen, the paralegal will draft the articles of partnership.

Once established, small businesses often rely on their lawyer to represent them in other transactions. If contracts are required for the operation of the business, the business will employ the attorney to draft these contracts. Here, the paralegal often is the first person to complete a draft of the contract. If a sale or purchase of real estate is required by the business, the attorney is looking to represent the small business and to complete or review the necessary documents. Again, the paralegal for these attorneys often is called upon to prepare drafts of these documents.

In addition, small businesses sometimes sue or are sued. The lawyer will represent the small business in these lawsuits. Most of these lawsuits are in state court, although some are tried in federal court. Because these lawyers are sole practitioners or work for small law firms, they often need the assistance of a paralegal to prepare the law case.

Thus, paralegals often work in smaller law firms representing local businesses and individuals. The paralegals in these law firms usually are involved in all aspects of the legal services provided to small-business clients. Work in small law firms will continue to be a substantial source of jobs for paralegals, particularly those who live in small communities across the country, as well as those who work for smaller law firms in metropolitan areas that derive a substantial amount of their work representing small businesses and their owners.

GENERAL PARTNERSHIP

General, or ordinary, partnerships have been recognized since ancient times. The English common law of partnerships governed early U.S. partnerships. The individual states expanded the body of partnership law.

A **general partnership**, or **partnership**, is a voluntary association of two or more persons for carrying on a business as co-owners for profit. The formation of a partnership creates certain rights and duties among partners and with third parties. These rights and duties are established in the **partnership agreement** and by law. General partners, or **partners**, are personally liable for the debts and obligations of the partnership (see Exhibit 18.3).

General partnership
A voluntary association of two or more persons for carrying on a business as co-owners for profit. Also called a *partnership*.

Uniform Partnership Act

In 1914, the National Conference of Commissioners on Uniform State Laws (a group of lawyers, judges, and legal scholars) promulgated the **Uniform Partnership Act (UPA)**, which codifies partnership law. Its goal was to establish consistent partnership law that would be uniform throughout the United States. The UPA has been adopted in whole or in part by 48 states, the District of Columbia, Guam, and the Virgin Islands.

Uniform Partnership Act (UPA)
A model act that codifies partnership law. Most states have adopted the UPA in whole or in part.

The UPA covers most problems that arise in the formation, operation, and dissolution of ordinary partnerships. Other rules of law or equity govern if there is no applicable provision of the UPA [UPA § 5].

Exhibit 18.3 **General partnership**

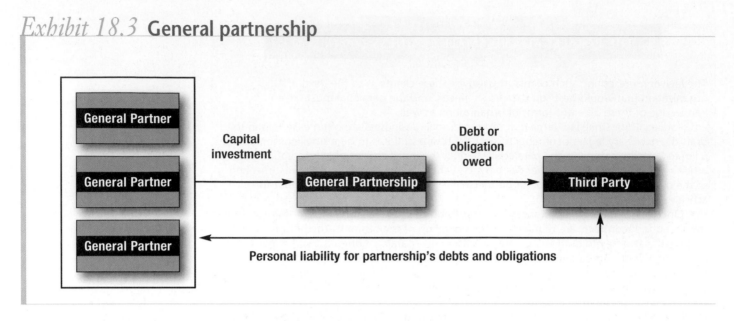

The UPA adopted the **entity theory** of partnership, which considers partnerships as separate legal entities. As such, partnerships can hold title to personal and real property, transact business in the partnership name, and the like.

Formation of a Partnership

A business must meet four criteria to qualify as a partnership under the Uniform Partnership Act [UPA Section 6(1)]. It must be

1. an association of two or more persons.
2. carrying on a business.
3. as co-owners.
4. for profit.

Partnerships are voluntary associations of two or more persons. All partners must agree to the participation of each co-partner. A person cannot be forced to be a partner or to accept another person as a partner. The UPA definition of "person" includes natural persons, partnerships (including limited partnerships), corporations, and other associations. A business—trade, occupation, or profession—must be carried on. To qualify as a partnership, the organization or venture must have a profit motive even though the business does not actually have to make a profit.

A general partnership may be formed with little or no formality. Co-ownership of a business is essential to create a partnership. The most important factor in determining co-ownership is whether the parties share the business's profits and management responsibility.

Receipt of a share of business profits is *prima facie* evidence of a partnership because nonpartners usually are not given the right to share in the business's profits. No inference of the existence of a partnership is drawn if profits are received in payment of

1. a debt owed to a creditor in installments or otherwise,
2. wages owed to an employee,
3. rent owed to a landlord,
4. an annuity owed to a widow, widower, or representative of a deceased partner,
5. interest owed on a loan, or
6. consideration for the sale of goodwill of a business [UPA Section 7].

An agreement to share losses of a business is strong evidence of a partnership.

The right to participate in the management of a business is important evidence for determining the existence of a partnership, but it is not conclusive evidence because the right to participate in management is sometimes given to employees, creditors, and others. If a person is given the right to share in profits, losses, and management of a business, it is compelling evidence of the existence of a partnership.

One of the most fruitful sources of ruin to men of the world is the recklessness or want of principle of partners, and it is one of the perils to which every man exposes himself who enters into partnership with another.

Malins, V.C.
Mackay v. Douglas, *14 Eq. 106 at 118*
(1872)

The Partnership Agreement

The agreement to form a partnership may be oral, written, or implied from the conduct of the parties. It may even be created inadvertently. No formalities are necessary, although a few states require general partnerships to file certificates of partnership with an appropriate government agency. Partnerships that exist for more than one year or are authorized to deal in real estate must be in writing under the Statute of Frauds. It is good practice for partners to put their partnership agreement in writing. A written document is important evidence of the terms of the agreement, particularly if a dispute arises among the partners.

A written partnership agreement is called a partnership agreement or **articles of partnership**. The partners can agree to almost any terms in their partnership agreement, except terms that are illegal. The articles of partnership can be short and simple or long and complex. If the agreement fails to provide for an essential term or

checklist ☑️   PARTNERSHIP AGREEMENT

The partnership agreement should contain the following information:

- ☐ the firm name

- ☐ names and addresses of the partners

- ☐ principal office of the partnership

- ☐ nature and scope of the partnership business

- ☐ duration of the partnership

- ☐ capital contributions of each partner

- ☐ the division of profits and losses among the partners

- ☐ the salaries, if any, to be paid to partners

- ☐ duties of the partners regarding management of the partnership

- ☐ limitations, if any, on the authority of partners to bind the partnership

- ☐ provisions for the admission and withdrawal of partners from the firm and the terms, conditions, and notices required for withdrawal

- ☐ provisions for continuing the partnership upon withdrawal of a partner, death of a partner, or other dissolution of the partnership

- ☐ any other provisions deemed relevant by the partners

contingency, the provisions of the UPA control. Thus, the UPA acts as a gap-filling device to the partners' agreement.

Contract Liability

As a legal entity, a partnership must act through its agents—that is, its partners. Contracts entered into with suppliers, customers, lenders, or others on the partnership's behalf are binding on the partnership.

Under the UPA, partners have **joint liability** for the contracts and debts of the partnership [UPA Section 15(b)]. This means that a third party who sues to recover on a partnership contract or debt must name all of the partners in the lawsuit. If the lawsuit is successful, the plaintiff can collect the entire amount of the judgment against any or all of the partners. If the third party's suit does not name all of the partners, the judgment cannot be collected against any of the partners or the partnership assets. Similarly, releasing any partner from the lawsuit releases them all. A partner who is made to pay more than his or her proportionate share of contract liability may seek **indemnification** from the partnership and from those partners who have not paid their share of the loss.

Tort Liability

While acting on partnership business, a partner or an employee of the partnership may commit a tort that causes injury to a third person. This tort could be caused by a negligent act, a breach of trust (such as embezzlement from a customer's account), a breach of fiduciary duty, defamation, fraud, or other intentional tort. The partnership is liable if the act is committed while the person is acting within the ordinary course of partnership business or with the authority of his or her co-partners.

Under the UPA partners have **joint and several liability** for torts and breaches of trust [UPA Section 15(a)]. This is so even if a partner did not participate in commission of the act. This type of liability permits a third party to sue one or more of the partners separately. Judgment can be collected only against the partners who are sued.

Joint and several liability
Tort liability of a partnership in which the partners are liable together and separately. This means that the plaintiff can sue one or more of the partners separately. If successful, the plaintiff can recover the entire amount of the judgment from any or all of the defendant–partners.

PERSONAL LIABILITY OF GENERAL PARTNERS

The court applied the doctrine of joint and several liability in the following situation: Jose Pena and Joseph Antenucci were both medical doctors who were partners in a medical practice. Both doctors treated Elaine Zuckerman during her pregnancy. Her son, Daniel Zuckerman, was born with severe physical problems. Elaine, as Daniel's mother and natural guardian, brought a medical malpractice suit against both doctors.

The jury found that Pena was guilty of medical malpractice but that Antenucci was not. The amount of the verdict totaled $4 million. The Trial Court entered judgment against Pena but not against Antenucci. The plaintiffs made a posttrial motion for judgment against both defendants.

Is Antenucci jointly and severally liable for the medical malpractice of his partner, Pena? The court said yes.

The court noted that a partnership is liable for the tortious act of a partner, and a partner is jointly and severally liable for tortious acts chargeable to the partnership. When a tort is committed by the partnership, the wrong is imputable to all of the partners jointly and severally, and an action may be brought against all or any of them in their individual capacities or against the partnership as an entity. Therefore, even though the jury found that defendant Antenucci was not guilty of malpractice in his treatment of the patient, but that defendant Pena, his partner, was guilty of malpractice in his treatment of the patient, they were then both jointly and severally liable for the malpractice committed by defendant Pena by operation of law.

Source: Zuckerman v. Antenucci, 478 N.Y.S. 2d 578, 1984 N.Y. Misc. Lexis 3283 (N.Y. 1984)

The partnership and partners who are made to pay tort liability may seek indemnification from the partner who committed the wrongful act. A release of one partner does not discharge the liability of other partners.

Consider this example: Suppose Nicole, Jim, and Maureen form a partnership. Assume that Jim, while on partnership business, causes an automobile accident that injures Kurt, a pedestrian. Kurt suffers $100,000 in injuries. At his option, Kurt can sue Nicole, Jim, or Maureen separately, or any two of them, or all of them.

Dissolution of Partnerships

The duration of a partnership can be for a fixed term (e.g., five years) or until a specific undertaking is accomplished (e.g., until a real estate development is completed), or it can be for an unspecified term. A partnership with a fixed duration is called a **partnership for a term.** A partnership with no fixed duration is called a **partnership at will.**

Although a partner has the *power* to withdraw and dissolve the partnership at any time, he or she may not have the *right* to do so. For example, a partner who withdraws from a partnership before expiration of the term stated in the partnership agreement does not have the right to do so. The partner's action causes a **wrongful dissolution** of the partnership. The partner is liable for damages caused by wrongful dissolution of the partnership.

LIMITED PARTNERSHIP

Limited partnerships are statutory creations that have been used since the Middle Ages. They include both general (manager) and limited (investor) partners. Today, all states have enacted statutes that provide for the creation of limited partnerships. In most states these partnerships are called **limited partnerships** or *special partnerships*. Limited partnerships are used for business ventures such as investing in real estate, drilling oil and gas wells, investing in movie productions, and the like.

Limited partnership
A special form of partnership that is formed only if certain formalities are followed. A limited partnership has both general and limited partners.

Revised Uniform Limited Partnership Act

In 1916 the National Conference of Commissioners on Uniform State Laws, a group composed of lawyers, judges, and legal scholars, promulgated the **Uniform Limited Partnership Act (ULPA).** The ULPA contains a set of provisions for the formation, operation, and dissolution of limited partnerships. Most states originally enacted this law.

In 1976, the National Conference on Uniform State Laws promulgated the **Revised Uniform Limited Partnership Act (RULPA),** which provides a more modern comprehensive law for the formation, operation, and dissolution of limited partnerships. This law supersedes the ULPA in the states that have adopted it. The RULPA provides the basic foundation for our discussion of limited partnership law.

Revised Uniform Limited Partnership Act (RULPA)
A 1976 revision of the ULPA that provides a more modern, comprehensive law for the formation, operation, and dissolution of limited partnerships.

General and Limited Partners

Limited partnerships have two types of partners:

1. **general partners**, who invest capital, manage the business, and are personally liable for partnership debts
2. **limited partners,** who invest capital but do not participate in management and are not personally liable for partnership debts beyond their capital contribution.

Exhibit 18.4 illustrates a limited partnership. A limited partnership must have at least one or more general partners and one or more limited partners [RULPA Section 101 (7)]. There are no restrictions on the number of general or limited partners allowed in a limited partnership. Any person may be a general or limited partner. This

General partners
Partners in a limited partnership who invest capital, manage the business, and are personally liable for partnership debts.

Limited partners
Partners in a limited partnership who invest capital but do not participate in management and are not personally liable for partnership debts beyond their capital contribution.

Exhibit 18.4 **Limited partnership**

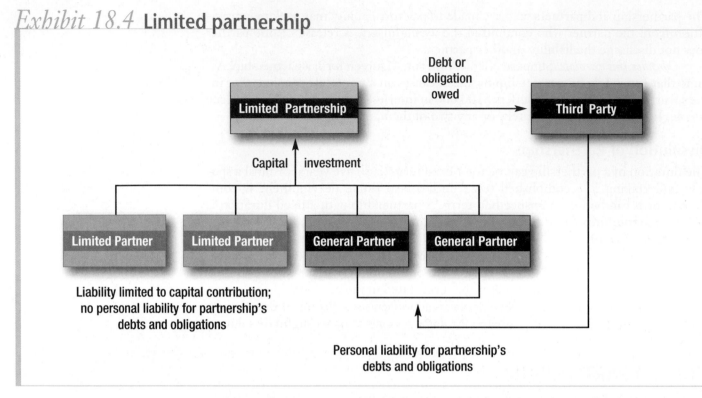

includes natural persons, partnerships, limited partnerships, trusts, estates, associations, and corporations. A person may be both a general and a limited partner in the same limited partnership.

Formation of Limited Partnerships

The creation of a limited partnership is formal and requires public disclosure. The entity must comply with the statutory requirements of the Revised Uniform Limited Partnership Act or other state statutes.

Under the RULPA, two or more persons must execute and sign a **certificate of limited partnership** [RULPA Sections 201 and 206]. The certificate must contain the following information:

1. name of the limited partnership
2. general character of the business
3. address of the principal place of business, and name and address of the agent to receive service of legal process
4. name and business address of each general and limited partner
5. the latest date upon which the limited partnership is to dissolve
6. amount of cash, property, or services (and description of property or services) contributed by each partner, and any contributions of cash, property, or services promised to be made in the future
7. any other matters that the general partners determine to include

The certificate of limited partnership must be filed with the secretary of state of the appropriate state and, if required by state law, with the county recorder in the county or counties in which the limited partnership carries on business. The limited partnership is formed when the certificates of limited partnership is filed.

Limited Partnership Agreement

Although not required by law, the partners of a limited partnership often draft and execute a **limited partnership agreement** (also called the **articles of limited partnership**) that sets forth the rights and duties of the general and limited partner(s), terms

Limited partnership agreement A document that sets forth the rights and duties of the general and limited partners, the terms and conditions regarding the operation, termination, and dissolution of the partnership, and so on.

and conditions regarding the operation, termination, and dissolution of the partnership, and so on. Where there is no such agreement, the certificate of limited partnership serves as the articles of limited partnership.

The limited partnership agreement may specify how profits and losses from the limited partnership are to be allocated among the general and limited partners. If there is no such agreement, the RULPA provides that profits and losses from a limited partnership are shared on the basis of the value of the partner's capital contribution [RULPA: Section 503]. A limited partner is not liable for losses beyond his or her capital contribution.

In addition, it is good practice to establish voting rights in the limited partnership agreement or certificate of limited partnership. The limited partnership agreement can provide which transactions must be approved by which partners (i.e., general, limited, or both). General and limited partners may be given unequal voting rights. A sample limited partnership agreement is set forth in Exhibit 18.5.

> *It is when merchants dispute about their own rules that they invoke the law.*
>
> J. Brett
> Robinsone v. Mollett *(1875)*

Exhibit 18.5 Sample limited partnership agreement

LIMITED PARTNERSHIP AGREEMENT

1. Introduction. This agreement of Limited Partnership dated January 2, 2007 by and between John Weston, Wai Chan, and Susan Martinez (General Partners) and Shari Berkowitz, Raymond Wong, and Harold Johnson (Limited Partners).

   The General Partners and Limited Partners agree to form a Limited Partnership (Partnership) pursuant to the provisions of the California Revised Limited Partnership Act on the terms and conditions hereinafter set forth.

2. Name of Partnership. The name of the Partnership shall be "The Wilshire Investment Company, a California Limited Partnership." The business of the Partnership shall be conducted in that name.

3. Principal Place of Business. The principal office of the Partnership shall be at 4000 Wilshire Boulevard, Los Angeles, California 90010 or at such other place within California as may be determined from time to time by the General Partners.

4. Purpose of the Partnership. The Partnership shall be engaged in the business of buying, selling, and developing commercial and industrial real estate and such activities as are related or incidental thereto.

5. Agent for Service of Process. The name of the agent for service of process is Frederick Friendly, whose address is 2500 Century Park East, Suite 600, Los Angeles, California 90067.

6. Term of Partnership. The term of the Partnership shall commence on the date on which the Partnership's Certificate of Limited Partnership is filed by the Secretary of State of California and shall continue until it terminates in accordance with the provisions of this Agreement.

7. Certificate of Limited Partnership. The General Partners shall immediately execute a Certificate of Limited Partnership and cause that Certificate to be filed in the office of the secretary of state of California. The General Partners shall also record a certified copy of the Certificate in the office of the county recorder of every county in which the Partnership owns real property.

8. Members of the Partnership.

   (a) The names and addresses of each original General Partner are as follows:

NAME	John Weston	ADDRESS	500 Ocean Boulevard, Los Angeles, California
	Wai Chan		700 Apple Road, Seattle, Washington
	Susan Martinez		800 Palm Drive, Miami, Florida

   (b) The names and addresses of each original Limited Partner are as follows:

NAME	Shari Berkowitz	ADDRESS	700 Apple Street, New York, New York
	Raymond Wong		900 Flower Avenue, San Francisco, California
	Harold Johnson		300 Oil Field Road, Houston, Texas

9. General Partners' Capital Contributions. The General Partners shall make the following contributions to the Partnership's capital no later than January 2, 2007.

CASH	John Weston	$60,000
PROPERTY	Wai Chan	$30,000
	Susan Martinez	$30,000

   No interest will be paid on any balances in the General Partners' capital accounts.

10. Limited Partners' Capital Contributions. The Limited Partners shall make the following contributions to the Partnership's capital no later than January 2, 2007.

CASH	Shari Berkowitz	$100,000
	Raymond Wong	$ 50,000
	Harold Johnson	$ 50,000

    No interest will be paid on any balances in the Limited Partners' capital accounts.

(continued)

Exhibit 18.5 **Sample limited partnership agreement** *(continued)*

11. Additional Capital Contributions from Limited Partners. The General Partners may call for additional cash contributions to the Partnership's capital from the Limited Partners. The aggregate of all additional capital contributions made by the Limited Partners pursuant to this Paragraph shall not exceed 100 percent of the original capital contributions made by them pursuant to Paragraph 10 of this Agreement. Notice of the call shall be made by registered mail, return receipt requested, and shall be deemed made when posted. The Limited Partners' additional capital contribution must be made no later than 60 days following the call.

12. Division of Profits. Each Partner shall receive the following share of the net profits of the Partnership:

	PARTNER	PERCENT
General Partners:	John Weston	30%
	Wai Chan	15%
	Susan Martinez	15%
Limited Partners:	Shari Berkowitz	20%
	Raymond Wong	10%
	Harold Johnson	10%

13. Sharing of Losses. Each Partner shall bear a share of the losses of the Partnership equal to the share of the profits to which he or she is entitled. The share of the losses of each Partner shall be charged against his contribution to the capital of the Partnership.

The Limited Partners will not be liable for any Partnership debts or losses beyond the amounts to be contributed to them pursuant to Paragraphs 10 and 11 of this Agreement.

After giving effect to the share of losses chargeable against the capital contributions of Limited Partners, the remaining Partnership losses shall be borne by the General Partners in the same proportions in which, between themselves, they are to share profits.

14. Management of Partnership. The General Partners shall have the sole and exclusive control of the Limited Partnership.

The General Partners shall have an equal voice in the management of the Partnership, and each shall devote his or her full time to the conduct of the Partnership's business.

The General Partners shall have the power and authority to take such action from time to time as they may deem to be necessary, appropriate, or convenient in connection with the management and conduct of the business and affairs of the Partnership, including, without limitation, the power to

(a) Acquire property, including real and personal property.

(b) Dispose of Partnership property.

(c) Borrow or lend money.

(d) Make, deliver, or accept commercial paper.

(e) Pledge, mortgage, encumber, or grant a security interest in the Partnership properties as security for repayment of loans.

(f) Take any and all other action permitted by law that is customary in or reasonably related to the conduct of the Partnership business or affairs.

15. Limited Partners Not to Manage Business. The Limited Partners will not manage the business of the Partnership or assist in its management.

16. Partnership Books and Records. The Partnership books of account will be kept in accordance with generally accepted accounting principles. The books and supporting records will be maintained at the Partnership's principal office and will be examined by the Partnership's certified public accountants at least annually. The Partnership's fiscal year shall start on January 1 and close on December 31.

17. General Partners' Salaries. The General Partners shall each receive a salary of $60,000 per annum, payable in monthly installments, as compensation for managing the Partnership. No increases shall be made in the General Partners' salaries without the written consent of a majority of the Limited Partners.

18. Admission of New General Partners. No new General Partners will be admitted to the Partnership without the written consent of all the General Partners and Limited Partners as to both his or her admission and the terms on which the new General Partner is admitted.

19. Admission of New Limited Partners. No new Limited Partners will be admitted to the Partnership without the written consent of all the General Partners and Limited Partners as to both his or her admission and the terms on which the new Limited Partner is admitted.

20. No Sale or Assignment of or Granting Lien on Partnership Interest by General Partner. Without the written consent of all the General Partners and Limited Partners, no General Partner shall assign, mortgage, or give a security interest in his or her Partnership interest.

21. Right of Limited Partner to Assign Partnership Interest or Substitute New Limited Partner. Upon 30 days' written notice to the General Partners, a Limited Partner can assign his or her interest in the Partnership's profits to a third party. Such assignment shall not constitute a substitution of the third party as a new Limited Partner in the place of the assignor. A Limited Partner may substitute a third party in his or her place as a new Limited Partner only with the consent in writing of all the General Partners and Limited Partners.

22. Effect of Death, Disability, or Retirement of a General Partner. The death, retirement, or permanent disability of a General Partner (the withdrawing General Partner) that makes it impossible for him or her to carry out his or her duties under this Agreement shall terminate the Partnership.

Exhibit 18.5 **Sample limited partnership agreement (*continued*)**

If a General Partner survives, the remaining General Partners may continue the Partnership business and may purchase the interest of the withdrawing General Partner in the assets and goodwill of the Partnership. The remaining General Partners have the option, exercisable by them at any time within 30 days after the date on which the withdrawing General Partner ceases to be a General Partner, to purchase the withdrawing General Partner's interest by paying to the person legally entitled thereto the value of that interest as shown on the last regular accounting of the Partnership preceding the date on which the General Partner ceased to be a General Partner, together with the full unwithdrawn portion of the withdrawing General Partner's distributive share of any net profits earned by the Partnership between the date of that accounting and the date on which the withdrawing General Partner ceased to be a General Partner of the Partnership.

23. Duties of Remaining Purchasing General Partners. Upon the purchase of a withdrawing General Partner's interest, the remaining General Partners shall assume all obligations of the Partnership and shall hold the withdrawing General Partner, the personal representative and estate of the withdrawing General Partner, and the property of the withdrawing General Partner free and harmless from all liability for those obligations.

The remaining General Partners shall immediately amend the Certificate of Limited Partnership and shall file such amendment with the office of the Secretary of State, and shall cause to be prepared, filed, served, and published all other notices required by law to protect the withdrawing General Partner or the personal representative and estate of the withdrawing General Partner from all liability for the future obligations of the Partnership business.

24. Effect of Death of Limited Partner or Substitution of Limited Partner. The death of a Limited Partner or the substitution of a new Limited Partner for a Limited Partner shall not affect the continuity of the Partnership or the conduct of its business.

25. Voluntary Dissolution. A General Partner may terminate the Partnership at any time upon 120 days written notice to each Limited Partner. Upon termination of the Partnership, it shall be liquidated in accordance with Paragraph 26 of this Agreement.

26. Liquidation of Partnership. If the Partnership is liquidated, its assets, including its goodwill and name, shall be sold in the manner designed to produce the greatest return. The proceeds of the liquidation shall be distributed in the following order:

   (a) To creditors of the Partnership including Partners who are creditors to the extent permitted by law, in satisfaction of liabilities of the Partnership
   (b) To Partners in payment of the balances in their income accounts
   (c) To Partners in payment of the balances in their capital accounts
   (d) To Partners in payment of the remainder of the proceeds

27. Certificate of Dissolution. Upon dissolution of the Partnership, the General Partners shall execute and file in the office of the Secretary of State a Certificate of Dissolution. If dissolution occurs after a sole General Partner ceases to be a General Partner, the Limited Partners conducting the winding up of the Partnership's affairs shall file the Certificate of Dissolution.

28. Entire Agreement. This Agreement contains the entire understanding among the Partners and supersedes any prior written or oral agreements between them respecting the subject matter contained herein. There are no representations, agreements, arrangements, or understandings, oral or written, between and among the Partners relating to the subject matter of this Agreement that are not fully expressed herein.

29. Controlling Law. This Agreement shall be interpreted under the law of the State of California. Further, each Partner consents to the jurisdiction of the courts of the State of California.

30. Service of Notices. Service of notice upon the Partnership will be made by registered or certified mail, return receipt requested, addressed to the Partnership's principal place of business.

Service of notice upon any or all Partners will be made by certified mail, return receipt requested, addressed to the addresses given in this Agreement or such other addresses as a Partner may from time to time give to the Partnership.

31. Severability. If any provisions of this Agreement shall be declared by a court of competent jurisdiction to be invalid, void, or unenforceable, the remaining provisions shall continue in full force and effect.

32. Arbitration of Disputes. Any controversy concerning this Agreement will be settled by arbitration according to the rules of the American Arbitration Association, and judgment upon the award may be entered and enforced in any court.

GENERAL PARTNER _____   LIMITED PARTNER _____

GENERAL PARTNER _____   LIMITED PARTNER _____

ACCOUNTING FIRMS OPERATING AS LLPS

Prior to the advent of the limited liability partnership (LLP) form of doing business, accounting firms operated as general partnerships. As such, the general partners were personally liable for the debt and obligations of the general partnership. In large accounting firms, this personal liability was rarely imposed because the general partnership usually carried sufficient liability insurance to cover most awards to third-party plaintiffs in negligence tort actions. Creditors usually extended credit to the large accounting firms based on the reputation of the firms and the fact that these large accounting firms had sufficient capital in the partnership to meet most loan obligations.

Beginning in the early 1980s, large accounting firms were hit with many large court judgments. These cases were brought in conjunction with the failure of large savings banks and commercial banks and the failure of other large firms that accountants had audited. Many of these firms failed because of fraud by their major owners and officers. The shareholders and creditors of these failed companies sued the auditors, alleging that the auditors had been negligent in not catching the fraud. Many juries agreed and awarded large sums against the accounting firms.

Sometimes the accounting firm's liability insurance was not enough to cover the judgment, thus imposing personal liability on the partners. General partners in accounting firms became worried that the inability of the profession to shield itself from such liability jeopardized the profession.

In response, in the 1990s, state legislatures created a new form of business, the limited liability partnership (LLP). This entity was created particularly for accountants, lawyers, and other professionals to offer their services under an umbrella of limited liability. The partners of an LLP have limited liability up to their capital contribution. But the partners do not have personal liability for the debts and liabilities of the LLP.

Once LLPs were permitted by law, most accounting firms changed their status from general partnerships to LLPs. The signs and letterhead of the Big Four accounting firms prominently announce that the accounting firm is an "LLP." Many accounting firms other than the Big Four also have changed to LLP status, as have many law firms. The LLP form of business has transformed how accountants, lawyers, and other professionals offer their services.

LIMITED LIABILITY COMPANY (LLC)

Limited liability company (LLC)
An unincorporated business entity that combines the most favorable attributes of general partnerships, limited partnerships, and corporations.

A majority of states have approved a new form of business entity called a **limited liability company (LLC).** An LLC is an unincorporated business entity that combines the most favorable attributes of general partnerships, limited partnerships, and corporations. An LLC may elect to be taxed as a partnership. The owners, usually called **members,** can manage the business and have limited liability. Many entrepreneurs who begin new businesses chose the LLC as their legal form for conducting business.

Uniform Limited Liability Company Act

Uniform Limited Liability Company Act (ULLCA)
A model act that provides comprehensive and uniform laws for the formation, operation, and dissolution of LLCs.

In 1995, the National Conference of Commissioners on Uniform State Laws (a group of lawyers, judges, and legal scholars) issued the **Uniform Limited Liability Company Act (ULLCA).** The ULLCA codifies limited liability company law. Its goal is to establish comprehensive LLC law that is uniform throughout the United States.

The ULLCA covers most problems that arise in the formation, operation, and termination of LLCs. The ULLCA is not law unless a state adopts it as its LLC statute. Many states have adopted all or part of the ULLCA as their limited liability company law.

Limited liability companies are creatures of state law, not federal law. Limited liability companies can be created only pursuant to the laws of the state in which the LLC is being organized. These statutes, commonly referred to as limited liability company codes, regulate the formation, operation, and dissolution of LLCs. The state legislature may amend its LLC statute at any time. The courts interpret state LLC statutes to decide LLC and member disputes.

Exhibit 18.7 Limited liability company (LLC)

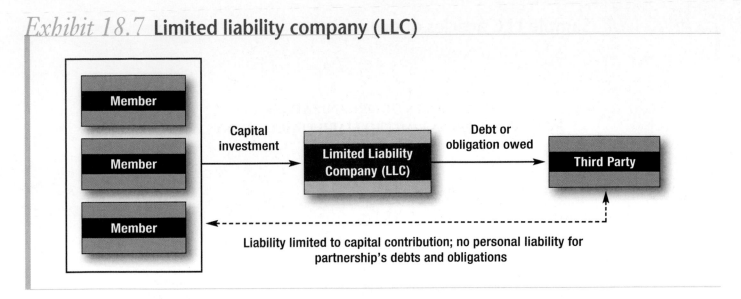

Members' Limited Liability

The general rule is that members are not personally liable to third parties for the debts, obligations, and liabilities of an LLC beyond their capital contribution. Members are said to have limited liability (see Exhibit 18.7). The debts, obligations, and liabilities of an LLC, whether arising from contracts, torts, or otherwise, are solely those of the LLC [ULLCA Section 303(a)].

Consider this example: Jasmin, Shan-Yi, and Vanessa form an LLC and each contributes $25,000 in capital. The LLC operates for a period of time during which it borrows money from banks and purchases goods on credit from suppliers. After some time, the LLC experiences financial difficulty and goes out of business. If the LLC fails with $500,000 in debts, each of the members will lose her capital contribution of $25,000 but will not be personally liable for the rest of the unpaid debts of the LLC.

Formation of an LLC

Forming an LLC is similar to organizing a corporation. Two or more persons (which include individuals, partnerships, corporations, and associations) may form an LLC for any lawful purpose. To form an LLC, **articles of organization** must be filed with the appropriate state office, usually the Secretary of State's office (see Exhibit 18.8). The articles of organization must state the LLC's name, duration, and other information required by statute or that the organizers deem important to include. The name of an LLC must contain the words Limited Liability Company or the abbreviation *L.L.C.* or *L.C.*

> **Articles of organization**
> The formal document that must be filed with the secretary of state to form an LLC.

The owners of an LLC usually are called **members**, although in some states they are referred to as shareholders. Members of an LLC may enter into an **operating agreement** that regulates the affairs of the company and the conduct of its business and governs relations among the members, managers, and company [ULLCA Section 103(a)]. The operating agreement may be amended by the approval of all members unless otherwise provided in the agreement. The operating agreement and amendments may be oral but usually are written.

> **Member**
> An owner of an LLC.

> **Operating agreement**
> An agreement entered into by members that governs the affairs and business of the LLC and the relations among members, managers, and the LLC.

Partnership Taxation for LLCs

Effective January 1, 1997, the IRS adopted "Check-the-box" regulations, making it easier for LLCs to be taxed as partnerships. These regulations provide that a business entity falls into one of the following categories:

1. *Per se corporations:* corporations incorporated under state law and taxed as corporations for federal income tax purposes.

Exhibit 18.8 **Sample LLC articles of organization**

ARTICLES OF ORGANIZATION
FOR FLORIDA LIMITED LIABILITY COMPANY

ARTICLE I – NAME

The name of the Limited Liability Company is

iCitrusSystems.com
_____

ARTICLE II – ADDRESS

The mailing address and street address of the principal office of the Limited Liability Company is

3000 Dade Boulevard
_____

Suite 200
_____

Miami Beach, Florida 33139
_____

ARTICLE III – DURATION

The period of duration for the Limited Liability Company shall be

50 years
_____

ARTICLE IV – MANAGEMENT

The Limited Liability Company is to be managed by a manager and the name and address of such manager is

Susan Escobar
_____

1000 Collins Avenue
_____

Miami Beach, Florida 33141
_____

_____

Thomas Blandford

_____

Pam Rosales

2. *Eligible entities:* entities other than *per se* corporations. Eligible entities include unincorporated businesses with two or more owners, such as LLCs, LLPs, limited partnerships, and general partnerships. An eligible entity is taxed as a partnership unless it elects to be taxed as a corporation.
3. *Single-owner entities:* entities that are taxed as sole proprietorships unless the owner elects to be taxed as a corporation.

DREAMWORKS SKG, LLC

In 1995, Steven Spielberg, Jeffrey Katzenberg, and David Geffen formed DreamWorks SKG, a major movie and recording production company. Spielberg's fame and money came from directing films such as *E. T.*, Katzenberg was a leading executive at Disney, and Geffen built and sold Geffen Records. These multimillionaire multimedia giants combined their talents to form a formidable entertainment company.

Interestingly, DreamWorks was hatched as a Delaware limited liability company, or LLC. The organizers chose an LLC because it is taxed as a partnership and the profits (or losses) flow directly to the owners, but like a corporation, the owners are protected from personal liability beyond their capital contributions.

DreamWorks issued several classes of stock, or interests. The three principals put up $100 million ($33.3 million each) for "SKG" stock, which grants the principals 100 percent voting control and 67 percent of the firm's profits. In addition, each principal has a seven-year employment contract that pays him $1 million annually, plus other fringe benefits and perquisites on terms that are customary for similarly situated executives in the entertainment industry.

DreamWorks raised the other $900 million of its $1 billion capital from other investors, who received a third of future profits. The other investors were issued the following classes of stock:

Class	Investment
A	*Outside investors.* Class A stock was sold to big investors with more than $20 million to invest. Microsoft's co-founder, Paul Allen, purchased $500 million of Class A stock. Class A investors got seats on the board of directors.
S	*Outside investors.* Class S stock was issued for smallish, "strategic" investments with other companies for cross-marketing purposes.
E	*Employees.* Employees were granted the right to participate in an employee stock purchase plan.

The **check-the-box regulations** have default rules that provide that eligible entities, such as an LLC, are treated as partnerships with flow-through taxation unless an election is made to be taxed as a corporation. This election is made by filing Form 8832 with the IRS and must be signed by all owners or a manager who is given authority to sign such an election. The check-the-box regulations make it easier for LLCs to obtain partnership taxation status for federal income tax purposes. Most states automatically apply the federal classification rules for state income tax purposes, although a few do not.

CORPORATION

Corporations are the dominant form of business organization in the United States, generating more than 85 percent of the country's gross business receipts. Corporations range in size from one owner to thousands of owners. Owners of corporations are called **shareholders**. Exhibit 18.9 depicts the hierarchy of a corporation.

A corporation is a separate *legal entity* (or *legal person*) for most purposes. Corporations are treated, in effect, as artificial persons created by the state that can sue or be sued in their own names, enter into and enforce contracts, hold title to and transfer property, and be found civilly and criminally liable for violations of law. Corporations cannot be put in prison, so the normal criminal penalty is the assessment of a fine, loss of a license, or other sanction.

Corporations have the following unique characteristics:

- *Limited liability of shareholders.* As separate-legal entities, corporations are liable for their own contracts and debts. Generally, the shareholders

Corporation
A fictitious legal entity that is created according to statutory requirements.

Shareholders
The owners of corporations, whose ownership interests are evidenced by stock certificates.

Exhibit 18.9 **Corporation**

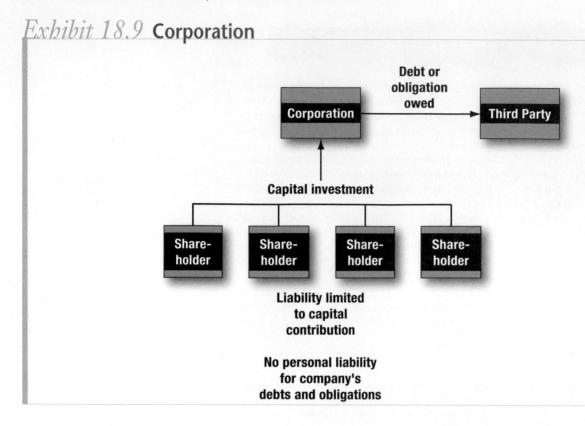

have only limited liability. They are liable only to the extent of their capital contributions (see Exhibit 18.9).

■ *Free transferability of shares.* Corporate shares are freely transferable by the shareholder, by sale, assignment, pledge, or gift, unless they are issued pursuant to certain exemptions from securities registration. Shareholders may agree among themselves on restrictions on the transfer of shares. National securities markets, such as the New York Stock Exchange, the American Stock Exchange, and NASDAQ, have been developed for the organized sale of securities.

■ *Perpetual existence.* Corporations exist in perpetuity unless a specific duration is stated in the corporation's articles of incorporation. The existence of a corporation can be terminated voluntarily by the shareholders. Corporations may be terminated involuntarily by the corporation's creditors if an involuntary petition for bankruptcy against the corporation is granted. The death, insanity, or bankruptcy of a shareholder, a director, or an officer of the corporation does not affect its existence.

■ *Centralized management.* The board of directors makes policy decisions concerning the operation of the corporation. Members of the board of directors are elected by the shareholders. The directors, in turn, appoint **corporate officers** to run the corporation's day-to-day operations. Together, the directors and the officers form the corporate "management."

Revised Model Business Corporation Act

Revised Model Business, Corporation Act (RMBCA)
A 1984 revision of the MBCA that arranged the provisions of the original act more logically, revised the language to be more consistent, and made substantial changes in the provisions.

The Committee on Corporate Laws of the American Bar Association drafted the Model Business Corporation Act (MBCA) in 1950. The model act was intended to provide a uniform law regulating the formation, operation, and termination of corporations.

In 1984, the committee completely revised the MBCA and issued the **Revised Model Business Corporation Act (RMBCA)**. Certain provisions of the RMBCA have been amended since 1984. The RMBCA arranged the provisions of the Act more logically, revised the language of the Act to be more consistent, and made substantial changes in the provisions of the model act.

Many states have adopted all or part of the RMBCA as their corporation codes. The RMBCA serves as the basis for our discussion of corporation law in this book.

Classifications of Corporations

A private, for-profit corporation is a **domestic corporation** in the state in which it is incorporated. It is a **foreign corporation** in all other states and jurisdictions. Suppose a corporation is incorporated in Texas and does business in Montana. The corporation is a domestic corporation in Texas and a foreign corporation in Montana. An **alien corporation** is a corporation that is incorporated in another country.

Domestic corporation
A corporation in the state in which it was formed.

Incorporation Procedure

Corporations are creatures of statute. Thus, the organizers of the corporation must comply with the state's incorporation statute to form a corporation. Although relatively similar, the procedure for **incorporation** varies somewhat from state to state.

Selecting a State for Incorporation

A corporation can be incorporated in only one state even though it can do business in all other states in which it qualifies to do business. In choosing a **state of incorporation,** the incorporators, directors, and/or shareholders must consider the corporation law of the states under consideration.

For the sake of convenience, most corporations (particularly small ones) choose as the state for incorporation the state in which the corporation will be doing most of its business. Large corporations generally opt to incorporate in the state with the laws that are most favorable to the corporation's internal operations.

Articles of Incorporation

The **articles of incorporation** or **corporate charter,** are the basic governing document of the corporation. They must be drafted and filed with, and approved by, the state before the corporation can be officially incorporated. Under the RMBCA [§ 2.02(a)], the articles of incorporation must include:

Articles of incorporation
The basic governing document of the corporation. This document must be filed with the secretary of state of the state of incorporation.

(1) the name of the corporation
(2) the number of shares the corporation is authorized to issue
(3) the address of the corporation's initial registered office and the name of the initial registered agent
(4) the name and address of each incorporator

The articles of incorporation also may include provisions concerning

1. the period of duration, which may be perpetual
2. the purpose or purposes for which the corporation is organized
3. limitation or regulation of the powers of the corporation
4. regulation of the affairs of the corporation
5. any provision that otherwise would be contained in the corporation's bylaws.

The RMBCA provides that corporate existence begins when the articles of incorporation are filed. The secretary of state's filing of the articles of incorporation is *conclusive proof* that the incorporators satisfied all conditions to incorporations. The corollary to this rule is that failure to file articles of incorporation is conclusive proof of the nonexistence of the corporation.

The articles of incorporation can be amended to contain any provision that could have been lawfully included in the original document. After the amendment is approved by the shareholders, the corporation must file articles of amendment with the secretary of state [RMBCA Section 10.06]. Exhibit 18.10 shows sample articles of incorporation.

THE PARALEGAL AND CORPORATIONS

Many paralegals work for large law firms that represent corporate America. Major corporations operate across America, and transnational corporations operate throughout the world. These corporations are huge, and they control an enormous proportion of the economy. Large corporations usually hire large law firms to represent them in all types of legal work. Sometimes large corporations hire boutique law firms to represent them in specialized areas of the law—for instance, patent law.

The largest law firms of America have hundreds of lawyers. The law firm itself typically is divided into different practice groups, including transactional work, real estate, securities regulation, environmental law, employment law, mergers and acquisitions, and so forth. Therefore, corporations can find most of the law talent they need in large law firms that serve corporate clients.

Paralegals who work for large law firms typically are assigned to one of the areas of the law practiced by the law firm. Therefore, the paralegals who work for these large law firms often become experts in one area of law—the type of law practiced by the attorney or attorneys to whom they have been assigned.

Transactional work takes up most of large firms' legal services provided to clients. This may consist of drafting the complex contracts the client needs. These contracts generally are negotiated with the help of the lawyers, then drafted by the lawyers. The contracts may be sales contracts, purchase contracts, service contracts, licenses, leases, and other contracts and agreements.

Major corporations need securities lawyers to represent them in issuing securities to the public, lawyers to represent them in negotiating collective bargaining agreements with labor unions, drafting the agreements for stock option and pension plans, consummating mergers with other corporations, and the like. Paralegals who work for these lawyers acquire expertise in these areas of practice.

Corporations also require lawyers to represent them in proceedings at administrative agencies, such as the federal Environmental Protection Agency (EPA), the federal Food and Drug Administration (FDA), the Securities and Exchange Commission (SEC), the Equal Employment Opportunity Commission, and other federal and state administrative agencies. Paralegals who work in these areas must acquire knowledge of administrative law that is practiced before these administrative agencies.

Many corporations operate in foreign markets. These law firms have lawyers who are experts in import law and export law, as well as specialists representing multinational corporations in their dealings in individual countries. Large law firms have international groups in America that provide these services. Large law firms also have opened offices in other countries to provide these services. Therefore, large law firms that represent multinational corporations offer an opportunity for paralegals in the international law area.

For paralegals, then, these large law firms offer tremendous employment opportunities. These large law firms seem to pay the highest salaries but also tend to demand the most hours of work from paralegals. Because large law firms are located almost solely in urban areas, these employment opportunities can be expected to be found in large cities.

Corporations themselves usually have a corporate law department; the corporation has its own legal department consisting of lawyers who are employees of the corporation. These in-house attorneys provide all sorts of legal services to the large corporation. In many instances, a large corporation uses its own attorneys to handle many of its legal needs.

In-house legal departments of corporations offer another employment opportunity for paralegals: Paralegals who work in legal departments of large corporations are employees of the corporation and, therefore, often participate in special employee benefits such as stock option plans. Corporate legal departments will continue to offer excellent employment opportunities for paralegals. Again, though, many corporate legal offices are located at the head office of the corporation in urban areas.

Corporate America will continue to employ substantial numbers of paralegals. These paralegals may work for the large law firms that represent corporate America or for the large national and multinational corporations themselves.

Exhibit 18.10 **Sample articles of incorporation**

ARTICLES OF INCORPORATION

OF

THE BIG CHEESE CORPORATION

ONE: The name of this corporation is:

THE BIG CHEESE CORPORATION

TWO: The purpose of this corporation is to engage in any lawful act or activity for which a corporation may be organized under the General Corporation Law of California other than the banking business, the trust company business, or the practice of a profession permitted to be incorporated by the California Corporations Code.

THREE: The name and address in this state of the corporation's initial agent for service of process is:

Nikki Nguyen, Esq.   1000 Main Street, Suite 800
Los Angeles, California 90010

FOUR: This corporation is authorized to issue only one class of shares which shall be designated common stock. The total number of shares it is authorized to issue is 1,000,000 shares.

FIVE: The names and addresses of the persons who are appointed to act as the initial directors of this corporation are:

Shou-Yi Kang	100 Maple Street	Los Angeles, California 90005
Frederick Richards	200 Spruce Road	Los Angeles, California 90006
Jessie Qilan	300 Palm Drive	Los Angeles, California 90007
Richard Eastin	400 Willow Lane	Los Angeles, California 90008

SIX: The liability of the directors of the corporation from monetary damages shall be eliminated to the fullest extent possible under California law.

SEVEN: The corporation is authorized to provide indemnification of agents (as defined in Section 317 of the Corporations Code) for breach of duty to the corporation and its stockholders through bylaw provisions or through agreements with the agents, or both, in excess of the indemnification otherwise permitted by Section 317 of the Corporations Code, subject to the limits on such excess indemnification set forth in Section 204 of the Corporations Code.

IN WITNESS WHEREOF, the undersigned, being all the persons named above as the initial directors, have executed these Articles of Incorporation.

_____

_____

_____

Dated: January 2, 2007

Corporate Bylaws

Corporate bylaws
A detailed set of rules that are adopted by the board of directors after the corporation is incorporated, containing provisions for managing the business and the affairs of the corporation.

In addition to the articles of incorporation, corporations are governed by their **corporate bylaws**. Either the incorporators or the initial directors can adopt the bylaws of the corporation. The **bylaws** are much more detailed than are the articles of incorporation. Bylaws may contain any provision for managing the business and affairs of the corporation that are not inconsistent with law or the articles of incorporation [RMBCA Section 2.06]. They do not have to be filed with any government official. The bylaws are binding on the directors, officers, and shareholders of the corporation.

The bylaws govern the internal management structure of the corporation. Typically, they specify the time and place of the annual shareholders' meeting, how special meetings of shareholders are called, the time and place of annual and monthly board of directors' meetings, how special meetings of the board of directors are called, the notice required for meetings, the quorum necessary to hold a shareholders' or board of directors' meeting, the required vote necessary to enact a corporate matter, the corporate officers and their duties, committees of the board of directors and their duties, where the records of the corporation are to be kept, directors' and shareholders' inspection rights of corporate records, procedure for transferring shares of the corporation, and such.

The board of directors has the authority to amend the bylaws unless the articles of incorporation reserve that right for the shareholders. The shareholders of the corporation have the absolute right to amend the bylaws even though the bylaws also may be amended by the board of directors. Sample provisions of corporate bylaws are set forth in Exhibit 18.11.

Organizational Meeting

Organizational meeting
A meeting that must be held by the initial directors of the corporation after the articles of incorporation are filed.

An **organizational meeting** of the initial directors of the corporation must be held after the articles of incorporation are filed. At this meeting the directors must adopt the bylaws, elect corporate officers, and transact other business that may come before the meeting [RMBCA Section 2.05]. The latter category includes matters such as accepting share subscriptions, approving the form of the stock certificate, authorizing issuance of the shares, ratifying or adopting promoters' contracts, selecting a bank, choosing an auditor, forming committees of the board of directors, fixing the salaries of officers, hiring employees, authorizing the filing of applications for government licenses to transact the business of the corporation, and empowering corporate officers to enter into contracts on behalf of the corporation. Exhibit 18.12 contains sample **corporate resolutions** from an organizational meeting of the board of directors of a corporation.

S Corporations

S corporation
A corporation that has elected S corporation status. An S corporation pays no federal income tax at the corporate level. The gains or losses of an S corporation flow-through to the shareholders.

In 1982, Congress enacted the Subchapter S Revision Act. The Act divided all corporations into two groups: **S corporations,** which are those that elect to be taxed under Subchapter S, and **C corporations,** which are all other corporations [26 U.S.C. Sections 6242 et seq.].

If a corporation elects to be taxed as an S Corporation, it pays no federal income tax at the corporate level. As in a partnership, the corporation's income or loss flows to the shareholders' individual income tax returns. Thus, this election is particularly advantageous if (1) the corporation is expected to have losses that can be offset against other income of the shareholders, or (2) the corporation is expected to make profits and the shareholders' income tax brackets are lower than the corporation's. Profits are taxed to the shareholders even if the income is not distributed. The shares retain other attributes of the corporate form, including limited liability.

Corporations that meet the following criteria can elect to be taxed as S corporations:

1. The corporation must be a domestic corporation.
2. The corporation cannot be a member of an affiliated group.

Exhibit 18.11 **Sample provisions from corporate bylaws**

BYLAWS OF
THE BIG CHEESE CORPORATION

ARTICLE I   Offices

Section 1. Principal Executive Office. The corporation's principal executive office shall be fixed and located at such place as the Board of Directors (herein called the "Board") shall determine. The Board is granted full power and authority to change said principal executive office from one location to another.

Section 2. Other Offices. Branch or subordinate offices may be established at any time by the Board at any place or places.

ARTICLE II   Shareholders

Section 1. Annual Meetings. The annual meetings of shareholders shall be held on such date and at such time as may be fixed by the Board. At such meetings, directors shall be elected and any other proper business may be transacted.

Section 2. Special Meetings. Special meetings of the shareholders may be called at any time by the Board, the Chairman of the Board, the President, or by the holders of shares entitled to cast not less than ten percent of the votes at such meeting. Upon request in writing to the Chairman of the Board, the President, any Vice President or the Secretary by any person (other than the Board) entitled to call a special meeting of shareholders, the officer forthwith shall cause notice to be given to the shareholders entitled to vote that a meeting will be held at a time requested by the person or persons calling the meeting, not less than thirty-five nor more than sixty days after the receipt of the request. If the notice is not given within twenty days after receipt of the request, the persons entitled to call the meeting may give the notice.

Section 3. Quorum. A majority of the shares entitled to vote, represented in person or by proxy, shall constitute a quorum at any meeting of shareholders. If a quorum is present, the affirmative vote of a majority of the shares represented and voting at the meeting (which shares voting affirmatively also constitute at least a majority of the required quorum) shall be the act of the shareholders, unless the vote of a greater number or voting by classes is required by law or by the Articles, except as provided in the following sentence. The shareholders present at a duly called or held meeting at which a quorum is present may continue to do business until adjournment, notwithstanding the withdrawal of enough shareholders to leave less than a quorum, if any action taken (other than adjournment) is approved by at least a majority of the shares required to constitute a quorum.

ARTICLE III   Directors

Section 1. Election and Term of Office. The directors shall be elected at each annual meeting of the shareholders, but if any such annual meeting is not held or the directors are not elected thereat, the directors may be elected at any special meeting of shareholders held for that purpose. Each director shall hold office until the next annual meeting and until a successor has been elected and qualified.

Section 2. Quorum. A majority of the authorized number of directors constitutes a quorum of the Board for the transaction of business. Every act or decision done or made by a majority of the directors present at a meeting duly held at which a quorum is present shall be regarded as the act of the Board, unless a greater number be required by law or by the Articles. A meeting at which a quorum is initially present may continue to transact business notwithstanding the withdrawal of directors, if any action taken is approved by at least a majority of the required quorum for such meeting.

Section 3. Participation in Meetings by Conference Telephone. Members of the Board may participate in a meeting through use of conference telephone or similar communications equipment, so long as all members participating in such meeting can hear one another.

Section 4. Action Without Meeting. Any action required or permitted to be taken by the Board may be taken without a meeting if all members of the Board shall individually or collectively consent in writing to such action. Such consent or consents shall have the same effect as a unanimous vote of the Board and shall be filed with the minutes of the proceedings of the Board.

Exhibit 18.12 **Sample corporate resolutions from an organizational meeting**

MINUTES OF FIRST MEETING
OF
BOARD OF DIRECTORS
OF
THE BIG CHEESE CORPORATION
January 2, 2007
10:00 A.M.

The Directors of said corporation held their first meeting on the above date and at the above time pursuant to required notice.

The following Directors, constituting a quorum of the Board of Directors, were present at such meeting:

Shou-Yi Kang
Frederick Richards
Jessie Quian
Richard Eastin

Upon motion duly made and seconded, Shou-Yi was unanimously elected Chairman of the meeting and Frederick Richards was unanimously elected Secretary of the meeting.

1. Articles of Incorporation and Agent for Service of Process

The Chairman stated that the Articles of Incorporation of the Corporation were filed in the office of the California Secretary of State. The Chairman presented to the meeting a certified copy of the Articles of Incorporation. The Secretary was directed to insert the copy in the Minute Book. Upon motion duly made and seconded, the following resolution was unanimously adopted.

RESOLVED, that the agent named as the initial agent for service of process in the Articles of Incorporation of this corporation is hereby confirmed as this corporation's agent for the purpose of service of process.

2. Bylaws

The matter of adopting Bylaws for the regulation of the affairs of the corporation was next considered. The Secretary presented to the meeting a form of Bylaws, which was considered and discussed. Upon motion duly made and seconded, the following recitals and resolutions were unanimously adopted:

WHEREAS, there has been presented to the directors a form of Bylaws for the regulation of the affairs of this corporation; and

WHEREAS, it is deemed to be in the best interests of this corporation that said Bylaws be adopted by this Board of Directors as the Bylaws of this corporation;

NOW, THEREFORE, BE IT RESOLVED, that Bylaws in the form presented to this meeting are adopted and approved as the Bylaws of this corporation until amended or repealed in accordance with applicable law.

RESOLVED FURTHER, that the Secretary of this corporation is authorized and directed to execute a certificate of the adoption of said Bylaws and to enter said Bylaws as so certified in the Minute Book of this corporation, and to see that a copy of said Bylaws is kept at the principal executive or business office of this corporation in California.

3. Corporate Seal

The secretary presented for approval a proposed seal of the corporation. Upon motion duly made and seconded, the following resolution was unanimously adopted:

RESOLVED, that a corporate seal is adopted as the seal of this corporation in the form of two concentric circles, with the name of this corporation between the two circles and the state and date of incorporation within the inner circle.

4. Stock Certificate

The Secretary presented a proposed form of stock certificate for use by the corporation. Upon motion duly made and seconded, the following resolution was unanimously adopted:

RESOLVED, that the form of stock certificate presented to this meeting is approved and adopted as the stock certificate of this corporation.

The secretary was instructed to insert a sample copy of the stock certificate in the Minute Book immediately following these minutes.

5. Election of officers

The Chairman announced that it would be in order to elect officers of the corporation. After discussion and upon motion duly made and seconded, the following resolution was unanimously adopted:

RESOLVED, that the following persons are unanimously elected to the offices indicated opposite their names

Title	Name
Chief Executive Officer	Shou-Yi Kang
President	Frederick Richards
Secretary and Vice President	Jessie Quian
Treasurer	Richard Eastin

There being no further business to come before the meeting, on motion duly made, seconded and unanimously carried, the meeting was adjourned.

3. The corporation can have no more than 75 shareholders.
4. Shareholders must be individuals, estates, or certain trusts. Corporations and partnerships cannot be shareholders.
5. Shareholders must be citizens or residents of the United States. Nonresident aliens cannot be shareholders.
6. The corporation cannot have more than one class of stock. Shareholders do not have to have equal voting rights.
7. No more than 20 percent of the corporation's income can be from passive investment income.

An S corporation election is made by filing a **Form 2553** with the Internal Revenue Service (IRS). The election can be rescinded by shareholders who collectively own at least a majority of the shares of the corporation. If the election is rescinded, however, another S Corporation election cannot be made for five years. Exhibit 18.13 contains sample Form 2553, "Election by a Small Business Corporation."

Shareholders

Common stock is an equity security that represents the residual value of the corporation. Common stock has no preferences. That is, creditors and preferred shareholders must receive their required interest and dividend payments before **common shareholders** receive anything. Common stock does not have a fixed maturity date. If the corporation is liquidated, the creditors and preferred shareholders are paid the value of their interests first, and the common shareholders are paid the value of their interest (if any) last. Corporations may issue different classes of common stock [RMBCA Section 6.01 (a) and (b)].

Common stock
A type of equity security that represents the residual value of the corporation.

Common stockholder
A person who owns common stock.

Rights and Duties of Common Shareholders

Persons who own common stock are called common shareholders. A common stockholder's investment in the corporation is represented by a common stock certificate. Common shareholders have the right to elect directors and to vote on mergers and other important matters. In return for their investment, common shareholders receive dividends declared by the board of directors.

A corporation's shareholders *own* the corporation. Nevertheless, they are not agents of the corporation (i.e., they cannot bind the corporation to any contracts), and the only management duties they have are the right to vote on matters such as the election of directors and the approval of fundamental changes in the corporation.

Disregard of the Corporate Entity

Shareholders of a corporation generally have limited liability (i.e., they are liable for the debts and obligations of the corporation only to the extent of their capital contribution). But if a shareholder or shareholders dominate a corporation and misuse it for improper purposes, a court of equity can **disregard the corporate entity** and hold the shareholders of a corporation personally liable for the corporation's debts and obligations. This doctrine, commonly referred to as **piercing the corporate veil**, is often resorted to by unpaid creditors who are trying to collect from shareholders a debt owed by the corporation. The piercing the corporate veil doctrine is also called the **alter-ego doctrine** because the corporation has become the alter ego of the shareholder.

Piercing the corporate veil
A doctrine that says that if a shareholder dominates a corporation and misuses it for improper purposes, a court of equity can disregard the corporate entity and hold the shareholder personally liable for the corporation's debts and obligations.

Courts will pierce the corporate veil if (1) the corporation has been formed without sufficient capital—called *thin capitalization*—or (2) the corporation and its shareholders have not maintained separateness (e.g., commingling of personal and corporate assets, failure to hold required shareholders' meetings, failure to maintain corporate records and books). The courts examine this doctrine on a case-by-case basis.

Exhibit 18.13 **Election by a small business corporation—form 2553**

Form **2553** (Rev. March 2005) Department of the Treasury Internal Revenue Service	**Election by a Small Business Corporation** (Under section 1362 of the Internal Revenue Code) ▶ See Parts II and III on back and the separate instructions. ▶ **The corporation may either send or fax this form to the IRS. See page 2 of the instructions.**	OMB No. 1545-0146

Notes: 1. *Do not file* **Form 1120S,** *U.S. Income Tax Return for an S Corporation, for any tax year before the year the election takes effect.*

2. *This election to be an S corporation can be accepted only if all the tests are met under* **Who May Elect** *on page 1 of the instructions; all shareholders have signed the consent statement; an officer has signed this form; and the exact name and address of the corporation and other required form information are provided.*

Part I	**Election Information**		

Please Type or Print	Name (see instructions)	**A** Employer identification number
	Number, street, and room or suite no. (If a P.O. box, see instructions.)	**B** Date incorporated
	City or town, state, and ZIP code	**C** State of incorporation

D Check the applicable box(es) if the corporation, after applying for the EIN shown in **A** above, changed its name ☐ or address ☐

E Election is to be effective for tax year beginning (month, day, year) . . . . ▶   /   /

F Name and title of officer or legal representative who the IRS may call for more information	**G** Telephone number of officer or legal representative ( )

H If this election takes effect for the first tax year the corporation exists, enter month, day, and year of the **earliest** of the following: (1) date the corporation first had shareholders, (2) date the corporation first had assets, or (3) date the corporation began doing business . . . . ▶   /   /

I Selected tax year: Annual return will be filed for tax year ending (month and day) ▶..

If the tax year ends on any date other than December 31, except for a 52-53-week tax year ending with reference to the month of December, complete Part II on the back. If the date you enter is the ending date of a 52-53-week tax year, write "52-53-week year" to the right of the date.

J Name and address of each shareholder or former shareholder required to consent to the election. (See the instructions for column K)	**K** Shareholders' Consent Statement. Under penalties of perjury, we declare that we consent to the election of the above-named corporation to be an S corporation under section 1362(a) and that we have examined this consent statement, including accompanying schedules and statements, and to the best of our knowledge and belief, it is true, correct, and complete. We understand our consent is binding and may not be withdrawn after the corporation has made a valid election. (Sign and date below.)		**L** Stock owned or percentage of ownership (see instructions)		**M** Social security number or employer identification number (see instructions)	**N** Share-holder's tax year ends (month and day)
	Signature	Date	Number of shares or percentage of ownership	Date(s) acquired		

Under penalties of perjury, I declare that I have examined this election, including accompanying schedules and statements, and to the best of my knowledge and belief, it is true, correct, and complete.

Signature of officer ▶   Title ▶   Date ▶

For Paperwork Reduction Act Notice, see page 4 of the instructions.   Cat. No. 18629R   Form **2553** (Rev. 3-2005)

Exhibit 18.13 **Election by a small business corporation—form 2553**

Form 2553 (Rev. 3-2005)

Page **2**

Part II   **Selection of Fiscal Tax Year** (All corporations using this part must complete item O and item P, Q, or R.)

O   Check the applicable box to indicate whether the corporation is:

    1. ☐ A new corporation **adopting** the tax year entered in item I, Part I.

    2. ☐ An existing corporation **retaining** the tax year entered in item I, Part I.

    3. ☐ An existing corporation **changing** to the tax year entered in item I, Part I.

P   Complete item P if the corporation is using the automatic approval provisions of Rev. Proc. 2002-38, 2002-22 I.R.B. 1037, to request **(1)** a natural business year (as defined in section 5.05 of Rev. Proc. 2002-38) or **(2)** a year that satisfies the ownership tax year test (as defined in section 5.06 of Rev. Proc. 2002-38). Check the applicable box below to indicate the representation statement the corporation is making.

    1. Natural Business Year ▶ ☐ I represent that the corporation is adopting, retaining, or changing to a tax year that qualifies as its natural business year as defined in section 5.05 of Rev. Proc. 2002-38 and has attached a statement verifying that it satisfies the 25% gross receipts test (see instructions for content of statement). I also represent that the corporation is not precluded by section 4.02 of Rev. Proc. 2002-38 from obtaining automatic approval of such adoption, retention, or change in tax year.

    2. Ownership Tax Year ▶ ☐ I represent that shareholders (as described in section 5.06 of Rev. Proc. 2002-38) holding more than half of the shares of the stock (as of the first day of the tax year to which the request relates) of the corporation have the same tax year or are concurrently changing to the tax year that the corporation adopts, retains, or changes to per item I, Part I, and that such tax year satisfies the requirement of section 4.01(3) of Rev. Proc. 2002-38. I also represent that the corporation is not precluded by section 4.02 of Rev. Proc. 2002-38 from obtaining automatic approval of such adoption, retention, or change in tax year.

Note: *If you do not use item P and the corporation wants a fiscal tax year, complete either item Q or R below. Item Q is used to request a fiscal tax year based on a business purpose and to make a back-up section 444 election. Item R is used to make a regular section 444 election.*

Q   Business Purpose—To request a fiscal tax year based on a business purpose, check box Q1. See instructions for details including payment of a user fee. You may also check box Q2 and/or box Q3.

    1. Check here ▶ ☐ if the fiscal year entered in item I, Part I, is requested under the prior approval provisions of Rev. Proc. 2002-39, 2002-22 I.R.B. 1046. Attach to Form 2553 a statement describing the relevant facts and circumstances and, if applicable, the gross receipts from sales and services necessary to establish a business purpose. See the instructions for details regarding the gross receipts from sales and services. If the IRS proposes to disapprove the requested fiscal year, do you want a conference with the IRS National Office?

    ☐ Yes   ☐ No

    2. Check here ▶ ☐ to show that the corporation intends to make a back-up section 444 election in the event the corporation's business purpose request is not approved by the IRS. (See instructions for more information.)

    3. Check here ▶ ☐ to show that the corporation agrees to adopt or change to a tax year ending December 31 if necessary for the IRS to accept this election for S corporation status in the event (1) the corporation's business purpose request is not approved and the corporation makes a back-up section 444 election, but is ultimately not qualified to make a section 444 election, or (2) the corporation's business purpose request is not approved and the corporation did not make a back-up section 444 election.

R   Section 444 Election—To make a section 444 election, check box R1. You may also check box R2.

    1. Check here ▶ ☐ to show the corporation will make, if qualified, a section 444 election to have the fiscal tax year shown in item I, Part I. To make the election, you must complete **Form 8716**, Election To Have a Tax Year Other Than a Required Tax Year, and either attach it to Form 2553 or file it separately.

    2. Check here ▶ ☐ to show that the corporation agrees to adopt or change to a tax year ending December 31 if necessary for the IRS to accept this election for S corporation status in the event the corporation is ultimately not qualified to make a section 444 election.

Part III   **Qualified Subchapter S Trust (QSST) Election Under Section 1361(d)(2)***

Income beneficiary's name and address	Social security number
Trust's name and address	Employer identification number

Date on which stock of the corporation was transferred to the trust (month, day, year) . . . . ▶   /   /

In order for the trust named above to be a QSST and thus a qualifying shareholder of the S corporation for which this Form 2553 is filed, I hereby make the election under section 1361(d)(2). Under penalties of perjury, I certify that the trust meets the definitional requirements of section 1361(d)(3) and that all other information provided in Part III is true, correct, and complete.

_____   _____

Signature of income beneficiary or signature and title of legal representative or other qualified person making the election   Date

*Use Part III to make the QSST election only if stock of the corporation has been transferred to the trust on or before the date on which the corporation makes its election to be an S corporation. The QSST election must be made and filed separately if stock of the corporation is transferred to the trust **after** the date on which the corporation makes the S election.

Form **2553** (Rev. 3-2005)

Board of Directors

Board of directors
A panel of decision makers, the members of which are elected by a corporation's shareholders.

The **board of directors** of a corporation is responsible for formulating the policy decisions affecting the management, supervision, and control of the operation of the corporation [RMBCA Section 8.01]. Such policy decisions include deciding the business or businesses in which the corporation should be engaged, selecting and removing the top officers of the corporation, determining the capital structure of the corporation, declaring dividends and the like.

Typically, boards of directors are composed of inside directors and outside directors. An **inside director** is a person who is also an officer of the corporation. For example, the president of a corporation often sits as a director of the corporation. An

ETHICAL *Perspective*

Duty Not to Use Confidential Information

Mr. Nickolas Drovski is a paralegal who works at a very large law firm that represents major corporate clients. Mr. Drovski works directly for Ms. Lana Ross, a senior partner of the law firm and an expert in mergers and acquisitions law.

One day Ms. Ross asks Mr. Drovski to accompany her to a meeting at the corporate offices of MicroHard Corporation, a client of the law firm. The corporation is one of the largest multinational corporations in the United States. Ms. Cybil Wong, the Chief Executive Officer (CEO) of MicroHard Corporation, and other top corporate officers of the corporation, attend the meeting.

At the meeting, Ms. Wong and the other executives disclose that they want MicroHard Corporation to make a secret tender offer to purchase the stock of Quail Technology Inc. from the shareholders of Quail Technology Inc. Ms. Wong explains that Quail Technology Inc. holds many patents that would be beneficial to MicroHard Corporation. Ms. Wong discloses that it wants Ms. Ross and her law firm to draft the documents necessary to make this secret tender offer. The drafting of these documents will take three weeks. Ms. Ross agrees, on behalf of her law firm, to represent MicroHard Corporation and draft the legal documents necessary for MicroHard Corporation's acquisition of Quail Technology Inc.

Ms. Wong further discloses that the purchase price that MicroHard Corporation will offer for each share of Quail Technology Inc. stock in the tender offer will be $50 per share. Quail Technology Inc.'s stock is currently priced at $20 per share on the New York Stock Exchange.

Ms. Wong states that preparation of the legal documents for the tender offer is an utmost secret and must remain so while Ms. Ross and her law firm prepare the necessary documents for the tender offer. Ms. Ross assures Ms. Wong that she and the personnel of her law firm will keep the tender offer secret while they draft the necessary legal documents for the tender offer. Mr. Drovski, the paralegal, has sat through the entire meeting and has heard everything that has been said.

Later that day, Mr. Drovski, the paralegal, calls a securities broker and purchases 1,000 shares of stock of Quail Technology Inc. Three weeks later Ms. Ross and the law firm finish preparing the legal documents and MicroHard Corporation's tender offer for the shares of Quail Technology Inc. is made public. Mr. Drovski sells his 1,000 shares of Quail Technology Inc. stock at $50 each and makes a profit of $30,000 on the transaction.

Mr. Drovski has violated his professional duty as a paralegal. Section EC-1.5 (c) of the *Model Code of Ethics and Professional Responsibility and Guidance for Enforcement* (Model Code) of the National Federation of Paralegal Associations, Inc. (NFPA) states:

> *A paralegal shall not use confidential information to the advantage of the paralegal or of a third person.*

Mr. Drovski used the confidential information about a client of the law firm that he works for to make a profit on confidential information and therefore has violated his ethical duty as a paralegal. In addition, Mr. Drovski has violated federal securities laws by engaging in insider trading. Therefore he could face criminal charges for his illegal action.

Source: Reprinted by permission from the National Federation of Paralegal Associations, Inc., **www.paralegals.org.**

outside director is a person who sits on the board of directors of a corporation but is not an officer of that corporation. Outside directors often are officers and directors of other corporations, bankers, lawyers, professors, and others. Outside directors usually are selected for their business knowledge and expertise.

The directors can act only as a board. They cannot act individually on the corporation's behalf. Every director has the right to participate in any meeting of the board of directors. Each director has one vote. Directors cannot vote by proxy.

Regular meetings of the board of directors are held at the times and places established in the bylaws. Such meetings can be held without notice. The board can call special meetings as provided in the bylaws [RMBCA Section 8.20(a)]. They typically are convened for reasons such as issuing new shares, considering proposals to merge with other corporations, adopting maneuvers to defend against hostile takeover attempts, and the like.

The board of directors may act without a meeting if all of the directors sign written consents that set forth the actions taken. Such consent has the effect of a unanimous vote. The RMBCA permits meetings of the board to be held via conference calls.

The law does not permit the stockholders to create a sterilized board of directors.

Collins, J.
Manson v. Curtis *(1918)*

Corporate Officers

The board of directors has the authority to appoint the **officers of the corporation.** The officers are elected by the board of directors at such time and by such manner as prescribed in the corporation's bylaws. The directors can delegate certain management authority to the officers of the corporation.

At minimum, most corporations have the following officers: (1) a president, (2) one or more vice presidents, (3) a secretary, and (4) a treasurer. The bylaws or the board of directors can authorize duly appointed officers the power to appoint assistant officers. The same individual may simultaneously hold more than one office in the corporation [RMBCA Section 8.40]. The duties of each officer are specified in the

Officers

Employees of a corporation who are appointed by the board of directors to manage the day-to-day operations of the corporation.

DELAWARE AMENDS CORPORATION CODE TO RECOGNIZE ELECTRONIC COMMUNICATIONS

The state of Delaware leads the nation as the site for incorporation of the United States' largest corporations. This is the result of the Delaware corporation code itself, as well as the expertise of the Delaware courts in resolving corporate disputes. To keep this leadership position, in 2000 the state legislature amended the Delaware General Corporation law to recognize evolving electronic technology. The major changes to the law are:

- Delivery of notices to stockholders may be made electronically if the stockholder consents to the delivery of notice in this form.
- Proxy solicitation for shareholder votes may be made by electronic transmission.
- The shareholder list of a corporation that must be made available during the 10 days prior to a stockholder meeting may be made available either at the principal place of business of the corporation or by posting the list on an electronic network.
- Stockholders who are not physically present at a meeting may be deemed present, participate in, and vote at the meeting by electronic communication; a meeting may be held solely by electronic communication without a physical location.
- The election of directors of the corporation may be held by electronic transmission.
- Directors' actions by unanimous consent may be taken by electronic transmission.

The use of electronic transmissions, electronic networks, and communication by email will make the operation and administration of corporate affairs more efficient in Delaware. Other states, too, have amended their corporation codes to permit electronic filing of documents and the use of electronic communications between directors, officers, and shareholders.

bylaws of the corporation. Officers of the corporation have such authority as may be provided in the bylaws of the corporation or as determined by resolution of the board of directors.

The hierarchy of the ownership, and control of a corporation, is set forth in Exhibit 18.14.

Directors' and Officers' Duty of Loyalty

Duty of loyalty
A responsibility of directors and officers not to act adversely to the interests of the corporation and to subordinate their personal interests to those of the corporation and its shareholders.

The **duty of loyalty** requires directors and officers to subordinate their personal interests to those of the corporation and its shareholders. Justice Benjamin Cardozo defined this duty of loyalty as follows:

> A corporate director or officer owes loyalty and allegiance to the corporation—a loyalty that is undivided and an allegiance that is influenced by no consideration other than the welfare of the corporation. Any adverse interest of a director or officer will be subjected to scrutiny rigid and uncompromising. He may not profit at the expense of his corporation and in conflict with its rights; he may not for personal gain divert unto himself the opportunities that in equity and fairness belong to the corporation.
>
> Many forms of conduct permissible in a workaday world for those acting at arm's length are forbidden to those bound by fiduciary ties. Not honesty alone, but the punctilio of an honor the most sensitive, is then the standard of behavior. As to this there has developed a tradition that is unbending and inveterate. [*Meinhard v. Salmon*, 164 N.E. 545, 546 (N.Y. App. 1928)]

The director is really a watchdog, and the watchdog has no right, without the knowledge of his master, to take a sop from a possible wolf.

L.J. Bowen
Re The North Australian Territory Co. Ltd.
(1891)

Among common breaches of the duty of loyalty are corporate director or officer competing with the corporation without board of directors' approval, secretly dealing with the corporation, secretly usurping a corporate opportunity, or making secret profits from bribes. If a director or officer breaches his or her duty of loyalty and makes a secret profit on a transaction, the corporation can sue the director or officer to recover the secret profit.

Directors' and Officers' Duty of Care

Duty of care
A responsibility of corporate directors and officers to use care and diligence when acting on behalf of the corporation.

The **duty of care** requires corporate directors and officers to use *care and diligence* when acting on behalf of the corporation. To meet this duty, the directors and officers must discharge their duties (1) in good faith, (2) with the care that an *ordinary*

Exhibit 18.14 **Hierarchy of corporation**

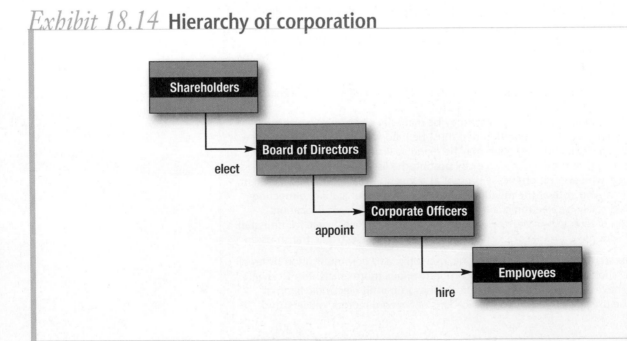

prudent person in a like position would use under similar circumstances, and (3) in a manner that he or she reasonably believes to be in the best interests of the corporation [RMBCA Sections 8.30 (a) and 8.42(a)].

A director or officer who breaches this duty of care is personally liable to the corporation and its shareholders for any damages caused by the breach. Such breaches, which normally are caused by **negligence**, often involve a director's or officer's failure to (1) make a reasonable investigation of a corporate matter, (2) attend board meetings on a regular basis, (3) properly supervise any subordinate who causes a loss to the corporation through embezzlement and such, or (4) stay adequately informed about corporate affairs. Breaches are examined by the courts on a case-by-case basis.

The determination of whether a corporate director or officer has met his or her duty of care is measured as of the time the decision is made. The benefit of hindsight is not a factor. Therefore, the directors and officers are not liable to the corporation or its shareholders for honest mistakes of judgment. This is called the **business judgment rule**.

Consider this example: Suppose, after conducting considerable research and investigation, the directors of a major automobile company decide to produce a large, expensive automobile. When the car is introduced to the public for sale, few of the automobiles are sold because the public is interested in buying smaller, less expensive automobiles. Because this was an honest mistake of judgment on the part of corporate management personnel, their judgment is shielded by the business judgment rule.

FRANCHISE

A **franchise** is established when one party—the **franchisor** or **licensor**—licenses another party—the **franchisee** or **licensee**— to use the franchisor's trade name, trademarks, commercial symbols, patents, copyrights, and other property in the distribution

Negligence
Failure of a corporate director or officer to exercise the duty of care while conducting the corporation's business.

Business judgment rule
A rule stating that directors and officers are not liable to the corporation or its shareholders for honest mistakes of judgment.

Franchise
An arrangement that is established when one party licenses another party to use the franchisor's trade name, trademarks, commercial symbols, patents, copyrights, and other property in the distribution and selling of goods and services.

MULTINATIONAL CORPORATIONS

In the past, the size, power, and range of activities of corporations were limited. This changed at the beginning of the twentieth century, when corporations won the right to own stock in each other. National corporate networks soon followed. Eventually, parent corporations, mostly American, expanded these networks overseas by setting up subsidiary corporations under the laws of other countries. These international networks, or **multinational corporations**, are made up of companies of different nationalities that constitute a single economic unit connected by shareholding, managerial control, or contractual agreement.

The Ford Motor Company is an example of a national multinational firm. Organized in the United States at the beginning of the twentieth century, Ford always has viewed the entire world as its market. The company's policy is for the American parent to own and control all of its overseas subsidiaries. Ford's European subsidiaries are all owned entirely by the American parent. The Mitsubishi Group is another example of this organizational format. It is actually made up of several Japanese companies that use joint directors' meetings to coordinate their activities in Japan and overseas.

The Royal Dutch/Shell Group is an example of an international multinational corporation. In 1907, the Dutch and British parents each formed a wholly owned holding company in its respective country. Each then transferred the ownership of the operating subsidiary to the holding company and exchanged shares in the holding companies. The Dutch parent held 60 percent of each holding company, and the British parent held 40 percent. In addition, the management and operation of the two companies were organized to function as a single economic unit.

Exhibit 18.16 **Sample provisions from a franchise agreement**

FRANCHISE AGREEMENT

Agreement, this 2nd day of January, 2004, between ALASKA PANCAKE HOUSE, INC., an Alaska corporation located in Anchorage, Alaska (hereinafter called the Company) and PANCAKE SYRUP COMPANY, INC., a Michigan corporation located in Detroit, Michigan (hereinafter called the Franchisee), for one KLONDIKE PANCAKE HOUSE restaurant to be located in the City of Mackinac Island, Michigan.

RECITALS

A.   The Company is the owner of proprietary and other rights and interests in various service marks, trademarks, and trade names used in its business including the trade name and service mark "KLONDIKE PANCAKE HOUSE."

B.   The Company operates and enfranchises others to operate restaurants under the trade name and service mark "KLONDIKE PANCAKE HOUSE" using certain recipes, formulas, food preparation procedures, business methods, business forms, and business policies it has developed. The Company has also developed a body of knowledge pertaining to the establishment and operation of restaurants. The Franchisee acknowledges that he does not presently know these recipes, formulas, food preparation procedures, business methods, or business policies, nor does the Franchisee have these business forms or access to the Company's body of knowledge.

C.   The Franchisee intends to enter the restaurant business and desires access to the Company's recipes, formulas, food preparation procedures, business methods, business forms, business policies, and body of knowledge pertaining to the operation of a restaurant. In addition, the Franchisee desires access to information pertaining to new developments and techniques in the Company's restaurant business.

D.   The Franchisee desires to participate in the use of the Company's rights in its service marks and trademarks in connection with the operation of one restaurant to be located at a site approved by the Company and the Franchisee.

E.   The Franchisee understands that information received from the Company or from any of its officers, employees, agents, or franchisees is confidential and has been developed with a great deal of effort and expense. The Franchisee acknowledges that the information is being made available to him so that he may more effectively establish and operate a restaurant.

F.   The Company has granted, and will continue to grant others, access to its recipes, formulas, food preparation procedures, business methods, business forms, business policies, and body of knowledge pertaining to the operation of restaurants and information pertaining to new developments and techniques in its business.

G.   The Company has and will continue to license others to use its service marks and trademarks in connection with the operation of restaurants at Company-approved locations.

H.   The Franchise Fee and Royalty constitute the sole consideration to the Company for the use by the Franchisee of its body of knowledge, systems, and trademark rights.

I.   The Franchisee acknowledges that he received the Company's franchise offering prospectus at or prior to the first personal meeting with a Company representative and at least ten (10) business days prior to the signing of this Agreement and that he has been given the opportunity to clarify provisions he did not understand and to consult with an attorney or other professional advisor. Franchisee represents he understands and agrees to be bound by the terms, conditions, and obligations of this Agreement.

J.   The Franchisee acknowledges that he understands that the success of the business to be operated by him under this Agreement depends primarily upon his efforts and that neither the Company nor any of its agents or representatives have made any oral, written, or visual representations or projections of actual or potential sales, earnings, or net or gross profits. Franchisee understands that the restaurant operated under this Agreement may lose money or fail.

AGREEMENT

Acknowledging the above recitals, the parties hereto agree as follows:

1. Upon execution of this Agreement, the Franchisee shall pay to the Company a Franchise Fee of $30,000 that shall not be refunded in any event.

2. The Franchisee shall also pay to the Company, weekly, a Royalty equal to eight (8%) percent of the gross sales from each restaurant that he operates throughout the term of this Agreement. "Gross sales" means all sales or revenues derived from the Franchisee's location exclusive of sales taxes.

3. The Company hereby grants to the Franchisee:
   a. Access to the Company's recipes, formulas, food preparation procedures, business methods, business forms, business policies, and body of knowledge pertaining to the operation of a restaurant.
   b. Access to information pertaining to new developments and techniques in the Company's restaurant business.
   c. License to use of the Company's rights in and to its service marks and trademarks in connection with the operation of one restaurant to be located at a site approved by the Company and the Franchisee.

(continued)

Exhibit 18.16 **Sample provisions from a franchise agreement** (*continued*)

4. The Company agrees to:
   a. Provide a training program for the operator of restaurants using the Company's recipes, formulas, food preparation procedures, business methods, business forms, and business policies. The Franchisee shall pay all transportation, lodging, and other expenses incurred in attending the program. The Franchisee must attend the training program before opening his restaurant.
   b. Provide a Company Representative that the Franchisee may call upon for consultation concerning the operation of his business.
   c. Provide the Franchise with a program of assistance that shall include periodic consultations with a Company Representative, publish a periodical advising of new developments and techniques in the Company's restaurant business, and grant access to Company personnel for consultations concerning the operation of his business.
5. The Franchisee agrees to:
   a. Begin operation of a restaurant within 365 days. The restaurant will be at a location found by the Franchisee and approved by the Company. The Company or one of its designees will lease the premises and sublet them to the Franchisee at cost. The Franchisee will then construct and equip his unit in accordance with Company specifications contained in the Operating Manual. Upon written request from the Franchisee, the Company will grant a 180-day extension that is effective immediately upon receipt of the request. Under certain circumstances, and at the sole discretion of the Company, the Company may grant additional time in which to open the business. In all instances, the location of each unit must be approved by the Company and the Franchisee. If the restaurant is not operating within 365 days, or within any approved extensions, this Agreement will automatically expire.
   b. Operate his business in compliance with applicable laws and governmental regulations. The Franchisee will obtain at his expense, and keep in force, any permits, licenses, or other consents required for the leasing, construction, or operation of his business. In addition, the Franchisee shall operate his restaurant in accordance with the Company's Operation Manual, which may be amended from time to time as a result of experience, changes in the law, or changes in the marketplace. The Franchisee shall refrain from conducting any business or selling any products other than those approved by the Company at the approved location.
   c. Be responsible for all costs of operating his unit, including but not limited to, advertising, taxes, insurance, food products, labor, and utilities. Insurance shall include, but not be limited to, comprehensive liability insurance including products liability coverage in the minimum amount of $1,000,000. The Franchisee shall keep these policies in force for the mutual benefit of the parties. In addition, the Franchisee shall save the Company harm from any claim of any type that arises in connection with the operation of his business.

BANKRUPTCY AND THE BANKRUPTCY ABUSE PREVENTION AND CONSUMER PROTECTION ACT OF 2005

The extension of credit from creditors to debtors in commercial and personal transactions is important to the viability of the U.S. and world economics. On occasion, however, borrowers become overextended and are unable to meet their debt obligations. Federal bankruptcy law provides methods for debtors to be relieved of some debt in order to obtain a "fresh start."

Prior to 2005, the most recent overhaul of federal bankruptcy law occurred in 1978. The 1978 law was structured to make it easier for debtors to be relieved of much of their debt by declaring bankruptcy. The 1978 act was deemed "debtor friendly" because it allowed many debtors to escape from their unsecured debts.

After a decade of lobbying by credit card companies and banks, Congress enacted the **Bankruptcy Abuse Prevention and Consumer Protection Act of 2005**. The 2005 act makes it much more difficult for debtors to escape from their debts under federal bankruptcy law. The 2005 act, which has been criticized by consumer groups for being too "creditor friendly," has been praised by many businesses, banks, and credit card issuers.

Bankruptcy Abuse Prevention and Consumer Protection Act of 2005
A federal act that substantially amended federal bankruptcy law. It makes it more difficult for debtors to file for bankruptcy and have their unpaid debts discharged.

Types of Bankruptcy

Four special chapters of the Bankruptcy Code provide different types of bankruptcy under which individual and business debtors may be granted remedy. These four types of bankruptcies established by the 2005 act are:

Chapter	Type of Bankruptcy
Chapter 7	Liquidation
Chapter 11	Reorganization
Chapter 12	Adjustment of debts of a family farmer or fisherman with regular income
Chapter 13	Adjustment of debts of an individual with regular income

Bankruptcy courts
Special federal courts that hear and decide bankruptcy cases.

Congress created a system of federal **bankruptcy courts**. These special courts are necessary because the number of bankruptcies would overwhelm the federal district courts. The bankruptcy courts are part of the federal court system, and one bankruptcy court is attached to each of the 96 U.S. district courts located across the country.

Bankruptcy Procedure

The Bankruptcy Code provides procedures and requirements for filing petitions for bankruptcy, defines the bankruptcy estate, provides certain protections to debtors during the course of bankruptcy, and establishes the rights of creditors.

THE PARALEGAL AND BANKRUPTCY LAW

For years, many paralegals have worked in the area of federal bankruptcy law. In the past, the majority of bankruptcy filings were for Chapter 7 liquidation bankruptcy. This type of bankruptcy was easy to file, and debtors were usually able to walk away from most of their unsecured credit such as credit card debt. This type of bankruptcy was "debtor friendly." Chapter 7 bankruptcy required the completion of forms, and was procedurally oriented. Paralegals were important in completing these forms and assisting in the completion of the bankruptcy proceeding.

However, the Bankruptcy Abuse Prevention and Consumer Protection Act of 2005 was enacted to make it more difficult for debtors to obtain Chapter 7 liquidation bankruptcy. The new act establishes detailed income and means tests that must be met before a debtor qualifies for Chapter 7 bankruptcy. The new law is designed to force many debtors into Chapter 13 bankruptcy, a form of rehabilitation bankruptcy that requires debtors to use part of their future income to pay off some of their preexisting debts. The 2005 Act also establishes certain requirements that must be met by a debtor before qualifying for Chapter 13 bankruptcy. The 2005 Act is said to be "creditor friendly."

The 2005 Act provides for Chapter 12 bankruptcy, a special type of rehabilitation bankruptcy designed for family farmers and family fisherman. In addition, the 2005 Act also made some changes to Chapter 11 bankruptcy, a form of bankruptcy usually used by large corporations to reorganize their financial structure. Chapter 11 is a very complicated form of bankruptcy, and requires a special knowledge of debtor and creditor rights. The 2005 Act also made some procedural changes to federal bankruptcy law.

What does this mean for paralegals either working in or interested in working in the bankruptcy field? The area of federal bankruptcy law is more complex than before. This will require that the paralegal learn substantive knowledge of the different forms of bankruptcy and how to determine who qualifies for each form of bankruptcy. Second, the procedures for filing and maintaining a bankruptcy are also more detailed. Therefore, paralegals that work in the bankruptcy field will be required to acquire a greater knowledge of bankruptcy procedures than before.

In the future, many paralegals will find opportunities to work in the field of bankruptcy law. Lawyers and paralegals will be called upon to assist debtors as well as creditors in bankruptcy proceedings. The bankruptcy field will continue to offer jobs for the well-educated and well-trained paralegal professional.

The 2005 act added a new provision that requires an individual filing for bankruptcy to receive prepetition and postpetition credit and financial counseling. The debtor must receive prepetition credit counseling within 180 days prior to the debtor filing his or her petition for bankruptcy. In addition, the 2005 act requires that before an individual debtor receives a discharge in a Chapter 7 or Chapter 13 bankruptcy, the debtor must attend a personal financial management course.

A bankruptcy case is commenced when a **petition** is filed with the bankruptcy court. A debtor can file a **voluntary petition** in Chapter 7 (liquidation), Chapter 11 (reorganization), Chapter 12 (family farmer or fisherman), and Chapter 13 (adjustment of debts) bankruptcy cases.

A creditor or creditors can file an **involuntary petition** and place a debtor into bankruptcy in Chapter 7 (liquidation) and Chapter 11 (reorganization) cases if certain requirements are met. An involuntary petition cannot be filed in Chapter 12 (family farmer or fisherman) or Chapter 13 (adjustment of debts)

The 2005 act places a new burden on attorneys who represent debtors in bankruptcy. The 2005 act requires the attorney to certify the accuracy of the information contained in the bankruptcy petition and the schedules, under penalty of perjury. If there are any factual discrepancies, the attorney is subject to monetary fines and sanctions. Many attorneys may no longer be willing to represent debtors in bankruptcy because of this rule.

A creditor must file a **proof of claim** stating the amount of his or her claim against the debtor. The proof of claim must be timely filed, which generally means within six months of the first meeting of the creditors. A secured creditor whose claim exceeds the value of the collateral may submit a proof of claim and become an unsecured claimant as to the difference. An equity security holder (e.g., a shareholder of a corporation) must file a **proof of interest.**

A **trustee** must be appointed in the following types of bankruptcy cases: Chapter 7 (liquidation), Chapter 12 (family farmer or family fisherman), and Chapter 13 (adjustment of debts). A trustee may be appointed in a Chapter 11 (reorganization) case upon a showing of fraud, dishonesty, incompetence, or gross mismanagement of the affairs of the debtor by current management. Once appointed, a trustee becomes a legal representative of the debtor's estate.

Petition
A document filed with the bankruptcy court that starts a bankruptcy proceeding.

"I will pay you some, and, as most debtors do, promise you indefinitely."
William Shakespeare
Henry IV, Pt. 11 (1597)

Trustee
A legal representative of a debtor's estate.

The Bankruptcy Estate

The **bankruptcy estate** is created upon the commencement of a bankruptcy case. It includes all the debtor's legal and equitable interests in real, personal, tangible, and intangible property, wherever located, that exist when the petition is filed, and all interests of the debtor and the debtor's spouse in community property. Gifts, inheritances, life insurance proceeds, and property from divorce settlements that the debtor is entitled to receive within 180 days after the petition is filed become part of the bankruptcy estate.

Earnings from services performed by an individual debtor are not part of the bankruptcy estate in a Chapter 7 (liquidation) bankruptcy. However, the 2005 act provides that a certain amount of postpetition earnings from services performed by the debtor may be required to be paid as part of the completion of Chapter 12 (family farmer or family fisherman), Chapter 11 (reorganization), and Chapter 13 (adjustment of debts) cases.

Because the Bankruptcy Code is not designed to make the debtor a pauper, certain property is exempt from the bankruptcy estate. The debtor may retain exempt property. **Exempt property** is property of the debtor that he or she can keep and that does not become part of the bankruptcy estate. The creditors cannot claim this property. Federal bankruptcy law establishes federal exemptions, but permits states to enact their own exemptions.

Bankruptcy estate
A debtor's property and earnings that comprise the estate of a bankruptcy proceeding.

Exempt property
Property that may be retained by a debtor pursuant to federal or state law that does not become part of the bankruptcy estate.

Homestead exemption
Equity in a debtor's home that the debtor is permitted to retain.

The federal Bankruptcy Code permits homeowners to claim a **homestead exemption** in their principal residence. The 2005 act limits abusive homestead exemptions. The 2005 act provides that a debtor may not exempt an amount greater than $125,000 if the property was acquired by the debtor within 1,215 days (approximately three years and four months) before the filing of the petition for bankruptcy.

The 2005 act gives the bankruptcy court the power to void certain **fraudulent transfers** of the debtor's property and obligations incurred by the debtor within two years of the filing of the petition for bankruptcy.

Chapter 7: Liquidation

Chapter 7 liquidation
A form of bankruptcy in which the debtor's nonexempt property is sold for cash, the cash is distributed to the creditors, and any unpaid debts are discharged.

Chapter 7 liquidation bankruptcy (also called **straight bankruptcy**) is a familiar form of bankruptcy. In this type of bankruptcy proceeding, the debtor is permitted to keep a substantial portion of his or her assets (*exempt assets*), the debtor's nonexempt property is sold for cash and the cash is distributed to the creditors, and any of the debtor's unpaid debts are discharged. The debtor's future income cannot be reached to pay the discharged debt. Thus, a debtor would be left to start life anew without the burden of his or her prepetition debts.

The 2005 act substantially restricts the ability of many debtors to obtain a Chapter 7 liquidation bankruptcy. The 2005 act added certain *median income* and dollar-based *means* tests that must be met before a debtor is permitted to obtain a discharge of debts under Chapter 7. If these tests are not met, the 2005 act provides that the debtor's Chapter 7 proceeding may, with the debtor's consent, be dismissed or be converted to a Chapter 13 or Chapter 11 bankruptcy proceeding.

Chapter 7 discharge
The termination of the legal duty of a debtor to pay unsecured debts that remain unpaid upon the completion of a Chapter 7 proceeding.

In a Chapter 7 bankruptcy, the property of the estate is sold and the proceeds are distributed to satisfy allowed claims. The remaining unpaid debts that the debtor incurred prior to the date of the order for relief are discharged. **Discharge** means that the debtor is no longer legally responsible for paying those claims. Only individual debtors may be granted discharge. Unsecured claims are to be satisfied out of the bankruptcy estate in order of their statutory priority, as established by the Bankruptcy Code.

Consider this example: Suppose that at the time that Eric is granted Chapter 7 relief, he still owes $50,000 of unsecured debt that there is no money in the bankruptcy estate to pay. This debt is composed of credit card debt, an unsecured loan from a friend, and unsecured credit from a department store. This $50,000 of unsecured credit is discharged, which means Eric is relieved of this debt and is not legally liable for its repayment. The unsecured creditors must write off this debt.

Chapter 13: Adjustment of Debts of an Individual with Regular Income

Chapter 13 adjustment of debts of an individual with regular income
A rehabilitation form of bankruptcy that permits bankruptcy courts to supervise the debtor's plan for the payment of unpaid debts in installments over the plan period.

Chapter 13, which is called **adjustment of debts of an individual with regular income**, is a rehabilitation form of bankruptcy for individuals. Chapter 13 permits qualified debtors to propose a plan to pay all or a portion of the debts that he or she owes in installments over a specified period of time, pursuant to the requirements of Chapter 13. The bankruptcy court supervises the debtor's plan for the payment. A Chapter 13 proceeding can be initiated only by the voluntary filing of a petition by an individual debtor with regular income. The 2005 act establishes dollar limits on the secured and unsecured debt that a debtor may have in order to qualify to file for Chapter 13 bankruptcy.

The debtor must file a plan of payment and information about his or her finances, including a budget of estimated income and expenses during the period of the plan. The Chapter 13 plan may be either up to three years or up to five years, depending on requirements established by the 2005 Act. A Chapter 13 plan of payment may modify the rights of unsecured creditors and some secured creditors.

The court will grant an order discharging the debtor from all unpaid unsecured debts covered by the plan after all the payments required under the plan are com-

DISCHARGE OF STUDENT LOANS

During college and other professional schools, many students borrow money for their tuition and living expenses. Upon graduation, when a student might have large student loans and very few assets, the student might be inclined to file for bankruptcy in an attempt to have his or her student loans discharged.

To prevent such abuse of bankruptcy law, Congress amended the Bankruptcy Code to make it more difficult for students to have their student loans discharged in bankruptcy. Student loans are defined by the Bankruptcy Code to include loans made by or guaranteed by governmental units. The 2005 act added student loans made by nongovernmental commercial institutions, such as banks, as well as funds for scholarships, benefits, or stipends granted by educational institutions.

The Bankruptcy Code now states that student loans can be discharged in bankruptcy only if the nondischarge would cause an "undue hardship" to the debtor and his or her dependants. Undue hardship is construed strictly and would be difficult for a debtor to prove unless he or she could show severe physical or mental disability or that he or she is unable to pay for the basic necessities of food or shelter for himself or herself and any dependents.

Cosigners (e.g., parents who guarantee their child's student loan) must also meet the heightened undue hardship test to discharge their obligation.

---

pleted (which could be up to three years or up to five years). This is called a **Chapter 13 discharge**.

Chapter 11: Reorganization

Chapter 11 of the Bankruptcy Code provides a method for reorganizing a debtor's financial affairs under the supervision of the bankruptcy court. The goal of Chapter 11 is to reorganize the debtor with a new capital structure so that it will emerge from bankruptcy as a viable concern. This option is referred to as **reorganization bankruptcy.** The majority of Chapter 11 proceedings are filed by corporations that want to reorganize their capital structures by receiving discharge of a portion of their debts, obtain relief from burdensome contracts, and emerge from bankruptcy as going concerns.

In a Chapter 11 proceeding, the court will appoint a **creditors' committee** composed of representatives of the class of unsecured claims. The court may also appoint a committee of secured creditors and a committee of equity holders. Committees may appear at bankruptcy court hearings, participate in the negotiation of a plan of reorganization, assert objections to proposed plans of reorganization, and the like.

The filing of a Chapter 11 petition stays (i.e., suspends) actions by creditors to recover the debtor's property. This **automatic stay** suspends legal actions against the debtor or the debtor's property, including the ability of creditors to foreclose on assets given as collateral for their loans to the debtor. An automatic stay is extremely important to a business trying to reorganize under Chapter 11 because the debtor needs to keep its assets to stay in business.

Another major benefit of Chapter 11 bankruptcy is that the debtor is given the opportunity to accept or reject certain executory contracts and unexpired leases. An **executory contract or unexpired lease** is a contract or lease that has not been fully performed. For example, a contract to purchase or supply goods at a later date is an executory contract; a 20-year office lease that has 8 years left until it is completed is an unexpired lease.

The debtor has the exclusive right to file a **plan of reorganization** with the bankruptcy court within the first 120 days after the date of the order for relief. Under the 2005 act, this period may be extended up to 18 months. If the debtor fails to do so, any party of interest (e.g., a trustee, a creditor, an equity holder) may propose a plan.

Chapter 13 discharge
A discharge in a Chapter 13 case that is granted to the debtor after the debtor's plan of payment is completed (which could be up to three or up to five years).

Chapter 11 reorganization
A bankruptcy method that allows the reorganization of the debtor's financial affairs under the supervision of the bankruptcy court.

Executory contract or unexpired lease
A contract or lease that has not been fully performed. With the bankruptcy court's approval, executor contracts and unexpired leases may be rejected by a debtor in bankruptcy.

Plan of reorganization
A plan that sets forth a proposed new capital structure for the debtor to have when it emerges from Chapter 11 reorganization bankruptcy.

Confirmation
The bankruptcy court's approval of a plan of reorganization.

There must be **confirmation** of the plan of reorganization by the bankruptcy court for the debtor to be reorganized under Chapter 11. The bankruptcy court will confirm a plan of reorganization under the acceptance method if the plan is feasible (that is, the new reorganized company is likely to succeed other necessary requirements are met. If a class of creditors does not accept the plan, the plan can still be confirmed by the court, using the Bankruptcy Code's **cram-down provision.** In order for the court to confirm a plan over the objection of a class of creditors, certain requirements as established by bankruptcy law must be met.

Chapter 12: Family Farmer and Family Fisherman Bankruptcy

Chapter 12—adjustment of debts of a family farmer or family fisherman with regular income
A form of bankruptcy reorganization permitted to be used by family farmers and family fishermen.

The 2005 act establishes special definitions and rules that allow family farmers and family fisherman to file for bankruptcy reorganization under **Chapter 12—adjustment of debts of a family farmer or fisherman with regular income**. *Family farmer* and *family fisherman* are defined by the 2005 Act.

The family farmer or family fisherman debtor must file a plan of reorganization. Generally, the plan may provide for payments to creditors over a period no longer than three years, but the court can increase the period to up to five years based on a showing of cause. The plan of reorganization must be confirmed by the court before it becomes operable. The plan of reorganization can modify the rights of secured creditors and unsecured creditors.

Chapter 12 discharge
A discharge in a Chapter 12 case that is granted to a family farmer or family fisherman debtor after the debtor's plan of payment is completed (which is usually three years but could be up to five years).

Once the family farmer or family fisherman debtor has completed making all payments required by the plan (which is usually three years but could be up to five years), the bankruptcy court will grant the debtor discharge of all debts provided for by the plan. This is called a **Chapter 12 discharge**. For example, if the Chapter 12 plan calls for the debtor to pay 55 percent of the outstanding unsecured debt to the unsecured creditors, and this amount has been paid by the debtor during the plan period, the court will grant discharge of the unpaid 45 percent of this unsecured debt.

Legal Terminology

Summary

CHAPTER *18*   BUSINESS ORGANIZATIONS AND BANKRUPTCY LAW

Sole Proprietorship

Definition	A sole proprietorship is a form of business in which the owner and the business are one; the business is not a separate legal entity.
Business Name	A sole proprietorship can operate under the name of the sole proprietor, or a *trade name*. Operating under a trade name is commonly designated as *d.b.a. (doing business as)*. If a trade name is used, a *fictitious business name statement* must be filed with the appropriate state government office.
Liability	The sole proprietor is personally liable for the debts and obligations of the sole proprietorship.

General Partnership

Definition	A general partnership is an association of two or more persons to carry on as co-owners of a business for profit [UPA Section 6(1)].
Uniform Partnership Act (UPA)	The UPA is a model act that codifies partnership law. Most states have adopted all or part of the UPA.
Entity Theory of Partnerships	The entity theory holds that partnerships are *separate legal entities* that can hold title to personal and real property, transact business in the partnership name, and the like.
Taxation of Partnerships	Partnerships do not pay federal income taxes; the income and losses of partnerships flow onto individual partners' federal income tax returns.

Partnership Agreement	The partnership agreement establishes a general partnership and sets forth terms of the partnership. It is good practice to have a written partnership agreement that the partners sign.
Partners' Contract Authority	A contract entered into by a partner with a third party on behalf of a partnership is binding on the partnership.
Tort Liability	1. *Tort*: A partner causes injury to a third party by his or her negligent act, breach of trust, breach of fiduciary duty, or intentional tort. 2. *Partnership liability*: The partnership is liable to third persons who are injured by torts committed by a partner while he or she is acting within the ordinary course of partnership business. 3. *Joint and several liability of partners*: Partners are personally liable for torts committed by partners acting on partnership business. This liability is *joint and several*, which means that the plaintiff can sue one or more of the partners separately. If successful, the plaintiff can recover the entire amount of the judgment from any or all of the defendant-partners.
Dissolution of Partnerships	A dissolution is a change in the relation of the partners caused by any partner ceasing to be associated in carrying on the business [UPA Section 29]. Wrongful dissolution occurs when a partner withdraws from a partnership without having the *right* to do so at the time. The partner is liable for damages caused by wrongful dissolution of the partnership.

Limited Partnership

Uniform Limited Partnership Act (ULPA)	The ULPA is a 1916 model act that contains a uniform set of provisions for the formation, operation, and dissolution of limited partnerships.
Revised Uniform Limited Partnership Act (RULPA)	The RULPA is a 1976 revision of the ULPA that provides a more modern, comprehensive law for the formation, operation, and dissolution of limited partnerships.
General and Limited Partnerships	1. *General partners*: partners in a limited partnership who invest capital, manage the business, and are personally liable for partnership debts. 2. *Limited partners*: partners in a limited partnership who invest capital but do not participate in management and are not personally liable for partnership debts beyond their capital contributions.
Formation of Limited Partnerships	1. *Certificate of limited partnership*: a document that two or more persons must execute and sign that establishes a limited partnership. The certificate of limited partnership must be filed with the secretary of state of the appropriate state. 2. *Limited partnership agreement*: a document that sets forth the rights and duties of general and limited partners, the terms and conditions regarding the operation, termination, and dissolution of the partnership, and so on.
Liability of General and Limited Partners	1. *General partners*: General partners of a limited partnership have *unlimited personal liability* for the debts and obligations of the limited partnership. 2. *Limited partners*: Limited partners of a limited partnership are liable only for the debts and obligations of the limited partnership up to their capital contributions. 3. *Limited partners and management*: Limited partners have no right to participate in the management of the partnership. A limited partner is *liable as a general partner* if his or her participation in the control of the business is substantially the same as that of a general partner, but the limited partner is liable only to persons who reasonably believed him or her to be a general partner.

Limited Liability Partnership (LLP)

Definition	The LLP is a form of business in which there does not have to be a general partner who is personally liable for debts and obligations of the partnership. All partners are limited partners and stand to lose only their capital contribution should the partnership fail. LLPs are formed by accountants and other professionals as allowed by LLP law.
Partners	The partners are owners of an LLP.
Articles of Partnership	Articles of partnership constitute a document that the partners of an LLP must execute, sign, and file with the secretary of state of the appropriate state to form an LLP.
Taxation	An LLP does not pay federal income taxes unless it elects to do so. If an LLP is taxed as a partnership, the income and losses of the LLP flow onto individual partners' federal income tax returns.

Limited Liability Company (LLC)

Definition	The LLC is a special form of unincorporated business entity that combines the tax benefits of a partnership with the limited personal liability attribute of a corporation.
Members	Members are owners of an LLC.
Articles of Organization	Articles of organization constitute a document that owners of an LLC must execute, sign, and file with the secretary of state of the appropriate state to form an LLC.
Operating Agreement	An operating agreement is entered into among members that governs the affairs and business of the LLC and the relations among partners, managers, and the LLC.
Taxation	An LLC does not pay federal income taxes unless it elects to do so. If an LLC is taxed as a partnership, the income and losses of the LLP flow onto individual members' federal income tax returns.

Nature of the Corporation

Definition	A corporation is a legal entity created pursuant to the laws of the state of incorporation. A corporation is a separate legal entity—an *artificial person*—that can own property, sue and be sued, enter into contracts, and such.
Characteristics of Corporations	1. *Limited liability of shareholders:* Shareholders are liable for the debts and obligations of the corporation only to the extent of their capital contributions. 2. *Free transferability of shares:* Shares of a corporation are freely transferable by the shareholders unless they are expressly restricted. 3. *Perpetual existence:* Corporations exist in perpetuity unless a specific duration is stated in the corporation's articles of incorporation. 4. *Centralized management: Board of directors* of the corporation makes policy decisions of the corporation. Corporate *officers* appointed by the board of directors run the corporation's day-to-day operations. Together, the directors and officers form the corporation's management.
Business Corporation Acts	1. *Model Business Corporation Act (MBCA):* a model act drafted in 1950 that was intended to provide a uniform law for the regulation of corporations. 2. *Revised Model Business Corporation Act (RMBCA):* a revision of the MBCA promulgated in 1984 that arranged the provisions of the model to act more logically, revised the language to be more consistent, and made substantial changes that modernized the provisions of the Act.

Classifications of Corporations	1. *Domestic corporation*: a corporation in the state in which it is incorporated. 2. *Foreign corporation*: a corporation in any state other than the one in which it is incorporated. A domestic corporation often transacts business in states other than its state of incorporation; hence, it is a foreign corporation in these other states. A foreign corporation must obtain a *certificate of authority* from these other states to be able to transact intrastate business in those states. 3. *Alien corporation*: a corporation that is incorporated in another country. Alien corporations are treated as foreign corporations for most purposes.
Incorporation Procedure	Incorporation is the process of incorporating (forming) a new corporation. A corporation can be incorporated in only one state, although it can conduct business in other states.
Articles of Incorporation	1. The basic governing document of a corporation; must be filed with the secretary of state of the state of incorporation. This is a public document, also called the *corporate charter*. 2. The corporation code of each state sets out the information that must be included in the articles of incorporation. Additional information may be included in the articles of incorporation as deemed necessary or desirable by the incorporators.
Corporate Bylaws	Corporate bylaws are a detailed set of rules adopted by the board of directors after the corporation is formed, containing provisions for managing the business and affairs of the corporation. This document does not have to be filed with the secretary of state.
Organizational Meeting	An organizational meeting must be held by the initial directors of the corporation after the articles of incorporation are filed. At this meeting the directors adopt the bylaws, elect corporate officers, ratify promoters' contracts, adopt a corporate seal, and transact such other business as may come before the meeting.
Common Stock	Common stock is a type of equity security that represents the *residual value* of the corporation. Common stock has no preferences, and its shareholders are paid dividends and assets upon liquidation only after creditors and preferred shareholders have been paid. 1. *Common stockholder*: a person who owns common stock. 2. *Common stock certificate*: a document that represents the common shareholders' investment in the corporation.
Liability of Shareholders	1. Shareholders of corporations typically have *limited liability*; that is, they are liable for the debts and obligations of the corporation only to the extent of their capital contribution to the corporation. 2. Shareholders may be found *personally liable* for the debts and obligation of the corporation under the doctrine called *piercing the corporate veil*. Courts can disregard the corporate entity and hold shareholders personally liable for the debts and obligations of the corporation if (a) the corporation has been formed without sufficient capital (*thin capitalization*), or (b) separateness has not been maintained between the corporation and its shareholders (e.g., commingling of personal and corporate assets, failure to hold required shareholders' meetings, and such). Also called the *alter-ego doctrine*.
Board of Directors	The board of directors is a panel of decision makers for the corporation, the members of which are elected by the shareholders. The directors of a corporation are responsible for formulating the policy decisions affecting the corporation, such as deciding what businesses to engage in, determining the capital structure of the corporation, selecting and removing top officers of the corporation, and the like.

	1. *Inside director*: A member of the board of directors who is also an officer of the corporation.
	2. *Outside director*: A member of the board of directors who is not an officer of the corporation.
Meetings of the Board of Directors	1. *Regular meeting*: a meeting of the board of directors held at the time and place scheduled in the bylaws.
	2. *Special meeting*: a meeting of the board of directors convened to discuss an important or emergency matter, such as a proposed merger, a hostile takeover attempt, and such.
	3. *Written consents*: the board of directors acting without a meeting if all of the directors sign written consents that set forth the action taken.
Officers	*Officers*: Employees of the corporation who are appointed by the board of directors to manage the *day-to-day operations* of the corporation.
	1. *Duties of loyalty*: a duty that directors and officers have not to act adversely to the interests of the corporation and to subordinate their personal interests to those of the corporation and its shareholders.
	2. *Duty of Care*: a duty that corporate directors and officers have to use care and diligence when acting on behalf of the corporation. This duty is discharged if they perform their duties (a) in good faith, (b) with the care that an *ordinary prudent person* in a like position would use under similar circumstances, and (c) in a manner they reasonably believe to be in the best interests of the corporation.
	1. *Negligence*: failure of a corporate director or officer to exercise this duty of care when conducting the corporation's business.
	2. *Business judgment rule*: a rule that says directors and officers are not liable to the corporation or its shareholders for honest mistakes of judgment.

Franchise

Description	A franchise is established when one party licenses another party to use the franchisor's trade name, trademarks, commercial symbols, patents, copyrights, and other property in the distribution and selling of goods and services.
	1. *Franchisor*: the party who does the licensing in a franchise arrangement. Also called the *licensor*.
	2. *Franchisee*: the party who is licensed by the franchisor in a franchise arrangement. Also called the *licensee*.

Bankruptcy

Bankruptcy Law	1. **Bankruptcy Reform Act of 1978, as amended**. This federal statute establishes the requirements and procedures for filing for bankruptcy.
	2. **Bankruptcy Abuse Prevention and Consumer Protection Act of 2005**. This federal act substantially amends federal bankruptcy law. The 2005 act makes it more difficult for debtors to file for bankruptcy and have their unpaid debts discharged.
	3. **Bankruptcy courts**. Bankruptcy courts have exclusive jurisdiction to hear bankruptcy cases. A bankruptcy court is attached to each federal district court. Bankruptcy judges are appointed for 14-year terms.
Bankruptcy Procedure	1. **Filing of a petition**. The filing of a petition commences a bankruptcy case.
	a. Voluntary petition. A voluntary petition is filed by a debtor.
	b. Involuntary petition. An involuntary petition is filed by a creditor or creditors.
	2. **Proof of claims**. Each unsecured creditor must file proof of claim, stating the amount of its claim against the debtors.
Bankruptcy Estate	The *bankruptcy estate* includes:
	1. All the debtor's legal and equitable interests in real, personal, tangible, and intangible property at the time the petition is filed.
	2. Gifts, inheritances, life insurance proceeds, and property from divorce settlements that the debtor is entitled to receive within 180 days after the petition is filed.

Exempt Property	The Bankruptcy Code permits the debtor to retain certain property that does not become part of the bankruptcy estate. Exemptions are stipulated in federal and state law.
Chapter 7 Bankruptcy	**Chapter 7 bankruptcy:** A form of bankruptcy where the debtor's nonexempt property is sold for cash, the cash is distributed to the creditors, and any unpaid debts are discharged. Also called *liquidation bankruptcy*. **Median income and means tests:** The 2005 act establishes certain median income and means tests that a debtor must meet in order to qualify for Chapter 7 liquidation relief.
Types of Bankruptcy	1. **Chapter 7–Discharge:** A form of bankruptcy where the debtor's nonexempt property is sold, the proceeds are distributed to the creditors, and the debtor's legal obligation to pay unpaid debts is terminated. **Discharge** is available only to individuals. **Discharge of Student Loans:** A student loan may be discharged after it is due only if nondischarge would cause an *undue hardship* on the debtor or his or her family. 2. **Chapter 13–Consumer Debt Adjustment:** A rehabilitation form of bankruptcy that permits bankruptcy courts to supervise the debtor's plan for the repayment of unpaid debts by installment. Called *consumer debt adjustment*. The court will grant an order discharging the debtor from all unpaid debts covered by the plan only after all the payments required under the plan are completed. 3. **Chapter 11–Reorganization Bankruptcy:** A form of bankruptcy for reorganizing the debtor's financial affairs under the supervision of the bankruptcy court. The debtor files a plan of reorganization that sets forth the debtor's proposed new capital structure. A plan of reorganization must be confirmed by the bankruptcy court before it becomes effective. Upon confirmation of a plan of reorganization, the debtor is granted a discharge of all claims not included in the plan. The debtor's legal obligation to pay the discharged debts is terminated. 4. **Chapter 12–Family Farmer and Family Fisherman Bankruptcy:** A rehabilitation form of bankruptcy that provides a method for reorganizing the family farmer or family fisherman debtor's financial affairs under the supervision of the bankruptcy court.

▶ WORKING THE WEB

1. Use the website **http://google.com.html** or similar Internet search engine to find an Internet business that provides services to incorporate a corporation. Read the website you found and write a one-half page report on what you found, answering questions such as how fast a corporation can be formed and how much it costs.

2. Go to the website **http://www.microsoftcorporation.com.html**. Type the search term "Board of Directors." How many directors does the Microsoft Corporation have? Make a list of these directors and identify which directors are inside directors and which directors are outside directors.

3. Visit the website **http://www.business.gov/html**. Where the words "Access Additional Information by" appear on the screen, click on "Region." On the map that appears, click on your state, then click on "Starting a Business." Find out how to reserve a business or corporate name in your state. Write a one-page report about this process.

4. Visit the website **http://www.franchise.org/html**. Whose website is this? Find a franchise that you might be interested in. Write a one-page report about this franchise. In your report, answer questions such as: When was this franchise started? What investment is needed to purchase this franchise? What requirements must be met for obtaining this franchise?

5. Visit the website **http://www.sba.gov/regions/states.html**. Whose website is this? Click on your state on the map. Read "About Us." Write a one-half page report on what this organization does.

▶ CRITICAL THINKING AND WRITING QUESTIONS

1. Define *sole proprietorship*. Describe the liability of a sole proprietor.
2. What does the term *d.b.a. (doing business as)* mean? How is it obtained?
3. Define *general partnership*. Describe the liability of general partners.
4. What is the difference between *joint liability* and *joint and several liability*? Explain.
5. Define *limited partnership*. What is the liability exposure of a (a) general partner, and (b) a limited partner? Explain.
6. Define *limited liability partnership (LLP)*. Describe the liability of its partners.
7. Define *limited liability company (LLC)*. Describe the liability of its members.
8. Define *corporation*. Describe the liability of shareholders.
9. Describe the difference between a (a) domestic corporation, (b) foreign corporation, and (c) alien corporation.
10. Describe the following: (a) articles of incorporation, (b) bylaws, (3) organizational meeting.
11. Explain the difference between a C corporation and an S corporation. How is S corporation status obtained?
12. Describe the function of the board of directors of a corporation. What is the difference between an *inside director* and an *outside director*?
13. Define a corporate officer's and a director's duty of loyalty. Give examples of breaches of this duty.
14. Define a corporate officer's and a director's duty of care. When is this duty breached?
15. Define *franchise*. Who are the parties to a franchise?

▶ ETHICS ANALYSIS AND DISCUSSION QUESTIONS

1. May a paralegal be a partner in a law firm?
2. May a paralegal be a partner with a client of the law firm?
3. Because of the volume of work and an impending deadline, you are hired as a temporary paralegal in a large Wall Street law firm to work on a case involving a major corporate client. One of the lawyers tells you that the client soon will announce a major breakthrough that will lead to a highly profitable business opportunity. May a paralegal take advantage of inside information learned about a public corporate client to trade in stock of the client?

▶ DEVELOPING YOUR COLLABORATION SKILLS

Working on your own or with a group of other students, assigned by your instructor, review the scenario at the beginning of the chapter. As a group, discuss the following questions.

1. What is a sole proprietorship? Does this form of business satisfy the owners' requirements? Why or why not?
2. What is a general partnership? Does this form of business satisfy the owners' requirements? Why or why not?
3. What is a limited partnership? Does this form of business satisfy the owners' requirements? Why or why not?
4. What is a limited liability partnership (LLP)? Does this form of business satisfy the owners' requirements? Can this form of business be used by the owners?
5. What is a limited liability company (LLC)? Does this form of business satisfy the owners' requirements? Can this form of business be used by the owners?
6. What is a corporation? What is the difference between a C corporation and an S corporation? Does either of these satisfy the owners' requirements?

▶ PARALEGAL PORTFOLIO EXERCISE

Locate on the Internet or in the library a source that explains the requirements for preparing the articles of incorporation for a new corporation to be formed in your state. Prepare the articles of incorporation to form a new corporation in your state. Select a corporate name, and make up other information that is needed to complete the articles of incorporation.

▶LEGAL ANALYSIS AND WRITING CASES

Kinney Shoe Corp. v. Polan

939 F.2d 209 (1991) United States Court of Appeals, Fourth Circuit

FACTS

In 1984, Lincoln M. Polan formed Industrial Realty Company (Industrial), a West Virginia corporation. Polan was the sole shareholder of Industrial. Although a certificate of incorporation was issued, no organizational meeting was held and no officers were elected. Industrial issued no stock certificates because nothing was ever paid in to the corporation. Other corporate formalities were not observed.

Polan, on behalf of Industrial, signed a lease to sublease commercial space in a building controlled by Kinney Shoe Corporation (Kinney). The first rental payment to Kinney was made out of Polan's personal funds, and no further payments were made on the lease. Kinney filed suit against Industrial and obtained a judgment of $66,400 for unpaid rent. When the amount was unpaid by Industrial, Kinney sued Polan individually and sought to pierce the corporate veil to collect from Polan.

The District Court held for Polan. Kinney appealed.

Question

1. Is Polan personally liable for Industrial's debts?

National Lumber Co. v. Advance Development Corp.

732 S.W.2d 840, 1987 Ark. Lexis 2225 (Ark. 1987)

FACTS

Pat McGowan, Val Somers, and Brent Robertson were general partners of Vermont Place, a limited partnership formed on January 20, 1984, for the purpose of constructing duplexes on an undeveloped tract of land in Fort Smith, Arkansas. The general partners appointed McGowan and his company, Advance Development Corporation, to develop the project, including contracting with material men, mechanics, and other suppliers. None of the limited partners took part in the management or control of the partnership.

On September 3, 1984, Somers and Robertson discovered that McGowan had not been paying the suppliers. They removed McGowan from the partnership and took over the project. The suppliers sued the partnership to recover the money owed them. The partnership assets were not sufficient to pay all of their claims.

Question

1. Who is liable to the suppliers?

Singer v. Microhard.com, LLC et al.

Hypothetical

FACTS

Harold, Jasmine, Caesar, and Yuan form "Microhard.com, LLC," a limited liability company, to sell computer hardware and software over the Internet. Microhard.com, LLC hires Heather, a recent graduate of the University of Chicago and a brilliant software designer, as an employee. Heather's job is to design and develop software that will execute a computer command when the computer user thinks of the next command he or she wants to execute on the computer.

Using Heather's research, Microhard.com, LLC, develops the "Third Eye" software program that does this. Microhard.com, LLC, sends Heather to the annual Comdex Computer Show in Las Vegas, Nevada, to unveil this revolutionary software. Heather goes to Las Vegas and, while there, rents an automobile to get from the hotel to the computer show and to meet interested buyers at different locations in Las Vegas.

While Heather is driving from her hotel to the site of the Comdex Computer Show, she negligently causes an accident and runs over Harold Singer, a pedestrian. Singer, who suffers severe personal injuries, sues Microhard.com, LLC as well as Heather, Harold, Jasmine, Caesar, and Yuan to recover monetary damages for his injuries.

Question

1. Who is liable?

Billy v. Consolidated Mach. Tool Corp.

51 N.Y.2d 152, 412 N.E.2d 934, 432 N.Y.S.2d 879, 1980 N.Y. Lexis 2638 (N.Y.App. 1980)

FACTS

Joseph M. Billy was an employee of the USM Corporation, a publicly held corporation. On October 21, 1976, Billy was at work when a 4,600-pound ram from a vertical boring mill broke loose and crushed him to death.

Billy's widow brought suit against USM, alleging that the accident was caused by certain defects in the manufacture and design of the vertical boring mill and in the two moving parts directly involved in the accident, a metal lifting arm and the 4,600-pound ram.

Question

1. If Mrs. Billy's suit is successful, can the shareholders of USM Corporation be held personally liable for any judgment against USM?

Vernon v. Schuster, d/b/a Diversity Heating and Plumbing

688 N.E.2d 1172 (1997) Supreme Court of Illinois

FACTS

James Schuster was a sole proprietor doing business as (d.b.a.) Diversity Heating and Plumbing. Diversity Heating was in the business of selling, installing, and servicing heating and plumbing systems. George Vernon and others (Vernon) owned a building that needed a new boiler. In November 1989, Vernon hired Diversity Heating to install a new boiler in the building. Diversity Heating installed the boiler and gave a warranty that the boiler would not crack for 10 years.

On October 20, 1993, James Schuster died. On that date, James's son, Jerry Schuster, inherited his father's business and thereafter ran the business as a sole proprietorship under the d/b/a "Diversity Heating and Plumbing."

In February 1994, the boiler installed in Vernon's building broke and could not be repaired. Vernon demanded that Jerry Schuster honor the warranty and replace the boiler. When Jerry Schuster refused to do so, Vernon had the boiler replaced at the cost of $8,203 and sued Jerry Schuster to recover this amount for breach of warranty.

The Trial Court dismissed Vernon's complaint, but the Appellate Court reinstated the case. Jerry Schuster appealed to the Supreme Court of Illinois.

Question

1. Is Jerry Schuster liable for the warranty made by his father?

Zuckerman v. Antenucci

478 N.Y.S.2d 578 (1984) Supreme Court of New York

FACTS

Jose Pena and Joseph Antenucci, both medical doctors, were partners in a medical practice. Both doctors treated Elaine Zuckerman during her pregnancy. Her son, Daniel Zuckerman, was born with severe physical problems. Elaine, as Daniel's mother and natural guardian, brought this medical malpractice suit against both doctors.

The jury found that Pena was guilty of medical malpractice but that Antenucci was not. The amount of the verdict totaled $4 million. The Trial Court entered judgment against Pena but not against Antenucci. The plaintiffs made a posttrial motion for judgment against both defendants.

Question

1. Is Antenucci jointly and severally liable for the medical malpractice of his partner, Pena?

We're Associates Company v. Cohen, Stracher & Bloom, P.C.

478 N.Y.S.2d 670 (1984) Supreme Court of New York, Appellate Division

FACTS

Three lawyers, Howard R. Cohen, Richard L. Stracher, and Paul J. Bloom, formed a professional corporation, Cohen, Stracher & Bloom, P.C., to engage in the practice of law. The three men were the sole shareholders, directors, and officers of the corporation. The corporation entered into an agreement to lease office space from We're Associates Company (We're Associates) in a building in Lake Success, New York.

The lease was executed on behalf of the corporation "by Paul J. Bloom, Vice President."

We're Associates sued Cohen, Stracher & Bloom, P.C., and its three shareholders to recover $9,000 allegedly due and owing under the lease. The Trial Court dismissed the We're Associates case. Plaintiff We're Associates appealed.

Question

1. Are the three shareholders of the professional corporation liable for the lease obligation of the corporation?

Chelsea Industries, Inc. v. Gaffney

449 N.E.2d 320 1983 Mass. Lexis 1413 (Mass. Sup. 1983)

FACTS

Lawrence Gaffney was the president and general manager of Ideal Tape Co. Ideal, a subsidiary of Chelsea Industries, Inc., was engaged in the business of manufacturing pressure-sensitive tape. In 1975, Gaffney recruited three other Ideal executives to join him in starting a tape-manufacturing business. The four men remained at Ideal for the two years it took them to plan the new enterprise. During this time they used their positions at Ideal to travel around the country to gather business ideas, recruit potential customers, and pur-

chase equipment for their business. At no time did they reveal to Chelsea their intention to open a competing business.

In November 1977, the new business was incorporated as Action Manufacturing Co. When executives at Chelsea discovered the existence of the new venture, Gaffney and the others resigned from Chelsea. Chelsea sued them for damages.

Question

1. Who wins?

Kawaauhau v. Geiger

523 U.S. 57, 118 S.Ct. 974, 1998 U.S. Lexis 1595 Supreme Court of the United States

FACTS

Margaret Kawaauhau sought treatment from Dr. Paul Geiger for a foot injury. Dr. Geiger examined Kawaauhau and admitted her to the hospital to attend to the risks of infection. Although Dr. Geiger knew that intravenous penicillin would have been a more effective treatment, he prescribed oral penicillin, explaining that he thought that his patient wished to minimize the cost of her treatment. Dr. Geiger then departed on a business trip, leaving Kawaauhau in the care of other physicians. When Dr. Geiger returned, he discontinued all antibiotics because he believed that the infection had subsided. Kawaauhau's condition deteriorated over the next

few days, requiring the amputation of her right leg below the knee. Kawaauhau and her husband sued Dr. Geiger for medical malpractice. The jury found Dr. Geiger liable and awarded the Kawaauhaus $355,000 in damages. Dr. Geiger, who carried no malpractice insurance, filed for bankruptcy in an attempt to discharge the judgment. The bankruptcy court denied discharge, and the district court agreed. The Court of Appeals reversed and allowed discharge. The Kawaauhaus appealed to the U.S. Supreme Court.

Question

1. Is a debt arising from a medical malpractice judgment that is attributable to negligent or reckless conduct dischargeable in bankruptcy?

▶WORKING WITH THE LANGUAGE OF THE COURT CASE

United States v. WRW Corporation

986 F.2d 138 1993 U.S. App. Lexis 2307 (1993)
United States Court of Appeals, Sixth Circuit

Read the following case, excerpted from the Court of Appeals opinion. Review and brief the case. In your brief, answer the following questions.

1. Who was the plaintiff? What was it suing for?
2. Who were the defendants?

3. What is the doctrine of piercing the corporate veil?
4. Did the court find the defendants personally liable?

Peck, Judge

In 1985, civil penalties totaling $90,350 were assessed against WRW Corporation (WRW), a Kentucky corporation, for serious violations of safety standards under the Federal Mine Safety and Health Act (the Act) which resulted in the deaths of two miners. Following the imposition of civil penalties, WRW liquidated its assets and went out of business.

Three individual defendants, who were the sole shareholders, officers, and directors of WRW, were later indicted and convicted for willful violations of mandatory health and safety standards under the Act. Roger Richardson, Noah Woolum, and William Woolum each served prison sentences and paid criminal fines. After his release from prison, Roger Richardson filed for bankruptcy under Chapter 7 of the Bankruptcy Code.

The United States (the Government) brought this action in May of 1988 against WRW and Roger Richardson, Noah Woolum, and William Woolum to recover the civil penalties previously imposed against WRW. The District Court denied the individual defendants' motion to dismiss and granted summary judgment to the Government, piercing the corporate veil under state law and holding the individual defendants liable for the civil penalties assessed against WRW. For the reasons discussed herein, we affirm.

Having determined that the imposition of a $90,350 sanction upon the defendants does not violate principles of double jeopardy, we turn to the defendants' argument that the district court erred in holding the individual defendants liable for the penalty by piercing the corporate veil of WRW under Kentucky law.

The district court held that it was appropriate to pierce WRW's corporate veil under either an equity theory or an alter-ego theory, both of which are recognized under Kentucky law. Under either theory, the following factors must be considered when determining whether to pierce the corporate veil: (1) undercapitalization; (2) a failure to observe the formalities of corporate existence; (3) nonpayment or overpayment of dividends; (4) a siphoning off of funds by dominant shareholders; and (5) the majority shareholders having guaranteed corporate liabilities in their individual capacities.

The court first found that WRW was undercapitalized because it was incorporated with only $3,000 of capital, which the record indicates was insufficient to pay normal expenses associated with the operation of a coal mine. The District Court next found that WRW failed to observe corporate formalities, noting that no bylaws were produced by the defendants, and that all corporate actions taken by the individual defendants were without corporation authorization. Finally, although WRW never distributed any dividends to the individual defendants, and there was no evidence that the individual defendants siphoned off corporate funds, these factors alone do not mitigate against piercing the corporate veil in this case because WRW was never sufficiently capitalized and operated at a loss during its two years of active existence.

In addition to holding that the equities of this case support piercing the corporate veil, the District Court held that the corporate veil should be pierced under the "alter ego" theory, because WRW and the defendants did not have separate personalities. In light of the lack of observance of corporate formalities or distinction between the individual defendants and the corporation, we agree with the district court's conclusion that "there was a complete merger of ownership and control of WRW with the individual defendants."

The specific factual findings made by the District Court amply support piercing the corporate veil of WRW and holding the individual defendants liable for the penalty assessed against the corporate entity. For all of the foregoing reasons, the judgment of the district court is AFFIRMED. ■

CRIMINAL LAW

"It is better that ten guilty persons
escape, than that one innocent suffer."

*Sir William Blackstone,
Commentaries on the
Laws of England (1809)*

PARALEGALS AT WORK

You are a paralegal who works for a law firm that does criminal defense work. The law firm specializes in defending executives in white-collar criminal law matters. You work for Mr. Harold Josephson, a renowned attorney in the area of white-collar criminal defense. Mr. Josephson informs you that the law firm has been retained to represent Mr. Keith Day, an executive now facing criminal charges for alleged white-collar crimes. Mr. Josephson informs you that you will assist him in preparing the defense of Mr. Day.

Mr. Josephson explains the following facts and issues to you: Mr. Day was the founder and Chief Executive Officer (CEO) of the E-Run Corporation. The E-Run Corporation was one of the largest companies in the United States and operated an energy business. Mr. Day has been served a complaint, *United States v. Day*, wherein Mr. Day has been charged by the federal government with various crimes.

The complaint alleges that Mr. Day, as well as Mr. Don Shilling, E-Run Corporation's Chief Financial Officer (CFO), and other corporate officers agreed with each other to "cook the books" of the corporation to make the corporation seem like it was making huge profits when it was not. The complaint alleges that the executives failed to report on its financial statements large debts incurred by the corporation, causing the corporation to show a large financial profit when in fact the corporation was losing money. When the alleged misdeeds were discovered, the E-Run Corporation failed and had to declare bankruptcy. Shareholders lost their entire investment, and the creditors of the corporation were not paid.

In addition, the complaint alleges that Mr. Day, Mr. Shilling, and other corporate officers stole money directly from the corporation and diverted corporate cash and other property to their own personal bank accounts. Mr. Day is alleged to have used the mail, telephones, and computers to implement and operate the entire scheme. The complaint also alleges that Mr. Day had

After studying this chapter, you should be able to:

1. Define and list the essential elements of a crime.
2. Describe criminal procedure, including arrest, indictment, arraignment, and the criminal trial.
3. List and describe crimes against persons and property.
4. Define major white-collar crimes, such as embezzlement, fraud, and bribery.
5. Explain the constitutional safeguards against unreasonable searches and seizures.
6. Describe the Fifth Amendment's privilege against self-incrimination.
7. List and describe laws involving computer and Internet crimes.

purchased a restaurant and used the restaurant to hide and move the stolen money through it to make it seem that he had another business that generated the stolen property for him.

Mr. Josephson explains to you that the federal government had engaged in a wiretap of Mr. Day's and Mr. Shilling's telephones for twelve months but had failed to obtain a warrant to conduct the wiretap on Mr. Shilling's telephone.

Consider the issues involved as you read the chapter.

▶ INTRODUCTION FOR THE PARALEGAL

Paralegals often work for criminal lawyers, and therefore require knowledge of the criminal legal process. Some private lawyers specialize in representing clients accused of criminal wrongdoing. Other lawyers work for the government, either for the prosecution team that represents the government in the criminal lawsuit against the defendant, or for a government-appointed defense counsel representing defendants who cannot afford a private attorney to represent them.

For members of society to coexist peacefully and commerce to flourish, people and their property must be protected from injury by other members of society. Federal, state, and local governments' **criminal laws** are intended to accomplish this by providing an incentive for persons to act reasonably in society and imposing penalties on persons who violate them.

A person charged with a crime in the United States is *presumed innocent until proven guilty*. The **burden of proof** is on the government to prove that the accused is guilty of the crime charged. The accused must be found guilty "**beyond a reasonable doubt.**" Conviction requires a unanimous jury vote.

Further, a person charged with a crime in the United States is provided with substantial constitutional safeguards during the criminal justice process. These include the protections against unreasonable search and seizure, against self-incrimination, against double jeopardy, and against cruel and unusual punishment, and the right to a public jury trial.

This chapter covers criminal law and procedure. ■

DEFINITION OF A CRIME

Crime
A violation of a statute for which the government imposes a punishment.

A **crime** is defined as any act by an individual in violation of those duties that he or she owes to society and for the breach of which the law provides that the wrongdoer shall make amends to the public. Many activities have been considered crimes throughout the ages, whereas other crimes are of recent origin.

Penal Codes and Regulatory Statutes

Penal codes
Statutes that define crimes.

Regulatory statutes
Statutes, such as environmental laws, securities laws, and antitrust laws that provide for criminal violations and penalties.

Statutes are the primary source of criminal law. Most states have adopted comprehensive **penal codes** that define in detail the activities considered to be crimes within their jurisdiction and the penalties that will be imposed for committing these crimes. A comprehensive federal criminal code defines federal crimes (Title 18 of the U.S. Code). In addition, state and federal **regulatory statutes** often provide for criminal violations and penalties. The state and federal legislatures are adding to the list of crimes continually.

The penalty for committing a crime may be the imposition of a fine, imprisonment, both, or some other form of punishment (e.g., probation). Generally, imprisonment is imposed to

1. incapacitate the criminal so he or she will not harm others in society,
2. provide a means to rehabilitate the criminal,
3. deter others from similar conduct, and/or
4. inhibit personal retribution by the victim.

Parties to a Criminal Action

In a criminal lawsuit, the government (not a private party) is the **plaintiff**. A lawyer called the **prosecutor**, **district attorney**, or, in the federal system, **United States Attorney** represents the government. The accused is the **defendant**. The **defense attorney** represents the accused. If the accused cannot afford a defense lawyer, the government will provide one free of charge, called a **public defender**.

MARTHA STEWART GUILTY OF A CRIME

Martha Stewart is an icon of fine living. Through her company, Martha Stewart Living Omnimedia Inc. (Omnimedia), Stewart built a business conglomerate involved in publishing magazines and cookbooks, selling clothing and home-based merchandise, and producing a syndicated television program. She and her business became so successful that when the company went public in 1999, Stewart became an instant billionaire.

In 2003, Stewart's friend Sam Waksal, the primary owner of ImClone Systems Inc. (ImClone), received news that the U.S. Food and Drug Administration (FDA) had not given approval for ImClone to market a cancer-fighting drug. Waksal received this information one day before the news would be made public. Waksal and a number of his family members tried to sell their ImClone stock through a securities broker named Peter E. Bacanovic. Bacanovic was also Martha Stewart's stockbroker, and Stewart was a shareholder of ImClone.

Bacanovic had his assistant, Douglas Faneuil, notify Stewart of Waksal's activities. Stewart sold her ImClone stock at $58 per share. When the FDA's negative decision regarding the anticancer drug was released, ImClone stock fell in value. Stewart saved $45,000 by selling her ImClone stock early.

When the U.S. government investigated the substantial selling activity in ImClone stock prior to the public announcement of the FDA's adverse ruling, they netted the Waksal family and Martha Stewart. Sam Waksal pleaded guilty to insider trading and was sent to jail. When the federal government questioned Stewart about her sale of ImClone stock, she said that she had a prior $60 "sell order" (to sell the stock if it ever dropped to $60). Although both Bacanovic and Faneuil first collaborated this story, eventually Faneuil reached a plea bargain with the government and became a witness: He then told the government that the $60 sell order story was a lie and cover-up.

The U.S. government brought criminal charges against Stewart for criminal conspiracy, lying to the federal government, and obstruction of justice. Stewart pleaded the Fifth Amendment and did not testify at trial. The government called many witnesses, including Faneuil and several of Stewart's friends to whom she had talked to about the ImClone stock sale. One witness testified that Stewart told her that Stewart knew of Waksal's trading before she sold her ImClone stock and then stated "Isn't it nice to have brokers who tell you these things?"

The jury returned a verdict of guilty on all charges. On the day the judgment was announced, Stewart's Omnimedia stock plummeted, and Stewart lost about $100 million in one day. Stewart served four and a half months in jail.

Source: *United States v. Stewart* (2004).

checklist

CLASSIFICATION OF CRIMES

CLASSIFICATION	DESCRIPTION
• Felony	The most serious kinds of crimes. They are *mala in se* (inherently evil), and they usually are punishable by imprisonment.
• Misdemeanor	Crimes that are less serious than felonies. They are *mala prohibita* (prohibited by society), and they usually are punishable by fine and/or imprisonment for less than one year.
• Violation	Crimes that are neither felonies nor misdemeanors. Violations generally are punishable by a fine.

Classification of Crimes

All crimes can be classified as felonies, misdemeanors, or violations.

> The magnitude of a crime is proportionate to the magnitude of the injustice which prompts it. Hence, the smallest crimes may be actually the greatest.
>
> Aristotle
> The Rhetoric, *Bk. 1, Ch. XIV*

- *Felonies.* **Felonies** are the most serious kinds of crimes. They include crimes that are ***mala in se***—inherently evil. Most crimes against the person (murder, rape, and the like) and certain business-related crimes (such as embezzlement and bribery) are felonies in most jurisdictions.

  Felonies usually are punishable by imprisonment. In some jurisdictions, certain felonies (e.g., first-degree murder) are punishable by death. Federal law and some state laws require mandatory sentencing for specified crimes. Many statutes define different degrees of crimes (e.g., first-, second-, and third-degree murder) with each degree earning different penalties.

- *Misdemeanors.* **Misdemeanors** are less serious than felonies. They are crimes ***mala prohibita***—not inherently evil but prohibited by society. This category includes many crimes against property, such as robbery, burglary, and violations of regulatory statutes. Misdemeanors carry lesser penalties than felonies; they usually are punishable by fine and/or imprisonment for one year or less.

- *Violations.* Crimes such as traffic violations and jaywalking are neither felonies nor misdemeanors. Called **violations**, these crimes usually are punishable by a fine. Occasionally, a few days of imprisonment are imposed.

Essential Elements of a Crime

For a person to be found guilty of most crimes, a *criminal act* and *criminal intent* must be proven.

Criminal Act

Actus reus
"Guilty act"—the actual performance of the criminal act.

To commit a **criminal act**, the defendant must have actually performed the prohibited act. Under the common law, actual performance of the criminal act is called the ***actus reus*** (guilty act). Under the Model Penal Code, the prohibited act may be analyzed in terms of conduct, circumstances, and results. Killing someone without legal justification is an example of *actus reus*. Sometimes the omission of an act constitutes the requisite *actus reus*. For example, a crime has been committed if a taxpayer who is under a legal duty to file a tax return fails to do so. Merely thinking about committing a crime is not a crime, because no action has been taken.

checklist ✓

ELEMENTS OF AN INTENT CRIME

ELEMENT	DESCRIPTION
Actus reus	Guilty act
Mens rea	Evil intent

Criminal Intent

To be found guilty of a crime, the accused must be found to have possessed the requisite subjective state of mind, or **criminal intent** (i.e., specific or general intent) when the act was performed. This is called the *mens rea* (evil intent) under the traditional common law analysis and *culpable mental state* under the Model Penal Code. The Model Penal Code has four levels of culpable mental state:

1. Purposeful (or intentional)
2. Knowingly
3. Recklessly
4. With criminal negligence

Specific intent is found where the accused purposefully, intentionally, or with knowledge commits a prohibited act. *General intent* is found where there is a showing of recklessness or a lesser degree of mental culpability. The individual criminal statutes state whether the crime requires a showing of specific or general intent. Juries may infer an accused's intent from the facts and circumstances of the case. There is no crime if the requisite *mens rea* cannot be proven. Thus, no crime is committed if one person accidentally injures another person.

Most states provide for certain **non-intent crimes**. The crime of **involuntary manslaughter** is often imposed for reckless conduct. For example, if a driver of an automobile drives too fast (e.g., 20 miles over the speed limit) on a city street and hits and kills a pedestrian, the driver most likely would be found guilty of the crime of involuntary manslaughter and be sentenced to jail.

Mens rea
"Evil intent"—the possession of the requisite state of mind to commit a prohibited act.

Non-intent crime
A crime that imposes criminal liability without a finding of *mens rea* (intent).

Criminal Acts as Basis for Tort Actions

An injured party may bring a *civil tort action* against a wrongdoer who has caused the party injury during the commission of a criminal act. Civil lawsuits are separate from

MEET THE COURTHOUSE TEAM

District Attorney and Public Defender

In most jurisdictions, the individual who prosecutes criminal cases on behalf of the state is called the **district attorney (DA)** or prosecutor. In the federal system, the **United States Attorney** is the one who prosecutes federal criminal cases. The U.S. Attorney is appointed, whereas a district attorney usually is an elected official. Persons who are unable to afford private counsel to defend them in a criminal prosecution are appointed counsel by the court. This can be either a public defender, an attorney who is an employee of the government, or a private attorney appointed and compensated by the government.

the government's criminal action against the wrongdoer. In many cases, a person injured by a criminal act will not sue the criminal to recover civil damages. This is because the criminal is often *judgment-proof*—that is, the criminal does not have the money to pay a civil judgment.

CRIMINAL PROCEDURE

The court procedure for initiating and maintaining a criminal action is quite detailed. It encompasses both pretrial procedures and the actual trial. Pretrial criminal procedure consists of several distinct stages: *arrest, indictment* or *information, arraignment,* and possible *plea bargaining.*

THE PARALEGAL AND CRIMINAL LAW

The area of criminal law provides abundant opportunities for jobs for paralegals. The criminal law system in this country is extremely large and requires the services of thousands of lawyers and, thus, thousands of paralegals. The job opportunities for paralegals are quite varied in the area of criminal law.

Most of the crimes prosecuted in the United States involve violations of state laws. These include many physical crimes, such as assault, battery, robbery, rape, and such. In addition, many crimes involve illegal drug sales, fraud, and other violations of criminal law.

In each case when a defendant is charged with a state-law crime, the state brings the lawsuit against the alleged criminal. The lawsuits are brought by prosecutors of the local jurisdiction where the crime has been alleged to have been committed.

The prosecutors are lawyers who are state government employees. The prosecutor is responsible for investigating the alleged crime and for assembling the government's case against the defendant.

Many defendants in criminal cases cannot afford their own attorneys, so the government provides defense attorneys to represent the defendant in the criminal case. The defense attorneys frequently are government employees as well. These lawyers often are referred to as public defenders. Sometimes the court will appoint an attorney in private practice to represent a defendant. The government, of course, pays the private attorney's fees.

In criminal law cases paralegals work for both the prosecutor's office and for the defense attorneys. Paralegals typically are relied on heavily to conduct investigations and to prepare cases for hearings and for trial. Thus, many paralegals who work in the criminal law area work for the state government. Substantial job opportunities are available for paralegals in this criminal law area.

In addition, some defendants are charged with committing white-collar crimes, including criminal fraud, securities fraud, money laundering, racketeering, and such. White-collar criminal defendants can be charged with violating either state or federal criminal laws, depending on the crimes they are alleged to have committed.

In white-collar criminal law cases, the government employs lawyers to represent the government in its case against the accused. In state criminal law cases, the lawyers are state employees. In federal criminal law cases, these lawyers are federal government employees. On the other side, white-collar defendants often have sufficient funds to employ private attorneys to represent them in white-collar criminal law cases. If a defendant cannot afford his or her own private attorney, the government will provide the defendant with an attorney to represent him or her in the criminal law case.

White-collar criminal cases are often complex. These cases require substantial investigation, as well as preparation for trial. Paralegals are indispensable in preparing for these complex white-collar criminal cases. Therefore, many job opportunities are available for paralegals in white-collar criminal defense law firms.

There will always be criminals; therefore, there will always be a need for attorneys to represent the government on one side of the case and the defendant on the other side of the case. In a parallel fashion, there will always be a need for paralegals on the government prosecutor's side of the case, as well as the defendant's side of the case. The area of criminal law will remain an important source of employment for paralegals.

checklist ✓

CIVIL AND CRIMINAL LAW COMPARED

ISSUE	CIVIL LAW	CRIMINAL LAW
Party who brings the action	Plaintiff	Government
Trial by jury	Yes, except actions for equity	Yes
Burden of proof	Preponderance of evidence	Beyond a reasonable doubt
Jury vote	Judgment for plaintiff requires specific jury vote (e.g., 9 of 12 jurors)	Conviction requires unanimous jury vote
Sanctions and penalties	Monetary damages and equitable remedies (e.g., injunction, specific performance)	Imprisonment, capital punishment, fine, probation

Federal rules of criminal procedure govern all criminal proceedings in the courts of the United States (federal courts). [F.R.C.P. Rule 1]

Arrest

Before the police can arrest a person for committing a crime, they usually must obtain an **arrest warrant** based upon a showing of **probable cause**—the substantial likelihood that the person either committed or is about to commit a crime. If the police do not have time to obtain a warrant (e.g., if the police arrive during the commission of a crime, when a person is fleeing from the scene of the crime, or when it is likely that evidence will be destroyed), the police still may arrest the suspect. *Warrantless arrests*, too, are judged by the probable-cause standard. After a person is arrested, he or she is taken to the police station for *booking*—the administrative proceeding for recording the arrest, fingerprinting, and so on.

Arrest warrant
A document for a person's detainment based upon a showing of probable cause that the person committed the crime.

Indictment or Information

Accused persons must be formally charged with a crime before they can be brought to trial. This usually is done by the issuance of a *grand jury indictment* or a *magistrate's* (judge's) *information statement*. Evidence of serious crimes, such as murder, is usually presented to a **grand jury**. Grand juries consist of between 6 and 24 citizens who are charged with evaluating the evidence presented by the government. Grand jurors sit for a fixed time, such as one year. If the grand jury determines that there is sufficient evidence to hold the accused for trial, it issues an **indictment**. Note that the grand jury does not determine guilt. If an indictment is issued, the accused will be held for later trial.

For lesser crimes (burglary, shoplifting and such), the accused will be brought before a **magistrate (judge)**. A magistrate who finds that there is enough evidence to hold the accused for trial will issue **information**. The case against the accused is dismissed if neither an indictment nor information is issued.

Indictment
The charge of having committed a crime (usually a felony), based on the judgment of a grand jury.

Arraignment

If an indictment or information is issued, the accused is brought before a court for an **arraignment** proceeding during which the accused is (1) informed of the charges against him or her and (2) asked to enter a *plea*. The accused may plead *guilty, not guilty*, or *nolo contendere*. A plea of ***nolo contendere*** means that the accused agrees to

Arraignment
A hearing during which the accused is brought before a court and is (1) informed of the charges against him or her and (2) asked to enter a plea.

the imposition of a penalty but does not admit guilt. A *nolo contendere* plea cannot be used as evidence of liability against the accused at a subsequent civil trial. Corporate defendants often enter this plea. The government has the option of accepting a *nolo contendere* plea or requiring the defendant to plead guilty or not guilty. Depending on the nature of the crime, the accused may be released upon posting bail.

Plea Bargaining

Sometimes the accused and the government enter into a **plea bargain** agreement. The government engages in plea bargaining to save costs, avoid the risks of a trial, and prevent further overcrowding of the prisons. This arrangement allows the accused to admit to a lesser crime than charged. In return, the government agrees to impose a lesser penalty or sentence than might have been obtained had the case gone to trial. In the federal system, more than 90 percent plead guilty rather than go to trial.

CRIMINAL TRIAL

The criminal trial and the civil action trial have many similarities. The functions of the judge and jury are the same. The jury acts as the **trier of fact.** In cases in which the defendant exercises the right to proceed without a jury, also known as a **bench trial**, or **waiver trial**, the judge acts as the trier of fact. The judge also acts as the arbiter of procedural rules covering the conduct of the trial, and the judge ultimately is the one who applies the law to findings of fact, and guilt or innocence of the charges and who determines the sentence, fine, or other permitted forfeiture in cases of guilt. In some cases, such as murder trials, the jury also decides the sentence.

The order and presentation of evidence also are similar. The prosecution goes first and puts on its case, followed by the defense's presentation of its evidence. Motions for dismissal at the close of the prosecution's case also are similar to those in the civil action.

A significant difference is the concern in many cases to protect the record (the trial transcript). The defense counsel tends to be concerned especially with making appropriate objections on the record that can be used as the basis for an appeal. Prosecutors, too, are concerned that they not say anything on the record that the defendant can use as a basis for appeal in the event of a conviction.

Pretrial Discovery

At the present time in this country there is more danger that criminals will escape justice than that they will be subjected to tyranny.

J. Homes
Dissenting
Kepner v. United States (1904)

A limited amount of pretrial discovery is permitted, with substantial restrictions to protect the identity of government informants and to prevent intimidation of witnesses. Defense attorneys often file motions to suppress evidence, which ask the court to exclude evidence from trial that the defendant believes the government obtained in violation of the defendant's constitutional rights, statute, or procedural rule. The government is under an obligation to provide **exculpatory evidence** to the defense attorney.

Under the Federal Rules of Criminal Procedure Rule 16, upon the defendant's request, the government must disclose and make available for inspection, copying, or photographing any relevant written or recorded statements made by defendant within the possession, custody, or control of the government, the existence of which is known, or where the exercise of due diligence may become known to the attorney for the government.

Determination of Guilt

At a criminal trial, unlike a civil-action trial, all jurors must agree *unanimously* before the accused is found *guilty* of the crime charged. If even one juror disagrees (i.e., has reasonable doubt) about the guilt of the accused, the accused is not guilty of the crime charged. If all of the jurors agree that the accused did not commit the crime, the accused is *innocent* of the crime charged.

After trial, the following rules apply:

- If the defendant is found guilty, he or she may appeal.
- If the defendant is found innocent, the government cannot appeal.
- If the jury cannot come to a unanimous decision about the defendant's guilt, the jury is considered a **hung jury**. The government may choose to retry the case before a new judge and jury.

Hung jury
A jury that cannot come to a unanimous decision about the defendant's guilt. The government may choose to retry the case.

COMMON CRIMES

Many crimes are committed against persons and property. The most important types of crimes against persons and property are discussed in the following paragraphs.

Crimes Against the Person

Crimes against the person are the most heinous of crimes. The most common forms of crimes against the person are:

- *Assault:* threat of immediate harm or offensive conduct toward another person coupled with apparent present ability to execute the attempt. Actual physical contact is not necessary.
- *Battery:* harmful or offensive physical contact with another person without his consent (e.g., punching someone in the face without just cause).
- *Mayhem:* depriving another person of a member of his body (e.g., cutting off a person's finger).
- *Rape:* Sexual relations with a person by another person forcibly and against the other person's will.
- *Kidnaping:* the abduction and detention of a person against his will.
- *False imprisonment:* confinement or restraint of another person without authority or justification and without his/her consent.
- *Murder:* the unlawful killing of a human being by another with intent. There are several degrees of murder—such as first degree, second degree, and third degree—depending on the circumstances of the case.

  Sometimes a murder is committed during the commission of another crime even though the criminal did not originally intend to commit murder. Most state laws hold the perpetrator liable for the crime of murder in addition to the other crime. This is called the **felony murder rule**. The intent to commit the murder is inferred from the intent to commit the other crime. Many states also hold accomplices liable under this doctrine.

The convicted perpetrators of crimes against the person generally receive the harshest jail sentences for committing these crimes.

Robbery

At common law, **robbery** is defined as the taking of personal property from another person by the use of fear or force. For example, if a robber threatens to physically harm a storekeeper unless the victim surrenders the contents of the cash register, this is robbery. If a criminal pickpockets somebody's wallet, it is not robbery because there has been no use of force or fear. Robbery with a deadly weapon is considered *aggravated robbery* (or armed robbery) and carries a harsher penalty.

Burglary

At common law, **burglary** was defined as "breaking and entering a dwelling at night" with the intent to commit a felony. Modern penal codes have broadened this definition

On the Web, find the "Ten Most Wanted" fugitives that the United States Federal Bureau of Investigation (FBI) is seeking. Who is number one? What crimes is he or she wanted for? http://www.fbi.gov/html

to include daytime thefts and thefts from offices and commercial and other buildings. In addition, most modern definitions of burglary have abandoned the "breaking-in" element. Thus, unauthorized entering of a building through an unlocked door is sufficient. Aggravated burglary (or armed burglary) carries stiffer penalties.

Larceny

At common law, **larceny** is defined as the wrongful and fraudulent taking of another person's personal property. Most personal property—including tangible property, trade secrets, computer programs, and other business property—is subject to larceny. The stealing of automobiles and car stereos, pickpocketing, and such are larceny. Neither the use of force nor the entry of a building is required. Some states distinguish between *grand larceny* and *petit larceny*, depending on the value of the property taken.

Theft

Some states have dropped the distinction among the crimes of robbery, burglary, and larceny. Instead, these states group these crimes under the general crime of **theft.** Most of these states distinguish between *grand theft* and *petit theft*, depending upon the value of the property taken.

Receiving Stolen Property

It is a crime for a person to (1) knowingly **receive stolen property**, and (2) intend to deprive the rightful owner of that property. Knowledge and intent can be inferred from the circumstances. The stolen property can be any tangible property (e.g., personal property, money, negotiable instruments, stock certificates, and so on).

Arson

At common law, **arson** was defined as the malicious or willful burning of the dwelling of another person. Modern penal codes expanded this definition to include the burning of all types of private, commercial, and public buildings. Thus, in most states, an owner who burns his or her own building to collect insurance proceeds can be found liable for arson. If arson is found, the insurance company does not have to pay the proceeds of any insurance policy on the burned property.

Forgery

Forgery
The fraudulent making or alteration of a written document that affects the legal liability of another person.

The crime of **forgery** occurs if a written document is fraudulently made or altered and that change affects the legal liability of another person. Examples of forgery are counterfeiting, falsifying public records, and materially altering legal documents. One of the most common forms of forgery is the signing of another person's signature to a check or changing the amount of a check. Note that signing another person's signature without intent to defraud is not forgery. For instance, forgery has not been committed if one spouse signs the other spouse's payroll check for deposit in a joint checking or savings account at the bank.

Extortion

Extortion
Threat to expose something about another person unless that other person gives money or property. Often referred to as "blackmail."

The crime of **extortion** means the obtaining of property from another, with his or her consent, induced by wrongful use of actual or threatened force, violence, or fear. For example, extortion occurs when a person threatens to expose something about another person unless that other person gives money or property. The truth or falsity of the information is immaterial. Extortion of private persons is commonly called *blackmail*. Extortion of public officials is called *extortion "under color of official right."*

Credit-Card Crimes

Substantial purchases in the United States are made with credit cards. This poses a problem if someone steals and uses another person's credit cards. Many states have enacted statutes that make the misappropriation and use of credit cards a separate crime. In other states, credit-card crimes are prosecuted under the forgery statute.

Bad Checks

Many states have enacted *bad check legislation*, which makes it a crime for a person to make, draw, or deliver a check at a time when that person knows that funds in the account are insufficient to cover the amount of the check. Some states require proof that the accused intended to defraud the payee of the check.

WHITE-COLLAR CRIMES

Certain types of crime that are prone to be committed by businesspersons are often referred to as **white-collar crimes**. These crimes usually involve cunning and deceit rather than physical force. Many of the white-collar crimes are discussed in the paragraphs that follow.

White-collar crimes
Crimes usually involving cunning and deceit rather than physical force.

Embezzlement

Unknown at common law, the crime of **embezzlement** is now a statutory crime. Embezzlement is the fraudulent conversion of property by a person to whom that property was entrusted. Typically, embezzlement is committed by an employer's employees, agents, or representatives (e.g., accountants, lawyers, trust officers, treasurers). Embezzlers often try to cover their tracks by preparing false books, records, or entries.

Embezzlement
The fraudulent conversion of property by a person to whom that property was entrusted.

The key element here is that the stolen property was *entrusted* to the embezzler. This differs from robbery, burglary, and larceny, in which property is taken by someone not entrusted with the property.

Consider this example: Embezzlement has been committed if a bank teller absconds with money that was deposited by depositors. The employer (the bank) entrusted the teller to take deposits from its customers.

Criminal Fraud

Obtaining title to property through deception or trickery constitutes the crime of **criminal fraud**, also known as *false pretenses* or *deceit*.

Consider this example: Robert Anderson, a stockbroker, promises Mary Greenberg, a prospective investor, that he will use any money she invests to purchase interests in oil wells. Based on this promise, Ms. Greenberg decides to make the investment. Mr. Anderson never intended to invest the money. Instead, he used the money for his personal needs. This is criminal fraud.

Fraud includes the pretense of knowledge when knowledge there is none.

C. J. Cardozo
Ultramares Corp. v. Touche
(1931)

Mail and Wire Fraud

Federal law prohibits the use of mails or wires (e.g., telegraph or telephone) to defraud another person. These crimes are called **mail fraud** and **wire fraud**, respectively. The government often prosecutes a suspect under these statutes if there is insufficient evidence to prove the real crime that the criminal was attempting to commit or did commit. Wire fraud statutes also are used sometimes to prosecute Internet fraud.

Cyber Identity Fraud

For centuries, some people—for various purposes, mostly financial in nature—have attempted to take the identities of other persons. Today, taking on the identity of another can be extremely lucrative, earning the spoils of another's credit cards, bank accounts, Social Security benefits, and such. Use of new technology—computers and the Internet—has made **identity fraud** even easier. But a victim of such fraud is left with funds stolen, a dismanded credit history, and thousands of dollars in costs trying to straighten out the mess. Identity fraud is the fastest-growing financial fraud in America.

To combat such fraud, Congress passed the **Identity Theft and Assumption Deterrence Act of 1998**. This Act criminalizes identity fraud, making it a federal felony punishable with prison sentences ranging from 3 to 25 years. The Act also appoints a federal administrative agency, the Federal Trade Commission (FTC), to help victims restore their credit and erase the impact of the imposter. Law enforcement officials suggest the following steps to protect against identity fraud: Never put your Social Security number on any document unless it is legally required, obtain and review copies of your credit report at least twice each year, and use safe passwords (e.g., other than family names and birthdays) on bank accounts and other accounts that require personal identification numbers (PINs).

Bribery

Bribery
A crime in which one person gives another person money, property, favors, or anything else of value for a favor in return. Often referred to as a payoff or *kickback*.

Bribery is one of the most prevalent forms of white-collar crime. A bribe can be in the form of money, property, favors, or anything else of value. The crime of commercial bribery prohibits the payment of bribes to private persons and businesses. This type of bribe is often called a *kickback* or a *payoff*. Intent is a necessary element of this crime. The offeror of a bribe commits the crime of bribery when the bribe is tendered. The offeree is guilty of the crime of bribery when he or she accepts the bribe. The offeror can be found liable for the crime of bribery even if the person to whom the bribe is offered rejects the bribe.

Consider this example: Harriet Landers, as the purchasing agent for the ABCD Corporation, is in charge of purchasing equipment to be used by the corporation. Neal Brown, sales representative of a company that makes equipment that can be used by the ABCD Corporation, offers to pay her a 10 percent kickback if she buys equipment from him. She accepts the bribe and orders the equipment. Both parties are guilty of bribery.

At common law, the crime of bribery was defined as the giving or receiving of anything of value in corrupt payment for an "official act" by a public official. Public officials include legislators, judges, jurors, witnesses at trial, administrative agency personnel, and other government officials. Modern penal codes also make it a crime to bribe public officials. For example, a developer who is constructing an apartment building cannot pay the building inspector to overlook a building code violation.

Foreign Corrupt Practices Act

Foreign Corrupt Practices Act
A federal statute that makes it illegal for U.S. companies, or their officers, directors, agents, or employees, to bribe a foreign official or foreign political party official to influence the awarding of new business or the retention of continuous business activity.

It is well known that the payment of bribes is pervasive in conducting international business. To prevent U.S. companies from engaging in this type of conduct, the U.S. Congress enacted the **Foreign Corrupt Practices Act** of 1977 (FCPA) [15 U.S.C Section 78m]. The FCPA makes it illegal for U.S. companies, or their officers, directors, agents, or employees, to bribe a foreign official, a foreign political party official, or a candidate for foreign political office. A bribe is illegal only where it is meant to influence the awarding of new business or retaining a continuing business activity.

The FCPA imposes criminal liability where a person pays the illegal bribe himself or herself, or supplies a payment to a third party or an agent, knowing that it will be used as a bribe. A firm can be fined up to $2 million, and an individual can be fined up to $100,000 and imprisoned for up to five years for violations of the FCPA.

The 1988 amendments to the FCPA created two defenses. One excuses a firm or person charged with bribery under the FCPA if the firm or person can show that the payment was lawful under the written laws of that country. The other allows a defendant to show that a payment was a reasonable and *bona fide* expenditure related

HIDING MONEY IN OFFSHORE BANKS

Little did Christopher Columbus know in 1503, when he sailed past the Cayman Islands in the Caribbean, that these tiny islands would become a bastion of international finance in the late twentieth and early twenty-first centuries. These tiny islands of 35,000 people host about 600 banks with more than $500 million in deposits. Why is so much money being hoarded there? The answer is: bank secrecy laws.

Every nation has banking laws, but all banking laws are not equal. What the Cayman Islands banking law provides is confidentiality. In most instances, no party other than the depositor has the right to know the identity of the depositor, account number, or amount in the account. In fact, most accounts are held in the name of trusts instead of the depositor's actual name. This bank secrecy law has attracted many persons to park their ill-gotten gains in a Cayman Islands bank. Often the bank is no more than a lawyer's office.

Switzerland once was the primary location for depositing money that did not want to be found. After some pressure from the United States and other countries, however, Switzerland entered into memoranda of understanding, agreeing to cooperate with criminal investigations by these countries and to help uncover money deposited in Switzerland made through securities frauds and other crimes. Therefore, Switzerland has lost some of its luster as an international money hideout.

So Switzerland has been replaced by other places offering even more secret bank secrecy laws. The Cayman Islands is now the "Switzerland of the Caribbean," and there are several other bank secrecy hideouts around the world, including the Bahamas in the Caribbean, the country of Liechtenstein in Europe, the Isle of Jersey off Great Britain, and the micro-island of Niue in the South Pacific. These tiny countries and islands follow the adage: "Write a good law and they will come."

to the furtherance or execution of a contract. This latter exemption is difficult to interpret.

Some people argue that U.S. companies are placed at a disadvantage in international markets where commercial bribery is commonplace and firms from other countries are not hindered by laws similar to the FCPA.

RACKETEER INFLUENCED AND CORRUPT ORGANIZATIONS ACT (RICO)

Organized crime has a pervasive influence on many parts of the U.S. economy. In 1980, Congress enacted the Organized Crime Control Act. The **Racketeer Influenced and Corrupt Organizations Act (RICO)** is part of this Act [18 U.S.C. Sections 1961–1968]. Originally, RICO was intended to apply only to organized crime, but the broad language of the RICO statute has been used against nonorganized crime defendants as well. RICO, which provides for both criminal and civil penalties, is one of the most important laws affecting business today.

Racketeer Influenced and Corrupt Organizations Act (RICO)
A federal act that provides for both criminal and civil penalties for racketeering.

Criminal RICO

Criminal RICO makes it a federal crime to acquire or maintain an interest in, use income from, or conduct or participate in the affairs of an "enterprise" through a "pattern" of "racketeering activity." An "enterprise" is defined as a corporation, a partnership, a sole proprietorship, another business or organization, and the government. **Racketeering** consists of a number of specifically enumerated federal and state crimes, including activities such as gambling, arson, robbery, counterfeiting, dealing in narcotics, and so on. Business-related crimes, such as bribery, embezzlement, mail fraud, wire fraud, and the like, also are considered racketeering.

To prove a *pattern of racketeering*, the defendant must commit at least two predicate acts within a 10-year period. For example, committing two different frauds

---

CORPORATE CRIMINAL LIABILITY

A corporation is a fictitious legal person that is granted legal existence by the state only after meeting certain requirements. A corporation cannot act on its own behalf. Instead, it must act through *agents* such as managers, representatives, and employees.

The question of whether a corporation can be held criminally liable has intrigued legal scholars for some time. Originally, under the common law, it was generally held that corporations lacked the criminal mind (*mens rea*) to be held criminally liable. Modern courts, however, are more pragmatic. These courts have held that corporations are criminally liable for the acts of their managers, agents, and employees. In any event, because corporations cannot be put in prison, they usually are sanctioned with fines, loss of a license or franchise, and the like.

Corporate directors, officers, and employees are individually liable for crimes they personally commit, whether for personal benefit or on behalf of the corporation. In addition, under certain circumstances a corporate manager can be held criminally liable for the criminal activities of his or her subordinates. To be held criminally liable, the manager must have failed to supervise the subordinate appropriately. This is an evolving area of the law.

---

would be considered a pattern. Individual defendants found criminally liable for RICO violations can be fined up to $25,000 per violation, imprisoned for up to 20 years, or both. In addition, RICO provides for the *forfeiture* of any property or business interests (even interests in a legitimate business) that were gained because of RICO violations. This provision allows the government to recover investments made with monies derived from racketeering activities. The government also may seek civil penalties for RICO violations. These include injunctions, orders of dissolution, reorganization of business, and divestiture of the defendant's interest in an enterprise.

Law cannot persuade, where it cannot punish.

Thomas Fuller
Gnomologia (1732)

Civil RICO

Persons injured by a RICO violation can bring a private *civil* action against the violator to recover injury to business or property. A successful plaintiff may recover *treble damages* (three times actual loss) plus attorneys' fees.

Money Laundering Control Act

When criminals make money from illegal activities, they often are faced with the problem of having large sums of money and no record of how this money was earned. This could easily tip off the government to their illegal activities. To "wash" the money and make it look as though it was earned legitimately, many criminals purchase legitimate businesses and run the money through that business to clean it before the criminal receives the money. The legitimate business has "cooked the books," showing faked expenditures and receipts, in which the illegal money is buried. Restaurants, motels, and other cash businesses make excellent money laundries.

Money Laundering Control Act
A federal statute that makes money laundering a federal crime.

To address the problem of **money laundering**, the federal government enacted the **Money Laundering Control Act** [18 U.S.C. Section 1957]. This Act makes it a crime to:

- knowingly engage in a *monetary transaction* through a financial institution involving property worth more than $10,000. For example, this would include making deposits, making withdrawals, conducting transactions between accounts, or obtaining monetary instruments such as cashiers' checks, money orders, and travelers' checks from a bank or other financial institution.
- knowingly engage in a *financial transaction* involving the proceeds of an illegal activity. For example, this would include buying real estate, auto-

mobiles, personal property, intangible assets, or anything else of value with money obtained from illegal activities.

Thus, money laundering itself is now a federal crime. The money that is washed could have been made from illegal gambling operations, drug dealing, fraud, and other crimes, including white-collar crimes. Persons convicted of money laundering can be fined up to $500,000, or twice the value of the property involved, whichever is greater, and sentenced to up to 20 years in federal prison. In addition, violation of the Act subjects any property involved in or traceable to the offense to forfeiture to the government.

INCHOATE CRIMES

In addition to the substantive crimes discussed, a person can be held criminally liable for committing an **inchoate crime**, which includes incomplete crimes and crimes committed by nonparticipants. The most important inchoate crimes are discussed in the following paragraphs.

Criminal Conspiracy

When two or more persons enter into an *agreement* to commit a crime, it is termed **criminal conspiracy**. To be liable for a criminal conspiracy, the conspirators must take an *overt act* to further the crime. The crime itself does not have to be committed, however.

Criminal conspiracy
A crime in which two or more persons enter into an agreement to commit a crime and an overt act is taken to further the crime.

Consider this example: Two securities brokers agreed by telephone to commit a securities fraud. They also obtained a list of potential victims and prepared false financial statements necessary for the fraud. Because they entered into an agreement to commit a crime and took overt action, the brokers are guilty of the crime of criminal conspiracy even if they didn't carry out the securities fraud. The government usually brings criminal conspiracy charges if (1) the defendants have been thwarted in their efforts to commit the substantive crime, or (2) insufficient evidence is available to prove the substantive crime.

Attempt to Commit a Crime

The **attempt to commit a crime** is itself a crime.

For example: Suppose a person wants to kill his neighbor. He shoots at her but misses. The perpetrator is not liable for the crime of murder, but he is liable for the crime of attempted murder.

Aiding and Abetting the Commission of a Crime

Sometimes persons assist others in the commission of a crime. The act of **aiding and abetting** the commission of a crime is itself a crime. This concept, which is broad, encompasses rendering support, assistance, or encouragement to the commission of a crime. Harboring a criminal after he or she has committed a crime is also considered aiding and abetting.

Cyber Crimes

The Internet and Information Age ushered in a whole new world for education, business, and consumer transactions. But with it followed a new rash of cyber crimes. Prosecutors and courts wrestled over how to apply existing laws written in a nondigital age to new internet-related abuses.

In 1996, Congress responded by enacting the **Information Infrastructure Protection Act (IIP Act)**. In this federal law, Congress addressed computer related crimes as distinct offenses. The IIP Act provides protection for any computer attached to the Internet.

The IIP Act makes it a federal crime for anyone to intentionally access and obtain information from a protected computer without authorization. The IIP Act does not require that the defendant accessed a protected computer for commercial benefit. Thus, persons who transmit a computer virus over the Internet or hackers who trespass into Internet-connected computers may be criminally prosecuted under the IIP Act. Even merely observing data on a protected computer without authorization is sufficient to meet the requirement that the defendant has accessed a protected computer. Criminal penalties for violating the IIP Act include imprisonment for up to 10 years and fines.

The IIP Act gives the federal government a much needed weapon for directly prosecuting cyber-crooks, hackers, and others who enter, steal, destroy, or look at others' computer data without authorization.

CONSTITUTIONAL SAFEGUARDS

When our forefathers drafted the U.S. Constitution, they included provisions that protect persons from unreasonable government intrusion and provide safeguards for those accused of crimes. Although these safeguards originally applied only to federal cases, the Fourteenth Amendment's Due Process Clause made them applicable to state criminal law cases as well. The most important constitutional safeguards and privileges are discussed in the following paragraphs.

The criminal is to go free because the constable has blundered.

C.J. Cardozo
People v. Defore (1926)

Fourth Amendment Protection Against Unreasonable Searches and Seizures

The *Fourth Amendment* to the U.S. Constitution protects persons and corporations from overzealous investigative activities by the government. It protects the rights of the people from **unreasonable search and seizure** by the government and permits people to be secure in their persons, houses, papers, and effects.

Unreasonable search and seizure
Any search and seizure by the government that violates the Fourth Amendment.

"Reasonable" search and seizure by the government is lawful. **Search warrants** based on probable cause are necessary in most cases. These warrants specifically state the place and scope of the authorized search. General searches beyond the specified area are forbidden. **Warrantless searches** generally are permitted only (1) incident to arrest, (2) where evidence is in "plain view," or (3) where evidence likely will be destroyed. Warrantless searches also are judged by the probable-cause standard.

Exclusionary rule
A rule that says evidence obtained from an unreasonable search and seizure can generally be prohibited from introduction at a trial or administrative proceeding against the person searched.

Evidence obtained from an unreasonable search and seizure is considered tainted evidence ("fruit of a poisonous tree"). Under the **exclusionary rule**, such evidence can be prohibited from introduction at a trial or administrative proceeding against the person searched. This evidence, however, is freely admissible against other persons. The U.S. Supreme Court created a *good-faith exception* to the exclusionary rule. This exception allows evidence otherwise obtained illegally to be introduced as evidence against the accused if the police officers who conducted the unreasonable search reasonably believed they were acting pursuant to a lawful search warrant.

Generally, the government does not have the right to search business premises without a search warrant. But businesses in certain hazardous and regulated industries—such as sellers of firearms and liquor, coal mines, vehicle dismantling and automobile junkyards, and the like—are subject to warrantless searches if proper statutory procedures are met. A business also may give consent to search the premises, including employee desks and computers, because of the lack of privacy in those items.

Fifth Amendment Privilege Against Self-Incrimination

The *Fifth Amendment* to the U.S. Constitution provides that no person "shall be compelled in any criminal case to be a witness against himself." Thus, a person cannot be compelled to give testimony against himself or herself, although nontestimonial evidence (fingerprints, body fluids, and the like) may be required. A person who asserts this right is described as having "taken the Fifth." This protection applies to federal

ETHICAL Perspective

Duty Not to Assist in Criminal Activity and Duty to Report Criminal Activity

Mr. Alfred Bush is a paralegal who works at a white-collar criminal defense law firm. Mr. Bush works directly for Ms. Abigail Swanson, a partner at the law firm.

One day Ms. Swanson requests that Mr. Bush sit in on a meeting with her with a client of the firm. The client, Mr. John White, owns White Enterprises Inc. Mr. White explains that he and White Enterprises Inc. are under investigation by the federal government for engaging in criminal fraud, wire fraud, mail fraud, and racketeering. Mr. White has hired Ms. Swanson and her law firm to represent him and the company during the federal investigation and possible criminal lawsuit. At the meeting, Mr. White discloses that he wants "to get the cash out of White Enterprises and put it in a safe place" before the federal government goes any further with its investigation.

Ms. Swanson, who is an expert in white-collar criminal matters, tells Mr. White he can accomplish this if he starts another business that is secretly owned by Mr. White through a front, transfers the cash from White Enterprises to this new business, and then transfers the cash to a bank located in the Cayman Islands in a bank account in Mr. White's name. Ms. Swanson explains that the Cayman Islands has bank secrecy laws that prevent anyone, including the United States government, from discovering the owner of, and the amount of money in, bank accounts located in the Cayman Islands.

Mr. White asks Ms. Swanson if she will help him do this, and Ms. Swanson agrees. The actions that Mr. White proposes, and Ms. Swanson has agreed to help accomplish, would constitute criminal conspiracy, criminal fraud, money laundering, and other federal and state crimes.

What ethical duties does Mr. Bush, as a paralegal, owe in this case? Several provisions of the *Model Code of Ethics and Professional Responsibility and Guidance for Enforcement* (Model Code) of the National Federation of Paralegal Associations, Inc. (NFPA) provide guidance. The following sections are applicable:

> *EC-1.3(e) A paralegal shall not knowingly assist any individual with the commission of an act that is in direct violation of the Model Code/Model Rules and/or the rules and/or laws governing the jurisdiction in which the paralegal practices.*
>
> **Source:** *Reprinted by permission from The National Federation of Paralegal Associations, Inc., www.paralegals.org*

> *EC-1.3(f) If a paralegal possesses knowledge of future criminal activity, that knowledge must be reported to the appropriate authority immediately.*
>
> **Source:** *Reprinted by permission from The National Federation of Paralegal Associations, Inc., www.paralegals.org*

The above rules, and the law, prevent Mr. Bush from assisting Mr. White and Ms. Swanson in accomplishing the transfer of assets by a fraudulent scheme from White Enterprises to the bank in the Cayman Islands. If Mr. Bush helps accomplish this he would not only violate his duties as a paralegal, but would also violate federal and state criminal laws. Mr. Bush has a duty not to participate in this criminal scheme and also a duty to report Mr. White's and Ms. Swanson's fraudulent scheme to federal and state authorities.

cases and is extended to state and local criminal cases through the Due Process Clause of the Fourteenth Amendment.

The protection against **self-incrimination** applies only to natural persons who are accused of crimes. Therefore, artificial persons (such as corporations and partnerships) cannot raise this protection against incriminating testimony. Thus, business records of corporations and partnerships are not protected from disclosure, even if they incriminate individuals who work for the business. But certain "private papers" of businesspersons (such as personal diaries) are protected from disclosure. It is improper for a jury to infer guilt from the defendant's exercise of his or her constitutional right to remain silent.

Self-incrimination
The Fifth Amendment states that no person shall be compelled in any criminal case to be a witness against him- or herself.

Miranda Rights

Miranda **rights**
Rights that a suspect must be informed of before being interrogated, so that the suspect will not unwittingly give up his or her Fifth Amendment right.

Most people have not read and memorized the provisions of the U.S. Constitution. The U.S. Supreme Court recognized this fact when it decided the landmark case *Miranda v. Arizona* in 1966 [384 U.S. 436, 86 S.Ct. 1602, 16 L.Ed.2d 694, 1966 U.S. Lexis 2817]. In that case, the Supreme Court held that the Fifth Amendment privilege against self-incrimination is not useful unless a criminal suspect has knowledge of this right. Therefore, the Supreme Court required that the following warning—colloquially called the *Miranda* **rights**—be read to a criminal suspect before he or she is interrogated by the police or other government officials:

- You have the right to remain silent.
- Anything you say can and will be used against you.
- You have the right to consult a lawyer and to have a lawyer present with you during interrogation.
- If you cannot afford a lawyer, a lawyer will be appointed free of charge to represent you.

Any statements or confessions obtained from a suspect prior to being read his or her *Miranda* rights can be excluded from evidence at trial. In 2000, the U.S. Supreme Court upheld *Miranda* in *Dickerson v. United States* [530 U.S. 428, 120 S.Ct. 2326, 147 L.Ed.2d 405, 2000 U.S. Lexis 4305]. The Supreme Court stated, "We do not think there is justification for overruling *Miranda*. *Miranda* has become embedded in routine police practice to the point where the warnings have become part of our national culture."

Immunity from Prosecution

On occasion, the government wants to obtain information from a suspect who has asserted his or her Fifth Amendment privilege against self-incrimination. The government can try to achieve this by offering the suspect **immunity from prosecution**, in which the government agrees not to use any evidence given by a person who has been granted immunity against that person. Once immunity is granted, the suspect loses the right to assert his or her Fifth Amendment privilege.

Grants of immunity often are given when the government wants the suspect to give information that will lead to the prosecution of other, more important criminal suspects. Partial grants of immunity also are available. For example, a suspect may be granted immunity from prosecution for a serious crime but not a lesser crime, in exchange for information. Some persons who are granted immunity are placed in witness protection programs in which they are given a new identity, relocated, and found a job.

Attorney-Client Privilege and Other Privileges

Attorney–client privilege
A rule that says a client can tell his or her lawyer anything about the case without fear that the attorney will be called as a witness against the client.

To obtain a proper defense, the accused person must be able to tell his or her attorney facts about the case without fear that the attorney will be called as a witness against the accused. The **attorney–client privilege** is protected by the Fifth Amendment. Either the client or the attorney can raise this privilege. For the privilege to apply, the information must be told to the attorney in his or her capacity as an attorney, and not as a friend or neighbor or other such relationship.

The following privileges also have been recognized under the Fifth Amendment:

1. Psychiatrist/psychologist–patient privilege,
2. Priest/minister/rabbi–penitent privilege,
3. Spouse–spouse privilege, and
4. Parent–child privilege.

There are some exceptions. For example, a spouse or a child who is beaten by a spouse or a parent may testify against the accused.

Fifth Amendment Protection Against Double Jeopardy

The **Double Jeopardy Clause** of the Fifth Amendment protects persons from being tried twice for the same crime. For example, if the state tries a suspect for the crime of murder and the suspect is found innocent, the state cannot bring another trial against the accused for the same crime. But if the same criminal act involves several different crimes, the accused may be tried for each of the crimes without violating the double jeopardy clause. Suppose the accused kills two people during a robbery. The accused may be tried for two murders and for the robbery.

If the same act violates the laws of two or more jurisdictions, each jurisdiction may try the accused. For instance, if an accused person kidnaps a person in one state and brings the victim across a state border into another state, the act violates the laws of two states and the federal government. Thus, three jurisdictions can prosecute the accused without violating the double jeopardy clause.

Double Jeopardy Clause
A clause of the Fifth Amendment that protects persons from being tried twice for the same crime.

Sixth Amendment Right to a Public Jury Trial

The *Sixth Amendment* guarantees that criminal defendants have these rights:

1. The right to be tried by an impartial jury of the state or district in which the alleged crime was committed.
2. The right to confront (cross-examine) the witnesses against the accused.
3. The right to have the assistance of a lawyer.
4. The right to have a speedy trial.

The **Speedy Trial Act** requires that a criminal defendant be brought to trial within 70 days after indictment [18 U.S.C. Section 3161(c)(1)]. The court may grant continuances to serve the "ends of justice."

Eighth Amendment Protection Against Cruel and Unusual Punishment

The *Eighth Amendment* protects criminal defendants from **cruel and unusual punishment**. For example, it prohibits the torture of criminals. This clause, however, does not prohibit capital punishment.

Federal Antiterrorism Act

The devastating terrorist attacks on the World Trade Center in New York and the Pentagon in Washington, DC, on September 11, 2001, shocked the nation. The attacks were organized and orchestrated by terrorists who crossed nations' borders easily, secretly planned and prepared for the attacks undetected, and financed the attacks using money located in banks in the United States, Great Britain, and other countries. In response, Congress enacted the federal **Antiterrorism Act**, which assists the government in detecting, investigating, and prosecuting terrorists. The bill was signed into law on October 26, 2001, with many of the provisions set to expire in five years. In 2006, most of the provisions of the Act were reenacted as law. The Act contains the following main features:

- *Special Intelligence Court.* The Act authorizes the Special Intelligence Court to issue expanded wiretap orders and subpoenas to obtain evidence of suspected terrorism.
- *Nationwide search warrant.* The Act creates a nationwide search warrant to obtain evidence of terrorist activities.
- *Roving wiretaps.* The act permits "roving wiretaps" on a person suspected of involvement in terrorism so any telephone or electronic device used by the person may be monitored.

■ *Detention of noncitizens.* The Act gives the federal government authority to detain a nonresident in the United States for up to seven days without filing charges against that person. Nonresidents who are certified by a court as a threat to national security may be held for up to six months without a trial.

Legal Terminology

Actus reus   692
Aiding and abetting   703
Antiterrorism Act   707
Arraignment   695
Arrest warrant   695
Arson   697
Assault   697
Attempt to commit a crime   703
Attorney–client privilege   705
Battery   697
Bench trial (waiver trial)   695
Beyond a reasonable doubt   690
Bribery   700
Burden of proof   690
Burglary   697
Crime   690
Criminal act   692
Criminal conspiracy   703
Criminal fraud   699
Criminal intent   693
Criminal laws   690
Cruel and unusual punishment   707
Defendant   691
Defense attorney   691
District attorney (prosecutor)   693
Double Jeopardy Clause   707
Embezzlement   699
Exclusionary rule   704
Exculpatory evidence   695
Extortion   697

False imprisonment   697
Felony   692
Felony murder rule   697
Foreign Corrupt Practices Act   700
Forgery   697
Grand jury   695
Guilty   695
Hung jury   697
Identity fraud/Identity theft   700
Identity Theft and Assumption
  Deterrence Act of 1998   700
Immunity from prosecution   705
Inchoate crimes   703
Indictment   695
Information   695
Information Infrastructure Protection
  Act (IIP Act)   703
Involuntary manslaughter   693
Kidnapping   697
Larceny   697
Mail fraud   699
Mala in se   692
Mala prohibita   692
Mayhem   697
Mens rea   693
Miranda rights   705
Misdemeanor   692
Money laundering   702
Money Laundering Control Act   702

Murder   697
Nolo contendere   695
Non-intent crime   693
Not guilty   695
Penal code   690
Plaintiff   691
Plea bargain   695
Probable cause   695
Prosecutor (district attorney)   691
Public defender   691
Racketeer Influenced and Corrupt
  Organizations Act (RICO)   701
Racketeering   701
Rape   692
Receive stolen property   697
Regulatory statutes   690
Robbery   697
Search warrant   704
Self-incrimination   705
Speedy Trial Act   707
Theft   697
Trier of fact   695
United States Attorney   693
Unreasonable search and seizure   704
Violation   692
Waiver trial (bench trial)   695
Warrantless search   704
White-collar crime   699
Wire fraud   699

CHAPTER *19* CRIMINAL LAW

What Is a Crime?

Definition	A crime is any act done by a person in violation of those duties that he or she owes to society and for the breach of which the law provides a penalty.
Specifics of a Criminal Trial	1. The accused is *presumed innocent until proven guilty.* 2. The plaintiff (the government) bears the *burden of proof.* 3. The government must prove *beyond a reasonable doubt* that the accused is guilty of the crime charged. 4. The accused does not have to testify against himself or herself.
Penal Codes and Regulatory Statutes	Penal codes are state and federal statutes that define many crimes. Criminal conduct also is defined in many *regulatory statutes.*
Parties to a Criminal Lawsuit	1. *Plaintiff:* the government, which is represented by the *prosecuting attorney (or prosecutor).* 2. *Defendant:* the person or business accused of the crime, who is represented by a *defense attorney.*
Classification of Crimes	1. *Felonies:* the most serious kinds of crimes; *mala in se* (inherently evil); usually punishable by imprisonment. 2. *Misdemeanors:* less serious crimes; *mala prohibita* (prohibited by society); usually punishable by fine and/or imprisonment for less than one year. 3. *Violations:* not a felony or a misdemeanor; generally punishable by a fine.
Elements of a Crime	1. *Actus reas:* guilty act 2. *Mens rea:* evil intent

Criminal Procedure and Process

Pretrial Criminal Procedure	1. *Arrest:* The person is arrested pursuant to an *arrest warrant* based upon a showing of *probable cause,* or, where permitted, by a *warrentless* arrest. 2. *Indictment or information:* Grand juries issue *indictments;* magistrates (judges) issue *informations.* These formally charge the accused with specific crimes. 3. *Arraignment:* The accused is informed of the charges against him or her and enters a *plea* in court. The plea may be *not guilty, guilty,* or *nolo contendere.* 4. *Plea bargaining:* The government and the accused may negotiate a settlement agreement wherein the accused agrees to admit to a lesser crime than charged.

Criminal Trial

Outcomes	1. *Conviction:* requires unanimous vote of jury 2. *Innocent:* requires unanimous vote of jury 3. *Hung jury:* nonunanimous vote of the jury; the government may prosecute the case again
Appeal	1. *Defendant:* may appeal his or her conviction 2. *Plaintiff (government):* may not appeal a verdict of innocent

Common Crimes

Robbery	Robbery is the taking of personal property from another by fear or force.
Burglary	Burglary is the unauthorized entering of a building to commit a felony.
Larceny	Larceny is the wrongful taking of another's property other than from his or her person or building.

Crimes Against the Person

	Theft: the wrongful taking of another's property, whether by robbery, burglary, or larceny. *Receiving stolen property:* a person knowingly receiving stolen property with the intent to deprive the rightful owner of that property. *Arson:* the malicious and willful burning of another's building. *Forgery:* fraudulent making or altering of a written document that affects the legal liability of another person. *Extortion:* threat to expose something about another person unless that person gives up money or property. *Credit-card crimes:* the misappropriation or use of another person's credit card. *Bad-checks:* the making, drawing, or delivery of a check by a person when that person knows that there are insufficient funds in the account to cover the check.

White-Collar Crimes

Definition	White-collar crimes are those that are prone to be committed by businesspersons and involve cunning and trickery rather than physical force.
Embezzlement	Embezzlement is the fraudulent conversion of property by a person to whom the property was entrusted.
Criminal Fraud	Criminal fraud involves obtaining title to another's property through deception or trickery. Also called *false pretenses* or *deceit*.
Mail Fraud	Mail fraud is the use of mail to defraud another person.
Wire Fraud	Wire fraud is the use of wire (telephone or telegraph) to defraud another person.
Bribery	Bribery is the offer of payment of money or property or something else of value in return for an unwarranted favor. The payor of a bribe also is guilty of the crime of bribery. 1. *Commercial bribery* is the offer of a payment of a bribe to a private person or a business. This often is referred to as a *kickback* or *payoff*. 2. Bribery of a public official for an "official act" is a crime.
Cyber Identify Fraud	Cyber identity fraud is using computers, the Internet and other means to obtain and use another's credit cards, bank accounts, social security numbers, and such to commit fraud.
Identity Theft and Assumption Deterrence Act	Identity Theft and Assumption Deterrence Act of 1998 is a federal statute that makes identity fraud a federal crime and provides for prison sentences for violating the Act.
Foreign Corrupt Practices Act	A federal statute that makes it illegal for U.S. companies, or their officers, directors, agents, or employees, to bribe a foreign official or foreign political party official to influence the awarding of new business or the retention of continuous business activity.
Racketeer Influenced and Corrupt Organizations Act (RICO)	RICO makes it a federal crime to acquire or maintain an interest in, use income from, or conduct or participate in the affairs of an "enterprise" through a "pattern" of "racketeering activity." Criminal penalties include the *forfeiture* of any property or business interests gained by a RICO violation.

Inchoate Crimes

Definition	Inchoate crimes are crimes that are incomplete or are committed by nonparticipants.

Criminal Conspiracy	A criminal conspiracy consists of two or more persons entering into an *agreement* to commit a crime and taking some *overt act* to further the crime.
Money Laundering Control Act	A federal statute that makes money laundering a federal crime.
Attempt to Commit a Crime	The attempt to commit a crime is a crime even if the commission of the intended crime is unsuccessful.
Aiding and Abetting the Commission of a Crime	Aiding and abetting refer to rendering support, assistance, or encouragement to the commission of a crime, or knowingly harboring a criminal after he or she has committed a crime.

Constitutional Safeguards

Fourth Amendment Protection Against Unreasonable Searches and Seizures	The Fourth Amendment protects persons and corporations from *unreasonable searches and seizures*.
	1. *Reasonable searches and seizures* based on *probable cause* are lawful:
	  a. *Search warrant*: stipulates the place and scope of the search
	  b. *Warrantless search*: permitted only:
	    i. incident to an arrest
	    ii. where evidence is in plain view
	    iii. where it is likely that evidence will be destroyed
	2. *Exclusionary rule*: states that evidence obtained from an unreasonable search and seizure is *tainted evidence* that may not be introduced at a government proceeding against the person searched.
	3. *Business premises*: protected by the Fourth Amendment, except that certain *regulated industries* may be subject to warrantless searches authorized by statute.

Fifth Amendment Privilege Against Self-Incrimination	The Fifth Amendment provides that no person "shall be compelled in any criminal case to be a witness against himself." A person asserting this privilege is said to have "taken the Fifth."
	1. *Nontestimonial evidence*: evidence (e.g., fingerprints, body fluids, etc.) that is not protected.
	2. *Businesses*: a privilege that applies only to natural persons; business cannot assert the privilege.
	3. *Miranda rights*: a right of a criminal suspect to be informed of his or her Fifth Amendment rights before the suspect can be interrogated by the police or government officials.
	5. *Immunity from prosecution*: granted by the government to obtain otherwise privileged evidence; the government agrees not to use the evidence given against the person who gave it.
	6. *Attorney client privilege*: An accused's lawyer cannot be called as a witness against the accused.
	7. *Other privileges*: The following privileges have been recognized, with some limitations:
	  a. psychiatrist/psychologist–patient
	  b. priest/minister/rabbi–penitent
	  c. spouse–spouse: parent–child
	8. *Accountant–client privilege*: None recognized at the federal level. Some states recognize this privilege in state law actions.

Fifth Amendment Protection Against Double Jeopardy	The Fifth Amendment protects persons from being tried twice by the same jurisdiction for the same crime. If the act violates the laws of two or more jurisdictions, each jurisdiction may try the accused.

Sixth Amendment Right to a Public Jury Trial	The Sixth Amendment guarantees criminal defendants the following rights: 1. to be tried by an impartial jury 2. to confront the witness 3. to have the assistance of a lawyer 4. to have a speedy trial (Speedy Trial Law)
Eighth Amendment Protection Against Cruel and Unusual Punishment	The Eighth Amendment protects criminal defendants from cruel and unusual punishment. Capital punishment is permitted.

▶WORKING THE WEB

1. Using **http://www.google.com/html**, or similar Internet search engine, or using a legal Internet search service such as Westlaw or LexisNexis, find the Penal Code of your state. Find and describe the elements of and difference between the types of murder (e.g., first degree murder, second degree murder) in your state.

2. Go to the website **http://consumer.gov/idtheft/html**. Find the definition of the e-scam "phishing." Write a description of phishing. Is it a crime?

3. Visit the website **http://www.usdoj.gov/html**. Browse this website of the U.S. Department of Justice. Find a crime that the Department of Justice is investigating currently. Write a one-page report describing this crime.

4. Using **http://www.google.com**, or similar Internet search engine, or using a legal Internet search service such as Westlaw or LexisNexis, find your state's jury instruction for the crime of bribery. Print out this jury instruction.

5. Visit the website **http://www.ussc.gov/html**. Write a two-page report answering the following questions: What are federal sentencing guidelines? How did the U.S. Supreme Court's decision in *United States v. Booker* [543 U.S. 220, 125 S.Ct. 738, 160 L.Ed.2d 621, 2005 U.S. Lexis 628 (2005)] affect federal sentencing guidelines?

▶CRITICAL THINKING AND WRITING QUESTIONS

1. Define a crime. Who are the parties to a criminal action?

2. What is a penal code? Give an example of a crime defined by the penal code. What types of crimes are prohibited by regulatory statutes? Give an example of such a crime.

3. Describe the difference between the following classifications of crimes: felonies, misdemeanors, violations.

4. Define *actus reus*. Define *mens rea*. What is a non-intent crime? Give an example.

5. What are the differences between a criminal law and civil law? What is the jury vote required for each? What is the standard of proof required for each?

6. Define and explain the following: indictment, information, arraignment, plea bargain.

7. Define the following common crimes: (a) robbery, (b) burglary, (c) larceny, and (d) receiving stolen property.

8. Describe each of the following crimes: (a) forgery, (b) extortion, (c) bribery, and (d) embezzlement.

9. Define criminal fraud. What is mail fraud? What is wire fraud?

10. Describe the crime made unlawful by the Identity Theft and Assumption Deterrence Act.

11. Describe the crime made unlawful by the Foreign Corrupt Practices Act. Give an example.

12. Describe the crime made unlawful by the Racketeer Influenced and Corrupt Practices Act (RICO). Give an example.

13. Describe the crime made unlawful by the Money Laundering Control Act. Give an example of money laundering.

14. Explain the following inchoate crimes: (1) criminal conspiracy, (2) attempt to commit a crime, and (3) aiding and abetting the commission of a crime.

15. Describe corporate criminal liability.

16. What does the Fourth Amendment's protection against unreasonable search and seizure provide? What is required for there to be a reasonable search and seizure? What is a search warrant? What is unreasonable search and seizure? Explain the exclusionary rule.

17. What does the Fifth Amendment privilege against self-incrimination provide? Describe the *Miranda* rights. Describe the attorney–client privilege. What is immunity from prosecution?

18. Explain the Fifth Amendment's protection against double jeopardy.
19. Explain the Sixth Amendment's right to a public jury trial.
20. Explain the Eighth Amendment's protection against cruel and unusual punishment.
21. Explain the main provisions of the federal Antiterrorism Act.

ETHICS ANALYSIS AND DISCUSSION QUESTIONS

1. Is the information given to a paralegal by a criminal client covered under the Fifth Amendment when he or she interviews a criminal?
2. What obligation does a paralegal have to make available exculpatory evidence discovered during the investigation of a case?
3. You are working at a firm with a large client base that does not speak English. You are fluent in three languages, and you are asked to translate for a firm attorney during an interview of a client in a criminal case. You take notes as you translate to be sure you are translating what is said properly [*Von Bulow by Auersperg v. Von Bulow*, 811 F. 2nd 136 1987 U.S. App. Lexis 2048 (2nd Cir. 1987)] Are the notes covered under the work product doctrine? Does the attorney–client privilege apply to what you heard?

DEVELOPING YOUR COLLABORATION SKILLS

Working on your own or with a group of other students assigned by your instructor, review the scenario at the beginning of the chapter. As a group, discuss the following questions.

1. What is criminal conspiracy? Is the defendant Mr. Day guilty of conspiracy if the allegations against him are proven in court?

2. What is criminal fraud? What are the elements of criminal fraud? If the allegations in the complaint are proved, is Mr. Day guilty of the crime of fraud?
3. What other types of fraud could Mr. Day have committed? Explain.
4. Define the crime of racketeering. If the facts alleged are true, is Mr. Day guilty of this crime?

PARALEGAL PORTFOLIO EXERCISE

Prepare a memorandum, no longer than three pages, that discusses the criminal procedure for initiating a federal criminal case against a defendant in the U.S. District Court that serves the city in which your paralegal program is located.

LEGAL ANALYSIS AND WRITING CASES

Atwater v. Lago Vista, Texas

532 U.S. 318, 121 S.Ct. 1536, 149 L.Ed.2d 549 (2001)
Supreme Court of the United States

FACTS

Texas law requires that front-seat drivers and passengers wear seatbelts and that a driver secure any small child riding in front: In March 1997, Gail Atwater was driving her pickup truck in Lago Vista, Texas, with her three-year-old son and five-year-old daughter in the front seat. None were wearing seatbelts. Bart Turek, a Lago Vista police officer, observed the seatbelt violation and pulled Atwater over. A friend of Atwater's arrived at the scene and took charge of the children. Turek handcuffed Atwater, placed her in his squad car, and drove her to the police station. Atwater was booked, her mug shot was taken, and she was placed in a jail cell for about one hour until she was released on $310 bond.

Atwater ultimately pleaded no contest to the misdemeanor seatbelt offenses and paid a $50 fine. Atwater sued the City of Lago Vista and the police officer for compensatory and punitive damages for allegedly violating her Fourth Amendment right to be free from unreasonable seizure. The District Court ruled against Atwater, and the Court of Appeals affirmed. The U.S. Supreme Court granted certiorari to hear the appeal

Question

1. Does the Fourth Amendment permit police to make a warrantless arrest pursuant to a minor criminal offense?

City of Indianapolis v. Edmond

531 U.S. 32, 121 S.Ct. 447, 148 L.Ed.2d 333 (2000)
Supreme Court of the United States

FACTS

In August 1998, the police of the city of Indianapolis, Indiana, began to operate vehicle roadblock checkpoints on Indianapolis roads in an effort to interdict unlawful drugs. Once a car had been stopped, police questioned the driver and passengers and conducted an open-view examination of the vehicle from the outside. A narcotics-detection dog walked around outside each vehicle. The police conducted a search and seizure of the occupants and vehicle only if suspicion developed from the initial investigation. The overall "hit rate" of the program was approximately 9 percent.

James Edmond and Joel Palmer, each attorneys who had been stopped at one of Indianapolis's checkpoints, filed a lawsuit on behalf of themselves and the class of all motorists who had been stopped or were subject to being stopped at such checkpoints. They claimed that the roadblocks violated the Fourth Amendment to the Constitution. The District Court found for Indianapolis, but the Court of Appeals reversed. The U.S. Supreme Court granted certiorari to hear the appeal.

Question

1. Does Indianapolis's highway checkpoint program, whereby police, without individualized suspicion, stop vehicles for the primary purpose of discovering and interdicting illegal narcotics, violate the Fourth Amendment to the U.S. Constitution?

People v. Paulson

216 Cal.App.3d 1480, 265 Cal.Rptr. 579 1990 Cal. App. Lexis 10 (Cal.App. 1990)

FACTS

Lee Stuart Paulson owns the liquor license for "My House," a bar in San Francisco. The California Department of Alcoholic Beverage Control is the administrative agency that regulates bars in that state. The California Business and Professions Code, which the department administers, prohibits "any kind of illegal activity on licensed premises."

On February 11, 1988, an anonymous informer tipped the Department that narcotic sales were occurring on the premises of "My House" and that the narcotics were kept in a safe behind the bar on the premises.

A special department investigator entered the bar during its hours of operation, identified himself, and informed Paulson that he was conducting an inspection. The investigator, who did not have a search warrant, opened the safe without seeking Paulson's consent. Twenty-two bundles of cocaine, totaling 5.5 grams, were found in the safe. Paulson was arrested. At his criminal trial, Paulson challenged the lawfulness of the search.

Question

1. Was the warrantless search of the safe a lawful search?

Kyllo v. United States

533 U.S. 27, 121 S.Ct. 2038, 150 L.Ed.2d 94 Supreme Court of the United States

FACTS

In 1992, government agents suspected that marijuana was being grown in the home of Danny Kyllo, part of a triplex building in Florence, Oregon. Indoor marijuana growth typically requires high-intensity lamps. To determine whether an amount of heat was emanating from Kyllo's home consistent with the use of such lamps, federal agents used a thermal imager to scan the triplex. Thermal imagers detect infrared radiation and produce images of the radiation. The scan of Kyllo's home, which was performed from an automobile on the street, showed that the roof over the garage and a side wall of Kyllo's home were "hot." The federal agents concluded that Kyllo was using halide lights to grow marijuana in his house. The agents used this scanning evidence to obtain a search warrant authorizing a search of Kyllo's home. During the search, the agents found an indoor growing operation involving more than 100 marijuana plants.

Kyllo was indicted for manufacturing marijuana, a violation of federal criminal law. Kyllo moved to suppress the imaging evidence and the evidence it led to, arguing that it was an unreasonable search that violated the Fourth Amendment to the U.S. Constitution. The trial court disagreed with Kyllo and let the evidence be introduced and considered at trial. Kyllo then entered a conditional guilty plea and appealed the trial court's failure to suppress the challenged evidence. The court of appeals affirmed. The U.S. Supreme Court granted *certiorari* to hear the appeal.

Question

1. Is the use of a thermal-imaging device aimed at a private home from a public street to detect relative amounts of heat within the home a "search" within the meaning of the Fourth Amendment?

Center Art Galleries—Hawaii, Inc. v. United States

875 F.2d 747 1989 U.S. App. Lexis 6983 (9th Cir. 1989)

FACTS

The Center Art Galleries—Hawaii sells artwork. Approximately 20 percent of its business involves art by Salvador Dali. The federal government, which suspected the center of fraudulently selling forged Dali artwork, obtained identical search warrants for six locations controlled by the center. The warrants commanded the executing officer to seize items that were "evidence of violations of federal criminal law." The warrants did not describe the specific crimes suspected and did not stipulate that only items pertaining to the sale of Dali's work could be seized. There was no evidence of any criminal activity unrelated to that artist.

Question

1. Is the search warrant valid?

United States v. John Doe

465 U.S. 605, 104 S.Ct. 1237, 79 L.Ed.2d 552 1984 U.S. Lexis 169 (1984)

FACTS

John Doe is the owner of several sole-proprietorship businesses. In 1980, during the course of an investigation of corruption in awarding county and municipal contracts, a federal grand jury served several subpoenas on John Doe, demanding the production of certain business records. The subpoenas demanded the production of the following records: (1) general ledgers and journals, (2) invoices, (3) bank statements and canceled checks, (4) financial statements, (5) telephone-company records, (6) safe-deposit box records, and (7) copies of tax returns.

John Doe filed a motion in federal court seeking to quash the subpoenas, alleging that producing these business records would violate his Fifth Amendment privilege of not testifying against himself.

Question

1. Do the records have to be disclosed?

People v. Shaw

10 Cal.App.4th 969, 12 Cal Rptr.2d 665 1992 Cal.App. Lexis 1256 (Cal. App. 1992)

FACTS

In 1979, Leo Shaw, an attorney, entered into a partnership agreement with three other persons to build and operate an office building. From the outset, it was agreed that Shaw's role was to manage the operation of the building. Management of the property was Shaw's contribution to the partnership; the other three partners contributed the necessary capital.

In January 1989, the other partners discovered that the loan on the building was in default and that foreclosure proceedings were imminent. Upon investigation, they discovered that Shaw had taken approximately $80,000 from the partnership's checking account. After heated discussions, Shaw repaid $13,000. In May 1989, when no further payment was forthcoming, a partner filed a civil suit against Shaw and notified the police. The state filed a criminal complaint against Shaw on March 15, 1990. On April 3, 1990, Shaw repaid the remaining funds as part of a civil settlement.

At his criminal trial in November 1990, Shaw argued that the repayment of the money was a defense to the crime of embezzlement.

Question

1. Did Shaw act ethically in this case? Would your answer be different if he had really only "borrowed" the money and had intended to return it?

▶ WORKING WITH THE LANGUAGE OF THE COURT CASE

Department of Justice v. Landano

508 U.S. 165, 113 S.Ct. 2014, 124 L.Ed.2d 84, 1993 U.S. Lexis 3727 (1993) Supreme Court of the United States

Read the following case, excerpted from the U.S. Supreme Court's opinion. Review and brief the case. In your brief, answer the following questions:

1. Under what circumstances may a defendant obtain information under the Freedom of Information Act (FOIA)?
2. When may the government in a criminal case refuse to divulge information under the FOIA?
3. Is all information provided to the Federal Bureau of Investigation confidential and therefore not available under the FOIA?
4. Who has the burden of proof in FOIA cases?

O'Connor, J., delivered the opinion for a unanimous Court

Exemption 7(D) of the Freedom of Information Act, 5 U.S.C. Section 552 (FOIA), exempts from disclosure agency records "compiled for law enforcement purposes by criminal law enforcement authority in the course of a criminal investigation" if release of those records "could reasonably be expected to disclose" the identity of or information provided by a "confidential source" [Section 552(b)(7)(D)]. This case concerns the evidentiary showing that the Government must make to establish that a source is "confidential" within the meaning of Exemption 7(D). We are asked to decide whether the Government is entitled to a presumption that all sources supplying information to the Federal Bureau of Investigation (FBI or Bureau) in the course of a criminal investigation are confidential sources.

Respondent Vincent Landano was convicted in New Jersey state court for murdering Newark, New Jersey, police officer John Snow in the course of a robbery. The crime received considerable media attention. Evidence at trial showed that the robbery had been orchestrated by Victor Forni and a motorcycle gang known as "the Breed." There was testimony that Landano, though not a Breed member, had been recruited for the job. Landano always has maintained that he did not participate in the robbery, and that Forni, not he, killed Officer Snow. He contends that the prosecution withheld material exculpatory evidence in violation of *Brady v. Maryland*, 373 U.S. 83 (1963).

Landano apparently is currently pursuing a Brady claim in the state courts. Seeking evidence to support that claim, Landano filed FOIA requests with the FBI for information that the Bureau had compiled in the course of its involvement in the investigation of Officer Snow's murder. Landano sought release of the Bureau's files on both Officer Snow and Forni. The FBI released several hundred pages of documents. The Bureau redacted some of these, however, and withheld several hundred other pages altogether.

The information withheld under Exemption 7(D) included information provided by five types of sources: regular FBI informants; individual witnesses who were not regular informants; state and local law enforcement agencies; other local agencies; and private financial and commercial institutions. In the Government's view, all such sources should be presumed confidential. The deleted portions of the files were coded to indicate which type of source each involved.

Relying on legislative history, the court stated that a source is confidential within the meaning of Exemption 7(D) if the source received an explicit assurance of confidentiality or if there are circumstances "from which such an assurance could reasonably be inferred." An "assurance of confidentiality," the court said, is not a promise of absolute anonymity or secrecy, but "an assurance that the FBI would not directly or indirectly disclose the cooperation of the interviewee with the investigation unless such a disclosure is determined by the FBI to be important to the success of its law enforcement objective."

Exemption 7(D) permits the Government to withhold "records or information compiled for law enforcement purposes, but only to the extent that the production of such law enforcement records or information . . . could reasonably be expected to disclose the identity of a confidential source, including a state, local, or foreign agency or authority or any private institution which furnished information on a confidential basis, and, in the case of a record or information compiled by criminal law enforcement authority in the course of a criminal investigation, information furnished by a confidential source" [§ 552(b)(7)(D)]. The Government bears the burden of establishing that the exemption applies.

When FOIA was enacted in 1966, Exemption 7 broadly protected "'investigatory files compiled for law enforcement purposes except to the extent available by law to a private party.'" Congress adopted the current version of Exemption 7(D) in 1986. The 1986 amendment expanded "records" to "records or information," replaced the word "would" with the phrase "could reasonably be expected to," deleted the word "only" from before "confidential source," and clarified that a confidential source could be a state, local, or foreign agency or a private institution.

Under Exemption 7(D), the question is not whether the requested document is of the type that the agency usually treats as confidential, but whether the particular source spoke with an understanding that the communication would remain confidential. According to the Conference Report on the 1974 amendment, a source is confidential within the meaning of Exemption 7(D) if the source provided information under an express assurance of confidentiality or in circumstances from which such an assurance could be reasonably inferred. In this case, the Government has not attempted to demonstrate that the FBI made explicit promises of confidentiality to particular sources. That sort of proof apparently often is not possible: The FBI does not have a policy of discussing confidentiality with every source, and when such discussions do occur, agents do not always document them.

The precise question before us, then, is how the Government can meet its burden of showing that a source provided information on an implied assurance of confidentiality. The parties dispute two issues: the meaning of the word "confidential," and whether, absent specific evidence to the contrary, an implied assurance of confidentiality always can be inferred from the fact that a source cooperated with the FBI during a criminal investigation.

FOIA does not define the word "confidential." In common usage, confidentiality is not limited to complete anonymity or secrecy. A statement can be made "in confidence" even if the speaker knows the communication will be shared with limited others, as long as the speaker expects that the information will not be published indiscriminately. A promise of complete secrecy would mean that the FBI agent receiving the source's information could not share it even with other FBI personnel. Such information, of course, would be of little use to the Bureau.

We assume that Congress was aware of the Government's disclosure obligations under Brady and applicable procedural rules when it adopted Exemption 7(D). Congress also must have realized that some FBI witnesses would testify at trial. We therefore agree with the Court of Appeals that the word "confidential," as used in Exemption 7(D), refers to a degree of confidentiality less than total secrecy. A source should be deemed confidential if the source furnished information with the understanding that the FBI would not divulge the communication except to the extent the Bureau thought necessary for law enforcement purposes.

Considerations of "fairness" also counsel against the Government's rule. The Government acknowledges that its proposed presumption, though rebuttable in theory, is in practice all but irrebuttable. Once the FBI asserts that information was provided by a confidential source during a criminal investigation, the requester—who has no knowledge about the particular source or the information being withheld—very rarely will be in a position to offer persuasive evidence that the source in fact had no interest in confidentiality.

We agree with the Government that, when certain circumstances characteristically support an inference of confidentiality, the Government similarly should be able to claim exemption under Exemption 7(D) without detailing the circumstances surrounding a particular interview. Neither the language of Exemption 7(D) nor Reporters Committee, Page 178, however, supports the proposition that the category of all FBI criminal investigative sources is exempt.

But Congress did not expressly create a blanket exemption for the FBI; the language that it adopted requires every agency to establish that a confidential source furnished the information sought to be withheld under Exemption 7(D). In short, the Government offers no persuasive evidence that Congress intended for the Bureau to be able to satisfy its burden in every instance simply by asserting that a source communicated with the Bureau during the course of a criminal investigation. Had Congress meant to create such a rule, it could have done so much more clearly.

The Government has argued forcefully that its ability to maintain the confidentiality of all of its sources is vital to effective law enforcement. A prophylactic rule protecting the identities of all FBI criminal investigative sources undoubtedly would serve the Government's objectives, and would be simple for the Bureau and the courts to administer. But we are not free to engraft that policy choice onto the statute that Congress passed. For the reasons we have discussed, and consistent with our obligation to construe FOIA exemptions narrowly in favor of disclosure, we hold that the Government is not entitled to a presumption that a source is confidential within the meaning of Exemption 7(D) whenever the source provides information to the FBI in the course of a criminal investigation.

More narrowly defined circumstances, however, can provide a basis for inferring confidentiality. For example, when circumstances such as the nature of the crime investigated and the witness' relation to it support an inference of confidentiality, the Government is entitled to a presumption. In this case, the Court of Appeals incorrectly concluded that it lacked discretion to rely on such circumstances. Accordingly, we vacate the judgment of the Court of Appeals and remand the case for further proceedings consistent with this opinion. It is so ordered. ■

CYBER LAW AND INTELLECTUAL PROPERTY

"The Congress shall have the power . . .
to promote the Progress of Science and
useful Arts, by securing for limited Times
to Authors and Inventors the exclusive
Right to their respective Writings and
Discoveries."

Article 1, Section 8, Clause 8,
U.S. Constitution

PARALEGALS AT WORK

You are a paralegal for a boutique law firm that specializes in intellectual property and Internet law. The lawyers of the firm are known for their expertise in this area of the law. As a paralegal, you often work for different partners of the law firm, depending upon the needs of the firm.

One day, Ms. Maria Rodriquez, an intellectual property lawyer and partner at the firm, calls you into her office. Waiting in the office is a client, Mr. Geek Einstein. Ms. Rodriquez introduces you to Mr. Einstein and asks you to sit in on a meeting between them. Ms. Rodriquez cautions you that everything said is highly confidential.

Mr. Einstein goes on to explain that he has invented a new digital basketball shoe that will allow wearers of the shoe to jump at least 8 inches higher in the air than if they wore competing nondigital basketball shoes. Mr. Einstein describes his digital technology that, if imbedded in a shoe, allows a user to jump this high. Mr. Einstein goes on to explain that he believes no such digital technology exists, and that he is the first inventor of this technology.

Further, Mr. Einstein explains that he has determined a name he would like to call the basketball shoe—"Einstein+2". He also shows you a design he has drawn that he wants to be used as the logo for the shoe. The logo is an "E" with an "2" superimposed over it, using script writing. He also tells you that he has a new slogan—"Plus 2"—for the advertising campaign for the shoe.

Mr. Einstein shows you a ten-page *User's Manual* he has written that is to be inserted into each shoebox explaining how to use his new digital basketball shoe. In addition, Mr. Einstein explains that he would like to sell the shoe not only in stores but also over the Internet, using the website name "Einstein+2."

Consider the issues involved in this scenario as you read the chapter.

After studying this chapter, you should be able to:

1. Describe the business tort of misappropriating a trade secret.
2. Describe how an invention can be patented under patent laws and the penalties for patent infringement.
3. List the writings and other works that can be copyrighted, and describe the penalties for copyright infringement.
4. Describe the legal rights that computer and software designers have in their works.
5. Define *trademarks* and *service marks*, and describe the penalties for trademark infringement.
6. Explain the process for obtaining Internet domain names.
7. Describe the protections provided by the federal Anticybersquatting Act.

▶INTRODUCTION FOR THE PARALEGAL

Often, a paralegal will work in an area of the law that requires a unique and special expertise of statutory law. One of these areas is cyber law and intellectual property. Many boutique law firms or departments in large law firms specialize in intellectual property areas that involve patents, copyrights, trademarks, trade secrets, domain names, e-commerce, and Internet law. A paralegal who works for lawyers in these areas must have knowledge of the major statutes, cases, and issues of these law subjects.

The American economy is based on the freedom of ownership of property. In addition to real estate and personal property, intellectual property rights have value to both businesses and individuals. This is particularly the case in the modern Information Age, computers, and the Internet.

Trade secrets form the basis of many successful businesses, which are protected from misappropriation. Federal law provides protections for intellectual property rights, such as patents, copyrights, and trademarks. In addition, businesses and individuals may register domain names to use on the Internet. Anyone who infringes on these rights may be stopped from doing so and is liable for damages. Computers and computer software are accorded special protections from infringement.

Intellectual property rights and cyber law are two of the most important developing areas of the law. United States inventors and companies own valuable **intellectual property**—patents, trademarks, and copyrights—that are licensed worldwide. In addition, the area of Internet law, e-commerce, and domain names is exploding in use. Therefore, a paralegal has to acquire knowledge of these important areas of the law to conduct patent searches, do research in the areas of intellectual property rights and cyber law, and help prepare documents for the creation and transfer of intellectual property and the use of e-commerce contracts. His chapter covers trade secrets, patents, copyrights, trademarks, domain names, and cyber law. ■

TRADE SECRETS

Trade secret
A product formula, pattern, design, compilation of data, customer list, or other business secret.

Many businesses are successful because their **trade secrets** set them apart from their competitors. Trade secrets may be product formulas, patterns, designs, compilations of data, customer lists, or other business secrets. Many trade secrets either do not qualify to be—or simply are not—patented, copyrighted, or trademarked. Many states have adopted the Uniform Trade Secrets Act to give statutory protection to trade secrets.

State unfair competition laws allow the owner of a trade secret to bring a lawsuit for **misappropriation** against anyone who steals a trade secret. To be actionable, the defendant (often an employee of the owner or a competitor) must have obtained the trade secret through unlawful means such as theft, bribery, or industrial espionage. No tort has occurred if there is no misappropriation. For example, a competitor can lawfully discover a trade secret by performing reverse engineering (i.e., taking apart and examining a rival's product).

The owner of a trade secret is obliged to take all reasonable precautions to prevent others from discovering that secret. These precautions include fencing in buildings, placing locks on doors, hiring security guards, and the like. If the owner fails to take such actions, the secret is no longer subject to protection under state unfair competition laws.

Generally, a successful plaintiff in a trade secret action can:

1. recover the profits made by the offender from the use of the trade secret,
2. recover for damages, and
3. obtain an injunction prohibiting the offender from divulging or using the trade secret.

ECONOMIC ESPIONAGE ACT

Until recently—although stealing trade secrets exposes the offender to a civil lawsuit by the injured party to recover economic damages—the offender seldom faced criminal charges except under a few state laws. All of that changed with enactment of the federal **Economic Espionage Act** of 1996 [18 U.S.C. Sections 1831–1839], which makes it a federal crime to steal another's trade secrets.

Under the Espionage Act, it is a federal crime for any person to convert a trade secret to his or her benefit or for the benefit of others, knowing or intending that the Act would cause injury to the owner of the trade secret. Under the Espionage Act, the definition of *trade secret* is broad and covers any economic, business, financial, technical, scientific, or engineering information, including processes, software programs, and codes.

One of the major reasons for passing the Espionage Act was to address the ease of stealing trade secrets through espionage and using the Internet. For example, hundreds of pages of confidential information can be downloaded onto a small computer diskette, placed in someone's pocket, and taken from the legal owner. In addition, computer hackers can crack into a company's computers and steal customer lists, databases, formulas, and other trade secrets. The Espionage Act adds an important weapon to address and penalize computer and Internet espionage.

The Espionage Act provides for severe criminal penalties. An organization can be fined up to $5 million per criminal act. The Act imposes prison terms on individuals of up to 15 years per criminal violation.

PATENTS

Pursuant to the express authority granted in the U.S. Constitution [Article I, Section 8, clause 8, Congress enacted the **Federal Patent Statute** of 1952 [35 U.S.C. Sections 10 et seq.]. This law is intended to provide an incentive for inventors to invent and make their inventions public and to protect patented inventions from infringement. Federal patent law is exclusive; there are no state patent laws. The United States Court of Appeals for the Federal Circuit in Washington, D.C., was created in 1982 to hear patent appeals. The court was established to promote uniformity in patent law.

Federal Patent Statute
A federal statute that establishes the requirements for obtaining a patent and protects patented inventions from infringement.

Patenting an Invention

For an inventor to be granted a **patent**, a patent application must be filed with the **United States Patent and Trademark Office**. To be patented, the **invention** must be *novel*, *useful*, and *nonobvious*. In addition, only certain subject matters can be patented. Patentable subject matter includes (1) machines, (2) processes, (3) compositions of matter, (4) improvements to existing machines, processes, or compositions of matter, (5) designs for an article of manufacture, (6) asexually reproduced plants, and (7) living material invented by a person. Abstractions and scientific principles cannot be patented unless they are part of the tangible environment. For example, Einstein's theory of relativity ($E = MC^2$) cannot be patented.

Patent applicants must file a **patent application** containing a written description of the invention with the United States Patent and Trademark Office in Washington, D.C. If a patent is granted, the invention is assigned a patent number. Patent holders usually affix the word *Patent* or *Pat.* and the patent number to the patented article. If a patent application is filed but a patent has not yet been issued, the applicant usually places the words **patent pending** on the article. Any party can challenge either the issuance of a patent or the validity of an existing patent.

The patent system added the fuel of interest to the fire of genius.
Abraham Lincoln
Lectures on Discoveries, Inventions, and Improvements (1859)

THE PARALEGAL AND INTELLECTUAL PROPERTY

Paralegals can work in one of the most explosive areas of the law today: intellectual property rights. Lawyers and paralegals both have been able to find excellent positions in this dynamic area of the law, provided, however, that they learn significant knowledge of intellectual property laws and procedures.

Who does not recognize the business names "McDonald's Corporation" or "Microsoft Corporation"? And who does not know the famous phrases, "Diamonds are Forever" or, "Just Do It." These are examples of famous trademarks. Paralegals who work for lawyers that practice in the trademark field must know how to search for available names at the U.S. Patent and Trademark Office, as well as how to complete the necessary documents for obtaining or renewing trademarks.

The copyright area is similar in requiring paralegals who know how to work with copyright lawyers. Copyrights are an extremely important intellectual property right. Movies, books, screenplays, paintings, sculptures, and software can be copyrighted. Therefore, a paralegal must know how the U.S. Copyright Office works, how to check on the availability of proposed names and phrases, and how to complete the documentation for obtaining a copyright.

Of the intellectual property rights areas, the area of patent law is the most complex for lawyers and paralegals alike. Lawyers who practice in this area must pass a separate patent law examination. The determination of whether an invention, drug, biomedicine, or other innovation is patentable, or whether a patent exists on these, requires significant skill and knowledge. Drafting the patent application to be filed with the U.S. Patent and Trademark office is extremely complicated. Paralegals with science, biology, chemistry, engineering, or related education are indispensable in assisting patent lawyers.

A new form of intellectual property has developed with the advent of the Internet and the World Wide Web. Businesses and individuals can now sell and purchase goods and services using the Internet. Cyber law provides that businesses and individuals can operate using Web addresses and domain names. Domain names sometimes are valuable property rights. Many federal and state laws protect business and privacy rights involving the Internet. This area of the law offers paralegals a new avenue in which to apply their skills.

In addition, paralegals support lawyers who are engaged in lawsuits and arbitration proceedings that allege infringement of trademarks, copyrights, patents, or domain names. Paralegals support lawyers involved on both sides of these infringement cases. Therefore, paralegals who provide support in litigation and arbitration of intellectual property rights must know the area of the law involved as well as the procedures, pleadings, documents, discovery, and other issues involved in the dispute.

The area of intellectual property is a growing area of the law for lawyers and paralegals. Paralegals have a great opportunity to join this complex, yet dynamic area of the law.

Changes in Patent Law Mandated by GATT

In 1994, the **General Agreement on Tariffs and Trade (GATT)** established the **World Trade Organization (WTO)**, an international organization of which the United States is a member. GATT's intellectual property provisions, and implementing legislation passed by Congress, made the following important changes in U.S. patent law:

1. Patents are valid for *20 years*, instead of the previous term of 17 years.
2. The patent term begins to run from the date the patent application is *filed* instead of when the patent is issued, as was the case previously.

These changes, which became effective June 8, 1995, brought the U.S. patent system in harmony with the majority of other developed nations. The United States still follows the first-to-invent rule rather than the first-to-file rule that some other countries follow.

American Inventors Protection Act

In 1999, Congress enacted the **American Inventors Protection Act**. This statute, which was a watered-down version of the initial bill that was introduced, still made significant changes in federal patent law. The Act reorganized the U.S. Patent and Trademark Office (PTO) and granted the PTO new regulatory powers. The Act:

- permits an inventor to file a provisional application with the PTO pending the preparation and filing of a final and complete patent application. This part of the law grants "provisional rights" to an inventor for three months pending the filing of a final application.
- requires the PTO to issue a patent within three years after the filing of a patent application unless the applicant engages in dilatory activities.
- provides that non-patent holders may challenge a patent as overly broad by requesting a contested re-examination of the patent application by the PTO. This provides that the reexamination will be within the confines of the PTO; the decision of the PTO can be appealed to the U.S. Court of Appeals for the Federal Circuit in Washington, D.C.

The Act also upgrades the PTO Commissioner to an Assistant Secretary of Commerce with authority to advise the U.S. government on intellectual policy.

Patent Infringement

Patent holders own exclusive rights to use and exploit their patent. **Patent infringement** occurs when someone makes unauthorized use of another's patent. In a suit for patent infringement, a successful plaintiff can recover:

Patent infringement
Unauthorized use of another's patent. A patent holder may recover damages and other remedies against a patent infringer.

1. money damages equal to a reasonable royalty rate on the sale of the infringed articles,
2. other damages caused by the infringement (such as loss of customers),
3. an order requiring the destruction of the infringing article, and
4. an injunction preventing the infringer from such action in the future.

The court has the discretion to award up to treble damages if the infringement was intentional.

Public-Use Doctrine

Under the **public-use doctrine**, a patent may not be granted if the invention was used by the public for more than one year prior to filing of the patent application. This doctrine forces inventors to file their patent applications at the proper time. For example, suppose Cindy Parsons invents a new invention on January 1. She allows the public to use this invention and does not file a patent application until February of the following year. She has lost the right to patent her invention.

COPYRIGHTS

A **copyright** is the exclusive legal right to reproduce, publish, and sell a literary, musical, or artistic work. Congress enacted a federal copyright law pursuant to an express grant of authority in the U.S. Constitution [Article I, Section 8, clause 8]. This law protects the work of authors and other creative persons from the unauthorized use of their copyrighted materials and provides a financial incentive for authors to write, thereby increasing the number of creative works available in society. The **Copyright Revision Act** of 1976 governs copyright law [17 U.S.C. Sections 101 et seq.]. Federal copyright law is exclusive; there are no state copyright laws.

Copyright Revision Act
A federal statute that (1) establishes the requirements for obtaining a copyright and (2) protects copyrighted works from infringement.

INVENTOR WIPES FORD'S AND CHRYSLER'S WINDSHIELDS CLEAN

In 1967, Robert Kearns, a professor at Wayne State University in Detroit, Michigan, patented his design for the electronic intermittent windshield wiper for automobiles and other vehicles. He peddled his invention to many automobile manufacturers but never reached a licensing deal with any of them. In 1969, automobile manufacturers began producing cars with Kearns's invention. Virtually all cars sold in the United States today now have these wipers as standard equipment.

Kearns filed patent infringement lawsuits against Ford in 1978 and Chrysler in 1982. He later filed patent infringement cases against virtually all automobile manufacturers. The Ford case went to trial first. Kearns sought $325 million in damages from Ford. Ford alleged that Kearns's patents were not valid because of obviousness and prior art. The jury disagreed with Ford and decided that Kearns's patents were valid. The jury ordered Ford to pay $5.2 million, plus interest. In 1990, Ford settled by paying Kearns $10.2 million and agreeing to drop all appeals. This represented 50¢ per Ford vehicle that used the wiper system.

Kearns sought $468 million in damages from Chrysler. In that case, Kearns fired his lawyers and represented himself. This was at least the fourth law firm hired and fired in the course of Kearns's patent-infringement lawsuits. Kearns won a second victory: In 1991, the jury found that Chrysler had infringed Kearns's patents and awarded him $11.3 million. The court denied Kearns injunctive relief because his 17-year patents had expired years ago. The Court of Appeals affirmed the judgment, and the U.S. Supreme Court refused to hear Kearns's appeal. Kearns received more than $21 million from Chrysler, which amounted to 90¢ for every vehicle sold by Chrysler with the wiper system.

In 1993 and 1994, courts dismissed Kearns's lawsuits against 23 automobile manufacturers, including General Motors, Porsche, Nissan, Toyota, Honda, and Rolls Royce, among others, because Kearns failed to comply with court orders to disclose documents relevant to the cases. The District Court then ordered Kearns to pay his fired lawyers $6.4 million in contingency fees. Thus ended Kearns's 30-plus-year saga and legal battle with the automobile industry. In an interview Kearns stated, "The patent system is a fraud pure and simple."

PROTECTING A PATENT

Inventors spend years dreaming up new products and inventions, then file an application with the Patent and Trademark Office and wait to see if their patent is granted. The day the patent is issued is a cause for celebration—or is it? Ask Donald BonAsia. The young entrepreneur invented "forkchops"—two eating utensils with chopsticks on one end and a knife and fork on the other end. He spent two years and $7,500 to receive a patent on his invention.

But his worst fear became reality. Other manufacturers began copying his invention and selling them without seeking BonAsia's permission or paying him a royalty fee. BonAsia contacted a patent lawyer and found out the following: The normal cost to pursue a patent-infringement case through trial is $1.5 million, and $1 million if it settles near trial. Attorneys typically want more than $100,000 in retainer fees before filing a patent-infringement case. BonAsia discovered he had a patent but not enough money to protect it. BonAsia's plight is typical for small-time inventors who are under the misconception that a patent gives the holder an exclusive right to make the item. Wrong: What a patent gives the holder is the right to defend the patent and try to stop others from making the patented article.

Berne Convention on Copyright Notice

In 1989, the United States signed the **Berne Convention**. This international convention provides the copyright law that is now followed by most countries of the world. The convention made a major change in U.S. copyright law. Prior to 1989, to protect a copyright in a published work in the United States, the copyright holder had to place a copyright notice on the work, containing the following information:

1. Copyright holder's name
2. A "(c)" or "©" or "Copyright," or "copr."
3. The year the material was copyrighted

Under the Berne Convention, however, notice is not required on works entering the public domain on or after March 1, 1989. Although notice is now permissive, it is recommended that notice be placed on copyrighted works to defeat a defendant's claim of innocent infringement.

Registration of Copyrights

Only **tangible writings**—writings that can be physically seen—are subject to copyright registration and protection. The term *writing* has been defined broadly to include books, periodicals, and newspapers; lectures, sermons, and addresses; musical compositions; plays, motion pictures, radio and television productions; maps; works of art, including paintings, drawings, sculpture, jewelry, glassware, tapestry, and lithographs; architectural drawings and models; photographs, including prints, slides, and filmstrips; greeting cards and picture postcards; photoplays, including feature films, cartoons, newsreels, travelogues, and training films; and sound recordings published in the form of tapes, cassettes, compact disks, and phonograph albums.

To be protected under federal copyright law, the work must be the original work of the author. Published and unpublished works may be copyrighted and registered with the **United States Copyright Office** in Washington, D.C. **Registration** is permissive and voluntary and can be effected at any time during the term of the copyright. Registration itself does not create the copyright.

> The law in respect to literature ought to remain upon the same footing as that which regards the profits of mechanical inventions and chemical discoveries.
>
> William Wordsworth
> *Letter (1838)*

Copyright Term

The Founding Fathers decided to provide copyright protection in the U.S. Constitution when they granted Congress authority to secure for "limited times" to authors the exclusive right to their writings. In 1970, copyright law guaranteed 14 years of protection with a 14-year renewal. The period of protection has been extended several times since, and in 1998 stood at the life of the author plus 50 years. A corporation-owned copyright was good for 75 years from the date of publication, or 100 years from the date of creation, whichever was shorter.

After the copyright period runs out, the work enters the public domain, which means that anyone can publish the work without paying the prior copyright holder. Many small publishers and Internet sites were dedicated to publishing great works—and not-so-great works—once they entered the public domain. These publishers and Internet content providers waited anxiously as popular works such as A. A. Milne's *Winnie the Pooh*, Ernest Hemingway's *Three Stories and Ten Poems*, and the Walt Disney Company's first Mickey Mouse cartoon were set to enter the public domain. Cartoons starring Disney characters such as Donald Duck and Goofy were to follow shortly thereafter.

The Walt Disney Company was driven goofy at the prospect of its leading cartoon characters joining the likes of Santa Claus and Uncle Sam (both created by nineteenth-century cartoonist Thomas Nast) in the public domain. So the long arm of Disney went into action, lobbying Congress for a new copyright law that would increase the length of copyright protection for its characters. Disney, joined by the

MARTIN LUTHER KING, JR.'S "I HAVE A DREAM" SPEECH COPYRIGHTED

Martin Luther King, Jr., was a leader of the Civil Rights movement in the United States until he was shot and killed outside a Memphis, Tennessee, motel in 1968. King left behind a valuable legacy of intellectual property—speeches, letters, books and unpublished manuscripts. The ownership rights to this intellectual property were left to his family—his widow, Coretta Scott King, and their children.

Since King's death, there has been an ongoing conflict between his heirs and some of the media. King's heirs have taken the position that copyright law protects King's intellectual property left to them, whereas some of the media and others argue that because King was such an influential figure in history, his works belong in the public domain.

Under the Copyright Act of 1976, as authorized by Article I, Section 8 of the U.S. Constitution, the right to King's works belongs to his heirs. The Kings license—for a fee— these intellectual property rights. The Kings also protect these intellectual property rights from copyright infringement. For example, the family sued *USA Today* for publishing the entire text of King's most famous speech—"I have a Dream"—without permission.

Copyright law does not restrict the media from publishing works about King and his life, however. Writers can write articles and books about King's life, editors can publish photographs of him, professors can teach courses about him, and producers can make films about King. What they cannot do is use his words without the permission of the King family.

Although some members of the media and the public will continue to criticize the King family for their stand on this issue, copyright law gives King's heirs rights to his intellectual property for 75 years after his death.

American Society of Composers, Authors, and Publishers, and other publishing and entertainment companies, persuaded Congress to pass the **Copyright Term Extension Act of 1998 (CTEA)**. Although not restoring copyright protection to works already in the public domain, the Act added 20 years to existing copyrighted works and works to be copyrighted in the future. The Act grants the following copyright terms to the following copyright holders:

- *Individual copyright holder:* life of the author plus 70 years
- *Corporate copyright holder:* 95 years from the year of first publication or 120 years from the year of creation, whichever is shorter

Proponents assert that the law is good for the country because the United States is the world's leading exporter of intellectual property.

Copyright Infringement

Copyright infringement occurs when a party copies a substantial and material part of the plaintiff's copyrighted work without permission. The copying does not have to be either word-for-word or the entire work. A successful plaintiff can recover:

1. the profit made by the infringer from the copyright infringement,
2. damages suffered by the plaintiff,
3. an order requiring the impoundment and destruction of the infringing works, and
4. an injunction preventing the infringer from doing so in the future.

The court, at its discretion, can award statutory damages ranging from $200 for innocent infringement up to $100,000 for willful infringement in lieu of actual damages.

Copyright infringement
An act in which a party copies a substantial and material part of the plaintiff's copyrighted work without permission. A copyright holder may recover damages and other remedies against the infringer.

COPYRIGHTING SOFTWARE

The advent of new technology challenges the ability of laws to protect it. For example, the invention of computers and the writing of software programs caused problems for existing copyright laws. These laws had to be changed to afford protection to software.

In 1980, Congress enacted the **Computer Software Copyright Act**, which amended the Copyright Act of 1976. The 1980 amendments include computer programs in the list of tangible items protected by copyright law. The amendments define *computer program* broadly as "a set of statements or instructions to be used directly or indirectly in a computer in order to bring about a certain result" [17 U.S.C. Section 101].

A computer program is written first in programming language, which is called a "source code." It then is translated into another language, called an "object code," which is understood by the computer.

In an important decision, *Apple Computer, Inc. v. Franklin Computer Corp.*, 714 F.2d 1240 (3d Cir. 1983), the court held that object codes could be copyrighted. As with other works, the creator of a copyrightable software program obtains automatic copyright protection. The **Judicial Improvement Act of 1990** authorizes the Register of Copyright to accept and record any document pertaining to computer software, and to issue a certificate of recordation to the recorder.

Congress passed the **Semiconductor Chip Protection Act of 1984** to provide greater protection of the hardware components of a computer. This law protects masks that are used to create computer chips. A *mask* is an original layout of software programs that is used to create a semiconductor chip. This Act sometimes is referred to as the "Mask Work Act." Notice on the work is optional but when used must contain (1) the words *Mask Work* or the symbol *M* or (M), and (2) the name of the owner.

Source: [17 U.S.C. §§ 901–914]

ETHICAL *Perspective*

Mr. Frederick Aston, a paralegal, leaves his current employment at the law firm at which he has been working for years, to take a new paralegal position at a new law firm. Upon joining the new law firm, the firm provides Mr. Aston with a list of clients that the firm represents, and a list of the lawsuits and other matters in which the law firm represents clients, including the names of the adversarial party and opposing law firms that represent these clients.

As Mr. Aston reviews the list, he identifies a pending lawsuit where the prior law firm represents a client in a case against a client that is represented by his new law firm. Mr. Ashton worked on that case during his previous employment. Mr. Ashton immediately discloses this conflict of interest to the new law firm.

The *Model Code of Ethics and Professional Responsibility and Guidance for Enforcement* (Model Code) of the National Federation of Paralegal Associations, Inc. (NFPA) provides these professional standards:

EC-1.6(f) A paralegal shall not participate in or conduct work on any matter where a conflict of interest has been identified.

Source: Reprinted by permission from The National Federation of Paralegal Associations, Inc., www.paralegals.org

EC-1.6(g) In matters where a conflict of interest has been identified and the client consents to continued representation, a paralegal shall comply fully with the implementation and maintenance of an Ethical Wall.

Source: Reprinted by permission from The National Federation of Paralegal Associations, Inc., www.paralegals.org

This conflict must be disclosed to the client. If the client consents to still being represented by the law firm, an ethical wall must be established between Mr. Ashton and any proceedings of the case. This ethical wall must be maintained to prevent Mr. Ashton from disclosing any information from his previous employment, as well as to prevent Mr. Ashton from learning anything about the client's current employment with the new law firm.

NET ACT: CRIMINAL COPYRIGHT INFRINGEMENT

A copyright holder owns a valuable right and may sue an infringer in a civil lawsuit to recover damages and obtain injunctions and other remedies for copyright infringement. In 1997, Congress enacted the **No Electronic Theft Act (NET Act),** which criminalizes certain copyright infringement as well.

Congress passed the NET Act to directly criminalize copyright infringement. The NET Act prohibits any person from willfully infringing a copyright for the purpose of commercial advantage or financial gain, or by reproduction or distribution even without commercial advantage or financial gain, including by electronic means, where the retail value of the copyrighted work exceeds $1,000. Criminal penalties for violating the Act include imprisonment for up to one year and fines of up to $100,000.

Fair-Use Doctrine

Fair-use doctrine
A doctrine that permits certain limited use of a copyright by someone other than the copyright holder without the permission of the copyright holder.

The copyright holder's rights in the work are not absolute. The law permits certain limited unauthorized use of copyrighted materials under the **fair-use doctrine**. Protected under this doctrine are:

1. quotation of the copyrighted work for review or criticism or in a scholarly or technical work,
2. use in a parody or satire,
3. brief quotation in a news report,
4. reproduction by a teacher or student of a small part of the work to illustrate a lesson,
5. incidental reproduction of a work in a newsreel or broadcast of an event being reported, and
6. reproduction of a work in a legislative or judicial proceeding.

DIGITAL MILLENNIUM COPYRIGHT ACT

The Internet makes it easier for people to illegally copy and distribute copyrighted works. To combat this, software and entertainment companies developed "wrappers" and encryption technology to protect their copyrighted works from unauthorized access. Not to be outdone, software pirates and other Internet users devised ways to crack these wrappers and protection devices.

Seeing that they were losing the battle, software companies and the entertainment industry lobbied Congress to enact legislation that made illegal the cracking of their wrappers and selling of technology to do so. In 1998, Congress responded by enacting the **Digital Millennium Copyright Act (DMCA)** [17 U.S.C. Section 1201], which does the following:

- Prohibits unauthorized *access* to copyrighted digital works by circumventing the wrapper or encryption technology that protects the intellectual property.
- Prohibits the manufacture and distribution of technologies, products, or services designed primarily for the purpose of circumventing wrappers or encryption protection.

The DMCA imposes civil and criminal penalties. A successful plaintiff in a civil action can recover actual damages from first-time offenders and treble damages from repeat offenders, costs and attorney's fees, an order for the destruction of illegal products and devices, and an injunction against future violations by the offender. The following criminal penalties can be accessed:

- First-time violators can be fined up to $500,000 and imprisoned for up to 5 years.
- Subsequent violators can be fined up to $1 million and imprisoned up to 10 years.

The copyright holder cannot recover for copyright infringement where fair use is found.

TRADEMARKS

Trademark law is intended to (1) protect the owner's investment and goodwill in a **mark**, and (2) prevent consumers from being confused as to the origin of goods and services. In 1946, Congress enacted the **Lanham Trademark Act** to provide federal protection to trademarks, service marks, and other marks [15 U.S.C. Sections 1114 et seq.]. Congress passed the **Trademark Law Revision Act of 1988,** which amended trademark law in several respects. The amendments made it easier to register a trademark but harder to maintain it. States also may enact trademark laws.

Mark
The collective name for trademarks, service marks, certification marks, and collective marks that all can be trademarked.

Lanham Trademark Act
A federal statute that (1) establishes the requirements for obtaining a federal mark, and (2) protects marks from infringement.

Registration of Trademarks

Trademarks are registered with the United States Patent and Trademark Office in Washington, D.C. The original **registration** of a mark is valid for 10 years and can be renewed for an unlimited number of 10-year periods. The registration of a trademark, which is given nationwide effect, serves as constructive notice that the mark is the registrant's personal property. The registrant is entitled to use the registered trade mark symbol ® in connection with a registered trademark or service mark. Use of the symbol is not mandatory. Note that the frequently used notations "TM" and "SM" have no legal significance.

An applicant can register a mark if (1) it was in use in commerce (e.g., actually used in the sale of goods or services), or (2) the applicant verifies a bona fide intention to use the mark in commerce and actually does so within six months of its registration. Failure to do so during this period causes loss of the mark to the registrant. A party other than the registrant can submit an opposition to a proposed registration of a mark or to the cancellation of a previously registered mark.

Distinctiveness of a Mark

To qualify for federal protection, there must be **distinctiveness of a mark** or it must have acquired a **secondary meaning**. For example, a mark such as "Xerox" is *distinctive*. A term such as *English Leather*, which literally means leather processed in England, has taken on a secondary meaning as a trademark for an aftershave lotion. Words that are *descriptive* but have no secondary meaning cannot be trademarked. For example, the word *cola* alone could not be trademarked.

Marks That Can Be Trademarked

The following types of marks can be trademarked:

- *Trademarks.* A **trademark** is a distinctive mark, symbol, name, word, motto, or device that identifies the *goods* of a particular business. For example the words *Xerox, Coca-Cola*, and *IBM* are trademarks.
- *Service marks.* A **service mark** is used to distinguish the *services* of the holder from those of its competitors. Examples of service marks are the trade names *United Airlines, Marriott Hotels*, and *Weight Watchers*.
- *Certification marks.* A **certification mark** is used to verify that goods and services are of a certain quality or originate from specific geographical areas—for example, wines from the "Napa Valley" of California or "Florida" oranges. The owner of the mark usually is a nonprofit corporation that licenses producers that meet certain standards or conditions to use the mark.
- *Collective marks.* A **collective mark** is used by cooperatives, associations, and fraternal organizations. An example is "Boy Scouts of America."

Trademark
A distinctive mark, symbol, name, word, motto, or device that identifies the goods of a particular business.

Service mark
A mark that distinguishes the services of the holder from those of its competitors.

The following marks cannot be registered: (1) the flag or coat of arms of the United States or any state, municipality, or foreign nation, (2) marks that are immoral or scandalous, (3) geographical names standing alone (e.g., "South"), (4) surnames standing alone (note that a surname can be registered if it is accompanied by a picture or fanciful name, such as "Smith Brothers' Cough Drops," and (5) any mark that resembles a mark already registered with the federal Patent and Trademark Office.

Trademark Infringement

Trademark infringement
Unauthorized use of another's mark. The holder may recover damages and other remedies from the infringer.

The owner of a mark can sue a third party for the unauthorized use of a mark. To succeed in a **trademark infringement** case, the owner must prove that (1) the defendant infringed the plaintiff's mark by using it in an unauthorized manner, and (2) such use is likely to cause confusion, mistake, or deception of the public as to the origin of the goods or services. A successful plaintiff can recover:

1. the profits made by the infringer by the unauthorized use of the mark,
2. damages caused to the plaintiff's business and reputation.

checklist ☑ TYPES OF INTELLECTUAL PROPERTY PROTECTED BY FEDERAL LAW

TYPE	SUBJECT MATTER	TERM
• Patent	Inventions (e.g., machines; processes; compositions of matter; designs for articles of manufacture; and improvements to existing machines, processes). Invention must be 1. Novel 2. Useful 3. Nonobvious *Public* use *doctrine:* Patent will not be granted if the invention was used in public for more than one year prior to filing of the patent application.	Patents on articles of manufacture and processes: 20 years: design patents: 14 years.
• Copyright	Tangible writing (e.g., books, magazines, newspapers, lectures, operas, plays, screenplays, musical compositions, maps, works of art, lithographs, photographs, postcards, greeting cards, motion pictures, newsreels, sound recordings, computer programs, and mask works fixed to semiconductor chips). Writing must be the original work of the author. *Fair use doctrine:* It permits use of copyrighted material without consent for limited uses (e.g., scholarly work, parody or satire, and brief quotation in news reports).	Author (individual registrant): life of author plus 70 years. Work for hire (business registrant) for the shorter of either (1) 120 years from the date of creation or (2) 95 years from the date of first publication.
• Trademark	Marks (e.g., name, symbol, word, logo, or device). Marks include trademarks, service marks, certification marks, and collective marks. Mark must be distinctive or have acquired a secondary meaning. *Generic name:* A mark that becomes a common term for a product line or type of service loses its protection under federal trademark law.	Original registration: 10 years. Renewal registration: unlimited number of renewals for 10-year terms.

3. an order requiring the defendant to destroy all goods containing the unauthorized mark, and
4. an injunction preventing the defendant from such infringement in the future.

The court has discretion to award up to treble damages where intentional infringement is found.

Generic Names

Most companies promote their trademarks and service marks to increase the public's awareness of the availability and quality of their products and services. At some point in time, however, the public may begin to treat the mark as a common name to denote the type of product or service being sold, rather than as the trademark or trade name of an individual seller. A trademark that becomes a common term for a product line or type of service is called a **generic name**. Once that happens, the term loses its protection under federal trademark law because it has become *descriptive* rather than *distinctive*.

> **Generic name**
> A term for a mark that has become a common term for a product line or type of service and therefore has lost its trademark protection.

Examples of once trademarked names that have lost their trademark protection because they became generic names are *escalator, wind surfer, trampoline, nylon, cornflakes, lanolin, raisin bran, kerosene, toll house cookies*. The most famous brand name that is in jeopardy of someday becoming a generic name is the mark "Xerox." This is because many people use the word "xerox" to mean "copy" a document on a copy machine. The Xerox Corporation spends millions of dollars each year protecting its mark.

THE INTERNET AND DOMAIN NAMES

The **Internet**, or Net, is a collection of millions of computers that provide a network of electronic connections between the computers. The Internet was initiated in 1969 by the U.S. Department of Defense to create electronic communications for military and national defense purposes. Building on this start, in the 1980s the National Science Foundation, the federal government's main scientific and technical

---

BOOTLEGGING OF LIVE MUSIC OUTLAWED

In 1995, the United States joined more than 130 other countries and became a member of the World Trade Organization (WTO).

The WTO member nations adopted the international Agreement on Trade-Related Aspects of Intellectual Property Rights (TRIPS), which outlawed unauthorized taping of sounds or images of live musical performances. To enforce this agreement in the United States, the U.S. Congress enacted the following federal antibootlegging statutes:

- *18 U.S.C. Section 2319A*: This statute imposes criminal liability for the unauthorized taping of the sounds and images of live musical performances "knowingly and for purposes of commercial advantage or private financial gain." A first offense carries a prison term of up to five years; subsequent offenses carry prison terms of up to ten years. The court can order unauthorized recordings to be destroyed.
- *17 U.S.C. Section 1101*: This statute imposes civil liability for similar conduct but without the commercial advantage or private financial gain requirement. A successful plaintiff can recover actual damages and any profits made by the defendant, destruction of any unauthorized recordings, and an injunction against any future violations by the defendant.

It is important to note that both recording the sound of the concert and taking photographs of the performance are conduct outlawed by these statutes.

agency, established the Net to facilitate high-speed communications among research centers at academic and research institutions around the world.

Eventually, individuals and businesses began using the Internet for communicating information and data. In 1980, fewer than 250 computers were hooked to the Internet. Growth was rapid in the late 1990s and into the early 2000s, and today several hundred million computers are connected to the Internet. The Internet's evolution helped usher in the Information Age of today. Use of the Internet and the World Wide Web has required courts to apply existing laws to new technologies and has spurred the federal Congress and state legislatures to enact new laws to govern modern means of communication and the conduct of electronic business.

World Wide Web

The **World Wide Web** consists of millions of computers that support a standard set of rules for the exchange of information called *hypertext transfer protocol* (HTTP). Web-based documents are formatted using common coding languages such as *hypertext markup language* (HTML) and Java. Businesses and individuals can hook up to the Web by registering with a server such as America Online (AOL).

Individuals and businesses can have their own websites. A website is composed of electronic documents known as web pages. The websites and pages are stored on servers throughout the world. They are viewed by using Web browsing software such as Microsoft Internet Explorer and Netscape Navigator. Each website has a unique online address. Web pages can contain a full range of multimedia content, including text, images, video, sound, and animation. Web pages can include references, called *hyperlinks*, or *links*, to other web pages or websites.

The Web has made it extremely attractive to conduct commercial activities online. Companies such as Amazon.com and eBay are e-commerce powerhouses that sell all sorts of goods and services. And existing companies are increasingly selling their goods and services online as well. E-commerce over the Web will continue to grow dramatically.

Electronic Mail

Electronic mail, or **email**, is one of the most widely used applications for communication over the Internet. Using email, individuals can instantaneously communicate in electronic writing with one another around the world. Each person can have his or her own email address, which identifies the user by a unique address. Email will continue to grow in use, replacing telephone and paper correspondence and increasing new communication between persons.

Internet Domain Names

Domain name
A unique name that identifies an individual's or a company's Web site.

Each website is identified by a unique Internet **domain name.** For example, the domain name for the publisher of this book is www.prenhall.com. Domain names can be registered. The first step in **registration** of a domain name is to determine whether any other party already owns the name. For this purpose, InterNIC maintains a "Whois" database containing the domain names that have been registered. The InterNIC website is located online at www.internic.net. Domain names also can be registered at the website of Network Solutions, Inc., located online at www.networksolutions.com, as well as at other online sites. An applicant must complete a registration form, which can be done online. Registering a domain name for one year costs less than $50, and the fee may be paid by credit card online.

The most commonly used top-level extensions for domains names are set forth in Exhibit 20.1.

Electronic Communications Privacy Act

E-mail, computer data, and other electronic communications are sent daily by millions of people using computers and the Internet. Recognizing how the use of computer and

Our legal system faces no theoretical dilemma but a single continuous problem: how to apply to ever changing conditions the never changing principles of freedom.

Earl Warren (1995)

Exhibit 20.1 **Domain name extensions**

The most common **domain name extensions** include the following.

Extension	Used by
.com	represents the word *commercial*, and is the most widely used extension in the world. Most businesses prefer a .com domain name because it is a highly recognized business symbol.
.net	represents the word *network*, and is used most commonly by Internet service providers, Web-hosting companies, and other businesses that are involved directly in the infrastructure of the Internet. Some businesses also choose domain names with a .net extension.
.org	represents the word *organization* and is used primarily by nonprofit groups and trade associations.
.info	signifies a "resource" website. This unrestricted global name may be used by businesses, individuals, and organizations.
.biz	used for small-business websites.
.us	for U.S. websites. Many businesses choose this extension, which is a relatively new extension.
.cc	originally was the country code for Coco Keeling Islands but now is unrestricted and may be registered by anyone from any country. It often is registered by businesses.
.bz	originally was the country code for Belize but now is unrestricted and may be registered by anyone from any country. It is commonly used by small businesses.
.name	new extension for individuals, who can use it to register personalized domain names.
.museum	enables museums, museum associations, and museum professionals to register their own websites.
.coop	represents the word *cooperative* and may be used by cooperative associations around the world.
.aero	reserved exclusive for the aviation community. It enables organizations and individuals to reserve websites.
.pro	available to professionals, such as doctors, lawyers, consultants, and other professionals.
.edu	for educational institutions.

WEB DOMAIN NAMES SOLD FOR MILLIONS

What is a domain name worth? Some are worth plenty. Multimillion dollar prices are being paid for the most desirable names. Take the case of the domain name *business.com*. This name, which originally was registered as a domain name for less than $100, was sold for $150,000 in 1996. Many people thought this was an outrageous sum to pay for a domain name—that is, until it was resold in 1999 for $7.5 million.

Other domain names have been sold at high prices, too. *Wine.com* was sold for $3 million, *bingo.com* for $1 million, and *wallstreet.com* for $1 million. The all-time winner, however, is *sex.com*, which commanded the price of $12 million in 2006.

ARMANI OUTMANEUVERED FOR INTERNET DOMAIN NAME

G. A. Modefine S. A. is the owner of the famous "Armani" trademark under which it produces and sells upscale and high-priced apparel. The Armani label is recognized worldwide. But Modefine was surprised when it tried to register for the domain name. armani.com and found that it had been taken already. Modefine brought an arbitration action in the WIPO's Arbitration and Mediation Center against the domain name owner to recover the armani.com domain name under the UDRP. To win, Modefine had to prove that the domain name was identical or confusingly similar to its trademark, the owner who registered the name did not have a legitimate interest in the name, and the owner registered the name in bad faith.

The person who owned the domain name, Anand Ramnath Mani, appeared at the proceeding and defended his ownership rights. The arbitrator found that Modefine's trademark and Mr. Mani's domain name were identical but held that Mr. Mani had a legitimate claim to the domain name. The arbitrator wrote that it is "common practice for people to register domain names which are based upon initials and a name, acronyms, or otherwise variants of their full names." The court rejected Modefine's claim that Mr. Mani's offer to sell the name for $1,935 constituted bad faith. The arbitrator ruled against Modefine and permitted Mr. Mani to own the domain name armani.com.

Source: G.A.: Modefine S.A. v. A. R. Mani, WIPO, No. D2001-0537 (2001).

electronic communications raise special issues of privacy, the federal government enacted the **Electronic Communications Privacy Act (ECPA)**. The ECPA makes it a crime to intercept an "electronic communication" at the point of transmission, while in transit, when stored by a router or server, or after receipt by the intended recipient.

An electronic communication includes any transfer of signals, writings, images, sounds, data, or intelligence of any nature. The ECPA makes it illegal to access stored email, as well as email in transmission.

The ECPA provides that stored electronic communications may be accessed without violating the law by the following:

1. The party or entity providing the electronic communication service. The primary example would be an employer who can access stored email communications of employees using the employer's service.
2. Government and law enforcement entities that are investigating suspected illegal activity. Disclosure would be required only pursuant to a validly issued warrant.

The ECPA provides for criminal penalties. In addition, the ECPA provides that an injured party may sue for civil damages for violations of the Act.

Anticybersquatting Consumer Protection Act

Often, when companies and famous people try to register Internet domain names for their trademarked or famous names, they discover that someone else already has registered their domain name. This often happens when "cybersquatters" register Internet domain and try to hold famous companies and demand high ransom payments for the desired domain name.

In response, the U.S. Congress enacted the **Anticybersquatting Consumer Protection Act (ACPA)** [15 U.S.C. Section 1125(d)]. This Act provides that famous companies or persons can recover their domain name held by others if they can prove (1) that the name is famous, and (2) that the domain name was registered in bad faith. Thus, this law prohibits the act of **cybersquatting** if it is done in bad faith.

The first issue in applying the statute is whether the domain name is the famous name of someone else. Trademarked names qualify; nontrademarked names—such as those of famous actors, actresses, singers, sports figures, political figures, and such—also are protected. In determining bad faith, the law provides that courts may consider the extent to which the domain name resembles the holder's name or the famous person's name, whether goods or services are sold under the name, the holder's offer to sell or transfer the name, and whether the holder has acquired multiple Internet domain names of famous companies and persons.

The Act provides for the issuance of cease-and-desist orders and injunctions by the court. In addition, the law adds monetary penalties: A plaintiff has the option of seeking statutory damages of between $1,000 and $300,000 in lieu of proving damages. The ACPA gives owners of trademarks and persons with famous names a new weapon to attack the kidnapping of Internet domain names by cyberpirates.

Advice from the Field •••••••••••••••••••••••••••••••••

E-LAWYER.COM, AN ONLINE LEGAL SITE OFFERING ACCESS TO LICENSED ATTORNEYS, LAUNCHES IN FLORIDA

E-Lawyer.com

A Florida law firm has combined the power of the Internet with traditional in-office legal services to launch E-lawyer.com. The website provides online access to wills, powers of attorney, and a variety of advanced medical planning services, plus unlimited one-year access to licensed attorneys.

"I believe in the power of the Internet to improve delivery of legal services to people who might not otherwise see a lawyer because of procrastination, privacy, or other reasons," said Louis N. Larsen, president and founder of E-lawyer.com. "However, creating a will, obtaining a power of attorney, or appointing someone to make health care decisions for you are serious matters that require professional judgment. That's why E-lawyer. com provides access to licensed attorneys as part of its service."

Larsen, whose office is in Stuart, Fla., near Port St. Lucie, explained the E-lawyer.com process this way:

1. Clients log in to the secure E-lawyer.com site to create, review, and revise documents.
2. They are guided through a user-friendly online interview to help with decision making. The interview is specific to Florida and contains frequently asked legal questions and provides answers.
3. Before, during, and after the interview, clients may contact an attorney using E-lawyer.com's secure Client Message Center.
4. A staff attorney licensed in Florida responds to all questions.

5. After questions are answered, documents and instructions are printed on acid-free paper and shipped by First-Class mail within 48 hours.

Larsen said he plans to roll-out E-lawyer.com nationwide within a few years but at present offers it in Florida only. Development efforts are under way to offer services in Minnesota and Missouri next.

"My vision of providing people with a better experience than other online legal sites means it will take longer to establish E-lawyer.com links in every state," he explained. "But ensuring that licensed attorneys are available everywhere, E-lawyer.com launches means you won't see disclaimers such as 'Our website is not a law firm and is not a substitute for an attorney.'"

Larsen explained that the E-lawyer.com system provides a measure of safety and security not available with a "do-it-yourself" will kit or a website run by paralegals or laypersons. The E-lawyer.com website has recently gone live after a two-year development period, which involved integrating the latest document assembly and user interface programming technology.

Larsen, a board-certified trial attorney, received his law degree from the University of Miami and has been a trial lawyer in Florida for more than 13 years. His partner in E-lawyer.com is Jeffrey M. Kirsch, who has been practicing civil law since 1982.

"E-Lawyer.com, an Online Legal Site Offering Access to Licensed Attorneys, Launches in Florida." Reprinted with permission from E-Lawyer.com

Legal Terminology

American Inventors Protection
Act   723

Anticybersquatting Consumer
Protection Act (ACPA)   736

Berne Convention   725

Certification mark   729

Collective mark   729

Computer Software Copyright
Act   727

Copyright   723

Copyright infringement   726

Copyright Revision Act   723

Copyright Term Extension Act   726

Cybersquatting   726

Digital Millennium Copyright Act
(DMCA)   728

Distinctiveness of a mark   729

Domain name   732

Domain name extensions   733

Economic Espionage Act   721

Electronic Communications Privacy
Act (ECPA)   734

Electronic mail (email)   732

Fair-use doctrine   728

Federal Patent Statute   721

General Agreement on Tariffs and
Trade (GATT)   722

Generic name   731

Intellectual property   720

Internet   731

Invention   721

Judicial Improvement Act
of 1990   727

Lanham Trademark Act   729

Misappropriation   720

No Electronic Theft Act
(NET Act)   728

Patent   721

Patent application   721

Patent infringement   723

Patent pending   721

Public-use doctrine   723

Registration (of a copyright)   725

Registration (of a domain name)   732

Registration (of a trademark)   729

Secondary meaning   729

Semiconductor Chip
Protection Act of 1934   727

Service mark   729

Tangible writings   725

Trade secret   720

Trademark   729

Trademark infringement   730

Trademark Law Revision Act
of 1988   729

United States Copyright Office   725

United States Patent and Trademark
Office   721

World Trade Organization
(WTO)   722

World Wide Web   732

Summary

CHAPTER *20*   CYBERLAW AND INTELLECTUAL PROPERTY

Trade Secrets

Definition	A *trade secret* is a product formula, pattern, design, compilation of data, customer list, or other business secret that makes a business successful. The owner of a trade secret must take reasonable precautions to prevent its trade secret from being discovered by others.
Misappropriation	Misappropriation is a tort in which another's trade secret is obtained through unlawful means such as theft, bribery, or espionage. A successful plaintiff can recover profits, damages, and an injunction against the offender.
Economic Espionage Act	The Federal Economic Espionage Act makes it a crime for any person to convert a trade secret for his or another's benefit, knowing or intending to cause injury to the owners of the trade secret.

Patents

Federal Patent Statute	Patent law is exclusively federal law; there are no state patent laws.
Scope	Patentable subject matter includes inventions such as machines; processes; compositions of matter; improvements to existing machines, processes, or compositions of matter; designs for articles of manufacture; asexually reproduced plants; and living matter invented by humans.
Criteria	To be patented an invention must be: 1. Novel 2. Useful 3. Nonobvious

Patent Application	An application containing a written description of the invention must be filed with the United States Patent and Trademark Office in Washington, D.C.
Term	Patents are valid for 20 years.
Public-use Doctrine	A patent may not be granted if the invention was used by the public for more than one year prior to filing the patent application.
Patent Infringement	The patent holder may recover damages and other remedies against a person who makes unauthorized use of another's patent.
American Inventors Protection Act	The American Inventors Protection Act: 1. permits an inventor to file a *provisional application* with the U.S. Patent and Trademark Office three months pending the filing of a final patent application to gain "provisional rights." 2. requires the PTO to issue a patent within three years after the filing of a patent application.
Patent Appeal	The United States Court of Appeals for the Federal Circuit in Washington, D.C., hears patent appeals.

Copyrights

Scope	Copyright law is exclusively federal law; there are no state copyright laws. Only tangible writings can be copyrighted. These include books, newspapers, addresses, musical compositions, motion pictures, works of art, architectural plans, greeting cards, photographs, sound recordings, computer programs, and mask works fixed in semiconductor chips.

Copyright Revision Act
Copyright Laws

	Judicial Improvement Act Semiconductor Chip Protection Act Computer Software Copyright Act Copyright Term Extension Act
Requirements for Copyright	The writing must be the original work of the author.
Copyright Registration	Copyright registration is permissive and voluntary. Published and unpublished works may be registered with the United States Copyright Office in Washington, D.C. Registration itself does not create the copyright.
Term	Copyrights are for the following terms: 1. *Individual holder:* Life of the author plus 70 years 2. *Corporate holder:* Either (1) 120 years from the date of creation, or (2) 95 years from the date of publication, whichever is shorter.
Copyright Infringement	The copyright holder may recover damages and other remedies against a person who copies a substantial and material part of a copyrighted work without the holder's permission.
Fair-use Doctrine	The fair-use doctrine permits use of copyrighted material without the consent of the copyright holder for limited uses (e.g., scholarly work, parody or satire, and brief quotation in news reports).
Digital Millennium Copyright Act (DMCA)	The federal DMCA, enacted in 1998, provides civil and criminal penalties that 1. prohibit the manufacture and distribution of technologies, products, or services primarily designed for the purpose of circumventing wrappers or encryption protection. 2. prohibit unauthorized *access* to copyrighted digital works by circumventing the wrapper or encryption technology that protects the intellectual property.
No Electronic Theft Act (NET Act)	The federal Net Act makes it a crime for a person to willfully infringe a copyright work exceeding $1,000 in retail value, even without commercial advantages or financial gain.

Trademarks

Mark	Referred to collectively as trademarks, a mark consists of the trade name, symbol, word, logo, design, or device that distinguishes the owner's good or services.
Trademark Registration	Marks are registered with the United States Patent and Trademark Office in Washington, D.C.
Types of Marks	1. *Trademark:* identifies goods of a particular business 2. *Service mark:* identifies services of a particular business 3. *Certification mark:* certifies that goods or services are of a certain quality or origin 4. *Collective mark:* used by cooperatives, associations, and fraternal organizations
Requirements for a Trademark	The mark must either 1. be *distinctive*, or 2. have acquired a *secondary meaning*. The mark must have been used in commerce or the holder must intend to use the mark in commerce and actually do so within six months after registering the mark.
Term	The original registration of a mark is valid for 10 years and can be renewed for an unlimited number of 10-year periods.
Trademark Infringement	The mark holder may recover damages and other remedies from a person who makes unauthorized use of another's registered mark.
Generic Name	A generic name is a mark that becomes a common term for a product line or type of service loses its protection under federal trademark law.

The Internet and Domain Names

Internet	The Internet is a collection of millions of computers that provide a network of electronic connections between computers.
World Wide Web	The www is an electronic connection of computers that support a standard set of rules for the exchange of information called hypertext transfer protocol (HTTP).
Electronic Mail (email)	Email is electronic written communication between individuals using computers connected to the Internet.
Domain Name	The domain name is a unique name that identifies an individual's or company's website.
Electronic Communications Privacy Act	The Electronic Communications Privacy Act is a federal statute that makes it a federal crime to intercept an electronic communication at the point of transmission, while in transit, when stored by a router or server, or after receipt by the intended recipient.
Anticybersquatting Consumer Protection Act	The Anticybersquatting Consumer Protection Act is a federal statute that permits a court to issue cease-and-desist orders and injunctions and to award monetary damages against anyone who has registered a domain name (1) of a famous name (2) in bad faith.

▶ WORKING THE WEB

1. Go to the website **http://networksolutions. com.html.** Pick an Internet domain name you would be interested in registering. Check to see if this name is available? What is the cost of registering an Internet domain name?

2. Visit the website **http://www.uspto.gov/ html.** Select "Trademarks" and click on "search." Select a name in which you are interested to determine whether a trademark or service mark is available for that name. Select "New User Form Search" and search

to see if this name is available. What are the results of your search?

3. Visit the website **http://1web.loc.gov/ copyright/html.** Click on "Frequently Asked Questions (FAQ)." Click on "What is a copyright?" Write a one-page report on what a copyright is and what protection is afforded a copyright.

4. Visit the website **http://www.inta.org/html.** Describe this association and the mission of

the association. Read about the E-Learning courses this association offers.

5. Visit the website **http://coca-cola.com. html.** Search this website and find the history of the "Coca-Cola" trademark. Write a half-page history of the trademark. Find and list five other trademarks that the Coca-Cola Company owns.

▶ CRITICAL THINKING AND WRITING QUESTIONS

1. What is intellectual property?
2. What is a trade secret? How is a trade secret protected? For how long a time is protection available? Explain.
3. What does the Economic Espionage Act provide? What does the Digital Millennium Copyright Act (DMCA) provide?
4. What is a patent? What can be patented? What are the statutory requirements for a patent? How is a patent obtained?
5. Explain patent infringement. What types of remedies are available for patent infringement?
6. Explain the public-use doctrine. Give an example.
7. What is a copyright? What can be copyrighted? How is a copyright obtained?
8. Explain copyright infringement. What types of remedies are available for copyright infringement?
9. Explain the fair-use doctrine. Give an example.
10. What is a mark? What are the requirements for obtaining a mark?
11. Describe the difference between: (1) trademark, (2) service mark, (3) certification mark, and (4) collective mark.
12. What is a generic name. Give an example.
13. What is the Internet? What is email? What does the Electronic Communications Privacy Act (ECPA) do?
14. What is an Internet domain name? How is a domain name registered?
15. What is cybersquatting? Describe the protection afforded by the Anticybersquatting Consumer Protection Act (ACPA).

▶ ETHICS ANALYSIS AND DISCUSSION QUESTIONS

1. Does a paralegal working in the area of intellectual property law have any ethical obligation to obtain specialized training or education?
2. Are memoranda of law and other reports prepared by a paralegal protected by copyright law? To whom do the rights belong—the paralegal, the client, or the firm?
3. You are not a lawyer but, under regulations issued by the Commissioner of Patents with the approval of the Secretary of Commerce pursuant to 35 U.S.C. Section 31, you are authorized to practice before the United States Patent Office [*Sperry v. Florida ex rel. Florida Bar*, 373 U.S. 379, 83 S.Ct. 1322, 10 L.Ed.2d 428, 1963 U.S. Lexis 2486 (1963)]. May you represent patent applicants, prepare and prosecute their applications, and advise them in connection with their applications in Florida?

▶ DEVELOPING YOUR COLLABORATION SKILLS

With a group of other students, selected by you or as assigned by your instructor, review the Paralegals and Work at the beginning of the chapter. As a group, discuss the following questions.

1. What type of protection can Mr. Einstein obtain for his new invention? How is this protection obtained? How long does this protection last?
2. What type of protection can Mr. Einstein obtain for the name of the shoe, the logo he has designed, and the slogan he has developed? How is this protection obtained? How long does this protection last?
3. What type of protection can Mr. Einstein obtain for his *User's Manual*? How is this protection obtained? How long does this protection last?
4. What type of protection is available to protect Mr. Einstein's proposed website name? How is this protection obtained? How long does this protection last?

▶ PARALEGAL PORTFOLIO EXERCISE

Go to the website **http://www.loc.gov/copyright.html.** Find and print out the proper form and instructions for obtaining a copyright for a nondramatic literary work. Read the instructions for completing this form. Complete the form as if you are the writer of the nondramatic literary work to be registered. Make up whatever information is necessary to complete the form. Search the website and determine where the form is to be submitted and the fee that must be paid to submit the form.

▶LEGAL ANALYSIS AND WRITING CASES

J.E.M. Ag Supply, Inc., dba Farm Advantage, Inc. v. Pioneer Hi-Bred International, Inc.

534 U.S. 124, 122 S.Ct. 593, 151 L.Ed.2d 508 Supreme Court of the United States

FACTS

Pioneer Hi-Bred International, Inc. (Pioneer) has obtained seventeen patents that cover the company's inbred and hybrid corn and corn seed products. A hybrid plant patent protects the plant, its seeds, variants, mutants, and modifications of the hybrid. Pioneer sells its patented hybrid seeds under a limited label license that provides: "License is granted solely to produce grain and/or forage." The license states that it "does not extend to the use of seed from such crop or the progeny thereof for propagation or seed multiplication." The license strictly prohibits "the use of such seed or progeny thereof for propagation or seed multiplication or for production or development of a hybrid or different variety of seed."

J.E.M. Ag Supply, Inc., doing business as Farm Advantage, Inc., purchased patented hybrid seeds from Pioneer in bags bearing this license agreement. Pioneer sued Farm Advantage, alleging that Farm Advantage infringed its patent and violated the license by creating seed from the hybrid corn products it grew from Pioneer's patented hybrid seed. Farm Advantage filed a counter-claim of patent invalidity, arguing that Pioneer hybrid plant seed patents are not patentable subject matter. The District Court granted summary judgment to Pioneer, and the Court of Appeals affirmed. The U.S. Supreme Court agreed to hear the appeal.

Question

1. Are sexually reproducing hybrid plants patentable subject matter?

Castle Rock Entertainment, Inc. v. Carol Publishing Group, Inc.

150 F.3d 132 (1998) United States Court of Appeals, Second Circuit

FACTS

Castle Rock Entertainment, Inc., is the producer and copyright owner of the successful "Seinfeld" television series. For years, Seinfeld was the highest-rated show on television. The series revolved around petty tribulations in the lives of four single, adult friends in New York: Jerry Seinfeld, George Costanza, Elaine Benes, and Cosmo Kramer.

To take advantage of the public interest in Seinfeld, Carol Publishing Group, Inc. published a book written by Beth Golub, entitled *The Seinfeld Aptitude Test* (SAT). The 132-page book contained 643 questions and answers about events and characters in 84 TV episodes of Seinfeld. These included 211 multiple-choice questions, 93 matching questions, and a number of short-answer questions. The correct answers to these questions have as their source fictional moments in Seinfeld episodes, and 41 questions contain exact dialogue from Seinfeld. The name "Seinfeld" appears prominently on front and back covers of the SAT, and pictures of the principal actors in Seinfeld appear on the cover and throughout the book.

In February 1995, Castle Rock filed this action against Carol Publishing and Golub alleging federal copyright infringement. Castle Rock made a motion for summary judgment, alleging that no facts were in dispute and that the court could make a decision as a matter of law whether copyright infringement occurred. The trial court agreed that no facts were in dispute that required a jury's determination. The court, therefore, considered the undisputed evidence that the defendants had violated Castle Rock's copyrights of Seinfeld, and awarded damages and issued an injunction enjoining the defendants from publishing *The Seinfeld Aptitude Test*. The court granted Castle Rock's motion for summary judgment. The defendants appealed.

Question

1. Is Castle Rock entitled to a summary judgment on its copyright infringement claim?

Acuson Corp. v. Aloka Co., Ltd.

209 Cal.App. 435, 257 Cal.Rptr. 368, 1989 Cal.App. Lexis 317, 10 U.S.P.Q.2d (BNA) 1814 (Cal.App. 1989)

FACTS

Acuson Corporation, a Delaware corporation, and Aloka Co., Ltd., a Japanese company, are competitors that both manufacture ultrasonic imaging equipment, a widely used medical diagnostic tool. The device uses sound waves to produce moving images of the inside of a patient's body, which a computer processes into an image that is displayed on a video monitor. Acuson's unit provides finer resolution than Aloka's unit. Both companies have sold many units to hospitals and medical centers.

In November 1985, Aloka decided to purchase an Acuson unit. Aloka had another company make the actual purchase because it was concerned that Acuson would not sell the unit to a competitor. After the unit was shipped to Tokyo, Aloka's engineers partially dismantled the Acuson unit. They recorded their observations in notebooks. When Acuson discovered that Aloka had purchased one of its units, it sued Aloka, seeking an injunction and return of the unit.

Question

1. Is Aloka liable for misappropriation of a trade secret?

E. & J. Gallo Winery v. Spider Webs Ltd.

286 F.3d 270, 2002 U.S. App. Lexis 5928 (2002) United States Court of Appeals, Fifth Circuit

FACTS

Emest and Julio Gallo Winery (Gallo) is a famous maker of wines that is located in California. The company registered the trademark "Ernest & Julio Gallo" in 1964 with the United States Patent and Trademark Office. The company has spent over $500 million promoting its brand name and has sold more than 4 billion bottles of wine. Its name has taken on a secondary meaning as a famous trademark name.

In 1999, Steve, Pierce, and Fred Thumann created Spider Webs Ltd., a limited partnership, to register Internet domain names. Spider Webs registered more than 2,000 Internet domain names, including ernestandjuliogallo.com. Spider Webs is in the business of selling some of its domain names.

Gallo filed suit against Spider Webs Ltd. and the Thumanns, alleging violation of the federal ACPA. The District Court held in favor of Gallo and ordered Spider Webs to transfer the domain name ernestandjuliogallo.com to Gallo. Spider Webs Ltd. appealed.

Question

1. Did Spider Webs Ltd. and the Thumanns act in bad faith in registering the Internet domain name ernestandjuliogallo.com?

Coca-Cola Company v. Francis Net

Hypothetical

FACTS

Francis Net, a freshman in college and computer expert, browses websites for hours each day. One day she thinks to herself, "I can make money registering domain names and selling them for a fortune." She recently saw an advertisement for Classic Coke, a cola drink produced and marketed by the Coca-Cola Company. The Coca-Cola Company has a famous trademark for the term *Classic Coke* and has spent millions of dollars advertising this brand and making the term famous throughout the United States and the world.

Francis goes to the website www.networksolutions.com, an Internet domain name registration service, to see if the Internet domain name classiccoke.com has been taken. She discovers that it is available, so she immediately registers the Internet domain name classiccoke.com for herself and pays the $70 registration fee with her credit card.

Coca Cola Company decides to register the Internet domain name classiccoke.com but discovers that Francis Net has already registered the domain name. Coca Cola Company contacts Francis, who demands $500,000 for the name. Coca Cola Company sues Francis to prevent Francis from using the Internet domain name classiccoke.com and to recover it from her under the federal Anticybersquatting Consumer Protection Act.

Question

1. Who wins?

Macy's Department Stores et al. v. BluePeace.org

Hypothetical

FACTS

BluePeace.org is a new environmentalist group that has decided that expounding its environmental causes over the Internet is the best and most efficient way to spend its time and money to advance its environmental causes. To draw attention to its websites, BluePeace.org comes up with catchy Internet domain names. One is macyswear us.org; another is exxonvaldezesseals.org; and another is generalmotorscrashesdummies. org.

The macyswearus.org website first shows beautiful women dressed in mink coats sold by Macy's Department Stores, and then goes into graphic photos of minks being slaughtered and skinned and made into the coats. The exxonvaldezesseals.org website first shows a beautiful pristine bay in Alaska with the Exxon Valdez oil tanker quietly sailing through the waters, and then shows photos of the ship breaking open and spewing forth oil, and then seals who are good with oil suffocating and dying on the shoreline. The website generalmotorscrashesdummies.org shows a General Motors automobile involved in normal crash tests with dummies, followed by photographs of automobile accident scenes where people lie bleeding and dying after accidents involving General Motors automobiles.

Macy's Department Stores, the Exxon Oil Company, and the General Motors Corporation sue BluePeace.org for violating the federal Anticybersquatting Consumer Protection Act.

Question

1. Who wins? Has BluePeace.org acted unethically in this case?

▶WORKING WITH THE LANGUAGE OF THE COURT CASE

Feist Publications, Inc. v. Rural Telephone Service Co., Inc.

499 U.S. 340, 111 S.Ct. 1282, 113 L.Ed.2d 358 1991
U.S. Lexis 1856 (1991) Supreme Court of the United States

Read the following case, excerpted from the U.S. Supreme Court's opinion. Review and brief the case. In your brief, answer the following questions.

1. Who was the plaintiff? Who was the defendant?
2. What had the defendant done that caused the plaintiff to sue?

3. What is the issue in this case?
4. What was the decision of the U.S. Supreme Court?

O'Connor, S., delivered the opinion of the Court.

Rural Telephone Service Company is a certified public utility that provides telephone service to several communities in northwest Kansas. It is subject to a state regulation that requires all telephone companies operating in Kansas to issue annually an updated telephone directory. Accordingly, as a condition of its monopoly franchise, Rural publishes a typical telephone directory, consisting of white pages and yellow pages. The white pages list in alphabetical order the names of Rural's subscribers, together with their towns and telephone numbers. The yellow pages list Rural's business subscribers alphabetically by category and feature classified advertisements of various sites. Rural distributes its directory free of charge to its subscribers, but earns revenue by selling yellow pages advertisements.

Feist Publications, Inc. is a publishing company that specializes in areawide telephone directories. Unlike a typical directory, which covers only a particular calling area, Feist's areawide directories cover a much larger geographical range, reducing the need to call directory assistance or consult multiple directories. The Feist directory that is the subject of this litigation covers 11 different telephone service areas in 15 counties and contains 46,878 white pages listings—compared to Rural's approximately 7,700 listings.

Of the 11 telephone companies, only Rural refused to license its listings to Feist. Rural's refusal created a problem for Feist, as omitting these listings would have left a gaping hole in its areawide directory,

rendering it less attractive to potential yellow pages advertisers. Unable to license Rural's white pages listings, Feist used them without Rural's consent.

Rural sued for copyright infringement in the District Court for the District of Kansas, taking the position that Feist, in compiling its own directory, could not use the information contained in Rural's white pages. The District Court granted summary judgment to Rural, explaining that "courts have consistently held that telephone directories are copyrightable" and citing a string of lower court decisions. In an unpublished opinion, the Court of Appeals for the Tenth Circuit affirmed "for substantially the reasons given by the district court."

This case concerns the interaction of two well-established propositions. The first is that facts are not copyrightable; the other, that compilations of facts generally are. The key to resolving the tension lies in understanding why facts are not copyrightable. The *sine qua non* of copyright is originality. To qualify for copyright protection, a work must be original to the author. Original, as the term is used in copyright, means only that the work was independently created by the author (as opposed to copied from other works), and that it possesses at least some minimal degree of creativity.

Originality is a constitutional requirement. The source of Congress' power to enact copyright laws is Article 1, Section 8, C. 8, of the Constitution, which authorizes Congress to "secure for limited Times to Authors . . . the exclusive Right to their respective Writings." It is this bedrock principle of copyright that mandates the law's seemingly disparate treatment of facts and factual compilations.

No one may claim originality as to facts. This is because facts do not owe their origin to an act of authorship. The distinction is one between creation and discovery: The first person to find and report a particular fact has not created the fact; he or she has merely discovered its existence.

If the selection and arrangement of facts are original, these elements of the work are eligible for copyright protection. No matter how original the format, however, the facts themselves do not become original through association.

There is no doubt that Feist took from the white pages of Rural's directory a substantial amount of factual information. At a minimum, Feist copied the names, towns, and telephone numbers of 1,309 of Rural's subscribers. Not all copying, however, is copyright infringement. Two elements must be proven: (1) ownership of a valid copyright, and (2) copying of constituent elements of the work that are original. The first element is not at issue here: Feist appears to concede that Rural's directory, considered as a whole, is subject to a valid copyright because it contains some foreword text, as well as original material in its yellow pages advertisements.

The question is whether Rural has proven the second element. In other words, did Feist, by taking 1,309 names, towns, and telephone numbers from Rural's white pages, copy anything that was "original" to Rural? Certainly, the raw data do not satisfy the originality requirement. Rural may have been the first to discover and report the names, towns, and telephone numbers of its subscribers, but these data do not "owe their origin" to Rural. The question that remains is whether Rural selected, coordinated, or arranged these copyrightable facts in an original way. The selection, coordination, and arrangement of Rural's white pages do not satisfy the minimum constitutional standards for copyright protection. Rural's selection of listings could not be more obvious: It publishes the most basic information—name, town, and telephone number—about each person who applies to it for telephone service. This is "selection" of a sort, but it lacks the modicum of creativity necessary to transform mere selection into copyrightable expression. Rural extended sufficient effort to make the white pages directory useful, but insufficient creativity to make it original.

The judgment of the Court of Appeals is Reversed. ■

How to Brief a Case

CRITICAL LEGAL THINKING

Judges apply legal reasoning in reaching a decision in a case. In doing so, the judge must specify the issue presented by the case, identify the key facts in the case and the applicable law, and then apply the law to the facts to come to a conclusion that answers the issue presented. This process is called **critical legal thinking.** Skills of analysis and interpretation are important in deciding legal cases.

Key Terms

Before embarking upon the study of law, the student should be familiar with the following key legal terms:

> *Plaintiff*   The party who originally brought the lawsuit.
>
> *Defendant*   The party against whom the lawsuit has been brought.
>
> *Petitioner or Appellant*   The party who has appealed the decision of the trial court or lower court. The petitioner may be either the plaintiff or the defendant, depending on who lost the case at the trial court or lower court level.
>
> *Respondent or Appellee*   The party who must answer the petitioner's appeal. The respondent may be either the plaintiff or the defendant, depending upon which party is the petitioner. In some cases, both the plaintiff *and* the defendant may disagree with the trial court's or lower court's decision and both parties may appeal the decision.

Briefing a Case

"Briefing" a case is important to clarify the legal issues involved and to gain a better understanding of the case.

The student must summarize (brief) the court's decision in no more than 400 words (some professors may shorten or lengthen this limit). The format is highly structured, consisting of five parts, each of which is numbered and labeled:

Part	Maximum Words
1. Case name and citation	25
2. Summary of key facts in the case	125
3. Issue presented by the case, stated as a one-sentence question answerable only by *yes* or *no*	25
4. Holding—the court's resolution of the issue	25
5. A summary of the court's reasoning justifying the holding	200
Total words	400

1. Case Name and Citation

The name of the case is placed at the beginning of each briefed case. The case name usually contains the names of the parties to the lawsuit. If there are multiple plaintiffs or defendants, however, some of the names of the parties may be omitted from the case name. Abbreviations often are used in case names.

The case citation—which consists of a number plus the year in which the case was decided, such as "126 L.Ed.2d 295 (1993)"—is set forth below the case name. The case citation identifies the book in the law library in which the case may be found. For example, the case in the above citation may be found in volume 126 of the *Supreme Court Reporter Lawyer's Edition (Second)*, page 295. The name of the court that decided the case appears below the case name.

2. Summary of Key Facts in the Case

The important facts of a case are stated briefly. Extraneous facts and facts of minor importance are omitted from the brief. The facts of the case usually can be found at the beginning of the case, but not necessarily. Important facts may be found throughout the case.

3. Issue Presented by the Case

It is crucial in briefing a case to identify the issue presented to the court to decide. The issue on appeal is most often a legal question, although questions of fact sometimes are the subject of an appeal. The issue presented in each case usually is quite specific and should be asked in a one-sentence question that is answerable only by a *yes* or *no*. For example, the issue statement, "Is Mary liable?" is too broad. A more proper statement of the issue would be, "Is Mary liable to Joe for breach of the contract made between them based on her refusal to make the payment due on September 30?"

4. Holding

The holding is the decision reached by the present court. It should be *yes* or *no*. The holding also states which party won.

5. Summary of the Court's Reasoning

When an appellate court or supreme court issues a decision—which often is called an *opinion*—the court normally states the reasoning it used in reaching its decision. The rationale for the decision may be based on the specific facts of the case, public policy, prior law, or other matters. In stating the reasoning of the court, the student should reword the court's language into the student's own language. This summary of the court's reasoning should pick out the meat of the opinions and weed out the nonessentials.

Following are two U.S. Supreme Court opinions for briefing. The case is presented in the language of the U.S. Supreme Court. A "Brief of the Case" follows each of the two cases. A third case, from the New York State Court of Appeals, also is included for briefing.

▶CASE 1

For Briefing

Harris v. Forklift Systems, Inc.	**CASE NAME**
510 U.S. 17, 114 S.Ct. 367, 126 L.Ed.2d 295	**CITATION** 1993 U.S. LEXIS 7155 (1993)
	COURT **Supreme Court of the United States**

OPINION OF THE COURT. O'CONNOR, JUSTICE

FACTS. Teresa Harris worked as a manager at Forklift Systems, Inc., an equipment rental company, from April 1985 until October 1987. Charles Hardy was Forklift's president. Throughout Harris's time at Forklift, Hardy often insulted her because of her gender and often made her the target of unwanted sexual innuendos. Hardy told Harris on several occasions, in the presence of other employees, "You're a woman, what do you know" and "We need a man as the rental manager"; at least once, he told her she was "a dumb-ass woman." Again in front of others, he suggested that the two of them "go to the Holiday Inn to negotiate Harris' raise." Hardy occasionally asked Harris and other female employees to get coins from his front pants pocket. He threw objects on the ground in front of Harris and other women, and asked them to pick the objects up. He made sexual innuendos about Harris' and other women's clothing.

In mid-August 1987, Harris complained to Hardy about his conduct. Hardy said he was surprised that Harris was offended, claimed he was only joking, and apologized. He also promised he would stop and based on his assurance Harris stayed on the job. But in early September, Hardy began anew: While Harris was arranging a deal with one of Forklift's customers, he asked her, again in front of other employees, "What did you do, promise the guy some sex Saturday night?" On October 1, Harris collected her paycheck and quit.

LOWER COURTS' OPINIONS. Harris then sued Forklift, claiming that Hardy's conduct had created an abusive work environment for her because of her gender. The United States District Court for the Middle District of Tennessee found this to be "a close case," but held that Hardy's conduct did not create an abusive environment. The court found that some of Hardy's comments offended Harris, and would offend the "reasonable woman," but that they were not "so severe as to be expected to seriously affect Harris' psychological well-being." A reasonable woman manager under like circumstances would have been offended by Hardy, but his conduct would not have risen to the level of interfering with that person's work performance. The United States Court of Appeals for the Sixth Circuit affirmed in a brief unpublished decision.

ISSUE. We granted certiorari to resolve a conflict among the Circuits on whether conduct, to be actionable as "abusive work environment" harassment, must "seriously affect an employee's psychological well-being" or lead the plaintiff to "suffer injury."

STATUTE BEING INTERPRETED. Title VII of the Civil Rights Act of 1964 makes it "an unlawful employment practice for an employer . . . to discriminate against any individual with respect to his compensation, terms, conditions, or privileges of employment, because of such individual's race, color, religion, sex, or national origin." 42 U.S.C. §2000e-2(a)(1).

U.S. SUPREME COURT'S REASONING. When the workplace is permeated with discriminatory intimidation, ridicule, and insult that is sufficiently severe or pervasive to alter the conditions of the victim's employment and create an abusive working environment, Title VII is violated. This standard takes a middle path between making actionable any conduct that is merely offensive and requiring the conduct to cause a tangible psychological injury. Mere utterance of an epithet which engenders offensive feelings in an employee does not sufficiently affect the conditions of employment to implicate Title VII. Conduct that is not severe or pervasive enough to create an objectively hostile or abusive work environment—an environment that a reasonable person would find hostile or abusive—is beyond Title VII's purview. Likewise, if the victim does not subjectively perceive the environment to be abusive, the conduct has not actually altered the conditions of the victim's employment, and there is no Title VII violation.

But Title VII comes into play before the harassing conduct leads to a nervous breakdown. A discriminatorily abusive work environment, even one that does not seriously affect employees' psychological well-being, can and often will detract from employees' job performance, discourage employees from remaining on the job, or keep them from advancing in their careers. Moreover, even without regard to these tangible effects, the very fact that the discriminatory conduct was so severe or pervasive that it created a work environment abusive to employees because of their race, gender, religion, or national origin offends Title VII's broad rule of workplace equality.

HOLDING. We therefore believe the district court erred in relying on whether the conduct "seriously affected plaintiff's psychological well-being" or led her to "suffer injury." Such an inquiry may needlessly focus the factfinder's attention on concrete psychological harm, an element Title VII does not require. So long as the environment would reasonably be perceived, and is perceived, as hostile or abusive, there is no need for it also to be psychologically injurious. This is not, and by its nature cannot be, a mathematically precise test. But we can say that whether an environment is "hostile" or "abusive" can be determined only by looking at all the circumstances.

We therefore reverse the judgment of the Court of Appeals, and remand the case for further proceedings consistent with this opinion.

CONCURRING OPINION. GINSBURG, JUSTICE
The critical issue, Title VII's text indicates, is whether members of one sex are exposed to disadvantageous terms or conditions of employment to which members of the other sex are not exposed. The adjudicator's inquiry should center, dominantly, on whether the discriminatory conduct has reasonably interfered with the plaintiff's work performance. To show such interference, the plaintiff need not prove that his or her tangible productivity has declined as a result of the harassment.

Brief of the Case: *Harris v. Forklift Systems, Inc.*

1. Case Name, Citation, and Court

Harris v. Forklift Systems, Inc.
126 L.Ed.2d. 295 (1993)
United States Supreme Court

2. Summary of the Key Facts

A. While Harris worked at Forklift, Hardy continually insulted her because of her gender and made her the target of unwanted sexual innuendos.

B. This conduct created an abusive and hostile work environment, causing Harris to terminate her employment.

C. Harris sued Forklift, alleging sexual harassment in violation of Title VII of the Civil Rights Act of 1964, which makes it an unlawful employment practice for an employer to discriminate in employment because of an individual's sex.

3. The Issue

Must an employee prove that she suffered psychological injury before she can prove a Title VII claim for sexual harassment against her employer?

4. The Holding

No. The Supreme Court remanded the case for further proceedings consistent with its opinion.

5. Summary of the Court's Reasoning

The Supreme Court held that a workplace that is permeated with discriminatory intimidation, ridicule, and insult so severe that it alters the conditions of the victim's employment creates an abusive and hostile work environment that violates Title VII. The Court held that the victim is not required to prove that she suffered tangible psychological injury to prove her Title VII claim. The Court noted that Title VII comes into play before the harassing conduct leads the victim to have a nervous breakdown.

▶**CASE 2**

For Briefing

PGA Tour, Inc. v. Martin	**CASE NAME**
121 S.Ct. 1879, 149 L.Ed.2d 904 (2001)	**CITATION** **2001 U.S. LEXIS 4115**
	COURT **Supreme Court of the United States**

OPINION OF THE COURT. STEVEN, JUSTICE

ISSUE. This case raises two questions concerning the application of the Americans with Disabilities Act of 1990 [42 U.S.C. § 12101 *et seq.*] to a gifted athlete: first, whether the Act protects access to professional golf tournaments by a qualified entrant with a disability; and second, whether a disabled contestant may be denied the use of a golf cart because it would "fundamentally alter the nature" of the tournaments to allow him to ride when all other contestants must walk.

FACTS. Petitioner PGA TOUR, Inc., a nonprofit entity formed in 1968, sponsors and cosponsors professional golf tournaments conducted on three annual tours. About 200 golfers participate in the PGA TOUR; about 170 in the NIKE TOUR; and about 100 in the SENIOR PGA TOUR. PGA TOUR and NIKE TOUR tournaments typically are 4-day events, played on courses leased and operated by petitioner. The revenues generated by television, admissions, concessions, and contributions from cosponsors amount to about $300 million a year, much of which is distributed in prize money. The "Conditions of Competition and Local Rules," often described as the "hard card," apply specifically to petitioner's professional tours. The hard cards for the PGA TOUR and NIKE TOUR require players to walk the golf course during tournaments, but not during open qualifying rounds. On the SENIOR PGA TOUR, which is limited to golfers age 50 and older, the contestants may use golf carts. Most seniors, however, prefer to walk.

RESPONDENT. Casey Martin is a talented golfer. As an amateur, he won 17 Oregon Golf Association junior events before he was 15, and won the state championship as a high school senior. He played on the Stanford University golf team that won the 1994 National Collegiate Athletic Association (NCAA) championship. As a professional, Martin qualified for the NIKE TOUR in 1998 and 1999, and based on his 1999 performance, qualified for the PGA TOUR in 2000. In the 1999 season, he entered 24 events, made the cut 13 times, and had 6 top-10 finishes, coming in second twice and third once.

Martin is also an individual with a disability as defined in the Americans with Disabilities Act of 1990 (ADA or Act). Since birth he has been afflicted with Klippel-Trenaunay-Weber Syndrome, a degenerative circulatory disorder that obstructs the flow of blood from his right leg back to his heart. The disease is progressive; it causes severe pain and has atrophied his right leg. During the latter part of his college career, because of the progress of the disease, Martin could no longer walk an 18-hole golf course. Walking not only caused him pain, fatigue, and anxiety, but also created a significant risk of hemorrhaging, developing blood clots, and fracturing his tibia so badly that an amputation might be required.

When Martin turned pro and entered the petitioner's Qualifying-School, the hard card permitted him to use a cart during his successful progress through the first two stages. He made a request, supported by detailed medical records, for permission to use a golf cart during the third stage. Petitioner refused to review those records, or to waive its walking rule for the third stage. Martin therefore filed this action.

DISTRICT COURT'S DECISION 994 F.SUPP. 1242 [DISTRICT: OREGON (1998)]. At trial, petitioner PGA TOUR did not contest the conclusion that Martin has a disability covered by the ADA, or the fact that his disability prevents him from walking the course during a round of golf. Rather, petitioner asserted that the condition of walking is a substantive rule of competition, and that waiving it as to any individual for any reason would fundamentally alter the nature of the competition. Petitioner's evidence included the testimony of a number of experts, among them some of the greatest golfers in history. Arnold Palmer, Jack Nicklaus, and Ken Venturi explained that fatigue can be a critical factor in a tournament, particularly on the last day when psychological pressure is at a maximum. Their testimony makes it clear that, in their view, permission to use a cart might well give some players a competitive advantage over other players who must walk.

The judge found that the purpose of the rule was to inject fatigue into the skill of shot-making, but that the fatigue injected "by walking the course cannot be deemed significant under normal circumstances." Furthermore, Martin presented evidence, and the judge found, that even with the use of a cart, Martin must walk over a mile during an 18-hole round, and that the fatigue he suffers from coping with his disability is "undeniably greater" than the fatigue his able-bodied competitors endure from walking the course. As a result, the judge concluded that it would "not fundamentally alter the nature of the PGA Tour's game to accommodate him with a cart." The judge accordingly entered a permanent injunction requiring petitioner to permit Martin to use a cart in tour and qualifying events.

COURT OF APPEALS DECISION 204 F.3D 994 [9TH CIRCUIT (2000)]. The Court of Appeals concluded that golf courses remain places of public accommodation during PGA tournaments. On the merits, because there was no serious dispute about the fact that permitting Martin to use a golf cart was both a reasonable and a necessary solution to the problem of providing him access to the tournaments, the Court of Appeals regarded the central dispute as whether such permission would "fundamentally alter" the nature of the PGA TOUR or NIKE TOUR. Like the District Court, the Court of Appeals viewed the issue not as "whether use of carts generally would fundamentally alter the competition, but whether the use of a cart by

Martin would do so." That issue turned on "an intensively fact-based inquiry," and, the court concluded, had been correctly resolved by the trial judge. In its words, "all that the cart does is permit Martin access to a type of competition in which he otherwise could not engage because of his disability."

FEDERAL STATUTE BEING INTERPRETED. Congress enacted the ADA in 1990 to remedy widespread discrimination against disabled individuals. To effectuate its sweeping purpose, the ADA forbids discrimination against disabled individuals in major areas of public life, among them employment (Title I of the Act), public services (Title II), and public accommodations (Title III). At issue now is the applicability of Title III to petitioner's golf tours and qualifying rounds, in particular to petitioner's treatment of a qualified disabled golfer wishing to compete in those events.

U.S. SUPREME COURT'S REASONING. It seems apparent, from both the general rule and the comprehensive definition of "public accommodation," that petitioner's golf tours and their qualifying rounds fit comfortably within the coverage of Title III, and Martin within its protection. The events occur on "golf courses," a type of place specifically identified by the Act as a public accommodation. Section 12181(7)(L). In this case, the narrow dispute is whether allowing Martin to use a golf cart, despite the walking requirement that applies to the PGA TOUR, the NIKE TOUR, and the third stage of the Qualifying-School, is a modification that would "fundamentally alter the nature" of those events.

As an initial matter, we observe that the use of carts is not itself inconsistent with the fundamental character of the game of golf. From early on, the essence of the game has been shot-making—using clubs to cause a ball to progress from the teeing ground to a hole some distance away with as few strokes as possible. Golf carts started appearing with increasing regularity on American golf courses in the 1950's. Today they are everywhere. And they are encouraged. For one thing, they often speed up play, and for another, they are great revenue producers. There is nothing in the Rules of Golf that either forbids the use of carts, or penalizes a player for using a cart.

Petitioner, however, distinguishes the game of golf as it is generally played from the game that it sponsors in the PGA TOUR, NIKE TOUR, and the last stage of the Qualifying-School—golf at the "highest level." According to petitioner, "the goal of the highest-level competitive athletics is to assess and compare the performance of different competitors, a task that is meaningful only if the competitors are subject to identical substantive rules." The waiver of any possibly "outcome-affecting" rule for a contestant would violate this principle and therefore, in petitioner's view, fundamentally alter the nature of the highest level athletic event. The walking rule is one such rule, petitioner submits, because its purpose is "to inject the element of fatigue into the skill of shot-making," and thus its effect may be the critical loss of a stroke. As a consequence, the reasonable modification Martin seeks would fundamentally alter the nature of petitioner's highest level tournaments.

The force of petitioner's argument is, first of all, mitigated by the fact that golf is a game in which it is impossible to guarantee that all competitors will play under exactly the same conditions or that an individual's ability will be the sole determinant of the outcome. For example, changes in the weather may produce harder greens and more head winds for the tournament leader than for his closest pursuers. A lucky bounce may save a shot or two. Whether such happenstance events are more or less probable than the likelihood that a golfer afflicted with Klippel-Trenaunay-Weber Syndrome would one day qualify for the NIKE TOUR and PGA TOUR, they at least demonstrate that pure chance may have a greater impact on the outcome of elite golf tournaments than the fatigue resulting from the enforcement of the walking rule.

Further, the factual basis of petitioner's argument is undermined by the District Court's finding that the fatigue from walking during one of petitioner's 4-day tournaments cannot be deemed significant. The District Court credited the testimony of a professor in physiology and expert on fatigue, who calculated the calories expended in walking a golf course (about five miles) to be approximately 500 calories—"nutritionally less than a Big Mac." What is more, that energy is expended over a 5-hour period, during which golfers have numerous intervals for rest and refreshment. In fact, the expert concluded, because golf is a low intensity activity, fatigue from the game is primarily a psychological phenomenon in which stress and motivation are the key ingredients. And even under conditions of severe heat and humidity, the critical factor in fatigue is fluid loss rather than exercise from walking. Moreover, when given the option of using a cart, the majority of golfers in petitioner's tournaments have chosen to walk, often to relieve stress or for other strategic reasons. As NIKE TOUR member Eric Johnson testified, walking allows him to keep in rhythm, stay warmer when it is chilly, and develop a better sense of the elements and the course than riding in a cart. As we have demonstrated, the walking rule is at best peripheral to the nature of petitioner's athletic events, and thus it might be waived in individual cases without working a fundamental alteration.

HOLDING AND REMEDY. Under the ADA's basic requirement that the need of a disabled person be evaluated on an individual basis, we have no doubt that allowing Martin to use a golf cart would not fundamentally alter the nature of petitioner's tournaments. As we have discussed, the purpose of the walking rule is to subject players to fatigue, which in turn may influence the outcome of tournaments. Even if the rule does serve that purpose, it is an uncontested finding of the District Court that Martin "easily endures greater fatigue even with a cart than his able-bodied competitors do by walking." The purpose of the walking rule is therefore not compromised in the slightest by allowing Martin to use a cart. A modification that provides an exception to a peripheral tournament rule without impairing its purpose cannot be said to "fundamentally alter" the tournament. What it can be said to do, on the other hand, is to allow Martin the chance to qualify for and compete in the athletic events petitioner offers to those members of the public who have the skill and desire to enter. That is exactly what the ADA requires. As a result, Martin's request for a waiver of the walking rule should have been granted.

The judgment of the Court of Appeals is affirmed. It is so ordered.

DISSENTING OPINION. SCALIA, JUSTICE

In my view, today's opinion exercises a benevolent compassion that the law does not place it within our power to impose. The judgment distorts the text of Title III, the structure of the ADA, and common sense. I respectfully dissent.

The Court, for its part, assumes that conclusion for the sake of argument, but pronounces respondent to be a "customer" of the PGA TOUR or of the golf courses on which it is played. That seems to me quite incredible. The PGA TOUR is a professional sporting event, staged for the entertainment of a live and TV audience. The professional golfers on the tour are no more "enjoying" (the statutory term) the entertainment that the tour provides, or the facilities of the golf courses on which it is held, than professional baseball players "enjoy" the baseball games in which they play or the facilities of Yankee Stadium. To be sure, professional baseball players *participate* in the games, and *use* the ballfields, but no one in his right mind would think that they are *customers* of the American League or of Yankee Stadium. They are themselves the entertainment that the customers pay to watch. And professional golfers are no different. A professional golfer's practicing his profession is not comparable to John Q. Public's frequenting "a 232-acre amusement area with swimming, boating, sun bathing, picnicking, miniature golf, dancing facilities, and a snack bar."

Having erroneously held that Title III applies to the "customers" of professional golf who consist of its practitioners, the Court then erroneously answers—or to be accurate simply ignores   a second question. The ADA requires covered businesses to make such reasonable modifications of "policies, practices, or procedures" as are necessary to "afford" goods, services, and privileges to individuals with disabilities; but it explicitly does not require "modifications that would fundamentally alter the nature" of the goods, services, and privileges. Section 12182(b)(2)(A)(ii). In other words, disabled individuals must be given *access* to the same goods, services, and privileges that others enjoy.

A camera store may not refuse to sell cameras to a disabled person, but it is not required to stock cameras specially designed for such persons. It is hardly a feasible judicial function to decide whether shoe stores should sell single shoes to one-legged persons and if so at what price, or how many Braille books the Borders or Barnes and Noble bookstore chains should stock in each of their stores. Eighteen-hole golf courses, 10-foot-high basketball hoops, 90-foot baselines, 100-yard football fields—all are arbitrary and none is essential. The only support for any of them is tradition and (in more modern times) insistence by what has come to be regarded as the ruling body of the sport—both of which factors support the PGA TOUR's position in the present case. One can envision the parents of a Little League player with attention deficit disorder trying to convince a judge that their son's disability makes it at least 25% more difficult to hit a pitched ball. (If they are successful, the only thing that could prevent a court order giving a kid four strikes would be a judicial determination that, in baseball, three strikes are metaphysically necessary, which is quite absurd.)

Agility, strength, speed, balance, quickness of mind, steadiness of nerves, intensity of concentration—these talents are not evenly distributed. No wild-eyed dreamer has ever suggested that the managing bodies of the competitive sports that test precisely these qualities should try to take account of the uneven distribution of God-given gifts when writing and enforcing the rules of competition. And I have no doubt Congress did not authorize misty-eyed judicial supervision of such revolution. The year was 2001, and "everybody was finally equal." K. Vonnegut, Harrison Bergeron, in *Animal Farm and Related Readings* 129 (1997).

Brief of the Case: *PGA TOUR, Inc. v. Martin*

1. Case Name, Citation, and Court

PGA TOUR, Inc. v. Martin
121 S.Ct. 1879, 2001 LEXIS 415 (2001)
Supreme Court of the United States

2. Summary of the Key Facts

A. PGA TOUR, Inc. is a nonprofit organization that sponsors professional golf tournaments.

B. The PGA establishes rules for its golf tournaments. A PGA rule requires golfers to walk the golf course, and not use golf carts.

C. Casey Martin is a professional golfer who suffers from Klippel-Trenaunay-Weber Syndrome, a degenerative circulatory disorder that atrophied Martin's right leg and causes him pain, fatigue, and anxiety when walking.

D. When Martin petitioned the PGA to use a golf cart during golf tournaments, the PGA refused.

E. Martin sued the PGA, alleging discrimination against a disabled individual in violation of the American with Disabilities Act of 1990, a federal statute.

3. Issue

Does the Americans with Disabilities Act require the PGA to accommodate Martin by permitting him to use a golf cart while playing in PGA golf tournaments?

4. Holding

Yes. The Supreme Court held that the PGA must allow Martin to use a golf cart when competing in PGA golf tournaments. Affirmed.

5. Court's Reasoning

The Supreme Court held that:

    A. Martin was disabled and covered by the Act.

    B. Golf courses are "public accommodations" covered by the Act.

    C. The use of golf carts is not a fundamental characteristic of the game of golf.

    D. Other than the PGA rule, no Rule of Golf forbids the use of golf carts.

    E. It is impossible to guarantee all players in golf will play under the exact same conditions, so allowing Martin to use a golf cart gives him no advantage over other golfers.

    F. Martin, because of his disease, will probably suffer more fatigue playing golf using a golf cart than other golfers will suffer without using a cart.

    G. The PGA's "walking rule" is only peripheral to the game of golf and not a fundamental part of golf.

    H. Allowing Martin to use a golf cart will not fundamentally alter the PGA's highest-level professional golf tournaments.

▶ CASE 3

For Briefing

Palsgraf v. Long Island R.R. Co.
248 N.Y. 339 (1928)

CASE NAME
CITATION   **162 N.E. 99**
COURT Court of Appeals of the State of New York

OPINION OF THE COURT. CARDOZO, Ch. J.

FACTS. Plaintiff was standing on a platform of defendant's railroad after buying a ticket to go to Rockaway Beach. A train stopped at the station, bound for another place. Two men ran forward to catch it. One of the men reached the platform of the car without mishap, though the train was already moving. The other man, carrying a package, jumped aboard the car, but seemed unsteady as if about to fall. A guard on the car, who had held the door open, reached forward to help him in, and another guard on the platform pushed him from behind. In this act, the package was dislodged, and fell upon the rails. It was a package of small size, about fifteen inches long, and was covered by a newspaper. In fact it contained fireworks, but there was nothing in its appearance to give notice of its contents. The fireworks when they fell exploded. The shock of the explosion threw down some scales at the other end of the platform, many feet away. The scales struck the plaintiff, causing injuries for which she sues.

    The conduct of the defendant's guard, if a wrong in its relation to the holder of the package, was not a wrong in its relation to the plaintiff, standing far away. Relatively to her it was not negligence at all. Nothing in the situation gave notice that the falling package had in it the potency of peril to persons thus removed. Negligence is not actionable unless it involves the invasion of a legally protected interest, the violation of a right. "Proof of negligence in the air, so to speak, will not do" (Pollock, *Torts* [11th ed.], p. 455; *Martin v. Herzog*, 228 N.Y. 164, 170; cf. Salmond, Torts [6th ed.], p.24). "Negligence is the absence of care, according to the circumstances" (WILLES, J., in *Vaughan v. Taff Vale Ry. Co.*, 5 H. & N. 679, 688; 1 Beven, Negligence [4th ed.], 7; *Paul v. Consol. Fireworks Co.*, 212 N.Y. 117; *Adams v. Bullock*, 227 N.Y. 208, 211; *Parrott v. Wells-Fargo Co.*, 15 Wall. [U.S.] 524). The plaintiff as she stood upon the platform of the station might claim to be protected against intentional invasion of her bodily security. Such invasion is not charged. She might claim to be protected against unintentional invasion by conduct involving in the thought of reasonable men an unreasonable hazard that such invasion would ensue. These, from the point of view of the law, were the bounds of her immunity, with perhaps some rare exceptions, survivals for the most part of ancient forms of liability, where conduct is held to be at the peril of the actor (*Sullivan v. Dunham*, 161 N.Y. 290 Page 342). If no hazard was apparent to the eye of ordinary vigilance, an act innocent and harmless, at least to outward seeming, with reference to her, did not take to itself the quality of a tort because it happened to be a wrong, though apparently not one involving the risk of bodily insecurity, with reference to some one else. "In every instance, before negligence can be predicated of a given act, back of the act must be sought and found a duty to the individual complaining, the observance of which would have averted or avoided the injury" (McSHERRY, C.J., in *W. Va. Central R. Co. v. State*, 96 Md. 652, 666; cf. *Norfolk & Western Ry. Co. v. Wood*, 99 Va. 156, 158, 159; *Hughes v. Boston & Maine R.R. Co.*, 71 N.H. 279, 284; *U.S. Express Co. v. Everest*, 72 Kan. 517; *Emry v. Roanoke Nav. Co.*, 111 N.C. 94, 95; *Vaughan v. Transit Dev. Co.*, 222 N.Y. 79; *Losee v. Clute*, 51 N.Y. 494; *DiCaprio v. N.Y.C.R.R. Co.*, 231 N.Y. 94; 1 Shearman & Redfield on Negligence, § 8, and cases cited; Cooley on Torts [3d ed.], p. 1411; Jaggard on Torts, vol. 2, p. 826; Wharton, *Negligence*, § 24; Bohlen, *Studies in the Law of Torts*, p. 601). "The ideas of negligence and duty are strictly correlative" (BOWEN, L.J., in *Thomas v. Quartermaine*, 18 Q.B.D. 685, 694). The plaintiff sues in her own right for a wrong personal to her, and not as the vicarious beneficiary of a breach of duty to another.

A different conclusion will involve us, and swiftly too, in a maze of contradictions. A guard stumbles over a package which has been left upon a platform. It seems to be a bundle of newspapers. It turns out to be a can of dynamite. To the eye of ordinary vigilance, the bundle is abandoned waste, which may be kicked or trod on with impunity. Is a passenger at the other end of the platform protected by the law against the unsuspected hazard concealed beneath the waste? If not, is the result to be any different, so far as the distant passenger is concerned, when the guard stumbles over a valise which a truckman or a porter has left upon the walk? The passenger far away, if the victim of a wrong at all, has a cause of action, not derivative, but original and primary. His claim to be protected against invasion of his bodily security is neither greater nor less because the act resulting in the invasion is a wrong to another far removed. In this case, the rights that are said to have been violated, the interests said to have been invaded, are not even of the same order. The man was not injured in his person nor even put in danger. The purpose of the act, as well as its effect, was to make his person safe. If there was a wrong to him at all, which may very well be doubted, it was a wrong to a property interest only, the safety of his package. Out of this wrong to property, which threatened injury to nothing else, there has passed, we are told, to the plaintiff by derivation or succession a right of action for the invasion of an interest of another order, the right to bodily security. The diversity of interests emphasizes the futility of the effort to build the plaintiff's right upon the basis of a wrong to some one else. The gain is one of emphasis, for a like result would follow if the interests were the same. Even then, the orbit of the danger as disclosed to the eye of reasonable vigilance would be the orbit of the duty. One who jostles one's neighbor in a crowd does not invade the rights of others standing at the outer fringe when the unintended contact casts a bomb upon the ground. The wrongdoer as to them is the man who carries the bomb, not the one who explodes it without suspicion of the danger. Life will have to be made over, and human nature transformed, before prevision so extravagant can be accepted as the norm of conduct, the

customary standard to which behavior must conform. The argument for the plaintiff is built upon the shifting meanings of such words as "wrong" and "wrongful," and shares their instability. What the plaintiff must show is "a wrong" to herself, i.e., a violation of her own right, and not merely a wrong to some one else, nor conduct "wrongful" because unsocial, but not "a wrong" to any one. We are told that one who drives at reckless speed through a crowded city street is guilty of a negligent act and, therefore, of a wrongful one irrespective of the consequences. Negligent the act is, and wrongful in the sense that it is unsocial, but wrongful and unsocial in relation to other travelers, only because the eye of vigilance perceives the risk of damage. If the same act were to be committed on a speedway or a race course, it would lose its wrongful quality. The risk reasonably to be perceived defines the duty to be obeyed, and risk imports relation; it is risk to another or to others within the range of apprehension (Seavey, Negligence, Subjective or Objective, 41 H.L. Rv. 6; *Boronkay v. Robinson & Carpenter*, 247 N.Y. 365). This does not mean, of course, that one who launches a destructive force is always relieved of liability if the force, though known to be destructive, pursues an unexpected path. "It was not necessary that the defendant should have had notice of the particular method in which an accident would occur, if the possibility of an accident was clear to the ordinarily prudent eye" (*Munsey v. Webb*, 231 U.S. 150, 156; *Condran v. Park & Tilford*, 213 N.Y. 341, 345; *Robert v. U.S.E.F. Corp.*, 240 N.Y. 474, 477). Some acts, such as shooting, are so imminently dangerous to any one who may come within reach of the missile, however unexpectedly, as to impose a duty of prevision not far from that of an insurer. Even today, and much oftener in earlier stages of the law, one acts sometimes at one's peril (Jeremiah Smith, Tort and Absolute Liability, 30 H.L. Rv. 328; Street, *Foundations of Legal Liability*, vol. 1, pp. 77, 78). Under this head, it may be, fall certain cases of what is known as transferred intent, an act willfully dangerous to A resulting by misadventure in injury to B (*Talmage v. Smith*, 101 Mich. 370, 374) These cases aside, wrong is defined in terms of the natural or probable, at least when unintentional (*Parrot v. Wells-Fargo Co.* [The Nitro-Glycerine Case], 15 Wall. [U.S.] 524). The range of reasonable apprehension is at times a question for the court, and at times, if varying inferences are possible, a question for the jury. Here, by concession, there was nothing in the situation to suggest to the most cautious mind that the parcel wrapped in newspaper would spread wreckage through the station. If the guard had thrown it down knowingly and willfully, he would not have threatened the plaintiff's safety, so far as appearances could warn him. His conduct would not have involved, even then, an unreasonable probability of invasion of her bodily security. Liability can be no greater where the act is inadvertent.

Negligence, like risk, is thus a term of relation. Negligence in the abstract, apart from things related, is surely not a tort, if indeed it is understandable at all (BOWEN, L.J., in *Thomas v. Quartermaine*, 18 Q.B.D. 685, 694). Negligence is not a tort unless it results in the commission of a wrong, and the commission of a wrong imports the violation of a right, in this case, we are told, the right to be protected against interference with one's bodily security. But bodily security is protected, not against all forms of interference or aggression, but only against some. One who seeks redress at law does not make out a cause of action by showing without more that there has been damage to his person. If the harm was not willful, he must show that the act as to him had possibilities of danger so many and apparent as to entitle him to be protected against the doing of it though the harm was unintended. Affront to personality is still the keynote of the wrong. Confirmation of this view will be found in the history and development of the action on the case. Negligence as a basis of civil liability was unknown to mediaeval law (8 Holdsworth, *History of English Law*, p. 449; Street, *Foundations of Legal Liability*, vol. 1, pp. 189, 190). For damage to the person, the sole remedy was trespass, and trespass did not lie in the absence of aggression, and that direct and personal (Holdsworth, op. cit. p. 453; Street, op. cit. vol. 3, pp. 258, 260, vol. 1, pp. 71, 74.) Liability for other damage, as where a servant without orders from the master does or omits something to the damage of another, is a plant of later growth (Holdsworth, op. cit. 450, 457; Wigmore, *Responsibility or Tortious Acts*, vol. 3, *Essays in Anglo-American Legal History*, 520, 523, 526, 533). When it emerged out of the legal soil, it was thought of as a variant of trespass, an offshoot of the parent stock. This appears in the form of action, which was known as trespass on the case (Holdsworth, op. cit. p. 449; cf. *Scott v. Shepard*, 2 Wm. Black. 892; Green, *Rationale of Proximate Cause*, p. 19). The victim does not sue derivatively, or by right of subrogation, to vindicate an interest invaded in the person of another. Thus to view his cause of action is to ignore the fundamental difference between tort and crime (Holland, *Jurisprudence* [12th ed.], p. 328). He sues for breach of a duty owing to himself.

The law of causation, remote or proximate, is thus foreign to the case before us. The question of liability is always anterior to the question of the measure of the consequences that go with liability. If there is no tort to be redressed, there is no occasion to consider what damage might be recovered if there were a finding of a tort. We may assume, without deciding, that negligence, not at large or in the abstract, but in relation to the plaintiff, would entail liability for any and all consequences, however novel or extraordinary (*Bird v. St. Paul F. & M. Ins. Co.*, 224 N.Y. 47, 54; *Ehrgott v. Mayor, etc., of N Y*, 96 N.Y. 264; *Smith v. London & S.W. Ry. Co.*, L.R. 6 C.P. 14; 1 Beven, Negligence, 106; Street, op. cit. vol. 1, p. 90; Green, *Rationale of Proximate Cause*, pp. 88, 118; cf. *Matter of Polemis*, L.R. 1921, 3 K.B. 560; 44 *Law Quarterly Review*, 142). There is room for argument that a distinction is to be drawn according to the diversity of interests invaded by the act, as where conduct negligent in that it threatens an insignificant invasion of an interest in property results in an unforeseeable invasion of an interest of another order, as, e.g., one of bodily security. Perhaps other distinctions may be necessary. We do not go into the question now. The consequences to be followed must first be rooted in a wrong.

HOLDING. The judgment of the Appellate Division and that of the Trial Term should be reversed, and the complaint dismissed, with costs in all courts.

DISSENTING OPINION. ANDREWS, J.
Assisting a passenger to board a train, the defendant's servant negligently knocked a package from his arms. It fell between the platform and the cars. Of its contents the servant knew and could know nothing. A violent explosion followed. The concussion broke some scales standing a considerable distance away. In falling they injured the plaintiff, an intending passenger.

Upon these facts may she recover the damages she has suffered in an action brought against the master? The result we shall reach depends upon our theory as to the nature of negligence. Is it a relative concept—the breach of some duty owing to a particular person or to particular persons? Or where there is an act which unreasonably threatens the safety of others, is the doer liable for all its proximate consequences, even where they result in injury to one who would generally be thought to be outside the radius of danger? This is not a mere dispute as to words. We might not believe that to the average mind the dropping of the bundle would seem to involve the probability of harm to the plaintiff standing many feet away whatever might be the case as to the owner or to one so near as to be likely to be struck by its fall. If, however, we adopt the second hypothesis we have to inquire only as to the relation between cause and effect. We deal in terms of proximate cause, not of negligence.

Negligence may be defined roughly as an act or omission which unreasonably does or may affect the rights of others, or which unreasonably fails to protect oneself from the dangers resulting from such acts. Here I confine myself to the first branch of the definition. Nor do I comment on the word "unreasonable." For present purposes it sufficiently describes that average of conduct that society requires of its members.

There must be both the act or the omission, and the right. It is the act itself, not the intent of the actor, that is important. (*Hover v. Barkhoof*, 44 N.Y. 113; *Mertz v. Connecticut Co.*, 217 N.Y. 475.) In criminal law both the intent and the result are to be considered. Intent again is material in tort actions, where punitive damages are sought, dependent on actual malice—not on merely reckless conduct. But here neither insanity nor infancy lessens responsibility. (*Williams v. Hays*, 143 N.Y. 442.)

As has been said, except in cases of contributory negligence, there must be rights which are or may be affected. Often though injury has occurred, no rights of him who suffers have been touched. A licensee or trespasser upon my land has no claim to affirmative care on my part that the land be made safe. (*Meiers v. Koch Brewery*, 229 N.Y. 10.) Where a railroad is required to fence its tracks against cattle, no man's rights are injured should he wander upon the road because such fence is absent. (*DiCaprio v. N.Y.C.R.R.*, 231 N.Y. 94.) An unborn child may not demand immunity from personal harm. (*Drobner v. Peters*, 232 N.Y. 220.)

But we are told that "there is no negligence unless there is in the particular case a legal duty to take care, and this duty must be one which is owed to the plaintiff himself and not merely to others." (*Salmond Torts* [6th ed.], 24.) This, I think too narrow a conception. Where there is the unreasonable act, and some right that may be affected there is negligence whether damage does or does not result. That is immaterial. Should we drive down Broadway at a reckless speed, we are negligent whether we strike an approaching car or miss it by an inch. The act itself is wrongful. It is a wrong not only to those who happen to be within the radius of danger but to all who might have been there—a wrong to the public at large. Such is the language of the street. Such the language of the courts when speaking of contributory negligence. Such again and again their language in speaking of the duty of some defendant and discussing proximate cause in cases where such a discussion is wholly irrelevant on any other theory. (*Perry v. Rochester Line Co.*, 219 N.Y. 60.) As was said by Mr. Justice HOLMES many years ago, "the measure of the defendant's duty in determining whether a wrong has been committed is one thing, the measure of liability when a wrong has been committed is another." (*Spade v. Lynn & Boston R.R. Co.*, 172 Mass. 488.) Due care is a duty imposed on each one of us to protect society from unnecessary danger, not to protect A, B or C alone.

It may well be that there is no such thing as negligence in the abstract. "Proof of negligence in the air, so to speak, will not do." In an empty world negligence would not exist. It does involve a relationship between man and his fellows. But not merely a relationship between man and those whom he might reasonably expect his act would injure. Rather, a relationship between him and those whom he does in fact injure. If his act has a tendency to harm some one, it harms him a mile away as surely as it does those on the scene. We now permit children to recover for the negligent killing of the father. It was never prevented on the theory that no duty was owing to them. A husband may be compensated for the loss of his wife's services. To say that the wrongdoer was negligent as to the husband as well as to the wife is merely an attempt to fit facts to theory. An insurance company paying a fire loss recovers its payment of the negligent incendiary. We speak of subrogation—of suing in the right of the insured. Behind the cloud of words is the fact they hide, that the act, wrongful as to the insured, has also injured the company. Even if it be true that the fault of father, wife or insured will prevent recovery, it is because we consider the original negligence not the proximate cause of the injury. (Pollock, *Torts* [12th ed.], 463.)

In the well-known *Polemis* case (1921, 3 K.B. 560), SCRUTTON, L.J., said that the dropping of a plank was negligent for it might injure "workman or cargo or ship." Because of either possibility the owner of the vessel was to be made good for his loss. The act being wrongful the doer was liable for its proximate results. Criticized and explained as this statement may have been, I think it states the law as it should be and as it is. (*Smith v. London & Southwestern Ry. Co.*, [1870-71] 6 C.P. 14; *Anthony v. Slaid*, 52 Mass. 290; *Wood v. Penn. R.R.Co.*, 177 Penn. St. 306; *Trashansky v. Hershkovitz*, 239 N.Y. 452.)

The proposition is this. Every one owes to the world at large the duty of refraining from those acts that may unreasonably threaten the safety of others. Such an act occurs. Not only is he wronged to whom harm might reasonably be expected to result, but he also who is in fact injured, even if he be outside what would generally be thought the danger zone. There needs be duty due the one complaining but this is not a duty to a particular individual because as to him harm might be expected. Harm to some one being the natural result of the act, not only that one alone, but all those in fact injured may complain. We have never, I think, held otherwise. Indeed in the Di Caprio case we said that a breach of a general ordinance defining the degree of care to be exercised in one's calling is evidence of negligence as to every one. We did not limit this statement to those who might be expected to be exposed to danger. Unreasonable risk being taken, its consequences are not confined to those who might probably be hurt.

If this be so, we do not have a plaintiff suing by "derivation or succession." Her action is original and primary. Her claim is for a breach of duty to herself—not that she is subrogated to any

right of action of the owner of the parcel or of a passenger standing at the scene of the explosion.

The right to recover damages rests on additional considerations. The plaintiff's rights must be injured, and this injury must be caused by the negligence. We build a dam, but are negligent as to its foundations. Breaking, it injures property down stream. We are not liable if all this happened because of some reason other than the insecure foundation. But when injuries do result from our unlawful act we are liable for the consequences. It does not matter that they are unusual, unexpected, unforeseen and unforeseeable. But there is one limitation. The damages must be so connected with the negligence that the latter may be said to be the proximate cause of the former.

These two words have never been given an inclusive definition. What is a cause in a legal sense, still more what is a proximate cause, depend in each case upon many considerations, as does the existence of negligence itself. Any philosophical doctrine of causation does not help us. A boy throws a stone into a pond. The ripples spread. The water level rises. The history of that pond is altered to all eternity. It will be altered by other causes also. Yet it will be forever the resultant of all causes combined. Each one will have an influence. How great only omniscience can say. You may speak of a chain, or if you please, a net. An analogy is of little aid. Each cause brings about future events. Without each the future would not be the same. Each is proximate in the sense it is essential. But that is not what we mean by the word. Nor on the other hand do we mean sole cause. There is no such thing.

Should analogy be thought helpful, however, I prefer that of a stream. The spring, starting on its journey, is joined by tributary after tributary. The river, reaching the ocean, comes from a hundred sources. No man may say whence any drop of water is derived. Yet for a time distinction may be possible. Into the clear creek, brown swamp water flows from the left. Later, from the right comes water stained by its clay bed. The three may remain for a space, sharply divided. But at last, inevitably no trace of separation remains. They are so commingled that all distinction is lost.

As we have said, we cannot trace the effect of an act to the end, if end there is. Again, however, we may trace it part of the way. A murder at Sarajevo may be the necessary antecedent to an assassination in London twenty years hence. An overturned lantern may burn all Chicago. We may follow the fire from the shed to the last building. We rightly say the fire started by the lantern caused its destruction.

A cause, but not the proximate cause. What we do mean by the word "proximate" is, that because of convenience, of public policy, of a rough sense of justice, the law arbitrarily declines to trace a series of events beyond a certain point. This is not logic. It is practical politics. Take our rule as to fires. Sparks from my burning haystack set on fire my house and my neighbor's. I may recover from a negligent railroad. He may not. Yet the wrongful act as directly harmed the one as the other. We may regret that the line was drawn just where it was, but drawn somewhere it had to be. We said the act of the railroad was not the proximate cause of our neighbor's fire. Cause it surely was. The words we used were simply indicative of our notions of public policy. Other courts think differently. But somewhere they reach the point where they cannot say the stream comes from any one source.

Take the illustration given in an unpublished manuscript by a distinguished and helpful writer on the law of torts. A chauffeur negligently collides with another car which is filled with dynamite, although he could not know it. An explosion follows. A, walking on the sidewalk nearby, is killed. B, sitting in a window of a building opposite, is cut by flying glass. C, likewise sitting in a window a block away, is similarly injured. And a further illustration. A nursemaid, ten blocks away, startled by the noise, involuntarily drops a baby from her arms to the walk. We are told that C may not recover while A may. As to B it is a question for court or jury. We will all agree that the baby might not. Because, we are again told, the chauffeur had no reason to believe his conduct involved any risk of injuring either C or the baby. As to them he was not negligent.

But the chauffeur, being negligent in risking the collision, his belief that the scope of the harm he might do would be limited is immaterial. His act unreasonably jeopardized the safety of any one who might be affected by it. C's injury and that of the baby were directly traceable to the collision. Without that, the injury would not have happened. C had the right to sit in his office, secure from such dangers. The baby was entitled to use the sidewalk with reasonable safety.

The true theory is, it seems to me, that the injury to C, if in truth he is to be denied recovery, and the injury to the baby is that their several injuries were not the proximate result of the negligence. And here not what the chauffeur had reason to believe would be the result of his conduct, but what the prudent would foresee, may have a bearing. May have some bearing, for the problem of proximate cause is not to be solved by any one consideration.

It is all a question of expediency. There are no fixed rules to govern our judgment. There are simply matters of which we may take account. We have in a somewhat different connection spoken of "the stream of events." We have asked whether that stream was deflected—whether it was forced into new and unexpected channels. (*Donnelly v. Piercy Contracting Co.*, 222 N.Y. 210.) This is rather rhetoric than law. There is in truth little to guide us other than common sense.

There are some hints that may help us. The proximate cause, involved as it may be with many other causes, must be, at the least, something without which the event would not happen. The court must ask itself whether there was a natural and continuous sequence between cause and effect. Was the one a substantial factor in producing the other? Was there a direct connection between them, without too many intervening causes? Is the effect of cause on result not too attenuated? Is the cause likely, in the usual judgment of mankind, to produce the result? Or by the exercise of prudent foresight could the result be foreseen? Is the result too remote from the cause, and here we consider remoteness in time and space. (*Bird v. St. Paul F. & M. Ins. Co.*, 224 N.Y. 47, where we passed upon the construction of a contract—but something was also said on this subject.) Clearly we must so consider, for the greater the distance either in time or space, the more surely do other causes intervene to affect the result. When a lantern is overturned the firing of a shed is a fairly direct consequence. Many things contribute to the spread of the conflagration—the force of the wind, the direction and width of streets, the character of intervening structures, other factors. We draw an uncertain and wavering line, but draw it we must as best we can.

Once again, it is all a question of fair judgment, always keeping in mind the fact that we endeavor to make a rule in each case that will be practical and in keeping with the general understanding of mankind.

Here another question must be answered. In the case supposed it is said, and said correctly, that the chauffeur is liable for the direct effect of the explosion although he had no reason to suppose it would follow a collision. "The fact that the injury occurred in a different manner than that which might have been expected does not prevent the chauffeur's negligence from being in law the cause of the injury." But the natural results of a negligent act—the results which a prudent man would or should foresee—do have a bearing upon the decision as to proximate cause. We have said so repeatedly. What should be foreseen? No human foresight would suggest that a collision itself might injure one a block away. On the contrary, given an explosion, such a possibility might be reasonably expected. I think the direct connection, the foresight of which the courts peak, assumes prevision of the explosion, for the immediate results of which, at least, the chauffeur is responsible.

It may be said this is unjust. Why? In fairness he should make good every injury flowing from his negligence. Not because of tenderness toward him we say he need not answer for all that follows his wrong. We look back to the catastrophe, the fire kindled by the spark, or the explosion. We trace the consequences—not indefinitely, but to a certain point. And to aid us in fixing that point we ask what might ordinarily be expected to follow the fire or the explosion.

This last suggestion is the factor which must determine the case before us. The act upon which defendant's liability rests is knocking an apparently harmless package onto the platform. The act was negligent. For its proximate consequences the defendant is liable. If its contents were broken, to the owner; if it fell upon and crushed a passenger's foot, then to him. If it exploded and injured one in the immediate vicinity, to him also as to A in the illustration. Mrs. Palsgraf was standing some distance away. How far cannot be told from the record—apparently twenty-five or thirty feet. Perhaps less. Except for the explosion, she would not have been injured. We are told by the appellant in his brief "it cannot be denied that the explosion was the direct cause of the plaintiff's injuries." So it was a substantial factor in producing the result—there was here a natural and continuous sequence—direct connection. The only intervening cause was that instead of blowing her to the ground the concussion smashed the weighing machine which in turn fell upon her. There was no remoteness in time, little in space. And surely, given such an explosion as here it needed no great foresight to predict that the natural result would be to injure one on the platform at no greater distance from its scene than was the plaintiff. Just how no one might be able to predict. Whether by flying fragments, by broken glass, by wreckage of machines or structures no one could say. But injury in some form was most probable.

Under these circumstances I cannot say as a matter of law that the plaintiff's injuries were not the proximate result of the negligence. That is all we have before us. The court refused to so charge. No request was made to submit the matter to the jury as a question of fact, even would that have been proper upon the record before us.

The judgment appealed from should be affirmed, with costs.

Appendix B

Model Rules of Professional Conduct

CLIENT–LAWYER RELATIONSHIP
Rule 1.6 Confidentiality of Information

(a) A lawyer shall not reveal information relating to the representation of a client unless the client gives informed consent, the disclosure is impliedly authorized in order to carry out the representation or the disclosure is permitted by paragraph (b).

(b) A lawyer may reveal information relating to the representation of a client to the extent the lawyer reasonably believes necessary:

    (1) to prevent reasonably certain death or substantial bodily harm;

    (2) to prevent the client from committing a crime or fraud that is reasonably certain to result in substantial injury to the financial interests or property of another and in furtherance of which the client has used or is using the lawyer's services;

    (3) to prevent, mitigate or rectify substantial injury to the financial interests or property of another that is reasonably certain to result or has resulted from the client's commission of a crime or fraud in furtherance of which the client has used the lawyer's services;

    (4) to secure legal advice about the lawyer's compliance with these Rules;

    (5) to establish a claim or defense on behalf of the lawyer in a controversy between the lawyer and the client, to establish a defense to a criminal charge or civil claim against the lawyer based upon conduct in which the client was involved, or to respond to allegations in any proceeding concerning the lawyer's representation of the client; or

    (6) to comply with other law or a court order.

ABA *Model Rules of Professional Conduct*, 2004 Edition. © 2003 by the American Bar Association. Reprinted with permission.
Copies of the ABA *Model Rules of Professional Conduct*, 2004 Edition, are available from Service Center, American Bar Association. 321 North Clark Street, Chicago, IL 60610, 1-800-285-2221.

CLIENT–LAWYER RELATIONSHIP
Rule 1.6 Confidentiality of Information—Comment

[1] This Rule governs the disclosure by a lawyer of information relating to the representation of a client during the lawyer's representation of the client. See Rule 1.18 for the lawyer's duties with respect to information provided to the lawyer by a prospective client, Rule 1.9(c)(2) for the lawyer's duty not to reveal information relating to the lawyer's prior representation of a former client and Rules 1.8(b) and 1.9(c)(1) for the lawyer's duties with respect to the use of such information to the disadvantage of clients and former clients.

[2] A fundamental principle in the client-lawyer relationship is that, in the absence of the client's informed consent, the lawyer must not reveal information relating to the representation. See Rule 1.0(e) for the definition of informed consent. This contributes to the trust that is the hallmark of the client-lawyer relationship. The client is thereby encouraged to seek legal assistance and to communicate fully and

frankly with the lawyer even as to embarrassing or legally damaging subject matter. The lawyer needs this information to represent the client effectively and, if necessary, to advise the client to refrain from wrongful conduct. Almost without exception, clients come to lawyers in order to determine their rights and what is, in the complex of laws and regulations, deemed to be legal and correct. Based upon experience, lawyers know that almost all clients follow the advice given, and the law is upheld.

[3] The principle of client-lawyer confidentiality is given effect by related bodies of law: the attorney-client privilege, the work product doctrine, and the rule of confidentiality established in professional ethics. The attorney-client privilege and work-product doctrine apply in judicial and other proceedings in which a lawyer may be called as a witness or otherwise required to produce evidence concerning a client. The rule of client-lawyer confidentiality applies in situations other than those where evidence is sought from the lawyer through compulsion of law. The confidentiality rule, for example, applies not only to matters communicated in confidence by the client but also to all information relating to the representation, whatever its source. A lawyer may not disclose such information except as authorized or required by the Rules of Professional Conduct or other law. See also Scope.

[4] Paragraph (a) prohibits a lawyer from revealing information relating to the representation of a client. This prohibition also applies to disclosures by a lawyer that do not in themselves reveal protected information but could reasonably lead to the discovery of such information by a third person. A lawyer's use of a hypothetical to discuss issues relating to the representation is permissible so long as there is no reasonable likelihood that the listener will be able to ascertain the identity of the client or the situation involved.

Authorized Disclosure

[5] Except to the extent that the client's instructions or special circumstances limit that authority, a lawyer is impliedly authorized to make disclosures about a client when appropriate in carrying out the representation. In some situations, for example, a lawyer may be impliedly authorized to admit a fact that cannot properly be disputed or to make a disclosure that facilitates a satisfactory conclusion to a matter. Lawyers in a firm may, in the course of the firm's practice, disclose to each other information relating to a client of the firm, unless the client has instructed that particular information be confined to specified lawyers.

Disclosure Adverse to Client

[6] Although the public interest is usually best served by a strict rule requiring lawyers to preserve the confidentiality of information relating to the representation of their clients, the confidentiality rule is subject to limited exceptions. Paragraph (b)(1) recognizes the overriding value of life and physical integrity and permits disclosure reasonably necessary to prevent reasonably certain death or substantial bodily harm. Such harm is reasonably certain to occur if it will be suffered imminently or if there is a present and substantial threat that a person will suffer such harm at a later date if the lawyer fails to take action necessary to eliminate the threat. Thus, a lawyer who knows that a client has accidentally discharged toxic waste into a town's water supply may reveal this information to the authorities if there is a present and substantial risk that a person who drinks the water will contract a life-threatening or debilitating disease and the lawyer's disclosure is necessary to eliminate the threat or reduce the number of victims.

[7] Paragraph (b)(2) is a limited exception to the rule of confidentiality that permits the lawyer to reveal information to the extent necessary to enable affected persons or appropriate authorities to prevent the client from committing a crime or fraud, as defined in Rule 1.0(d), that is reasonably certain to result in substantial injury to the financial or property interests of another and in furtherance of which the client has used or is using the lawyer's services. Such a serious abuse of the client-lawyer relationship by the client forfeits the protection of this Rule. The client can, of

course, prevent such disclosure by refraining from the wrongful conduct. Although paragraph (b)(2) does not require the lawyer to reveal the client's misconduct, the lawyer may not counsel or assist the client in conduct the lawyer knows is criminal or fraudulent. See Rule 1.2(d). See also Rule 1.16 with respect to the lawyer's obligation or right to withdraw from the representation of the client in such circumstances, and Rule 1.13(c), which permits the lawyer, where the client is an organization, to reveal information relating to the representation in limited circumstances.

[8] Paragraph (b)(3) addresses the situation in which the lawyer does not learn of the client's crime or fraud until after it has been consummated. Although the client no longer has the option of preventing disclosure by refraining from the wrongful conduct, there will be situations in which the loss suffered by the affected person can be prevented, rectified or mitigated. In such situations, the lawyer may disclose information relating to the representation to the extent necessary to enable the affected persons to prevent or mitigate reasonably certain losses or to attempt to recoup their losses. Paragraph (b)(3) does not apply when a person who has committed a crime or fraud thereafter employs a lawyer for representation concerning that offense.

[9] A lawyer's confidentiality obligations do not preclude a lawyer from securing confidential legal advice about the lawyer's personal responsibility to comply with these Rules. In most situations, disclosing information to secure such advice will be impliedly authorized for the lawyer to carry out the representation. Even when the disclosure is not impliedly authorized, paragraph (b)(4) permits such disclosure because of the importance of a lawyer's compliance with the Rules of Professional Conduct.

[10] Where a legal claim or disciplinary charge alleges complicity of the lawyer in a client's conduct or other misconduct of the lawyer involving representation of the client, the lawyer may respond to the extent the lawyer reasonably believes necessary to establish a defense. The same is true with respect to a claim involving the conduct or representation of a former client. Such a charge can arise in a civil, criminal, disciplinary or other proceeding and can be based on a wrong allegedly committed by the lawyer against the client or on a wrong alleged by a third person, for example, a person claiming to have been defrauded by the lawyer and client acting together. The lawyer's right to respond arises when an assertion of such complicity has been made. Paragraph (b)(5) does not require the lawyer to await the commencement of an action or proceeding that charges such complicity, so that the defense may be established by responding directly to a third party who has made such an assertion. The right to defend also applies, of course, where a proceeding has been commenced.

[11] A lawyer entitled to a fee is permitted by paragraph (b)(5) to prove the services rendered in an action to collect it. This aspect of the rule expresses the principle that the beneficiary of a fiduciary relationship may not exploit it to the detriment of the fiduciary.

[12] Other law may require that a lawyer disclose information about a client. Whether such a law supersedes Rule 1.6 is a question of law beyond the scope of these Rules. When disclosure of information relating to the representation appears to be required by other law, the lawyer must discuss the matter with the client to the extent required by Rule 1.4. If, however, the other law supersedes this Rule and requires disclosure, paragraph (b)(6) permits the lawyer to make such disclosures as are necessary to comply with the law.

[13] A lawyer may be ordered to reveal information relating to the representation of a client by a court or by another tribunal or governmental entity claiming authority pursuant to other law to compel the disclosure. Absent informed consent of the client to do otherwise, the lawyer should assert on behalf of the client all nonfrivolous claims that the order is not authorized by other law or that the information sought is protected against disclosure by the attorney-client privilege or other applicable law. In the event of an adverse ruling, the lawyer must consult with the client about the possibility of appeal to the extent required by Rule 1.4. Unless review is sought, however, paragraph (b)(6) permits the lawyer to comply with the court's order.

[14] Paragraph (b) permits disclosure only to the extent the lawyer reasonably believes the disclosure is necessary to accomplish one of the purposes specified. Where practicable, the lawyer should first seek to persuade the client to take suitable action to obviate the need for disclosure. In any case, a disclosure adverse to the client's interest should be no greater than the lawyer reasonably believes necessary to accomplish the purpose. If the disclosure will be made in connection with a judicial proceeding, the disclosure should be made in a manner that limits access to the information to the tribunal or other persons having a need to know it and appropriate protective orders or other arrangements should be sought by the lawyer to the fullest extent practicable.

[15] Paragraph (b) permits but does not require the disclosure of information relating to a client's representation to accomplish the purposes specified in paragraphs (b)(1) through (b)(6). In exercising the discretion conferred by this Rule, the lawyer may consider such factors as the nature of the lawyer's relationship with the client and with those who might be injured by the client, the lawyer's own involvement in the transaction and factors that may extenuate the conduct in question. A lawyer's decision not to disclose as permitted by paragraph (b) does not violate this Rule. Disclosure may be required, however, by other Rules. Some Rules require disclosure only if such disclosure would be permitted by paragraph (b). See Rules 1.2(d), 4.1(b), 8.1 and 8.3. Rule 3.3, on the other hand, requires disclosure in some circumstances regardless of whether such disclosure is permitted by this Rule. See Rule 3.3(c).

Acting Competently to Preserve Confidentiality

[16] A lawyer must act competently to safeguard information relating to the representation of a client against inadvertent or unauthorized disclosure by the lawyer or other persons who are participating in the representation of the client or who are subject to the lawyer's supervision. See Rules 1.1, 5.1 and 5.3.

[17] When transmitting a communication that includes information relating to the representation of a client, the lawyer must take reasonable precautions to prevent the information from coming into the hands of unintended recipients. This duty, however, does not require that the lawyer use special security measures if the method of communication affords a reasonable expectation of privacy. Special circumstances, however, may warrant special precautions. Factors to be considered in determining the reasonableness of the lawyer's expectation of confidentiality include the sensitivity of the information and the extent to which the privacy of the communication is protected by law or by a confidentiality agreement. A client may require the lawyer to implement special security measures not required by this Rule or may give informed consent to the use of a means of communication that would otherwise be prohibited by this Rule.

Former Client

[18] The duty of confidentiality continues after the client-lawyer relationship has terminated. See Rule 1.9(c)(2). See Rule 1.9(c)(1) for the prohibition against using such information to the disadvantage of the former client.

CLIENT–LAWYER RELATIONSHIP
Rule 1.7 Conflict of Interest: Current Clients

(a) Except as provided in paragraph (b), a lawyer shall not represent a client if the representation involves a concurrent conflict of interest. A concurrent conflict of interest exists if:

    (1) the representation of one client will be directly adverse to another client; or

    (2) there is a significant risk that the representation of one or more clients will be materially limited by the lawyer's responsibilities to another client, a former client or a third person or by a personal interest of the lawyer.

(b) Notwithstanding the existence of a concurrent conflict of interest under paragraph (a), a lawyer may represent a client if:

    (1) the lawyer reasonably believes that the lawyer will be able to provide competent and diligent representation to each affected client;

    (2) the representation is not prohibited by law;

    (3) the representation does not involve the assertion of a claim by one client against another client represented by the lawyer in the same litigation or other proceeding before a tribunal; and

    (4) each affected client gives informed consent, confirmed in writing.

CLIENT–LAWYER RELATIONSHIP

Rule 1.7 Conflict of Interest: Current Clients—Comment

General Principles

[1] Loyalty and independent judgment are essential elements in the lawyer's relationship to a client. Concurrent conflicts of interest can arise from the lawyer's responsibilities to another client, a former client or a third person or from the lawyer's own interests. For specific Rules regarding certain concurrent conflicts of interest, see Rule 1.8. For former client conflicts of interest, see Rule 1.9. For conflicts of interest involving prospective clients, see Rule 1.18. For definitions of "informed consent" and "confirmed in writing," see Rule 1.0(e) and (b).

    [2] Resolution of a conflict of interest problem under this Rule requires the lawyer to: 1) clearly identify the client or clients; 2) determine whether a conflict of interest exists; 3) decide whether the representation may be undertaken despite the existence of a conflict, i.e., whether the conflict is consentable; and 4) if so, consult with the clients affected under paragraph (a) and obtain their informed consent, confirmed in writing. The clients affected under paragraph (a) include both of the clients referred to in paragraph (a)(1) and the one or more clients whose representation might be materially limited under paragraph (a)(2).

    [3] A conflict of interest may exist before representation is undertaken, in which event the representation must be declined, unless the lawyer obtains the informed consent of each client under the conditions of paragraph (b). To determine whether a conflict of interest exists, a lawyer should adopt reasonable procedures, appropriate for the size and type of firm and practice, to determine in both litigation and non-litigation matters the persons and issues involved. See also Comment to Rule 5.1. Ignorance caused by a failure to institute such procedures will not excuse a lawyer's violation of this Rule. As to whether a client-lawyer relationship exists or, having once been established, is continuing, see Comment to Rule 1.3 and Scope.

    [4] If a conflict arises after representation has been undertaken, the lawyer ordinarily must withdraw from the representation, unless the lawyer has obtained the informed consent of the client under the conditions of paragraph (b). See Rule 1.16. Where more than one client is involved, whether the lawyer may continue to represent any of the clients is determined both by the lawyer's ability to comply with duties owed to the former client and by the lawyer's ability to represent adequately the

remaining client or clients, given the lawyer's duties to the former client. See Rule 1.9. See also Comments [5] and [29].

[5] Unforeseeable developments, such as changes in corporate and other organizational affiliations or the addition or realignment of parties in litigation, might create conflicts in the midst of a representation, as when a company sued by the lawyer on behalf of one client is bought by another client represented by the lawyer in an unrelated matter. Depending on the circumstances, the lawyer may have the option to withdraw from one of the representations in order to avoid the conflict. The lawyer must seek court approval where necessary and take steps to minimize harm to the clients. See Rule 1.16. The lawyer must continue to protect the confidences of the client from whose representation the lawyer has withdrawn. See Rule 1.9(c).

Identifying Conflicts of Interest: Directly Adverse

[6] Loyalty to a current client prohibits undertaking representation directly adverse to that client without that client's informed consent. Thus, absent consent, a lawyer may not act as an advocate in one matter against a person the lawyer represents in some other matter, even when the matters are wholly unrelated. The client as to whom the representation is directly adverse is likely to feel betrayed, and the resulting damage to the client-lawyer relationship is likely to impair the lawyer's ability to represent the client effectively. In addition, the client on whose behalf the adverse representation is undertaken reasonably may fear that the lawyer will pursue that client's case less effectively out of deference to the other client, i.e., that the representation may be materially limited by the lawyer's interest in retaining the current client. Similarly, a directly adverse conflict may arise when a lawyer is required to cross-examine a client who appears as a witness in a lawsuit involving another client, as when the testimony will be damaging to the client who is represented in the lawsuit. On the other hand, simultaneous representation in unrelated matters of clients whose interests are only economically adverse, such as representation of competing economic enterprises in unrelated litigation, does not ordinarily constitute a conflict of interest and thus may not require consent of the respective clients.

[7] Directly adverse conflicts can also arise in transactional matters. For example, if a lawyer is asked to represent the seller of a business in negotiations with a buyer represented by the lawyer, not in the same transaction but in another, unrelated matter, the lawyer could not undertake the representation without the informed consent of each client.

Identifying Conflicts of Interest: Material Limitation

[8] Even where there is no direct adverseness, a conflict of interest exists if there is a significant risk that a lawyer's ability to consider, recommend or carry out an appropriate course of action for the client will be materially limited as a result of the lawyer's other responsibilities or interests. For example, a lawyer asked to represent several individuals seeking to form a joint venture is likely to be materially limited in the lawyer's ability to recommend or advocate all possible positions that each might take because of the lawyer's duty of loyalty to the others. The conflict in effect forecloses alternatives that would otherwise be available to the client. The mere possibility of subsequent harm does not itself require disclosure and consent. The critical questions are the likelihood that a difference in interests will eventuate and, if it does, whether it will materially interfere with the lawyer's independent professional judgment in considering alternatives or foreclose courses of action that reasonably should be pursued on behalf of the client.

Lawyer's Responsibilities to Former Clients and Other Third Persons

[9] In addition to conflicts with other current clients, a lawyer's duties of loyalty and independence may be materially limited by responsibilities to former clients under Rule 1.9 or by the lawyer's responsibilities to other persons, such as fiduciary duties arising from a lawyer's service as a trustee, executor or corporate director.

Personal Interest Conflicts

[10] The lawyer's own interests should not be permitted to have an adverse effect on representation of a client. For example, if the probity of a lawyer's own conduct in a transaction is in serious question, it may be difficult or impossible for the lawyer to give a client detached advice. Similarly, when a lawyer has discussions concerning possible employment with an opponent of the lawyer's client, or with a law firm representing the opponent, such discussions could materially limit the lawyer's representation of the client. In addition, a lawyer may not allow related business interests to affect representation, for example, by referring clients to an enterprise in which the lawyer has an undisclosed financial interest. See Rule 1.8 for specific Rules pertaining to a number of personal interest conflicts, including business transactions with clients. See also Rule 1.10 (personal interest conflicts under Rule 1.7 ordinarily are not imputed to other lawyers in a law firm).

[11] When lawyers representing different clients in the same matter or in substantially related matters are closely related by blood or marriage, there may be a significant risk that client confidences will be revealed and that the lawyer's family relationship will interfere with both loyalty and independent professional judgment. As a result, each client is entitled to know of the existence and implications of the relationship between the lawyers before the lawyer agrees to undertake the representation. Thus, a lawyer related to another lawyer, e.g., as parent, child, sibling or spouse, ordinarily may not represent a client in a matter where that lawyer is representing another party, unless each client gives informed consent. The disqualification arising from a close family relationship is personal and ordinarily is not imputed to members of firms with whom the lawyers are associated. See Rule 1.10.

[12] A lawyer is prohibited from engaging in sexual relationships with a client unless the sexual relationship predates the formation of the client-lawyer relationship. See Rule 1.8(j).

Interest of Person Paying for a Lawyer's Service

[13] A lawyer may be paid from a source other than the client, including a co-client, if the client is informed of that fact and consents and the arrangement does not compromise the lawyer's duty of loyalty or independent judgment to the client. See Rule 1.8(f). If acceptance of the payment from any other source presents a significant risk that the lawyer's representation of the client will be materially limited by the lawyer's own interest in accommodating the person paying the lawyer's fee or by the lawyer's responsibilities to a payer who is also a co-client, then the lawyer must comply with the requirements of paragraph (b) before accepting the representation, including determining whether the conflict is consentable and, if so, that the client has adequate information about the material risks of the representation.

Prohibited Representations

[14] Ordinarily, clients may consent to representation notwithstanding a conflict. However, as indicated in paragraph (b), some conflicts are nonconsentable, meaning that the lawyer involved cannot properly ask for such agreement or provide representation on the basis of the client's consent. When the lawyer is representing more than one client, the question of consentability must be resolved as to each client.

[15] Consentability is typically determined by considering whether the interests of the clients will be adequately protected if the clients are permitted to give their informed consent to representation burdened by a conflict of interest. Thus, under paragraph (b)(1), representation is prohibited if in the circumstances the lawyer cannot reasonably conclude that the lawyer will be able to provide competent and diligent representation. See Rule 1.1 (competence) and Rule 1.3 (diligence).

[16] Paragraph (b)(2) describes conflicts that are nonconsentable because the representation is prohibited by applicable law. For example, in some states substantive

law provides that the same lawyer may not represent more than one defendant in a capital case, even with the consent of the clients, and under federal criminal statutes certain representations by a former government lawyer are prohibited, despite the informed consent of the former client. In addition, decisional law in some states limits the ability of a governmental client, such as a municipality, to consent to a conflict of interest.

[17] Paragraph (b)(3) describes conflicts that are nonconsentable because of the institutional interest in vigorous development of each client's position when the clients are aligned directly against each other in the same litigation or other proceeding before a tribunal. Whether clients are aligned directly against each other within the meaning of this paragraph requires examination of the context of the proceeding. Although this paragraph does not preclude a lawyer's multiple representation of adverse parties to a mediation (because mediation is not a proceeding before a "tribunal" under Rule 1.0(m)), such representation may be precluded by paragraph (b)(1).

Informed Consent

[18] Informed consent requires that each affected client be aware of the relevant circumstances and of the material and reasonably foreseeable ways that the conflict could have adverse effects on the interests of that client. See Rule 1.0(e) (informed consent). The information required depends on the nature of the conflict and the nature of the risks involved. When representation of multiple clients in a single matter is undertaken, the information must include the implications of the common representation, including possible effects on loyalty, confidentiality and the attorney-client privilege and the advantages and risks involved. See Comments [30] and [31] (effect of common representation on confidentiality).

[19] Under some circumstances it may be impossible to make the disclosure necessary to obtain consent. For example, when the lawyer represents different clients in related matters and one of the clients refuses to consent to the disclosure necessary to permit the other client to make an informed decision, the lawyer cannot properly ask the latter to consent. In some cases the alternative to common representation can be that each party may have to obtain separate representation with the possibility of incurring additional costs. These costs, along with the benefits of securing separate representation, are factors that may be considered by the affected client in determining whether common representation is in the client's interests.

Consent Confirmed in Writing

[20] Paragraph (b) requires the lawyer to obtain the informed consent of the client, confirmed in writing. Such a writing may consist of a document executed by the client or one that the lawyer promptly records and transmits to the client following an oral consent. See Rule 1.0(b). See also Rule 1.0(n) (writing includes electronic transmission). If it is not feasible to obtain or transmit the writing at the time the client gives informed consent, then the lawyer must obtain or transmit it within a reasonable time thereafter. See Rule 1.0(b). The requirement of a writing does not supplant the need in most cases for the lawyer to talk with the client, to explain the risks and advantages, if any, of representation burdened with a conflict of interest, as well as reasonably available alternatives, and to afford the client a reasonable opportunity to consider the risks and alternatives and to raise questions and concerns. Rather, the writing is required in order to impress upon clients the seriousness of the decision the client is being asked to make and to avoid disputes or ambiguities that might later occur in the absence of a writing.

Revoking Consent

[21] A client who has given consent to a conflict may revoke the consent and, like any other client, may terminate the lawyer's representation at any time. Whether revoking consent to the client's own representation precludes the lawyer from continuing

to represent other clients depends on the circumstances, including the nature of the conflict, whether the client revoked consent because of a material change in circumstances, the reasonable expectations of the other client and whether material detriment to the other clients or the lawyer would result.

Consent to Future Conflict

[22] Whether a lawyer may properly request a client to waive conflicts that might arise in the future is subject to the test of paragraph (b). The effectiveness of such waivers is generally determined by the extent to which the client reasonably understands the material risks that the waiver entails. The more comprehensive the explanation of the types of future representations that might arise and the actual and reasonably foreseeable adverse consequences of those representations, the greater the likelihood that the client will have the requisite understanding. Thus, if the client agrees to consent to a particular type of conflict with which the client is already familiar, then the consent ordinarily will be effective with regard to that type of conflict. If the consent is general and open-ended, then the consent ordinarily will be ineffective, because it is not reasonably likely that the client will have understood the material risks involved. On the other hand, if the client is an experienced user of the legal services involved and is reasonably informed regarding the risk that a conflict may arise, such consent is more likely to be effective, particularly if, e.g., the client is independently represented by other counsel in giving consent and the consent is limited to future conflicts unrelated to the subject of the representation. In any case, advance consent cannot be effective if the circumstances that materialize in the future are such as would make the conflict nonconsentable under paragraph (b).

Conflicts in Litigation

[23] Paragraph (b)(3) prohibits representation of opposing parties in the same litigation, regardless of the clients' consent. On the other hand, simultaneous representation of parties whose interests in litigation may conflict, such as coplaintiffs or codefendants, is governed by paragraph (a)(2). A conflict may exist by reason of substantial discrepancy in the parties' testimony, incompatibility in positions in relation to an opposing party or the fact that there are substantially different possibilities of settlement of the claims or liabilities in question. Such conflicts can arise in criminal cases as well as civil. The potential for conflict of interest in representing multiple defendants in a criminal case is so grave that ordinarily a lawyer should decline to represent more than one codefendant. On the other hand, common representation of persons having similar interests in civil litigation is proper if the requirements of paragraph (b) are met.

[24] Ordinarily a lawyer may take inconsistent legal positions in different tribunals at different times on behalf of different clients. The mere fact that advocating a legal position on behalf of one client might create precedent adverse to the interests of a client represented by the lawyer in an unrelated matter does not create a conflict of interest. A conflict of interest exists, however, if there is a significant risk that a lawyer's action on behalf of one client will materially limit the lawyer's effectiveness in representing another client in a different case; for example, when a decision favoring one client will create a precedent likely to seriously weaken the position taken on behalf of the other client. Factors relevant in determining whether the clients need to be advised of the risk include: where the cases are pending, whether the issue is substantive or procedural, the temporal relationship between the matters, the significance of the issue to the immediate and long-term interests of the clients involved, and the clients' reasonable expectations in retaining the lawyer. If there is significant risk of material limitation, then absent informed consent of the affected clients, the lawyer must refuse one of the representations or withdraw from one or both matters.

[25] When a lawyer represents or seeks to represent a class of plaintiffs or defendants in a class-action lawsuit, unnamed members of the class are ordinarily not considered to be clients of the lawyer for purposes of applying paragraph (a)(1) of this Rule. Thus, the lawyer does not typically need to get the consent of such a person before representing a client suing the person in an unrelated matter. Similarly, a lawyer seeking to represent an opponent in a class action does not typically need the consent of an unnamed member of the class whom the lawyer represents in an unrelated matter.

Nonlitigation Conflicts

[26] Conflicts of interest under paragraphs (a)(1) and (a)(2) arise in contexts other than litigation. For a discussion of directly adverse conflicts in transactional matters, see Comment [7]. Relevant factors in determining whether there is significant potential for material limitation include the duration and intimacy of the lawyer's relationship with the client or clients involved, the functions being performed by the lawyer, the likelihood that disagreements will arise and the likely prejudice to the client from the conflict. The question is often one of proximity and degree. See Comment [8].

[27] For example, conflict questions may arise in estate planning and estate administration. A lawyer may be called upon to prepare wills for several family members, such as husband and wife, and, depending upon the circumstances, a conflict of interest may be present. In estate administration the identity of the client may be unclear under the law of a particular jurisdiction. Under one view, the client is the fiduciary; under another view the client is the estate or trust, including its beneficiaries. In order to comply with conflict of interest rules, the lawyer should make clear the lawyer's relationship to the parties involved.

[28] Whether a conflict is consentable depends on the circumstances. For example, a lawyer may not represent multiple parties to a negotiation whose interests are fundamentally antagonistic to each other, but common representation is permissible where the clients are generally aligned in interest even though there is some difference in interest among them. Thus, a lawyer may seek to establish or adjust a relationship between clients on an amicable and mutually advantageous basis; for example, in helping to organize a business in which two or more clients are entrepreneurs, working out the financial reorganization of an enterprise in which two or more clients have an interest or arranging a property distribution in settlement of an estate. The lawyer seeks to resolve potentially adverse interests by developing the parties' mutual interests. Otherwise, each party might have to obtain separate representation, with the possibility of incurring additional cost, complication or even litigation. Given these and other relevant factors, the clients may prefer that the lawyer act for all of them.

Special Considerations in Common Representation

[29] In considering whether to represent multiple clients in the same matter, a lawyer should be mindful that if the common representation fails because the potentially adverse interests cannot be reconciled, the result can be additional cost, embarrassment, and recrimination. Ordinarily, the lawyer will be forced to withdraw from representing all of the clients if the common representation fails. In some situations, the risk of failure is so great that multiple representation is plainly impossible. For example, a lawyer cannot undertake common representation of clients where contentious litigation or negotiations between them are imminent or contemplated. Moreover, because the lawyer is required to be impartial between commonly represented clients, representation of multiple clients is improper when it is unlikely that impartiality can be maintained. Generally, if the relationship between the parties has already assumed antagonism, the possibility that the clients' interests can be adequately served by common representation is not very good. Other relevant factors are whether the lawyer subsequently will represent both parties on a continuing basis and whether the situation involves creating or terminating a relationship between the parties.

[30] A particularly important factor in determining the appropriateness of common representation is the effect on client-lawyer confidentiality and the attorney-client privilege. With regard to the attorney-client privilege, the prevailing rule is that, as between commonly represented clients, the privilege does not attach. Hence, it must be assumed that if litigation eventuates between the clients, the privilege will not protect any such communications, and the clients should be so advised.

[31] As to the duty of confidentiality, continued common representation will almost certainly be inadequate if one client asks the lawyer not to disclose to the other client information relevant to the common representation. This is so because the lawyer has an equal duty of loyalty to each client, and each client has the right to be informed of anything bearing on the representation that might affect that client's interests and the right to expect that the lawyer will use that information to that client's benefit. See Rule 1.4. The lawyer should, at the outset of the common representation and as part of the process of obtaining each client's informed consent, advise each client that information will be shared and that the lawyer will have to withdraw if one client decides that some matter material to the representation should be kept from the other. In limited circumstances, it may be appropriate for the lawyer to proceed with the representation when the clients have agreed, after being properly informed, that the lawyer will keep certain information confidential. For example, the lawyer may reasonably conclude that failure to disclose one client's trade secrets to another client will not adversely affect representation involving a joint venture between the clients and agree to keep that information confidential with the informed consent of both clients.

[32] When seeking to establish or adjust a relationship between clients, the lawyer should make clear that the lawyer's role is not that of partisanship normally expected in other circumstances and, thus, that the clients may be required to assume greater responsibility for decisions than when each client is separately represented. Any limitations on the scope of the representation made necessary as a result of the common representation should be fully explained to the clients at the outset of the representation. See Rule 1.2(c).

[33] Subject to the above limitations, each client in the common representation has the right to loyal and diligent representation and the protection of Rule 1.9 concerning the obligations to a former client. The client also has the right to discharge the lawyer as stated in Rule 1.16.

Organizational Clients

[34] A lawyer who represents a corporation or other organization does not, by virtue of that representation, necessarily represent any constituent or affiliated organization, such as a parent or subsidiary. See Rule 1.13(a). Thus, the lawyer for an organization is not barred from accepting representation adverse to an affiliate in an unrelated matter, unless the circumstances are such that the affiliate should also be considered a client of the lawyer, there is an understanding between the lawyer and the organizational client that the lawyer will avoid representation adverse to the client's affiliates, or the lawyer's obligations to either the organizational client or the new client are likely to limit materially the lawyer's representation of the other client.

[35] A lawyer for a corporation or other organization who is also a member of its board of directors should determine whether the responsibilities of the two roles may conflict. The lawyer may be called on to advise the corporation in matters involving actions of the directors. Consideration should be given to the frequency with which such situations may arise, the potential intensity of the conflict, the effect of the lawyer's resignation from the board, and the possibility of the corporation's obtaining legal advice from another lawyer in such situations. If there is material risk that the dual role will compromise the lawyer's independence of professional judgment, the lawyer should not serve as a director or should cease to act as the corporation's lawyer when conflicts of interest arise. The lawyer should advise the other members of the

board that in some circumstances matters discussed at board meetings while the lawyer is present in the capacity of director might not be protected by the attorney-client privilege and that conflict of interest considerations might require the lawyer's recusal as a director or might require the lawyer and the lawyer's firm to decline representation of the corporation in a matter.

ADVOCATE
Rule 3.3 Candor toward the Tribunal

(a) A lawyer shall not knowingly:
   (1) make a false statement of fact or law to a tribunal or fail to correct a false statement of material fact or law previously made to the tribunal by the lawyer;
   (2) fail to disclose to the tribunal legal authority in the controlling jurisdiction known to the lawyer to be directly adverse to the position of the client and not disclosed by opposing counsel; or
   (3) offer evidence that the lawyer knows to be false. If a lawyer, the lawyer's client, or a witness called by the lawyer, has offered material evidence and the lawyer comes to know of its falsity, the lawyer shall take reasonable remedial measures, including, if necessary, disclosure to the tribunal. A lawyer may refuse to offer evidence, other than the testimony of a defendant in a criminal matter, that the lawyer reasonably believes is false.

(b) A lawyer who represents a client in an adjudicative proceeding and who knows that a person intends to engage, is engaging or has engaged in criminal or fraudulent conduct related to the proceeding shall take reasonable remedial measures, including, if necessary, disclosure to the tribunal.

(c) The duties stated in paragraphs (a) and (b) continue to the conclusion of the proceeding, and apply even if compliance requires disclosure of information otherwise protected by Rule 1.6.

(d) In an ex parte proceeding, a lawyer shall inform the tribunal of all material facts known to the lawyer that will enable the tribunal to make an informed decision, whether or not the facts are adverse.

ADVOCATE
Rule 3.3 Candor toward the Tribunal—Comment

[1] This Rule governs the conduct of a lawyer who is representing a client in the proceedings of a tribunal. See Rule 1.0(m) for the definition of "tribunal." It also applies when the lawyer is representing a client in an ancillary proceeding conducted pursuant to the tribunal's adjudicative authority, such as a deposition. Thus, for example, paragraph (a)(3) requires a lawyer to take reasonable remedial measures if the lawyer comes to know that a client who is testifying in a deposition has offered evidence that is false.

[2] This Rule sets forth the special duties of lawyers as officers of the court to avoid conduct that undermines the integrity of the adjudicative process. A lawyer acting as an advocate in an adjudicative proceeding has an obligation to present the client's case with persuasive force. Performance of that duty while maintaining confidences of the client, however, is qualified by the advocate's duty of candor to the tribunal. Consequently, although a lawyer in an adversary proceeding is not required to present an impartial exposition of the law or to vouch for the evidence submitted in a cause, the lawyer must not allow the tribunal to be misled by false statements of law or fact or evidence that the lawyer knows to be false.

Representations by a Lawyer

[3] An advocate is responsible for pleadings and other documents prepared for litigation, but is usually not required to have personal knowledge of matters asserted therein, for litigation documents ordinarily present assertions by the client, or by someone on the client's behalf, and not assertions by the lawyer. Compare Rule 3.1. However, an assertion purporting to be on the lawyer's own knowledge, as in an affidavit by the lawyer or in a statement in open court, may properly be made only when the lawyer knows the assertion is true or believes it to be true on the basis of a reasonably diligent inquiry. There are circumstances where failure to make a disclosure is the equivalent of an affirmative misrepresentation. The obligation prescribed in Rule 1.2(d) not to counsel a client to commit or assist the client in committing a fraud applies in litigation. Regarding compliance with Rule 1.2(d), see the Comment to that Rule. See also the Comment to Rule 8.4(b).

Legal Argument

[4] Legal argument based on a knowingly false representation of law constitutes dishonesty toward the tribunal. A lawyer is not required to make a disinterested exposition of the law, but must recognize the existence of pertinent legal authorities. Furthermore, as stated in paragraph (a)(2), an advocate has a duty to disclose directly adverse authority in the controlling jurisdiction that has not been disclosed by the opposing party. The underlying concept is that legal argument is a discussion seeking to determine the legal premises properly applicable to the case.

Offering Evidence

[5] Paragraph (a)(3) requires that the lawyer refuse to offer evidence that the lawyer knows to be false, regardless of the client's wishes. This duty is premised on the lawyer's obligation as an officer of the court to prevent the trier of fact from being misled by false evidence. A lawyer does not violate this Rule if the lawyer offers the evidence for the purpose of establishing its falsity.

[6] If a lawyer knows that the client intends to testify falsely or wants the lawyer to introduce false evidence, the lawyer should seek to persuade the client that the evidence should not be offered. If the persuasion is ineffective and the lawyer continues to represent the client, the lawyer must refuse to offer the false evidence. If only a portion of a witness's testimony will be false, the lawyer may call the witness to testify but may not elicit or otherwise permit the witness to present the testimony that the lawyer knows is false.

[7] The duties stated in paragraphs (a) and (b) apply to all lawyers, including defense counsel in criminal cases. In some jurisdictions, however, courts have required counsel to present the accused as a witness or to give a narrative statement if the accused so desires, even if counsel knows that the testimony or statement will be false. The obligation of the advocate under the Rules of Professional Conduct is subordinate to such requirements. See also Comment [9].

[8] The prohibition against offering false evidence only applies if the lawyer knows that the evidence is false. A lawyer's reasonable belief that evidence is false does

not preclude its presentation to the trier of fact. A lawyer's knowledge that evidence is false, however, can be inferred from the circumstances. See Rule 1.0(f). Thus, although a lawyer should resolve doubts about the veracity of testimony or other evidence in favor of the client, the lawyer cannot ignore an obvious falsehood.

[9] Although paragraph (a)(3) only prohibits a lawyer from offering evidence the lawyer knows to be false, it permits the lawyer to refuse to offer testimony or other proof that the lawyer reasonably believes is false. Offering such proof may reflect adversely on the lawyer's ability to discriminate in the quality of evidence and thus impair the lawyer's effectiveness as an advocate. Because of the special protections historically provided criminal defendants, however, this Rule does not permit a lawyer to refuse to offer the testimony of such a client where the lawyer reasonably believes but does not know that the testimony will be false. Unless the lawyer knows the testimony will be false, the lawyer must honor the client's decision to testify. See also Comment [7].

Remedial Measures

[10] Having offered material evidence in the belief that it was true, a lawyer may subsequently come to know that the evidence is false. Or, a lawyer may be surprised when the lawyer's client, or another witness called by the lawyer, offers testimony the lawyer knows to be false, either during the lawyer's direct examination or in response to cross-examination by the opposing lawyer. In such situations or if the lawyer knows of the falsity of testimony elicited from the client during a deposition, the lawyer must take reasonable remedial measures. In such situations, the advocate's proper course is to remonstrate with the client confidentially, advise the client of the lawyer's duty of candor to the tribunal, and seek the client's cooperation with respect to the withdrawal or correction of the false statements or evidence. If that fails, the advocate must take further remedial action. If withdrawal from the representation is not permitted or will not undo the effect of the false evidence, the advocate must make such disclosure to the tribunal as is reasonably necessary to remedy the situation, even if doing so requires the lawyer to reveal information that otherwise would be protected by Rule 1.6. It is for the tribunal then to determine what should be done—making a statement about the matter to the trier of fact, ordering a mistrial or perhaps nothing.

[11] The disclosure of a client's false testimony can result in grave consequences to the client, including not only a sense of betrayal but also loss of the case and perhaps a prosecution for perjury. But the alternative is that the lawyer cooperate in deceiving the court, thereby subverting the truth-finding process which the adversary system is designed to implement. See Rule 1.2(d). Furthermore, unless it is clearly understood that the lawyer will act upon the duty to disclose the existence of false evidence, the client can simply reject the lawyer's advice to reveal the false evidence and insist that the lawyer keep silent. Thus the client could in effect coerce the lawyer into being a party to fraud on the court.

Preserving Integrity of Adjudicative Process

[12] Lawyers have a special obligation to protect a tribunal against criminal or fraudulent conduct that undermines the integrity of the adjudicative process, such as bribing, intimidating or otherwise unlawfully communicating with a witness, juror, court official or other participant in the proceeding, unlawfully destroying or concealing documents or other evidence or failing to disclose information to the tribunal when required by law to do so. Thus, paragraph (b) requires a lawyer to take reasonable remedial measures, including disclosure if necessary, whenever the lawyer knows that a person, including the lawyer's client, intends to engage, is engaging or has engaged in criminal or fraudulent conduct related to the proceeding.

Duration of Obligation

[13] A practical time limit on the obligation to rectify false evidence or false statements of law and fact has to be established. The conclusion of the proceeding is a reasonably definite point for the termination of the obligation. A proceeding has concluded within the meaning of this Rule when a final judgment in the proceeding has been affirmed on appeal or the time for review has passed.

Ex Parte Proceedings

[14] Ordinarily, an advocate has the limited responsibility of presenting one side of the matters that a tribunal should consider in reaching a decision; the conflicting position is expected to be presented by the opposing party. However, in any ex parte proceeding, such as an application for a temporary restraining order, there is no balance of presentation by opposing advocates. The object of an ex parte proceeding is nevertheless to yield a substantially just result. The judge has an affirmative responsibility to accord the absent party just consideration. The lawyer for the represented party has the correlative duty to make disclosures of material facts known to the lawyer and that the lawyer reasonably believes are necessary to an informed decision.

Withdrawal

[15] Normally, a lawyer's compliance with the duty of candor imposed by this Rule does not require that the lawyer withdraw from the representation of a client whose interests will be or have been adversely affected by the lawyer's disclosure. The lawyer may, however, be required by Rule 1.16(a) to seek permission of the tribunal to withdraw if the lawyer's compliance with this Rule's duty of candor results in such an extreme deterioration of the client-lawyer relationship that the lawyer can no longer competently represent the client. Also see Rule 1.16(b) for the circumstances in which a lawyer will be permitted to seek a tribunal's permission to withdraw. In connection with a request for permission to withdraw that is premised on a client's misconduct, a lawyer may reveal information relating to the representation only to the extent reasonably necessary to comply with this Rule or as otherwise permitted by Rule 1.6.

LAW FIRMS AND ASSOCIATIONS
Rule 5.3 Responsibilities Regarding Nonlawyer Assistants

With respect to a nonlawyer employed or retained by or associated with a lawyer:

(a) a partner, and a lawyer who individually or together with other lawyers possesses comparable managerial authority in a law firm shall make reasonable efforts to ensure that the firm has in effect measures giving reasonable assurance that the person's conduct is compatible with the professional obligations of the lawyer;

(b) a lawyer having direct supervisory authority over the nonlawyer shall make reasonable efforts to ensure that the person's conduct is compatible with the professional obligations of the lawyer; and

(c) a lawyer shall be responsible for conduct of such a person that would be a violation of the Rules of Professional Conduct if engaged in by a lawyer if:

(1) the lawyer orders or, with the knowledge of the specific conduct, ratifies the conduct involved; or

(2) the lawyer is a partner or has comparable managerial authority in the law firm in which the person is employed, or has direct supervisory authority over the person, and knows of the conduct at a time when its consequences can be avoided or mitigated but fails to take reasonable remedial action.

LAW FIRMS AND ASSOCIATIONS
Rule 5.3 Responsibilities Regarding Nonlawyer Assistants—Comment

[1] Lawyers generally employ assistants in their practice, including secretaries, investigators, law student interns, and paraprofessionals. Such assistants, whether employees or independent contractors, act for the lawyer in rendition of the lawyer's professional services. A lawyer must give such assistants appropriate instruction and supervision concerning the ethical aspects of their employment, particularly regarding the obligation not to disclose information relating to representation of the client, and should be responsible for their work product. The measures employed in supervising nonlawyers should take account of the fact that they do not have legal training and are not subject to professional discipline.

[2] Paragraph (a) requires lawyers with managerial authority within a law firm to make reasonable efforts to establish internal policies and procedures designed to provide reasonable assurance that nonlawyers in the firm will act in a way compatible with the Rules of Professional Conduct. See Comment [1] to Rule 5.1. Paragraph (b) applies to lawyers who have supervisory authority over the work of a nonlawyer. Paragraph (c) specifies the circumstances in which a lawyer is responsible for conduct of a nonlawyer that would be a violation of the Rules of Professional Conduct if engaged in by a lawyer.

LAW FIRMS AND ASSOCIATIONS
Rule 5.5 Unauthorized Practice of Law; Multijurisdictional Practice of Law

(a) A lawyer shall not practice law in a jurisdiction in violation of the regulation of the legal profession in that jurisdiction, or assist another in doing so.

(b) A lawyer who is not admitted to practice in this jurisdiction shall not:

(1) except as authorized by these Rules or other law, establish an office or other systematic and continuous presence in this jurisdiction for the practice of law; or

(2) hold out to the public or otherwise represent that the lawyer is admitted to practice law in this jurisdiction.

(c) A lawyer admitted in another United States jurisdiction, and not disbarred or suspended from practice in any jurisdiction, may provide legal services on a temporary basis in this jurisdiction that:

(1) are undertaken in association with a lawyer who is admitted to practice in this jurisdiction and who actively participates in the matter;

(2) are in or reasonably related to a pending or potential proceeding before a tribunal in this or another jurisdiction, if the lawyer, or a person the lawyer is as-

sisting, is authorized by law or order to appear in such proceeding or reasonably expects to be so authorized;

    (3) are in or reasonably related to a pending or potential arbitration, mediation, or other alternative dispute resolution proceeding in this or another jurisdiction, if the services arise out of or are reasonably related to the lawyer's practice in a jurisdiction in which the lawyer is admitted to practice and are not services for which the forum requires pro hac vice admission; or

    (4) are not within paragraphs (c)(2) or (c)(3) and arise out of or are reasonably related to the lawyer's practice in a jurisdiction in which the lawyer is admitted to practice.

(d) A lawyer admitted in another United States jurisdiction, and not disbarred or suspended from practice in any jurisdiction, may provide legal services in this jurisdiction that:

    (1) are provided to the lawyer's employer or its organizational affiliates and are not services for which the forum requires pro hac vice admission; or

    (2) are services that the lawyer is authorized to provide by federal law or other law of this jurisdiction.

LAW FIRMS AND ASSOCIATIONS
Rule 5.5 Unauthorized Practice of Law; Multijurisdictional Practice of Law—Comment

[1] A lawyer may practice law only in a jurisdiction in which the lawyer is authorized to practice. A lawyer may be admitted to practice law in a jurisdiction on a regular basis or may be authorized by court rule or order or by law to practice for a limited purpose or on a restricted basis. Paragraph (a) applies to unauthorized practice of law by a lawyer, whether through the lawyer's direct action or by the lawyer assisting another person.

    [2] The definition of the practice of law is established by law and varies from one jurisdiction to another. Whatever the definition, limiting the practice of law to members of the bar protects the public against rendition of legal services by unqualified persons. This Rule does not prohibit a lawyer from employing the services of paraprofessionals and delegating functions to them, so long as the lawyer supervises the delegated work and retains responsibility for their work. See Rule 5.3.

    [3] A lawyer may provide professional advice and instruction to nonlawyers whose employment requires knowledge of the law; for example, claims adjusters, employees of financial or commercial institutions, social workers, accountants and persons employed in government agencies. Lawyers also may assist independent nonlawyers, such as paraprofessionals, who are authorized by the law of a jurisdiction to provide particular law-related services. In addition, a lawyer may counsel nonlawyers who wish to proceed pro se.

    [4] Other than as authorized by law or this Rule, a lawyer who is not admitted to practice generally in this jurisdiction violates paragraph (b) if the lawyer establishes an office or other systematic and continuous presence in this jurisdiction for the practice of law. Presence may be systematic and continuous even if the lawyer is not physically present here. Such a lawyer must not hold out to the public or otherwise represent that the lawyer is admitted to practice law in this jurisdiction. See also Rules 7.1(a) and 7.5(b).

    [5] There are occasions in which a lawyer admitted to practice in another United States jurisdiction, and not disbarred or suspended from practice in any jurisdiction,

may provide legal services on a temporary basis in this jurisdiction under circumstances that do not create an unreasonable risk to the interests of their clients, the public or the courts. Paragraph (c) identifies four such circumstances. The fact that conduct is not so identified does not imply that the conduct is or is not authorized. With the exception of paragraphs (d)(1) and (d)(2), this Rule does not authorize a lawyer to establish an office or other systematic and continuous presence in this jurisdiction without being admitted to practice generally here.

[6] There is no single test to determine whether a lawyer's services are provided on a "temporary basis" in this jurisdiction, and may therefore be permissible under paragraph (c). Services may be "temporary" even though the lawyer provides services in this jurisdiction on a recurring basis, or for an extended period of time, as when the lawyer is representing a client in a single lengthy negotiation or litigation.

[7] Paragraphs (c) and (d) apply to lawyers who are admitted to practice law in any United States jurisdiction, which includes the District of Columbia and any state, territory or commonwealth of the United States. The word "admitted" in paragraph (c) contemplates that the lawyer is authorized to practice in the jurisdiction in which the lawyer is admitted and excludes a lawyer who while technically admitted is not authorized to practice, because, for example, the lawyer is on inactive status.

[8] Paragraph (c)(1) recognizes that the interests of clients and the public are protected if a lawyer admitted only in another jurisdiction associates with a lawyer licensed to practice in this jurisdiction. For this paragraph to apply, however, the lawyer admitted to practice in this jurisdiction must actively participate in and share responsibility for the representation of the client.

[9] Lawyers not admitted to practice generally in a jurisdiction may be authorized by law or order of a tribunal or an administrative agency to appear before the tribunal or agency. This authority may be granted pursuant to formal rules governing admission pro hac vice or pursuant to informal practice of the tribunal or agency. Under paragraph (c)(2), a lawyer does not violate this Rule when the lawyer appears before a tribunal or agency pursuant to such authority. To the extent that a court rule or other law of this jurisdiction requires a lawyer who is not admitted to practice in this jurisdiction to obtain admission pro hac vice before appearing before a tribunal or administrative agency, this Rule requires the lawyer to obtain that authority.

[10] Paragraph (c)(2) also provides that a lawyer rendering services in this jurisdiction on a temporary basis does not violate this Rule when the lawyer engages in conduct in anticipation of a proceeding or hearing in a jurisdiction in which the lawyer is authorized to practice law or in which the lawyer reasonably expects to be admitted pro hac vice. Examples of such conduct include meetings with the client, interviews of potential witnesses, and the review of documents. Similarly, a lawyer admitted only in another jurisdiction may engage in conduct temporarily in this jurisdiction in connection with pending litigation in another jurisdiction in which the lawyer is or reasonably expects to be authorized to appear, including taking depositions in this jurisdiction.

[11] When a lawyer has been or reasonably expects to be admitted to appear before a court or administrative agency, paragraph (c)(2) also permits conduct by lawyers who are associated with that lawyer in the matter, but who do not expect to appear before the court or administrative agency. For example, subordinate lawyers may conduct research, review documents, and attend meetings with witnesses in support of the lawyer responsible for the litigation.

[12] Paragraph (c)(3) permits a lawyer admitted to practice law in another jurisdiction to perform services on a temporary basis in this jurisdiction if those services are in or reasonably related to a pending or potential arbitration, mediation, or other alternative dispute resolution proceeding in this or another jurisdiction, if the services arise out of or are reasonably related to the lawyer's practice in a jurisdiction in which the lawyer is admitted to practice. The lawyer, however, must obtain admission pro

hac vice in the case of a court-annexed arbitration or mediation or otherwise if court rules or law so require.

[13] Paragraph (c)(4) permits a lawyer admitted in another jurisdiction to provide certain legal services on a temporary basis in this jurisdiction that arise out of or are reasonably related to the lawyer's practice in a jurisdiction in which the lawyer is admitted but are not within paragraphs (c)(2) or (c)(3). These services include both legal services and services that nonlawyers may perform but that are considered the practice of law when performed by lawyers.

[14] Paragraphs (c)(3) and (c)(4) require that the services arise out of or be reasonably related to the lawyer's practice in a jurisdiction in which the lawyer is admitted. A variety of factors evidence such a relationship. The lawyer's client may have been previously represented by the lawyer, or may be resident in or have substantial contacts with the jurisdiction in which the lawyer is admitted. The matter, although involving other jurisdictions, may have a significant connection with that jurisdiction. In other cases, significant aspects of the lawyer's work might be conducted in that jurisdiction or a significant aspect of the matter may involve the law of that jurisdiction. The necessary relationship might arise when the client's activities or the legal issues involve multiple jurisdictions, such as when the officers of a multinational corporation survey potential business sites and seek the services of their lawyer in assessing the relative merits of each. In addition, the services may draw on the lawyer's recognized expertise developed through the regular practice of law on behalf of clients in matters involving a particular body of federal, nationally-uniform, foreign, or international law.

[15] Paragraph (d) identifies two circumstances in which a lawyer who is admitted to practice in another United States jurisdiction, and is not disbarred or suspended from practice in any jurisdiction, may establish an office or other systematic and continuous presence in this jurisdiction for the practice of law as well as provide legal services on a temporary basis. Except as provided in paragraphs (d)(1) and (d)(2), a lawyer who is admitted to practice law in another jurisdiction and who establishes an office or other systematic or continuous presence in this jurisdiction must become admitted to practice law generally in this jurisdiction.

[16] Paragraph (d)(1) applies to a lawyer who is employed by a client to provide legal services to the client or its organizational affiliates, i.e., entities that control, are controlled by, or are under common control with the employer. This paragraph does not authorize the provision of personal legal services to the employer's officers or employees. The paragraph applies to in-house corporate lawyers, government lawyers, and others who are employed to render legal services to the employer. The lawyer's ability to represent the employer outside the jurisdiction in which the lawyer is licensed generally serves the interests of the employer and does not create an unreasonable risk to the client and others because the employer is well situated to assess the lawyer's qualifications and the quality of the lawyer's work.

[17] If an employed lawyer establishes an office or other systematic presence in this jurisdiction for the purpose of rendering legal services to the employer, the lawyer may be subject to registration or other requirements, including assessments for client protection funds and mandatory continuing legal education.

[18] Paragraph (d)(2) recognizes that a lawyer may provide legal services in a jurisdiction in which the lawyer is not licensed when authorized to do so by federal or other law, which includes statute, court rule, executive regulation or judicial precedent.

[19] A lawyer who practices law in this jurisdiction pursuant to paragraphs (c) or (d) or otherwise is subject to the disciplinary authority of this jurisdiction. See Rule 8.5(a).

[20] In some circumstances, a lawyer who practices law in this jurisdiction pursuant to paragraphs (c) or (d) may have to inform the client that the lawyer is not licensed to practice law in this jurisdiction. For example, that may be required when the

representation occurs primarily in this jurisdiction and requires knowledge of the law of this jurisdiction. See Rule 1.4(b).

[21] Paragraphs (c) and (d) do not authorize communications advertising legal services to prospective clients in this jurisdiction by lawyers who are admitted to practice in other jurisdictions. Whether and how lawyers may communicate the availability of their services to prospective clients in this jurisdiction is governed by Rules 7.1 to 7.5.

Appendix C

National Federation of Paralegal Associations, Inc.
Model Code of Ethics and Professional Responsibility and Guidelines for Enforcement

PREAMBLE

The National Federation of Paralegal Associations, Inc. ("NFPA") is a professional organization comprised of paralegal associations and individual paralegals throughout the United States and Canada. Members of NFPA have varying backgrounds, experiences, education, and job responsibilities that reflect the diversity of the paralegal profession. NFPA promotes the growth, development, and recognition of the paralegal profession as an integral partner in the delivery of legal services.

In May 1993 NFPA adopted its Model Code of Ethics and Professional Responsibility ("Model Code") to delineate the principles for ethics and conduct to which every paralegal should aspire.

Many paralegal associations throughout the United States have endorsed the concept and content of NFPA's Model Code through the adoption of their own ethical codes. In doing so, paralegals have confirmed the profession's commitment to increase the quality and efficiency of legal services, as well as recognized its responsibilities to the public, the legal community, and colleagues.

Paralegals have recognized, and will continue to recognize, that the profession must continue to evolve to enhance their roles in the delivery of legal services. With increased levels of responsibility comes the need to define and enforce mandatory rules of professional conduct. Enforcement of codes of paralegal conduct is a logical and necessary step to enhance and ensure the confidence of the legal community and the public in the integrity and professional responsibility of paralegals.

In April 1997 NFPA adopted the Model Disciplinary Rules ("Model Rules") to make possible the enforcement of the Canons and Ethical Considerations contained in the NFPA Model Code. A concurrent determination was made that the Model Code of Ethics and Professional Responsibility, formerly aspirational in nature, should be recognized as setting forth the enforceable obligations of all paralegals.

The Model Code and Model Rules offer a framework for professional discipline, either voluntarily or through formal regulatory programs.

§1 NFPA Model Disciplinary Rules and Ethical Considerations

1.1 A Paralegal Shall Achieve and Maintain a High Level of Competence.

Ethical Considerations

EC-1.1 (a) A paralegal shall achieve competency through education, training, and work experience.

EC-1.1 (b) A paralegal shall aspire to participate in a minimum of twelve (12) hours of continuing legal education, to include at least one (1) hour of ethics education, every two (2) years in order to remain current on developments in the law.

EC-1.1 (c) A paralegal shall perform all assignments promptly and efficiently.

1.2 A Paralegal Shall Maintain a High Level of Personal and Professional Integrity.

Ethical Considerations

EC-1.2 (a) A paralegal shall not engage in any ex parte communications involving the courts or any other adjudicatory body in an attempt to exert undue influence or to obtain advantage or the benefit of only one party

EC-1.2 (b) A paralegal shall not communicate, or cause another to communicate, with a party the paralegal knows to be represented by a lawyer in a pending matter without the prior consent of the lawyer representing such other party.

EC-1.2 (c) A paralegal shall ensure that all timekeeping and billing records prepared by the paralegal are thorough, accurate, honest, and complete.

EC-1.2 (d) A paralegal shall not knowingly engage in fraudulent billing practices. Such practices may include, but are not limited to: inflation of hours billed to a client or employer; misrepresentation of the nature of tasks performed; and/or submission of fraudulent expense and disbursement documentation.

EC-1.2 (e) A paralegal shall be scrupulous, thorough, and honest in the identification and maintenance of all funds, securities, and other assets of a client and shall provide accurate accounting as appropriate.

EC-1.2 (f) A paralegal shall advise the proper authority of non-confidential knowledge of any dishonest or fraudulent acts by any person pertaining to the handling of the funds, securities or other assets of a client. The authority to whom the report is made shall depend on the nature and circumstances of the possible misconduct, (e.g., ethics committees of law firms, corporations and/or paralegal associations, local or state bar associations, local prosecutors, administrative agencies, etc.). Failure to report such knowledge is in itself misconduct and shall be treated as such under these rules.

1.3 A Paralegal Shall Maintain a High Standard of Professional Conduct.

Ethical Considerations

EC-1.3 (a) A paralegal shall refrain from engaging in any conduct that offends the dignity and decorum of proceedings before a court or other adjudicatory body and shall be respectful of all rules and procedures.

EC-1.3 (b) A paralegal shall avoid impropriety and the appearance of impropriety and shall not engage in any conduct that would adversely affect his/her fitness to practice. Such conduct may include, but is not limited to: violence, dishonesty, interference with the administration of justice, and/or abuse of a professional position or public office.

EC-1.3
(c)
Should a paralegal's fitness to practice be compromised by physical or mental illness, causing that paralegal to commit an act that is in direct violation of the Model Code/Model Rules and/or the rules and/or laws governing the jurisdiction in which the paralegal practices, that paralegal may be protected from sanction upon review of the nature and circumstances of that illness.

EC-1.3
(d)
A paralegal shall advise the proper authority of non-confidential knowledge of any action of another legal professional that clearly demonstrates fraud, deceit, dishonesty, or misrepresentation. The authority to whom the report is made shall depend on the nature and circumstances of the possible misconduct (e.g., ethics committees of law firms, corporations and/or paralegal associations, local or state bar associations, local prosecutors, administrative agencies, etc.). Failure to report such knowledge is in itself misconduct and shall be treated as such under these rules.

EC-1.3
(e)
A paralegal shall not knowingly assist any individual with the commission of an act that is in direct violation of the Model Code/Model Rules and/or the rules and/or laws governing the jurisdiction in which the paralegal practices.

EC-1.3
(f)
If a paralegal possesses knowledge of future criminal activity, that knowledge must be reported to the appropriate authority immediately.

1.4 A Paralegal Shall Serve the Public Interest by Contributing to the Improvement of the Legal System and Delivery of Quality Legal Services, Including Pro Bono Publico Services.

Ethical Considerations

EC-1.4
(a)
A paralegal shall be sensitive to the legal needs of the public and shall promote the development and implementation of programs that address those needs.

EC-1.4
(b)
A paralegal shall support efforts to improve the legal system and access thereto and shall assist in making changes.

EC-1.4
(c)
A paralegal shall support and participate in the delivery of Pro Bono Publico services directed toward implementing and improving access to justice, the law, the legal system or the paralegal and legal professions.

EC-1.4
(d)
A paralegal should aspire annually to contribute twenty-four (24) hours of Pro Bono Publico services under the supervision of an attorney or as authorized by administrative, statutory or court authority to:

1. persons of limited means; or
2. charitable, religious, civic, community, governmental and educational organizations in matters that are designed primarily to address the legal needs of persons with limited means; or
3. individuals, groups or organizations seeking to secure or protect civil rights, civil liberties or public rights.

The twenty-four (24) hours of Pro Bono Publico services contributed annually by a paralegal may consist of such services as detailed in this EC-1.4(d), and/or administrative matters designed to develop and implement the attainment of this aspiration as detailed above in EC-1.4(a) or (c), or any combination of the two.

1.5 A Paralegal Shall Preserve all Confidential Information Provided by the Client or Acquired from Other Sources Before, During, and After the Course of the Professional Relationship.

Ethical Considerations

EC-1.5
(a)
A paralegal shall be aware of and abide by all legal authority governing confidential information in the jurisdiction in which the paralegal practices.

EC-1.5 (b) A paralegal shall not use confidential information to the disadvantage of the client.

EC-1.5 (c) A paralegal shall not use confidential information to the advantage of the paralegal or of a third person.

EC-1.5 (d) A paralegal may reveal confidential information only after full disclosure and with the client's written consent; or, when required by law or court order; or, when necessary to prevent the client from committing an act that could result in death or serious bodily harm.

EC-1.5 (e) A paralegal shall keep those individuals responsible for the legal representation of a client fully informed of any confidential information the paralegal may have pertaining to that client.

EC-1.5 (f) A paralegal shall not engage in any indiscreet communications concerning clients.

1.6 A Paralegal Shall Avoid Conflicts of Interest and Shall Disclose any Possible Conflict to the Employer or Client, as Well as to the Prospective Employers or Clients.

Ethical Considerations

EC-1.6 (a) A paralegal shall act within the bounds of the law, solely for the benefit of the client, and shall be free of compromising influences and loyalties. Neither the paralegal's personal or business interest, nor those of other clients or third persons, should compromise the paralegal's professional judgment and loyalty to the client.

EC-1.6 (b) A paralegal shall avoid conflicts of interest that may arise from previous assignments, whether for a present or past employer or client.

EC-1.6 (c) A paralegal shall avoid conflicts of interest that may arise from family relationships and from personal and business interests.

EC-1.6 (d) In order to be able to determine whether an actual or potential conflict of interest exists, a paralegal shall create and maintain an effective recordkeeping system that identifies clients, matters, and parties with which the paralegal has worked.

EC-1.6 (e) A paralegal shall reveal sufficient non-confidential information about a client or former client to reasonably ascertain if an actual or potential conflict of interest exists.

EC-1.6 (f) A paralegal shall not participate in or conduct work on any matter where a conflict of interest has been identified.

EC-1.6 (g) In matters where a conflict of interest has been identified and the client consents to continued representation, a paralegal shall comply fully with the implementation and maintenance of an Ethical Wall.

1.7 A Paralegal's Title Shall be Fully Disclosed.

Ethical Considerations

EC-1.7 (a) A paralegal's title shall clearly indicate the individual's status and shall be disclosed in all business and professional communications to avoid misunderstandings and misconceptions about the paralegal's role and responsibilities.

EC-1.7 (b) A paralegal's title shall be included if the paralegal's name appears on business cards, letterhead, brochures, directories, and advertisements.

EC-1.7 (c) A paralegal shall not use letterhead, business cards or other promotional materials to create a fraudulent impression of his/her status or ability to practice in the jurisdiction in which the paralegal practices.

EC-1.7
(d)
A paralegal shall not practice under color of any record, diploma, or certificate that has been illegally or fraudulently obtained or issued or which is misrepresentative in any way.

EC1.7
(e)
A paralegal shall not participate in the creation, issuance, or dissemination of fraudulent records, diplomas, or certificates.

1.8 A Paralegal Shall Not Engage in the Unauthorized Practice of Law.

Ethical Considerations

EC-1.8
(a)
A paralegal shall comply with the applicable legal authority governing the unauthorized practice of law in the jurisdiction in which the paralegal practices.

§2 NFPA Guidelines for the Enforcement of the Model Code of Ethics and Professional Responsibility

2.1 Basis for Discipline

2.1(a)   Disciplinary investigations and proceedings brought under authority of the Rules shall be conducted in accord with obligations imposed on the paralegal professional by the Model Code of Ethics and Professional Responsibility.

2.2 Structure of Disciplinary Committee

2.2(a)   The Disciplinary Committee ("Committee") shall be made up of nine (9) members including the Chair.

2.2(b)   Each member of the Committee, including any temporary replacement members, shall have demonstrated working knowledge of ethics/professional responsibility-related issues and activities.

2.2(c)   The Committee shall represent a cross-section of practice areas and work experience. The following recommendations are made regarding the members of the Committee.

1) At least one paralegal with one to three years of law-related work experience.
2) At least one paralegal with five to seven years of law related work experience.
3) At least one paralegal with over ten years of law related work experience.
4) One paralegal educator with five to seven years of work experience; preferably in the area of ethics/professional responsibility.
5) One paralegal manager.
6) One lawyer with five to seven years of law-related work experience.
7) One lay member.

2.2(d)   The Chair of the Committee shall be appointed within thirty (30) days of its members' induction. The Chair shall have no fewer than ten (10) years of law-related work experience.

2.2(e)   The terms of all members of the Committee shall be staggered. Of those members initially appointed, a simple majority plus one shall be appointed to a term of one year, and the remaining members shall be appointed to a term of two years. Thereafter, all members of the Committee shall be appointed to terms of two years.

2.2(f)   If for any reason the terms of a majority of the Committee will expire at the same time, members may be appointed to terms of one year to maintain continuity of the Committee.

2.2(g)   The Committee shall organize from its members a three-tiered structure to investigate, prosecute, and/or adjudicate charges of misconduct. The members shall be rotated among the tiers.

2.3 Operation of Committee

2.3(a)   The Committee shall meet on an as-needed basis to discuss, investigate, and/or adjudicate alleged violations of the Model Code/Model Rules.

2.3(b)   A majority of the members of the Committee present at a meeting shall constitute a quorum.

2.3(c)   A Recording Secretary shall be designated to maintain complete and accurate minutes of all Committee meetings. All such minutes shall be kept confidential until a decision has been made that the matter will be set for hearing as set forth in Section 6.1 below.

2.3(d)   If any member of the Committee has a conflict of interest with the Charging Party, the Responding Party, or the allegations of misconduct, that member shall not take part in any hearing or deliberations concerning those allegations. If the absence of that member creates a lack of a quorum for the Committee, then a temporary replacement for the member shall be appointed.

2.3(e)   Either the Charging Party or the Responding Party may request that, for good cause shown, any member of the Committee not participate in a hearing or deliberation. All such requests shall be honored. If the absence of a Committee member under those circumstances creates a lack of a quorum for the Committee, then a temporary replacement for that member shall be appointed.

2.3(f)   All discussions and correspondence of the Committee shall be kept confidential until a decision has been made that the matter will be set for hearing as set forth in Section 6.1 below.

2.3(g)   All correspondence from the Committee to the Responding Party regarding any charge of misconduct and any decisions made regarding the charge shall be mailed certified mail, return receipt requested, to the Responding Party's last known address and shall be clearly marked with a "Confidential" designation.

2.4 Procedure for the Reporting of Alleged Violations of the Model Code/Disciplinary Rules

2.4(a)   An individual or entity in possession of non-confidential knowledge or information concerning possible instances of misconduct shall make a confidential written report to the Committee within thirty (30) days of obtaining same. This report shall include all details of the alleged misconduct.

2.4(b)   The Committee so notified shall inform the Responding Party of the allegation(s) of misconduct no later than ten (10) business days after receiving the confidential written report from the Charging Party.

2.4(c)   Notification to the Responding Party shall include the identity of the Charging Party, unless, for good cause shown, the Charging Party requests anonymity.

2.4(d)   The Responding Party shall reply to the allegations within ten (10) business days of notification.

2.5 Procedure for the Investigation of a Charge of Misconduct

2.5(a)   Upon receipt of a Charge of Misconduct ("Charge"), or on its own initiative, the Committee shall initiate an investigation.

2.5(b)   If, upon initial or preliminary review, the Committee makes a determination that the charges are either without basis in fact or, if proven, would not constitute professional misconduct, the Committee shall dismiss the allegations of misconduct. If such determination of dismissal cannot be made, a formal investigation shall be initiated.

2.5(c)   Upon the decision to conduct a formal investigation, the Committee shall:

1) mail to the Charging and Responding Parties within three (3) business days of that decision notice of the commencement of a formal investigation. That notification shall be in writing and shall contain a complete explanation of all Charge(s), as well as the reasons for a formal investigation and shall cite the applicable codes and rules;

2) allow the Responding Party thirty (30) days to prepare and submit a confidential response to the Committee, which response shall address each charge specifically and shall be in writing; and

3) upon receipt of the response to the notification, have thirty (30) days to investigate the Charge(s). If an extension of time is deemed necessary, that extension shall not exceed ninety (90) days.

2.5(d)   Upon conclusion of the investigation, the Committee may:

1) dismiss the Charge upon the finding that it has no basis in fact;

2) dismiss the Charge upon the finding that, if proven, the Charge would not constitute Misconduct;

3) refer the matter for hearing by the Tribunal; or

4) in the case of criminal activity, refer the Charge(s) and all investigation results to the appropriate authority.

2.6 Procedure for a Misconduct Hearing Before a Tribunal

2.6(a)   Upon the decision by the Committee that a matter should be heard, all parties shall be notified and a hearing date shall be set. The hearing shall take place no more than thirty (30) days from the conclusion of the formal investigation.

2.6(b)   The Responding Party shall have the right to counsel. The parties and the Tribunal shall have the right to call any witnesses and introduce any documentation that they believe will lead to the fair and reasonable resolution of the matter.

2.6(c)   Upon completion of the hearing, the Tribunal shall deliberate and present a written decision to the parties in accordance with procedures as set forth by the Tribunal.

2.6(d)   Notice of the decision of the Tribunal shall be appropriately published.

2.7 Sanctions

2.7(a)   Upon a finding of the Tribunal that misconduct has occurred, any of the following sanctions, or others as may be deemed appropriate, may be imposed upon the Responding Party, either singularly or in combination:

1) letter of reprimand to the Responding Party; counseling;

2) attendance at an ethics course approved by the Tribunal; probation;

3) suspension of license/authority to practice; revocation of license/authority to practice;

4) imposition of a fine; assessment of costs; or

5) in the instance of criminal activity, referral to the appropriate authority.

2.7(b)   Upon the expiration of any period of probation, suspension, or revocation, the Responding Party may make application for reinstatement. With the application for reinstatement, the Responding Party must show proof of having complied with all aspects of the sanctions imposed by the Tribunal.

2.8 Appellate Procedures

2.8(a)   The parties shall have the right to appeal the decision of the Tribunal in accordance with the procedure as set forth by the Tribunal.

DEFINITIONS

"Appellate Body" means a body established to adjudicate an appeal to any decision made by a Tribunal or other decision-making body with respect to formally-heard Charges of Misconduct.

"Charge of Misconduct" means a written submission by any individual or entity to an ethics committee, paralegal association, bar association, law enforcement agency, judicial body, government agency, or other appropriate body or entity, that sets forth non-confidential information regarding any instance of alleged misconduct by an individual paralegal or paralegal entity.

"Charging Party" means any individual or entity who submits a Charge of Misconduct against an individual paralegal or paralegal entity.

"Competency" means the demonstration of: diligence, education, skill, and mental, emotional, and physical fitness reasonably necessary for the performance of paralegal services.

"Confidential Information" means information relating to a client, whatever its source, that is not public knowledge nor available to the public. ("Non-Confidential Information" would generally include the name of the client and the identity of the matter for which the paralegal provided services.)

"Disciplinary Hearing" means the confidential proceeding conducted by a committee or other designated body or entity concerning any instance of alleged misconduct by an individual paralegal or paralegal entity.

"Disciplinary Committee" means any committee that has been established by an entity such as a paralegal association, bar association, judicial body, or government agency to: (a) identify, define, and investigate general ethical considerations and concerns with respect to paralegal practice; (b) administer and enforce the Model Code and Model Rules and; (c) discipline any individual paralegal or paralegal entity found to be in violation of same.

"Disclose" means communication of information reasonably sufficient to permit identification of the significance of the matter in question.

"Ethical Wall" means the screening method implemented in order to protect a client from a conflict of interest. An Ethical Wall generally includes, but is not limited to, the following elements: (1) prohibit the paralegal from having any connection with the matter; (2) ban discussions with or the transfer of documents to or from the paralegal; (3) restrict access to files; and (4) educate all members of the firm, corporation, or entity as to the separation of the paralegal (both organizationally and physically) from the pending matter. For more information regarding the Ethical Wall, see the NFPA publication entitled "The Ethical Wall—Its Application to Paralegals."

"Ex parte" means actions or communications conducted at the instance and for the benefit of one party only, and without notice to, or contestation by, any person adversely interested.

"Investigation" means the investigation of any charge(s) of misconduct filed against an individual paralegal or paralegal entity by a Committee.

"Letter of Reprimand" means a written notice of formal censure or severe reproof administered to an individual paralegal or paralegal entity for unethical or improper conduct.

"Misconduct" means the knowing or unknowing commission of an act that is in direct violation of those Canons and Ethical Considerations of any and all applicable codes and/or rules of conduct.

"Paralegal" is synonymous with "Legal Assistant" and is defined as a person qualified through education, training, or work experience to perform substantive legal work that requires knowledge of legal concepts and is customarily, but not exclusively, performed by a lawyer. This person may be retained or employed by a lawyer, law office, governmental agency, or other entity or may be authorized by administrative, statutory, or court authority to perform this work.

"Pro Bono Publico" means providing or assisting to provide quality legal services in order to enhance access to justice for persons of limited means; charitable, religious, civic, community, governmental, and educational organizations in matters that are designed primarily to address the legal needs of persons with limited means; or individuals, groups or organizations seeking to secure or protect civil rights, civil liberties or public rights.

"Proper Authority" means the local paralegal association, the local or state bar association, Committee(s) of the local paralegal or bar association(s), local prosecutor, administrative agency, or other tribunal empowered to investigate or act upon an instance of alleged misconduct.

"Responding Party" means an individual paralegal or paralegal entity against whom a Charge of Misconduct has been submitted.

"Revocation" means the recision of the license, certificate or other authority to practice of an individual paralegal or paralegal entity found in violation of those Canons and Ethical Considerations of any and all applicable codes and/or rules of conduct.

"Suspension" means the suspension of the license, certificate or other authority to practice of an individual paralegal or paralegal entity found in violation of those Canons and Ethical Considerations of any and all applicable codes and/or rules of conduct.

"Tribunal" means the body designated to adjudicate allegations of misconduct.

Model Standards and Guidelines for Utilization of Legal Assistants—Paralegals

Table of Contents:

INTRODUCTION

The purpose of this annotated version of the National Association of Legal Assistants, Inc. Model Standards and Guidelines for the Utilization of Legal Assistants (the "Model," "Standards" and/or the "Guidelines") is to provide references to the existing case law and other authorities where the underlying issues have been considered. The authorities cited will serve as a basis upon which conduct of a legal assistant may be analyzed as proper or improper.

The Guidelines represent a statement of how the legal assistant may function. The Guidelines are not intended to be a comprehensive or exhaustive list of the proper duties of a legal assistant. Rather, they are designed as guides to what may or may not be proper conduct for the legal assistant. In formulating the Guidelines, the reasoning and rules of law in many reported decisions of disciplinary cases and unauthorized practice of law cases have been analyzed and considered. In addition, the provisions of the American Bar Association's Model Rules of Professional Conduct, as well as the ethical promulgations of various state courts and bar associations, have been considered in the development of the Guidelines.

These Guidelines form a sound basis for the legal assistant and the supervising attorney to follow. This Model will serve as a comprehensive resource document and as a definitive, well-reasoned guide to those considering voluntary standards and guidelines for legal assistants.

I
PREAMBLE

Proper utilization of the services of legal assistants contributes to the delivery of cost-effective, high-quality legal services. Legal assistants and the legal profession should be assured that measures exist for identifying legal assistants and their role in assisting attorneys in the delivery of legal services. Therefore, the National Association of Legal Assistants, Inc., hereby adopts these Standards and Guidelines as an educational document for the benefit of legal assistants and the legal profession.

Comment

The three most frequently raised questions concerning legal assistants are (1) How do you define a legal assistant; (2) Who is qualified to be identified as a legal assistant; and (3) What duties may a legal assistant perform? The definition adopted in 1984 by the National Association of Legal Assistants answers the first question. The Model sets forth minimum education, training, and experience through standards which will assure that an individual utilizing the title "legal assistant" or "paralegal" has the qualifications to be held out to the legal community and the public in that capacity. The Guidelines identify those acts which the reported cases hold to be proscribed and give examples of services which the legal assistant may perform under the supervision of a licensed attorney.

These Guidelines constitute a statement relating to services performed by legal assistants, as defined herein, as approved by court decisions and other sources of authority. The purpose of the Guidelines is not to place limitations or restrictions on the legal assistant profession. Rather, the Guidelines are intended to outline for the legal profession an acceptable course of conduct. Voluntary recognition and utilization of the Standards and Guidelines will benefit the entire legal profession and the public it serves.

II
DEFINITION

The National Association of Legal Assistants adopted the following definition in 1984:

> Legal assistants, also known as paralegals, are a distinguishable group of persons who assist attorneys in the delivery of legal services. Through formal education, training, and experience, legal assistants have knowledge and expertise regarding the legal system and substantive and procedural law which qualify them to do work of a legal nature under the supervision of an attorney.

In recognition of the similarity of the definitions and the need for one clear definition, in July 2001, the NALA membership approved a resolution to adopt the definition of the American Bar Association as well. The ABA definition reads as follows:

> A legal assistant or paralegal is a person qualified by education, training or work experience who is employed or retained by a lawyer, law office, corporation, governmental agency or other entity who performs specifically delegated substantive legal work for which a lawyer is responsible. (Adopted by the ABA in 1997)

Comment

These definitions emphasize the knowledge and expertise of legal assistants in substantive and procedural law obtained through education and work experience. They further define the legal assistant or paralegal as a professional working under the supervision of an attorney as distinguished from a non-lawyer who delivers services directly to the public without any intervention or review of work product by an attorney. Such unsupervised services, unless authorized by court or agency rules, constitute the unauthorized practice of law.

Statutes, court rules, case law, and bar association documents are additional sources for legal assistant or paralegal definitions. In applying the Standards and Guidelines, it is important to remember that they were developed to apply to the legal assistant as defined herein. Lawyers should refrain from labeling those as paralegals or legal assistants who do not meet the criteria set forth in these definitions and/or the definitions set forth by state rules, guidelines or bar associations. Labeling secretaries and other administrative staff as legal assistants/paralegals is inaccurate.

For billing purposes, the services of a legal secretary are considered part of overhead costs and are not recoverable in fee awards. However, the courts have held that fees for paralegal services are recoverable as long as they are not clerical functions, such as organizing files, copying documents, checking docket, updating files, checking court dates, and delivering papers. As established in *Missouri v. Jenkins*, 491 U.S.274, 109 S.Ct. 2463, 2471, n.10 (1989) tasks performed by legal assistants must be substantive in nature which, absent the legal assistant, the attorney would perform.

There are also case law and Supreme Court Rules addressing the issue of a disbarred attorney serving in the capacity of a legal assistant.

III
STANDARDS

A legal assistant should meet certain minimum qualifications. The following standards may be used to determine an individual's qualifications as a legal assistant:

1. Successful completion of the Certified Legal Assistant (CLA)/Certified Paralegal (CP) certifying examination of the National Association of Legal Assistants, Inc.;
2. Graduation from an ABA approved program of study for legal assistants;
3. Graduation from a course of study for legal assistants which is institutionally accredited but not ABA approved, and which requires not less than the equivalent of 60 semester hours of classroom study;
4. Graduation from a course of study for legal assistants, other than those set forth in (2) and (3) above, plus not less than six months of in-house training as a legal assistant;
5. A baccalaureate degree in any field, plus not less than six months in-house training as a legal assistant;
6. A minimum of three years of law-related experience under the supervision of an attorney, including at least six months of in-house training as a legal assistant; or
7. Two years of in-house training as a legal assistant.

For purposes of these Standards, "in-house training as a legal assistant" means attorney education of the employee concerning legal assistant duties and these Guidelines. In addition to review and analysis of assignments, the legal assistant should receive a reasonable amount of instruction directly related to the duties and obligations of the legal assistant.

Comment

The Standards set forth suggest minimum qualifications for a legal assistant. These minimum qualifications, as adopted, recognize legal related work backgrounds and formal education backgrounds, both of which provide the legal assistant with a broad base in exposure to and knowledge of the legal profession. This background is necessary to assure the public and the legal profession that the employee identified as a legal assistant is qualified.

The Certified Legal Assistant (CLA) /Certified Paralegal (CP) examination established by NALA in 1976 is a voluntary nationwide certification program for legal assistants. (*CLA and CP are federally registered certification marks owned by NALA.*) The CLA/CP designation is a statement to the legal profession and the public that the legal assistant has met the high levels of knowledge and professionalism required by NALA's certification program. Continuing education requirements, which all certified legal assistants must meet, assure that high standards are maintained. The CLA/CP designation has been recognized as a means of establishing the qualifications of a legal assistant in supreme court rules, state court and bar association standards, and utilization guidelines.

Certification through NALA is available to all legal assistants meeting the educational and experience requirements. Certified Legal Assistants may also pursue advanced certification in specialty practice areas through the APC, Advanced Paralegal Certification, credentialing program. Legal assistants/paralegals may also pursue certification based on state laws and procedures in California, Florida, Louisiana, and Texas.

IV
GUIDELINES

These Guidelines relating to standards of performance and professional responsibility are intended to aid legal assistants and attorneys. The ultimate responsibility rests with an attorney who employs legal assistants to educate them with respect to the duties they are assigned and to supervise the manner in which such duties are accomplished.

Comment

In general, a legal assistant is allowed to perform any task which is properly delegated and supervised by an attorney, as long as the attorney is ultimately responsible to the client and assumes complete professional responsibility for the work product.

ABA Model Rules of Professional Conduct, Rule 5.3 provides:

With respect to a non-lawyer employed or retained by or associated with a lawyer:

(a) a partner in a law firm shall make reasonable efforts to ensure that the firm has in effect measures giving reasonable assurance that the person's conduct is compatible with the professional obligations of the lawyer;

(b) a lawyer having direct supervisory authority over the non-lawyer shall make reasonable efforts to ensure that the person's conduct is compatible with the professional obligations of the lawyer; and

(c) a lawyer shall be responsible for conduct of such a person that would be a violation of the rules of professional conduct if engaged in by a lawyer if:

 (1) the lawyer orders or, with the knowledge of the specific conduct ratifies the conduct involved; or

 (2) the lawyer is a partner in the law firm in which the person is employed, or has direct supervisory authority over the person, and knows of the conduct at a time when its consequences can be avoided or mitigated but fails to take remedial action.

There are many interesting and complex issues involving the use of legal assistants. In any discussion of the proper role of a legal assistant, attention must be directed to what constitutes the practice of law. Proper delegation to legal assistants is further complicated and confused by the lack of an adequate definition of the practice of law.

Kentucky became the first state to adopt a Paralegal Code by Supreme Court Rule. This Code sets forth certain exclusions to the unauthorized practice of law:

> For purposes of this rule, the unauthorized practice of law shall not include any service rendered involving legal knowledge or advice, whether representation, counsel or advocacy, in or out of court, rendered in respect to the acts, duties, obligations, liabilities or business relations of the one requiring services where:
> A. The client understands that the paralegal is not a lawyer;
> B. The lawyer supervises the paralegal in the performance of his or her duties; and
> C. The lawyer remains fully responsible for such representation including all actions taken or not taken in connection therewith by the paralegal to the same extent as if such representation had been furnished entirely by the lawyer and all such actions had been taken or not taken directly by the attorney. Paralegal Code, Ky.S.Ct.R3.700, Sub-Rule 2.

South Dakota Supreme Court Rule 97-25 Utilization Rule a(4) states:

> The attorney remains responsible for the services performed by the legal assistant to the same extent as though such services had been furnished entirely by the attorney and such actions were those of the attorney.

GUIDELINE 1

Legal assistants should:

1. Disclose their status as legal assistants at the outset of any professional relationship with a client, other attorneys, a court or administrative agency or personnel thereof, or members of the general public;
2. Preserve the confidences and secrets of all clients; and
3. Understand the attorney's Rules of Professional Responsibility and these Guidelines in order to avoid any action which would involve the attorney in a violation of the Rules, or give the appearance of professional impropriety.

Comment

Routine early disclosure of the paralegal's status when dealing with persons outside the attorney's office is necessary to assure that there will be no misunderstanding as to the responsibilities and role of the legal assistant. Disclosure may be made in any way that avoids confusion. If the person dealing with the legal assistant already knows of his/her status, further disclosure is unnecessary. If at any time in written or oral communication the legal assistant becomes aware that the other person may believe the legal assistant is an attorney, immediate disclosure should be made as to the legal assistant's status.

The attorney should exercise care that the legal assistant preserves and refrains from using any confidence or secrets of a client, and should instruct the legal assistant not to disclose or use any such confidences or secrets.

The legal assistant must take any and all steps necessary to prevent conflicts of interest and fully disclose such conflicts to the supervising attorney. Failure to do so may jeopardize both the attorney's representation of the client and the case itself.

Guidelines for the Utilization of Legal Assistant Services adopted December 3, 1994 by the Washington State Bar Association Board of Governors states:

> Guideline 7: A lawyer shall take reasonable measures to prevent conflicts of interest resulting from a legal assistant's other employment or interest insofar as such other employment or interests would present a conflict of interest if it were that of the lawyer.

In Re Complex Asbestos Litigation, 232 Cal. App. 3d 572 (Cal. 1991), addresses the issue wherein a law firm was disqualified due to possession of attorney-client confidences by a legal assistant employee resulting from previous employment by opposing counsel.

In Oklahoma, in an order issued July 12, 2001, in the matter of *Mark A. Hayes, M.D. v. Central States Orthopedic Specialists, Inc.*, a Tulsa County District Court Judge disqualified a law firm from representation of a client on the basis that an ethical screen was an impermissible device to protect from disclosure confidences gained by a nonlawyer employee while employed by another law firm. In applying the same rules that govern attorneys, the court found that the Rules of Professional Conduct pertaining to confidentiality apply to nonlawyers who leave firms with actual knowledge of material, confidential information, and a screening device is not an appropriate alternative to the imputed disqualification of an incoming legal assistant who has moved from one firm to another during ongoing litigation and has actual knowledge of material, confidential information. The decision was appealed and the Oklahoma

Supreme Court determined that, under certain circumstances, screening is an appropriate management tool for non-lawyer staff.

In 2004 the Nevada Supreme Court also addressed this issue at the urging of the state's paralegals. The Nevada Supreme Court granted a petition to rescind the Court's 1997 ruling in *Ciaffone v. District Court*. In this case, the court clarified the original ruling, stating "mere opportunity to access confidential information does not merit disqualification." The opinion stated instances in which screening may be appropriate, and listed minimum screening requirements. The opinion also set forth guidelines that a district court may use to determine if screening has been or may be effective. These considerations are:

1. substantiality of the relationship between the former and current matters
2. the time elapsed between the matters
3. size of the firm
4. number of individuals presumed to have confidential information
5. nature of their involvement in the former matter
6. timing and features of any measures taken to reduce the danger of disclosure
7. whether the old firm and the new firm represent adverse parties in the same proceeding rather than in different proceedings.

The ultimate responsibility for compliance with approved standards of professional conduct rests with the supervising attorney. The burden rests upon the attorney who employs a legal assistant to educate the latter with respect to the duties which may be assigned and then to supervise the manner in which the legal assistant carries out such duties. However, this does not relieve the legal assistant from an independent obligation to refrain from illegal conduct. Additionally, and notwithstanding that the Rules are not binding upon non-lawyers, the very nature of a legal assistant's employment imposes an obligation not to engage in conduct which would involve the supervising attorney in a violation of the Rules.

The attorney must make sufficient background investigation of the prior activities and character and integrity of his or her legal assistants.

Further, the attorney must take all measures necessary to avoid and fully disclose conflicts of interest due to other employment or interests. Failure to do so may jeopardize both the attorney's representation of the client and the case itself.

Legal assistant associations strive to maintain the high level of integrity and competence expected of the legal profession and, further, strive to uphold the high standards of ethics.

NALA's Code of Ethics and Professional Responsibility states "A legal assistant's conduct is guided by bar associations' codes of professional responsibility and rules of professional conduct."

GUIDELINE 2

Legal assistants should not:

1. Establish attorney-client relationships; set legal fees; give legal opinions or advice; or represent a client before a court, unless authorized to do so by said court; nor
2. Engage in, encourage, or contribute to any act which could constitute the unauthorized practice law.

Comment

Case law, court rules, codes of ethics and professional responsibilities, as well as bar ethics opinions now hold which acts can and cannot be performed by a legal assistant. Generally, the determination of what acts constitute the unauthorized practice of law is made by state supreme courts.

Numerous cases exist relating to the unauthorized practice of law. Courts have gone so far as to prohibit the legal assistant from preparation of divorce kits and assisting in preparation of bankruptcy forms and, more specifically, from providing basic information about procedures and requirements, deciding where information should be placed on forms, and responding to questions from debtors regarding the interpretation or definition of terms.

Cases have identified certain areas in which an attorney has a duty to act, but it is interesting to note that none of these cases state that it is improper for an attorney to have the initial work performed by the legal assistant. This again points out the importance of adequate supervision by the employing attorney.

An attorney can be found to have aided in the unauthorized practice of law when delegating acts which cannot be performed by a legal assistant.

GUIDELINE 3

Legal assistants may perform services for an attorney in the representation of a client, provided:

1. The services performed by the legal assistant do not require the exercise of independent professional legal judgment;
2. The attorney maintains a direct relationship with the client and maintains control of all client matters;
3. The attorney supervises the legal assistant;
4. The attorney remains professionally responsible for all work on behalf of the client, including any actions taken or not taken by the legal assistant in connection therewith; and
5. The services performed supplement, merge with, and become the attorney's work product.

Comment

Paralegals, whether employees or independent contractors, perform services for the attorney in the representation of a client. Attorneys should delegate work to legal assistants commensurate with their knowledge and experience and provide appropriate instruction and supervision concerning the delegated work, as well as ethical acts of their employment. Ultimate responsibility for the work product of a legal assistant rests with the attorney. However, a legal assistant must use discretion and professional judgment and must not render independent legal judgment in place of an attorney.

The work product of a legal assistant is subject to civil rules governing discovery of materials prepared in anticipation of litigation, whether the legal assistant is viewed as an extension of the attorney or as another representative of the party itself. Fed.R.Civ.P. 26 (b) (3) and (5).

GUIDELINE 4

In the supervision of a legal assistant, consideration should be given to

1. Designating work assignments that correspond to the legal assistant's abilities, knowledge, training, and experience;
2. Educating and training the legal assistant with respect to professional responsibility, local rules and practices, and firm policies;
3. Monitoring the work and professional conduct of the legal assistant to ensure that the work is substantively correct and timely performed;
4. Providing continuing education for the legal assistant in substantive matters through courses, institutes, workshops, seminars and in-house training; and
5. Encouraging and supporting membership and active participation in professional organizations.

Comment

Attorneys are responsible for the actions of their employees in both malpractice and disciplinary proceedings. In the vast majority of cases, the courts have not censured attorneys for a particular act delegated to the legal assistant, but rather, have been critical of and imposed sanctions against attorneys for failure to adequately supervise the legal assistant. The attorney's responsibility for supervision of his or her legal assistant must be more than a willingness to accept responsibility and liability for the legal assistant's work. Supervision of a legal assistant must be offered in both the procedural and substantive legal areas. The attorney must delegate work based upon the education, knowledge, and abilities of the legal assistant and must monitor the work product and conduct of the legal assistant to insure that the work performed is substantively correct and competently performed in a professional manner.

Michigan State Board of Commissioners has adopted Guidelines for the Utilization of Legal Assistants (April 23, 1993). These guidelines, in part, encourage employers to support legal assistant participation in continuing education programs to ensure that the legal assistant remains competent in the fields of practice in which the legal assistant is assigned.

The working relationship between the lawyer and the legal assistant should extend to cooperative efforts on public service activities wherever possible. Participation in pro bono activities is encouraged in ABA Guideline 10.

GUIDELINE 5

Except as otherwise provided by statute, court rule or decision, administrative rule or regulation, or the attorney's rules of professional responsibility, and within the preceding parameters and proscriptions, a legal assistant may perform any function delegated by an attorney, including, but not limited to the following:

1. Conduct client interviews and maintain general contact with the client after the establishment of the attorney-client relationship, so long as the client is aware of the status and function of the legal assistant, and the client contact is under the supervision of the attorney.
2. Locate and interview witnesses, so long as the witnesses are aware of the status and function of the legal assistant.
3. Conduct investigations and statistical and documentary research for review by the attorney.
4. Conduct legal research for review by the attorney.
5. Draft legal documents for review by the attorney.
6. Draft correspondence and pleadings for review by and signature of the attorney.
7. Summarize depositions, interrogatories and testimony for review by the attorney.
8. Attend executions of wills, real estate closings, depositions, court or administrative hearings and trials with the attorney.
9. Author and sign letters providing the legal assistant's status is clearly indicated and the correspondence does not contain independent legal opinions or legal advice.

Comment

The United States Supreme Court has recognized the variety of tasks being performed by legal assistants and has noted that use of legal assistants encourages cost-effective delivery of legal services, *Missouri v. Jenkins*, 491 U.S.274, 109 S.Ct. 2463, 2471, n.10 (1989). In *Jenkins*, the court further held that legal assistant time should be included in compensation for attorney fee awards at the market rate of the relevant community to bill legal assistant time.

Courts have held that legal assistant fees are not a part of the overall overhead of a law firm. Legal assistant services are billed separately by attorneys, and decrease litigation expenses. Tasks performed by legal assistants must contain substantive legal work under the direction or supervision of an attorney, such that if the legal assistant were not present, the work would be performed by the attorney.

In *Taylor v. Chubb*, 874 P.2d 806 (Okla. 1994), the Court ruled that attorney fees awarded should include fees for services performed by legal assistants and, further, defined tasks which may be performed by the legal assistant under the supervision of an attorney including, among others: interview clients; draft pleadings and other documents; carry on legal research, both conventional and computer aided; research public records; prepare discovery requests and responses; schedule depositions and prepare notices and subpoenas; summarize depositions and other discovery responses; coordinate and manage document production; locate and interview witnesses; organize pleadings, trial exhibits and other documents; prepare witness and exhibit lists; prepare trial notebooks; prepare for the attendance of witnesses at trial; and assist lawyers at trials.

Except for the specific proscription contained in Guideline 1, the reported cases do not limit the duties which may be performed by a legal assistant under the supervision of the attorney.

An attorney may not split legal fees with a legal assistant, nor pay a legal assistant for the referral of legal business. An attorney may compensate a legal assistant based on the quantity and quality of the legal assistant's work and value of that work to a law practice.

CONCLUSION

These Standards and Guidelines were developed from generally accepted practices. Each supervising attorney must be aware of the specific rules, decisions, and statutes applicable to legal assistants within his/her jurisdiction.

ADDENDUM

For further information, the following cases may be helpful to you:

Duties
Taylor v. Chubb, 874 P.2d 806 (Okla. 1994)
McMackin v. McMackin, 651 A.2d 778 (Del.Fam Ct 1993)

Work Product
Fine v. Facet Aerospace Products Co., 133 F.R.D. 439 (S.D.N.Y. 1990)

Unauthorized Practice of Law
Akron Bar Assn. v. Green, 673 N.E.2d 1307 (Ohio 1997)
In Re Hessinger & Associates, 192 B.R. 211 (N.D. Calif. 1996)
In the Matter of Bright, 171 B.R. 799 (Bkrtcy. E.D. Mich)
Louisiana State Bar Assn v. Edwins, 540 So.2d 294 (La. 1989)

Attorney/Client Privilege
In Re Complex Asbestos Litigation, 232 Cal. App. 3d 572 (Calif. 1991)
Makita Corp. v. U.S., 819 F.Supp. 1099 (CIT 1993)

Conflicts
In Re Complex Asbestos Litigation, 232 Cal. App. 3d 572 (Calif. 1991)
Makita Corp. v. U.S., 819 F.Supp. 1099 (CIT 1993)
Phoenix Founders, Inc., v. Marshall, 887 S.W.2d 831 (Tex. 1994)
Smart Industries v. Superior Court, 876 P.2d 1176 (Ariz. App. Div.1 1994)

Supervision
Matter of Martinez, 754 P.2d 842 (N.M. 1988)
State v. Barrett, 483 P.2d 1106 (Kan. 1971)

Hayes v. Central States Orthopedic Specialists, Inc., 2002 OK 30, 51 P.3d 562

Liebowitz v. Eighth Judicial District Court of Nevada Nev Sup Ct., No 39683, November 3, 2003 clarified in part and overrules in part *Ciaffone v. District Court*, 113 Nev 1165, 945. P2d 950 (1997)

Fee Awards

In Re Bicoastal Corp., 121 B.R. 653 (Bktrcy.M.D.Fla. 1990)

In Re Carter, 101 B.R. 170 (Bkrtcy.D.S.D. 1989)

Taylor v. Chubb, 874 P.2d 806 (Okla.1994)

Missouri v. Jenkins, 491 U.S. 274, 109 S.Ct. 2463, 105 L.Ed.2d 229 (1989) 11 U.S.C.A.§ 330

McMackin v. McMackin, Del.Fam.Ct. 651 A.2d 778 (1993)

Miller v. Alamo, 983 F.2d 856 (8th Cir. 1993)

Stewart v. Sullivan, 810 F.Supp. 1102 (D.Hawaii 1993)

In Re Yankton College, 101 B.R. 151 (Bkrtcy. D.S.D. 1989)

Stacey v. Stroud, 845 F.Supp. 1135 (S.D.W.Va. 1993)

Court Appearances

Louisiana State Bar Assn v. Edwins, 540 So.2d 294 (La. 1989)

In addition to the above referenced cases, you may contact your state bar association for information regarding guidelines for the utilization of legal assistants that may have been adopted by the bar, or ethical opinions concerning the utilization of legal assistants. The following states have adopted a definition of "legal assistant" or "paralegal" either through bar association guidelines, ethical opinions, legislation or case law:

Legislation	**Cases (Cont.)**	**Bar Association Activity (Cont.)**
California	South Carolina	Iowa
Florida	Washington	Kansas
Illinois		Kentucky
Indiana	**Guidelines**	Massachusetts
Maine		Michigan
Pennsylvania	Colorado	Minnesota
	Connecticut	Missouri
Supreme Court Cases or Rules	Georgia	Nevada
	Idaho	New Mexico
Kentucky	New York	New Hampshire
New Hampshire	Oregon	North Carolina
New Mexico	Utah	North Dakota
North Dakota	Wisconsin	Ohio
Rhode Island		Oregon
South Dakota	**Bar Association Activity**	Rhode Island
Virginia		South Carolina
	Alaska	South Dakota
Cases	Arizona	Tennessee
	Colorado	Texas
Arizona	Connecticut	Virginia
New Jersey	Florida	Wisconsin
Oklahoma	Illinois	

Appendix E

Effective Learning: *How to Study*

Everyone learns differently. Some people seem to absorb information like a sponge while others must work hard to soak up any information. Although some people truly do have photographic memories, they are few and far between. Most likely, the people who seem to absorb information "like a sponge" have learned how to maximize their learning experiences. Most of us do not take the time to figure out how we learn best and, as a result, probably spend more time than necessary to achieve the same results as more proficient learners.

Have you ever wondered how some people who are just average students seem to always get A's? If you were to ask them, they probably would tell you that they spend more time than most people studying and preparing, or that they have learned how to study more effectively and efficiently in the time they have available. A good starting point is to determine how you learn best and work out methods to maximize the time and effort you have available.

LEARNING STYLES

A learning style is the way you learn most effectively. Everyone has his or her own learning style, and there are no "better" or "correct" ways to learn. Somewhere in your school career you may have been given tests—such as the Hogan/Champagne Personal Style Indicator or the Kolb Learning Style Inventory—to determine your personal learning styles. These and similar assessments are available through most school advisors and guidance counselors. If you want help in determining your learning styles, take the initiative for your own success and make an appointment with someone who can administer an assessment.

Learning styles fall into these categories:

- independent (competitive) versus collaborative
- structured versus unstructured
- auditory versus visual
- spatial versus verbal
- practical versus creative
- applied versus conceptual
- factual versus analytical
- emotional versus logical

This sounds like a lot to consider, but taking a few minutes to determine which learning style best suits you can save you countless hours of frustration—hours that could be better devoted to studying or other activities.

Independent Versus Collaborative

Do you prefer to work with a group or independently? Some people like to avoid all distractions by working alone. Others prefer to work in a study group and share information.

If you prefer to work independently, you may want to obtain additional course information from study guides and computer-assisted instruction. You may prefer lecture-format classes to small discussion courses. If you prefer to work collaboratively, you may wish to form study groups early in the semester or find a tutor to work with, and you should choose courses that include small discussion groups or group projects.

Structured Versus Unstructured

Structured learners feel more comfortable when they formalize their study habits—for example, by selecting a definite time and place in which to study every day. If you are a structured learner, you may find it useful to create "to-do" lists and keep a written schedule of classes, study times, and activities.

Unstructured learners tend to resist formalizing their study plan and try to avoid feeling "locked-in." They tend to procrastinate. Procrastinators need to find ways to give more structure to their learning activities. One method is to join a study group of students who are more organized.

Auditory Versus Visual

Auditory learners learn best by listening. Visual learners learn best from what they see. Visual learners cannot always learn everything by listening to lectures or by reading and watching video presentations. Auditory learners may find it more efficient to listen to lectures and then read related material. Visual learners may do better reading the book first, and then attending lectures. Auditory learners may also find group discussion and study group activities beneficial.

Spatial Versus Verbal

Spatial learners are better then verbal learners at reading and interpreting maps, charts, and other graphics. Verbal learners prefer to read words than to interpret graphics. Spatial learners need to create and incorporate their own diagrams, maps, timelines, and other graphics into their notes.

Verbal learners need to translate or obtain translations of graphics into words. A useful technique for verbal learners is to take notes that describe the material, including the graphics, in such a way that a visually impaired student could understand the graphic representation from the verbal description. Teaming up with a visually impaired student may be mutually beneficial.

Practical Versus Creative

Practical learners tend to be methodical and systematic. They prefer specific instruction that is directed and focused. Creative learners prefer experimentation and creative activities. Practical learners may benefit from creating an organized study plan for each course, including detailed "to-do" lists and a calendar. For creative learners, courses that allow writing and other creative approaches may be more satisfying.

Applied Versus Conceptual

Applied learners want to know how information can be transferred to given situations. Conceptual learners are not so much concerned with the application as with the underlying concepts. Applied learners need to focus on ways in which the ideas presented in courses and lectures can be applied. Taking notes that include examples for applying the concepts helps them recall the concepts later. Conceptual learners may find it useful to consider the concepts in a broader context than that of the narrow lecture presentation.

Factual Versus Analytical

Factual learners are good with details and enjoy learning interesting and unusual facts. They prefer objective tests. Analytical learners like to break down a topic into its component parts to understand how the parts relate to each other. Analytical learners prefer essay exams that allow them to demonstrate how their knowledge relates to the question. Factual learners may want to make lists of facts, which they can associate with prior knowledge. Analytical learners may want to analyze the organization as they read a textbook, looking for trends and patterns.

Emotional Versus Logical

Emotional learners tend to prefer human-interest stories to material that presents just facts and logic. Logical learners want to understand the factual basis, including statistics, of an argument. Emotional learners may find that reading biographical sketches helps them understand factual subjects.

PUTTING IT ALL TOGETHER

1. *Understand yourself.* From the previous list of types of learners, select the descriptions in each category that best fit your style of learning. Look back at courses and classes you have taken in which you have done well or that you enjoyed the most. You may see a pattern that will help you understand your learning style.

2. *Set goals.* Determine your personal and occupational goals. Do you want a career working with people or with things? Do you want a professional career working directly with people or behind the scenes supporting others? What courses will help you acquire the skills and knowledge you need to achieve these goals?

3. *Make a plan.* Your educational path should lead to a goal. It may be a personal goal to be an outstanding parent or partner, or it may be a goal to be a generalist or a specialist in an occupation or profession. To achieve these goals, you will have to focus on courses that give you the necessary skills and knowledge. Within the courses may be options that accommodate your learning style, such as large lecture classes versus small-group discussion classes, face-to-face courses versus distance-learning courses, and so on.

  Create a personal plan that allows for flexibility as your goals or interests change. A good foundation will allow you more flexibility in courses and curriculum. Don't be afraid to admit that you did not enjoy some courses you expected to enjoy or that you enjoyed some classes you didn't think would give you pleasure. These insights may help you fine-tune your personal and professional goals.

4. *Check your progress.* Periodically assess how well you are doing in individual classes, as well as in your overall program of study. Use the opportunity to assess why you are doing better than you expected in some classes and not as well in others. You may have to adjust your overall plan or merely your learning methods. Or outside influences such as work, family, or personal issues may be interfering with your learning. Periodic self-assessment is the first step in modifying your goals.

5. *Make adjustments.* As your goals change, so will your plan. Don't be afraid to make the adjustments necessary to achieve your goals or to change your goals as your interests change. Life rarely follows a straight path. Be adaptable and make adjustments when necessary.

SCHEDULING TIME

Most people use a calendar to keep track of information such as birthdays, appointments, or upcoming events. Calendars may include vacations, concerts, and other special events or activities. Depending on your personal style, you might include "to-do" lists or an hour-by-hour schedule of classes and other activities. Scheduling school and study time is helpful to most students.

Whichever method works best for you, use it to track the amount of time you spend in all of your activities so you can budget your time more accurately. When scheduling, keep in mind that the power of concentration has a limitation for everyone. Don't schedule so many activities that they exceed your mental or physical abilities.

SUPPLEMENTAL LEARNING AIDS

1. *Study guides.* Many textbooks have a study guide that will give you additional information, including sample tests and quizzes. Your instructor may or may not require the use of a study guide. If you need additional reinforcement, you may want to purchase a study guide even if it is not a required part of the course.

2. *Flash cards.* Flash cards are available in college bookstores for many courses. But you will learn more by preparing your own and customizing them to the course you are taking. On the front side of an index card, write a word, phrase, or concept, and write the definition or explanation on the reverse side. With a properly prepared set of flash cards, you may not have to refer to the text or your notes when studying for a test.

3. *Companion websites.* Many publishers offer companion websites for their textbooks. These websites frequently are available on the publisher's website without cost or for a nominal fee. Often these websites are the equivalent of an online study guide. Others offer self-tests. The publisher may post information that has become available since the publication of the textbook.

4. *Outlining.* Few people have a photographic memory or the ability to absorb material on one reading. The following approach can help you use your textbook effectively.

  a. *How long is the chapter?* Before you start, check the length of the chapter and your reading assignment. Most textbooks are filled with graphics and illustrations that reduce the amount of actual reading time to a manageable level.
  b. *Scan the chapter.* Look over the material quickly to get a sense of what will be covered.
  c. *Chapter objectives.* At the beginnings of each chapter, most textbooks list what you should learn from reading the chapter. These chapter objectives help you focus on important topics, information, and themes.
  d. *Read the chapter.* Quickly read through the chapter to get an overall sense of the material and how the sections relate to each other.
  e. *Underline the important items.* After you have done this go back over the material and underline in pencil the items you believe are important.
  f. *Go to class.* From the instructor's lecture and class discussion, you may find that what you think is important changes.
  g. *Highlight the important material.* After class, use a highlighter to highlight what you now believe to be the important information in the text. You probably will find that it is substantially less than what you underlined in pencil.
  h. *Make your flash cards.* From the highlighted information, create a set of flash cards for each chapter.

5. *Tutors.* Not everyone can afford the luxury of a personal tutor, but most colleges and universities have a tutoring center or offer some form of tutoring assistance. If you are having difficulty, don't be afraid to ask for help before it is too late. At the beginning of the semester determine what personalized help is available for each course. You may not need to use this information, but having it available will reduce your anxiety and panic if you realize that you need some help.

Don't be afraid to ask your instructor for help. Your instructor wants you to succeed. If you are doing everything you can to be successful in a class, the instructor should be more than happy to help you or direct you for help.

6. *Study groups.* If you are the type of learner who benefits from working with others, form a study group at the beginning of each semester in each course. After the first class, ask if others wish to form a study group, or post a notice on the course bulletin board website.

One advantage of study groups is the opportunity to share class notes as well as ideas. Verbal learners can benefit from having visual learners in the study group to interpret and explain charts, graphs, and maps. Study groups can motivate procrastinators to complete tasks on time.

7. *Tests.* Most students suffer from some form of test anxiety. At the beginning of each course, ask the instructor for the exam schedule and the type of tests he or she will be giving. Some schools maintain copies of all tests that students can use for practice. If your school does not maintain these, ask your instructors if they will make available sample tests and quizzes. Practice tests may be available in the study guide for the text or on a companion website. If you are in a study group, members can prepare practice tests as part of test preparation.

For more detailed information about study skills, see *Effective Study Skills: Maximizing Your Academic Potential,* by Judy M. Roberts (Prentice Hall, 1998).

Appendix F

The Constitution of the United States of America

PREAMBLE

We the People of the United States, in Order to form a more perfect Union, establish Justice, insure domestic Tranquility, provide for the common defense, promote the general Welfare, and secure the Blessings of Liberty to ourselves and our Posterity, do ordain and establish this Constitution for the United States of America.

ARTICLE I

Section 1. All legislative Powers herein granted shall be vested in a Congress of the United States, which shall consist of a Senate and House of Representatives.

Section 2. The House of Representatives shall be composed of Members chosen every second Year by the People of the several States, and the Electors in each State shall have the Qualifications requisite for Electors of the most numerous Branch of the State Legislature.

No Person shall be a Representative who shall not have attained to the Age of twenty five Years, and been seven Years a Citizen of the United States, and who shall not, when elected, be an Inhabitant of that State in which he shall be chosen.

Representatives and direct Taxes shall be apportioned among the several States which may be included within this Union, according to their respective Numbers, which shall be determined by adding to the whole Number of free Persons, including those bound to Service for a Term of Years, and excluding Indians not taxed, three fifths of all other Persons. The actual Enumeration shall be made within three Years after the first Meeting of the Congress of the United States, and within every subsequent Term of ten Years, in such Manner as they shall by Law direct. The Number of Representatives shall not exceed one for every thirty Thousand, but each State shall have at Least one Representative; and until such enumeration shall be made, the State of New Hampshire shall be entitled to chuse three, Massachusetts eight, Rhode Island and Providence Plantations one, Connecticut five, New York six, New Jersey four, Pennsylvania eight, Delaware one, Maryland six, Virginia ten, North Carolina five, South Carolina five, and Georgia three.

When vacancies happen in the Representation from any State, the Executive Authority thereof shall issue Writs of Election to fill such Vacancies.

The House of Representatives shall chuse their Speaker and other Officers; and shall have the sole Power of Impeachment.

Section 3. The Senate of the United States shall be composed of two Senators from each State, chosen by the Legislature thereof for six Years; and each Senator shall have one Vote.

Immediately after they shall be assembled in Consequence of the first Election, they shall be divided as equally as may be into three Classes. The Seats of the Senators of the first Class shall be vacated at the Expiration of the second Year, of the second Class at the Expiration of the fourth Year, and of the third Class at the Expiration

To exercise exclusive Legislation in all Cases whatsoever, over such District (not exceeding ten Miles square) as may, by Cession of particular States, and the Acceptance of Congress, become the Seat of the Government of the United States, and to exercise like Authority over all Places purchased by the Consent of the Legislature of the State in which the Same shall be, for the Erection of Forts, Magazines, Arsenals, dockYards, and other needful Buildings;—And

To make all Laws which shall be necessary and proper for carrying into Execution the foregoing Powers, and all other Powers vested by this Constitution in the Government of the United States, or in any Department or Officer thereof.

Section 9. The Migration or Importation of such Persons as any of the States now existing shall think proper to admit, shall not be prohibited by the Congress prior to the Year one thousand eight hundred and eight, but a Tax or duty may be imposed on such Importation, not exceeding ten dollars for each Person.

The Privilege of the Writ of Habeas Corpus shall not be suspended, unless when in Cases of Rebellion or Invasion the public Safety may require it.

No Bill of Attainder or ex post facto Law shall be passed.

No Capitation, or other direct, Tax shall be laid, unless in Proportion to the Census or enumeration herein before directed to be taken.

No Tax or Duty shall be laid on Articles exported from any State.

No Preference shall be given by any Regulation of Commerce or Revenue to the Ports of one State over those of another; nor shall Vessels bound to, or from, one State, be obliged to enter, clear, or pay Duties in another.

No Money shall be drawn from the Treasury, but in Consequence of Appropriations made by Law; and a regular Statement and Account of the Receipts and Expenditures of all public Money shall be published from time to time.

No Title of Nobility shall be granted by the United States: And no Person holding any Office of Profit or Trust under them, shall, without the Consent of the Congress, accept of any present, Emolument, Office, or Title, of any kind whatever, from any King, Prince, or foreign State.

Section 10. No State shall enter into any Treaty, Alliance, or Confederation; grant Letters of Marque and Reprisal; coin Money; emit Bills of Credit; make any Thing but gold and silver Coin a Tender in Payment of Debts; pass any Bill of Attainder, ex post facto Law, or Law impairing the Obligation of Contracts, or grant any Title of Nobility.

No State shall, without the Consent of the Congress, lay any Imposts or Duties on Imports or Exports, except what may be absolutely necessary for executing it's inspection Laws: and the net Produce of all Duties and Imposts, laid by any State on Imports or Exports, shall be for the Use of the Treasury of the United States; and all such Laws shall be subject to the Revision and Controul of the Congress.

No State shall, without the Consent of Congress, lay any Duty of Tonnage, keep Troops, or Ships of War in time of Peace, enter into any Agreement or Compact with another State, or with a foreign Power, or engage in War, unless actually invaded, or in such imminent Danger as will not admit of delay.

ARTICLE II

Section 1. The executive Power shall be vested in a President of the United States of America. He shall hold his Office during the Term of four Years, and, together with the Vice President, chosen for the same Term, be elected, as follows:

Each State shall appoint, in such Manner as the Legislature thereof may direct, a Number of Electors, equal to the whole Number of Senators and Representatives to which the State may be entitled in the Congress: but no Senator or Representative, or Person holding an Office of Trust or Profit under the United States, shall be appointed an Elector.

The Electors shall meet in their respective States, and vote by Ballot for two Persons, of whom one at least shall not be an Inhabitant of the same State with themselves. And they shall make a List of all the Persons voted for, and of the Number of Votes for each; which List they shall sign and certify, and transmit sealed to the Seat of the Government of the United States, directed to the President of the Senate. The President of the Senate shall, in the Presence of the Senate and House of Representatives, open all the Certificates, and the Votes shall then be counted. The Person having the greatest Number of Votes shall be the President, if such Number be a Majority of the whole Number of Electors appointed; and if there be more than one who have such Majority, and have an equal Number of Votes, then the House of Representatives shall immediately chuse by Ballot one of them for President; and if no Person have a Majority, then from the five highest on the List the said House shall in like Manner chuse the President. But in chusing the President, the Votes shall be taken by States, the Representation from each State having one Vote; A quorum for this purpose shall consist of a Member or Members from two thirds of the States, and a Majority of all the States shall be necessary to a Choice. In every Case, after the Choice of the President, the Person having the greatest Number of Votes of the Electors shall be the Vice President. But if there should remain two or more who have equal Votes, the Senate shall chuse from them by Ballot the Vice President.

The Congress may determine the Time of chusing the Electors, and the Day on which they shall give their Votes; which Day shall be the same throughout the United States.

No Person except a natural born Citizen, or a Citizen of the United States, at the time of the Adoption of this Constitution, shall be eligible to the Office of President; neither shall any Person be eligible to that Office who shall not have attained to the Age of thirty five Years, and been fourteen Years a Resident within the United States.

In Case of the Removal of the President from Office, or of his Death, Resignation, or Inability to discharge the Powers and Duties of the said Office, the Same shall devolve on the Vice President, and the Congress may by Law provide for the Case of Removal, Death, Resignation or Inability, both of the President and Vice President, declaring what Officer shall then act as President, and such Officer shall act accordingly, until the Disability be removed, or a President shall be elected.

The President shall, at stated Times, receive for his Services, a Compensation, which shall neither be increased nor diminished during the Period for which he shall have been elected, and he shall not receive within that Period any other Emolument from the United States, or any of them.

Before he enter on the Execution of his Office, he shall take the following Oath or Affirmation:—"I do solemnly swear (or affirm) that I will faithfully execute the Office of President of the United States, and will to the best of my Ability, preserve, protect and defend the Constitution of the United States."

Section 2. The President shall be Commander in Chief of the Army and Navy of the United States, and of the Militia of the several States, when called into the actual Service of the United States; he may require the Opinion, in writing, of the principal Officer in each of the executive Departments, upon any Subject relating to the Duties of their respective Offices, and he shall have Power to grant Reprieves and Pardons for Offences against the United States, except in Cases of Impeachment.

He shall have Power, by and with the Advice and Consent of the Senate, to make Treaties, provided two thirds of the Senators present concur; and he shall nominate, and by and with the Advice and Consent of the Senate, shall appoint Ambassadors, other public Ministers and Consuls, Judges of the supreme Court, and all other Officers of the United States, whose Appointments are not herein otherwise provided for, and which shall be established by Law: but the Congress may by Law vest the Appointment of such inferior Officers, as they think proper, in the President alone, in the Courts of Law, or in the Heads of Departments.

The President shall have Power to fill up all Vacancies that may happen during the Recess of the Senate, by granting Commissions which shall expire at the End of their next Session.

Section 3. He shall from time to time give to the Congress Information of the State of the Union, and recommend to their Consideration such Measures as he shall judge necessary and expedient; he may, on extraordinary Occasions, convene both Houses, or either of them, and in Case of Disagreement between them, with Respect to the Time of Adjournment, he may adjourn them to such Time as he shall think proper; he shall receive Ambassadors and other public Ministers; he shall take Care that the Laws be faithfully executed, and shall Commission all the Officers of the United States.

Section 4. The President, Vice President and all civil Officers of the United States, shall be removed from Office on Impeachment for, and Conviction of, Treason, Bribery, or other high Crimes and Misdemeanors.

ARTICLE III

Section 1. The judicial Power of the United States shall be vested in one supreme Court, and in such inferior Courts as the Congress may from time to time ordain and establish. The Judges, both of the supreme and inferior Courts, shall hold their Offices during good Behaviour, and shall, at stated Times, receive for their Services a Compensation, which shall not be diminished during their Continuance in Office.

Section 2. The judicial Power shall extend to all Cases, in Law and Equity, arising under this Constitution, the Laws of the United States, and Treaties made, or which shall be made, under their Authority;—to all Cases affecting Ambassadors, other public Ministers and Consuls;—to all Cases of admiralty and maritime Jurisdiction;—to Controversies to which the United States shall be a Party;—to Controversies between two or more States;—between a State and Citizens of another State;—between Citizens of different States;—between Citizens of the same State claiming Lands under Grants of different States, and between a State, or the Citizens thereof, and foreign States, Citizens or Subjects.

In all Cases affecting Ambassadors, other public Ministers and Consuls, and those in which a State shall be Party, the supreme Court shall have original Jurisdiction. In all the other Cases before mentioned, the supreme Court shall have appellate Jurisdiction, both as to Law and Fact, with such Exceptions, and under such Regulations as the Congress shall make.

The Trial of all Crimes, except in Cases of Impeachment, shall be by Jury; and such Trial shall be held in the State where the said Crimes shall have been committed; but when not committed within any State, the Trial shall be at such Place or Places as the Congress may by Law have directed.

Section 3. Treason against the United States, shall consist only in levying War against them, or in adhering to their Enemies, giving them Aid and Comfort. No Person shall be convicted of Treason unless on the Testimony of two Witnesses to the same overt Act, or on Confession in open Court.

The Congress shall have Power to declare the Punishment of Treason, but no Attainder of Treason shall work Corruption of Blood, or Forfeiture except during the Life of the Person attainted.

ARTICLE IV

Section 1. Full Faith and Credit shall be given in each State to the public Acts, Records, and judicial Proceedings of every other State. And the Congress may by general Laws prescribe the Manner in which such Acts, Records and Proceedings shall be proved, and the Effect thereof.

Section 2. The Citizens of each State shall be entitled to all Privileges and Immunities of Citizens in the several States.

A Person charged in any State with Treason, Felony, or other Crime, who shall flee from Justice, and be found in another State, shall on Demand of the executive Authority of the State from which he fled, be delivered up, to be removed to the State having Jurisdiction of the Crime.

No Person held to Service or Labour in one State, under the Laws thereof, escaping into another, shall, in Consequence of any Law or Regulation therein, be discharged from such Service or Labour, but shall be delivered up on Claim of the Party to whom such Service or Labour may be due.

Section 3. New States may be admitted by the Congress into this Union; but no new State shall be formed or erected within the Jurisdiction of any other State; nor any State be formed by the Junction of two or more States, or Parts of States, without the Consent of the Legislatures of the States concerned as well as of the Congress.

The Congress shall have Power to dispose of and make all needful Rules and Regulations respecting the Territory or other Property belonging to the United States; and nothing in this Constitution shall be so construed as to Prejudice any Claims of the United States, or of any particular State.

Section 4. The United States shall guarantee to every State in this Union a Republican Form of Government, and shall protect each of them against Invasion; and on Application of the Legislature, or of the Executive (when the Legislature cannot be convened), against domestic Violence.

ARTICLE V

The Congress, whenever two thirds of both Houses shall deem it necessary, shall propose Amendments to this Constitution, or, on the Application of the Legislatures of two thirds of the several States, shall call a Convention for proposing Amendments, which, in either Case, shall be valid to all Intents and Purposes, as Part of this Constitution, when ratified by the Legislatures of three fourths of the several States, or by Conventions in three fourths thereof, as the one or the other Mode of Ratification may be proposed by the Congress; Provided that no Amendment which may be made prior to the Year One thousand eight hundred and eight shall in any Manner affect the first and fourth Clauses in the Ninth Section of the first Article; and that no State, without its Consent, shall be deprived of its equal Suffrage in the Senate.

ARTICLE VI

All Debts contracted and Engagements entered into, before the Adoption of this Constitution, shall be as valid against the United States under this Constitution, as under the Confederation.

This Constitution, and the Laws of the United States which shall be made in Pursuance thereof; and all Treaties made, or which shall be made, under the Authority of the United States, shall be the supreme Law of the Land; and the Judges in every State shall be bound thereby, any Thing in the Constitution or Laws of any State to the Contrary notwithstanding.

The Senators and Representatives before mentioned, and the Members of the several State Legislatures, and all executive and judicial Officers, both of the United States and of the several States, shall be bound by Oath or Affirmation, to support this

Constitution; but no religious Test shall ever be required as a Qualification to any Office or public Trust under the United States.

ARTICLE VII

The Ratification of the Conventions of nine States, shall be sufficient for the Establishment of this Constitution between the States so ratifying the Same.

AMENDMENTS TO THE CONSTITUTION OF THE UNITED STATES

[Amendments I-X make up the Bill of Rights]

AMENDMENT I

Congress shall make no law respecting an establishment of religion, or prohibiting the free exercise thereof; or abridging the freedom of speech, or of the press; or the right of the people peaceably to assemble, and to petition the Government for a redress of grievances.

AMENDMENT II

A well regulated Militia, being necessary to the security of a free State, the right of the people to keep and bear Arms, shall not be infringed.

AMENDMENT III

No Soldier shall, in time of peace be quartered in any house, without the consent of the Owner, nor in time of war, but in a manner to be prescribed by law.

AMENDMENT IV

The right of the people to be secure in their persons, houses, papers, and effects, against unreasonable searches and seizures, shall not be violated, and no Warrants shall issue, but upon probable cause, supported by Oath or affirmation, and particularly describing the place to be searched, and the persons or things to be seized.

AMENDMENT V

No person shall be held to answer for a capital, or otherwise infamous crime, unless on a presentment or indictment of a Grand Jury, except in cases arising in the land or naval forces, or in the Militia, when in actual service in time of War or public danger; nor shall any person be subject for the same offence to be twice put in jeopardy of life or limb; nor shall be compelled in any criminal case to be a witness against himself, nor be deprived of life, liberty, or property, without due process of law; nor shall private property be taken for public use, without just compensation.

AMENDMENT VI

In all criminal prosecutions, the accused shall enjoy the right to a speedy and public trial, by an impartial jury of the State and district wherein the crime shall have been committed, which district shall have been previously ascertained by law, and to be informed of the nature and cause of the accusation; to be confronted with the witnesses against him; to have compulsory process for obtaining witnesses in his favor, and to have the Assistance of Counsel for his defence.

AMENDMENT VII

In suits at common law, where the value in controversy shall exceed twenty dollars, the right of trial by jury shall be preserved, and no fact tried by a jury, shall be otherwise reexamined in any Court of the United States, than according to the rules of the common law.

AMENDMENT VIII

Excessive bail shall not be required, nor excessive fines imposed, nor cruel and unusual punishments inflicted.

AMENDMENT IX

The enumeration in the Constitution, of certain rights, shall not be construed to deny or disparage others retained by the people.

AMENDMENT X

The powers not delegated to the United States by the Constitution, nor prohibited by it to the States, are reserved to the States respectively, or to the people.

AMENDMENT XI

The Judicial power of the United States shall not be construed to extend to any suit in law or equity, commenced or prosecuted against one of the United States by Citizens of another State, or by Citizens or Subjects of any Foreign State.

AMENDMENT XII

The Electors shall meet in their respective states and vote by ballot for President and Vice-President, one of whom, at least, shall not be an inhabitant of the same state with themselves; they shall name in their ballots the person voted for as President, and in distinct ballots the person voted for as Vice-President, and they shall make distinct lists of all persons voted for as President, and of all persons voted for as Vice-President, and of the number of votes for each, which lists they shall sign and certify, and transmit sealed to the seat of the government of the United States, directed to the President of the Senate;—the President of the Senate shall, in the presence of the Senate and House of Representatives, open all the certificates and the votes shall then be counted;—The person having the greatest number of votes for President, shall be the President, if such number be a majority of the whole number of Electors appointed; and if no person have such majority, then from the persons having the highest numbers not exceeding three on the list of those voted for as President, the House of Representatives shall choose immediately, by ballot, the President. But in choosing the President, the votes shall be taken by states, the representation from each state having one vote; a quorum for this purpose shall consist of a member or members from two-thirds of the states, and a majority of all the states shall be necessary to a choice. [And if the House of Representatives shall not choose a President whenever the right of choice shall devolve upon them, before the fourth day of March next following, then the Vice-President shall act as President, as in case of the death or other constitutional disability of the President.—]* The person having the greatest number of votes as Vice-President, shall be the Vice-President, if such number be a majority of the whole number of Electors appointed, and if no person have a majority, then from the two highest numbers on the list, the Senate shall choose the Vice-President; a quorum for the purpose shall consist of two-thirds of the whole number of Senators, and a majority of the whole number shall be necessary to a choice. But no person constitutionally ineligible to the office of President shall be eligible to that of Vice-President of the United States.

AMENDMENT XIII

Section 1. Neither slavery nor involuntary servitude, except as a punishment for crime whereof the party shall have been duly convicted, shall exist within the United States, or any place subject to their jurisdiction.

Section 2. Congress shall have power to enforce this article by appropriate legislation.

AMENDMENT XIV

Section 1. All persons born or naturalized in the United States, and subject to the jurisdiction thereof, are citizens of the United States and of the State wherein they reside. No State shall make or enforce any law which shall abridge the privileges or immunities of citizens of the United States; nor shall any State deprive any person of life, liberty, or property, without due process of law; nor deny to any person within its jurisdiction the equal protection of the laws.

Section 2. Representatives shall be apportioned among the several States according to their respective numbers, counting the whole number of persons in each State, excluding Indians not taxed. But when the right to vote at any election for the choice of electors for President and Vice-President of the United States, Representatives in Congress, the Executive and Judicial officers of a State, or the members of the Legislature thereof, is denied to any of the male inhabitants of such State, being twenty-one years of age,* and citizens of the United States, or in any way abridged, except for participation in rebellion, or other crime, the basis of representation therein shall be reduced in the proportion which the number of such male citizens shall bear to the whole number of male citizens twenty-one years of age in such State.

Section 3. No person shall be a Senator or Representative in Congress, or elector of President and Vice-President, or hold any office, civil or military, under the United States, or under any State, who, having previously taken an oath, as a member of Congress, or as an officer of the United States, or as a member of any State legislature, or as an executive or judicial officer of any State, to support the Constitution of the United States, shall have engaged in insurrection or rebellion against the same, or given aid or comfort to the enemies thereof. But Congress may by a vote of two-thirds of each House, remove such disability.

Section 4. The validity of the public debt of the United States, authorized by law, including debts incurred for payment of pensions and bounties for services in suppressing insurrection or rebellion, shall not be questioned. But neither the United States nor any State shall assume or pay any debt or obligation incurred in aid of insurrection or rebellion against the United States, or any claim for the loss or emancipation of any slave; but all such debts, obligations and claims shall be held illegal and void.

Section 5. The Congress shall have the power to enforce, by appropriate legislation, the provisions of this article.

AMENDMENT XV

Section 1. The right of citizens of the United States to vote shall not be denied or abridged by the United States or by any State on account of race, color, or previous condition of servitude—

Section 2. The Congress shall have the power to enforce this article by appropriate legislation.

AMENDMENT XVI

The Congress shall have power to lay and collect taxes on incomes, from whatever source derived, without apportionment among the several States, and without regard to any census or enumeration.

AMENDMENT XVII

The Senate of the United States shall be composed of two Senators from each State, elected by the people thereof, for six years; and each Senator shall have one vote. The electors in each State shall have the qualifications requisite for electors of the most numerous branch of the State legislatures.

When vacancies happen in the representation of any State in the Senate, the executive authority of such State shall issue writs of election to fill such vacancies: Provided, That the legislature of any State may empower the executive thereof to make temporary appointments until the people fill the vacancies by election as the legislature may direct.

This amendment shall not be so construed as to affect the election or term of any Senator chosen before it becomes valid as part of the Constitution.

AMENDMENT XVIII

Section 1. After one year from the ratification of this article the manufacture, sale, or transportation of intoxicating liquors within, the importation thereof into, or the exportation thereof from the United States and all territory subject to the jurisdiction thereof for beverage purposes is hereby prohibited.

Section 2. The Congress and the several States shall have concurrent power to enforce this article by appropriate legislation.

Section 3. This article shall be inoperative unless it shall have been ratified as an amendment to the Constitution by the legislatures of the several States, as provided in the Constitution, within seven years from the date of the submission hereof to the States by the Congress.

AMENDMENT XIX

The right of citizens of the United States to vote shall not be denied or abridged by the United States or by any State on account of sex.

Congress shall have power to enforce this article by appropriate legislation.

AMENDMENT XX

Section 1. The terms of the President and the Vice President shall end at noon on the 20th day of January, and the terms of Senators and Representatives at noon on the 3d day of January, of the years in which such terms would have ended if this article had not been ratified; and the terms of their successors shall then begin.

Section 2. The Congress shall assemble at least once in every year, and such meeting shall begin at noon on the 3d day of January, unless they shall by law appoint a different day.

Section 3. If, at the time fixed for the beginning of the term of the President, the President elect shall have died, the Vice President elect shall become President. If a President shall not have been chosen before the time fixed for the beginning of his term, or if the President elect shall have failed to qualify, then the Vice President elect shall act as President until a President shall have qualified; and the Congress may by law provide for the case wherein neither a President elect nor a Vice President shall have qualified, declaring who shall then act as President, or the manner in which one who is to act shall be selected, and such person shall act accordingly until a President or Vice President shall have qualified.

Section 4. The Congress may by law provide for the case of the death of any of the persons from whom the House of Representatives may choose a President whenever the right of choice shall have devolved upon them, and for the case of the death of any of the persons from whom the Senate may choose a Vice President whenever the right of choice shall have devolved upon them.

Section 5. Sections 1 and 2 shall take effect on the 15th day of October following the ratification of this article.

Section 6. This article shall be inoperative unless it shall have been ratified as an amendment to the Constitution by the legislatures of three-fourths of the several States within seven years from the date of its submission.

AMENDMENT XXI

Section 1. The eighteenth article of amendment to the Constitution of the United States is hereby repealed.

Section 2. The transportation or importation into any State, Territory, or Possession of the United States for delivery or use therein of intoxicating liquors, in violation of the laws thereof, is hereby prohibited.

Section 3. This article shall be inoperative unless it shall have been ratified as an amendment to the Constitution by conventions in the several States, as provided in the Constitution, within seven years from the date of the submission hereof to the States by the Congress.

AMENDMENT XXII

Section 1. No person shall be elected to the office of the President more than twice, and no person who has held the office of President, or acted as President, for more than two years of a term to which some other person was elected President shall be elected to the office of President more than once. But this Article shall not apply to any person holding the office of President when this Article was proposed by Congress, and shall not prevent any person who may be holding the office of President, or acting as President, during the term within which this Article becomes operative from holding the office of President or acting as President during the remainder of such term.

Section 2. This article shall be inoperative unless it shall have been ratified as an amendment to the Constitution by the legislatures of three-fourths of the several States within seven years from the date of its submission to the States by the Congress.

AMENDMENT XXIII

Section 1. The District constituting the seat of Government of the United States shall appoint in such manner as Congress may direct:

A number of electors of President and Vice President equal to the whole number of Senators and Representatives in Congress to which the District would be entitled if it were a State, but in no event more than the least populous State; they shall be in addition to those appointed by the States, but they shall be considered, for the purposes of the election of President and Vice President, to be electors appointed by a State; and they shall meet in the District and perform such duties as provided by the twelfth article of amendment.

Section 2. The Congress shall have power to enforce this article by appropriate legislation.

AMENDMENT XXIV

Section 1. The right of citizens of the United States to vote in any primary or other election for President or Vice President, for electors for President or Vice President, or for Senator or Representative in Congress, shall not be denied or abridged by the United States or any State by reason of failure to pay poll tax or other tax.

Section 2. The Congress shall have power to enforce this article by appropriate legislation.

AMENDMENT XXV

Section 1. In case of the removal of the President from office or of his death or resignation, the Vice President shall become President.

Section 2. Whenever there is a vacancy in the office of the Vice President, the President shall nominate a Vice President who shall take office upon confirmation by a majority vote of both Houses of Congress.

Section 3. Whenever the President transmits to the President pro tempore of the Senate and the Speaker of the House of Representatives his written declaration that he is unable to discharge the powers and duties of his office, and until he transmits to them a written declaration to the contrary, such powers and duties shall be discharged by the Vice President as Acting President.

Section 4. Whenever the Vice President and a majority of either the principal officers of the executive departments or of such other body as Congress may by law provide, transmit to the President pro tempore of the Senate and the Speaker of the House of Representatives their written declaration that the President is unable to discharge the powers and duties of his office, the Vice President shall immediately assume the powers and duties of the office as Acting President.

Thereafter, when the President transmits to the President pro tempore of the Senate and the Speaker of the House of Representatives his written declaration that no inability exists, he shall resume the powers and duties of his office unless the Vice President and a majority of either the principal officers of the executive department or of such other body as Congress may by law provide, transmit within four days to the President pro tempore of the Senate and the Speaker of the House of Representatives their written declaration that the President is unable to discharge the powers and duties of his office. Thereupon Congress shall decide the issue, assembling within forty-eight hours for that purpose if not in session. If the Congress, within twenty-one days after receipt of the latter written declaration, or, if Congress is not in session, within twenty-one days after Congress is required to assemble, determines by two-thirds vote of both Houses that the President is unable to discharge the powers and duties of his office, the Vice President shall continue to discharge the same as Acting President; otherwise, the President shall resume the powers and duties of his office.

AMENDMENT XXVI

Section 1. The right of citizens of the United States, who are eighteen years of age or older, to vote shall not be denied or abridged by the United States or by any State on account of age.

Section 2. The Congress shall have power to enforce this article by appropriate legislation.

AMENDMENT XXVII

No law, varying the compensation for the services of the Senators and Representatives, shall take effect, until an election of representatives shall have intervened.

Appendix G

Internet Resources

Courts—Alternative Dispute Resolution—Government

U.S. Courts	www.uscourts.gov
U.S. Tax Court	www.ustaxcourt.gov/ustcweb.htm
U.S. Court of Federal Claims	www.uscfc.uscourts.gov/
U.S. Court of International Trade	www.uscit.gov/
U.S Court for the Federal Circuit	www.fedcir.gov/
U.S. Supreme Court	www.supremecourtus.gov
National Mediation Board	www.nmb.gov
American Arbitration Association	www.adr.org
Pacer System	http://pacer.psc.uscourts.gov/
U.S. Court of Appeals	www.uscourts.gov/courtsofappeals.html
Internal Revenue Service	www.irs.gov
Government Printing Office	www.gpo.gov/
Code of Federal Regulations	www.access.gpo.gov/nara/cfr/index.html

Legal Research

VersusLaw	www.versuslaw.com/
Lexis	www.lexisnexis.com/
Westlaw	www.westlaw.com/
Library of Congress	www.loc.gov
Loislaw	www.loislaw.com
Cornell University LII	www.law.cornell.edu/citation
ALWD Manual	www.alwd.org

Legal Organizations

American Bar Association	www.abanet.org
National Federation of Paralegal Associations, Inc.	www.paralegals.org
National Association of Legal Assistants	www.nala.org
American Association of Legal Administrators	www.alanet.org/home.html
American Association for Paralegal Education	www.aafpe.org
ABA Standing Committee on Legal Assistants	www.abanet.org/legalassts
Legal Nurse Consultants	www.aalnc.org

State Bar Associations

Alabama	www.alabar.org
Alaska	www.alaskabar.org
Arizona	www.azbar.org.org
Arkansas	www.arkbar.org
California	www.calbar.org
Colorado	www.cobar.org
Connecticut	www.ctbar.org
Delaware	www.dsba.org
District of Columbia	www.dcbar.org
Florida	www.flabar.org
Georgia	www.gabar.org
Hawaii	www.hsba.org
Idaho	www2.state.id.us/isb/
Illinois	www.isba.org
Indiana	www.inbar.org
Iowa	www.iowabar.org
Kansas	www.ksbar.org
Kentucky	www.kybar.org
Louisiana	www.lsba.org
Maine	www.maine.org
Maryland	www.msba.org
Massachusetts	www.massbar.org
Michigan	www.michbar.org
Minnesota	www.mnbar.org
Mississippi	www.msbar.org
Missouri	www.mobar.org
Montana	www.montanabar.org
Nebraska	www.nebar.org
Nevada	www.nvbar.org
New Hampshire	www.nhbar.org
New Jersey	www.njsba.com
New Mexico	www.nmbar.org
New York	www.nysba.org
North Carolina	www.ncbar.com
North Dakota	www.sband.org
Ohio	www.ohiobar.org
Oklahoma	www.okbar.org
Oregon	www.osbar.org
Pennsylvania	www.pa-bar.org
Rhode Island	www.ribar.com
South Carolina	www.scbar.org
South Dakota	www.sdbar.org
Tennessee	www.tba.org

Texas	www.texasbar.com
Utah	www.utahbar.org
Vermont	www.vtbar.org
Virginia	www.vsb.org
Washington	www.wsba.org
West Virginia	www.wvbar.org
Wisconsin	www.wisbar.org
Wyoming	www.wyomingbar.org

Other

Religious calendar	www.interfaithcalendar.org/
AOL	www.aol.com
Compuserve	www.compuserve.com
The Affiliate	www.futurelawoffice.com/practice.html
Adobe Systems	www.adobe.com
Mapquest	www.mapquest.com

Internet Search Engines

AltaVista	www.altavista.com
Ask Jeeves	www.askjeeves.com
Dogpile	www.dogpile.com
Excite	www.excite.com
Google	www.google.com
Metacrawler	www.metacrawler.com
Netscape	www.netscape.com
Yahoo!	www.yahoo.com
Findlaw	www.findlaw.com

Glossary of Spanish Equivalents for Important Legal Terms

a priori   Desde antes, del pasado.

AAA   Siglas para **American Arbitration Association** Asociación de Arbitraje.

ABA   Siglas para **American Bar Association** Colegio de Abogados Estadounidenses.

accept   Aceptar, admitir, aprobar, recibir reconocer.

accession   Accesión, admisión, aumento, incremento.

accord   Acuerdo, convenio, arreglo, acordar, conceder.

acquittal   Absolución, descargo, veredicto de no culpable.

act   Acto, estatuto, decreto, actuar, funcionar.

actionable   Justiciable, punible, procesable.

adjourn   Levantar, posponer, suspender la sesión.

adjudicate   Adjudicar, decidir, dar fallo a favor de, sentenciar, declarar.

administrative   Administrativo, ejecutivo.

administrative agency   Agencia administrativa.

administrative hearing   Juicio administrativo.

administrative law   Derecho administrativo.

administrative law judge   Juez de derecho, Administrativo.

administrator   Administrador.

admit   Admitir, conceder, reconocer, permitir entrada, confesar, asentir.

adverse   Adverso, contrario, opuesto.

adverse possession   Posesión adversa.

advice   Consejo, asesoramiento, notificación.

affected class   Clase afectada, grupo iscriminado.

affidavit   Declaración voluntaria, escrita y bajo uramento, afidávit, atestiguación, testificata.

affirmative action   Acción positiva.

affirmative defense   Defensa justificativa.

after acquired property   Propiedad adquirida con garantía adicional.

against   En contra.

agency   Agencia, oficina, intervención.

agent   Agente, representante autorizado.

aggrieved party   Parte dañada, agraviada, perjudicada.

agreement   Acuerdo, arreglo, contrato, convenio, pacto.

alibi   Coartada.

alien   Extranjero, extraño, foráneo.

annul   Anular, cancelar, invalidar, revocar, dejar sin efecto.

answer   Contestación, réplica, respuesta, alegato.

antecedent   Antecedente, previo, preexistente.

appeal   Apelar, apelación.

appear   Aparecer, comparecer.

appellate court   Tribunal de apelaciones.

appellate jurisdiction   Competencia de apelación.

applicable   Aplicable, apropiado, pertinente a, lo que puede ser aplicado.

arraign   Denunciar, acusar, procesar, instruir de cargos hechos.

arrears   Retrasos, pagos atrasados, decursas.

arrest   Arresto, arrestar, aprehensión, aprehender, detener.

arson   Incendio intencional.

articles of incorporation   Carta de organización corporativa.

assault   Agresión, asalto, ataque, violencia carnal, agredir, atacar, acometer.

assault and battery   Amenazas y agresión, asalto.

assign   Asignar, ceder, designar, hacer cesión, traspasar, persona asignada un derecho.

attachment   Secuestro judicial.

attorney   Abogado, consejero, apoderado.

award   Fallo, juicio, laudo, premio.

bail   Caución, fianza.

bail bondsman   Fiador, fiador judicial.

bailee   Depositario de bienes.

bailment   Depósito, encargo, depósito mercantil, depósito comercial.

bailment   For hire, depósito oneroso.

bailor   Fiador.

bankruptcy   Bancarrota, quiebra, insolvencia.

battery   Agravio, agresión.

bearer bond   Título mobiliario.

bearer instrument   Título al portador.

bench   Tribunal, los jueces, la magistratura.

Excerpted from *Dictionary of Legal Terms: English/Spanish, Spanish/English*, by Figueroa and Connolly. © 2004 Prentice Hall. Used with permission of Pearson Education, Inc., Upper Saddle River, NJ.

beneficiary Beneficiario, legatario.

bequeath Legar.

bilateral contract Contrato bilateral.

bill of lading Póliza de embarque, boleto de carga, documento de tránsito.

bill of rights Las primeras diez enmiendas a la Constitución de los Estados Unidos de América.

binder Resguardo provisional, recibo para garantizar el precio de un bien inmueble.

birth certificate Acta de nacimiento, partida de nacimiento, certificado de nacimiento.

blue sky laws Estatutos para prevenir el fraude en la compraventa de valores.

bond Bono, título, obligación, deuda inversionista, fianza.

booking Término dado en el cuartel de policía al registro de arresto y los cargos hechos al arrestado.

breach of contract Violación, rotura, incumplimiento de contrato.

brief Alegato, escrito memorial.

burglary Escalamiento, allanamiento de morada.

buyer Comprador.

bylaws Estatutos sociales, reglamentos internos.

capacity to contract Capacidad contractual.

case Causa, caso, acción legal, proceso, proceso civil, asunto, expediente.

case law Jurisprudencia.

cashier's check Cheque bancario.

cease and desist order Orden judicial de cese.

censure Censura.

certificate of deposit Certificado de depósito.

certified check Cheque certificado.

certify Certificar, atestiguar.

charge Cobrar, acusar, imputar.

charitable trust Fideicomiso caritativo.

chattel Bienes muebles, bártulos.

cheat Fraude, engaño, defraudador, trampa, tramposo, estafar.

check Cheque, talón, comprobación.

cite Citación, citar, referir, emplazar.

citizenship Ciudadanía.

civil action Acción, enjuiciamiento civil, demanda.

civil law Derecho civil.

Claims Court Tribunal federal de reclamaciones.

client Cliente.

closing arguments Alegatos de clausura.

closing costs Gastos ocasionados en la venta de bienes raíces.

clue Pista, indicio.

codicil Codicilo.

coercion Coerción, coacción.

collateral Colateral, auxiliar, subsidiario, seguridad colateral, garantía prendaria.

collect Cobrar, recobrar, recaudar.

collision Choque, colisión.

common law Derecho consuetudinario.

comparative negligence Negligencia comparativa.

compensatory damages Indemnización compensatoria por daños y perjuicios, daños compensatorios.

competency Competencia, capacidad legal.

concurrent conditions Condiciones concurrentes.

concurrent jurisdiction Jurisdicción simultanea, conocimiento acumulativo.

concurrent sentences Sentencias que se cumplen simultáneamente.

concurring opinion Opinión coincidente.

condemn Condenar, confiscar, expropiar.

condition precedent Condición precedente.

condition subsequent Condición subsecuente.

confession Confesión, admisión.

confidential Confidencial, íntimo, secreto.

confiscation Confiscación, comiso, decomiso.

consent decree Decreto por acuerdo mutuo.

consequential damages Daños especiales.

consideration Contraprestación.

consolidation Consolidación, unión, concentración.

constructive delivery Presunta entrega.

contempt of court Desacato, contumacia o menosprecio a la corte.

contract Contrato, convenio, acuerdo, pacto.

contributory negligence Negligencia contribuyente.

conversion Conversión, canje.

conviction Convicción, fallo de culpabilidad, convencimiento, sentencia condenatoria, condena.

copyright Derecho de autor, propiedad literaria, propiedad intelectual, derecho de impresión.

corroborate Corroborar, confirmar.

counterclaim Contrademanda, excepción de compensación.

counteroffer Contra oferta.

courts Cortes o tribunales establecidas por la constitución.

covenant for quiet enjoyment Convenio de disfrute y posesión pacífica.

creditor Acreedor.

crime Crimen, delito.

criminal act Acto criminal.

criminal law Derecho penal.

cross examination Contrainterrogatorio, repregunta.

cure Curar, corregir.

damages Daños y perjuicios, indemnización pecuniaria.

DBA Sigla para **doing business as** En negociación comercial.

deadly force Fuerza mortífera.

debt Deuda, débito.

debtor Deudor.

decision Decisión judicial, fallo, determinación auto, sentencia.

deed Escritura, título de propiedad, escritura de traspaso.

defamation   Difamación, infamación.

default   Incumplir, faltar, no comparecer, incumplimiento.

defendant   Demandado, reo, procesado, acusado.

delinquent   Delincuente, atrasado en pagos, delictuoso.

denial   Denegación, negación, denegatoria.

deponent   Deponente, declarante.

deportation   Deportación, destierro.

deposition   Deposición, declaración bajo juramento.

detain   Detener, retardar, retrasar.

devise   Legado de bienes raíces.

direct examination   Interrogatorio directo, interrogatorio a testigo propio.

directed verdict   Veredicto expedido por el juez, veredicto por falta de pruebas.

disaffirm   Negar, rechazar, repudiar, anular.

discharge   Descargo, cumplimiento, liberación.

disclose   Revelar.

discovery   Revelación de prueba, exposición reveladora.

discriminate   Discriminar.

dismiss   Despedir, desechar, desestimar.

dissenting opinion   Opinión en desacuerdo.

dissolution   Disolución, liquidación.

diversity of citizenship   Diversidad de ciudadanías, ciudadanías diferentes.

dividend   Acción librada, dividendo.

divorce   Divorcio, divorciar.

docket   Orden del día, lista de casos en la corte.

double jeopardy   Non bis in idem.

driving under the influence   Manejar bajo los efectos de bebidas alcohólicas o drogas.

duress   Coacción.

earnest money   Arras, señal.

easement   Servidumbre.

edict   Edicto, decreto, auto.

embezzlement   Malversación de fondos.

eminent domain   Dominio eminente.

encroachment   Intrusión, usurpación, invasión, uso indebido.

encumbrance   Gravamen, afectación, cargo.

enforce   Hacer cumplir, dar valor, poner en efecto.

entitlement   Derecho, título.

equal protection clause   Cláusula de protección de igualdad ante la ley.

equal protection of the law   Igualdad ante la ley.

equity   Equidad. Derecho equitativo.

escheat   Reversión al estado al no haber herederos.

estate   Bienes, propiedad, caudal hereditario, cuerpo de la herencia, caudal, derecho, título, interés sobre propiedad.

estop   Impedir, detener, prevenir.

ethics   Sistema ético.

eviction   Evicción, desalojo, desalojamiento, desahucio, lanzamiento.

evidence   Testimonio, prueba, pruebas documentales, pieza de prueba.

examination   Examen, reconocimiento, interrogatorio.

executed contract   Contrato firmado, contrato ejecutado.

execution   Ejecución, desempeño, cumplimiento.

executory contract   Contrato por cumplirse.

executory interests   Intereses futuros.

exempt   Franquear, exentar, exencionar, eximir, libre, franco, exento, inmune.

exoneration   Exoneración, descargo, liberación.

expert witness   Testigo perito.

express contract   Contrato explícito.

expropriation   Expropiación, confiscación.

eyewitness   Testigo ocular o presencial.

fact   Hecho falsificado.

failure to appear   Incomparecencia.

fault   Falta, defecto, culpa, negligencia.

fee   Honorarios, retribución, cuota, cargo, derecho, dominio, asesoría, propiedad, bienes raíces.

fee simple estate   Propiedad en dominio pleno.

felon   Felón, autor de un delito.

felony   Delito mayor o grave.

fiduciary   Fiduciario.

find against   Fallar o decidir en contra.

find for   Fallar o decidir a favor.

finding   Determinación de los hechos.

fine   Multa, castigo.

fixture   Accesorio fijo.

foreclose   Entablar juicio hipotecario, embargar bienes hipotecados.

forgery   Falsificación.

franchise   Franquicia, privilegio, patente, concesión social, derecho de votar.

fraud   Fraude, engaño, estafa, trampa, embuste, defraudación.

full disclosure   Revelación completa.

garnishment   Embargo de bienes.

gift   Regalo, dádiva, donación.

gift causa mortis   Donación de propiedad en expectativa de muerte.

gift inter vivos   Donación entre vivos.

gift tax   Impuesto sobre donaciones.

good and valid consideration   Causa contractual válida.

good faith   Buena fe.

goods   Mercaderías, bienes, productos.

grace period   Período de espera.

grantee   Concesionario, cesionario.

grantor   Otorgante, cesionista.

grievance   Agravio, injuria, ofensa, queja formal.

gross negligence   Negligencia temeraria, negligencia grave.

habitation   Habitación, lugar donde se vive.

harassment   Hostigamiento.

hearing   Audiencia, vista, juicio.

hearsay   Testimonio de oídas.

holder   Tenedor, poseedor.

holding   Decisión, opinión, tenencia posesión, asociación, grupo industrial.

holographic will   Testamento hológrafo.

homeowner   Propietario, dueño de casa.

homestead   Casa, solariega, hogar, heredad, excepción de embargo, bien de familia.

hung jury   Jurado sin veredicto.

identify   Identificar, verificar, autenticar.

illegal   Ilegal, ilícito, ilegítimo.

illegal entry   Entrada ilegal.

illegal search   Registro domiciliario, allanamiento ilegal, cacheo ilegal.

immunity   Inmunidad, exención.

implied warranty   Garantía implícita.

impossibility of performance   Imposibilidad de cumplimiento.

impound   Embargar, incautar, confiscar, secuestrar.

inadmissible   Inadmisible, inaceptable.

income   Ingreso, ganancia, entrada, renta, rédito.

incriminate   Incriminar, acriminar.

indictment   Procesamiento, acusación por jurado acusatorio, inculpatoria.

indorsement   Endose, endoso, respaldo, garantía.

informant   Informador, denunciante, delator.

information   Información, informe, acusación por el fiscal, denuncia.

informed consent   Conformidad por información.

inherit   Heredar, recibir por herencia.

injunction   Mandato judicial, amparo, prohibición judicial, interdicto.

innocent   Inocente, no culpable.

inquiry   Indagatoria judicial, pesquisa.

insufficient evidence   Prueba insuficiente.

interrogation   Interrogación.

interstate commerce   Comercio interestatal.

intestate   Intestado, intestar, sin testamento.

intestate succession   Sucesión hereditaria.

investigation   Investigación, indagación, encuesta.

issue   Emisión, cuestión, punto, edición, número, tirada, sucesión, descendencia, resultado, decisión.

jail   Cárcel, calabozo, encarcelar.

joint tenancy   Condominio.

judge   Magistrado, juez, juzgar, adjudicar, enjuiciar, fallar.

judgment   Sentencia, fallo, juicio, decisión, dictamen, criterio.

judicial proceeding   Proceso o diligencia judicial.

judicial review   Revisión judicial.

jump bail   Fugarse bajo fianza.

jurisdiction   Jurisdicción, fuero competencia.

jury   Jurado

landlord   Arrendatario, propietario.

larceny   Hurto, latrocinio, ladronicio.

law   Ley, derecho.

lease   Contrato de arrendamiento, arrendamiento, arriendo, contrato de locación, arrendar, alquilar.

leasehold estate   Bienes forales.

legatee   Legatario, asignatario.

lender   Prestamista.

lessee   Arrendatario, locatario, inquilino.

lessor   Arrendatario, arrendador, arrendante, locador.

letter of credit   Letra de crédito.

liability   Responsiva, responsabilidad.

libel   Libelo por difamación por escrito.

license   Licencia, permiso, privilegio, matrícula, patente, título, licenciar, permitir.

lien   Gravamen, derecho prendario o de retención, embargo preventivo.

life estate   Hipoteca legal, dominio vitalicio.

limited liability company   Sociedad de responsabilidad limitada.

limited partnership   Sociedad en comandita, sociedad comanditaria.

litigated   Pleiteado, litigado, sujeto a litigación.

majority opinion   Opinión que refleja la mayoría de los miembros de la corte de apelaciones.

maker   Otorgante, girador.

malice   Malicia, malignidad, maldad.

malpractice   Incompetencia profesional.

manslaughter   Homicidio sin premeditación.

material witness   Testigo esencial.

mechanics lien   Gravamen de construcción.

mediation   Mediación, tercería, intervención, interposición.

medical examiner   Médico examinador.

merger   Fusión, incorporación, unión, consolidación.

minor   Menor, insignificante, pequeño, trivial.

misdemeanor   Delito menor, fechoría.

mitigation of damages   Mitigación de daños, minoración, atenuación.

monetary damages   Daños pecuniarios.

mortgage   Hipoteca, gravamen, hipotecar, gravar.

motion to dismiss   Petición para declaración sin lugar.

motion to suppress   Moción para suprimir, reprimir o suspender.

motive   Motivo.

murder   Asesinato, asesinar, homicidio culposo.

naturalization   Naturalización.

negligence   Negligencia, descuido, imprudencia.

negotiable   Negociable.

negotiate   Negociar, agenciar, hacer efectivo, traspasar, tratar.

net assets   Haberes netos.

notice   Aviso, notificación, advertencia, conocimiento.

novation   Novación, delegación de crédito.

nuisance   Daño, molestia, perjuicio.

nuncupative will   Testamento abierto.

oath   Juramento.

objection   Objeción, oposición, disconformidad, recusación, impugnación, excepción, réplica, reclamación.

obstruction of justice   Encubrimiento activo.

offer   Oferta, ofrecimiento, propuesta, ofrecer, proponer.

omission   Omisión, falla, falta.

opinion   Opinión, dictamen, decisión de la corte.

oral argument   Alegato oral.

order instrument   Instrumento de pago a la orden.

owe   Deber, estar en deuda, adeudo.

owner   Dueño, propietario, poseedor.

pain and suffering   Angustia mental y dolor físico.

pardon   Perdón, indulto, absolución, indultar, perdonar.

parol evidence rule   Principio que prohíbe la modificación de un contrato por prueba verbal.

parole   Libertad vigilada.

partnership   Sociedad, compañía colectiva, aparcería, consorcio, sociedad personal.

patent   Patente, obvio, evidente, aparente, privilegio de invención, patentar.

penalty   Pena, multa, castigo, penalidad, condena.

pending   Pendiente, en trámite, pendiente de, hasta que.

per capita   Por cabeza.

performance   Cumplimiento, desempeño, ejecución, rendimiento.

perjury   Perjurio, testimonio falso, juramento falso.

personal property   Bienes personales, bienes mobiliarios.

plea bargain   Declaración de culpabilidad concertada.

plea of guilty   Alegación de culpabilidad.

pleadings   Alegatos, alegaciones, escritos.

pledge   Prenda, caución, empeño, empeñar, dar en prenda, pignorar.

police power   Poder policial.

policy   Póliza, escritura, práctica política.

possession   Posesión, tenencia, goce, disfrute.

possibility of reverter   Posibilidad de reversión.

power of attorney   Poder de representación, poder notarial, procura.

precedent   Precedente, decisión previa por el mismo tribunal.

preemptive right   Derecho de prioridad.

prejudicial   Dañoso, perjudicial.

preliminary hearing   Audiencia preliminar.

premeditation   Premeditación.

presume   Presumir, asumir como hecho basado en la experiencia, suponer.

prevail   Prevalecer, persuadir, predominar, ganar, triunfar.

price discrimination   Discriminación en el precio.

principal   Principal, jefe, de mayor importancia, valor actual.

privileged communication   Comunicación privilegiada.

privity   Coparticipación, intereses comunes.

procedural   Procesal.

proceeds   Ganancias.

profit   Ganancia, utilidad, lucro, beneficio.

prohibited   Prohibido.

promise   Promesa.

promissory estoppel   Impedimento promisorio.

promissory note   Pagaré, vale, nota de pago.

proof   Prueba, comprobación, demostración.

prosecutor   Fiscal, abogado público acusador.

proximate cause   Causa relacionada.

proxy   Poder, delegación, apoderado, mandatario.

punishment   Pena, castigo.

punitive damages   Indemnización punitiva por daños y perjuicios, daños ejemplares.

qualification   Capacidad, calidad, preparación.

qualified indorsement   Endoso limitado endoso con reservas.

quasi contract   Cuasicontrato.

query   Pregunta, interrogación.

question of fact   Cuestión de hecho.

question of law   Cuestión de derecho.

quiet enjoyment   Uso y disfrute.

quitclaim deed   Escritura de traspaso de finiquito.

race discrimination   Discriminación racial.

rape   Estupro, violación, ultraje, rapto, violar.

ratification   Ratificación, aprobación, confirmación.

ratify   Aprobar, confirmar, ratificar, convalidar, adoptar.

real property   Bienes raíces, bienes inmuebles, arraigo.

reasonable doubt   Duda razonable.

rebut   Rebatir, refutar, negar, contradecir.

recognizance   Obligación impuesta judicialmente.

recordation   Inscripción oficial, grabación.

recover   Recobrar, recuperar, obtener como resultado de decreto.

redress   Reparación, compensación, desagravio, compensar, reparar, satisfacer, remediar.

regulatory agency   Agencia reguladora.

reimburse   Reembolsar, repagar, compensar, reintegrar.

rejoinder   Respuesta, réplica, contrarréplica.

release   Descargo, liberación, librar, relevar, descargar, libertar.

relevance   Relevancia.

remainder   Resto, restante, residuo, derecho expectativo a un bien raíz.

remedy   Remedio, recurso.

remuneration   Remuneración, compensación.

reply   Réplica, contestación, contestar, responder.

reprieve   Suspensión de la sentencia, suspensión, indulto, indultar, suspender.

reprimand   Reprender, regañar, reprimenda, represión.

repudiate   Repudiar, renunciar, rechazar.

rescission   Rescisión, abrogación, cancelación de un contrato.

respondeat superior   Responsabilidad civil al supervisor.

respondent   Apelado, demandado.

restitution   Restitución, devolución.

restraining order   Inhibitoria, interdicto, orden de amparo.

retain   Retener, emplear, guardar.

reversion   Reversión, derecho de sucesión.

revocation   Revocación, derogación, anulación.

reward   Premio.

right of first refusal   Retracto arrendaticio.

right of subrogation   Derecho de sustituir.

right of survivorship   Derecho de supervivencia entre dueños de propiedad mancomunada.

right to work laws   Leyes que prohíben la filiación sindical como requisito para poder desempeñar un puesto, derecho de trabajo.

rights   Derechos.

robbery   Robo, atraco.

ruling   Determinación oficial, auto judicial.

sale   Venta.

sale on approval   Venta por aprobación.

satisfaction   Satisfacción, liquidación, cumplimiento, pago, finiquito.

scope of authority   Autoridad explícitamente otorgada o implícitamente concedida.

search and seizure   Allanamiento, registro e incautación.

search warrant   Orden de registro o de allanamiento.

secured party   Persona con interés asegurado.

secured transaction   Transacción con un interés asegurado.

securities   Valores, títulos, obligaciones.

security agreement   Acuerdo que crea la garantía de un interés.

security deposit   Deposito de seguridad.

seize   Arrestar, confiscar, secuestrar, incautar.

settlement   Arreglo, composición, ajuste, liquidación, componenda, acomodo.

sex discrimination   Discriminación sexual.

sexual harassment   Acoso sexual.

shoplifting   Ratería en tiendas.

signature   Firma.

slander   Calumnia, difamación oral, calumniar.

source of income   Fuente de ingresos.

specific performance   Prestación específica contractual.

split decision   Decisión con opiniones mixtas.

spousal abuse   Abuso conyugal.

stare decisis   Vinculación con decisiones judiciales anteriores.

state of mind   Estado de ánimo, estado mental.

statement   Alegación, declaración, relato, estado de cuentas.

statutory foreclosure   Ejecución hipotecaria estatutaria.

statutory law   Derecho estatutario.

statutory rape   Estupro, violación de un menor de edad.

steal   Robar, hurtar, robo, hurto.

stock   Acciones, capital, existencias, semental.

stock option   Opción de comprar o vender acciones.

stop payment order   Suspensión de pago.

strict liability   Responsabilidad rigurosa.

sublease   Subarriendo, sublocación, subarrendar.

subpoena   Citación, citatorio, comparendo, cédula de citación, citación judicial, subpoena.

sue   Demandar, procesar.

summary judgment   Sentencia sumaria.

summon   Convocar, llamar, citar.

suppress   Suprimir, excluir pruebas ilegalmente obtenidas, reprimir, suspender.

surrender   Rendir, entregar, entrega, rendirse, entregarse.

surviving spouse   Cónyuge sobreviviente.

suspect   Sospecha, sospechar, sospechoso.

tangible evidence   Prueba real.

tangible property   Propiedad tangible, bienes tangibles.

tenancy at sufferance   Tenencia o posesión por tolerancia.

tenancy at will   Tenencia o inquilinato sin plazo fijo.

tenancy by the entirety   Tenencia conyugal.

tenancy for life   Tenencia vitalicia.

tenancy for years   Inquilinato por tiempo fijo.

tender   Propuesta, oferta, presentar.

testator   Testador.

testify   Atestar, atestiguar, dar testimonio.

theft   Hurto.

title   Título, derecho de posesión, rango, denominación.

tort   Agravio, torticero, entuerto, daño legal, perjuicio, acto ilícito civil.

Totten trust   Fideicomiso bancario Totten.

trade name   Nombre comercial, marca de fábrica, marca comercial.

trademark   Marca registrada, marca industrial.

transgression   Ofensa, delito, transgresión.

trespass   Transgresión, violación de propiedad ajena, translimitación, traspasar, violar, infringir, transgredir.

trial court   Tribunal de primera instancia.

trust   Fideicomiso, confianza, confidencia, confianza, crédito, combinación, consorcio, grupo industrial.

truth   Verdad, verdadero, veracidad.

try   Probar, juzgar.

ultra vires   Mas allá de la facultad de actuar.

unanimous verdict   Veredicto unánime.

unbiased   Imparcial, neutral.

unconditional pardon   Perdón, amnistía, indulto incondicional.

unconscionable   Reprochable, repugnante, desmedido.

under arrest   Arrestado, bajo arresto.

underwrite   Subscribir, asegurar, firmar.

undisclosed   Escondido, no revelado.

undue influence   Influencia indebida, coacción, abuso de poder.

unenforceable   Inejecutable.

unilateral contract   Contrato unilateral.

unlawful   Ilegal, ilícito, ilegítimo.

unsound mind   Privado de razón, de mente inestable.

usury   Usura, agiotaje, logrería.

vagrancy   Vagancia, vagabundeo.

validity   Validez, vigencia.

valuable consideration   Causa contractual con cierto valor, causa contractual onerosa.

venue   Partido judicial.

verbal contract   Contrato verbal.

verbatim   Al pié de la letra.

verdict   Veredicto, fallo, sentencia, decisión.

victim   Víctima.

voidable   Anulable, cancelable.

wage   Salario, jornal, sueldo.

waive   Renunciar, ceder, suspender, abdicar.

waiver   Renunciar, desistir, ceder, suspender, abdicar, renuncia.

warrant   Autorización, resguardo, comprobante, certificado, justificación, decisión judicial.

warranty   Garantía, seguridad.

warranty of habitability   Garantía de habitabilidad.

welfare   Asistencia pública.

will   Testamento, voluntad.

willful misconduct   Mala conducta intencional.

withhold   Retener, detener.

witness   Testigo, declarante, atestar, testificar, atestiguar.

writ of attachment   Mandamiento de embargo.

writ of certiorari   Pedimento de avocación.

writ of execution   Auto de ejecución, ejecutoria.

Appendix I

Additional Commentaries on the ABA Model Rules of Professional Conduct

CLIENT-LAWYER RELATIONSHIP
RULE 1.5 FEES - COMMENT

Reasonableness of Fee and Expenses

[1] Paragraph (a) requires that lawyers charge fees that are reasonable under the circumstances. The factors specified in (1) through (8) are not exclusive. Nor will each factor be relevant in each instance. Paragraph (a) also requires that expenses for which the client will be charged must be reasonable. A lawyer may seek reimbursement for the cost of services performed in-house, such as copying, or for other expenses incurred in-house, such as telephone charges, either by charging a reasonable amount to which the client has agreed in advance or by charging an amount that reasonably reflects the cost incurred by the lawyer.

Basis or Rate of Fee

[2] When the lawyer has regularly represented a client, they ordinarily will have evolved an understanding concerning the basis or rate of the fee and the expenses for which the client will be responsible. In a new client-lawyer relationship, however, an understanding as to fees and expenses must be promptly established. Generally, it is desirable to furnish the client with at least a simple memorandum or copy of the lawyer's customary fee arrangements that states the general nature of the legal services to be provided, the basis, rate or total amount of the fee and whether and to what extent the client will be responsible for any costs, expenses or disbursements in the course of the representation. A written statement concerning the terms of the engagement reduces the possibility of misunderstanding.

[3] Contingent fees, like any other fees, are subject to the reasonableness standard of paragraph (a) of this Rule. In determining whether a particular contingent fee is reasonable, or whether it is reasonable to charge any form of contingent fee, a lawyer must consider the factors that are relevant under the circumstances. Applicable law may impose limitations on contingent fees, such as a ceiling on the percentage allowable, or may require a lawyer to offer clients an alternative basis for the fee. Applicable law also may apply to situations other than a contingent fee, for example, government regulations regarding fees in certain tax matters.

Terms of Payment

[4] A lawyer may require advance payment of a fee, but is obliged to return any unearned portion. See Rule 1.16(d). A lawyer may accept property in payment for services, such as an ownership interest in an enterprise, providing this does not involve acquisition of a proprietary interest in the cause of action or subject matter of the litigation contrary to Rule 1.8 (i). However, a fee paid in property instead of money may be subject to the requirements of Rule 1.8(a) because such fees often have the essential qualities of a business transaction with the client.

[5] An agreement may not be made whose terms might induce the lawyer improperly to curtail services for the client or perform them in a way contrary to the client's interest. For example, a lawyer should not enter into an agreement whereby services are to be provided only up to a stated amount when it is foreseeable that more extensive services probably will be required, unless the situation is adequately explained to the client. Otherwise, the client might have to bargain for further assistance in the midst of a proceeding or transaction. However, it is proper to define the extent of services in light of the client's ability to pay. A lawyer should not exploit a fee arrangement based primarily on hourly charges by using wasteful procedures.

Prohibited Contingent Fees

[6] Paragraph (d) prohibits a lawyer from charging a contingent fee in a domestic relations matter when payment is contingent upon the securing of a divorce or upon the amount of alimony or support or property settlement to be obtained. This provision does not preclude a contract for a contingent fee for legal representation in connection with the recovery of post-judgment balances due under support, alimony or other financial orders because such contracts do not implicate the same policy concerns.

Division of Fee

[7] A division of fee is a single billing to a client covering the fee of two or more lawyers who are not in the same firm. A division of fee facilitates association of more than one lawyer in a matter in which neither alone could serve the client as well, and most often is used when the fee is contingent and the division is between a referring lawyer and a trial specialist. Paragraph (e) permits the lawyers to divide a fee either on the basis of the proportion of services they render or if each lawyer assumes responsibility for the representation as a whole. In addition, the client must agree to the arrangement, including the share that each lawyer is to receive, and the agreement must be confirmed in writing. Contingent fee agreements must be in a writing signed by the client and must otherwise comply with paragraph (c) of this Rule. Joint responsibility for the representation entails financial and ethical responsibility for the representation as if the lawyers were associated in a partnership. A lawyer should only refer a matter to a lawyer whom the referring lawyer reasonably believes is competent to handle the matter. See Rule 1.1.

[8] Paragraph (e) does not prohibit or regulate division of fees to be received in the future for work done when lawyers were previously associated in a law firm.

Disputes over Fees

[9] If a procedure has been established for resolution of fee disputes, such as an arbitration or mediation procedure established by the bar, the lawyer must comply with the procedure when it is mandatory, and, even when it is voluntary, the lawyer should conscientiously consider submitting to it. Law may prescribe a procedure for determining a lawyer's fee, for example, in representation of an executor or administrator, a class or a person entitled to a reasonable fee as part of the measure of damages. The lawyer entitled to such a fee and a lawyer representing another party concerned with the fee should comply with the prescribed procedure.

CLIENT-LAWYER RELATIONSHIP
RULE 1.15 SAFEKEEPING PROPERTY - COMMENT

[1] A lawyer should hold property of others with the care required of a professional fiduciary. Securities should be kept in a safe deposit box, except when some other form of safekeeping is warranted by special circumstances. All property that is the property of clients or third persons, including prospective clients, must be kept separate from the lawyer's business and personal property and, if monies, in one or more trust accounts. Separate trust accounts may be warranted when administering estate monies or acting in similar fiduciary capacities. A lawyer should maintain on a current basis books and records in accordance with generally accepted accounting practice and comply with any recordkeeping rules established by law or court order. See, e.g., ABA Model Financial Recordkeeping Rule.

[2] While normally it is impermissible to commingle the lawyer's own funds with client funds, paragraph (b) provides that it is permissible when necessary to pay bank service charges on that account. Accurate records must be kept regarding which part of the funds are the lawyer's.

[3] Lawyers often receive funds from which the lawyer's fee will be paid. The lawyer is not required to remit to the client funds that the lawyer reasonably believes represent fees owed. However, a lawyer may not hold funds to coerce a client into accepting the lawyer's contention. The disputed portion of the funds must be kept in a trust account and the lawyer should suggest means for prompt resolution of the dispute, such as arbitration. The undisputed portion of the funds shall be promptly distributed.

[4] Paragraph (e) also recognizes that third parties may have lawful claims against specific funds or other property in a lawyer's custody, such as a client's creditor who has a lien on funds recovered in a personal injury action. A lawyer may have a duty under applicable law to protect such third-party claims against wrongful interference by the client. In such cases, when the third-party claim is not frivolous under applicable law, the lawyer must refuse to surrender the property to the client until the claims are resolved. A lawyer should not unilaterally assume to arbitrate a dispute between the client and the third party, but, when there are substantial grounds for dispute as to the person entitled to the funds, the lawyer may file an action to have a court resolve the dispute.

[5] The obligations of a lawyer under this Rule are independent of those arising from activity other than rendering legal services. For example, a lawyer who serves only as an escrow agent is governed by the applicable law relating to fiduciaries even though the lawyer does not render legal services in the transaction and is not governed by this Rule.

[6] A lawyers' fund for client protection provides a means through the collective efforts of the bar to reimburse persons who have lost money or property as a result of dishonest conduct of a lawyer. Where such a fund has been established, a lawyer must participate where it is mandatory, and, even when it is voluntary, the lawyer should participate.

CLIENT-LAWYER RELATIONSHIP
RULE 1.18 DUTIES TO PROSPECTIVE CLIENT - COMMENT

[1] Prospective clients, like clients, may disclose information to a lawyer, place documents or other property in the lawyer's custody, or rely on the lawyer's advice. A lawyer's discussions with a prospective client usually are limited in time and depth and leave both the prospective client and the lawyer free (and sometimes required) to proceed no further. Hence, prospective clients should receive some but not all of the protection afforded clients.

[2] Not all persons who communicate information to a lawyer are entitled to protection under this Rule. A person who communicates information unilaterally to a lawyer, without any reasonable expectation that the lawyer is willing to discuss the possibility of forming a client-lawyer relationship, is not a "prospective client" within the meaning of paragraph (a).

[3] It is often necessary for a prospective client to reveal information to the lawyer during an initial consultation prior to the decision about formation of a client-lawyer relationship. The lawyer often must learn such information to determine whether there is a conflict of interest with an existing client and whether the matter is one that the lawyer is willing to undertake. Paragraph (b) prohibits the lawyer from using or revealing that information, except as permitted by Rule 1.9, even if the client or lawyer decides not to proceed with the representation. The duty exists regardless of how brief the initial conference may be.

[4] In order to avoid acquiring disqualifying information from a prospective client, a lawyer considering whether or not to undertake a new matter should limit the initial interview to only such information as reasonably appears necessary for that purpose. Where the information indicates that a conflict of interest or other reason for non-representation exists, the lawyer should so inform the prospective client or decline the representation. If the prospective client wishes to retain the lawyer, and if consent is possible under Rule 1.7, then consent from all affected present or former clients must be obtained before accepting the representation.

[5] A lawyer may condition conversations with a prospective client on the person's informed consent that no information disclosed during the consultation will prohibit the lawyer from representing a different client in the matter. See Rule 1.0(e) for the definition of informed consent. If the agreement expressly so provides, the prospective client may also consent to the lawyer's subsequent use of information received from the prospective client.

[6] Even in the absence of an agreement, under paragraph (c), the lawyer is not prohibited from representing a client with interests adverse to those of the prospective client in the same or a substantially related matter unless the lawyer has received from the prospective client information that could be significantly harmful if used in the matter.

[7] Under paragraph (c), the prohibition in this Rule is imputed to other lawyers as provided in Rule 1.10, but, under paragraph (d)(1), imputation may be avoided if the lawyer obtains the informed consent, confirmed in writing, of both the prospective and affected clients. In the alternative, imputation may be avoided if the conditions of paragraph (d)(2) are met and all disqualified lawyers are timely screened and written notice is promptly given to the prospective client. See Rule 1.0(k) (requirements for screening procedures). Paragraph (d)(2)(i) does not prohibit the screened lawyer from receiving a salary or partnership share established by prior independent agreement, but that lawyer may not receive compensation directly related to the matter in which the lawyer is disqualified.

[8] Notice, including a general description of the subject matter about which the lawyer was consulted, and of the screening procedures employed, generally should be given as soon as practicable after the need for screening becomes apparent.

[9] For the duty of competence of a lawyer who gives assistance on the merits of a matter to a prospective client, see Rule 1.1. For a lawyer's duties when a prospective client entrusts valuables or papers to the lawyer's care, see Rule 1.15.

Glossary

Citation A reference to the source of the information.

Citator An index of cases.

Cite checking The process of verifying proper citation form
in a document.

Civil Rights Act of 1866 A federal statute enacted after the
Civil War that says all persons "have the same right . . . to mak
and enforce contracts . . . as is enjoyed by white persons." It
prohibits racial and national origin employment discriminatio

Codicil A separate document that must be executed to amen
will. It must be executed with the same formalities as a will.

Collective bargaining The act of negotiating contract term
between an employer and the members of a union.

"Coming and going" rule A rule that says a principal is
generally not liable for injuries caused by its agents and emplo
while they are on their way to and from work.

Commerce Clause A clause of the U.S. Constitution that gr
Congress the power "to regulate commerce with foreign natio
and among the several states, and with Indian tribes."

Common interest privilege To permit a client to share
confidential information with the attorney for another who sl
a common legal interest.

Common law Developed by judges who issued their opinic
when deciding a case. The principles announced in these case
became precedent for later judges deciding similar cases.

Common-law marriage A type of marriage recognized in s
states where a marriage license has not been issued but certai
requirements are met.

Common law of contracts Contract law developed primar
by state courts.

Common stock A type of equity security that represents th
residual value of the corporation.

Common stockholder A person who owns common stock

Community property A form of ownership in which each
spouse owns an equal one-half share of the income of both
spouses and the assets acquired during the marriage.

Comparative negligence A doctrine under which damage
apportioned according to fault.

Compensatory damages An award of money intended to
compensate a nonbreaching party for loss of the bargain.
Compensatory damages place the nonbreaching party in the
position as if the contract had been fully performed by resto
the "benefit of the bargain."

Complaint The document the plaintiff files with the cour
serves on the defendant to initiate a lawsuit.

Complete performance A situation in which a party to a
contract renders performance exactly as required by the cor
Complete performance discharges that party's obligations u
the contract.

Complex litigation Cases involving many parties as in a
action or multiple or complex legal issues.

Computer addresses and locations The modern equiva
a person's telephone number is the email address. Pages on
Internet also have addresses known as the Uniform Resour
Locator (URL), made up of three parts: protocol, compute
path.

ABA Model Rules of Professional Conduct A recommended
set of ethics and professional conduct guidelines for lawyers,
prepared by American Bar Association, originally released in
1983; prior release was Model Code of Professional Conduct.

Abatement If the property the testator leaves is not sufficient to
satisfy all the beneficiaries named in a will and there are both
general and residuary bequests, the residuary bequest is abated
first (i.e., paid last).

Acceptance A manifestation of assent by the offeree to the
terms of the offer in a manner invited or required by the offer as
measured by the objective theory of contracts.

Actus reus "Guilty act"—the actual performance of the criminal
act.

Ademption A principle that says if a testator leaves a specific
devise of property to a beneficiary, but the property is no longer
in the estate when the testator dies, the beneficiary receives
nothing.

Administrative law judges (ALJ) A judge, presiding over
administrative proceedings, who decides questions of law and fact
concerning the case.

Administrative Procedure Act (APA) An act that establishes
certain administrative procedures that federal administrative
agencies must follow in conducting their affairs.

Administrative subpoena An order that directs the subject of
the subpoena to disclose the requested information.

Adoption A situation in which a person becomes the legal
parent of a child who is not his or her biological child.

Age Discrimination In Employment Act (ADEA) A federal
statute that prohibits age discrimination practices against
employees who are age 40 and older.

Agency A principal–agent relationship; the fiduciary
relationship "which results from the manifestation of consent by
one person to another that the other shall act in his behalf and
subject to his control, and consent by the other so to act."

Agency adoption An adoption that occurs when a person
adopts a child from a social service organization of a state.

Agency by ratification An agency that occurs when (1) a
person misrepresents him or herself as another's agent when in
fact he or she is not and (2) the purported principal ratifies the
unauthorized act.

Agent A party who agrees to act on behalf of another.

Agreement The manifestation by two or more persons of the
substance of a contract.

Air pollution Pollution caused by factories, homes, vehicles,
and the like that affects the air.

ALS The basic certification for legal professional of NALS.

Alternative dispute resolution (ADR) Methods of resolving
disputes other than litigation.

ALWD Association of Legal Writing Directors is a society for
professors who coordinate legal writing instruction.

American Association for Paralegal Education (AAfPE)
National organization of paralegal educators and institutions
offering paralegal education programs.

American Bar Association (ABA) Largest professional legal
organization in the United States.

Americans with Disabilities Act (ADA) A federal statute that
imposes obligations on employers and providers of public
transportation, telecommunications, and public accommodations
to accommodate individuals with disabilities.

Amicus curia Briefs submitted by interested parties who do not
have standing in the action as a "friend of the court."

Annulment An order of the court declaring that a marriage did
not exist.

Apparent agency Agency that arises when a principal creates
the appearance of an agency that in actuality does not exist.

Appeal The act of asking an appellate court to overturn a
decision after the trial court's final judgment has been entered.

Appellant The appealing party in an appeal. Also known as
petitioner.

Appellee The responding party in an appeal. Also known as
respondent.

Application software Applications programs are software that
perform generic tasks such as word processing.

Arbitration A form of ADR in which the parties choose an
impartial third party to hear and decide the dispute.

Arraignment A hearing during which the accused is brought
before a court and is (1) informed of the charges against him or
her and (2) asked to enter a plea.

Arrest warrant A document for a person's detainment based
upon a showing of probable cause that the person committed the
crime.

Article 2 (Sales) of the UCC An article of the UCC that
governs the sale of goods.

Article 2A (Leases) of the UCC An article of the UCC that
governs the lease of goods.

Articles of incorporation The basic governing document of the corporation. This document must be filed with the secretar[y] of state of the state of incorporation.

Articles of limited liability partnership A public document that must be filed with the secretary of state to form a limited liability partnership.

Articles of organization The formal document that must be filed with the secretary of state to form an LLC.

Associate's degree A college degree in science (AS), arts (AA) applied arts (AAS), generally requiring two years of full-time st[udy].

Association of Legal Administrators (ALA) An association law office managers.

Assumption of the risk A defense a defendant can use again[st a] plaintiff who knowingly and voluntarily enters into or particip[ates] in a risky activity that results in injury.

Attestation The action of a will being witnessed by the required number of competent people.

Attorney–client privilege A rule that says a client can tell h[is or] her lawyer anything about the case without fear that the attor[ney] will be called as a witness against the client.

Bachelor's degree A college degree generally requiring fou[r] years of full-time study.

Backup of data Making a copy of critical files and program[s in] case of a loss of the original computer files.

Bailee A holder of goods who is not a seller or a buyer (e.g., warehouse or common carrier).

Bailment A transaction in which an owner transfers his or h[er] personal property to another to be held, stored, delivered, or some other purpose. Title to the property does not transfer.

Bailor The owner of property in a bailment.

Bankruptcy Abuse Prevention and Consumer Protection [Act] of 2005 A federal act that substantially amended federal bankruptcy law. It makes it more difficult for debtors to file f[or] bankruptcy and have their unpaid debts discharged.

Bankruptcy courts Special federal courts that hear and dec[ide] bankruptcy cases.

Bankruptcy estate A debtor's property and earnings that comprise the estate of a bankruptcy proceeding.

Bench opinions The initial version of a decision issued fro[m] the bench of the court.

Beneficiary A person or organization designated in the wil[l who] receives all or a portion of the testator's property at the time [of] the testator's death.

Bicameral In the American system a legislature of a house [of] representatives and a senate.

Bill of Rights The first 10 amendments to the Constitutio[n.] They were added to the U.S. Constitution in 1791.

Board of directors A panel of decision makers, the memb[ers of] which are elected by a corporation's shareholders.

Bona fide occupational qualification (BFOQ) Lawful employment discrimination that is based on a protected [class] (other than race or color) and is *job-related* and *a business necessity*. This exception is narrowly interpreted by the c[ourts.]

Breach of contract A contracting party's failure to perfor[m an] absolute duty owed under a contract.

Cooperative A form of co-ownership of a multiple-dwelling building in which a corporation owns the building and the residents own shares in the corporation.

Co-ownership (concurrent ownership) A situation in which two or more persons own a piece of real property. Also called *concurrent ownership*.

Copyright infringement An act in which a party copies a substantial and material part of the plaintiff's copyrighted work without permission. A copyright holder may recover damages and other remedies against the infringer.

Copyright Revision Act A federal statute that (1) establishes the requirements for obtaining a copyright and (2) protects copyrighted works from infringement.

Corporate bylaws A detailed set of rules that are adopted by the board of directors after the corporation is incorporated, containing provisions for managing the business and the affairs of the corporation.

Corporation A fictitious legal entity that is created according to statutory requirements.

Counteroffer A response by an offeree that contains terms and conditions different from or in addition to those of the offer. A counteroffer terminates an offer.

Court accounting An accounting with the local court that administers or supervises trust and estate matters. These reports are designed to show that the fiduciary has properly administered the estate or trust.

Covenant An unconditional promise to perform.

Cover letter A brief letter sent with a document identifying the intended recipient and the purpose of the attachment.

Crime A violation of a statute for which the government imposes a punishment.

Criminal conspiracy A crime in which two or more persons enter into an agreement to commit a crime and an overt act is taken to further the crime.

Critical legal thinking The process of identifying the issue, the material facts, and the applicable law and applying the law to come to a conclusion.

Cross-complaint Filed by the defendant against the plaintiff to seek damages or some other remedy.

Database program A database program is an electronic repository of information of all types that can be sorted and presented in a meaningful manner.

Deathbed will Oral will that is made dying declaration before a witness during the testator's last illness.

Decree of divorce A court order that terminates a marriage.

Deed A writing that describes a person's ownership interest in a piece of real property.

Defect Something wrong, inadequate, or improper in manufacture, design, packaging, warning, or safety measures of a product.

Defect in design A flaw that occurs when a product is improperly designed.

Defendant The party who files the answer.

Defendant's case Process by which the defendant calls witnesses and introduces evidence to (1) rebut the plaintiff's evidence, (2) prove affirmative defenses, and (3) prove allegations made in a cross-complaint.

Deposition Oral testimony given by a party or witness prior to trial. The testimony is given under oath and is transcribed.

Dicta Court comments on issues not directly related to the holding and therefore not having precedential effect.

Discovery A legal process during which both parties engage in various activities to elicit facts of the case from the other party and witnesses prior to trial.

Diversity of citizenship A case between (1) citizens of different states, (2) a citizen of a state and a citizen or subject of a foreign country, and (3) a citizen of a state and a foreign country where a foreign country is the plaintiff.

Divorce An order of the court that terminates a marriage.

Domain name A unique name that identifies an individual's or a company's Web site.

Domestic corporation A corporation in the state in which it was formed.

Donee A person who receives a gift.

Donor A person who gives a gift.

Double Jeopardy Clause A clause of the Fifth Amendment that protects persons from being tried twice for the same crime.

Dual-purpose mission An errand or another act that a principal requests of an agent while the agent is on his or her own personal business.

Due Process Clause A clause that provides that no person shall be deprived of "life, liberty, or property" without due process of the law.

Duty not to willfully or wantonly injure The duty an owner or renter of real property owes a trespasser to prevent intentional injury or harm to the trespasser when the trespasser is on his or her premises.

Duty of candor Honesty to the court.

Duty of care A responsibility of corporate directors and officers to use care and diligence when acting on behalf of the corporation.

Duty of loyalty A responsibility of directors and officers not to act adversely to the interests of the corporation and to subordinate their personal interests to those of the corporation and its shareholders.

Duty of ordinary care The duty an owner or renter of real property owes an invitee or a licensee to prevent injury or harm when the invitee or licensee steps on the owner's premises.

Easement A given or required right to make limited use of someone else's land without owning or leasing it.

E-commerce The sale of goods and services by computer over the Internet.

E-contract A contract that is entered into by email and over the World Wide Web.

Elder law Advocacy for the elderly.

Electronic Signature in Global and National Commerce Act A federal statute that recognizes that electronic contracts, or e-contracts, meet the writing requirement of the Statute of Frauds and gives electronic signatures, or e-signatures, the same force and effect as pen-inscribed signatures on paper.

Embezzlement The fraudulent conversion of property by a person to whom that property was entrusted.

Eminent domain   The government's power to take private property for public use, provided that just compensation is paid to the private property holder.

Employer–employee relationship   A relationship that results when an employer hires an employee to perform some form of physical service.

Encryption   Encryption is technology that allows computer users to put a "lock" around information to prevent discovery by others.

Environmental Impact Statement (EIS)   A document that must be prepared by the federal government, which analyzes the adverse impact that a federal government action will have on the environment.

Environmental Law   An area of the law dealing with the protection of the environment.

Environmental Protection Agency (EPA)   A federal administrative agency responsible for enforcing most federal environmental protection laws.

Equal Employment Opportunity Commission (EEOC)   A federal administrative agency responsible for enforcing most federal antidiscrimination laws.

Equal Pay Act of 1963   A federal statute that protects both sexes from pay discrimination based on sex. It extends to jobs that require equal skill, equal effort, equal responsibility, and similar working conditions.

Equal Protection Clause   A clause that provides that state, local, and federal governments cannot deny to any person the "equal protection of the laws."

Equitable distribution   A law used by many states where the court orders a *fair distribution* of marital property to the divorcing spouses.

Establishment Clause   A clause to the First Amendment that prohibits the government from either establishing a state religion or promoting one religion over another.

Estate (estate in land)   Ownership rights in real property; the bundle of legal rights of the owner to possess, use, and enjoy the property.

Ethical guidelines   Rules of minimally acceptable professional conduct.

Ethical obligation   A minimum standard of conduct usually within one's profession.

Ethical wall   An environment in which an attorney or a paralegal is isolated from a particular case or client to avoid a conflict of interest or to protect a client's confidences and secrets.

Exclusionary rule   A rule that says evidence obtained from an unreasonable search and seizure can generally be prohibited from introduction at a trial or administrative proceeding against the person searched.

Executory contract or unexpired lease   A contract or lease that has not been fully performed. With the bankruptcy court's approval, executor contracts and unexpired leases may be rejected by a debtor in bankruptcy.

Exempt property   Property that may be retained by a debtor pursuant to federal or state law that does not become part of the bankruptcy estate.

Expert witness   A person qualified by education or experience to render an opinion based on a set of facts.

Express agency   An agency that occurs when a principal and an agent expressly agree to enter into an agency agreement with each other.

Express contract   An agreement that is expressed in written or oral words.

Express trust   A trust created voluntarily by the settlor.

Extortion   Threat to expose something about another person unless that other person gives money or property. Often referred to as "blackmail."

Facts   Information or details.

Fair Labor Standards Act (FLSA)   A federal act enacted in 1938 to protect workers that prohibits child labor and establishes minimum wage and overtime pay requirements.

Fair-use doctrine   A doctrine that permits certain limited use of a copyright by someone other than the copyright holder without the permission of the copyright holder.

Federal administrative agencies   Agencies established by legislative and executive branches of federal and state governments.

Federal Patent Statute   A federal statute that establishes the requirements for obtaining a patent and protects patented inventions from infringement.

Federal question   A case arising under the U.S. Constitution, treaties, or federal statutes and regulations.

Federal Trade Commission (FTC)   A federal administrative agency responsible for enforcing the Federal Trade Commission Act.

Fee simple absolute (fee simple)   A type of ownership of real property that grants the owner the fullest bundle of legal rights that a person can hold in real property.

Fee simple defeasible (qualified fee)   A type of ownership of real property that grants the owner all the incidents of a fee simple absolute except that it may be taken away if a specified condition occurs or does not occur.

File attachment   The attachment is a popular method for transmitting text files, and occasionally graphic images, by attaching the file to an email.

File extension   When a file is saved, a file extension (a period followed by three characters) is added to the end of the filename to identify the program or format in which the file has been saved.

Final order rule   A rule that says the decision of an administrative agency must be final before judicial review can be sought.

Finding tools   Publications used to find primary and secondary sources.

Firewalls   Programs designed to limit access to authorized users and applications.

Fixtures   Goods that are affixed to real estate so as to become part thereof.

Food and Drug Administration (FDA)   A federal administrative agency that administers and enforces the federal Food, Drug, and Cosmetic Act (FDCA) and other federal consumer protection laws.

Food, Drug, and Cosmetic Act (FDCA)   A federal statute enacted in 1938 that provides the basis for the regulation of much of the testing, manufacture, distribution, and sale of foods, drugs, cosmetics, and medicinal products.

Foreign Corrupt Practices Act   A federal statute that makes it illegal for U.S. companies, or their officers, directors, agents, or employees, to bribe a foreign official or foreign political party official to influence the awarding of new business or the retention of continuous business activity.

Forgery   The fraudulent making or alteration of a written document that affects the legal liability of another person.

Franchise   An arrangement that is established when one party licenses another party to use the franchisor's trade name, trademarks, commercial symbols, patents, copyrights, and other property in the distribution and selling of goods and services.

Franchise agreement   An agreement that a franchisor and a franchisee enter into that sets forth the terms and conditions of the franchise.

Free Exercise Clause   A clause to the First Amendment that prohibits the government from interfering with the free exercise of religion in the United States.

Freedom of Information Act   A law that was enacted to give the public access to most documents in the possession of federal administrative agencies.

Freedom of speech   The right to engage in oral, written, and symbolic speech protected by the First Amendment.

Freehold estate   An estate in which the owner has a present possessory interest in the real property.

Frolic and detour   A situation in which an agent does something during the course of his or her employment to further his or her own interests rather than the principal's interests.

Fully disclosed agency   An agency in which the contracting third party knows (1) that the agent is acting for a principal and (2) the identity of the principal.

Functional resume format   Lists a summary of the individual's qualifications with current experience, and education without any emphasis on dates of employment.

Future interest   The interest that the grantor retains for him- or herself or a third party.

Gap-filling rule   A rule that says an open term can be "read into" a sales or lease contract.

General government regulation   Government regulation that applies to many industries collectively.

General law practice   A general law practice is one that handles all types of cases.

General partners   Partners in a limited partnership who invest capital, manage the business, and are personally liable for partnership debts.

General partnership   A voluntary association of two or more persons for carrying on a business as co-owners for profit. Also called a partnership.

General-jurisdiction trial court (courts of record)   A court that hears cases of a general nature that are not within the jurisdiction of limited-jurisdiction trial courts.

Generic name   A term for a mark that has become a common term for a product line or type of service and therefore has lost its trademark protection.

Gift   A voluntary transfer of title to property without payment of consideration by the donee. To be a valid gift, three elements must be shown: (1) *donative intent*, (2) *delivery*, and (3) *acceptance*.

Gift promise   A promise that is unenforceable because it lacks consideration.

GlobalCite   Loislaw's tool for searching cases containing references to another case.

Good Samaritan law   A state statute that relieves medical professionals from liability for ordinary negligence when they stop and render aid to victims in emergency situations.

Government employment   Working for federal, state, and local government agencies and authorities.

Government in the Sunshine Act   An act that was enacted to open certain federal administrative agency meetings to the public.

Grantee   The party to whom an interest in real property is transferred.

Grantor (trustor)   The person who creates a living trust. Also called the *trustor*.

Grantor   The party who transfers an ownership interest in real property.

Hacking   Unauthorized access to a computer or computer network.

Hazardous waste   Substances that may cause or significantly contribute to an increase in mortality or serious illness or pose a hazard to human health or the environment if managed improperly.

Headnotes   The syllabus or summary of the points of law prepared by the editorial staff of a publisher.

Highest state court   The top court in a state court system; it hears appeals from intermediate state courts and certain trial courts.

Holding   The actual decision on the specific point of law the court was asked to decide.

Holographic will   Will that is entirely handwritten and signed by the testator.

Homestead exemption   Equity in a debtor's home that the debtor is permitted to retain.

Hung jury   A jury that cannot come to a unanimous decision about the defendant's guilt. The government may choose to retry the case.

Illegal contract   A contract to perform an illegal act. Cannot be enforced by either party to the contract.

Immaterial facts   A fact not essential to the matter or issue at hand.

Implied attorney–client relationship   Implied attorney–client relationship may result when a prospective client divulges confidential information during a consultation with an attorney for the purpose of retaining the attorney, even if actual employment does not result.

Implied-in-fact contract   A contract in which agreement between parties has been inferred from their conduct.

Implied warranty of habitability   A warranty that provides that leased premises must be fit, safe, and suitable for ordinary residential use.

***In personam* jurisdiction**   Jurisdiction over the parties to a lawsuit.

***In rem* jurisdiction**   Jurisdiction to hear a case because of jurisdiction over the property of the lawsuit.

Income beneficiary   Person or entity to be paid income from the trust.

Independent adoption An adoption in which there is a private arrangement between the biological parents and adoptive parents.

Independent contractor A person or business that is not an employee and is employed by a principal to perform a certain task on his or her behalf.

Indictment The charge of having committed a crime (usually a felony), based on the judgment of a grand jury.

Infancy doctrine A doctrine that allows minors to disaffirm (cancel) most contracts they have entered into with adults.

Inferior performance A situation in which a party fails to perform express or implied contractual obligations and impairs or destroys the essence of the contract.

Injunction A court order that prohibits a person from doing a certain act.

Intellectual property Protection of intellectual property interests like patents, trademarks, and copyrights.

Intentional infliction of emotional distress A tort that occurs when a person's extreme and outrageous conduct intentionally or recklessly causes severe emotional distress to another person. Also known as the tort of outrage.

Intentional torts A category of torts that requires that the defendant possessed the intent to do the act that caused the plaintiff's injuries.

***Inter vivos* trust** A trust that is created while the settlor is alive.

Intermediate appellate court An intermediate court that hears appeals from trial courts.

International Paralegal Management Association A North American association for legal assistant managers.

Internet The Internet or the World Wide Web is a group of computers linked together with the added ability to search all the connections for information.

Internet (Web) browsers An Internet or Web browser is a software program that allows a person to use a computer to access the Internet. The two most popular Web browsers are Microsoft Internet Explorer and Netscape.

Internet search engine An Internet search engine is a program designed to take a word or set of words and locate websites on the Internet.

Internet service providers (ISP) The company providing the connection between the user and the internet.

Interrogatories Written questions submitted by one party to another party. The questions must be answered in writing within a stipulated time.

Intestacy statute A state statute that specifies how a deceased's property will be distributed if he or she dies without a will or if the last will is declared void and there is no prior valid will.

Intestate The state of having died without leaving a will.

Invasion of the right to privacy A tort that constitutes the violation of a person's right to live his or her life without being subjected to unwarranted and undesired publicity.

IOLTA account Where the amount is too small to earn interest, court rules require the funds be deposited into a special interest-bearing account, and the interest generally paid to support legal aid projects (Interest on Lawyers Trust Accounts).

Issue The legal matter in dispute.

Joint and several liability Tort liability of a partnership in which the partners are liable together and separately. This means that the plaintiff can sue one or more of the partners separately. If successful, the plaintiff can recover the entire amount of the judgment from any or all of the defendant–partners.

Joint tenancy A form of co-ownership that includes the right of survivorship.

Judgment The official decision of the court.

Judicial branch The court system.

Judicial decision A ruling about an individual lawsuit issued by federal and state courts.

Jury instructions (charges) Instructions given by the judge to the jury that informs them of the law to be applied in the case.

Just Compensation Clause A clause of the U.S. Constitution that requires the government to compensate the property owner, and possibly others, when the government takes property under its power of eminent domain.

KeyCite Westlaw's tool for searching cases containing references to another case.

Land use control or land use regulation The collective term for the laws that regulate the possession, ownership, and use of real property.

Landlord An owner who transfers a leasehold.

Lanham Trademark Act A federal statute that (1) establishes the requirements for obtaining a federal mark, and (2) protects marks from infringement.

Large law offices Large law offices are an outgrowth of traditional law offices that have expanded over the years, adding partners and associates along the way.

Law That which must be obeyed and followed by citizens subject to sanctions or legal consequences; a body of rules of action or conduct prescribed by controlling authority, and having binding legal force.

Leading question A question which suggests the answer.

Lease A transfer of the right to the possession and use of real property for a set term in return for certain consideration; the rental agreement between a landlord and a tenant.

Leasehold A tenant's interest in property.

Legal research The process for finding the answer to a legal question.

Legally enforceable A contract in which if one party fails to perform as promised, the other party can use the court system to enforce the contract and recover damages or other remedy.

Legislative branch The part of the government that consists of Congress (the Senate and the House of Representatives).

Libel A false statement that appears in a letter, newspaper, magazine, book, photograph, movie, video, or other media.

License A contract that transfers limited rights in intellectual property and informational rights.

Licensee A party who is granted limited rights in or access to intellectual property or informational rights owned by a licensor.

Licensing agreement A detailed and comprehensive written agreement between a licensor and a licensee that sets forth the express terms of their agreement.

Licensor   An owner of intellectual property or informational rights who transfers rights in the property or information to the licensee.

Life estate   An interest in land for a person's lifetime; upon that person's death, the interest will be transferred to another party.

Limited liability company (LLC)   An unincorporated business entity that combines the most favorable attributes of general partnerships, limited partnerships, and corporations.

Limited liability partnership (LLP)   A form of partnership in which all partners are limited partners and there are no general partners.

Limited partners   Partners in a limited partnership who invest capital but do not participate in management and are not personally liable for partnership debts beyond their capital contribution.

Limited partnership   A special form of partnership that is formed only if certain formalities are followed. A limited partnership has both general and limited partners.

Limited partnership agreement   A document that sets forth the rights and duties of the general and limited partners, the terms and conditions regarding the operation, termination, and dissolution of the partnership, and so on.

Lineal descendants   The testator's children, grandchildren, great-grandchildren, and so on.

Liquidated damages   Damages to which parties to a contract agree in advance should be paid if the contract is breached.

Living trust   A method for holding property during a person's lifetime and distributing the property upon that person's death. Also called a *grantor's trust* and a *revocable trust*.

Local area network   A network of computers at one location.

Long-arm statute   A statute that extends a state's jurisdiction to nonresidents who were not served a summons within the state.

Lost property   Property that the owner leaves somewhere because of negligence, carelessness, or inadvertence.

Mandatory authority   Court decisions that are binding on all lower courts.

Marital property   Property acquired during the course of marriage using income earned during the marriage, and separate property that has been converted to marital property.

Mark   The collective name for trademarks, service marks, certification marks, and collective marks that all can be trademarked.

Marriage   A legal union between spouses that confers certain legal rights and duties upon the spouses and upon the children born of the marriage.

Marriage license   A legal document issued by a state certifying that two people are married.

Material breach   A breach that occurs when a party renders inferior performance of his of her contractual duties.

Material facts   A fact significant or essential to the issue.

Mediation   A form of negotiation in which a neutral third party assists the disputing parties in reaching a settlement of their dispute.

Mediator   A neutral third party who assists the disputing parties in reaching a settlement of their dispute. The mediator cannot make a decision or an award.

Member   An owner of an LLC.

Memorandum   A working legal document for the legal team for use in preparation and presentation of a case.

Mens rea   "Evil intent," the possession of the requisite state of mind to commit a prohibited act.

Merchant protection statute   A state statute that allows merchants to stop, detain, and investigate suspected shoplifters without being held liable for false imprisonment if (1) there are reasonable grounds for the suspicion, (2) suspects are detained for only a reasonable time, and (3) investigations are conducted in a reasonable manner.

Minitrial   A voluntary private proceeding in which the lawyers for each side present a shortened version of their case to representatives of the other side, and usually to a neutral third party, in an attempt to reach a settlement of the dispute.

Minor breach   A breach that occurs when a party renders substantial performance of his or her contractual duties.

Miranda rights   Rights that a suspect must be informed of before being interrogated, so that the suspect will not unwittingly give up his or her Fifth Amendment right.

Mirror image rule   A rule that states that for an acceptance to exist, the offeree must accept the terms as stated in the offer.

Misappropriation of the right to publicity   A tort in which one party appropriates a person's name or identity for commercial purposes.

Mislaid property   Property that an owner voluntarily places somewhere and then inadvertently forgets.

Mitigation of damages   A nonbreaching party's legal duty to avoid or reduce damages caused by a breach of contract.

Model guidelines for the utilization of legal assistant services   A set of guidelines by ABA policy-making body, the House of Delegates, intended to govern conduct of lawyers when utilizing paralegals or legal assistants.

Modem   A device to translate electrical signals to allow computers to communicate with each other.

Monetary damages   An award of money.

Money Laundering Control Act   A federal statute that makes money laundering a federal crime.

Moonlighting   Working for more than one firm or attorney.

Moral obligation   An obligation based on one's own conscience.

Narrative opportunity   A question that allows the giving of a full explanation.

National Association of Legal Assistants (NALA)   Professional organization for legal assistants that provides continuing education and professional certification for paralegals, incorporated in 1975.

National Association of Legal Secretaries (NALS)   Since 1999 an association for legal professionals, originally formed in 1949 as an association for legal secretaries.

National Federation of Paralegal Associations (NFPA)   Professional organization of state and local paralegal associations founded in 1974.

National Labor Relations Board (NLRB)   A federal administrative agency that oversees union elections, prevents employers and unions from engaging in illegal and unfair labor practices, and enforces and interprets certain federal labor laws.

Negligence   Failure of a corporate director or officer to exercise the duty of care while conducting the corporation's business.

Negligence per se   Tort where the violation of a statute or ordinance constitutes the breach of the duty of care.

Negotiation A procedure in which the parties to a dispute engage in negotiations to try to reach a voluntary settlement of their dispute.

Network administrator The network administrator usually is the person with the highest-level access to the network file server.

Network file server A separate computer in a network that acts as the traffic cop of the system controlling the flow of data.

Network rights and privileges Rights or privileges determine who has access to the server, the data stored on the server, and the flow of information between connections.

Networking The establishment of contact with others with whom questions and information are shared.

No-fault divorce A divorce recognized by the law of a state whereby neither party is blamed for the divorce.

Non-intent crime A crime that imposes criminal liability without a finding of *mens rea* (intent).

Nurse paralegals or legal nurse consultants Nurses who have gained medical work experience and combine it with paralegal skills.

Objective rule A rule stating that if an engagement is broken off, the prospective bride must return the engagement ring, regardless of which party broke off the engagement.

Occupational Safety and Health Act A federal act enacted in 1970 that promotes safety in the workplace.

offer The manifestation of willingness to enter into a bargain, so made as to justify another person in understanding that his assent to that bargain is invited and will conclude it.

Offeree The party to whom an offer to enter into a contract is made.

Offeror The party who makes an offer to enter into a contract.

Office software suites This software consists of commonly used office software programs that manage data and database programs; manipulate financial or numeric information; spreadsheet programs; or display images and graphics presentation programs.

Officers Employees of a corporation who are appointed by the board of directors to manage the day-to-day operations of the corporation.

Open-ended question Questions that usually do not have a yes or no answer.

Operating agreement An agreement entered into by members that governs the affairs and business of the LLC and the relations among members, managers, and the LLC.

Operating system The operating system is a basic set of instructions to the computer on how to handle basic functions—how to process input from "input devices" such as the keyboard and mouse, the order in which to process information, and what to show on the computer monitor.

Organizational meeting A meeting that must be held by the initial directors of the corporation after the articles of incorporation are filed.

Paperless office An office with electronic documents.

Paralegal (legal assistant) A person qualified by education, training, or work experience who is employed or retained by a lawyer, law office, corporation, governmental agency, or other entity who performs specifically delegated substantive legal work for which a lawyer is responsible; equivalent term is legal assistant.

Paralegal Advanced Competency Exam (PACE) National Association of Paralegal Association's certification program that requires the paralegal to have two years of experience and a bachelor's degree and have completed a paralegal course at an accredited school.

Paralegal manager Someone who hires, supervises, trains, and evaluates paralegals.

Parallel citation The citation to the same case in a different publication.

Partially disclosed agency An agency in which the contracting third party knows that the agent is acting for a principal but does not know the identity of the principal.

Partnership Two or more natural or artificial (corporation) persons who have joined together to share ownership and profit or loss.

Patent infringement Unauthorized use of another's patent. A patent holder may recover damages and other remedies against a patent infringer.

Paternity action A legal proceeding that determines the identity of the father of a child.

Penal codes Statutes that define crimes.

Per capita distribution A distribution of the estate that makes each grandchild and great-grandchild of the deceased inherit equally with the children of the deceased.

Per stirpes distribution A distribution of the estate that makes grandchildren and great-grandchildren of the deceased inherit by representation of their parent.

Periodic tenancy A tenancy created when a lease specifies intervals at which payments are due but does not specify the length of the lease.

Personal property Tangible property such as automobiles, furniture, and equipment, and intangible property such as securities, patents, and copyrights.

Persuasive authority Court decisions the court is not required to follow but are well reasoned and from a respected court.

Petition A document filed with the bankruptcy court that starts a bankruptcy proceeding.

Petition for certiorari A petition asking the Supreme Court to hear one's case.

Petition for divorce A document filed with the proper state court that commences a divorce proceeding.

Picketing The action of strikers walking in front of the employer's premises carrying signs announcing their strike.

Piercing the corporate veil A doctrine that says that if a shareholder dominates a corporation and misuses it for improper purposes, a court of equity can disregard the corporate entity and hold the shareholder personally liable for the corporation's debts and obligations.

Plaintiff The party who files the complaint.

Plaintiff's case Process by which the plaintiff calls witnesses and introduces evidence to prove the allegations contained in his or her complaint.

Plan of reorganization A plan that sets forth a proposed new capital structure for the debtor to have when it emerges from Chapter 11 reorganization bankruptcy.

Pleadings The paperwork that is filed with the court to initiate and respond to a lawsuit.

PLS The advanced certification for legal professionals of NALS.

Pocket parts An update to a book that is a separate document that slips into a pocket in the back of the main volume.

Pour-over will A will that, upon the grantor's death, distributes the grantor's property that is not in the living will.

Power of attorney An express agency agreement that is often used to give an agent the power to sign legal documents on behalf of the principal.

PP Professional Paralegal certification of NALS.

Precedent Prior case law that is controlling.

Prenuptial agreement A contract entered into prior to marriage that specifies how property will be distributed upon the termination of the marriage or death of a spouse.

Pretrial motion A motion a party can make to try to dispose of all or part of a lawsuit prior to trial.

Primary authority The actual law itself.

Primary source of law The actual law itself.

Principal A party who employs another person to act on his or her behalf.

Principal–agent relationship A relationship in which an employer hires an employee and gives that employee authority to act and enter into contracts on his or her behalf.

Privilege A special legal right.

Privileged communication A communication that the person has a right to be kept confidential based on the relationship with the other party such as attorney and client.

Pro bono Working without compensation on behalf of individuals and organizations that otherwise could not afford legal assistance.

Probate (settlement of estate) The process of a deceased's property being collected, debts and taxes being paid, and the remainder of the estate being distributed.

Production of documents Request by one party to another party to produce all documents relevant to the case prior to the trial.

Products liability The liability of manufacturers, sellers, and others for the injuries caused by defective products.

Proprietary school Private, as opposed to public, institution, generally for profit, offering training and education.

Protocol In a URL the required format of the web address.

Quasi-contract An equitable doctrine whereby a court may award monetary damages to a plaintiff for providing work or services to a defendant even though no actual contract existed.

Quasi in rem (attachment) jurisdiction Jurisdiction allowed a plaintiff who obtains a judgment in one state to try to collect the judgment by attaching property of the defendant located in another state.

Racketeer Influenced and Corrupt Organizations Act (RICO) A federal act that provides for both criminal and civil penalities for racketeering.

Real property The land itself as well as buildings, trees, soil, minerals, timber, plants, and other things permanently affixed to the land.

Reformation An equitable doctrine that permits the court to rewrite a contract to express the parties' true intentions.

Regulatory statutes Statutes, such as environmental laws, securities laws, and antitrust laws that provide for criminal violations and penalties.

Rejection Express words or conduct by the offeree that rejects an offer. Rejection terminates the offer.

Relevant facts Facts crucial to the case and having legal significance.

Religious discrimination Discrimination against a person solely because of his or her religion or religious practices.

Remainder (remainderman) A right of possession that returns to a third party upon the expiration of a limited or contingent estate.

Remainder beneficiary Person or entity to receive the trust *corpus* upon termination of the trust.

Reply Filed by the original plaintiff to answer the defendant's cross-complaint.

Res ipsa loquitur Tort where the presumption of negligence arises because (1) the defendant was in exclusive control of the situation, and (2) the plaintiff would not have suffered injury but for someone's negligence. The burden switches to the defendant(s) to prove they were not negligent.

Respondeat superior A rule that says an employer is liable for the tortious conduct of its employees or agents while they are acting within the scope of its authority.

Restatement of the law third torts A legal treatise with suggested rules of laws relating to torts.

Resulting trust A trust that is implied from the conduct of the parties.

Resume A short description of a person's education, a summary of work experience, and other related and supporting information that potential employers use in evaluating a person's qualifications for a position in a firm or an organization.

Retainer A payment at the beginning of the handling of a new matter for a client. This amount may be used to offset the fees for services rendered or costs advanced on behalf of the client.

Reversion A right of possession that returns to the grantor after the expiration of a limited or contingent estate.

Revised Model Business, Corporation Act (RMBCA) A 1984 revision of the MBCA that arranged the provisions of the original act more logically, revised the language to be more consistent, and made substantial changes in the provisions.

Revised Uniform Limited Partnership Act (RULPA) A 1976 revision of the ULPA that provides a more modern, comprehensive law for the formation, operation, and dissolution of limited partnerships.

Revocation Withdrawal of an offer by the offeror which terminates the offer.

S corporation A corporation that has elected S corporation status. An S corporation pays no federal income tax at the corporate level. The gains or losses of an S corporation flow-through to the shareholders.

Sale The passing of title from a seller to a buyer for a price. Also called a conveyance.

Screening interview Limited first contact with a prospective new client.

Search query Specific words used in a computerized search.

Secondary authority Writings that explain the law.

Secondary source of law Writings about the law.

Section 7 of the NLRA A law that gives employees the right to join together and form a union.

Self employment Working independently either as a freelance paralegal for different lawyers or, when authorized by state or federal law, performing services for the public.

Self-incrimination The Fifth Amendment states that no person shall be compelled in any criminal case to be a witness against him- or herself.

Separate property Property owned by a spouse prior to marriage, as well as inheritances and gifts received by a spouse during the marriage.

Service mark A mark that distinguishes the services of the holder from those of its competitors.

Settlement agreement A written document signed by divorcing parties that evidences their agreement settling property rights and other issues of their divorce.

Settlor, trustor, or transferor Person who creates a trust.

Sex discrimination Discrimination against a person solely because of his or her sex.

Sexual harassment Lewd remarks, touching, intimidation, posting of pinups, and other verbal or physical conduct of a sexual nature that occur on the job.

Shareholders The owners of corporations, whose ownership interests are evidenced by stock certificates.

Slander Oral defamation of character.

Slip opinion A copy of the opinion sent to the printer.

Small offices Small-office arrangements range from individual practitioners sharing space to partnerships.

Sole proprietorship A form of business in which the owner is actually the business; the business is not a separate legal entity.

Solo practice One lawyer practicing alone without the assistance of other attorneys.

Specialty applicaton programs Specialty programs combine many of the basic functions found in software suites, word processing, database management, spreadsheets and graphic presentations to perform law office, case, and litigation management.

Specialty practice A specialty practice is involved in practice in one area of law.

Specific government regulation Government regulation that applies to individual industries.

Specific performance A remedy that orders the breaching party to perform the acts promised in the contract. Specific performance usually is awarded in cases where the subject matter is unique, such as in contracts involving land, heirlooms, and paintings.

Spoliation of evidence Destruction of evidence.

Spousal support Payments made by one divorced spouse to the other divorced spouse. Also called *alimony*.

Spreadsheet programs Programs that permit the calculation and presentation of financial information in a grid format of rows and columns.

Stare decisis The legal principle that prior case law should apply unless there is a substantial change in society necessitating a change in the case law.

Statute Written law enacted by the legislative branch of the federal and state governments that establishes certain courses of conduct that the covered parties must adhere to.

Statute of frauds A state statute that requires certain types of contracts to be in writing.

Statute of limitations A time limit within which a case must be brought or lose the right to seek redress in court.

Statute of Wills A state statute that establishes the requirements for making a valid will.

Strict liability A tort doctrine that makes manufacturers, distributors, wholesalers, retailers, and others in the chain of distribution of a defective product liable for the damages caused by the defect irrespective of fault.

Strike Cessation of work by union members to obtain economic benefits or correct an unfair labor practice.

Subject-matter jurisdiction Jurisdiction over the subject matter of a lawsuit.

Substantial performance Performance by a contracting party that deviates only slightly from complete performance.

Substantive rule A rule issued by an administrative agency that has much the same power as a statute: It has the force of law and must be adhered to by covered persons and businesses.

Summons A court order directing the defendant to appear in court and answer the complaint.

Supremacy Clause A clause of the U.S. Constitution that establishes that the federal Constitution, treaties, federal laws, and federal regulations are the supreme law of the land.

Syllabus In a court opinion a headnote for the convenience of the reader.

Tenancy at sufferance A tenancy created when a tenant retains possession of property after the expiration of another tenancy or a life estate without the owner's consent.

Tenancy at will A tenancy created by a lease that may be terminated at any time by either party.

Tenancy by the entirety A form of co-ownership of real property that can be used only by married couples.

Tenancy for years A tenancy created when the landlord and the tenant agree on a specific duration for a lease.

Tenancy in common A form of co-ownership in which the interest of a surviving tenant in common passes to the deceased tenant's estate and not to the co-tenants.

Tenant The party to whom a leasehold is transferred.

Testamentary trust A trust created by will: the trust comes into existence when the settlor dies.

Testator or testatrix The person who makes a will.

Thermal pollution Pollution created by heated water or material being discharged into waterways. It upsets the ecological balance and decreases the oxygen content.

Third-party documents Documents prepared by a third party in the ordinary course of business that would have been prepared in similar form if there was no litigation.

Title VII of the Civil Rights Act of 1964 A title of a federal statute enacted to eliminate job discrimination based on five protected classes: *race, color, religion, sex, and national origin.*

Toxic substances Chemicals used for agricultural, industrial, and mining uses that cause injury to humans, birds, animals, fish, and vegetation.

Track changes Track Changes, as found in MS word, shows the original text, the deleted text, and the new text as well as a strike through for deleted text, underlining or highlighting of new text, as well as margin notes on the document.

Trade secret   A product formula, pattern, design, compilation of data, customer list, or other business secret.

Trademark   A distinctive mark, symbol, name, word, motto, or device that identifies the goods of a particular business.

Trademark infringement   Unauthorized use of another's mark. The holder may recover damages and other remedies from the infringer.

Treaty   A compact made between two or more nations.

Trial notebook   A summary of the case tabbed for each major activity, witness, or element of proof.

Trier of fact   The jury in a jury trial; the judge where there is not a jury trial.

Trust   A legal arrangement established when one person transfers title to property to another person to be held and used for the benefit of a third person.

Trust accounts   The funds of the client.

Trust *corpus* or trust *res*   The property and assets held in trust.

Trustee   Person or entity that holds legal title to the trust corpus and manages the trust for the benefit of the beneficiary or beneficiaries.

U.S. Courts of Appeals   The federal court system's intermediate appellate courts.

U.S. District Courts   The federal court system's trial courts of general jurisdiction.

U.S. Supreme Court   The Supreme Court was created by Article III of the U.S. Constitution. The Supreme Court is the highest court in the land. It is located in Washington, DC.

Unauthorized Practice of Law (UPL)   Giving legal advice, if legal rights may be affected, by anyone not licensed to practice law.

Undisclosed agency   An agency in which the contracting third party does not know of either the existence of the agency or the principal's identity.

Undue influence   Occurs where one person takes advantage of another person's mental, emotional, or physical weakness and unduly persuades that person to make a will; the persuasion by the wrongdoer must overcome the free will of the testator.

Uniform Commercial Code (UCC)   A comprehensive statutory scheme that includes laws covering aspects of commercial transactions.

Uniform Computer Information Transactions Act (UCITA)   A model state law that creates contract law for the licensing of information technology rights.

Uniform Gift to Minors Act or Revised Uniform Gift to Minors Act   Acts that establish procedures for adults to make gifts of money and securities to minors.

Uniform Limited Liability Company Act (ULLCA)   A model act that provides comprehensive and uniform laws for the formation, operation, and dissolution of LLCs.

Uniform Partnership Act (UPA)   A model act that codifies partnership law. Most states have adopted the UPA in whole or in part.

Unintentional tort/negligence   A doctrine that says a person is liable for harm that is the foreseeable consequence of his or her actions.

Universal citation format   A system for citation relying on the courts to number the paragraphs in their opinions.

Universal Resource Locator (URL)   The address of a site on the internet.

Unprotected speech   Speech that is not protected by the First Amendment and may be forbidden by the government.

Unpublished opinions   Cases which the court does not feel have precedential effect and are limited to a specific set of facts.

Unreasonable search and seizure   Any search and seizure by the government that violates the Fourth Amendment.

V.Cite   VersusLaw's tool for searching cases containing references to another case.

Vendor-specific citation format   Citation format of a legal publisher adopted by a court.

Venue   A concept that requires lawsuits to be heard by the court with jurisdiction that is nearest the location in which the incident occurred or where the parties reside.

Verdict   Decision reached by the jury.

Voir dire   Process whereby prospective jurors are asked questions by the judge and attorneys to determine if they would be biased in their decision.

Water pollution   Pollution of lakes, rivers, oceans, and other bodies of water.

White-collar crimes   Crimes usually involving cunning and deceit rather than physical force.

Wide area network   A wide area network is a network of networks. Each network is treated as if it were a connection on the network.

Will   A declaration of how a person wants his or her property to be distributed upon death.

Wireless network   A wireless network uses wireless technology instead of wires for connecting to the network.

Workers' compensation acts   Laws that compensate workers and their families if workers are injured in connection with their jobs.

Work-product doctrine   A qualified immunity from discovery for "work product of the lawyer" except on a substantial showing of "necessity or justification" of certain written statements and memoranda prepared by counsel in representation of a client, generally in preparation for trial.

Work-related test   A test that says if an agent commits an intentional tort within a work-related time or space, the principal is liable for any injury caused by the agent's intentional tort.

Workstation   A computer connected to a network that is used for access consisting of a monitor, input device, and computer.

Writ of certiorari   An official notice that the Supreme Court will review one's case.

Wrongful termination of an agency   The termination of an agency contract in violation of the terms of the agency contract. In this situation, the nonbreaching party may recover damages from the breaching party.

Zoning ordinances   Local laws that are adopted by municipalities and local governments to regulate land use within their boundaries.

Index

Case Index

Index

Subject Index